1986-87
Accredited Institutions of Postsecondary Education

1986-87 Accredited Institutions of Postsecondary Education Programs Candidates

A directory of accredited institutions, professionally accredited programs, and candidates for accreditation

Edited by Sherry S. Harris

Published for the Council on Postsecondary Accreditation

American Council on Education
Washington, D.C.

American Council on Education
One Dupont Circle
Washington, D.C. 20036

Printed in the United States of America

printing number

1 2 3 4 5 6 7 8 9 10

Library of Congress Cataloging in Publication Data

The Library of Congress has catalogued this
serial as follows:

Accredited institutions of postsecondary education, programs,
candidates / published for the Council on Postsecondary Accreditation.— —Washington, D.C.: American Council on Education.

v.; 24 cm.

Annual.
Began with issue for 1976-77.
A directory of accredited institutions, professionally accredited programs, and candidates for accreditation.
Description based on: 1980-81.
Spine title: Accredited institutions of postsecondary education

ISSN 0270-1715 = Accredited institutions of postsecondary education, programs, candidates.

1. Education, Higher—United States—Directories. I. Council on Postsecondary Accreditation. II. American Council on Education. III. Title: Accredited institutions of postsecondary education.
[DNLM: L901 A172]

L901.A48 378.73 81-641495
AACR 2 MARC-S

Contents

About This Directory

Accredited Institutions of Postsecondary Education is an annual publication of the American Council on Education for the Council on Postsecondary Accreditation. Neither COPA nor the American Council is an accrediting body; the listings in the directory are supplied by the numerous national and regional accrediting groups that have been evaluated by COPA and recognized as meeting acceptable levels of quality and performance.

The institutions and programs listed, in turn, have been evaluated by the recognized accreditors and determined by their peers to meet acceptable levels of educational quality.

Those institutions designated as "candidate for accreditation" have achieved initial recognition from the appropriate accrediting commission or association. The designation "candidate" means that an institution is progressing toward accreditation, but that does not assure the achievement of accredited status.

Most of the data contained in each entry has been provided by the individual accrediting bodies. They, in turn, have had an opportunity to verify the listings as near publication deadline (August 1, 1986) as possible

The user of the directory is cautioned that the entries show only accredited institutions and indicate the professional programs within those institutions that have sought and attained specialized accreditation. *The listings do not indicate all curricula offered by an institution.* For example, curricula in anthropology, English, physics, and many other disciplines are not listed because no recognized specialized accreditation exists in those fields. The absence of a particular discipline or course of study in these listings does not necessarily mean that it is not offered at that institution, nor that it is not a quality program if offered.

Also, the user is reminded that the process of accreditation is an ongoing one and that institutions and programs are accredited (or dropped from accredited status) throughout the year. Information about the accredited status of a specific institution or program beyond what is given should be sought directly from the appropriate accrediting body. (Addresses, names and telephone numbers of persons to contact are given on page 446.)

Please take time to review the section on how to use this directory and interpret the listings (Page ix). For further clarification regarding entries in the directory, please contact COPA at The Council on Postsecondary Accreditation, One Dupont Circle, Suite 305, Washington, D.C. 20036, Tel. (202) 452-1433

Additional copies of this directory may be ordered directly from:

Macmillan Publishing Company, Inc.
Front & Brown Streets
Riverside, New Jersey 08075

HOW TO USE THIS DIRECTORY

Initial entry into the directory should be through the index, which lists some 5,000 accredited institutions alphabetically by institutional name. The main body of the directory lists institutions alphabetically by state. Information for the individual listings is arranged as follows (not all categories are listed for each institution):

UNIVERSITY OF THE UNITED STATES
(1) Washington 20010. (2) Public (federal): (3) branches Teachers College, 200 Capitol Hill, N.E.; Technical College, 400 Wisc. Ave., N.W. (4) 1940/1975 (MSA/CHE). (5) Qtr. plan. (6) Degrees: A, B, P, M, D. (7) Prof. Accred.: Art, Chemistry, Engineering, Engineering Technology (civil, electrical, mechanical), Journalism, Law, Medicine, Teacher Education (e, s, p). (8) Pres. George J. Samuels. (9) Enroll.: 8,632 (f.t. 3,210 m., 2,690 w.) (10) 202/333-3725

1. Name and address of institution.
2. Brief statement of (*a*) control (public or private, with religious relationship where appropriate); (*b*) type of institution; (*c*) type of student body (no indication means coeducational).
3. Branch campuses or affiliated institutions where appropriate.
4. Dates of first accreditation or of admission to candidate category and of latest renewal or reaffirmation of this status, and by which accrediting body. (Consult association publications for dates of interruption in or limitations on accredited status.)
5. Type of academic calendar at accredited institutions.
6. Level of degrees offered by accredited institutions.
7. Specialized accreditation by 52 professional agencies in 102 fields.
8. Name of the chief executive officer.
9. Fall 1985 enrollment. Figures are included to provide indication of relative size and composition of student body and indicate total number enrolled and, in parentheses, men and women attending full time.
10. Telephone numbers.

Abbreviations

A—associate degree or equivalent

Accounting (Type A)—Baccalaureate degree with a concentration in accounting

Accounting (Type B)—MBA with an emphasis in accounting

Accounting (Type C)—Masters degree in accounting

B—bachelor's degree

D—doctoral degree

e—elementary education curriculum

4-1-4—academic year of two 4-month terms with 1-month intersession

4-4-x—academic year of two 4-month terms with one term of flexible length

f.t—full-time

FTE—full-time equivalent

M—master's degree

P—first professional degree, i.e., those degrees such as J.D., M.D., or M. Div. requiring six years after high school

p—school service personnel curriculum

Qtr.—quarter calendar of four academic terms, each of about 11 weeks

s—secondary school curriculum

Sem.—semester calendar of two academic terms, together comprising about 34 weeks

3-3—academic year of three terms with students enrolled in three courses a term

Tri.—trimester academic calendar of three 15-week terms, with students generally attending two of the three

Key to Institutional Accrediting Bodies*

AABC	American Association of Bible Colleges
ABHES	Accrediting Bureau of Health Education Schools
AICS	Association of Independent Schools and Colleges
ATS	Association of Theological Schools
MSA/CHE	Middle States Association of Colleges and Schools/Commission on Higher Education
NATTS	National Association of Trade and Technical Schools
NHSC	National Home Study Council
NEASC-CIHE	New England Association of Schools and Colleges-Commission on Institutions of Higher Education
NEASC-CVTCI	New England Association of Schools and Colleges-Commission on Vocational, Technical, Career Institutions
NCA	North Central Association of Colleges and Schools
NASC	Northwest Association of Schools and Colleges
SACS-Comm. on Coll.	Southern Association of Colleges and Schools-Commission on Colleges
SACS-COEI	Southern Association of Colleges and Schools-Commission on Occupational Education Institutions
WASC-Sr.	Western Association of Schools and Colleges-Accrediting Commission for Senior Colleges
WASC-Jr.	Western Association of Schools and Colleges-Accrediting Commission for Junior Colleges

* Complete information on page 446.

1986-87 Accredited Institutions of Postsecondary Education

Accredited Institutions

ALABAMA

Alabama Agricultural and Mechanical University
P.O. Box 285, Normal 35762. Public (state) liberal arts. 1963/1984 (SACS-Comm. on Coll.). Sem. plan. Degrees: A,B,M. *Prof. Accred.:* Engineering Technology (civil, electrical/electronics, mechanical drafting and design, mechanical technology), Home Economics, Social Work (B), Teacher Education (*e,s,p*). Pres. Douglas Covington.
Enroll.: 3,457
(205) 859-7011

Alabama Aviation and Technical College
P.O. Box 1279, Ozark 36361. Public (state). 1973/1981 (SACS-COEI). Courses of varying lengths. Degrees: AAT. Pres. James G. Sasser.
Enroll.: FTE 354
(205) 774-5113

Branch Campus
246 Club Manor Dr., Mobile 36615.

Alabama State University
Montgomery 36195. Public liberal arts college. 1966/1980 (SACS-Comm. on Coll.). Sem. plan. Degrees: A,B,M. *Prof. Accred.:* Music, Teacher Education (*e,s,p*). Pres. Leon Howard.
Enroll.: FTE 3,629
(205) 293-4100

Alabama Technical College
1001 E. Broad St., Gadsden 35999. Public (state). 1972/1982 (SACS-COEI). Courses of varying lengths. Degrees: AAT. Pres. Robert W. Howard.
Enroll.: FTE 519
(205) 547-5451

Branch Campus
600 Valley St., Gadsden 35902.

Alexander City State Junior College
P.O. Box 699, Alexander City 35010. Public. 1969/1984 (SACS-Comm. on Coll.). Qtr. plan. Degrees: A. Pres. W. Byron Causey.
Enroll.: FTE 925
(205) 234-6346

Athens State College
Athens 35611. Public (state) liberal arts. 1955/1979 (SACS-Comm. on Coll.). 4-1-4 plan. Degrees: B. Pres. James R. Chasteen.
Enroll.: FTE 1,133
(205) 232-1802

Atmore State Technical Institute
P.O. Box 1119, Atmore 36504. Public (state). 1978/1983 (SACS-COEI). Courses of varying lengths. Certificates. Dir. Malcolm A. Jones.
Enroll.: FTE 342
(205) 368-8118

Auburn University Central Office
Auburn University 36849. Public (state). Pres. James E. Martin.
(205) 826-4000

Auburn University Main Campus
Auburn University 36849. Public (state). 1922/1984 (SACS-Comm. on Coll.). Qtr. plan. Degrees: B,P,M,D. *Prof. Accred.:* Architecture (B), Art, Business (B,M), Construction Education, Dietetics, Engineering (aerospace, agricultural, chemical, civil, electrical, industrial, materials, mechanical), Engineering Technology (textile management and technology), Forestry, Home Economics, Interior Design, Landscape Architecture (B), Medical Technology, Music, Nursing (B), Pharmacy, Psychology, Rehabilitation Counseling, Social Work, Speech Pathology and Audiology, Teacher Education (*e,s,p*), Veterinary Medicine. Pres. James E. Martin.
Enroll.: 18,346
(205) 826-4000

Auburn University at Montgomery
Montgomery 36193. 1968/1978 (SACS-Comm. on Coll.). Degrees: B,M. *Prof. Accred.:* Nursing (B), Teacher Education (*e,s,p*). Chanc. James O. Williams.
Enroll.: FTE 4,191
(205) 271-9300

Bessemer State Technical College
P.O. Box 308, Bessemer 35021. Public (state). 1972/1982 (SACS-COEI). Courses of varying lengths. Degrees: AAT. *Prof. Accred.:* Dental Assisting. Pres. W. Michael Bailey.
Enroll.: FTE 1,172
(205) 428-6391

Birmingham College of Allied Health
916 S. 18th St., Birmingham 35205. Private. 1980/1982 (ABHES). 32-week program. Diplomas. *Prof. Accred.:* Medical Assisting. Dir. of Ed. Dorothy Forsythe.
Enroll.: f.t. 90
(205) 933 -8097

Birmingham-Southern College
800 Eighth Ave., W., Birmingham 35254. Private (United Methodist) liberal arts. 1922/1984 (SACS-Comm. on Coll.). 4-1-4 plan. Degrees: B,M. *Prof. Accred.:* Music, Nursing (B), Teacher Education (*e,s*). Pres. Neal R. Berte.
Enroll.: FTE 1,455
(205) 226-4600

Booker T. Washington Junior College of Business
1527 Fifth Ave., N., Birmingham 35203. Private. 1954/1981 (AICS). Qtr. plan. Degrees: A, diplomas. Pres/Dir. Mrs. M.L. Gaston.
Enroll.: 308 (*f.t.* 44 m., 264 w.)
(205) 252-4181

Brewer State Junior College
Fayette 35555. Public. 1973/1978 (SACS-Comm. on Coll.). Qtr. plan. Degrees: A. Pres. Tommy M. Boothe.
Enroll.: FTE 611
(205) 932-3221

CAPPS College
2970 Cottage Hill Rd., Suite 150, P.O. Box 6553, Mobile 36606. Private. 1986 (ABHES). Courses of varying lengths. Diplomas. *Prof. Accred.:* Medical Assisting. Admin. Bruce G. Capps.
Enroll.: f.t. 27
(205) 473-1393

C. A. Fredd State Technical College
3401 32nd Ave., Tuscaloosa 35401. Public (state). 1973/1983 (SACS-COEI). Courses of varying lengths. Certificates. Dir. Norman C. Cephus.
Enroll.: FTE 321
(205) 758-3361

Carver State Technical Institute
414 Stanton St., Mobile 36617. Public (state). 1975/1985 (SACS-COEI). Courses of varying lengths. Certificates. Dir. Earl Roberson, Sr.
Enroll.: FTE 284
(205) 478-1296

Chattahoochee Valley State Community College
Phenix City 36867. Public 2-year. 1976/1982 (SACS-Comm. on Coll.). Qtr. plan. Degrees: A. *Prof. Accred.:* Nursing (A). Pres. James E.Owen.
Enroll.: FTE 1,160
(205) 297-4981

Chauncey Sparks State Technical College
P.O. Drawer 580, Eufaula 36027. Public (state). 1973/1983 (SACS-COEI). Courses of varying lengths. Certificates. Dir. Motier Cope.
Enroll.: FTE 295
(205) 687-3543

Coastal Training Institute
77 University Blvd., Mobile 36608. Private business. 1978/1981 (AICS); 1985 (SACS-COEI). Courses of varying lengths. Diplomas. Pres. Elizabeth Kammer Bandy.
Enroll.: FTE 3,042
(205) 343-7652

Branch Campus
1809 Government St., Mobile 36606.

Branch Campus
3738 Atlanta Hwy., Montgomery 36109. Dir. Mac McGilberry.
(205) 279-6241

Branch Campus
3500 N. Pace Blvd., Pensacola, FL 32505. Dir. Carolyn McCants.
(904) 434-3505

Branch Campus
2001 Canal St., Suite 101, New Orleans, LA 70112.

Branch Campus
2460 Terry Rd., Jackson, MS 39204. Dir. Mac McGilberry.
(601) 371-2900

Branch Campus
1710 Market St., Pascagoula, MS 39567. Dir. Carol Hunt.
(601) 762-2020

*Community College of the Air Force
Maxwell Air Force Base 36112. Public (federal) technical for Air Force. 1980 (SACS-Comm. on Coll.). Courses of varying lengths. Degrees: A. *Prof. Accred.:* Assistant to the Primary Care Physician, Dental Assisting, Dental Laboratory Technology, Medical Laboratory Technology, Optometric Technology, Radiography, Surgical Technology. Pres. Col. Rodney V. Cox, Jr.
Enroll.: FTE 83,415
(205) 293-7847

Concordia College
P.O. Box 1329, Selma 36702. Private (Lutheran) junior. 1983 (SACS-Comm. on Coll.). Sem. plan. Degrees: A. Pres. Julius Jenkins.
Enroll.: FTE 321
(205) 875-1550

Debbie's School of Beauty Culture
911 Third Ave., N., Birmingham 35202. Private. 1984 (SACS-COEI). Courses of varying lengths. Certificates. Pres. Deborah Howell.
Enroll.: FTE 144

Branch Campus
2064 Cambellton Rd., Atlanta, GA 30314.

Branch Campus
2917 North Central, Indianapolis, IN 46205.

Branch Campus
1408 N. Kings Hwy., St. Louis, MO 63113.

Branch Campus
11336 Chimney Rock, Houston, TX 77035.

Branch Campus
10340 Eastex Freeway, Houston, TX 77093.

Douglas MacArthur State Technical College
1708 N. Main St., Opp 36467. Public (state). 1972/1982 (SACS-COEI). Courses of varying lengths. Degrees: AAT. Pres. Raymond V. Chisum.
Enroll.: FTE 362
(205) 493-3573

Draughons Junior College
122 Commerce St., Montgomery 36104. Private business. 1954/1983 (AICS). Qtr. plan. Degrees: A. Dean Conley D. Siler.
Enroll.: 651 (*f.t.* 89 m., 562 w.)
(205) 263-1013

*Accreditation includes a complex of technical and management programs offered at various Air Force bases.

Ed E. Reid State Technical College
P.O. Box 588, Evergreen 36401. Public (state). 1972/1982 (SACS-COEI). Courses of varying lengths. Degrees: AAT. Pres. Wiley Salter.
Enroll.: FTE 329
(205) 578-1313

Enterprise State Junior College
P.O. Box 1300, Enterprise 36331. Public. 1969/1984 (SACS-Comm. on Coll.). Qtr. plan. Degrees: A. Pres. Joseph D. Talmadge.
Enroll.: FTE 1,891
(205) 347-2623

The Extension Course Institute of the United States Air Force
Gunter Air Force Sta., Montgomery 36118. Public (federal) home study. 1975/1981 (NHSC). Commandant Col. Ralph O. Clemens, Jr.
(205) 279-4252

Faulkner University
5345 Atlanta Hwy., Montgomery 36193-4601. Private (Church of Christ) liberal arts. 1971/1984 (SACS-Comm. on Coll.). Qtr. plan. Degrees: A,B. Pres. Ernest Cleavenger.
Enroll.: FTE 1,575
(205) 272-5820

Gadsden Business College
P.O. Box 1544, Gadsden 35901. Private. 1962/1985 (AICS). Qtr. plan. Certificates. Pres. Richard E. Beecham.
Enroll.: 303 (*f.t.* 27 m., 276 w.)
(205) 546-2863

Branch Campus
631 S. Wilmer, Anniston 36201. Dir. Ray A. Reese.
(205) 237-7517

Gadsden State Junior College
P.O. Box 1544, Gadsden 35902. Public. 1968/1982 (SACS-Comm. on Coll.). Qtr. plan. Degrees: A. *Prof. Accred.:* Medical Laboratory Technology, Nursing (A), Radiography. Pres. James McEwen.
Enroll.: FTE 2,625
(205) 547-5451

George C. Wallace State Community College
Dothan 36303 . Public. 1969/1984 (SACS-Comm. on Coll.). Qtr. plan. Degrees: A. *Prof. Accred.:* Medical Laboratory Technology, Nursing (A), Respiratory Therapy. Pres. Nathan L. Hodges.

Enroll.: FTE 2,405
(205) 983-3521

GEORGE C. WALLACE STATE COMMUNITY COLLEGE
P.O. Box 250, Hanceville 35077. Public (state) technical. 1978/1984 (SACS-Comm. on Coll.). Courses of varying lengths. Degrees: AAT. *Prof. Accred.:* Dental Assisting, Medical Laboratory Technology (A), Medical Record Technology, Nursing (A), Radiography, Respiratory Therapy. Pres. James C. Bailey.
Enroll.: FTE 2,764
(205) 352-6403

GEORGE CORLEY WALLACE STATE COMMUNITY COLLEGE
P.O. Drawer 1049, Selma 36702-1049. Public. 1974/1979 (SACS-Comm. on Coll.). Qtr. plan. Degrees: A. *Prof. Accred.:* Nursing (A), Practical Nursing. Pres. Charles L. Byrd.
Enroll.: FTE 1,259
(205) 875-2634

HARRY M. AYERS STATE TECHNICAL COLLEGE
1801 Coleman Rd., Anniston 36201. Public (state). 1972/1982 (SACS-COEI). Courses of varying lengths. Degrees: AAT. Pres. Pierce C. Cain.
Enroll.: FTE 542
(205) 831-4540

HEALTH CARE TRAINING INSTITUTE EXTENSION
2233 Fourth Ave., N., Birmingham 35203. Private. 1983 (NATTS). Qtr. plan. Diplomas. Dir. Darlene Mosley.
Enroll.: 228
(205) 252-6396

HEALTH CARE TRAINING INSTITUTE EXTENSION
305 N. Water St., P.O. Box 1066, Mobile 36603-1066. Private. 1984 (NATTS). Qtr. plan. Diplomas. Dir. Judy Johnston.
(205) 433-5042

HEALTH CARE TRAINING INSTITUTE EXTENSION
505-507 Montgomery St., Montgomery 36104. Private. 1984 (NATTS). Qtr. plan. Diplomas. Dir. Tommy Garrett.
(205) 262-3131

HERZING INSTITUTE
1218 S. 20th St., Birmingham 35205. Private. 1971/1983 (NATTS). Courses of varying lengths. Diplomas, certificates. Dir. Don Lewis.
Enroll.: 520
(205) 933-8536

HOBSON STATE TECHNICAL COLLEGE
P.O. Box 489, Thomasville 36784. Public (state). 1972/1982 (SACS-COEI). Courses of varying lengths. Degrees: AAT. Pres. Hoyt Jones.
Enroll.: FTE 382
(205) 636-4429

HUFFSTETLER COLLEGE
P.O. Box 1334, Mobile 36633. Private business. 1985 (AICS). Course of varying lengths. Certificates, diplomas. Pres. Kenneth L. Furby.
(205) 432-2276

HUNTINGDON COLLEGE
1500 E. Fairview Ave., Montgomery 36194-6201. Private (United Methodist) liberal arts. 1928/1979 (SACS-Comm. on Coll.). Sem. plan. Degrees: A,B. *Prof. Accred.:* Music. Pres. Allen K. Jackson.
Enroll.: FTE 685
(205) 265-0511

J. F. DRAKE STATE TECHNICAL COLLEGE
3421 Meridian St., N., Huntsville 35811. Public
(state). 1971/1981 (SACS-COEI). Courses of varying lengths. Degrees: AAT. Pres. Johnny L. Harris.
Enroll.: FTE 503
(205) 539-8161

J. F. INGRAM STATE TECHNICAL COLLEGE
P.O. Box 209, Deatsville 36022. Public (state). 1977/1982 (SACS-COEI). Courses of varying lengths. Degrees: AAT. Pres. Murry Gregg.
Enroll.: FTE 776
(205) 285-5177

JACKSONVILLE STATE UNIVERSITY
Jacksonville 36265. Public. 1935/1983 (SACS-Comm. on Coll.). Sem. plan. Degrees: B,M. *Prof. Accred.:* Nursing, Teacher Education (*e,s,p*). Pres. Harold McGee.
Enroll.: FTE 6,025
(205) 231-5781

JAMES H. FAULKNER STATE JUNIOR COLLEGE
Bay Minette 36507. Public. 1970/1985 (SACS-Comm. on Coll.). Qtr. plan. Degrees: A. *Prof. Accred.:* Dental Assisting. Pres. Gary Branch.

Enroll.: FTE 1,471
(205) 937- 9581

JEFFERSON DAVIS STATE JUNIOR COLLEGE
Brewton 36426. Public. 1968/1985 (SACS-Comm. on Coll.). Qtr. plan. Degrees: A. Pres. George R. McCormick.
Enroll.: FTE 725
(205) 867-4832

JEFFERSON STATE JUNIOR COLLEGE
Pinson Valley Parkway at 2601 Carson Rd., Birmingham 35215. Public. 1968/1985 (SACS-Comm.on Coll.). Qtr. plan. Degrees: A. *Prof. Accred.:* Engineering Technology (electronic), Medical Laboratory Technology (A), Medical Record Technology, Nursing (A), Radiography. Pres. Judy M. Merritt.
Enroll.: FTE 4,846
(205) 853-1200

JOHN C. CALHOUN STATE COMMUNITYCOLLEGE
P.O. Box 2216, Decatur 35602. Public. 1968/1982 (SACS-Comm. on Coll.). Qtr . plan. Degrees: A, certificates. *Prof. Accred.:* Dental Assisting, Medical Record Technology, Nursing (A), Practical Nursing. Pres. James R. Chasteen.
Enroll.: FTE 6,004
(205) 353-3102

JOHN M. PATTERSON STATE TECHNICAL COLLEGE
3920 Troy Hwy., Montgomery 36116. Public (state). 1972/1982 (SACS-COEI). Courses of varying lengths. Degrees: AAT. Pres. J. L. Taunton.
Enroll.: FTE 607
(205) 288-1080

JUDSON COLLEGE
Marion 36756. Private (Southern Baptist) liberal arts for women. 1925/1984 (SACS-Comm. on Coll.). Sem. plan. Degrees: B. *Prof. Accred.:* Music. Pres. N.H. McCrummen.
Enroll.: FTE 350
(205) 683-6161

LAWSON STATE COMMUNITY COLLEGE
3060 Wilson Rd., Birmingham 35221. Public. 1968/1982 (SACS-Comm. on Coll.). Qtr. plan. Degrees: A. *Prof. Accred.:* Nursing (A). Pres. Jesse J. Lewis.
Enroll.: FTE 1,552
(205) 925-1666

LIVINGSTON UNIVERSITY
Livingston 35470. Public (state) liberal arts. 1938/1984 (SACS-Comm. on Coll.). Qtr. plan. Degrees: B,M. *Prof. Accred.:* Nursing (A), Teacher Education (*e,s*). Pres. Asa N. Green.
Enroll.: FTE 1,346
(205) 652-9661

LURLEEN B. WALLACE STATE JUNIOR COLLEGE
Andalusia 36420. Public. 1972/1976 (SACS-Comm. on Coll.). Qtr. plan. Degrees: A. Pres. William H. McWhorter.
Enroll.: FTE 678
(205) 222-6591

MARION MILITARY INSTITUTE
Marion 36756. Private junior college for men. 1926/1984 (SACS-Comm. on Coll.). Sem. plan. Degrees: A. Pres. Gen. Clyde Spence.
Enroll.: FTE 347
(205) 683-9911

MILES COLLEGE
Birmingham 35208. Private (Christian Methodist Espiscopal) liberal arts. 1969/1983 (SACS-Comm. on Coll.). Sem. plan. Degrees: B. Pres. W. Clyde Williams.
Enroll.: FTE 573
(205) 923-2771

MOBILE COLLEGE
P.O. Box 13220, Mobile 36613. Private (Southern Baptist) liberal arts. 1968/1983 (SACS-Comm. on Coll.). Sem. plan. Degrees: A,B,M. *Prof. Accred.:* Nursing (A,B). Pres. Michael A. Magnoli.
Enroll.: FTE 777
(205) 675-5990

MUSCLE SHOALS STATE TECHNICAL COLLEGE
P.O. Box 2545, Muscle Shoals 35662. Public (state) technical. 1973/1981 (SACS-COEI). Courses of varying lengths. Certificates. Dir. Hugo A. Barton.
Enroll.: FTE 609
(205) 381-2813

N. F. NUNNELLEY STATE TECHNICAL COLLEGE
P.O. Box 389, Childersburg 35044. Public (state) technical. 1973/1983 (SACS-COEI). Courses of varying lengths. Degrees: AAT. Dir. James H. Cornell.
Enroll.: FTE 457
(205) 378-2461

National Career College
222 Gordon Dr., Decatur 35602. Private business. 1978/1984 (AICS). Qtr. plan. Diplomas. Dir. Carol L. Johnson.
Enroll.: 661 (*f.t.* 68 m., 593 w.)
(205) 353-6243

National Career College
3527 Memorial Pkwy., N.W., Huntsville 35810. Private business. 1984 (AICS). Qtr. plan. Diplomas. Dir. Susan Provlik.
Enroll.: 661 (*f.t.* 68m m., 593 w.)
(205) 859-9460

National Career College
1351 McFarland Blvd ., E., Tuscaloosa 35405. Private business. 1984 (AICS). Qtr. plan. Diplomas. Dir. Carol Patton Pradat.
Enroll.: f.t. 71
(205) 758-9091

National Education Center/National Institute of Technology Campus
1900 28th Ave., S., Homewood 35209. 1972/1977 (NATTS). Qtr. plan. Degrees: A, diplomas. Dir. Robert Lott.
Enroll.: 59 (*f.t.* 50 m., 9 w.)
(205) 871-2131

New World College of Business
1031 Noble St., Anniston 36201. Private. 1979 (AICS). Qtr. plan. Certificates, diplomas. Pres. Barbara Turner.
Enroll.: 431 (*f.t.* 85 m., 346 w.)
(205) 236-7578

Branch Campus
434-440 Broad St., Gadsden 35901. Dir. J. Robert Guthrie.
(205) 543-1060

North Alabama College of Commerce
2820 Holmes Ave., W., Huntsville 35816. Private. 1959/1982 (AICS); 1979/1984 (SACS-COEI). Qtr. plan. Certificates, diplomas. Pres. John Tabor Butler.
Enroll.: FTE 193
(205) 539-0428

Northeast Alabama State Junior College
Rainsville 35986. Public. 1969/1984 (SACS-Comm. on Coll.). Qtr. plan. Degrees: A. *Prof. Accred.:* Nursing (A). Pres. Charles M. Pendley.
Enroll.: FTE 891
(205) 228-6001

Northwest Alabama State Junior College
Phil Campbell 35581. Public. 1967/1982 (SACS-Comm. on Coll.). Qtr. plan. Degrees: A. *Prof. Accred.:* Nursing (A). Pres. Charles W. Brittnell.
Enroll.: 1,020
(205) 993-5331

Northwest Alabama State Technical College
P.O. Drawer 9, Hamilton 35570. Public (state) technical. 1972/1982 (SACS-COEI). Courses of varying lengths. Degrees: AAT. Pres. Wayne Cobb.
Enroll.: FTE 450
(205) 921-3177

Oakwood College
Huntsville 35896. Private (Seventh-day Adventist) liberal arts. 1958/1981 (SACS-Comm. on Coll.). Qtr. plan. Degrees: A,B. *Prof. Accred.:* Teacher Education (*e,s*). Pres. Emerson A. Cooper.
Enroll.: 1,330
(205) 837-1630

Opelika State Technical College
1701 Lafayette Pkwy., Opelika 36803. Public (state). 1971/1981 (SACS-COEI). Courses of varying lengths. Degrees: AAT. Pres. Robert G. Brown.
Enroll.: FTE 444
(205) 745-6437

Patrick Henry State Junior College
Monroeville 36460. Public. 1970/1985 (SACS-Comm. on Coll.). Qtr. plan. Degrees: A. Pres. James R. Allen.
Enroll.: FTE 600
(205) 575-3156

Prince Institute of Professional Studies
6001 E. Shirley Ln., Montgomery 36117. Private. 1984 (AICS). 2-year program. Diplomas. Dir. Sara Prince.
Enroll.: 71
(205) 271-1670

R.E.T.S. Electronic Institute
2812 12th Ave., N., Birmingham 35234. Private. 1980 (NATTS). Sem. plan. Degrees: A. Vice Pres. Gene D. Smythe.
Enroll.: 928
(205) 251-7962

Riley College
4129 Ross Clark Cir., N.W., P.O. Box 7001, Dothan 36302. Private business. 1975/1981

(AICS); 1983 (SACS-COEI). Qtr. plan. Certificates, diplomas. Pres. Peggy Rice.
Enroll.: FTE 318
(205) 794-4296

Branch Campus
2530 E. South Blvd., Montgomery 36108.

S. D. Bishop State Junior College
Mobile 36690. Public. 1970/1974 (SACS-Comm. on Coll.). Qtr. plan. Degrees: A. *Prof. Accred.:* Nursing (A). Pres. Yvonne Kennedy.
Enroll.: 1,351
(205) 690-6412

Samford University
800 Lakeshore Dr., Birmingham 35229. Private (Southern Baptist). 1920/1975 (SACS-Comm. on Coll.). Sem. plan. Degrees: A,B,P,M. *Prof. Accred.:* Law, Medical Record Administration, Music, Nursing (A,B), Pharmacy, Teacher Education (*e,s,p*). Pres. Thomas E. Corts.
Enroll.: FTE 3,696
(205) 870-2011

Shelton State Community College
202 Skyland Blvd., Tuscaloosa 35404. Public (state) technical. 1979/1984 (SACS-Comm. on Coll.). Qtr. plan. Degrees: A. Pres. Leo Sumner.
Enroll.: FTE 2,786
(205) 556-1165

Snead State Junior College
Boaz 35957. Public. 1941/1983 (SACS-Comm. on Coll.). Qtr. plan. Degrees: A. Pres. William H. Osborn.
Enroll.: FTE 1,072
(205) 593-5120

Southeastern Bible College
2901 Pawnee Ave., Birmingham 35256. Private (Interdenominational) professional. 1962/1983 (AABC). Sem. plan. Degrees: B. Pres. James G. Kallam.
Enroll.: 127
(205) 251-2311

Southeastern School of Cosmetology
1844 Bessemer Rd., Birmingham 35208. Private. 1983 (SACS-COEI). Courses of varying lengths. Certificates. Dir. Shirley E. Parker.
Enroll.: FTE 189

Southern Junior College of Business
1710 First Ave., N., Birmingham 35203. Private junior. 1969/1981 (AICS); 1980 (SACS-Comm. on Coll.). Qtr. plan. Degrees: A, certificates, diplomas. Pres. Kenneth C. Horne, Jr.
Enroll.: FTE 1,488
(205) 251-2821

Branch Campus
2015–2019 Highland Ave., Birmingham 35205. Dir. Ann S. Horne.
(205) 933-8242

Branch Campus
1001 Airport Rd., S.W., Huntsville 35802. Dir. James E. Lott.
(205) 882-3082

Southern Technical College
1900 Crestwood Blvd., Birmingham 35210. Private. 1981 (SACS-COEI). Courses of varying lengths. Certificates. Dir. John Dyer.
Enroll.: FTE 140
(205) 781-2191

Branch Campus
122 E. Broad, Texarkana, AR 77502.

Branch Campus
3780 I-55, N., Jackson, MS 39216.

Southern Union State Junior College
Wadley 36276. Public. 1970/1975 (SACS-Comm. on Coll.). Qtr. plan. Degrees: A. *Prof. Accred.:* Nursing (A). Pres. Richard Federinko.
Enroll.: FTE 1,463
(205) 395-2211

Southern Vocational College
209 Althea St., Tuskegee 36083. Private. 1983 (SACS-COEI). Courses of varying lengths. Certificates, diplomas. Pres. Lawrence F. Haygood, Jr.
Enroll.: FTE 85
(205) 727-1440

Southwest State Technical College
925 Dauphin Island Pkwy., Mobile 36605. Public (state). 1972/1982 (SACS-COEI). Courses of varying lengths. Degrees: AAT. Pres. Donald S. Jefferies.
Enroll.: FTE 670
(205) 479-7476

Spring Hill College
4307 Old Shell Rd., Mobile 36608. Private (Roman Catholic) liberal arts. 1922/1985 (SACS-Comm. on Coll.). Sem. plan. Degrees: B,M. Pres. Rev. Paul S. Tipton, S.J.
Enroll.: FTE 1,005
(205) 460-2121

STILLMAN COLLEGE
P.O. Drawer 1430, Tuscaloosa 35403. Private (Presbyterian, U.S.) liberal arts. 1953/1981 (SACS-Comm. on Coll.). Sem. plan. Degrees: B. Pres. Cordell Wynn.
Enroll.: FTE 718
(205) 349-4240

TALLADEGA COLLEGE
Talledega 35160. Private liberal arts. 1931/1978 (SACS-Comm. on Coll.). Sem. plan. Degrees: B. *Prof. Accred.:* Social Work (B). Pres. Paul Mohr.
Enroll.: FTE 482
(205) 362-0206

TRENHOLM STATE TECHNICAL COLLEGE
1225 Air Base Blvd., Montgomery 36108. Public (state). 1972/1982 (SACS-COEI). Courses of varying lengths. Degrees: AAT. *Prof. Accred.:* Dental Assisting, Practical Nursing. Pres. Thad McClammy.
Enroll.: FTE 2,355
(205) 264-8426

TROY STATE UNIVERSITY-CENTRAL OFFICE
Troy 36082. Administration for three campuses. Public. Pres. Ralph W. Adams.
(205) 566-3000

TROY STATE UNIVERSITY-MAIN CAMPUS
Public liberal arts and teachers. 1934/1983 (SACS-Comm. on Coll.). Qtr. plan. Degrees: A,B,M. *Prof. Accred.:* Nursing (A,B), Teacher Education (*e,s,p*). Pres. Ralph W. Adams.
Enroll.: FTE 6,423
(205) 566-3000

TROY STATE UNIVERSITY AT DOTHAN/ FORT RUCKER
227 N. Foster St., Dothan 36302. Public liberal arts and teachers. 1985 (SACS-Comm. on Coll.). Qtr. plan. Degrees: A.B,M. Vice Pres. R. M. Paul.
Enroll.: FTE 1,127
(205) 793-1445

TROY STATE UNIVERSITY IN MONTGOMERY
P.O. Drawer 4419, Montgomery 36195-5701. Public liberal arts and teachers. 1983 (SACS-Comm. on Coll.). Qtr. plan. Degrees: A,B,M. Vice Pres. Millard E. Elrod.
Enroll.: FTE 1,421
(205) 834-1400

TUSKEGEE UNIVERSITY
Tuskegee 36088. Private university. 1933/1978 (SACS-Comm. on Coll.). Sem. plan. Degrees: B,P,M,D. *Prof. Accred.:* Architecture (M), Dietetics, Engineering (civil, electrical, mechanical), Medical Technology, Nursing (B), Occupational Therapy, Radiography, Social Work (B), Veterinary Medicine. Pres. Benjamin F. Payton.
Enroll.: 3,201
(205) 727-8011

TWENTIETH CENTURY COLLEGE
352 Government St., Mobile 36602. Private business. 1966/1978 (AICS). Courses of varying lengths. Certificates, diplomas. Pres. John P. Hornung.
Enroll.: 611 (*f.t.* 17 m., 594 w.)
(205) 438-9837

U.S. ARMY AVIATION CENTER AND SCHOOL
ATTN: ATZQ-CG (Bldg. 114), Fort Rucker 36362. Public (federal) technical. 1975/1985 (SACS-COEI). Courses of varying lengths. Certificates. Commandant Maj. Gen. Ellis D. Parker.
Enroll.: FTE 5,072
(205) 255-3320

U.S. ARMY CHEMICAL SCHOOL
ATTN: ATZN-CM-F, Fort McClellan 36205. Public (federal) technical. 1978/1983 (SACS-COEI). Courses of varying lengths. Certificates. Commandant Maj. Gen. Gerald G. Watson.
*Enroll.:*FTE 1,327
(205) 664-2182

U.S. ARMY MILITARY POLICE SCHOOL/ TRAINING CENTER
Fort McClellan 36205. Public (federal). 1976/1981 (SACS-COEI). Courses of varying lengths. Certificates. Commandant Brig. Gen. David H. Stern.
Enroll.: FTE 3,094
(205) 238-4311

U.S. ARMY ORDNANCE MISSILE AND MUNITIONS CENTER AND SCHOOL
Redstone Arsenal 35897. Public (federal) technical. 1975/1985 (SACS-COEI). Courses of varying lengths. Certificates. Commandant Col. Paul A. Wilbur.
Enroll.: FTE 2,573
(205) 876-2498

UNITED STATES SPORTS ACADEMY
917 Western American Cir., Mobile 36608. Private professional. 1983 (SACS-Comm. on Coll.). Qtr. plan. Degrees: M. Pres. Thomas P. Rosandich.
Enroll.: FTE 2,069
(205) 343-7700

UNIVERSITY OF ALABAMA SYSTEM
University 35486. Public (state). Chanc. Thomas A. Bartlett.
(205) 348-5121

UNIVERSITY OF ALABAMA AT BIRMINGHAM
Birmingham 35294. Public (state). 1970/1984 (SACS-Comm. on Coll.). Qtr. plan. Degrees: A,B,P,M,D. *Prof. Accred.:* Accounting (Type A), Business (B,M), Cytotechnology, Dental Assisting, Dental Hygiene, Dental Laboratory Technology, Dentistry, Dietetics, EMT-Paramedic, Engineering (civil, electrical, materials, mechanical), Health Services Administration, Medical Assistant, Medical Laboratory Technology, Medical Record Administration, Medical Record Technology, Medical Technology, Medicine, Nuclear Medicine Technology, Nurse Anesthesia Education, Nursing (B,M), Occupational Therapy, Optometric Technology, Optometry, Physical Therapy, Psychology, Public Health, Radiation Therapy Technology, Radiography, Rehabilitation Counseling, Social Work (B), Surgeon's Assistant, Teacher Education (*e,s,p*). Pres. S. Richardson Hill, Jr.
Enroll.: FTE 11,457
(205) 934-4011

UNIVERSITY OF ALABAMA IN HUNTSVILLE
Huntsville 35899. Public (state). 1970/1985 (SACS-Comm. on Coll.). Tri. plan. Degrees: A,B,M,D. *Prof. Accred.:* EMT-Paramedic, Engineering (electrical, industrial and systems, mechanical), Nursing (B,M). Pres. John C. Wright.
Enroll.: FTE 4,884
(205) 895-6120

UNIVERSITY OF ALABAMA
University 35486. Public (state). 1897/1984 (SACS-Comm. on Coll.). Sem. plan. Degrees: B,P,M,D. *Prof. Accred.:* Accounting (Type A,C), Business (B,M), Dietetics, Engineering (aerospace, chemical, civil, electrical, industrial, mechanical, metallurgical, mineral), Engineering Technology (civil, electrical), Home Economics, Interior Design, Journalism, Law, Librarianship, Music, Psychology, Rehabilitation Counseling, Social Work (B,M), Speech Pathology and Audiology, Teacher Education (*e,s,p*). Pres. Joab L. Thomas.
Enroll.: 14.005
(205) 348-6010

UNIVERSITY OF MONTEVALLO
Montevallo 35115. Public (state) liberal arts and professional. 1925/1980 (SACS-Comm. on Coll.). Sem. plan. Degrees: B,M. *Prof. Accred.:* Home Economics, Music, Social Work (B), Speech Pathology and Audiology, Teacher Education (*e,s*). Pres. James F. Vickrey, Jr.
Enroll.: FTE 2,349
(205) 665-6000

UNIVERSITY OF NORTH ALABAMA
Florence 35632-0001. Public liberal arts and teachers college. 1934/1982 (SACS-Comm. on Coll.). Sem. plan. Degrees: B,M. *Prof. Accred.:* Nursing (B), Social Work (B), Teacher Education (*e,s*). Pres. Robert Miller Guillot.
Enroll.: FTE 4,991
(205) 766-4100

UNIVERSITY OF SOUTH ALABAMA
Mobile 36688. Public (state) liberal arts. 1968/1983 (SACS-Comm. on Coll.). Qtr. plan. Degrees: B,P,M,D. *Prof. Accred.:* Business (B,M), Cytotechnology, Engineering (chemical, electrical, mechanical), Medical Technology, Medicine, Music, Nursing (B,M), Physical Therapy, Radiography, Respiratory Therapy, Speech Pathology and Audiology, Teacher Education (*e,s,p*). Pres. Frederick P. Whiddon.
Enroll.: FTE 7,418
(205) 460-6101

WALKER COLLEGE
Jasper 35501. Private junior. 1959/1980 (SACS-Comm. on Coll.). Sem. plan. Degrees: A. *Prof. Accred.:* Nursing (A). Pres. David J. Rowland.
Enroll.: FTE 588
(205) 387-0511

WALKER STATE TECHNICAL COLLEGE
Drawer K, Sumiton 35148. Public (state). 1973/1983 (SACS-COEI). Courses of varying lengths. Certificates. Dir. Harold Wade.
Enroll.: FTE 629
(205) 648-3271

ALASKA

Alaska Bible College
P.O. Box 289, Glenn-Allen 99588. Private (Interdenominational) professional. 1982 (AABC). Sem. plan. Degrees: A,B. Pres. Eugene Mayhew.
Enroll.: 40
(907) 822-3201

Alaska Business College
5159 Old Seward Hwy., Suite 102, Anchorage 99503. Private. 1970/1982 (AICS). Qtr. plan. Certificates, diplomas. Pres. Bettye L. Smith.
Enroll.: 389 (*f.t.* 30 m., 359 w.)
(907) 561-1905

Alaska Pacific University
4101 University Ave., Anchorage 99508. Private (United Methodist). 1981 (NASC). Tri. plan. Degrees: A,B,M. Pres. Glenn A. Olds.
Enroll.: 1,328
(907) 561-1266

*Anchorage Community College
Anchorage 99508-4670. Public junior. 1972/1979 (NASC). Sem. plan. Degrees: A, certificates. *Prof. Accred.:* Dental Assisting, Dental Hygiene, Medical Laboratory Technology, Nursing (A), Practical Nursing. Chanc. Herbert Lyon.
Enroll.: 12,209
(907) 786-1101

*Islands Community College
P.O. Box 490, Sitka 99835. Public junior. 1983 (NASC). Sem. plan. Degrees: A. Campus Pres. Jerry L. Harris.
Enroll.: 909
(907) 646-6653

*Kenai Peninsula Community College
Soldotna 99669. Public junior. 1974/1984 (NASC). Sem. plan. Degrees: A. Pres. Lester T. Vierra.
Enroll.: 1,607
(907) 262-5801

*Ketchikan Community College
Ketchikan 99901. Public junior. 1979/1984 (NASC). Sem. plan. Degrees: A. Pres. John C. Menzie.
Enroll.: 653
(907) 225-6177

*Member of the University of Alaska system

*Kodiak Community College
Kodiak 99615. Public junior. 1974/1984 (NASC). Sem. plan. Degrees: A. Pres. Carolyn Floyd.
Enroll.: 1,061
(907) 486-4161

*Kuskokwim Community College
Bethel 99559. Public junior. 1974/1983 (NASC). Sem. plan. Degrees: A. Pres. Linwood Laughy.
Enroll.: 656
(907) 543-2621

*Matanuska-Susitna Community College
Palmer 99645. Public junior. 1974/1985 (NASC). Sem. plan. Degrees: A. Pres. Alvin Okeson.
Enroll.: 1,296
(907) 745-9726

*Northwest Community College
Nome 99762. Public junior. 1984 (NASC). Sem. plan. Degrees A. Interim Campus Pres. Lucien Johnson.
Enroll.: 395
(907) 443-2201

Sheldon Jackson College
Sitka 99835. Private (United Presbyterian) liberal arts. 1966/1978 (NASC). 4-1-4 plan. Degrees: A,B. Pres. Michael E. Kaelke.
Enroll.: 266
(907) 747-5231

*Tanana Valley Community College
Fairbanks 99712. Public junior. 1983 (NASC). Sem. plan. Degrees: A. Campus Pres. Michael Metty.
Enroll.: 2,671
(907) 474-7812

University of Alaska System Office
Bunnell Bldg., Tanana Dr., Fairbanks 99701. Public (state). Sem. plan. Pres. Donald O'Dowd.
(907) 479-7211

University of Alaska, Anchorage
Anchorage 99508. 1974/1979 (NASC). Degrees: B,M. *Prof. Accred.:* Engineering (civil), Nursing (B), Social Work (B).Chanc. David L. Outcalt.

*Member of the University of Alaska system

Enroll.: 4,581
(907) 786-1413

UNIVERSITY OF ALASKA, FAIRBANKS
Fairbanks 99701. 1934/1984 (NASC). Sem. plan. Degrees: B,M,D. *Prof. Accred.:* Engineering (civil, electrical, geological, mechanical, mining), Journalism, Music. Chanc. Patrick J. O'Rourke.
Enroll.: 5,299
(907) 474-7112

UNIVERSITY OF ALASKA, JUNEAU
11120 Glacier Hwy., Juneau 99801. 1983 (NASC); accreditation includes Juneau-Douglas Community College. Sem. plan. Degrees: A,B,M. Chanc. Michael E. Paradise.
Enroll.: 2,108
(909) 789-4425

AMERICAN SAMOA

AMERICAN SAMOA COMMUNITY COLLEGE
Mapusaga Campus, Pago Pago 96799. Public (state) junior. 1976/1986 (WASC-Jr.). Sem. plan. Degrees: A. Pres. Eneliko Sofa'i.
Enroll.: 868
Overseas (684) 639-9155

ARIZONA

ABC Technical and Trade Schools
3781 E. Aviation Hwy., Tucson 85713. Private. 1977/1983 (NATTS). Courses of varying lengths. Certificates. Pres. E. B. Kessler.
Enroll.: 363
(602) 748-7073

ABC Welding School
2117 E. Buckeye Rd., Phoenix 85034. Private. 1978/1980 (NATTS). Courses of varying lengths. Certificates, diplomas. Ed. Dir. Torch Hall.
Enroll.: 312
(602) 244-0387

Academy of Business
3320 W. Cheryl Dr., Suite 115, Phoenix 85051. Private. 1984 (AICS). Courses of varying lengths. Certificates. Dir. Toby Jalowsky.
Enroll.: 42
(602) 942-4141

Academy of Drafting
1131 W. Broadway, Tempe 85282. Private. 1973/1978 (NATTS). Courses of varying lengths. Certificates. Pres. Francis J. Cody.
Enroll.: 35 (*f.t.* 24 m., 3 w.)
(602) 967-7813

Adelphi Institute
1917 W. Glendale Ave., Phoenix 85021. Private business. 1973/1981 (AICS). Sem. plan. Certificates, diplomas. Pres. Albert Terranova.
Enroll.: 7,415 (*f.t.* 2,263 m., 5,152 w.)
(602) 246-6550

Branch Campus
1255 W. Baseline Rd., Mesa 85202. Dir. Jule Goldberg.
(602) 831-1611

Branch Campus
230 S. Euclid St., Anaheim, CA 92802. Dir. Philip Faden.
(714) 758-8844

Branch Campus
111 N. La Brea Blvd., Inglewood, CA 90301. Dir. Steve Collins.
(818) 785-1555

Branch Campus
1633 Long Beach Blvd., Long Beach, CA 90815. Dir. Carl Pearse.
(213) 622-8585

Branch Campus
634 S. Spring St., Los Angeles, CA 90013. Dir. William A. Taylor.

Branch Campus
798 W. Fourth St., San Bernardino, CA 92410. Dir. Ken Hendershot.
(714) 381-6565

Branch Campus
428 C. St., Suite 300, San Diego, CA 92101. Dir. Edward Miller.
(619) 233-6969

Branch Campus
617 W. 17th St., Santa Ana, CA 92706. Dir. Jean Knight Heck.
(714) 835-2828

Branch Campus
14540 Sherman Way, Van Nuys, CA 91405. Dir. Craig Deonik.
(818) 785-1555

Branch Campus
475 Broadway, Gary, IN 46402. Dir. Adlee Hodges.
(219) 886-0101

Branch Campus
32-03 Steinway St., Astoria NY 11103. Dir. Danny L. Cesco.
(718) 545-8932

Branch Campus
1024 Fulton St., Brooklyn, NY 11238. Dir. Phillipe Doinel.
(212) 636-5858

Branch Campus
1712 Kings Hwy., Brooklyn, NY 11229. Dir. Barbara Reisfeld.
(212) 336-7200

Branch Campus
425 MacDonald Ave., Brooklyn, NY 11218. Dir. Frederick S. Hershinson.
(212) 438-5500

Branch Campus
601 Eighth Ave., New York, NY 10036. Dir. Thomas C. Creasy.
(212) 736-4453

Al Collins Graphic Design School
605 E. Gilbert Dr., P.O. Box 3178, Tempe 85281. Private. 1981 (NATTS). Courses of varying lengths. Certificates. Dir. Al Collins.

Arizona

Enroll.: 245
(602) 966-3000

American Graduate School of International Management, Thunderbird Campus
Glendale 85306. Private professional graduate only. 1969/1985 (NCA). Sem. plan. Degrees: M. Pres. William Voris.
Enroll.: FTE 1,099
(602) 978-7200

American Institute of Court Reporting
1313 N. Second St., Phoenix 85004. Private. 1981 (AICS). Qtr. plan. Certificates, diplomas. Exec. Dir. Ann Faulkner Kennedy.
Enroll.: 200 (*f.t.* 23 m., 177 w.)
(602) 252-4986

American Technical Center
3400 W. Osborn Rd., Phoenix 85017. Private. 1983 (NATTS). Courses of varying lengths. Certificates. Pres. George Milhoan.
Enroll.: 45
(602) 278-0971

Apollo College of Medical and Dental Careers
8503 N. 27th Ave., Phoenix 85051. Private. 1979 (NATTS). Courses of varying lengths. Diplomas. *Prof. Accred.:* Medical Assisting. Pres. and Dir. Margaret M. Carlson.
Enroll.: 239 (*f.t.* 2 m., 237 w.)
(602) 864-1571

Apollo College of Medical and Dental Careers
630 W. Southern Ave., Mesa 85202. 1986 (ABHES). Certificates. *Prof. Accred.:* Medical Assisting. Dir. Margaret M. Carlson.
Enroll.: 405 (*f.t.* 5 m., 400 w.)
(602) 831-6585

Arizona Academy of Medical and Dental Assistants
212 S. Montezuma St., Prescott 86301. Private. 1982 (ABHES). Courses of varying lengths. Certificates. *Prof. Accred.:* Medical Assisting. Dir. Betty L. McCarty.
(602) 778-4382

Arizona Barber/Styling College
3650 W. Camelback, Suite #7, Phoenix 85019. Phoenix 85019. Private. 1984 (NATTS). Courses of varying lengths. Certificates. Pres. Kenneth J. Brech.
Enroll.: 20
(602) 973-1785

Arizona Career College
1005 N. First St., Phoenix 85004. Private business. 1977/1982 (AICS). Courses of varying lengths. Certificates. Dir. Bob Jobes.
Enroll.: 257 (*f.t.* 62 m., 195 w.)
(602) 254-7301

Branch Campus
1621 W. University Dr., Mesa 85201. Dir. Barbara Willis.
(602) 834-3931

Arizona College of Medical-Dental Careers
4020 N. 19th St., Phoenix 85015. Private. 1974/1981 (ABHES). Courses of varying lengths. Diplomas. *Prof. Accred.:* Medical Assisting. Dir. Nancy Kushner.
(602) 277-1451

Arizona College of Medical-Dental Careers
3975 N. Tucson Blvd., Tucson 85716. Private. 1971/1977 (NATTS). Courses of varying lengths. Diplomas. *Prof. Accred.:* Medical Assisting, Respiratory Therapy Technology. Dir. Albert J. Chevalier.
Enroll.: 117 (*f.t.* 33 m., 84 w.)
(602) 323-3146

Arizona College of the Bible
2045 W. Northern Ave., Phoenix 85021. Private (Interdenominational). 1981 (AABC). Sem. plan. Degrees: A,B, certificates, diplomas. Pres. Leonard W. Fleming.
Enroll.: 178
(602) 995-2670

Arizona Institute of Business and Technology
10202 N. 19th Ave., Phoenix 85021. Private. 1982 (AICS). Courses of varying lengths. Certificates, diplomas. Dir. Logan P. Bauer.
Enroll.: 123 (*f.t.* 60 m., 63 w.)
(602) 242-6265

Arizona Institute of Electrolysis
4151 N. Granite Reef Rd., Suite A, Scottsdale 85251. Private. 1983 (NATTS). Courses of varying lengths. Certificates. Dir. Gail J. Walker.
Enroll.: 7
(602) 949-7055

Arizona State University
Tempe 85287. Public. 1931/1983 (NCA). Sem. plan. Degrees: B,P,M,D. *Prof. Accred.:* Architecture (B,M), Business (B,M), Construction Education, Engineering (chemical, civil,

computer systems, electrical, engineering mechanics, engineering science, industrial, mechanical-interdisciplinary studies, mechanical-special studies), Engineering Technology (aeronautical, electronic, manufacturing, mechanical, welding), Health Services Administration, Journalism, Law, Music, Nursing (B,M), Psychology, Social Work (B,M), Speech Pathology and Audiology, Teacher Education (*e,s,p*). Pres. J. Russell Nelson.
Enroll.: FTE 30,342
(602) 965-9011

ARIZONA WESTERN COLLEGE
Yuma 85364. Public (county) junior. 1968/1979 (NCA). Sem. plan. Degrees: A. *Prof. Accred.:* Nursing (A). Pres. James Carruthers.
Enroll.: FTE 1,766
(602) 726-1000

BAILIE SCHOOL OF BROADCAST
2108 E. Thomas Rd., #130, Phoenix 85016. Private. 1973/1978 (NATTS). Courses of varying lengths. Diplomas. Dir. Larry Blodgett.
Enroll.: 126
(602) 957-3626

BIOSYSTEMS INSTITUTE
1701 S. 52nd St., Tempe 85282. Private. 1978/1985 (NATTS); 1983 (NHSC). Courses of varying lengths. Certificates. *Prof. Accred.:* Respiratory Therapy. Admin. Jeannine Faucher.
Enroll.: 119
(602) 244-9301

CENTRAL ARIZONA COLLEGE
Coolidge 85228. Public (district) 2-year institutions. Accreditation includes Signal Peak Campus, Coolidge 85228; Aravaipa Campus, Winkleman 85292. 1973/1986 (NCA). Sem. plan. Degrees: A. *Prof. Accred.:* EMT-Paramedic, Medical Record Technology, Nursing (A). Pres. Dwayne Gerkin.
Enroll.: FTE 1,591
(602) 723-4141

CHAPARRAL CAREER COLLEGE
5001 E. Speedway, Tucson 85712. Private business. 1969/1983 (AICS). Qtr. plan. Degrees: A, diplomas. Pres. A. Lauren Rhude.
Enroll.: 887 (*f.t.* 156 m., 731 w.)
(602) 327-6866

BRANCH CAMPUS
3212 N. Oracle, Tucson 85705. Dir. Ralph Lewis.
(602) 888-4750

CLINTON TECHNICAL INSTITUTE/ MOTORCYCLE MECHANICS INSTITUTE CAMPUS
2844 W. Deer Valley Rd., Phoenix 85027. Private. 1979 (NATTS). Courses of varying lengths. Certificates. Dir. John C. White.
Enroll.: 252 (*f.t.* 248 m., 4 w.)
In AZ (602) 869-9644 Toll Free (800) 528-7995

COCHISE COLLEGE
Douglas 85607. Public (district) junior; accreditation includes Sierra Vista Campus. 1969/1984 (NCA). Sem. plan. Degrees: A. *Prof. Accred.:* Nursing (A). Pres. Dan Rehurek.
Enroll.: FTE 2,086
(602) 364-7943

*COLLEGE OF GANADO
Ganado 86505. Private junior. 1979/1985 (NCA). 4-1-4 plan. Degrees: A. Acting Pres. Robert Johns.
Enroll.: FTE 136
(602) 755-3442

CRESTWOOD CAREER ACADEMY
2103 E. Southern Ave., Tempe 85282. Private. 1985 (ABHES). 28-week program. Certificates. Pres. Frances D. Keller.
Enroll.: 16
(602) 820-1232

DEVRY INSTITUTE OF TECHNOLOGY
2149 W. Dunlap Ave., Phoenix 85021. Private. 1968/1979 (NATTS); 1981 (NCA). Tri. plan. Degrees: A,B, diplomas. *Prof. Accred.:* Engineering Technology (electronics). Pres. James A. Dugan.
Enroll.: 3,475 (*f.t.* 2,854 m., 552 w.)
(602) 870-9222

EASTERN ARIZONA COLLEGE
6100 Church St., Thatcher 85552. Public (district) junior. 1966/1986 (NCA). Sem. plan. Degrees: A. Pres. Gherald L. Hoopes, Jr.
Enroll.: FTE 1,586
(602) 428-1133

GRAND CANYON COLLEGE
3300 W. Camelback Rd., Phoenix 85017. Private (Southern Baptist) liberal arts and teachers. 1968/1982 (NCA). 4-1-4 plan. Degrees: B. *Prof. Accred.:* Nursing (B). Pres. Bill Williams.
Enroll.: FTE 1,489
(602) 249-3300

*Accreditation on Probation

Health Careers Institute
3320 W. Flower, Phoenix 85017. Private. 1982 (ABHES). Courses of varying lengths. Diplomas. *Prof. Accred.:* Medical Assisting, Medical Laboratory Technology. Pres. Ila G. Jarol.
Enroll.: 119
(602) 241-9217

Branch Campus
4444 E. Grant Rd., Tucson 85712. 1983 (ABHES). *Prof. Accred.:* Medical Assisting, Medical Laboratory Technology. Dir. Mary Yablonski.
Enroll.: 60
(602) 795-2865

Extension
3228 S. Fairlane, Tempe 85282.

High-Tech Institute
4021 N. 30th St., Phoenix 85016. Private. 1984 (NATTS). Courses of varying lengths. Certificates. Dir. Marilyn Pobiak.
(602) 954-9400

ITT Technical Institute
4837 E. McDowell Rd., Phoenix 85008. Private. 1977 (NATTS). Courses of varying lengths. Diplomas. Pres. Kenneth A. Gabbert.
(602) 252-2331

Extension
1840 E. Benson Hwy., Tucson 85714. Dir. John Cisler.
(602) 294-2944

Institute of Medical-Dental Technology at Mesa
240 W. First St., Mesa 85201. Private. 1980 (NATTS). Courses of varying lengths. Diplomas. Admin. Leonard Karp.
Enroll.: f.t. 30 w.
(602) 969-5505

International Training, Ltd.,
2123 S. Priest Rd., Suite 201, Tempe 85282. Private. 1985 (NATTS). Courses of varying lengths. Diplomas. Dir. Tom Yocum.
(602) 894-0907

Lamson Business College
5320 E. Pima, Tucson 85712. Private. 1977/1985 (AICS). Qtr. plan. Certificates, diplomas. Dir. Jane Gibson.
Enroll.: 702 (*f.t.* 272 m., 430 w.)
(602) 327-6851

Lamson College
4425 W. Olive, Glendale 85302. Private business. 1966/1984 (AICS). Qtr. plan. Degrees: A, certificates, diplomas. Dir. Bernie Fortunoff.
Enroll.: 628 (*f.t.* 73 m., 555 w.)
(602) 841-2067

Lamson College
1313 N. Second St., Suite 100, Phoenix 85004. Private business. 1966/1984 (AICS). Qtr. plan. Degrees: A, certificates, diplomas. Dir. Dennis Del Valle.
Enroll.: 358 (*f.t.* 41 m., 317 w.)
(602) 258-7947

Lamson College
2300 E. Broadway, Tempe 85282. Private business. 1981/1984 (AICS). Qtr. plan. Degrees: A, certificates, diplomas. Ed. Dir. James W. Cox.
Enroll.: 683 (*f.t.* 63 m., 620 w.)
(602) 968-7211

The Laural School
2538 N. Eighth St., Phoenix 85006. Private home study. 1980 (NHSC). Dir. Laura Fabricant.
(602) 992-3460

Long Medical Institute
4126 N. Black Canyon Hwy., Phoenix 85017. Private. 1981 (NATTS). Courses of varying lengths. Diplomas. *Prof. Accred.:* Respiratory Therapy Technology. Gen. Mgr. Diane Mauck.
Enroll.: 93 (*f.t.* 16 m., 77 w.)
(602) 279-9333

Maricopa County Community College District
System office, 3910 E. Washington, Phoenix 85034. Public (district) 2-year institutions. Sem. plan. Degrees: A. Chanc. Paul A. Elsner.
(602) 244-8355
The accreditation of Phoenix College, first accredited in 1928, was transferred to Maricopa County Junior College District in 1966 (NCA). The following were formerly accredited as part of Maricopa County Junior College District:

Glendale Community College
Glendale 85302. 1967/1984 (NCA). *Prof. Accred.:* Engineering Technology (electronic), Nursing (A). Pres. John R. Waltrip.
Enroll.: FTE 3,971
(602) 934-2211

MARICOPA TECHNICAL COMMUNITY COLLEGE
Phoenix 85004. 1971/1982 (NCA). *Prof. Accred.:* Radiography, Respiratory Therapy, Respiratory Therapy Technology, Surgical Technology. Pres. Myrna Harrison.
Enroll.: FTE 1,107
(602) 275-8500

MESA COMMUNITY COLLEGE
Mesa 85202. 1967/1985 (NCA). *Prof. Accred.:* Nursing (A). Pres. Wallace A. Simpson.
Enroll.: FTE 7,302
(602) 833-1261

PHOENIX COLLEGE
Phoenix 85013. 1928/1977 (NCA). *Prof. Accred.:* Dental Assisting, Dental Hygiene, Engineering Technology (electronic), Medical Laboratory Technician, Medical Record Technology, Nursing (A). Pres. William E. Berry.
Enroll.: FTE 5,452
(602) 264-2492

RIO SALADO COMMUNITY COLLEGE
135 N. Second Ave., Phoenix 85002. 1981 (NCA). Pres. Charles Green.
Enroll.: FTE 2,799
(602) 244-8355

SCOTTSDALE COMMUNITY COLLEGE
Scottsdale 85253. 1975/1980 (NCA). *Prof. Accred.:* Nursing (A). Pres. Arthur W. DeCabooter.
Enroll.: FTE 3,621
(602) 941-0999

SOUTH MOUNTAIN COMMUNITY COLLEGE
7050 S. 24th St., Phoenix 85040. 1984 (NCA). Degrees A. Pres. Raul Cardenas.
Enroll.: FTE 657
(602) 243-6661

MODERN SCHOOLS OF AMERICA, INC.
2538 N. Eighth St., Phoenix 85006. Private home study. 1980 (NHSC). Dir. Paul Fabricant.
(602) 990-8346

MOHAVE COMMUNITY COLLEGE
Kingman 86401. Public junior. Accreditation includes Kingman, Lake Havasu, and Mohave Valley Campuses. 1981/1986 (NCA). Sem. plan. Degrees: A. Pres. Charles W. Hall.
Enroll.: FTE 1,041
(602) 757-4331

MOUNTAIN STATES TECHNICAL INSTITUTE
3120 N. 34th Dr., Phoenix 85017. Private. 1979/1980 (NATTS). Courses of varying lengths. Diplomas. Dir. Ernest L. Gaddie.
Enroll.: 220 (*f.t.* 180 m., 40 w.)
(602) 269-7555

NATIONAL EDUCATION CENTER-ARIZONA AUTOMOTIVE INSTITUTE CAMPUS
6829 N. 46th Ave., Glendale 85301. Private. 1972/1983 (NATTS). Qtr. plan. Diplomas. Dir. Allan J. Reed.
Enroll.: 1,175
(602) 934-7273

NATIONAL EDUCATION CENTER-BRYMAN CAMPUS
9215 N. Black Canyon Rd., Phoenix 85021. Private. 1973/1977 (NATTS). Modular courses. Diplomas. *Prof. Accred.:* Medical Assisting. Dir. George C. Ballew.
Enroll.: 102 (*f.t.* 2 m., 100 w.)
(602) 861-9200

NAVAJO COMMUNITY COLLEGE
Tsaile 86556. Public junior. 1976/1984 (NCA). Sem. plan. Degrees: A. Pres. Dean C. Jackson.
Enroll.: FTE 1,200
(602) 724-3311

NORTH AMERICAN COLLEGE
1777 W. Camelback, Phoenix 85015. Private business. 1982 (AICS). Courses of varying lengths. Certificates, diplomas. Dir. John Hammond.
Enroll.: 411 (*f.t.* 131 m., 280 w.)
(602) 248-0648

NORTHERN ARIZONA UNIVERSITY
Flagstaff 86001. Public (state). 1930/1978 (NCA). Sem. plan. Degrees: A,B,M,D. *Prof. Accred.:* Business (B,M), Dental Hygiene, Engineering (civil, computer science and engineering, electrical, mechanical), Engineering Technology (civil, electrical, mechanical), Forestry, Music, Nursing (B), Physical Therapy, Radiologic Technology, Teacher Education (*e,s,p*). Pres. Eugene Hughes.
Enroll.: FTE 10,393
(602) 523-3232

NORTHLAND PIONEER COLLEGE
Holbrook 86025. Public junior; accreditation includes centers at Holbrook, Oraibi, Saint Johns, Showlow, Snowflake, Springerville, and Winslow. 1980 (NCA). Sem. plan. Degrees: A, certificates. Pres. Marvin Vasher.

Enroll.: 1,505
(602) 524-6111

NORTHWEST SCHOOLS
PHOENIX TRAINING CENTER
1700 E. Thomas Rd., Phoenix 85016. Private; resident training site. 1985 (NHSC). Exec. Dir. James Hockman.
(602) 277-6062

THE PARALEGAL INSTITUTE
1315 W. Indian School Rd., Phoenix 85065. Private home study. 1979/1983 (NHSC). Pres. John W. Morrison.
(602) 263-7950.

PEDIGREE PROFESSIONAL SCHOOL FOR DOG GROOMING EXTENSION
3781 E. Technical Dr., Suite 5, Tucson 85713. Private. 1985 (NATTS). Courses of varying lengths. Certificates. Pres. E. B. Kessler.
(602) 748-7073

PHOENIX INSTITUTE OF TECHNOLOGY
2555-B E. University Dr., Phoenix 85034. Private. 1976/1979 (NATTS). Qtr. plan. Diplomas. V. Pres. Ray Sevy.
Enroll.: 1,350
(602) 244-8111

PHOENIX TECHNICAL AND TRADE SCHOOL
603 S. First Ave., Phoenix 85003. Private. 1976/1982 (NATTS). Courses of varying lengths. Certificates, diplomas. Dir. Mike Kessler.
Enroll.: 220 (*f.t.* 212 m., 8 w.)
(602) 252-7304

PIMA COUNTY COMMUNITY COLLEGE DISTRICT
Tucson 85709. Public (district) junior. Accreditation includes Community Campus, Downtown Campus, East Education Center, West Campus. 1975/1984 (NCA). Sem. plan. Degrees: A. *Prof. Accred.:* Dental Assisting, Dental Laboratory Technology, Nursing (A), Radiography, Respiratory Therapy. Pres. S. James Manilla.
Enroll.: FTE 9,709
(602) 884-6047

PIMA MEDICAL INSTITUTE
1010 N. Alvernon Way, P.O. Box 18451, Tucson 85711. Private. 1982 (ABHES). Courses of varying lengths. Diplomas. *Prof. Accred.:* Medical Assisting, Medical Laboratory Assisting. Chairman Richard L. Luebke.
Enroll.: 238(602) 326-1600

EXTENSION
5501 N. Oracle Ave., Tucson 85704.

PLAZA THREE ACADEMY
4343 N. 16th St., Phoenix 85016. Private. 1977/1984 (NATTS). Courses of varying lengths. Certificates. Pres. Richard Rogers.
Enroll.: 800 (*f.t.* 34 m., 138 w.)
(602) 264-9703

EXTENSION
6367 E. Tanque Verde Rd., Suite 100, Tucson 85715.
(602) 745-2500

PRESCOTT COLLEGE
220 Grove Ave., Prescott 86301. Private liberal arts. 1984 (NCA). 4-1-4 plan. Degrees: B. Pres. Ralph Bohrson.
Enroll.: FTE 198
(602) 778-2090

THE REFRIGERATION SCHOOL, INC.
4210 E. Washington St., Phoenix 85034. Private. 1973/1978 (NATTS). Courses of varying lengths. Diplomas. Dir. Ola Lee Loney.
Enroll.: 250 (*f.t.* 246 m., 4 w.)
(602) 275-7133

ROBERTO-VENN SCHOOL OF LUTHIERY
5445 E. Washington St., Phoenix 85034. Private technical. 1979 (NATTS). Courses of varying lengths. Certificates. Dir. John H. Roberto.
Enroll.: 21 (*f.t.* 19 m., 2 w.)
(602) 267-9241

ST. JOHN'S ACADEMY, INC.
2007 W. Peoria, Phoenix 85029. Private. 1983 (NATTS). Courses of varying lengths. Diplomas. Pres. Barbara St. John.
Enroll.: 25
(602) 997-6369

SOUTH WEST ACADEMY OF TECHNOLOGY
1043 E. Indian School Rd., Phoenix 85014; (Mailing Address: P.O. Box 30617, Phoenix 85046). Private. 1983 (NATTS). Courses of varying lengths. Certificates. Dir. Harry E. Wujastyk.
Enroll.: 9
(602) 277-0847

*SOUTHWESTERN CONSERVATIVE BAPTIST BIBLE COLLEGE
2625 E. Cactus Rd., Phoenix 85032. Private (Baptist) professional. 1977 (AABC). Sem. plan. Degrees: B. Pres. Wesley A. Olsen.

*Candidate for Accreditation by Regional Accrediting Commission

Enroll.: 138
(602) 992-6101

SOUTHWESTERN MEDICAL SOCIETY ACADEMY
2021 North Central Ave., Phoenix 85004. Private. 1979 (NATTS). Courses of varying lengths. Certificates. *Prof. Accrd.:* Medical Assisting. Dir. Carole Miller.
Enroll.: 325 (*f.t.* 6 m., 319 w.)
(602) 252-5696

BRANCH CAMPUS
2115 E. Southern Ave., Tempe 85282.
(602) 820-4055

STERLING SCHOOL
810 E. Indian School Rd., Phoenix 85014. Private business. 1981/1984 (AICS). Courses of varying lengths. Certificates, diplomas. Dir. Ruby Sterling.
Enroll.: 33 (*f.t.* 8 m., 25 w.)
(602) 277-5276

TUCSON COLLEGE OF BUSINESS
7830 E. Broadway, Tucson 85710. Private. 1966/1978 (AICS). Courses of varying lengths. Certificates, diplomas. Pres. M. A. Mikhail.
Enroll.: 1,517 (*f.t.* 683 m., 834 w.)
(602) 206-3261

UNITED STATES ARMY INTELLIGENCE CENTER AND SCHOOL
Fort Huachuca 85613. Public (federal). 1980/1985 (NCA). Courses of varying lengths. Certificates. Commander Brig. Gen. Richard W. Wilmot.
Enroll.: 4,593
(602) 538-2223

UNIVERSAL TECHNICAL INSTITUTE
3121 W. Weldon Ave., Phoenix 85017. Private. 1968/1983 (NATTS). Courses of varying lengths. Certificates. Pres. Robert I. Sweet.
Enroll.: 1,325 (*f.t.* 1,315 m., 10 w.)
(602) 264-4164

UNIVERSITY OF ARIZONA
Tucson 85721. Public (state). 1917/1980 (NCA). Sem plan. Degrees: B,P,M,D. *Prof. Accred.:* Architecture(B), Business (B,M), Dietetics, Engineering (aerospace, agricultural, chemical, civil, electrical, geological, mechanical, metallurgical, mining, nuclear), Forestry, Journalism, Landscape Architecture (B), Law, Librarianship, Medical Laboratory Technology, Medical Technology, Medicine, Music, Nuclear Medicine Technology, Nursing (B,M), Pharmacy, Psychology, Radiation Therapy Technology, Rehabilitation Counseling, Speech Pathology and Audiology, Teacher Education (*e,s,p*). Pres. Henry Koffler.
Enroll.: FTE 25,438
(602) 621-2211

UNIVERSITY OF PHOENIX
2525 N. Third St., Phoenix 85004. Private professional. 1978/1982 (NCA). Sem. plan; also 8-wk. sessions year round. Degrees: B,M. Pres. Harold J. O'Donnell.
Enroll.: FTE 4,152
(602) 258-3666

WESTERN INTERNATIONAL UNIVERSITY
10202 N. 19th Ave., Phoenix 85021. Private 1984 (NCA). Tri. plan. Degrees: B,M. Chanc. Robert S. Webber.
Enroll.: FTE 282
(602) 943-2311

YAVAPAI COLLEGE
1100 E. Sheldon, Prescott 86301. Public (district) junior. 1975/1980 (NCA). Accreditation includes Verde Valley Center, Clarkdale. Sem. plan. Degrees: A. *Prof. Accred.:* Nursing (A). Pres. Paul D. Walker.
Enroll.: FTE 1,610
(602) 445-7300

ARKANSAS

AMERICAN COLLEGE
3448 N. College, Fayetteville 72703. Private business. 1972/1985 (AICS). Courses of varying lengths. Degrees: A, diplomas. Dir. Mary Z. Pate.
Enroll.: 3,542 (*f.t.* 429 m., 3,113 w.)
(501) 442-2364

BRANCH CAMPUS
2840 Florida Blvd., Baton Rouge, LA 70802. Dir. W. E. Butler.
(504) 346-8545

BRANCH CAMPUS
2025 Canal St., Suite 210, New Orleans, LA 70112. Dir. Dorris G. Perry.
(504) 822-1900

BRANCH CAMPUS
820 Cotton St., Shreveport, LA 71101. Dir. Arthur Lovett.
(318) 424-1000

BRANCH CAMPUS
2906 N. State St., Suite 250, Jackson, MS 39216. Dir. Dave Redd.
(601) 362-0909

BRANCH CAMPUS
2301 S. Congress, Suite 27, Austin, TX 78704. Dir. Chris Miteff.
(512) 462-0044

BRANCH CAMPUS
410 S. Main St., Suite 201, San Antonio, TX 78204. Dir. Chris Miteff.
(512) 271-7222

AMERICAN COLLEGE
115 Central Mall, Fort Smith 72913. Private business. 1984 (AICS). Courses of varying lengths. Degrees: A, diplomas. Executive Dir. J. Michael Shelton.
(501) 452-5556

ARKANSAS COLLEGE
Batesville 72501. Private (Presbyterian, U.S.) liberal arts. 1959/1982 (NCA). 4-1-4 plan. Degrees: B. *Prof. Accred.:* Medical Technology, Teacher Education (*e,s,p*). Pres. Dan C. West.
Enroll.: FTE 498
(501) 793-9813

ARKANSAS STATE UNIVERSITY-SYSTEM OFFICE
State University 72467. Public. Pres. Eugene W. Smith.
(501) 882-6452.

ARKANSAS STATE UNIVERSITY-MAIN CAMPUS
State University 72467. Public. 1928/1983 (NCA). Sem. plan. Degrees: A,B,M. *Prof. Accred.:* Business (B,M), Engineering (agricultural), Journalism, Medical Technology, Music, Nursing (A,B), Radiography, Rehabilitation Counseling, Social Work (B), Teacher Education (*e,s,p*). Pres. Eugene W. Smith.
Enroll.: FTE 6,758
(501) 972-3030

ARKANSAS STATE UNIVERSITY–BEEBE BRANCH
Beebe 72012. 1971/1982 (NCA). Sem. plan. Degrees: A. Chanc. William Owen.
Enroll.: FTE 536
(501) 882-6452

ARKANSAS TECH UNIVERSITY
Russellville 72801. Public (state) liberal arts. 1930/1981 (NCA). Sem. plan. Degrees: A,B,M. *Prof. Accred.:* Medical Assistant, Medical Record Administration, Music, Nursing (B), Teacher Education (*e,s*). Pres. Kenneth G. Kersh.
Enroll.: FTE 2,776
(501) 968-0237

CAPITAL CITY BUSINESS COLLEGE
K-Mart Shopping Center, Hwy. 64 E., Russellville 72801. Private. 1973/1985 (AICS). Qtr. plan. Certificates, diplomas. Dir. Kim Bradford.
Enroll.: 374 (*f.t.* 90 m., 284 w.)
(501) 968-1825

BRANCH CAMPUS
908 Broadway, Kansas City, MO 64105. Dir. Stanley E. Howard.
(816) 474-5997

BRANCH CAMPUS
411 N. Tenth St., Suite 210, St. Louis, MO 63101. Dir. Nancy Burstein.
(314) 436-5041.

*CAPITAL CITY JUNIOR COLLEGE
P.O. Box 4818, Little Rock 72214. Private. 1966/1980 (AICS). Qtr. plan. Degrees: A, certificates, diplomas. Dir. Kenneth D. Sullivan.
Enroll.: FTE 430
(501) 562-0700

*Candidate for Accreditation by Regional Accrediting Commission

*Central Baptist College
CBC Station, Conway 72032. Private (Baptist) professional. 1977 (AABC). Sem. plan. Degrees: A,B. Pres. James Ray Raines.
Enroll.: 179
(501) 329-6872

College of the Ozarks
Clarksville 72830. Private (United Presbyterian) liberal arts. 1931/1983 (NCA). 4-1-4 plan. Degrees: B. *Prof. Accred.:* Teacher Education (*e,s,p*). Pres. Fritz H. Ehren.
Enroll.: FTE 632
(501) 754-3839

Draughon School of Business
P.O. Box 11, Little Rock 72203. Private. 1953/1984 (AICS). Courses of varying lengths. Certificates, diplomas. Dir. L.E. Burford.
Enroll.: 310 (*f.t.* 80 m., 230 w.)
(501) 372-2128

East Arkansas Community College
Forrest City 72335. Public 2-year. 1979/1982 (NCA). Sem. plan. Degrees: A. Pres. Bob C. Burns.
Enroll.: FTE 572
(501) 633-4480

Eastern College of Health Vocations
6423 Forbing Rd., Little Rock 72209. Private. 1981 (ABHES). Courses of varying lengths. Diplomas. *Prof. Accred.:* Medical Assisting. Dir. Teresa Bour.
(501) 568-0211

Branch Campus
2748 Metairie Lawn Dr., Metarie, LA 70002. Pres. Sue Dalto.
(504) 834-8644

Garland County Community College
No. One College Dr., Mid-America Park, Hot Springs 71901. Public junior. 1981/1986 (NCA). Sem. plan. Degrees: A. *Prof. Accred.:* Medical Laboratory Technology, Nursing (A), Radiography. Pres. Gerald H. Fisher.
Enroll.: FTE 725
(501) 767-9371

Harding University
Searcy 72143. Private (Churches of Christ) liberal arts. 1954/1985 (NCA). Sem plan. Degrees: B,M. *Prof. Accred.:* Music, Nursing (B), Social Work (B), Teacher Education (*e,s*). Pres. Clifton L. Ganus, Jr.
Enroll.: FTE 2,689
(501) 268 6161

*Candidate for Accreditation by Regional Accrediting Commission

Henderson State University
Arkadelphia 71923. Public liberal arts and teachers. 1934/1982 (NCA). Sem. plan. Degrees: A,B,M. *Prof. Acccred.:* Music, Nursing (B), Teacher Education (*e,s,p*). Pres. Charles D. Dunn.
Enroll.: FTE 2,417
(501) 246-5511

Hendrix College
Conway 72032. Private (United Methodist) liberal arts. 1924/1979 (NCA). Sem. plan. Degrees: B. *Prof. Accred.:* Music, Teacher Education (*e,s*). Pres. Joe B. Hatcher.
Enroll.: FTE 989
(501) 329-6811

John Brown University
Siloam Springs 72761. Private liberal arts college. 1962/1982 (NCA). Sem. plan. Degrees: B. *Prof. Accred.:* Teacher Education (*e,s*). Pres. John E. Brown, III.
Enroll.: FTE 780
(501) 524-3131

Mississippi County Community College
Blytheville 72316. Public junior. 1980/1985 (NCA). Sem. plan. Degrees: A. Pres. John Sullins.
Enroll.: FTE 749
(501) 762-1020

National Education Center—Arkansas College of Technology Campus
9720 Rodney Parham, Little Rock 72207. Private. 1972/1977 (NATTS). Qtr. plan. Degrees: A, certificates. Admin. Dir. Lyle Groth.
Enroll.: 635 (*f.t.* 445 m., 149 w.)
(501) 224-8200

New Tyler Barber College
1221 E. Seventh St., N. Little Rock 72114. Private. 1984 (NATTS). Courses of varying lengths. Certificates. Pres. Daniel Bryant.
(501) 375-0377

North Arkansas Community College
Harrison 72601. Public 2-year. 1979 (NCA). Sem. plan. Degrees: A. Pres. William Bert Baker.
Enroll.: FTE 1,041
(501) 743-3000

Ouachita Baptist University
Arkadelphia 71923. Private (Southern Baptist). 1927/1980 (NCA). Sem. plan. Degrees:

B,M. *Prof. Accred.:* Music, Teacher Education (*e,s*). Pres. Daniel R. Grant.
Enroll.: FTE 1,161
(501) 246-4531

PHILANDER SMITH COLLEGE
812 West 13th St., Little Rock 72202. Private (United Methodist) liberal arts. 1949/1984 (NCA). Sem. plan. Degrees: B. Pres. Hazo W. Carter., Jr.
Enroll.: FTE 487
(501) 375-9845

PHILLIPS COUNTY COMMUNITY COLLEGE
Helena 72342. Public (district) junior. 1972/1985 (NCA). Sem. plan. Degrees: A. *Prof. Accred.:* Medical Laboratory Technology (A), Nursing (A). Pres. John W. Easley.
Enroll.: FTE 1,018
(501) 338-6474

SHORTER COLLEGE
North Little Rock 72114. Private junior. 1981 (NCA). Sem. plan. Degrees: A. Pres. John L. Phillips.
Enroll.: FTE 103

SOUTH CENTRAL CAREER COLLEGE
3901 McCain Park Dr., North Little Rock 72116. Private business. 1979/1982 (AICS). Qtr. plan. Certificates, diplomas. Pres. Fred A. Ellis.
Enroll.: 881 (*f.t.* 173 m., 708 w.)
(501) 758-6800

BRANCH CAMPUS
Jefferson Square Ctr., 208 Olive St., Pine Bluff 71603-5439. Dir. of Admissions Joni Hagan.
(501) 848-3400

SOUTHERN ARKANSAS UNIVERSITY—CENTRAL OFFICE
Magnolia 71753. Public (state). Pres. Harold T. Brinson.
(501) 234-5120

SOUTHERN ARKANSAS UNIVERSITY—MAIN CAMPUS
Magnolia 71753. Public (state) liberal arts and teachers. 1929/1983 (NCA). Sem. plan. Degrees: A,B,M. *Prof. Accred.:* Medical Laboratory Technology, Music, Nursing (A), Teacher Education (*e,s*). Pres. Harold T. Brinson.
Enroll.: FTE 1,788
(501) 234-5120

SOUTHERN ARKANSAS UNIVERSITY—EL DORADO BRANCH
300 S. West Ave., El Dorado 71730. Public (state) community. 1983 (NCA). Sem. plan. Degrees: A. Chanc. Ben Whitfield.
Enroll.: FTE 346
(501) 862-8131

SOUTHERN ARKANSAS UNIVERSITY—TECHNICAL BRANCH
SAU Tech Sta., East Camden 71701. Public (state) 2-year. 1980/1985 (NCA). Sem. plan. Degrees: A. *Prof. Accred.:* Dental Assisting. Chanc. George J. Brown.
Enroll.: FTE 444
(501) 574-0741

SOUTHERN BAPTIST COLLEGE
Walnut Ridge 72476. Private (Southern Baptist). 1963/1984 (NCA). Sem. plan. Degrees: A,B. Pres. D. Jack Nicholas.
Enroll.: FTE 355
(501) 886-6741

UNIVERSITY OF ARKANSAS—CENTRAL OFFICE
Admin. Bldg. 425, Fayetteville 72702. Pres. Ray Thornton.
(501) 575-2000

UNIVERSITY OF ARKANSAS AT FAYETTEVILLE
Fayetteville 72701. Public (state). 1924/1976 (NCA). Accreditation includes Graduate Institute ofTechnology, Graduate School of Social Work, Law School and Medical Center at Little Rock. Sem. plan. Degrees: A,B,P,M,D. *Prof. Accred.:* Accounting (Type A,C), Architecture (B), Business (B,M), Cytotechnology, Dental Hygiene, Dietetics, Engineering (agricultural, chemical, civil, electrical, industrial, mechanical), Home Economics, Journalism, Landscape Architecture (B), Law, Medicine, Music, Nursing (A,B), Pharmacy, Psychology, Radiography, Respiratory Therapy, Speech Pathology, Surgical Technology, Teacher Education (*e,s,p*). Chanc. Daniel E. Ferritor.
Enroll.: FTE 12,570
Medical Center: *Enroll.:* 1,421 (*f.t.* 642 m., 617 w.)
(501) 575-2000

UNIVERSITY OF ARKANSAS AT LITTLE ROCK
33rd St. and University Ave., Little Rock 72204. 1929/1980 (NCA). Sem. plan. Degrees: A,B,P,M. *Prof. Accred.:* Business

(B,M), Dental Hygiene, Engineering Technology (electronics), Health Administration, Journalism, Law (ABA only), Medical Technology, Music, Nursing (A,B,M), Social Work (M), Speech Pathology and Audiology, Teacher Education (*e,s*). Chanc. James H. Young.
Enroll.: FTE 7,001
(501) 569-3000

UNIVERSITY OF ARKANSAS AT MONTICELLO
Monticello 71655. Public (state) liberal arts and technological. 1928/1985 (NCA). Sem. plan. Degrees: B. *Prof. Accred.:* Forestry, Nursing (A), Teacher Education (*e,s*). Chanc. Fred J. Taylor.
Enroll.: FTE 1,621
(501) 367-6811

UNIVERSITY OF ARKANSAS AT PINE BLUFF
Pine Bluff 71601. Public (state) liberal arts and professional. 1950/1982 (NCA). Sem. plan. Degrees: B. *Prof. Accred.:* Home Economics, Music, Nursing (B), Teacher Education (*e,s*). Acting Chanc. J. B. Johnson.
Enroll.: FTE 2,412
(501) 535-6700

UNIVERSITY OF CENTRAL ARKANSAS
Conway 72032. Public liberal arts and teachers. 1931/1985 (NCA). School of Health Sciences at Little Rock. Sem. plan. Degrees: B,M. *Prof. Accred.:* Business (B), Music, Nursing (B), Occupational Therapy, Physical Therapy, Teacher Education (*e,s,p*). Pres. Jefferson D. Farris, Jr.
Enroll.: FTE 5,829
(501) 329-2931

WESTARK COMMUNITY COLLEGE
Fort Smith 72903. Public (district). 1973/1985 (NCA). Sem. plan. Degrees: A. *Prof. Accred.:* Medical Technology, Nursing (A), Surgical Technology. Pres. Joel Stubblefield.
Enroll.: fte 2,035
(501) 785-4241

CALIFORNIA

ABC Colleges
2213 Kern St., Fresno 93721. Private business. 1976/1984 (AICS). Courses of varying lengths. Certificates. Adm. N. M. Stamoulis.
Enroll.: 148 (*f.t.* 33 m., 115 w.)
(209) 268-4481

AMS College
10025 Shoemaker Ave., Santa Fe Springs 90670. Private. 1980 (NATTS); 1983 (NHSC). Qtr. plan. Certificates. Chairman Charles R. Ochsner.
Enroll.: 44 (*f.t.* 42 m., 2 w.)
(213) 944-0121 or Toll Free: (800) 423-4678

Academy International
P.O. Box 90859, Santa Barbara 93190. Private. 1972/1980 (NATTS). Courses of varying lengths. Diplomas. Admin. Greg Fahlman.
Enroll.: 38
(805) 965-5264

*Academy of Art College
540 Powell St., San Francisco 94108. Independent. 1972/1981 (NATTS). Sem. plan. Degrees: B, certificates, diplomas. *Prof. Accred.:* Art, Interior Design. Pres. Donald A. Haight.
Enroll.: 1,689 (*f.t.* 586 m., 683 w.)
(415) 673-4200

Academy of Stenographic Arts
347 Dolores St., San Francisco 94110. Private. 1978/1984 (AICS). Courses of varying lengths. Certificates. Pres. Thomas Kerrins.
Enroll.: 604 (*f.t.* 25 m., 579 w.)
(415) 861-0635

Academy Pacific Business and Travel College
6253 Hollywood Blvd., Hollywood 90028. Private. 1968/1978 (NATTS). Courses of varying lengths. Diplomas. Pres. Marsha Toy.
Enroll.: 227 (*f.t.* 122 m., 105 w.)
(213) 462-3211

Airco Technical Institute
189 W. Victoria St., Long Beach 90805. Private. 1985 (NATTS). Courses of varying lengths. Certificates. Dir. Edward J. Miller.
(213) 604-8511

*Candidate for Accreditation by Regional Accrediting Commission

Airco Technical Institute
8383 Capwell Dr., Oakland 94621. Private. 1981 (NATTS). Courses of varying lengths. Certificates. Dir. Craig A. Wood.
Enroll.: 320 (*f.t.* 300 m., 20 w.)
(415) 562-8980

Allan Hancock College
800 S. College Dr., Santa Maria 93454. Public (district) junior. 1952/1986 (WASC-Jr.). Sem. plan. Degrees: A. *Prof. Accred.:* Medical Assisting. Supt.-Pres. Gary R. Edelbrock.
Enroll.: 6,654
(805) 922-6966

American Academy of Dramatic Arts West
2550 Paloma St., Pasadena 91107. Private 2-yr. professional. 1981/1986 (WASC-Jr.). Sem. plan. Degrees: A, certificates. Dir. George C. Cuttingham.
Enroll.: 212
(818) 798-0777

*American Baptist Seminary of the West
2515 Hillegass St., Berkeley 94704. Private (American Baptist Convention) professional; graduate only. Sem. plan. Degrees: P,M,D. *Prof. Accred.:* Theology (1938/1985, ATS). Pres. Wesley H. Brown.
Enroll.: 127
(415) 841-1905

American Business College—Technical Division
5952 El Cajon Blvd., San Diego 92115. Private. 1970/1981 (NATTS). Courses of varying lengths. Certificates, diplomas. Pres. Frank E. Hollar.
Enroll.: 485 (*f.t.* 342 m., 142 w.)
(619) 582-1319

Branch Campus
1541 Broadway, San Diego 92101.
(619) 239-4138

American College of Optics
3630 Wilshire Blvd., Second Floor, Los Angeles 90020-1597. 1983 (ABHES). Courses of varying lengths. Certificates. Pres. David A. Pyle.
(213) 383-2862

*Candidate for Accreditation by Regional Accrediting Commission

AMERICAN CONSERVATORY THEATRE
450 Geary St., San Francisco 94102. Independent professional. 1984 (WASC-Sr.). Sem. plan. Degrees: M. Dir. Lawrence Hecht.
Enroll.: FTE 62
(415) 771-3880

AMERICAN FILM INSTITUTE CENTER FOR ADVANCED FILM STUDIES
2021 N. Western Ave., Los Angeles 90027. Private professional; graduate only. 1982. Sem. plan. Degrees: M. *Prof. Accred.:* Art. Dirs. Jean Firstenberg and Antoine Vellani.
Enroll.: 130 (*f.t.* 92 m., 38 w.)
(213) 856-7600

AMERICAN INSTITUTE OF TECHNOLOGY
1490 Island Ave., San Diego 92101. Private. 1985 (NATTS). Courses of varying lengths. Certificates. Dir. Brad Landeberjer.
(619) 235-6238

AMERICAN RIVER COLLEGE
4700 College Oak Dr., Sacramento 95841. Public (district) junior. 1959/1984 (WASC-Jr.). Sem. plan. Degrees: A. *Prof. Accred.:* Medical Assisting, Respiratory Therapy. Pres. Queen F. Randall.
Enroll.: 17,413
(916) 484-8011

AMERICAN SCHOOL OF DIAMOND CUTTING
14599 E. Whittier Blvd., Whittier 90605. Private. 1972/1976 (NATTS). 10-month course. Certificates. Dir. Jeffrey Lopez.
Enroll.: 17 (*f.t.* 15 m., 2 w.)
(213) 945-7751

AMERICAN TECHNICAL COLLEGE FOR CAREER TRAINING
191 S. "E" St., San Bernardino 92401. Private. 1971/1982 (NATTS). Courses of varying lengths. Certificates. Dir. Steve S. Hu.
Enroll.: 21 (*f.t.* 5 m., 16 w.)
(714) 885-3857

AMERICAN TECHNICAL INSTITUTE
6843 Lennox Ave., Van Nuys 91405. Private. 1980/1982 (NATTS). Courses of varying lengths. Certificates. Pres. Gary P. Booth.
Enroll.: 290
(818) 988-7054

ORANGE COUNTY BRANCH
15062 Jackson St., Midway City 92655.
(714) 891-9211

ANDON COLLEGE AT MODESTO
1314 H St., Modesto 95354. Private. 1985 (ABHES). Courses of varying lengths. Certificates. *Prof. Accred.:* Medical Assisting. Pres. Donald J. Bogue.
(209) 529-6011

ANDON COLLEGE AT STOCKTON
(Extension)
1201 N. El Dorado St., Stockton 95202.

ANTELOPE VALLEY COLLEGE
3041 West Ave. K, Lancaster 93534. Public (district) junior. 1952/1986 (WASC-Jr.). Sem. plan. Degrees: A. *Prof. Accred.:* Radiology. Interim Supt./Pres. Byron Cooper.
Enroll.: 6,649
(805) 943-3241

*ARMSTRONG UNIVERSITY
2222 Harold Way, Berkeley 94704. Proprietary business and law. 1963/1981 (WASC-Sr.). Qtr. plan. Degrees: A,B,P,M. Pres. John E. Armstrong.
Enroll.: FTE 421
(415) 848-2500

ART CENTER COLLEGE OF DESIGN
1700 Lida St., Pasadena 91103. Independent professional. 1955/1983 (WASC-Sr.). Tri. plan. Degrees: B,M. *Prof. Accred.:* Art. Pres. David R. Brown.
Enroll.: FTE 1,191
(818) 557-1700

ASSOCIATED TECHNICAL COLLEGE
1670 W. Wilshire Blvd., Los Angeles 90017. Private. 1969/1975 (NATTS). Courses of varying lengths. Certificates, diplomas. Pres. Samuel Romano.
Enroll.: 708 (*f.t.* 213 m., 495 w.)
(213) 484-2444

EXTENSION
1101 S. Anaheim Blvd., Anaheim 92805. Dir. William Bennedetti.
(714) 520-9701

EXTENSION
630 Ash St., San Diego 92805. Dir. Ken McNalley.
(619) 234-2181

AUTO BODY INSTITUTE
2961 "K" St., P.O.Box 13686, San Diego 92113. Private. 1982 (NATTS). Courses of varying lengths. Diplomas. Pres. Gene Golliet.
Enroll.: 29 (*f.t.* 28 m., 1 w.)
(714) 231-0052

*Accreditation on Probation

Azusa Pacific University
Citrus Ave. and Alosta, Azusa 91702. Independent liberal arts. 1964/1982 (WASC-Sr.). 4-4-1 plan. Degrees: A,B,M. *Prof. Accred.:* Nursing (B), Social Work. Pres. Paul E. Sago.
Enroll.: FTE 2,174
(818) 969-3434

Bailie School of Broadcast
1875 S. Bascom Ave., Suite 410, Campbell 95008. Private. 1976 (NATTS). Courses of varying lengths. Diplomas. Dir. Tom Hart.
Enroll.: 42 (*f.t.* 31 m., 11 w.)
(408) 298-7300

Bailie School of Broadcast
420 Taylor, San Francisco 94102. Private. 1985 (NATTS). Courses of varying lengths. Diplomas. Dir. James A. Trudeau.
Enroll.: 100
(415) 441-0707

Bakersfield College
1801 Panorama Dr., Bakersfield 93305. Public (district) junior. 1952/1985 (WASC-Jr.). Sem. plan. Degrees: A. *Prof. Accred.:* Dental Assisting, Radiologic Technology. Pres. Richard L. Wright.
Enroll.: 9,549
(805) 395-4011

Barclay College
777 12th St., Suite 300, Sacramento 95814. Private business. 1979/1985 (AICS). Courses of varying lengths. Certification Dir. Zoe Smith.
Enroll.: 157 (*f.t.* 26 m., 131 w.)
(916) 448-8118

Branch Campus
5172 Orange Ave., Cypress 90630. Dir. Charles S. Shrader.
(714) 827-5853

Branch Campus
504 N. Mountain View, San Bernardino 92401. Dir. Wilma E. Smith.
(714) 381-1445

Branch Campus
10403 International Plaza Drive, St. Ann, MO 63074. Dir. Mac N. Callis.
(314) 426-4200

Barstow College
2700 Barstow Rd., Barstow 92311. Public (district) junior. 1962/1984 (WASC-Jr.). Sem. plan. Degrees: A. Pres. J. W. Edwin Spear.
Enroll.: 1,776
(619) 252-2411

Bay City College Dental-Medical Assistants
211 Sutter St., 10th Floor, San Francisco 94108. Private. 1969/1978 (NATTS). Courses of varying lengths. Certificates, diplomas. *Prof. Accred.:* Medical Assisting. Pres. Sarah A. Davis.
Enroll.: 178 (*f.t.* 66 m., 112 w.)
(415) 434-0626

Bay-Valley Tech
2550 Scott Blvd., Santa Clara 95050. Private. 1976/1983 (NATTS). Qtr. plan. Courses of varying lengths. Degrees: A, certificates, diplomas. Dir. Keith P. Binkle, Jr.
Enroll.: 479 (*f.t.* 294 m., 70 w.)
(408) 727-1060

Bethany Bible College
800 Bethany Dr., Scotts Valley 95066. Independent (Assemblies of God) professional. 1959/1978 (AABC); 1966/1985 (WASC-Sr.) 4-1-4 plan. Degrees: A,B. Pres. Richard B. Foth.
Enroll.: FTE 468
(408) 438-3800

Biola University
13800 Biola Ave., La Mirada 90639. Independent liberal arts and professional. 1948/1978 (AABC); 1961/1983 (WASC-Sr.). 4-1-4 plan. Degrees: B,P,M,D. *Prof. Accred.:* Music, Nursing (B), Psychology, Theology. Pres. Clyde Cook.
Enroll.: FTE 2,577
(213) 944-0351

Brooks College
4825 E. Pacific Coast Hwy., Long Beach 90804. Private 2-year. 1976 (NATTS); 1977/1982 (WASC-Jr.). Qtr. plan. Degrees: A, diplomas. Dir. of Admin. Steven B. Sotraidis.
Enroll.: 892
(213) 597-6611

Brooks Institute
801 Alston Rd., Santa Barbara, 93108. Private senior business. 1984 (AICS). Tri. plan. Degrees: A,B,M. Pres. Ernest H. Brooks, III.
Enroll.: 689
(805) 969-2291

Bryan College of Court Reporting
2511 Beverly Blvd., Los Angeles 90057. Private. 1971/1983 (AICS). Courses of varying lengths. Certificates. Pres. James T. Patterson.
Enroll.: 543 (*f.t.* 48 m., 495 w.)
(213) 484-8850

BUTTE COLLEGE
3536 Butte Campus Dr., Oroville 95965. Public (district) junior. 1972/1986 (WASC-Jr.). Sem. plan. Degrees: A. *Prof. Accred.:* Respiratory Therapy. Pres. Wendell L. Reeder.
Enroll.: 6,647
(916) 895-2484

CABRILLO COLLEGE
6500 Soquel Dr., Aptos 95003. Public (district) junior. 1961/1984 (WASC-Jr.). Sem. plan. Degrees: A. *Prof. Accred.:* Dental Assisting, Dental Hygiene, Radiologic Technology. Pres. Robert F. Agrella.
Enroll.: 9,391

CABRILLO SCHOOL OF NURSING
5509 E. Cajon Blvd., San Diego 92115. Private. 1978/1985 (ABHES). Courses of 28 Wks. Diplomas. *Prof. Accred.*: Medical Assisting. Pres. Henry Salas.
Enroll.: 91
(714) 582-4801

EXTENSION
713 Broadway, Chula Vista 92010.
(408) 425-6000

CALIFORNIA BAPTIST COLLEGE
8432 Magnolia Ave., Riverside 92504. Independent (Southern Baptist) liberal arts. 1961/1982 (WASC-Sr.). Early sem. plan with inter-term. Degrees: B,M. *Prof. Accred.:* Music. Pres. Russell R. Tuck.
Enroll.: FTE 527
(714) 689-5771

CALIFORNIA COLLEGE FOR RESPIRATORY THERAPY
1810 State St., San Diego 92101. Private. 1980 (NATTS); 1981 (NHSC). Courses of varying lengths. Degrees: A, certificates. Pres. Dale Bean.
Enroll.: 73 (*f.t.* 32 m., 41 w.)
(619) 232-3784

CALIFORNIA COLLEGE OF ARTS AND CRAFTS
5212 Broadway, Oakland 94618. Independent professional. 1954/1984 (WASC-Sr.). Tri. plan. Degrees: B,M. *Prof. Accred.:* Art, Interior Design. Pres. Neil J. Hoffman.
Enroll.: FTE 995
(415) 653-8118

CALIFORNIA COLLEGE OF MORTUARY SCIENCE
Merged with Cypress College February 1977.

*CALIFORNIA COLLEGE OF PODIATRIC MEDICINE
1210 Scott St., San Francisco 94115. Mailing address: P.O. Box 7855, Rincon Annex, San Francisco 94120. Private professional. 1961/1983 (WASC-Sr.). Sem. plan. Degrees: B,P,M,D. *Prof. Accred.:* Podiatry. Pres. Simon Lane.
Enroll.: FTE 447
(415) 563-3444

CALIFORNIA CULINARY ACADEMY
625 Polk St., San Francisco 94102. Private. 1982 (NATTS). Courses of varying lengths. Certificates. Pres. Danielle Carlisle.
Enroll.: 265
(415) 543-2764

CALIFORNIA FAMILY STUDY CENTER
4400 Riverside Dr., Burbank 91505. Private. 1983 (WASC-Sr.). Sem. plan. Degrees: M. Pres. Edwin S. Cox.
Enroll.: FTE 232
(818) 843-0711

CALIFORNIA INSTITUTE
4365 Atlantic Ave., Long Beach 90807. Private. 1982 (ABHES). 9-month program. Diplomas. Pres. Ronald V. Avery.
Enroll.: 20
(213) 426-7031

CALIFORNIA INSTITUTE OF INTEGRAL STUDIES
765 Ashbury St., San Francisco 94117. Independent; graduate only. 1981/1984 (WASC-Sr.). Sem. plan. Degrees: M,D. Pres. John H. Broomfield.
Enroll.: FTE 262
(415) 753-6100

CALIFORNIA INSTITUTE OF TECHNOLOGY
1201 E. California Blvd., Pasadena 91125. Independent. 1949/1985 (WASC-Sr.). Qtr. plan. Degrees: B,M,D. *Prof. Accred.:* Engineering (chemical, engineering and applied science, environmental engineering science). Pres. Marvin L. Goldberger.
Enroll.: FTE 1,839
(818) 356-6811

CALIFORNIA INSTITUTE OF THE ARTS
24700 McBean Pkwy., Valencia 91355. Independent professional. 1955/1981 (WASC-Sr.). Sem. plan. Degrees: B,M. *Prof. Accred.:* Art, Music. Pres. Robert J. Fitzpatrick.

*Accreditation on Probation

Enroll.: FTE 826
(805) 255-1050

California Lutheran University
Thousand Oaks 91360. Independent (American Lutheran Church and Lutheran Church in America) liberal arts. 1962/1984 (WASC-Sr.). 4-1-4 plan. Degrees: B,M. Pres. Jerry H. Miller.
Enroll.: FTE 1,790
(805) 492-2411

California Maritime Academy
P.O. Box 1392, Vallejo 94590. Public (state) professional. 1977/1982 (WASC-Sr.). Tri. plan. Degrees: B. *Prof. Accred.:* Engineering Technology (marine). Pres. John J. Ekelund.
Enroll.: FTE 403
(707) 644-5601

California Paramedical and Technical College
3745 Long Beach Blvd., Long Beach 90807. Private. 1980 (NATTS). Courses of varying lengths. Diplomas. *Prof. Accred.:* Medical Assisting, Respiratory Therapy Technology, Surgical Technology. Dir. Julia Morally.
Enroll.: 412 (*f.t.* 122 m., 290 w.)
(213) 426-9359

Branch Campus
4550 LaSierra Ave., Riverside 92505.
(714) 687-9006

*California Polytechnic State University, San Luis Obispo
San Luis Obispo 93407. 1951/1985 (WASC-Sr.). Qtr. plan. Degrees: B,M. *Prof. Accred.:* Architecture (B,M), Business (B), Construction Management, Engineering (aeronautical, agricultural, architectural, civil, electrical, electronic, environmental, industrial, mechanical, metallurgical), Engineering Technology (air conditioning and refrigeration, electronic, manufacturing processes, mechanical, welding), Home Economics, Landscape Architecture (B). Pres. Warren J. Baker.
Enroll.: FTE 14,660
(805) 546-0111

California School of Court Reporting
1201 N. Main St., Santa Ana 92701. Private. 1979/1985 (AICS). Courses of varying lengths. Certificates. Pres. Virginia Wilcke.
Enroll.: 526 (*f.t.* 10 m., 516 w.)
(714) 541-6892

*Member California State University System

Branch Campus
3510 Adams, Riverside 92504.
(714) 359-0293

California School of Professional Psychology
2152 Union St., San Francisco 94123. Central administration for the campuses in Berkeley, Fresno, Los Angeles, and San Diego. Independent professional. Pres. John R. O'Neil.
(415) 346-4500

California School of Professional Psychology—Berkeley
1900 Addison St., Berkeley 94704. 1977/1980 (WASC-Sr.). Sem. plan. Degrees: M,D. *Prof. Accred.:* Psychology. Prov. Edward F. Bourg.
Enroll.: FTE 297
(415) 548-5415

California School of Professional Psychology—Fresno
1350 M St., Fresno 93721. 1977/1980 (WASC-Sr.). Sem. plan. Degrees: M,D. *Prof. Accred.:* Psychology. Prov. W. Gary Cannon.
Enroll.: FTE 152
(209) 486-8420

California School of Professional Psychology—Los Angeles
2235 Beverly Blvd., Los Angeles 90057. 1977/1980 (WASC-Sr.) Sem. plan. Degrees: M,D. *Prof. Accred.:* Psychology. Prov. Connell F. Persico.
Enroll.: FTE 339
(213) 483-7034

California School of Professional Psychology—San Diego
3974 Sorrento Valley Blvd., San Diego 92121. 1977/1980 (WASC-Sr.). Sem. plan. Degrees: M,D. *Prof. Accred.:* Psychology. Prov. Joanne E. Callan.
Enroll.: FTE 302
(619) 452-1664

*California State College, Bakersfield
9001 Stockdale Hwy., Bakersfield 93311-1099. 1970/1985 (WASC-Sr.). Qtr. plan. Degrees: B,M. *Prof. Accred.:* Business (B,M), Medical Technology, Nursing (B). Pres. Tomas A. Arciniega.
Enroll.: FTE 2,929
(805) 833-2011

*Member California State University System

*CALIFORNIA STATE POLYTECHNIC UNIVERSITY, POMONA
3801 W. Temple Ave., Pomona 91768. 1970/1985 (WASC-Sr.). Qtr. plan. Degrees: B,M. *Prof. Accred.:* Architecture (B,M), Engineering (aerospace, agricultural, chemical, civil, electrical, industrial, mechanical), Engineering Technology, Landscape Architecture (B,M), Social Work (B). Pres. Hugh O. LaBounty, Jr.
Enroll.: FTE 14,159
(714) 598-4726

CALIFORNIA STATE UNIVERSITY SYSTEM
400 Golden Shore Dr., Long Beach 90802. Coordinating agency for 19 public state colleges, universities, and The Consortium. Chanc. W. Ann Reynolds.
(213) 590-5506

*CALIFORNIA STATE UNIVERSITY, CHICO
First and Normal Sts., Chico 95929. 1949/1984 (WASC-Sr.). Sem. plan. Degrees: B,M. *Prof. Accred.:* Art, Business (B,M), Dietetics, Engineering (civil, electrical and electronic, mechanical), Home Economics, Music, Nursing (B), Social Work (B), Speech Pathology, Teacher Education (*e,s,p*). Pres. Robin S. Wilson.
Enroll.: FTE 12,892
(916) 895-INFO

*CALIFORNIA STATE UNIVERSITY, DOMINGUEZ HILLS
1000 E. Victoria, Carson 90747. 1965/1983 (WASC-Sr.). Qtr. plan. Degrees: B,M. *Prof. Accred.:* Art, Medical Technology, Music, Teacher Education (*e,s,p*). Pres. Richard Butwell.
Enroll.: FTE 5,450
(213) 516-3696

*CALIFORNIA STATE UNIVERSITY, FRESNO
Shaw and Cedar Aves., Fresno 93740. 1949/1984 (WASC-Sr.). Sem. plan. Degrees: B,M. *Prof. Accred.:* Business (B,M), Engineering (civil, electrical, industrial, mechanical, surveying and photogrammetry), Home Economics, Journalism, Music, Nursing (B,M), Physical Therapy, Rehabilitation Counseling, Social Work (B,M), Speech Pathology, Teacher Education (*e,s,p*). Pres. Harold H. Haak.
Enroll.: FTE 13,904
(209) 294-4240

*Member California State University System

*CALIFORNIA STATE UNIVERSITY, FULLERTON
800 N. State College Blvd., Fullerton 92634. 1961/1981 (WASC -Sr.). Sem. plan. Degrees: B,M. *Prof. Accred.:* Art, Business (B,M), Engineering (civil, electrical, mechanical), Journalism, Music, Nursing (B), Speech Pathology, Teacher Education (*e,s,p*). Pres. Jewel Plummer Cobb.
Enroll.: FTE 16,652
(714) 773-2011

*CALIFORNIA STATE UNIVERSITY, HAYWARD
Hayward 94542. 1961/1984 (WASC-Sr.) Qtr. plan. Degrees: B,M. *Prof. Accred.:* Art, Business (B,M), Music, Nursing (B), Teacher Education (*e,s,p*). Pres. Ellis E. McCune.
Enroll.: FTE 9,460
(415) 881-3000

*CALIFORNIA STATE UNIVERSITY, LONG BEACH
1250 Bellflower Blvd., Long Beach 90840. 1957/1982 (WASC-Sr.). Sem. plan. Degrees: B,M. *Prof. Accred.:* Art, Business (B,M), Engineering (civil, computer science and engineering, electrical, materials engineering, mechanical, ocean), Home Economics, Interior Design, Journalism, Music, Nursing (M), Physical Therapy, Social Work (B). Speech Pathology and Audiology, Pres. Stephen Horn.
Enroll.: FTE 23,376
(213) 498-4111

*CALIFORNIA STATE UNIVERSITY, LOS ANGELES
5151 State University Dr., Los Angeles 90032. 1954/1985 (WASC-Sr.). Qtr. plan. Degrees: B,P,M,D in Special Education offered jointly with UCLA. *Prof. Accred.:* Art, Business (B,M), Dietetics, Engineering (civil, electrical, mechanical), Home Economics, Music, Nursing (B,M), Social Work (B), Teacher Education (*e,s,p*). Pres. James M. Rosser.
Enroll.: FTE 13,919
(213) 224-0111

*CALIFORNIA STATE UNIVERSITY, NORTHRIDGE
18111 Nordhoff St., Northridge 91330. 1958/1985 (WASC-Sr.). Sem. plan. Degrees: B,M. *Prof. Accred.:* Business (B,M), Community Health Education, Engineering, Health Services Administration, Home Economics, Journalism, Music, Physical Therapy, Ra-

*Member California State University System

diography, Speech Pathology. Pres. James W. Cleary.
Enroll.: FTE 20,701
(818) 885-1200

*CALIFORNIA STATE UNIVERSITY, SACRAMENTO
6000 J St., Sacramento 95819. 1951/1985 (WASC-Sr.). Sem. plan. Degrees: B,M. *Prof. Accred.:* Art, Business (B,M), Engineering (civil, electrical, mechanical), Engineering Technology (construction, mechanical), Home Economics, Music, Nursing, Rehabilitation Counseling, Social Work (B,M), Speech Pathology and Audiology, Teacher Education (*e,s,p*). Pres. Donald R. Gerth.
Enroll.: FTE 18,161
(916) 278-6011

*CALIFORNIA STATE UNIVERSITY, SAN BERNARDINO
5500 State University Pkwy., San Bernardino 92407. 1965/1984 (WASC-Sr.). Qtr. plan. Degrees: B,M. *Prof. Accred.:* Art, Nursing (B). Pres. Anthony H. Evans.
Enroll.: FTE 4,909
(714) 887-7201

*CALIFORNIA STATE UNIVERSITY, STANISLAUS
801 Monte Vista, Turlock 95380. 1963/1984 (WASC-Sr.). 4-1-4 plan. Degrees: B,M. *Prof. Accred.:* Art, Music, Speech Pathology. Pres. John W. Moore.
Enroll.: FTE 3,412
(209) 667-3201

CALIFORNIA WESTERN SCHOOL OF LAW
350 Cedar St., San Diego 92101. Private professional. 1962 (ABA); 1967 (AALS). Sem. plan. Degrees: P. *Prof. Accred.:* Law. Dean Ernest C. Friesen.
Enroll.: 667 (*f.t.* 493 m., 174 w.)
(714) 239-0391

CALWEST COLLEGE
1095 E. Shaw Ave., Fresno 93701. Private. 1984 (ABHES). Courses of varying lengths. Certificates. *Prof. Accred.:* Medical Assisting. Pres. Grace W. Lim.
(209) 225-3838

CAÑADA COLLEGE
4200 Farm Hill Blvd., Redwood City 94061. Public (district) junior. 1970/1986 (WASC-Jr.). Sem. plan. Degrees: A. *Prof. Accred.:* Radiograpy. Pres. Robert Stiff.
Enroll.: 7,088
(415) 364-1212

*Member California State University System

CATHERINE COLLEGE
1700 W. Burbank Blvd., Burbank 91506. 1984 (AICS). Courses of varying lengths. Certificates. Dir. Ione Gamrat.
(818) 954-9570

CENTER FOR EARLY EDUCATION. *See* COLLEGE FOR DEVELOPMENTAL STUDIES/ CENTER FOR EARLY EDUCATION

CERRITOS COLLEGE
11110 E. Alondra Blvd., Norwalk 90650. Public (district) junior. 1959/1985 (WASC-Jr.). Sem. plan. Degrees: A. *Prof. Accred.:* Dental Assisting, Dental Hygiene, Medical Assisting, Medical Record Technology, Physical Therapy. Pres. Wilford M. Michael.
Enroll.: 18,327
(213) 860-2451

CERRO COSO COMMUNITY COLLEGE
300 College Heights Blvd., Ridgecrest 93555. Public (district) junior. 1975/1985 (WASC-Jr.). Sem. plan. Degrees: A. Pres. Raymond A. McCue.
Enroll.: 3,163
(619) 375-5001

CHABOT COLLEGE
25555 Hesperian Blvd., Hayward 94545. Public (district) junior. 1963/1986 (WASC-Jr.). Qtr. plan. Degrees: A. *Prof. Accred.:* Dental Assisting, Dental Hygiene, Medical Assisting, Medical Record Technology. Pres. Howard B. Larson.
Enroll.: 17,882
(415) 786-6600

CHAFFEY COMMUNITY COLLEGE
5885 Haven Ave., Rancho Cucamonga 91701. Public (district) junior. 1952/1982 (WASC-Jr.). Qtr. plan. Degrees: A. *Prof. Accred.:* Dental Assisting, Nursing (A), Radiography. Pres. Jerry W. Young.
Enroll.: 10,200
(714) 987-1737

CHAPMAN COLLEGE
333 N. Glassell, Orange 92666. Independent (Disciples of Christ) liberal arts. 1956/1981 (WASC-Sr.). 4-1-4 plan. Degrees: A,B,M. *Prof. Accred.:* Social Work (B). Pres. G.T. Smith.
Enroll.: FTE 4,143
(714) 997-6611

Christ College, Irvine
1530 Concordia, Irvine 92715. Independent (Lutheran Church-Missouri Synod) liberal arts. 1981/1985 (WASC-Sr.). Qtr. plan. Degrees: A,B. Pres. D. Ray Halm.
Enroll.: FTE 419
(714) 854-8002

Christian Heritage College
2100 Greenfield Dr., El Cajon 92021. Independent (Scott Memorial Baptist Church), liberal arts. 1984 (WASC-Sr.). Sem. plan. Degrees: B. Pres. Earl Mills.
Enroll.: FTE 372
(619) 440-3043

Church Divinity School of the Pacific
2451 Ridge Rd., Berkeley 94709. Independent (Protestant Episcopal) professional; graduate only. 1978/1984 (WASC-Sr.). Qtr. plan. Degrees: P,M,D. *Prof. Accred.:* Theology (1945/1984, ATS). Dean and Pres. William W. Pregnall.
Enroll.: 102
(415) 848-3282

Citrus College
1000 W. Foothill Blvd., Glendora 91740. Public (district) junior. 1952/1982 (WASC-Jr.). Sem. plan. Degrees: A. *Prof. Accred.:* Dental Assisting. Pres. Louis E. Zellers.
Enroll.: 8,641
(818) 335-0521

Claremont Colleges
See Claremont Graduate School, Claremont McKenna College, Harvey Mudd College, Pitzer College, Pomona College and Scripps College. The coordinating agency for the Claremont Colleges is the Claremont University Center, Claremont 91711. Pres. John D. Maguire.
(714) 621-8000

Claremont Graduate School
Claremont 91711. Independent, graduate only; one of the Claremont Colleges. 1949/1982 (WASC-Sr.). Sem. plan. Degrees: M,D. Pres. John D. Maguire.
Enroll.: FTE 755
(714) 621-8068

Claremont McKenna College
Claremont 91711. Independent liberal arts; one of the Claremont Colleges. 1949/1985 (WASC-Sr.). Sem. plan. Degrees: B. Pres. Jack L. Stark.
Enroll.: FTE 838
(714) 621-8111

Clayton Career College
1414 N. Winchester Blvd., San Jose 95128. Private. 1973/1978 (NATTS). Qtr. plan. Diplomas. *Prof. Accred.:* Dental Assisting, Medical Assisting. Pres. William F. Cates.
Enroll.: 175 (*f.t.* 4 m., 171 w.)
(408) 244-8777

Clayton Career College
6850 Van Nuys Blvd., Van Nuys 91405. Private. 1976/1982 (ABHES). Courses of varying lengths. Certificates. *Prof. Accred.:* Medical Assisting. Pres. Dennis C. Day.
Enroll.: 96
(818) 780-5252

Cleveland Chiropractic College
590 N. Vermont Ave., Los Angeles 90004. Private professional. 1985. Sem. plan. Degrees: P. *Prof. Accred.:* Chiropractic Education. Pres. Carl Cleveland, Jr.
Enroll.: 608 (*f.t.* 446 m., 162 w.)
(213) 660-6166

Coastline Community College
11460 Warner Ave., Fountain Valley 92708. Public (district) junior. 1978/1983 (WASC-Jr.). Sem. plan. Degrees: A. Pres. William M. Vega.
Enroll.: 11,386
(714) 546-7600

Cogswell College
10420 Bubb Rd., Cupertino 95014. Independent technical. 1977/1982 (WASC-Sr.). Qtr. plan. Degrees: A,B. *Prof. Accred.:* Engineering Technology (civil, electronic, mechanical, structural). Pres. Sandra J. Basel.
Enroll.: FTE 171
(408) 252-5550

Coleman College
7380 Parkway Dr., La Mesa 92041. Private senior college of business. 1967/1982 (AICS). Qtr. plan. Degrees: A,B. Ch. of the Board Coleman Furr.
Enroll.: 1,908 (*f.t.* 1,256 m., 652 w.)
(619) 465-3990

College for Developmental Studies
563 N. Alfred St., Los Angeles 90048. Independent. Early childhood education, including teacher training. 1964/1981 (WASC-Sr.). Sem. plan. Degrees: A,M, certificates, credential. Pres. Estelle Shane.
Enroll.: FTE 37
(213) 852-1321

College of Alameda
555 Atlantic Ave., Alameda 94501. Public (district) junior. 1973/1983 (WASC-Jr.). Sem. plan. Degrees: A. *Prof. Accred.:* Dental Assisting, Medical Assisting. Pres. Donald R. Hongisto.
Enroll.: 5,155
(415) 522-7221

College of the Canyons
26455 N. Rockwell Canyon Rd., Valencia 91355. Public (district) junior. 1972/1985 (WASC-Jr.). Sem. plan. Degrees: A. Supt.-Pres. Ramon F. LaGrandeur.
Enroll.: 3,527
(805) 259-7800

College of the Desert
43-500 Monterey Ave., Palm Desert 92260. Public (district) junior. 1963/1982 (WASC-Jr.). Sem. plan. Degrees: A. *Prof. Accred.:* Nursing (A), Respiratory Therapy. Pres. ——.
Enroll.: 4,599
(619) 346-8041

College of Notre Dame
Belmont 94002. Independent (Roman Catholic) liberal arts. 1955/1985 (WASC-Sr.). 4-1-4 plan. Degrees: B, M. *Prof. Accred.:* Music, Teacher Education (*e,s*). Pres. Sister Veronica Skillin.
Enroll.: FTE 760
(415) 593-1601

College of Oceaneering
272 S. Fries Ave., Wilmington 90744. Private. 1973/1980 (NATTS); 1982 (WASC-Jr). Courses of varying lengths. Degrees: A, certificates, diplomas. Pres. James T. Joiner.
Enroll.: 120
(213) 834-2501

College of Osteopathic Medicine of the Pacific
352 Pomona Mall E., Pomona 91766. Private professional. 1978. Sem. plan. Degrees: P. *Prof. Accred.:* Osteopathy. Pres. Philip Pumerantz.
Enroll.: 236 (*f.t.* 187 m., 49 w.)
(714) 623-6116

College of Recording Arts
665 Harrison St., San Francisco 94107. Private. 1974/1984 (NATTS). Sem. plan. Diplomas. Pres. Leo de Gar Kulka.
Enroll.: 70 (*f.t.* 58 m., w.)
(415) 781-6306

College of the Redwoods
7351 Tompkins Hill Rd., Eureka 95501. Public (district) junior. 1967/1984 (WASC-Jr.). Sem. plan. Degrees: A. *Prof. Accred.:* Dental Assisting. Pres. D. Donald Weichert.
Enroll.: 8,012
(707) 443-8411

College of San Mateo
1700 W. Hillsdale Blvd., San Mateo 94402. Public (district) junior. 1952/1984 (WASC-Jr.). Sem. plan. Degrees: A. *Prof. Accred.:* Dental Assisting, Nursing (A). Pres. Lois A. Callahan.
Enroll.: 13,503
(415) 574-6161

College of the Sequoias
915 S. Mooney Blvd., Visalia 93277. Public (district) junior. 1952/1984 (WASC-Jr.). Sem. plan. Degrees: A. Pres. Lincoln H. Hall.
Enroll.: 7,519
(209) 733-2050

College of the Siskiyous
800 College Ave., Weed 96094. Public (district) junior. 1961/1982 (WASC-Jr.). Sem. plan. Degrees: A. Pres. Eugene Schumacher.
Enroll.: 4,856
(916) 938-4462

Color Me A Season, Inc.
1070 A Shary Cir., Concord 94518. Private combination home study and resident. 1985 (NHSC). Pres. Dean Kentner.
(415) 676-9184

Columbia College
P.O. Box 1849, Columbia 95310. Public (district) junior. 1972/1985 (WASC-Jr.). Sem. plan. Degrees: A. Pres. Dean Cunningham.
Enroll.: 2,309
(209) 533-5100

Columbia College
925 N. La Brea Ave., Los Angeles 90038. Private technical. 1980 (NATTS). Qtr. plan. Degrees: A, B, diplomas. Pres. Ernest Baumeister.
Enroll.: 425 (*f.t.* 265 m., 80 w.)
(213) 851-0550

Columbia School of Broadcasting
5858 Hollywood Blvd., Fourth Floor, Hollywood 90028-5619 Private home study. 1972/1982 (NHSC). Pres. Art Mandelbaum.
(213) 469-8321

COMPTON COMMUNITY COLLEGE
1111 E. Artesia Blvd., Compton 90221. Public (district) junior. 1952/1983 (WASC-Jr.). Sem. plan. Degrees: A. Pres. Edison O. Jackson.
Enroll.: 3,543
(213) 637-2660

COMPUTER LEARNING CENTER OF LOS ANGELES
3130 Wilshire Blvd., Los Angeles 90010. Private. 1970/1980 (NATTS). Courses of varying lengths. Diplomas. Dir. Floyd M. Haugen.
Enroll.: 510 (*f.t.* 180 m., 120 w.)
(213) 386-6311

BRANCH CAMPUS
1240 S. State College Blvd., Anaheim 92806. Dir. Tyrone Rosenthal.
Enroll.: 119 (*f.t.* 92 m., 27 w.)
(714) 956-8060

COMPUTER LEARNING CENTER
661 Howard St., San Francisco 91405. 1985 (AICS). Courses of varying lengths. Diplomas. Dir. Barbara Gordon.
(415) 495-0880

*CONDIE JUNIOR COLLEGE OF BUSINESS AND TECHNOLOGY
One W. Campbell Ave., Campbell 95008. Private. 1974/1984 (AICS). Qtr. plan. Degrees: A, diplomas. Dir. Wayne Wilson.
Enroll.: 1,378 (*f.t.* 825 m., 553 w.)
(408) 866-6666

CONSOLIDATED WELDING SCHOOLS
4343 E. Imperial Hwy., Lynwood 90262. Private. 1985 (NATTS). Courses of varying lengths. Certificates. Dir. Robert Swanson.
(213) 638-0418

**†CONSORTIUM OF THE CALIFORNIA STATE UNIVERSITY SYSTEM
400 Golden Shore, Long Beach 90802. Public liberal arts and professional. 1976/1982 (WASC-Sr.). Sem. plan. Degrees: B,M. *Prof. Accred.:* Nursing (B). Dir. Joan T. Cobin
Enroll.: FTE 593
(213) 590-5696

CONTRA COSTA COLLEGE
2600 Mission Bell Dr., San Pablo 94806. Public (district) junior. 1952/1984 (WASC-Jr.). Sem. plan. Degrees: A. *Prof. Accred.:* Dental Assisting. Pres. D. Candy Rose.
Enroll.: 6,707
(415) 235-7800

CONTROL DATA INSTITUTE
1780 W. Lincoln Ave., Anaheim 92801. Private. 1969/1980 (NATTS). Courses of varying lengths. Certificates. Dir. Donald E. Scherer.
Enroll.: 430 (*f.t.* 220 m., 60 w.)
(714) 635-2770

CONTROL DATA INSTITUTE
5630 Arbor Vitae St., Los Angeles 90045. Private. 1968/1978 (NATTS). Courses of varying lengths. Certificates. Dir. E. M. Reardon.
Enroll.: 450 (*f.t.* 302 m., 148 w.)
(213) 642-2345

CONTROL DATA INSTITUTE
1930 Market St., San Francisco 94102. Private. 1969/1979 (NATTS). Courses of varying lengths. Certificates. Dir. Herb Liberman.
Enroll.: 628 (*f.t.* 284 m., 122 w.)
(415) 864-1156

BRANCH CAMPUS
5206 Benito St., Montclair 91763. Dir. Donald Scherer.
(714) 621-6867

EXTENSION
660 J St., Sacramento 95814.
(916) 447-5282

CONTROL DATA INSTITUTE
20301 Ventura Blvd., Suite 330, Woodland Hills 91364. Private. 1985 (NATTS). Courses of varying lengths. Certificates. Dir. Barbara Jackson.
(213) 992-3344

COSUMNES RIVER COLLEGE
8401 Center Pkwy., Sacramento 95823. Public (district) junior. 1972/1986 (WASC-Jr.). Sem. plan . Degrees: A. Pres. Marc E. Hall.
Enroll.: 7,211
(916) 686-7451

CRAFTON HILLS COLLEGE
11711 Sand Canyon Rd., Yucaipa 92399. Public (district) junior. 1975/1985 (WASC-Jr.). Sem. plan. Degrees: A. *Prof. Accred.:* EMT-Paramedic, Respiratory Therapy Technology. Pres. Donald L. Singer.
Enroll.: 3,376
(714) 794-2161

*Candidate for Accreditation by Regional Accrediting Commission
**Member California State University System
†Accreditation on Probation through June 30, 1987

Criss College
1238 E. Katella Ave., Anaheim 92805. Private business. 1969/1981 (AICS). Qtr. plan. Certificates, diplomas. Pres. Donald Hecht.
Enroll.: 470 (*f.t.* 157 m., 313 w.)
(714) 634-1001

Branch Campus
179 Roymar Rd., Oceanside 92055. Dir. Marty Cockell.
(619) 757-3729

Cuesta College
P.O. Box 8106, San Luis Obispo 93403. Public (district) junior. 1968/1986 (WASC-Jr.). Sem. plan . Degrees: A. Pres. Frank R. Martinez.
Enroll.: 5,883
(805) 544-2943

Cuyamaca College
2950 Jamacha Rd., El Cajon 92020. Public (district) junior. 1980/1985 (WASC-Jr.). Sem. plan. Degrees: A. Pres. Samuel M. Ciccati.
Enroll.: 2,528
(619) 464-1980

Cypress College
9200 Valley View St., Cypress 90630. Public (district) junior. 1968/1986 (WASC-Jr.). Sem. plan. Degrees: A. *Prof. Accred.:* Dental Assisting, Dental Hygiene, Dental Laboratory Technology, Medical Assisting, Medical Record Technology, Radiography. Pres. Jack A. Scott.
Enroll.: 12,912
(714) 826-2220

D-Q University–Lower Division
P.O. Box 409, Davis 95617. Private junior college emphasizing American Indian and Chicano cultures. 1977/1982 (WASC-Jr.). Sem. plan. Degrees: A. Pres. Carlos Cordero.
Enroll.: 197
(916) 758-0470

DeAnza College
21250 Stevens Creek Blvd., Cupertino 95014. Public (district) junior. 1969/1982 (WASC-Jr.). Sem. plan. Degrees: A. *Prof. Accred.:* Medical Assisting, Physical Therapy. Pres. A. Robert DeHart.
Enroll.: 22,522
(408) 996-4560

Deep Springs College
Deep Springs via Dyer, Nevada 89010. Private junior for men. 1952/1982 (WASC-Jr.). 14-week trimester. Degrees: A. Dir. Brandt Kehoe.
Enroll.: f.t. 21 m.
(619) 872-2000

Defense Language Institute, Foreign Language Center
Presidio of Monterey 93944. Public (federal) technical. 1979/1984 (WASC-Jr.). Year-round program. Certificates. Commandant Col. Monte R. Bullard, USA.
Enroll.: f.t. 3,571
(408) 647-5324

Dental Technology Institute
969 N. Tustin Ave., Orange 92667. Private. 1976/1984 (NATTS). Courses of varying lengths. Diplomas. Dir. Donna M. Kent.
Enroll.: 103 (*f.t.* 18 m., 7 w.)
(714) 997-3052

DeVry Institute of Technology
12801 Crossroads Pkwy., S., City of Industry 91744. Private. 1983 (NCA); 1984 (NATTS, Extension of Phoenix, AZ). Tri. plan. Degrees: A,B, diplomas. *Prof. Accred.:* Engineering Technology. Pres. Paul R. McGuirk.
Enroll.: 760
(213) 699-9927

Diablo Valley College
321 Golf Club Rd., Pleasant Hill 94523. Public (district) junior. 1952/1986 (WASC-Jr.). Sem. plan. Degrees: A. Pres. Phyllis L. Wiedman.
Enroll.: 17,147
(415) 685-1230

Dick Grove Music Workshops
12754 Ventura Blvd., Studio City 91604. Private music trade school. 1979. Sem. plan. Certificates, diplomas. *Prof. Accred.:* Music. Pres. Dick Grove.
Enroll.: 800
(213) 985-0905

Dickinson-Warren Business College
2210 Harold Way, Berkeley 94704. Private. 1979/1982 (AICS). Courses of varying lengths. Certificates. Pres. Ramon Flores.
Enroll.: 319 (*f.t.* 64 m., 255 w.)
(415) 843-1973

Branch Campus
1001 S. 57th St., Richmond 94801. Dir. Roger L. Chretian.
(415) 236-5627

Dominican College of San Rafael
San Rafael 94901. Independent (Roman Catholic) liberal arts. 1949/1982 (WASC-Sr.).

Sem. plan. Degrees: B,M. Pres. Barbara Korpan Bundy.
Enroll.: FTE 561
(415) 457-4440

DOMINICAN SCHOOL OF PHILOSOPHY AND THEOLOGY
(*Formerly* ST. ALBERT'S COLLEGE)
2401 Ridge Rd., Berkeley 94709. Independent (Roman Catholic) seminary. 1964/1983 (WASC-Sr.). Sem. plan. Degrees: B,P,M. *Prof. Accred.:* Theology (1978/1983, ATS). Pres. Paul Philibert, O.P.
Enroll.: FTE 78
(415) 849-2030

DON BOSCO TECHNICAL INSTITUTE
1151 San Gabriel Blvd., Rosemead 91770. Private (Roman Catholic) 2-year. 1972/1984 (WASC-Jr.). Sem. plan. Degrees: A. Pres. Rev. Nicholas Reina, SDB.
Enroll.: 284
(818) 280-0451

EAST LOS ANGELES COLLEGE
1301 Brooklyn Ave., Monterey Park 91754. Public (district) junior. 1952/1981 (WASC-Jr.). Sem. plan. Degrees: A. *Prof. Accred.:* Medical Assisting, Medical Record Technology, Respiratory Therapy. Pres. Arthur D. Avila.
Enroll.: 12,364
(213) 265-8650

EDISON TECHNICAL INSTITUTE
4629 Van Nuys Blvd., Sherman Oaks 91403. Private. 1985 (NATTS). Courses of varying lengths. Certificates. Dir. E. C. Alvarez.
(818) 788-7141

EL CAMINO COLLEGE
16007 S. Crenshaw Blvd., Torrance 90506. Public (district) junior. 1952/1985 (WASC-Jr.). Sem. plan. Degrees: A. *Prof. Accred.:* Medical Assisting, Radiography, Respiratory Therapy. Pres. Rafael L. Cortada.
Enroll.: 24,476
(213) 532-3670

EL DORADO COLLEGE
2181 El Camino Real, Suite 102, Oceanside 92054. Private business. 1980/1985 (AICS). Qtr. plan. Certificates, diplomas. Dir. Anthony J. Pitale.
Enroll.: 427 (*f.t.* 45 m., 382 w.)
(619) 433-3660

BRANCH
1901 Pacific Ave., West Covina 91793. Dir. Joan E. Muse.
(213) 960-5173

ELEGANCE INTERNATIONAL—ACADEMY OF PROFESSIONAL MAKEUP
3912 Wilshire Blvd., Los Angeles 90010. Private. 1978/1984 (NATTS). Sem. plan. Diplomas. Pres. Wynna Miller.
Enroll.: 110
(213) 385-4026

EMPIRE COLLEGE
3033 Cleveland Ave., Suite 107, Santa Rosa 95401. Private. 1969/1981 (AICS). Sem. plan. Certificates, diplomas. CEO Dorothe D. Hutchinson.
Enroll.: 471 (*f.t.* 32 m., 439 w.)
(707) 546-4000

ESTELLE HARMON ACTORS' WORKSHOP
522 N. La Brea Ave., Los Angeles 90036. Private. 1976/1981 (NATTS). Qtr. plan. Certificates. Diplomas. Dir. Estelle Harmon.
Enroll.: 175
(213) 931-8137

EVERGREEN VALLEY COLLEGE
3095 Yerba Buena Rd., San Jose 95135. Public (district) junior. 1977/1982 (WASC-Jr.). Sem. plan. Degrees: A. *Prof. Accred.:* Nursing (A). Pres. Gerald H. Strelitz.
Enroll.: 6,714
(408) 270-7900

FASHION CAREERS OF CALIFORNIA
1923 Morena Blvd., San Diego 92110. Private. 1983 (AICS). Courses of varying lengths. Certificates. Dir. Patricia G. O'Connor.
Enroll.: 184 (*f.t.* 15 m., 169 w.)
(619) 275-4700

THE FASHION INSTITUTE OF DESIGN AND MERCHANDISING
818 W. Seventh St., Los Angeles 90017. Private 2-year. 1972/1984 (AICS); 1978/1983 (WASC-Jr.). Qtr. plan. Degrees: A. *Prof. Accred.:* Interior Design. Pres. Tonian Thomas Hohberg.
Enroll.: 2,723 (*f.t.* 236 m., 1,969 w.)
(213) 624-1200

BRANCH CAMPUS
790 Market Street, San Francisco 94102. Dir. Hollace Wood.
(415) 433-6691

Branch Campus
3850 S. Plaza Dr., Santa Ana 92704. Acting Dir. Laura Soloff.
(714) 546-0903

Branch Campus
13701 Riverside Dr., Sherman Oaks 91403. Dir. Laura Soloff.
(213) 872-1411

Feather River College
P O. Box 1110, Quincy 95971. Public (district) junior. 1973/1983 (WASC-Jr.). Sem. plan. Degrees: A. Pres. Joseph Brennan.
Enroll.: 1,408
(916) 283-0202

Federico College
555 N. Van Ness, Fresno 93728. Private. 1985 (NATTS). Courses of varying lengths. Diplomas. Pres. Samuel Federico.

Fielding Institute
2112 Santa Barbara St., Santa Barbara 93105. Independent professional, graduate only. 1982 (WASC-Sr.). Tri. plan. Degrees: M,D. Pres. Frederic M. Hudson.
Enroll.: FTE 615
(805) 687-1099

Foothill College
12345 El Monte Rd., Los Altos Hills 94022. Public (district) junior. 1959/1983 (WASC-Jr.). Qtr. plan. Degrees: A. *Prof. Accred.:* Dental Assisting, Dental Hygiene, Radiation Therapy, Radiography. Pres. Thomas H. Clements.
Enroll.: 12,893
(415) 960-4600

Franciscan School of Theology
1712 Euclid Ave., Berkeley 94709. Independent (Roman Catholic) professional; graduate only. 1975/1983 (WASC-Sr.). Sem. plan. Degrees: P,M. *Prof. Accred.:* Theology (1975/1983, ATS). Pres. Xavier Harris, O.F.M.
Enroll.: 116
(415) 848-5232

Fresno City College
1101 E. University Ave., Fresno 93741. Public (district) junior. 1952/1983 (WASC-Jr.). Sem. plan. Degrees: A. *Prof. Accred.:* Dental Hygiene, Radiography, Respiratory Therapy. Pres. Clyde C. McCully.
Enroll.: 13,222
(209) 442-4600

Fresno Pacific College
1717 S. Chestnut, Fresno 93702. Independent (Mennonite Brethren) liberal arts. 1961/1985 (WASC-Sr.). Qtr. plan. Degrees: A,B,M. Pres. Richard Kriegbaum.
Enroll.: FTE 693
(209) 251-7194

Fuller Theological Seminary
135 N. Oakland Ave., Pasadena 91101-1790. Independent (multidenominational) professional; graduate only. 1969/1985 (WASC-Sr.). Qtr. plan. Degrees: P,M,D. *Prof. Accred.:* Psychology, Theology (1957/1980, ATS). Pres. David A. Hubbard.
Enroll.: FTE 1,445
(818) 449-1745

Fullerton College
321 E. Chapman Ave., Fullerton 92634. Public (district) junior. 1952/1982 (WASC-Jr.). Sem. plan. Degrees: A. Pres. Philip W. Borst.
Enroll.: 16,596
(714) 871-8000

Galen College of Medical and Dental Assistants
1325 N. Wishon, Fresno 93728. Private. 1974/1979 (NATTS). Courses of varying lengths. Diplomas. Pres. Stella Cord.
Enroll.: 248 (*f.t.* 4 m., 244 w.)
(209) 264-9726

Branch
3746 W. Mineral King, Suite C, Visalia 93277. Dir. David A. Loescher.
(209) 732-2217

Extension
1800 Westwind, Building "L", Bakersfield 93301. Dir. John Cowan.
(805) 324-1499

Extension
1604 Ford Ave., Suite 10, Modesto 95350.
(209) 527-5084

Gavilan College
5055 Santa Teresa Blvd., Gilroy 95020. Public (district) junior. 1952/1984 (WASC-Jr.). Sem. plan. Degrees: A. Pres. John Holleman.
Enroll.: 2,479
(408) 847-1400

Gemological Institute of America
1660 Stewart St., Santa Monica 90404. Private. 1965/1982 (NHSC); 1973/1978 (NATTS). Courses of varying lengths. Certificates, diplomas. Pres. Raymond Page.
Enroll.: 983 (*f.t.* 659 m., 224 w.)
(213) 829-2991

GLENDALE COLLEGE OF BUSINESS AND PARAMEDICAL
335 N. Brand Blvd., Glendale 91203. Private. 1986 (ABHES). 28-week program. Diplomas. *Prof. Accred.:*Medical Assisting. Exec. Dir. Gloria Green.
Enroll.: 9
(818) 243-1131

GLENDALE COMMUNITY COLLEGE
1500 N. Verdugo Rd., Glendale 91208. Public (district) junior. 1952/1982 (WASC-Jr.). Sem. plan. Degrees: A. Acting Pres. John A. Davitt.
Enroll.: 10,196
(213) 240-1000

GOLDEN GATE BAPTIST THEOLOGICAL SEMINARY
Strawberry Point, Mill Valley 94941. Independent (Southern Baptist) professional; graduate only. 1971/1981 (WASC-Sr.). Sem. plan. Degrees: P,M,D. *Prof. Accred.:* Music, Theology (1962/1981, ATS). Acting Pres. Harold Graves.
Enroll.: FTE 525
(415) 388-8080

GOLDEN GATE UNIVERSITY
536 Mission St., San Francisco 94105. Independent business and public administration, law. 1959/1980 (WASC-Sr.). Tri. plan (sem. plan in law school). Degrees: A,B,P,M,D. *Prof. Accred.:* Law. Pres. Otto Butz.
Enroll.: FTE 5,771
(415) 442-7000

GOLDEN STATE SCHOOL
195 W. Benedict St., P.O. Box 5807, San Bernardino 92408. Private. 1981 (NATTS). Courses of varying lengths. Certificates, diplomas. Dir. William F. Rabenaldt.
Enroll.: 107 (*f.t.* 97 m., 5 w.)
(714) 884-0479

BAKERSFIELD EXTENSION
3916 S. Chester, Bakersfield 93307. Dir. James M. Creech.
(805) 833-0123

OXNARD EXTENSION
1910 Sunkist Circle, P.O. Box 5098, Oxnard 93030. Dir. Larry Owens.
Enroll.: 21
(805) 587-3975

GOLDEN WEST COLLEGE
15744 Golden West St., Huntington Beach 92647. Public (district) junior. 1969/1982 (WASC-Jr.). Sem. plan. Degrees: A. *Prof. Accred.:* Nursing (A). Acting Pres. Fred Garcia.
Enroll.: 15,000
(714) 892-7711

GRADUATE THEOLOGICAL UNION
2465 Le Conte Ave., Berkeley 94709. Independent institution offering graduate instruction in theology in conjunction with member institutions. 1966/1983. (WASC-Sr.). Sem. plan. Degrees: M,D. *Prof. Accred.:* Theology (1969/1978, ATS). Pres. Rev. Michael J. Blecker.
Enroll.: FTE 373
(415) 841-9811

GRANTHAM COLLEGE OF ENGINEERING
10570 Humboldt St., P.O. Box 539, Los Alamitos 90720. Private home study. 1961/1985 (NHSC). Courses of varying lengths. Degrees: A,B. Pres. Donald J. Grantham.
(213) 493-4421

GROSSMONT COLLEGE
8800 Grossmont College Dr., El Cajon 92020. Public (district) junior. 1963/1985 (WASC-Jr.). Sem. plan. Degrees: A. *Prof. Accred.:* Engineering Technology (biomedical, electronic), Respiratory Therapy. Pres. Ivan L. Jones.
Enroll.: 13,472
(619) 465-1700

HARTNELL COLLEGE
156 Homestead Ave., Salinas 93901. Public (district) junior. 1952/1984 (WASC-Jr.). Sem. plan. Degrees: A. Pres. James R. Hardt.
Enroll.: 5,630
(408) 758-8211

HARVEY MUDD COLLEGE
Claremont 91711. Independent science and engineering; one of the Claremont Colleges. 1959/1982 (WASC-Sr.). Sem. plan. Degrees: B,M. *Prof Accred.:* Engineering. Pres. D. Kenneth Baker.
Enroll.: 545
(714) 621-8000, Ext. 3843

HEALD COLLEGES
Central administration office, 1388 Sutter St., San Francisco 94109. Pres. James E. Deitz.
(415) 474-8711

HEALD COLLEGE-HAYWARD
22730 Mission Blvd., Hayward 94541. Private. 1983 (WASC-Jr.). Qtr. plan. Certificates, Diplomas. Dir. F. William King.

Enroll.: 237
(415) 886-3101

HEALD COLLEGE-MARTINEZ (FORMERLY HEALD COLLEGE-OAKLAND
2860 Howe Rd., Martinez 94553. Private 2-year. 1984 (WASC-Jr.). Qtr. plan. Degrees: A. Dir. Louis J. Collins.
Enroll.: 430
(415) 228-9000

HEALD COLLEGE-OAKLAND
505 14th St., Oakland 94612. Private. 1984 (WASC-Jr.). Qtr. plan. Certificates, diplomas. Dir. Ronald C. Hayes.
Enroll.: 250
(415) 444-0201

HEALD COLLEGE-ROHNERT PARK
100 Professional Center Dr., Rohnert Park 94928. Private. 1986 (WASC-Jr.). Qtr. plan. Degrees: A, certificates, diplomas. Dir. M. Douglas Ketchter.
Enroll.: 245
(707) 584-5900

HEALD COLLEGE-SACRAMENTO
2401 J St., Sacramento 95816. Private. 1983 (WASC-Jr.). Qtr. plan. Degrees: A, certificates, diplomas. Dir. J. Robert Evans.
Enroll.: 509
(916) 444-2320

HEALD COLLEGE-SAN DIEGO (FORMERLY KELSEY-JENNEY COLLEGE
620 C St., San Diego 92101. Private. 1983 (WASC-Jr.). Qtr. plan. Certificates, diplomas. Dir. Nelson E. Melchior.
Enroll.: 230
(619) 233-7418

HEALD COLLEGE-SAN JOSE
684 El Paseo de Saratoga, San Jose 95130. Private. 1983 (WASC-Jr.). Qtr. plan. Certificates, diplomas. Dir. Joseph E. Militano.
Enroll.: 963
(408) 370-2400

HEALD COLLEGE-WALNUT CREEK
2085 N. Broadway, Walnut Creek 94596. Private. 1983 (WASC-Jr.). Qtr. plan. Degrees: A, certificates, diplomas. Vice Pres./Dir. William B. Collins.
Enroll.: 432
(415) 933-2436

HEALD COLLEGE (BUSINESS DIVISION)-SAN FRANCISCO
1453 Mission St., San Francisco 94103. Private. 1983 (WASC-Jr.). Qtr. plan. Degrees: A, certificates, diplomas. Dir. David B. Raulston.
Enroll.: 818
(415) 673-5500

HEALD COLLEGE (TECHNICAL DIVISION)-SAN FRANCISCO
150 Fourth St., San Francisco 94103. 1983 (WASC-Jr.). Qtr. plan. Degrees: A, certificates, diplomas. Dir. David B. Raulston.
Enroll.: 793
(415) 441-5555

HEALD 4C'S COLLEGE (FORMERLY CENTRAL CALIFORNIA COMMERCIAL COLLEGE)
1545 Fulton St., Fresno 93721. Private. 1983 (WASC-Jr.). Qtr. plan. Degrees: A, certificates, diplomas. Dir. Robert D. Myers.
Enroll.: 451
(209) 438-4222

HEBREW UNION COLLEGE–JEWISH INSTITUTE OF RELIGION
3077 University Ave., Los Angeles 90007. Independent (Reform Judaism) school of religion; parent institution at Cincinnati, Ohio. 1960/1985 (WASC-Sr.). Sem. plan. Degrees: B,M,D. Exec. Vice Pres. Uri D. Herscher.
Enroll.: FTE 59
(213) 749-3424

HEMPHILL SCHOOLS/HELIX INSTITUTION
1543 W. Olympic Blvd., Los Angeles 90015-3894. Private home study; courses available in Spanish only. 1966/1982 (NHSC). Pres. Arturo Delgado.
(213) 381-1898

HELIX INSTITUTION
A Division of Hemphill Schools. Courses in computer programming written in the English language.

HOLLYWOOD SCRIPTWRITING INSTITUTE
1300 Cahuenga Blvd., Hollywood 90028. Private home study. 1985 (NHSC). Courses of varying lengths. Certificates. Dir. Donna Lee.
(213) 737-4482

HOLY FAMILY COLLEGE
159 Washington Blvd., Mailing Address: P.O. Box 3426, Fremont 94539-0342. Independent (Roman Catholic) upper division preprofessional for women. 1973/1983 (WASC-Sr.). Sem. plan. Degrees: B. Pres. Sister M. Jeanette Kelly, S.H.F.
Enroll.: FTE 51
(415) 651-1639

Holy Names College
3500 Mountain Blvd., Oakland 94619. Independent (Roman Catholic) liberal arts. 1949/1985 (WASC-Sr.) Tri. plan and weekend college. Degrees: B,M. *Prof. Accred.:* Music, Nursing (B). Pres. Sister Lois A. MacGillivray, S.N.J.M.
Enroll.: FTE 476
(415) 436-0111

*Humboldt State University
Arcata 95521. 1949/1985 (WASC-Sr.). Qtr. plan. Degrees: B,M. *Prof. Accred.:* Art, Engineering (environmental resources), Forestry, Journalism, Music, Nursing (B). Pres. Alistair W. McCrone.
Enroll.: FTE 5,809
(707) 826-3011

Humphreys College
6650 Inglewood St., Stockton 95207. Private junior. 1972/1985 (WASC-Jr.). Qtr. plan. Degrees: A,B,P. Pres. Robert G. Humphreys.
Enroll.: 400
(209) 478-0800

ITT Technical Institute (Extension)
7100 Knott Ave., Buena Park 90620. Private. 1983 (NATTS). Qtr. plan. Degrees: A. Dir. Cindy Norman.
(714) 523-9080

ITT Technical Institute
8374 Hercules St., La Mesa 92401. Private. 1983 (NATTS). Qtr. plan. Degrees: A. Dir. Robert Hammond.
(619) 462-0682

ITT Technical Institute
2007 O St., Sacramento 95814. Private. 1979/1982 (AICS). Qtr. plan. Degrees: A. Dir. Kenneth Potter
Enroll.: 679
(916) 444-0345

ITT Technical Institute (Extension)
6723 Van Nuys Blvd., Van Nuys 91405-4620. Private. 1983 (NATTS). Qtr. plan. Degrees: A. Dir. James E. Cobis, Sr.
(818) 989-1177

ITT Technical Institute
1530 W. Cameron Ave., West Covina 91790. 1982 (NATTS). Qtr. plan. Degrees: A. Dir. William H. Fennelly.
Enroll.: 150
(213) 960-8681

*Member California State University System

Immaculate Heart College
Los Angeles 90027. (Closed August 31, 1980. Accreditation terminated June 30, 1981.)

Imperial Valley College
P.O. Box 158, Imperial 92251. Public (district) junior. 1952/1984 (WASC-Jr.). Sem. plan. Degrees: A. Pres. John A. DePaoli, Jr.
Enroll.: 3,181
(619) 352-8320

Institute of Computer Technology
3200 Wilshire Blvd., Los Angeles 90010. Private. 1985 (NATTS). Courses of varying lengths. Diplomas. Dir. K. C. You.
(213) 381-3333

International Dealer's School (Extension)
2772 Artesia Blvd., Redondo Beach 90278. Private. 1984 (NATTS). Courses of varying lengths. Certificates, diplomas. Dir. Gary Mahoney.
(213) 371-1223

Irvine College of Business
16591 Noyes Ave., Irvine 92714. Private. 1977/1983 (AICS). Courses of varying lengths. Certificates. Pres. W. D. Polick.
Enroll.: 332 (*f.t.* 21 m., 311 w.)
(714) 863-1145

Jesuit School of Theology
1735 LeRoy Ave., Berkeley 94709. Independent (Roman Catholic), professional; graduate only; a participating school of the Graduate Theological Union. 1971/1983 (WASC-Sr.). Qtr. plan. Degrees: P,M. *Prof. Accred.:* Theology (1971/1983, ATS). Acting Pres. T. Howland Sanks, S.J.
Enroll.: FTE 143
(415) 841-8804

John F. Kennedy University
12 Altarinda Rd., Orinda 94563. Independent liberal arts and professional; upper division and graduate only. 1977/1985 (WASC-Sr.). Qtr. plan. Degrees: B,P,M. Pres. Donald J. MacIntyre.
Enroll.: FTE 1,326
(415) 254-0200

John Tracy Clinic
806 W. Adams Blvd., Los Angeles 90007. Private home study. 1965/1982 (NHSC). Exec. Dir. Edgar L. Lowell; Dir. of Corres. Ed. Sandra Meyer.
(213) 748-5481

Kings River Community College
995 N. Reed Ave., Reedley 93654. Public (district) junior. 1952/1983 (WASC-Jr.). Sem. plan. Degrees: A. *Prof. Accred.:* Dental Assisting. Pres. Abel B. Sykes, Jr.
Enroll.: 3,571
(209) 638-3641

L.I.F.E. Bible College
1100 Glendale Blvd., Los Angeles 90026. Private (International Four Square Gospel) professional. 1980/1985 (AABC). Sem. plan. Degrees: B. Pres. Jack E. Hamilton.
Enroll.: 456
(213) 413-1234

Laguna Beach School of Art
2222 Laguna Canyon Rd., Laguna Beach 92651. Private professional 3-year program. 1984. Certificates. *Prof. Accred.:* Art. Dir. Patricia Caldwell.
(714) 497-3309

Lake Tahoe Community College
P.O. Box 14445, South Lake Tahoe 95702. Public (district) junior. 1979/1984 (WASC-Jr.). Qtr. plan. Degrees: A. Pres. James W. Duke.
Enroll.: 1,468
(916) 541-4660

Laney College
900 Fallon St., Oakland 94619. Public (district) junior. 1956/1986 (WASC-Jr.). Sem. plan. Degrees: A. Pres. Odell Johnson.
Enroll.: 9,651
(916) 464-3133

Lassen College
Hwy. 139, P.O. Box 3000, Susanville 96130. Public (district) junior. 1952/1985 (WASC-Jr.). Sem. plan. Degrees: A. Pres. Virginia Holten.
Enroll.: 1,969
(916) 257-6181

Laurenwood College
2621 K St., Sacramento 95816. Private business. 1971/1984 (AICS). Courses of varying lengths. Diplomas. Dean Angela J. Ivey.
Enroll.: 238 (*f.t.* 17 m., 221 w.)
(916) 448-6782

Lawton College for Medical and Dental Assistants
950 S. Bascom Ave., San Jose 95128. Private. 1976/1982 (NATTS). Courses of varying lengths. Certificates. *Prof. Accred.:* Medical Assisting. Dir. Krishna Naicker.
Enroll.: 60 (*f.t.* 5 m., 55 w.)
(408) 288-8400

Lifetime Career Schools, Inc.
2251 Barry Ave., Los Angeles 90064. Private home study. 1957/1982 (NHSC). Pres. Norman A. Morris.
(213) 478-0617

Loma Linda University
Loma Linda 92350. Independent (Seventh-day Adventist) liberal arts and professional. 1960/1980 (WASC-Sr.); accreditation includes La Sierra Campus in Riverside. Qtr. plan. Degrees: A,B,P,M,D. *Prof. Accred.:* Cytotechnology, Dental Assisting, Dental Hygiene, Dentistry, Diagnostic Medical Sonography, Dietetics, Medical Record Administration, Medical Technology, Medicine, Nuclear Medicine Technology, Nursing (A,B,M), Occupational Therapy, Physical Therapy, Public Health, Radiation Therapy Technology, Radiography, Respiratory Therapy, Social Work (B). Pres. Norman J. Woods.
Enroll.: FTE 3,886
(714) 824-4300

Long Beach City College
4901 E. Carson St., Long Beach 90808. Public (district) junior. 1952/1985 (WASC-Jr.). Sem. plan. Degrees: A. *Prof. Accred.:* Medical Assisting, Nursing (A), Radiography, Respiratory Therapy. Pres. John T. McCuen.
Enroll.: 22,973
(213) 420-4111

Long Beach College of Business
236 E. Third St., P.O. Box 530, Long Beach 90801. Private. 1972/1977 (AICS). Courses of varying lengths. Diplomas. Chairman of the Board J. E. Taylor, Jr.
Enroll.: 854 (*f.t.* 342 m., 512 w.)
(213) 436-3621

Los Angeles Business College
707 S. Broadway, Suite 400, Los Angeles 90014. Private. 1972/1984 (AICS). Qtr. Plan. Degrees: A, certificates, diplomas. Pres. Donald Martin.
Enroll.: 423 (*f.t.* 75 m., 348 w.)
(213) 629-3581

Los Angeles City College
855 N. Vermont Ave., Los Angeles 90029. Public (district) junior. 1952/1985 (WASC-Jr.). Sem. plan. Degrees: A. *Prof. Accred.:* Dental Assisting, Dental Hygiene, Dental Laboratory Technology, Nuclear Medicine

Technology, Nursing (A), Radiography. Pres. Stelle K. Feuers.
Enroll.: 13,516
(213) 669-4000

*Los Angeles College of Chiropractic
16200 E. Amber Valley Drive, P.O. Box 1166, Whittier 90609. Private professional. 1966/1980. Sem. plan. Degrees: P. *Prof. Accred.:* Chiropractic Education. Pres. E. Maylon Drake.
Enroll.: 862
(213) 947-8755

Los Angeles Harbor College
1111 Figueroa Place, Wilmington 90744. Public (district) junior. 1952/1985 (WASC - Jr.). Sem. plan. Degrees: A. Pres. James L. Heinselman.
Enroll.: 7,763
(213) 518-1000

Los Angeles Mission College
1212 San Fernando Rd., San Fernando 91340. Public (district) junior. 1978/1984 (WASC-Jr.). Sem. plan. Degrees: A. Pres. Lowell J. Erickson.
Enroll.: 6,626
(818) 365-8271

Los Angeles Pierce College
6201 Winnetka Ave., Woodland Hills 91371. Public (district) junior. 1952/1984 (WASC-Jr.). Sem. plan. Degrees: A. *Prof. Accred.:* Nursing (A). Pres. David B. Wolf.
Enroll.: 17,135
(818) 347-0551

Los Angeles Southwest College
1600 W. Imperial Hwy., Los Angeles 90047. Public (district) junior. 1970/1983 (WASC-Jr.). Sem. plan. Degrees: A. Acting Pres. Thomas Lakin.
Enroll.: 2,873
(213) 777-2225

Los Angeles Trade-Technical College
400 W. Washington Blvd., Los Angeles 90015. Public (district) junior. 1952/1982 (WASC-Jr.). Sem. plan. Degrees: A. *Prof. Accred.:* Surgical Technology. Pres. Thomas L. Stevens, Jr.
Enroll.: 11,888
(213) 746-0800

Los Angeles Valley College
5800 Fulton Ave., Van Nuys 91401. Public (district) junior. 1952/1984 (WASC-Jr.). Sem. plan. Degrees: A. *Prof. Accred.:* Nursing (A), Respiratory Therapy. Pres. Mary E. Lee.
Enroll.: 17,701
(818) 781-1200

Los Medanos College
2700 E. Leland Rd., Pittsburg 94565. Public (district) junior. 1977/1982 (WASC -Jr.). Sem. plan. Degrees: A. Pres. Chester H. Case.
Enroll.: 4,493
(415) 439-2181

Louise Salinger Academy of Fashion
101 Jessie St., San Francisco 94105. Private. 1971/1977 (NATTS). Qtr. plan. Degrees: A,B, diplomas. V. Pres. Esther Herschelle.
Enroll.: 64 (*f.t.* 6 m., 28 w.)
(415) 362-8060

Loyola Marymount University
Loyola Blvd. at W. 80th Street, Los Angeles 90045. Independent (Roman Catholic) liberal arts and professional. 1949/1983 (WASC-Sr.). Sem. plan. Degrees: B,P,M. *Prof. Accred.:* Business (B), Engineering (civil, electrical, mechanical), Law. Pres. James N. Loughran, S.J.
Enroll.: FTE 5,461
(213) 642-2700

Marymount Palos Verdes College
30800 Palos Verdes Dr. E., Rancho Palos Verdes 90274. Private (Roman Catholic) junior. 1971/1984 (WASC-Jr.). 4-1-4 plan. Degrees: A. Pres. Thomas D. Wood.
Enroll.: 892
(213) 377-5501

MTD Business College
22505 Montgomery St., Hayward 94541. Private. 1975/1984 (ABHES). Courses of varying lengths. Certificates. *Prof. Accred.:* Medical Assisting. Dir. Marie Ladd.
Enroll.: 30
(415) 538-6151

Extension
667 Mission St., San Francisco 92270.

MTI-Western Business College
2731 Capitol Ave., Sacramento 95816. Private. 1975/1981 (AICS). Courses of varying lengths. Diplomas. Pres. John Zimmerman.
Enroll.: 1,014 (*f.t.* 318 m., 696 w.)
(916) 442-8933

Maric College of Medical Careers
7202 Princess View Dr., San Diego 92120. Private. 1981 (NATTS). 28-wk. courses. Cer-

*Candidate for Accreditation by Regional Accrediting Commission

tificates. *Prof. Accred.:* Medical Assisting. Pres. Richard I. Lyles.
Enroll.: 124 (*f.t.* 14 m., 110 w.)
(619) 583-8232

NORTH COUNTY CAMPUS
1300 Rancheros Dr., San Marco 92069. *Prof. Accred.:* Medical Assisting. Dir. James Trent.
(619) 747-1555

MARIN COMMUNITY COLLEGE
Kentfield 94904. Public (district). 1952/1985 (WASC-Jr.). Accreditation reflects consolidation of College of Marin, Kentfield, and Indian Valley Colleges, Novato, into Marin Community College. Sem. plan. Degrees: A. *Prof. Accred.:* Dental Assisting, Nursing (A). Pres. Myrna R. Miller.
Enroll.: 9,617
(415) 457-8811

THE MASTER'S COLLEGE
21726 W. Placerita Canyon Rd., Newhall 91322. Independent (Baptist) liberal arts. 1975/1985 (WASC-Sr.). Sem plan. Degrees: B. Pres. John R. MacArthur, Jr.
Enroll.: FTE 421
(805) 259-3540

MASTERS DESIGN AND TECHNICAL CENTER
3350 Scott Blvd., Santa Clara 95054. Private. 1984 (NATTS). Courses of varying lengths. Certificates. Pres. Darryl Lindsey.
(408) 727-2955

MED-HELP TRAINING SCHOOL
1079 Boulevard Way, Walnut Creek 94595. Private. 1981 (NATTS). Courses of varying lengths. Certificates. Dir. Elaine Reschke.
Enroll.: 48 (*f.t.* 14 m., 34 w.)
(415) 934-1947

MEDICAL SERVICES TRAINING CENTER
1963 N. "E" St., San Bernardino 92405. Private. 1983 (ABHES). Courses of varying lengths. Certificates. *Prof. Accred.:* Medical Assisting. Dir. Robert A. Krasney.
(714) 885-0036

MENDOCINO COLLEGE
P.O. Box 3000, Ukiah 95482. Public (district) junior. 1980/1985 (WASC-Jr.). Sem. plan. Degrees: A. Pres. Leroy R. Lowery.
Enroll.: 3,285
(707) 462-3000

MENLO COLLEGE
1000 El Camino Real, Atherton 94025. Independent business administration, computer information, and mass communication. 1952/1982 (WASC-Sr.). 4-1-4 plan. Degrees: A,B. Pres. Richard F. O'Brien.
Enroll.: 645
(415) 323-6141

MENNONITE BRETHREN BIBLICAL SEMINARY
4824 E. Butler at Chestnut, Fresno 93727. Independent (Mennonite Brethren) professional; graduate only. 1972/1982 (WASC-Sr.). 4-1-4 plan. Degrees: P,M. *Prof. Accred.:* Theology (1977/1981, ATS). Pres. Elmer A. Martens.
Enroll.: 119
(209) 251-8628

MERCED COLLEGE
3600 M St., Merced 95348. Public (district) junior. 1965/1983 (WASC-Jr.). Sem. plan. Degrees: A. *Prof. Accred.:* Dental Assisting, Dental Laboratory Technology, Radiography. Pres. Tom K. Harris, Jr.
Enroll.: 6,322
(209) 384-6000

MERIT COLLEGE OF COURT REPORTING
7101 Sepulveda Blvd., Van Nuys 91406. Private. 1972/1984 (AICS). Courses of varying lengths. Diplomas. Pres. M. William Gumpert.
Enroll.: 773 (*f.t.* 105 m., 668 w.)
(213) 988-6640

MERRITT COLLEGE
12500 Campus Dr., Oakland 94619. Public (district) junior. 1956/1981 (WASC-Jr.). Sem. plan. Degrees: A. *Prof. Accred.:* Radiography. Pres. Norma J. Tucker.
Enroll.: 6,023
(415) 531-4911

MICROWAVE TRAINING INSTITUTE
444 Castro St., Mountain View 94041. Private. 1984 (NATTS). Courses of varying lengths. Certificates. Dir. Allan W. Scott.
(415) 696-7363

MILLS COLLEGE
Oakland 94613. Independent liberal arts for women, graduate school coeducational. 1949/1981 (WASC-Sr.). Sem. plan. Degrees: B,M. Pres. Mary S. Metz.
Enroll.: FTE 896
(415) 430-2255

MIRA COSTA COLLEGE
One Barnard Dr., Oceanside 92056. Public (district) junior. 1952/1982 (WASC-Jr.). Sem. plan. Degrees: A. Pres. H. Deon Holt.

California

Enroll.: 5,509
(619) 757-2121

MISSION COLLEGE
3000 Mission College Blvd., Santa Clara 95054. Public (district) junior. 1979/1984 (WASC-Jr.). Sem. plan. Degrees: A. Pres. Betty Dean.
Enroll.: 8,799
(408) 988-2200

MODESTO JUNIOR COLLEGE
435 College Ave., Modesto 95350. Public (district) junior. 1952/1983 (WASC-Jr.). Sem. plan. Degrees: A. *Prof. Accred.:* Dental Assisting, EMT-Paramedic Training, Medical Assisting, Nursing (A), Respiratory Therapy Technology. Pres. Tom Van Groningen.
Enroll.: 9,550
(209) 575-6067

MOLER BARBER COLLEGE
3500 Broadway, Oakland 94611. Private. 1980 (NATTS). Courses of varying lengths. Certificates. Owner Willie C. McHenry.
Enroll.: 36 (*f.t.* 18 m., 18 w.)
(415) 652-4917

MOLER BARBER COLLEGE
727 J St., Sacramento 95814. Private. 1980 (NATTS). Courses of varying lengths. Diplomas. Dir. Jame s A. Murray, Jr.
Enroll.: 52 (*f.t.* 29 m., 22 w.)
(916) 441-0072

MOLER BARBER SCHOOL
50 Mason St., San Francisco 94102. Private. 1980 (NATTS). Courses of varying lengths. Diplomas. Pres. Donald Forfang.
Enroll.: 25 (*f.t.* 12 m., 11 w.)
(415) 362-5885

MOLER BARBER COLLEGE
324 E. Market St., Stockton 95202. Private. 1980 (NATTS). Courses of varying lengths. Diplomas. Dir. James A. Murry, Jr.
Enroll.: 10 (*f.t.* 5 m., 5 w.)
(209) 465-3218

MONTEREY INSTITUTE OF INTERNATIONAL STUDIES
425 Van Buren, Monterey 93940. Independent language-based. Upper division and graduate only. 1961/1985 (WASC-Sr.). Qtr. plan. Degrees: B, M. Pres. William G. Craig.
Enroll.: FTE 383
(408) 649-3113

MONTEREY PENINSULA COLLEGE
980 Fremont, Monterey 93940. Public (district) junior. 1952/1982 (WASC-Jr.). Sem. plan. Degrees: A. *Prof. Accred.:* Dental Assisting, Medical Assisting. Pres. Samuel A. Ferguson.
Enroll.: 5,325
(408) 646-4000

MOORPARK COLLEGE
7075 Campus Rd., Moorpark 93021. Public (district) junior. 1969/1982 (WASC-Jr.). Sem. plan. Degrees: A. Pres. W. Ray Hearon.
Enroll.: 9,023
(805) 529-2321

MOUNT ST. MARY'S COLLEGE
12001 Chalon Rd., Los Angeles 90049. Independent (Roman Catholic) liberal arts primarily for women; includes Doheny Campus, 10 Chester Pl., Los Angeles 90007. 1949/1981 (WASC-Sr.). 4-1-4 plan. Degrees: A, B, M. *Prof. Accred.:* Music, Nursing (A, B), Physical Therapy. Pres. Sister Magdalen Coughlin, C.S.J.
Enroll.: FTE 1,044
(213) 476-2237

MT. SAN ANTONIO COLLEGE
1100 N. Grand Ave., Walnut 91789. Public (district) junior. 1952/1982 (WASC-Jr.). Sem. plan. Degrees: A. *Prof. Accred.:* Radiography, Respiratory Therapy, Respiratory Therapy Technology. Pres. John D. Randall.
Enroll.: 20,314
(714) 594-5611

MT. SAN JACINTO COLLEGE
1499 N. State St., San Jacinto 92383. Public (district) junior. 1965/1983 (WASC-Jr.). Sem. plan. Degrees: A. Pres. Dennis M. Mayer.
Enroll.: 3,136
(714) 654-8011

MUSICIANS' INSTITUTE
6757 Hollywood Blvd., Hollywood 90028. Private professional. 1980. 1-year program. Certificates. *Prof. Accred.:* Music. Pres. Patrick Hicks.
Enroll: 167 (*f.t.* 140)
(213) 462-1384

NAPA VALLEY COLLEGE
2277 Napa-Vallejo Highway, Napa 94558. Public (district) junior. 1952/1986 (WASC-Jr.). Sem. plan. Degrees: A. *Prof. Accred.:* Respiratory Therapy. Pres. William H. Feddersen.
Enroll.: 4,892
(707) 253-3095

NATION COLLEGE
50 Mark West Springs Rd., Santa Rosa 95401. Private business. 1979 (AICS). Courses of varying lengths. Certificates, diplomas. CEO Steven Bagley.
Enroll.: 245 (*f.t.* 19 m., 226 w.)
(707) 527-7827

NATIONAL BROADCASTING SCHOOL
5738 Marconi Ave., Suite B-1, Carmichael 95608. Private. 1985 (NATTS). Courses of varying lengths. Certificates, diplomas. Dir. Todd J. Shipper.
(916) 487-2346

NATIONAL BUSINESS INSTITUTE
4300 Central Ave., Riverside 92506. Private. 1982 (AICS). Courses of varying lengths. Certificates, diplomas. Dir. Ken Murakami.
Enroll.: 305 (*f.t.* 149 m., 156 w.)
(714) 787-9300

NATIONAL EDUCATION CENTER
1380 S. Sanderson Ave., Anaheim 92806. Private. 1985 (NATTS). Courses of varying lengths. Certificates, diplomas. *Prof. Accred.:* Medical Assisting. Dir. Albert DiStefano.
(714) 758-0330

NATIONAL EDUCATION CENTER—BRYMAN CAMPUS
1120 N. Brookhurst Rd., Anaheim 92801. Private. 1973/1978 (NATTS). Courses of varying lengths. Diplomas. Dir. Albert DiStefano.
Enroll.: 275 (*f.t.* 25 m., 250 w.)
(714) 778-6500

NATIONAL EDUCATION CENTER—BRYMAN CAMPUS
20835 Sherman Way, Canoga Park 91306. Private. 1974/1979 (NATTS). Courses of varying lengths. Diplomas. *Prof. Accred.:* Medical Assisting. Dir. Susan Young.
Enroll.: 140 (*f.t.* 5 m., 115 w.)
(818) 887-7911

NATIONAL EDUCATION CENTER—BRYMAN CAMPUS
5350 Atlantic Ave., Long Beach 90805. Private. 1968/1979 (NATTS). Courses of varying lengths. Diplomas. Dir. Pam Burns.
Enroll.: 205
(213) 422-6007

NATIONAL EDUCATION CENTER—BRYMAN CAMPUS
1017 Wilshire Blvd., Los Angeles 90017. Private. 1973/1978 (NATTS). Courses of varying lengths. Diplomas. Dir. Beverly Yourstone.
Enroll.: 161 (*f.t.* 4 m., 137 w.)
(213) 481-1640

NATIONAL EDUCATION CENTER—BRYMAN CAMPUS
3505 N. Hart Ave., Rosemead 91770. Private. 1968/1978 (NATTS). Courses of varying lengths. Diplomas. Dir. George Ballew.
Enroll.: 170 (*f.t.* 1 m., 169 w.)
(818) 573-5470

NATIONAL EDUCATION CENTER—BRYMAN CAMPUS
731 Market St., San Francisco 94103. Private. 1972/1978 (NATTS). Courses of varying lengths. Diplomas. Dir. Edward M. Reardon.
Enroll.: 260 (*f.t.* 3 m., 257 w.)
(415) 777-2500

NATIONAL EDUCATION CENTER—BRYMAN CAMPUS
2015 Naglee Ave., San Jose 95128. Private. 1973/1978 (NATTS). Courses of varying lengths. Certificates. Dir. Diane Donnelly.
Enroll.: 140 (*f.t.* 3 m., 137 w.)
(408) 275-8800

NATIONAL EDUCATION CENTER—BRYMAN CAMPUS
4212 W. Artesia Blvd., Torrance 90504. Private. 1973/1981 (NATTS). Qtr. plan. Diplomas. *Prof. Accred.:* Medical Assisting. Dir. Richard Laub.
Enroll.: 160
(213) 542-6951

NATIONAL EDUCATION CENTER—SAWYER CAMPUS
10474 Santa Monica Blvd., Los Angeles 90025. Private business. 1972/1984 (AICS). Courses of varying lengths. Certificates. Dir. Dianne Maddock.
Enroll.: 1,467 (*f.t.* 870 m., 597 w.)
(213) 479-0911

NATIONAL EDUCATION CENTER—SAWYER CAMPUS
2415 K St., Sacramento 95816. Private business. 1973/1986 (AICS). Courses of varying lengths. Certificates. Dir. Barry Helgoth.
Enroll.: 612 (*f.t.* 126 m., 486 w.)
(916) 444-3936

California

NATIONAL EDUCATION CENTER—SKADRON CAMPUS
1200 N. E St., San Bernardino 92405. Private business. 1962/1985 (AICS). Qtr. plan. Degrees: A. Acting Dir. Ron Garrison.
Enroll.: 1,116 (*f.t.* 390 m., 726 w.)
(714) 885-3896

NATIONAL EDUCATION CORPORATION
1300 Bristol St., Newport Beach 92660. Private. Business, trade, and home study courses of varying lengths. AICS, NATTS, NHSC. Pres. H. David Bright.
(714) 546-7360

EXTENSION
National Education Center/National Institute of Tech Campus 5172 Orange Ave., Cypress 90630. Dir. Mona Maassarani.
(714) 952-8713

NORTH AMERICAN CORRESPONDENCE SCHOOLS
1300 Bristol St., Newport Beach 92660. A division accredited by NHSC. Private home study courses. Pres. David Crowther.
(714) 546-7360

THE BARTON SCHOOL A branch of NORTH AMERICAN CORRESPONDENCE SCHOOLS, NEWPORT BEACH.

POLICE SCIENCES INSTITUTE A branch of NORTH AMERICAN CORRESPONDENCE SCHOOLS, NEWPORT BEACH.

NATIONAL TECHNICAL COLLEGE
12001 Victory Blvd., North Hollywood 91606. Private. 1984 (ABHES).Courses of varying lengths. Certificates, diplomas. Pres. Anatoly Bidny.

EXTENSION
600 S. Spring St., Los Angeles 90013.

NATIONAL TECHNICAL SCHOOLS
4000 S. Figueroa St., Los Angeles 90037. Private. 1967/1983 (NATTS); 1957/1982 (NHSC). Courses of varying lengths. Degrees: A, certificates, diplomas. Pres. Robert Parma.
Enroll.: 922 (*f.t.* 489 m., 2 w.)
(213) 234-9061

NATIONAL UNIVERSITY
4141 Camino del Rio S., San Diego 92108. Independent. 1977/1982 (WASC-Sr.). 12-term plan. Degrees: A,B,P,M. Pres. David Chigos.
Enroll.: FTE 8,536
1-800 NAT-UNIV

NAVAL AMPHIBIOUS SCHOOL
Coronado 92155. Public (federal) technical. 1979/1985 (WASC-Jr.). Courses of varying lengths. Certificates. Commanding Officer Capt. J. L. Harken, U.S.N.
Enroll.: 1,542
(619) 437-2236

NAVAL COMBAT SYSTEMS TECHNICAL SCHOOLS COMMAND
Mare Island, Vallejo 94592. Public (federal) technical. 1986 (WASC-Jr.). Courses of varying lengths. Certificates. Commanding Officer Capt. T. E. Kilpatrick, U.S.N.
(707) 554-8550

NAVAL CONSTRUCTION TRAINING CENTER
Port Hueneme 93043. Public (federal) technical. 1979/1984 (WASC-Jr.). Courses of varying lengths. Certificates. Cmdr. Gary E. Monroe, U.S.N.
Enroll.: 400
(805) 982-3193

NAVAL SCHOOL PHYSICAL DISTRIBUTION MANAGEMENT
Oakland 94625. Public (federal) technical. 1986 (WASC-Jr.). Courses of varying lengths. Certificates. Commanding Officer Capt. J. W. Lunn, U.S.N.
Enroll.: 1,409
(415) 466-2155

NAVAL POSTGRADUATE SCHOOL
Monterey 93940. Public (federal) science and technology; upper division and graduate only. 1955/1985 (WASC-Sr.). Qtr. plan. Degrees: B,M,D. *Prof. Accred.:* Engineering (aeronautical, electrical, mechanical). Supt. Robert H. Shumaker.
Enroll.: FTE 1,668
(408) 626-2411

NAVY SERVICE SCHOOL COMMAND
San Diego 92133. Public (federal). 1985 (WASC-Jr.). Courses of varying lengths. Certificates. Commanding Officer Capt. V. O. Young, U.S.N.
Enroll.: 4,687
(619) 225-3416

NEW COLLEGE OF CALIFORNIA
777 Valencia St., San Francisco 94110. Independent liberal arts and law. 1976/1985 (WASC-Sr.). Sem. plan. Degrees: B,P,M. Pres. Mildred M. Henry.
Enroll.: FTE 638
(415) 626-1696

NORTH COUNTY COLLEGE
463 N. Midway Dr., Escondido 92027. Private business. 1979/1982 (AICS). Qtr. plan. Certificates, diplomas. Pres. Dean Petersen.
Enroll.: 428 (*f.t.* 76 m., 352 w.)
(619) 747-7204

BRANCH CAMPUS
5440 Morehouse Dr., San Diego 92121. Vice Pres. Wayne D. Gray.
(619) 450-1091

NORTHROP UNIVERSITY
5800 W. Arbor Vitae St., Inglewood 90306. Independent technological, business, and law. 1960/1985 (WASC-Sr.). Qtr. plan. Degrees: A,B,P,M. *Prof. Accred.:* Engineering (aerospace, electronic, mechanical), Engineering Technology (aircraft maintenance). Pres. B. J. Shell.
Enroll.: FTE 1,003
(213) 641-3470

NORTH-WEST COLLEGE OF MEDICAL AND DENTAL ASSISTANTS
739 E. Walnut, Pasadena 91101. Private. 1976/1982 (NATTS). Courses of varying lengths. Diplomas. *Prof. Accred.:* Medical Assisting. Exec. Dir. Marsha Fuerst.
(213) 796-5815

NORTH-WEST COLLEGE OF MEDICAL AND DENTAL ASSISTANTS
134 W. Holt Ave., Pomona 91768. Private. 1976/1982 (NATTS). Courses of varying lengths. Diplomas. *Prof. Accred.:* Medical Assisting. Exec. Dir. Marsha Fuerst.
Enroll.: 100 (*f.t.* 3 m., 97 w.)
(714) 623-1552

NORTH-WEST COLLEGE OF MEDICAL AND DENTAL ASSISTANTS
2121 W. Garvey Ave., West Covina 91790. Private. 1973/1979 (NATTS). Courses of varying lengths. Diplomas. *Prof. Accred.:* Medical Assisting. Exec. Dir. Marsha Fuerst.
Enroll.: 100 (*f.t.* 4 m., 96 w.)
(213) 962-3495

OAKLAND COLLEGE OF COURT REPORTING
343 19th St., Oakland 94612. Private. 1982 (AICS). Courses of varying lengths. Certificates, diplomas. Dir. Frank Hutchinson.
Enroll.: 236 (*f.t* 22 m., 214 w.)
(415) 465-3184

OAKLAND COLLEGE OF DENTAL-MEDICAL ASSISTANTS
388 17th St., Oakland 94612. Private. 1968/1978 (NATTS). Courses of varying lengths. Diplomas. *Prof. Accred.:* Medical Assisting. Pres. Sarah A. Davis.
Enroll.: 131 (*f.t.* 21 m., 110 w.)
(415) 832-6955

OCCIDENTAL COLLEGE
1600 Campus Rd., Los Angeles 90041. Independent liberal arts. 1949/1985 (WASC-Sr.). 3-term plan. Degrees: B,M. Pres. Richard C. Gilman.
Enroll.: FTE 1,630
(213) 259-2974

OHLONE COLLEGE
43600 Mission Blvd., Fremont 94539. Public (district) junior. 1970/1985 (WASC-Jr.). Sem. plan. Degrees: A. *Prof. Accred.:* Medical Assisting, Nursing (A), Respiratory Therapy, Respiratory Therapy Technology. Pres. Peter L . Blomerley.
Enroll.: 7,214
(415) 659-6000

ORANGE COAST COLLEGE
2701 Fairview Rd., Costa Mesa 92628. Public (district) junior. 1952/1985 (WASC-Jr.). Sem. plan. Degrees: A. *Prof. Accred.:* Dental Assisting, Dental Laboratory Technology, EEG Technology, Medical Assisting, Radiation Therapy Technology, Radiography, Respiratory Therapy. Pres. Donald R. Brousard.
Enroll.: 21,925
(714) 432-0202

ORANGE COUNTY BUSINESS COLLEGE
1401 S. Anaheim Blvd., Anaheim 92805. Private. 1973/1979 (AICS). Courses of varying lengths. Certificates, diplomas. Dir. G. E. Kerlin.
Enroll.: 280 (*f.t.* 41 m., 239 w.)
(714) 772-6941

OTIS ART INSTITUTE OF PARSONS SCHOOL OF DESIGN
2401 Wilshire Blvd., Los Angeles 90057. Independent professional, upper division and graduate only. 1956/1980 (WASC-Sr.). Sem. plan. Degrees: B,M. *Prof. Accred.:* Art. Dean Roger Workman.
Enroll.: FTE 713
(213) 251-0500

OXNARD COLLEGE
4000 S. Rose Ave., Oxnard 93033. Public (district) junior. 1978/1983 (WASC-Jr.). Sem. plan. Degrees: A. Pres. Edward Robings.
Enroll.: 7,214
(805) 488-0911

Pacific Christian College
2500 E. Nutwood Ave., Fullerton 92631. Independent (Christian Churches and Churches of Christ) liberal arts. 1963/1984 (AABC); 1969/1983 (WASC-Sr.). 4-1-4 plan. Degrees: A,B,M. Pres. Knofel L. Staton.
Enroll.: 414
(714) 879-3901

Pacific Coast College
6562 Stanford Ave., Garden Grove 92645. Private. 1972/1977 (NATTS). Courses of varying lengths. Diplomas. *Prof. Accred.:* Medical Assisting, Respiratory Therapy Technology. Dir. Beverly Howard.
Enroll.: 187 (*f.t.* 15 m., 172 w.)
(714) 898-5669.

Pacific Coast College
323 W. Eighth St., Los Angeles 90014. Private. 1976/1981 (NATTS). Courses of varying lengths. Diplomas. Pres. Diane Gluchow.
Enroll.: 316 (*f.t.* 144 m., 96 w.)
(213) 622-2371

Pacific Coast College—Los Angeles Campus
198 S. Alvarado St., Los Angeles 90057. Private. 1972/1982 (NATTS). Courses of varying lengths. Diplomas. Admin. Charles Schrader.
Enroll.: 250 (*f.t.* 40 m., 185 w.)
(213) 413-3390

West Los Angeles Campus (Branch)
6330 Arizona Circle, West Los Angeles 90045. Private. 1982 (NATTS). Courses of varying lengths. Diplomas. *Prof. Accred.:* Practical Nursing.Admin. Milton D. Morrison.
Enroll.: 70 (*f.t.* 4 m., 66 w.)
(213) 417-8922

Pacific Coast College
7655 Convoy Ct., San Diego 92111. Private junior. 1982 (AICS). Qtr. plan. Degrees: A. Ex. Dir. Beth Wilson..
Enroll.: 492 (*f.t.* 98 m., 394 w.)
(714) 560-4146

Branch Campus
7227 Broadway, Lemon Grove 92045. Exec. Dir. Peggy Taylor.
(619) 460-7227

Pacific Coast College
12519 E. Washington Blvd., Whittier 90602. Private business. 1976/1985 (AICS). Courses of varying lengths. Certificates. Dir. Phyllis Lorenzen.
Enroll.: 572 (*f.t.* 96 m., 476 w.)
(213) 692-0246

Pacific Coast Technical Institute
1740 Orangethorpe Pk.,Anaheim 92801. Private. 1975/1979 (NATTS). Courses of varying lengths. Diplomas. Dir. Bob Lord.
Enroll.: 291 (*f.t.* 274 m., 5 w.)
(714) 879-1053

Pacific Coast Technical Institute
9722 E. Firestone Blvd., Downey 90241. Private. 1973/1978 (NATTS). Courses of varying lengths. Diplomas. Dir. Bob Lord.
Enroll.: 276 (*f.t.* 230 m., 6 w.)
(213) 923-9489

Pacific Coast Technical Institute
14620 Keswick, Van Nuys 91405. Private. 1984 (NATTS). Courses of varying lengths. Diplomas. Dir. Paul Lehrer.
(213) 781-9500

Pacific College of Medical and Dental Careers
4411 30th St., San Diego 92116. Private. 1969/1979 (NATTS). Courses of varying lengths. Diplomas. *Prof. Accred.:* Medical Assisting. Dir. Sheldon Wolpoff.
Enroll.: f.t. 232 w.
(619) 280-5005

Pacific Lutheran Theological Seminary
2770 Marin Ave., Berkeley 94708. Private (Lutheran Church in America and American Lutheran Church) professional; graduate only. Qtr. plan. Degrees: P,M,D. *Prof. Accred.:* Theology (1964/1976, ATS). Pres. Walter M. Stuhr.
Enroll.: 166
(415) 524-5264

Pacific Oaks College
5 Westmoreland Pl., Pasadena 91103. Independent professional; upper division and graduate only. 1959/1985 (WASC-Sr.). Sem. plan. Degrees: B,M. Pres. Katherine Gabel.
Enroll.: FTE 355
(818) 795-9161

Pacific School of Religion
1798 Scenic Ave., Berkeley 94709. Independent (interdenominational) professional; graduate only. Member of the Graduate Theological Union. 1971/1983 (WASC-Sr.). Qtr. plan. Degrees: P,M,D. *Prof. Accred.:*

Theology (1938/1983, ATS). Pres. Neely D. McCarter.
Enroll.: 232
(415) 848-0528

PACIFIC TRAVEL SCHOOL
2515 N. Main St., Santa Ana 92701. Private. 1968/1978 (NATTS). Courses of varying lengths. Diplomas. Dir. J. R. McClure.
Enroll.: 480 (*f.t.* 30 m., 210 w.)
(714) 543-9495

PACIFIC UNION COLLEGE
Angwin 94508. Independent (Seventh-day Adventist) liberal arts. 1951/1983 (WASC-Sr.). Qtr . plan. Degrees: A,B,M. *Prof. Accred.*: Music, Nursing (A,B), Social Work (B). Pres. Malcom Maxwell.
Enroll.: FTE 1,316
(707) 965-6303

PALMER COLLEGE OF CHIROPRACTIC-WEST
1095 Dunford Way, Sunnyvale 94087. Private professional. 1985. Sem . plan. Degrees: P. *Prof. Accred.*: Chiropractic Education. Pres. John Miller.
Enroll.: FTE 530
(408) 244-8907

PALO VERDE COLLEGE
811 W. Chanslorway, Blythe 92225. Public (district) junior. 1952/1985 (WASC-Jr.). Sem. plan. Degrees: A. Pres. Kirk Avery.
Enroll.: 730
(619) 922-6168

PALOMAR COLLEGE
1140 W. Mission Rd., San Marcos 92069. Public (district) junior. 1952/1986 (WASC-Jr.). Sem. plan. Degrees: A. *Prof. Accred.*: Dental Assisting, Nursing (A). Pres. George R. Boggs
Enroll.: 12,766
(619) 744-1150

PASADENA CITY COLLEGE
1570 E. Colorado Blvd., Pasadena 91106. Public (district) junior. 1952/1986 (WASC-Jr.). Sem. plan. Degrees: A. *Prof. Accred.*: Dental Assisting, Dental Hygiene, Dental Laboratory Technology, Medical Assisting, Nursing (A), Radiography. Supt.-Pres. John W. Casey.
Enroll.: ,17,908
(818) 578-7123

PATRICIA STEVENS FASHION COLLEGE
541 Mission Valley Ctr. W., San Diego 92108. Private. 1980/1983 (AICS). Courses of varying lengths. Certificates. Dir. Ernine L. Merino.
Enroll.: 299 (*f.t.* 7 m., 292 w.)
(619) 298-0242

PATTEN COLLEGE
2433 Coolidge Ave., Oakland 94601. Independent (Christian Evangelical Church of America) liberal arts and professional. 1980/1983 (WASC-Sr.). Sem. plan. Degrees: A,B. Pres. Priscilla C. Patten.
Enroll.: FTE 98
(415) 533-8303

PEPPERDINE UNIVERSITY
24255 Pacific Coast Hwy., Malibu 90265. (Includes campuses at Los Angeles and Malibu). Independent (Church of Christ) liberal arts and professional. 1952/1983 (WASC-Sr.). Tri-plan. Degrees: B,P,M,D. *Prof. Accred.*: Law, Music. Pres. David Davenport.
Total Enroll.: FTE 4,999
(213) 456-4000

PITZER COLLEGE
Claremont 91711. Independent liberal arts; one of the Claremont Colleges. 1965/1983 (WASC-Sr.). Sem. plan. Degrees: B. Pres. Frank L. Ellsworth.
Enroll.: FTE 720
(619) 621-8000

PLATT COLLEGE
6250 El Cajon Blvd., San Diego 92115. Private. 1985 (NATTS). Courses of varying lengths. Certificates. Dir. Marshall Payn.
(619) 265-0107

POINT LOMA NAZARENE COLLEGE
3900 Lomaland Dr., San Diego 92106. Independent (Church of Nazarene) liberal arts. 1949/1985 (WASC-Sr.). Qtr. plan. Degrees: A,B,M. *Prof. Accred.*: Nursing (B). Pres. Jim L. Bond.
Enroll.: FTE 1,685
(619) 222-6474

POLYTECHNICAL INSTITUTE
890 Pomeroy Ave., Santa Clara 95051. Private. 1980 (NATTS). Courses of varying lengths. Certificates, diplomas. Pres. William L. Karr.
Enroll.: 60 (*f.t.* 50 m., 1 w.)
(408) 247-8818

POMONA COLLEGE
Claremont 91711. Independent liberal arts; one of the Claremont Colleges. 1949/1983

(WASC-Sr.). Early sem. plan. Degrees: B. Pres. David Alexander.
Enroll.: FTE 1,359
(714) 621-8000

PORTERVILLE COLLEGE
900 S. Main St., Porterville 93257. Public (district) junior. 1952/1984 (WASC-Jr.). Sem. plan. Degrees: A. Pres. Paul D. Alcantra.
Enroll.: 763
(209) 781-3130

PRACTICAL SCHOOLS
3290 E. Carpenter, Anaheim 92806. Private. 1973/1979 (NATTS). Courses of varying lengths. Diplomas. Pres. Marlyn B. Sheehan.
Enroll.: 156 (*f.t.* 106 m., 10 w.)
(714) 630-9614

QUEEN OF THE HOLY ROSARY COLLEGE
P.O. Box 3908, 43326 Mission Blvd., Mission San Jose 94539. Private (Roman Catholic) junior. 1979/1985 (WASC-Jr.). Sem. plan. Degrees: A. Dean Sister Mary Paul Mohegan.
Enroll.: 232 (*f.t.* 10 w.)
(415) 657-2468

RANCHO ARROYO VOCATIONAL TECHNICAL INSTITUTE
9880 Jackson Rd., Sacramento 95826. Private. 1985 (NATTS). Courses of varying lengths. Certificates. Admin. Frank Howard.
(916) 362-1125

RANCHO SANTIAGO COLLEGE (FORMERLY SANTA ANA COLLEGE)
17th at Bristol St., Santa Ana 92706. Public (junior). 1952/1985 (WASC-Jr.). Sem. plan. Degrees: A. Pres. Robert Jensen.
Enroll.: 20,843
(714) 667-3000

RAND GRADUATE SCHOOL OF POLICY STUDIES
1700 Main St., Santa Monica 90406. Independent, graduate only. 1975/1985 (WASC-Sr.). Qtr. plan. Degrees: D. Dean Charles Wolf, Jr.
Enroll.: FTE 57
(213) 393-0411

RIO HONDO COLLEGE
3600 Workman Mill Rd., Whittier 90608. Public (district) junior. 1967/1985 (WASC-Jr.). Sem. plan. Degrees: A. *Prof. Accred.:* Dental Assisting, Respiratory Therapy. Pres. Herbert M. Sussman.
Enroll.: 10,872
(213) 692-0921

RIVERSIDE CITY COLLEGE
4800 Magnolia Ave., Riverside 92506. Public (district) junior. 1952/1984 (WASC-Jr.). Sem. plan. Degrees: A. *Prof. Accred.:* Dental Laboratory Technology, Nursing (A). Pres. Charles A. Kane.
Enroll.: 13,408
(714) 684-3240

ROSSTON SCHOOL OF MEN'S HAIR DESIGN
1814 W. Lincoln Ave., Anaheim 92804. Private. 1976/1981 (NATTS). Courses of varying lengths. Certificates, diplomas. Pres. Ross L. Alloway.
Enroll.: 60 (*f.t.* 42 m., 18 w.)
(800) 821-4934

ROSSTON SCHOOL OF MEN'S HAIR DESIGN
717 Pine Ave., Long Beach 90813. Private. 1976/1981 (NATTS). Courses of varying lengths. Diplomas. Pres. Ross L. Alloway.
Enroll.: 25 (*f.t.* 18 m., 7 w.)
1-(800) 821-4934

ROSSTON SCHOOL OF MEN'S HAIR DESIGN
230 E. Third St., Long Beach 90802. Private. 1975/1980 (NATTS). Courses of varying lengths. Certificates, diplomas. Mgr. Bob Warsella.
Enroll.: 60 (*f.t.* 42 m., 18 w.)
(213) 437-5551

ROSSTON SCHOOL OF MEN'S HAIR DESIGN
29 W. Colorado Blvd., Pasadena 91105. Private. 1976/1981 (NATTS). Courses of varying lengths. Diplomas. Pres. Ross L. Alloway.
Enroll.: 25 (*f.t.* 18 m., 7 w.)
(213) 792-7216

ROSSTON SCHOOL OF MEN'S HAIR DESIGN
18330 Sherman Way, Reseda 91335. Private. 1976/1981 (NATTS). Courses of varying lengths. Certificates, diplomas. Pres. Ross L. Alloway.
Enroll.: 25 (*f.t.* 18 m., 7 w.)
(800) 821-4934

ROSSTON SCHOOL OF MEN'S HAIR DESIGN
637 W. Fifth St., San Bernardino 92401. Private. 1976/1981 (NATTS). Courses of varying lengths. Certificates, diplomas. Pres. Jerry A. Anderson.
Enroll.: 25 (*f.t.* 18 m., 7 w.)
(800) 821-4934

Royal Hair Institute
5924 Whittier Blvd., Los Angeles 90022. Private. 1979 (NATTS). Courses of varying lengths. Certificates. Pres. Loran Keller.
Enroll.: 68 (*f.t.* 34 m., 34 w.)
(213) 724-1087

Sacramento City College
3835 Freeport Blvd., Sacramento 95822. Public (district) junior. 1952/1986 (WASC-Jr.). Sem. plan. Degrees: A. *Prof. Accred.:* Dental Assisting, Dental Hygiene, Nursing (A). Pres. Carl C. Andersen.
Enroll.: 13,051
(916) 449-7111

Saddleback College
28000 Marguerite Pkwy., Mission Viejo 92692. Public (district) junior. 1971/1983 (WASC-Jr.). Sem. plan. Degrees: A. Chanc. Richard Sneed.
Enroll.: 21,493
(714) 831-4500

Saint John's College
5118 E. Seminary Rd., Camarillo 93010. Independent (Roman Catholic, Archdiocese of Los Angeles) liberal arts. 1951/1981 (WASC-Sr.). Sem. plan. Degrees: B. Pres. Sylvester Ryan.
Enroll.: FTE 126
(805) 482-4697

Saint John's Seminary
5012 E. Seminary Road, Camarillo 93010. Independent (Roman Catholic). 1951/1981 (WASC-Sr.). Sem. plan. Degrees: P,M. *Prof. Accred.:* Theology (1976/1981, ATS). Rector Charles E. Miller, C.M.
Enroll.: 135
(805) 482-2755

Saint Joseph's College Seminary
(*Formerly* St. Patrick's College)
P.O. Box 7009, Mountain View 94039. Independent (Roman Catholic, Diocese of San Jose) pre-professional for men. 1954/1985 (WASC-Sr.). Qtr. plan. Degrees: B. Pres. Gerald D. Coleman, S.S.
Enroll.: FTE 107
(415) 967-9501

Saint Mary's College of California
Moraga 94575. Independent (Roman Catholic, Christian Brothers) liberal arts. 1949/1985 (WASC-Sr.). 4-1-4 plan. Degrees: A,B,M. Pres. Mel Anderson, F.S.C.
Enroll.: FTE 2,853
(415) 376-4411

Saint Patrick's Seminary
320 Middlefield Rd., Menlo Park 94025. Independent (Roman Catholic) professional; graduate only. 1971/1984 (WASC-Sr.). Sem. plan. Degrees: P,M. *Prof. Accred.:* Theology (1971/1984, ATS). Rector-Pres. Howard P. Bleichner, S.S.
Enroll.: f.t. 82 m.
(415) 325-5621

Samuel Merritt College of Nursing
370 Hawthorne Ave., Oakland 94609. Independent, professional. 1984 (WASC-Sr.). 4-1-4 plan. Degrees: A,B. Pres. Sharon Diaz.
Enroll.: FTE 278
(415) 420-6011

San Bernardino Valley College
701 S. Mt. Vernon Ave., San Bernardino 92410. Public (district) junior. 1952/1986 (WASC-Jr.). Sem. plan. Degrees: A. Pres. Arthur M. Jensen.
Enroll.: 10,742
(714) 888-6511

San Diego College for Medical and Dental Assistants
5952 El Cajon Blvd., San Diego 92115. Private. 1969/1980 (NATTS). Courses of varying lengths. Certificates, diplomas. Pres. Frank E. Hollar.
Enroll.: 115 (*f.t.* 10 m., 105 w.)
(619) 582-1319

San Diego City College
1313 Twelfth Ave., San Diego 92101. Public (district) junior. 1952/1982 (WASC-Jr.). Sem. plan. Degrees: A. Pres. Allen J. Repashy.
Enroll.: 11,616
(619) 230-2400

San Diego Golf Academy
P.O. Box 3050, Rancho Santa Fe 92067. Private. 1982 (AICS). Sem. plan. Certificates, diplomas. Exec. Dir. Tim Somerville.
Enroll.: 107 (*f.t.* 102 m., 5 w.)
(619) 756-2486

San Diego Mesa College
7250 Mesa College Dr., San Diego 92111. Public (district) junior. 1966/1982 (WASC-Jr.). Sem. plan. Degrees: A. *Prof. Accred.:* Dental Assisting, Medical Assisting, Medical Record Technology, Radiography. Pres. Allen Brooks.
Enroll.: 17,989
(619) 560-2600

San Diego Miramar College
10440 Black Mountain Rd., San Diego 92126. Public (district) junior. 1982 (WASC-Jr.). Sem. plan. Degrees: A. Pres. George F. Yee.
Enroll.: 3,616
(619) 693-6800

*San Diego State University
5402 College Ave., San Diego 92182. 1949/1984 (WASC-Sr.). Sem. plan. Degrees: B,M; also D in chemistry, ecology, and genetics in cooperation with U.C. campuses at San Diego, Riverside, and Berkeley, respectively; and D in education with a multicultural component in cooperation with the Claremont Graduate School. *Prof. Accred.:* Accounting (Type A,C), Art, Business (B,M), Engineering (aerospace, civil, electrical, mechanical), Health Services Administration, Home Economics, Interior Design, Journalism, Music, Nursing (B,M), Public Health, Rehabilitation Counseling, Social Work (B,M), Speech Pathology and Audiology, Teacher Education (*e,s,p*). Pres. Thomas B. Day.
Enroll.: FTE 26,196
(619) 265-5200

San Francisco Art Institute
800 Chestnut St., San Francisco 94133. Independent professional. 1954/1984 (WASC-Sr.). Sem. plan. Degrees: B,M. *Prof. Accred.:* Art. Pres. Stephen J. Goldstine.
Enroll.: FTE 558
(415) 771-7020

San Francisco Barber College
64 Sixth St., San Francisco 94103. Private. 1984 (NATTS). Courses of varying lengths. Certificates. Pres. Frank Yorkis.
(415) 621-6802

San Francisco College of Mortuary Science
1450 Post St., San Francisco 94109. Private professional. 1962/1982 (WASC-Jr.). Tri. plan. Degrees: A. Pres. Michael C. Hawkins.
Enroll.: 40
(415) 567-0674

San Francisco Community College District
33 Gough St., San Francisco 94103. Public (district) junior. 1952/1983 (WASC-Jr.). Chanc. Hilary K. L. Hsu.

*Member California State University System

Enroll.: 28,405 (*f.t.* 4,328 m., 3,748 w.)
(415) 239-3000

City College of San Francisco
50 Phelan Ave., San Francisco 94112. Public (district) junior. 1952/1983 (WASC-Jr.). Sem. plan. Degrees: A. *Prof. Accred.:* Dental Assisting, Dental Laboratory Technology, Engineering Technology (electrical-electronics, electromechanical, mechanical), Medical Assisting, Medical Record Technology, Nursing (A), Radiation Therapy, Radiography. Pres. Carlos B. Ramirez.
Enroll.: 22,416
(415) 239-3303

Community College Centers
33 Gough St., San Francisco 94103. Sem. plan. Certificates. Pres. Rena Merritt Bancroft.
Enroll.: 33,536
(415) 239-3000

Alemany Community College Center

Chinatown-North Beach Center

Downtown Center

Galileo Community College Center

John Adams Community College Center

John O'Connell Community College Center

Mission Community College Center

Pacific Heights Community College Center

Skills Center Community College Center

San Francisco Conservatory of Music
1201 Ortega St., San Francisco 94122. Independent professional. 1960/1983 (WASC-Sr.). Sem. plan. Degrees: B,M. *Prof. Accred.:* Music. Pres. Milton Salkind.
Enroll.: 200
(415) 564-8086

*San Francisco State University
1600 Holloway Ave., San Francisco 94132. 1949/1982 (WASC-Sr.). Sem. plan. Degrees: B,M; also D in special education offered jointly with U.C. Berkeley. *Prof. Accred.:* Art, Business (B,M), Engineering, Home Economics, Journalism, Medical Technology, Music, Nursing (B), Rehabilitation

*Member of California State University System

Counseling, Social Work (B,M), Speech Pathology and Audiology, Teacher Education (*e,s,p*). Pres. Chia-Wei Woo.
Enroll.: FTE 18,413
(415) 469-2141

San Francisco Theological Seminary
2 Kensington Rd., San Anselmo 94960. Independent (Presbyterian (U.S.A.)) professional; graduate only. Member of the Graduate Theological Union. 1973/1984 (WASC-Sr.). Sem. plan. Degrees: P,M,D. *Prof. Accred.:* Theology (1938/1983, ATS). Pres. J. Randolph Taylor.
Enroll.: FTE 429
(415) 453-2280

San Joaquin Delta College
5151 Pacific Ave., Stockton 95207. Public (district) junior. 1952/1986 (WASC-Jr.). Sem. plan. Degrees: A, certificates. *Prof. Accred.:* Nursing (A), Vocational Nursing. Pres. Lawrence A. DeRicco.
Enroll.: 15,296
(209) 474-5020

San Joaquin Valley College
211 Real Rd., Suite 201, Bakersfield 93309. Private. 1985 (NATTS). Courses of varying lengths. Diplomas. *Prof. Accred.:* Medical Assisting, Respiratory Therapy Technology. Pres. Robert F. Perry.
(805) 834-0126

San Joaquin Valley College
4706 W. Mineral King Ave., Suite K, Visalia 93291. Private. 1981 (NATTS). Courses of varying lengths. Diplomas. *Prof. Accred.:* Medical Assisting, Respiratory Therapy Technology. Pres. Robert F. Perry.
Enroll.: 100 (*f.t.* 10 m., 90 w.)
(209) 732-6426

Extension
333 N. Bond, Fresno 93726.
(209) 229-7800

San Jose Bible College
P.O. Box 1090, San Jose 95108. Private (Christian Churches) professional. 1969/1979 (AABC). Qtr. plan. Degrees: B. Pres. Bryce Jessup.
Enroll.: 180
(408) 293-9058

San Jose City College
2100 Moorpark Ave., San Jose 95128. Public (district) junior. 1953/1981 (WASC-Jr.). Sem. plan. Degrees: A. *Prof. Accred.:* Dental Assisting, Nursing (A). Pres. Byron Skinner.
Enroll.: 11,423
(408) 298-2181

*San Jose State University
125 S. Seventh St., San Jose 95192-0135. 1949/1984 (WASC-Sr.). Sem. plan. Degrees: B,M. *Prof. Accred.:* Art, Business (B,M), Community Health Education, Engineering (chemical, civil, electrical, industrial and systems, materials, mechanical), Home Economics, Journalism, Librarianship, Music, Nursing (B,M), Occupational Therapy, Public Health, Social Work (B,M), Speech Pathology, Teacher Education (*e,s,p*). Pres. Gail Fullerton.
Enroll.: FTE 18,862
(408) 277-2000

Santa Barbara Business College
2005 Eye St., Bakersfield 93301. Private. 1985 (AICS). Qtr. plan. Diplomas. Dir. Linda Jones.
(805) 322-3006

Santa Barbara Business College
740 State St., Santa Barbara 93101. Private. 1976/1979 (AICS). Qtr. plan. Diplomas. Pres. Dean Johnston.
Enroll.: 1,213 (*f.t.* 215 m., 998 w.)
(805) 963-8681

Santa Barbara Business College
305 E. Plaza Dr., Santa Maria 93454. Private. 1985 (AICS). Qtr. plan. Diplomas. Dir. Carol Gastiger.
(805) 922-8256

Branch Campus
4333 Hansen Ave., Fremont 94537. Dir. Gloria Mereer.
(415) 793-4342

Santa Barbara City College
721 Cliff Dr., Santa Barbara 93109. Public (district) junior. 1952/1986 (WASC-Jr.). Sem. plan. Degrees: A. *Prof. Accred.:* Nursing (A), Radiography. Pres. Peter R. MacDougall.
Enroll.: 9,760
(805) 965-0581

Santa Clara University
Santa Clara 95053. Independent (Roman Catholic) liberal arts and professional. 1949/1983 (WASC-Sr.). Qtr. plan. Degrees:

*Member California State University System

B,P,M,D. *Prof. Accred.:* Business (B,M), Engineering (civil, electrical, mechanical), Law, Music. Pres. Rev. William J. Rewak, S.J.
Enroll.: FTE 6,214
(408) 554-4764

SANTA MONICA COLLEGE
1900 Pico Blvd., Santa Monica 90405. Public (district) junior. 1952/1986 (WASC-Jr.). Sem. plan. Degrees: A. *Prof. Accred.:* Respiratory Therapy. Pres. Richard L. Moore.
Enroll.: 19,722
(213) 450-5150

SANTA ROSA JUNIOR COLLEGE
1501 Mendocino Ave., Santa Rosa 95401. Public (district) junior. 1952/1986 (WASC-Jr.). Sem. plan. Degrees: A. *Prof. Accred.:* Dental Assisting, Nursing (A), Radiography. Pres. Roy G. Mikalson.
Enroll.: 21,587
(707) 527-4415

SAWYER COLLEGE AT POMONA
1021 E. Holt Ave., Pomona 91767. Private. 1967/1985 (AICS). Courses of varying lengths. Certificates. Pres. Sondra Orlowski.
Enroll.: 789 (*f.t.* 113 m., 676 w.)
(714) 629-2534

SAWYER COLLEGE AT VENTURA
470 E. Thompson Blvd., Ventura 93001. Private. 1969/1981 (AICS). Courses of varying lengths. Certificates, diplomas. Pres. Doreen E.Adamache.
Enroll.: 865 (*f.t.* 208 m., 657 w.)
(805) 648-6877

SAWYER COLLEGE OF BUSINESS
5507 El Cajon Blvd., San Diego 92115. Private. 1973/1985 (AICS). Courses of varying lengths. Certificates, diplomas. Exec. Dir. Berta Cuaron.
Enroll.: 789 (*f.t.* 174 m., 615 w.)
(619) 286-4770

SAWYER COLLEGE OF BUSINESS
3120 De La Cruz Blvd., Santa Clara 95054. Private. 1973/1984 (AICS).Courses of varying lengths. Certificates. Pres. Roy O. Hurd.
Enroll.: 682 (*f.t.* 102 m., 580 w.)
(408) 988-1880

SAYBROOK INSTITUTE (*Formerly* HUMANISTIC PSYCHOLOGY INSTITUTE)
1772 Vallejo St., San Francisco 94123. Independent, professional. 1984 (WASC-Sr.). Sem. plan. Degrees: M,D. Pres. Donald E. Polkinghorne.
Enroll.: FTE 163
(415) 441-5034

SCHOOL OF THEOLOGY AT CLAREMONT
1325 N. College Ave., Claremont 91711. Independent (United Methodist) professional; graduate only. 1971/1984 (WASC-Sr.). Sem. plan. Degrees: P,M,D. *Prof. Accred.:* Theology (1944/1979, ATS). Pres. Richard W. Cain.
Enroll.: FTE 177
(714) 626-3521

SCRIPPS COLLEGE
Claremont 91711. Independent liberal arts for women; one of the Claremont Colleges. 1949/1983 (WASC-Sr.). Sem. plan. Degrees: B. Pres. John H. Chandler
Enroll.: FTE 602
(714) 621-8000

SEQUOIA INSTITUTE
420 Whitney Pl., Fremont 94539. Private. 1976/1984 (NATTS). Courses of varying lengths. Certificates. Dir. Kenneth Heineman.
Enroll.: 200 (*f.t.* 194 m., 6 w.)
(415) 490-6900

SHASTA COLLEGE
P.O. Box 6006, Redding 96099. Public (district) junior. 1952/1984 (WASC-Jr.). Sem. plan. Degrees: A. Pres. Kenneth B. Cerreta.
Enroll.: 8,343
(916) 241-3523

SIERRA COLLEGE OF BUSINESS
225 W. Eighth St., Suite 1200, Los Angeles 90014. Private. 1968/1981 (AICS). Qtr. plan. Degrees: A. Pres. Adela Stubblefield Kettle.
Enroll.: 1,679 (*f.t.* 517 m., 1,162 w.)
(213) 628-2322

SIERRA COMMUNITY COLLEGE
5000 Rocklin Rd., Rocklin 95677. Public (district) junior. 1952/1985 (WASC-Jr.). Sem. plan. Degrees: A. Pres. Gerald C. Angove.
Enroll.: 9,257
(916) 624-3333

SIERRA VALLEY BUSINESS COLLEGE
258 N. Blackstone Ave., Fresno 93701. Private. 1981 (AICS). Courses of varying lengths. Certificates. Pres. Donald Goodpaster.
Enroll.: 260 (*f.t.* 23 m., 237 w.)
(209) 486-3550

SIERRA-WESTLAND COLLEGE
390 W. Westland Ave., Clovis 93612. Private. 1979 (AICS). Courses of varying lengths. Certificates. Pres. John W. Hatch.
Enroll.: 566
(209) 297-8900

BRANCH CAMPUS
6060 Sunrise Vista Dr., Citrus Heights 95610. Admin. Steven D. Bagley.
(916) 922-5636

SIMPSON COLLEGE
801 Silver Ave., San Francisco 94134. Independent (Christian and Missionary Alliance) liberal arts. 1952/1981 (AABC); 1969/1981 (WASC-Sr.). 4-1-4 plan. Degrees: B,M. Pres. Mark W. Lee.
Enroll.: FTE 277
(415) 334-7400

SKYLINE COLLEGE
3300 College Dr., San Bruno 94066. Public (district) junior. 1971/1984 (WASC-Jr.). Sem. plan. Degrees: A. *Prof. Accred.:* Respiratory Therapy. Pres. Linda Graef Salter.
Enroll.: 7,393
(415) 355-7000

SOLANO COMMUNITY COLLEGE
4000 Suisun Valley Rd., Suisun City 94585. Public (district) junior. 1952/1985 (WASC-Jr.). Sem. plan. Degrees: A. Pres. Marjorie Blaha.
Enroll.: 7,541
(707) 864-7000

*SONOMA STATE UNIVERSITY
1801 E. Cotati Ave., Rohnert Park 94928. 1963/1984 (WASC-Sr.). Sem. plan. Degrees: B,M. *Prof. Accred.:* Art, Music, Nursing (B). Pres. David W. Benson.
Enroll.: FTE 3,953
(707) 664-2156

SOUTH BAY COLLEGE
13430 Hawthorne Blvd., Hawthorne 90250. Private business. 1972/1984 (AICS). Courses of varying lengths. Diplomas. Dean Edwin Williams.
Enroll.: 885 (*f.t.* 292 m., 593 w.)
(213) 679-2531

BRANCH CAMPUS
13851 E. Garvey Ave., Baldwin Park 91706. Dean Paul E. Hammond.
(213) 962-6656

*Member California State University System

BRANCH CAMPUS
15211 S. Hawthorne Blvd., Lawndale 90260. Dean Mary Taylor.
(213) 978-4519

BRANCH CAMPUS
501 Pine Ave., Long Beach 90802. Dean Marcus Hawkins.
(213) 435-3385

BRANCH CAMPUS
1725 Beverly Blvd., Los Angeles 90026. Dean Harrison Johnson.
(213) 483-3493

BRANCH CAMPUS
1835 S. LaCienega Blvd., Los Angeles 90035. Dir. Geraldine Deamovchet-Smith.
(213) 204-0248

SOUTH COAST COLLEGE OF COURT REPORTING
8341 Garden Grove Blvd., Garden Grove 92644. Private. 1984 (AICS). Courses of varying lengths. Diplomas. Dir Jerry A. Jordan.
(714) 636-8322

SOUTHERN CALIFORNIA COLLEGE
55 Fair Dr., Costa Mesa 92626. Independent (Assemblies of God) liberal arts. 1964/1985 (WASC-Sr.). 4-1-4 plan. Degrees: B,M. Pres. Wayne E. Kraiss.
Enroll.: FTE 841
(714) 556-3610

SOUTHERN CALIFORNIA COLLEGE OF MEDICAL AND DENTAL CAREERS
1717 S. Brookhurst St., Anaheim 92804. Private. 1968/1979 (NATTS). Courses of varying lengths. Certificates, diplomas. Dir. Allene Tumelty.
Enroll.: 456 (*f.t.* 60 m., 396 w.)
(714) 635-3450

SOUTHERN CALIFORNIA COLLEGE OF OPTOMETRY
2575 Yorba Linda Blvd. Fullerton 92631-1699. Independent professional. 1961/1984 (WASC-Sr.). Qtr. plan. Degrees: A,B,P. *Prof. Accred.:* Optometric Technology, Optometry. Pres. Richard L. Hopping.
Enroll.: FTE 398
(714) 870-7226

SOUTHERN CALIFORNIA INSTITUTE OF ARCHITECTURE
1800 Berkeley St., Santa Monica 90404. 1977. Sem. plan. Degrees: B. *Prof. Accred.:* Architecture (B,M). Dir. Raymond Kappe.

Enroll.: 363 (*f.t.* 254 m., 79 w.)
(213) 829-3482

SOUTHLAND CAREERS INSTITUTE
15610 S. Crenshaw Blvd., Gardena 90249. Private. 1974/1983 (ABHES). Courses of varying lengths. Diplomas. *Prof. Accred.:* Medical Assisting. Dir. Marilyn Curtis.
Enroll.: 85 (*f.t.* 24 m., 61 w.)
(213) 770-0162

SOUTHLAND CAREERS INSTITUTE
846 S. Union Ave., Los Angeles 90017. Private. 1973/1979 (NATTS). Courses of varying lengths. Certificates, diplomas. *Prof. Accred.:* Medical Assisting. Dir. Robert Kasold.
Enroll.: 718 (*f.t.* 143 m., 574 w.)
(213) 388-0625

SOUTHLAND CAREERS INSTITUTE
512 W. Beverly Blvd., Montebello 90640. Private. 1983 (ABHES). Courses of varying lengths. Certificates, diplomas. *Prof. Accred.:* Medical Assisting. Dir. Lyn Frazier.
Enroll.: 119 (*f.t.* 89 m., 30 w.)
(213) 723-1672

SOUTHWEST TRADE SCHOOL
334 Rancheros Dr., San Marcos 92069. Private. 1983 (NATTS). Courses of varying lengths. Certificates. Pres. John H. Stinton.
Enroll.: 85
(619) 744-8730

SOUTHWESTERN COLLEGE
900 Otay Lakes Rd., Chula Vista 92010. Public (district) junior. 1964/1986 (WASC-Jr.). Sem. plan. Degrees: A. Interim Pres. Raymond F. Ellerman.
Enroll.: 10,027
(619) 421-6700

SOUTHWESTERN UNIVERSITY SCHOOL OF LAW
675 S. Westmoreland Ave., Los Angeles 90005. Private professional. 1970 (ABA); 1974 (AALS). Sem. plan. Degrees: P. *Prof. Accred.:* Law. Pres. Leigh H. Taylor.
Enroll.: 1,311 (*f.t.* 505 m., 263 w.)
(213) 380-4800

STANFORD UNIVERSITY
Stanford 94305. Independent. 1949/1981 (WASC-Sr.). Qtr. plan. Degrees: B,P,M,D. *Prof. Accred.:* Assistant to the Primary Care Physician, Business (M), Engineering (aeronautics and astronautics, chemical, civil, electrical, industrial, mechanical, petroleum), Law, Medical Technology, Medicine, Nursing, Radiation Therapy. Pres. Donald Kennedy.
Enroll.: FTE 12,131
(415) 723-2300

STARR KING SCHOOL FOR THE MINISTRY
2441 LeConte Ave., Berkeley 94709. Private (Unitarian Universalist) professional; graduate only by virtue of participation in the Graduate Theological Union. Sem. plan. Degrees: P,M. *Prof. Accred.:* Theology (1978/1983, ATS). Pres. Gordon B. McKeeman.
Enroll.: 52 (*f.t.* 28 m., 24 w.)
(415) 845-6232

STUDIO SEVEN FASHION CAREER COLLEGE
261 E. Rowland Ave., Covina 91723. Private. 1977/1984 (NATTS). Qtr. plan. Diplomas. Dir. Leslie Stevenson.
Enroll.: 75 (*f.t.* 3 m., 72 w.)
(818) 331-6351

SYSTEMS AND PROGRAMMING DEVELOPMENT INSTITUTE
5525 Wilshire Blvd., Los Angeles 90036. Private. 1984 (NATTS). Courses of varying lengths. Certificates. Pres. Jose Segura.
(213) 937-7734

TAFT COLLEGE
29 Emmons Park Dr., Taft 93268. Public (district) junior. 1952/1986 (WASC-Jr.). Sem. plan. Degrees: A. Pres. David Cothrun.
Enroll.: 857
(805) 763-4282

TECHNICAL HEALTH CAREERS SCHOOL, INC.
1843 W. Imperial Hwy., Los Angeles 90047. Private. 1982 (ABHES). Courses of varying lengths. Certificates. *Prof. Accred.:* Medical Assisting. Exec. Dir. Sharon L. Hughes.
(213) 757-0273

TECHNICAL TRAINING CENTER
One W. Campbell Ave., Campbell 95008. Private. 1985 (NATTS). Courses of varying lengths. Certificates. Dir. James Harris.
(408) 374-8235

THOMAS AQUINAS COLLEGE
10000 N. Ojai Rd., Santa Paula 93060. Independent liberal arts. 1980 (WASC-Sr.). Sem. plan. Degrees: B. Pres. Ronald P. McArthur.
Enroll: FTE 125
(805) 525- 4417

TOTAL TECHNICAL INSTITUTE (EXTENSION)
3180 Newberry Dr., Suite 110, San Jose 95118. Private. 1985 (NATTS). Courses of

varying lengths. Diplomas. Dir. Nina R. Bouley.
(408) 978-8787

Transwestern Institute of Word Processing
1645 W. Beverly Blvd., Los Angeles 90026. Private. 1981 (AICS). Qtr. plan. Certificates, diplomas. Pres. Henry Feltenberg.
Enroll.: 1,006 (*f.t.* 177 m., 829 w.)
(213) 483-1880

Branch Campus
4250 Long Beach Blvd., Long Beach 90807. Dir. LaDene Snook.
(213) 483-1880

Travel and Trade Career Institute
3635 Atlantic Ave., Long Beach 90807. Private. 1968/1977 (NATTS). Courses of varying lengths. Diplomas. Pres. Randy M. Erickson.
Enroll.: 160 (*f.t.* 85 m., 75 w.)
(213) 426-8841.

Truck Marketing Institute
1056 Eugenia Pl., P.O. Box 188, Carpinteria 93013. Private home study. 1968/1985 (NHSC). Dir. James E. Godfrey.
(805) 684-4558

United College of Business
6690 Sunset Blvd., Hollywood 90028. Private. 1971/1984 (AICS). Courses of varying lengths. Degrees: A, certificates, diplomas. Dir. of Ed. John Scott.
Enroll.: 3,619 (*f.t.* 1,447 m., 2,172 w.)
(213) 461-8565

Branch Campus
8524 Firestone Blvd., Downey 92041. Dir. Roslyn Mentzer.
(213) 862-3455

United Health Careers Institute
600 N. Sierra Way, San Bernardino 92401. Private. 1968/1978 (NATTS). Sem. plan, courses of varying lengths. Certificates, diplomas. *Prof. Accred.*: Practical Nursing. Dir. Thomas G. Beckerle.
Enroll.: 371 (*f.t.* 20 m., 351 w.)
(714) 884-8891

United States International University
10455 Pomerado Rd., San Diego 92131. Independent liberal arts and professional. Accreditation covers programs in England, Kenya, and Mexico. 1956/1984 (WASC-Sr.). Qtr. plan. Degrees: A,B,P,M,D. Pres. William C. Rust.
Enroll.: FTE 3,497
(619) 271-4300

University of California
Berkeley 94720. Public (state). Central administration for nine University of California campuses and Hastings College of Law. Pres. David P. Gardner.
(415) 642-1441

University of California, Berkeley
Berkeley 94720. 1949/1985 (WASC-Sr.). Sem. plan. Degrees: B,P,M,D. *Prof. Accred.:* Architecture (M), Business (B,M), Dietetics, Engineering (chemical, civil, computer science, electrical, industrial engineering and operations research, mechanical, mineral, naval architecture, nuclear), Forestry, Health Services Administration, Journalism, Landscape Architecture (M), Law, Librarianship, Optometry, Psychology, Public Health, Social Work (M). Chanc. I. M. Heyman.
Enroll.: 28,982
(415) 642-6000

University of California, Davis
Davis 95616. 1954/1982 (WASC-Sr.). Qtr. plan. Degrees: B,P,M,D. *Prof. Accred.:* Assistant to the Primary Care Physician, Engineering (aeronautical science, agricultural, chemical, civil, electrical—general; computers; electonics, circuits, and signal processing; solid state, microwaves, and quantum—options , mechanical), Landscape Architecture (B), Law, Medical Technology, Medicine, Nuclear Medicine Technology, Psychology, Veterinary Medicine. Chanc. James H. Meyer.
Enroll.: 19,055
(916) 752-1011

University of California, Hastings College of Law
San Francisco 94102. 1900/1949 (AALS); 1939 (ABA). Sem. plan. Degrees: P. *Prof. Accred.:* Law. Dean Bert Prunty.
Enroll.: 1,519 (*f.t.* 807 m., 674 w.)
(415) 565-4600

University of California, Irvine
Irvine 92717. 1965/1981 (WASC-Sr.). Qtr. plan. Degrees: B,P,M,D. *Prof. Accred.:* Engineering (civil, electrical, mechanical), Medical Technology, Medicine. Chanc. Jack W. Peltason.
Enroll.: 12,108
(714) 856-5011

University of California, Los Angeles
405 Hilgard Ave., Los Angeles 90024. 1949/1984 (WASC-Sr.). Qtr. plan. Degrees: B,P, M,D. *Prof. Accred.:* Architecture (M), Assistant to the Primary Care Physician, Business (M), Dentistry, Engineering (aerospace, chemical, civil, electrical, materials science, mechanical, unified), Health Services Administration, Interior Design, Law, Librarianship, Medical Record Administration, Medical Technology, Medicine, Nurse Anesthesia Education, Nursing (B,M), Psychology, Public Health, Radiation Therapy, Radiography, Social Work (M), Specialist in Blood Bank Technology. Chanc. Charles E. Young.
Enroll.: 31,051
(213) 825-4321

University of California, Riverside
Riverside 92521. 1956/1983 (WASC-Sr.). Qtr. plan. Degrees: B,M,D. Chanc. Theodore L. Hullar
Enroll.: FTE 5,257
(714) 787-1012

University of California, San Diego
La Jolla 92093. 1964/1981 (WASC-Sr.). Qtr. plan. Degrees: B,P,M,D. *Prof. Accred.:* Engineering (chemical, electrical), EMT-Paramedic Training, Medicine, Radiation Therapy Technology. Chanc. Richard C. Atkinson.
Enroll.: FTE 14,851
(619) 452-2230

University of California, San Francisco
Third Ave. and Parnassus, San Francisco 94143. 1976/1981 (WASC-Sr.). Qtr. plan. Degrees: B,P,M,D. *Prof. Accred.:* Cytotechnology, Dental Hygiene, Dentistry, Dietetics, Medicine, Medical Technology, Nuclear Medicine Technology, Nursing (B,M), Pharmacy, Physical Therapy, Psychology, Radiography. Chanc. Julius R. Krevans.
Enroll.: FTE 3,612
(415) 666-9000

University of California, Santa Barbara
Santa Barbara 93106. 1949/1981 (WASC-Sr.). Qtr. plan. Degrees: B,M,D. *Prof. Accred.:* Engineering (chemical, electrical, mechanical, nuclear), Psychology, Speech Pathology and Audiology. Chanc. Robert A. Huttenback.
Enroll.: 17,415
(805) 961-2311

University of California, Santa Cruz
Santa Cruz 95064. 1965/1981 (WASC-Sr.). Qtr. plan. Degrees: B,M,D. Chanc. Robert. L. Sinsheimer.
Enroll.: FTE 7,616
(408) 429-0111

University of Judaism
15600 Mulholland Dr., Los Angeles 90077. Independent. 1961/1984 (WASC-Sr.). Sem. plan. Degrees: A,B,M. Pres. David L. Lieber.
Enroll.: FTE 133
(213) 476-9777

University of La Verne
1950 Third St., La Verne 91750. Independent liberal arts and professional. 1955/1980 (WASC-Sr.). Accreditation includes law-related programs at La Verne and San Fernando Valley campuses. 4-1-4 plan. Degrees: B,P,M,D. Pres. Stephen Morgan.
Enroll.: FTE 3,993
(714) 593-3511

University of the Pacific
3601 Pacific Ave., Stockton 95211. Independent liberal arts and professional. 1949/1982 (WASC-Sr.). 4-1-4 plan. Degrees: B,P,M,D. *Prof. Accred.:* Art , Business (B), Dentistry, Engineering (civil, computer, electrical), Law, Music, Pharmacy, Speech Pathology, Teacher Education (*e,s,p*). Pres. Stanley E. McCaffrey.
Enroll.: FTE 5,323
(209) 946-2011

University of Redlands
Redlands 92373. Independent liberal arts and professional. 1949/1982 (WASC-Sr.). 4-1-4 plan. Degrees: B,M. *Prof. Accred.:* Music. Pres. Douglas R. Moore.
Enroll.: FTE 2,565
(714) 793-2121

University of San Diego
Alcala Pk., San Diego 92110. Independent (Roman Catholic) liberal arts and professional. 1956/1983 (WASC-Sr.). 4-1-4 plan. Degrees: B,P,M,D. *Prof. Accred.:* Business (B,M), Law, Nursing (B,M). Pres. Author E. Hughes.
Enroll.: FTE 4,462
(619) 291-6480

University of San Francisco
2 130 Fulton St., Ignatian Heights, San Francisco 94117-1080. Independent (Roman Catholic) liberal arts and professional. 1949/1981 (WASC-Sr.). Sem. plan. Degrees: B,P,M,D. *Prof. Accred.:* Business (B,M), Law, Nursing. Pres. Rev. John J. LoSchiavo, S.J.
Enroll.: FTE 6,210
(415) 666-6136

University of Southern California
University Park, Los Angeles 90007. Independent liberal arts and professional. 1949/1981 (WASC-Sr.). Sem. plan. Degrees: B,P,M,D. *Prof. Accred.:* Architecture (B,M), Business (B,M), Dental Hygiene, Dentistry, Engineering (aerospace, chemical, civil, civil engineering/building sciences, electrical, industrial and systems, mechanical, petroleum), Health Services Administration, Journalism, Law, Librarianship, Medical Technology, Medicine, Music, Nursing (B), Occupational Therapy, Pharmacy, Physical Therapy, Physician's Assistant, Psychology, Radiation Therapy, Social Work (M), Teacher Education (*e,s,p*). Pres. James H. Zumberge.
Enroll.: 23,691
(213) 743-2311

University of West Los Angeles
12201 Washington Pl., Los Angeles 90066. Independent; paralegal and law. 1983 (WASC-Sr.). Tri. plan. Degrees: B,P. Pres. Bernard S. Jefferson.
Enroll.: FTE 440
(213) 313-1011

Valley College of Medical & Dental Careers
4150 Lankershim Blvd., North Hollywood 91602. Private. 1973/1979 (NATTS). Courses of varying lengths. Diplomas. *Prof. Accred.:* Respiratory Therapy Technology. Pres. Ben F. Ostergren.
Enroll.: 230
(213) 766-8151

Valley Commercial College
910 12th St., Modesto 95354. Private. 1970/1983 (AICS). Courses of varying lengths. Certificates, diplomas. Pres. Gregory L. Martin.
Enroll.: 378 (*f.t.* 85 m., 293 w.)
(209) 578-0616

Branch Campus
1752 E. Bullard, Fresno 93710. Dir. Barbara J. Martin.
(209) 436-1138

Van Nuys College of Business
8041 Van Nuys Blvd., Van Nuys 91402. Private. 1972/1984 (AICS). Courses of varying lengths. Diplomas. Chairman of the Board J. E. Taylor, Jr.
Enroll.: 789 (*f.t.* 346 m., 443 w.)
(213) 782-0550

Ventura College
4667 Telegraph Rd., Ventura 93003. Public (district) junior. 1952/1985 (WASC-Jr.). Sem. plan. Degrees: A. Pres. Robert W. Long.
Enroll.: 10,725
(805) 642-3211

Victor Valley College
18422 Bear Valley Rd., P.O. Drawer 00, Victorville 92392. Public (district) junior. 1963/1982 (WASC-Jr.). Sem. plan. Degrees: A. *Prof. Accred.:* Nursing (A), Respiratory Therapy. Pres. Ruth Johnson.
Enroll.: 4,080
(619) 245-4271

Video Technical Institute (Extension)
2828 Junipero Ave., Long Beach 90806. Private. 1985 (NATTS). Courses of varying lengths. Certificates. Dir. Maurice Crowley.
(213) 595-1660

Vista College
2020 Milvia St., Suite 200, Berkeley 94704. Public (district) junior. 1981 (WASC-Jr.). Sem. plan. Degrees: A. Acting Pres. Santiago Wood.
Enroll.: 3,995
(415) 841-8431

Watterson College
815 Oxnard Blvd., Oxnard 93030. Private. 1979/1985 (AICS). Courses of varying lengths. Certificates. Dir. Sandra Grunewald.
Enroll.: 1,565 (*f.t.* 164 m., 1,401 w.)
(805) 656-5566

Branch Campus
5337 Truxton Ave., Bakersfield 93309. Dir. Robert Patty.
(805) 323-1747

Branch Campus
1600 Sawtelle Ave., Los Angeles 90025. Dir. Ronald Provencio.
(213) 473-4551

Watterson College
1165 E. Colorado Blvd., Pasadena 91106. Private. 1953/1984 (AICS). Qtr. plan. Certificates. Dir. Carol Kurtzman.
Enroll.: 1,164 (*f.t.* 138 m., 1,026 w.)
(213) 449-3990

Branch Campus-Pasadena
1422 S. Azusa Ave., West Covina 91790. Dir. William Lockwood.
(818) 919-8701

Watterson College
5121 Van Nuys Blvd., Sherman Oaks 91403 Private. 1966/1984 (AICS). Qtr. plan. Certificates, diplomas. Dir. Mary L. Williams.
Enroll.: 1,139 (*f.t.* 119 m., 1,020 w.)
(213) 990-4070

Branch Campus-Sherman Oaks
3838 W. Martin Luther King Blvd., Los Angeles 90008. Dir. Rhoda James.
(213) 299-2966

Branch Campus-Sherman Oaks
453 S. Spring St., Los Angeles 90013. Dir. Craig Deonik.
(213) 623-7811

Branch Campus
41 E. 12th St., National City 92050. Dir. Carol Nelson.
(619) 474-8017

Webster Career College
222 S. Hill St., Suite 400, Los Angeles 90012. Private. 1969/1983 (AICS). Qtr. plan. Diplomas. *Prof. Accred.:* Medical Assisting. Pres. Harold Chuang.
Enroll.: 1,939 (*f.t.* 691 m., 1,248 w.)
(213) 625-1201

Branch Campus
16620 Bellflower Blvd., Bellflower 90706. Dir. Johnny Wilson.
(213) 804-1064

Branch Campus
1975 Long Beach Blvd., Long Beach 90806. Dir. Lourine Hodge.
(213) 599-2122

West Coast Christian College
6901 N. Maple Ave., Fresno 93710. Private (Church of God) junior and professional. 1976 (AABC); 1976/1986 (WASC-Jr.). Sem. plan. Degrees: A,B. Pres. Hubert P. Black.
Enroll.: 249
(209) 299-7201

West Coast University
440 S. Shatto Pl., Los Angeles 90020. Independent; science, engineering, and management; evening only. 1963/1982 (WASC-Sr.); accreditation includes branch campuses in Orange, San Diego and Santa Barbara Counties. Tri. plan. Degrees: B,M. *Prof. Accred.:* Engineering (electrical, mechanical). Pres. Robert M. L. Baker, Jr.
Enroll.: FTE 1,264
(213) 487-4433

West Hills Community College
300 Cherry Lane, Coalinga 93210. Public (district) junior. 1952/1983 (WASC-Jr.). Sem. plan. Degrees: A. Pres. ———.
Enroll.: 1,694
(209) 935-0801

West Los Angeles College
4800 Freshman Dr., Culver City 90230. Public (district) junior. 1971/1984 (WASC-Jr.). Sem. plan. Degrees: A. *Prof. Accred.:* Dental Hygiene. Acting Pres. Linda Thor.
Enroll.: 13,170
(408) 867-2200

West Valley College
14000 Fruitvale Ave., Saratoga 95070. Public (district) junior. 1966/1985 (WASC-Jr.). Sem. plan. Degrees: A. *Prof. Accred.:* Medical Assisting. Pres. Dale A. Johnston.
Enroll.: 13,170
(408) 867-2200

Western Career College
4000 El Camino Ave., Sacramento 95821. Private. 1972/1979 (NATTS). Courses of varying lengths. Diplomas. *Prof. Accred.:* Medical Assisting. Dir. Richard G. Nathanon.
Enroll.: 383 (*f.t.* 5 m., 378 w.)
(916) 481-1922

Branch Campus
170 Bay Fair Mall, San Leandro 94578.
(415) 276-3888

Western State University College of Law Central Office
1111 N. State College Blvd., Fullerton 92631. Proprietary law school. Pres. William B. Lawless.
(714) 738-1000

Western State University College of Law of Orange County
1111 N. State College Blvd., Fullerton 92631. Proprietary law school. 1976/1982 (WASC-

Sr.). Sem. plan. Degrees: B,P. Dean O. Keith Snyder.
Enroll.: FTE 1,183
(714) 738-1000

Western State University College of Law of San Diego
2121 San Diego Ave., San Diego 92110. Proprietary law school. 1976/1982 (WASC-Sr.). Sem. plan. Degrees: B,P. Dean and Dir. Ross B. Lipsker.
Enroll.: FTE 472
(619) 297-9700

Western Technical College
5434 Van Nuys Blvd., Van Nuys 91401. Private. 1968/1978 (NATTS). Courses of varying lengths. Certificates, diplomas. *Prof. Accred.:* Medical Assisting. Dir. Samuel Romano.
Enroll.: 203 (*f.t.* 56 m., 147 w.)
(818) 783-6520

Western Truck Driving School
300 Richards Blvd., Sacramento 95814. Private. 1980 (NATTS). Courses of varying lengths. Certificates. Pres. Everett G. Nord.
(916) 448-8388

Westminster Theological Seminary in California
1725 Bear Valley Pkwy., P.O. Box 2215, Escondido 92025. Independent professional. 1984 (WASC-Sr.). 4-1-4 plan. Degrees: B,M,P,D. Pres. Robert B. Strimple.
Enroll.: FTE 86
(619) 480-8474

Westmont College
955 La Paz Rd., Santa Barbara 93108. Independent liberal arts. 1957/1984 (WASC-Sr.). 4-1-4 plan. Degrees: B. Pres. David K. Winter.
Enroll.: FTE 1,195
(805) 969-5051

Whittier College
Whittier 90608. Independent liberal arts and law. 1949/1985 (WASC-Sr.). 4-1-4 modular curriculum. Degrees: B,P,M. *Prof. Accred.:* Law, Social Work (B). Pres. Eugene S. Mills.
Enroll.: FTE 1,428
(213) 693-0771

Wilshire Computer College
2140 W. Olympic Blvd., Suite 503, Los Angeles 90006. Private. 1985 (AICS). Courses of varying lengths. Certificates. Pres. Peter M. Chung.
(213) 388-7008

Branch Campus
15751 Brookhurst St., Suite 132, Westminster 92683. Dir. Soon Chung.
(714) 839-1701

Woodbury University
1027 Wilshire Blvd., Los Angeles 90017. Independent professional business and design. 1961/1982 (WASC-Sr.). Qtr. plan. Degrees: B,M. *Prof. Accred.:* Interior Design. Pres. Wayne L. Miller.
Enroll.: FTE 831
(213) 482-8491

World College West
101 S. San Antonio Rd., Petaluma 94952. Independent liberal arts. 1981/1984 (WASC-Sr.). Qtr. plan. Degrees: B. Pres. Richard M. Gray.
Enroll.: FTE 83
(707) 765-4502

Wright Institute
2728 Durant Ave., Berkeley 94704. Independent, professional psychology. 1977 (WASC-Sr.). Sem. plan. Degrees: D. Pres. Peter Dybwad.
Enroll.: FTE 150
(415) 841-9230

Yeshiva Ohr Elchonon Chabad/West Coast Talmudic Seminary
7215 Waring Ave., Los Angeles 90046. Private professional. 1983. Degrees: B of Regigious Studies. *Prof. Accred.:* Rabbinical and Talmudic Education. Pres. D. Weiss.
Enroll.: 42
(213) 937-3763

Yuba College
2088 N. Beale Rd., Marysville 95901. Public (district) junior. 1952/1984 (WASC-Jr.). Sem. plan. Degrees: A, certificates. *Prof. Accred.:* Radiography. Pres. Patricia L. Wirth.
Enroll.: 7,934
(916) 741-6700

COLORADO

ACADEMY OF FLORAL DESIGN
7350 N. Broadway, Denver 80221. Private business. 1983 (AICS). Courses of varying lengths. Certificates. Pres. Sharon Tinlin.
(303) 426-1808

ADAMS STATE COLLEGE
Alamosa 81102. Public liberal arts and teachers. 1950/1981 (NCA). Qtr. plan. Degrees: B,M. *Prof. Accred.:* Teacher Education (*e,s,p*). Pres. William M. Fulkerson, Jr.
Enroll.: 1,838
(303) 589-7341

ADELPHI BUSINESS COLLEGE
824 S. Union Blvd., Colorado Springs 80910. Private. 1969/1985 (AICS). Qtr. plan. Diplomas. Dir. Robert J. Luff.
Enroll.: 654 (*f.t.* 226 m., 428 w.)
(303) 475-1700

AIMS COMMUNITY COLLEGE
P.O. Box 69, Greeley 80632. Public (district) junior. 1977/1982 (NCA). Qtr. plan. Degrees: A. *Prof. Accred.:* Radiography. Pres. George R. Conger.
Enroll.: FTE 3,159
(303) 339-2211

AMERICAN DIESEL & AUTOMOTIVE SCHOOL
1002 S. Jason St., Denver 80223. Private. 1981 (NATTS). Qtr. plan. Diplomas. Pres. Mel Jones.
Enroll.: 113 (*f.t.* 112 m., 1 w.)
(303) 778-6772

ARAPAHOE COMMUNITY COLLEGE
Littleton 80120. Public (district) junior. 1970/1982 (NCA). Qtr. plan. Degrees: A. *Prof. Accred.:* Medical Laboratory Technology (A), Medical Record Technology. Pres. James F. Weber.
Enroll.: FTE 2,893
(303) 797-5700

BAILIE SCHOOL OF BROADCAST
1100 Stout, Denver 80204. Private. 1974/1979 (NATTS). Courses of varying lengths. Diplomas. Dir. John Hendrickson.
Enroll.: 75 (*f.t.* 60 m., 15 w.)
(303) 592-1234

BARNES BUSINESS COLLEGE
150 N. Sheridan Blvd., Denver 80226. Private. 1953/1981 (AICS). Qtr. plan. Certificates, diplomas. Dir. Vernon Lowery.
Enroll.: 2,484 (*f.t.* 482 m., 2,002 w.)
(303) 922-8454

BEL-REA INSTITUTE OF ANIMAL TECHNOLOGY
1681 S. Dayton St., Denver 80231. Private. 1975/1981 (NATTS). Qtr. plan. Degrees: A. Dir. Marc Schapiro.
Enroll.: 100 (*f.t.* 10 m., 90 w.)
(303) 751-8700

BIOSYSTEMS INSTITUTE (EXTENSION)
5250 Leetsdale Dr., Suite 206, Denver 80222. Private. 1983 (NATTS). Courses of varying lengths. Certificates. Admin. Kathy Metcalf.
Enroll.: 30
(303) 393-1063

*BLAIR JUNIOR COLLEGE
828 Wooten Rd., Colorado Springs 80915. Private junior. 1953/1982 (AICS). Qtr. plan. Degrees: A. Dir. Tom Twardowski.
Enroll.: 496
(303) 574-1082

CAPITOL CITY BARBER COLLEGE (EXTENSION)
1523 S. Nevada Ave., Colorado Springs 80906. Private. 1985 (NATTS). Courses of varying lengths. Certificates. Dir. Allen Hossfeld.
(303) 633-2400

CAPITOL CITY BARBER COLLEGE (EXTENSION)
1631 S. Prairie Ave., Pueblo 81005. Private. 1985 (NATTS). Courses of varying lengths. Certificates. Dir. Allen Hossfeld.
(303) 561-2600

CERTIFIED WELDING SCHOOL, INC.
3701 S. Kalamath, Englewood 80110. Private. 1975/1980 (NATTS). Courses of varying lengths. Certificates, diplomas. Pres. Gordon Bay.
Enroll.: 223
(303) 781-7845

COLORADO AERO TECH
10851 W. 120th Ave., Broomfield 80020. Private. 1972/1980 (NATTS). Courses of varying lengths. Certificates. Dir. Leroy Broesder.
Enroll.: 560 (*f.t.* 525 m., 35 w.)
(303) 466-1714

*Candidate for Accreditation by Regional Accrediting Commission

Colorado Barber College
3101 W. 14th Ave., Denver 80204. Private. 1981 (NATTS). Courses of varying lengths. Diplomas. Pres. Frank Landeen, Jr.
Enroll.: 30 (*f.t.* 12 m., 22 w.)
(303) 623-9185

Colorado Christian College
180 S. Garrison St., Lakewood 80226. Private. 1981/1986 (NCA); 1985 (AABC). Sem. plan. Degrees: B. Pres. Joe L. Wall.
Enroll.: FTE 313
(303) 238-5386

Colorado College
Colorado Springs 80903. Private liberal arts. 1915/1978 (NCA). Sem. plan. Degrees: B,M. *Prof. Accred.:* Music. Pres. Gresham Riley.
Enroll.: FTE 1,920
(303) 473-2233

Colorado College of Medical and Dental Careers
445 Grant, Denver 80203. Private. 1969/1979 (NATTS). Courses of varying lengths. Diplomas. Dir. Richard K. Shepard.
Enroll.: 300 (*f.t.* 10 m., 290 w.)
(303) 778-8681

Colorado Institute of Art
200 E. Ninth Ave., Denver 80203. Private. 1977/1983 (NATTS). Qtr. plan. Degrees: A, diplomas. Pres. Cheryl Murphy.
Enroll.: 1,100 (*f.t.* 490 m., 635 w.)
(303) 837-0825

Colorado Mountain College
Glenwood Springs 81602. Public (district) junior. 1974/1985 (NCA). Accreditation includes Steamboat Springs Alpine Campus. Qtr. plan. Degrees: A. Pres. Gordon L. Snowbarger.
FTE 996
(303) 945-8691

East Campus
Leadville 80461. Vice-Pres. Arlynn D. Anderson
(303) 486-2015

West Campus
Glenwood Springs 81601. Vice-Pres. Rodney D. Anderson.
(303) 945-7481

Colorado Northwestern Community College
Rangely 81648. Public (district) junior. 1976/1979 (NCA). Sem. plan. Degrees: A. *Prof. Accred.:* Dental Hygiene. Pres. James H. Bos.
Enroll.: FTE 290
(303) 675-2261

Colorado School of Dog Grooming
95 S. Wadsworth Blvd., Lakewood 80226. Private. 1985 (NATTS). Courses of varying lengths. Certificates. Dir. Madeleine Athanasiou.
(303)234-0401

Colorado School of Mines
Golden 80401. Public (state) technological. 1929/1983 (NCA). Sem. plan. Degrees: B,M,D. *Prof. Accred.:* Engineering (chemical and petroleum refining, engineering physics, geological, geophysical, metallurgical, mining, petroleum). Pres. George S. Ansell.
Enroll.: FTE 2,718
(303) 273-3000

Colorado School of Trades
1575 Hoyt St., Lakewood 80215. Private. 1973/1980 (NATTS). Courses of varying lengths. Certificates. Dir. John T. Snyder.
Enroll.: 312 (*f.t.* 310 m., 2 w.)
(303) 233-4697

Colorado State University
Fort Collins 80523. Public. 1925/1984 (NCA). Sem. plan. Degrees: B,P,M,D. *Prof. Accred.:* Business (B,M), Construction Education, Engineering (agricultural, chemical, civil, electrical, engineering science, environmental, mechanical), Forestry, Journalism, Landscape Architecture (B), Music, Occupational Therapy, Psychology, Social Work (B), Speech Pathology and Audiology, Teacher Education (*s,p*), Veterinary Medicine. Pres. Philip Austin.
Enroll.: 18,084
(303) 491-1101

Colorado Technical College
655 Elkton Dr., Colorado Springs 80907. Private. 1980/1984 (NCA). Qtr. plan. Degrees: A,B. *Prof. Accred.:* Engineering Technology (biomedical, electronic, solar energy). Pres. David O'Donnell.
Enroll.: FTE 346
(303) 598-0200

Community College of Denver
Denver 80204. Public (state) junior. 1975/1982 (NCA). Qtr. plan. Degrees: A. *Prof. Accred.:* Nuclear Medicine Technology,

Nursing (A), Radiation Therapy, Radiation Therapy Technology, Radiography, Surgical Technology. Pres. Myer Titus.
Enroll.: FTE 1,129
(303) 629-2419

CONTROL DATA INSTITUTE (EXTENSION)
720 S. Colorado Blvd., Denver 80222. Private. 1985 (NATTS). Courses of varying lengths. Certificates. Dir. Paul J. Stonely.
(303) 691-9756

DENVER ACADEMY OF COURT REPORTING
1000 Speer Blvd., Denver 80204. Private business. 1982 (AICS). Qtr. plan. Certificates, diplomas. Pres. Charles W. Jarstfer.
Enroll.: 164 (*f.t.* 16 m., 148 w.)
(303) 825-6119

DENVER AUTOMOTIVE AND DIESEL COLLEGE
460 S. Lipan St., Denver 80223. Private. 1968/1977 (NATTS). Courses of varying lengths. Diplomas. Dir. Joe Crutchfield.
Enroll.: 714 (*f.t.* 706 m., 8 w.)
(800) 525-8956

DENVER CONSERVATIVE BAPTIST SEMINARY
P.O. Box 10,000, University Park Sta., Denver 80210. Private (Conservative Baptist) professional; graduate only. 1972/1982 (NCA). Qtr. plan. Degrees: P,M,D. *Prof. Accred.:* Theology (1970/1981, ATS). Pres. Haddon W. Robinson.
Enroll.: 558
(303) 761-2482

DENVER INSTITUTE OF TECHNOLOGY
The Educational Plaza, 7350 N. Broadway, Denver 80221. Private. 1973/1978 (NATTS). Qtr. plan. Courses of varying lengths. Degrees: A. Pres. R. Wade Murphree.
Enroll.: 619 (*f.t.* 495 m., 124 w.)
(303) 426-1808

DENVER PARALEGAL INSTITUTE
2150 W. 29th Ave., Denver 80211. Private. 1979 (NATTS). Courses of varying lengths. Certificates. Dir. Lorie Bartlett.
Enroll.: 134 (*f.t.* 13 m., 83 w.)
(303) 480-1697

DENVER TECHNICAL COLLEGE
5250 Leetsdale Dr., Denver 80222. Private. 1979 (NATTS). Courses of varying lengths. Degrees: A, certificates. Pres. M. A. Schledorn.
Enroll.: 89 (*f.t.* 52 m., 19 w.)
(303) 329-3000

DESIGN FLORAL SCHOOL, INC.
3945-47 Tennyson, Denver 80212. Private. 1978/1985 (NATTS). Courses of varying lengths. Certificates. Dir. B. J. Clay.
Enroll.: 22 (*f.t.* 2 m., 20 w.)
(303) 458-6100

ELECTRONIC TECHNICAL INSTITUTE
1070 Bannock St., Denver 80204. Private. 1968/1985 (NATTS). Courses of varying lengths. Degrees: A, diplomas. Pres. Howard Killmer.
Enroll.: 162 (*f.t.* 136 m., 15 w.)
(303) 629-6225

BRANCH CAMPUS
4765 Oakland St., Denver 80239.
(303) 373-3060

FORT LEWIS COLLEGE
Durango 81301. Public (state) liberal arts. 1958/1976 (NCA). Tri. plan. Degrees: A,B. *Prof. Accred.:* Business (B), Music, Teacher Education (*e,s*). Pres. Bernard S. Adams.
Enroll.: FTE 3,563
(303) 247-7661

FRONT RANGE COMMUNITY COLLEGE
Westminster 80030. Public (state) junior. 1975/1982 (NCA). Qtr. plan. Degrees: A. *Prof. Accred.:* Dental Assisting, Nursing (A), Respiratory Therapy. Interim Pres. Donald Mankenberg.
Enroll.: FTE 2,706 (*f.t.* 1,002 m., 865 w.)
(303) 466-8811

ITT TECHNICAL INSTITUTE (EXTENSION)
2121 S. Blackhawk St., Aurora 80014. Private. 1984 (NATTS). Courses of varying lengths. Certificates. Dir. Patricia O'Brien.
(303) 695-1913

ILIFF SCHOOL OF THEOLOGY
2201 S. University Blvd., Denver 80210. Private (United Methodist) professional; graduate only. 1973/1978 (NCA). Qtr. plan. Degrees: P,M,D. *Prof. Accred.:* Theology (1938/1988, ATS). Pres. Donald E. Messer.
Enroll.: 358
(303) 744-1287

INTERIOR DESIGN INTERNSHIP
Denver 80222. Private professional. 1977. Sem. plan. Certificates. *Prof. Accred.:* Interior Design. Dir. Edward A. Jensen.

INTERNATIONAL TRAINING, LTD.
HAIRCUTTING AND STYLING COLLEGE
2186 D South Colorado Blvd., Denver 80010. Private. 1980 (NATTS). Courses of varying lengths. Diplomas. Dir. Lanora Mattern.

Enroll.: 21 (*f.t.* 13 m., 8 w.)
(303) 343-6233

LAMAR COMMUNITY COLLEGE
Lamar 81052. Public (state) junior. 1976/1982 (NCA). Qtr. plan. Degrees: A. Pres. Marvin E. Lane.
Enroll.: FTE 364
(303) 336-2248

LORETTO HEIGHTS COLLEGE
3001 S. Federal Blvd., Denver 80236. Private (Roman Catholic) liberal arts. 1926/1984 (NCA). Sem. plan. Degrees: B. *Prof. Accred.:* Nursing (B), Teacher Education (*e,s*). Pres. Thomas K. Craine.
Enroll.: FTE 544
(303) 936-8441

MESA COLLEGE
Grand Junction 81502. Public (state). 1957/1984 (NCA). Sem. plan. Degrees: A,B. *Prof. Accred.:* Dental Assisting, Nursing (A,B), Radiography. Pres. John U. Tomlinson.
Enroll.: FTE 1,472
(303) 248-1020

METROPOLITAN STATE COLLEGE
Denver 80204. Public liberal arts. 1971/1976 (NCA). Qtr. plan. Degrees: B. *Prof. Accred.:* Engineering Technology (civil and environmental, electronics, mechanical), Music, Nursing (B), Teacher Education (*e,s*). Pres. Paul J. Magelli.
Enroll.: FTE 9,751
(303) 629-3220

MILE HI COLLEGE
6464 W. 14th Ave., Lakewood 80214. Private business. 1977/1983 (AICS). Qtr. plan. Diplomas. Pres. William L. Wilson.
Enroll.: 421 (*f.t.* 38 m., 383 w.)
(303) 233-7973

BRANCH CAMPUS
227 San Pedro Dr., N.E., Albuquerque, NM 87108. Dir. Nora Glenn.
(505) 266-9955

MORGAN COMMUNITY COLLEGE
Fort Morgan 80701. Public. 1980/1983 (NCA). Qtr. plan. Degrees: A. Pres. Larry Carter.
Enroll.: FTE 387
(303) 867-8564

NAZARENE BIBLE COLLEGE
P.O. Box 15749, Colorado Springs 80935. Private (Church of the Nazarene) junior. 1976 (AABC). Qtr. plan. Degrees: A. Pres. Jerry Lambert.
Enroll.: 436
(303) 596-5110

NORTHEASTERN JUNIOR COLLEGE
Sterling 80751. Public (county). 1964/1984 (NCA). Qtr. plan. Degrees: A. Pres. Marvin W. Weiss.
Enroll.: FTE 1,646
(303) 522-6600

OTERO JUNIOR COLLEGE
La Junta 81050. Public (county). 1967/1977 (NCA). Qtr. plan. Degrees: A. *Prof. Accred.:* Nursing (A). Pres. W. L. McDivitt.
Enroll.: FTE 535
(303) 384-8721

*PARKS COLLEGE
7350 N. Broadway, Suite P-300, Denver 80221. Private business. 1962/1984 (AICS). Qtr. plan. Degrees: A, certificates, diplomas. *Prof. Accred.:* Medical Assisting. Dir. Morgan Landry.
Enroll.: 1,813 (*f.t.* 725 m., 1,088 w.)
(303) 430-8511

PIKES PEAK COMMUNITY COLLEGE
Colorado Springs 80906. Public (state) junior. 1975/1980 (NCA). Sem. plan. Degrees: A. *Prof. Accred.:* Dental Assisting, Nursing (A). Pres. Cecil L. Groves.
Enroll.: FTE 3,519
(303) 576-7711

PIKES PEAK INSTITUTE OF MEDICAL TECHNOLOGY
820 Arcturus Dr., Colorado Springs 80906. Private. 1971/1983 (ABHES). 18-month program. Diplomas. *Prof. Accred.:* Medical Assisting, Medical Laboratory Technology. Pres. Alice E. Johnson.
Enroll.: 109
(303) 471-0814

PUEBLO COLLEGE OF BUSINESS
4035 Fortino Blvd., Pueblo 81008. Private business. 1969/1981 (AICS). Qtr. plan. Certificates, diplomas. Pres. E.R. Dill.
Enroll.: 436 (*f.t.* 76 m., 360 w.)
(303) 545-3100

PUEBLO COMMUNITY COLLEGE
Pueblo 81004. Public (state) junior. 1979/1981 (NCA). Sem. plan. Degrees: A. *Prof. Accred.:* Radiography, Respiratory Therapy. Interim Pres. P. Anthony Zeiss.

*Candidate for Accreditation by Regional Accrediting Commission.

Enroll.: FTE 1,082
(303) 549-3325

Red Rocks Community College
12600 W. Sixth Ave., Golden 80401. Public (state). 1975/1985 (NCA). Sem. plan. Degrees: A, certificates. Pres. Richard Wilson.
Enroll.: FTE 1,858
(303) 988-6160

Regis College
3539 West 50th Ave., Denver 80221. Private (Roman Catholic) liberal arts. 1922/1979 (NCA). Sem. plan. Degrees: A,B,M. Pres. Rev. David M. Clarke, S.J.
Enroll.: FTE 2,746
(303) 458-4100

Rocky Mountain College of Art and Design
1441 Ogden St., Denver 80218. Private. 1977/1984 (NATTS). Qtr. plan. Degrees: A. Dir. Steven M. Steele.
Enroll.: 150 (*f.t.* 42 m., 63 w.)
(303) 832-1557

St. Thomas Theological Seminary
1300 S. Steele St., Denver 80210. Private (Roman Catholic) theology for men. 1961/1984 (NCA). Qtr. plan. Degrees: P.M. *Prof. Accred.:* Theology (1970/1984, ATS). Rector-Pres. Rev. John E. Rybolt, C.M.
Enroll.: 118
(303) 722-4687

Technical Trades Institute
2315 E. Pikes Peak Ave., Colorado Springs 80909. Private. 1983 (NATTS). Courses of varying lengths. Diplomas. Dir. E. R. Dill.
Enroll.: 152
(303) 632-7626

Technical Trades Institute (Extension)
772 Horizon Dr., Grand Junction 81506. Private. 1985 (NATTS). Courses of varying lengths. Certificates. Dir. Grant Fleming.
(303) 245-8101

Trinidad State Junior College
Trinidad 81082. Public (county). 1962/1981 (NCA). Qtr. plan. Degrees: A. *Prof. Accred.:* Nursing (A). Pres. Thomas W. Sullivan.
Enroll.: FTE 930
(303) 846-5541

United States Air Force Academy
USAF Academy 80840. Public (federal) military and technological. 1959/1979 (NCA). Sem. plan. Degrees: B. *Prof. Accred.:* Engineering (aeronautical, astronautical, civil, electrical, engineering mechanics, engineering science). Lt. Maj. Gen. Winfield W. Scott, Jr.
Enroll.: 4,522 (*f.t.* 3,988 m., 584 w.)
(303) 472-4140

University of Colorado
Central Office, Boulder 80309. Public (state). Pres. E. Gordon Gee.
(303) 492-0111

University of Colorado at Boulder
Boulder 80309. 1913/1983 (NCA). Sem. plan. Degrees: B,P,M,D. *Prof. Accred.:* Architecture (M), Business (B,M), Engineering (aerospace engineering sciences, architectural, chemical, civil, electrical, electrical engineering and computer science, mechanical), Health Services Administration, Journalism, Law, Music, Pharmacy, Psychology, Speech Pathology and Audiology, Teacher Education (*e,s,p*). Chanc. James Corbridge.
Enroll.: FTE 19,881
(303) 492-8908

University of Colorado at Colorado Springs
Colorado Springs 80933. 1970/1977 (NCA). Degrees: B,M. *Prof. Accred.:* Engineering (electrical). Chanc. Dwayne C. Nuzum.
Enroll.: FTE 3,250
(303) 593-3119

University of Colorado at Denver
Denver 80202. 1970/1984 (NCA). Degrees: B,P,M. *Prof. Accred.:* Business (B,M), Dental Hygiene, Engineering (civil, electrical, mechanical), Landscape Architecture (M), Music, Nursing (B,M). Chanc. Glendon Drake.
Enroll.: FTE 2,832
(303) 629-2643

University of Colorado Health Sciences Center
4200 E. Ninth Ave., Denver 80262. 1913/1981 (NCA). Qtr. plan in Medical School; sem. in Dental and Nursing Schools. Degrees: B, P,M,D. *Prof. Accred.:* Assistant to the Primary Care Physician, Dentistry, Medical Technology, Medicine, Nursing (B,M), Physical Therapy. Chanc. Bernard W. Nelson.
Enroll.: FTE 1,475
(303) 492-7682

University of Denver
2301 S. Gaylord, Denver 80208. Private (United Methodist); accreditation includes

Colorado Women's College. 1914/1983 (NCA). Qtr. plan. Degrees: A,B,P,M,D. *Prof. Accred.:* Art, Business (B,M), Law, Librarianship, Music, Psychology, Social Work (M), Speech Pathology and Audiology, Teacher Education (*e,s,p*). Chanc. Dwight M. Smith.
Enroll.: FTE 6,321
(303) 871-2000

UNIVERSITY OF NORTHERN COLORADO
Greeley 80639. Public (state). 1916/1985 (NCA). Qtr. plan. Degrees: B,M,D. *Prof. Accred.:* Music, Nursing (B), Psychology, Rehabilitation Counseling, Speech Pathology and Audiology, Teacher Education (*e,s,p*). Pres. Robert C. Dickeson.
Enroll.: FTE 8,233
(303) 351-2121

UNIVERSITY OF SOUTHERN COLORADO
Pueblo 81001. Public liberal arts and technological. 1951/1984 (NCA). Qtr. plan. Degrees: A,B,M. *Prof. Accred.:* Engineering Technology (civil, electronics, mechanical, metallurgical), Music, Nursing (A,B), Radiography, Respiratory Therapy, Social Work (B), Teacher Education (*e,s,p*). Interim Pres. Robert C. Shirley.
Enroll.: FTE 3,849
(303) 549-2306

WESTERN BIBLE COLLEGE
16075 W. Belleview Ave., Morrison 80465. Private (Interdenominational) professional. 1974 (AABC). Sem. plan. Degrees: A,B. Pres. Joe Wall.
Enroll.: 164
(303) 697-8135

WESTERN STATE COLLEGE OF COLORADO
Gunnison 81230. Public liberal arts. 1915/1985 (NCA). Sem. plan. Degrees: B,M. *Prof. Accred.:* Music, Teacher Education (*e,s,p*). Pres. J. Gilbert Hause.
Enroll.: FTE 2,276
(303) 943-2114

YESHIVA TORAS CHAIM TALMUDIC SEMINARY
1400 Quitman St., Denver 80204. Private professional. 1979/1985. Degrees: B of Judaic Studies; B of Talmudic Law. *Prof. Accred.:* Rabbinical and Talmudic Education. Pres. S. Beren.
Enroll.: 49 (*f.t.* 34 m., 0 w.)
(303) 629-8200

CONNECTICUT

Academy for Business Careers
1315 Dixwell Ave., Hamden 06514. Private. 1974/1980 (AICS). Sem. plan. Diplomas. Pres. Janet S. Arena.
Enroll.: 499 (*f.t.* 54 m., 445 w.)
(203) 288-7474

Branch Campus
50 Washington St., Norwalk 06854. Dir. Tina Santella.
(203) 853-4070

Albertus Magnus College
New Haven 06511. Private (Roman Catholic) liberal arts. 1932/1981. (NEASC-CIHE). Sem. plan. Degrees: A,B. Pres. Sister Julia McNamara, O.P.
Enroll.: 440
(203) 773-8850

Asnuntuck Community College
Enfield 06082. Public (state) junior. 1976/1986 (NEASC-CIHE). Sem. plan. Degrees: A. Exec. Dean Harvey S. Irlen.
Enroll.: 1,980
(203) 745-1603

Berkeley Divinity School
New Haven 06511. Private (Episcopal) (professional; graduate only by virtue of affiliation with Yale University Divinity School). Dean James E. Annand.
(203) 436-3636

Branford Hall School of Business
9 Business Park Dr., Branford 06405. Private. 1977/1980 (AICS). Courses of varying lengths. Certificates. Pres. Nelson Bernabucci.
Enroll.: 363 (*f.t.* 49 m., 314 w.)
(203) 488-2525

Briarwood College
2279 Mount Vernon Rd., Southington 06489. Private business. 1982 (NEASC-CVTCI). Sem. plan. Degrees: A, diplomas. *Prof. Accred.:* Dental Assisting. Pres. John J. LeConche.
Enroll.: 467
(203) 628-4751

Bridgeport Engineering Institute
Bridgeport 06606. Private professional. 1977/1985 (NEASC-CIHE). Tri. plan. Degrees: A,B. Pres. William Krummel.
Enroll.: 869
(203) 366-1565

Business Careers Institute
177 Columbus Blvd., New Britain 06051. Private. 1970/1981 (AICS). Sem. plan. Certificates. Dir. David Kravet.
Enroll.: 102 (*f.t.* 7 m., 95 w.)
(203) 223-6563

Butler Business School
2710 North Ave., Bridgeport 06604. Private. 1979/1985 (AICS). Courses of varying lengths. Certificates, diplomas. Pres. Morton S. Butler.
Enroll.: 295 (*f.t.* 4 m., 291 w.)
(203) 333-3601

*Central Connecticut State University
New Britain 06050. Public liberal arts and teachers. 1947/1979 (NEASC-CIHE). Sem. plan. Degrees: A,B,M. *Prof. Accred.:* Nurse Anesthesia Education, Nursing (B), Teacher Education (*e,s*). Pres. F. Don James.
Enroll.: 13,510
(203) 827-7203

Charter Oak College/Board for State Academic Awards
340 Capitol Ave., Hartford 06106. Public (state) nonteaching liberal arts. Established to administer external degrees and grant collegiate credit. 1981 (NEASC-CIHE). Degrees: A,B. Pres. Bernard Shea.
Enroll.: 782
(203) 566-7230

Computer Processing Institute
111 Ash St., East Hartford 06108. Private business. 1971/1983 (AICS). Courses of varying lengths. Diplomas. Pres. David S. Shefrin.
Enroll.: 6,834 (*f.t.* 4,387 m., 2,447 w.)
(203) 528-9211

Branch Campus
803 Broad St., Bridgeport 06604. Dir. Robert Moir.
(203) 377-6714

Branch Campus
19 Commonwealth Ave., Woburn, MA 01801. Dir. John Pirroni.
(617) 933-1771

Branch Campus
E-81, Route 4 West, Paramus, NJ 07652. Dir. Randy Proto.
(201) 843-4465

*Member Connecticut State University System

Connecticut Academy
11-13 W. Washington St., South Norwalk 06854. Private. 1984 (ABHES); 1985 (NATTS). Courses of varying lengths. Certificates. Dir. Nicholas Koloniaris.
(203) 838-0286

Connecticut Business Institute
605 Broad St., Stratford 06497. Private. 1972/1985 (AICS). Tri. plan. Certificates, diplomas. Pres. Emanuel Pallant.
Enroll.: 582 (*f.t.* 27 m., 555 w.)
(203) 377-1775

Connecticut College
New London 06320. Private liberal arts. 1932/1977 (NEASC-CIHE). Sem. plan. Degrees: B,M. Pres. Oakes Ames.
Enroll.: 1,911
(203) 447-1911

Connecticut Institute of Hair Design
305 Church St., Naugatuck 06770. Private. 1980 (NATTS). Courses of varying lengths. Diplomas. Dir. John Varanelli.
Enroll.: 30 (*f.t.* 2 m., 28 w.)
(203) 729-1593

Connecticut School of Electronics
586 Boulevard, P.O. Box 7308, New Haven 06519. Private. 1968/1984 (NATTS). Sem. plan. Certificates, diplomas. Pres. Albert J. Marcarelli.
Enroll.: 623 (*f.t.* 596 m., 27 w.)
(203) 624-2121

Connecticut State University
Central office, P.O. Box 2008, New Britain 06050. Public. Pres. Dallas K. Beal.
(203) 827-7700

County Schools, Inc.
3787 Main St., Bridgeport 06606. Private home study. 1976/1982 (NHSC). Dir. Joseph M. Monaco.
(203) 374-6187

Data Institute
525 Burnside Ave., East Hartford 06108. Private business. 1983 (AICS). Courses of varying lengths. Certificates. Exec. Dir. Mark Scheinberg.
Enroll.: 135 (*f.t.* 24 m., 111 w.)
(203) 528-4111

Diesel Technology Institute
105 Phoenix Ave., Enfield 06082. Private. 1982 (NATTS). Courses of varying lengths. Certificates. Pres. Arthur Bertrand.
(203) 745-2010

East Coast Welding Technical School
179 Cross Road, Waterford 06385. Private. 1981 (NATTS). Courses of varying lengths. Certificates. Dir. James D. Corvello.
Enroll.: 75 (*f.t.* 66 m., 1 w.)
(203) 447-3115

*Eastern Connecticut State University
Willimantic 06226. Public liberal arts and teachers. 1958/1981 (NEASC-CIHE). Sem. plan. Degrees: A,B,M. Pres. Charles R. Webb.
Enroll.: 3,873
(203) 456-2231

Fairfield University
Fairfield 06430. Private (Roman Catholic) liberal arts. 1953/1978 (NEASC-CIHE). Sem. plan. Degrees: B,M. Pres. Rev. Aloysius P. Kelley, S.J.
Enroll.: 7,246
(203) 254-4000

Greater Hartford Community College
Hartford 06105. Public (state) junior. 1975/1986 (NEASC-CIHE). Sem. plan. Degrees: A. *Prof. Accred.:* Nursing (A). Exec. Dean Walter Markiewicz.
Enroll.: 3,430
(203) 549-4200

Greater New Haven State Technical College
88 Bassett Rd., North Haven 06473. Public 2-year. 1983 (NEASC-CVTCI). Sem. plan. Degrees: A. Pres. Thomas J. Sullivan.
Enroll.: 875
(203) 789-7499

Hartford College for Women
Hartford 06105. Private junior. 1962/1983 (NEASC-CIHE). Sem. plan. Degrees: A. Pres. M. Kathleen McGrory.
Enroll.: 394
(203) 236-1215

Hartford Conservatory of Music and Dance
Hartford 06105. Private professional 2-year for music and dance. 1979/1985 (NEASC-CVTCI). Sem. plan. Diplomas. Dir. Edward DeGroat.
Enroll.: 43
(203) 246-2588

*Member Connecticut State University System

Hartford Graduate Center
Hartford 06120. Private; graduate only. 1966/1983 (NEASC-CIHE). Sem. plan. Degrees: M. Pres. Robert L. Cole.
Enroll.: 2,239
(203) 549-3600

Hartford Modern School of Welding
184 Ledyard St., Hartford 06114. Private. 1975/1980 (NATTS). Courses of varying lengths. Certificates. Pres. Robert L. Annecharico.
Enroll.: 219 (*f.t.* 208 m., 11 w.)
(203) 249-7576

Hartford Secretarial School
19 Woodland St., Hartford 06105. Private business. 1979/1985 (AICS). Qtr. plan. Certificates, diplomas. Dir. Janet E. Fox.
Enroll.: 168 (*f.t.* 0 m., 168 w.)
(203) 522-2888

Hartford Seminary
77 Sherman St., Hartford 06105. Private (Interdenominational); graduate only. 1983 (NEASC-CIHE). Sem. plan. Degrees: M,D. *Prof. Accred.:* Theology (1938/1983, ATS). Pres. Michael Rion.
Enroll.: 143
(203) 232-4451

Hartford State Technical College
401 Flatbush Ave., Hartford 06106. Public 2-year technical. 1970/1984 (NEASC-CVTCI). Qtr. plan. Degrees: A. *Prof. Accred.:* Engineering Technology (civil, electrical, manufacturing, mechanical) Pres. Kenneth E. DeRego.
Enroll.: 1,484
(203) 527-4111

Hartford Technical Institute
424 Homestead Ave., Hartford 06112. Private. 1981 (NATTS). Courses of varying lengths. Certificates, diplomas. Pres. Robert M. Meyers.
Enroll.: 130 (*f.t.* 43 m., 2 w.)
(203) 249-8688

Holy Apostles College and Seminary
Cromwell 06416. Private (Roman Catholic) liberal arts for men. 1979/1986 (NEASC-CIHE). Sem. plan. Degrees: A,B,M. Pres.-Rector V. Rev. Leo J. Ovian, M.S.A.
Enroll.: 171
(203) 635-5311

Housatonic Community College
Bridgeport 06608. Public (state) junior. 1972/1985 (NEASC-CIHE). Sem. plan. Degrees: A. *Prof. Accred.:* Medical Laboratory Technology (A). Pres. Vincent S. Darnowski.
Enroll.: 2,386
(203) 579-6400

Huntington Institute
193 Broadway, Norwich 06360. Private business. 1980/1986 (AICS). Courses of varying lengths. Certificates. Dir. Judith K. Leonard.
Enroll.: 164 (*f.t.* 1 m., 163 w.)
(203) 886-0507

Branch Campus
204 State St., North Haven 06473.
(203) 288-8945

Katharine Gibbs School
142 East Ave., Norwalk 06851. Private business. 1975/1986 (AICS). Sem. plan. Degrees: A. Dir. Sandra Krakoff.
Enroll.: *f.t.* 847 w.
(203) 838-4173

MTA School
64 Oakland Ave., East Hartford 06108. Branch of MTA, Inc., Middletown, PA. Private. Combination home study and resident programs in truck driving and diesel mechanics. 1982 (NHSC); accredited as an Extension of the New England Technical Institute 1983 (NATTS). Pres. William R. Yocom.
(203) 289-6421

Manchester Community College
Manchester 06040. Public (state) junior. 1971/1982 (NEASC-CIHE). Sem. plan. Degrees: A. *Prof. Accred.:* Medical Laboratory Technology, Respiratory Therapy, Surgical Technology. Pres. William E. Vincent.
Enroll.: 6,231
(203) 646-4900

Mattatuck Community College
Waterbury 06708. Public (state) junior. 1973/1983 (NEASC-CIHE). Sem. plan. Degrees: A. *Prof. Accred.:* Nursing (A), Radiography. Pres. Richard L. Sanders.
Enroll.: 4,496
(203) 757-9661

Middlesex Community College
Middletown 06457. Public (state) junior. 1973/1983 (NEASC-CIHE). Sem. plan. Degrees: A. *Prof. Accred.:* Radiography.
Pres. Robert A. Chapman.
Enroll.: 2,690
(203) 344-3001

Mitchell College
New London 06320. Private junior. 1956/1983 (NEASC-CIHE). Sem. plan. Degrees: A. Pres. Robert C. Weller.
Enroll.: 921
(203) 443-2811

Mohegan Community College
Norwich 06360. Public (state) junior. 1973/1983 (NEASC-CIHE). Sem. plan. Degrees: A. *Prof. Accred.:* Nursing (A). Pres. John D. Hurd.
Enroll.: 2,099
(203) 886-1931

Morse School of Business
275 Asylum St., Hartford 06103. Private. 1953/1984 (AICS). Courses of varying lengths. Diplomas. Pres. Michael S. Taub.
Enroll.: 1,759 (*f.t.* 459 m., 1,300 w.)
(203) 522-2261

New England Technical Institute of Connecticut
99 John Downey Dr., New Britain 06051. Private. 1983 (NATTS). 66-week program. Diplomas. Dir. Joseph J. Skarzynski.
Enroll.: 150
(203) 225-8641

New England Tractor Trailer Training of Connecticut
Main St., Somers 06071. Private. 1982 (NATTS). 4-week courses. Diplomas. Pres. Arlan Greenberg.
Enroll.: 50
(203) 749-0711

New London School of Business
231 Captain's Walk, New London 06320. Private. 1979/1985 (AICS). Courses of varying lengths. Certificates. Dir. Leonard Fuller.
Enroll.: 248 (*f.t.* 1 m., 247 w.)
(203) 443-7441

Northwestern Connecticut Community College
Winsted 06098. Public (state) junior. 1971/1983 (NEASC-CIHE). Sem. plan. Degrees: A. Pres. Booker T. DeVaughan, Jr.
Enroll.: 2,344
(203) 379-8543

Norwalk Community College
Norwalk 06854. Public (state) junior. 1973/1982 (NEASC-CIHE). Sem. plan. Degrees: A. *Prof. Accred.:* Nursing (A). Pres. William H. Schwab.
Enroll.: 3,357
(203) 853-2040

Norwalk State Technical College
Norwalk 06854. Public 2-year technical. 1970/1984 (NEASC-CVTCI). Qtr. plan. Degrees: A. *Prof. Accred.:* Engineering Technology (architectural, chemical, civil, computer, electrical, electro-mechanical, manufacturing, mechanical). Pres. William M. Krummel.
Enroll.: 1,662
(203) 838-0601

*Paier College of Art, Inc.
Six Prospect Ct., Hamden 06511. Private. 1970/1976 (NATTS). Sem. plan. Degrees: B, certificates, diplomas. Pres. Edward T. Paier.
Enroll.: 391 (*f.t.* 91 m., 149 w.)
(203) 777-3851

Porter and Chester Institute (Branch)
138 Weymouth St., Enfield 06082. Private. 1980 (NATTS). Qtr. plan. Diplomas. Exec. Dir. Wil Brown.
Enroll.: 280 (*f.t.* 240 m., 40 w.)
(203) 741-2561

Porter and Chester Institute
2139 Silas Deane Hwy., P.O. Box 330, Rocky Hill 06067. Private. 1973/1976 (NATTS). Qtr. plan. Diplomas. Exec. Dir. Henry J. Kamerzel.
Enroll.: 300 (*f.t.* 220 m., 30 w.)
(203) 529-2519

Porter and Chester Institute
670 Lordship Blvd., P.O. Box 364, Stratford 06497. Private. 1972/1977 (NATTS). Qtr. plan. Diplomas. Exec. Dir. Wil Brown.
Enroll.: 290 (*f.t.* 205 m., 15 w.)
(203) 375-4463

Porter and Chester Institute
625 Wolcott St., Waterbury 06705. Private technical. 1979 (NATTS). Qtr. plan. Diplomas. Exec. Dir. Wil Brown.
Enroll.: 140 (*f.t.* 105 m., 15 w.)
(203) 575-1244

Post College
Waterbury 06708. Private liberal arts. 1972/1985 (NEASC-CIHE). Sem. plan. Degrees: A,B. Pres. N. Patricia Yarborough.
Enroll.: 1,507
(203) 755-0121

Propersi Institute of Art
581 W. Putnam Ave., Greenwich 06830. Private. 1980 (NATTS). Sem. plan. Diplomas. Dir. August J. Propersi.

*Candidate for Accreditation by Regional Accrediting Commission

Connecticut

Enroll.: 33 (*f.t.* 21 m., 24 w.)
(203) 869-4430

QUINEBAUG VALLEY COMMUNITY COLLEGE
Danielson 06239. Public (state) junior. 1978/1985 (NEASC-CIHE). Sem. plan. Degrees: A. Pres. Robert E. Miller
Enroll.: 1,131
(203) 774-1160

QUINNIPIAC COLLEGE
Hamden 06518. Private liberal arts and professional. 1958/1980 (NEASC-CIHE). Sem. plan. Degrees: A,B,M. *Prof. Accred.:* Diagnostic Medical Sonography, Medical Technology, Nuclear Medicine Technology, Nursing (A), Occupational Therapy, Physical Therapy, Radiography, Respiratory Therapy. Interim Pres. Carl N. Hansen.
Enroll.: 3,139
(203) 288-5251

RENSSELAER POLYTECHNIC INSTITUTE
See Hartford Graduate Center

ROFFLER ACADEMY FOR HAIRSTYLISTS
454 Park St., Hartford 06106. Private. 1977 (NATTS). Courses of varying lengths. Diplomas. Pres. Barbara Kamholtz.
Enroll.: 42 (*f.t.* 11 m., 31 w.)
(203) 522-2359

SACRED HEART UNIVERSITY
Bridgeport 06606. Private (Roman Catholic) liberal arts college. 1969/1983 (NEASC-CIHE). Sem. plan. Degrees: A,B,M. *Prof. Accred.:* Nursing (B). Social Work (B). Pres. Robert A. Preston.
Enroll.: 5,014
(203) 371-7900

SAINT ALPHONSUS COLLEGE
Suffield 06078. Private (Roman Catholic, Congregation of Most Holy Redeemer) seminary. 1968/1979 (NEASC-CIHE). Sem. plan with 6-week postsession. Degrees: B. Pres. Rev. Patrick McGarrity, C.SS.R.
Enroll.: 52
(203) 668-7393

SAINT JOSEPH COLLEGE
West Hartford 06117. Private (Roman Catholic) liberal arts for women, graduate school coeducational. 1938/1976 (NEASC-CIHE). Sem. plan. Degrees: B,M. *Prof. Accred.:* Dietetics, Social Work (B). Pres. Sister M. Paton Ryan, R.S.M.
Enroll.: 1,223
(203) 232-4571

SOUTH CENTRAL COMMUNITY COLLEGE
60 Sargent Dr., New Haven 06511. Public (state) junior. 1981/1983 (NEASC-CIHE). Sem. plan. Degrees: A. *Prof. Accred.:* Nuclear Medicine Technology, Radiation Therapy Technology, Radiography. Pres. Antonio Perez.
Enroll.: 2,254
(203) 789-7028

*SOUTHERN CONNECTICUT STATE UNIVERSITY
New Haven 06515. Public liberal arts and teachers. 1952/1986 (NEASC-CIHE). Sem. plan. Degrees: A,B,M. *Prof. Accred.:* Librarianship, Nurse Anesthesia Education, Nursing (B), Social Work (B), Speech Pathology, Teacher Education (*e,s,p*). Pres. Michael J. Adanti.
Enroll.: 10,733
(203) 397-4000

STONE SCHOOL
55 Church St., New Haven 06510. Private business. 1953/1984 (AICS). Qtr. plan. Diplomas. Dir. Lynn Carlson.
Enroll.: *f.t.* 498 w.
(203) 624-0121

TECHNICAL CAREERS INSTITUTE
11 Kimberly Ave., West Haven 06516. Private. 1974/1979 (NATTS). Courses of varying lengths. Certificates. Dir. Anthony D'Agostino.
Enroll.: 1,100 (*f.t.* 850 m., 50 w.)
(203) 932-2282

BRANCH
605 Day Hill Rd., Windsor 06095. Dir. Bradley R. Baran.
(203) 688-8351

THAMES VALLEY STATE TECHNICAL COLLEGE
Norwich 06360. Public 2-year technical. 1970/1980 (NEASC-CVTCI). Qtr. plan. Degrees: A. *Prof. Accred.:* Engineering Technology (chemical, electrical, manufacturing, mechanical). Acting Pres. George D. Harris.
Enroll.: 693
(203) 886-0177

TRINITY COLLEGE
Hartford 06106. Private liberal arts. 1929/1976 (NEASC-CIHE). Sem. plan. Degrees: B,M. *Prof. Accred.:* Pres. James F. English, Jr.

*Member Connecticut State University System

Enroll.: 2,158
(203) 527-3151

TUNXIS COMMUNITY COLLEGE
Farmington 06032. Public (state) junior. 1975/1984 (NEASC-CIHE). Sem. plan. Degrees: A. *Prof. Accred.:* Dental Assisting, Dental Hygiene. CEO-Exec. Dean Eduardo J. Marti.
Enroll.: 3,043
(203) 677-7701

UNITED STATES COAST GUARD ACADEMY
New London 06320. Public (federal) professional. 1952/1980 (NEASC-CIHE). Sem. plan. Degrees: B. *Prof. Accred.:* Engineering (civil, electrical, marine, ocean). Supt. Rear Adm. Edward Nelson, Jr., USCG.
Enroll.: 790
(203) 444-8444

UNIVERSITY OF BRIDGEPORT
Bridgeport 06602. Private. 1951/1986 (NEASC-CIHE). Sem. plan. Degrees: A,B,M,D. *Prof. Accred.:* Art, Business (B,M), Dental Hygiene, Engineering (electrical, mechanical), Law, Music, Nursing (A,B). Pres. Leland W. Miles.
Enroll.: 6,337
(203) 576-4000

UNIVERSITY OF CONNECTICUT
Storrs 06268. Public (state). 1931/1977 (NEASC-CIHE). Medical School at Hartford. 2-year branch campuses at Groton, Hartford, Stamford, Waterbury. Sem. plan. Degrees: B,P,M,D. *Prof. Accred.:* Accounting (Type A,B), Art, Business (B,M), Community Health, Cytotechnology, Dentistry, Dietetics, Engineering (chemical, civil, computer science, electrical, mechanical), Engineering Technology (mechanical), Law, Medicine, Music, Nursing (B,M), Pharmacy, Physical Therapy, Psychology, Social Work (M), Speech Pathology and Audiology, Teacher Education (*e,s,p*). Pres. John T. Casteen, III.
Enroll.: 23,486
(203) 486-2000

UNIVERSITY OF HARTFORD
200 Bloomfield Ave., West Hartford 06117. Private. 1961/1982 (NEASC-CIHE). Sem. plan. Degrees: A,B,M,D. *Prof. Accred.:* Art, Engineering (civil, electrical, mechanical), Engineering Technology (electronic), Medical Technology, Music, Respiratory Therapy, Teacher Education (*e,s,p*). Pres. Stephen J. Trachtenberg.
Enroll.: 7,611
(203) 243-4100

UNIVERSITY OF NEW HAVEN
West Haven 06516. Private. 1966/1981 (NEASC-CIHE). Sem. plan. Degrees: A,B,M. *Prof. Accred.:* Engineering (civil, electrical, industrial, mechanical). Pres. Phillip S. Kaplan.
Enroll.: 7,762
(203) 932-7000

WATERBURY STATE TECHNICAL COLLEGE
Waterbury 06708. Public 2-year technical. 1970/1984 (NEASC-CVTCI). Qtr. plan. Degrees: A. *Prof. Accred.:* Engineering Technology (chemical, electrical, manufacturing, mechanical). Pres. Charles A. Ekstrom.
Enroll.: 1,765
(203) 575-8078

WESLEYAN UNIVERSITY
Middletown 06457. Private liberal arts college. 1929/1980 (NEASC-CIHE). Sem. plan. Degrees: B,M,D. Pres. Colin G. Campbell.
Enroll.: 3,252
(203) 347-9411

*WESTERN CONNECTICUT STATE UNIVERSITY
Danbury 06810. Public liberal arts and teachers. 1954/1984 (NEASC-CIHE). Sem. plan. Degrees: A,B,M. *Prof. Accred.:* Nursing (B). Pres. Stephen Feldman.
Enroll.: 5,778
(203) 797-4347

WESTLAWN SCHOOL OF YACHT DESIGN
733 Summer St., Stamford 06904. Private home study. 1971/1982 (NHSC). Pres. Jules G. Fleder.
(203) 359-0500

YALE UNIVERSITY
New Haven 06520. Private. 1929/1979 (NEASC-CIHE). Sem. plan. Degrees: B,P,M,D. *Prof. Accred.:* Architecture (M), Assistant to the Primary Care Physician, Dietetics, Engineering (chemical, electrical, mechanical), Forestry, Health Services Administration, Law, Medicine, Music, Nursing (M), Psychology, Public Health, Theology. Pres. Benno C. Schmidt, Jr.
Enroll.: 10,920
(203) 436-4771

*Member Connecticut State University System

DELAWARE

Brandywine College of Widener University
P.O. Box 7139, Wilmington 19803. Private. 1972/1986 (MSA/CHE). Sem. plan. Degrees: A,B. Dean Andrew A. Bushko; Pres. Robert J. Bruce.
Enroll.: 608 (*f.t.* 169 m., 402 w.)
(302) 478-3000

Delaware Law School of Widener University
Wilmington 19802. Private professional. 1975/1986. Sem. plan. Degrees: P. *Prof. Accred.:* Law (ABA only). Dean J. Kirkland Grant; Pres. Robert J. Bruce.
Enroll.: 914 (*f.t.* 375 m., 195 w.)
(302) 658-8531

Delaware State College
1200 Dupont Hwy., Dover 19901. Public liberal arts and teachers. 1945/1982 (MSA/CHE). Sem. plan. Degrees: B,M. *Prof. Accred.:* Social Work (B). Pres. Luna I. Mishoe.
Enroll.: 2,151 (*f.t.* 757 m., 876 w.)
(302) 736-5201

Delaware Technical and Community College—Central Office
P.O. Box 897, Dover 19901. Public (state) 2-year technological. Qtr. plan. Degrees: A, certificates. Pres. John R. Kotula.
(302) 736-5321

Southern Campus
P.O. Box 610, Georgetown 19947. 1972/1983 (MSA/CHE). *Prof. Accred.:* Medical Laboratory Technology (A), Occupational Therapy, Practical Nursing, Respiratory Therapy. Vice Pres./Campus Dir. Jack F. Owens.
Enroll.: 1,798 (*f.t.* 340 m., 569 w.)
(302) 856-5400

Terry Campus
1832 N. Dupont Pkwy., Dover 19901. 1978/1983 (MSA/CHE). Acting Vice Pres./Campus Dir. William Pfeifer.
Enroll.: 1,395 (*f.t.* 220 m., 238 w.)
(302) 736-5321

Wilmington/Stanton Campuses
Wilmington Campus, 333 Shipley St., Wilmington 19801. 1972/1983 (MSA/CHE); Stanton Campus, 400 Stanton-Christiana Rd., Newark 19702. 1972/1983 (MSA/CHE). *Prof. Accred.:* Dental Assisting, Dental Hygiene, Nuclear Medicine Technology, Nursing (A), Occupational Therapy, Practical Nursing. Vice Pres./Campus Dir. John H. Jones.
Enroll.: 4,288 (*f.t.* 779 m., 818 w.)
(302) 571-5391 (Wilmington)
(302) 454-3917 (Stanton)

Dorothea B. Lane Schools
1800 Pennsylvania Ave., Wilmington 19806. Private business. 1983 (AICS). Courses of varying lengths. Certificates. Dir. Louis Mene.
(302) 654-9797

Branch Campus
Maryland Executive Park, York Bldg., 8600 LaSalle Rd., Towson, MD 21204. Dir. Karen A. Paglia.
(301) 296-0900

Branch Campus
1730 Walton Rd., Blue Bell, PA 19422. Dir. Arlene Rosales.
(215) 825-7272

Branch Campus
2121 Eisenhower Ave., Alexandria, VA 22314.
(703) 683-2066

Branch Campus
505 Charlotte St., Fredericksburg, VA 22401. Dir. Bonnie T. Andrews.
(703) 373-1721

Goldey Beacom College
4701 Limestone Rd., Wilmington 19808. Private. 1976/1981 (MSA/CHE). Sem. plan. Degrees: A,B. Pres. William R. Baldt.
Enroll.: 1,896 (*f.t.* 213 m., 694 w.)
(302) 998-8814

Harris Careers Institute
301-B E. Lea Blvd., Wilmington 19802. Private. 1985 (ABHES). 26-week program. Diplomas. Dir. Burton Braverman.
(302) 764-4488

USA Training Academy, Inc.
955 S. Chapel St., P.O. Box 9439, Newark 19714. Private; combination home study-resident. 1974/1984 (NHSC). Pres. Paul L. Teeven.
(302) 731-1555

Dorothea B. Lane School (Branch)
955 S. Chapel St., P.O. Box 9439, Newark 19714. A division.
(302) 731-1555

Branch
Resident training site. Ellyson Industrial Park, 9300 Sturdevant St., Box 16, Pensacola, FL 32504. Dir. Arlo Moore.
(904) 478-2490

Branch
Resident truck driving training site. 2721 Thompson La., Clarksville, TN 37040.
(615) 552-0515

University of Delaware
Newark 19716. Public (state). 1921/1981 (MSA/CHE). 4-1-4 plan. Degrees: A,B,P,M,D. *Prof. Accred.:* Accounting (Type A), Business (B,M), Dietetics, Engineering (chemical, civil, electrical, mechanical), Engineering Technology (agricultural), Medical Technology, Music, Nursing (B,M), Physical Therapy, Psychology. Pres. E. Arthur Trabant.
Enroll.: 18,162 (*f.t.* 6,269 m., 7,797 w.)
(302) 451-2000

Wesley College
120 N. State St., Dover 19901. Private (United Methodist) liberal arts. 1950/1978 (MSA/CHE). Sem. plan. Degrees: A,B. *Prof. Accred.:* Medical Technology, Nursing (A). Pres. Reed M. Stewart.
Enroll.: 1,083 (*f.t.* 252 m., 298 w.)
(302) 736-2300

Wilmington College
New Castle 19720. Private liberal arts. 1975/1985 (MSA/CHE). Sem. plan. Degrees: A,B,M. Pres. Audrey K. Doberstein.
Enroll.: 971 (*f.t.* 142 m., 120 w.)
(302) 328-9401

DISTRICT OF COLUMBIA

AMERICAN UNIVERSITY
Massachusetts and Nebraska Aves., N.W., Washington 20016. Private (United Methodist). 1928/1984 (MSA/CHE). Sem. plan. Degrees: A,B,P,M,D. *Prof. Accred.:* Journalism, Law, Music, Nursing (B), Psychology, Teacher Education (*e,s*). Pres. Richard Berendzen.
Enroll.: 11,014 (*f.t.* 2,944 m., 3,493 w.)
(202) 885-1000

BENJAMIN FRANKLIN UNIVERSITY
1100 16th St., N.W., Washington 20036. Private senior business. 1979/1983 (AICS). Tri. plan. Degrees: A,B,M. Pres. Marthajane Kennedy.
Enroll.: 256 (*f.t.* 167 m., 89 w.)
(202) 737-2262

BROOK-WEIN BUSINESS INSTITUTE
1003 K St., N.W., Suite 400, Washington 20001. Private. 1978/1982 (AICS). Qtr. plan. Certificates, diplomas. Pres. Iva Brookin Carter.
Enroll.: 462 (*f.t.* 67 m., 395 w.)
(202) 659-5411

CATHOLIC UNIVERSITY OF AMERICA
Fourth St. and Michigan Ave., N.E., Washington 20064. Private (Roman Catholic). 1921/1980 (MSA/CHE). Sem. plan. Degrees: B,P,M,D. *Prof. Accred.:* Architecture (M), Engineering (chemical, civil, electrical, mechanical), Law, Librarianship, Medical Technology, Music, Nursing (B,M), Psychology, Social Work (B,M), Speech Pathology, Teacher Education (*e*), Theology. Pres. William J. Byron, S.J.
Enroll.: 6,633 (*f.t.* 2,105 m., 2,100 w.)
(202) 635-5100

CORCORAN SCHOOL OF ART
Washington 20006. Private professional. 1985 (MSA/CHE). Sem. plan. Degrees: A,B, diplomas. *Prof. Accred.:* Art. Dean William Barrett.
Enroll.: 194 (*f.t.* 104 m., 131 w.)
(202) 628-9484

CULINARY SCHOOL OF WASHINGTON
1050 Connecticut Ave., N.W., Washington 20036. Private. 1982 (NATTS). Sem. plan. Diplomas. Pres. Mary Ann Kibarian.
Enroll.: 200 (*f.t.* 140 m., 60 w.)
(202) 745-2665

DE SALES SCHOOL OF THEOLOGY
721 Lawrence St., N.E., Washington 20017. Private (Roman Catholic) graduate only. Member Cluster of Independent Theological Schools (CITS) and Washington Theological Union. 1976/1986 (MSA/CHE). Sem. plan. Degrees: P,M. *Prof. Accred.:* Theology (1976/1986, ATS). Pres. V. Rev. William J. Ruhl, O.S.F.S.
Enroll.: 26 (*f.t.* 21 m.)
(202) 269-9412

DEFENSE INTELLIGENCE COLLEGE
Washington 20301-6111. Public (Dept. of Defense) graduate only. 1983/1986 (MSA/CHE). Qtr. plan and courses of varying lengths. Degrees: M, certificates, diplomas. Commandant Col. John D. Macartney, USAF.
Enroll.: 1,095 (*f.t.* 91 m., 13 w.)
(202) 373-3344

DOMINICAN HOUSE OF STUDIES
487 Michigan Ave., N.E., Washington 20017. Private (Roman Catholic) graduate for men. 1976/1986 (MSA/CHE). Sem. plan. Degrees: P,M. *Prof. Accred.:* Theology (1976/1986, ATS). Pres. Rev. J.A. DiNoia, O.P.
Enroll.: *f.t.* 43 m.
(202) 529-5300

GALLAUDET COLLEGE
800 Florida Ave., N.E., Washington 20002. Private liberal arts institution for the deaf. 1957/1986 (MSA/CHE). Sem. plan. Degrees: A,B,M,D. *Prof. Accred.:* Audiology, Rehabilitation Counseling, Social Work (B), Teacher Education (*e,s*). Pres. Jerry C. Lee.
Enroll.: 1,844 (*f.t.* 678 m., 1,000 w.)
(202) 651-5000

GEORGE WASHINGTON UNIVERSITY
Washington 20052. Private. 1922/1977 (MSA/CHE). Sem. plan. Degrees: A,B,P,M,D. *Prof. Accred.:* Assistant to the Primary Care Physician, Business (B,M), Engineering (civil, computer science, electrical, mechanical), Health Services Administration, Law, Medical Technology, Medicine, Music, Nuclear Medical Technology, Nurse Anesthesia Education, Psychology, Radiation Therapy Technology, Rehabilitation Counseling, Speech Pathology and Audiology, Teacher Education (*e,s,p*). Pres. Lloyd H. Elliott.
Enroll.: 18,790 (*f.t.* 5,340 m., 4,412 w.)
(202) 676-6000

Georgetown School of Science and Arts, Ltd.
2461 Wisconsin Ave., N.W., Washington 20007. Private. 1981/1982 (ABHES). Courses of varying lengths. Diplomas. *Prof. Accred.:* Medical Assisting, Medical Laboratory Technology. Pres. and Dir. James L. Greenberg.
Enroll.: 139 (*f.t.* 23 m., 53 w.)
(202) 965-5100

Georgetown University
37th and O Sts. N.W., Washington 20057. Private (Roman Catholic). 1921/1982 (MSA/CHE). Sem. plan. Degrees: B,P,M,D. *Prof. Accred.:* Business (B), Dentistry, Law, Medicine, Nursing (B), Radiography. Pres. Rev. Timothy S. Healy, S.J.
Enroll.: 11,985 (*f.t.* 5,188 m., 4,288 w.)
(202) 625-0100

Hannah Harrison Career School Practical Nursing Program
4470 MacArthur Blvd., N.W., Washington 20007. Private (YWCA). 1980. Courses of varying lengths. Diplomas. *Prof. Accred.:* Practical Nursing, Respiratory Therapy. Dir. Jane Pown.
(202) 333-3500

Howard University
2400 Sixth St., N.W., Washington 20059; School of Religion, 1240 Randolph St., N.E., Washington 20017. Private (federal government support). 1921/1984 (MSA/CHE). Sem. plan. Degrees: B,P,M,D. *Prof. Accred.:* Architecture (B), Art, Assistant to the Primary Care Physician, Business (B,M), Dental Hygiene, Dentistry, Dietetics, Engineering (civil, electrical, mechanical), Health Services Administration, Home Economics, Law, Medicine, Medical Technology, Music, Nursing (B,M), Occupational Therapy, Pharmacy, Physical Therapy, Psychology, Radiation Therapy, Radiation Therapy Technology, Radiography, Social Work (B,M), Speech Pathology, Theology. Pres. James E. Cheek.
Enroll.: 11,184 (*f.t.* 4,138 m., 5,103 w.)
(202) 636-6100

HumRRO Technical Education Center
1400 Eye St., N.W., Washington 20005. Private. 1985 (NATTS). Courses of varying lengths. Certificates, diplomas. Dir. Roger J. Williams.
(202) 842-4106

Jefferson Business College
P.O.Box 19170, Washington 20036. Private business. 1979/1982 (AICS). Courses of varying lengths. Certificates, diplomas. Dir. Dennis Madej.
Enroll.: 228 (*f.t.* 37 m., 191 w.)
(202) 293-9200

Branch Campus
233 Schermerhorn St., Brooklyn, NY 11201.
(718) 802-9500

Branch Campus
215 Broad St., Elizabeth NJ 07208. Dir. Judith Trisker.
(201) 965-2100

Margaret Murray Washington Career Center
First and P Sts., N.W., Washington 20001. Public. Dental Assisting Program. 1981. 1-year course. Certificates. *Prof. Accred.:*Dental Assisting. Coord. Mrs. Hosetta Reid.
(202) 673-7224

Marine Corps Institute
Located at Marine Barracks, 8th and Eye Sts, S.E., Washington 20390. Public (federal) home study. 1977/1983 (NHSC). Dir. Lt. Col. J. M. D. Holladay.
(202) 433-2632

McGraw-Hill Continuing Education Center
3939 Wisconsin Ave., N.W., Washington 20016. Private home study. 1956/1983 (NHSC). Pres. Martin E. Kenney, Jr.
(202) 244-1600

NRI Schools
Washington 20016. A division.

Mount Vernon College
2100 Foxhall Rd., N.W., Washington 20007. Private for women, liberal arts. 1958/1977 (MSA/CHE). Modular plan. Degrees: A,B. *Prof. Accred.:* Interior Design. Pres. Jane C. Evans.
Enroll.: 457 (*f.t.* 387 w.)
(202) 331-0400

Oblate College
391 Michigan Ave., N.E., Washington 20017-1578. Private (Roman Catholic). 1966/1986 (MSA/CHE). Sem. plan. Degrees: B,M. *Prof. Accred.:* Theology (1976/1986, ATS). Pres. Rev. Joseph C. Schwab, O.M.I.
Enroll.: 41 (*f.t.* 38 m., 2 w.)
(202) 529-6544

Smith Business School
1010 Vermont Ave., N.W., Washington 20005. Private. 1979/1985 (AICS). Courses of vary-

ing lengths. Certificates, diplomas. Pres. Lois H. Smith.
Enroll.: 938 (*f.t.* 162 m., 776 w.)
(202) 638-1700

SOUTHEASTERN UNIVERSITY
501 Eye St., S.W., Washington 20024. Private. 1977 (MSA/CHE). Sem. plan. Degrees: A,B,M, certificates. Pres. W. Robert Higgins.
Enroll.: 1,597 (*f.t.* 554 m., 308 w.)
(202) 488-8162

STRAYER COLLEGE
1100 Vermont Ave., N.W., Washington 20005. Private senior business. 1959/1985 (AICS); 1981/1985 (MSA/CHE). Qtr. plan. Degrees: A,B, certificates, diplomas. Pres. Charles E. Palmer, Jr..
Enroll.: 1,226 (*f.t.* 330 m., 403 w.)
(202) 467-6966

BRANCH CAMPUS
3045 Columbia Pike, Arlington, VA 22204.
(703) 892-5100

THE THEATRE SCHOOL
1556 Wisconsin Ave., N.W., Washington 20007. Private. 1980 (NATTS). Sem. plan. Diplomas. Pres. C. Wayne Rudisill.
Enroll.: 65 (*f.t.* 40 m., 25 w.)
(202) 333-2202

TRINITY COLLEGE
Michigan Ave. and Franklin St., N.E., Washington 20017. Private (Roman Catholic) liberal arts for women, graduate school coeducational. 1921/1986 (MSA/CHE). Sem. plan. Degrees: B,M. Pres. Donna M. Jurick.
Enroll.: 941 (*f.t.* 1 m., 441 w.)
(202) 939-5000

UNIVERSITY OF THE DISTRICT OF COLUMBIA
4200 Connecticut Ave., N.W., Washington, D.C. 20008. Public (federal) system. 1979/1985 (MSA/CHE). Acting Pres. Claude Ford.
Total
Enroll.: 12,080 (*f.t.* 2,288 m., 2,189 w.)
(202) 282-7300

GEORGIA/HARVARD STREET CAMPUS
11th and Harvard Sts., N.W., Washington 20009. Public (federal) teacher education. 1943/1985 (MSA/CHE). Sem. plan. Degrees: B,M. (202) 673-7021

MOUNT VERNON SQUARE CAMPUS
929 E St., N.W., Washington 20005. Public (federal) liberal arts. 1974/1985 (MSA/CHE). Sem. plan. Degrees: A,B,M. *Prof. Accred.:* Speech Pathology.
(202) 282-7300

VAN NESS CAMPUS
4200 Connecticut Ave., N. W., Washington 20008. Public (federal) technological. 1971/1985 (MSA/CHE). Sem. plan. Degrees: A,B. *Prof. Accred.:* Engineering (civil, electrical), Engineering Technology (architectural, civil, construction management, digital and electromechanical systems, electromechanical, electronic, mechanical), Nursing (A,B), Radiography, Respiratory Therapy, Social Work (B).
(202) 282-7300

WASHINGTON SCHOOL FOR SECRETARIES
2020 K St., N.W., Washington 20006. Private business. 1954/1979 (AICS). Courses of varying lengths. Certificates. Dir. Barbara N. Thomas.
Enroll.: 1,329 (*f.t.* 86 m., 1,243 w.)
(202) 457-1800

WESLEY THEOLOGICAL SEMINARY
4500 Massachusetts Ave., N.W., Washington 20016. Private (United Methodist) professional; graduate only. 1975/1981 (MSA/CHE). Sem. plan. Degrees: P,M,D. *Prof. Accred.:* Theology (1940/1984, ATS). Pres. G. Douglass Lewis.
Enroll.: 380 (*f.t.* 31 m., 29 w.)
(202) 885-8600

FLORIDA

AMERICAN CAREER TRAINING/TRAVEL SCHOOL
4699 N. Federal Hwy., Suite 106, Pompano Beach 33064. Private; combination home study and resident. 1985 (NHSC). Pres. Joseph Calareso.
(305) 946-5551

AMERICAN CAREERS INSTITUTE
4331 N. Federal Hwy., Suite 204 A, Fort Lauderdale 33308. Private business. 1985 (SACS-COEI). Courses of varying lengths. Certificates, diplomas. Pres. Demetrios Bonaros.
Enroll.: FTE 99
(305) 486-0721

AMERICAN MEDICAL TRAINING INSTITUTE
10700 Caribbean Blvd., Miami 33189. Private technical. 1979/1985 (ABHES). Courses of varying lengths. Diplomas. *Prof. Accred.:* Medical Assisting. Admin. James K. Brodie.
Enroll.: 57
(305) 253-8028

AMERICAN VOCATIONAL SCHOOL
2900 W. 12th Ave., Hialeah 33012. Private. 1985 (SACS-COEI). Courses of varying lengths. Certificates, diplomas. Pres. Pedro Capote.
Enroll.: FTE 99

APEX TECHNICAL SCHOOL
3501 N.W. Ninth Ave., Oakland Park 33309. Private. 1985 (NATTS). Courses of varying lengths. Certificates. Dir. John R. Cann.
(305) 563-5899

ART INSTITUTE OF FORT LAUDERDALE
3000 E. Las Olas Blvd., Fort Lauderdale 33316. Private. 1971/1976 (NATTS). Qtr. plan. Degrees: A. Pres. Mark K. Wheeler.
Enroll.: 1,240 (*f.t.* 489 m., 744 w.)
(305) 463-3000

ATLANTIC VOCATIONAL CENTER
4700 Coconut Creek Pkwy., Coconut Creek 33066. Public (state) technical. 1978/1983 (SACS-COEI). Courses of varying lengths. Certificates. *Prof. Accred.:* Practical Nursing. Dir. Glenn S. Sanderson.
Enroll.: FTE 888
(305) 974-7600

AUBREY WILLIS SCHOOL
P.O. Drawer 15190, 5840 W. Concord Ave., Orlando 32858. Private home study. 1980 (NHSC). Pres. David Pennington.
(305) 299-3690

AUTOMOTIVE TRANSMISSION SCHOOL
453 E. Okeechobee Rd., Hialeah 33010. Private. 1985 (NATTS). Courses of varying lengths. Certificates. Dir. Manuel J. Safon.
(305) 888-4898

BAPTIST BIBLE INSTITUTE
1306 College Dr., Graceville 32440. Private (Southern Baptist). 1981 (SACS-Comm. on Coll.). Sem. plan. Degrees: B. Pres. Joseph P. Dubose, Jr.
Enroll.: 344
(904) 263-3261

BARNA INSTITUTE
1050 N.E. Fifth Terrace, Ft. Lauderdale 33304. Private technical. 1984 (SACS-COEI). Courses of varying lengths. Certificates. Dir. Patricia Araujo-Wetstein.
Enroll.: FTE 99

BARRY UNIVERSITY
11300 N.E. Second Ave., Miami Shores 33161. Private (Roman Catholic) liberal arts. 1947/1983 (SACS-Comm. on Coll.). Sem. plan. Degrees: B,M (candidate for D). *Prof. Accred.:* Dietetics, Medical Assisting, Medical Laboratory Technology, Nursing (B), Social Work (B,M). Pres. Sister Jeanne O'Laughlin, O.P.
Enroll.: 3,184
(305) 758-3392

BAY AREA ACADEMY OF BUSINESS
4508 Oak Fair Blvd., Suite 20, Tampa 33610. Private. 1979/1982 (AICS). Courses of varying lengths. Certificates. Exec. Dir. Sharon B. Jones.
Enroll.: 142 (*f.t.* 8 m., 134 w.)
(813) 621-8074

BAY AREA VOCATIONAL-TECHNICAL SCHOOL
1976 Lewis Turner Blvd., Fort Walton Beach 32548. Public (state). 1979/1984 (SACS-COEI). Courses of varying lengths. Certificates. Dir. Edward V. Baker.
Enroll.: FTE 518
(904) 862-0169

BETHUNE-COOKMAN COLLEGE, INC.
640 Second Ave., Daytona Beach 32015. Private liberal arts. 1947/1980 (SACS-Comm.

on Coll.). Sem. plan. Degrees: B. *Prof. Accred.:* Medical Technology, Teacher Education (*e,s*). Pres. Oswald P. Bronson, Sr.
Enroll.: 1,685
(904) 255-1401

BREVARD COMMUNITY COLLEGE
Cocoa 32922. Public (district) junior. 1963/1983 (SACS-Comm. on Coll.). Tri. plan. Degrees: A. *Prof. Accred.:* Dental Assisting, Medical Laboratory Technology (A), Radiography, Respiratory Therapy Technology. Pres. Maxwell C. King.
Enroll.: 11,790
(305) 632-1111

BROWARD COMMUNITY COLLEGE
225 E. Las Olas Blvd., Fort Lauderdale 33301. Public (district) junior. 1963/1983 (SACS-Comm. on Coll.). Tri. plan. Degrees: A. *Prof. Accred.:* Dental Assisting, Medical Assisting, Medical Laboratory Technology (A), Nursing (A), Radiography, Respiratory Therapy, Respiratory Therapy Technology. Pres. A. Hugh Adams.
Enroll.: 14,403
(305) 761-7400

BURNSIDE-OTT AVIATION
Tamiami Airport, 14100 S.W. 129th St., Miami 33186. Private. 1985 (NATTS). Courses of varying lengths. Certificates, diplomas. Pres. Stanley Sidicane.
(305) 235-0855

CAMBRIDGE ACADEMY
1553 N.E. Arch Ave., Jensen Beach 33457. Private home study. 1982 (NHSC). Pres. James K. Isenhour.
(305) 334-7155

CAREER TRAINING INSTITUTE
3399 S. Orange Blossom Trail, Orlando 32805. Private. 1980 (NATTS). Time clock plan. Diplomas. Pres. Jack E. Carter.
Enroll.: 42 (*f.t.* 12 m., 27 w.)
(305) 843-3980

EXTENSION
107 W. Main St., Leesburg 32809. Dir. Thomas J. Voldness.
(904) 326-5734

CAREY TECHNICAL INSTITUTE
901 N.W. 54th St., Miami 33127. Private business. 1985 (SACS-COEI). Courses of varying lengths. Certificates, diplomas. Dir. Barbara M. Carey.
Enroll.: FTE 128

CENTRAL FLORIDA COMMUNITY COLLEGE
P.O. Box 1388, Ocala 32678. Public (district) junior. 1964/1985 (SACS-Comm. on Coll.). Sem. plan. Degrees: A. Pres. Henry Goodlett.
Enroll.: 3,293
(904) 237-2111

CENTRAL FLORIDA COMPUTER INSTITUTE
7129 University Blvd., Winter Park 32792. Private. 1985 (NATTS). Courses of varying lengths. Certificates. Dir. Donna R. Miller.
(305) 671-2272

CHAPMAN SCHOOL OF SEAMANSHIP
4343 S.E. St. Lucie Blvd., Stuart 33494. Private. 1983 (NATTS). Courses of varying lengths. Certificates. Pres. Jennifer J. Castle.
Enroll.: 30
(305) 283-8130

CHARLOTTE VOCATIONAL-TECHNICAL CENTER
1468 Toledo Blade Blvd., Port Charlotte 33948. Public (state). 1983 (SACS-COEI). Courses of varying lengths. Certificates. Dir. Roseann Keller Samson.
Enroll.: FTE 457
(813) 629-6819

CHARRON-WILLIAMS COLLEGE
255 S.W. Eighth St., Miami 33130. Private business. 1962/1983 (AICS); 1984 (SACS-COEI). Courses of varying lengths. Diplomas. Dir. Irving Goldstein.
Enroll.: FTE 136
(305) 854-9770

CHARRON-WILLIAMS COLLEGE—PARAMEDICAL DIVISION
Sunrise Executive Bldg., 6289 W. Sunrise Blvd., Suite 265, Fort Lauderdale 33301. Private business. 1974/1979 (ABHES). Also recognized as a branch campus by AICS and 1984 (SACS-COEI). 12-month program. Diplomas. *Prof. Accred.:* Medical Assisting. Dir. Manny Sion.
Enroll.: 66
(305) 584-4980

CHIPOLA JUNIOR COLLEGE
Marianna 32446. Public (district). 1957/1977 (SACS-Comm. on Coll.). Sem. plan. Degrees: A. Pres. James R. Richburg.
Enroll.: 1,323
(904) 526-2761

CLEARWATER CHRISTIAN COLLEGE
3400 Gulf-to-Bay Blvd., Clearwater 33519. Private. 1984 (SACS.- Comm. on Coll.).

Sem. plan. Degrees: A,B. Pres. Arthur E. Steele.
Enroll.: FTE 212
(813) 726-1153

THE COLLEGE OF BOCA RATON
3601 N. Military Tr., Boca Raton 33431. Private junior. 1964/1983 (SACS-Comm. on Coll.). Sem. plan. Degrees: A, (candidate for B and M). Pres. Donald E. Ross.
Enroll.: 832
(305) 994-0770

COLLEGE OF THE PALM BEACHES
660 Fern St., West Palm Beach 33401. Private. 1986 (AICS). Courses of varying lengths. Degrees: A, diplomas. Exec. Dir. Don W. Schaefer.
Enroll.: 11
(305) 833-5575

COLLIER COUNTY VOCATIONAL-TECHNICAL CENTER
3702 Estey Ave., Naples 33942. Public (state). 1980/1985 (SACS-COEI). Courses of varying lengths. Certificates. Dir. William G. Perry.
Enroll.: FTE 454
(813) 774-6635

COMPUTECH INSTITUTE
9708 Coral Way, 24th St., S.W., Miami 33165. Private. 1983 (SACS-COEI). Courses of varying lengths. Certificates. Dir. Maria R. Izquierdo.
Enroll.: FTE 328
(305) 592-1341

BRANCH CAMPUS
4206 W. 12th Ave., Hialeah 33012.

DATAMERICA INSTITUTE
1101 S.W. 27th Ave., Miami 33135. Private. 1984 (NATTS). Courses of varying lengths. Certificates. Dir. Avelino Rodriguez.
Enroll.: FTE 209
(305) 649-8227

DAYTONA BEACH COMMUNITY COLLEGE
P.O. Box 1111, Daytona Beach 32015. Public (district) junior. 1963/1983 (SACS-Comm. on Coll.). Sem. plan. Degrees: A. *Prof. Accred.:* Dental Assisting, Medical Record Technology, Nursing (A), Respiratory Therapy, Respiratory Therapy Technology, Surgical Technology. Pres. Charles H. Polk.
Enroll.: 10,553
(904) 255-8131

DEFENSE EQUAL OPPORTUNITY MANAGEMENT INSTITUTE
DOMI/DSO, Patrick AFB, Cocoa Beach 32925. Public (federal). 1983 (SACS-COEI). Courses of varying lengths. Certificates. Dir. Col. Roland A. Goodman.
Enroll.: FTE 169
(305) 494-6208

ECKERD COLLEGE
4200 54th Ave., S., Petersburg 33711. Private (Presbyterian, U.S.) liberal arts. 1963/1980 (SACS-Comm. on Coll.). 4-1-4 plan. Degrees: B. (Candidate for Level III). Pres. Peter H. Armacost.
Enroll.: 1,382
(813) 867-1166

EDISON COMMUNITY COLLEGE
8099 College Pkwy., Fort Myers 33907. Public (district). 1964/1981 (SACS-Comm. on Coll.). Tri. plan. Degrees: A. *Prof. Accred.:* Respiratory Therapy. Pres. David G. Robinson.
Enroll.: 4,078
(813) 489-9300

EDWARD WATERS COLLEGE
1658 Kings Rd., Jacksonville 32209. Private (African Methodist Episcopal) liberal arts and teachers. 1979/1984 (SACS-Comm. on Coll.). Sem. plan. Degrees: B. Pres. Cecil Wayne Cone.
Enroll.: 683
(904) 355-3030

EMBRY-RIDDLE AERONAUTICAL UNIVERSITY
Star Rt., Box 540, Bunnell 32010. Private technological. 1968/1983 (SACS-Comm. on Coll.). Campuses at Daytona Beach, FL and Prescott, AZ. Tri. plan. Degrees: A,B,M. *Prof. Accred.:* Engineering (aeronautical), Engineering Technology (air craft maintenance). Pres. Kenneth L. Tallman, Lt. General, USAF (Ret.).
Enroll.: 7,695
(904) 673-3180

ENGINE TECHNICAL INSTITUTE/PRATT AND WHITNEY AIRCRAFT
P.O. Box 2691, West Palm Beach 33402. Private. 1983 (SACS-COEI). Courses of varying lengths. Certificates. Dir. Joseph F. Manning.
Enroll.: FTE 378
(305) 840-7260

ERWIN VOCATIONAL-TECHNICAL CENTER
2010 E. Hillsborough Ave., Tampa 33610. Public (state). 1981 (SACS-COEI). Courses

of varying lengths. Certificates. *Prof. Accred.:* Medical Laboratory Technology, Respiratory Therapy Technology, Surgical Technology. Dir. Boyd Wilborn.
Enroll.: FTE 1,007
(813) 238-2141

BRANCH CAMPUS
105 W. Ross Ave., Tampa 33602.

FLAGLER CAREER INSTITUTE
3225 University Blvd., S., Jacksonville 32216. Private. 1984 (NATTS). Qtr. plan. Degrees: A. *Prof. Accred.:* Respiratory Therapy, Respiratory Therapy Technology. Dir. Michael F. Hoffman.
(904) 721-1622

EXTENSION
2125 Biscayne Blvd., Miami 33137. 1979 (NATTS). *Prof. Accred.:* Respiratory Therapy, Respiratory Therapy Technology. Dir. Vickie S. McNair.
Enroll.: 685 (*f.t.* 329 m., 356 w.)
(305) 573-0260

BRANCH CAMPUS
4100 Hospital Dr., Suite 304, Plantation 33317. Dir. Joseph Servick.
(305) 583-4111

BRANCH CAMPUS
845 S. Ponce de Leon St., St. Augustine 32084. Branch Dir. Gene Meadows.
(904) 824-4366

FLAGLER COLLEGE
P.O. Box 1027, St. Augustine 32085. Private liberal arts. 1973/1978 (SACS-Comm. on Coll.). Sem. plan. Degrees: B. Pres. William L. Proctor.
Enroll.: 1,018
(904) 829-6481

FLIGHT SAFETY INTERNATIONAL
P.O. Box 2708, Municipal Airport, Vero Beach 32960. Private. 1975/1980 (NATTS). Courses of varying lengths. Certificates. Mgr. Stephen T. Blanchard.
Enroll.: 251 (*f.t.* 247 m., 4 w.)
(305) 567-5178

FLORIDA AGRICULTURAL AND MECHANICAL UNIVERSITY
Tallahassee 32307. Public (state). 1935/1978 (SACS-Comm. on Coll.). Sem. plan. Degrees: B,P,M,D. *Prof. Accred.:* Architecture (M), Engineering Technology (civil, electronic), Medical Record Administration, Nursing (B), Pharmacy, Physical Therapy, Social Work (B), Teacher Education (*e,s,p*). Pres. Frederick S. Humphries.
Enroll.: 4,600
(904) 599-3000

FLORIDA ATLANTIC UNIVERSITY
Boca Raton 33431. Public (state); upper division and graduate only. 1965/1982 (SACS-Comm. on Coll.). Sem. plan. Degrees: B,M,D. *Prof. Accred.:* Business (B,M), Engineering (electrical, mechanical, ocean), Medical Technology, Music, Nursing (B), Social Work (B), Teacher Education (*e,s,p*). Pres. Helen Popovich
Enroll.: 6,756
(305) 393-3000

FLORIDA CHRISTIAN COLLEGE
1011 Oceola Blvd., Kissimmee 32742. Private (Christian Church/Church of Christ). 1985 (AABC). Sem. plan. Degrees: A,B. Pres. Marion Henderson.
Enroll.: 115
(305) 847-8966

FLORIDA COLLEGE
Temple Terrace 33617. Private junior. 1954/1976 (SACS-Comm. on Coll.). Sem. plan. Degrees: A. Pres. Bob F. Owen.
Enroll.: 378
(813) 988-5131

FLORIDA COLLEGE OF BUSINESS
434 E. Atlantic Blvd., Pompano Beach 33060. Private. 1977/1980 (AICS). Qtr. plan. Diplomas. Dir. David Penna.
Enroll.: 1,341 (*f.t.* 182 m., 1,159 w.)
(305) 942-7900

BRANCH CAMPUS
2990 N.W. 81st Ter., Miami 33147. Dir. Michael Beauregard.
(305) 696-6312

BRANCH CAMPUS
405 E. Polk, Tampa 33602. Dir. Matthew Dickard.
(813) 221-4200

FLORIDA COLLEGE OF MEDICAL AND DENTAL CAREERS
6250 N. Andrews Ave., Fort Lauderdale 33309. Private. 1985 (NATTS). Sem. plan. Diplomas. Dir. Janet R. Bertz.
Enroll.: 125
(305) 491-0828

FLORIDA COLLEGE OF MEDICAL AND DENTAL CAREERS
7820 Arlington Expressway, Suite 120, Jacksonville 32211. Private. 1977/1983 (NATTS). Sem. plan. Diplomas. Dir. Jeanette Erdel.
Enroll.: 226 (*f.t.* 2 m., 224 w.)
(904) 725-0525

FLORIDA COLLEGE OF MEDICAL AND DENTAL CAREERS
3500 E. Fletcher, No. 301, Tampa 33612. Private. 1981 (NATTS). Courses of varying lengths. Diplomas. Dir. Mark Dugan.
Enroll.: 104
(813) 977-8800.

FLORIDA INSTITUTE OF CAREERS
140 S.E. 15th St., Pompano Beach 33060 . Private business. 1981 (AICS). Qtr. plan. Certificates, diplomas. Pres. Burton Braverman.
Enroll.: 155 (*f.t.* 4 m., 151 w.)
(305) 946-5656

BRANCH CAMPUS
3218 S. University Dr., Miramar 33025. Dir. Nina Pierce.
(305) 432-2004

FLORIDA INSTITUTE OF TECHNOLOGY
150 W. University Blvd., Melbourne 32901. Private technological. 1964/1985 (SACS-Comm. on Coll.). Qtr. plan. Degrees: A,B,M,D. *Prof. Accred.:* Engineering (chemical, civil, computer, electrical, mechanical, ocean), Psychology, Social Work. Pres. ———.
Enroll.: 5,392
(305) 768-8000

FLORIDA INSTITUTE OF ULTRASOUND, INC.
P.O. Box 15135, 8800 University Pkwy., Bldg. A, Suite 4, Pensacola 32514. Private. 1985 (ABHES). 23-week program. Certificates. *Prof. Accred.:* Diagnostic Medical Sonography. Dir. J. Jay Crittenden.
(904) 478-7300

FLORIDA INTERNATIONAL UNIVERSITY
Tamiami Trail, Miami 33199. Public (state) liberal arts; upper division only. 1974/1985 (SACS-Comm. on Coll.). Qtr. plan. Degrees: B,M (candidate for D). *Prof. Accred.:* Accounting (Type A,C), Business (B,M), Construction Education, Dietetics, Medical Record Administration, Medical Technology, Nursing (B), Occupational Therapy, Physical Therapy, Social Work (B). Pres. ———.
Enroll.: 11,178
(305) 554-2000

FLORIDA JUNIOR COLLEGE AT JACKSONVILLE
501 W. State St., Jacksonville 32202. Public (district). 1969/1984 (SACS-Comm. on Coll.). Tri. plan. Degrees: A. *Prof. Accred.:* Dental Assisting, Dental Hygiene, Medical Laboratory Technology (A), Nursing (A), Respiratory Therapy. Pres. Charles C. Spence.
Enroll.: 13,353
(904) 632-3000

FLORIDA KEYS COMMUNITY COLLEGE
Key West 33040. Public (district) junior. 1968/1982 (SACS-Comm. on Coll.). Tri. plan. Degrees: A. Pres. William A. Seeker.
Enroll.: 889
(305) 296-9081

FLORIDA MEMORIAL COLLEGE
15800 N.W. 42nd Ave., Miami 33054. Private (American Baptist) liberal arts. 1951/1982 (SACS-Comm. on Coll.). Sem. plan. Degrees: B. Pres. Willie C. Robinson.
Enroll.: 1,758
(305) 625-4141

FLORIDA PROGRAMMING EDUCATIONAL CENTER
8360 Flagler St., No. 102, Miami 33144. Private business. 1985 (AICS). Courses of varying lengths. Certificates, diplomas. Pres. Carlos Rossie.
(305) 387-3614

FLORIDA SOUTHERN COLLEGE
111 Lake Hollingsworth Dr., Lakeland 33802. Private (United Methodist) liberal arts. 1935/1977 (SACS-Comm. on Coll.). Sem. plan. Degrees: B,M. Pres. Robert A. Davis.
Enroll.: 2,304
(813) 680-4111

FLORIDA STATE UNIVERSITY
Tallahassee 32306. Public (state). 1915/1984 (SACS-Comm. on Coll.). Sem. plan. Degrees: A,B,M,D. *Prof. Accred.:* Accounting (Type A,C), Business (B,M), Home Economics, Interior Design, Law, Librarianship, Music, Nursing (B), Psychology, Rehabilitation Counseling, Social Work (B,M), Speech Pathology and Audiology, Teacher Education (*e,s,p*). Pres. Bernard F. Sliger.
Enroll.: 20,271
(904) 644-2525

FLORIDA TECHNICAL COLLEGE
1819 N. Semoran Blvd., Orlando 32807. Private business. 1982 (AICS). Courses of

varying lengths. Certificates, diplomas. Pres. Neil R. Euliano.
Enroll.: 1,465 (*f.t.* 865 m., 600 w.)
(305) 678-5600

BRANCH CAMPUS
8711 Lone Star Rd., Jacksonville 32211.
(904) 724-2229

BRANCH CAMPUS
4308 56th St., N., Tampa 33610.
(813) 621-5700

FORT LAUDERDALE COLLEGE
1401 E. Broward Blvd., Fort Lauderdale 33301. Private senior business. 1968/1981 (AICS). Qtr. plan. Degrees: A,B. Pres. J. Robert Couch.
Enroll.: 593 (*f.t.* 318 m., 275 w.)
(305) 462-3761

FORT MYERS BUSINESS ACADEMY
2235 First St., Fort Myers 33901. Private. 1984 (AICS). Qtr. plan. Diplomas. Pres. Thomas E. Langford.
Enroll.: f.t. 21
(813) 334-4766

*GARCES COMMERCIAL COLLEGE
1301 S.W. First St., Miami 33135. Private business. 1976/1980 (AICS). Qtr. plan. Diplomas. Pres. Elena Nespereira.
Enroll.: FTE 535
(305) 643-1044

BRANCH CAMPUS
391 E. Eighth St., Hialeah 33010. Dir. Olga Vinas.
(305) 885-5334.

BRANCH CAMPUS
5385 N.W. 36th St., Miami Springs 33166. Dir. Juan Almeida.
(305) 871-6535

GEORGE STONE VOCATIONAL-TECHNICAL CENTER
2400 Longleaf Dr., Pensacola 32506. Public (state). 1981 (SACS-COEI). Courses of varying lengths. Certificates. Dir. Waymon Wynn.
Enroll.: FTE 603
(904) 944-1424

GEORGE T. BAKER AVIATION SCHOOL
3275 N.W. 42nd Ave., Miami 33142. Public (local) technical. 1978/1983 (SACS-COEI). Courses of varying lengths. Certificates. Dir. Vincent V. Pavicic.
Enroll.: FTE 597
(305) 871-3143

GULF COAST COMMUNITY COLLEGE
Panama City 32401. Public (district). 1962/1980 (SACS-Comm. on Coll.). Sem. plan. Degrees: A. *Prof. Accred.:* Dental Assisting, Nursing (A), Respiratory Therapy Technology. Pres. Lawrence Worley Tyree.
Enroll.: 2,849
(904) 769-1551

HAMMEL COLLEGE
4000 NW 12th St., Ft. Lauderdale 33313. Private business. 1985 (AICS). Courses of varying lengths. Diplomas. Pres. Dale Hansen.
(305) 581-2223

HILLSBOROUGH COMMUNITY COLLEGE
P.O. Box 22127, Tampa 33630. Public (district) junior. 1971/1975 (SACS-Comm. on Coll.). Modified Tri. plan. Degrees: A. *Prof. Accred.:* Medical Record Technology, Nuclear Medicine Technology, Radiation Therapy Technology, Radiography. Pres. Andreas A. Paloumpis.
Enroll.: 8,165
(813) 879-7222

HUMANITIES CENTER SCHOOL OF THERAPUTIC MASSAGE
3565 Cypress Ter., Pinellas Park 33565. Private. 1984 (NATTS). Courses of varying lengths. Certificates. Dir. Sherry L. Fears.
(813) 522-1697 or
(813) 527-6882

ITT TECHNICAL INSTITUTE
11211 N. Nebraska Ave., Tampa 33612. Private. 1982 (NATTS). Qtr. plan. Degrees: A, certificates, diplomas. Dir. Larry Graphman.
Enroll.: 125
(813) 977-2700

INDIAN RIVER COMMUNITY COLLEGE
3209 Virginia Ave., Fort Pierce 33450. Public (district) junior. 1963/1983 (SACS-Comm. on Coll.). Sem. plan. Degrees: A. *Prof. Accred.:* Dental Assisting, Dental Laboratory Technology, Medical Laboratory Technology, Nursing (A), Radiography. Pres. Herman A. Heise.
Enroll.: 5,873
(305) 464-2000

*Candidate for Accreditation by Regional Accrediting Commission

INSTITUTE OF SECURITY & TECHNOLOGY
1120 N.W. 159th Dr., Miami 33169. Private. 1985 (NATTS). Courses of varying lengths. Certificates. Dir. Claude Korvela.
(305) 685-1067

INTERNATIONAL CAREER INSTITUTE
1050 N.E. Fifth Ter., Ft. Lauderdale 33304. Private. 1984 (SACS-COEI). Courses of varying lengths. Certificates. Dir. Elizabeth Parave.
Enroll.: FTE 10

INTERNATIONAL FINE ARTS COLLEGE
1737 N. Bayshore Dr., Miami 33132. Private. 1979/1984 (SACS-Comm. on Coll.). Qtr. plan. Degrees: A. Pres. Edward Porter.
Enroll.: 284
(305) 373-4684

INTERNATIONAL TECHNICAL INSTITUTE
8407 Laurel Fair Circle, Tampa 33610. Private. 1973/1978 (NATTS). Qtr. plan and courses of varying lengths. Degrees: A, diplomas. Pres. Larry J. Nero.
Enroll.: 450 (*f.t.* 275 m., 175 w.)
(813) 621-3566

JACKSONVILLE UNIVERSITY
University Blvd., Jacksonville 32211. Private. 1961/1983 (SACS-Comm. on Coll.). Tri. plan. Degrees: B,M. *Prof. Accred.:* Music. Pres. Frances Bartlett Kinne.
Enroll.: 1,898
(904) 744-3950

JONES COLLEGE
5353 Arlington Expressway, Jacksonville 32211-5588. Private senior business. 1957/1982 (AICS). Qtr. plan. Degrees: A,B, certificates, diplomas. Ch. of the Board Jack H. Jones.
Enroll.: 3,706 (*f.t.* 1,101 m., 2,605 w.)
(904) 743-1122

JONES COLLEGE MEDICAL EDUCATION CENTER-WEST CAMPUS
1195 Edgewood Ave., South Jacksonville 32205. Private. 1978/1980 (NATTS). Sem. plan and courses of varying lengths. Diplomas. Dir. Betty J. Tapp.
Enroll.: 250 (*f.t.* 15 m., 235 w.)
(904) 743-1122

KEISER INSTITUTE OF TECHNOLOGY
4861 N. Dixie Hwy., Suite 200, Ft. Lauderdale 33334. Private technical. 1981 (NATTS); 1984 (SACS-COEI). Courses of varying lengths. Certificates. *Prof. Accred.:* Medical Assisting, Medical Laboratory Technology. Pres. Arthur Keiser.
Enroll.: FTE 385
(305) 776-4456

LAKE CITY COMMUNITY COLLEGE
Route 7, Box 378, Lake City 32055. Public (district) junior. 1964/1980 (SACS-Comm. on Coll.). Sem. plan. Degrees: A. Pres. Muriel K. Heimer.
Enroll.: 2,550
(904) 752-1822

LAKE COUNTY AREA VOCATIONAL-TECHNICAL CENTER
2001 Kurt St., Eustis 32726. Public (state). 1974/1984 (SACS-COEI). Courses of varying lengths. Certificates. Dir. Maxine Felts.
Enroll.: FTE 796
(904) 357-8222

LAKE-SUMTER COMMUNITY COLLEGE
Leesburg 32748. Public (district) junior. 1965/1980 (SACS-Comm. on Coll.). Tri. plan. Degrees: A. Pres. Robert S. Palinchak.
Enroll.: 1,118
(904) 787-3747

LAKELAND COLLEGE OF BUSINESS AND FASHION
P.O. Box 3612, Lakeland 33802. Private junior. 1961/1984 (AICS). Qtr. plan. Degrees: A. Pres. Eugene Roberts.
Enroll.: 436 (*f.t.* 145 m., 291 w.)
(813) 858-1444

BRANCH CAMPUS
5700 S.W. 34th St., Suite 301, Gainesville 32608. Pres. Ronald W. McFaddin.
(904) 377-8989

LEE COUNTY AREA VOCATIONAL-TECHNICAL SCHOOL
3800 Michigan Ave., Fort Myers 33901. Public (local). 1978/1983 (SACS-COEI). Courses of varying lengths. Certificates. Dir. Ronald E. Pentiuk.
Enroll.: FTE 800
(813) 334-4544

LINDSEY HOPKINS TECHNICAL EDUCATION CENTER
750 N.W. 20th St., Miami 33127. Public (state). 1972/1982 (SACS-COEI). Courses of varying lengths. Certificates. *Prof. Accred.:* Dental Assisting, Dental Laboratory Technology, Medical Assisting, Practical Nursing. Dir. John T. Coursey.

Enroll.: FTE 2,295
(305) 350-3254

LIVELY AREA VOCATIONAL-TECHNICAL CENTER
500 N. Appleyard Dr., Tallahassee 32304. Public (state). 1977/1982 (SACS-COEI). Courses of varying lengths. Certificates. *Prof. Accred.:* Surgical Technology. Dir. James H. Joyce.
Enroll.: FTE 1,489
(904) 576-3181

BRANCH CAMPUS
Florida State Hospital

BRANCH CAMPUS
Lively Agribusiness Center

BRANCH CAMPUS
Lively Aviation Center

BRANCH CAMPUS
Lively Criminal Justice Training Academy

MBC MEDICAL EDUCATION CENTER
8313 W. Hillsborough Ave., Bldg. 2, Suite 3, Tampa 33615. Private 1985 (ABHES). 9-month program. Certificates. *Prof. Accred.:* Medical Assisting. Pres. Paul R. Bell.
(813) 885-7067

MANATEE AREA VOCATIONAL-TECHNICAL CENTER
5603 34th St., W., Bradenton 33507. Public (state). 1980/1985 (SACS-COEI). Courses of varying lengths. Certificates. Dir. Donald McBride.
Enroll.: FTE 602
(813) 755-2641

MANATEE COMMUNITY COLLEGE
Bradenton 33506. Public (district). 1963/1984 (SACS-Comm. on Coll.). Sem. plan. Degrees: A. *Prof. Accred.:* Dental Assisting, Medical Laboratory Technology, Nursing (A), Radiography, Respiratory Therapy. Pres. Stephen J. Korcheck.
Enroll.: 4,308
(813) 755-1511

MARTIN TECHNICAL COLLEGE
1901 N.W. Seventh St., Miami 33125. Private. 1978 (NATTS). Courses of varying lengths. Certificates, diplomas. Dir. Fernando A. Alvarez.
Enroll.: 45 (*f.t.* 28 m., 17 w.)
(305) 541-8140

MASTER SCHOOL OF BARTENDING
824 S.W. 24th St., Fort Lauderdale 33315. Private. 1983 (NATTS). 2-week course. Diplomas. Vice Pres. Judi Snelling.
Enroll.: 20
(305) 467-8829

BRANCH CAMPUS
4315 N.W. Seventh St., Miami 33126.
(305) 373-3036

BRANCH CAMPUS
2525 Old Okeechobee Rd., No. 11, West Palm Beach 33409.
(305) 684-2916

MEDICAL ARTS TRAINING CENTER
111 N.W. 183rd St., Miami 33169. Private. 1978 (ABHES). Courses of varying lengths. Certificates *Prof. Accred.:* Medical Assisting. Pres. Lauren Hemedinger.
Enroll.: 24
(305) 625-2020

MIAMI CHRISTIAN COLLEGE
2300 N.W. 135th St., Miami 33167. Private (Interdenominational) professional. 1975/1979 (AABC). Sem. plan. Degrees: A,B. Pres. George S. Pearson.
Enroll.: 211
(305) 685-7431

MIAMI-DADE COMMUNITY COLLEGE
11011 S. W. 104 St., Miami 33176. Public (district) junior. 1964/1985 (SACS-Comm. on Coll.). Sem. plan. Degrees: A. *Prof. Accred.:* Dental Hygiene, EEG Technology, Medical Laboratory Technology (A), Medical Record Technology, Nursing (A), Optometric Technology, Radiography, Respiratory Therapy, Respiratory Therapy Technology. Pres. Robert H. McCabe.
Enroll.: 31,414
(305) 347-2500

MIAMI LAKES TECHNICAL EDUCATION CENTER
5780 N.W. 158th St., Miami Lakes 33014. Public (state). 1983 (SACS-COEI). Courses of varying lengths. Certificates. Dir. M. Gene Stansell.
Enroll.: FTE 1,063
(305) 557-1100

MIAMI TECHNICAL COLLEGE
1001 Southwest First St., Miami 33130. Private. 1980 (NATTS). Sem. plan. Diplomas. Pres. Robert Piacenti.

Enroll.: 84 (*f.t.* 54 m., 30 w.)
(305) 324-6831

MID-FLORIDA TECHNICAL INSTITUTE
2900 W. Oak Ridge Rd., Orlando 32809. Public (state). 1974/1984 (SACS-COEI). Courses of varying lengths. Certificates. Dir. Robert J. Clark.
Enroll.: FTE 5,617
(305) 855-5880

MIRROR LAKE/TOMLINSON ADULT VOCATIONAL CENTER
709 Mirror Lake Dr., N. St. Petersburg 33701. Public (state). 1973/1983 (SACS-COEI). Courses of varying lengths. Certificates. *Prof. Accred.:* Medical Assisting. Dir. Elliott L. Carr.
Enroll.: FTE 291
(813) 821-4593

MORRIS JUNIOR COLLEGE OF BUSINESS
4635 N. Harbor City Blvd., Melbourne 32935. Private junior. 1966/1980 (AICS). Qtr. plan. Degrees: A, diplomas. Pres. William T. Morris.
Enroll.: 561 (*f.t.* 158 m., 403 w.)
(305) 254-6459

NATIONAL EDUCATION CENTER—BAUDER FASHION COLLEGE CAMPUS
4801 N. Dixie Hwy., Fort Lauderdale 33334. Private. 1970/1976 (NATTS). Qtr. plan. Degrees: A, diplomas. *Prof. Accred.:* Interior Design. Pres. Erik Brumme.
Enroll.: 531 (*f.t.* 18 m., 513 w.)
(305) 491-7171

NATIONAL EDUCATION CENTER—TAMPA TECHNICAL INSTITUTE CAMPUS
3920 E. Hillsborough Ave., Tampa 33610. Private. 1968/1978 (NATTS). Qtr. plan. Degrees: A. Dir. Robert DeVito.
Enroll.: 2,091 (*f.t.* 1,652 m., 439 w.)
(813) 238-0455

NATIONAL INSTITUTE OF TECHNOLOGY
Twelfth Ave. at N. G St., Lake Worth 33460. Private 2-year. 1981 (NATTS). Sem. plan. Degrees: A, diplomas. Dir. Victor C. Richard.
Enroll.: 50
(305) 586-2593

NATIONAL SCHOOL OF TECHNOLOGY, INC.
16150 N.E. 17th Ave., North Miami Beach 33162. Private. 1978 (ABHES); 1983 (NATTS). Courses of 24-weeks plus externship. Diplomas. *Prof. Accred.:* Medical Assisting. Exec. Dir. Roland C. Graff.
Enroll.: 30
(305) 949-9500

NATIONAL TRAINING, INC.
1543 Kingsley Ave., P.O. Box 1389, Orange Park 32073. Private; combination home study-resident program in truck driving. 1982 (NHSC). Pres. Larry S. Lark.
(904) 264-6664

NAVAL DIVING AND SALVAGE TRAINING CENTER
Panama City 32407. Public (federal). 1983 (SACS-COEI). Courses of varying lengths. Certificates. Dir. Cmdr. P. F. Fawcett.
Enroll.: FTE 190
(904) 234-4651

NAVAL TECHNICAL TRAINING CENTER—CORRY STATION
Pensacola 32511. Public (federal) technical. 1975/1985 (SACS-COEI). Courses of varying lengths. Certificates. Cmdr. Capt. David C. Gill.
Enroll.: FTE 2,228
(904) 452-6558

NEW ENGLAND INSTITUTE OF TECHNOLOGY AT PALM BEACH
1126 53rd Ct., West Palm Beach 33407. Private. 1984 (NATTS). Qtr. plan. Degrees: A. Pres. Richard I. Gouse.
(305) 842-8324

NEW IMAGE CENTER TRAVEL SCHOOL
15015 N. Florida, Tampa 33612. Private. 1985 (NATTS). Courses of varying lengths. Certificates. Pres. Carroll Gossage.
(813) 961-4326

NORTH FLORIDA JUNIOR COLLEGE
1000 Turner Davis Dr., Madison 32340. Public (district). 1963/1973 (SACS-Comm. on Coll.). Sem. plan. Degrees: A. Pres. Robert Ramsay.
Enroll.: 821 (*f.t.* 152 m., 195 w.)
(904) 973-2288

NORTH TECHNICAL EDUCATION CENTER
7071 Garden Rd., Riviera Beach 33404. Public (state). 1976/1981 (SACS-COEI). Courses of varying lengths. Certificates. Dir. Patricia I. Nugent.
Enroll.: FTE 504
(305) 848-0692

NOVA UNIVERSITY
3301 College Ave., Fort Lauderdale 33314. Private liberal arts and professional. 1971/

1985 (SACS-Comm. on Coll.). Sem. plan. Degrees: B,P,M,D. *Prof. Accred.:* Law (ABA only), Psychology. Pres. Abraham S. Fischler.
Enroll.: 6,620
(305) 475-7300

Okaloosa-Walton Junior College
100 College Blvd., Niceville 32578. Public (district). 1965/1981 (SACS-Comm. on Coll.). Sem. plan. Degrees: A. Pres. J.E. McCracken.
Enroll.: 3,376
(904) 678-5111

Orlando College
5500-5800 Diplomat Cir., Orlando 32810. Private, senior business. 1957/1981 (AICS). Qtr. plan. Degrees: A,B, certificates, diplomas. Dir. Eugene Wells.
Enroll.: 1,954 (*f.t.* 749 m., 1,205 w.)
(305) 628-5870

Orlando Vocational-Technical Center
301 W. Amelia St., Orlando 32801. Public (state). 1983 (SACS-COEI). Courses of varying lengths. Certificates. Dir. Wilbur S. Gary.
Enroll.: FTE 1,374
(305) 425-2756

Palm Beach Atlantic College
1101 S. Olive Ave., West Palm Beach 33401. Private liberal arts. 1972/1978 (SACS-Comm. on Coll.). Tri. plan. Degrees: B. Pres. Claude H. Rhea, Jr.
Enroll.: 991
(305) 833-8592

Palm Beach Junior College
Lake Worth 33461. Public (district). 1942/1981 (SACS-Comm. on Coll.). Tri. plan. Degrees: A. *Prof. Accred.:* Dental Assisting, Dental Hygiene, Dental Laboratory Technology. Pres. Edward M. Eissey.
Enroll.: 7,707
(305) 439-8000

Pasco-Hernando Community College
2401 State Hwy. 41 N., Dade City 33525. Public (district) 2-year. 1974/1979 (SACS-Comm. on Coll.). Sem. plan. Degrees: A. Pres. Milton O. Jones.
Enroll.: 2,140
(904) 567-6701

Pensacola Junior College
Pensacola 32504. Public (district). 1956/1976 (SACS-Comm. on Coll.). Sem. plan. Degrees: A. *Prof. Accred.:* Dental Assisting, Dental Hygiene, Dental Laboratory Technology, Respiratory Therapy, Respiratory Therapy Technology. Pres. Horace E. Hartsell.
Enroll.: 9,912
(904) 476-5410

Pinellas Vocational-Technical Institute
6100 154th Ave., N., Clearwater 33520. Public (state). 1970/1985 (SACS-COEI). Courses of varying lengths. Certificates. Dir. Robert G. Wagner.
Enroll.: FTE 1,561
(813) 531-3531

Polk Community College
999 Avenue H, N.E., Winter Haven 33881. Public (district) junior. 1965/1980 (SACS-Comm. on Coll.). Tri. plan. Degrees: A. *Prof. Accred.:* Nursing (A), Radiography. Pres. Maryly Vanleer Peck.
Enroll.: 3,079
(813) 297-1000

Porter and Chester Institute (Extension)
9914 N.W. Second Ave., Miami 33269. Private. 1984 (NATTS). Courses of varying lengths. Certificates. Pres. Wil Brown.
(305) 652-9323

The Poynter Institute for Media Studies
801 Third St., S., St. Petersburg 33701. Private. 1983 (SACS-COEI). Courses of varying lengths. Certificates. Pres. Robert J. Haiman.
Enroll.: FTE 413
(813) 821-9494

Prospect Hall College
1725 Monroe St., Hollywood 33020. Private business. 1971/1980 (AICS). Qtr. plan. Degrees: A, certificates, diplomas. Ch. of the Board. Joseph S. Pace.
Enroll.: 805 (*f.t.* 347 m., 458 w.)
(305) 923-8100

R.E.T.S. Technical Training Centers
201 W. Sunrise Blvd., Ft. Lauderdale 33311. Private. 1984 (NATTS). Courses of varying lengths. Certificates. Pres. David L. Withers.
(305) 764-3432

Branch Campus
One N.E. 19th St., Miami 33132.
(305) 573-1600

RIDGE VOCATIONAL-TECHNICAL CENTER
7700 State Rd. 544, Winter Haven 33881. Public (state). 1982 (SACS-COEI). Courses of varying lengths. Certificates. Dir. Bill Hampton.
Enroll.: FTE 1,092
(813) 422-6402

RINGLING SCHOOL OF ART AND DESIGN
1111 27th St., Sarasota 33580. Private professional. 1979/1985 (SACS-Comm. on Coll.). Sem. plan. Degrees: B, certificates. *Prof. Accred.:* Art. Pres. Arland F. Christ-Janer.
Enroll.: 388
(813) 351-4614

ROBERT MORGAN VOCATIONAL-TECHNICAL INSTITUTE
18180 S.W. 122nd Ave., Miami 33177. Public (state). 1983. (SACS-COEI). Courses of varying lengths. Certificates. Dir. John Leyva.
Enroll.: FTE 1,386
(305) 253-9920

ROFFLER HAIR DESIGN COLLEGE
2242 W. Broward Blvd., Ft. Lauderdale 33312. Private. 1979 (NATTS). Clock hours. Diplomas. Dir. Stewart A. Smith.
Enroll.: 24 (*f.t.* 9 m., 15 w.)
(305) 584-4730

ROFFLER HAIR DESIGN COLLEGE
5863 University Blvd. W., Jacksonville 32216. Private. 1983 (NATTS). Clock hours. Diplomas. Pres. Stewart A. Smith, Jr.
Enroll.: 25
(904) 731-5060

ROFFLER HAIR DESIGN COLLEGE
9328 Miller Rd., Miami 33165. Private 1978/1985 (NATTS). Clock hours. Diplomas. Dir. Anthony Sanchez.
Enroll.: 18 (*f.t.* 7 m., 10 w.)
(305) 279-9627

EXTENSION
5433 Lake Howell Rd., Winter Park 32792. Private. 1984 (NATTS). Courses of varying lengths. Diplomas. Dir. Glen Blount.
(305) 657-0700

ROFFLER HAIR DESIGN COLLEGE
1964 W. Tennessee, #14, Tallahassee 32304. Private. 1983 (NATTS). Courses of varying lengths. Diplomas. Dir. Stewart A. Smith.
(904) 576-2174

EXTENSION
1412 W. Fairfield Dr., Pensacola 32501. Dir. Larry Bryant.
(904) 433-6547

BRANCH CAMPUS
7545 W. Waters Ave., Tampa 33614.
(813) 884-2717

ROFFLER HAIR DESIGN COLLEGE
8851 N. 56th St., Temple Terrace 33617. Private. 1981 (NATTS). Courses of varying lengths. Diplomas. Dir. Dwayne Adams.
Enroll.: 21 (*f.t.* 8 m., 13 w.)
(813) 985-8785

BRANCH CAMPUS
2626 U.S. Hwy. 92 E., Lakeland 33801.
(813) 666-2887

ROFFLER HAIR DESIGN COLLEGE
4645 Gun Club Rd., West Palm Beach 33406. 1982 (NATTS). Courses of varying lengths. Diplomas. Dir. James McFarland.
Enroll.: 20
(305) 683-1233

ROLLINS COLLEGE
1000 Holt Ave., Winter Park 32789. Private liberal arts. 1927/1984 (SACS-Comm. on Coll.). 4-1-4 plan. Degrees: A,B,M. *Prof. Accred.:* Business (M), Music. Pres. Thaddeus Seymour.
Enroll.: 2,797
(305) 646-2000

ROSS MEDICAL EDUCATION CENTER
1490 S. Military Trail, Suite 11, West Palm Beach 33406. Private. 1985 (NATTS). Courses of varying lengths. Certificates. Dir. Debra Stern.
(305) 433-1288

ST. AUGUSTINE TECHNICAL CENTER
Collins Ave. at Delmonte, St. Augustine 32084. Public (state). 1980/1985 (SACS-COEI). Courses of varying lengths. Certificates. Dir. R. E. Upton.
Enroll.: FTE 1,292
(904) 824-4401

ST. JOHN VIANNEY COLLEGE SEMINARY
2900 S.W. 87th Ave., Miami 33165. Private (Roman Catholic, Archdiocese of Miami) for men. 1980 (SACS-Comm. on Coll.). Sem. plan. Degrees: A,B. Pres. Bernard Kirlin.
Enroll.: *f.t.* 66 m.
(305) 223-4561

ST. JOHNS RIVER COMMUNITY COLLEGE
5001 St. Johns Ave., Palatka 32077. Public (district) junior. 1963/1983 (SACS-Comm. on Coll.). Tri. plan. Degrees: A. Pres. Robert L. McLendon, Jr.

Enroll.: 928
(904) 328-1571

SAINT LEO COLLEGE
P.O. Box 2187, St. Leo 33574. Private (Roman Catholic) liberal arts and teachers. 1967/1981 (SACS-Comm. on Coll.). Tri. plan. Degrees: A,B. *Prof. Accred.:* Social Work (B). Pres. M. Daniel Henry.
Enroll.: 3,317
(904) 588-8200

ST. PETERSBURG JUNIOR COLLEGE
P.O. Box 13489, St. Petersburg 33733. Public (district); second campus at Clearwater. 1931/1980 (SACS-Comm. on Coll.). Sem. plan. Degrees: A. *Prof. Accred.:* Dental Assisting, Dental Hygiene, Engineering Technology (electronics), Medical Laboratory Technology, Nursing (A), Optometric Technology, Radiography, Respiratory Therapy. Pres. Carl M. Kuttler, Jr.
Enroll.: 11,779
(813) 341-3600

ST. PETERSBURG VOCATIONAL-TECHNICAL INSTITUTE
910 34th St., St. Petersburg 33711. Public (state). 1975/1985 (SACS-COEI). Courses of varying lengths. Certificates. *Prof. Accred.:* Respiratory Therapy Technology. Dir. Warren Laux.
Enroll.: FTE 1,237
(813) 895-3671

ST. THOMAS UNIVERSITY
16400 N.W. 32nd Ave., Miami 33054. Private (Roman Catholic) liberal arts. 1968/1983 (SACS-Comm on Coll.). Sem. plan. Degrees: A,B,M. Pres. Father Patrick H. O'Neill.
Enroll.: 2,918
(305) 625-6000

SAINT VINCENT DE PAUL REGIONAL SEMINARY
P.O. Box 460, Boynton Beach 33425. Private (Roman Catholic, Vincentian Fathers); upper division, professional and graduate only. 1968/1984 (SACS-Comm. on Coll.). Sem. plan. Degrees: B,P,M. *Prof. Accred.:* Theology (1984, ATS). Rector-Pres. Joseph Cunningham.
Enroll.: 104 (*f.t.* 89 m.)
(305) 732-4424

SANTA FE COMMUNITY COLLEGE
P.O. Box 1530, Gainesville 32601. Public (county). 1968/1982 (SACS-Comm. on Coll.). Qtr. plan. Degrees: A. *Prof. Accred.:* Dental Assisting, Dental Hygiene, Nuclear Medicine Technology, Perfusion, Radiography, Respiratory Therapy. Pres. Alan J. Robertson.
Enroll.: 6,414
(904) 395-5000

SARASOTA COUNTY VOCATIONAL-TECHNICAL CENTER
4748 Beneva Rd., Sarasota 33583. Public (state). 1971/1981 (SACS-COEI). Courses of varying lengths. Certificates. *Prof. Accred.:* Medical Assisting, Medical Laboratory Technology, Respiratory Therapy. Dir. Steve Harvey.
Enroll.: FTE 1,916
(813) 924-1365

BRANCH CAMPUS
2300 Janie Poe Dr., Sarasota 33580.

BRANCH CAMPUS
1001 S. Washington Blvd., Rm. 109, Sarasota 33577.

BRANCH CAMPUS
East Turin St., Venice 33595.

SEMINOLE COMMUNITY COLLEGE
Sanford 32771. Public (county). 1969/1983 (SACS-Comm. on Coll.). Tri. plan. Degrees: A. *Prof. Accred.:* Respiratory Therapy Technology. Pres. Earl Weldon.
Enroll.: 6,359
956 (*f.t.* 894 m., (305) 323-1450

SER——JOBS FOR PROGRESS
888 N.W. 27th , Miami 33125. Private. 1985 (SACS-COEI). Courses of varying lengths. Certificates. Dir. Melvin Chaves.
Enroll.: FTE 24

SERVICE SCHOOL COMMAND—NAVAL TRAINING CENTER
Orlando 32813. Public (federal) technical. 1976/1981 (SACS-COEI). Courses of varying lengths. Certificates. Cmdr. Capt. H. L. Pabst.
Enroll.: FTE 1,012
(305) 646-4122

SHERIDAN VOCATIONAL-TECHNICAL CENTER
5400 Sheridan St., Hollywood 33021. Public (state). 1974/1984 (SACS-COEI). Courses of varying lengths. Certificates. *Prof. Accred.:* Medical Laboratory Technology, Practical Nursing. Dir. Ann Robb.
Enroll.: FTE 1,354
(305) 963-8616

South Florida Community College
Avon Park 33825. Public (state). 1968/1982 (SACS-Comm. on Coll.). Tri. plan. Degrees: A. Pres. Catherine P. Cornelius.
Enroll.: 1,995
(813) 453-6661

South Technical Education Center
1300 S.W. 30th Ave., Boynton Beach 33435. Public (state). 1980/1985 (SACS-COEI). Courses of varying lengths. Certificates. Dir. Leonard Goforth.
Enroll.: FTE 1,055
(305) 737-7400

Southeastern Academy
2333 E. Spacecoast Pkwy., Drawer 1768, Kissimmee 32741. Private; combination home study and resident. 1977/1982 (NHSC). Degrees: A, diplomas. Pres. David L. Peoples.
(305) 847-4444

*Southeastern College of the Assemblies of God
1000 Longfellow Blvd., Lakeland 33801. Private (Assembly of God) professional. 1954/1983 (AABC). Sem. plan. Degrees: B. Pres. James E. Hennesy.
Enroll.: 1,043
(813) 665-4404

Southeastern College of Osteopathic Medicine
1750-60 Northeast 168th St., North Miami Beach 33162. Private professional. 1980. Sem. plan. Degrees: P. *Prof. Accred.:* Osteopathy. Pres. Morton Terry.
Enroll.: 100 (*f.t.* 79 m., 21 w.)
(305) 949-4000

Southern Career Institute
1692 N.W. Madrid Way, Boca Raton 33432. Private home study. 1979/1984 (NHSC). Pres. R. W. Beaver.
(305) 368-2522

Southern College
5600 Lake Underhill Rd., Orlando 32807. Private business; recognized candidate for junior college. 1970/1980 (AICS). Qtr. plan. Diplomas. *Prof. Accred.:* Dental Assisting, Dental Laboratory Technology. Vice Pres. Daniel F. Moore.
Enroll.: 1,339 (*f.t.* 436 m., 903 w.)
(305) 273-1000

*Candidate for Accreditation by Regional Accrediting Commission

Southern Technical Institute
221 W. Oakland Park Blvd., Oakland Park 33311. Private. 1983 (ABHES). 34-week program. Diplomas. *Prof. Accred.:* Medical Assisting. Pres. Michael L. Hook.
(305) 564-4677

Branch Campus
Honey Hill Shopping Ctr., 1994 N.W. Second Ave., North Miami 33161. *Prof. Accred.:* Medical Assisting. Dir. Barbara Franklin.
(305) 651-7515

State University of Florida
System office, 107 W. Gaines St., Tallahassee 32301. Public (state). Chanc. Charles Reed.
(904) 488-4234

Stenotype Institute of Jacksonville
500 Ninth Ave., N., Jacksonville Beach 32250. Private business. 1968/1981 (AICS); 1980 (NHSC). Courses of varying lengths. Diplomas. Pres. Thyra D. Ellis.
Enroll.: 76 (*f.t.* 3 m., 73 w.)
(904) 246-7466

Stetson University
P.O. Box 8358, DeLand 32720. Private (Southern Baptist). 1932/1981 (SACS-Comm. on Coll.). 4-1-4 plan. Degrees: B,P,M,D. *Prof. Accred.:* Law, Music. Pres. H. Douglas Lee.
Enroll.: 2,545
(904) 734-4121

Sunstate College of Hair Design, Inc.
1650 N. Missouri Ave., Largo 33540. Private. 1978/1984 (NATTS). Courses of varying lengths. Diplomas. Dir. Kenneth F. Stone.
Enroll.: 54 (*f.t.* 18 m., 36 w.)
(813) 584-0475

Extension
4901 Palm Beach Blvd., Suite 12, Fort Myers 33905.
(813) 694-6979

Extension
1805 34th St. N., St. Petersburg 33713. Dir. Gayl E. McCanless.
(813) 327-0999

Branch Campus
4424 Bee Ridge Rd., Sarasota 33583.
(813) 377-4880

Branch Campus
1805 34th St., N., St. Petersburg 33713.
(813) 327-0999

SUWANEE-HAMILTON AREA VOCATIONAL, TECHNICAL AND ADULT CENTER
415 Pinewood Dr., S.W., Live Oak 32060. Public (state). 1973/1985 (SACS-COEI). Courses of varying lengths. Certificates. Dir. Bill McMillian.
Enroll.: FTE 203
(904) 362-2252

SYSTEMS TECHNOLOGY INSTITUTE
130 E. Altamonte Dr., Suite 24-A, Altamonte Springs 32701. Private. 1984 (SACS-COEI). Courses of varying lengths. Certificates. Dir. James H. Walton.
Enroll.: FTE 63

TALLAHASSEE COMMUNITY COLLEGE
444 Appleyard Dr., Tallahassee 32304-2895. Public (district) junior. 1969/1984 (SACS-Comm. on Coll.). Sem. plan. Degrees: A. *Prof. Accred.:* Dental Hygiene, Radiography, Respiratory Therapy. Pres. James H. Hinson, Jr.
Enroll.: 3,573
(904) 576-5181

TAMPA COLLEGE
3319 W. Hillsborough Ave., Tampa 33614. Private senior business. 1966/1981 (AICS). Qtr. plan. Degrees: A,B, certificates, diplomas. Dir./Vice Pres. David Zorn.
Enroll.: 3,777 (*f.t.* 1,526 m., 2,251 w.)
(813) 879-6000

BRANCH CAMPUS
15000 U.S. Hwy. 19 South, Clearwater 33546. Dir. Karen Ehmig.
(813) 530-9495

TOM P. HANEY VOCATIONAL-TECHNICAL CENTER
3016 Highway 77, Panama City 32405. Public (state). 1977/1982 (SACS-COEI). Courses of varying lengths. Certificates. Dir. Marion Riviere.
Enroll.: FTE 663
(904) 769-2191

BRANCH CAMPUS
Tyndall A.F.B., FL 32403.

TOTAL TECHNICAL INSTITUTE
2880 N.W. 62nd St., Fort Lauderdale 33309. Private. 1982 (NATTS). Courses of varying lengths. Diplomas. Dir. George Klein.
Enroll.: 1126
(305) 973-4760

TRAVIS VOCATIONAL-TECHNICAL CENTER
3225 Winterlake Rd., Eaton Park 33830. Public (state). 1978/1983 (SACS-COEI). Courses of varying lengths. Certificates. Dir. Thaliah S. Harris.
Enroll.: FTE 766
(904) 769-2191

ULTISSIMA BEAUTY INSTITUTE AT HIALEAH
510 W. 29th St., Hialeah 33012. Private. 1983/1985 (SACS-COEI). Courses of varying lengths. Certificates. Dir. Frank Catapano.
Enroll.: FTE 1,703
(305) 888-5078

BRANCH CAMPUS
551 N.E. 81st, Miami 33131.

BRANCH CAMPUS
9203 N. Florida, Tampa 33612.

BRANCH CAMPUS
3911 St. Timothy Ln., St. Ann, MO 63074.

BRANCH CAMPUS
26 North Oaks Plaza, St. Louis, MO 63121.

UNITED COLLEGE
500 W. 29th St., Hialeah 33012. Private. 1985 (SACS-COEI). Sem. plan. Certificates, diplomas. *Prof. Accred.:* Medical Assisting. Dir. Lee Dixon.
Enroll.: FTE 670
(305) 883-8931

UNITED COLLEGE
720 N.W. 27th Ave., Miami 33125. Private. 1985 (SACS-COEI). Sem. plan. Certificates, diplomas. Dir. Marta Sosa.
Enroll.: FTE 67

UNITED COLLEGE
9203 N. Florida Ave., Tampa 33612. Private business. 1982 (SACS-COEI) Sem. plan. Certificates, diplomas. *Prof. Accred.:* Medical Assisting. Pres. Frank Catapano.
Enroll.: 3,908
(813) 933-9675

BRANCH CAMPUS
551 N.E. 81st, Miami 33131.

BRANCH CAMPUS
4401 Hampton Ave., St. Louis, MO 63121.

BRANCH CAMPUS
26 North Oaks Plaza, St. Louis, MO 63121.

BRANCH CAMPUS
151 Lawrence St., Brooklyn, NY 11201.
(212) 624-7557

BRANCH CAMPUS
329-34 E. 149th St., Bronx, NY 10451.
(212) 665-9600

Branch Campus
47 Mineola Blvd., Mineola, NY 11501. Dir. Harriet Rubenstein.
(516) 294-8344

Branch Campus
22 W. 34th St., New York, NY 10001. Dr. Frank Catapano.
(212) 564-5777

Branch Campus
161 W. 66th St., New York, NY 10023.
(212) 496-8651

Branch Campus
95-20 63rd Rd., Rego Park, NY 11374. Dir. Fran S. Marks.
(212) 459-5550

United Electronics Institute
4202 Spruce St., Tampa 33607. Private. 1973/1985 (NATTS). Qtr. plan. Degrees: A. Exec. Dir. George E. Glenn.
Enroll.: 1,120 (*f.t.* 1,030 m., 90 w.)
(813) 875-3717

United Truck Master
3250 U.S. Hwy. 19 N., Suite 201, Clearwater 33575. Private; combination home study and resident course. 1985 (NHSC). Pres. George L. Eyler.
(813) 784-0660

Branch
Florida State Fair and Expo Park, E. of Tampa on I-4, Exit U.S. 301, Tampa 33680. Resident training site.
(813) 621-7821

*University of Central Florida
P.O. Box 25000, Orlando 32816. Public (state) liberal arts and professional. 1970/1985 (SACS-Comm. on Coll.). Sem. plan. Degrees: B,M,D. *Prof. Accred.:* Accounting (Type A,C), Business (B,M), Engineering (civil, electrical, engineering mathematics and computer systems, environmental, industrial, mechanical), Engineering Technology (design, electronics, operations technology), Medical Record Administration, Medical Technology, Music, Nursing (B), Radiography, Respiratory Therapy, Social Work (B), Teacher Education (*p*). Pres. Trevor Colbourn.
Enroll.: 11,688
(305) 275-2000

*Member State University of Florida System

*University of Florida
Gainesville 32611. Public (state). 1913/1983 (SACS-Comm. on Coll.). Qtr. plan. Degrees: A,B,P,M,D. *Prof. Accred.:* Accounting (Type A,B,C), Architecture (M), Assistant to the Primary Care Physician, Business (B,M), Construction Education, Dentistry, Dietetics, Engineering (aerospace, agricultural, ceramics, chemical, civil, coastal and oceanographic, computer and information sciences, electrical, engineering science, environmental, industrial, mechanical, metallurgical, nuclear and systems), Forestry, Health and Hospital Administration, Interior Design, Journalism, Landscape Architecture (B), Law, Medical Technology, Medicine, Music, Nursing (B,M), Occupational Therapy, Pharmacy, Physical Therapy, Psychology, Rehabilitation Counseling, Specialist in Blood Bank Technology, Speech Pathology and Audiology, Teacher Education (*e,s,p*), Veterinary Medicine. Pres. Marshall M. Criser.
Enroll.: 32,453
(904) 392-0223

University of Miami
Coral Gables 33124. Private. 1940/1976 (SACS-Comm. on Coll.). Sem. plan. Degrees: B,P,M,D. *Prof. Accred.:* Accounting (Type A,C). Architecture (B), Business (B,M), Cytotechnology, Engineering (architectural, civil, electrical, industrial, mechanical), Health Administration, Histologic Technology, Law, Medical Technology, Medicine, Music, Nuclear Medicine Technology, Nursing (B,M), Physical Therapy, Psychology, Public Health, Radiation Therapy Technology, Radiography, Teacher Education (*e,s,p*). Pres. Edward T. Foote, II.
Enroll.: 12,748
(305) 284-2211

*University of North Florida
4567 St. Johns Bluff Rd., Jacksonville 32216. Public (state); upper division only. 1974/1979 (SACS-Comm. on Coll.). Sem. plan. Degrees: B,M. *Prof. Accred.:* Business (B,M), Nursing (B). Pres. Curtis L. McCray.
Enroll.: 12,228
(904) 646-2666

*University of South Florida
4202 E. Fowler Ave., Tampa 33620. Public (state). 1963/1984 (SACS-Comm. on Coll.).

*Member State University of Florida System

Branch campuses at St. Petersburg and Sarasota. Qtr. plan. Degrees: B,P,M,D. *Prof. Accred.:* Accounting (Type A,C), Business (B,M), Engineering (chemical, electrical, industrial, mechanical, structures, material and fluids), Journalism, Librarianship, Medicine, Nursing (B), Psychology, Rehabilitation Counseling, Social Work (B), Speech Pathology and Audiology. Pres. John L. Brown.
Enroll.: 20,354
(813) 974-2011

UNIVERSITY OF TAMPA
Tampa 33606. Private liberal arts college. 1951/1974 (SACS-Comm. on Coll.). Sem. plan. Degrees: B,M. *Prof. Accred.:* Music. Pres. Richard D. Cheshire.
Enroll.: 1,745
(813) 253-3333

*UNIVERSITY OF WEST FLORIDA
Pensacola 32504. Public (state) liberal arts college; upper division only. 1969/1985 (SACS-Comm. on Coll.). Qtr. plan. Degrees: B,M. *Prof. Accred.:* Music, Nursing (B), Social Work (B). Pres. James A. Robinson.
Enroll.: 6,396
(904) 474-2000

VALENCIA COMMUNITY COLLEGE
P.O. Box 3028, Orlando 32802. Public (district). 1969/1983 (SACS-Comm. on Coll.). Tri. plan. Degrees: A. *Prof. Accred.:* Dental Hygiene, Medical Laboratory Technology, Nursing (A), Respiratory Therapy. Pres. Paul C. Gianini, Jr.
Enroll.: 8,523
(305) 299-5000

VOCATIONAL TRAINING CENTER
1835 W. Flagler St., Miami 33125. Public (state). 1984 (SACS-COEI). Courses of varying lengths. Certificates. Dir. Luis Hernandez.
Enroll.: FTE 1,076

WARNER SOUTHERN COLLEGE
5301 U.S. Hwy. 27S, Lake Wales 33853. Private liberal arts. 1977/1982 (SACS-Comm. on Coll.). Sem. plan. Degrees: A,B. Pres. Leroy M. Fulton.
Enroll.: 304 (*f.t.* 138 m., 147 w.)
(813) 638-1426

WASHINGTON HOLMES AREA VOCATIONAL-TECHNICAL CENTER
209 Hoyt St., Chipley 32428. Public (state). 1976/1981 (SACS-COEI). Courses of varying lengths. Certificates. Dir. Wayne C. Saunders.
Enroll.: FTE 651
(904) 638-1180

*Member State University of Florida System

WEBBER COLLEGE
Babson Park 33827. Private 4-year business. 1981 (SACS-Comm. on Coll.). Sem. plan. Degrees: A,B. Pres. Gale W. Cleven.
Enroll.: 283
(813) 638-1431

WEST TECHNICAL EDUCATION CENTER
2625 State Rd. 715, Belle Glade 33430. Public (state). 1984 (SACS-COEI). Courses of varying lengths. Certificates. Dir. Myron W. Cost.
Enroll.: FTE 318

WESTSIDE VOCATIONAL-TECHNICAL CENTER
731 E. Story Rd., Winter Garden 32787. Public (state). 1981 (SACS-COEI). Courses of varying lengths. Certificates. Dir. Walt Cobb.
Enroll.: FTE 562
(305) 656-2851

WILFRED ACADEMY
2137 W. Buffalo Ave., Tampa 33607. Private. 1983 (SACS-COEI). 1200 clock hours. Certificates. Pres. John M. Haffner.
Enroll.: FTE 340
(813) 872-6242

BRANCH CAMPUS
1001 W. Oakland Park Blvd., Ft. Lauderdale 33311.

BRANCH CAMPUS
4578 W. 12th Ave., Hialeah 33162.

BRANCH CAMPUS
6562 Bird Rd., Miami 33155.

BRANCH CAMPUS
1102 S.W. 27th Ave., Miamii 33125.

BRANCH CAMPUS
1024 N.E. 163rd St., North Miami Beach 33162.

BRANCH CAMPUS
1013 E. Colonial Dr., Orlando 32803.

BRANCH CAMPUS
3301 Third Ave., St. Petersburg 33713.

BRANCH CAMPUS
1645 N. Vine St., Hollywood, CA 90028.

BRANCH CAMPUS
513 S. Broadway, Los Angeles, CA 90013.

WITHLACOOCHEE VOCATIONAL AND ADULT EDUCATIONAL CENTER
1201 W. Main St., Inverness 32650. Public (state). 1984 (SACS-COEI). Courses of varying lengths. Certificates. Dir. Roland W. Best.
Enroll.: FTE 445

GEORGIA

*Abraham Baldwin Agricultural College
Tifton 31793. Public (state) junior. 1953/1975 (SACS-Comm. on Coll.). Qtr. plan. Degrees: A. *Prof. Accred.:* Nursing (A). Pres. Wayne C. Curtis.
Enroll.: 1,926
(912) 386-3236

Agnes Scott College
Decatur 30030. Private liberal arts for women. 1907/1984 (SACS-Comm. on Coll.). Qtr. plan. Degrees: B. Pres. Ruth A. Schmidt.
Enroll.: 510
(404) 371-6000

Akers Computerized Learning Centers
5600 Roswell Rd., N.E., Atlanta 30342. Private. 1984 (AICS). Courses of varying lengths. Certificates. Pres. Lynn R. Akers.
Enroll.: 698
(404) 843-0014

Branch Campus
480 N. Thomas St., Athens 30601. Dir. Ralph Towler.
(404) 548-9800

Branch Campus
2121 New Market Pkwy., Bldg. 5, Suite 152, Marietta 30062. Dir. Mike Campbell.
(404) 951-2367

Branch Campus
2191 Northlake Pkwy., Tucker 30084. Dir. of Instruction Pandora Law.
(404) 939-6008

Albany Area Vocational-Technical School
1021 Lowe Rd., Albany 31708. Public (state). 1974/1984 (SACS-COEI). Courses of varying lengths. Certificates. *Prof. Accred.:* Dental Assisting, Radiography. Dir. Nathaniel Cross.
Enroll.: FTE 1,552
(912) 888-1320

*Albany Junior College
2400 Gillionville Rd., Albany 31707. Public (state) junior. 1968/1983 (SACS-Comm. on Coll.). Qtr. plan. Degrees: A. *Prof. Accred.:* Dental Hygiene, Medical Laboratory Technology (A), Nursing (A). Pres. B. R. Tilley.
Enroll.: 2,020
(912) 888-8705

*Member Georgia State University System

*Albany State College
Albany 31705. Public (state) liberal arts and professional. 1951/1978 (SACS-Comm. on Coll.). Qtr. plan. Degrees: B,M. *Prof. Accred.:* Nursing (B), Teacher Education (*e,s*). Pres. Billy C. Black.
Enroll.: 2,130
(912) 439-4600

The American College for the Applied Arts
3330 Peachtree Rd., N.E., Atlanta 30326. Private technical. 1978/1983 (SACS-COEI). 2- and 4-year programs. Degrees: A,B. Dir. Rafael A. Lago.
Enroll.: FTE 186
(404) 231-9000

Branch Campus
1651 Westwood Blvd., Los Angeles, CA 90024.
(213) 470-2000

Andrew College
Cuthbert 31740. Private (United Methodist) junior. 1927/1974 (SACS-Comm. on Coll.). Qtr. plan. Degrees: A. Pres. Morris Wray.
Enroll.: 268
(912) 732-2171

*Armstrong State College
11935 Abercorn St., Savannah 31419. Public (state) liberal arts. 1968/1982 (SACS-Comm. on Coll.). Qtr. plan. Degrees: A,B,M. *Prof. Accred.:* Dental Hygiene, Medical Record Technology, Medical Technology, Music, Nursing (A,B), Radiography, Respiratory Therapy, Teacher Education (*e,s,p*). Pres. Robert A. Burnett.
Enroll.: 2,459
(912) 927-5258

Art Institute of Atlanta
3376 Peachtree Rd., N.E., Atlanta 30326. Private. 1972/1977 (NATTS); 1985 (SACS-Comm. on Coll.). Qtr. plan. Degrees: A, diplomas. Pres. Gerald Murphy.
Enroll.: 1,261
(404) 266-1341

Extension
Art Institute of Seattle, 906 E. Pine St., Seattle, WA 98122. Pres. Jess D. Cauthorn.
(206) 322-0596

*Member Georgia State University System

Athens Area Vocational-Technical School
U.S. Hwy. 29 North, Athens 30610. Public (state). 1973/1983 (SACS-COEI). Courses of varying lengths. Certificates. *Prof. Accred.:* Respiratory Therapy Technology. Dir. Kenneth C. Eason.
Enroll.: FTE 1,308
(404) 549-2360

Atlanta Area Technical School
1560 Stewart Ave., S.W., Atlanta 30310. Public (state). 1971/1981 (SACS-COEI). Courses of varying lengths. Certificates. *Prof. Accred.:* Dental Assisting, Dental Laboratory Technology, Medical Laboratory Technology. Dir. Betty Campbell.
Enroll.: FTE 7,879
(404) 758-9451

Branch Campus
4191 Northside Dr., Atlanta 30342.

Atlanta Christian College
2605 Ben Hill Rd., East Point 30344. Private (Church of Christ) professional. 1965/1984 (AABC). Sem. plan. Degrees: B. Pres. James C. Donovan.
Enroll.: 152
(404) 761-8861

The Atlanta College of Art
1280 Peachtree St., N.E., Atlanta 30309. Private professional. 1969/1984 (SACS-Comm. on Coll.). Sem. plan. Degrees: B. *Prof. Accred.:* Art. Pres. Ofelia Garcia.
Enroll.: 233
(404) 898-1164

Atlanta College of Medical & Dental Careers
1240 W. Peachtree St., N.W., Atlanta 30309. Private. 1978/1983 (SACS-COEI). Qtr. plan, courses of varying lengths. Diplomas. *Prof. Accred.:* Dental Laboratory Technology, Medical Assisting, Medical Laboratory Technology. Exec. Dir. Manny Correia.
Enroll.: FTE 242
(404) 873-1701

Branch Campus
120 Copeland Rd., N.E., Atlanta 30342.

Atlanta Job Corps Center
239 West Lake Ave., N.W., Atlanta 30367. Public (federal). 1985 (SACS-COEI). Courses of varying lengths. Diplomas. Dir. Willie Barnes.
Enroll.: FTE 483

*Atlanta Junior College
1630 Stewart Ave., S.W., Atlanta 30310. Public (state) junior. 1976/1981 (SACS-Comm. on Coll.). Qtr. plan. Degrees: A. Pres. Edwin A. Thompson.
Enroll.: 1,258
(404) 656-6441

Atlanta University
223 Chestnut St., S.W., Atlanta 30314. Private, graduate only; together with Clark College, Morehouse College, Morris Brown College, Spelman College, and the Interdenominational Theological Center forms the Atlanta University Center. 1932/1978 (SACS-Comm. on Coll.). Sem. plan. Degrees: M,D. *Prof. Accred.:* Business (M), Librarianship, Social Work (M), Teacher Education (*e,s,p*). Pres. Luther S. Williams.
Enroll.: 758
(404) 681-0251

Augusta Area Vocational-Technical School
3116 Deans Bridge Rd., Augusta 30906. Public (state). 1973/1983 (SACS-COEI). Courses of varying lengths. Certificates. *Prof. Accred.:* Dental Assisting, Dental Laboratory Technology, Medical Assisting, Medical Laboratory Technology. Dir. Jack B. Patrick.
Enroll.: FTE 1,458
(404) 793-3326

Branch Campus
2704 Benson Rd., Augusta 30906.

Branch Campus
1399 Walton Way, Augusta 30901.

*Augusta College
2500 Walton Way, Augusta 30910. Public (state) liberal arts. 1967/1981 (SACS-Comm. on Coll.). Qtr. plan. Degrees: A,B,M. *Prof. Accred.:* Music, Nursing (A), Teacher Education (*e,s,*). Pres. George A. Christenberry.
Enroll.: 3,413
(912) 737-1400

*Bainbridge Junior College
P.O. Box 953, Bainbridge 31717. Public (state). 1975/1980 (SACS-Comm. on Coll.). Qtr. plan. Degrees: A. Pres. Edward D. Mobley.
Enroll.: 522
(912) 246-7642

*Member Georgia State University System

Balin Institute of Technology
1359-B Spring St., N.W., Atlanta 30309. Private. 1972/1984 (NATTS); 1981 (SACS-COEI). Courses of varying lengths. Diplomas. Dir. Jeanne Lubow.
Enroll.: FTE 72
(404) 874-5278

Branch Campus
3301 W. Lincoln Ave., Anaheim, CA 92801.

Branch Campus
3355 Mission Ave., No. B9, Oceanside, CA 92054.

Bauder Fashion College
Phipps Plaza, 3500 Peachtree Rd., N.E., Atlanta 30326. Private. 1973/1981 (NATTS); 1985 (SACS-Comm. on Coll.). Courses of varying lengths. Degrees: A. Pres. John E. Kettle.
Enroll.: 536
(404) 237-7573

BellSouth Services Learning Centers
1447 N.E. Expwy., Atlanta 30029. Private. 1984 (SACS-COEI). Courses of varying lengths. Certificates. Dir. J. R. Baugus.
Enroll.: FTE 1,206

Branch Campus
1034 W. College Ave., Decatur 30030.

Branch Campus
75 Bagby Dr., Birmingham, AL 35201.

Branch Campus
4951 Richard Rd., Jacksonville, FL 32207.

Branch Campus
18560 N. W. 27th Ave., Miami, FL 33055.

Branch Campus
8601 W. Sunrise Blvd., Plantation, FL 33322.

Branch Campus
909 S. Jefferson Davis Pkwy., New Orleans, LA 70125.

Branch Campus
Southern National Ctr., Charlotte, NC 28230.

Branch Campus
2814 Firestone Dr., Greensboro, NC 27406.

Branch Campus
1415 Henderson St., Columbia, SC 29201.

Branch Campus
443 Donaldson Pike, Nashville, TN 37214.

Ben Hill-Irwin Area Vocational-Technical School
P.O. Box 1096, Fitzgerald 31750. Public (state). 1973/1983 (SACS-COEI). Courses of varying lengths. Certificates. Dir. Edgar B. Greene.
Enroll.: FTE 342
(912) 468-7487

Berry College
Mount Berry 30149. Private liberal arts. 1957/1978 (SACS-Comm. on Coll.). Qtr. plan. Degrees: A,B,M. *Prof. Accred.:* Music, Teacher Education (*e,s*). Pres. Gloria M. Shatto.
Enroll.: 1,351
(404) 232-5374

Branell College
401 West Peachtree St., N.E., Suite 1800, Atlanta 30308. Private business. 1972/1985 (AICS). Courses of varying lengths. Certificates. Pres. F. Jack Henderson.
Enroll.: 1,005 (*f.t.* 160 m., 845 w.)
(404) 525-5633

Branch Campus
3401 West End St., Nashville, TN 37203. Dir. Susan Strader.
(615) 297-1100

Brenau College
Gainesville 30501. Private liberal arts. 1947/1981 (SACS-Comm. on Coll.). Qtr. plan. Degrees: B,M. *Prof. Accred.:* Nursing (B). Pres. John S. Burd.
Enroll.: 1,745
(404) 534-6299

Brewton-Parker College
Mt. Vernon 30445. Private (Southern Baptist) junior. 1962/1975 (SACS-Comm. on Coll.). Qtr. plan. Degrees: A, (candidate for B). Pres. Y. Lynn Holmes.
Enroll.: 1,068
(912) 583-2241

Brown College of Court Reporting and Business
1776 Peachtree St., N.W., Suite 220 S., Atlanta 30309. Private. 1976/1982 (AICS); 1984 (SACS-COEI). Courses of varying lengths. Certificates. Dir. Harold O. Sasser.
Enroll.: FTE 100
(404) 876-1227

*Brunswick Junior College
Brunswick 31523. Public (state). 1965/1981 (SACS-Comm. on Coll.). Qtr. plan. Degrees: A. *Prof. Accred.:* Medical Laboratory Technology, Nursing (A), Radiography, Respira-

*Member Georgia State University System

tory Therapy Technology. Pres. John W. Teel.
Enroll.: 1,758
(912) 264-7235

CARROLL COUNTY AREA VOCATIONAL-TECHNICAL SCHOOL
997 S. Hwy. 16, Carrollton 30117. Public (state). 1973/1983 (SACS-COEI). Courses of varying lengths. Certificates. Dir. Wendell Hoomes.
Enroll.: FTE 517
(404) 834-3391

CITIZENS' HIGH SCHOOL
5582 Peachtree Rd., Atlanta 30341. Private home study. 1984 (NHSC). Pres. Roy Linderman.
(404) 455-8358

CLARK COLLEGE
240 Chestnut St., S.W., Atlanta 30314. Private (United Methodist) liberal arts; member of Atlanta University Center. 1941/1978 (SACS-Comm. on Coll.). Sem. plan. Degrees: B. *Prof. Accred.:* Social Work (B), Teacher Education (*e,s*). Pres. Elias Blake, Jr.
Enroll.: 1,814
(404) 681-3080

*CLAYTON JUNIOR COLLEGE
P.O. Box 285, Morrow 30260. Public (state). 1971/1975 (SACS-Comm. on Coll.). Qtr. plan. Degrees: A. *Prof. Accred.:* Dental Hygiene, Nursing (A). Pres. Harry S. Downs.
Enroll.: 3,260
(404) 961-3400

COLUMBIA THEOLOGICAL SEMINARY
701 Columbia Dr., Decatur 30031. Private (Presbyterian, U.S.A.) professional; graduate only. 1983 (SACS-Comm. on Coll.). Qtr. plan. Degrees: P,M,D. *Prof. Accred.:* Theology (1938/1982, ATS). Pres. J. Davison Philips.
Enroll.: 485
(404) 378-8821

COLUMBUS AREA VOCATIONAL-TECHNICAL SCHOOL
928 45th St., Columbus 31995. Public (state). 1972/1982 (SACS-COEI). Courses of varying lengths. Certificates. Dir. W. G. Hartline.
Enroll.: FTE 1,930
(404) 322-1425

*Member Georgia State University System

BRANCH CAMPUS
2601 Courtland Ave., Columbus 31907.
(404) 561-2889

BRANCH CAMPUS
5330 Transport Blvd., Columbus 31907.
(404) 563-0800

*COLUMBUS COLLEGE
Columbus 31993. Public (state) liberal arts. 1970/1985 (SACS-Comm. on Coll.). Qtr. plan. Degrees: A,B,M. *Prof. Accred.:* Dental Hygiene, Medical Technology, Music, Nursing (A), Teacher Education (*e,s*). Pres. Francis J. Brooke.
Enroll.: 3,872
(404) 568-2001

CONTROL DATA INSTITUTE
3379 Peachtree Rd., N.E., Suite 400, Atlanta 30326. Private. 1976/1982 (NATTS); 1978/1983 (SACS-COEI). Courses of varying lengths. Certificates. Dir. William Polmear.
Enroll.: FTE 274
(404) 261-7700

COOSA VALLEY VOCATIONAL-TECHNICAL SCHOOL
112 Hemlock St., Rome 30161. Public (state). 1972/1982 (SACS-COEI). Courses of varying lengths. Certificates. Dir. Charles E. Earle.
Enroll.: FTE 430
(404) 235-1142

COUNTY SCHOOLS, INC
Rt. 3, Box 273, McDonough 30253. Private home study. 1981 (NHSC). Pres.———.

COVENANT COLLEGE
Lookout Mountain, Tennessee 37350. Private (Reformed Presbyterian) liberal arts. 1971/1975 (SACS-Comm. on Coll.). Sem. plan. Degrees: A,B. Pres. Martin Essenburg.
Enroll.: 498
(404) 820-1560

CRANDALL JUNIOR COLLEGE
1283 Adams St., Macon 31201. Private junior business. 1969/1980 (AICS). Qtr. plan. Degrees: A, certificates, diplomas. Pres. Linda H. Godwin.
Enroll.: 1,237 (*f.t.* 395 m., 842 w.)
(912) 745-6593

*DALTON JUNIOR COLLEGE
213 N. College Dr., Dalton 30720. Public (state). 1969/1984 (SACS-Comm. on Coll.). Qtr. plan. Degrees: A. *Prof. Accred.:* Med-

*Member Georgia State University System

ical Laboratory Technology, Medical Record Technology, Nursing (A). Pres. Derrell C. Roberts.
Enroll.: 1,386
(404) 278-3113

DALTON VOCATIONAL SCHOOL OF HEALTH OCCUPATIONS
1221 Elkwood Dr., Dalton 30720. Public (state) technical. 1975/1985 (SACS-COEI). Courses of varying lengths. Certificates. Dir. Sue M. Pack.
Enroll.: FTE 67
(404) 278-8922

DEKALB COMMUNITY COLLEGE
3251 Panthersville Rd., Decatur 30089. Public (county) junior. 1965/1982 (SACS-Comm. on Coll.). Qtr. plan. Degrees: A. *Prof. Accred.:* Dental Hygiene, Medical Laboratory Technology (A), Nursing (A), Surgical Technology. Pres. Marvin M. Cole.
Enroll.: 11,485
(404) 244-2360

DEVRY INSTITUTE OF TECHNOLOGY
250 N. Arcadia Ave., Decatur 30030. Private. 1971/1978 (NATTS); 1981 (NCA). Tri. plan. Degrees: A,B, certificates, diplomas. *Prof. Accred.:* Engineering Technology (electronics). Pres. William Weaver.
Enroll.: 2,758 (*f.t.* 2,041 m., 463 w.)
(404) 292-7900

DRAUGHON'S JUNIOR COLLEGE
709 Mall Blvd., Savannah 31406. Private junior business. 1975/1983 (AICS); 1985 (SACS-Comm. on Coll.). Qtr. plan. Degrees: A. Pres. John T. South, III.
Enroll.: 898
(912) 355-3133

BRANCH CAMPUS
2925 Tenth Ave., North, Lake Worth, FL 33461. Dir. Vincent J. Zambito.
(305) 439-5333

*EMANUEL COUNTY JUNIOR COLLEGE
Swainsboro 30401. Public (state). 1975/1980 (SACS-Comm. on Coll.). Qtr. plan. Degrees: A. Pres. Willie D. Gunn.
Enroll.: 518
(404) 237-7831

EMMANUEL COLLEGE AND SCHOOL OF CHRISTIAN MINISTRY
P.O. Box 128, Franklin Springs 30639. Private (Pentecostal Holiness) junior and professional. 1967/1981 (SACS-Comm. on Coll.) for A degree only; 1979 (AABC). Qtr. plan. Degrees: A,B. Pres. David R. Hopkins.
Enroll.: 342
(404) 245-7226

EMORY UNIVERSITY
Atlanta 30322. Private (United Methodist). 1917/1983 (SACS-Comm. on Coll.). Qtr. plan. Degrees: B,P,M,D. *Prof. Accred.:* Assistant to the Primary Care Physician, Business (B,M), Community Health/Preventive Medicine, Cytotechnology, Dentistry, Dietetics, Law, Librarianship, Medical Technology, Medicine, Music, Nuclear Medicine Technology, Nursing (B,M), Physical Therapy, Psychology, Radiography, Respiratory Therapy Technology, Theology. Pres. James T. Laney.
Enroll.: 7,838
(404) 727-6123

*FLOYD JUNIOR COLLEGE
P.O. Box 1864, Rome 30163. Public (state). 1972/1976 (SACS-Comm. on Coll.). Qtr. plan. Degrees: A. *Prof. Accred.:* Medical Laboratory Technology, Nursing (A). Pres. David B. McCorkle.
Enroll.: 1,278
(404) 295-6328

*FORT VALLEY COLLEGE
State College Dr., Fort Valley 31030. Public (state) liberal arts and teachers. 1951/1979 (SACS-Comm. on Coll.). Qtr. plan. Degrees: A,B,M. *Prof. Accred.:* Engineering Technology (electronic), Home Economics, Rehabilitation Counseling, Teacher Education (*e,s,p*). Pres. Luther Burse.
Enroll.: 2,078
(912) 825-6211

*GAINESVILLE JUNIOR COLLEGE
P.O. Box 1358, Gainesville 30503. Public (state). 1968/1982 (SACS-Comm. on Coll.). Qtr. plan. Degrees: A. Pres. J. Foster Watkins.
Enroll.: 1,634
(404) 535-6239

*GEORGIA COLLEGE
Milledgeville 31061. Public (state) liberal arts. 1925/1984 (SACS-Comm. on Coll.). Qtr. plan. Degrees: A,B,M. *Prof. Accred.:* Home Economics, Music, Nursing (B), Teacher Education (*e,s*). Pres. Edwin G. Speir, Jr.

*Member Georgia State University System

*Member Georgia State University System

Enroll.: 3,145
(912) 453-4054

*Georgia Institute of Technology
225 North Ave., N.W., Atlanta 30332. Public (state) technological. 1923/1984 (SACS-Comm. on Coll.). Qtr. plan. Degrees: B,M,D. *Prof. Accred.:* Architecture (M), Business (B,M), Engineering (aerospace, ceramic, chemical, civil, electrical, engineering science, industrial, mechanical, metallurgy, nuclear, textile). Pres. Joseph M. Pettit.
Enroll.: 10,675
(404) 894-2000

Georgia Medical Education Preparation Center
828 Peachtree St., N.W., Suite 206, Atlanta 30308. Private. 1985 (ABHES). 28-week course. Diplomas. *Prof. Accred.:* Medical Assisting. Dir. Ginger Gibbs.
(404) 873-2864

Georgia Military College
Milledgeville 31061. Private junior. 1940/1975 (SACS-Comm. on Coll.). Qtr. plan. Degrees: A. Pres. William P. Acker.
Enroll.: 1,133
(912) 453-3481

*Georgia Southern College
Statesboro 30460. Public (state) liberal arts and teachers. 1935/1984 (SACS-Comm. on Coll.). Qtr. plan. Degrees: A,B,P,M. *Prof. Accred.:* Business (B,M), Engineering Technology (civil, electrical, mechanical), Home Economics, Music, Nursing (B), Teacher Education (*e,s,p*). Pres. Dale W. Lick.
Enroll.: 6,489
(912) 681-5211

*Georgia Southwestern College
Americus 31709. Public (state) liberal arts. 1968/1983 (SACS-Comm. on Coll.). Qtr. plan. Degrees: A,B,M. *Prof. Accred.:* Nursing (A,B), Teacher Education (*e,s*). Pres. William H. Capitan.
Enroll.: 2,268
(912) 928-1279

*Georgia State University
University Plaza, Atlanta 30303. Public. 1952/1977 (SACS-Comm. on Coll.). Qtr. plan. Degrees: A,B,M,D. *Prof. Accred.:* Art, Business (B,M), Dietetics, Health Services Administration, Law (ABA only), Medical Technology, Music, Nursing (B,M), Physical Therapy, Psychology, Rehabilitation Counseling, Respiratory Therapy, Respiratory Therapy Technology, Social Work (B), Teacher Education (*e,s,p*). Pres. Noah N. Langdale, Jr.
Enroll.: 18,209
(404) 658-2000

Georgia State University System
Board of Regents, 244 Washington St., S.W., Atlanta 30334. Public (state). Chanc. H. Dean Propst.
(404) 656-2200

*Gordon Junior College
Barnesville 30204. Public (state). 1941/1975 (SACS-Comm. on Coll.). Qtr. plan. Degrees: A. *Prof. Accred.:* Nursing (A). Pres. Jerry M. Williamson.
Enroll.: 1,424
(404) 358-1700

Griffin Spalding County Area Vocational-Technical School
501 Varsity Rd., Griffin 30223. Public (state). 1971/1981 (SACS-COEI). Courses of varying lengths. Certificates. Dir. Coy L. Hodges.
Enroll.: FTE 399
(404) 227-1322

Health Care Training Institute
806 Peachtree St., N.E., Atlanta 30308. Private. 1985 (NATTS). Courses of varying lengths. Certificates. Dir. Doris Perry.
(404) 876-4303

Houston Vocational Center
1311 Corder Rd., Warner Robins 31056. Public (local). 1978/1983 (SACS-COEI). Courses of varying lengths. Certificates. Dir. Neal Rumble.
Enroll.: FTE 295
(912) 922-4231

Branch Campus
Beatrice St., Warner Robins 31056.
(912) 929-4039

Interdenominational Theological Center
671 Beckwith St., S.W., Atlanta 30314. Private (Interdenominational) professional; graduate only; member of Atlanta University Center. 1984 (SACS-Comm. on Coll.). Sem. plan. Degrees: P,M,D. *Prof. Accred.:* Theology (1960/1984, ATS). Pres. James H. Costen.

*Member Georgia State University System

*Member Georgia State University System

Enroll.: 304
(404) 522-1772

*KENNESAW COLLEGE
P.O. Box 444, Marietta 30061. Public (state) liberal arts. 1968/1980 (SACS-Comm. on Coll.). Qtr. plan. Degrees: A,B; candidate for M. *Prof. Accred.:* Music, Nursing (A), Teacher Education (*e,s*). Pres. Betty Lentz Siegel.
Enroll.: 4,929
(404) 429-2700

KERR BUSINESS COLLEGE
3011 Hogansville Rd., P.O. Box 976, La-Grange 30241. Private. 1976/1985 (AICS). Qtr. plan. Certificates. Vice Pres. Dennis Kerr.
Enroll.: 172 (*f.t.* 11 m., 161 w.)
(404) 884-1751

BRANCH CAMPUS
2623 Washington Rd., Bldg. B, P.O. Box 1986, Augusta 30903. Vice Pres. Fred Randall Kerr.
(404) 738-5046

BRANCH CAMPUS
P.O. Box 450329, Atlanta 30345. Vice Pres. Fred Randall Kerr.
(404) 934-3353

KO'WETA BEAUTY SCHOOLS
8-B Franklin St., Newnan 30263. Private. 1983/1985 (SACS-COEI). 1,500 hours. Certificates. Dir. Bill J. Maxwell.
Enroll.: FTE 27
(404) 251-4592

LAGRANGE COLLEGE
601 Broad St., LaGrange 30240. Private (United Methodist) liberal arts. 1946/1982 (SACS-Comm. on Coll.). Qtr. plan. Degrees: A,B,M. *Prof. Accred.:* Nursing (A). Pres. Walter Y. Murphy.
Enroll.: 890
(404) 882-2911

LANIER AREA TECHNICAL SCHOOL
P.O. Box 58, Oakwood 30566. Public (state). 1972/1982 (SACS-COEI). Courses of varying lengths. Certificates. *Prof. Accred.:* Medical Laboratory Technology. Dir. Joe E. Hill.
Enroll.: FTE 480
(404) 536-8884

BRANCH CAMPUS
Whitman St., P.O. Box 1172, Toccoa 30577.

*Member Georgia State University System

LIFE CHIROPRACTIC COLLEGE
1269 Barclay Cir., Suite A, Marietta 30060. Private professional. 1985 (SACS-Comm on Coll.). Sem. plan. Degrees: P. *Prof. Accred.:* Chiropractic Education. Pres. Sid Williams.
Enroll.: FTE 1,563
(404) 424-0554

MABLE BAILEY FASHION COLLEGE
1332 13th St., Columbus 31901. Private. 1983 (SACS-COEI). Courses of varying lengths. Certificates. Dir. Mable Bailey.
Enroll.: FTE 39
(404) 324-4295

MACON AREA VOCATIONAL-TECHNICAL SCHOOL
3300 Macon Tech Dr., Macon 31206. Public (state). 1973/1978 (SACS-COEI). Courses of varying lengths. Certificates. *Prof. Accred.:* Medical Laboratory Technology. Dir. Ben C. Brewton, Jr.
Enroll.: FTE 962
(912) 781-0551

BRANCH CAMPUS
1065 Anthony Rd., Macon 31204.

*MACON JUNIOR COLLEGE
Macon 31297. Public (state). 1970/1985 (SACS-Comm. on Coll.). Qtr. plan. Degrees: A. *Prof. Accred.:*Dental Hygiene, Nursing (A). Pres. S. Aaron Hyatt.
Enroll.: 1,187
(912) 474-2700

MARIETTA-COBB AREA VOCATIONAL-TECHNICAL SCHOOL
980 S. Cobb Dr., Marietta 30060. Public (state). 1973/1983 (SACS-COEI). Courses of varying lengths. Certificates. Dir. H. D. Crimm.
Enroll.: FTE 851
(404) 422-1660

MASSEY BUSINESS COLLEGE
120 Ralph McGill Blvd., N.E., Atlanta 30308. Private. 1977/1983 (AICS). Qtr. plan. Degrees: A. Acting Dir. Joe M. Brown.
Enroll.: 1,015 (*f.t.* 287 m., 728 w.)
(404) 872-1900

BRANCH CAMPUS
5299 Roswell Rd., Atlanta 30342.
(404) 256-3533

*Member Georgia State University System

Meadows College of Business
P,O. Box 173, Albany 31706. Private. 1976/1986 (AICS). Qtr. plan. Certificates. Dir. Michael Davis.
Enroll.: 252 (*f.t.* 51 m., 201 w.)
(912) 883-1736

Meadows College of Business
1170 Brown Ave., Columbus 31906. Private junior. 1974/1983 (AICS). Qtr. plan. Degrees. A, certificates. Pres. William F. Meadows, Jr.
Enroll.: 749 (*f.t.* 288 m., 461 w.)
(404) 327-7668

*Medical College of Georgia
Augusta 30912. Public (state) professional. 1973/1979 (SACS-Comm. on Coll.). Qtr. plan. Degrees: A,B,P,M,D. *Prof. Accred.:* Assistant to the Primary Care Physician, Dental Hygiene, Dentistry, Diagnostic Medical Sonography, Medical Record Administration, Medical Technology, Medicine, Nuclear Medicine Technology, Nursing (B,M), Occupational Therapy, Physical Therapy, Radiation Therapy, Radiography, Respiratory Therapy. Pres. Jesse L. Steinfeld.
Enroll.: 2,047
(404) 828-0211

Mercer University-Macon
Macon 31207. Private (Southern Baptist) 1911/1984 (SACS-Comm. on Coll.). Qtr. plan. Degrees: B,P,M,D. *Prof. Accred.:* Law, Medicine, Music, Teacher Education (*e,s*). Chanc. Rufus C. Harris. Pres. R. Kirby Godsey.
Enroll.: 2,569
(912) 744-2700

Mercer University-Atlanta
3001 Mercer University Dr., Atlanta 30341. Private (Southern Baptist) liberal arts; accreditation includes Southern School of Pharmacy. 1973/1978 (SACS-Comm. on Coll.). Qtr. plan. Degrees: B,P,M,D. *Prof. Accred.:* Music, Pharmacy. Pres. R. Kirby Godsey.
Enroll.: 1,951
(404) 688-6291

*Middle Georgia College
Cochran 31014. Public (state) junior. 1933/1979 (SACS-Comm. on Coll.). Qtr. plan. Degrees: A. *Prof. Accred.:*Nursing (A). Pres. Louis C. Alderman, Jr.
Enroll.: 1,490
(912) 934-6221

Morehouse College
830 Westview Dr., S.W., Atlanta 30314. Private liberal arts for men; member of Atlanta University Center. 1932/1978 (SACS-Comm. on Coll.). Sem. plan. Degrees: B. Pres. Hugh M. Gloster.
Enroll.: 2,046
(404) 681-2800

*The Morehouse School of Medicine
720 Westview Dr., S.W., Atlanta 30310. Private professional. 1981. *Prof. Accred.:* Medicine. Sem. plan. Degrees: P. Pres. and Dean Louis W. Sullivan.
Enroll.: 127
(404) 752-1500

Morris Brown College
634 Martin Luther King, Jr. Dr., S.W., Atlanta 30314. Private (African Methodist Episcopal) liberal arts; member of Atlanta University Center. 1941/1979 (SACS-Comm. on Coll.). Sem. plan. Degrees: B. Pres. Calvert H. Smith.
Enroll.: 1,0721
(404) 525-7831

Moultrie Area Vocational-Technical School
P.O. Box 520, Moultrie 31776. Public (state). 1974/1984 (SACS-COEI). Courses of varying lengths. Certificates. Dir. Jack N. Gay.
Enroll.: FTE 310
(912) 985-2297

Branch Campus
302 E. 14th St., Tifton 31794.

The Music Business Institute
3376 Peachtree Rd., N.E., Atlanta 30326. Private technical. 1981 (SACS-COEI). Courses of varying lengths. Certificates. Dir. Mert Paul.
Enroll.: FTE 279
(404) 231-3303

Branch Campus
1701 S.E. 17th St., Ft. Lauderdale, FL 33316.

Branch Campus
2829 West N.W. Hwy., Dallas, TX 75220.

*Member Georgia State University System

*Candidate for Accreditation by Regional Accrediting Commission

National Education Center—Bryman Campus
1789 Peachtree Rd., N.E., Atlanta 30309. Private. 1973/1979 (NATTS). Courses of varying lengths. Diplomas. *Prof. Accred.:* Medical Assisting. Dir. Sandra R. Ashley.
Enroll.: 160 (*f.t.* 4 m., 156 w.)
(404) 876-6741

Navy Supply Corps School
Athens 30606. Public (federal) technical. 1981 (SACS-COEI). Courses of varying lengths. Certificates. Commanding Officer Capt. Earnest E. Fava.
Enroll.: FTE 450
(404) 549-6620

*North Georgia College
Dahlonega 30597. Public (state) liberal arts and teachers. 1948/1976 (SACS-Comm. on Coll.). Qtr. plan. Degrees: A,B,M. *Prof. Accred.:* Nursing (A), Teacher Education (*e,s*). Pres. John H. Owen.
Enroll.: 1,908
(404) 864-3391

North Georgia Technical and Vocational School
Georgia Hwy. 197 N., Clarksville 30523. Public (state). 1972/1982 (SACS-COEI). Courses of varying lengths. Certificates. *Prof. Accred.:* Medical Laboratory Technology. Dir. James H. Marlowe.
Enroll.: FTE 667
(404) 754-2131

O.R.M. Word Processing Training School
82 Piedmont Ave., N.E., Atlanta 30303. Private. 1983 (SACS-COEI). Courses of varying lengths. Certificates. Dir. Florence V. Black.
Enroll.: FTE 90
(404) 874-2504

Branch Campus
3860 M. L. King, Jr. Blvd., Suite 103, Los Angeles, CA 90008.

Oglethorpe University
4484 Peachtree Rd., N.E., Atlanta 30319. Private liberal arts. 1950/1975 (SACS-Comm. on Coll.). Sem. plan. Degrees: B,M. Pres. Manning M. Pattillo, Jr.
Enroll.: 874
(404) 261-1441

*Member Georgia State University System

Paine College
1235 15th St., Augusta 30910. Private (United Methodist and Christian Methodist Episcopal) liberal arts. 1944/1981 (SACS-Comm. on Coll.). Sem. plan. Degrees: B. Pres. William H. Harris.
Enroll.: 667
(404) 722-4471

Phillips College
745 Greenee St., Augusta 30902. Private junior business. 1973/1985 (AICS). Qtr. plan. Degrees: A, certificates, diplomas. Pres. J. L. Wasson.
Enroll.: 1,407 (*f.t.* 595 m., 812 w.)
(404) 724-7719

Phillips College
1622 13th Ave., Columbus 31901. Private junior business. 1972/1980 (AICS). Qtr. plan. Degrees: A, certificates, diplomas. Pres. Joyce Meadows.
Enroll.: 1,307 (*f.t.* 733 m., 574 w.)
(404) 327-4381

Phillips College of Atlanta
1010 W. Peachtree St., N.W., Atlanta 30309. Private business. 1973/1979 (AICS); 1979/1984 (SACS-COEI). Qtr. plan. Certificates, diplomas. Dir. Patrick D. Turner.
Enroll.: FTE 197
(404) 873-1981

Phillips College of Atlanta-Northside
1901 Montreal Rd., Suite 134, Atlanta 30084. Private business. 1979/1984 (SACS-COEI); 1985 (AICS). Qtr. plan. Certificates, diplomas. Dir. Charles H. Feistkorn.
Enroll.: FTE 71
(404) 496-5800

Pickens Area Vocational-Technical School
240 Burnt Mountain Rd., Jasper 30143. Public (state). 1971/1981 (SACS-COEI). Courses of varying lengths. Certificates. Dir. Tom Harrison.
Enroll.: FTE 341
(404) 692-3411

Piedmont College
Demoresmi30535. Private (Independent) liberal arts. 1965/1975 (SACS-Comm. on Coll.). Qtr. plan. Degrees: B. Pres. D. Garen Simmons.
Enroll.: 368
(404) 778-8301

PORTFOLIO CENTER
125 Bennett St., N.W., Atlanta 30309. Private technical. 1982 (SACS-COEI). Courset of varying lengths. Certificates. Dir. Ronald Seichrist.
Enroll.: FTE 132
(404) 892-1559

REINHARDT COLLEGE
Waleska 30183. Private (United Methodist) junior. 1953/1977 (SACS-Comm. on Coll.). Qtr. plan. Degrees: A. Pres. Floyd A. Falany.
Enroll.: 477
(404) 479-1454

RUTLEDGE COLLEGE
571 Ashby St., S.W., Atlanta 30310. Private business. 1972/1982 (AICS). Courses of varying lengths. Certificates. Dir. Jerome Evans.
Enroll.: 987 (*f.t.* 98 m., 889 w.)
(404) 753-4891

SAMVERLY COLLEGE (EXTENSION)
87 Pryor St., S.W., Atlanta 30303-4553. Private. 1985 (NATTS). Courses of varying lengths. Certificates. Dir. Beverly Purdie.
(404) 659-2645

SAVANNAH AREA VOCATIONAL-TECHNICAL SCHOOL
5717 White Bluff Rd., Savannah 31499. Public (state). 1972/1982 (SACS-COEI). Courses of varying lengths. Certificates. Dir. Billy Hair.
Enroll.: FTE 778
(912) 352-1464

SAVANNAH COLLEGE OF ART AND DESIGN
342 Bull St., Savannah 31401. Private. 1983 (SACS-Comm. on Coll.). Qtr. plan. Degrees B. Pres. Richard G. Rowan.
Enroll.: 809
(912) 236-7458

*SAVANNAH STATE COLLEGE
Savannah 31404. Public (state) liberal arts and professional. 1951/1981 (SACS-Comm. on Coll.). Qtr. plan. Degrees: A, B, M. *Prof. Accred.:* Engineering Technology (civil, electrical, mechanical), Social Work (B). Pres. Wendell G. Rayburn.
Enroll.: 2,184
(912) 356-2240

SHORTER COLLEGE
Rome 30161. Private (Southern Baptist) liberal arts. 1923/1982 (SACS-Comm. on Coll.). Sem. plan. Degrees: B. *Prof. Accred.:* Music. Pres. George L. Balentine.
Enroll.: 693
(404) 291-2121

*Member Georgia State University System

*SOUTH GEORGIA COLLEGE
Douglas 31533. Public (state) junior. 1934/1976 (SACS-Comm. on Coll.). Qtr. plan. Degrees: A. Pres. Edward D. Jackson, Jr.
Enroll.: 1,123
(912) 384-1100

SOUTH GEORGIA TECHNICAL AND VOCATIONAL SCHOOL
P.O. Box 1088, Americus 31709. Public (state). 1973/1983 (SACS-COEI). Courses of varying lengths. Certificates. Dir. Dea Pounders.
Enroll.: FTE 329
(912) 928-0283

SOUTHEASTERN CENTER FOR PHOTOGRAPHIC ARTS
1935 Cliff Valley Way, Suite 210, Atlanta 30329. Private. 1983 (SACS-COEI). Courses of varying lengths. Certificates. Dir. Neil Chaput de Saintonge.
Enroll.: FTE 17
(404) 231-5323

*SOUTHERN TECHNICAL INSTITUTE
1112 Clay St., Marietta 30060. Public (state). 1972/1977 (SACS-Comm. on Coll.). Qtr. plan. Degrees: A, B. *Prof. Accred.:* Engineering Technology (apparel, architectural, civil, electrical, industrial, mechanical, textile). Pres. Stephen R. Cheshier.
Enroll.: 3,112
(912) 356-7230

SPELMAN COLLEGE
350 Spelman Lane, S.W., Atlanta 30314. Private liberal arts for women; member of Atlanta University Center. 1932/1979 (SACS-Comm. on Coll.). Sem. plan. Degrees: B. *Prof. Accred.:* Music, Teacher Education (*e,s*). Pres. Donald M. Stewart.
Enroll.: 1,581
(404) 681-3643

SWAINSBORO AREA VOCATIONAL-TECHNICAL SCHOOL
201 Kite Rd., Swainsboro 30401. Public (state). 1973/1983 (SACS-COEI). Courses of varying lengths. Certificates. Dir. Donald Speir.
Enroll.: FTE 731
(912) 237-6465

*Member Georgia State University System

THOMAS AREA TECHNICAL SCHOOL
P.O. Box 1578, Thomasville 31799. Public (state). 1973/1983 (SACS-COEI). Courses of varying lengths. Certificates. *Prof. Accred.*: Radiography, Respiratory Therapy Technology. Dir. Charles R. DeMott.
Enroll.: FTE 723
(912) 228-2389

THOMAS COLLEGE
1501 Millpond Rd., Thomasville 31792. Private 2-year. 1984 (SACS-Comm. on Coll.). Qtr. plan. Degrees: A. Pres. H. Douglas Meyers.
Enroll.: FTE 363
(912) 226-1621

TIFT COLLEGE OF MERCER UNIVERSITY
Forsyth 31029. Private (Southern Baptist) liberal arts primarily for women. 1946/1982 (SACS-Comm. on Coll.). Qtr. plan. Degrees: B. Pres. O. Suthern Sims, Jr.
Enroll.: 468
(912) 994-1916

TOCCOA FALLS COLLEGE
Toccoa Falls 30598. Private (Christian and Missionary Alliance) professional. 1957/1977 (AABC); 1983 (SACS-Comm. on Coll.). Sem. plan. Degrees: A,B. Pres. Paul L. Alford.
Enroll.: 575
(404) 886-6831

TOTAL TECHNICAL INSTITUTE (EXTENSION)
6185-C Jimmy Carter Blvd., Norcross 30071. Private. 1984 (NATTS). Courses of varying lengths. Certificates. Dir. George Klein.
(404) 449-9012

TROUP COUNTY AREA VOCATIONAL-TECHNICAL SCHOOL
Fort Dr., LaGrange 30240. Public (state). 1973/1983 (SACS-COEI). Courses of varying lengths. Certificates. *Prof. Accred.*: Radiography. Dir. Roger Slater.
Enroll.: FTE 250
(404) 882-3273

TRUETT MCCONNELL COLLEGE
Cleveland 30528. Private (Southern Baptist) junior. 1966/1980 (SACS-Comm. on Coll.). Qtr. plan. Degrees: A. *Prof. Accred.*: Music. Pres. Ronald Weitman.
Enroll.: 695
(800) 342-8857

TURNER JOB CORPS CENTER
1601 Elmer Darosa Ave., Albany 31708. Public (district). 1984 (SACS-COEI). Courses of varying lengths. Certificates. Dir. Lonnie L. Hall.
Enroll.: FTE 1,442

U.S. ARMY INFANTRY SCHOOL
Fort Benning ATSH-SE-TSD 31905. Public (federal) technical 1975/1985 (SACS-COEI). Courses of varying lengths. Certificates. Commandant L.T.C. P. Burney.
Enroll.: FTE 7,390
(404) 545-1008

U.S. ARMY SIGNAL CENTER AND SCHOOL
Fort Gordon 30905. Public (federal) technical. 1976/1981 (SACS-COEI). Courses of varying lengths. Certificates. Commandant Maj. Gen. T. D. Rodgers.
Enroll.: FTE 8,778
(404) 791-7795

*UNIVERSITY OF GEORGIA
Athens 30602. Public (state). 1909/1981 (SACS-Comm. on Coll.). Qtr. plan. Degrees: A,B,P,M,D. *Prof. Accred.*: Art, Business (B,M), Engineering (agricultural), Forestry, Home Economics, Interior Design, Journalism, Landscape Architecture (B), Law, Music, Pharmacy, Psychology, Rehabilitation Counseling, Social Work (B,M), Speech Pathology, Teacher Education (*e,s,p*), Veterinary Medicine. Pres. Henry King Stanford.
Enroll.: 25,005
(404) 542-3030

UPSON COUNTY AREA VOCATIONAL-TECHNICAL SCHOOL
P. O. Box 1089, Thomaston 30286. Public (state). 1973/1983 (SACS-COEI). Courses of varying lengths. Certificates. Dir. Leon Barnes.
Enroll.: FTE 219
(404) 647-9616

VALDOSTA AREA VOCATIONAL-TECHNICAL SCHOOL
Rte. 1, Box 202, Val-Tech Rd., Valdosta 31602. Public (state). 1974/1984 (SACS-COEI). Courses of varying lengths. Certificates. *Prof. Accred.*: Medical Laboratory Technology, Radiography. Dir. James Bridges.
Enroll.: FTE 480
(912) 247-3335

*VALDOSTA STATE COLLEGE
Valdosta 31698. Public liberal arts and teachers. 1929/1980 (SACS-Comm. on Coll.). Qtr. plan. Degrees: A,B,M. *Prof. Accred.*: Busi-

*Member Georgia State University System

ness (B), Music, Nursing (B), Teacher Education (*e,s*). Pres. Hugh C. Bailey.
Enroll.: 5,592
(912) 333-5800

WALKER COUNTY AREA VOCATIONAL-TECHNICAL SCHOOL
Rt. 2, Box 185, Rock Spring 30739. Public (state). 1972/1982 (SACS-COEI). Courses of varying lengths. Certificates. Dir. Edward R. Bickrey.
Enroll.: FTE 635
(404) 764-1016

*WAYCROSS JUNIOR COLLEGE
2001 Francis St., Waycross 31501. Public (state). 1978/1983 (SACS-Comm. on Coll.). Qtr. plan. Degrees: A. Pres. James M. Dye.
Enroll.: 369
(912) 284-6130

WAYCROSS-WARE COUNTY AREA VOCATIONAL-TECHNICAL SCHOOL
1701 Carswell Ave., Waycross 31501. Public (state). 1972/1982 (SACS-COEI). Courses of varying lengths. Certificates. *Prof. Accred.:* Medical Laboratory Technology, Radiography. Dir. Joseph R. Miller.
Enroll.: FTE 400
(912) 283-2002

*Member Georgia State University System

BRANCH CAMPUS
Wayne Memorial Hospital, Jesup 31545.

WESLEYAN COLLEGE
4760 Forsyth Rd., Macon 31297. Private (United Methodist) liberal arts for women. 1919/1984 (SACS-Comm. on Coll.). 4-1-4 plan. Degrees: B. *Prof. Accred.:* Music, Teacher Education (*e,s*). Pres. Robert K. Ackerman.
Enroll.: 342
(912) 477-1110

*WEST GEORGIA COLLEGE
Carollton 30118. Public (state) liberal arts and professional. 1963/1983 (SACS-Comm. on Coll.). Qtr. plan. Degrees: A,B,M. *Prof. Accred.:* Business (B), Music, Nursing (A), Teacher Education (*e,s,p*). Pres. Maurice K. Townsend.
Enroll.: 5,944
(404) 834-1311

YOUNG HARRIS COLLEGE
Young Harris 30582. Private (United Methodist) junior. 1938/1981 (SACS-Comm. on Coll.). Qtr. plan. Degrees: A. Pres. D. Ray Farley.
Enroll.: 378
(404) 379-3112

*Member Georgia State University System

GUAM

GUAM COMMUNITY COLLEGE
P.O. Box 23069, Guam Main Facility, Guam, M.I. 96921. Public (territorial) junior. 1979/1984 (WASC-Jr.). Sem. plan. Degrees: A. Prov. Peter R. Nelson.
Enroll.: 1,832
(671) 734-4311

INTERNATIONAL BUSINESS COLLEGE OF GUAM
P.O. Box 3783, Agana 96910. Private. 1978/1986 (AICS). Qtr. plan. Certificates, diplomas. Dir. Dennis M. Wible.
Enroll.: 615 (*f.t.* 171 m., 444 w.)
(671) 646-6901

†UNIVERSITY OF GUAM
UOG Station, Mangilao 96913. Public (territorial) liberal arts and professional. 1963/1978 (WASC-Sr.). Sem. plan. Degrees: A,B,M. Pres. Jose Q. Cruz.
Enroll.: FTE 2,140
011-671-734-2177

†Accreditation on Probation

HAWAII

BRIGHAM YOUNG UNIVERSITY—HAWAII CAMPUS
(Formerly Church College of Hawaii) Laie, Oahu 96762. Independent (Church of Jesus Christ of Latter-day Saints) liberal arts and occupational. 1959/1981 (WASC-Sr.). Sem. plan. Degrees: A,B. *Prof. Accred.:* Social Work (B). Pres. Alton L. Wade.
Enroll.: FTE 1,826
(808) 293-3700

CANNON'S INTERNATIONAL BUSINESS COLLEGE
1500 Kapiolani Blvd., Honolulu 96814. Private; recognized candidate for junior college. 1954/1986 (AICS). Qtr. plan. Diplomas. Pres. Evelyn A. Schemmel.
Enroll.: 1,638 (*f.t.* 359 m., 1,279 w.)
(808) 955-1500

CHAMINADE UNIVERSITY OF HONOLULU
3140 Waialae Ave., Honolulu 96816. Independent (Roman Catholic) liberal arts and professional. 1960/1981 (WASC-Sr.). Sem. plan. Degrees: A,B,M. Pres. Rev. Raymond A. Roesch, S.M.
Enroll.: FTE 1,538
(808) 735-4711

HAWAII BUSINESS COLLEGE
111 N. King St., Honolulu 96817. Private. 1976/1983 (AICS). Courses of varying lengths. Certificates. Pres. Mitsuru Omori.
Enroll.: 657 (*f.t.* 113 m., 544 w.)
(808) 524-4014

HAWAII COMMUNITY COLLEGE
(*See* University of Hawaii at Hilo)

HAWAII INSTITUTE OF HAIR DESIGN
1124 Fort St. Mall, Suite 201, Honolulu 96813. Private. 1978/1985 (NATTS). Courses of varying lengths. Certificates, diplomas. Pres. Leo Williams.
Enroll.: 85 (*f.t.* 14 m., 70 w.)
(808) 533-6496

†HAWAII LOA COLLEGE
45-045 Kamehameha Hwy., Kaneohe, Oahu 96744. Independent (Episcopal, United Church of Christ, United Methodist, United Presbyterian) liberal arts. 1971/1982 (WASC-Sr.). 4-4-4 plan. Degrees: B. Pres. Marvin J. Anderson.
Enroll.: FTE 387
(808) 235-3641

HAWAII PACIFIC COLLEGE
1166 Fort St., Honolulu 96813. Independent liberal arts and business. 1973/1983 (WASC-Sr.). Sem. plan. Degrees: A,B. Pres. Chatt G. Wright.
Enroll.: FTE 2,618
(808) 544-0200

*HONOLULU COMMUNITY COLLEGE
874 Dillingham Blvd., Honolulu 96817. Public (state) junior. 1970/1985 (WASC-Jr.). Sem. plan. Degrees: A. Prov. Peter R. Kessinger.
Enroll.: 4,535
(808) 845-9225

KANSAI GAIDAI HAWAII COLLEGE
5257 Kalanianaole Hwy., Honolulu 96821. Private 2-year. 1985 (WASC-Jr.). Qtr. plan. Diplomas. Prov. Andrew Dykstra.
Enroll.: 81
(808) 377-5402

*KAPIOLANI COMMUNITY COLLEGE
620 Pensacola St., Honolulu 96814. Public (state) junior. 1970/1985 (WASC-Jr.). Sem. plan. Degrees: A. *Prof. Accred.:* Dental Assisting, Medical Assisting, Medical Laboratory Technology, Radiography, Respiratory Therapy, Respiratory Therapy Techonolgy. Prov. John E. Morton.
Enroll.: 3,234
(808) 531-4654

*KAUAI COMMUNITY COLLEGE
3-1901 Kaumualii Hwy., Lihue, Kauai 96766. Public (state) junior. 1971/1984 (WASC-Jr.). Sem. plan. Degrees: A. *Prof. Accred.:* Nursing (A). Prov. David Iha.
Enroll.: 1,159
(808) 245-8311

*LEEWARD COMMUNITY COLLEGE
96-045 Ala Ike, Pearl City 96782. Public (state) junior. 1971/1984 (WASC-Jr.). Sem. plan. Degrees: A. Prov. Melvyn K. Sakaguchi.
Enroll.: 5,645
(808) 455-0011

*MAUI COMMUNITY COLLEGE
310 Kaahumanu Ave., Kahului 96732. Public (state) junior. 1970/1985 (WASC-Jr.). Sem. plan. Degrees: A. Prov. Alma K. Henderson.

†Accreditation on Probation through June 1988

*Member of the University of Hawaii system

Enroll.: 2,055
(808) 244-9181

MED-ASSIST SCHOOL OF HAWAII, INC.
1164 Bishop St., Suite 612, Honolulu 96813. Private. 1978/1983 (ABHES). 25-week courses, plus externship. Diplomas. *Prof. Accred.:* Medical Assisting. Pres. J. Gary Hawthorne.
Enroll.: 42
(808) 524-3363

UNIVERSITY OF HAWAII
2444 Dole St., Honolulu 96822. Central administration for University of Hawaii System. Public liberal arts and professional. Pres. Albert J. Simone.
(808) 948-8207

*UNIVERSITY OF HAWAII AT HILO
1400 Kapiolani St., Hilo 96720. Public (state); accreditation includes Hawaii Community College, College of Arts and Crafts, and College of Agriculture. 1976/1984 (WASC-Sr.). Sem. plan. Degrees: A,B. Chanc. Edward J. Kormondy.
Enroll.: FTE 2,578
(808) 961-9311

*UNIVERSITY OF HAWAII AT MANOA
2500 Campus Rd., Honolulu 96822. Public (state). 1952/1985 WASC-Sr.). Sem. plan. Degrees: A,B,P,M,D. *Prof. Accred.:* Architecture (B,M), Business (B,M), Dental Hygiene, Dietetics, Engineering (civil, electrical, mechanical, ocean), Journalism, Law (ABA only), Librarianship, Medical Technology, Medicine, Music, Nursing (A,B,M), Psychology, Public Health, Rehabilitation Counseling, Social Work (B,M). Chanc. Albert J. Simone.
Enroll.: 15,250
(808) 948 -8111

*Member of the University of Hawaii system

UNIVERSITY OF HAWAII COMMUNITY COLLEGES
2327 Dole St., Honolulu 96822. Central administration for six community colleges and the Employment Training Office. Public liberal arts and vocational. Chanc. Joyce S. Tsunoda.
(808) 948-7313

*WEST OAHU COLLEGE
96-043 Ala Ike, Pearl City 96782. Public (state) liberal arts; upper division only. 1981 (WASC-Sr.). Sem. plan. Degrees: B. Chanc. Edward J. Kormondy.
Enroll.: FTE 245
(808) 456-5921

*WINDWARD COMMUNITY COLLEGE
45-720 Keaahala Rd., Kaneohe 96744. Public (state) junior. 1977/1985 (WASC-Jr.). Sem. plan. Degrees: A. Prov. Peter T. Dyer.
Enroll.: 1,540
(808) 235-0077

*Member of the University of Hawaii system

IDAHO

AERO TECHNICIANS
P.O. Box 7, Rexburg-Madison Co. Airport, Rexburg 83440-0007. Private. 1975/1980 (NATTS). Sem. plan. Certificates, diplomas. Pres. Eldon C. Hart.
Enroll.: 75 (*f.t.* 35 m., 10 w.)
(208) 356-4446

AMERICAN INSTITUTE OF MEDICAL -DENTAL TECHNOLOGY
Emerald Professional Park, 6152 Emerald, Boise 83704. Private. 1982 (ABHES). 28-week program. Diplomas. *Prof. Accred.:* Medical Assisting. Dir. J. L. Groothius.
Enroll.: 53
(208) 377-8080

BOISE STATE UNIVERSITY
Boise 83725. Public liberal arts and teachers. 1941/1984 (NASC). Sem. plan. Degrees: A,B,M. *Prof. Accred.:* Business (B,M), Dental Assisting, Medical Record Technology, Music, Nursing (A,B), Radiography, Respiratory Therapy, Social Work (B), Teacher Education (*e,s*). Pres. John H. Keiser.
Enroll.: 10,401
(208) 385-1202

COLLEGE OF IDAHO
Caldwell 83605. Private (United Presbyterian) liberal arts. 1922/1982 (NASC). 4-1-4 plan. Degrees: B,M. Pres. Arthur H. DeRosier, Jr.
Enroll.: 905
(208) 459-5011

COLLEGE OF SOUTHERN IDAHO
P.O. Box 1238, Twin Falls 83303-1238. Public (district) junior. 1968/1984 (NASC). Sem. plan. Degrees: A. *Prof. Accred.:* Nursing (A). Pres. Gerald R. Meyerhoeffer.
Enroll.: 1,946
(208) 733-9554

EASTERN IDAHO VOCATIONAL-TECHNICAL SCHOOL
2299 E. 17th St., Idaho Falls 83401. Public (district) 2-year. 1982 (NASC). Modified qtr. plan. Certificates. *Prof Accred.:* Dental Assisting, Dental Laboratory Technology. Pres. John E. Christofferson.
Enroll.: 319
(208) 524-3000

IDAHO STATE UNIVERSITY
Pocatello 83209-0009. Public. 1923/1984 (NASC). Sem. plan. Degrees: A,B,M,D. *Prof. Accred.:* Business (B,M), Construction Education, Dental Hygiene, Engineering (general), Music, Nursing (B,M), Pharmacy, Radiography, Social Work (B), Speech Pathology and Audiology, Teacher Education (*e,s,p*). Pres. Richard Bowen.
Enroll.: 7,031
(208) 236-0211

LEWIS-CLARK STATE COLLEGE
Lewiston 83501. Public (state) 4-year liberal arts and teachers college. 1964/1978 (NASC). Sem. plan. Degrees: A,B. *Prof. Accred.:* Nursing (A), Teacher Education (*e,s*). Pres. Lee A. Vickers.
Enroll.: 2,018
(208) 799-2216

LINK'S SCHOOL OF BUSINESS
970 Lusk St., Boise 83706. Private. 1985 (NATTS). Qtr. plan. Diplomas. Dir. Burton L. Waite.
Enroll.: 973 (*f.t.* 382 m., 591 w.)
(208) 344-8376

NORTH IDAHO COLLEGE
Coeur d'Alene 83814. Public (district) junior. 1947/1983 (NASC). Sem. plan. Degrees: A. *Prof. Accred.:* Nursing (A). Pres. Barry Schuler.
Enroll.: 2,235
(208) 769-3301

NORTHWEST NAZARENE COLLEGE
Nampa 83651. Private (Nazarene) liberal arts. 1930/1977 (NASC) Qtr. plan. Degrees: A,B,M. *Prof. Accred.:* Music, Social Work (B), Teacher Education (*e,s*). Pres. Gordon Wetmore.
Enroll.: 1,178
(208) 467-8777

RICKS COLLEGE
Rexburg 83440. Private (Latter-day Saints) junior. 1936/1979 (NASC). Sem. plan. Degrees: A. *Prof. Accred.:* Engineering Technology (design and drafting, electronics, manufacturing, welding), Music, Nursing (A). Pres. Joseph J. Christensen.
Enroll.: 6,880
(208) 356-2011

UNIVERSITY OF IDAHO
Moscow 83843. Public (state). 1918/1984 (NASC). Sem. plan. Degrees: B,P,M,D. *Prof. Accred.:* Architecture (B), Dietetics, Engineering (argicultural, chemical, civil, elec-

trical, geological, mechanical, metallurgical, mining), Forestry, Landscape Architecture (B), Law, Music, Teacher Education (*e,s,p*).
Pres. Richard D. Gibb.
Enroll.: 8,848
(208) 885-6365

ILLINOIS

Airco Technical Institute
1201 W. Adams St., Chicago 60607. Private. 1981 (NATTS). Courses of varying lengths. Certificates, diplomas. Dir. Gary McGee.
Enroll.: 100 (*f.t.* 95 m., 5 w.)
(312) 666-5590

Alfred Adler Institute
159 N. Dearborn St., Chicago 60601. Private professional and graduate only. 1978/1984 (NCA). Qtr. plan. Degrees: M. Pres. Randall Thompson.
Enroll.: FTE 30
(312) 346-3458

American Academy of Art
220 S. State St., Chicago 60604. Private. 1974/1979 (NATTS). Sem. plan. Degrees: A. Dir. I. Shapiro.
Enroll.: 735 (*f.t.* 186 m., 222 w.)
(312) 939-3883

American Conservatory of Music
Chicago 60605. Private professional. 1928/1978. Sem. plan. Degrees: B,M,D. *Prof. Accred.:* Music. Pres. Leo E. Heim.
Enroll.: 339 (*f.t.* 98 m., 59 w.)
(312) 263-4161

American Institute of Occupational Trades
2323 N. Pulaski Rd., Chicago 60639. Private. 1980 (NATTS). Courses of varying lengths. Diplomas. Dir. John J. Freeman.
Enroll.: 440 (*f.t.* 150 m., 10 w.)
(312) 489-2828

American Medical Record Association
875 N. Michigan Ave., Suite 1850, Chicago 60611. Private home study. 1970/1985 (NHSC). Dir. Ind. Study Margaret Amatayakul.
(312) 787-2672

American School
850 E. 58th St., Chicago 60637. Private home study. 1956/1982 (NHSC). Pres. William Wright.
(312) 947-3300

American Vocational School
102 N. Center, Bloomington 61701. Private. 1983 (NATTS). 26-week courses. Diplomas. Pres. Freddie H. Clark.
Enroll.: 30
(309) 828-5151

Assurance Corporation Technical Institute
1924 W. Chicago Ave., Chicago 60622. Private. 1986 (AICS). 20-week program. Diplomas. Dir. Pedro A. Galva.
Enroll.: 23
(312) 278-0042

Augustana College
Rock Island 61201. Private (Lutheran in America) liberal arts. 1913/1978 (NCA). Qtr. plan. Degrees: B,M. *Prof. Accred.:* Music, Social Work (B), Teacher Education (*e,s*). Pres. Thomas Tredway.
Enroll.: 2,101
(309) 794-7208

Aurora University
Aurora 60507. Private (Advent Christian) liberal arts. 1938/1986 (NCA). Sem. plan. Degrees: B,M. *Prof. Accred.:* Nursing (B). Pres. Alan J. Stone.
Enroll.: FTE 980
(312) 892-6431

Barat College
Lake Forest 60045. Private (Roman Catholic) liberal arts. 1943/1985 (NCA). Sem. plan. Degrees: B. Pres. Richard Soter.
Enroll.: FTE 436
(312) 234-3000

Belleville Area College
Belleville 62221. Public (district) junior. 1961/1983 (NCA). Sem. plan. Degrees: A. *Prof. Accred.:* Engineering Technology (electronics), Medical Assisting, Medical Laboratory Technology (A), Medical Record Technology, Nursing (A), Radiography, Respiratory Therapy Technology. Pres. Bruce R. Wissore.
Enroll.: FTE 5,581
(618) 235-2700

Bethany Theological Seminary
Oak Brook 60521. Private (Brethren) professional; graduate only. 1971/1982 (NCA). Qtr. plan. Degrees: P,M,D. *Prof. Accred.:* Theology (1940/1981, ATS). Pres. Warren F. Groff.
Enroll.: FTE 128
(312) 620-2200

Black Hawk College
Moline 61265. Public (district) community. Sem. plan. Chanc. Richard J. Puffer.
(309) 796-1311

BLACK HAWK COLLEGE—EAST CAMPUS
Kewanee 61443. 1975/1982 (NCA). Sem. plan. Degrees: A. Pres. ———.
Enroll.: FTE 590
(309) 852-5671

BLACK HAWK COLLEGE—QUAD CITIES CAMPUS
Moline 61265. 1951/1975 (NCA). Sem. plan. Degrees: A. *Prof. Accred.:* Dental Assisting, Nursing (A), Radiography, Respiratory Therapy, Respiratory Therapy Technology. Pres. Charles Laws.
Enroll.: FTE 2,893
(309) 796-1311

BLACKBURN COLLEGE
Carlinville 62626. Private (United Presbyterian) liberal arts. 1918/1976 (NCA). Sem. plan. Degrees: B. Pres. William F. Denman.
Enroll.: FTE 455
(217) 854-3231

BRADLEY UNIVERSITY
Peoria 61625. Private. 1913/1981 (NCA). Sem. plan. Degrees: A,B,M. *Prof. Accred.:* Accounting (Type A), Art, Business (B,M), Construction Education, Engineering (civil, electrical, industrial, mechanical), Engineering Technology (electrical, manufacturing technology—operations and mechanical design option), Music, Nursing (B), Teacher Education (*e,s,p*). Pres. Martin G. Abegg.
Enroll.: FTE 4,257
(309) 676-7611

BRYANT AND STRATTON COLLEGE
Suite 420, Merchandise Mart, Chicago 60654. Private business. 1982/1984 (AICS). Courses of varying lengths. Certificates, diplomas. Pres. Colleen Colby Kurtz.
Enroll.: 554 (*f.t.* 216 m., 338 w.)
(312) 670-0058

CARL SANDBURG COLLEGE
Galesburg 61401. Public (district) community. 1974/1980 (NCA). Qtr. plan. Degrees: A. *Prof. Accred.:* Radiography. Pres. Jack W. Fuller.
Enroll.: FTE 1,147
(309) 344-2518

CATHERINE COLLEGE
Two N. LaSalle, Mezzanine Level, Chicago 60602. Private business. 1969/1981 (AICS). Courses of varying lengths. Certificates. Pres. Richard Otto.
Enroll.: 2,233 (*f.t.* 2 m., 2231 w.)
(312) 263-7800

CATHOLIC THEOLOGICAL UNION
5401 S. Cornell, Chicago 60615. Private (Roman Catholic) professional; graduate only. 1972/1982 (NCA). Qtr. plan. Degrees: P,M. *Prof. Accred.:* Theology (1972/1981, ATS). Pres. Rev. John E. Linnan, C.S.V.
Enroll.: 290
(312) 324-8000

CENTRAL ILLINOIS BARBER AND BEAUTY COLLEGE
566 N. Water St.,P.O. Box 1304, Decatur 62523. Private. 1980 (NATTS). Courses of varying lengths. Diplomas. Dir. Richard Dean Blancett.
Enroll.: 27 (*f.t.* 16 m., 11 w.)
(217) 428-4299

CHICAGO COLLEGE OF COMMERCE
36 Wabash Ave., Chicago 60603. Private. 1968/1980 (AICS). Qtr. plan. Degrees: A. Ch. of the Board Mae S. Glassbrenner.
Enroll.: 770 (*f.t.* 38 m., 732 w.)
(312) 236-3312

CHICAGO COLLEGE OF OSTEOPATHIC MEDICINE
5200 S. Ellis Ave., Chicago 60615. Private professional. 1901/1975. Sem. plan. Degrees: P. *Prof. Accred.:* Osteopathy. Pres. Thaddeus P. Kawalek.
Enroll.: 395 (*f.t.* 304 m., 91 w.)
(312) 947-3000

CHICAGO INSTITUTE OF TECHNOLOGY
1412 W. Washington Blvd., Chicago 60607. Private. 1983 (ABHES). Courses of varying lengths. Certificates. Dir. Earle L. Ciaglia.
(312) 829-4123

CHICAGO SCHOOL OF AUTOMATIC TRANSMISSIONS
1717 S. Wabash Ave., Chicago 60616. Private. 1985 (NATTS). Courses of varying lengths. Certificates. Dir. Herman L. James, Sr.

CHICAGO SCHOOL OF PROFESSIONAL PSYCHOLOGY
410 S. Michigan Ave., Chicago 60605. Private. 1984 (NCA). Sem. plan. Degrees: P. Pres. Jeffrey C. Grip.
Enroll.: FTE 78
(312) 786-9443

CHICAGO STATE UNIVERSITY
Chicago 60628. Public liberal arts and teachers. 1941/1983 (NCA). Tri. plan. Degrees: B,M. *Prof. Accred.:* Dietetics, Medical Re-

cord Administration, Nursing (B), Occupational Therapy, Radiation Therapy Technology, Teacher Education (*e,s,p*). Pres. George E. Ayers..
Enroll.: FTE 4,645
(312) 995-2400

THE CHICAGO THEOLOGICAL SEMINARY
Chicago 60637. Private (United Church of Christ) professional; graduate only. 1982 (NCA). Qtr. plan. Degrees: P,M,D. *Prof. Accred.:* Theology (1938/1981, ATS). Pres. Kenneth B. Smith.
Enroll.: FTE 151
(312) 752-5757

CHRIST SEMINARY—SEMINEX
5430 S. University Ave., Chicago 60615. Private. (Association of Evangelical Lutheran Churches) professional; graduate only. Sem. plan. Degrees: P,M,D. *Prof. Accred.:* Theology (1976/1980, ATS). Pres. John J. Tietjen.
Enroll.: 102
(312) 288-0800

CITY COLLEGES OF CHICAGO
30 E. Lake, Chicago 60601. Public (district) community colleges. Sem. plan. Degrees: A. Chanc. Salvatore G. Rotella.
(312) 781-9330

The following were formerly accredited as part of Chicago City Junior College, which was first accredited in 1941 (NCA).

CHICAGO CITY-WIDE COLLEGE
30 E. Lake, Chicago 60601. 1980/1985 (NCA). Degrees: A. *Prof. Accred.:* Radiation Therapy Technology. Pres. Mark D. Warden.
Enroll.: FTE 3,433
(312) 781-9430

HARRY S. TRUMAN COLLEGE
1145 W. Wilson Ave., Chicago 60640. 1967/1977 (NCA). Degrees: A. *Prof. Accred.:* Medical Record Technology. Pres. Wallace B. Appelson.
Enroll.: FTE 2,942
(312) 878-1700

KENNEDY-KING COLLEGE
6800 S. Wentworth Ave., Chicago 60621. 1967/1985 (NCA). Degrees: A. Pres. Ewen M. Akin, Jr.
Enroll.: FTE 3,580
(312) 962-3200

LOOP COLLEGE
30 E. Lake St., Chicago 60601. 1967/1980 (NCA). Degrees: A. *Prof. Accred.:* Dental Assisting. Pres. Bernice Miller.
Enroll.: FTE 4,492
(312) 781-9430

MALCOLM X COLLEGE
1900 W. Van Buren St., Chicago 60612. 1967/1971 (NCA). Degrees: A. *Prof. Accred.:* Radiography, Respiratory Therapy. Pres. James C. Griggs.
Enroll.: FTE 3409
(312) 738-5818

OLIVE-HARVEY COLLEGE
10001 S. Woodlawn Ave., Chicago 60628. 1967/1985 (NCA). Degrees: A. Pres. Homer D. Franklin.
Enroll.: FTE 2,678
(312) 568-3700

RICHARD J. DALEY COLLEGE
7500 S. Pulaski Rd., Chicago 60652. 1967/1985 (NCA). Degrees: A. Pres. William P. Conway.
Enroll.: FTE 3,782
(312) 735-3000

WILBUR WRIGHT COLLEGE
3400 N. Austin Ave., Chicago 60634. 1967/1971 (NCA). Degrees: A. *Prof. Accred.:* Radiography. Pres. Ernest V. Clements.
Enroll.: FTE 3,019
(312) 777-7900

COLLEGE OF AUTOMATION
209 W. Jackson Blvd., Suite 1200, Chicago 60606. Private business. 1969/1981 (AICS). Sem. plan. Degrees: A, diplomas. Pres. James S. White.
Enroll.: 922 (*f.t.* 442 m., 480 w.)
(312) 987-9575

COLLEGE OF DUPAGE
Glen Ellyn 60137. Public (district) community. 1932/1984 (NCA); accreditation includes Open College. Qtr. plan. Degrees: A. *Prof. Accred.:* Medical Record Technology, Nuclear Medicine Technology, Nursing (A), Radiography, Respiratory Therapy Technology. Pres. Harold D. McAninch.
Enroll.: FTE 11,470
(312) 858-2800

COLLEGE OF LAKE COUNTY
Grayslake 60030. Public (district) community. 1974/1982 (NCA). Sem. plan. Degrees: A. *Prof. Accred.:* Dental Assisting, Medical

Laboratory Technology (A), Medical Record Technology, Nursing (A), Radiography. Pres. ———.
Enroll.: FTE 4,387
(312) 223-6601

College of St. Francis
Joliet 60435. Private (Roman Catholic) liberal arts. 1938/1980 (NCA). Sem. plan. Degrees: B,M. *Prof. Accred.:* Social Work (B). Pres. John C. Orr.
Enroll.: FTE 1,790
(815) 740-3369

Columbia College
Chicago 60605. Private liberal arts. 1974/1981 (NCA). Sem. plan.jDegrees: B,M Pres. Mirron Alexandroff.
Enroll.: FTE 4,459
(312) 663-1600

Computer Learning Center
200 E. Ontario St., Chicago 60611. Private. 1985 (AICS). Courses of varying lengths. Diplomas. Pres. Robert Goodrich.
(312) 664-1000

Concordia College
River Forest 60305. Private (Lutheran-Missouri Synod) for training of parochial school teachers. 1950/1982 (NCA). Qtr. plan. Degrees: B,M. *Prof. Accred.:* Teacher Education (*e,s,p*). Pres. Eugene L. Krentz.
Enroll.: 1,171
(312) 771-8300

Control Data Institute
200 N. Michigan Ave., Chicago 60601. Private. 1972/1983 (NATTS). Courses of varying lengths. Certificates. Dir. R. F. Blumenstein.
Enroll.: 340 (*f.t.* 221 m., 119 w.)
(312) 454-6888

Branch
1072 Tower La., Bensenville 60106. Dir. James W. Jackson.
(312) 595-2805

Cortez W. Peters Business College
1633 W. 95th St., Chicago 60643. Private. 1982 (AICS). Courses of varying lengths. Certificates, diplomas. Pres. Frank Harris.
Enroll.: 308 (*f.t.* 32 m., 276 w.)
(312) 779-6350

Coyne-American Institute
1235 W. Fullerton Ave., Chicago 60614. Private. 1965/1980 (NATTS). Qtr. plan. Diplomas. Dir. John J. Freeman.
Enroll.: 800 (*f.t.* 425 m., 20 w.)
(312) 935-2520

Danville Area Community College
Danville 61832. Public (district) community. 1967/1982 (NCA). Sem. plan. Degrees: A. Pres. Ronald K. Lingle.
Enroll.: FTE 1,972
(217) 443-1811

DeLourdes College
353 N. River Rd., Des Plaines 60016. Private (Roman Catholic) liberal arts. 1982/1985 (NCA). Sem. plan. Degrees: B. Pres./Dean Sister Mary Canisia.
Enroll.: 64
(312) 298-6942

DePaul University
25 E. Jackson Blvd., Chicago 60604. Private (Roman Catholic) liberal arts and professional; accreditation includes Goodman School of Drama. 1925/1977 (NCA). Qtr. plan. (sem. plan in law school). Degrees: B,P,M,D. *Prof. Accred.:* Accounting (Type A,B,C), Business (B,M), Law, Music, Nursing (B,M), Psychology, Radiography, Teacher Education (*e,s,p*). Pres. Rev. John T. Richardson, C.M.
Enroll.: FTE 8,948
(312) 341-8850

DeVry, Inc., A Bell and Howell Company
2201 W. Howard St., Evanston 60202. Private technical. 1981/1984 (NCA). Accreditation includes DeVry Institute of Technology, Phoenix, AZ; Atlanta, GA; Chicago, IL; Woodbridge, NJ; and Irving, TX. Tri. plan. Degrees: A,B. Pres. Philip A. Clement.
Enroll.: FTE 23,572
(312) 328-8100

DeVry Institute of Technology
3300 N. Campbell, Chicago 60618. Private. 1967/1982 (NATTS); 1981 (NCA). Tri. plan. Degrees: A,B,M, certificates, diplomas. *Prof. Accred.:* Engineering Technology (electronics). Pres. E. Arthur Stunard.
Enroll.: 4,837 (*f.t.* 3,214 m., 578 w.)
(312) 929-8500

DeVry Institute of Technology
2000 S. Finley Rd., Lombard 60148. Private. 1982 (NCA); 1984 (NATTS, Extension of Chicago). Tri. plan. Degrees: A,B, certificates, diplomas. Pres. Thomas F. Davisson
Enroll.: 3,130
(312) 953-1300

Dr. William M. Scholl College of Podiatric Medicine
1001 N. Dearborn St., Chicago 60610. Private professional. 1985 (NCA). Sem. plan. Degrees: P. *Prof. Accred.:* Podiatry. Pres. George B. Geppner.
Enroll.: 503
(312) 664-3301

DuPage Horticultural School
1017 W. Roosevelt Rd., P.O. Box 342, West Chicago 60185. Private. 1979 (NATTS). Courses of varying lengths. Certificates. Dir. Mike Richardson.
Enroll.: 29 (*f.t.* 19 m., 10 w.)
(312) 231-3414

East-West University
816 S. Michigan Ave., Chicago 60605. Private technical. 1983 (NCA). Qtr. plan. Degrees: A,B. Chanc. M. Wasi Khan.
Enroll.: FTE 454
(312) 939-0111

Eastern Illinois University
Charleston 61920. Public (state). 1915/1985 (NCA). Sem. plan. Degrees: B,M. *Prof. Accred.:* Home Economics, Music, Speech Pathology, Teacher Education (*e,s,p*). Pres. Stanley G. Rives.
Enroll.: FTE 9,748
(217) 581-2011

Elgin Community College
Elgin 60120. Public (district). 1968/1979 (NCA). Sem. plan. Degrees: A. *Prof. Accred.:* Dental Assisting, Nursing (A). Pres. Searle Charles.
Enroll.: FTE 2,588
(312) 697-1000

Elmhurst College
Elmhurst 60126. Private (United Church of Christ) liberal arts. 1924/1979 (NCA). 4-1-4 plan. Degrees: B. *Prof. Accred.:* Nursing (B), Teacher Education (*e,s*). Pres. Ivan E. Frick.
Enroll.: FTE 2,468
(312) 279-4100

The English Language Institute of America
332 S. Michigan Ave., Suite 963, Chicago 60604. Private home study. 1981 (NHSC). Vice Pres. Graham Dunbar.
(312) 663-0880

Eureka College
Eureka 61530. Private (Disciples of Christ) liberal arts. 1924/1985 (NCA). Year of four 8-week terms. Degrees: B. Pres. George A. Hearne.
Enroll.: FTE 445
(309) 467-3721

Felician College
Chicago 60659. Private (Roman Catholic) 2-year liberal arts for women. 1977/1982 (NCA). 4-1-4 plan. Degrees: A. Pres. Sister Mary Bonita Willow.
Enroll.: FTE 201
(312) 539-1919

First Business School
500 Davis St., Evanston 60201. Private. 1982/1985 (AICS). Qtr. plan. Certificates, diplomas. Vice Pres. Eileen L. O'Gara.
Enroll.: 162 (*f.t.* 19 m., 143 w.)
(312) 492-1898

Branch Campus
111 Green Bay Rd., Wilmette 60091. Dir. Marjory Margraf.
(312) 256-0375

Forest Institute of Professional Psychology
1717 Rand Rd., Des Plaines 60016. Private. 1983 (NCA). Tri. plan. Degrees: B,M,D. Pres. Robert V. Moriarty.
Enroll.: 185
(312) 635-4175

Garrett-Evangelical Theological Seminary
Evanston 60201. Private (United Methodist) professional; graduate only. 1972/1978 (NCA). Qtr. plan. Degrees: P,M,D. *Prof. Accred.:* Theology
(1938/1978, ATS). Pres. Neal F. Fisher.
Enroll.: 332
(312) 866-3900

Gem City College
700 State St., Quincy 62301; mailing address P.O. Box 179, Quincy 62306. Private business and technical. 1954/1982 (AICS); 1969/1974 (NATTS). Courses of varying lengths. Degrees: A, certificates, diplomas. *Prof. Accred.:* Medical Assisting. Pres. Floyd W. Marshall.
Enroll.: 1,418 (*f.t.* 194 m., 1,224 w.)
(217) 222-0391

Governors State University
University Park 60466. Public liberal arts; upper division and graduate only. 1975/1984 (NCA). Tri. plan. Degrees: B,M. *Prof. Accred.:* Health Services Administration, Med-

ical Technology, Nursing (B). Pres. Leo Goodman-Malamuth, II.
Enroll.: FTE 2,258
(312) 534-5000

GREENVILLE COLLEGE
Greenville 62246. Private (Free Methodist) liberal arts. 1948/1986 (NCA). 4-1-4 plan. Degrees: B. *Prof. Accred.:* Teacher Education (*e,s*). Pres. W. Richard Stephens.
Enroll.: FTE 585
(618) 664-1840

THE HADLEY SCHOOL FOR THE BLIND
700 Elm St., Winnetka 60093. Private home study. 1958/1985 (NHSC). Pres. Robert Winn.
(312) 446-8111

THE HARRINGTON INSTITUTE OF INTERIOR DESIGN
410 S. Michigan Ave., Chicago 60605. Private. 1978. 3-year program. Degrees: A. *Prof. Accred.:* Interior Design. Dean Robert C. Marks.
Enroll.: 372 (*f.t.* 39 m., 163 w.)
(312) 939-4975

HIGHLAND COMMUNITY COLLEGE
Freeport 61032. Public (district). 1973/1981 (NCA). Sem. plan. Degrees: A. Pres. Joseph Piland.
Enroll.: FTE 1,291
(815) 235-6121

ITT TECHNICAL INSTITUTE
5150 W. Roosevelt Rd., Chicago 60650. Private. 1967/1972 (NATTS). Courses of varying lengths. Diplomas. Dir. William N. Griffin.
Enroll.: 400
(312) 779-6350

ILLINOIS BENEDICTINE COLLEGE
Lisle 60532. Private (Roman Catholic) liberal arts. 1958/1986 (NCA). Sem. plan. Degrees: B,M. *Prof. Accred.:* Nursing (B). Pres. Richard C. Becker.
Enroll.: 1,323
(312) 960-1500

ILLINOIS CENTRAL COLLEGE
East Peoria 61635. Public (district) community. 1972/1982 (NCA). Sem. plan. Degrees: A. *Prof. Accred.:* Dental Assisting, Dental Hygiene, Medical Laboratory Technology (A), Medical Record Technology, Music, Nursing (A), Practical Nursing, Radiography, Surgical Technology. Pres. Leon H. Perley.
Enroll.: FTE 5,989
(309) 694-5431

ILLINOIS COLLEGE
Jacksonville 62650. Private (United Presbyterian and United Church of Christ) liberal arts. 1913/1985 (NCA). Sem. plan. Degrees: B. Pres. Donald C. Mundinger.
Enroll.: FTE 749
(217) 245-7126

ILLINOIS COLLEGE OF OPTOMETRY
3241 S. Michigan Ave., Chicago 60616. Private professional. 1969/1980 (NCA). Qtr. plan. Degrees: B,P. *Prof. Accred.:* Optometry. Pres. Boyd B. Banwell.
Enroll.: FTE 539
(312) 225-1700

ILLINOIS EASTERN COMMUNITY COLLEGES
Olney 62450. Public (district): accreditation includes Frontier Community College, Fairfield 62837; Lincoln Trail College, Robinson 62454; Olney Central College, Olney 62450; Wabash Valley College, Mount Carmel 62863. 1974/1984 (NCA). Qtr. plan. Degrees: A. *Prof. Accred.:* Dental Assisting, Nursing (A). Chanc. Harry V. Smith, Jr.
Enroll.: FTE 4,591
(618) 393-2982

ILLINOIS INSTITUTE OF TECHNOLOGY
3300 S. Federal St., Chicago 60616. Private university. 1941/1977 (NCA). Sem. plan. Degrees: B,M,D. *Prof. Accred.:* Architecture (B), Art, Engineering (chemical, civil, electrical, mechanical, metallurgical), Law, Psychology, Rehabilitation Counseling. Pres. Thomas L. Martin, Jr.
Enroll.: FTE 4,538
(312) 567-3001

ILLINOIS MEDICAL TRAINING CENTER
162 N. State St., Chicago 60601. Private. 1979 (NATTS). Courses of varying lengths. Diplomas. *Prof. Accred.:* Medical Assisting. Dir. John R. Gibson.
Enroll.: 404 (*f.t.* 84 m., 320 w.)
(312) 782-2061

ILLINOIS SCHOOL OF COMMERCE
17 N. State St., Chicago 60602. Private. 1981 (AICS). Qtr. plan. Certificates, diplomas. Pres. Thomas S. Ross.
Enroll.: 1,705 (*f.t.* 492 m., 1,213 w.)
(312) 782-9200

Illinois School of Professional Psychology
14 E. Jackson Blvd., Chicago 60604. Private. 1981/1984 (NCA). Sem. plan. Degrees: D. *Prof. Accred.:*Psychology. Pres. James D. McHolland.
Enroll.: FTE 195
(312) 341-1198

*Illinois State University
Normal 61761. Public. 1913/1985 (NCA). Sem. plan. Degrees: B,M,D. *Prof. Accred.:* Art, Business (B,M), Home Economics, Medical Record Administration, Music, Social Work (B), Speech Pathology and Audiology, Teacher Education (*e,s,p*). Pres. Lloyd J. Watkins.
Enroll.: FTE 18,873
(309) 438-5677

Illinois Technical College
506 S. Wabash, Chicago 60605. Private. 1969/1979 (NATTS); 1985 (NCA). Sem. plan. Degrees: A, certificates, diplomas. Pres. Harold M. Rabin.
Enroll.: FTE 369
(312) 922-9000

Illinois Valley Community College
Oglesby 61348. Public (district). 1929/1978 (NCA). Sem. plan.jDegrees: A. *Prof. Accred.:* Dental Assisting, Nursing (A). Pres. Alfred Wisgoski.
Enroll.: FTE 2,171
(815) 224-2720

Illinois Wesleyan University
P.O. Box 2900, Bloomington 61701. Private (United Methodist). 1916/1973 (NCA). Sem. plan. Degrees: B,M. *Prof. Accred.:* Music, Nursing (B), Teacher Education (*e*). Pres. Wayne W. Anderson.
Enroll.: FTE 1,568
(309) 556-3151

International Academy of Merchandising and Design
350 N. Orleans, Chicago 60654. Private. 1981 (AICS). Qtr. plan. Degrees: A, diplomas. Pres. Clem Stein, Jr.
Enroll.: 794 (*f.t.* 61 m., 733 w.)
(312) 828-0202

Branch Campus
211 Mariner Sq. Park, 200 S. Hooder Blvd., Tampa, FL 33609. Dir. Michael Santoro.
(813) 875-8585

*Member Regency Universities System

Branch Campus
9001 State Line Rd., Kansas City, MO 64114. Dir. Charles F. Higgins.
(816) 363-3456

Jacksonville Business and Careers Institute
1429 S. Main St., P.O. Box 786, Jacksonville 62650. Private. 1981 (AICS). Qtr. plan. Certificates, diplomas. Pres. Floyd E. Becker.
Enroll.: 300 (*f.t.* 33 m., 267 w.)
(217) 243-7421

Branch Campus
300 S. Grand, Suite 241, St. Louis, MO 63103. Dir. Patricia Stringer.
(314) 531-2025

John A. Logan College
Carterville 62918. Public (district) community. 1972/1977 (NCA). Sem. plan. Degrees: A. *Prof. Accred.:* Dental Assisting, Nursing (A). Pres. Harold R. O'Neil.
Enroll.: FTE 1,977
(618) 985-3741

John Marshall Law School
Chicago 60604. Private professional. 1951 (ABA); 1979 (AALS). Sem. plan. Degrees: P,M. *Prof. Accred.:* Law. Dean Leonard J. Schrager.
Enroll.: 1,651 (*f.t.* 656 m., 250 w.)
(312) 427-2737

John Wood Community College
Quincy 62301. Public (district) junior. 1980/1986 (NCA). Sem. plan. Degrees: A. Pres. Paul R. Heath.
Enroll.: FTE 1,412
(217) 224-6500

Joliet Junior College
Joliet 60436. Public (district) community. 1917/1984 (NCA). Sem. plan. Degrees: A. *Prof. Accred.:* Nursing (A). Pres. Raymond A. Pietak.
Enroll.: FTE 4,897
(815) 729-9020

Judson College
Elgin 60120. Private (Baptist) liberal arts. 1973/1978 (NCA). Tri. plan. Degrees: B. Pres. Harm A. Weber.
Enroll.: FTE 442
(312) 695-2500

Kankakee Community College
Kankakee 60901. Public (district). 1974/1984 (NCA). 4-1-4 plan. Degrees: A. *Prof. Accred.:* Medical Laboratory Technology, Ra-

Illinois

diography, Respiratory Therapy Technology. Pres. Lilburn H. Horton, Jr.
Enroll.: FTE 1,674
(815) 933-0211

KASKASKIA COLLEGE
Centralia 62801. Public (district) community. 1964/1981 (NCA). Sem. plan. Degrees: A. *Prof. Accred.:* Dental Assisting, Nursing (A), Radiography. Pres. Bruce G. Stahl.
Enroll.: FTE 1,735
(618) 532-4646

KELLER GRADUATE SCHOOL OF MANAGEMENT
Chicago 60606. Private professional. 1977/1986 (NCA). Qtr. plan. Degrees: M. Chairman and CEO Dennis J. Keller.
Enroll.: FTE 643
(312) 454-0880

KENDALL COLLEGE
Evanston 60201. Private (United Methodist) liberal arts. 1962/1983 (NCA). 4-1-4 plan. Degrees: A,B. Pres. Andrew N. Cothran.
Enroll.: FTE 234
(*f.t.* (312) 866-1300

KISHWAUKEE COLLEGE
Malta 60150. Public (district) community. 1974/1979 (NCA). Sem. plan. Degrees: A. *Prof. Accred.:* Radiography. Pres. Norman L. Jenkins.
Enroll.: FTE 1,546
(815)825-2086

KNOX COLLEGE
Galesburg 61401. Private liberal arts. 1913/1979 (NCA). 3-3-3 plan. Degrees: B. Pres. John P. McCall.
Enroll.: FTE 930
(309) 343-0112

LAKE FOREST COLLEGE
Lake Forest 60045. Private (United Presbyterian) liberal arts. 1913/1977 (NCA). Modified 3-3 plan. Degrees: B,M. *Prof. Accred.:* Pres. Eugene Hotchkiss, III.
Enroll.: FTE 1,115
(312) 234-3100

LAKE FOREST GRADUATE SCHOOL OF MANAGEMENT
Lake Forest 60045. Private graduate only. 1978/1986 (NCA). Qtr. plan. Degrees: M. Pres. Maurice F. Dunne, Jr.
Enroll.: FTE 415
(312) 234-5005

LAKE LAND COLLEGE
Mattoon 61938. Public (district) community. 1973/1978 (NCA). Qtr. plan. Degrees: A, certificates. *Prof. Accred.:* Dental Assisting, Dental Hygiene, Practical Nursing. Pres. David Schultz.
Enroll.: FTE 2,195
(217) 235-3131

LEWIS AND CLARK COMMUNITY COLLEGE
Godfrey 62035. Public (district). 1971/1986 (NCA). Sem. plan. Degrees: A. *Prof. Accred.:* Dental Assisting, Medical Laboratory Technology (A), Nursing (A). Pres. J. Neil Admire.
Enroll.: FTE 2,624
(618) 466-3411

LEWIS UNIVERSITY
Romeoville 60441. Private (Roman Catholic) liberal arts. 1963/1982 (NCA). 4-1-4 plan. Degjrees: B,P,M. *Prof. Accred.:* Nursing (B). Pres. Brother David Delahanty, F.S.C.
Enroll.: FTE 2,069
(815) 838-0500

LINCOLN CHRISTIAN COLLEGE
P.O. Box 178, Lincoln 62656. Private (Church of Christ) professional. 1954/1985 (AABC). Sem. plan. Degrees: B. Pres. Charles A. McNeely.
Enroll.: 346
(217) 732-3168

LINCOLN COLLEGE
Lincoln 62656. Private junior. 1929/1986 (NCA). 4-1-4 plan. Degrees: A. Pres. Jack D. Nutt.
Enroll.: FTE 1,025
(217) 732-3155

LINCOLN LAND COMMUNITY COLLEGE
Springfield 62708. Public (district). 1973/1983 (NCA). Sem. plan. Degrees: A. *Prof. Accred.:* Dental Assisting, Nursing (A), Radiography, Respiratory Therapy. Pres. Robert L. Poorman.
Enroll.: FTE 3,258
(217) 786-2273

LINCOLN TECHNICAL INSTITUTE
7320 W. Agatite Ave., Norridge 60656. Private. 1971/1985 (NATTS). Courses of varying lengths. Certificates, diplomas. Dir. Jack B. Wendt.
Enroll.: 258 (*f.t.* 252 m., 6 w.)
(312) 625-1535

BRANCH
8920 S. Cicero Ave., Oak Lawn 60453. Dir. Kenneth R. Ruff.
(312) 423-9000

LOYOLA UNIVERSITY OF CHICAGO
820 N. Michigan Ave., Chicago 60611. Private (Roman Catholic). 1921/1985 (NCA). Branch campuses: Niles College, Chicago Jesuit School of Theology, Erikson Institute for Early Childhood Development, Medical Center at Hines, Rome Center of Liberal Arts. Sem. plan (qtr. plan in selected programs). Degrees: B,P,M,D. *Prof. Accred.:* Business (B,M), Dental Hygiene, Dentistry, Law, Medical Technology, Medicine, Nursing (B,M), Psychology, Social Work (B,M), Teacher Education (*e,s,p*), Theology. Pres. Rev. Raymond C. Baumhart, S.J.
Enroll.: FTE 11,022
(312) 670-2820

LUTHERAN SCHOOL OF THEOLOGY AT CHICAGO
Chicago 60615. Private (Lutheran Church in America) professional; graduate only. 1982 (NCA). Qtr. plan. Degrees: P,M,D. *Prof. Accred.:* Theology (1945/1981, ATS). Pres. William E. Lesher.
Enroll.: 321
(312) 667-3500

MSTA BUSINESS COLLEGE
1307 S. Wabash Ave., Chicago 60605. Private business. 1976/1979 (AICS). Courses of varying lengths. Diplomas. Pres. James M. Graham.
Enroll.: 1,681 (*f.t.* 250 m., 1,431 w.)
(312) 922-0083

MACCORMAC JUNIOR COLLEGE
Chicago 60604. Private. 1979/1982 (NCA). Qtr. plan. Degrees: A. Pres. Gordon C. Borchardt.
Enroll.: FTE 536
(312) 922-1884

MACMURRAY COLLEGE
Jacksonville 62650. Private (United Methodist) liberal arts. 1921/1978 (NCA). 4-1-4 plan. Degrees: B. *Prof. Accred.:* Nursing (B). Pres. B. G. Stephens.
Enroll.: FTE 615
(217) 245-6151

MALLINCKRODT COLLEGE
1041 Ridge Rd., Wilmette 60091. Private (Roman Catholic) liberal arts. 1979/1982 (NCA). Sem. plan. Degrees: A. Pres. and Dean Sister M. Marcella Ripper.
Enroll.: FTE 129
(312) 256-1094

MARION ADULT EDUCATION AND CAREER TRAINING CENTER
128 S. Paulina St., Chicago 60616. Private. 1977/1981 (AICS). Qtr. plan. Degrees: A, diplomas. *Prof. Accred.:* Respiratory Therapy Technology. Pres. ———.
Enroll.: 540 (*f.t.* 151 m., 389 w.)
(312) 733-1104

MARYCREST COLLEGE, INC.
185 N. St. Joseph Ave., Kankakee 60901. Private business. 1979/1983 (AICS). Qtr. plan. Certificates, diplomas. Pres. Joseph Thiel.
Enroll.: 45
(815) 932-8724

MCCORMICK THEOLOGICAL SEMINARY
Chicago 60637. Private (Presbyterian, U.S.A.) professional; graduate only. 1982 (NCA). Qtr. plan. Degrees: P,M,D. *Prof. Accred.:* Theology. (1938/1981, ATS). Pres. David Ramage, Jr.
Enroll.: 539
(312) 241-7800

MCHENRY COUNTY COLLEGE
Crystal Lake 60014. Public (district) community. 1976/1981 (NCA). Sem. plan. Degrees: A. Acting Pres. Robert C. Bartlett.
Enroll.: FTE 1,327
(815) 455-3700

MCKENDREE COLLEGE
Lebanon 62254. Private (United Methodist) liberal arts. Accreditation includes centers at Belleville Area, Kaskaskia, Lewis and Clark, Mattoon, Olney, and Rend Lake Colleges; Scott AFB; and Kentucky Centers at Fort Knox/Elizabethtown and Louisville. 1970/1981 (NCA). 4-1-4 plan. Degrees: B. *Prof. Accred.:* Nursing (B). Pres. Gerrit J. TenBrink.
Enroll.: FTE 647
(618) 537-4481

MEADVILLE/LOMBARD THEOLOGICAL SCHOOL
Chicago 60637. Private (Unitarian Universalist) professional; graduate only. Qtr. plan. Degrees: P,M,D. *Prof. Accred.:* Theology (1940/1981, ATS). Dean Gene Reeves.
Enroll.: 36 (*f.t.* 24 m., 10 w.)
(312) 753-3195

Mennonite College of Nursing
804 N. East St., Bloomington 61701. Private. 1986 (NCA). Qtr. plan. Degrees: B. Vice Pres. for Nursing Education Kathleen Hogan.
Enroll.: FTE 128
(309) 827-4664

Metropolitan Business College
2654 W. 95th St., Evergreen Park 60642. Private. 1961/1984 (AICS). Tri. plan. Degrees: A, certificates, diplomas. Pres. Kenneth A. Lorino.
Enroll.: 71 (*f.t.* 18 m., 53 w.)
(312) 424-3000

Branch Campus
700 W. 63rd St., Chicago 60621. Dir. Milton Kobus.
(312) 874-1000

Midstate College
244 S.W. Jefferson St., Peoria 61602. Private junior/Business. 1962/1980 (AICS); 1982 (NCA). Qtr. plan. Degrees: A. Pres. R. Dale Bunch.
Enroll.: FTE 429
(309) 673-6365

Midwest College of Engineering
Lombard 60148. Private professional. 1978/1984 (NCA). Qtr. plan. Degrees: B,M. Pres. Albert Budlong.
Enroll.: FTE 120
(312) 627-6850

Millikin University
Decatur 62522. Private. (United Presbyterian) liberal arts and professional college. 1914/1977 (NCA). 4-1-4 plan. Degrees: B. *Prof. Accred.:* Music, Nursing (B), Teacher Education (*e,s*). Pres. J. Roger Miller.
Enroll.: FTE 1,478
(217) 424-6211

Moler Hairstyling College
1685 N. Farnsworth Ave., Aurora 60505. Private. 1982 (NATTS). Courses of varying lengths. Certificates. Pres./Dir. Kenneth M. Edwards.
(312) 851-7505

Branch Campus
1469 N. Milwaukee Ave., Chicago 60622.
(312) 278-3830

Branch Campus
1557 N. Milwaukee Ave., Chicago 60622.
(312) 342-2933

Moler Hairstyling College
924 W. Jefferson St., Joliet 60435. Private. 1982 (NATTS). Courses of varying lengths. Certificates. Pres./Dir. Kenneth M. Edwards.
(815) 725-2225

Monmouth College
Monmouth 61462. Private (United Presbyterian) liberal arts. 1913/1978 (NCA). 3-3-3 plan. Degrees: A,B. Pres. Bruce Haywood.
Enroll.: FTE 693
(309) 457-2011

Moody Bible Institute
820 N. LaSalle St., Chicago 60610. Private (Interdenominational) professional. 1951/1982 (AABC). Sem. plan. Degrees: B. *Prof. Accred.:* Music. Pres. George Sweeting.
Enroll.: 1,330
(312) 329-4000

Moraine Valley Community College
Palos Hills 60465. Public (district). 1975/1980 (NCA). Sem. plan. Degrees: A. *Prof. Accred.:* Medical Laboratory Technology (A), Medical Record Technology, Nursing (A), Radiography, Respiratory Therapy, Respiratory Therapy Technology, Surgical Technology. Pres. Fred Gaskin.
Enroll.: FTE 6,761
(312) 974-4300

Morrison Institute of Technology
Morrison 61270. Private 2-year. 1976. Sem. plan. Degrees: A. *Prof. Accred.:* Engineering Technology (architectural and building, design and drafting, highway engineering). Pres. Richard C. Parkinson.
Enroll.: 290 (*f.t.* 250 m., 40 w.)
(815) 772-7218

Morton College
Cicero 60650. Public (district) community. 1927/1984 (NCA). Sem. plan. Degrees: A. *Prof. Accred.:* Dental Assisting. Pres. Charles P. Ferro.
Enroll.: FTE 1,513
(312) 656-8000

Mundelein College
6363 Sheridan Rd., Chicago 60660. Private (Roman Catholic) liberal arts primarily for women. 1940/1977 (NCA). 3-3 plan. Degrees: B,M. *Prof. Accred.:* Teacher Education (*e,s*). Pres. Sr. Mary Brenan Breslin.
Enroll.: FTE 826
(312) 262-8100

Music Center of the North Shore
300 Green Bay Rd., Winnetka 60093. Community professional. 1978. Courses of varying lengths. Certificates. *Prof. Accred.:* Music. Exec. Dir. Kalman Novak.
Enroll.: 1,243 (*f.t.* 0)
(312) 446-3822

NAES College
Chicago 60659. Private. 1984 (NCA). Sem. plan. Degrees: B. Pres. Faith Smith.
Enroll.: FTE 42
(312) 761-5000

National College of Chiropractic
Lombard 60148. Private professional. 1981/1986 (NCA). Tri. plan. Degrees: P. *Prof. Accred.:* Chiropractic Education. Pres. Lee E. Arnold.
Enroll.: FTE 877
(312) 629-2000

National College of Education
Evanston 60201. Private liberal arts and teachers. Accreditation includes Urban Campus at Chicago. 1946/1983 (NCA). Qtr. plan. Degrees: B,M,D. *Prof. Accred.:* Radiation Therapy Technology, Teacher Education (*e*). Pres. Orley R. Herron.
Enroll.: FTE 2,398
(312) 256-5150

National Education Center/The Bryman School
1132 Lake St., Oak Park 60301. Private. 1973/1978 (NATTS). Courses of varying lengths. Diplomas. Dir. Michael P. Sullivan.
Enroll.: 986 (*f.t.* 184 m., 902 w.)
(312) 383-9360

Extension
17 N. State St., Suite 1800, Chicago 60602. Dir. Frank S. Jordan.
(312) 368-4911

National Safety Council, Safety Training Institute
444 N. Michigan Ave., Chicago 60611. Private home study. 1962/1983 (NHSC). Mgr. Carlton D. Piepho.
(312) 527-4800

National Technical College
909 W. Montrose St., Chicago 60613. Private. 1986 (ABHES). 30-week program. Diplomas. Dir. Peter M. Friguletto.
(312) 472-1202

North Central College
Naperville 60566. Private (United Methodist) liberal arts. 1914/1980 (NCA). 3-3 plan. Degrees: B.M. *Prof. Accred.:* Music. Pres. Gael D. Swing.
Enroll.: FTE 1,426
(312) 420-3434

North Park College and Theological Seminary
5125 N. Spaulding Ave., Chicago 60625. Private (Evangelical Covenant) liberal arts and theology. 1926/1986 (NCA). 3-3 plan. Degrees: B,P,M. *Prof. Accred.:* Music, Nursing (B), Theology. Acting Pres. Patrick A. Lattore.
Enroll.: FTE 1,034
(312) 583-2700

Northeastern Illinois University
5500 N. St. Louis Ave., Chicago 60625. Public liberal arts and teachers. 1961/1980 (NCA). Tri. plan. Degrees: B,M . *Prof. Accred.:* Art, Librarianship, Music, Teacher Education (*e,s,p*). Pres. Gordon Lamb.
Enroll.: FTE 6,142
(312) 583-4050

Northeastern Technical Institute
14840 S. Dixie Hwy., P.O. Box 70, Posen 60469. Private. 1984 (NATTS). Courses of varying lengths. Diplomas. Pres. Roger Dehaven.
(312) 396-1470

Northern Baptist Theological Seminary
Lombard 60148. Private (American Baptist), professional; graduate only. 1947/1982 (NCA). Qtr. plan. Degrees: P,M,D. *Prof. Accred.:* Theology (1968/1981, ATS). Pres. William R. Myers.
Enroll.: FTE 204
(312) 620-2101

*Northern Illinois University
DeKalb 60115. Public (state). 1915/1984 (NCA). Sem. plan. Degrees: B,M,D. *Prof. Accred.:* Accounting (Type A,C), Art, Business (B,M), Home Economics, Journalism, Law, Librarianship, Nursing (B,M), Physical Therapy, Psychology, Rehabilitation Counseling, Speech Pathology and Audiology, Teacher Education (*e,s,p*). Pres. John La-Tourette.
Enroll.: FTE 19,313
(815) 753-1271

*Member Regency Universities System

Northwestern Business College
4829 N. Lipps, Chicago 60630. Private. 1974/1985 (AICS). Qtr. plan. Degrees: A, certificates, diplomas. Dir. Lawrence Schumacher.
Enroll.: 925 (*f.t.* 223 m., 702 w.)
(312) 777-4220

Northwestern University
Evanston 60201. Private. 1913/1985 (NCA). Sem. plan. Degrees: B,P,M,D. *Prof. Accred.:* Business (M), Dental Hygiene, Dentistry, Engineering (biomedical, chemical, civil, electrical, environmental, industrial, materials science, mechanical, nuclear), Health Services Administration, Law, Medicine, Music, Nursing (B,M), Physical Therapy, Psychology, Respiratory Therapy, Speech Pathology and Audiology. Pres. Arnold R. Weber.
Enroll.: FTE 13,814
(312) 492-7456

Oakton Community College
1600 E. Golf Rd., Des Plaines 60016. Public (district). 1976/1981 (NCA). Sem. plan. Degrees : A. *Prof. Accred.:* Medical Laboratory Technology (A), Medical Record Technology, Radiation Technology, Radiography. Pres. Thomas TenHoeve.
Enroll.: FTE 4,142
(312) 635-1600

Olivet Nazarene College
Kankakee 60901. Private (Nazarene) liberal arts. 1956/1985 (NCA). Sem. plan. Degrees: A,B,M. *Prof. Accred.:* Music, Nursing (B), Teacher Education (*e,s*). Pres. A. Leslie Parrott.
Enroll.: FTE 1,538
(815) 939-5011

Parkland College
Champaign 61820. Public (district) community. 1972/1982 (NCA). Qtr. plan. Degrees: A, certificates. *Prof. Accred.:* Dental Assisting, Dental Hygiene, Engineering Technology (electronics), Nursing (A), Practical Nursing, Radiography, Respiratory Therapy, Respiratory Therapy Technology. Pres. William M. Staerkel.
Enroll.: FTE 4,043
(217) 351-2231

Parks College of St. Louis University
Cahokia 62206. Private (Roman Catholic); branch of St. Louis University. 1970/1975 (NCA). Tri. plan. Degrees: B. *Prof. Accred.:* Engineering (aerospace). Vice Pres. Paul A. Whelan.
Enroll.: FTE 997
(618) 337-7500

Prairie State College
Chicago Heights 60411. Public (district) community. 1965/1985 (NCA). Sem. plan. Degrees: A. *Prof. Accred.:* Dental Assisting, Dental Hygiene, Technical Nursing. Pres. W. Harold Garner.
Enroll.: FTE 2,510
(312) 756-3110

Principia College
Elsah 62028. Private (Christian Science) liberal arts. 1923/1985 (NCA). Qtr. plan. Degrees: B. Pres. John E. G. Boyman.
Enroll.: FTE 695
(618) 374-2131

Quincy College
Quincy 62301. Private (Roman Catholic) liberal arts. 1954/1985 (NCA). Sem. plan. Degrees: B,M. *Prof. Accred.:* Music. Pres. Rev. James Toal.
Enroll.: FTE 738
(217) 222-8020

Quincy Technical Schools
501 N. Third St., Quincy 62301. Private. 1977/1983 (NATTS). Qtr. plan. Diplomas. Pres. W. G. Dubuque.
Enroll.: 349 (*f.t.* 255 m., 15 w.)
(217) 224-0600

Ray College of Design
401 N. Wabash St., Chicago 60611. Private. 1975/1980 (NATTS). Sem. plan. Degrees: A, diplomas. Pres. Wade F. Ray.
Enroll.: 386 (*f.t.* 123 m., 263 w.)
(312) 280-3500

Regency Universities System
616 Myers Bldg., Springfield 62701. Public (state). Chanc. William R. Monat.
(217) 782-3770

Rend Lake College
Ina 62846. Public (district) community. 1969/1982 (NCA). Sem. plan. Degrees: A. *Prof. Accred.:* Nursing (A). Pres. Harry J. Braun.
Enroll.: FTE 1,566
(618) 437-5321

Richland Community College
2425 Federal Dr., Decatur 62526. Public (district). 1978/1981 (NCA). Qtr. plan. Degrees: A. Pres. Howard E. Brown.

Enroll.: FTE 1,418
(217) 875-7200

ROBERT MORRIS COLLEGE
College Ave., Carthage 62321. Private business. 1969/1981 (AICS); 1986 (NCA). Qtr. plan, courses of varying lengths. Degrees: A, certificates. *Prof. Accred.:* Dental Assisting, Medical Assisting. Pres. Richard Pickett.
Enroll.: FTE 2,173
(217) 357-2121

BRANCH CAMPUS
180 N. LaSalle St., Chicago 60601. Vice Pres. Janet S. Day.
(312) 836-4888

ROCK VALLEY COLLEGE
Rockford 61101. Public (district) community. 1971/1984 (NCA). Sem. plan. Degrees: A. *Prof. Accred.:* Dental Assisting, Respiratory Therapy. Pres. Karl J. Jacobs.
Enroll.: FTE 3,044
(815) 654-4260

ROCKFORD BUSINESS COLLEGE
319 W. Jefferson St., Rockford 61101. Private. 1968/1986 (AICS). Qtr. plan. Diplomas. Pres. David G. Swank.
Enroll.: 776 (*f.t.* 66 m., 710 w.)
(815) 965-8616

ROCKFORD COLLEGE
Rockford 61101. Private liberal arts. 1913/1984 (NCA). 4-1-4 plan. Degrees: A,B, M. Pres. Norman L. Stewart.
Enroll.: FTE 906
(815) 226-4010

ROOSEVELT UNIVERSITY
430 S. Michigan Ave., Chicago 60605. Private. 1946/1986 (NCA). Sem. plan. Degrees: A,B,M. *Prof. Accred.:* Music, Social Work (B), Teacher Education (*e,s,p*). Pres. Rolf A. Weil.
Enroll.: FTE 3,320
(312) 341-3500

ROSARY COLLEGE
River Forest 60305. Private (Roman Catholic) liberal arts. 1919/1985 (NCA). Sem. plan. Degrees: B,M. *Prof. Accred.:* Librarianship. Pres. Sister Jean Murray.
Enroll.: FTE 991
(312) 366-2490

RUSH UNIVERSITY
Chicago 60612. Private professional. 1974/1978 (NCA). Qtr. plan. Degrees: B,P,M,D. *Prof. Accred.:* Dietetics, Health Systems Management, Medical Technology, Medicine, Nurse Anesthesia Education, Nursing (B,M), Psychology, Radiation Therapy. Pres. Leo M. Henikoff.
Enroll.: FTE 1,042
(312) 942-5474

ST. MARY OF THE LAKE SEMINARY
Mundelein 60060. Private (Roman Catholic) professional. Sem. plan. Degrees: P,M. *Prof. Accred.:* Theology (1972/1982, ATS). Pres. Gerald F. Kicanas.
Enroll.: 227
(312) 566-6401

SAINT XAVIER COLLEGE
103rd and Central Park Ave., Chicago 60655. Private (Roman Catholic) liberal arts. 1937/1984 (NCA). 4-1-4 plan. Degrees: B,M. *Prof. Accred.:* Nursing (B,M). Pres. Ronald O. Champagne.
Enroll.: FTE 1,680
(312) 779-3300

*SANGAMON STATE UNIVERSITY
Springfield 62708. Public liberal arts; upper division and graduate only. 1975/1982 (NCA). Sem. plan. Degrees: B,M. *Prof. Accred.:* Medical Technology, Nursing (B), Rehabilitation Counseling. Pres. Durward Long.
Enroll.: FTE 1,889
(217) 786-6634

SAUK VALLEY COLLEGE
Dixon 61021. Public (district) community. 1972/1985 (NCA). Sem. plan. Degrees: A. *Prof. Accred.:* Medical Laboratory Technology (A), Radiography. Interim Pres. Herbert Phillips.
Enroll.: FTE 1,300
(815) 288-5511

SAWYER SECRETARIAL SCHOOL
130 N. Marion St., Oak Park 60301. Private business. 1973/1980 (AICS). Courses of varying lengths. Certificates. Dir. Lorraine Phillips.
Enroll.: 553 (*f.t.* 19 m., 534 w.)
(312) 383-6833

THE SCHOOL OF THE ART INSTITUTE OF CHICAGO
Michigan Ave. at Adams St., Chicago 60603. Private professional; affiliated with The Art Institute of Chicago. Dean and Acting Dir. Roger Gilmore. 1936/1982 (NCA). Sem. plan.

*Member Regency Universities System

Degrees: B,M. *Prof. Accred.:* Art. Pres. Anthony Jones.
Enroll.: FTE 1,366
(312) 443-3709

SEABURY-WESTERN THEOLOGICAL SEMINARY
Evanston 60201. Private (Episcopal) professional; graduate only. 1981 (NCA). Sem. plan. Degrees: P,M. *Prof. Acc red.:* Theology. (1938/1981, ATS). President Mark Sisk.
Enroll.: FTE 71
(312) 328-9300

SHAWNEE COLLEGE
Ullin 62992. Public (district) 2-year. 1974/1982 (NCA). Sem. plan. Degrees: A. *Prof. Accred.:* Nursing (A). Pres. Loren E. Klaus.
Enroll.: FTE 905
(618) 634-2242

SHERWOOD CONSERVATORY OF MUSIC
1014 S. Michigan Ave., Chicago 60605. Private professional. 1936/1977. Sem. plan. Degrees: B. *Prof. Accred.:* Music. Pres. David M. Blodgett.
Enroll.: 45 (*f.t.* 16 m., 14 w.)
(312) 427-6267

SOUTHEASTERN ILLINOIS COLLEGE
Harrisburg 62946. Public (district) community. 1976/1980 (NCA). Sem. plan. Degrees: A. *Prof. Accred.:* Nursing (A). Pres. Harry W. Abell.
Enroll.: FTE 1,369
(618) 252-4411

SOUTHERN ILLINOIS UNIVERSITY SYSTEM OFFICE
111 Small Group Housing, Carbondale 62901. Public (state). Chanc. Lawrence K. Pettit.
(618) 536-3331

SOUTHERN ILLINOIS UNIVERSITY—CARBONDALE
Carbondale 62901. Medical center in Springfield. Public (state). 1913/1979 (NCA). Sem. plan. Degrees: A,B,P,M,D. *Prof. Accred.:* Accounting (Type A), Art, Business (B,M), Dental Hygiene, Dental Laboratory Technology, Engineering (electrical sciences and systems, engineering mechanics, mining, thermal and environmental), Engineering Technology (civil, electrical, mechanical), Forestry, Interior Design, Journalism, Law, Medicine, Music, Nursing (A), Psychology, Rehabilitation Counseling, Respiratory Therapy, Social Work (B), Speech Pathology, Teacher Education (*e,s,p*). Pres. Albert Somit.
Enroll.: FTE 19,859
(618) 453-2341

SOUTHERN ILLINOIS UNIVERSITY—EDWARDSVILLE
Edwardsville 62026. 1969/1980 (NCA). Qtr. plan. Degrees: A,B,M,D. *Prof. Accred.:* Business (B,M), Dentistry, Engineering (civil, electrical), Journalism, Music, Nursing (B), Social Work (B), Speech Pathology, Teacher Education (*e,s,p*). Pres. Earl E. Lazerson.
Enroll.: FTE 8,222
(618) 692-2475

SOUTHWEST SCHOOL OF BUSINESS
8030 S. Kedzie Ave., Chicago 60652. Private. 1984 (AICS). Courses of varying lengths. Certificates, diplomas. Pres. Joseph B. Nichols.
Enroll.: 130 (*f.t.* 60)
(312) 436-5050

SPARKS COLLEGE
131 S. Morgan St., Shelbyville 62565. Private business. 1954/1980 (AICS). Courses of varying lengths. Diplomas. Pres. Roger R. Sparks.
Enroll.: 188 (*f.t.* 8 m., 180 w.)
(217) 774-5112

SPERTUS COLLEGE OF JUDAICA
Chicago 60605. Private (Jewish) liberal arts and teachers. 1971/1976 (NCA). Qtr. plan. Degrees: B,M. Pres. Howard A. Sulkin.
Enroll.: FTE 173
(312) 922-9012

SPOON RIVER COLLEGE
Canton 61520. Public (district) community. 1977/1982 (NCA). Sem. plan. Degrees: A. Pres. Robert N. Rue.
Enroll.: FTE 1,147
(309) 647-4645

SPRINGFIELD COLLEGE IN ILLINOIS
Springfield 62702. Private (Roman Catholic) junior. 1933/1982 (NCA). 4-1-4 plan. Degrees: A. Pres. Sister Francis Marie Thrailkill, O.S.U.
Enroll.: FTE 332
(217) 525-1420

STATE COMMUNITY COLLEGE OF EAST ST. LOUIS
East St. Louis 62201. Public (state). 1978/1986 (NCA). Qtr. plan. Degrees: A. Pres. Johnny Hill.
Enroll.: FTE 981
(618) 274-6666

SUPERIOR TECHNICAL INSTITUTE
P.O. Box 70, Posen 60469. Private. 1984 (NATTS). Courses of varying lengths. Certificates. Pres. Roger Dehaven.
(312) 396-1470

TAYLOR BUSINESS INSTITUTE
250 S. Wacker Dr., #900, Chicago 60606. Private. 1973/1986 (AICS). Courses of varying lengths. Certificates. Dir. Janice C. Parker.
Enroll.: 1,836 (*f.t.* 459 m., 1,377 w.)
(312) 822-9560

TELSHE YESHIVA-CHICAGO
3535 W. Foster Ave., Chicago 60625. Private professional. 1976/1983. Sem. plan. Degrees: First and Second Rabbinic. *Prof. Accred.:* Rabbinical and Talmudic Education. Pres. Rabbi A. Levin.
Enroll.: 83 (*f.t.* 71 m., 0 w.)
(312) 463-7738

THORNTON COMMUNITY COLLEGE
South Holland 60473. Public (district). 1933/1981 (NCA). Sem. plan. Degrees: A, certificates. *Prof. Accred.:* Music, Nursing (A), Practijcal Nursing, Radiography. Pres. James L. Evanko.
Enroll.: FTE 3,753
(312) 596-2000

TODAY'S EDUCATIONAL NETWORK
127 N. Dearborn St., Suite 325, Chicago 60602. Private business. 1984 (AICS). Courses of varying lengths. Diplomas. Pres./Dir. Sharon Lee Golz.
Enroll.: f.t. 45
(312) 726-8203

TRAINCO BUSINESS SCHOOL
407 S. Dearborn St., Chicago 60605. Private. 1980 (AICS). Courses of varying lengths. Certificates. Dir. Roseann Comes.
Enroll.: 1,676 (*f.t.* 726 m., 950 w.)
(312) 939-3317

TRINITY CHRISTIAN COLLEGE
Palos Heights 60463. Private (Christian Reformed) liberal arts. 1976/1981 (NCA). Sem. plan. Degrees: B. Pres. Kenneth B. Bootsman.
Enroll.: FTE 482
(312) 597-3000

TRINITY COLLEGE
2077 Half Day Rd., Deerfield 60015. Private (Evangelical Free Church) liberal arts and professional. 1969/1984 (NCA). Sem. plan. Degrees: B. Pres. Kenneth M. Meyer.
Enroll.: FTE 575
(312) 948-8980

TRINITY EVANGELICAL DIVINITY SCHOOL
Deerfield 60015. Private (Evangelical Free Church) professional; graduate only. 1969/1986 (NCA). Qtr. plan. Degrees: P,M,D. *Prof. Accred.:* Theology (1973/1983, ATS). Pres. Rev. Kenneth M. Meyer.
Enroll.: 1,039
(312) 945-8800

TRITON COLLEGE
River Grove 60171. Public (district) community. 1972/1983 (NCA). Sem. plan. Degrees: A, certificates. *Prof. Accred.:* Dental Assisting, Dental Laboratory Technology, Medical Assisting, Medical Laboratory Technology (A), Nuclear Medicine Technology, Nursing (A), Optometric Technology, Practical Nursing, Radiography, Respiratory Therapy, Surgical Technology. Interim Pres. Richard Fonte.
Enroll.: FTE 8,393
(312) 456-0300

UNIVERSITY OF CHICAGO
5801 S. Ellis Ave., Chicago 60637. Private. 1913/1986 (NCA). Qtr. plan. Degrees: B,P,M,D. *Prof. Accred.:* Accounting (Type B), Business (M), Health Services Administration, Law, Librarianship, Medicine, Social Work (M), Theology. Pres. Hanna H. Gray.
Enroll.: FTE 8,409
(312) 962-8001

UNIVERSITY OF HEALTH SCIENCES–THE CHICAGO MEDICAL SCHOOL
3333 S. Green Bay Rd., North Chicago 60664. Private professional. 1980/1983 (NCA). Degrees: A,B,P,M,D. *Prof. Accred.:* Medical Technology, Medicine, Physical Therapy, Psychology. CEO Herman M. Finch.
Enroll.: FTE 812
(312) 578-3000

UNIVERSITY OF ILLINOIS
Urbana 61801. Public (state) system. Qtr. plan at Chicago. Sem. plan at Urbana—Champaign. Pres. Stanley O. Ikenberry.
(217) 333-1000

UNIVERSITY OF ILLINOIS AT CHICAGO
Chicago 60680. 1970/1977 (NCA). Degrees: B,P,M,D. *Prof. Accred.:* Architecture (B,M), Art, Business (B,M), Dentistry, Diagnostic

Medical Sonography, Dietetics, Engineering (bioengineering, chemical, communication, computer and information systems, electrical, engineering mechanics, fluids, industrial, mechanical analysis and design, metallurgy, structural engineering and materials, thermomechanical and energy conversion), Medical Record Administration, Medical Technology, Medicine, Nursing (B,M), Occupational Therapy, Pharmacy, Physical Therapy, Psychology, Public Health, Radiography, Social Work (B,M), Specialist in Blood Bank Technology. Chanc. Donald N. Langenberg.
Enroll.: FTE 21,777
(312) 996-3000

UNIVERSITY OF ILLINOIS AT URBANA—CHAMPAIGN
Urbana 61801. 1913/1979 (NCA). Degrees: B,P,M,D. *Prof. Accred.:* Accounting (Type A,C), Architecture (M), Art, Business (B,M), Community Health Education, Engineering (aeronautical and astronautical, agricultural, ceramic, chemical, civil, electrical, engineering mechanics, general, industrial, mechanical, metallurgical, nuclear), Forestry, Home Economics, Journalism, Landscape Architecture (B,M), Law, Librarianship, Music, Psychology, Social Work (B,M), Speech Pathology and Audiology, Teacher Education (*e,s,p*), Veterinary Medicine. Chanc. Thomas E. Everhart.
Enroll.: FTE 33,274
(217) 333-1000

VANDERCOOK COLLEGE OF MUSIC
Chicago 60616. Private professional. 1972/1983 (NCA). Sem. plan. Degrees: B,M. *Prof. Accred.:* Music. Pres. James Gilworth.
Enroll.: FTE 100
(312) 225-6288

WASHINGTON BUSINESS INSTITUTE
624 S. Michigan Ave., Suite 1410, Chicago 60605. Private. 1984 (AICS). Courses of varying lengths. Certificates, diplomas. Pres. Robert Triplett.
Enroll.: 80
(312) 663-1851

WAUBONSEE COMMUNITY COLLEGE
Sugar Grove 60554. Public (district) junior. 1972/1986 (NCA). Sem. plan. Degrees: A. Pres. John J. Swalec.
Enroll.: FTE 2,145
(312) 466-4811

WESTERN ILLINOIS UNIVERSITY
Macomb 61455. Public (state). 1913/1981 (NCA). Sem. plan. Degrees: B,M. *Prof. Accred.:* Business (B,M), Music, Speech Pathology and Audiology, Teacher Education (*e,s,p*). Pres. Leslie F. Malpass.
Enroll.: FTE 10,028
(309) 298-1824

WHEATON COLLEGE
Wheaton 60187. Private liberal arts. 1913/1984 (NCA). Sem. plan. Degrees: B,M. *Prof. Accred.:*Music, Teacher Education (*e,s*). Pres. Richard J. Chase.
Enroll.: FTE 2,495
(312) 260-5000

WILLIAM RAINEY HARPER COLLEGE
Palatine 60067. Public (district) community. 1971/1981 (NCA). Sem. plan. Degrees: A. *Prof. Accred.:* Dental Hygiene, Music, Nursing (A). Pres. James J. McGrath.
Enroll.: FTE 7,522
(312) 397-3000

INDIANA

ACADEMY OF HAIR DESIGN
2150 Lafayette Rd., Indianapolis 46222. Private. 1982 (NATTS). Courses of varying lengths. Diplomas. Dir. Jack Hale.
Enroll.: 23 (*f.t.* 4 m., 19 w.)
(317) 637-7227

ACME INSTITUTE OF TECHNOLOGY
504 W. Calvert St., P.O. Box 2708, South Bend 46613. Private. 1985 (NATTS). Courses of varying lengths. Diplomas. Dir. Herbert F. Bowman.
(219) 233-5792

ANCILLA COLLEGE
Donaldson 46513. Private (Roman Catholic) junior. 1973/1978 (NCA). Sem. plan. Degrees: A. Pres.-Dean Sister Virginia Kampweth.
Enroll.: FTE 281
(219) 936-8898

ANDERSON COLLEGE
1100 E. Fifth Ave., Anderson 46012. Private (Church of God) liberal arts and graduate theology. 1946/1979 (NCA). Sem. plan. Degrees: A,B,P. *Prof. Accred.:* Music, Nursing (A), Social Work (B), Teacher Education (*e,s*), Theology. Pres. Robert A. Nicholson.
Enroll.: FTE 1,897
(317) 649-9071

ARISTOTLE COLLEGE OF MEDICAL AND DENTAL TECHNOLOGY
5514 E. Fall Creek Pkwy., Indianapolis 46226. Private technical. 1980 (ABHES). 28-week program. Diplomas. *Prof. Accred.:* Medical Assisting. Pres. H. Dayle Boyt.
Enroll.: f.t. 37
(317) 547-9661

BRANCH CAMPUS
6152 Cleveland Ave., P.O. Box 29365, Columbus, OH 43229. *Prof. Accred.:* Medical Assisting.
(614) 891-1800

ASSOCIATED MENNONITE BIBLICAL SEMINARIES
See Goshen Biblical Seminary and Mennonite Biblical Seminary

BALL STATE UNIVERSITY
Muncie 47306. Public. 1925/1974 (NCA). Qtr. plan. Degrees: A,B,M,D. *Prof. Accred.:* Architecture (B), Business (B,M), Home Economics, Journalism, Landscape Architecture (B), Librarianship, Music, Nuclear Medicine Technology, Nursing (B,M), Psychology, Radiography, Respiratory Therapy, Social Work (B), Speech Pathology and Audiology, Teacher Education (*e,s,p*). Pres. John E. Worthen.
Enroll.: FTE 15,653
(317) 285-5555

BETHEL COLLEGE
Mishawaka 46544. Private (United Missionary) liberal arts. 1971/1986 (NCA). Sem. plan. Degrees: B. Pres. James A. Bennett.
Enroll.: 387
(219) 259-8511

BUTLER UNIVERSITY
4600 Sunset Ave., Indianapolis 46208. Private. 1915/1983 (NCA). Sem. plan. Degrees: B,M. *Prof. Accred.:* Music, Pharmacy, Teacher Education (*e,s*). Pres. John G. Johnson.
Enroll.: FTE 2,793
(317) 283-9201

CALUMET COLLEGE
2400 New York Ave., Whiting 46394. Private (Roman Catholic) liberal arts. 1968/1986 (NCA). Sem. plan. Degrees: A,B. Acting Pres. Rev. Ronald J. Schiml.
Enroll.: FTE 631
(219) 473-4333

CHRISTIAN THEOLOGICAL SEMINARY
Indianapolis 46208. Private (Christian Church, Disciples of Christ) professional; graduate only. 1973/1978 (NCA). Sem. plan. Degrees: P,M,D. *Prof. Accred.:* Theology (1944/1978, ATS). Acting Pres. Richard D. N. Dickinson.
Enroll.: 359
(317) 924-1331

CLARK COLLEGE
1840 N. Meridian St., Indianapolis 46202. Private junior/business. 1969/1985 (AICS). Qtr. plan. Degrees: A, certificates. *Prof. Accred.:* Medical Assisting. Pres. James Lamers.
Enroll.: 1984 (*f.t.* 603 m., 1,381 w.)
(317) 923-3933

COMMONWEALTH BUSINESS COLLEGE
8995 State Rt. 39 N., LaPorte 46350. Private. 1978/1984 (AICS). Qtr. plan. Degrees: A, certificates, diplomas. Dir. Steven C. Smith.

Enroll.: FTE 1,306
(219) 362-3338

BRANCH CAMPUS
Lower Level, Executive Plaza, 8400 Louisiana St., Merrillville 46410.
(219) 769-3321

BRANCH CAMPUS
3218 E. 35th St. Court, Davenport, IA 52807. Dir. Joseph J. Hernandez.
(319) 359-3936

CONCORDIA THEOLOGICAL SEMINARY
Fort Wayne 46825. Private (Lutheran-Missouri Synod) professional; graduate only. 1981 (NCA). Qtr. plan. Degrees: P,M,D. *Prof. Accred.:* Theology (1968/1986, ATS). Pres. Robert D. Preus.
Enroll.: 538
(219) 482-9611

DEFENSE INFORMATION SCHOOL
Ft. Benjamin Harrison, Indianapolis 46216. Public (federal). 1979/1984 (NCA). Courses of varying lengths. Certificates. Commandant Col. Edward M. McDonald.
Enroll.: FTE 1,914
(317) 542-4046

DEPAUW UNIVERSITY
Greencastle 46135. Private (United Methodist). 1915/1978 (NCA). 4-1-4 plan. Degrees: B,M. *Prof. Accred.:* Music, Nursing (B), Teacher Education (*e,s*). Pres. Robert G. Bottoms.
Enroll.: FTE 2,329
(317) 653-9721

EARLHAM COLLEGE
Richmond 47374. Private (Friends) liberal arts. 1915/1984 (NCA). 3-3 plan. Degrees: B,P,M. *Prof. Accred.:* Teacher Education (*e,s*), Theology. Pres. Richard J. Wood.
Enroll.: FTE 1,008
(317) 962-6561

ELKHART INSTITUTE OF TECHNOLOGY
516 S. Main St., Elkhart 46516. Private. 1969/1985 (ABHES). 18-month program. Degrees: A, diplomas. *Prof. Accred.:* Medical Assisting, Medical Laboratory Technology. Pres. J. Richard Miller.
Enroll.: 23
(219) 295-5900

BRANCH CAMPUS
905 Third Ave., Huntington, WV 25701.
(304) 529-1072

EVANSVILLE SCHOOL OF PRACTICAL NURSING
1900 Stringtown Rd., Evansville 47711. Public technical. 1981. 11-month program. Certificates. *Prof. Accred.:* Practical Nursing. Dir. Joyce Stevens.
Enroll.: 62

FORT WAYNE BIBLE COLLEGE
1025 W. Rudisill Blvd., Fort Wayne 46807. Private (Missionary Church) liberal arts and professional. 1948/1985 (AABC); 1985 (NCA) Sem. plan. Degrees: A,B. Pres. Harvey R. Bostrom.
Enroll.: FTE 314
(219) 456-2111

FRANKLIN COLLEGE OF INDIANA
Franklin 46131. Private (American Baptist) liberal arts. 1915/1982 (NCA). 4-1-4 plan. Degrees: B. Pres. William B. Martin.
Enroll.: FTE 678
(317) 736-8441

GOSHEN BIBLICAL SEMINARY
3003 Benham Ave., Elkhart 46517. Private (Mennonite) professional; graduate only. 1974/1979 (NCA). Sem. plan. Degrees: P,M. *Prof. Accred.:* Theology (1958/1979, ATS). Pres. Marlin E. Miller.
Enroll.: 130
(219) 295-3726

GOSHEN COLLEGE
Goshen 46526. Private (Mennonite) liberal arts. 1941/1985 (NCA). Tri. plan. Degrees: B. *Prof. Accred.:* Nursing (B), Social Work (B), Teacher Education (*e,s*). Pres. Victor Stoltzfus.
Enroll.: FTE 863
(219) 533-3161

GRACE COLLEGE
Winona Lake 46590. Private (National Fellowship of Brethren Churches) liberal arts. 1976/1984 (NCA). Sem. plan. Degrees: B. Pres. John J. Davis.
Enroll.: FTE 730
(219) 267-8191

GRACE THEOLOGICAL SEMINARY
Winona Lake 46590. Private (National Fellowship of Brethren Churches) professional; graduate only. 1982 (NCA). Sem. plan. Degrees: P,M. Pres. John J. Davis.
Enroll.: FTE 258
(219) 372-5100

Hanover College
Hanover 47243. Private (United Presbyterian) liberal arts. 1915/1979 (NCA). 4-4-1 plan. Degrees: B. Pres. John E. Horner.
Enroll.: FTE 1,007
(812) 866-2151

Huntington College
Huntington 46750. Private (United Brethren in Christ) liberal arts and theology. 1961/1984 (NCA). 4-1-4 plan. Degrees: B,M. Pres. Eugene B. Habecker.
Enroll.: FTE 419
(219) 356-6000

ITT Technical Institute
5115 Oak Grove Rd., Evansville 47715. Private/Business. 1967/1979 (NATTS). Qtr. plan. Degrees: A. Dir. Harry E. Strong.
Enroll.: 450 (*f.t.* 467 m., 22 w.)
(812) 479-1441

ITT Technical Institute
4919 Coldwater Rd., Fort Wayne 46825. Private. 1968/1978 (NATTS). Qtr. plan. Degrees: A, diplomas. Pres. Jack Bainter.
Enroll.: 1,215 (*f.t.* 1,181 m., 34 w.)
(219) 484-4107

Branch Campus
2121 South Blackhawk St., Aurora, CO 80014. 1984 (NATTS). Dir. Patricia O'Brien.

ITT Technical Institute
9511 Angola Ct., Indianapolis 46268. Private. 1967/1984 (NATTS). Qtr. plan. Degrees: A, certificates, diplomas. Dir. Marvin L. Copes.
Enroll.: 1,683
(317) 875-8640

Indiana Barber/Styling College
5536 E. Washington St., Indianapolis 46219. Private. 1973/1978 (NATTS). Courses of varying lengths. Diplomas. Pres. Kenneth L. Fleener.
Enroll.: 75 (*f.t.* 40 m., 35 w.)
(317) 356-8222

Indiana Business College
802 N. Meridian St., Indianapolis 46204. Private. 1980/1985 (AICS). Courses of varying lengths. Certificates. Dir. Michael L. Skaggs.
Enroll.: 2,271 (*f.t.* 285 m., 1,986 w.)
(317) 634-8337

Branch Campus
145 W. 14th St., Anderson 46016-1695. Dir. John K. Boggs.
(317) 644-7514

Branch Campus
641 Washington St., Columbus 47201. Dir. William J. Weisner.
(812) 376-3510

Branch Campus
102 1/2 E. Taylor St., P.O. Box 354, Kokomo 46901. Dir. William E. Shockley.
(317) 459-5681

Branch Campus
217-219 N. Sixth St., Lafayette 47902. Dir. Kay V. Ringen.
(317) 742-7204

Branch Campus
1011/2 S. Washington St., Marion 46952. Dir. George L. Roberds.
(317) 662-7497

Branch Campus
809 N. Walnut St., Muncie 47305. Dir. John K. Boggs.
(317) 288-8681

Branch Campus
35 S. Eighth St., Richmond 47374. Dir. Ronald L. Wickett.
(317) 962-5205

Branch Campus
618 Wabash St., Terre Haute 47807. Dir. Ronald E. Fishback.
(812) 232-4458

Branch Campus
Fifth and Main Sts., P.O. Box 24, Vincennes 47591. Dir. Bill F. Sheppard.
(812) 882-2550

Indiana Institute of Technology
1600 E. Washington Blvd., Fort Wayne 46803. Private technological. 1962/1984 (NCA). Qtr. plan. Degrees: B. Pres. Donald J. Andorfer.
Enroll.: FTE 415
(219) 422-5561

Indiana State University
Central office, 217 N. Sixth St., Terre Haute 47809. Pres. Richard G. Landini.
Enroll.: FTE 9,913
(812) 232-6311

Indiana State University—Terre Haute
Terre Haute 47809. Public. 1915/1980 (NCA). Sem. plan. Degrees: B,M,D. *Prof. Accred.:* Art, Business (B,M), Dietetics, Interior Design, Medical Laboratory Technology (A), Medical Technology, Music, Nursing (A,B),

Psychology, Speech Pathology, Teacher Education (*e,s,p*). Pres. Richard G. Landini.
Enroll.: FTE 9,480
(812) 232-6311

INDIANA UNIVERSITY
Central office, Bryan Hall, Bloomington 47405. Pres. John W. Ryan.
(812) 332-0211

INDIANA UNIVERSITY—BLOOMINGTON
Bloomington 47405. Public (state). 1913/1977 (NCA). Sem. plan. Degrees: A,B,P,M,D. *Prof. Accred.:* Business (B,M), Health Services Administration, Journalism, Law, Librarianship, Medical Technology, Music, Optometric Technology, Optometry, Physical Therapy, Psychology, Speech Pathology and Audiology, Teacher Education (*e,s,p*). Vice Pres. Kenneth R. R. GrosLouis.
Enroll.: FTE 32,816
(812) 337-4602

INDIANA UNIVERSITY EAST
Richmond 47374. 1971/1982 (NCA). Degrees: A. Chanc. Glenn A. Goerke.
Enroll.: FTE 641
(317) 966-8261

INDIANA UNIVERSITY AT KOKOMO
Kokomo 46902. 1969/1984 (NCA). Degrees: A,B. *Prof. Accred.:* Engineering Technology (electrical), Nursing (A), Teacher Education (*e*). Chanc. Hugh L. Thompson.
Enroll.: FTE 1,235
(317) 453-2000

INDIANA UNIVERSITY NORTHWEST
Gary 46408. 1969/1984 (NCA). Degrees: A,B,M. *Prof. Accred.:* Business (B,M), Dental Assisting, Medical Record Technology, Nursing (A), Radiography, Respiratory Therapy, Teacher Education (*e,s*). Chanc. Peggy G. Elliott.
Enroll.: FTE 2,654
(219) 980-6700

INDIANA UNIVERSITY AT SOUTH BEND
South Bend 46634. 1969/1980 (NCA). Degrees: A,B,M. *Prof. Accred.:* Dental Assisting, Dental Hygiene, Teacher Education (*e,s,p*). Chanc. Lester M. Wolfson.
Enroll.: FTE 2,827
(219) 237-4220

INDIANA UNIVERSITY SOUTHEAST
New Albany 47150. 1969/1980 (NCA). Degrees: A,B,M. Chanc. Leon Rand.
Enroll.: FTE 2,615
(812) 945-2731

INDIANA UNIVERSITY—PURDUE UNIVERSITY AT FORT WAYNE
Fort Wayne 46805. 1969/1980 (NCA). Degrees: A,B,M,. *Prof. Accred.:* Dental Assisting, Dental Hygiene, Dental Laboratory Technology, Engineering (electrical, mechanical), Engineering Technology (architectural, civil, construction, electrical, industrial, mechanical drafting design, mechanical, mechanical-manufacturing option), Nursing (A,B), Teacher Education (*e,s,p*). Chanc. Thomas P. Wallace.
Enroll.: FTE 5,716
(219) 482-5121

INDIANA UNIVERSITY—PURDUE UNIVERSITY AT INDIANAPOLIS
1701 N. Pennsylvania St., Indianapolis 46202. 1969/1973 (NCA). Degrees: A,B,M. *Prof. Accred.:* Art, Cytotechnology, Dental Assisting, Dental Hygiene, Dentistry, Dietetics, Engineering Technology (civil, electrical, industrial, mechanical, mechanical drafting design), Health Administration, Law, Medical Record Administration, Medical Technology, Medicine, Music, Nuclear Medicine Technology, Nursing (A,B,M), Occupational Therapy, Physical Therapy, Psychology, Radiation Therapy, Radiography, Respiratory Therapy, Social Work (B,M). Vice Pres. Glenn W. Irwin, Jr.
Enroll.: 14,255
(317) 264-4417

INDIANA VOCATIONAL TECHNICAL COLLEGE
Central office, One W. 26th St., Indianapolis 46206. Public (state) 2-year. Pres. Gerald I. Lamkin.
(317) 872-3210

INDIANA VOCATIONAL TECHNICAL COLLEGE–CENTRAL INDIANA TECHNICAL INSTITUTE
Indianapolis 46202. 1977/1982 (NCA). Qtr. plan. Degrees: A, certificates. *Prof. Accred.:* Medical Assisting, Medical Laboratory Technology (A), Practical Nursing, Radiography, Respiratory Therapy, Surgical Technology. Vice Pres. and Dean Meredith Carter.
Enroll.: FTE 2,552
(317) 929-4882

INDIANA VOCATIONAL TECHNICAL COLLEGE–COLUMBUS TECHNICAL INSTITUTE
Columbus 47201. 1978/1981 (NCA). Qtr. plan. Degrees: A. *Prof. Accred.:* Respiratory Therapy Technology. Vice Pres. and Dean Homer B. Smith.
Enroll.: FTE 1,242
(812) 372-9925

INDIANA VOCATIONAL TECHNICAL COLLEGE–EASTCENTRAL TECHNICAL INSTITUTE
Muncie 47302. 1979/1984 (NCA). Qtr. plan. Degrees: A. *Prof. Accred.:* Medical Assisting. Vice Pres. and Dean Richard L. Davidson.
Enroll.: FTE 1,066
(317) 289-2291

INDIANA VOCATIONAL TECHNICAL COLLEGE–KOKOMO TECHNICAL INSTITUTE
Kokomo 46901. 1978/1982 (NCA). Qtr. plan. Degrees: A. *Prof. Accred.:* Medical Assisting. Vice Pres. and Charles E. Hefley.
Enroll.: FTE 913
(317) 459-0561

INDIANA VOCATIONAL TECHNICAL COLLEGE—LAFAYETTE TECHNICAL INSTITUTE
Lafayette 47903. 1980/1984 (NCA). Degrees: A. *Prof. Accred.:* Dental Assisting, Medical Assisting, Medical Laboratory Technology (A), Respiratory Therapy, Surgical Technology. Vice Pres. and Dean Thomas E. Reckerd.
Enroll.: FTE 862
(317) 477-7401

INDIANA VOCATIONAL TECHNICAL COLLEGE–NORTHCENTRAL TECHNICAL INSTITUTE
South Bend 46619. 1977/1982 (NCA). Qtr. plan. Degrees: A. *Prof. Accred.:* Medical Assisting. Vice Pres. and Dean Carl F. Lutz.
Enroll.: 1,116
(219) 289-7001

INDIANA VOCATIONAL TECHNICAL COLLEGE–NORTHEAST TECHNICAL INSTITUTE
Fort Wayne 46805. 1977/1982 (NCA). Qtr. plan. Degrees: A. *Prof. Accred.:* Medical Assisting, Respiratory Therapy Technology. Vice Pres. and Dean Jon L. Rupright.
Enroll.: FTE 1,572
(219) 482-9171

INDIANA VOCATIONAL TECHNICAL COLLEGE–NORTHWEST TECHNICAL INSTITUTE
Gary 46409. 1981 (NCA). Qtr. plan. Degrees: A. *Prof. Accred.:* Medical Assisting, Respiratory Therapy, Surgical Technology. Vice Pres. and Dean Mearle R. Donica.
Enroll.: FTE 2,222
(219) 981-1111

INDIANA VOCATIONAL TECHNICAL COLLEGE–SOUTHCENTRAL TECHNICAL INSTITUTE
Sellersburg 47171. 1980/1985 (NCA). Qtr. plan. Degrees: A. *Prof. Accred.:* Surgical Technology. Vice Pres and Dean Carl F. Scott.
Enroll.: 913
(812) 246-3301

INDIANA VOCATIONAL TECHNICAL COLLEGE–SOUTHEAST TECHNICAL INSTITUTE
Madison 47250. 1981 (NCA). Qtr. plan. Degrees: A. *Prof. Accred.:* Medical Assisting. Vice Pres. and Dean Gregory K. Flood.
Enroll.: FTE 382
(812) 265-2580

INDIANA VOCATIONAL TECHNICAL COLLEGE–SOUTHWEST TECHNICAL INSTITUTE
Evansville 47710. 1977/1981 (NCA). Qtr. plan. Degrees: A. *Prof. Accred.:* Medical Assisting. Vice Pres. and Dean H. Victor Baldi.
Enroll.: FTE 1,051
(812) 426-2865

INDIANA VOCATIONAL TECHNICAL COLLEGE–WABASH VALLEY TECHNICAL INSTITUTE
Terre Haute 47802. 1977/1985 (NCA). Qtr. plan. Degrees: A. *Prof. Accred.:* Medical Assisting, Radiography. Vice Pres. and Dean Sam Borden.
Enroll.: FTE 1,236
(812) 299-1121

INDIANA VOCATIONAL TECHNICAL COLLEGE–WHITEWATER TECHNICAL INSTITUTE
Richmond 47374. 1981 (NCA). Qtr. plan. Degrees: A. *Prof. Accred.:* Medical Laboratory Technology. Vice Pres. and Dean Judith A. Redwine.
Enroll.: FTE 560
(317) 966-2656

International Business College
3811 Old Illinois Rd., Fort Wayne 46804. Private junior/business. 1953/1981 (AICS). Sem. and Qtr. plans. Degrees: A, certificates, diplomas. Pres . A. W. Conti.
Enroll.: 620 (*f.t.* 167 m., 453 w.)
(219) 432-8702

Branch Campus
7205 Shadeland Sta., Indianapolis 46256. Dir. Lowell E. Frame.
(317) 841-6400

Interstate Technical Institute
2402 Medford Dr., Fort Wayne 46803. Private. 1972/1980 (NATTS). Qtr. plan. Degrees: A. Dir. F. H. Hurt.
Enroll.: f.t. 143 m.
(219) 749-8583

Lincoln Technical Institute
1201 Stadium Dr., Indianapolis 46202. Private. 1968/1978 (NATTS). Courses of varying lengths. Degrees: A, certificates, diplomas. Dir. James W. Jackson.
Enroll.: 1,150 (*f.t.* 1,136 m., 14 w.)
(317) 632-5553

Lockyear College
209 N.W. Fifth St., P.O. Box 923, Evansville 47706-0923. Private junior/business. 1953/1981 (AICS). Qtr. plan. Degrees: A, certificates, diplomas. Pres. C. Ray Noblett, Jr.
Enroll.: 1,177 (*f.t.* 348 m., 829 w.)
(812) 425-8157

Branch Campus
5330 E. 38th St., Indianapolis 46218. Dir. Tony Payne.
(317) 546-9500

Manchester College
North Manchester 46962. Private (Church of Brethren) liberal arts. 1932/1983 (NCA). 4-1-4 plan. Degrees: B,M. *Prof. Accred.:* Social Work (B), Teacher Education (*e,s*). Pres. William P. Robinson.
Enroll.: FTE 927
(219) 982-2141

Marian College
3200 Cold Spring Rd., Indianapolis 46222. Private (Roman Catholic) liberal arts. 1956/1986 (NCA). Sem. plan. Degrees: B. *Prof. Accred.:* Radiography, Teacher Education (*e,s*). Pres. Louis C. Gatto.
Enroll.: FTE 855
(317) 929-0213

Marion College
Marion 46952. Private (Wesleyan Methodist) liberal arts. 1966/1981 (NCA). Sem. plan. Degrees: B,M. *Prof. Accred.:* Medical Laboratory Technology (A), Nursing (B), Social Work (B). Pres. James P. Hill, Jr.
Enroll.: FTE 887
(317) 674-6901

Mennonite Biblical Seminary
3003 Benham Ave., Elkhart 46517. Private (Mennonite) professional; graduate only. 1974/1979 (NCA). Sem. plan. Degrees: P,M. *Prof. Accred.:* Theology (1964/1979, ATS). Pres. Henry Poettcker.
Enroll.: FTE 85
(219) 295-3726

Michiana College of Commerce
1530 E. Jackson Rd., South Bend 46614. Private. 1961/1981 (AICS). Qtr. plan. Degrees: A, diplomas. Pres. David Krueper.
Enroll.: 430 (*f.t.* 66 m., 364 w.)
(219) 233-3191

Muncie School of Practical Nursing
Ball Memorial Hospital, 2300 W. Gilbert St., Muncie 47303. Private. 1981. 1-year program. Certificates. *Prof. Accred.:* Practical Nursing. Dir. Anita S. Haney.
Enroll.: 30

National Barber Stylist College
2051 W. Washington St., Indianapolis 46222. Private. 1973/1984 (NATTS). Courses of varying lengths. Certificates. Registrar Nancy L. Goode.
Enroll.: 75 (*f.t.* 40 m., 35 w.)
(317) 634-6950

Oakland City College
Oakland City 47660. Private (Baptist) liberal arts. 1977/1985 (NCA). Qtr. plan. Degrees: B,M. Pres. James W. Murray.
Enroll.: FTE 529
(812) 749-4781

Pontiac Business Institute
47 E. Washington, Indianapolis 46204. Private. 1985 (AICS). Qtr. plan. Certificates, diplomas. Dir. Margaret Strommen.
(317) 634-2901

Professional Careers Institute, Inc.
2611 Waterfront Pkwy. E. Drive, Indianapolis 46224. Private. 1970/1980 (NATTS). Courses of varying lengths. Certificates. *Prof. Accred.:* Dental Assisting, Medical Assisting. Pres. Richard H. Weiss.

Enroll.: f.t. 206 w.
(317) 229-6001

PURDUE UNIVERSITY
West Lafayette 47907. Public (state). 1913/1980 (NCA). Sem. plan. Degrees: A,B,P,M,D. *Prof. Accred.:* Business (B,M), Construction Education, Dietetics, Engineering (aeronautical and astronautical, agricultural, chemical, civil, computer and electrical, construction and management, electrical, industrial, electrical, mechanical, surveying), Forestry, Interior Design, Landscape Architecture (B), Nursing (B), Pharmacy, Psychology, Speech Pathology and Audiology, Teacher Education (*e,s,p*), Veterinary Medicine. Pres. Steven C. Beering.
Enroll.: FTE 30,744
(317) 494-4600

PURDUE UNIVERSITY REGIONAL CAMPUSES
(Central office) West Lafayette 47907. Dean G. Walter Bergren.

PURDUE UNIVERSITY—CALUMET CAMPUS
Hammond 46323. 1969/1983 (NCA). Degrees: A,B,M. *Prof. Accred.:* Engineering (electrical, mechanical), Engineering Technology (architectural, civil, construction, electrical, industrial, mechanical), Nursing (A,B), Teacher Education (*e,s*). Chanc. Richard J. Combs.
Enroll.: FTE 4,696
(219) 844-0520

INDIANA UNIVERSITY—PURDUE UNIVERSITY AT INDIANAPOLIS
See Indiana University.

PURDUE UNIVERSITY—NORTH CENTRAL CAMPUS
Westville 46391. 1971/1981 (NCA). Degrees: A. *Prof. Accred.:* Nursing (A), Radiography. Chanc. Dale W. Alspaugh.
Enroll.: FTE 1,400
(219) 785-2541

ROSE-HULMAN INSTITUTE OF TECHNOLOGY
5500 Wabash Ave., Terre Haute 47803. Private science and engineering for men. 1916/1982 (NCA). Qtr. plan. Degrees: B,M. *Prof. Accred.:* Engineering (chemical, civil, electrical, mechanical). Pres. Samuel F. Hulbert.
Enroll.: FTE 1,331
(812) 877-1511

SAILWRIGHT ACADEMY
Route 1, Columbia City 46725. Private home study. 1981 (NHSC). Pres. James Grant.
(219) 244-6715

SAINT FRANCIS COLLEGE
Fort Wayne 46808. Private (Roman Catholic) liberal arts. 1957/1986 (NCA). Sem. plan. Degrees: B,M. *Prof. Accred.:* Business, Social Work (B), Teacher Education (*e,s*). Pres. Sister M. JoEllen Scheetz.
Enroll.: FTE 740
(219) 432-3551

SAINT JOSEPH'S COLLEGE
Rensselaer 47978. Private (Roman Catholic) liberal arts. 1932/1982 (NCA). Sem. plan. Degrees: B,M. *Prof. Accred.:* Teacher Education (*e,s*). Pres. Rev. Charles H. Banet.
Enroll.: FTE 847
(219) 866-7111

SAINT MARY-OF-THE-WOODS COLLEGE
Saint Mary-of-the-Woods 47876. Private (Roman Catholic) liberal arts for women. 1919/1986 (NCA). Sem. plan. Degrees: B,M. *Prof. Accred.:* Music. Pres. Sister Barbara Doherty, S.P.
Enroll.: FTE 464
(812) 535-4141

SAINT MARY'S COLLEGE
Notre Dame 46556. Private (Roman Catholic) liberal arts primarily for women. 1922/1976 (NCA). Sem. plan. Degrees: B. *Prof. Accred.:* Art, Music, Nursing (B), Teacher Education (*e,s*). Pres. William A. Hickey.
Enroll.: FTE 1,806
(219) 284-4328

SAINT MEINRAD COLLEGE
St. Meinrad 47577. Private (Roman Catholic, Order of St. Benedict) liberal arts primarily for seminarians. 1961/1981 (NCA). Sem. plan. Degrees: B. Pres./Rector V. Rev. Daniel Buechlein, O.S.B.
Enroll.: FTE 169
(812) 357-6522

ST. MEINRAD SCHOOL OF THEOLOGY
St. Meinrad 47577. Private (Roman Catholic) professional; graduate only. 1979/1984 (NCA). Sem. plan. Degrees: P,M. *Prof. Accred.:* Theology (1968/1983, ATS). Pres./Rector Daniel Buechlein, O.S.B.
Enroll.: FTE 151
(812) 357-6611

SAWYER COLLEGE OF BUSINESS
6040 Hohman Ave., Hammond 46320. Private. 1982 (AICS). Qtr. plan. Certificates, diplomas. Pres. Ronald J. Adams.
Enroll.: 546 (*f.t.* 8 m., 538 w.)
(219) 931-0436

BRANCH CAMPUS
3803 E. Lincoln Hwy., Merrillville 46410. Dir. Mary Jo Dixon.
(219) 736-0436

SUPERIOR TRAINING SERVICES
334 Founders Rd., P.O. Box 68115, Indianapolis 46468. Address all inquiries to: 1817 N. Seventh St., Phoenix, AZ 85067. Private; combination home study-resident courses in tractor-trailer driving and heavy equipment operation. 1980/1985 (NHSC). Chairman Gary Eyler; Pres. Kenneth Wittington.
(317) 872-7274

ARIZONA TRAINING SITE BRANCH CAMPUS
Apache Junction 85220. Heavy equipment training site. 1982 (NHSC).
(602) 228-2973

ARIZONA TRAINING SITE BRANCH CAMPUS
27th Ave. and Thomas Rd., Phoenix 85008. Truck driving site.
(602) 275-8869

CALIFORNIA TRAINING SITE BRANCH CAMPUS
140 W. Agua Mansa Rd., P.O. Box 606, Rialto, CA 92376. Heavy equipment and truck-driver training site. 1982 (NHSC).

INDIANA TRAINING SITE BRANCH CAMPUS
Camp Atterbury, Edinburgh, IN 96124. Heavy equipment and truck-driver training site. 1985 (NHSC).

EXTENSION PENNSYLVANIA TRAINING SITE
Box 9, Deer Lake Camp., Fleetville, PA 18420. Truck driving training site. 1984 (NHSC).
(717) 945-5135

TAYLOR UNIVERSITY
Upland 46989. Private liberal arts college. 1947/1977 (NCA). Sem. plan. Degrees: B. *Prof. Accred.:* Music, Social Work (B), Teacher Education (*e,s*). Pres. Jay L. Kesler.
Enroll.: FTE 1,345
(317) 998-2751

TRANSPORT CAREERS, INC.
325 N. Taylor Rd., Garrett 46738. Private home study. 1977 (NHSC). Pres. H. B. Orr.
(219) 357-4171

TRI-STATE UNIVERSITY
Angola 46703. Private business and engineering. 1966/1985 (NCA). Qtr. plan. Degrees: B. *Prof. Accred.:* Engineering (aeronautical, chemical, civil, electrical, mechanical), Engineering Technology (drafting and design). Pres. Beaumont Davison.
Enroll.: FTE 934
(219) 665-3141

UNITED STATES ARMY SOLDIER SUPPORT INSTITUTE
Fort Benjamin Harrison 46216. Public (federal). 1980/1985 (NCA). Courses of varying lengths. Certificates. Commandant Major Gen. Maurice O. Edmonds.
Enroll.: FTE 2,500
(317) 542-4566

UNIVERSITY OF EVANSVILLE
Evansville 47702. Private (United Methodist). Overseas program: Harlaxton, Grantham, England. 1931/1986 (NCA). Qtr. plan. Degrees: A,B,M. *Prof. Accred.:* Engineering (electrical, mechanical), Music, Nursing (A,B,M), Physical Therapy, Teacher Education (*e,s*). Pres. Wallace B. Graves.
Enroll.: FTE 4,033
(812) 477-6241

UNIVERSITY OF INDIANAPOLIS
1400 E. Hanna Ave., Indianapolis 46227. Private (United Methodist) liberal arts. 1947/1978 (NCA). Qtr. plan. Degrees: A,B,M. *Prof. Accred.:* Music, Nursing (A), Physical Therapy, Teacher Education (*e,s*). Pres. Gene E. Sease.
Enroll.: FTE 1,768
(317) 788-3211

UNIVERSITY OF NOTRE DAME
Notre Dame 46556. Private (Roman Catholic). 1913/1984 (NCA). Sem. plan. Degrees: B,P,M,D. *Prof. Accred.:* Accounting (Type A), Architecture (B), Business (B,M), Engineering (aerospace, chemical, civil, electrical, mechanical, metallurgical), Law, Music, Psychology, Theology. Pres. Rev. Theodore M. Hesburgh, C.S.C.
Enroll.: FTE 9,686
(219) 283-6385

*UNIVERSITY OF SOUTHERN INDIANA
Evansville 47712. Public (state). 1974/1979 (NCA). Sem. plan. Degrees: A,B,M. *Prof. Accred.:* Dental Assisting, Dental Hygiene, Dental Laboratory Technology, Engineering Technology (civil, electrical, mechanical, metallurgical), Radiography, Respiratpru Therapy, Teacher Educatiom (*e,s*,. Pres. David L. Rice.

*Member Indiana State University System

Indiana

Enroll.: FTE 2,785
(219) 283-6385

VALPARAISO UNIVERSITY
Valparaiso 46383. Private (The Lutheran Church—Missouri Synod). 1929/1978 (NCA). Sem. plan. Degrees: A,B,P,M. *Prof. Accred.:* Engineering (civil, electrical, mechanical), Law, Music, Nursing (B), Social Work (B), Teacher Education (*e,s*). Pres. Robert V. Schnabel.
Enroll.: FTE 3,603
(219) 464-5000

VINCENNES UNIVERSITY
Vincennes 47591. Public (county and state) junior college. Accreditation includes Center at Jasper. 1958/1976 (NCA). Sem. plan. Degrees: A, certificates. *Prof. Accred.:* Art, Nursing (A), Practical Nursing, Respiratory Therapy. Pres. Phillip M. Summers.
Enroll.: FTE 5,397
(812) 882-3350

WABASH COLLEGE
Crawfordsville 47933. Private liberal arts for men. 1913/1983 (NCA). Sem. plan. Degrees: B. *Prof. Accred.:* Pres. Lewis S. Salter.
Enroll.: FTE 844
(317) 362-1400

IOWA

American Institute of Business
2500 Fleur Dr., Des Moines 50321. Private junior. 1959/1985 (AICS); 1986 (NCA). Qtr. plan. Degrees: A. Pres. Keith Fenton.
Enroll.: 1,963 (*f.t.* 537 m., 1,426 w.)
(515) 244-4221

American Institute of Commerce
Duck Creek Plaza, Bettendorf 52722. Private. 1957/1981 (AICS). Qtr. plan. Degrees: A, diplomas. Pres. John Huston.
Enroll.: 1,156 (*f.t.* 205 m., 951 w.)
(319) 355-6456

Briar Cliff College
Sioux City 51104. Private (Roman Catholic) liberal arts. 1945/1985 (NCA). 3-3 plan. Degrees: B. *Prof. Accred.:* Nursing (B), Social Work (B). Pres. ———.
Enroll.: FTE 1,079
(712) 279-5400

Buena Vista College
Storm Lake 50588. Private (United Presbyterian) liberal arts. 1952/1981 (NCA). Sem. plan. Degrees: B. *Prof. Accred.:* Social Work (B), Teacher Education (*e,s*). Pres. Keith G. Briscoe.
Enroll.: FTE 2,009
(712) 749-2103

Business Institute of Technology
P.O. Box 887, Cedar Falls 50613-0887. Private. 1983 (AICS). Qtr. plan. Degrees: A, certificates, diplomas. Pres. Rebecca A. Kusel.
Enroll.: 122
(319) 277-1235

Cedar Rapids School of Hairstyling
1531 First Ave., S.E., Cedar Rapids 52402. Private. 1977/1983 (NATTS). Courses of varying lengths. Diplomas. Pres. T. L. Millis.
Enroll.: 20 (*f.t.* 7 m., 13 w.)
(319) 362-1488

Central University of Iowa
Pella 50219. Private (Reformed Church in America) liberal arts college. 1942/1984 (NCA). 3-3 plan. Degrees: B. *Prof. Accred.:* Music, Teacher Education (*e,s*). Pres. Kenneth J. Weller.
Enroll.: FTE 1,565
(515) 628-4151

Clarke College
Dubuque 52001. Private (Roman Catholic) liberal arts primarily for women. 1918/1984 (NCA). Sem. plan. Degrees: B,M. *Prof. Accred.:* Music, Social Work (B), Teacher Education (*e,s*). Pres. Sister Catherine Dunn.
Enroll.: FTE 642
(319) 588-6385

Coe College
1220 First Ave., Cedar Rapids 52402. Private (United Presbyterian) liberal arts. 1913/1977 (NCA). 4-1-4 plan. Degrees: B. *Prof. Accred.:* Music, Nursing (B). Pres. John E. Brown.
Enroll.: FTE 1,026
(319) 399-8686

Cornell College
Mount Vernon 52314. Private (United Methodist) liberal arts. 1913/1983 (NCA). Sem. plan. Degrees: B. *Prof. Accred.:* Music. Pres. David G. Marker.
Enroll.: FTE 1,092
(319) 895-8811

Des Moines Area Community College
Ankeny 50021. Public (district). Accreditation includes Ankeny Campus, Boone Campus, and Urban Center at Des Moines. 1974/1983 (NCA). Qtr.plan. Degrees: A, certificates. *Prof. Accred.:* Dental Assisting, Dental Hygiene, Medical Assisting, Medical Laboratory Technology (A), Practical Nursing, Respiratory Therapy, Surgical Technology. Supt.-Pres. Joseph A. Borgen.
Enroll.: FTE 5,065
(515) 964-6260

Divine Word College
Epworth 52045. Private (Roman Catholic, Divine Word Missionaries) liberal arts and seminary. 1970/1986 (NCA). Sem. plan. Degrees: B. Pres. Rev. John J. Donaghey, S.V.D.
Enroll.: FTE 58
(319) 876-3353

Dordt College
Sioux Center 51250. Private (Christian Reformed) liberal arts. 1969/1981 (NCA). Sem. plan. Degrees: B. Pres. John B. Hulst.
Enroll.: FTE 1,008
(712) 722-3771

Drake University
26th St. and University Ave., Des Moines 50311. Private. 1913/1982 (NCA). Sem. plan. Degrees: B,P,M,D. *Prof. Accred.:* Art, Business (B,M), Journalism, Law, Medical Tech-

nology, Music, Nurse Anesthesia Education, Pharmacy, Teacher Education (*e,s,p*). Pres. Michael Ferrari.
Enroll.: FTE 4,459
(515) 271-2199

EASTERN IOWA COMMUNITY COLLEGE DISTRICT
Central office, Davenport 52803. Public (district) junior; accreditation includes Clinton Community College; Muscatine Community College; Scott Community College, including Bettendorf Campus and Palmer Campus, Davenport. 1983 (NCA). Qtr. plan. Degrees: A. *Prof. Accred.:* Radiography, Surgical Technology. Chanc. ———.
(319) 322-5015

FAITH BAPTIST BIBLE COLLEGE
1900 N.W. Fourth St., Ankeny 50021. Private. (Baptist) professional. 1969/1979 (AABC). Sem. plan. Degrees: B. Pres. Gordon L. Shipp.
Enroll.: 295
(515) 964-0601

GRACELAND COLLEGE
Lamoni 50140. Private (Reorganized Latter Day Saints) liberalarts. 1920/1977 (NCA). 4-1-4 plan. Degrees: A,B. *Prof. Accred.:* Nursing (B), Teacher Education (*e,s,*). Pres. Barbara Higdon.
Enroll.: FTE 957
(515) 784-5000

GRAND VIEW COLLEGE
Des Moines 50316. Private (Lutheran in America) liberal arts. 1959/1985 (NCA). 4-1-4 plan. Degrees: A,B. *Prof. Accred.:* Nursing (B). Pres. Karl Frederick Langrock.
Enroll.: FTE 1,097
(515) 263-2800

GRINNELL COLLEGE
Grinnell 50112. Private liberal arts. 1913/1978 (NCA). Sem. plan. Degrees: B. Pres. George A. Drake.
Enroll.: FTE 1,360
(515) 236-2587

HAMILTON BUSINESS COLLEGE
100 First St., N.W., Mason City 50401. Private. 1957/1980 (AICS). Qtr. plan. Diplomas. Dir. Kay Holland.
Enroll.: 1,060 (*f.t.* 182 m., 878 w.)
(515) 423-2530

HAMILTON BUSINESS COLLEGE
1924 D St., S.W., Cedar Rapids 52404. Private. 1985 (AICS). Courses of varying lengths. Certificates, diplomas. Dir. James Mullen.
(319) 363-0481

BRANCH CAMPUS
3675 S. Noland Rd., Suite #300, Independence, MO 64055. Dir. Mary Ann Mooee.
(816) 833-4430

HAMILTON TECHNICAL COLLEGE
425 E. 59th St., P.O. Box 2674, Davenport 52807. Private. 1974/1979 (NATTS). Sem. plan. Degrees: A. Dir. Charles L. Hamilton.
Enroll.: 498 (*f.t.* 470 m., 28 w.)
(319) 386-3570

HAWKEYE INSTITUTE OF TECHNOLOGY
Waterloo 50704. Public 2-year technical. 1975/1980 (NCA). Qtr. plan. Degrees: A. *Prof. Accred.:* Dental Assisting, Dental Hygiene, Engineering Technology (civil), Medical Laboratory Technology A), Respiratory Therapy Technology. Supt. John E. Hawse.
Enroll.: FTE 2,071
(319) 296-2320

INDIAN HILLS COMMUNITY COLLEGE
Ottumwa 52501. Public (state) junior. 1977/1983 (NCA). Qtr. plan. Degrees: A. *Prof. Accred.:* Medical Record Technology, Radiography. Pres. Lyle Adrian Hellyer.
Enroll.: FTE 670
(515) 683-5111

CENTERVILLE CAMPUS
Centerville 52544. Dir. Richard Sharp.
Enroll.: 316 (*f.t.* 161 m., 126 w.)
(515) 856-2143

IOWA CENTRAL COMMUNITY COLLEGE
Fort Dodge 50501. Public (district) junior. Accreditation includes centers at Eagle Grove, Fort Dodge, and Webster City. 1974/1984 (NCA). Sem. plan. Degrees: A. *Prof. Accred.:* Dental Assisting, Medical Assisting. Supt. Harvey D. Martin.
Enroll.: FTE 2,760
(515) 576-3103

IOWA LAKES COMMUNITY COLLEGE
Estherville 51334. Public (district) junior. Accreditation includes centers at Estherville and Emmetsburg. 1976/1981 (NCA). Qtr. plan. Degrees: A. Supt. Richard H. Blacker.
Enroll.: FTE 2,747
(712) 362-2601

IOWA SCHOOL OF BARBERING AND HAIRSTYLING
603 E. Sixth St., Des Moines 50316. Private. 1975/1980 (NATTS). Courses of varying lengths. Diplomas. Pres. T. L. Millis.
Enroll.: 32 (*f.t.* 15 m., 17 w.)
(515) 244-0971

IOWA STATE UNIVERSITY
Ames 50011. Public. 1916/1976 (NCA). Sem. plan. Degrees: A,B,P,M,D. *Prof. Accred.:* Architecture (M), Dietetics, Engineering (aerospace, agricultural, ceramic, chemical, civil, computer, construction, electrical, engineering science, industrial, mechanical, metallurgical, nuclear, surveying), Engineering Technology (construction, electronics, mechanical, nuclear), Forestry, Health Administration, Home Economics, Interior Design, Journalism, Landscape Architecture (B), Music, Psychology, Social Work (B), Teacher Education (*e,s,p*), Veterinary Medicine. Pres. Gordon P. Eaton.
Enroll.: FTE 24,672
(515) 294-2042

IOWA VALLEY COMMUNITY COLLEGE DISTRICT
Marshalltown 50158. Public (city) junior. Sem. plan. Degrees: A. Dist. Supt. John J. Prihoda.
(515) 752-4643

ELLSWORTH COMMUNITY COLLEGE
Iowa Falls 50126. 1963/1982 (NCA). Dean Duane R. Lloyd.
Enroll.: FTE 895
(515) 648-4611

MARSHALLTOWN COMMUNITY COLLEGE
Marshalltown 50158. 1966/1982 (NCA). *Prof. Accred.:* Dental Assisting, Medical Assisting, Surgical Technology. Dean Paul L. Kegel.
Enroll.: FTE 992
(515) 752-7106

IOWA WESLEYAN COLLEGE
Mount Pleasant 52641. Private (United Methodist) liberal arts. 1916/1981 (NCA). 4-1-4 plan. Degrees: B. *Prof. Accred.:* Nursing (B). Pres. Dr. Robert J. Prins.
Enroll.: FTE 652
(319) 385-8021

IOWA WESTERN COMMUNITY COLLEGE DISTRICT
Council Bluffs 51501. Public (district) junior. Accreditation includes Clarinda Center. 1975/1984 (NCA). Qtr. plan. Degrees: A. *Prof. Accred.:* Dental Assisting, Medical Assisting, Surgical Technology. Supt.-Pres. Robert D. Looft.
Enroll.: FTE 1,932
(712) 325-3201

KIRKWOOD COMMUNITY COLLEGE
Cedar Rapids 52406. Public (district) junior. 1970/1980 (NCA). Qtr. plan. Degrees: A. *Prof. Accred.:* Dental Assisting, Dental Laboratory Technology, Medical Assisting, Medical Record Technology, Respiratory Therapy. Supt./Acting. Norman R. Nielsen
Enroll.: FTE 4,590
(319) 398-5411

LINCOLN TECHNICAL INSTITUTE
2501 Vine St., West Des Moines 50265. Private. 1971/1982 (NATTS). Sem. plan. Diplomas. Dir. Terry Johnson.
Enroll.: *f.t.* 349 m.
(515) 225-8433

LORAS COLLEGE
Dubuque 52001. Private (Roman Catholic) liberal arts. 1917/1980 (NCA). Sem. plan. Degrees: B,M. *Prof. Accred.:* Social Work (B), Teacher Education (*e,s*). Pres. Pasquale di Pasquale, Jr.
Enroll.: FTE 1,793
(319) 588-7103

LUTHER COLLEGE
Decorah 52101. Private (American Lutheran) liberal arts. 1915/1979 (NCA). 4-1-4 plan. Degrees: B. *Prof. Accred.:* Music, Nursing (B), Social Work (B), Teacher Education (*e,s*). Pres. Hugh George Anderson.
Enroll.: FTE 2,034
(319) 387-1001

MAHARISHI INTERNATIONAL UNIVERSITY
Fairfield 52556. Private liberal arts. 1980/1985 (NCA). Sem. plan. Degrees: B,M,D. Pres. Bevan Morris.
Enroll.: FTE 726
(515) 472-5031

MARYCREST COLLEGE
Davenport 52804. Private (Roman Catholic) liberal arts. 1955/1986 (NCA). Sem. plan. Degrees: B,M. *Prof. Accred.:* Nursing (B), Social Work (B). Pres. Sr. Anne Therese Collins.
Enroll.: FTE 1,038
(319) 326-9221

MORNINGSIDE COLLEGE
Sioux City 51106. Private (United Methodist) liberal arts. 1913/1984 (NCA). Sem. plan.

Degrees: A,B,M. *Prof. Accred.:* Music, Social Work (B), Teacher Education (*e,s*). Pres. Miles Tommeraasen.
Enroll.: FTE 1,257
(712) 247-5100

MOUNT MERCY COLLEGE
Cedar Rapids 52402. Private (Roman Catholic) liberal arts. 1932/1973 (NCA). 4-1-4 plan. Degrees: B. *Prof. Accred.:* Nursing (B), Social Work (B). Pres. Thomas R. Feld.
Enroll.: FTE 1,075
(319) 363-8213

MOUNT SAINT CLARE COLLEGE
Clinton 52732. Private (Roman Catholic) liberal arts. 1950/1984 (NCA). Sem. plan. Degrees: A,B. Pres. Rev. Charles E. Lang.
Enroll.: FTE 300
(319) 242-4023

NATIONAL EDUCATION CENTER—NATIONAL INSTITUTE OF TECHNOLOGY CAMPUS
1119 Fifth St., West Des Moines 50265. Private. 1968/1979 (NATTS). Qtr. plan. Degrees: A, diplomas. Dir. Michael C. Akerman.
Enroll.: 302 (*f.t.* 251 m., 51 w.)
(515) 223-1486

NORTH IOWA AREA COMMUNITY COLLEGE
Mason City 50401. Public (district) junior. 1919/1984 (NCA). Sem. plan. Degrees: A. Supt. David L. Buettner.
Enroll.: FTE 2,016
(515) 423-1264

NORTHEAST IOWA TECHNICAL INSTITUTE
Calmar 52132. Public (district) junior. 1977/1982 (NCA). Qtr. plan. Degrees: A. Supt./Pres. Clyde Kramer
Enroll.: FTE 1,125
(319) 562-3263

NORTHWEST IOWA TECHNICAL COLLEGE
Sheldon 51201. Public (district) junior. 1980/1985 (NCA). Qtr. plan. Degrees: A. Supt. C. E. Martin.
Enroll.: FTE 470
(712) 324-2587

NORTHWESTERN COLLEGE
Orange City 51041. Private (Reformed Church in America) liberal arts and teachers. 1953/1986 (NCA). Sem. plan. Degrees: A, B. *Prof. Accred.:* Teacher Education (*e,s*). Pres. James Bultman.
Enroll.: FTE 843
(712) 737-4821

OPEN BIBLE COLLEGE
2633 Fleur Dr., Des Moines 50321. Private (Open Bible Standard) professional. 1977 (AABC). Sem. plan. Degrees: A,B. Pres. Dennis M. Schmidt.
Enroll.: 72
(515) 283-0476

PALMER COLLEGE OF CHIROPRACTIC
1000 Brady St., Davenport 52803. Private professional. 1984 (NCA). Sem. plan. Degrees: P. *Prof. Accred.:* Chiropractic Education. Pres. J. F. McAndrews.
Enroll.: FTE 1,690
(319) 326-9600

ST. AMBROSE COLLEGE
Davenport 52803. Private (Roman Catholic) liberal arts. 1927/1978 (NCA). Sem. plan. Degrees: B,M. Pres. William J. Bakrow.
Enroll.: FTE 1,684
(319) 324-1681

SIMPSON COLLEGE
Indianola 50125. Private (United Methodist) liberal arts. 1913/1986 (NCA). 4-1-4 plan. Degrees: B. *Prof. Accred.:* Music, Teacher Education (*e,s*). Pres. Robert E. McBride.
Enroll.: FTE 982
(515) 961-1611

SOUTHEASTERN COMMUNITY COLLEGE
West Burlington 52655. Public (district) junior; accreditation includes all locations. 1974/1982 (NCA). Qtr. plan. Degrees: A. *Prof. Accred.:* Medical Assisting. Supt. R. Gene Gardner.
Enroll.: FTE 1,215
(319) 752-2731

SOUTHWESTERN COMMUNITY COLLEGE
Creston 50801. Public (district) junior. 1975/1983 (NCA). Sem. plan. Degrees: A. Supt. Richard L. Byerly.
Enroll.: FTE 689
(515) 782-7081

SPENCER SCHOOL OF BUSINESS
217 W. Fifth St., Spencer 51301. Private. 1972/1984 (AICS). Qtr. plan. Diplomas. Pres. James R. Grove.
Enroll.: 643 (*f.t.* 51 m., 592 w.)
(712) 262-7290

UNIVERSITY OF DUBUQUE
Dubuque 52001. Private (United Presbyterian) liberal arts. 1921/1984 (NCA). Sem. plan. Degrees: B. *Prof. Accred.:* Music, Nursing

(B), Social Work (B), Teacher Education (*e,s*). Pres. Walter F. Peterson.
Enroll.: FTE 793
(319) 589-3223

UNIVERSITY OF DUBUQUE—THEOLOGICAL SEMINARY
Dubuque 52001. Private (Presbyterian, U.S.A.) professional; graduate only. 1976/1980 (NCA). 4-1-4 plan. Degrees: P,M,D. *Prof. Accred.:* Theology (1944/1980, ATS). Pres. Walter F. Peterson.
Enroll.: 170
(319) 589-2222

UNIVERSITY OF IOWA
Iowa City 52242. Public (state). 1913/1978 (NCA). Sem. plan. Degrees: B,P,M,D. *Prof. Accred.:* Assistant to the Primary Care Physician, Business (B,M), Dental Hygiene, Dentistry, Dietetics, Engineering (chemical, civil, electrical, industrial, mechanical), Health Services Administration, Home Economics, Journalism, Law, Librarianship, Medical Technology, Medicine, Music, Nuclear Medicine Technology, Nursing (B,M), Pharmacy, Physical Therapy, Psychology, Rehabilitation Counseling, Social Work (B,M), Speech Pathology and Audiology, Teacher Education (*e,s,p*). Pres. James O. Freedman.
Enroll.: 24,832
(319) 353-3120

UNIVERSITY OF NORTHERN IOWA
Cedar Falls 50614. Public (state). 1913/1981 (NCA). Sem. plan. Degrees: B,M,D. *Prof. Accred.:* Art, Home Economics, Music, Social Work (B), Speech Pathology, Teacher Education (*e,s,p*). Pres. Constantine W. Curris.
Enroll.: FTE 9,356
(319) 273-2566

*UNIVERSITY OF OSTEOPATHIC MEDICINE AND HEALTH SCIENCES
3200 Grand Ave., Des Moines 50312. Private professional. 1901/1975. Sem. plan. Degrees: B. *Prof. Accred.:* Osteopathy, Physician's Assistant, Podiatry. Pres. J. Leonard Azneer.
Enroll.: FTE 1,053
(515) 271-1400

UPPER IOWA UNIVERSITY
Fayette 52142. Private liberal arts college. 1913/1982 (NCA). 4-1-4 plan. Degrees: B. Pres. James R. Rocheleau.
Enroll.: FTE 873
(319) 425-3311

VENNARD COLLEGE
University Park 52595. Private (Interdenominational) professional. 1948/1974 (AABC). Sem. plan. Degrees: A,B. Pres. Merne A. Harris.
Enroll.: 174
(515) 673-8391

WALDORF COLLEGE
Forest City 50436. Private (American Lutheran) junior. 1948/1979 (NCA). Sem. plan. Degrees: A. Pres. Walter E. Hamm.
Enroll.: FTE 441
(515) 582-2450

WARTBURG COLLEGE
Waverly 50677. Private (American Lutheran) liberal arts. 1948/1977 (NCA). 4-4-1 plan. Degrees: B. *Prof. Accred.:* Music, Social Work (B). Pres. Robert L. Vogel.
Enroll.: FTE 1,254
(319) 352-8200

WARTBURG THEOLOGICAL SEMINARY
Dubuque 52001. Private (American Lutheran) professional; graduate only. 1976 (NCA). 4-1-4 plan. Degrees: P,M,D. *Prof. Accred.:* Theology (1944/1976, ATS). Pres. Roger W. Fjeld.
Enroll.: 248
(319) 589-0200

WESTERN IOWA TECH COMMUNITY COLLEGE
P.O. Box 265, Sioux City 51102. Public junior. 1977/1985 (NCA). Qtr. plan. Degrees: A. *Prof. Accred.:* Dental Assisting, Surgical Technology. Supt. Robert H. Kiser.
Enroll.: FTE 1,348
(712) 276-0380

WESTMAR COLLEGE
Le Mars 51031. Private (United Methodist) liberal arts. 1953/1986 (NCA). 4-1-4 plan. Degrees: B. Pres. Arthur W. Richardson.
Enroll.: FTE 466
(712) 546-7081

WILLIAM PENN COLLEGE
Oskaloosa 52577. Private (Friends) liberal arts. 1913/1981 (NCA). Sem. plan. Degrees: B. *Prof. Accred.:* Teacher Education (*e,s*). Pres. John D. Wagoner.
Enroll.: FTE 484
(515) 673-8311

*Candidate for Accreditation by Regional Accrediting Commission

KANSAS

Allen County Community College
Iola 66749. Public (district). 1974/1982 (NCA). Sem. plan. Degrees: A. Pres. Hugh L. Haire.
Enroll.: FTE 702
(316) 365-5116

Baker University
Baldwin City 66006. Private (United Methodist) liberal arts college. 1913/1985 (NCA). 4-1-4 plan. Degrees: B,M. *Prof. Accred.:* Teacher Education (*e,s*). Pres. Ralph M. Tanner.
Enroll.: FTE 771
(913) 594-6451

Barton County Community College
Great Bend 67530. Public (district). 1974/1985 (NCA). Sem. plan. Degrees: A. *Prof. Accred.:* Medical Labroratory Technology (A), Nursing (A). Pres. Jimmie L. Downing.
Enroll.: FTE 1,810
(316) 792-2701

Benedictine College
Atchison 66002. Private (Roman Catholic, Benedictine Order) liberal arts and theology. 1971/1985 (NCA). 4-1-4 plan. Degrees: B. *Prof. Accred.:* Music, Teacher Education (*e,s*). Pres. Rev. Gerard Senecal, O.S.B.
Enroll.: FTE 821
(913) 367-6110

Bethany College
Lindsborg 67456. Private (Lutheran in America) liberal arts. 1932/1980 (NCA). 4-1-4 plan. Degrees: B. *Prof. Accred.:* Music, Social Work (B), Teacher Education (*e,s*). Pres. Peter J. Ristuben.
Enroll.: FTE 816
(913) 227-3311

Bethel College
North Newton 67117. Private (General Mennonite) liberal arts. 1938/1979 (NCA). 4-1-4 plan. Degrees: B. *Prof. Accred.:* Nursing (B), Social Work (B). Pres. Harold J. Schultz.
Enroll.: FTE 604
(316) 283-2500

The Brown Mackie College
126 S. Santa Fe, Salina 67401. Private business. 1953/1985 (AICS); 1980/1984 (NCA). Qtr. plan. Certificates, diplomas. Pres. M. Gary Talley.
Enroll.: FTE 328
(913) 825-5422

Branch Campus
8000 W. 110th St., Overland Park 66210. Dir. John C. Miller.
(913) 451-3856

Bryan Institute
1004 S. Oliver, Wichita 67218. Private. 1971/1983 (NATTS). Courses of varying lengths. Diplomas. *Prof. Accred.:* Medical Assisting. Pres. Brian Dickinson.
Enroll.: 154 (*f.t.* 60 m., 84 w.)
(316) 685-2284

Extension
9400 Nall Ave., Overland Park 66207: mailing address; P.O. Box 4460, zip 66204. *Prof. Accred.:* Medical Assisting. Dir. Terry Facht.
(913) 341-9201

Butler County Community College
El Dorado 67042. Public (district). 1970/1980 (NCA). Sem. plan. Degrees: A. *Prof. Accred.:* Nursing (A). Pres. Carl L. Heinrich.
Enroll.: FTE 1,879
(316) 321-5083

Capitol City Barber College
812 N. Kansas Ave., Topeka 66608. Private. 1982 (NATTS). Courses of varying lengths. Diplomas. Dir. Gary Croucher.
Enroll.: 15 (*f.t.* 7 m., 8 w.)
(913) 234-5401

Central Baptist Theological Seminary
Seminary Heights, Kansas City 66102. Private (American Baptist) professional and graduate only. 1979/1985 (NCA). Sem. plan. Degrees: P,M. *Prof. Accred.:* Theology (1962/1984, ATS). Pres. William F. Keucher.
Enroll.: 135
(913) 371-5313

Central College
McPherson 67460. Private (Free Methodist) junior. 1975/1980 (NCA). 4-1-4 plan. Degrees: A. Pres. Dorsey Brause.
Enroll.: FTE 265
(316) 241-0723

Central College
2502 E. Douglas, Wichita 67214. Private business and technical. 1966/1984 (AICS). Qtr. plan. Diplomas. Dir. Alvin J. Hennessy.
Enroll.: 315 (*f.t.* 112 m., 139 w.)
(316) 684-5138

CLIMATE CONTROL INSTITUTE
3030 N. Hillside, Wichita 67219. Private. 1976/1980 (NATTS). Courses of varying lengths. Certificates. Pres. D.J. Hampton.
Enroll.: 85 (*f.t.* 49 m.)
(316) 686-7355

CLOUD COUNTY COMMUNITY COLLEGE
Concordia 66901. Public (county) junior. 1977/1980 (NCA). Sem. plan. Degrees: A. *Prof. Accred.:* Nursing (A). Pres. James P. Ihrig.
Enroll.: FTE 903
(913) 243-1435

COFFEYVILLE COMMUNITY COLLEGE
Coffeyville 67337. Public (district). 1972/1983 (NCA). Sem. plan. *Prof. Accred.:* Medical Laboratory Technology (A). Degrees: A. Pres. Dan Kinney.
Enroll.: FTE 670
(316) 251-4350

COLBY COMMUNITY COLLEGE
Colby 67701. Public (district) junior. 1972/1985 (NCA). Sem. plan. Degrees: A, certificates. *Prof. Accred.:* Practical Nursing. Pres. James H. Tangeman.
Enroll.: FTE 952
(913) 462-3984

CONTROL DATA INSTITUTE
Gateway Centre Tower II, Fourth and State, Suite 800, Kansas City 66101. Private. 1985 (NATTS). Courses of varying lengths. Certificates. Pres. Arthur L. Kimbrough.
(913) 321-3400

COWLEY COUNTY COMMUNITY COLLEGE
Arkansas City 67005. Public (district). 1975/1980 (NCA). Sem. plan. Degrees: A. Pres. Gwen A. Nelson.
Enroll.: FTE 831
(316) 442-0430

CRANFORD SCHOOL OF BUSINESS
1600 N. Lorraine, Hutchinson 67501. Private. 1966/1984 (AICS). Courses of varying lengths. Certificates, diplomas. Dir. Nevada Dauber.
Enroll.: 111 (*f.t.* 11 m., 100 w.)
(316) 663-4419

DODGE CITY COMMUNITY COLLEGE
Dodge City 67801. Public (county). 1966/1976 (NCA). Sem. plan. Degrees: A, certificates. *Prof. Accred.:* Nursing (A), Practical Nursing. Pres. Gay R. Dahn.
Enroll.: FTE 891
(316) 225-1321

DONNELLY COLLEGE
1236 Sandusky Ave., Kansas City 66102. Private (Roman Catholic) junior. 1958/1979 (NCA). Sem. plan. Degrees: A. Pres. Rev. Raymond J. Davern.
Enroll.: FTE 529
(913) 621-6070

ELECTRONIC COMPUTER PROGRAMMING INSTITUTE
401 E. Douglas, Commerce Plaza, L/L, Wichita 67202. Private. 1972/1983 (NATTS). Courses of varying lengths. Certificates. Dir. Walter S. Johnson.
Enroll.: 62 (*f.t.* 22 m., 15 w.)
(316) 263-0276

EMPORIA STATE UNIVERSITY
Emporia 66801. Public liberal arts and teachers. 1915/1985 (NCA). Sem. plan. Degrees: B,M.S *Prof. Accred.:* Journalism, Music, Rehabilitation Counseling, Teacher Education (*e,s,p*). Pres. Robert E. Glennen, Jr.
Enroll.: FTE 4,357
(316) 343-1200

FORT HAYS STATE UNIVERSITY
Hays 67601. Public liberal arts and teachers. 1915/1982 (NCA). Sem. plan. Degrees: B,M. *Prof. Accred.:* Music, Nursing (B), Radiography, Teacher Education (*e,s,p*). Pres. G. W. Tomanek.
Enroll.: FTE 4,258
(913) 628-5880

FORT SCOTT COMMUNITY COLLEGE
Fort Scott 66701. Public (district). 1976/1981 (NCA). Sem. plan. Degrees: A. Pres. Richard D. Hedges.
Enroll.: FTE 614
(316) 223-2700

FRIENDS BIBLE COLLEGE
P.O. Box 288, Haviland 67059. Private (Friends) professional. 1975/1985 (AABC). Sem. plan. Degrees: A,B. Pres. Robin Johnston.
Enroll.: 99
(316) 862-5252

FRIENDS UNIVERSITY
Wichita 67213. Private (Friends) liberal arts college. 1915/1986 (NCA). Sem. plan. Degrees: B,M. *Prof. Accred.:* Music, Teacher Education (*e,s*). Pres. Richard Felix.
Enroll.: FTE 720
(316) 261-5800

GARDEN CITY COMMUNITY COLLEGE
Garden City 67846. Public (district). 1975/1985 (NCA). Sem. plan. Degrees: A. *Prof. Accred.:* Nursing (A). Pres. Thomas Saffell.
Enroll.: FTE 1,055
(316) 276-7611

HASKELL INDIAN JUNIOR COLLEGE
P.O. Box H-1305 Lawrence 66044. Public (state). 1979/1984 (NCA). Sem. plan. Degrees: A. *Prof. Accred.:* Dental Assisting. Pres. Gerald E. Gipp.
Enroll.: FTE 876
(913) 841-2000

HESSTON COLLEGE
Hesston 67062. Private (Mennonite) junior. 1964/1984 (NCA). 4-1-4 plan. Degrees: A. *Prof. Accred.:* Nursing (A), Respiratory Therapy. Pres. Kirk Alliman.
Enroll.: FTE 491
(316) 327-4221

HIGHLAND COMMUNITY COLLEGE
Highland 66035. Public (district). 1977/1982 (NCA). Sem. plan. Degrees: A. Pres. Larry Devane.
Enroll.: FTE 648
(913) 442-3238

HUTCHINSON COMMUNITY COLLEGE
Hutchinson 67501. Public (county and state). 1960/1984 (NCA). Sem. plan. Degrees: A. *Prof. Accred.:* Medical Record Technology, Nursing (A), Radiography. Pres. James H. Stringer.
Enroll.: FTE 1,666
(316) 663-3500

INDEPENDENCE COMMUNITY COLLEGE
Independence 67301. Public (district). 1957/1978 (NCA). Sem. plan. Degrees: A. Pres. Thomas R. Burke.
Enroll.: FTE 571
(316) 331-4100

JOHNSON COUNTY COMMUNITY COLLEGE
Overland Park 66210. Public (district). 1975/1980 (NCA). Sem. plan. Degrees: A. *Prof. Accred.:* Dental Hygiene, Nursing (A). Pres. Charles J. Carlsen.
Enroll.: FTE 4,197
(913) 888-8500

KANSAS CITY COLLEGE OF MEDICAL AND DENTAL CAREERS
660 College Blvd., Suite 100, Overland Park 66211. Private. 1984 (NATTS). Courses of varying lengths. Certificates. *Prof. Accred.:* Medical Assisting. Dir. Mike Savely.
(913) 491-6350

KANSAS CITY KANSAS COMMUNITY COLLEGE
7250 State Ave., Kansas City 66112. Public (county and state). 1951/1986 (NCA). Sem. plan. Degrees: A. *Prof. Accred.:* Nursing (A). Pres. Alton L. Davies.
Enroll.: FTE 2,526
(913) 334-1100

KANSAS NEWMAN COLLEGE
3100 McCormick Ave., Wichita 67213. Private (Roman Catholic) liberal arts. 1967/1977 (NCA). Sem. plan. Degrees: B. *Prof. Accred.:* Nursing (A,B). Pres. Rev. Robert Giroux, O.S.B.
Enroll.: FTE 526
(316) 942-4291

KANSAS SCHOOL OF HAIRSTYLING
1207 E. Douglas Ave., Wichita 67211. Private. 1984 (NATTS). Courses of varying lengths. Certificates. Dir. George Helterbrand.
(316) 264-4891

KANSAS STATE UNIVERSITY
Manhattan 66506. Public. 1916/1982 (NCA). Sem. plan. Degrees: B,P,M,D. *Prof. Accred.:* Architecture (B), Business (B,M), Construction Education, Dietetics, Engineering (agricultural, architectural, chemical, civil, electrical, industrial, mechanical, nuclear), Engineering Technology (computer, electronic, environmental, mechanical, production management), Home Economics, Interior Design, Journalism, Landscape Architecture (B,M), Music, Social Work (B), Speech Pathology, Teacher Education (*e,s,p*), Veterinary Medicine. Pres. Jon Wefald.
Enroll.: FTE 15,996
(913) 532-6222

KANSAS TECHNICAL INSTITUTE
Salina 67401. Public (state) 2-year. 1980/1985(NCA). Sem. plan. Degrees: A. *Prof. Accred.:* Engineering Technology (civil, computer, electronic, mechanical). Pres. Anthony L. Tilmans.
Enroll.: FTE 437
(913) 825-0275

KANSAS WESLEYAN UNIVERSITY
Salina 67401. Private (United Methodist) liberal arts college. 1916/1985 (NCA). 4-1-4 plan. Degrees: B. Pres. Rev. Marshall P. Stanton.

Enroll.: FTE 437
(913) 827-5541

LABETTE COMMUNITY COLLEGE
Parsons 67357. Public (district). 1976/1981 (NCA). Sem. plan. Degrees: A. *Prof. Accred.:* Nursing (A), Radiography, Respiratory Therapy, Respiratory Therapy Technology . Pres. Gery Hochanadel.
Enroll.: FTE 1,206
(316) 421-6700

MANHATTAN CHRISTIAN COLLEGE
1407 Anderson, Manhattan 66502. Private (Churches of Christ) liberal arts and professional. 1948/1976 (AABC). Sem. plan. Degrees: A,B. Pres. Kenneth D. Cable.
Enroll.: 171
(913) 539-3571

MARYMOUNT COLLEGE
Salina 67401. Private (Roman Catholic) liberal arts. 1932/1982 (NCA). 3-3 plan. Degrees: B. *Prof. Accred.:* Music, Nursing (B), Teacher Education (*e,s*). Pres. Dan C. Johnson.
Enroll.: FTE 519
(913) 825-2101

MCPHERSON COLLEGE
McPherson 67460. Private (Church of Brethren) liberal arts. 1921/1983 (NCA). 4-1-4 plan. Degrees: B. Pres. Paul W. Hoffman.
Enroll.: FTE 487
(316) 241-0731

MID-AMERICA NAZARENE COLLEGE
Olathe 66061. Private (Nazarene) liberal arts. 1974/1979 (NCA). 4-1-4 plan. Degrees: B. *Prof. Accred.:* Nursing (B). Pres. Donald Owens.
Enroll.: FTE 498
(913) 782-3750

NEOSHO COUNTY COMMUNITY COLLEGE
Chanute 66720. Public (district). 1976/1986 (NCA). Sem. plan. Degrees: A. Pres. J. C. Sanders.
Enroll.: FTE 477
(316) 431-2820

NORTH CENTRAL KANSAS AREA VOCATIONAL TECHNICAL SCHOOL
Beloit 67420. Public 2-year. 1981 (NCA). Qtr. plan. Certificates. *Prof. Accred.:* Practical Nursing. Dir. Robert J. Severance.
Enroll.: FTE 455
(913) 738-2276

OTTAWA UNIVERSITY
Ottawa 66067. Private (American Baptist) liberal arts. Accreditation includes College Without Campus program, Phoenix, AZ and Kansas City, MO. 1914/1984 (NCA). Sem. plan. Degrees: B. Pres. Wilbur D. Wheaton.
Enroll.: FTE 767
(913) 242-5200

PITTSBURG STATE UNIVERSITY
Pittsburg 66762. Public liberal arts and professional. 1915/1983 (NCA). Sem. plan. Degrees: B,M. *Prof. Accred.:* Engineering Technology (construction, electronics, manufacturing, mechanical design, plastics), Music, Nursing (B), Social Work (B), Teacher Education (*e,s,p*). Pres. Donald W. Wilson.
Enroll.: FTE 4,404
(316) 231-7000

PLATT COLLEGE
10990 Quivira Rd., Overland Park 66210. Private business. 1979/1982 (AICS). Courses of varying lengths. Certificates. Pres. Frank T. Ollin.
Enroll.: 981 (*f.t.* 355 m., 626 w.)
(913) 469-6000

PLATT COLLEGE
2010 California, Topeka 66607. Private business. 1984 (AICS). Qtr. plan. Certificates, diplomas. Pres. Oscar L. Adams, Jr.
Enroll.: 337
(913) 232-6352

PRATT COMMUNITY COLLEGE
Pratt 67124. Public (district). 1976/1981 (NCA). Sem. plan. Degrees: A. Pres. John Gwaltney.
Enroll.: FTE 751
(316) 672-5641

ST. JOHN'S COLLEGE
Winfield 67156. Private (Lutheran-Missouri Synod) primarily training for church service. 1961/1984 (NCA). 4-1-4 plan. Degrees: A,B. Pres. Erich H. Helge.
Enroll.: 251
(316) 221-4000

SAINT MARY COLLEGE
Leavenworth 66048. Private (Roman Catholic) liberal arts primarily for women. 1928/1977 (NCA). Sem. plan. Degrees: B. *Prof. Accred.:* Music, Nursing (B), Teacher Education (*e,s*). Pres. Sister Mary Janet McGilley.
Enroll.: FTE 560
(913) 682-5151

SAINT MARY OF THE PLAINS COLLEGE
Dodge City 67801. Private (Roman Catholic) liberal arts. 1963/1984 (NCA). 4-1-4 plan. Degrees: B. *Prof. Accred.:* Music, Nursing (A,B), Social Work (B), Teacher Education (*e,s*). Pres. Michael J. McCarthy.
Enroll.: FTE 497
(316) 225-4171

SEWARD COUNTY COMMUNITY COLLEGE
Liberal 67901. Public (district). 1975/1980 (NCA). Sem. plan. Degrees: A, certificates. *Prof. Accred.:* Medical Laboratory Technology (A), Nursing (A), Practical Nursing. Pres. ———.
Enroll.: FTE 634
(316) 624-1951

SOUTHWESTERN COLLEGE
Winfield 67156. Private (United Methodist) liberal arts. 1918/1986 (NCA). 4-1-4 plan. Degrees: B,M. *Prof. Accred.:* Music, Social Work (B). Pres. Bruce Blake.
Enroll.: FTE 502
(316) 221-4150

STERLING COLLEGE
Sterling 67579. Private (United Presbyterian) liberal arts. 1928/1977 (NCA). 4-1-4 plan. Degrees: B. *Prof. Accred.:* Teacher Education (*e,s*). Pres. Robert A. Veitch.
Enroll.: FTE 430
(316) 278-2173

TABOR COLLEGE
Hillsboro 67063. Private (Mennonite Brethren) liberal arts. 1965/1985 (NCA). Sem. plan. Degrees: B. *Prof. Accred.:* Music, Social Work (B). Pres. Vernon Janzen.
Enroll.: FTE 368
(316) 947-3121

TOPEKA TECHNICAL COLLEGE
3600 S. Topeka Blvd., Topeka 66611. Private. 1971/1982 (NATTS). Qtr. plan. Diplomas. Dir. Jerry Barnett.
Enroll.: 125 (*f.t.* 74 m., 51 w.)
(913) 266-3180

U.S. ARMY COMMAND AND GENERAL STAFF COLLEGE
Fort Leavenworth 66027. Public (federal). 1976/1985 (NCA). Sem. plan. Degrees: M. Commandant Lt. Gen. Gerald T. Bartlett.
Enroll.: FTE 1,000
(913) 684-2960

UNITED TECHNICAL INSTITUTE
1301 S. Handley, Wichita 67213. Private. 1984 (NATTS). Courses of varying lengths. Certificates. Pres. R. P. Cooper.
(316) 263-7939

UNIVERSITY OF KANSAS
Lawrence 66045. Public (state). Accreditation includes Medical Center at Kansas City. 1913/1985 (NCA). Sem. plan. Degrees: B,P,M,D. *Prof. Accred.:* Architecture (B,M), Art, Business (B,M), Cytotechnology, Dietetics, Engineering (aerospace, architectural, chemical, civil, electrical, engineering physics, mechanical, petroleum), Journalism, Law, Medical Record Administration, Medical Technology, Medicine, Music, Nuclear Medicine Technology, Nurse Anesthesia Education, Nursing (B,M), Occupational Therapy, Pharmacy, Physical Therapy, Psychology, Radiation Therapy, Radiation Therapy Technology, Radiography, Respiratory Therapy, Social Work (B,M), Speech Pathology and Audiology, Teacher Education (*e,s,p*). Chanc. Gene A. Budig.
Enroll.: FTE 21,182
(913) 864-2700

WASHBURN UNIVERSITY OF TOPEKA
17th and College Sts., Topeka 66621. Public (city). 1913/1978 (NCA). Sem. plan. Degrees: B,P,M. *Prof. Accred.:* Law, Music, Nursing (B), Radiography, Social Work (B), Teacher Education (*e,s,p*). Pres. John L. Green, Jr.
Enroll.: 4,972 (*f.t.* (913) 295-6300

WICHITA AUTOMOTIVE AND ELECTRONIC INSTITUTE
4011 E. 31st St., S., Wichita 67210. Private. 1972/1982 (NATTS). Courses of varying lengths. Diplomas. Dir. John Poston.
Enroll.: 350 (*f.t.* 345 m., 5 w.)
(316) 682-6548

WICHITA BUSINESS COLLEGE
501 E. Pawnee, Suite 515, Wichita 67211. Private. 1963/1984 (AICS). Qtr. plan. Certificates, diplomas. Pres. R. W. Sparrow.
Enroll.: 425 (*f.t.* 106 m., 319 w.)
(316) 263-1261

WICHITA STATE UNIVERSITY
1845 Fairmont, Wichita 67208. Public. 1927/1982 (NCA). Sem. plan. Degrees: B,M,D. *Prof. Accred.:* Assistant to the Primary Care Physician, Business (B,M), Dental Hygiene, Engineering (aeronautical, electrical, industrial, mechanical), Engineering Technology,

Medical Technology, Music, Nursing (B,M), Physical Therapy, Respiratory Therapy, Social Work (B), Speech Pathology and Audiology, Teacher Education (*e,s,p*). Pres. Warren B. Armstrong.
Enroll.: FTE 11,010
(316) 689-3001

WICHITA TECHNICAL INSTITUTE
942 S. West St., Wichita 67213. Private. 1971/1983 (NATTS). Courses of varying lengths. Certificates, diplomas. Pres. Paul D. Moore.
Enroll.: 87 (*f.t.* 83 m., 4 w.)
(316) 943-2241

KENTUCKY

ALICE LLOYD COLLEGE
Pippa Passes 41844. Private liberal arts. 1952/1982 (SACS-Comm. on Coll.). Sem. plan. Degrees: A, B. Pres. Jerry C. Davis.
Enroll.: 524
(606) 368-2101

ASBURY COLLEGE
Wilmore 40390. Private liberal arts and teachers. 1940/1978 (SACS-Comm. on Coll.). Qtr. plan. Degrees: B. *Prof. Accred.:* Music. Pres. John N. Oswalt.
Enroll.: 1,041
(606) 858-3511

ASBURY THEOLOGICAL SEMINARY
Wilmore 40390. Private (Interdenominational) professional; graduate only. 1984 (SACS-Comm. on Coll.). Sem. plan. Degrees: P, M, D. *Prof. Accred.:* Theology (1946/1954; 1960/1984, ATS). Pres. David L. McKenna.
Enroll.: 726
(606) 858-3581

BALLARD COUNTY AREA VOCATIONAL EDUCATION CENTER
Route 1, Barlow 42024. 1975/1985 (SACS-COEI). Courses of varying lengths. Certificates. Dir. Donald G. Wells.
Enroll.: FTE 119
(502) 665-5112

BELLARMINE COLLEGE
2001 Newburg Rd., Louisville 40205. Private (Roman Catholic) liberal arts. 1949/1977 (SACS-Comm. on Coll.). Sem. plan. Degrees: A, B, M. Pres. Eugene V. Petrik.
Enroll.: 1,830
(502) 452-8211

BEREA COLLEGE
Berea 40404. Private liberal arts. 1926/1985 (SACS-Comm. on Coll.). 4-1-4 plan. Degrees: B. *Prof. Accred.:* Nursing (B), Teacher Education *(e,s)*. Pres. John B. Stephenson.
Enroll.: 1,523
(606) 986-9341

BOWLING GREEN JUNIOR COLLEGE OF BUSINESS
1141 State St., Bowling Green 42101. Private. 1972/1982 (AICS). Qtr. plan. Degrees: A. *Prof. Accred.:* Medical Assisting. Pres. J. R. Rippetoe.
Enroll.: 1,809 (*f.t.* 696 m., 1,113 w.)
(502) 842-6556

BRANNON BUSINESS SCHOOL
P.O. Box 6, Paducah 42002. 1985 (SACS-COEI). Courses of varying lengths. Certificates. Dir. Mary Ruth Brannon.
Enroll.: FTE 118

BRESCIA COLLEGE
Owensboro 42301. Private (Roman Catholic) liberal arts. 1957/1979 (SACS-Comm. on Coll.). Sem. plan. Degrees: A, B. Pres. Sister Mary Ruth Genre.
Enroll.: 594
(502) 685-3131

CAMPBELLSVILLE COLLEGE
Campbellsville 42718. Private (Southern Baptist) liberal arts. 1963/1984 (SACS-Comm. on Coll.). Sem. plan. Degrees: A, B. Pres. William R. Davenport.
Enroll.: 579
(502) 465-8158

CARL D. PERKINS JOB CORPS CENTER
Box G-ll, Goble Roberts Rd., Prestonsburg 41653. 1985 (SACS-COEI). Courses of varying lengths. Certificates. Dir. Kermit L. Berry.
Enroll.: FTE 175

CENTRE COLLEGE OF KENTUCKY
Danville 40422. Private liberal arts. 1904/1985 (SACS-Comm. on Coll.). Year of two 13-week and one 6½-week terms. Degrees: B. Pres. Richard L. Morrill.
Enroll.: 746
(606) 236-5211

COMMUNICATIONS INSTITUTE
5702 Outer Loop, Louisville 40219. Private. 1983 (SACS-COEI). 600 hours. Certificates. Dir. Chris Phillips.
Enroll.: FTE 23
(502) 969-3032

CUMBERLAND COLLEGE
Williamsburg 40769. Private (Southern Baptist) liberal arts and teachers. 1964/1985 (SACS-Comm. on Coll.). Sem. plan. Degrees: A, B, M. *Prof. Accred.:* Music. Pres. James H. Taylor.
Enroll.: 1,902
(606) 549-2200

DRAUGHON'S JUNIOR COLLEGE OF BUSINESS
P.O. Box 2376, Paducah 42002-2376. Private junior. 1966/1985 (AICS). Qtr. plan. Degrees: A, diplomas. Dir. Clifton Phillips.
Enroll.: 1,178 (*f.t.* 397 m., 781 w.)
(502) 443-8478

BRANCH CAMPUS
1102 S. Virginia, Hopkinsville 42240. Dir. Ron McPherson.
(502) 886-1302

BRANCH CAMPUS
1317 N.E. Fourth Ave., Ft. Lauderdale, FL 33304. Dir. David Spriggs.
(305) 764-4660

EARLE C. CLEMENTS JOB CORPS CENTER
Morganfield 42437. Private. 1983 (SACS-COEI). Courses of varying lengths. Certificates. Dir. Gerald A. Oettle.
Enroll.: FTE 959
(502) 389-2419

EASTERN KENTUCKY UNIVERSITY
Richmond 40475. Public (state). 1928/1975 (SACS-Comm. on Coll.). Sem. plan. Degrees: A,B,M. *Prof. Accred.:* EMT-Paramedic Training, Interior Design, Medical Assisting, Medical Laboratory Technology (A), Medical Record Administration, Medical Record Technology, Medical Technology, Music, Nursing (A,B), Social Work (B), Speech Pathology, Teacher Education (*e,s,p*). Pres. H. Hanley Funderburk, Jr.
Enroll.: 11,784
(606) 622-0111

FUGAZZI COLLEGE
406 Lafayette Ave., Lexington 40502-2140 . Private business. 1957/1981 (AICS). Qtr. plan. Degrees: A, certificates, diplomas. *Prof. Accred.:* Medical Assisting. Dir. Earl Boardman.
Enroll.: 277 (*f.t.* 92 m., 185 w.)
(606) 266-0401

GEORGETOWN COLLEGE
Georgetown 40324. Private (Southern Baptist) liberal arts. 1919/1982 (SACS-Comm. on Coll.). Sem. plan. Degrees: B,M. Pres. W. Morgan Patterson.
Enroll.: 1,067
(502) 863-8011

GRAYSON COUNTY AREA VOCATIONAL EDUCATION CENTER
Route 5, Leitchfield 42754. Public. 1974/1982 (SACS-COEI). Courses of varying lengths. Certificates. Dir. Morris Craig.
Enroll.: FTE 73
(502) 259-3195

HEALTH CAREERS INSTITUTE
317 Guthrie Green, Louisville 40202. Private technical. 1983 (ABHES). 52-week course. Diplomas. *Prof. Accred.:* Medical Assisting. Dir. Michael Bewley.
Enroll.: 23
(502) 585-5193

INSTITUTE OF ELECTRONIC TECHNOLOGY
P.O. Box 1113, 509 S. 30th St., Paducah 42001. Private. 1968/1984 (NATTS). Sem. plan. Degrees: A. Dir. Lee Hicklin.
Enroll.: 252 (*f.t.* 242 m., 10 w.)
(502) 444-9676

KENTUCKY CHRISTIAN COLLEGE
617 Carol Malone Blvd., Grayson 41143. Private (Church of Christ) liberal arts and professional. 1962/1981 (AABC); 1984 (SACS-Comm. on Coll.). Sem. plan. Degrees: B. Pres. L. Palmer Young.
Enroll.: 430
(606) 474-6613

KENTUCKY COLLEGE OF BARBERING AND HAIRSTYLING
1230 S. Third St., Louisville 40203. Private. 1983 (NATTS). Courses of varying lengths. Diplomas. Dir. Charles Thompson.
Enroll.: 35
(502) 634-0521

KENTUCKY COLLEGE OF BUSINESS
628 E. Main St., Lexington 40508. Private junior. 1970/1984 (AICS). Qtr. plan. Degrees: A, certificates, diplomas. Pres. Richard G. Wood.
Enroll.: 1,016 (*f.t.* 294 m., 722 w.)
(606) 253-0621

BRANCH CAMPUS
6616 Dixie Hwy., Florence 41042. Dir. Carolyn Fries.
(606) 625-6510

BRANCH CAMPUS
640 S. Mayo Trail, Pikeville 41501. Dir. Rene Little.
(606) 432-5477

KENTUCKY POLYTECHNIC INSTITUTE
7410 LaGrange Rd., Louisville 40222. Private. 1984 (SACS-COEI). Courses of varying lengths. Certificates. Dir. Gary J. Rivoli.
Enroll.: FTE 82
(502) 426-7744

KENTUCKY STATE UNIVERSITY
Frankfort 40601. Public liberal arts and teachers. 1939/1979 (SACS-Comm. on Coll.). Sem. plan. Degrees: A,B,M. *Prof. Accred.:* Music, Nursing (A), Social Work (B), Teacher Education (*e,s*). Pres. Raymond M. Burse.
Enroll.: 1,693
(502) 227-6000

KENTUCKY WESLEYAN COLLEGE
Owensboro 42301. Private (United Methodist) liberal arts. 1948/1977 (SACS-Comm. on Coll.). Sem. plan. Degrees:A,B. Pres. Luther W. White, III.
Enroll.: 746
(502) 926-3111

LEES COLLEGE
Jackson 41339. Private (Presbyterian, U.S.). 1951/1979 (SACS-Comm. on Coll.). Sem. plan. Degrees: A. Pres. Troy R. Eslinger.
Enroll.: 269
(606) 666-7521

LEXINGTON THEOLOGICAL SEMINARY
631 S. Limestone St., Lexington 40508. Private (Christian Church, Disciples of Christ) professional; graduate only. 1984 (SACS-Comm. on Coll.). 4-1-4 plan. Degrees: P,M,D. *Prof. Accred.:* Theology (1938/1984, ATS). Pres. W. Daniel Cobb.
Enroll.: 185
(606) 252-0361

LINDSEY WILSON COLLEGE
Columbia 42728. Private (United Methodist) junior. 1951/1985 (SACS-Comm. on Coll.). Sem. plan. Degrees: A. Pres. John B. Begley.
Enroll.: 480
(502) 384-2126

LOUISVILLE COLLEGE
1512 Crums Lane, Louisville 40216. Private. 1978 (NATTS). Courses of varying lengths. Diplomas. *Prof. Accred.:* Dental Laboratory Technology, Medical Assisting, Medical Laboratory Technology. Dir. Carole A. Fuller.
Enroll.: 115 (*f.t.* 5 m., 110 w.)
(502) 361-1607

LOUISVILLE PRESBYTERIAN THEOLOGICAL SEMINARY
1044 Alta Vista Rd., Louisville 40205. Private (Presbyterian, U.S.A.) professional; graduate only. 1973/1978 (SACS-Comm. on Coll.). 4-1-4 plan. Degrees: P,M,D. *Prof. Accred.:* Theology (1938/1978, ATS). Pres. John M. Mulder.
Enroll.: 216
(502) 895-3411

LOUISVILLE TECHNICAL INSTITUTE
3901 Atkinson Dr., Atkinson Square, Louisville 40218. Private. 1974/1983 (NATTS). Qtr. plan. Degrees: A, certificates, diplomas. Dir. Kenneth Votteler.
Enroll.: 400
(502) 456-6509

MIDWAY COLLEGE
Midway 40347. Private junior for women. 1949/1984 (SACS-Comm. on Coll.). Sem. plan. Degrees: A. *Prof. Accred.:* Medical Laboratory Technician, Nursing (A). Pres. Robert Botkin.
Enroll.: 316
(606) 846-4421

MOREHEAD STATE UNIVERSITY
Morehead 40351. Public. 1930/1980 (SACS-Comm. on Coll.). Sem. plan. Degrees: A,B,M. *Prof. Accred.:* Medical Assisting, Music, Nursing (A), Radiography, Social Work (B), Teacher Education (*e,s,p*). Pres. ———.
Enroll.: 5,587
(606) 783-2221

MURRAY STATE UNIVERSITY
Murray 42071. Public. 1928/1984 (SACS-Comm. on Coll.). Sem. plan. Degrees: A,B,M. *Prof. Accred.:* Business (B,M), Engineering Technology (civil, computer, construction, electrical, manufacturing), Medical Laboratory Technology (A), Music, Nursing (B), Social Work (B), Speech Pathology, Teacher Education (*e,s,p*). Pres. Kala M. Stroup.
Enroll.: 6,412
(502) 762-3011

NATIONAL EDUCATION CENTER—KENTUCKY COLLEGE OF TECH CAMPUS
3947 Park Dr., Louisville 40216. Private. 1968/1981 (NATTS). Qtr. plan. Degrees: A. Dir. Richard Dewhirst
Enroll.: 981 (*f.t.* 881 m., 100 w.)
(502) 447-7777

NEW IMAGE COLLEGE OF COSMETOLOGY
109 E. Sixth St., Corbin 40701. Private. 1984 (SACS-COEI). Courses of varying lengths. Certificates. Dir. Wanda Powers.
Enroll.: FTE 33
(606) 528-1490

NORTHERN KENTUCKY UNIVERSITY
Highland Heights 41076. Public (state). 1973/1978 (SACS-Comm. on Coll.). Sem. plan.

Degrees: A,B,P,M. *Prof. Accred.:* Law, Nursing (A,B), Radiography, Social Work (B). Pres. Leon E. Boothe.
Enroll.: 6,557
(606) 572-5100

OWENSBORO JUNIOR COLLEGE OF BUSINESS
1515 E. 18th St., Owensboro 42301. Private junior. 1969/1984 (AICS). Tri. plan. Degrees: A, certificates, diplomas. Pres. Lenda Wilson.
Enroll.: 528 (*f.t.* 124 m., 404 w.)
(502) 926-4040

PIKEVILLE COLLEGE
Pikeville 41501. Private (United Presbyterian) liberal arts. 1961/1982 (SACS-Comm. on Coll.). Sem. plan. Degrees: A,B. Pres. William H. Owens.
Enroll.: 494
(606) 432-9200

PURCHASE TRAINING CENTER
Route 2, Mayfield 42066. Private. 1985 (SACS-COEI). Courses of varying lengths. Certificates. Dir. Edward W. Spencer.
Enroll.: FTE 23

R.E.T.S. ELECTRONIC INSTITUTE
4146 Outer Loop, Louisville 40219. Private. 1978 (NATTS). Sem. plan. Degrees: A. Pres. Larry F. Sample.
Enroll.: 844 (*f.t.* 787 m., 57 w.)
(502) 968-7191

ST. CATHARINE COLLEGE
St. Catharine 40061. Private (Roman Catholic) junior. 1957/1978 (SACS-Comm. on Coll.). Sem. plan. Degrees: A. Pres. Sister Delores Enderle.
Enroll.: 147
(606) 336-9303

SOUTHERN BAPTIST THEOLOGICAL SEMINARY
2825 Lexington Rd., Louisville 40280. Private (Southern Baptist) professional; graduate only. 1968/1983 (SACS-Comm. on Coll.). 4-1-4 plan. Degrees: P,M,D. *Prof. Accred.:* Music, Theology (1938/1983, ATS). Pres. Roy L. Honeycutt.
Enroll.: 2,316
(502) 897-4011

SOUTHWESTERN COLLEGE OF BUSINESS (BRANCH)
2929 S. Dixie Hwy., Crestview Hills 41017. Private. 1986 (ABHES). 44-week program Diplomas. *Prof. Accred.:* Medical Assisting. Pres. Gary Wright.
Enroll.: 29
(606) 341-6633

SPALDING UNIVERSITY
851 S. Fourth St., Louisville 40203. Private (Roman Catholic) liberal arts. 1938/1975 (SACS-Comm. on Coll.). Sem. plan. Degrees: A,B,M. *Prof. Accred.:* Dietetics, Nursing (B), Social Work (B). Pres. Sister Eileen M. Egan.
Enroll.: 718
(502) 585-9911

SPENCERIAN COLLEGE
914 E. Broadway, Louisville 40204. Private business. 1954/1981 (AICS); 1977/1982 (SACS-COEI). Qtr. plan. Degrees: A, certificates, diplomas. *Prof. Accred.:* Medical Assisting. Exec. Dir. David Gray.
Enroll.: FTE 415
(502) 584-7105

SUE BENNETT COLLEGE
London 40741. Private (United Methodist) junior. 1932/1985 (SACS-Comm. on Coll.). Sem. plan. Degrees: A. Pres. John E. Patterson
Enroll.: 269
(606) 864-2238

SULLIVAN JUNIOR COLLEGE OF BUSINESS
Watterson Expy. and Bardstown Rd., P.O. Box 33-308, Louisville 40232. Private. 1965/1982 (AICS); 1979/1984 (SACS-Comm. on Coll.). Qtr. plan. Degrees: A. Pres. A. R. Sullivan.
Enroll.: 1,360
(502) 456-6504

BRANCH CAMPUS
2659 Regency Rd., Lexington 40503. Dir. Bill Noel.
(606) 276-4357

THOMAS MORE COLLEGE
2771 Turkey Foot Rd., Crestview Hills 41017. Private (Roman Catholic) liberal arts. 1959/1981 (SACS-Comm. on Coll.). Sem. plan. Degrees: A,B. *Prof. Accred.:* Nursing (B), Social Work (B). Pres. Charles J. Bensman.
Enroll.: 886
(606) 341-5800

TRANSYLVANIA UNIVERSITY
300 N. Broadway, Lexington 40508. Private liberal arts. 1915/1983 (SACS-Comm. on Coll.). Qtr. plan. Degrees: B. Pres. Charles Shearer.

Enroll.: 798
(606) 233-8120

TRI-STATE BEAUTY ACADEMY
219 W. Main St., Morehead 40351. Private. 1983 (SACS-COEI). 1800 hours. Certificates. Dir. Betty Stucky.
Enroll.: FTE 49
(606) 784-9335

UNION COLLEGE
Barbourville 40906. Private (United Methodist) liberal arts. 1932/1984 (SACS-Comm. on Coll.). Sem. plan. Degrees: A,B,M. Pres. Jack C. Phillips.
Enroll.: 640
(606) 546-4151

U.S. ARMY ARMOR CENTER AND SCHOOL
2369 Old Ironsides Ave., Fort Knox 40121. Public (federal) technical. 1976/1981 (SACS-COEI). Courses of varying lengths. Certificates. Commandant Maj. Gen. Frederic J. Brown.
Enroll.: FTE 10,925
(502) 624-7445

UNIVERSITY SYSTEM OF KENTUCKY
Lexington 40506. Pres. Otis Singletary.
(606) 257-9000

UNIVERSITY OF KENTUCKY
Lexington 40506. Public (state). 1915/1982 (SACS-Comm. on Coll.). Sem. plan. Degrees: B,P,M,D. *Prof. Accred.:* Architecture (B), Assistant to the Primary Care Physician, Business (B,M), Dental Laboratory Technology, Dentistry, Dietetics, Engineering (agricultural, chemical, civil, electrical, mechanical, metallurgical, mining), Forestry, Home Economics, Interior Design, Journalism, Landscape Architecture (B), Law, Librarianship, Medical Technology, Medicine, Music, Nursing (B,M), Pharmacy, Physical Therapy, Psychology, Radiation Therapy Technology, Rehabilitation Counseling, Social Work (B,M), Teacher Education (*e,s,p*). Pres. Otis A. Singletary.
Enroll.: 17,853
(606) 257-9000

COMMUNITY COLLEGE SYSTEM
Central Office, 305 Euclid Ave., Lexington 40506. Chanc. Charles T. Wethington.
(606) 257-9000

ASHLAND COMMUNITY COLLEGE
1400 College Dr., Ashland 41101. 1957/1981 (SACS-Comm. on Coll.). Degrees: A. Dir. Robert L. Goodpaster.
Enroll.: 1,500
(606) 329-2999

ELIZABETHTOWN COMMUNITY COLLEGE
Elizabethtown 42701. 1964/1981 (SACS-Comm. on Coll.). Degrees: A. *Prof. Accred.:* Nursing (A). Dir. James S. Owen.
Enroll.: 1,491
(502) 769-2371

HAZARD COMMUNITY COLLEGE
Hazard 41701. 1968/1981 (SACS-Comm. on Coll.). Degrees: A. *Prof. Accred.:* Dental Hygiene. Dir. G. Edward Hughes.
Enroll.: 500
(606) 436-5721

HENDERSON COMMUNITY COLLEGE
Henderson 42420. 1960/1981 (SACS-Comm. on Coll.). Degrees: A. *Prof. Accred.:* Medical Laboratory Technology. Dir. Patrick R. Lake.
Enroll.: 2,345
(502) 827-1867

HOPKINSVILLE COMMUNITY COLLEGE
Hopkinsville 42240. 1965/1981 (SACS-Comm. on Coll.). Degrees: A. Dir. Thomas L. Riley.
Enroll.: 871
(502) 886-3921

JEFFERSON COMMUNITY COLLEGE
109 E. Broadway, Louisville 40202. 1968/1981 (SACS-Comm. on Coll.). Degrees: A. *Prof. Accred.:* Medical Laboratory Technology (A), Nursing (A), Respiratory Therapy. Dir. Ronald J. Horvath.
Enroll.: 4,540
(502) 584-0181

LEXINGTON COMMUNITY COLLEGE
Lexington 40506-0235. 1965/1981 (SACS-Comm. on Coll.). Degrees: A. *Prof. Accred.:* Dental Hygiene, Dental Laboratory Technology, Nursing (A), Physical Therapy, Radiography, Respiratory Therapy. Dir. Sharon B. Jaggard.
Enroll.: 1,889
(606) 257-4831

MADISONVILLE COMMUNITY COLLEGE
Madisonville 42431. 1968/1981 (SACS-Comm. on Coll.). Degrees: A. *Prof. Accred.:* Dental Hygiene, Respiratory Therapy. Dir. Arthur D. Stumpf.
Enroll.: 858
(502) 821-2250

MAYSVILLE COMMUNITY COLLEGE
Maysville 41056. 1968/1981 (SACS-Comm. on Coll.). Degrees: A. Dir. James Shires.

Enroll.: 588
(606) 759-7141

PADUCAH COMMUNITY COLLEGE
P.O. Box 7380, Paducah 42002. 1932/1981 (SACS-Comm. on Coll.). Degrees: A. *Prof. Accred.:* Nursing (A). Dir. Donald J. Clemens.
Enroll.: 1,365
(502) 442-6131

PRESTONSBURG COMMUNITY COLLEGE
H.C. 69, Box 230, Prestonsburg 41653. 1964/1981 (SACS-Comm. on Coll.). Degrees: A. Dir. Henry A. Campbell, Jr.
Enroll.: 1,009
(606) 886-3863

SOMERSET COMMUNITY COLLEGE
Somerset 42501. 1965/1981 (SACS-Comm. on Coll.). Degrees: A. *Prof. Accred.:* Medical Laboratory Technology (A). Dir. Richard G. Carpenter.
Enroll.: 784
(606) 678-8174

SOUTHEAST COMMUNITY COLLEGE
Cumberland 40823. 1960/1981 (SACS-Comm. on Coll.). Degrees: A. *Prof. Accred.:* Dental Hygiene. Dir. Vivian Blevins.
Enroll.: 482
(606) 589-2145

UNIVERSITY OF LOUISVILLE
2301 S. Third St., Louisville 40292. Public (state). 1915/1976 (SACS-Comm. on Coll.). Sem. plan. Degrees: Certificates, A,B,P,M,D. *Prof. Accred.:* Business (B), Cytotechnology, Dental Assisting, Dental Hygiene, Dentistry, Engineering (chemical, civil, electrical, engineering mathematics and computer science, industrial, mechanical), Health Administration, Law, Medical Technology, Medicine, Music, Nuclear Medicine Technology, Nursing (B,M), Physical Therapy, Psychology, Radiography, Respiratory Therapy, Respiratory Therapy Technology, Social Work (M), Speech Pathology and Audiology, Teacher Education (*e,s,p*). Pres. Donald C. Swain.
Enroll.: 15,150
(502) 588-5555

VOCATIONAL EDUCATION REGION 1 (PURCHASE)
1400 H. C. Mathis Dr., Paducah 42001. Public (state) technical. 1975/1985 (SACS-COEI). Courses of varying lengths. Certificates. Regional Dir. Ray D. Brown.
Enroll.: FTE 1,086
(502) 444-8355

WEST KENTUCKY STATE VOCATIONAL-TECHNICAL SCHOOL
Prof. Accred.: Radiography, Respiratory Therapy Technology. Prin. William D. Houston.

FULTON COUNTY AREA VOCATIONAL EDUCATION CENTER
Coor. James M. Everett.

MAYFIELD AREA VOCATIONAL EDUCATION CENTER

MURRAY AREA VOCATIONAL EDUCATION CENTER
Coor. James Lawson.

PADUCAH AREA VOCATIONAL EDUCATION CENTER

VOCATIONAL EDUCATION REGION 2 (PENNYRILE)
645 W. Center St., Madisonville 42431. Public (state) technical. 1971/1981 (SACS-COEI). Courses of varying lengths. Certificates. *Prof. Accred.:* Medical Laboratory Technology, Radiography, Respiratory Therapy. Regional Dir. Bill M. Hatley.
Enroll.: FTE 1,126
(502) 821-7070

MADISONVILLE STATE VOCATIONAL-TECHNICAL SCHOOL
Prin. Jack Ford.

EDDYVILLE VOCATIONAL EDUCATION CENTER
Coor. Jim Creekmur.

HEALTH OCCUPATIONS SCHOOL
Coor. James C. Whitledge.

CALDWELL COUNTY AREA VOCATIONAL EDUCATION CENTER
Coor. Kenny Creekmur.

CHRISTIAN COUNTY AREA VOCATIONAL EDUCATION CENTER
Coor. Dwight Borum.

MUHLENBERG COUNTY AREA VOCATIONAL EDUCATION CENTER
Coor. Fred Coots, Jr.

WEBSTER COUNTY AREA VOCATIONAL EDUCATION CENTER
Coor. James Pfeffer.

VOCATIONAL EDUCATION REGION 3 (GREEN RIVER)
P.O. Box 1677, 1905 Southeastern Pkwy., Owensboro 42302. Public (state) technical. 1973/1983 (SACS-COEI). Courses of varying lengths. Certificates. Regional Dir. W. O. Jackson.
Enroll.: FTE 1,348
(502) 684-7201

DAVIESS COUNTY STATE VOCATIONAL-TECHNICAL SCHOOL
Prin. Ray Gillaspie.

HENDERSON COUNTY AREA VOCATIONAL EDUCATION CENTER
Coor. Louis Joiner.

OHIO COUNTY AREA VOCATIONAL EDUCATION CENTER
Coor. Ray Price.

OWENSBORO STATE VOCATIONAL-TECHNICAL SCHOOL
Prin. Martin Cecil.

UNION COUNTY AREA VOCATIONAL EDUCATION CENTER
Coor. James Holland.

VOCATIONAL EDUCATION REGION 4 (BARREN RIVER)
P.O. Box 1868, Bowling Green 42101. Public (state) technical. 1972/1982 (SACS-COEI). Courses of varying lengths. Certificates. Regional Dir. Joe D. Hunt.
Enroll.: FTE 1,281
(502) 781-3854

BARRON COUNTY AREA VOCATIONAL EDUCATION CENTER

BOWLING GREEN STATE VOCATIONAL-TECHNICAL SCHOOL
Prof. Accred.: Radiography, Surgical Technology. Prin. Robert Bierman.

GLASCOW SCHOOL FOR HEALTH OCCUPATIONS
Coor. Rebecca Forrest.

MONROE COUNTY AREA VOCATIONAL EDUCATION CENTER
Coor. Robert Bierman.

RUSSELLVILLE AREA VOCATIONAL EDUCATION CENTER
Coor. Maurice Grayson.

VOCATIONAL EDUCATION REGION 5 (ELIZABETHTOWN)
505 University Dr., Elizabethtown 42701. Public (state) technical. 1974/1982 (SACS-COEI). Courses of varying lengths. Certificates. Regional Dir. Roye S. Wilson.
Enroll.: FTE 908
(502) 769-2326

ELIZABETHTOWN STATE VOCATIONAL-TECHNICAL SCHOOL
Prin. Neil Ramer.

BRECKINRIDGE COUNTY AREA VOCATIONAL EDUCATION CENTER
Coor. Wayne A. Spencer.

MARION COUNTY AREA VOCATIONAL EDUCATION CENTER
Coor. John Coyle.

MEADE COUNTY AREA VOCATIONAL EDUCATION CENTER
Coor. Betty Johnson.

NELSON COUNTY AREA VOCATIONAL EDUCATION CENTER
Coor. John T. Kromer.

VOCATIONAL EDUCATION REGIONS 6 AND 8 (JEFFERSON)
8911 Shelbyville Rd., Louisville 40222. Public (state) technical. 1973/1983 (SACS-COEI). Courses of varying lengths. Certificates. Regional Dir. Bill L. Evans.
Enroll.: FTE 1,653
(502) 267-7491

JEFFERSON STATE VOCATIONAL-TECHNICAL SCHOOL AND MANPOWER SKILL CENTER
Prin. James Woodrow.

AHRENS VOCATIONAL EDUCATION CENTER

BULLITT COUNTY AREA VOCATIONAL EDUCATION CENTER
Coor. Dennis Scarbrough.

FAIRDALE VOCATIONAL EDUCATION CENTER

JEFFERSON TOWN VOCATIONAL EDUCATION CENTER
Dir. Jim Floyd.

LAGRANGE VOCATIONAL EDUCATION CENTER
Coor. Robert Schneider.

LUTHER LUCKETT VOCATIONAL EDUCATION CENTER
Dir. ———.

OLDHAM COUNTY VOCATIONAL EDUCATION CENTER
Dir. ———.

PEEWEE VALLEY VOCATIONAL EDUCATION CENTER
Teacher-Coor. Margaret Moore.

PLEASURE RIDGE PARK VOCATIONAL EDUCATION CENTER

SCOTT DETRICK VOCATIONAL EDUCATION CENTER

SHELBY COUNTY AREA VOCATIONAL EDUCATION CENTER
Coor. Ruth Bunch.

WESTPORT ROAD VOCATIONAL EDUCATION CENTER

VOCATIONAL EDUCATION REGION 7 (NORTHERN KENTUCKY)
1025 Amsterdam Rd., Covington 41011. Public (state) technical. 1973/1983 (SACS-COEI). Courses of varying lengths. Certificates. Regional Dir. John G. Corwin.
Enroll.: FTE 1,409
(606) 292-2760

NORTHERN KENTUCKY STATE VOCATIONAL TECHNICAL SCHOOL
Prin. Edward Burton.

BOONE COUNTY AREA VOCATIONAL EDUCATIONAL CENTER
Coor. Ralph Rollins.

CAMPBELL COUNTY AREA VOCATIONAL EDUCATION CENTER
Coor. Kenneth McCormick.

CARROLL COUNTY AREA VOCATIONAL EDUCATION CENTER
Coor. Donald W. Garner.

KENTON COUNTY AREA VOCATIONAL EDUCATION CENTER
Coor. James Barnes.

NORTHERN CAMPBELL COUNTY VOCATIONAL-TECHNICAL SCHOOL
Guidance Counselor Robert Green.

NORTHERN KENTUCKY HEALTH OCCUPATIONS CENTER

VOCATIONAL EDUCATION REGION 9 (BUFFALO TRACE-GATEWAY)
32 S. Christy, Morehead 40351. Public (state) technical. 1975/1983 (SACS-COEI). Courses of varying lengths. Certificates. Regional Dir. John Vansant.
Enroll.: FTE 659
(606) 784-7541

MAYSVILLE AREA VOCATIONAL EDUCATION CENTER
Coor. Charles Lee.

MONTGOMERY COUNTY AREA VOCATIONAL EDUCATION CENTER
Coor. Norma Wilevaloughby.

MOREHEAD TREATMENT CENTER
Acting Supt. Mike Murphy.

MORGAN COUNTY AREA VOCATIONAL EDUCATION CENTER
Coor. Wil552552lis Lyon.

ROWAN STATE VOCATIONAL-TECHNICAL SCHOOL
Coor. Clifford Wells.

VOCATIONAL EDUCATION REGION 10 (FIVCO)
4818 Roberts Dr., Ashland 41101. Public (state) technical. 1971/1984 (SACS-COEI). Courses of varying lengths. Certificates. Regional Dir. Charles E. Chattin.
Enroll.: FTE 816
(606) 928-6427

ASHLAND STATE VOCATIONAL TECHNICAL SCHOOL
Prin. Howard Moore.

GREENUP COUNTY AREA VOCATIONAL EDUCATION CENTER
Coor. Helen Spears.

RUSSELL VOCATIONAL EDUCATION CENTER
Coor. Charles Sammons.

VOCATIONAL EDUCATION REGION 11 (BIG SANDY)
313 Third St., Paintsville 41240. Public (state) technical. 1974/1984 (SACS-COEI). Courses of varying lengths. Certificates. Regional Dir. Bronelle Skaggs.
Enroll.: FTE 1,310
(606) 789-3115

MAYO STATE VOCATIONAL-TECHNICAL SCHOOL
Prin. Jesse Conley.

BELFRY AREA VOCATIONAL EDUCATION CENTER

GARTH AREA VOCATIONAL EDUCATION CENTER

MARTIN COUNTY AREA VOCATIONAL EDUCATION CENTER
Coor. Robert L. Allen.

MILLARD AREA VOCATIONAL EDUCATION CENTER

PHELPS AREA VOCATIONAL EDUCATION CENTER

VOCATIONAL EDUCATION REGION 12 (KENTUCKY RIVER)
101 Vo-Tech Dr., Hazard 41701. Public (state) technical. 1973/1983 (SACS-COEI). Courses of varying lengths. Certificates. Regional Dir. Walter Prater.
Enroll.: FTE 1,782
(606) 436-3101

HAZARD STATE VOCATIONAL-TECHNICAL SCHOOL
Prin. Connie W. Johnson.

BREATHITT COUNTY AREA VOCATIONAL EDUCATION CENTER
Coor. Sam Herald.

KNOTT COUNTY AREA VOCATIONAL EDUCATION CENTER
Coor. Walter Davidson.

LEE COUNTY AREA VOCATIONAL EDUCATION CENTER
Coor. Kenneth Blanton.

LESLIE COUNTY AREA VOCATIONAL EDUCATION CENTER
Coor. Hubert L. Holbrook.

LETCHER COUNTY AREA VOCATIONAL EDUCATION CENTER
Coor. James G. Estep.

VOCATIONAL EDUCATION REGION 13 (CUMBERLAND VALLEY)
333 North Main St., London 40701, Public (state) technical. 1975/1985 (SACS-COEI). Courses of varying lengths. Certificates. Regional Dir. Stuart Hodges.
Enroll.: FTE 1,641
(606) 546-9274

HARLAN STATE VOCATIONAL-TECHNICAL SCHOOL
Prin. Harve J. Couch.

LAUREL COUNTY STATE VOCATIONAL-TECHNICAL SCHOOL
Prin. R. V. Holcomb.

BELL COUNTY AREA VOCATIONAL EDUCATION CENTER
Coor. Stuart W. Hodges.

CLAY COUNTY AREA VOCATIONAL EDUCATION CENTER
Coor. Bill White.

CORBIN AREA VOCATIONAL EDUCATION CENTER
Coor. Ronnie Partin.

CUMBERLAND VALLEY HEALTH OCCUPATIONS CENTER
Coor. Mildred G. Winkler.

HARRY SPARKS VOCATIONAL SCHOOL
Coor. Lloyd Cain.

KNOX COUNTY AREA VOCATIONAL EDUCATION CENTER
Coor. Charles Frazier.

VOCATIONAL EDUCATION REGION 14 (LAKE CUMBERLAND)
P. O. Box 110, Somerset 42501. Public (state) technical. 1974/1984 (SACS-COEI). Courses of varying lengths. Certificates. Regional Dir. W. L. Ford.
Enroll.: FTE 1,034
(606) 679-2225

SOMERSET STATE VOCATIONAL-TECHNICAL SCHOOL
Prin. J. P. McCarty.

CASEY COUNTY AREA VOCATIONAL EDUCATION CENTER
Coor. Philip Dillon.

CLINTON COUNTY AREA VOCATIONAL EDUCATION CENTER
Coor. Preston Sparks.

GREEN COUNTY AREA VOCATIONAL EDUCATION CENTER
Coor. Jerry O. Rogers.

RUSSELL COUNTY AREA VOCATIONAL EDUCATION CENTER
Coor. Clifford Wilson.

WAYNE COUNTY AREA VOCATIONAL EDUCATION CENTER
Coor. Gerald Sloan.

VOCATIONAL EDUCATION REGION 15 (BLUEGRASS)
1093 S. Broadway, Suite 9, Lexington 40504. Public (state) technical. 1972/1982 (SACS-COEI). Courses of varying lengths. Certificates. Regional Dir. Ann C. Vescio.
Enroll.: FTE 3,147
(606) 252-3418

CENTRAL KENTUCKY STATE VOCATIONAL-TECHNICAL SCHOOL
Prin. Patrick White.

BLACKBURN VOCATIONAL CENTER
Coor. Clyde Carroll.

Clark County Area Vocational Education Center
Coor. Larry Sutton.

Danville School of Health Occupations
Coor. Moseill Jester.

Garrard County Area Vocational Education Center
Coor. Gabriel U. Gabriel.

Harrison County Area Vocational Education Center
Coor. James Plummer.

Harrodsburg Area Vocational Education Center
Coor. L. Hughes Jones.

Madison County Area Vocational Education Center

Northside Area Vocational Education Center
Coor. W. Thomas Wilson.

Southside Area Vocational Education Center
Coor. Luther Spotts.

Vogue College of Hair Design
2331 Alexandria Pike, Highland Heights 41076. Private. 1983 (SACS-COEI). Courses of varying lengths. Certificates. Dir. Albert Frank Knight.
Enroll.: FTE 91
(606) 781-1111

Branch Campus
111 W. Second St., Maysville 41056.

Branch Campus
Branch Campus
919 Ohio Pike, Cincinnati, OH 45245.

Watterson College
Breckinridge La., Louisville 40218. Private junior. 1965/1982 (AICS); 1982 (SACS-Comm. on Coll.) Breckinridge campus only. Qtr. plan. Degrees: A. *Prof. Accred.:* Dental Assisting, Medical Assistant, Medical Laboratory Technology. Pres. Burton Lipson.
Enroll.: 4757
(502) 491-5000

Branch Campus
1015 W. Chestnut St., Louisville 40203. Dir. Vikki Leone.
(502) 585-1670

Branch Campus
18 Forsyth St., N.W., Atlanta, GA 30303. Dir. Ray Ross.
(404) 589-0314

Branch Campus
4418 Edmondson Ave., Baltimore, MD 21229. Dir. Michael Larson.
(301) 945-3200

Branch Campus
1408 N. Kingshighway, St. Louis, MO 63113. Dir. Fred Richards.
(314) 367-4844

Branch Campus
8900 Manchester Rd., St. Louis, MO 63144. Dir. Paul St. Pierre.
(314) 962-6700

Branch Campus
4500 N. Tryon St., Charlotte, NC 28213. Dir. Larry Sample.
(704) 598-9000

Branch Campus
1415 N. Broad St., Philadelphia, PA 19122. Dir. Shelby Levy.
(215) 236-6655

Branch Campus
5800 N. Marvine St., Philadelphia, PA 19141. Dir. Charles Catley.
(215) 548-7200

Western Kentucky University
Bowling Green 42101. Public (state). 1926/1984 (SACS-Comm. on Coll.). Sem. plan. Degrees: A,B,M. *Prof. Accred.:* Business (B), Dental Hygiene, Engineering Technology (civil, electrical, environmental, mechanical), Journalism, Medical Record Technology, Music, Nursing (A,B), Social Work (B), Teacher Education (*e,s,p*). Pres. Kern Alexander.
Enroll.: 9,918
(502) 745-0111

LOUISIANA

ARCADIANA TECHNICAL COLLEGE
102 Savonne Dr., P.O. Box 5633, Scott 70583. Private. 1985 (AICS). Courses of varying lengths. Certificates, diplomas. Gen Mgr. Phillip Vinciguerra.
(318) 235-7327

BRANCH CAMPUS
1015 Sixth St., Lake Charles 70601.
(318) 433-4488

ALEXANDRIA VOCATIONAL-TECHNICAL INSTITUTE
4311 S. MacArthur Dr., Alexandria 71302. Public (state). 1976/1981 (SACS-COEI). Courses of varying lengths. Certificates. Dir. Walter L. Lemoine.
Enroll.: FTE 445
(318) 487-5443

AMERICO TECHNICAL INSTITUTE
264 Harbor Cir., New Orleans 70126. Private. 1985 (SACS-COEI). Courses of varying lengths. Certificates. Dir. Danny L. Bedford
Enroll.: FTE 115
(504) 246-4105

ASCENSION VOCATIONAL-TECHNICAL SCHOOL
P.O. Box 38, Sorrento 70778. Public (state). 1982 (SACS-COEI). Courses of varying lengths. Certificates. Dir. Charles A. Tassin.
Enroll.: FTE 122
(504) 675-5397

AUDUBON COLLEGE
3901 Tulane Ave., New Orleans 70119. Private business. 1976/1979 (AICS). Courses of varying lengths. Diplomas. Dir. Grover N. Craft.
Enroll.: 428 (*f.t.* 134 m., 294 w.)
(504) 486-6141

AVOYELLES VOCATIONAL-TECHNICAL INSTITUTE
P.O. Box 307, Cottonport 71327. Public (state). 1979/1984 (SACS-COEI). Courses of varying lengths. Certificates. Dir. Ward Nash.
Enroll.: FTE 148
(318) 876-2401

AYERS INSTITUTE
1431 Wilkinson St., Shreveport 71103. Private business. 1963/1980 (AICS). Courses of varying lengths. Certificates, diplomas. Pres. R. G. Hammett.
Enroll.: 181 (*f.t.* 105 m., 76 w.)
(318) 221-1853

BASTROP VOCATIONAL-TECHNICAL SCHOOL
P.O. Box 1120, Bastrop 71221. Public (state). 1981 (SACS-COEI). Courses of varying lengths. Certificates. Dir. Don R. Wood.
Enroll.: FTE 179
(318) 281-8954

BATON ROUGE SCHOOL OF COMPUTERS
9255 Interline Dr., Baton Rouge 70809. Private. 1982 (NATTS). Courses of varying lengths. Diplomas. Pres. Betty Truxillo.
Enroll.: 214 (*f.t.* 100 m., 1143 w.)
(504) 923-2525

BATON ROUGE VOCATIONAL-TECHNICAL INSTITUTE
3250 N. Acadian Thruway, Baton Rouge 70805. Public (state). 1973/1981 (SACS-COEI). Courses of varying lengths. Certificates. *Prof. Accred.:* Medical Laboratory Technology. Dir. Dan B. Riggs.
Enroll.: FTE 984
(504) 355-5621

BAYOU TECHNICAL INSTITUTE
2760 Toulouse St., New Orleans 70119. Private. 1980 (NATTS). Courses of varying lengths. Certificates. Pres. Albert B. Murphy, Jr.
Enroll.: 49 (*f.t.* 48 m., 1 w.)
(504) 486-6628

BIGGERS COLLEGES
601 Papworth Ave., Suite 200, Metairie 70005. Private business. 1982/1984 (AICS). Courses of varying lengths. Certificates, diplomas. Dir. Virgene Koehler Biggers.
Enroll.: 32 (*f.t.* 13 w.)
(504) 831-3333

BOSSIER PARISH COMMUNITY COLLEGE
2719 Airline Dr., N., Bossier City 71111. Public. 1983 (SACS-Comm. on Coll.). Sem. plan. Degrees: A. Chanc. Douglas Peterson.
Enroll.: 727
(318) 746-9851

CAMERON COLLEGE
2740 Canal St., New Orleans 70179 Private technical. 1982 (SACS-COEI). Courses of varying lengths. Certificates. Dir. Eleanor Cameron.
Enroll.: FTE 746
(504) 821-5881

CENTENARY COLLEGE OF LOUISIANA
2911 Centenary Blvd., P.O. Box 4188, Shreveport 71131-0188. Private (United

Methodist) liberal arts. 1925/1976 (SACS-Comm. on Coll.). 4-1-4 plan. Degrees: B,M. *Prof. Accred.:* Music. Pres. Donald A. Webb.
Enroll.: 586
(318) 869-5011

COMMERCIAL COLLEGE OF BATON ROUGE
5677 Florida Blvd., Baton Rouge 70806. Private. 1972/1984 (AICS). Courses of varying lengths. Diplomas. Dir. Ernest Etheredge.
Enroll.: 510 (*f.t.* 139 m., 371 w.)
(504) 927-3470

COMMERCIAL COLLEGE OF SHREVEPORT
2640 Youree Dr., Shreveport 71104. Private. 1971/1983 (AICS). Courses of varying lengths. Certificates. Dir. Brent Henley.
Enroll.: 706 (*f.t.* 240 m., 466 w.)
(318) 865-6571

CONCORDIA VOCATIONAL-TECHNICAL SCHOOL
E. E. Wallace Blvd., Ferriday 71334. Public (state). 1980/1985 (SACS-COEI). Courses of varying lengths. Certificates. Dir. Ray King.
Enroll.: FTE 123
(318) 757-6501

CRESCENT CITY TECH
6600 Plaza Dr., New Orleans 70127. Private. 1981 (SACS-COEI). Courses of varying lengths. Certificates. Dir. Edward G. Venanzi.
Enroll.: FTE 44
(504) 522-5666

DELGADO COMMUNITY COLLEGE
501 City Park Ave., New Orleans 70119. Public (city). 1971/1975 (SACS-Comm. on Coll.). Sem. plan. Degrees: A. *Prof. Accred.:* Radiography, Respiratory Therapy, Respiratory Therapy Technology. Pres. Harry J. Boyer.
Enroll.: 5,435
(504) 483-4400

DELTA COLLEGE
7290 Exchange Pl., Baton Rouge 70806. Private business. 1973/1979 (AICS). Qtr. plan. Certificates, diplomas. Pres. Billy B. Clark.
Enroll.: 916 (*f.t.* 257 m., 659 w.)
(504) 927-7780

BRANCH CAMPUS
511 West Bank Expressway, Gretna 70053. Dir. Jerian Hix.
(504) 362-5445

BRANCH CAMPUS
734 Martin Behrman Ave., Metairie 70005. Dir. Andrew Decell.
(504) 838-8823

DELTA-OUACHITA VOCATIONAL-TECHNICAL SCHOOL
609 Vocational Pkwy., West Monroe 71291. Public (state). 1976/1981 (SACS-COEI). Courses of varying lengths. Certificates. Dir. George W. Muse.
Enroll.: FTE 414
(318) 323-3491

DELTA SCHOOL OF BUSINESS
517 Broad St., Lake Charles 70601. Private. 1976/1982 (AICS). Courses of varying lengths. Certificates. Pres. Gary Holt.
Enroll.: 504 (*f.t.* 64 m., 440 w.)
(318) 439-5765

DELTA SCHOOL OF COMMERCE
P.O. Box 1528, Alexandria 71301. Private. 1970/1983 (AICS). Qtr. plan. Diplomas. Pres. John F. McCray.
Enroll.: 634 (*f.t.* 57 m., 577 w.)
(318) 442-9586

BRANCH CAMPUS
814 W. Congress, Lafayette 71501. Dir. Phillip Mayeaux.
(318) 235-1147

BRANCH CAMPUS
102 S. Grand St., Monroe 71201. Dir. Keith Edwards.
(318) 322-8870

BRANCH CAMPUS
3475 Fannin St., Beaumont, TX 77701. Dir. Kenneth A. Webb.
(409) 833-6161

DELTA SCHOOLS
1900 Cameron St., Lafayette 70506. Private business. 1971/1986 (AICS). Courses of varying lengths. Certificates. Pres. Peggy Fassio.
Enroll.: 709 (*f.t.* 166 m., 370 w.)
(318) 232-4641

BRANCH CAMPUS
404 Admiral Doyle St., New Iberia 70560. Dir. Peggy Fassio.
(318) 365-7348

DIESEL DRIVING ACADEMY
P.O.Box 36949, Shreveport 71109. Private. 1982 (SACS-COEI). Courses of varying lengths. Certificates. Dir. Philip O. Johnson.

Enroll.: FTE 152
(318) 636-6300

DILLARD UNIVERSITY
2601 Gentilly Blvd., New Orleans 70122. Private (United Church of Christ and United Methodist) liberal arts. 1937/1979 (SACS-Comm. on Coll.). Sem. plan. Degrees: B. *Prof. Accred.:* Music, Nursing (B). Pres. Samuel D. Cook.
Enroll.: 1,212
(504) 283-8822

DRAUGHON BUSINESS COLLEGE
427 Edward St., Shreveport 71101. Private. 1954/1982 (AICS). Qtr. plan. Certificates, diplomas. Acting Admin. Terry F. Schultz.
Enroll.: 445 (*f.t.* 146 m., 299 w.)
(318) 222-5778

EASTERN COLLEGE OF HEALTH VOCATIONS BRANCH
2748 Metairie Lawn Dr., Metairie 70002. Private. 40-week program. Diplomas. *Prof. Accred.:* Medical Assisting. Pres. Sue Dalto.
Enroll.: 57
(504) 834-8644

ELAINE P. NUNEZ VOCATIONAL-TECHNICAL SCHOOL
3700 La Fontaine St., Chalmette 70043. Public (state). 1983 (SACS-COEI). Courses of varying lengths. Certificates. Dir. John J. Kane.
Enroll.: FTE 355
(504) 277-8111

BRANCH CAMPUS
901 Delery St., New Orleans 70177.

EVANGELINE AREA TRI-PARISH VOCATIONAL TECHNICAL SCHOOL
P.O.Box 68, St. Martinville 70582. Public (state). 1974/1984 (SACS-COEI). Courses of varying lengths. Certificates. Dir. Prosper Chretien.
Enroll.: FTE 232
(318) 394-6466

FLORIDA PARISHES VOCATIONAL SCHOOL
P.O. Box 130, Greensburg 70441. Public (state). 1977/1983 (SACS-COEI). Courses of varying lengths. Certificates. Dir. Thomas J. Dykes.
Enroll.: FTE 185
(504) 222-4251

FOLKES VOCATIONAL-TECHNICAL SCHOOL
P.O. Box 808, Jackson 70748. Public (state). 1981 (SACS-COEI). Courses of varying lengths. Certificates. Dir. Edward J. Daigle.
Enroll.: 190
(504) 643-2636

BRANCH CAMPUS
Highway 68, Jackson 70748.

BRANCH CAMPUS
Highway 61, Wakefield 70784.

GRAMBLING STATE UNIVERSITY
Grambling 71245. Public (state) liberal arts and professional. 1949/1980 (SACS-Comm. on Coll.). Sem. plan. Degrees: A,B,M. *Prof. Accred.:* Music, Teacher Education (*e,s*). Pres. Joseph B. Johnson.
Enroll.: 4,495
(318) 274-3811

GULF AREA VOCATIONAL-TECHNICAL SCHOOL
1115 Clover St., Abbeville 70510. Public (state). 1975/1985 (SACS-COEI). Courses of varying lengths. Certificates. Dir. Albert Robin, Jr.
Enroll.: FTE 287
(318) 893-4984

HAMMOND AREA VOCATIONAL SCHOOL
P.O. Box 489, Hammond 70404. Public (state). 1975/1985 (SACS-COEI). Courses of varying lengths. Certificates. Dir. Thomas Spangler.
Enroll.: FTE 223
(504) 345-0731

HUEY P. LONG MEMORIAL VOCATIONAL SCHOOL
303 S. Jones St., Winnfield 71438. Public (state). 1977/1982 (SACS-COEI). Courses of varying lengths. Certificates. Dir. Donald R. Purser.
Enroll.: FTE 146
(318) 628-4342

BRANCH CAMPUS
E. Bradford St., Jena 71342.

INSTITUTE OF ELECTRONIC TECHNOLOGY
3521 Florida St., Bldg. B, Kenner 70062. Private. 1983 (SACS-COEI). Courses of varying lengths. Certificates. Dir. Julian G. Thompson.
Enroll.: FTE 228
(504) 469-8601

INSURANCE ACHIEVEMENT, INC.
7330 Highland Rd., Baton Rouge 70808-6609. Private home study. 1980/1985 (NHSC). Pres. R. Robert Rackley.
(504) 766-9828

INTERNATIONAL TECHNICAL INSTITUTE, INC.
13944 Airline Hwy., Baton Rouge 70816. Private. 1981 (NATTS). Courses of varying lengths. Certificates. Pres. Earl J. Martin, Jr.
Enroll.: 194 (*f.t.* 80 m., 5 w.)
(504) 292-4230

J.M. FRAZIER, SR., VOCATIONAL-TECHNICAL SCHOOL
555 Julia St., Baton Rouge 70821. Public (state). 1983 (SACS-COEI). Courses of varying lengths. Certificates. Dir. B. J. Brumfield.
Enroll.: FTE 237
(504) 342-6828

JEFFERSON DAVIS VOCATIONAL-TECHNICAL SCHOOL
1230 N. Main St., Jennings 70546. Public (state). 1976/1981 (SACS-COEI). Courses of varying lengths. Certificates. Dir. Nolan Ackoury.
Enroll.: FTE 121
(318) 824-4812

JEFFERSON PARISH VOCATIONAL-TECHNICAL SCHOOL
5200 Blair Dr., Metairie 70001. Public (state). 1975/1984 (SACS-COEI). Courses of varying lengths. Certificates. Dir. John L. D'Aubin.
Enroll.: FTE 627
(504) 733-5250

JEFFERSON PARISH WEST BANK VOCATIONAL-TECHNICAL SCHOOL
475 Manhattan Blvd., Harvey 70058. Public (state). 1982 (SACS-COEI). Courses of varying lengths. Certificates. Dir. Thomas M. Tebbe
Enroll.: FTE 386
(504) 361-6464

BRANCH CAMPUS
501 Texaco La., Harvey 70058.

LAFAYETTE REGIONAL VOCATIONAL-TECHNICAL INSTITUTE
1101 Bertrand Dr., Lafayette 70506. Public (state) technical. 1981 (SACS-COEI). Courses of varying lengths. Certificates. *Prof. Accred.:* Medical Laboratory Technology. Dir. Shelton Cobb.
Enroll.: FTE 704
(318) 235- 5541

LAKE PROVIDENCE VOCATIONAL-TECHNICAL SCHOOL
P.O. Box 368, Lake Providence 71254. Public (state). 1980/1985 (SACS-COEI). Courses of varying lengths. Certificates. Dir. Lynn Payne.
Enroll.: FTE 71
(318) 559-0864

LOUISIANA BUSINESS COLLEGE
1125 Forsythe Ave., Monroe 71201. Private. 1965/1982 (AICS). Courses of varying lengths. Certificates. Admin. Joyce Beatty.
Enroll.: 446 (*f.t.* 89 m., 357 w.)
(318) 325-8261

LOUISIANA COLLEGE
Pineville 71360. Private (Southern Baptist) liberal arts. 1923/1981 (SACS-Comm. on Coll.). Sem. plan. Degrees: B. *Prof. Accred.:* Music. Pres. Robert L. Lynn.
Enroll.: 970
(318) 487-7011

LOUSIANA MARINE AND PETROLEUM INSTITUTE
Station 1 Box 10251, Houma 70363. Public (state). 1985 (SACS-COEI). Courses of varying lengths. Certificates. Dir. V. J. Gianelloni, III.
Enroll.: FTE 56

LOUISIANA STATE UNIVERSITY SYSTEM
Baton Rouge 70803-8402. Public university. Sem. plan. Pres. Allen A. Copping.
(504) 388-6977

LOUISIANA STATE UNIVERSITY AND AGRICULTURAL AND MECHANICAL COLLEGE
Baton Rouge 70803-8402. 1913/1984 (SACS-Comm. on Coll.). Degrees: B,P,M,D. *Prof. Accred.:* Architecture (B), Art, Business (B,M), Construction Education, Engineering (agricultural, chemical, civil, electrical, industrial, mechanical, petroleum), Forestry, Home Economics, Interior Design, Journalism, Landscape Architecture (B), Law, Librarianship, Music, Psychology, Respiratory Therapy, Social Work (M), Speech Pathology, Teacher Education (*e,s,p*), Veterinary Medicine. Chanc. James H. Wharton.
Enroll.: 27,540
(504) 388-3202

LOUISIANA STATE UNIVERSITY MEDICAL CENTER AT NEW ORLEANS
New Orleans 70112. 1931/1984 (SACS-Comm. on Coll.). Degrees: A,B,P,M,D. *Prof. Accred.:* Cytotechnology, Dental Hygiene, DentaljAssisting, Dental Laboratory Technology, Dentistry, EEG Technology, Medical Technology, Medicine, Nursing (A,B,M),

Occupational Therapy, Physical Therapy, Respiratory Therapy, Speech Pathology and Audiology. Chanc. Perry G. Rigby.
Enroll.: 2,477
(504) 568-4800

LOUISIANA STATE UNIVERSITY AT ALEXANDRIA
Alexandria 71301. 1960/ 1984 (SACS-Comm. on Coll.). Degrees: A. *Prof. Accred.:* Nursing (A). Chanc. James W. Firnberg.
Enroll.: 1,651
(318) 473-6400

LOUISIANA STATE UNIVERSITY AT EUNICE
P.O. Box 1129, Eunice 70535. 1967/1984 (SACS-Comm. on Coll.). Degrees: A. *Prof. Accred.:* Respiratory Therapy Technician. Chanc. Anthony Mumphrey.
Enroll.: 1,110
(318) 457-7311

LOUISIANA STATE UNIVERSITY IN SHREVEPORT
8515 Youree Dr., Shreveport 71115. 1975/ 1984 (SACS-Comm. on Coll.). Degrees: A,B,P,M. *Prof. Accred.:* Medicine, Speech Pathology and Audiology, Teacher Education (*e,s*). Chanc. E. Grady Bogue.
Enroll.: 3,881
(318) 797-5000

UNIVERSITY OF NEW ORLEANS
Lake Front, New Orleans 70148. Public part of Louisiana State University System. 1958/ 1984 (SACS-Comm. on Coll.). Degrees:A, B,M,D. *Prof. Accred.:* Accounting (Type A), Business (B,M), Engineering (civil, electrical, mechanical), Music, Teacher Education (*e,s,p*). Chanc. Cooper R. Mackin.
Enroll.: 12,788
(504) 286-6000

LOUISIANA TECH UNIVERSITY
Ruston 71272. Public (state). 1927/1984 (SACS-Comm. on Coll.). Qtr. plan. Degrees: A,B,M,D. *Prof. Accred.:* Accounting (Type A,B,C), Architecture (B), Art, Business (B,M), Dietetics, Engineering (agricultural, biomedical, chemical, civil, electrical, industrial, mechanical, petroleum), Engineering Technology (construction, electrical), Forestry, Interior Design, Medical Record Administration, Medical Record Technology, Music, Nursing (A), Speech Pathology, Teacher Education (*e,s,p*). Pres. F. Jay Taylor.
Enroll.: 9,833
(318) 257-0211

LOYOLA UNIVERSITY
6363 St. Charles Ave., New Orleans 70118. Private (Roman Catholic). 1929/1985 (SACS-Comm. on Coll.). Sem. plan. Degrees: B,P,M. *Prof. Accred.:* Business (B,M), Dental Hygiene, Law, Music, Nursing (B), Teacher Education (*e,s,p*). Pres. Rev. James C. Carter, S.J.
Enroll.: 4,193
(504) 865-2011

MCNEESE STATE UNIVERSITY
Lake Charles 70609. Public liberal arts. 1954/ 1975 (SACS-Comm. on Coll.). Sem. plan. Degrees: A,B,M. *Prof . Accred.:* Engineering, Music, Nursing (B), Radiography, Teacher Education (*e,s,p*). Pres. Jack Doland.
Enroll.: 6,704
(318) 437-5000

MEADOWS-DRAUGHON COLLEGE
3030 Canal St., New Orleans 70119. Private business. 1964/1980 (AICS). Qtr. plan. Certificates, diplomas. Dir. Douglas Stromberg.
Enroll.: 552 (*f.t.* 78 m., 474 w.)
(504) 822-1092

MEMORIAL AREA VOCATIONAL SCHOOL
P.O. Box 725, New Roads 70760. Public (state). 1976/1981 (SACS-COEI). Courses of varying lengths. Certificates. Dir. Cosby D. Joiner.
Enroll.: FTE 378
(504) 638-8613

BRANCH CAMPUS
Louisiana State Penitentary, Angola 70712.
(504) 655-4411

BRANCH CAMPUS
P.O. Box 26, St. Gabriel 70776.
(504) 642-5529

BRANCH CAMPUS
P.O. Box 174, St. Gabriel 70776.
(504) 642-3306

NATCHITOCHES—CENTRAL AREA VOCATIONAL-TECHNICAL SCHOOL
P.O. Box 657, Natchitoches 71457. Public (state). 1982 (SACS-COEI). Courses of varying lengths. Certificates. Dir. Huey Rachal.
Enroll.: FTE 277
(318) 357-0822

BRANCH CAMPUS
P.O. Box 755, Coushatta 71019.
(318) 932-5317

New Orleans Baptist Theological Seminary
3939 Gentilly Blvd., New Orleans 70126-9988. Private (Southern Baptist) professional; graduate only. 1965/1975 (SACS-Comm. on Coll.). Sem. plan. Degrees: A,P,M,D. *Prof. Accred.:* Music, Theology (1954/1986, ATS). Pres. Landrum P. Leavell, II.
Enroll.: 1,896
(504) 282-4455

Nicholls State University
Thibodaux 70301. Public liberal arts and teachers. 1964/1985 (SACS-Comm. on Coll.). Sem. plan. Degrees: A,B,M. *Prof. Accred.:* Business (B), Home Economics, Music, Nursing (A), Teacher Education (*e,s*). Pres. Donald J. Ayo.
Enroll.: 6,294
(504) 446-8111

North American Education Center
4173 Government St., Baton Rouge 70806. Private. 1983 (SACS-COEI). 576 hours. Certificates. Dir. Stanley Holloway.
Enroll.: FTE 22
(504) 291-2873

Branch Campus
6910 N. Holmes St., Kansas City, MO 64118.

Branch Campus
44 Court, Brooklyn, NY 11201.

Branch Campus
1225 N. Expressway, Brownsville, TX 78502.

Branch Campus
607 Calle Del Norte, Suite 6I, Laredo, TX 78041.

North Central Area Vocational-Technical School
605 N. Boundary, West, Farmerville 71241. Public (state). 1979/1984 (SACS-COEI). Courses of varying lengths. Certificates. Dir. Irving D. Adkins.
Enroll.: FTE 94
(318) 368-3179

Northeast Louisiana University
Monroe 71209. Public (state). 1955/1978 (SACS-Comm. on Coll.). Sem. plan. Degrees: A,B,M,D. *Prof. Accred.:* Business (B,M), Construction Education, Dental Hygiene, Home Economics, Music, Nursing (B), Occupational Therapy, Pharmacy, Radiography, Social Work (B), Teacher Education (*e,s,p*). Pres. Dwight Del Vines.
Enroll.: 9,856
(318) 342-2011

Northeast Louisiana Vocational School
1710 Warren St., Winnsboro 71295. Public (state). 1976/1981 (SACS-COEI). Courses of varying lengths. Certificates. Dir. Kenneth Bridges
Enroll.: FTE 149
(318) 435-5096

Northwest Louisiana Vocational-Technical School
P.O. Box 835, Minden 71055. Public (state). 1975/1985 (SACS-COEI). Courses of varying lengths. Certificates. Dir. Robert A. Alost.
Enroll.: FTE 252
(318) 377-6832

Branch Campus
First S.E and Reynolds Sts., Springhill 71075.

Northwestern State University of Louisiana
Natchitoches 71497. Public liberal arts and professional. 1941/1975 (SACS-Comm. on Coll.). Sem. plan. Degrees: A,B,M,D. *Prof. Accred.:* Music, Nursing (A,B,M), Radiography, Social Work (B), Teacher Education (*e,s,p*). Pres. Joseph J. Orze.
Enroll.: 4,382
(318) 357-6361

Notre Dame Seminary—School of Theology
2901 S. Carrollton Ave., New Orleans 70118. Private (Roman Catholic) graduate only. 1951/1979 (SACS-Comm. on Coll.). Sem. plan. Degrees: P,M. Theology (1979/1986, ATS). Pres. John C. Favalora.
Enroll.: 112
(504) 866-7426

Oakdale Vocational-Technical School
P.O. Drawer EM, Oakdale 71463. Public (state). 1983 (SACS-COEI). Courses of varying lengths. Certificates. Dir. Charles L. Baggett.
Enroll.: FTE 113
(318) 335-3944

Ochsner School of Allied Health Sciences
1516 Jefferson Hwy., New Orleans 70121. Private technical. 1978/1983 (SACS-COEI). Courses of varying lengths. Certificates. Dir. Edward D. Frohlich.
Enroll.: FTE 99
(504) 837-3265

Our Lady of Holy Cross College
New Orleans 70114. Private (Roman Catholic) liberal arts and teacher's college. 1972/1976 (SACS-Comm. on Coll.). Sem. plan. Degrees: A,B. Acting Pres. Sister Mary Charles Clement.
Enroll.: 425
(504) 394-7744

Phillips Junior College
1333 S. Clearview Pkwy., New Orleans 70121. Private. 1974/1986 (AICS). Courses of varying lengths. Degrees: A, diplomas. *Prof. Accred.:*Medical Assisting. Pres. Jerry Adams.
Enroll.: 1,920 (*f.t.* 607 m., 1,313 w.)
(504) 734-0123

Branch Campus
5201 Westbank Expwy., Marrero 70072. Dir. Georjean Crosley.
(504) 348-1182

Port Sulphur Vocational-Technical School
P.O. Drawer 944, Port Sulphur 70083. Public (state). 1985 (SACS-COEI). Courses of varying lengths. Certificates. Dir. Vera B. Mailhes.
Enroll.: FTE 87

Portside Vocational-Technical School
3233 Rosedale Rd., Port Allen 70767. Public (state). 1981 (SACS-COEI). Courses of varying lengths. Certificates. Dir. James V. Soileau.
Enroll.: FTE 80
(504) 342-5061

R.E.T.S. Training Center
3605 Division St., Metairie 70002. Private. 1976/1985 (NATTS). Qtr. plan. Diplomas. Pres. Harold M. Zlatnicky.
Enroll.: 364 (*f.t.* 170 m., 24 w.)
(504) 888-6848

River Parishes Vocational-Technical School
P. O. Drawer AQ, Reserve 70084. Public (state). 1984 (SACS-COEI). Courses of varying lengths. Certificates. Dir. J. J. Zeringue.
Enroll.: FTE 180

Robinson Business College
604 Jack McEnery St., Monroe 71201. Private. 1966/1984 (AICS). Sem. plan. Diplomas. Dir. B. D. Robinson.
Enroll.: 88 (*f.t.* 14 m., 74 w.)
(318) 323-7515

Ruston Vocational-Technical School
1010 James St., Ruston 71270. Public (state). 1982 (SACS-COEI). Courses of varying lengths. Certificates. Dir. F. L. Ellerman.
Enroll.: FTE 116
(318) 255-6152

Sabine Valley Vocational-Technical School
P.O. Box 790, Many 71449. Public (state). 1977/1982 (SACS-COEI). Courses of varying lengths. Certificates. Dir. David B. Crittenden.
Enroll.: FTE 149
(318) 256-5663

Saint Bernard Parish Community College
100 E. Judge Perez Dr., Chalmette 70043. Public 2-year. 1985 (SACS-Comm. on Coll.). Sem. plan. Degrees: A. Pres. Elizabeth A. Zimmermann.
Enroll.: 344

Saint Joseph Seminary College
St. Benedict 70457. Private (Roman Catholic, Order of St. Benedict) liberal arts. 1969/1983 (SACS-Comm. on Coll.). Sem. plan. Degrees: B. Pres. Rev. Pius Lartigue.
Enroll.: 132
(504) 892-1800

Shreveport-Bossier Vocational Technical Center
2010 N. Market, Shreveport 71137. Public (state). 1976/1981 (SACS-COEI). Courses of varying lengths. Certificates. Dir. Bill H. Cates.
Enroll.: FTE 663
(318) 226-7816

Sidney N. Collier Memorial Vocational-Technical Institute
3727 Louisa St., New Orleans 70126. Public (state). 1977/1982 (SACS-COEI). Courses of varying lengths. Certificates. Dir. Levi Lewis.
Enroll.: FTE 260
(504) 945-8080

Slidell Vocational-Technical School
1000 Canulette Rd., Slidell 70458. Public (state). 1974/1983 (SACS-COEI). Courses of varying lengths. Certificates. Dir. George W. Foster.
Enroll.: FTE 264
(504) 643-9610

SOUTH LOUISIANA VOCATIONAL-TECHNICAL INSTITUTE
201 St. Charles St., Houma 70360. Public (state). 1975/1985 (SACS-COEI). Courses of varying lengths. Certificates. Dir. F. Travis Lavigne, Jr.
Enroll.: FTE 204
(504) 873-7773

SOUTHEASTERN LOUISIANA UNIVERSITY
Hammond 70402. Public (state) liberal arts and professional. 1946/1984 (SACS-Comm. on Coll.). Sem. plan. Degrees: A,B,M. *Prof. Accred.:* Home Economics, Medical Technology, Music, Nursing (B), Social Work (B), Teacher Education (*e,s,p*). Pres. J. Larry Crain.
Enroll.: 7,814
(504) 549-2280

SOUTHERN TECHNICAL COLLEGE
105 Patriot Ave., Lafayette 70503. Private. 1966/1980 (AICS). Qtr. plan. Certificates, diplomas. Dir. C. W. Stewart.
Enroll.: 2,050 (*f.t.* 1,013 m., 1,037 w.)
(318) 981-4010

BRANCH CAMPUS
119 Second St., Hot Springs, AR 71901. Dir. John Dyer.
(501) 623-2651

BRANCH CAMPUS
7800 Interstate Dr., Little Rock, AR 72209. Co-Dirs. Thomas DuPriest and William King.
(501) 565-7000

SOUTHERN UNIVERSITY AND AGRICULTURAL AND MECHANICAL COLLEGE SYSTEM
Baton Rouge 70813. Public (state). Pres. Joffre T. Whisenton.
(504) 771-4500

SOUTHERN UNIVERSITY AND AGRICULTURAL AND MECHANICAL COLLEGE
Baton Rouge 70813. Public (state). 1938/1980 (SACS-Comm. on Coll.). Sem. plan. Degrees: A,B,P,M. *Prof. Accred.:* Architecture (B), Engineering (civil, electrical, mechanical), Home Economics, Law (ABA only), Music, Social Work (B), Teacher Education (*e,s*). Chanc. Wesley C. McLure.
Enroll.: 10,872
(504) 771-4500

SOUTHERN UNIVERSITY IN NEW ORLEANS
6400 Press Dr., New Orleans 70126. 1958/1980 (SACS-Comm. on Coll.). Degrees: A,B,M. *Prof. Accred.:* Social Work (B). Chanc. Emmett W. Bashful.
Enroll.: 2,461
(504) 282-4401

SOUTHERN UNIVERSITY AT SHREVEPORT
Shreveport 71107. 1964/1980 (SACS-Comm. on Coll.). Degrees: A. Chanc. Leonard C. Barnes.
Enroll.: 537
(318) 674-3300

SOUTHWEST LOUISIANA VOCATIONAL-TECHNICAL SCHOOL
1933 W. Huchinson Ave., Crowley 70526. Public (state). 1976/1981 (SACS-COEI). Courses of varying lengths. Certificates. Dir. Richard A. Arnaud.
Enroll.: FTE 683
(318) 783-3723

BRANCH CAMPUS
404 W. 12th St., Crowley 70526.
(318) 537-3135

SOWELA TECHNICAL INSTITUTE
P.O. Box 16950, Lake Charles 70616. Public (state). 1971/1981 (SACS-COEI). Courses of varying lengths. Certificates. Dir. Earl L. Hammett.
Enroll.: FTE 2,178
(318) 491-2680

SPENCER COLLEGE
2902 Florida Blvd., Baton Rouge 70802. Private business. 1966/1980 (AICS). Qtr. plan. Certificates, diplomas. Pres. Sharon B. Burke.
Enroll.: 859 (*f.t.* 185 m., 674 w.)
(504) 383-7701

SULLIVAN VOCATIONAL-TECHNICAL INSTITUTE
1710 Sullivan Dr., Bogalusa 70427. Public (state). 1973/1983 (SACS-COEI). Courses of varying lengths. Certificates. Dir. M. J. Murphy.
Enroll.: FTE 427
(504) 735-8291

T. H. HARRIS VOCATIONAL-TECHNICAL SCHOOL
337 E. South St., Opelousas 70570. Public (state). 1970/1985 (SACS-COEI). Courses of varying lengths. Certificates. Dir. Ceasor Veazie.
Enroll.: FTE 667
(318) 942-4902

Tallulah Vocational-Technical School
Old Highway 65 S., Tallulah 71282. Public (state). 1980/1985 (SACS-COEI). Courses of varying lengths. Certificates. Dir. Patrick T. Murphy.
Enroll.: FTE 120
(318) 574-4820

Teche Area Vocational-Technical School
P.O. Box 1057, New Iberia 70561. Public (state). 1976/1981 (SACS-COEI). Courses of varying lengths. Certificates. Dir. Henry G. Segura.
Enroll.: FTE 301
(318) 365-6672

Tulane University
New Orleans 70118. Private; College of Arts and Sciences for men, Newcomb College for women, others coeducational. 1903/1979 (SACS-Comm. on Coll.). Sem. plan. Degrees: B,P,M,D. *Prof. Accred.:* Architecture (B), Art, Business (B,M), Engineering (biomedical, chemical, civil, electrical, mechanical), Health Services Administration, Law, Medicine, Music (Newcomb College), Public Health, Social Work (M). Pres. Eamon M. Kelly.
Enroll.: 8,931
(504) 865-5000

University of Southwestern Louisiana
P.O. Box 41008, Lafayette 70504. Public (state). 1925/1980 (SACS-Comm. on Coll.). Sem. plan. Degrees: A,B,M,D. *Prof. Accred.:* Architecture (B), Engineering (chemical, civil, electrical, mechanical, petroleum), Medical Record Administration, Music, Nursing (B), Speech Pathology, Teacher Education (*e,s,p*). Pres. Ray P. Authement.
Enroll.: 14,339
(318) 231-6000

Ville Platte Vocational-Technical School
P.O. Box 296, Ville Platte 70586. Public (state). 1981 (SACS-COEI). Courses of varying lengths. Certificates. Dir. C. B. Coreil.
Enroll.: FTE 161
(318) 363-2197

WKG-TV Video Electronic College
141 Ocean Dr., Baton Rouge 70806. Private. 1984 (SACS-COEI). Courses of varying lengths. Certificates. Dir. R. M. Fletcher
Enroll.: FTE 57

Branch Campus
6420 Richmond Ave., Suite 350, Houston, TX 77057.

West Louisiana Vocational-Technical School
Route 2, Box 25, Leesville 71446. Public (state). 1983 (SACS-COEI). Courses of varying lengths. Certificates. Dir. Alferd V. Davis.
Enroll.: FTE 215
(318) 537-3135

Branch Campus
502 S. Pine, DeRidder 70634.

Westbank Business College
4633 Westbank Expressway, Marrero 70072. Private. 1980 (AICS). Courses of varying lengths. Certificates. Dir. Bill Nettle.
Enroll.: 423 (*f.t.* 75 m., 348 w.)
(504) 347-8411

Westside Vocational-Technical School
1201 Bayou Rd., Plaquemine 70764. Public (state). 1974/1984 (SACS-COEI). Courses of varying lengths. Certificates. Dir. Alfred S. Bell.
Enroll.: FTE 231
(504) 687-6392

Xavier University of Louisiana
7325 Palmetto St., New Orleans 70125. Private (Roman Catholic). 1937/1979 (SACS-Comm. on Coll.). Sem. plan. Degrees: B,M. *Prof. Accred.:* Music, Pharmacy. Pres. Norman C. Francis.
Enroll.: 1,865
(504) 486-7411

Young Memorial Vocational-Technical School
P.O. Box 2148, Morgan City 70381. Public (state) technical. 1976/1981 (SACS-COEI). Courses of varying lengths. Certificates. Dir. Lyman J. Wilson.
Enroll.: FTE 266
(504) 384-6526

MAINE

ANDOVER COLLEGE
901 Washington Ave., The Educational Ctr., Portland 04103. Private junior. 1970/1980 (AICS). Qtr. plan. Degrees: A, certificates, diplomas. Pres. Lee C. Jenkins.
Enroll.: 761 (*f.t.* 277 m., 484 w.)
(207) 772-4675

BANGOR THEOLOGICAL SEMINARY
Bangor 04401. Private (United Church of Christ) professional; graduate only. 1968/1982 (NEASC-CIHE). Sem. plan. Degrees: P,M. *Prof. Accred.:* Theology (1974/1986, ATS). Pres. Malcolm L. Warford.
Enroll.: 123
(207) 942-6781

BATES COLLEGE
Lewiston 04240. Private liberal arts. 1929/1979 (NEASC-CIHE). Sem. plan. Degrees: B. Pres. Thomas Hedley Reynolds.
Enroll.: 1,519
(207) 786-6255

*BEAL COLLEGE
629 Main St., Bangor 04401. Private junior. 1966/1983 (AICS). Sem. (days) and Tri. (evenings) plans. Degrees: A, diplomas. *Prof. Accred.:* Medical Assisting. Pres. Allen Stehle.
Enroll.: 933 (*f.t.* 206 m., 727 w.)
(207) 947-4591

BRANCH CAMPUS
275 Bath Rd., Brunswick 04011. Dir. David Tibbetts.
(207) 729-4373

BOWDOIN COLLEGE
Brunswick 04011. Private liberal arts. 1929/1976 (NEASC-CIHE). Sem. plan. Degrees: B,M. Pres. A. LeRoy Greason.
Enroll.: 1,399
(207) 725-8731

CASCO BAY COLLEGE
477 Congress St., Portland 04101. Private junior. 1968/1986 (AICS). Sem. (days) and Tri. (evenings) plans. Degrees: A, diplomas. Pres. Gene F. Stearns.
Enroll.: 566 (*f.t.* 121 m., 445 w.)
(207) 772-0196

*Candidate for Accreditation by Regional Accrediting Commission

CENTRAL MAINE MEDICAL CENTER SCHOOL OF NURSING
Lewiston 04240. Private 2-year technical. 1978 (NEASC-CVTCI). Sept./June plan. Degrees: A. Pres. Fay E. Ingersoll.
Enroll.: 59
(207) 795-2840

CENTRAL MAINE VOCATIONAL-TECHNICAL INSTITUTE
Auburn 04210. Public (state) 2-year. 1976 (NEASC-CVTCI). Qtr. plan. Degrees: A, certificates. *Prof. Accred.:* Engineering Technology (architectural and civil). Dir. Nelson J. Megna.
Enroll.: 1,486
(207) 784-2385

COLBY COLLEGE
Waterville 04901. Private liberal arts. 1929/1978 (NEASC-CIHE). 4-1-4 plan. Degrees: B,M. Pres. William R. Cotter.
Enroll.: 1,696
(207) 872-3214

COLLEGE OF THE ATLANTIC
Bar Harbor 04609. Private liberal arts. 1976/1985 (NEASC-CIHE). Tri. plan. Degrees: B. Pres. Louis Rabineau.
Enroll.: 132
(207) 288-5015

EASTERN MAINE VOCATIONAL-TECHNICAL INSTITUTE
Bangor 04401. Public (state) 2-year technical. 1973/1983 (NEASC-CVTCI). Qtr. plan. Degrees: A. *Prof. Accred.:* Engineering Technology (environmental control), Medical Laboratory Technology (A), Radiography. Dir. Allen R. Campbell.
Enroll.: 871
(207) 942-5217

HUSSON COLLEGE
Bangor 04401. Private 4-year business. 1974/1986 (NEASC-CIHE). Sem. plan. Degrees: A,B,M, certificates, diplomas. Pres. Delmont N. Merrill.
Enroll.: 1,516
(207) 947-1121

KENNEBEC VALLEY VOCATIONAL-TECHNICAL INSTITUTE
Fairfield 04937. Public (state) 2-year. 1979 (NEASC-CVTCI). Sem. plan. Degrees: A.

Prof. Accred.: Nursing (A), Respiratory Therapy Technology. Dir. Barbara W. Woodlee.
Enroll.: 543
(207) 453-9762

MAINE MARITIME ACADEMY
Castine 04421. Public (state) professional. 1971/19851 (NEASC-CIHE). Sem. plan. Degrees: B,M. Supt. Rear Adm. Sayre A. Swarztrauber.
Enroll.: 600
(207) 326-4311

MID-STATE COLLEGE
Route 4, Box 484, Auburn 04210. Private business. 1970/1983 (AICS). Sem. plan. Diplomas. Pres. Allen T. Stehle.
Enroll.: 373 (*f.t.* 91 m., 282 w.)
(207) 783-1478

BRANCH CAMPUS
218 Water St., Augusta 04330. Dir. Val Landry.
(207) 623-3962

MR. RICHARD'S HAIRSTYLING ACADEMY
41 Broad St., Auburn 04210. Private. 1981 (NATTS). Courses of varying lengths. Diplomas. Dir. Richard Pepin.
Enroll.: 16 (*f.t.* 2 m., 14 w.)
(207) 783-9326

NORTHERN MAINE VOCATIONAL-TECHNICAL INSTITUTE
Presque Isle 04769. Public (state) 2-year technical. 1975/1985 (NEASC-CVTCI). Qtr. plan. Degrees: A. Dir. James C. Patterson.
Enroll.: FTE 1,353
(207) 769-2461

PORTLAND SCHOOL OF ART
Portland 04101. Private 4-year professional. 1978/1985 (NEASC-CIHE). Sem. plan. Degrees: B. *Prof. Accred.:* Art. Pres. Peter Hero
Enroll.: 400
(207) 775-3052

SAINT JOSEPH'S COLLEGE
North Windham 04062. Private (Roman Catholic) liberal arts. 1961/1985 (NEASC-CIHE). Sem. plan. Degrees: B. *Prof. Accred.:* Nursing (B). Pres. Anthony R. Santoro.
Enroll.: 4,358
(207) 892-6766

SOUTHERN MAINE VOCATIONAL-TECHNICAL INSTITUTE
South Portland 04106. Public (state) 2-year technical. 1974/1985 (NEASC-CVTCI). Qtr. plan. Degrees: A. *Prof. Accred.:* Radiation Therapy Technology, Respiratory Respiratory Therapy Technology. Dir. Wayne H. Ross.
Enroll.: 1,018
(207) 799-7303

THOMAS COLLEGE
Waterville 04901. Private liberal arts and business. 1969/1986 (NEASC-CIHE). Sem. plan. Degrees: A,B,M. Pres. Cyril M. Joly.
Enroll.: 832
(207) 873-0771

*UNITY COLLEGE
Unity 04988. Private liberal arts. 1974/1984 (NEASC-CIHE). Modular plan. Degrees: A,B. Pres. James L. Caplinger.
Enroll.: 283
(207) 948-3131

UNIVERSITY OF MAINE
Central office, 107 Maine Ave., Bangor 04401-1805. Public (state). Chanc. Jack E. Freeman.
(207) 947-0336

UNIVERSITY OF MAINE AT AUGUSTA
Augusta 04330. Public (state) 2-year. 1973/1985 (NEASC-CIHE). Sem. plan. Degrees: A,B. *Prof. Accred.:* Medical Laboratory Technology (A), Nursing (A). Interim Pres. George P. Connick.
Enroll.: 3,368
(207) 622-7131

UNIVERSITY OF MAINE AT FARMINGTON
Farmington 04938. Public (state) liberal arts and teachers college. 1958/1982 (NEASC-CIHE). Sem. plan. Degrees: A,B. *Prof. Accred.:* Teacher Education (*e,s*). Pres. Judith A. Sturnick.
Enroll.: 2,140
(207) 778-3501

UNIVERSITY OF MAINE AT FORT KENT
Fort Kent 04743. Public (state) liberal arts and teachers college. 1970/1986 (NEASC-CIHE). Sem. plan. Degrees: A,B. Pres. Richard J. Spath.
Enroll.: 656
(207) 834-3162

UNIVERSITY OF MAINE AT MACHIAS
Machias 04654. Public (state) liberal arts and teachers college. 1970/1984 (NEASC-CIHE). Sem. plan. Degrees: A,B. Pres. Frederic A. Reynolds.

*Accreditation on Probation

Enroll.: 834
(207) 255-3313

University of Maine at Orono
Orono 04469. Public (state). 1929/1977 (NEASC-CIHE). Sem. plan. Degrees: A,B,M,D. *Prof. Accred.:* Art, Business (B,M), Dental Hygiene, Engineering (agricultural, chemical, civil, electrical, engineering physics, mechanical, surveying), Engineering Technology (civil, electrical, mechanical), Forestry, Home Economics, Music, Psychology, Social Work (B), Teacher Education (*e,s,p*). Pres. Arthur M. Johnson.
Enroll.: 11,180
(207) 581-1110

University of Maine at Presque Isle
Presque Isle 04769. Public (state) liberal arts and teachers college. 1968/1984 (NEASC-CIHE). Sem. plan. Degrees: A,B. *Prof. Accred.:* Medical Laboratory Technology (A). Pres. ———.
Enroll.: 1,210
(207) 764-0311

University of Southern Maine
Portland 04103. Public liberal arts and professional. 1960/1981 (NEASC-CIHE). Degrees: A,B,P,M,D. *Prof. Accred.:* Art, Law, Music, Nursing (B), Social Work (B), Teacher Education (*e,s*). Pres. Robert L. Woodbury.
Enroll.: 8,769
(207) 780-4480

University of New England
Biddeford 04005. Private liberal arts and professional; accreditation includes New England College of Osteopathic Medicine. 1966/1983 (NEASC-CIHE). 4-1-4 plan. Degrees: B,P. *Prof. Accred.:* Nurse Anesthesia Education, Occupational Therapy, Osteopathy, Physical Therapy. Pres. Charles W. Ford.
Enroll.: 934
(207) 283-0171

Washington County Vocational-Technical Institute
Calais 04619. Public (state) 2-year. 1976/1979 (NEASC-CVTCI). Qtr. plan. Certificates. Dir. Ronald P. Renaud.
Enroll.: 210
(207) 454-2144

Westbrook College
Portland 04103. Private liberal arts. 1934/1984 (NEASC-CIHE). 4-1-4 plan. Degrees: A,B. *Prof. Accred.:* Dental Hygiene, Medical Assistant, Nursing (A,B). Pres. Thomas B. Courtice.
Enroll.: 1,138
(207) 797-7261

YDI Schools, Inc.
Main St., Blue Hill 04614. Private home study. 1978/1984 (NHSC). Degrees: A, certificates. Dir. Robert E. Wallstrom.
(207) 374-5551

MARYLAND

Abbie Business Institute
186 Thomas Jefferson Dr., Suite 203, Frederick 21701-4315. Private. 1984 (AICS). Courses of varying lengths. Certificates. Dir. Darlene T. Carver.
Enroll.: 29 (*f.t.* 17)
(301) 694-0211

Airco Technical Institute
121 Kane St., Baltimore 21224. Private. 1974/1979 (NATTS). Courses of varying lengths. Diplomas. Dir. James H. Ethridge.
Enroll.: 364 (*f.t.* 338 m., 26 w.)
(301) 633-4300

Allegany Community College
Willow Brook Rd., Cumberland 21502. Public (county) junior. 1965/1985 (MSA/CHE). Sem. plan. Degrees: A. *Prof. Accred.:* Dental Assisting, Dental Hygiene, Medical Laboratory Technology (A), Respiratory Therapy. Pres. Donald L. Alexander.
Enroll.: 225 (*f.t.* 492 m., 729 w.)
(301) 724-7700

Anne Arundel Community College
101 College Pkwy., Arnold 21012. Public (county) junior. 1968/1984 (MSA/CHE). Sem. plan. Degrees: A. *Prof. Accred.:* Nursing (A). Pres. Thomas E. Florestano.
Enroll.: 9,270 (*f.t.* 1,138 m., 1,043 w.)
(301) 647-7100

Arundel Institute of Technology
1808 Edison Hwy., Baltimore 21213. Private. 1971/1983 (NATTS). Qtr. plan. Diplomas. Dir. Manfred Bloch.
Enroll.: 223 (*f.t.* 192 m., 31 w.)
(301) 327-6640

Baltimore Hebrew College
5800 Park Heights Ave., Baltimore 21215. Private teacher preparatory and professional. 1974/1984 (MSA/CHE). Sem. plan. Degrees: B,M,D. Pres. Leivy Smolar.
Enroll.: 251 (*f.t.* 35 m., 101 w.)
(301) 578-6900

Baltimore's International Culinary Arts Institute
19-21 S. Gray St., Baltimore 212026. Private. 1985 (NATTS). Courses of varying lengths. Diplomas. Dir. Roger Chylurski.
(301) 752-4710

Bowie State College
Bowie 20715. Public liberal arts and teachers. 1961/1981 (MSA/CHE). Sem. plan. Degrees: B,M. *Prof. Accred.:* Social Work (B), Teacher Education (*e,s,p*). Pres. James E. Lyons, Sr.
Enroll.: 2,524 (*f.t.* 602 m., 741 w.)
(301) 464-3000

Broadcasting Institute of Maryland
7200 Harford Rd., Baltimore 21234. Private. 1980 (NATTS). Sem. plan. Diplomas. Pres. John C. Jeppi.
Enroll.: 114 (*f.t.* 67 m., 47 w.)
(301) 254-2770

Capitol Institute of Technology
11301 Springfield Rd., Laurel 20708. Private 4-year technological. 1976/1986 (MSA/CHE). Qtr. plan. Degrees: A,B. *Prof. Accred.:* Engineering Technology (electronics). Pres. G. William Troxler.
Enroll.: 1,079 (*f.t.* 452 m., 46 w.)
(301) 953-0060

Catonsville Community College
Catonsville 21228. Public (county) junior. 1966/1986 (MSA/CHE). Sem. plan. Degrees: A. Pres. John M. Kingsmore.
Enroll.: 10,856 (*f.t.* 1,171 m., 1,063 w.)
(301) 455-6050

Cecil Community College
North East 21901. Public 2-year. 1974/1985 (MSA/CHE). Sem. plan. Degrees: A. *Prof. Accred.:* Nursing (A). Pres. Robert L. Gell.
Enroll.: 1,310 (*f.t.* 99 m., 162 w.)
(301) 287-6060

Charles County Community College
La Plata 20646. Public (county) junior. 1969/1984 (MSA/CHE). Sem. plan. Degrees: A. *Prof. Accred.:* Practical Nursing. Pres. John M. Sine.
Enroll.: 4,462 (*f.t.* 265 m., 404 w.)
(301) 870-3008

Chesapeake Business Institute
5408 Silver Hill Rd., Forestville 20747. Private. 1978/1982 (AICS). Courses of varying lengths. Certificates, diplomas. Pres. Charles Harrington.
Enroll.: 401 (*f.t.* 24 m., 377 w.)
(301) 420-1624

Branch Campus
9135 Piscataway Rd., Clinton 20735. Dir. Lynn Johnson.
(301) 856-1560

Chesapeake College
Wye Mills 21679. Public (regional) junior. 1970/1985 (MSA/CHE). Sem. plan. Degrees: A. *Prof. Accred.:* Medical Laroratory Technology (A), Radiography. Pres. Robert C. Schleiger.
Enroll.: 2,022 (*f.t.* 153 m., 308 w.)
(301) 822-5400

College of Notre Dame of Maryland
4701 N. Charles St., Baltimore 21210. Private (Roman Catholic) liberal arts primarily for women. 1925/1980 (MSA/CHE). 4-1-4 plan. Degrees: B,M. Pres. Sister Kathleen Feeley, SSND.
Enroll.: 1,712 (*f.t.* 0 m., 487 w.)
(301) 435-0100

Columbia Union College
Takoma Park 20912. Private (Seventh-day Adventist) liberal arts. 1942/1985 (MSA/CHE). Accreditation includes nursing program in Kettering, OH. Tri. plan. Degrees: A,B. *Prof. Accred.:* Medical Laboratory Technician, Medical Technology, Nursing (B), Respiratory Therapy. Pres. William Loveless.
Enroll.: 927 (*f.t.* 148 m., 212 w.)
(301) 270-9200

Community College of Baltimore
Liberty Campus, 2901 Liberty Heights Ave., Baltimore 21215; Harbor Campus, Lombard and Market Sts., Baltimore 21202. Public (city) junior. 1963/1980 (MSA/CHE). Sem. plan. Degrees: A. *Prof. Accred.:* Dental Assisting, Dental Hygiene, Dental Laboratory Technology, Medical Record Technology, Nursing (A), Respiratory Therapy. Pres. Joseph Durham.
Enroll.: 5,847 (*f.t.* 584 m., 1,416 w.)
(301) 396-0203

Control Data Institute
1777 Reisterstown Rd., Commerce Centre East, No. 150, Baltimore 21208. 1981/1983 (NATTS). Courses of varying lengths. Certificates. Dir. Thomas Grimm.
Enroll.: 176 (*f.t.* 100 m., 76 w.)
(301) 486-4676

Coppin State College
2500 W. North Ave., Baltimore 21216. Public teachers. 1962/1978 (MSA/CHE). Sem. plan. Degrees: B,M. *Prof. Accred.:* Nursing (B), Rehabilitation Counseling, Social Work (B), Teacher Education (*e,s*). Pres. Calvin W. Burnett.
Enroll.: 2,355 (*f.t.* 555 m., 1,089 w.)
(301) 383-4500

Diesel Institute of America
5600 Columbia Park Rd., Cheverly 20785. Private. 1980 (NATTS). Courses of varying lengths. Diplomas. Dir. Jeff Monsein.
Enroll.: 250 (*f.t.* 248 m., 2 w.)
(301) 322-7400

Extension
515 S. Haven St., Baltimore 21224. 1985 (NATTS). Pres. Alvin Himelblau.
(301) 522-6600

Extension
P.O. Box 69, Grantsville 21536. 1983 (NATTS). Pres. Sheldon Monsein.
(301) 895-5138

Dundalk Community College
Dundalk 21221. Public (district) junior. 1975/1986 (MSA/CHE). 4-1-4 plan. Degrees: A. Pres. Philip R. Day, Jr.
Enroll.: 3,241 (*f.t.* 212 m., 253 w.)
(301) 282-6700

Essex Community College
Baltimore County 21237. Public (county) junior. 1966/1982 (MSA/CHE). Sem. plan. Degrees: A. *Prof. Accred.:* Assistant to the Primary Care Physician, Dental Assisting, Medical Laboratory Technology (A), Music, Nuclear Medicine Technology, Nursing (A), Radiography. Pres. John E. Ravekes.
Enroll.: 9,706 (*f.t.* 1,267 m., 1,115 w.)
(301) 682-6000

Fleet Business School
1939 Lincoln Dr., Annapolis 21401. Private. 1971/1983 (AICS). Qtr. plan. Certificates, diplomas. Pres./Dir. James Graves.
Enroll.: 316 (*f.t.* 9 m., 307 w.)
(301) 268-7511

Frederick Community College
7932 Oppossumtown Pk., Frederick 21701. Public (district) junior. 1971/1986 (MSA/CHE). Sem. plan. Degrees: A. *Prof. Accred.:* Dental Assisting. Pres. Lee J. Betts.
Enroll.: 3,076 (*f.t.* 388 m., 439 w.)
(301) 694-5240

Frostburg State College
Frostburg 21532. Public liberal arts and teachers. 1953/1986 (MSA/CHE). Sem. plan. Degrees: B,M. Pres. Herbert F. Reinhard.
Enroll.: 3,715 (*f.t.* 1,507 m., 1,349 w.)
(301) 689-4000

Garrett Community College
Box 151, McHenry 21541. Public (district) junior. 1975/1980 (MSA/CHE). Sem. plan. Degrees: A. Pres. Stephen J. Herman.
Enroll.: 553 (*f.t.* 112 m., 100 w.)
(301) 387-6666

Goucher College
Dulaney Rd., Towson, 21204. Private liberal arts primarily for women. 1921/1983 (MSA/CHE). 4-1-4 plan. Degrees: B,M. Pres. Rhoda M. Dorsey.
Enroll.: 907 (*f.t.* 3 m., 740 w.)
(301) 337-6000

Hagerstown Business College
441-449 N. Potomac St., P.O. Box 2809, Hagerstown 21741. Private junior. 1968/1981 (AICS). Qtr. plan. Degrees: A, certificates. Pres. Dudley Bryant.
Enroll.: 333 (*f.t.* 9 m., 324 w.)
(301) 739-2670

Hagerstown Junior College
Hagerstown 21740-6590. Public (county). 1968/1984 (MSA/CHE). Sem. plan. Degrees: A. *Prof. Accred.:* Radiography. Pres. Norman Shea.
Enroll.: 2,484 (*f.t.* 463 m., 424 w.)
(301) 790-2800

Harford Community College
Bel Air 21014. Public (county). 1967/1982 (MSA/CHE). Sem. plan. Degrees: A. *Prof. Accred.:* Histologic Technology, Nursing (A). Pres. Alfred C. O'Connell.
Enroll.: 4,306 (*f.t.* 467 m., 527 w.)
(301) 836-4000

Home Study International
6940 Carroll Ave., Takoma Park 20912. Private home study. 1967/1979 (NHSC). Pres. D. W. Holbrook.
(202) 722-6570

Hood College
Frederick 21701. Private liberal arts primarily for women. 1922/1974 (MSA/CHE). Sem. plan. Degrees: B,M. *Prof. Accred.:* Dietetics, Home Economics, Radiography, Social Work (B). Pres. Martha E. Church.
Enroll.: 1,711 (*f.t.* 33 m., 758 w.)
(301) 663-3131

Howard Community College
Columbia 21044. Public (county) junior. 1975/1985 (MSA/CHE). Sem. plan. Degrees: A. *Prof. Accred.:* Nursing (A), Optometric Technology. Pres. Dwight A. Burrill.
Enroll.: 3,380 (*f.t.* 357 m., 363 w.)
(301) 992-4800

Johns Hopkins University
Baltimore 21218. Private. 1921/1984 (MSA/CHE). Sem. plan. Degrees: A,B,P,M,D. *Prof. Accred.:* Cytotechnology, Engineering (biomedical, chemical, electrical, engineering mechanics, materials science and engineering), Medicine, Public Health. Pres. Steven Muller.
Enroll.: 9,955 (*f.t.* 3,134 m., 1,788 w.)
(301) 338-8000

Katharine Gibbs School
11300 Rockville Pike, Rockville 20852. Private business. 1969/1984 (AICS). Qtr. plan. Diplomas. Dir. Patricia Spencer.
Enroll.: 385 (*f.t.* 2 m., 383 w.)
(301) 881-6000

Lincoln Technical Institute
3200 Wilkens Ave., Baltimore 21229. Private. 1968/1979 (NATTS). Courses of varying lengths. Diplomas. Dir. Michael Iannacone.
Enroll.: 319 (*f.t.* 206 m., 6 w.)
(301) 646-5480

Lincoln Technical Institute
7800 Central Ave., P.O. Box 8502, Capitol Heights 20743. Private. 1968/1978 (NATTS). Courses of varying lengths. Certificates, diplomas. Dir. Louis R. Hernandez.
Enroll.: 967 (*f.t.* 818 m., 39 w.)
(301) 336-7250

Loyola College
4501 N. Charles St., Baltimore 21210. Private (Roman Catholic) liberal arts. 1931/1985 (MSA/CHE). Day undergraduate 4-1-4 plan; Evening undergraduate and graduate Sem. plan. Degrees: B,M. Pres. Rev. Joseph A. Sellinger, S.J.
Enroll.: 5,157 (*f.t.* 1,364 m., 1,546 w.)
(301) 323-1010

The Maryland College of Art and Design
10500 Georgia Ave., Silver Spring 20902. Private 2-year professional. 1983. Degrees: A, certificates. *Prof. Accred.:* Art. Interim Pres. Richard Weikart.
Enroll.: 110 (*f.t.* 28 m., 24 w.)
(301) 649-4454

Maryland Drafting Institute
2045 University Blvd., E., Langley Park 20783. Private. 1969/1979 (NATTS). Courses

of varying lengths. Certificates, diplomas. Dir. of Admin. C. B. Sawyer.
Enroll.: 200 (*f.t.* 80 m., 20 w.)
(301) 439-7776

MARYLAND INSTITUTE, COLLEGE OF ART
1300 W. Mt. Royal Ave., Baltimore 21217. Private professional. 1967/1983 (MSA/CHE). Sem. plan. Degrees: B,M. *Prof. Accred.:* Art. Pres. Fred Lazarus, IV.
Enroll.: 1,428 (*f.t.* 290 m., 450 w.)
(301) 669-9200

THE MEDIX SCHOOL
1406 Crain Hwy. S., Suite 100, Glen Burnie 21061. Private. 1976/1978 (NATTS). Courses of varying lengths. Certificates. *Prof. Accred.:* Medical Assisting. Dir. Donna Parker.
Enroll.: f.t. 300 w.
(301) 766-2000

BRANCH CAMPUS
8719 Colesville Rd., Silver Spring 20910. 1981 (NATTS). Qtr. plan. Certificates. *Prof. Accred.:* Medical Assisting. Dir. John Kolotos. Armbruster.
Enroll.: 200 w.
(301) 587-3000

MONTGOMERY COLLEGE—SYSTEM OFFICE
Rockville 20850. Public (county) junior. Pres. Robert E. Parilla.
(301) 279-5000

MONTGOMERY COLLEGE—GERMANTOWN CAMPUS
20200 Observation Dr., Germantown 20874. Public (county) junior. 1980 (MSA/CHE). Sem. plan. Degrees: A. Prov. Stanley M. Dahlman.
Enroll.: 2,559 (*f.t.* 255 m., 233 w.)
(301) 972-2000

MONTGOMERY COLLEGE—ROCKVILLE CAMPUS
Rockville 20850. Public (county) junior. 1968/1983 (MSA/CHE). Sem. plan. Degrees: A. *Prof. Accred.:* Dental Assisting, Dental Laboratory Technology, Engineering Technology (electronic), Music. Prov. Antoinette P. Hastings.
Enroll.: 12,555 (*f.t.* 2,234 m., 1,743 w.)
(301) 279-5000

MONTGOMERY COLLEGE—TAKOMA PARK CAMPUS
Takoma Park 20912. Public (county) junior. 1950/1983 (MSA/CHE). Sem. plan. Degrees: A. *Prof. Accred.:* Medical Assisting, Medical Laboratory Technology (A), Nursing (A), Radiography. Prov. O. Robert Brown.
Enroll.: 4,107 (*f.t.* 436 m., 561 w.)
(301) 587-4090

MORGAN STATE UNIVERSITY
Hillen Rd. and Cold Spring Lane, Baltimore 21239. Public liberal arts. 1925/1982 (MSA/CHE). Sem. plan. Degrees: B,M,D. *Prof. Accred.:* Art, Social Work (B), Teacher Education (*e,s*). Pres. Earl C. Richardson.
Enroll.: 3,907 (*f.t.* 1,433 m., 1,671 w.)
(301) 444-3333

MOUNT SAINT MARY'S COLLEGE AND SEMINARY
Emmitsburg 21727. *Private (Roman Catholic, Archdiocese of Baltimore) liberal arts and theology. 1922/1985 (MSA/CHE). Sem. plan. Degrees: B,P,M. Pres. Robert J. Wickenheiser.*
Enroll.: 1,777 (*f.t.* 845 m., 697 w.)
(301) 447-6122

NATIONAL TECHNICAL INSTITUTE
4703 Decatur St., Edmonston 20781. Private. 1977/1984 (NATTS). Courses of varying lengths. Diplomas. Pres. A. A. Mueller.
Enroll.: 100
(301) 277-2286

NATIONAL TRAINING SYSTEMS, INC.
7140 Virginia Manor Court, P.O. Box 2719, Laurel 20708. Private; combination home study-resident courses in tractor-trailer driving and diesel mechanics. 1981 (NHSC). Pres. Charles Longo.
(301) 792-7270

NAVAL HEALTH SCIENCES EDUCATION AND TRAINING COMMAND
Naval Medical Command, National Capital Region, Bethesda 20814. Public (federal) technical. 1984 (SACS-COEI). Courses of varying lengths. Certificates. Commandant Capt. Leon P. Georges, MC.
Enroll.: FTE 4,072

BRANCH CAMPUS
Field Medical Service School, Camp Pendleton, CA 92055.

BRANCH CAMPUS
Naval Medical Command, Northwest Region, Oakland, CA 94627.

BRANCH CAMPUS
Naval Medical Command, Southwest Region, San Diego, CA 92134.

BRANCH CAMPUS
Naval Underseas Medical Institute, Groton, CT 06349.

BRANCH CAMPUS
Naval Medical Command, Pensacola, FL 32508.

BRANCH CAMPUS
Naval Medical Command, Northeast Region, Great Lakes, IL.

BRANCH CAMPUS
Field Medical Service School, Camp Lejeune, NC 28542.

BRANCH CAMPUS
Naval Medical Command, Mid-Atlantic Region, Portsmouth, VA 23708.

BRANCH CAMPUS
Naval Medical Command, Yorktown, VA 23690.

NER ISRAEL RABBINICAL COLLEGE
Mount Wilson La., Baltimore 21208. Private professional. 1974/1981. Sem. plan. Degrees: B,M,D of Talmudic Law. *Prof. Accred.:* Rabbinical and Talmudic Education. Vice Pres. and CEO Herman N. Neuberger.
Enroll.: 342 (*f.t.* 337 m., 0 w.)
(301) 484-7200

PSI INSTITUTE OF WASHINGTON (EXTENSION)
1310 Apple Ave., Silver Spring 20910. Private. 1985 (NATTS). Courses of varying lengths. Certificates. Dir. Burl Dicken.
(301) 589-0900

PTC CAREER INSTITUTE-BALTIMORE (EXTENSION)
5818 Reisterstown Rd., Baltimore 21215. Private. 1985 (NATTS). Courses of varying lengths. Certificates. Dir. Robert Sweitzer.
(301) 538-1210

PTC CAREER INSTITUTE-WASHINGTON (EXTENSION)
8113 Fenton St., Silver Spring 20910. Private. 1985 (NATTS). Courses of varying lengths. Certificates. Dir. Nancy Baker.
(301) 588-3703

PEABODY INSTITUTE OF THE JOHNS HOPKINS UNIVERSITY
1 E. Mount Vernon Pl., Baltimore 21202. Private professional 1955/1983 (MSA/CHE). Sem. plan. Degrees: B,M,D. *Prof. Accred.:* Music. Dir. Robert O. Pierce.
Enroll.: 434 (*f.t.* 167 m., 166 w.)
(301) 659-8100

PRINCE GEORGE'S COMMUNITY COLLEGE
301 Largo Rd., Largo 20772. Public (county) junior. 1969/1985 (MSA/CHE). Sem. plan. Degrees: A. *Prof. Accred.:* Dental Assisting, Engineering Technology (electronics), Medical Laboratory Technology (A), Nuclear Medicine Technology, Nursing (A), Radiography. Pres. Robert I. Bickford.
Enroll.: 12,781 (*f.t.* 1,695 m., 1,754 w.)
(301) 336-6000

PROFESSIONAL INSTITUTE OF COMMERCIAL ART
4020 Clarks La., Baltimore 21215. Private. 1973/1978 (NATTS).jCourses of varying lengths. Diplomas. Dir. Mary Fleck Wise.
Enroll.: 60 (*f.t.* 28 m., 18 w.)
(301) 358-6311

R.E.T.S. ELECTRONIC SCHOOL
511 Russell St., (Baltimore-Washington Pkwy.), Baltimore 21230. Private. 1973/1978 (NATTS). Qtr. plan, courses of varying lengths. Certificates, diplomas. Pres. H. V. Leslie.
Enroll.: 420 (*f.t.* 324 m., 17 w.)
(301) 727-6863

ST. JOHN'S COLLEGE
Annapolis 21401. Private liberal arts. 1923/1984 (MSA/CHE) Sem. plan. Degrees: B,M. Pres. William M. Dyal, Jr.
Enroll.: 405 (*f.t.* 227 m., 166 w.)
(301) 263-2371

ST. MARY'S COLLEGE OF MARYLAND
St. Mary's City 20686. Public (state) liberal arts. 1959/1984 (MSA/CHE). 4-1-4 plan. Degrees: B. *Prof. Accred.:* Music. Pres. Edward T. Lewis.
Enroll.: 1,426 (*f.t.* 524 m., 633 w.)
(301) 863-7100

ST. MARY'S SEMINARY AND UNIVERSITY
5400 Roland Ave., Baltimore 21210. Private (Roman Catholic) professional; graduate only. 1951/1981 (MSA/CHE). Qtr. plan. Degrees: B,P,M. *Prof. Accred.:* Theology (1971/1981, ATS). Pres. Robert F. Leavitt, S.S.
Enroll.: 491
(301) 323-3200

SALISBURY STATE COLLEGE
Salisbury 21801. Public liberal arts and teachers. 1956/1986 (MSA/CHE). Sem. plan. Degrees: B,M. *Prof. Accred.:* Medical Tech-

nology, Nursing (B), Social Work (B). Pres. Thomas E. Bellavance.
Enroll.: 4,507 (*f.t.* 1,477 m., 1,744 w.)
(301) 543-6000

SOJOURNER-DOUGLASS COLLEGE
500 N. Caroline St., Baltimore 21205. Private for applied social sciences. 1980/1985 (MSA/CHE). Sem. plan. Degrees: B. Pres. Charles W. Simmons.
Enroll.: 446 (*f.t.* 113 m., 316 w.)
(301) 276-0306

THE STRATFORD SCHOOL
311 E. Pennsylvania Ave., Towson 21204. Private business. 1979/1982 (AICS). Courses of varying lengths. Certificates, diplomas. Dir. Lois O'Brien.
Enroll.: 577 (*f.t.* 60 m., 517 w.)
(301) 825-2566

BRANCH CAMPUS
15952 Shady Grove Rd., Gaithersburg 20877. Dir. Patrick H. Martin.
(301) 963-6400

STRAYER BUSINESS COLLEGE
10 N. Calvert St., Baltimore 21202. Private business. 1959/1982 (AICS). Courses of varying lengths. Certificates, diplomas. Dir. Charles E. Palmer, Jr.
Enroll.: 693 (*f.t.* 37 m., 656 w.)
(301) 539-5629

TESST ELECTRONIC SCHOOL
51122 Baltimore Ave., Hyattsville 20781. Private. 1975/1980 (NATTS). Sem. plan. Diplomas. Admin. Wayne Moore.
Enroll.: 300 (*f.t.* 280 m., 20 w.)
(301) 864-5750

TEMPLE SCHOOL OF MARYLAND
8635 Colesville Rd., Silver Spring 20910. Private. 1969/1981 (AICS). Qtr. plan. Certificates, diplomas. *Prof. Accred.:* Medical Assisting, Medical Laboratory Technology. Dir. David Wheeler.
Enroll.: 842 (*f.t.* 155 m., 687 w.)
(301) 588-1800

TOWSON STATE UNIVERSITY
Towson 21204. Public liberal arts and teachers. 1949/1985 (MSA/CHE). 4-1-4 plan. Degrees: B,M. *Prof. Accred.:* Music, Nursing (B), Occupational Therapy, Teacher Education (*e,s*). Pres. Hoke L. Smith.
Enroll.: 14,987 (*f.t.* 4,032 m., 5,411 w.)
(301) 321-2000

UNIFORMED SERVICES UNIVERSITY OF THE HEALTH SCIENCES SCHOOL OF MEDICINE
Bethesda 20814-4799. Public (federal) professional. 1984 (MSA-CHE). Sem. plan. Degrees: P,M,D. *Prof. Accred.:* Medicine, Public Health. Pres. Jay P. Sanford.
Enroll.: 736 (*f.t.* 553 m., 183 w.)
(301) 295-3100

U.S. ARMY ORDNANCE CENTER AND SCHOOL
Aberdeen Proving Ground 21005. Public (federal) technical. 1978/1983 (SACS-COEI). Courses of varying lengths. Certificates. Cmdr. Maj. Gen. William E. Potts.
Enroll.: FTE 3,396

UNITED STATES NAVAL ACADEMY
Annapolis 21402. Public (federal) military. 1947/1986 (MSA/CHE). Sem. plan. Degrees: B. *Prof. Accred.:* Engineering (aerospace, electrical, marine, mechanical, naval architecture, ocean, systems). Supt. RADM Charles R. Larson, U.S.N.
Enroll.: 4,584 (*f.t.* 4,260 m., 324 w.)
(301) 267-6100

UNIVERSITY OF BALTIMORE
1420 N. Charles St., Baltimore 21201. Public (state); business and liberal arts, upper division. 1971/1983 (MSA/CHE). Sem. plan. Degrees: B,P,M. *Prof. Accred.:* Business (B), Law (ABA only). Pres. H. Mebane Turner.
Enroll.: 5,188 (*f.t.* 1,275 m., 923 w.)
(301) 625-3000

UNIVERSITY OF MARYLAND
(System), central administration at Adelphi 20783. Public (state). (MSA/CHE). Five independent campus units located throughout the State. Sem. plan. Degrees: A,B,P,M,D. Pres. John S. Toll.
(301) 853-3600

UNIVERSITY OF MARYLAND AT BALTIMORE (UMAB)
Baltimore 21201. 1921/1986 (MSA/CHE). Degrees: B,P,M,D. *Prof. Accred.:* Dental Hygiene, Dentistry, Law, Medical Technology, Medicine, Nursing (B,M), Pharmacy, Physical Therapy, Radiography, Social Work (B,M). Chanc. Edward N. Brandt, Jr.
Enroll.: 4,621 (*f.t.* 1,458 m., 2,109 w.)
(301) 528-6975

UNIVERSITY OF MARYLAND, BALTIMORE COUNTY (UMBC)
Catonsville 21228. 1966/1986 (MSA/CHE). Degrees: B,M,D. *Prof. Accred.:* Social Work. Chanc. Michael K. Hooker.

Enroll.: 8,448 (*f.t.* 2,948 m., 3,104 w.)
(301) 455-1000

University of Maryland at College Park (UMCP)
College Park 20742. 1921/1986 (MSA/CHE). Degrees: B,M,D. *Prof. Accred.:* Architecture (B,M), Business (B,M), Engineering (aerospace, agricultural, chemical, civil, electrical, fire protection, mechanical, nuclear), Journalism, Librarianship, Music, Psychology, Rehabilitation Counseling, Speech Pathology and Audiology, Teacher Education (e,s,p). Chanc. John B. Slaughter.
Enroll.: 38,679 (*f.t.* 15,374 m., 13,463 w.)
(301) 454-3311

University of Maryland Eastern Shore (UMES)
Princess Anne 21853. 1937/1986 (MSA/CHE). Degrees: B,M,D. *Prof. Accred.:* Physical Therapy. Chanc. William P. Hytche.
Enroll.: 1,264 (*f.t.* 474 m., 582 w.)
(301) 651-2200

University of Maryland, University College (UMUC)
College Park 20742. 1947/1986 (MSA/CHE). (Offers instruction at approximately 50 Centers in Maryland and operates the overseas program). Degrees: A,B,M. Chanc. T. Benjamin Massey.
Enroll.: 36,289 (*f.t.* 3,493 m., 2,302 w.)
(301) 985-7000

Villa Julie College
Green Spring Valley Rd., Stevenson 21153. Private. 1962/1982 (MSA/CHE). Sem. plan. Degrees: A,B. *Prof. Accred.:* Medical Laboratory Technology. Pres. Carolyn Manuszak.
Enroll.: 1,079 (*f.t.* 48 m., 635 w.)
(301) 486-7000

Washington Bible College
6511 Princess Garden Pkwy., Lanham 20706. Private (Interdenominational) professional. 1962/1980 (AABC). Sem. plan. Degrees: B. Pres. Harry E. Fletcher.
Enroll.: 389
(301) 552-1400

Washington College
Chestertown 21620. Private liberal arts. 1925/1984 (MSA/CHE). Sem. plan. Degrees: B,M. Pres.S. Douglass Cater.
Enroll.: 797 (*f.t.* 392 m., 352 w.)

Washington Theological Union
Silver Spring 20903-3699. Private coeducational institution cosponsored by 7 Roman Catholic groups offering graduate theological programs. 1973/1983 (MSA/CHE). 4-1-4 plan. Degrees: P,M. *Prof. Accred.:* Theology (1973/1976, ATS). Pres. Vincent D. Cushing, O.F.M.
Enroll.: 325
(301) 439-0551

Western Maryland College
Westminster 21157. Independent liberal arts. 1922/1983 (MSA/CHE). 4-1-5 plan. Degrees: B,M. *Prof. Accred.:* Music, Social Work (B). Pres. Robert H. Chambers, III.
Enroll.: 1,666 (*f.t.* 519 m., 649 w.)
(301) 848-7000

Woodbridge Business Institute
Route 50 at Tilghman Rd., Shoppers World, P.O. Box 277, Salisbury 21801. Private. 1982 (AICS). Qtr. plan. Certificates, diplomas. Dir. Dawn K. Foskey.
Enroll.: 105 (*f.t.* 2 m., 103 w.)
(301) 749-3317

Wor-Wic Tech Community College
1202 Old Ocean City Rd., Salisbury 21801. Public (district) 2-year. 1980/1985 (MSA/CHE). Sem. plan. Degrees: A. *Prof. Accred.:* Radiography. Pres. Arnold H. Maner.
Enroll.: 745 (*f.t.* 39 m., 123 w.)
(301) 749-8181

Yorktowne Business Institute
4601 Calvert Rd., College Park 20740. Private. 1982 (AICS). Courses of varying lengths. Certificates, diplomas. Dir. Eugene Buccelli.
Enroll.: 1,813 (*f.t.* 813 m., 1,000 w.)
(301) 779-1903

Branch Campus
91 Aquahart Rd., Glen Burnie 21061. Dir. Robert Newman.
(301) 787-1060

Branch Campus
2121 Brightseat Rd., Landover Mall, Landover 20785. Dir. Joan McMenomey.
(301) 345-0613

MASSACHUSETTS

AMERICAN INTERNATIONAL COLLEGE
Springfield 01109. Private liberal arts and professional. 1933/1984 (NEASC-CIHE). Sem. plan. Degrees: B,M,D. *Prof. Accred.:* Nursing (B), Teacher Education (*e,s*). Pres. Harry J. Courniotes.
Enroll.: 1,873
(413) 737-7000

AMERICAN INSTITUTE OF BANKING
Boston 02114. Private. 1985 (NEASC-CVTCI). Sem. plan. Degrees: A Pres. Robert A. Regan.
Enroll.: 1,960
(617) 227-1774

AMHERST COLLEGE
Amherst 01002. Private liberal arts. 1929/1978 (NEASC-CIHE). Sem. plan. Degrees: B. Pres. Peter R. Pouncey.
Enroll.: 1,554
(413) 542-2000

ANDOVER NEWTON THEOLOGICAL SCHOOL
Newton Centre 02159. Private (United Church of Christ and American Baptist) professional; graduate only. 1978 (NEASC-CIHE). Sem. plan. Degrees: P,M,D. *Prof. Accred.:* Theology (1938/1978, ATS). Pres. George W. Peck.
Enroll.: 449
(617) 964-1100

ANDOVER TRACTOR TRAILER SCHOOL, INC.
55 Hampshire Rd., Methuen 01844. Private home study and technical. 1977/1981 (NHSC); 1985 (NATTS). Courses of varying lengths. Certificates. Pres. Charles Liponis.
(617) 689-3400

ANNA MARIA COLLEGE
Paxton 01612. Private (Roman Catholic) liberal arts. 1955/1985 (NEASC-CIHE). Sem. plan. Degrees: A,B,M. *Prof. Accred.:* Medical Laboratory Technology, Music, Social Work (B). Pres. Sister Bernadette Madore, S.S.A.
Enroll.: 1,749
(617) 757-4586

AQUINAS JUNIOR COLLEGE
Milton 02186. Private business. 1975/1985 (NEASC-CVTCI). Modular plan. Degrees: A. *Prof. Accred.:* Medical Assisting. Pres. Dorothy Mulcahy Oppenheim.
Enroll.: f.t. 497 w.
(617) 696-3100

AQUINAS JUNIOR COLLEGE
Newton 02158. Private business. 1975/1985 (NEASC-CVTCI). Qtr. plan. Degrees: A. Pres. Sister Margaret Joyce, C.S.J.
Enroll.: 288 (*f.t.* 253 w.)
(617) 969-4400

THE ART INSTITUTE OF BOSTON
700 Beacon St., Boston 02215. Private professional; 3-year programs. 1982. Sem. plan. Diplomas. *Prof. Accred.:* Art. Pres. William H. Willis, Jr.
Enroll.: 420 (*f.t.* 240 m., 180 w.)
(617) 262-1223

ARTHUR D. LITTLE MANAGEMENT EDUCATION INSTITUTE, INC.
Cambridge 02140. Private specialized graduate. 1976/1980 (NEASC-CIHE). 10-month program. Degrees: M. Pres. Frank G. Feeley, III.
Enroll.: 171
(617) 864-5770

ASSOCIATED TECHNICAL INSTITUTE
345 W. Cummings Pk., Woburn 01801. Private. 1975/1979 (NATTS). Courses of varying lengths. Certificates. Pres. Brian Matza.
Enroll.: 285 (*f.t.* 128 m., 5 w.)
(617) 935-3838

ASSUMPTION COLLEGE
Worcester 01609. Private (Roman Catholic) liberal arts. 1949/1981 (NEASC-CIHE). Sem. plan. Degrees: A,B,M. *Prof. Accred.:* Nursing (B), Rehabilitation Counseling. Pres. Joseph H. Hagan.
Enroll.: 1,885
(617) 752-5615

ATLANTIC UNION COLLEGE
South Lancaster 01561. Private (Seventh-day Adventist) liberal arts. 1945/1978 (NEASC-CIHE). Sem. plan. Degrees: A,B. *Prof. Accred.:* Nursing (A), Teacher Education (*e, s*). Pres. Lawrence T. Geraty.
Enroll.: 617
(617) 365-4561

BABSON COLLEGE
Babson Park 02157. Private professional. 1950/1982 (NEASC-CIHE). Sem. plan. De-

grees: B,M. *Prof. Accred.:* Business (B,M). Pres. William R. Dill.
Enroll.: 3,180 (*f.t.* 1,104 m., 618 w.)
(617) 235-1200

BAY PATH JUNIOR COLLEGE
Longmeadow 01106. Private for women. 1965/1985 (NEASC-CIHE). Sem. plan. Degrees: A. *Prof. Accred.:* Medical Assistant. Pres. Jeannette T. Wright.
Enroll.: 687
(413) 567-0621

†BAY STATE JUNIOR COLLEGE
122 Commonwealth Ave., Boston 02116. Private. 1958/1980 (AICS). Sem. plan. Degrees: A, diplomas. *Prof. Accred.:* Medical Assisting. Pres. Thomas E. Langford.
Enroll.: 964 (*f.t.* 232 m., 732 w.)
(617) 236-8000

BECKER JUNIOR COLLEGE
Worcester 01609. Private. 1976 (NEASC-CVTCI). Sem. plan. Degrees: A. Pres. Lloyd H. Van Buskirk.
Enroll.: 1,280 (*f.t.* 23 m., 697 w.)
(617) 791-9241

BENTLEY COLLEGE
Waltham 02154. Private accounting. 1966/1981 (NEASC-CIHE). Sem. plan. Degrees: A,B,M. Pres. Gregory H. Adamian.
Enroll.: 8,085
(617) 891-2000

BERKLEE COLLEGE OF MUSIC
1140 Boylston St., Boston 02215. Private professional. 1973/1983 (NEASC-CIHE). Sem. plan. Degrees: B. Pres. Lee Eliot Berk.
Enroll.: 2,425
(617) 266-1400

BERKSHIRE CHRISTIAN COLLEGE
200 Stockbridge Rd., Lenox 01240. Private (Advent Christian) professional. 1959/1978 (AABC). Sem. plan. Degrees: B. Pres. Lloyd M. Richardson.
Enroll.: 103
(413) 637-0838

*BERKSHIRE COMMUNITY COLLEGE
Pittsfield 01201. Public (state) junior. 1964/1985 (NEASC-CIHE). Sem. plan. Degrees: A. *Prof. Accred.:* Nursing (A). Pres. Jonathan M. Daube.

†Candidate for Accreditation by Regional Accrediting Commission
*Member Massachusetts Board of Regents of Higher Education

Enroll.: 3,017
(617) 499 1660

BOSTON ARCHITECTURAL CENTER
Boston 02115. Private professional. 1971. Sem. plan. Degrees: B, certificates. *Prof. Accred.:* Architecture (B). Dir. Bernard P. Spring.
Enroll.: 1,361 (*f.t.* 519 m., 134 w.)
(617) 536-3170

BOSTON COLLEGE
Chestnut Hill 02167. Private (Roman Catholic) university. 1935/1976 (NEASC-CIHE). Sem. plan. Degrees: B,P,M,D. *Prof. Accred.:* Business (B,M), Law, Nursing (B,M), Social Work (M), Teacher Education (*e,s,p*). Pres. V. Rev. J. Donald Monan, S.J.
Enroll.: 14,208
(617) 552-8000

BOSTON CONSERVATORY
Boston 02215. Private music, drama, dance. 1968/1985 (NEASC-CIHE). Sem. plan. Degrees: B,M. *Prof. Accred.:* Music. Pres. William A. Seymour.
Enroll.: 420
(617) 536-6340

BOSTON UNIVERSITY
Boston 02215. Private. 1929/1979 (NEASC-CIHE). Sem. plan. Degrees: B,P,M,D. *Prof. Accred.:* Business (B,M), Dental Assisting, Dental Laboratory Technology, Dentistry, Engineering (aerospace, biomedical, computer, electrical, manufacturing, mechanical, systems), Health Services Administration, Law, Medicine, Music, Nursing (B,M), Occupational Therapy, Physical Therapy, Psychology, Public Health, Rehabilitation Counseling, Social Work (B,M), Speech Pathology, Teacher Education (*e,s,p*), Theology. Pres. John R. Silber.
Enroll.: 27,397
(617) 353-2000

BRADFORD COLLEGE
Bradford 01830. Private. 1931/1984 (NEASC-CIHE). 4-1-4 plan. Degrees: A,B. Pres. Arthur E. Levine.
Enroll.: 403
(617) 372-7161

BRANDEIS UNIVERSITY
Waltham 02254. Private. 1953/1977 (NEASC-CIHE). Sem. plan. Degrees: B,M,D. Pres. Evelyn E. Handler.
Enroll.: 3,476
(617) 647-2000

*BRIDGEWATER STATE COLLEGE
Bridgewater 02324. Public (state) liberal arts and teachers. 1953/1983 (NEASC-CIHE). Sem. plan. Degrees: B,M. *Prof. Accred.:* Social Work (B), Teacher Education (*e,s*). Pres. Gerald Indelicato.
Enroll.: 7,914
(617) 697-1200

*BRISTOL COMMUNITY COLLEGE
Fall River 02720. Public (state) junior. 1970/1984 (NEASC-CIHE). Sem. plan. Degrees: A. *Prof. Accred.:* Dental Hygiene, Medical Laboratory Technology (A), Nursing (A). Pres. Eileen F. Farley.
Enroll.: 4,730
(617) 678-2811

BROMS ACADEMY
1696 Main St., Holyoke 01041. Private. 1978 (NATTS). Courses of varying lengths. Diplomas. Pres. Anthony J. Giaquinto.
(413) 734-5802

BROMS ACADEMYL
150 Pleasant St., Worcester 01609. Private. 1978 (NATTS). Courses of varying lengths. Diplomas. Pres. Anthony J. Giaquinto.
(617) 753-5021

*BUNKER HILL COMMUNITY COLLEGE
Charlestown 02129. Public (state) junior. 1976/1985 (NEASC-CIHE). Sem. plan. Degrees: A. *Prof. Accred.:* Nuclear Medicine Technology, Nursing (A), Radiography. Pres. Harold E. Shively.
Enroll.: 6,977
(617) 241-8600

BURDETT SCHOOL
372 Stuart St., Boston 02116. Private business. 1954/1984 (AICS). Courses of varying lengths. Certificates, diplomas. Pres. Florence S. Tate.
Enroll.: 516 (*f.t.* 6 m., 510 w.)
(617) 267-7435

BUSINESS EDUCATION INSTITUTE
201 Park Ave., West Springfield 01089. Private. 1978/1982 (AICS). Courses of varying lengths. Diplomas. Pres. Marjorie O. Camp.
Enroll.: 428 (*f.t.* 140 m., 288 w.)
(413) 737-4708

BUTERA SCHOOL OF ART
111 Beacon St., Boston 02116. Private. 1977 (NATTS). Sem. plan. Diplomas. Dir. Joseph L. Butera.

*Member Massachusetts Board of Regents of Higher Education

Enroll.: 120 (*f.t.* 70 m., 50 w.)
(617) 536-4623

CAMBRIDGE COLLEGE/INSTITUTE OF OPEN EDUCATION
Cambridge 02138. Private. 1981/1986 (NEASC-CIHE). Sem. plan. Degrees: M. Pres. Eileen M. Brown.
Enroll.: 439
(617) 492-5108

CAMBRIDGE INSTITUTE FOR COMPUTER PROGRAMMING
132 Brookline Ave., Boston 02115. Private. 1982/1986 (AICS). Courses of varying lengths. Certificates, diplomas. Pres. A. William Markell.
Enroll.: 301 (*f.t.* 195 m., 106 w.)
(617) 536-1980

*CAPE COD COMMUNITY COLLEGE
West Barnstable 02668. Public (state) junior. 1967/1977 (NEASC-CIHE). Sem. plan. Degrees: A. *Prof. Accred.:* Dental Hygiene, Nursing (A). Pres. James F. Hall.
Enroll.: 4,586
(617) 362-2131

CATHERINE E. HINDS INSTITUTE OF ESTHETICS
880 Walnut St., Newton 02159. Private technical. 1982 (NATTS). Courses of varying lengths. Certificates. Dir. Catherine E. Hinds.
(617) 527-3200

CENTRAL NEW ENGLAND COLLEGE
768 Main St., Worcester 01610. Private technical. 1978/1985 (NEASC-CIHE); accreditation includes Worcester Junior College. Sem. plan. Degrees: A,B. Pres. Edward Paul Mattar, III.
Enroll.: 2,138
(617) 755-4314

CHAMBERLAIN SCHOOL OF RETAILING
90 Marlborough St., Boston 02116. Private. 1977/1984 (NATTS). Qtr. plan. Diplomas. Dir. of Placement Mary Troy.
Enroll.: 66 (*f.t.* 5 m., 59 w.)
(617) 536-0682

†CHAMBERLAYNE JUNIOR COLLEGE
128 Commonwealth Ave., Boston 02116. Private. 1969/1981 (AICS). Tri. plan. Degrees: A. *Prof. Accred.:* Interior Design. Pres. Matthew J. Malloy.

*Member Massachusetts Board of Regents of Higher Education
†Candidate for Accreditation by Regional Accrediting Commission

Enroll.: 1,332 (*f.t.* 453 m., 879 w.)
(617) 536-4500

CLARK UNIVERSITY
Worcester 01610. Private. 1929/1986 (NEASC-CIHE). Mod. plan. Degrees: B,M,D. *Prof. Accred.:* Business (B,M), Health Administration, Psychology. Pres. Richard P. Traina.
Enroll.: 3,226
(617) 793-7711

COLLEGE OF THE HOLY CROSS
Worcester 01610. Private (Roman Catholic) liberal arts. 1930/1980 (NEASC-CIHE). Sem. plan. Degrees: B,M. *Prof. Accred.:* Pres. Rev. John E. Brooks, S.J.
Enroll.: 2,548 (*f.t.* 1,272 m., 1,264 w.)
(617) 793-2011

COLLEGE OF OUR LADY OF THE ELMS
Chicopee 01013. Private (Roman Catholic) liberal arts for women. 1942/1982 (NEASC-CIHE). Sem. plan. Degrees: B. *Prof. Accred.:* Nursing (B), Social Work (B). Pres. Sister Mary Dooley, S.S.J.
Enroll.: 909
(413) 598-8351

COMPUTER LEARNING CENTER
5 Middlesex Ave., Sommerville 02145. Private. 1985 (AICS). Courses of varying lengths. Diplomas. Dir. Janet Gailun.
(617) 776-3500

CURRY COLLEGE
Milton 02186. Private liberal arts and teachers. 1970/1984 (NEASC-CIHE). Sem. plan. Degrees: B,M. *Prof. Accred.:* Nursing (B). Pres. William L. Boyle, Jr.
Enroll.: 1,244
(617) 333-0500

DEAN JUNIOR COLLEGE
Franklin 02038. Private. 1957/1981 (NEASC-CIHE). Sem. plan. Degrees: A. Pres. Richard E. Crockford.
Enroll.: 2,354
(617) 528-9100

DUDLEY HALL CAREER INSTITUTE
258-260 W. Main St., Dudley 01570. Private. 1981 (AICS). Qtr. plan. Certificates, diplomas. Pres. Richard C. Crance.
Enroll.: 188 (*f.t.* 5 m., 183 w.)
(617) 943-7113

EAST COAST AERO TECHNICAL SCHOOL
Hanscom Field, Box 426, Lexington 02173. Private. 1970/1981 (NATTS). Courses of varying lengths. Diplomas. Pres. John T. Griffin, Jr.
Enroll.: 494 (*f.t.* 487 m., 7 w.)
(617) 274-6400

EASTERN NAZARENE COLLEGE
23 E. Elm Ave., Quincy 02170. Private (Nazarene) liberal arts. 1943/1981 (NEASC-CIHE). 4-1-4 plan. Degrees: A,B,M. *Prof. Accred.:* Social Work (B). Pres. Stephen W. Nease.
Enroll.: 951
(617) 773-6350

ELEANOR F. ROBERTS INSTITUTE
19 Temple Pl., Second Fl., Boston 02111. Private. 1978/1984 (NATTS). Courses of varying lengths. Certificates, diplomas. Dir. Morris Zack.
Enroll.: 100 (*f.t.* 70 m., 30 w.)
(617) 266-7000

EMERSON COLLEGE
100 Beacon St., Boston 02116. Private liberal arts emphasizing speech and drama. 1950/1983 (NEASC-CIHE). Sem. plan. Degrees: B,M. Pres. Allen E. Koenig.
Enroll.: 2,295
(617) 578-8500

EMMANUEL COLLEGE
Boston 02115. Private (Roman Catholic) liberal arts primarily for women. 1933/1983 (NEASC-CIHE). Sem. plan. Degrees: B,M. Pres. Sister Janet Eisner, S.N.D.
Enroll.: 958
(617) 277-9340

ENDICOTT COLLEGE
Beverly 01915. Private for women. 1952/1980 (NEASC-CIHE). Sem. plan. Degrees: A. Pres. Carol A. Hawkes.
Enroll.: 1,047
(617) 927-0585

EPISCOPAL DIVINITY SCHOOL
Cambridge 02138. Private (Episcopal) professional; graduate only. Sem. plan. Degrees: P,M,D. *Prof. Accred.:* Theology (1938/1979, ATS). Dean Bishop Otis Charles.
Enroll.: 130
(617) 868-3450

ESSEX AGRICULTURAL AND TECHNICAL INSTITUTE
Hathorne 01937. Public (state) 2-year. 1979/1985 (NEASC-CVTCI). Sem. plan. Certificates. Dir. Raymond F. Potter.

Enroll.: 442
(617) 774-0050

Fisher Junior College
118 Beacon St., Boston 02116. Private. 1970/1984 (NEASC-CIHE). Sem. plan. Degrees: A. *Prof. Accred.:* Medical Assisting, Optometric Technology. Pres. Brian Donnelly.
Enroll.: 4,384
(617) 262-3240

*Fitchburg State College
Fitchburg 01420. Public. 1953/1986 (NEASC-CIHE). Sem. plan. Degrees: B,M. *Prof. Accred.:* Nursing (B). Pres. Vincent J. Mara.
Enroll.: 6,692
(617) 345-2151

*Framingham State College
Framingham 01701. Public liberal arts and teachers. 1950/1984 (NEASC-CIHE). Sem. plan. Degrees: B,M. *Prof. Accred.:* Dietetics, Home Economics. Pres. Paul D. Weller.
Enroll.: 3,258
(617) 620-1220

Franklin Institute of Boston
Boston 02116. Private 2-year technical. 1970/1980 (NEASC-CVTCI). Sem. plan. Degrees: A. *Prof. Accred.:* Engineering Technology (architectural, civil, computer, electrical, electronic, mechanical, medical electronics). Pres. Michael C. Mazzola.
Enroll.: 431
(617) 423-4630

GTE/Sylvania Technical School
95 Second Ave., Waltham 02554. Private. 1973/1978 (NATTS). Courses of varying lengths. Diplomas. Dir. Gerald M. Campbell.
Enroll.: 1,526 (*f.t.* 888 m., 109 w.)
(617) 890-7711

Gordon College
Wenham 01984. Private liberal arts. 1961/1982 (NEASC-CIHE). Tri. plan. Degrees: B. *Prof. Accred.:* Music. Pres. Richard F. Gross.
Enroll.: 1,073
(617) 927-2300

Gordon-Conwell Theological Seminary
South Hamilton 01982. Private (Interdenominational) professional; graduate only. 1985 (NEASC-CIHE). Sem. plan. Degrees: P,M.

*Member Massachusetts Board of Regents of Higher Education

Prof. Accred.: Theology (1964/1985, ATS). Pres. Robert E. Cooley.
Enroll.: 864
(617) 468-7111

*Greenfield Community College
Greenfield 01301. Public (state) junior. 1966/1981 (NEASC-CIHE). Sem. plan. Degrees: A. *Prof. Accred.:* Nursing (A). Pres. Theodore L. Provo.
Enroll.: 2,350
(413) 774-3131

Hallmark Institute of Photography
At the Airport, Turners Falls 01376. Private. 1982 (NATTS). Courses of varying lengths. Certificates. Dir. Paul R. Turnbull.
(413) 863-2478

Hampshire College
Amherst 01002. Private liberal arts. 1974/1978 (NEASC-CIHE). 4-1-4 plan. Degrees: B. Pres. Adele Smith Simmons.
Enroll.: 1,000
(413) 549-4600

Harvard University
Cambridge 02138. Private; undergraduate division for men, graduate and professional schools coeducational. 1929/1977 (NEASC-CIHE). Sem. plan. Degrees: A,B,P,M,D. *Prof. Accred.:* Architecture (M), Business (M), Dentistry, Engineering (engineering science), Health Policy and Management, Landscape Architecture (M), Law, Medicine, Psychology, Teacher Education (*e,s,p*), Theology. Pres. Derek C. Bok.
Enroll.: 24,848
(617) 495-1000

Radcliffe College
Cambridge 02138. Private liberal arts for women; affiliate of Harvard. 1929/1977 (NEASC-CIHE). Sem. plan. Degrees: B. Pres. Matina S. Horner.

Hebrew College
Brookline 02146. Private (Jewish) teachers. 1955/1978 (NEASC-CIHE). Sem. plan. Degrees: B,M. Acting Pres. Michael Libenson.
Enroll.: 219
(617) 232 -8710

Hellenic College/Holy Cross Greek Orthodox Theological School
Brookline 02146. Private (Greek Orthodox) liberal arts and professional. 1974/1985

*Member Massachusetts Board of Regents of Higher Education

(NEASC-CIHE). Sem. plan. Degrees: B,P,M. *Prof. Accred.:* Theology (1974/1981, ATS). Pres. Thomas C. Lelon.
Enroll.: 224
(617) 731-3500

HICKOX SCHOOL
200 Tremont St., Boston 02116. Private business. 1968/1980 (AICS). Courses of varying lengths. Diplomas. Pres. S. Arthur Verenis.
Enroll.: 752911 (*f.t.* 77 m., 675 w.)
(617) 482-7655

*HOLYOKE COMMUNITY COLLEGE
Holyoke 01040. Public (state) junior. 1970/1986 (NEASC-CIHE). Sem. plan. Degrees: A. *Prof. Accred.:* Medical Record Technology, Nursing (A), Radiography. Pres. David M. Bartley.
Enroll.: 4,752
(413) 538-7000

ITT TECHNICAL INSTITUTE
45 Spruce St., Chelsea 02150. Private. 1968/1978 (NATTS). Courses of varying lengths. Diplomas. Center Dir. Jack Nickell.
Enroll.: 343 (*f.t.* 281 m., 62 w.)
(617) 889-3600

KATHARINE GIBBS SCHOOL
Five Arlington St., Boston 02188. Private junior. 1967/1983 (AICS). Sem. plan. Degrees: A, certificates, diplomas. Dir. Dolores L. Mitchell.
Enroll.: 916 *f.t.* (746 w.)
(617) 262-2250

KINYON-CAMPBELL BUSINESS SCHOOL
59 Linden St., New Bedford 02740. Private. 1971/1982 (AICS). Qtr. plan. Certificates, diplomas. Pres. Marjorie Daganhardt.
Enroll.: 584 (*f.t.* 61 m., 523 w.)
(617) 992-5448

LABOURÉ COLLEGE
Boston 02124. Private (Roman Catholic) nursing and allied health 2-year. 1975/1985 (NEASC-CVTCI). Sem. plan. Degrees: A. *Prof. Accred.:* EEG Technology, Nursing (A), Radiation Therapy Technology, Respiratory Therapy. Pres. Sister Maureen St. Charles, D.C.
Enroll.: 625
(617) 296-8300

*Member Massachusetts Board of Regents of Higher Education

LASELL JUNIOR COLLEGE
Newton 02166. Private for women. 1932/1983 (NEASC-CIHE). Sem. plan. Degrees: A. *Prof. Accred.:* Medical Assisting, Medical Laboratory Technology (A). Pres. Peter T. Mitchell.
Enroll.: 546
(617) 243-2000

LESLEY COLLEGE
Cambridge 02238. Private teachers for women, graduate school coeducational. 1952/1984 (NEASC-CIHE). Sem. plan. Degrees: A,B,M. Pres. Margaret A. McKenna.
Enroll.: 3,762
(617) 868-9600

LONGY SCHOOL OF MUSIC, INC.
One Follen St., Cambridge 02138. Private professional. 1979. Sem. plan. Certificates, diplomas. *Prof. Accred.:* Music. Dir. Roman Totenberg.
Enroll.: 520
(617) 876-0956

MGH INSTITUTE OF HEALTH PROFESSIONS
15 River St., Boston 02108-3402. Private professional. 1985 (NEASC-CIHE). Sem. plan. Degrees: M. Pres. Stephen N. Collier.
Enroll.: 91
(617) 726-8002

MARIAN COURT JUNIOR COLLEGE
35 Little's Point Rd., Swampscott 01907. Private (Roman Catholic, Sisters of Mercy). 1967/1982 (AICS); 1982 (NEASC-CVTCI). Sem. plan. Degrees: A. Interim Pres. Sister Joanne Bibeau, R.S.M.
Enroll.: 223
(617) 595-6768

*MASSACHUSETTS BAY COMMUNITY COLLEGE
Wellesley Hills 02181. Public (state) junior. 1967/1984 (NEASC-CIHE). Sem. plan. Degrees: A. *Prof. Accred.:* Medical Laboratory Technology, Medical Record Technology, Medical Technology, Radiography. Pres. Roger A. Van Winkle.
Enroll.: 4,937
(617) 237-1100

*Member Massachusetts Board of Regents of Higher Education

MASSACHUSETTS BOARD OF REGENTS OF HIGHER EDUCATION
System office, McCormack Bldg., Room 619, Ashburton Pl., Boston 02108. Interim Chanc. Joseph Finnegan.
(617) 727-7785

*MASSACHUSETTS COLLEGE OF ART
621 Huntington Ave., Boston 02115. Public (state) teachers and professional. 1954/1984 (NEASC-CIHE). Sem. plan. Degrees: B,M. *Prof. Accred.:* Art. Pres. John F. Nolan.
Enroll.: 3,330
(617) 232-1555

MASSACHUSETTS COLLEGE OF PHARMACY AND ALLIED HEALTH SCIENCES
179 Longwood Ave., Boston 02115. Private professional. 1974/1980 (NEASC-CIHE)-Boston Campus. Sem. plan. Degrees: A,B,M,D. *Prof. Accred.:* Nuclear Medicine Technology, Pharmacy. Pres. Raymond A. Gosselin.
Enroll.: 1,161
(617) 782-2800

MASSACHUSETTS INSTITUTE OF TECHNOLOGY
Cambridge 02139. Private university. 1929/1979 (NEASC-CIHE). Sem. plan. Degrees: B,M,D. *Prof. Accred.:* Architecture (M), Business (B,M), Engineering (aeronautics and astronautics, chemical, civil, computer science and engineering, electrical science and engineering, material science and engineering, mechanical, naval architecture and marine, nuclear, ocean). Pres. Paul E. Gray.
Enroll.: 9,577
(617) 253-1000

*MASSACHUSETTS MARITIME ACADEMY
Buzzards Bay 02532. Public (state) professional. 1974/1985 (NEASC-CIHE). Qtr. plan. Degrees: B. Pres. Rear Adm. John F. Aylmer, USN.
Enroll.: 820
(617) 759-5761

MASSACHUSETTS SCHOOL OF BARBERING AND MEN'S HAIRSTYLING
12454 Washington St., Boston 02118. Private. 1978/1985 (NATTS). Sem. plan. Certificates. Gen. Mgr. Richard Conragan.
Enroll.: 52 (*f.t.* 25 m., 27 w.)
(617) 482-6360

*Member Massachusetts Board of Regents of Higher Education

MASSACHUSETTS SCHOOL OF BARBERING AND MEN'S HAIRSTYLING
25 Exchange St., Lynn 01901. Private. 1980 (NATTS). Courses of varying lengths. Certificates. Vice Pres. James Papageorge.
Enroll.: 24 (*f.t.* 7 m., 37 w.)
(617) 593-1321

MASSACHUSETTS SCHOOL OF PROFESSIONAL PSYCHOLOGY
322 Sprague St., Dedham 02026. Private professional; graduate only. 1984 (NEASC-CIHE). Sem. plan. Degrees: D. Dean Bruce J. Weiss.
Enroll.: 83
(617) 329-6777

*MASSASOIT COMMUNITY COLLEGE
Brockton 02402. Public (state) junior; accreditation includes Blue Hills Regional Technical Institute. 1971/1980 (NEASC-CIHE). Sem. plan. Degrees: A. *Prof. Accred.:* Medical Laboratory Technology (A), Nursing (A), Respiratory Therapy. Pres. Gerard F. Burke.
Enroll.: 6,578
(617) 588-9100

MERRIMACK COLLEGE
North Andover 01845. Private (Roman Catholic) liberal arts. 1953/1981 (NEASC-CIHE). Sem. plan. Degrees: A,B. *Prof. Accred.:* Engineering (civil, electrical). Pres. Rev. John E. Deegan, O.S.A.
Enroll.: 3,643
(617) 683-7111

*MIDDLESEX COMMUNITY COLLEGE
Bedford 01730. Public (state) junior. 1973/1980 (NEASC-CIHE). Sem. plan. Degrees: A. *Prof. Accred.:*Dental Assisting, Dental Hygiene, Dental Laboratory Technology, Diagnostic Medical Sonography, Medical Assisting, Medical Laboratory Technology (A), Nursing (A), Radiation Therapy Technology, Radiography. Pres. James E. Houlihan, Jr.
Enroll.: 8,592
(617) 275-8910

MONTSERRAT COLLEGE OF ART
Beverly 01915. Private 4-year professional. 1982/1986 (NEASC-CVTCI). Sem. plan. *Prof. Accred.:* Art. Diplomas. Pres. James Davies.
Enroll.: 112
(617) 922-8222

*Member Massachusetts Board of Regents of Higher Education

MOUNT HOLYOKE COLLEGE
South Hadley 01075. Private liberal arts for women. 1929/1978 (NEASC-CIHE). Sem. plan. Degrees: B,M. Pres. Elizabeth T. Kennan.
Enroll.: 1,966
(413) 538-2000

MOUNT IDA COLLEGE
777 Dedham St., Newton Centre 02159. Private primarily for women. 1970/1984 (NEASC-CIHE). 12-6-12 plan. Degrees: A,B. *Prof. Accred.:* Dental Assisting, Medical Assisting. Pres. Bryan E. Carlson.
Enroll.: 839
(617) 969-7000

*MOUNT WACHUSETTS COMMUNITY COLLEGE
Gardner 01440. Public (state) junior. 1967/1984 (NEASC-CIHE). Sem. plan. Degrees: A. *Prof. Accred.:* Medical Laboratory Technology, Nursing (A) Pres. Arthur F. Haley.
Enroll.: 3,704
(617) 632-6600

NATIONAL EDUCATION CENTER—BRYMAN CAMPUS
323 Boylston St., Brookline 02146. Private. 1973/1980 (NATTS). Courses of varying lengths. Diplomas. Dir. Richard E. Brennan.
Enroll.: f.t. 200 w.
(617) 232-6035

NEW ENGLAND COLLEGE OF OPTOMETRY
424 Beacon St., Boston 02115. Private professional. 1976/1986 (NEASC-CIHE). Sem. plan. Degrees: B,P. *Prof. Accred.:* Optometric Technology, Optometry. Pres. Sylvio Dupuis.
Enroll.: 382
(617) 266-2030

NEW ENGLAND CONSERVATORY OF MUSIC
Boston 02115. Private professional. 1951/1977 (NEASC-CIHE). Sem. plan. Degrees: B,M. *Prof. Accred.:* Music. Pres. Laurence Lesser.
Enroll.: 741
(617) 262-1120

NEW ENGLAND INSTITUTE OF APPLIED ARTS AND SCIENCES
Boston 02215. Private. 1979 (NEASC-CVTCI). Sem. plan. Degrees: A. Pres. Victor F. Scalise, Jr.
Enroll.: 142
(617) 536-6970

*Member Massachusetts Board of Regents of Higher Education

NEW ENGLAND SCHOOL OF ACCOUNTING
155 Ararat St., Worcester 01606. Private. 1969/1981 (AICS). Sem. plan. Diplomas. Pres. John F. Albano.
Enroll.: 178 (*f.t.* 62 m., 116 w.)
(617) 853-8972

NEW ENGLAND SCHOOL OF ART AND DESIGN
28 Newbury St., Boston 02116. Private. 1968/1979 (NATTS). Sem. plan. Diplomas. *Prof. Accred.:* Interior Design. Pres. Christy Rufo.
Enroll.: 243 (*f.t.* 49 m., 121 w.)
(617) 536-0383

NEW ENGLAND SCHOOL OF LAW
Boston 02116. Private professional. 1969. Sem. plan. Degrees: P. *Prof. Accred.:* Law (ABA only). Dean Kenneth R. Evans.
Enroll.: 1,002 (*f.t.* 368 m., 222 w.)
(617) 267-9655

NEW ENGLAND SCHOOL OF PHOTOGRAPHY
537 Commonwealth Ave., Boston 02215. Private. 1981 (NATTS). Sem. plan. Diplomas. Pres. John H. Carruthers.
Enroll.: 177 (*f.t.* 84 m., 90 w.)
(617) 437-1868

NEW ENGLAND TRACTOR TRAILER TRAINING OF MASSACHUSETTS
542 E. Squantum St., P.O. Box 54, Quincy 02171. Private. 1982 (NATTS). 4-week program. Diplomas. Dir. Mark Greenberg. *Enroll.:* 60
(617) 328-0250

NEW STYLE BARBER SCHOOL
143 Pleasant St., Malden 02148. Private. 1979 (NATTS). Courses of varying lengths. Certificates. Pres. Anthony Clemente.
Enroll.: 30 (*f.t.* 6 m., 18 w.)
(617) 324-6799

NEWBURY COLLEGE
Boston 02115. Private. 1977/1984 (NEASC-CVTCI). Sem. plan. Degrees: A. Pres. Edward J. Tassinari.
Enroll.: 3,670
(617) 262-9350

NICHOLS COLLEGE
Dudley 01570. Private business. 1965/1984 (NEASC-CIHE). Sem. plan. Degrees: A,B,M. Pres. Lowell C. Smith.
Enroll.: 1,655
(617) 943-1560

*North Adams State College
North Adams 01247. Public teachers. 1953/1983 (NEASC-CIHE). 4-1-4 plan. Degrees: B,M. *Prof. Accred.:* Teacher Education (*e,s*). Pres. Catherine A. Tisinger.
Enroll.: 505
(413) 664-4511

North Bennet Street School
39 N. Bennet St., Boston 02113. Private. 1982 (NATTS). Courses of varying lengths. Diplomas. Dir. Thomas Williams.
Enroll.: 114 (*f.t.* 95 m., 19 w.)
(617) 227-0155

*North Shore Community College
Beverly 01915. Public (state) junior. 1969/1985 (NEASC-CIHE). Sem. plan. Degrees: A. *Prof. Accred.:* Nursing (A), Radiography, Respiratory Therapy. Pres. George Traicoff.
Enroll.: 8,047
(617) 927-4850

Northeast Broadcasting School
282 Marlborough St., Boston 02116. Private. 1972/1977 (NATTS). Sem. plan. Certificates. Pres. Victor S. Best.
Enroll.: 115 (*f.t.* 95 m., 20 w.)
(617) 267-7910

Northeast Institute of Industrial Technology
41 Phillips St., Boston 02114. Private. 1972/1977 (NATTS). Sem. plan. Certificates, diplomas. Pres. John W. Hoffman.
Enroll.: 663 (*f.t.* 312 m., 18 w.)
(617) 523-2813

Northeastern University
Boston 02115. Private. 1940/1979 (NEASC-CIHE). Modified quarter plan. Degrees: A,B,P,M,D. *Prof. Accred.:* Assistant to the Primary Care Physician, Business (B,M), Dental Assisting, Engineering (chemical, civil, electrical, industrial, mechanical), Engineering Technology (civil, electrical, mechanical, mechanical/structural), Law, Medical Laboratory Technology (A), Medical Record Administration, Medical Technology, Nursing (B), Perfusionist, Pharmacy, Physical Therapy, Radiography, Rehabilitation Counceling, Respiratory Therapy, Speech Pathology and Audiology, Teacher Education (*e,s,p*). Pres. Kenneth G. Ryder.
Enroll.: 39,191
(617) 437-2000

*Member Massachusetts Board of Regents of Higher Education

*Northern Essex Community College
100 Elliott St., Haverhill 01830. Public (state) junior. 1969/1986 (NEASC-CIHE). Sem. plan. Degrees: A. *Prof. Accred.:* Dental Assisting, Medical Record Technology, Nursing (A), Radiography, Respiratory Therapy, Respiratory Therapy Technology. Pres. John R. Dimitry.
Enroll.: 6,110
(617) 374-3900

Pedigree Professional School for Dog Grooming
Harbor Mall, Rt. 1A, Lynnway, Lynn 01901. Private. 1982 (NATTS). Courses of varying lengths. Certificates. Pres. Sandra M. Daniels.
Enroll.: 111 (*f.t.* 19 m., 92 w.)
(617) 599-6386

Pine Manor College
Chestnut Hill 02167. Private for women. 1939/1986 (NEASC-CIHE). Sem. plan. Degrees: A,B. Pres. Rosemary Ashby.
Enroll.: 585
(617) 731-7000

Pope John XXIII National Seminary
558 South Ave., Weston 02193. Private (Roman Catholic) professional; graduate only. Sem. plan. Degrees: P,M. *Prof. Accred.:* Theology (1983, ATS). Pres. Cornelius McRae.
Enroll.: 58
(617) 899-5500

Quincy Junior College
Quincy 02169. Public (municipal). 1980/1984 (NEASC-CIHE). Sem. plan. Degrees: A. *Prof. Accred.:* Dental Assisting, Dental Laboratory Technology, Nursing (A), Practical Nursing, Surgical Technology. Pres. O. Clayton Johnson.
Enroll.: 2,605
(617) 786-8777

*Quinsigamond Community College
Worcester 01606. Public (state) junior. 1967/1984 (NEASC-CIHE). Sem. plan. Degrees: A. *Prof. Accred.:* Dental Hygiene Nursing (A), Radiography, Respiratory Therapy. Pres. Clifford S. Peterson.
Enroll.: 4,777
(617) 853-2300

R.E.T.S. Electronic School
965 Commonwealth Ave., Boston 02215. Private. 1974/1979 (NATTS). Courses of

*Member Massachusetts Board of Regents of Higher Education

varying lengths. Certificates, diplomas. Dir. Henry J. Renzi.
Enroll.: 200 (*f.t.* 140 m., 10 w.)
(617) 783-1197

REGIS COLLEGE
Weston 02193. Private (Roman Catholic) liberal arts for women. 1933/1976 (NEASC-CIHE). Sem. plan. Degrees: B,M. *Prof. Accred.:* Social Work (B). Pres. Sister Therese Higgins, C.S.J.
Enroll.: 1,240
(617) 893-1820

*ROXBURY COMMUNITY COLLEGE
625 Huntington Ave., Boston 02115. Public (state) junior. 1981/1986 (NEASC-CIHE). Sem. plan. Degrees: A. Pres. Brunetta R. Wolfman.
Enroll.: 252
(617) 734-1960

ST. HYACINTH COLLEGE AND SEMINARY
Granby 01033. Private (Roman Catholic, Order of Friars Minor Conventual) for men. 1967/1978 (NEASC-CIHE). Sem. plan. Degrees: B. Pres. Rev. Germain Kopaczynski, O.F.M.Conv.
Enroll.: 41
(413) 467-7191

SAINT JOHN'S SCHOOL OF BUSINESS
511 Main St., West Springfield 01089. Private. 1981 (AICS). Qtr. plan. Certificates, diplomas. Dir. Kenneth C. Ballard.
Enroll.: 245 (*f.t.* 31 m., 214 w.)
(413) 781-0390

SAINT JOHN'S SEMINARY
Brighton 02135. Private (Roman Catholic). 1969/1980 (NEASC-CIHE). Sem. plan. Degrees: B,P,M. *Prof. Accred.:* Theology (1970/1980, ATS). Rector Rev. Thomas Daly.
Enroll.: 135
(617) 254-2610

*SALEM STATE COLLEGE
Salem 01907. Public liberal arts and professional. 1953/1984 (NEASC-CIHE). Sem. plan. Degrees: B,M. *Prof. Accred.:* Art, Nuclear Medicine Technology, Nursing (B), Social Work (B), Teacher Education (*e,s,p*). Pres. James T. Amsler.
Enroll.: 8,654
(617) 745-0556

*Member Massachusetts Board of Regents of Higher Education

SALTER SCHOOL
155 Ararat St., Worcester 01606. Private business. 1953/1983 (AICS). Sem. plan. Diplomas. CEO John F. Albano.
Enroll.: 370 (*f.t.* 13 m., 357 w.)
(617) 853-1074

SCHOOL OF THE MUSEUM OF FINE ARTS
230 The Fenway, Boston 02115. Private professional. 1948/1977. Sem. plan. Degrees: B,M, certificates, diplomas. *Prof. Accred.:* Art. Dean Bruce K. MacDonald.
Enroll.: 602 (*f.t.* 179 m., 340 w.)
(617) 267-9300

SIMMONS COLLEGE
Boston 02115. Private liberal arts and professional for women; graduate school coeducational. 1929/1981(NEASC-CIHE) Sem. plan. Degrees: B,M,D. *Prof. Accred.:* Librarianship, Medical Technology, Nursing (B,M), Physical Therapy, Social Work (M). Pres. William J. Holmes, Jr.
Enroll.: 3,138
(617) 738-2000

SIMON'S ROCK OF BARD COLLEGE
Great Barrington 01230. Private liberal arts. 1974/1984 (NEASC-CIHE). Sem. plan. Degrees: A,B. Pres. Leon Botstein.
Enroll.: 305
(413) 528-0771

SMITH COLLEGE
Northhampton 01063. Private liberal arts for women, graduate school coeducational. 1929/1977 (NEASC-CIHE). Sem. plan. Degrees: B,M,D. *Prof. Accred.:* Social Work (M). Pres. Mary Maples Dunn.
Enroll.: 2,485
(413) 584-2700

*SOUTHEASTERN MASSACHUSETTS UNIVERSITY
North Dartmouth 02747. Public (state) liberal arts and technological. 1964/1980 (NEASC-CIHE). Sem. plan. Degrees: B,M. *Prof. Accred.:* Art, Engineering (civil, computer, electrical, mechanical), Engineering Technology (electrical, mechanical), Medical Technology, Nursing (B). Pres. John R. Brazil.
Enroll.: 5,618
(617) 999-8615

*Member Massachusetts Board of Regents of Higher Education

SPRINGFIELD COLLEGE
Springfield 01109. Private liberal arts and professional. 1930/1980 (NEASC-CIHE). Qtr. plan. Degrees: B,M,D. *Prof. Accred.:* Rehabilitation Counseling, Teacher Education (*e*). Pres. Frank S. Falcone.
Enroll.: 2,358
(413) 787-3000

*SPRINGFIELD TECHNICAL COMMUNITY COLLEGE
Springfield 01105. Public (state) 2-year. 1971/1981 (NEASC-CIHE). Sem. plan. Degrees: A. *Prof. Accred.:* Dental Assisting, Dental Hygiene, Medical Assisting, Medical Laboratory Technology, Nuclear Medicine Technology, Nursing (A), Radiation Therapy Technology, Radiography, Surgical Technology. Pres. Andrew M. Scibelli.
Enroll.: 6,762
(413) 781-7822

STONEHILL COLLEGE
North Easton 02357. Private (Roman Catholic) liberal arts. 1959/1980 (NEASC-CIHE). Sem. plan. Degrees: B. *Prof. Accred.:* Teacher Education (*e*). Pres. Rev. Bartley MacPhaidin, C.S.C.
Enroll.: 2,786
(617) 238-1081

SUFFOLK UNIVERSITY
41 Temple St., Boston 02114. Private. 1952/1983 (NEASC-CIHE). Sem. plan. Degrees: A,B,P,M,D. *Prof. Accred.:* Law. Pres. Daniel H. Perlman.
Enroll.: 6,124
(617) 723-4700

SWAIN SCHOOL OF DESIGN
New Bedford 02740. Private professional. 1980. Sem. plan. Degrees: B. *Prof. Accred.:* Art. Pres. Bruce H. Yenawine.
Enroll.: 154 (*f.t.* 79 m., 68 w.)
(617) 997-7831

TRAVEL EDUCATION CENTER
93 Mt. Auburn St., Harvard Sq., Cambridge 02138. Private. 1979/1980 (NATTS). Courses of varying lengths. Certificates. Pres. Linda Paresky.
Enroll.: 99 (*f.t.* 3 m., 47 w.)
(617) 547-7750

*Member Massachusetts Board of Regents of Higher Education

TRAVEL SCHOOL OF AMERICA
1047 Commonwealth Ave., Boston 02215. Private. 1978 (NATTS). Courses of varying lengths. Certificates. Dir. Bernard Garber.
Enroll.: 340 (*f.t.* 31 m., 158 w.)
(617) 787-1214

TUFTS UNIVERSITY
Medford 02155. Medical School in Boston 02111. Private; College of Liberal Arts for men, Jackson College for women, others coeducational. 1929/1982 (NEASC-CIHE). Sem. plan. Degrees: B,P,M,D. *Prof. Accred.:* Dentistry, Engineering (chemical, civil, electrical, mechanical), Medicine, Occupational Therapy, Veterinary Medicine. Pres. Jean Mayer.
Enroll.: 5,967
(617) 628-5000

U.S. ARMY INTELLIGENCE SCHOOL
Fort Devens 01433. Public (federal) 2-year technological. 1976 (NEASC-CVTCI). Certificates. Cmdr. Col. Francis X. Toomey.
Enroll.: 547
(617) 796-2293

UNITED TECHNICAL SCHOOLS
17-23 Morgan St., Springfield 01107. Private. 1973/1979 (NATTS). Courses of varying lengths. Certificates. Pres. John M. Dooley.
Enroll.: 100 (*f.t.* 79 m., 1 w.)
(413) 733-0081

*UNIVERSITY OF LOWELL
Lowell 01854. Public (state). 1975/1982 (NEASC-CIHE). Sem. plan. Degrees: A,B,M,D. *Prof. Accred.:* Engineering (chemical, electrical, mechanical, plastics), Engineering Technology (civil, electronic, mechanical, nuclear), Medical Technology, Music, Nursing (B,M), Physical Therapy, Teacher Education (*e,s,p*). Pres. William T. Hogan.
Enroll.: 16,586
(617) 452-5000

UNIVERSITY OF MASSACHUSETTS CENTRAL OFFICE
250 Stuart St., Boston 02116. Public (state). Pres. David C. Knapp.
(617) 482-8400

UNIVERSITY OF MASSACHUSETTS AT AMHERST
Amherst 01003. Public (state). 1932/1985 (NEASC-CIHE); accreditation includes

*Member Massachusetts Board of Regents of Higher Education

Medical School at Worcester. Sem. plan. Degrees: A,B,P,M,D. *Prof. Accred.:* Art, Business (B,M), Engineering (chemical, civil, computer systems, electrical, environmental, engineering and options research, manufacturing, mechanical), Forestry, Health Administration, Interior Design, Landscape Architecture (M), Music, Nursing (B,M), Psychology, Public Health, Speech Pathology and Audiology, Teacher Education (*e,s,p*). Chanc. Joseph D. Duffey.
Enroll.: 27,156
(413) 545-0111

University of Massachusetts at Boston
Boston 02125. Public (state). 1972/1985 (NEASC-CIHE). Sem. plan. Degrees: B,M. Chanc. Robert A. Corrigan.
Enroll.: 11,496
(617) 929-7000

Wang Institute of Graduate Studies
Tyng Rd., Tyngsboro 01879. Private professional; graduate only. 1984 (NEASC-CIHE). Qtr. plan. Degrees: M. Pres. Edmund T. Cranch.
Enroll.: 57
(617) 649-9731

Wellesley College
Wellesley 02181. Private liberal arts for women. 1929/1979 (NEASC-CIHE). 4-1-4 plan. Degrees: B. *Prof. Accred.:* Pres. Nannerl O. Keohane.
Enroll.: 2,170
(617) 235-0320

Wentworth Institute of Technology
Boston 02115. Private technological 4-year. 1967/1983 (NEASC-CIHE). Sem. plan. Degrees: A,B. *Prof. Accred.:* Engineering Technology (aeronautical, architectural, civil, computer, electrical, electronic, mechanical, mechanical design, mechanical power, welding). Pres. Edward T. Kirkpatrick.
Enroll.: 4,855
(617) 442- 9010

Western New England College
Springfield 01119. Private liberal arts, business, and professional. 1965/1985 (NEASC-CIHE). Sem. plan. Degrees: B,P,M,D. *Prof. Accred.:* Engineering (electrical, industrial, mechanical), Law. Pres. Beverly White Miller.
Enroll.: 5,140
(413) 782-3111

*Westfield State College
Westfield 01086. Public (state) liberal arts and teachers. 1957/1981 (NEASC-CIHE). Sem. plan. Degrees: B,M. *Prof. Accred.:* Teacher Education (*e,s*). Acting Pres. John F. Nevins.
Enroll.: 4,607
(413) 568-3311

Weston School of Theology
Cambridge 02138. Private (Roman Catholic) professional; graduate only. Sem. plan. Degrees: P,M. *Prof. Accred.:* Theology (1968/1979, ATS). Pres. Edward M. O'Flaherty.
Enroll.: 181
(617) 492-1960

Wheaton College
Norton 02766. Private liberal arts for women. 1929/1979 (NEASC-CIHE). Sem. plan. Degrees: B. Pres. Alice F. Emerson.
Enroll.: 1,191
(617) 285-7722

Wheelock College
Boston 02215. Private teachers for women, graduate school coeducational. 1950/1985 (NEASC-CIHE). Tri. plan. Degrees: A,B,M. *Prof. Accred.:* Teacher Education (*e*). Pres. Daniel S. Cheever, Jr.
Enroll.: 1,706
(617) 734-5200

Williams College
Williamstown 01267. Private liberal arts. 1929/1978 (NEASC-CIHE). Sem. plan. Degrees: B,M. Pres. Francis C. Oakley.
Enroll.: 2,131
(413) 597-2233

Worcester Industrial Technical Institute
Worcester 01608. Public (state) 2-year. 1982/1985 (NEASC-CVTCI). Sem. plan. Certificates. Dir. John E. Lavin.
Enroll.: 386
(617) 799-1945

Worcester Polytechnic Institute
Worcester 01609. Private technological. 1937/1982(NEASC-CIHE). Sem. plan. Degrees: B,M,D. *Prof. Accred.:* Engineering (chemical, civil, electrical, mechanical). Pres. Jon C. Strauss.
Enroll.: 3,810
(617) 793-5000

*Member Massachusetts Board of Regents of Higher Education

*WORCESTER STATE COLLEGE
Worcester 01602. Public (state) liberal arts and teachers. 1957/1984 (NEASC-CIHE). Sem. plan. Degrees: B,M. *Prof. Accred.:* Nuclear Medicine Technology, Nursing (B), Speech Pathology. Pres. Philip D. Vairo.
Enroll.: 7,106
(617) 793-8000

*Member Massachusetts Board of Regents of Higher Education

MICHIGAN

ADELPHI TECHNICAL INSTITUTE
13301 E. Eight Mi. Rd., Warren 48089. Private, diesel and heavy-equipment mechanic school. 1981 (NATTS). Courses of varying lengths. Certificates. Dir. W. R. DeBusk.
Enroll.: 290
(313) 772-5100

BRANCH CAMPUS
20201 Hoover Rd., Detroit 48205. Dir. M. Loretta Watson.
(313) 522-9510

ADRIAN COLLEGE
110 S. Madison St., Adrian 49221. Private (United Methodist) liberal arts. 1916/1979 (NCA). Sem. plan. Degrees: B. *Prof. Accred.:* Teacher Education (*e,s*). Pres. Donald S. Stanton.
Enroll.: FTE 1,090
(517) 265-5161

ALBION COLLEGE
611 E. Porter St., Albion 49224. Private (United Methodist) liberal arts. 1915/1981 (NCA). Sem. plan. Degrees: B. *Prof. Accred.:* Music. Pres. Melvin L. Vulgamore.
Enroll.: FTE 1,565
(517) 629-5511

ALMA COLLEGE
Alma 48801. Private (United Presbyterian) liberal arts. 1916/1980 (NCA). 4-4-x plan. Degrees: B. *Prof. Accred.:* Music, Teacher Education (*e,s*). Pres. Oscar E. Remick.
Enroll.: FTE 998
(517) 463-7111

ALPENA COMMUNITY COLLEGE
Alpena 49707. Public (city) junior. 1963/1982 (NCA). Sem. plan. Degrees: A. Pres. Charles R. Donnelly.
Enroll.: FTE 535
(517) 356-9021

ANDREWS UNIVERSITY
Berrien Springs 49104. Private (Seventh-day Adventist) liberal arts and professional. 1922/1982 (NCA). Qtr. plan. Degrees: B,P,M,D. *Prof. Accred.:* Dietetics, Home Economics, Music, Nursing (B), Social Work (B), Teacher Education (*e,s,p*), Theology. Pres. W. Richard Lesher.
Enroll.: FTE 2,473
(616) 471-3100

AQUINAS COLLEGE
1607 Robinson Rd., Grand Rapids 49506. Private (Roman Catholic) liberal arts. 1946/1977 (NCA). Sem. plan. Degrees: B,M. Pres. Peter D. O'Connor.
Enroll.: FTE 1,818
(616) 459-8281

ARGUBRIGHT BUSINESS COLLEGE
67 W. Michigan Mall, Battle Creek 49017. Private. 1969/1982 (AICS). Sem. plan. Diplomas. Pres. James LaParl.
Enroll.: 355 (*f.t.* 66 m., 289 w.)
(616) 968-6105

BAKER COLLEGE
1110 Eldon Baker Dr., Flint 48507. Private. 1967/1982 (AICS); 1985/1986 (NCA). Qtr. plan. Degrees: A, certificates, diplomas. *Prof. Accred.:* Medical Assisting. Pres. Edward J. Kurtz.
Enroll.: FTE 2,187
(313) 744-4040

BRANCH CAMPUS
1020 S. Washington St., Owosso 48867. Dir. Edward J. Kurtz.
(517) 723-5251

BAY DE NOC COMMUNITY COLLEGE
Escanaba 49829. Public (district) junior. 1976/1981 (NCA). Sem. plan. Degrees: A. Pres. Dwight E. Link.
Enroll.: FTE 12,082
(906) 786-5802

CALVIN COLLEGE
3201 Burton St., S.E., Grand Rapids 49506. Private (Christian Reformed) liberal arts. 1930/1985 (NCA). 4-1-4 plan. Degrees: A,B,M. *Prof. Accred.:* Music, Teacher Education (*e,s,*). Pres. Anthony J. Diekema.
Enroll.: FTE 3,858
(616) 957-6000

CALVIN THEOLOGICAL SEMINARY
Grand Rapids 49506. Private (Christian Reformed) professional. Qtr. plan. Degrees: P,M. *Prof. Accred.:* Theology (1944/1978, ATS). Pres. James A. DeJong.
Enroll.: 235
(616) 949-2494

CAMBRIDGE BUSINESS SCHOOL
1529 Broadway, Detroit 48226. Private. 1977/1985 (AICS). Courses of varying lengths. Certificates, diplomas. Pres. Ted Jakub.

Enroll.: 1,280 (*f.t.* 164 m., 1,116 w.)
(313) 961-5105

BRANCH CAMPUS
18256 Grand River Ave., Detroit 48223. Dir. M. Loretta Watson.
(313) 272-0740

CAMBRIDGE CAREER CENTER
410 Cambridge, Royal Oak 48067. Private. 1985 (ABHES). Courses of varying lengths. Certificates, diplomas. Exec. Dir. Jose A. Rendon.
(313) 399-7531

CARNEGIE INSTITUTE
550 Stephenson Hwy., Suite 100, Troy 48083. Private. 1968/1980 (NATTS). Qtr. plan. Diplomas. *Prof. Accred.:* Medical Assistant. Pres. James F. McEachern.
Enroll.: 222 w.
(313) 589-1078

CENTER FOR HUMANISTIC STUDIES
40 E. Ferry Ave., Detroit 48202. Private professional; graduate only. 1984 (NCA). Qtr. plan. Degrees: P, M. Pres. Clark Moustakas.
Enroll.: FTE 58
(313) 875-7440

CENTRAL MICHIGAN UNIVERSITY
Mount Pleasant 48859. Public (state). 1915/1983 (NCA). Sem. plan. Degrees: B,M,D. *Prof. Accred.:* Business (B), Music, Speech Pathology and Audiology, Teacher Education (*e,s,p*). Acting Pres. Arthur E. Ellis.
Enroll.: FTE 15,153
(517) 774-3131

CHARLES STEWART MOTT COMMUNITY COLLEGE
1401 E. Court St., Flint 48503. Public (district) junior. 1926/1985 (NCA). Sem. plan. Degrees: A. *Prof. Accred.:* Dental Assisting, Dental Hygiene, Nursing (A), Respiratory Therapy, Respiratory Therapy Technology. Pres. David Moore.
Enroll.: FTE 5,097
(313) 762-0453

CHAUFFEURS TRAINING SCHOOL (EXTENSION)
19669 John R" St., Detroit 48203. Private. 1985 (NATTS). Courses of varying lengths. Certificates. Dir. James Van Vliet.
(313) 892-1300

*CLEARY COLLEGE
2170 Washtenaw Rd., Ypsilanti 48197. Private. 1968/1983 (AICS). Qtr. plan. Degrees: A,B, diplomas. *Prof. Accred.:* Medical Assisting. Pres. Harry Howard.
Enroll.: 1,447 (*f.t.* 283 m., 1,164 w.)
(313) 483-4400

COLLEGE OF ART AND DESIGN—CENTER FOR CREATIVE STUDIES
Detroit 48202. Private professional. 1977/1982 (NCA). Sem. plan. Degrees: B. *Prof. Accred.:* Art. Pres. Jerome L. Grove.
Enroll.: FTE 804
(313) 872-3118

CONCORDIA COLLEGE
Ann Arbor 48105. Private (Lutheran-Missouri Synod) liberal arts. 1968/1986 (NCA). Qtr. plan. Degrees: A,B. Pres. Rev. David G. Schmiel.
Enroll.: FTE 411
(313) 665-3691

CONTROL DATA INSTITUTE
21700 Northwestern Hwy., Tower 14, Suite 1401, Southfield 48075. Private. 1968/1979 (NATTS). Courses of varying lengths. Certificates. Dir. Norman L. Cohen.
Enroll.: 423 (*f.t.* 325 m., 98 w.)
(313) 552-6600

BRANCH CAMPUS
1946 N. 13th St., Toledo, OH 43624.
(419) 255-5969

CRANBROOK ACADEMY OF ART
Bloomfield Hills 48013. Private professional. 1960/1979 (NCA). Sem. plan. Degrees: B,M. *Prof. Accred.:* Art. Pres. Roy Slade.
Enroll.: FTE 131
(313) 645-3300

DAVENPORT COLLEGE
415 E. Fulton, Grand Rapids 49503. Private junior. 1976/1981 (NCA); 1981 (AICS). Qtr. plan. Degrees: A. *Prof. Accred.:* Medical Assisting. Pres. Donald W. Maine.
Enroll.: FTE 3,434
(616) 451-3511

BRANCH CAMPUS
4123 W. Main St., Kalamazoo 49007. *Prof. Accred.:* Medical Assisting. Dean C. Dexter Rohm.
(616) 382-2835

*Candidate for Accreditation by Regional Accrediting Commission

BRANCH CAMPUS
220 E. Kalamazoo, Lansing 48933. Dir. Don Colizzi.
(517) 484-2600

BRANCH CAMPUS
8120 Georgia St., Merrillville, IN 46410. Exec. Dir. Edward R. Bauer.
(219) 769-5556

BRANCH CAMPUS
6327 State Rd. 23, South Bend, IN 46635. *Prof. Accred.:* Medical Assisting. Dir. Edward R. Bauer.
(219) 277-8447

DELTA COLLEGE
University Center 48710. Public (county and district) junior. 1968/1984 (NCA). Sem. plan. Degrees: A. *Prof. Accred.:* Dental Assisting, Dental Hygiene, Engineering Technology (electronic, mechanical), Nursing (A), Radiography, Respiratory Therapy, Respiratory Therapy Technology. Pres. Donald J. Carlyon.
Enroll.: FTE 5,483
(517) 686-9201

DETROIT BUSINESS INSTITUTE
115 State St., Detroit 48226. Private. 1961/1981 (AICS). Qtr. plan. Certificates, diplomas. Exec. Vice Pres. Leon D. Gust.
Enroll.: 1,970 (*f.t.* 536 m., 1,434 w.)
(313) 962-6534

BRANCH CAMPUS
21700 Northwestern Hwy., Southfield 48075.
(313) 962-6534

DETROIT BUSINESS INSTITUTE
19100 Fort St., Riverview 48192. Private. 1983 (AICS). Qtr. plan. Certificates, diplomas. Dir. Kathleen Horon.
Enroll.: 840
(313) 479-0660

BRANCH CAMPUS
21700 Northwestern Hwy., Southfield 48075. Dir. Leon D. Gust.
(313) 962-6534

*DETROIT COLLEGE OF BUSINESS
4801 Oakman Blvd., Dearborn 48126. Private. 1961/1986 (AICS). Qtr. plan. Degrees: A,B, diplomas. Pres. Frank Paone.
Enroll.: 5,418 (*f.t.* 1,675 m., 3,743 w.)
(313) 582-6983

*Candidate for Accreditation by Regional Accrediting Commission

BRANCH CAMPUS
3115 Lawndale, Flint 48504. Dean Ralph E. Stingel, Jr.
(313) 239-1443

DETROIT COLLEGE OF LAW
Detroit 48201. Private professional. 1941 (ABA); 1946 (AALS). Sem. plan. Degrees: P. *Prof. Accred.:* Law. Dean John S. Abbott.
Enroll.: 841 (*f.t.* 303 m., 121 w.)
(313) 965-0150

DETROIT COMMUNITY MUSIC SCHOOL
200 E. Kirby St., Detroit 48202. Private professional. 1981. Courses of varying lengths. Certificates. *Prof. Accred.:* Music. Exec. Dir. John A. Smith.
(313) 831-2870

DETROIT ENGINEERING INSTITUTE
2030 Grand River, Detroit 48226. Private. 1967/1977 (NATTS). Qtr. plan. Certificates, diplomas. Pres. Peter Bercik.
Enroll.: 395 (*f.t.* 389 m., 6 w.)
(313) 961-7450

DETROIT INSTITUTE OF AERONAUTICS
Willow Run Airport, Box 809, Ypsilanti 48197. Private. 1976 (NATTS). Sem. plan. Diplomas. Pres. Lee R. Koepke.
Enroll.: 50 (*f.t.* 49 m., 1 w.)
(313) 483-3758

DETROIT INSTITUTE OF COMMERCE
4829 Woodward Ave., Detroit 48201. Private. 1971/1977 (AICS). Qtr. plan. Certificates, diplomas. Pres. Howard Weaver.
Enroll.: 476 (*f.t.* 76 m., 400 w.)
(313) 832-0200

DORSEY BUSINESS SCHOOL
31542 Gratiot Ave., Roseville 48066. Private. 1961/1984 (AICS). Qtr. plan. Certificates, diplomas. Pres. Dennis Stockemer.
Enroll.: 271 (*f.t.* 5 m., 266 w.)
(313) 296-3225

DORSEY BUSINESS SCHOOL
15755 Northline Rd., Southgate 48195. Private. 1972/1984 (AICS). Qtr. plan. Certificates, diplomas. Pres. Dennis Stockemer.
Enroll.: 472 (*f.t.* 32 m., 440 w.)
(313) 285-5400

DORSEY BUSINESS SCHOOL
750 Stephenson Hwy., Suite 105, Troy 48083. Private. 1984 (AICS). Courses of varying lengths. Certificates, diplomas. Dir. Adrienne Lapish.

Michigan

Enroll.: 245 (*f.t.* 0 m., 245 w.)
(313) 588-9660

BRANCH CAMPUS
24901 Northwestern Hwy., #202, Southfield 48075. Dir. Shirley Kennedy.
(313) 352-7830

DORSEY BUSINESS SCHOOL
34841 Veteran's Plaza, Wayne 48184. Private. 1984 (AICS). Courses of varying lengths. Certificates, diplomas. Dir. Jan Glotzbach.
Enroll.: 245 (*f.t.* 0 m., 245 w.)
(313) 595-1540

EASTERN MICHIGAN UNIVERSITY
Ypsilanti 48197. Public (state). 1915/1982 (NCA). Sem. plan. Degrees: B,M. *Prof. Accred.:* Business (B,M), Dietetics, Home Economics, Medical Technology, Music, Nursing (B), Occupational Therapy, Social Work (B), Speech Pathology, Teacher Education (*e,s,p*). Pres. John W. Porter.
Enroll.: FTE 14,602
(313) 487-1849

EDUCATIONAL INSTITUTE OF THE AMERICAN HOTEL AND MOTEL ASSOCIATION
1407 S. Harrison Rd., Suite 310, East Lansing 48823. Private home study. 1963/1983 (NHSC). Exec. Dir. E. Ray Swan.
(517) 353-5500

FASHION INSTITUTE OF AMERICA
20755 Greenfield, Suite 607, Southfield 48075. Private. 1982 (NATTS). Courses of varying lengths. Certificates. Pres. Diane E. Solomon.
(313) 559-9733

FERNDALE MEDICAL CAREERS, INC.
22720 Woodward Ave., Ferndale 48220. Private. 1986 (ABHES). Courses of varying lengths. Certificates. Pres. Ruth Evans Brett.
(313) 541-0686

FERRIS STATE COLLEGE
Big Rapids 49307. Public professional and technical. 1959/1983 (NCA). Qtr. plan. Degrees: A,B,P,M,D. *Prof. Accred.:* Dental Assisting, Dental Hygiene, Dental Laboratory Technology, Medical Assisting, Medical Laboratory Technology, Medical Record Administration, Medical Record Technology, Medical Technology, Nuclear Medicine Technology, Optometric Technology, Optometry, Pharmacy, Radiography, Respiratory Therapy. Pres. J. William Wenrich.
Enroll.: FTE 10,400
(616) 796-0461

FLINT INSTITUTE OF BARBERING
3214 Flushing Rd., Flint 48504. Private. 1972/1978 (NATTS). Courses of varying lengths. Diplomas. Pres. John L. Ayre.
Enroll.: 61 (*f.t.* 26 m., 35 w.)
(313) 232-4711

GMI ENGINEERING AND MANAGEMENT INSTITUTE
1700 W. Third Ave., Flint 48502. Private technological. 1962/1982 (NCA). Sem. plan. Degrees: B. *Prof. Accred.:* Engineering (electrical, industrial, mechanical). Pres. William B. Cottingham.
Enroll.: FTE 2,977
(313) 762-9864

GLEN OAKS COMMUNITY COLLEGE
Centreville 49032. Public (district) junior. 1975/1983 (NCA). Sem. plan. Degrees: A. Pres. Philip G. Ward.
Enroll.: FTE 299 (616) 467-9945

GOGEBIC COMMUNITY COLLEGE
Ironwood 49938. Public (county) junior. 1949/1978 (NCA). Sem. plan. Degrees: A. Pres. Carl R. Bennett.
Enroll.: FTE 527
(906) 932-4231

*GRACE BIBLE COLLEGE
P.O. Box 910, Grand Rapids 49509. Private (Grace Gospel Fellowship) professional. 1964/1983 (AABC). Sem. plan. Degrees: A,B. Pres. Samuel Vinton.
Enroll.: 126
(616) 538-2330

GRAND RAPIDS BAPTIST COLLEGE AND SEMINARY
Grand Rapids 49505. Private (Baptist) liberal arts and professional. 1977/1982 (NCA). Sem. plan. Degrees: A,B,P. Pres. Charles U. Wagner.
Enroll.: FTE 757
370 (*f.t.* 363 m., (616) 949-5300

GRAND RAPIDS EDUCATIONAL CENTER
2922 Fuller Ave., N.E., Northbrook Park Bldg. 2, Grand Rapids 49505. Private technical. 1978/1984 (NATTS); 1985 (ABHES). 6-month courses. Certificates. *Prof. Accred.:* Medical Assisting. Admin. Robert J. Malone.
Enroll.: *f.t.* 92 w.
(616) 364-8464

*Candidate for Accreditation by Regional Accrediting Commission

GRAND RAPIDS JUNIOR COLLEGE
143 Bostwick St., N.E., Grand Rapids 49503. Public (city). 1917/1985 (NCA). Sem. plan. Degrees: A, certificates. *Prof. Accred.:* Dental Assisting, Dental Hygiene, Practical Nursing, Radiography. Pres. Richard W. Calkins.
Enroll.: FTE 3.087
(616) 456-4895

GRAND VALLEY STATE COLLEGES
Allendale 49401. Public liberal arts. 1968/1979 (NCA). Sem. plan. Degrees: B, M. *Prof. Accred.:* Art, Music, Nursing (B), Physical Therapy. Pres. Arend D. Lubbers.
Enroll.: FTE 5,304
(616) 895-6611

GREAT LAKES BIBLE COLLEGE
P.O. Box 40060, Lansing 48901. Private (Church of Christ) professional. 1977 (AABC). Sem. plan. Degrees: A, B. Pres. Curtis D. Lloyd.
Enroll.: 155 (*f.t.* 79 m., 63 w.)
(517) 321-0242

GREAT LAKES JUNIOR COLLEGE OF BUSINESS
310 S. Washington Ave., Saginaw 48607. Private. 1965/1985 (AICS). Qtr. plan. Degrees: A, certificates, diplomas. Pres. Angelo Guerriero.
Enroll.: 644 (*f.t.* 130 m., 514 w.)
(517) 755-3444

BRANCH CAMPUS
701 N. Madison, Bay City 48706.
(517) 895-5234

HALLMARK COMPUTER TRAINING INSTITUTE
20770 Greenfield Rd., Oak Park 48237. Private. 1986 (AICS). Courses of varying lengths. Diplomas. Admin. David W. Spencer.
Enroll.: 318
(313) 968-1919

BRANCH CAMPUS
21 S. Glenwood, Pontiac 48058. Dir. David Kirby.
(313) 333-0404

HEATHKIT/ZENITH EDUCATIONAL SYSTEMS
Hilltop Rd., St. Joseph 49085. Private home study; a division of Heath Company, subsidiary of Zenith Radio Corporation. 1979/1984 (NHSC). Dir. Douglas M. Bonham.
(616) 982-3644

HENRY FORD COMMUNITY COLLEGE
5101 Evergreen Rd., Dearborn 48128. Public (city) junior. 1949/1985 (NCA). Sem. plan. Degrees: A. *Prof. Accred.:* Medical Assisting, Medical Record Technology, Nursing (A), Respiratory Therapy. Pres. Stuart M. Bundy.
Enroll.: FTE 8,066
(313) 271-2750

HIGHLAND PARK COMMUNITY COLLEGE
Glendale Ave. at Third St., Highland Park 48203. Public (city) junior. 1921/1982 (NCA). Sem. plan. Degrees: A. *Prof. Accred.:* Medical Laboratory Technology (A). Pres. Thomas Lloyd.
Enroll.: FTE 722
(313) 252-0475

HILLSDALE COLLEGE
Hillsdale 49242. Private liberal arts. 1915/1978 (NCA). Sem. plan. Degrees: B. Pres. George C. Roche, III.
Enroll.: FTE 922
(517) 437-7341

HOPE COLLEGE
Holland 49423. Private (Reformed Church in America) liberal arts. 1915/1984 (NCA). Sem. plan. Degrees: B. *Prof. Accred.:* Art, Chemistry, Music, Nursing (B), Teacher Education (*e,s*). Pres. Gordon J. Van Wylen.
Enroll.: FTE 2,288
(616) 392-5111

ITT TECHNICAL INSTITUTE
3013 Eastern Ave., S.E., Grand Rapids 49508. Private. 1969/1984 (NATTS). Qtr. plan. Diplomas. Dir. Calvin Harding.
Enroll.: 413 (*f.t.* 391 m., 22 w.)
(616) 452-1458

INSTITUTE OF MERCHANDISING AND DESIGN
116 W. Allegan St., Lansing 48933. Private. 1980 (NATTS). One- and two-year programs. Certificates, diplomas. Dir. Linda P. Knapp.
Enroll.: 38
(517) 484-3756

JACKSON BUSINESS INSTITUTE
234 S. Mechanic St., Jackson 49201. Private. 1953/1981 (AICS). Qtr. plan. Diplomas. Pres. Jack D. Bunce.
Enroll.: 434 (*f.t.* 57 m., 377 w.)
(517) 789-6123

JACKSON COMMUNITY COLLEGE
Jackson 49201. Public (district) junior. 1933/1976 (NCA). Sem. plan. Degrees: A. *Prof. Accred.:* Radiography. Pres. Clyde E. LeTarte.

Enroll.: FTE 2,673
(517) 787-0800

KALAMAZOO COLLEGE
Kalamazoo 49007. Private (American Baptist) liberal arts. 1915/1983 (NCA). Qtr. plan. Degrees: B. Pres. David W. Breneman.
Enroll.: FTE 1,115
(616) 383-8411

KALAMAZOO VALLEY COMMUNITY COLLEGE
Kalamazoo 49009. Public (district) junior. 1972/1976 (NCA). Sem. plan. Degrees: A. *Prof. Accred.:* Dental Hygiene, Medical Assisting, Respiratory Therapy, Respiratory Therapy Technology. Pres. Marilyn J. Schlack.
Enroll.: FTE 3,836
(616) 372-5200

KELLOGG COMMUNITY COLLEGE
Battle Creek 49016. Public (district) junior. 1965/1982 (NCA). Sem. plan. Degrees: A. *Prof. Accred.:* Dental Hygiene, Medical Laboratory Technology, Radiography. Pres. Richard F. Whitmore.
Enroll.: FTE 1,191
(616) 965-3931

KENDALL SCHOOL OF DESIGN
1110 College N.E., Grand Rapids 49503. Private. 1981/1984 (NCA). Sem. plan. Degrees: A,B, certificates. *Prof. Accred.:* Art, Interior Design. Pres. Phyllis I. Danielson.
Enroll.: FTE 605
(616) 451-2787

KIRTLAND COMMUNITY COLLEGE
Roscommon 48653. Public (district) junior. 1976/1981 (NCA). Sem. plan. Degrees: A. Pres. Raymond D. Homer.
Enroll.: FTE 815
(517) 275-5121

KRAINZ WOODS ACADEMY OF MEDICAL LABORATORY TECHNOLOGY
4327 E. Seven Mi. Rd., Detroit 48234. Private 2-year. 1973/1985 (ABHES). Qtr. plan. Diplomas. *Prof. Accred.:* Medical Laboratory Technology. Dir. Leophas Ford.
Enroll.: 20
(313) 366-5204

LAKE MICHIGAN COLLEGE
Benton Harbor 49022. Public (county) junior. 1962/1984 (NCA). Sem. plan. Degrees: A. *Prof. Accred.:* Dental Assisting, Medical Laboratory Technology (A), Nursing (A), Radiography. Pres. Anne E. Mulder.
Enroll.: FTE 25,014
(616) 927-3571

LAKE SUPERIOR STATE COLLEGE
Sault Ste. Marie 49783. Public liberal arts. 1968/1981 (NCA). Qtr. plan. Degrees: A,B,M. *Prof. Accred.:* Engineering Technology (computer, drafting and design, electronic, mechanical), Nursing (A,B). Pres. H. Erik Shaar.
Enroll.: FTE 2,403
(906) 632-6841

LANSING BARBER COLLEGE
315 Grand Ave., S., Lansing 48933. Private. 1985 (NATTS). Courses of varying lengths. Certificates. Dir. Robert Beckwith.
Enroll.: 36
(517) 484-9895

LANSING COMMUNITY COLLEGE
Lansing 48901. Public (district) junior. 1964/1984 (NCA). Qtr. plan. Degrees: A. *Prof. Accred.:* Cytotechnology, Dental Assisting, Dental Hygiene, Nursing (A), Radiography, Respiratory Therapy, Respiratory Therapy Technology. Pres. Philip J. Gannon.
Enroll.: FTE 9,578
(517) 483-1852

LANSING COMPUTER INSTITUTE
913 W. Holmes Rd., Suite 255, Lansing 48910. Private. 1985 (NATTS). Courses of varying lengths. Certificates. Dir. Virginia Hilbert.
(517) 332-3024

LAWRENCE INSTITUTE OF TECHNOLOGY
Southfield 48075. Private professional and technological. 1967/1981 (NCA). Qtr. plan. Degrees: A,B. *Prof. Accred.:* Architecture (B), Engineering (construction, electrical, mechanical), Engineering Technology (construction, electrical, industrial, mechanical). Pres. Richard E. Marburger.
Enroll.: FTE 4,393
(313) 356-0200

LEWIS COLLEGE OF BUSINESS
17370 Meyers, Detroit 48235. Private. 1978/1986 (NCA). Tri. plan. Degrees: A, certificates. Pres. Marjorie Harris.
Enroll.: FTE 268
(313) 862-6300

MACOMB COMMUNITY COLLEGE
145000 Twelve Mile Rd., Warren 48093-3896. Public (district) junior. Accreditation includes Macomb Community College—

Center Campus at Mount Clemens; Macomb Community College—South Campus at Warren. 1970/1980 (NCA). Sem. plan. Degrees: A. *Prof. Accred.:* Dental Assisting, Nursing (A), Respiratory Therapy, Respiratory Therapy Technology. Pres. Albert L. Lorenzo.
Enroll.: FTE 12,524
(313) 445-7000

MADONNA COLLEGE
Livonia 48150. Private (Roman Catholic) liberal arts. 1959/1985 (NCA). Sem. plan. Degrees: B,M. *Prof. Accred.:* Nursing (B), Social Work (B), Teacher Education (*e,s*). Pres. Sister Mary Francilene, C.S.S.F.
Enroll.: FTE 2,750
(313) 591-5000

MARYGROVE COLLEGE
8425 W. McNichols Rd., Detroit 48221. Private (Roman Catholic) liberal arts. 1926/1982 (NCA). Sem. plan. Degrees: B,M. *Prof. Accred.:* Radiography, Social Work (B), Teacher Education (*e,s*). Pres. John E. Shay, Jr.
Enroll.: FTE 946
(313) 862-8000

MEHARRY ALLIED HEALTH LEARNING CENTER
18100 Meyers Rd., Detroit 48235. Private. 1985 (ABHES). 44- and 42-week programs. Diplomas. Exec. Dir. Carolyn A. Worthy.
(313) 864-9087

MERCY COLLEGE OF DETROIT
8200 W. Outer Dr., Detroit 48219. Private (Roman Catholic) liberal arts. 1951/1980 (NCA). Sem. plan. Degrees: B,M. *Prof. Accred.:* Assistant to the Primary Care Physician, Dietetics, Medical Laboratory Technology (A), Medical Record Administration, Medical Record Technology, Medical Technology, Nursing (B), Respiratory Therapy, Social Work (B). Pres. Sister Maureen A. Fay, R.S.M.
Enroll.: FTE 1,807
(313) 592-6115

MICHIGAN CAREER INSTITUTE
14520 Gratiot Ave., Detroit 48205. Private. 1969/1979 (NATTS). Courses of varying lengths. Diplomas. Pres. James M. Meyer.
Enroll.: 533 (*f.t.* 295 m., 14 w.)
(313) 526-6600

MICHIGAN CHRISTIAN COLLEGE
Rochester 48063. Private (Church of Christ). 1974/1983 (NCA). Sem. plan. Degrees: A,B. Pres. Milton Fletcher.
Enroll.: FTE 322
(313) 651-5800

MICHIGAN PARAPROFESSIONAL TRAINING INSTITUTE
21800 Greenfield Rd., Oak Park 48237. Private. 1977 (ABHES). Courses of varying lengths. Certificates. *Prof. Accred.:* Medical Assisting, Medical Laboratory Technology, Radiography. Pres. Miguel A. Gonzalez-Prendes.
Enroll.: 187 (*f.t.* 25 m., 162 w.)
(313) 968-2460

BRANCH CAMPUS
29814 Smith Rd., Romulus 48174. *Prof. Accred.:* Medical Assisting, Medical Laboratory Technology.
(313) 721-1777

BRANCH CAMPUS
18600 Florence, Suite B-3, Roseville 48066. *Prof. Accred.:* Medical Assisting.
(313) 774-2727

MICHIGAN STATE UNIVERSITY
East Lansing 48824. Public. 1915/1975 (NCA). Qtr. plan. Degrees: B,P,M,D. *Prof. Accred.:* Accounting (Type A,B), Business (B,M), Engineering (agricultural, chemical, civil, electrical, mechanical), Forestry, Interior Design, Journalism, Landscape Architecture (B), Medical Technology, Medicine, Music, Nursing (M), Osteopathy, Psychology, Rehabilitation Counseling, Social Work (B,M), Speech Pathology and Audiology, Teacher Education (*e,s,p*), Veterinary Medicine. Pres. John A. DiBaggio.
Enroll.: FTE 38,051
(517) 355-6560

MICHIGAN TECHNICAL INSTITUTE
611 Church St., P.O. Box 8200, Ann Arbor 48107. Private. 1976/1983 (AICS). Courses of varying lengths. Certificates. Exec. Vice Pres. Nina M. Barwick.
Enroll.: 526 (*f.t.* 210 m., 316 w.)
(313) 769-4507

MICHIGAN TECHNOLOGICAL UNIVERSITY
Houghton 49931. Public (state). 1928/1978 (NCA). Qtr. plan. Degrees: A,B,M,D. *Prof. Accred.:* Engineering (chemical, civil, electrical, geological, materials science and en-

gineering, mechanical, mineral process, mining), Engineering Technology (civil, electrical, electromechanical), Forestry. Pres. Dale F. Stein.
Enroll.: FTE 6,433
(906) 487-1885

MID-MICHIGAN COMMUNITY COLLEGE
Harrison 48625. Public (district) junior. 1974/1982 (NCA). Sem. plan. Degrees: A. *Prof. Accred.:* Medical Laboratory Technology (A), Radiography. Pres. Eugene F. Schorzmann.
Enroll.: FTE 1,026
(517) 386-7792

MONROE COUNTY COMMUNITY COLLEGE
Monroe 48161. Public (district) junior. 1972/1980 (NCA). Sem. plan. Degrees: A. *Prof. Accred.:* Respiratory Therapy Technology. Pres. Gerald D. Welch.
Enroll.: FTE 1,464
(313) 242-7300

MONTCALM COMMUNITY COLLEGE
Sidney 48885. Public (district) junior. 1974/1979 (NCA). Sem. plan. Degrees: A. Pres. Donald C. Burns.
Enroll.: FTE 865
(517) 328-2111

MOTECH AUTOMOTIVE EDUCATION CENTER
35155 Industrial Rd., Livonia 48150. Private. 1976/1980 (NATTS). Sem. plan. Certificates. Dir. R. D. Henriksen.
Enroll.: 437 (*f.t.* 426 m., 11 w.)
(313) 522-9510

MUSKEGON BUSINESS COLLEGE
141 Hartford, Muskegon 49442. Private junior. 1953/1984 (AICS); 1984 (NCA). Qtr. plan. Degrees: A, certificates, diplomas. *Prof. Accred.:* Medical Assisting, Medical Record Technology. Pres. Robert D. Jewell.
Enroll.: FTE 1,205
(616) 726-4904

MUSKEGON COMMUNITY COLLEGE
Muskegon 49443. Public (county) junior. 1929/1984 (NCA). Sem. plan. Degrees: A. *Prof. Accred.:* Respiratory Therapy, Respiratory Therapy Technology. Pres. James L. Stevenson.
Enroll.: FTE 2,185
(616) 773-9131

NATIONAL EDUCATION CENTER/NATIONAL INSTITUTE OF TECH CAMPUS
15115 Deerfield, East Detroit 48021. Private. 1980 (NATTS). Qtr. plan. Diplomas. Dir. Gerry Kosentos.
Enroll.: 1,060 (*f.t.* 800 m., 100 w.)
(313) 779-5530

NATIONAL EDUCATION CENTER/NATIONAL INSTITUTE OF TECH CAMPUS
18000 Newburgh Rd., Livonia 48150. Private. 1970/1975 (NATTS). Qtr. plan. Certificates, diplomas. Dir. Sara Zarzycki.
Enroll.: 1,600 (*f.t.* 1,372 m., 245 w.)
(313) 464-7387

NATIONAL EDUCATION CENTER/NATIONAL INSTITUTE OF TECH CAMPUS
2620 Remico St., S.W., Wyoming 49509. Private. 1980 (NATTS). Qtr. plan. Diplomas. Dir. Reid Haglin.
Enroll.: 341 (*f.t.* 315 m., 9 w.)
(616) 538-3170

NAZARETH COLLEGE
Nazareth 49074. Private (Roman Catholic) liberal arts. 1940/1982 (NCA). Sem. plan. Degrees: B,M. *Prof. Accred.:* Nursing (B), Social Work (B), Teacher Education (*e*). Pres. Patrick B. Smith.
Enroll.: FTE 561
(616) 349-7783

NORTH CENTRAL MICHIGAN COLLEGE
Petoskey 49770. Public (district) junior. 1972/1985 (NCA). Sem. plan. Degrees: A. *Prof. Accred.:* Respiratory Therapy. Pres. A. D. Shankland.
Enroll.: FTE 857
(616) 347-3973

NORTHEASTERN SCHOOL OF COMMERCE
P.O. Box 819, 701 N. Madison Ave., Bay City 48706. Private. 1982 (AICS). Qtr. plan. Certificates, diplomas. Dir. Louis Bork
Enroll.: 121 (*f.t.* 65)
Enroll.: 285 (*f.t.* 14 m., 271 w.)
(517) 893-4502

NORTHERN MICHIGAN UNIVERSITY
Marquette 49855. Public (state). 1916/1985 (NCA). Sem. plan. Degrees: A,B,M. *Prof. Accred.:* Medical Laboratory Technology (A), Music, Nursing (B), Social Work (B), Speech Pathology, Teacher Education (*e,s,p*). Pres. James B. Appleberry.
Enroll.: FTE 6,123
(906) 227-2242

NORTHWESTERN MICHIGAN COLLEGE
Traverse City 49684. Public (county) junior. 1961/1980 (NCA). Qtr. plan. Degrees: A. *Prof. Accred.:* Dental Assisting. Pres. George Miller.

Enroll.: FTE 1,852
(616) 922-1010

NORTHWOOD INSTITUTE—MIDLAND CAMPUS
Midland 48640. Private business management. Accreditation includes Cedar Hill, TX and West Baden, IN campuses; A degrees only. 1974/1983 (NCA). Qtr. plan. Degrees: B. Pres. David E. Fry.
Enroll.: FTE 2,529
(517) 631-1600

OAKLAND COMMUNITY COLLEGE
Bloomfield Hills 48013. Public (district) junior. 1971/1981 (NCA). Tri. plan. Degrees: A. *Prof. Accred.:* Diagnostic Medical Sonography, Medical Laboratory Technology (A), Respiratory Therapy. Pres. R. Stephen Nicholson.
Total Enroll.: FTE 6,179
(313) 540-1500

AUBURN HILLS CAMPUS
Auburn Heights 48057. 1971/1976 (NCA). Prov. Christine Gram.
(313) 852-1000

HIGHLAND LAKES CAMPUS
Union Lake 48085. 1971/1976 (NCA). *Prof. Accred.:* Dental Assisting, Dental Hygiene, Medical Assisting. Prov. Ned A. Brodbeck.
(313) 363-7191

ORCHARD RIDGE CAMPUS
Farmington 48024. 1971/1976 (NCA). Prov. S. James Manilla.
(313) 476-9400

SOUTHEAST CAMPUS SYSTEM
Prov. Walter J. Fightmaster.
(313) 548-1252

OAKPARK CAMPUS Oakpark 48237. 1976 (NCA). Dean Thomas J. Krupa.

ROYAL OAK CAMPUS Royal Oak 48073. 1976 (NCA). Dean Ernest J. Chiakmakis.

OAKLAND UNIVERSITY
Rochester 48063. Public (state) liberal arts and professional. 1966/1983 (NCA). Tri. plan. Degrees: B,M,D. *Prof. Accred.:* Engineering (computer, electrical, mechanical, systems), Nursing (B), Perfusion, Physical Therapy, Teacher Education (*e,s,p*). Pres. Joseph E. Champagne.
Enroll.: FTE 9,007
(313) 377-3500

OLIVET COLLEGE
Olivet 49076. Private (United Church of Christ) liberal arts. 1913/1982 (NCA). Sem. plan. Degrees: B. Pres. Donald A. Morris.
Enroll.: FTE 675
(616) 749-7641

PAYNE-PULLIAM SCHOOL OF TRADE AND COMMERCE
2345 Cass Ave., Detroit 48201. Private business. 1978/1982 (AICS). Courses of varying lengths. Certificates, diplomas. Pres. Betty E. Pulliam.
Enroll.: 332 (*f.t.* 74 m., 258 w.)
(313) 963-4710

PHOTON SCHOOL OF WELDING
720 S. Hamilton, Saginaw 48602. Private. 1983 (NATTS). Courses of varying lengths. Certificates. Pres. Charles Garinger.
Enroll.: 45
(517) 791-1644

PONTIAC BUSINESS INSTITUTE
24 Market St., Mt. Clemens 48043. Private. 1986 (AICS). Qtr. plan. Certificates, diplomas. Dir. Helen McAllister.
(313) 465-6119

PONTIAC BUSINESS INSTITUTE
755 W. Drahner Rd., Oxford 48051. Private. 1979/1986 (AICS). Qtr. plan. Certificates, diplomas. Dir. Patricia Fischer.
Enroll.: 349 (*f.t.* 53 m., 296 w.)
(313) 628-4847

PONTIAC BUSINESS INSTITUTE
18 W. Lawrence St., Pontiac 48058. Private. 1962/1986 (AICS). Qtr. plan. Degrees: A. Vice Pres./Dir. Tina Lifsey.
Enroll.: 1,148 (*f.t.* 203 m., 945 w.)
(313) 333-7028

PORT HURON SCHOOL OF BUSINESS
3403 Lapeer Rd., Port Huron 48060. Private. 1979/1986 (AICS). Courses of varying lengths. Certificates, diplomas. Dir./Vice Pres. Dorothy Krupp.
Enroll.: 287 (*f.t.* 31 m., 256 w.)
(313) 984-5185

REFORMED BIBLE COLLEGE
1869 Robinson Rd., S.E., Grand Rapids 49506. Private (Reformed Churches) professional. 1964/1984 (AABC). Sem. plan. Degrees: A,B. Pres. Dick L. Van Halsema.
Enroll.: 191
(616) 458-0404

ROSS BUSINESS INSTITUTE
23400 Michigan Ave., Suite 221, Dearborn 48124. Private. 1983 (AICS). Qtr. plan. Certificates. Dir. Judith Sierota.
Enroll.: 1,048 (*f.t.* 215 m., 833 w.)
(313) 563-0640

BRANCH CAMPUS
21165 Gratiot Ave., E. Detroit 48021. Dir. Janice Waring.
(313) 774-7880

BRANCH CAMPUS
21700 Greenfield, Suite 254, Oak Park 48237. Dir. Kathleen Case.
(313) 968-1970

ROSS BUSINESS INSTITUTE
Detroit 48226. Private. 1977/1983 (AICS). Qtr. plan. Certificates. Pres. Howard J. Hulsman.
Enroll.: 177 (*f.t.* 8 m., 169 w.)
(313) 965-2122

THE ROSS MEDICAL EDUCATION CENTER
1007 S. Ballenger Hwy., Flint 48504. Private. 1978 (NATTS); 1983 (ABHES). Courses of varying lengths. Certificates, diplomas. *Prof. Accred.:* Medical Assisting. Pres. Chris Ossenmachen.
Enroll.: 139 (*f.t.* 1 m., 138 w.)
(313) 234-1674

BRANCH CAMPUS
4054 Bay Rd., Saginaw 48603. Exec. Dir. Susan Wood.
(517) 793-9800

THE ROSS MEDICAL EDUCATION CENTER
913 W. Holmes, Suite 260, Lansing 48910. Private. 1985 (NATTS). Courses of varying lengths. Certificates. *Prof. Accred.:* Medical Assisting. Dir. Debra Snetting.
Enroll.: f.t. 123 w.
(517) 887-0180

THE ROSS MEDICAL EDUCATION CENTER
29200 Vassar Dr., Suite 701, Livonia 48152. Private. 1979 (NATTS). Courses of varying lengths. Certificates, diplomas. *Prof. Accred.:* Medical Assisting. Exec. Dir. Roxanne Lopetrone.
Enroll.: 125 (*f.t.* 10 m., 115 w.)
(313) 478-8170

BRANCH CAMPUS
21700 Greenfield, Suite 272. Oak Park 48237. *Prof. Accred.:* Medical Assisting. Dir. Kathleen Case.
(313) 967-3100

THE ROSS MEDICAL EDUCATION CENTER
26417 Hoover Rd., Warren 48089. Private. 1981 (NATTS). Qtr. plan. Certificates, diplomas. *Prof. Accred.:* Medical Assisting. Pres. Janice Krupic.
Enroll.: 83 (*f.t.* 2 m., 81 w.)
(313) 758-7200

SACRED HEART SEMINARY
2701 Chicago Blvd., Detroit 48206. Private (Roman Catholic, Archdiocese of Detroit). 1960/1984 (NCA). Tri. plan. Degrees: B. Rector-Pres. V. Rev. Gerald Martin.
Enroll.: FTE 83
(313) 868-2700

SAGINAW VALLEY STATE COLLEGE
University Center 487byr10. Public (state) liberal arts. 1970/1980 (NCA). Tri. plan. Degrees: B,M. *Prof. Accred.:* Nursing (B), Social Work (B). Pres. Jack M. Ryder.
Enroll.: FTE 2,989
(517) 790-4042

ST. CLAIR COUNTY COMMUNITY COLLEGE
Port Huron 48060. Public (district) junior. 1930/1980 (NCA). Sem. plan. Degrees: A. Pres. Richard L. Norris.
Enroll.: FTE 2,202
(313) 984-3881

ST. JOHN'S PROVINCIAL SEMINARY
Plymouth 48170. Private (Roman Catholic) professional; graduate only. 1977/1982 (NCA). Sem. plan. Degrees: P,M. *Prof. Accred.:* Theology (1975/1982 ATS). Rector V. Rev. Robert H. Byrne.
Enroll.: 174
(313) 453-6200

SAINT MARY'S COLLEGE
Orchard Lake 48033. Private (Roman Catholic) liberal arts. 1976/1981 (NCA). Sem. plan. Degrees: B. Pres. Rev. Leonard F. Chrobot.
Enroll.: FTE 163
(313) 682-1885

SAWYER SCHOOL OF BUSINESS
26120 Van Dyke Ave., Center Line 48015. Private. 1973/1985 (AICS). Courses of varying lengths. Certificates, diplomas. Pres. Joseph T. Belliotti.
Enroll.: 612 (*f.t.* 12 m., 600 w.)
(313) 758-2300

SCHOOLCRAFT COLLEGE
Livonia 48152. Public (district) junior. 1968/1981 (NCA). Sem. plan. Degrees: A. *Prof.*

Accred.: Medical Laboratory Technology, Medical Record Technology. Pres. Richard W. McDowell.
Enroll.: FTE 4,277
(313) 591-6400

SIENA HEIGHTS COLLEGE
Adrian 49221. Private (Roman Catholic) liberal arts. 1940/1984 (NCA). Sem. plan. Degrees: B,M. Pres. Cathleen Real.
Enroll.: FTE 1,027
(517) 263-0731

SOUTHWESTERN MICHIGAN COLLEGE
Dowagiac 49047. Public (state) junior. 1971/1981 (NCA). 4-1-4 plan. Degrees: A. Pres. David C. Briegel.
Enroll.: 1,680
(616) 782-5911

SPECS HOWARD SCHOOL OF BROADCAST ARTS
16900 W. Eight Mi. Rd., One Northland Dr. Bldg., Southfield 48075. Private. 1978/1985 (NATTS). Monthly fixed class schedule. Diplomas. Exec. Dir. Specs Howard.
Enroll.: 157 (*f.t.* 119 m., 38 w.)
(313) 569-0101

SPRING ARBOR COLLEGE
Spring Arbor 49283. Private (Free Methodist) liberal arts. 1960/1985 (NCA). Sem. plan. Degrees: B. Pres. Kenneth H. Coffman.
Enroll.: FTE 963
(517) 750 -1200

SUOMI COLLEGE
Hancock 49930. Private (Lutheran in America) junior. 1969/1984 (NCA). Sem. plan. Degrees: A. Pres. Ralph J. Jalkanen.
Enroll.: FTE 663
(906) 482-5300

THOMAS M. COOLEY LAW SCHOOL
Lansing 48933. Private professional. 1975. Sem. plan. Degrees: P. *Prof. Accred.:* Law (ABA only). Dean Thomas E. Brennan.
Enroll.: 1,159 (*f.t.* 834 m., 281 w.)
(517) 371-5140

UNIVERSITY OF DETROIT
4001 W. McNichols Rd., Detroit 48221. Private (Roman Catholic). 1931/1985 (NCA). Tri. plan. Degrees: B,P,M,D. *Prof. Accred.:* Architecture (B), Business (B,M), Dental Hygiene, Dentistry, Engineering (chemical, civil, electrical, mechanical), Law, Nuclear Medicine Technology, Nurse Anesthesia Education, Social Work (B). Pres. Fr. Robert A. Mitchell, S.J.
Enroll.: FTE 4,117
(313) 927-1455

UNIVERSITY OF MICHIGAN
Central Office, Ann Arbor 48109. Public (state). Pres. Harold T. Shapiro.
(313) 764-1817

UNIVERSITY OF MICHIGAN—ANN ARBOR
Ann Arbor 48109. 1913/1980 (NCA). Tri. plan. Degrees: B,P,M,D. *Prof. Accred.:* Architecture (M), Art, Business (B,M), Dental Hygiene, Dentistry, Engineering (aerospace, chemical, civil, computer, electrical, engineering science, industrial and operations, materials, mechanical, metallurgical, naval architecture and marine, nuclear), Forestry, Health Services Administration, Landscape Architecture (M), Law, Librarianship, Medical Technology, Medicine, Music, Nurse Anesthesia Education, Nursing (B,M), Pharmacy, Physical Therapy, Psychology, Public Health, Social Work (M), Speech Pathology and Audiology, Teacher Education (*e,s,p*). Pres. Harold T. Shapiro.
Enroll.: FTE 32,172
(313) 764-6270

UNIVERSITY OF MICHIGAN—DEARBORN
Dearborn 48128. 1970/1984 (NCA). Tri. plan. Degrees: B. *Prof. Accred.:* Engineering (electrical, industrial and systems, mechanical), Teacher Education (*e,s*). Chanc. William A. Jenkins.
Enroll.: FTE 4,472
(313) 593-5500

UNIVERSITY OF MICHIGAN—FLINT
Flint 48503. 1970/1985 (NCA). Sem. plan. Degrees: B,M. *Prof. Accred.:* Business (B,M), Music, Nurse Anesthesia Education, Teacher Education (*e,s,p*). Chanc. Clinton B. Jones.
Enroll.: FTE 3,468
(313) 762-3322

WALSH COLLEGE OF ACCOUNTANCY AND BUSINESS ADMINISTRATION
Troy 48084. Private professional. 1975/1982 (NCA). Sem. plan. Degrees: B,M. Pres. Jeffery W. Barry.
Enroll.: FTE 917
(313) 689-8282

WASHTENAW COMMUNITY COLLEGE
Ann Arbor 48106. Public (district) junior. 1973/1981 (NCA). Sem. plan. Degrees: A.

Prof. Accred.: Dental Assisting, Radiography, Respiratory Therapy. Pres. Gunder A. Myran.
Enroll.: FTE 3,806
(313) 973-3300

*WAYNE COUNTY COMMUNITY COLLEGE
801 W. Fort St., Detroit 48226. Public (district) junior. 1976/1985 (NCA). Sem. plan. Degrees: A. *Prof. Accred.:* Dental Assisting, Dental Hygiene. Pres. Ronald J. Temple.
Enroll.: FTE 3,031
(313) 832-5500

WAYNE STATE UNIVERSITY
Detroit 48202. Public. 1915/1976 (NCA). Qtr. plan. Degrees: B,P,M,D.
Prof. Accred.: Business (B,M), Dietetics, Engineering (chemical, civil, electrical, industrial, mechanical, metallurgical), Law, Librarianship, Medical Technology, Medicine, Music, Nurse Anesthesia Education, Nursing (B,M), Occupational Therapy, Pharmacy, Physical Therapy, Psychology, Radiation Therapy, Social Work (B,M), Speech Pathology and Audiology, Teacher Education (*e,s,p*). Pres. David Adamany.
Enroll.: FTE 18,637
(313) 577-2424

WELDOR TRAINING CENTER
520 W. Eight Mile Rd., Ferndale 48220. Private. 1985 (NATTS). Courses of varying lengths. Certificates. Dir. Dennis Gilbert.
(313) 399-3388

WELDTECH WELDING EDUCATION CENTER
20201 Hoover Rd., Detroit 48205. Private. 1982 (NATTS). Courses of varying lengths. Certificates. Dir. Glen Knight.
Enroll.: 132 (*f.t.* 100 m., 10 w.)
(313) 267-3385

WEST SHORE COMMUNITY COLLEGE
Scottville 49454. Public (district) junior. 1974/1979 (NCA). Qtr. plan. Degrees: A. Pres. William M. Anderson.
Enroll.: FTE 306
(616) 845-6211

WESTERN MICHIGAN UNIVERSITY
Kalamazoo 49008. Public (state). 1915/1981 (NCA). Tri. plan. Degrees: B,M,D. *Prof. Accred.:* Art, Assistant to the Primary Care Physician, Business (B,M), Engineering (computer systems, electrical, industrial, mechanical), Music, Occupational Therapy, Social Work (B,M), Speech Pathology and Audiology, Teacher Education (*e,s,p*). Pres. Diether H. Haenicke.
Enroll.: FTE 15,034
(616) 383-1600

WESTERN THEOLOGICAL SEMINARY
Holland 49423. Private (Reformed) professional; graduate only. Sem. plan. Degrees: P,M. *Prof. Accred.:* Theology (1940/1982, ATS). Pres. Marvin D. Hoff.
Enroll.: 180
(616) 392-8555

WILLIAM TYNDALE COLLEGE
35700 W. Twelve Mi. Rd., Farmington Hills 48018. Private (Interdenominational) liberal arts and professional. 1954/1984 (AABC). Sem. plan. Degrees: B. Pres. William A. Shoemaker.
Enroll.: 336
(313) 553-7200

*Accreditation on Probation

MINNESOTA

Academy of Accountancy
4820 Excelsior Blvd., Suite 123, Minneapolis 55416. Private. 1976/1979 (AICS). Qtr. plan. Certificates. Dir. Philip Couch.
Enroll.: 226 (*f.t.* 126 m., 100 w.)
(612) 922-8900

Alexandria Area Technical Institute
Alexandria 56308. Public (state) 2-year. 1980/1984 (NCA). Qtr. plan. Degrees: A, certificates. *Prof. Accred.:* Interior Design, Medical Laboratory Technology. Dir. Frank Starke.
Enroll.: FTE 1,600
(612) 762-0221

Art Instruction Schools
500 S. Fourth St., Minneapolis 55415. Private home study. 1956/1981 (NHSC). Pres. Paul R. Phillips.
(612) 339-8721

Augsburg College
731 21st Ave., S., Minneapolis 55454. Private (American Lutheran) liberal arts. 1954/1977 (NCA). 4-1-4 plan. Degrees: B,M. *Prof. Accred.:* Nursing (B), Social Work (B), Teacher Education (*e,s*). Pres. Charles S. Anderson.
Enroll.: FTE 1,465
(612) 330-1212

Bethany Lutheran College
Mankato 56001. Private (Lutheran) junior. 1974/1979 (NCA). Sem. plan. Degrees: A. Pres. Marvin G. Meyer.
Enroll.: FTE 268
(507) 625-2977

Bethel College
3900 Bethel Dr., St. Paul 55112. Private (Baptist General Conference) liberal arts. 1959/1980 (NCA) 4-1-4 plan. Degrees: A,B. *Prof. Accred.:* Nursing (B), Social Work (B), Teacher Education (*e,s*). Pres. George K. Brushaber.
Enroll.: FTE 1,721
(612) 638-6400

Bethel Theological Seminary
3949 Bethel Dr., St. Paul 55112. Private (Baptist General Conference); professional; graduate only. 1976/1981 (NCA). Qtr. plan. Degrees: P,M,D. *Prof. Accred.:* Theology (1966/1981, ATS). Theological accreditation includes San Diego, CA campus. Dean Millard J. Erickson.
Enroll.: 504
(612) 638-6180

Brooks School of Barbering and Hairstyling
262 University Ave., St. Paul 55103. Private. 1981 (NATTS). Courses of varying lengths. Certificates, diplomas. Owner Arthur Brooks.
Enroll.: 30
(612) 222-4915

Carleton College
Northfield 55057. Private liberal arts. 1913/1979 (NCA). 3-3 plan. Degrees: B. *Prof. Accred.:* Art, Teacher Education (*s*). Pres. David H. Porter.
Enroll.: FTE 1,864
(507) 663-4000

College of Saint Benedict
Saint Joseph 56374. Private (Roman Catholic) liberal arts for women. 1933/1979 (NCA). 4-1-4 plan. Degrees: B. *Prof. Accred.:* Nursing (B), Social Work (B), Teacher Education (*e,s*). Pres. Sister Colman O'Connell, O.S.B.
Enroll.: FTE 1,879
(612) 363-5505

College of St. Catherine
2004 Randolph St., St. Paul 55105. Private (Roman Catholic) liberal arts for women. 1916/1974 (NCA). 4-1-4 plan. Degrees: B. *Prof. Accred.:* Music, Nursing (B), Occupational Therapy, Social Work (B), Teacher Education (*e,s*). Pres. Anita Pampusch.
Enroll.: FTE 1,990
(612) 690-6525

College of St. Scholastica
Kenwood Ave., Duluth 55811. Private (Roman Catholic) liberal arts. 1931/1983 (NCA). Qtr. plan. Degrees: B,M. *Prof. Accred.:* Medical Record Administration, Medical Technology, Nursing (B), Physical Therapy, Social Work (B). Pres. Daniel H. Pilon.
Enroll.: FTE 1,236
(218) 723-6033

College of Saint Teresa
Winona 55987. Private (Roman Catholic) liberal arts primarily for women. 1917/1983 (NCA). Qtr. plan. Degrees: B. *Prof. Accred.:* Music, Nursing (B), Social Work (B), Teacher Education (*e,s*). Pres. Sister Michaea Byron, O.S.F.

Enroll.: FTE 411
(507) 454-2930

College of St. Thomas
2115 Summit Ave., St. Paul 55105. Private (Roman Catholic) liberal arts for men, graduate school coeducational. 1916/1984 (NCA). Master's program in curriculum and instruction in CA accredited 1983 (WASC-Sr.). 4-1-4 plan. Degrees: B,M. *Prof. Accred.:* Music, Nurse Anesthesia Education, Social Work (B), Teacher Education (*s,p*). Pres. Msgr. Terrence J. Murphy.
Enroll.: FTE 5,143
(612) 647-5212

Concordia College
Moorhead 56560. Private (American Lutheran) liberal arts. 1927/1984 (NCA). Tri. plan. Degrees: B. *Prof. Accred.:* Music, Teacher Education (*e,s*). Pres . Paul J. Dovre.
Enroll.: FTE 2,481
(218) 299-3000

Concordia College
Hamline and Marshall Ave., St. Paul 55104. Private (Lutheran-Missouri Synod) liberal arts and teachers. 1959/1978 (NCA). Qtr. plan. Degrees: A,B. *Prof. Accred.:* Teacher Education (*e*). Pres. Alan Harre.
Enroll.: FTE 717
(612) 641-8211

Control Data Institute
1001 Washington Ave., N., Minneapolis 55401. Private. 1968/1978 (NATTS). Courses of varying lengths. Certificates. Dir. Gary Bettcher.
Enroll.: 417 (*f.t.* 278 m., 139 w.)
(612) 339-8282

Branch
245 E. Sixth St., St. Paul 55101.
(612) 292-2699

Crosier Seminary Junior College
Onamia 56359. Private (Roman Catholic) liberal arts. 1978 (NCA). Sem. plan. Degrees: A. Rector Rev. Eugene D. Plaisted.
Enroll.: FTE 14
(612) 532-3103

Dakota County Area Vocational Technical Institute
County Rd. 42, Rosemount 55068. Public (district) 2-year. 1981 (NCA). Qtr. plan. Degrees: A, diplomas. *Prof. Accred.:* Interior Design, Practical Nursing. Head of Program Elaine Meisch.
Enroll.: 3,266 (*f.t.* 993 m., 635 w.)

Dr. Martin Luther College
New Ulm 56073. Private (Evangelical Lutheran Synod). 1980/1985 (NCA). Sem. plan. Degrees: B. Pres. Rev. Lloyd O. Huebner.
Enroll.: FTE 755
181 (*f.t.* 446 m., (507) 354-8221

Duluth Business University
418 W. Superior St., Duluth 55802. Private. 1970/1981 (AICS). Qtr. plan. Diplomas. Pres. James R. Gessner.
Enroll.: 407 (*f.t.* 95 m., 312 w.)
(218) 722-3361

Dunwoody Industrial Institute
818 Wayzata Blvd., Minneapolis 55403. Private. 1972/1978 (NATTS). Courses of varying lengths. Diplomas. Pres. Warren Phillips.
Enroll.: 1,165 (*f.t.* 1,086 m., 79 w.)
(612) 374-5800

Globe College of Business
236 E. Fifth St., St. Paul 55101. Private. 1953/1984 (AICS). Qtr. plan. Diplomas. Pres. Helmer L. Myhre.
Enroll.: 531 (*f.t.* 163 m., 368 w.)
(612) 224-4378

Gustavus Adolphus College
St. Peter 56082. Private (Lutheran in America) liberal arts. 1915/1973 (NCA). 4-1-4 plan. Degrees: B. *Prof. Accred.:* Music, Nursing (B), Teacher Education (*e,s*). Pres. John S. Kendall.
Enroll.: FTE 2,174
(507) 931-8000

Hamline University
1536 Hewitt Ave., St. Paul 55104. Private (United Methodist) liberal arts college. 1914/1978 (NCA). 4-1-4 plan. Degrees: B,P,M. *Prof. Accred.:* Law, Music, Teacher Education (*e,s*). Pres. Charles J. Graham.
Enroll.: FTE 1,736
(612) 641-2202

Lakeland Medical-Dental Academy
1402 W. Lake St., Minneapolis 55408. Private. 1968/1978 (NATTS). Qtr. plan. Diplomas. *Prof. Accred.:* Dental Assisting, Medical Assisting, Medical Laboratory Technology. Dir. Joan Moffatt.
Enroll.: 110 (*f.t.* 5 m., 99 w.)
(612) 827-5656

Lowthian College
84 S. Tenth St., Minneapolis 55403. Private business. 1971/1983 (AICS). Courses of vary-

ing lengths. Certificates. Pres. Petrena Lowthian.
Enroll.: 267 (*f.t.* 0 m., 267 w.)
(612) 332-3361

LUTHER NORTHWESTERN THEOLOGICAL SEMINARY
2481 Como Ave., W., St. Paul 55108. Private (American Lutheran Church, Lutheran Church in America) professional; graduate only. 1979/1984 (NCA). Sem. plan. Degrees: P,M,D. *Prof. Accred.:* Theology (1944/1984, ATS). Pres. Lloyd Svendsbye.
Enroll.: FTE 621
(612) 641-3211

MACALESTER COLLEGE
St. Paul 55105. Private (United Presbyterian) liberal arts. 1913/1976 (NCA). 4-1-4 plan. Degrees: B. *Prof. Accred.:* Music, Teacher Education (*e,s*). Pres. Robert M. Gavin, Jr.
Enroll.: FTE 1,613
(612) 696-6000

MAYO FOUNDATION
200 First St., S.W., Rochester 55905. Private professional; affiliated academically with the University of Minnesota. 1984 (NCA). Sem. plan. Degrees: B,P,M,D. *Prof. Accred.:* Cytotechnology, Medicine, Nuclear Medicine Technology, Nurse Anesthesia Education, Physical Therapy, Radiation Therapy Technology, Radiography. CEO W. Eugene Mayberry.
Enroll.: FTE 1,299
(507) 284-3671

THE MCCONNELL SCHOOL
831 Second Ave., S., Minneapolis 55402. Private. 1967/1984 (NATTS). Courses of varying lengths. Diplomas. Pres. William McKay.
Enroll.: 266 (*f.t.* 14 m., 252 w.)
(612) 332-4238

MEDICAL INSTITUTE OF MINNESOTA
2309 Nicollet Ave., Minneapolis 55404. Private. 1985 (ABHES); 1985 (NATTS). Courses of varying lengths. Diplomas. *Prof. Accred.:* Medical Assisting, Medical Laboratory Technology. Pres. James D. Daras.
(612) 871-8481

MINNEAPOLIS BARBER SCHOOL
819 Hennepin Ave., S., Minneapolis 55403. Private. 1982 (NATTS). Courses of varying lengths. Certificates. Pres. Joseph Francis.
(612) 333-6010

MINNEAPOLIS BUSINESS COLLEGE
1711 W. County Rd. B, Roseville 55113. Private. 1962/1984 (AICS). Courses of varying lengths. Diplomas. Pres. Jim C. Zillman.
Enroll.: 294 (*f.t.* 31 m., 263 w.)
(612) 636-7406

MINNEAPOLIS COLLEGE OF ART AND DESIGN
133 E. 25th St., Minneapolis 55404. Private professional. 1960/1984 (NCA). Sem. plan. Degrees: B. *Prof. Accred.:* Art. Pres. G. Richard Slade.
Enroll.: FTE 515
(612) 870-3161

MINNEAPOLIS DRAFTING SCHOOL
3407 Chicago Ave., Minneapolis 55407. Private. 1972/1978 (NATTS). Qtr. plan. Certificates, diplomas. Dir. Robert X. Casserly.
Enroll.: 130 (*f.t.* 72 m., 22 w.)
(612) 824-8321

MINNESOTA BIBLE COLLEGE
920 Mayowood Rd., S.W., Rochester 55901. Private (Churches of Christ) professional. 1948/1983 (AABC). Qtr. plan. Degrees: A,B. Pres. Donald Lloyd.
Enroll.: 84
(507) 288-4563

MINNESOTA STATE BOARD FOR COMMUNITY COLLEGES
Central office. 301 Capitol Square, 550 Cedar St., St. Paul 55101. Public (state). Chanc. Gerald Christenson.
(612) 296-3990

ANOKA-RAMSEY COMMUNITY COLLEGE COON RAPIDS CAMPUS
11200 Mississippi Blvd., Coon Rapids 55433. 1975/1980 (NCA). Qtr. plan. Degrees: A. *Prof. Accred.:* Engineering Technology (electronic), Medical Assisting, Medical Record Technology, Nursing (A), Respiratory Therapy. Pres. Neil Christenson.
Enroll.: FTE 2,562
(612) 427-2600

CAMBRIDGE CENTER
West Highway 95, Cambridge 55008.
(612) 689-1536

ARROWHEAD COMMUNITY COLLEGE
1515 E. 25th St., Hibbing 55746. 1982/1984 (NCA). Pres. Philip Anderson.
Enroll.: 3,126
(218) 741-9200

HIBBING CAMPUS
Hibbing 55746. 1922/1980 (NCA). Qtr. plan. Degrees: A. Prov. Orville Olson.

Enroll.: FTE 2,469
(218) 262-6700

Itasca Campus
Grand Rapids 55744. 1975/1980 (NCA). Qtr. plan. Degrees: A. Prov. Lawrence Dukes.
Enroll.: FTE 2,469
(218) 327-1760

Mesabi Campus
Virginia 55792. 1925/1971 (NCA). Qtr. plan. Degrees: A. Prov. Richard N. Kohlhase.
Enroll.: FTE 2,469
(218) 749-7700

Rainy River Campus
International Falls 55649. 1976/1981 (NCA). Qtr. plan. Degrees: A. Prov. Raymond D. Berg.
Enroll.: FTE 2,469
(218) 285-7722

Vermillion Campus
Ely 55731. 1966/1981 (NCA). Qtr. plan. Degrees: A. Prov. Jon Harris.
Enroll.: FTE 2,469
(218) 365-3256

Austin Community College
Austin 55912. 1971/1985 (NCA). Qtr. plan. Degrees: A. *Prof.Accred.:* Nursing (A). Pres. James D. Flannery.
Enroll.: FTE 592
(507) 433-0508

Clearwater Community College
1414 College Way, Fergus Falls 56537. Pres. T. Alex Easton.
(218) 739-7500

Brainard Campus
Brainard 56401. 1977/1980 (NCA). Qtr. plan. Degrees: A. Prov. Sally Ihne.
Enroll.: FTE 519
(218) 828-2525

Fergus Falls Campus
Fergus Falls 56537. 1972/1976 (NCA). Qtr. plan. Degrees: A. *Prof.Accred.:* Histologic Technology, Medical Laboratory Technology. Prov. Daniel F. True.
Enroll.: FTE 567
(218) 739-7500

Northland Campus
Thief River Falls 56701. 1976/1981 (NCA). Qtr. plan. Degrees: A. Acting Prov. Allen Nichols.
Enroll.: FTE 505
(218) 749-7700

Inver Hills Community College
Inver Grove Heights 55075. 1976/1981 (NCA). Qtr. plan. Degrees: A. *Prof. Accred.:* Nursing (A), Radiography. Pres. Patrick Roche.
Enroll.: FTE 1,960
(612) 455-9621

Lakewood Community College
White Bear Lake 55110. 1974/1986 (NCA). Qtr. plan. Degrees: A. Pres. Jerry Owens.
Enroll.: FTE 2,320
(612) 779-3200

Minneapolis Community College
1501 Hennepin Ave., Minneapolis 55403. 1977/1986 (NCA). Qtr. plan. Degrees: A. *Prof. Accred.:* Nursing (A). Pres. Earl W. Bowman.
Enroll.: FTE 1,860
(612) 341-7000

Normandale Community College
Bloomington 55431. 1973/1985 (NCA). Qtr. plan. Degrees: A. *Prof. Accred.:* Dental Assisting, Dental Hygiene, Medical Assistant, Nursing (A). Pres. Dale A. Lorenz.
Enroll.: FTE 4,127
(612) 830-9300

North Hennepin Community College
7411 85th Ave. N., Brooklyn Park 55445. 1972/1986 (NCA). Qtr. plan. Degrees: A.*Prof. Accred.:* Nursing (A), Perfusion. Pres. John F. Helling.
Enroll.: FTE 2,670
(612) 425-4541

Rochester Community College
Rochester 55901. 1923/1981 (NCA). Qtr. plan. Degrees: A.*Prof. Accred.:* Engineering Technology (civil, electronics, mechanical), Medical Assisting, Nursing (A), Respiratory Therapy. Pres. Geraldine A.Evans.
Enroll.: FTE 2,175
(507) 285-7210

Willmar Community College
Willmar 56201. 1972/1985 (NCA). Qtr. plan. Degrees: A. Pres. Harold G. Conradi.
Enroll.: FTE 832
(612) 231-5102

Worthington Community College
Worthington 56187. 1973/1983 (NCA). Qtr. plan. Degrees: A. Pres. Joanne L. Pertz.
Enroll.: FTE 532
(507) 372-2107

MINNESOTA INSTITUTE OF MEDICAL AND DENTAL CAREERS
2915 Wayzata Blvd., Minneapolis 55405. Private. 1973/1980 (NATTS). Courses of varying lengths. Diplomas. *Prof. Accred.:* Dental Assisting. Dir. Linda Smaagaard.
Enroll.: f.t. 90 w.
(612) 374-2742

MINNESOTA SCHOOL OF BUSINESS
11 S. Fifth St., Minneapolis 55402. Private. 1953/1985 (AICS). Qtr. plan. Diplomas. Dir. Alan S. Crews.
Enroll.: 1,787 (*f.t.* 983 m., 804 w.)
(612) 338-6721

MINNESOTA STATE UNIVERSITY SYSTEM
Central office. St. Paul 55101. Public (state). Acting Chanc. Brendan J. McDonald.
(612) 296-2844

BEMIDJI STATE UNIVERSITY
Bemidji 56601. Public liberal arts and teachers. 1943/1984 (NCA). Qtr. plan. Degrees: A,B,M. *Prof. Accred.:* Social Work (B), Teacher Education (*e,s,p*). Pres. Lowell Gillett.
Enroll.: FTE 3,822
(218) 755-2800

MANKATO STATE UNIVERSITY
Mankato 56001. Public liberal arts and professional. 1916/1976 (NCA). Qtr. plan. Degrees: A,B,M. *Prof. Accred.:* Art, Dental Assisting, Dental Hygiene, Engineering Technology (electronics), Music, Nursing, Rehabilitation Counseling, Social Work (B), Teacher Education (*e,s,p*). Pres. Margaret R. Preska.
Enroll.: FTE 11,784
(507) 389-1111

METROPOLITAN STATE UNIVERSITY
St. Paul 55101. Public liberal arts. 1975/1985 (NCA). Qtr. plan. Degrees: B. Pres. Reatha Clark King.
Enroll.: FTE 1,326
(612) 296-4445

MOORHEAD STATE UNIVERSITY
1104 7th Ave. S., Moorhead 56560. Public liberal arts and teachers. 1916/1977 (NCA). Qtr. plan. Degrees: A,B,M. *Prof. Accred.:* Art, Music, Nursing (B), Social Work (B), Teacher Education (*e,s,p*). Pres. Roland Dille.
Enroll.: FTE 6,595
(218) 236-2243

ST. CLOUD STATE UNIVERSITY
St. Cloud 56301. Public liberal arts and professional. 1915/1977 (NCA). Qtr. plan. Degrees: A,B,M. *Prof. Accred.:* Art, Business (B,M), Music, Rehabilitation Counseling, Social Work (B), Teacher Education (*e,s,p*). Pres. ———.
Enroll.: FTE 10,806
(612) 255-2122

SOUTHWEST STATE UNIVERSITY
Marshall 56258. Public liberal arts. 1972/1983 (NCA). Qtr. plan. Degrees: B. Pres. Robert L. Carothers.
Enroll.: FTE 1,943
(507) 537-6272

WINONA STATE UNIVERSITY
Winona 55987. Public liberal arts and teachers. 1913/1986 (NCA). Qtr. plan. Degrees: A,B,M. *Prof. Accred.:* Music, Nursing (B), Teacher Education (*e,s,p*). Pres. Thomas F. Stark.
Enroll.: FTE 4,591
(507) 457-2017

MOLER BARBER SCHOOL OF HAIRSTYLING
1411 Nicollet Ave., Minneapolis 55403. Private. 1983 (NATTS). 37-week program. Certificates. Owner Don Mason.
Enroll.: 25
(612) 871-3754

NATIONAL EDUCATION CENTER/BROWN INSTITUTE CAMPUS
3123 E. Lake St., Minneapolis 55406. Private. 1967/1983 (NATTS). Courses of varying lengths. Degrees: A, certificates, diplomas. Dir. William Johnson.
Enroll.: 1,390 (*f.t.* 840 m., 305 w.)
(612) 721-2481

NORTH CENTRAL BIBLE COLLEGE
910 Elliot Ave., S., Minneapolis 55404. Private (Assembly of God) professional. 1964/1983 (AABC); 1986 (NCA). Sem. plan. Degrees: A,B. Pres. Don Argue.
Enroll.: 1,096
(612) 332-3491

NORTHERN TECHNICAL SCHOOL OF BUSINESS
2201 Blaisdell Ave., S., Minneapolis 55404. Private. 1973/1980 (AICS). Qtr. plan. Certificates. Dir. Roger A. Johnson.
Enroll.: 682 (*f.t.* 75 m., 607 w.)
(612) 874-6414

Northwest Technical Institute
11995 Singletree La., Eden Prairie 55344. Private. 1972/1978 (NATTS). Sem. plan. Degrees: A. Pres. Norris Nelson.
Enroll.: 49 (*f.t.* 38 m., 11 w.)
(612) 944-0080

Northwestern College
Roseville 55113. Private (church supported) liberal arts. 1978/1983 (NCA). Qtr. plan. Degrees: B. Pres. Donald O. Ericksen.
Enroll.: FTE 948
(612) 636-4840

*Northwestern College of Chiropractic
2501 W. 84th St., Bloomington 55431. Private professional. 1971/1979. Sem. plan. Degrees: P. *Prof. Accred.:* Chiropractic Education. Pres. Donald M. Cassata.
Enroll.: FTE 505
(612) 690-1735

Northwestern Electronics Institute
825 41st Ave., N.E., Columbia Heights 55421. Private. 1968/1978 (NATTS). Qtr. plan. Degrees: A, certificate, diploma. Pres. David L. Arneson.
Enroll.: 1,252 (*f.t.* 880 m., 70 w.)
(612) 781-4881

Rasmussen Business College
15 W. Fifth St., St. Paul 55102. Private. 1953/1978 (AICS). Courses of varying lengths. Certificates, diplomas. Dir. Kristi Waite.
Enroll.: 553 (*f.t.* 83 m., 470 w.)
(612) 222-4474

Branch Campus
Good Counsel Dr., Mankato 56001. Loretta Hazlett.
(507) 625-6556

Rochester Area Vocational-Technical Institute
332 16th St., S.E., Rochester 55904. Public practical nursing program. 1978. 11-month program. Diplomas. *Prof. Accred.:* Practical Nursing. Dir. Carol Backstrom.
(507) 285-8757

St. Cloud Area Vocational-Technical Institute
St. Cloud 56301. Public 2-year. 1985 (NCA). Qtr. plan. Degrees: A. *Prof. Accred.:* Practical Nursing. Dir. Don Hamerlinck.
Enroll.: FTE 1,606
(612) 252-0101

St. Cloud Business College
245 N. 37th Ave., St. Cloud 56301. Private. 1969/1981 (AICS). Qtr. plan. Diplomas. Pres. Kathleen M. Szczech.
Enroll.: 637 (*f.t.* 129 m., 508 w.)
(612) 251-5600

Saint John's University
Collegeville 56321. Private (Roman Catholic) liberal arts college and seminary for men. 1950/1979 (NCA). 4-1-4 plan. Degrees: B, P, M. *Prof. Accred.:* Social Work (B), Theology (1969/1979, ATS). Pres. Rev. Hilary D. Thimmesh, O.S.B.
Enroll.: FTE 1,886
(612) 363-2011

Saint Mary's College
Winona 55987. Private (Roman Catholic) liberal arts. 1934/1977 (NCA). Sem. plan. Degrees: B, M. *Prof. Accred.:* Nuclear Medicine Technology, Nurse Anesthesia Education. Pres. Brother Louis DeThomasis, F.S.C.
Enroll.: FTE 1,534
(507) 452-4430

St. Mary's Junior College
2600 S. 6th St., Minneapolis 55454. Private (Roman Catholic). 1971/1981 (NCA). Qtr. plan. Degrees: A. *Prof. Accred.:* Medical Laboratory Technology (A), Medical Record Technology, Nursing (A), Respiratory Therapy. Pres. Sister Anne Joachim Moore, C.S.J.
Enroll.: FTE 602
(612) 332-5521

St. Olaf College
Northfield 55057. Private (American Lutheran) liberal arts. 1915/1983 (NCA). 4-1-4 plan. Degrees: B. *Prof. Accred.:* Art, Music, Nursing (B), Teacher Education (*s*). Pres. Melvin D. George.
Enroll.: FTE 3,056
(507) 663-3000

St. Paul Barber School
211 W. Seventh St., St. Paul 55102. Private. 1982 (NATTS). Qtr. plan. Certificates. Pres. Jeff A. McWilliams.
Enroll.: 15 (*f.t.* 7 m., 8 w.)
(612) 222-1189

St. Paul Bible College
Bible College 55375. Private (Christian and Missionary Alliance) liberal arts and professional. 1950/1981 (AABC); 1980/1985 (NCA).

*Candidate for Accreditation by Regional Accrediting Association

Sem. plan. Degrees: A,B. Pres. L. John Eagen.
Enroll.: FTE 605
(612) 446-1411

SAINT PAUL SEMINARY
2260 Summit Ave., St. Paul 55105. Private (Roman Catholic); graduate and professional only. 1946/1985 (NCA). 4-1-4 plan. Degrees: P,M. *Prof. Accred.:* Theology (1974/1984, ATS). Rector-Pres. Charles L. Froehle.
Enroll.: FTE 75
(612) 698-0323

ST. PAUL TECHNICAL-VOCATIONAL INSTITUTE
235 Marshall Ave., St. Paul 55102. Public (local). 1983/1986 (NCA). Qtr. plan. Degrees: A, certificates, diplomas. Dir. Harlan H. Sheely.
Enroll.: FTE 2,400
(612) 221-1364

THE SCHOOL OF COMMUNICATION ARTS, INC.
2526 27th Ave., S., Minneapolis 55406. Private. 1978/1980 (NATTS). Sem. plan. Certificates. Dir. Roger Klietz.
Enroll.: 80 (*f.t.* 48 m., 32 w.)
(612) 721-5357

SCHOOL OF THE ASSOCIATED ARTS
344 Summit, St. Paul 55102. Private. 1978 (NATTS). Sem. plan. Degrees: B, certificates. Dir. Virginia Rahja.
Enroll.: 100 (*f.t.* 45 m., 55 w.)
(612) 224-3416 and 1-(800) 328-5893

UNITED THEOLOGICAL SEMINARY OF THE TWIN CITIES
New Brighton 55112. Private (United Church of Christ) professional; graduate only. 1977/1982 (NCA). Qtr. plan. Degrees: P,M,D. *Prof. Accred.:* Theology (1966/1982, ATS). Pres. Howard M. Mills.
Enroll.: FTE 126
(612) 633-4311

UNIVERSITY OF MINNESOTA
Central office. Minneapolis 55455. Public (state). Pres. Kenneth H. Keller.
(612) 373-2851

UNIVERSITY OF MINNESOTA—MINNEAPOLIS-ST. PAUL
Minneapolis 55455. Public (state). 1913/1976 (NCA). Qtr. plan. Degrees: A,B,P,M,D. *Prof. Accred.:* Architecture (B,M) Basic Medical Sciences, Business (B,M), Dental Hygiene, Dentistry, Dietetics, Engineering (aerospace engineering and mechanics, agricultural, chemical, civil, electrical, geo-engineering, materials science and engineering, mechanical, mineral), Forestry, Health Services Administration, Interior Design, Journalism, Landscape Architecture (B), Law, Librarianship, Medical Technology, Medicine, Music, Nurse Anesthesia Education, Nursing (B,M), Occupational Therapy, Pharmacy, Physical Therapy, Psychology, Public Health, Radiography, Radiation Therapy Technology, Social Work, Speech Pathology and Audiology, Teacher Education (*e,s,p*), Veterinary Medicine. Pres. Kenneth H. Keller.
Enroll.: FTE 42,568
(612) 373-2025

UNIVERSITY OF MINNESOTA—DULUTH
515 Darland, Administration Building, Duluth 55812. 1968/1978 (NCA). Degrees: A,B,M. *Prof. Accred.:* Basic Medical Sciences, Dental Hygiene, Music, Social Work (M), Speech Pathology, Teacher Education (*e,s,p*). Prov. Robert L. Heller.
Enroll.: FTE 6,610
(218) 726-8000

UNIVERSITY OF MINNESOTA—MORRIS
Morris 56267. 1970/1980 (NCA). Degrees: B. *Prof. Accred.:*Teacher Education (*e,s*). Prov. John Q. Imholte.
Enroll.: FTE 1,682
(612) 589-2211

UNIVERSITY OF MINNESOTA TECHNICAL COLLEGE–CROOKSTON
Crookston 56716. 1971/1984 (NCA). Degrees: A. Chanc. Donald G. Sargeant.
Enroll.: FTE 937
(218) 281-6510

UNIVERSITY OF MINNESOTA TECHNICALCOLLEGE—WASECA
Waseca 56093. 1975/1986 (NCA). Degrees: A. Chanc. Edward C. Frederick.
Enroll.: FTE 801
(507) 835-1000

WILLIAM MITCHELL COLLEGE OF LAW
St. Paul 55105. Private professional. 1938. Sem. plan. Degrees: P. *Prof. Accred.:* Law. Dean James Hogg.
Enroll.: 1,172 (*f.t.* 713 m., 459 w.)
(612) 227-9171

WILLMAR AREA VOCATIONAL-TECHNICAL INSTITUTE
Willmar 56201. Public (state). 1976/1985 (NCA). Qtr. plan. Certificates. *Prof. Accred.:* Medical Assisting, Practical Nursing. Dir. Ronald Erpelding.
Enroll.: FTE 1,418
(612) 235-5114

MISSISSIPPI

Alcorn State University
Lorman 39096. Public (state) teachers. 1948/1981 (SACS-Comm. on Coll.). Sem. plan. Degrees: A,B,M. *Prof. Accred.:* Music, Nursing (A,B), Teacher Education (*e,s*). Pres. Walter Washington.
Enroll.: 2,199
(601) 877-6100

Belhaven College
Jackson 39202. Private (Presbyterian, U.S.) liberal arts. 1946/1976 (SACS-Comm. on Coll.) Sem. plan. Degrees: B. *Prof. Accred.:*Music Pres. Newton Wilson.
Enroll.: 576
(601) 96859193

Blue Mountain College
P.O. Box 338, Blue Mountain 38610. Private (Southern Baptist) liberal arts primarily for women. 1927/1984 (SACS-Comm. on Coll.). Sem. plan. Degrees: B. Pres. E. Harold Fisher.
Enroll.: 304
(601) 685-4771

Clarke College
Newton 39345. Private (Southern Baptist) junior; a division of Mississippi College. 1952/1976 (SACS-Comm. on Coll.). Sem. plan. Degrees: A. Pres. Lewis Nobles.
Enroll.: 151
(601) 683-2061

Coahoma Junior College
Clarksdale 38614. Public (state). 1975/1980 (SACS-Comm. on Coll.). Sem. plan. Degrees: A. Pres. McKinley C. Martin.
Enroll.: 1,617
(601) 627-2571

Copiah-Lincoln Junior College
Wesson 39191. Public (district). 1936/1985 (SACS-Comm. on Coll.). Sem. plan. Degrees: A. *Prof. Accred.:* Medical Laboratory Technology, Radiography. Pres. Billy B. Thames.
Enroll.: 1,926
(601) 643-5101

Delta State University
Cleveland 38733. Public liberal arts and teachers. 1930/1984 (SACS-Comm. on Coll.). Sem. plan. Degrees:A,B,M,D. *Prof. Accred.:* Art, Home Economics, Music, Nursing (B), Social Work (B), Teacher Education (*e,s,p*). Pres. F. Kent Wyatt.
Enroll.: 2,892
(601) 846-3000

Draughon's Business College
502 North Street, P.O. Box 1192, Jackson 39205. Private. 1968/1980 (AICS). Courses of varying lengths. Diplomas. Pres. Milton White.
Enroll.: 321 (*f.t.* 19 m., 30 w.)
(601) 353-3826

East Central Junior College
Decatur 39327. Public (district). 1939/1981 (SACS-Comm. on Coll.) Sem. plan. Degrees: A. Pres. Eddie M. Smith.
Enroll.: 819
(601) 635-2111

East Mississippi Junior College
P.O. Box 158, Scooba 39358. Public (county). 1949/1975 (SACS-Comm. on Coll.). Sem. plan. Degrees: A. *Prof. Accred.:* Practical Nursing. Pres. Clois Cheatham.
Enroll.: 723
(601) 476-8442

Gulfport Job Corps Center
3300 20th St., Gulfport 39501. Public (state). 1985 (SACS-COEI). Courses of varying lengths. Certificates. Dir. E. M. Brennan.
Enroll.: FTE 350

Hinds Junior College
Raymond 39154. Public (county). 1928/1985 (SACS-Comm. on Coll.).Sem. plan. Degrees: A. *Prof. Accred.:* Dental Assisting, Medical Laboratory Technology (A), Medical Record Technology, Nursing (A), Respiratory Therapy, Respiratory Therapy Technology, Surgical Technology. Pres. V. Clyde Muse.
Enroll.: 7,645
(601) 857-5261

Holmes Junior College
Goodman 39079. Public (district). 1934/1974 (SACS-Comm. on Coll.). Sem. plan. Degrees: A. Pres. Murray R. Thorne.
Enroll.: 877
(601) 472-2312

Itawamba Junior College
Fulton 38843. Public (district). 1955/1977 (SACS-Comm. on Coll.). Sem. plan. Degrees: A. *Prof. Accred.:* Radiography, Res-

piratory Therapy, Respiratory Therapy Technology. Pres. W. O. Benjamin.
Enroll.: 4,004
(601) 862-3101

JACKSON BARBER AND HAIRSTYLING COLLEGE
852 W. Capitol St., Jackson 39203. 1980 (NATTS). Courses of varying lengths. Diplomas. Dir. Clinton Brock.
Enroll.: 17 (*f.t.* 7 m., 10 w.)
(601) 353-8122

JACKSON STATE UNIVERSITY
Jackson 39217. Public liberal arts and teachers. 1948/1981 (SACS-Comm. on Coll.). Sem. plan. Degrees: B,M,D. *Prof. Accred.:* Art, Journalism, Music, Rehabilitation Counseling, Social Work (B), Teacher Education (*e,s,p*). Pres. James A. Hefner.
Enroll.: 5,418
(601) 968-2121

JONES COUNTY JUNIOR COLLEGE
Ellisville 39437. Public (district). 1940/1976 (SACS-Comm. on Coll.). Qtr. plan. Degrees: A. Pres. T. Terrell Tisdale.
Enroll.: 2,785
(601) 477-9311

MARY HOLMES COLLEGE
P.O. Drawer 1257, West Point 39773. Private (United Presbyterian) 2-year. 1973/1978 (SACS-Comm. on Coll.). Sem. plan. Degrees: A. Interim Pres. Rev. Elbert L. Nelson, Jr.
Enroll.: 642
(601) 494-6820

MERIDIAN JUNIOR COLLEGE
5500 Hwy. 19 N., Meridian 39305. Public (city). 1942/1981 (SACS-Comm. on Coll.). Sem. plan. Degrees: A. *Prof. Accred.:* Dental Hygiene, Medical Laboratory Technology, Medical Record Technology, Nursing (A), Practical Nursing, Radiography, Respiratory Therapy. Pres. William F. Scaggs.
Enroll.: 3,750
(601) 483-8241

MILLSAPS COLLEGE
Jackson 39210. Private (United Methodist) liberal arts. 1912/1982 (SACS-Comm. on Coll.). Sem. plan. Degrees: B,M. Pres. George M. Harmon.
Enroll.: 1,133
(601) 354-5201

MISSISSIPPI COLLEGE
Clinton 39058. Private (Southern Baptist) liberal arts. 1922/1982 (SACS-Comm. on Coll.). Sem. plan. Degrees: B,P, M. *Prof. Accred.:* Law (ABA only), Music, Nursing (B), Teacher Education (*e,s,p*). Pres. Lewis Nobles.
Enroll.: 2,291
(601) 925-3000

MISSISSIPPI DELTA JUNIOR COLLEGE
Moorhead 38761. Public (county). 1930/1976 (SACS-Comm. on Coll.). Sem. plan. Degrees: A. *Prof. Accred.:* Medical Laboratory Technology (A), Nursing (A), Radiography. Pres. J. T. Hall.
Enroll.: 2,196
(601) 246-5631

MISSISSIPPI GULF COAST JUNIOR COLLEGE
Perkinston 39573. Public (district); campuses also at Gautier, Gulfport. 1929/1979 (SACS-Comm. on Coll.). Sem. plan. Degrees: A. *Prof. Accred.:* Medical Laboratory Technology (A), Nursing (A), Radiography, Respiratory Therapy, Respiratory Therapy Technology. Pres. Barry L. Mellinger.
Enroll.: 8,404
(601) 928-5211

MISSISSIPPI JOB CORPS CENTER
Harmony Rd., P.O. Box 817, Crystal Springs 39059. Public (state). 1984 (SACS-COEI). Courses of varying lengths. Certificates. Dir. Hugh Webb.
Enroll.: FTE 553

MISSISSIPPI STATE UNIVERSITY
Mississippi State 39762. Public. 1926/1983 (SACS-Comm. on Coll.). Sem. plan. Degrees: B,M,D. *Prof. Accred.:* Architecture (B), Art, Business (B,M), Engineering (aerospace, agricultural, biological, chemical, civil, electrical, industrial, mechanical, nuclear, petroleum), Forestry, Home Economics, Landscape Architecture (B), Rehabilitation Counseling, Teacher Education (*e,s,p*), Veterinary Medicine. Pres. Donald W. Zacharias.
Enroll.: 10,842
(601) 325-2323

MISSISSIPPI UNIVERSITY FOR WOMEN
Columbus 39701. Public liberal arts and teachers for women. 1921/1983 (SACS-Comm. on Coll.). Sem. plan. Degrees: A,B,M. *Prof. Accred.:* Home Economics, Music, Nursing (A,B), Speech Pathology and Audiology,

Teacher Education (*e,s*). Pres. James W. Strobel.
Enroll.: 1,802
(601) 329-4750

MISSISSIPPI VALLEY STATE UNIVERSITY
Itta Bena 38941. Public (state) teachers. 1968/1982 (SACS-Comm. on Coll.). Sem. plan. Degrees: B,M. *Prof. Accred.:* Art, Social Work (B), Teacher Education (*e,s,p*). Pres. Joe L. Boyer.
Enroll.: 2,280
(601) 254-9041

NAVAL CONSTRUCTION TRAINING CENTER
Building 343, Gulfport 39501. Public (federal) technical, 1975/1985 (SACS-COEI). Courses of varying lengths. Certificates. Commandant Cmdr. M. L. Frey.
Enroll.: FTE 667
(601) 865-2534

NAVAL TECHNICAL TRAINING CENTER
Naval Air Station, Meridian 39309. Public (federal) technical. 1976/1981 (SACS-COEI). Courses of varying lengths. Certificates. Commandant Cmdr. D. Miller.
Enroll.: FTE 1,498
(601) 679-2376

NORTHEAST MISSISSIPPI JUNIOR COLLEGE
Booneville 38829. Public (district). 1956/1980 (SACS-Comm. on Coll.). Sem. plan. Degrees: A. *Prof. Accred.:* Dental Hygiene, Medical Assisting, Medical Laboratory Technology (A), Nursing (A), Respiratory Therapy Technology. Pres. Harold T. White.
Enroll.: 2,212
(601) 728-7751

NORTHWEST MISSISSIPPI JUNIOR COLLEGE
Senatobia 38668. Public (district). 1953/1976 (SACS-Comm. on Coll.). Sem. plan. Degrees: A. *Prof. Accred.:* Engineering Technology (civil), Nursing (A). Pres. David M. Haraway.
Enroll.: 3,756
(601) 562-5262

PEARL RIVER JUNIOR COLLEGE
Poplarville 39470. Public (county) junior. 1929/1985 (SACS-Comm. on Coll.). Sem. plan. Degrees: A. *Prof. Accred.:* Respiratory Therapy Technology. Pres. Marvin R. White.
Enroll.: 1,731
(601) 795-4528

PHILLIPS JUNIOR COLLEGE OF THE MISSISSIPPI GULF COAST
942 E. Beach Blvd., Gulfport 39501. Private junior; recognized candidate for senior college accreditation. 1970/1982 (AICS). Qtr. plan. Degrees: A, certificates. Dir. Ann H. Gibson.
Enroll.: 1,626 (*f.t.* 748 m., 878 w.)
(601) 896-6465

PHILLIPS COLLEGE OF JACKSON
2680 Insurance Center Dr. at Lakeland, Jackson 39216. Private junior. 1975/1979 (AICS). Courses of varying lengths. Degrees: A, diplomas. Pres. Nan Thompson.
Enroll.: 1,385 (*f.t.* 542 m., 843 w.)
(601) 362-6341

REFORMED THEOLOGICAL SEMINARY
5422 Clinton Blvd., Jackson 39209. Private (Interdenominational) professional; graduate only. 1977/1982 (SACS-Comm. on Coll.). Sem. plan. Degrees: P,M.D. *Prof. Accred.:* Theology (1977/1983, ATS). Pres. Luder G. Whitlock, Jr.
Enroll.: 203
(601) 922-4988

RUST COLLEGE
Holly Springs 38635. Private (United Methodist) liberal arts. 1970/1984 (SACS-Comm. on Coll.). Mod. plan. Degrees:A,B. Pres. William A. McMillan.
Enroll.: 870
(601) 252-4661

SAMVERLY COLLEGE, BARBER/HAIRSTYLING
643 Washington Ave., Greenville 38701. Private. 1982 (NATTS). One-year course. Diplomas. Pres. Sam Purdie.
Enroll.: 20
(601) 378-2066

BRANCH CAMPUS
The Eastgate Shopping Mall, Rte. 8, Cleveland 38732.
(601) 846-0511

SOUTHWEST MISSISSIPPI JUNIOR COLLEGE
Summit 39666. Public (district). 1958/1980 (SACS-Comm. on Coll.). Sem. plan. Degrees: A. Pres. Horace Holmes.
Enroll.: 1,065
(601) 276-2000

TOUGALOO COLLEGE
Tougaloo 39174. Private liberal arts. 1953/1979 (SACS-Comm. on Coll.). Sem. plan. Degrees: B. Pres. J. Herman Blake.

Enroll.: 650
(601) 956-4941

UNIVERSITY OF MISSISSIPPI
University 38677. Public (state). 1895/1978 (SACS-Comm. on Coll.). Medical Center at Jackson. Sem. plan. (qtr. plan at Jackson). Degrees: B,P,M,D. *Prof. Accred.:* Accounting (Type A,C), Art, Business (B,M), Cytotechnology, Dental Hygiene, Dentistry, Engineering (chemical, civil, electrical, mechanical), Home Economics, Journalism, Law, Medical Record Administration, Medical Technology, Medicine, Music, Nuclear Medicine Technology, Nurse Anesthesia Education, Nursing (B,M), Pharmacy, Physical Therapy, Psychology, Radiography, Respiratory Therapy, Social Work (B), Speech Pathology and Audiology, Teacher Education (*e,s,p*). Chanc. R. Gerald Turner.
Enroll.: 8,691 Med. Ctr.: 1,782 (*f.t.* 977 m., 711 w.)
(601) 232-7211

UNIVERSITY OF SOUTHERN MISSISSIPPI
Hattiesburg 39406. Public (state). 1929/1985 (SACS-Comm. on Coll.). Qtr. plan. Degrees: B,M,D. *Prof. Accred.:* Accounting (Type A), Art, Business (B,M), Dietetics, Engineering Technology (architectural, construction, electronic, industrial, mechanical), Home Economics, Librarianship, Medical Technology, Music, Nursing (B,M), Psychology, Social Work (M), Speech Pathology and Audiology, Teacher Education (*e,s,p*). Pres. Aubrey K. Lucas.
Enroll.: 12,374
(601) 266-7011

WESLEY COLLEGE
P.O. Box 70, Florence 39073. Private (Congregational Methodist) professional. 1979 (AABC). Sem. plan. Degrees: A,B. Pres. Roman J. Miller.
Enroll.: 71
(601) 845-2265

WILLIAM CAREY COLLEGE
Hattiesburg 39401. Private (Southern Baptist) liberal arts. 1958/1978 (SACS-Comm. on Coll.). Sem. plan. Degrees: B,M. *Prof. Accred.:* Medical Technology, Music, Nursing (B). Pres. J. Ralph Noonkester.
Enroll.: 1,090
(601) 582-5051

WOOD JUNIOR COLLEGE
Mathiston 39752. Private (United Methodist). 1956/1979 (SACS-Comm. on Coll.). Sem. plan. Degrees: A. Pres. Felix Sutphin.
Enroll.: 306
(601) 263-8128

MISSOURI

AL-MED ACADEMY
10963 St. Charles Rock Rd., St. Louis 63074. Private. 1985 (ABHES). Courses of varying lengths. Diplomas. *Prof. Accred.:* Medical Assisting. Pres. C. Larkin Hicks.
(314) 739-4450

AQUINAS INSTITUTE
3642 Lindell Blvd., St. Louis 63108. Private (Roman Catholic) professional; graduate only. 1964/1982 (NCA). 4-1-4 plan. Degrees: B,P,M,D. *Prof. Accred.:* Theology (1968/1986, ATS). Pres. Rev. John F. Taylor, O.P.
Enroll.: FTE 51
(314) 658-3882

ASSEMBLIES OF GOD THEOLOGICAL SEMINARY
1445 Boonville Ave., Springfield 65802. Private (Assemblies of God) professional; graduate only. 1978 (NCA). 4-4-1-1 plan. Degrees: P,M. Exec. Vice Pres. James D. Brown.
Enroll.: FTE 276
(417) 862-3344

AVILA COLLEGE
11901 Wornall Rd., Kansas City 64145. Private (Roman Catholic) liberal arts. 1946/1978 (NCA). Sem. plan. Degrees: B,M. *Prof. Accred.:* Medical Technology, Nursing (B), Radiography, Social Work (B). Pres. Larry Kramer.
Enroll.: FTE 985
(816) 942-8400

BAPTIST BIBLE COLLEGE
628 E. Kearney, Springfield 65803. Private (Baptist)jprofessional. 1978 (AABC). Sem. plan. Degrees: A,B. Pres. A. V. Henderson.
Enroll.: 1,088
(417) 869-9811

BASIC INSTITUTE OF TECHNOLOGY
4455 Chippewa, St. Louis 63116. Private. 1974/1979 (NATTS). Qtr. plan. Degrees: A, diplomas. Dir. James A. Zoeller.
Enroll.: 227 (*f.t.* 218 m., 9 w.)
(314) 771-1200

BEREAN COLLEGE
1445 Boonville Ave., Sprigfield 65802. Private home study. 1985 (NHSC). Pres. J. Robert Ashcroft.
(417) 862-2781

BRYAN INSTITUTE
12184 Natural Bridge Rd., Bridgeton 63044. Private. 1980 (NATTS). Sem. plan. Diplomas. *Prof. Accred.:* Medical Assisting. Dir. Monika Wilson.
Enroll.: 97
(314) 291-0241

BRYAN INSTITUTE
103 E. Lockwood, Webster Groves 63119. Private. 1973/1978 (NATTS). Sem. plan. Diplomas. *Prof. Accred.:* Medical Assisting. Dir. Philip Kinen.
Enroll.: 178 (*f.t.* 8 m., 170 w.)
(314) 962-9111

CALVARY BIBLE COLLEGE
Kansas City 64147. Private (Independent) professional. 1961/1979 (AABC). Sem. plan. Degrees: A,B. Pres. Leslie Madison.
Enroll.: 322
(816) 322-0110

CARDINAL GLENNON COLLEGE
5200 Glennon Dr., St. Louis 63119. Private (Roman Catholic, Archdiocese of St. Louis) seminary. 1960/1982 (NCA). Sem. plan. Degrees: B. Pres. Patrick V. Harrity
Enroll.: FTE 75
(314) 644-0266

CENTRAL BIBLE COLLEGE
3000 N. Grant, Springfield 65803. Private (Assembly of God) professional. 1948/1985 (AABC). Sem. plan. Degrees: A,B. Pres. H. Maurice Lednicky.
Enroll.: 821
(417) 833-2551

CENTRAL CHRISTIAN COLLEGE OF THE BIBLE
1111 Urbandale Dr., E., Moberly 65270. Private (Christian Church) professional. 1982 (AABC). Sem. plan. Degrees: A,B. Pres. Lloyd M. Pelfrey.
Enroll.: 85
(816) 265-3900

CENTRAL METHODIST COLLEGE
Fayette 65248. Private (United Methodist) liberal arts. 1913/1981 (NCA). 4-1-4 plan. Degrees: B. *Prof. Accred.:* Medical Laboratory Technology (A), Music, Teacher Education (*e,s*). Pres. Joe A. Howell.
Enroll.: FTE 589
(816) 248-3391

Central Missouri State University
Warrensburg 64093. Public liberal arts and teachers. 1915/1984 (NCA). Qtr. plan. Degrees: A,B,M. *Prof. Accred.:* Music, Nursing (B), Speech Pathology and Audiology, Teacher Education (*e,s,p*). Pres. Ed. M. Elliott
Enroll.: FTE 8,226
(816) 429-4111

Cleveland Chiropractic College
6401 Rockhill Rd., Kansas City 64113. Private professional. 1984 (NCA). Tri. plan. Degrees: P. *Prof. Accred.:* Chiropractic Education. Pres. Carl Cleveland, III
Enroll.: FTE 419
(816) 333-8230

Columbia College
Tenth and Rogers, Columbia 65216. Private (Disciples of Christ). 1918/1983 (NCA). Sem. plan. Degrees: A,B. Pres. Donald B. Ruthenberg.
Enroll.: FTE 1,974
(314) 875-8700

Conception Seminary College
Conception 64433. Private (Roman Catholic, Order of St. Benedict). 1960/1984 (NCA). Sem. plan. Degrees: B. Pres.-Rector V. Rev. Isaac D. True, O.S.B.
Enroll.: FTE 93
(816) 944-2218

Concordia Seminary
St. Louis 63105. Private (Lutheran Church—Missouri Synod) professional; graduate only. 1978/1984 (NCA). Qtr. plan. Degrees: P,M,D. *Prof. Accred.:* Theology (1963/1983, ATS). Pres. Karl L. Barth.
Enroll.: FTE 530
(314) 721-5934

Control Data Institute
3694 W. Pine Blvd., Des Peres Hall, St. Louis 63108. Private. 1971/1982 (NATTS). Courses of varying lengths. Certificates. Dir. Christine Eldarrat.
Enroll.: 389 (*f.t.* 234 m., 155 w.)
(314) 534-8181

Cottey College
Nevada 64772. Private junior for women. 1918/1986 (NCA). Sem. plan. Degrees: A. *Prof. Accred.:* Music. Pres. Helen R. Washburn.
Enroll.: FTE 348
(417) 667-8181

Covenant Theological Seminary
St. Louis 63141. Private (Reformed Presbyterian Church) professional. 1973/1978 (NCA). Sem. plan. Degrees: M,D. *Prof. Accred.:* Theology
(1983, ATS). Pres. Paul D. Kooistra.
Enroll.: FTE 112
(314) 434-4044

Crowder College
Neosho 64850. Public (district) junior. 1977/1982 (NCA). Sem. plan. Degrees: A. Pres. Kent Farnsworth.
Enroll.: FTE 903
(417) 451-3226

Culver-Stockton College
Canton 63435. Private (Disciples of Christ) liberal arts. 1924/1981 (NCA). Sem. plan. Degrees: B. Pres. Robert Brown.
Enroll.: FTE 778
(314) 288-5221

Deaconess College of Nursing
6150 Oakland Ave., St. Louis 63136. Private professional. 1985 (NCA). Sem. plan. Degrees: B. Dean and CEO Patricia Afshar.
Enroll.: FTE 223
(314) 768-3040

DeVry Institute of Technology
11224 Holmes Rd., Kansas City 64131. Private. 1971/1984 (NATTS); 1982 (NCA). Tri. plan. Degrees: A,B, diplomas. *Prof. Accred.:* Engineering Technology (electronics). Pres. C. R. LeValley.
Enroll.: 2,141 (*f.t.* 1,622 m., 224 w.)
(816) 941-0430

Diamond Council of America
9140 Ward Pkwy., Kansas City 64114. Private home study. 1984 (NHSC). Exec. Dir. Jerry Fogel.
(816) 444-3500

Dickinson Junior College
3822 Summit, Kansas City 64111. Private. 1982 (AICS). Qtr. plan. Degrees: A, certificates, diplomas. Pres. James Miller, Jr.
Enroll.: 609 (*f.t.* 53 m., 556 w.)
(816) 931-7600

Branch Campus
5528 N.E. Antioch Rd., Kansas City 64119. Dir. Gail Luscombe.
(816) 452-4411

Branch Campus
Gateway Centre, Tower I, Suite 100, Kansas City, KS 66101. Dir. James Miller, Jr.
(913) 321-1900

BRANCH CAMPUS
2219 S. W. 74th, Suite 124, Oklahoma City, OK 73159. Dir. Pam. R. Brandeen.
(405) 681-2300

BRANCH CAMPUS
45-47 Garrett Rd., Upper Darby, PA 19082. Dir. Richard L. Wagner.
(215) 352-3000

BRANCH CAMPUS
485 Spencer La., San Antonio, TX 78201. Dir. Shirley Hecht.
(512) 732-3000

DRAUGHON BUSINESS COLLEGE
1258 E. Trafficway, Springfield 65802. Private. 1984 (AICS). Qtr. plan. Certificates, diplomas. Pres. James Leviner.
Enroll.: 727 (*f.t.* 220 m., 507 w.)
(417) 866-1926

BRANCH CAMPUS
P.O. Box 519, Joplin 64802. Dir. Wilson Wood.
(417) 624-3266

DRAUGHONS COLLEGE
3323 S. Kingshighway Blvd., St. Louis 63139. Private. 1972/1985 (AICS). Courses of varying lengths. Diplomas. Dean Daryl Veach.
Enroll.: 243 (*f.t.* 0 m., 243 w.)
(314) 832-5300

DRURY COLLEGE
Springfield 65802. Private (United Church of Christ) liberal arts. 1915/1986 (NCA). 4-1-4 plan. Degrees: B,M. *Prof. Accred.:* Teacher Education (*e,s*). Pres. John E. Moore, Jr.
Enroll.: FTE 1,719
(417) 865-8731

EAST CENTRAL JUNIOR COLLEGE
Union 63084. Public (district). 1976/1981 (NCA). Sem. plan. Degrees: A. *Prof. Accred.:* Dental Assisting. Pres. Donald D. Shook.
Enroll.: FTE 1,467
(314) 538-5193

EASTERN JACKSON COUNTY COLLEGE OF ALLIED HEALTH
808 S. 15th St., Blue Springs 64015. Private. 1984 (ABHES). Courses of varying lengths. Certificates. *Prof. Accred.:* Medical Assisting. Pres./Dir. Kathryn L. Harmon.
(816) 229-4720

EDEN THEOLOGICAL SEMINARY
St. Louis 63119. Private (United Church of Christ) professional; graduate only. 1973/1983 (NCA). 4-1-4 plan. Degrees: P,M,D. *Prof. Accred.:* Theology (1938/1978, ATS). Pres. ———.
Enroll.: FTE 123
(314) 961-3627

ELECTRONIC COMPUTER PROGRAMMING INSTITUTE
611 W. 39th St., Kansas City 64111. Private. 1971/1975 (NATTS). Courses of varying lengths. Certificates. Dir. Norman E. Capps.
Enroll.: 197 (*f.t.* 88 m., 47 w.)
(816) 561-7758

ELECTRONIC INSTITUTES
5605 Troost Ave., Kansas City 64110. Private. 1971/1977 (NATTS). Qtr. plan. Certificates. Dir. Larry Fajen.
Enroll.: 427 (*f.t.* 182 m., 32 w.)
(816) 361-5656

EVANGEL COLLEGE
Springfield 65802. Private (Assemblies of God) liberal arts. 1965/1978 (NCA). Sem. plan. Degrees: B. *Prof. Accred.:* Music, Teacher Education (*e,s*). Pres. Robert H. Spence.
Enroll.: FTE 1,569
(417) 865-2811

FARMLAND INDUSTRIES, INC.
Training Ctr., 5401 N. Oak, P.O. Box 7305, Dept. 23, Kansas City 64116. Private home study. 1980/1985 (NHSC). Manager Robert Schwindt.
(816) 459-6435

FONTBONNE COLLEGE
6800 Wydown Blvd., St. Louis 63105. Private (Roman Catholic) liberal arts for women. 1926/1985 (NCA). Sem. plan. Degrees: B,M. *Prof. Accred.:* Home Economics, Music, Teacher Education (*e*). Pres. Meneve Dunham.
Enroll.: FTE 684
(314) 862-3456

GENERAL EDUCATION AND TRAINING, INC.
12100 Grandview Rd., Grandview 64030. Private; combination home study/resident course. 1980 (NHSC). Pres. Richard G. Honan.
(816) 765-5400

GRADWOHL SCHOOL OF LABORATORY TECHNIQUE
3514 Lucas Ave., St. Louis 63103. Private. 1-year course. Diplomas. *Prof. Accred.:* Medical Laboratory Technology. Dir. Stanley Reitman.
Enroll.: 45 (*f.t.* 17 m., 28 w.)
(314) 533-9250

HAMILTON BUSINESS COLLEGE
3675 S. Noland Rd., Suite 300, Independence 64055. Private. 1985 (AICS). Courses of varying lengths. Diplomas. Dir. Mary Ann Moore.
(816) 833-4430

HANNIBAL-LAGRANGE COLLEGE
Hannibal 63401. Private (Southern Baptist) liberal arts. 1958/1985 (NCA). Sem. plan. Degrees: A,B. Pres. Larry L. Lewis.
Enroll.: FTE 478
(314) 221-3675

HARRIS-STOWE STATE COLLEGE
3026 Laclede, St. Louis 63103. Public (state) teachers. 1924/1984 (NCA). Sem. plan. Degrees: B. *Prof. Accred.:* Teacher Education (*e*). Pres. Henry Givens, Jr.
Enroll.: FTE 813
(314) 533-3366

HICKEY SCHOOL
6710 Clayton Rd., St. Louis 63117. Private business. 1968/1984 (AICS). Courses of varying lengths. Certificates. Pres. Edward Arrington.
Enroll.: 648 (*f.t.* 8 m., 640 w.)
(314) 644-2866

ITT TECHNICAL INSTITUTE
5303 E. 103rd St., Kansas City 64137. Private. 1977 (NATTS). Courses of varying lengths. Diplomas. Dir. Austin Morrill.
Enroll.: 214
(816) 765-0800

ITT TECHNICAL INSTITUTE
3750 Lindell Blvd., St. Louis 63108-3483. Private. 1968/1978 (NATTS). Courses of varying lengths. Degrees: A, diplomas. Dir. L. D. Cunningham.
Enroll.: 843
(314) 533-8700

INTERNATIONAL HAIR INSTITUTE—ST. LOUIS
415 S. Florissant Rd., Ferguson 63135. Private. 1985 (NATTS). Courses of varying lengths. Diplomas. Pres. Joseph A. Gentile.
(314) 524-3460

JAY TRUCK DRIVER TRAINING CENTER
5434 Natural Bridge Rd., St. Louis 63120. Private. 1982 (NATTS). Courses of varying lengths. Certificates. Pres. Steven H. Jay, Jr.
(314) 385-2600

EXTENSION
7600 Church Rd., Rte. 2, Box 199, Liberty 64068.
(816) 781-8600

EXTENSION
3500 E. Kearney, Springfield 65803.
(417) 831-3900

JEFFERSON COLLEGE
Hillsboro 63050. Public (district) junior. 1969/1979 (NCA). Sem. plan. Degrees: A. Pres. B. Ray Henry.
Enroll.: FTE 2,078
(314) 789-3951

KANSAS CITY ART INSTITUTE
4415 Warwick Blvd., Kansas City 64111. Private professional. 1964/1979 (NCA). Sem. plan. Degrees: B. *Prof. Accred.:* Art. Pres. George Parrino.
Enroll.: FTE 460
(816) 561-4852

KANSAS CITY COLLEGE OF MEDICAL AND DENTAL CAREERS
2928 Main St.-Penn Park Medical Ctr., Kansas City 64108. Private. 1977/1983 (NATTS). Qtr. plan. Diplomas. *Prof. Accred.:* Medical Assisting. Dir. Nancy Graham.
Enroll.: 170 (*f.t.* 15 m., 155 w.)
(816) 531-5223

KEMPER MILITARY SCHOOL AND COLLEGE
Boonville 65233. Private junior for men. 1927/1986 (NCA). Sem. plan. Degrees: A. Pres. Col. Roger D. Harms.
Enroll.: FTE 129
(816) 882-5623

KENRICK SEMINARY
St. Louis 63119. Private (Roman Catholic) professional; graduate only. 1973/1978 (NCA). Sem. plan. Degrees : P,M. *Prof. Accred.:* Theology (1973/1978, ATS). Pres. Rector Rev. Ronald Ransom, C.M.
Enroll.: FTE 77
(314) 961-4320

KIRKSVILLE COLLEGE OF OSTEOPATHIC MEDICINE
Kirksville 63501. Private professional. 1901/1975. Sem. plan. Degrees: P. *Prof. Accred.:* Osteopathy. Pres. Fred C. Tinning.

Enroll.: 544 (*f.t.* 451 m., 78 w.)
(816) 626-2121

LINCOLN UNIVERSITY
Jefferson City 65101. Public (state) liberal arts and professional. 1926/1977 (NCA). Sem. plan. Degrees: B,M. *Prof. Accred.:* Music. Pres. Thomas Miller Jenkins.
Enroll.: FTE 2,256
(314) 751-2325

LINDENWOOD COLLEGE
St. Charles 63301. Private (United Presbyterian) liberal arts. 1918/1984 (NCA). 4-1-4 plan. Degrees: B,M. *Prof. Accred.:* Teacher Education (*e,s*). Pres. James I. Spainhower.
Enroll.: FTE 1,263
(314) 723-7152

*LOGAN COLLEGE OF CHIROPRACTIC
P.O. Box 100, Chesterfield 63017. Private professional. 1978/1982. Sem. plan. Degrees: P. *Prof. Accred.:* Chiropractic Education. Pres. Beatrice B. Hagen.
Enroll.: FTE 686
(314) 227-2100

MARYVILLE COLLEGE
13550 Conway Rd., St. Louis 63141. Private liberal arts. 1941/1985 (NCA). 4-4-x plan. Degrees: A,B,M. *Prof. Accred.:* Interior Design, Nursing (A,B), Physical Therapy. Pres. Claudius Pritchard.
Enroll.: FTE 1,492
(314) 576-9330

MEDICAL PROFESSIONS INSTITUTE
9100 Lackland Rd., St. Louis 63114. Private. 1980 (ABHES). 36-week program. Diplomas. *Prof. Accred.:* Medical Assisting. Dir. Phyllis B. Ferris.
Enroll.: f.t. 10
(314) 429-3344

METRO BUSINESS COLLEGE OF CAPE GIRARDEAU
1452 N. Kingshighway, Cape Girardeau 63701. Private. 1979/1981 (AICS). Courses of varying lengths. Certificates. Pres. George R. Holske.
Enroll.: 270 (*f.t.* 15 m., 255 w.)
(314) 334-9181

BRANCH CAMPUS
314 Lafayette St., Jefferson City 65101. Dir. Patricia R. Singleton.
(314) 635-6600

*Candidate for Accreditation by Regional Accrediting Commission

BRANCH CAMPUS
Sixth and Adar, Rolla 65401. Dir. Dorothy Spadoni.
(314) 364-8464

BRANCH CAMPUS
4200 Lindell Blvd., St. Louis 63108. Dir. George R. Holske.
(314) 535-8900

THE METROPOLITAN COMMUNITY COLLEGES
Administrative center. 560 Westport Rd., Kansas City 64111. Public (district). 1918/1976 (NCA). Sem. plan. Degrees: A. Chanc. William J. Mann.
(816) 756-0220

LONGVIEW COMMUNITY COLLEGE
Lee's Summit 64063. 1972/1982 (NCA). *Prof. Accred:* Engineering Technology (electronic). Pres. Aldo Leker.
Enroll.: FTE 2,549
(816) 763-7777

MAPLE WOODS COMMUNITY COLLEGE
Kansas City 64156. 1972 (NCA). Pres. Stephen R. Brainard.
Enroll.: FTE 1,640
(816) 436-6500

PENN VALLEY COMMUNITY COLLEGE
Kansas City 64111. 1972/1976 (NCA) . *Prof. Accred.:* Dental Assisting, Medical Record Technology, Nursing (A), Radiography. Pres. Andrew V. Stevenson.
Enroll.: FTE 2,829
(816) 756-2800

PIONEER COMMUNITY COLLEGE
2700 E. 18th St., Kansas City 64111. 1980 (NCA). Pres. Zelema Harris.
Enroll.: FTE 300
(816) 753-4949

MIDWEST INSTITUTE OF MEDICAL ASSISTANTS
112 W. Jefferson, Suite 120, Kirkwood 63122. Private. 1977/1983 (NATTS). 6-month course. Diplomas. *Prof. Accred.:* Medical Assisting. Dir. Elizabeth Shreffler.
Enroll.: f.t. 45 w.
(314) 965-8363

MIDWESTERN BAPTIST THEOLOGICAL SEMINARY
Kansas City 64118. Private (Southern Baptist) professional; graduate only. 1971/1982 (NCA). Sem. plan. Degrees: P,M,D. *Prof. Accred.:* Theology (1964/1981, ATS). Pres. Milton U. Ferguson.

Enroll.: 593
(816) 453-4600

MINERAL AREA COLLEGE
Flat River 63601. Public (district) junior. 1971/1984 (NCA). Sem. plan. Degrees: A. *Prof. Accred.:* Dental Assisting. Pres. Dixie A. Kohn.
Enroll.: FTE 1,403
(314) 431-4593

MISSOURI BAPTIST COLLEGE
St. Louis 63141. Private (Southern Baptist) liberal arts. 1978/1985 (NCA). Sem. plan. Degrees: B. Pres. Patrick O. Copley.
Enroll.: FTE 415
(314) 434-1115

MISSOURI SCHOOL FOR DOCTORS' ASSISTANTS, INC.
10121 Manchester, St. Louis 63122. Private. 1970/1978 (NATTS). Courses of varying lengths. Certificates, diplomas. *Prof. Accred.:* Medical Assisting. Admin. Dir. Susan Day.
Enroll.: 132 (*f.t.* 1 m., 131 w.)
(314) 821-7700

MISSOURI SCHOOL OF BARBERING AND HAIRSTYLING—ST. LOUIS
91 Florissant Oaks Shopping Center, Florissant 63031. Private. 1980 (NATTS). Sem. plan. Diplomas. Pres. T. L. Millis.
Enroll.: 10 (*f.t.* 5 m., 5 w.)
(314) 839-0310

EXTENSION
3740 Noland Rd., Independence 64055. Dir. Michael Pardoe.
(816) 836-4118

EXTENSION
1215 Grand, Kansas City 64106. Dir. Edward J. Jones.
(816) 471-8639

MISSOURI SOUTHERN STATE COLLEGE
Joplin 64801. Public liberal arts and teachers. 1949/1981 (NCA). Sem. plan. Degrees: A,B. *Prof. Accred.:* Dental Assisting, Dental Hygiene, Nursing (A), Radiography. Pres. Julio S. Leon.
Enroll.: FTE 3,275
(417) 624-8181

MISSOURI TECHNICAL SCHOOL
9623 Saint Charles Rock Rd., Overland 63114. Private. 1985 (NATTS). Courses of varying lengths. Diplomas. Dir. James R. Long.
(314) 428-7700

MISSOURI VALLEY COLLEGE
Marshall 65340. Private (United Presbyterian) liberal arts. 1916/1983 (NCA). Sem. plan. Degrees: B. Pres. Earl J. Reeves.
Enroll.: FTE 545
(816) 886-6924

MISSOURI WESTERN STATE COLLEGE
St. Joseph 64507. Public (district). 1919/1980 (NCA). Sem. plan. Degrees: A,B. *Prof. Accred.:* Music, Nursing, (A), Social Work (B), Teacher Education (*e,s*). Pres. Janet Gorman Murphy.
Enroll.: FTE 3,135
(816) 271-4200

MOBERLY JUNIOR COLLEGE
Moberly 65270. Public (district) 2-year. 1980/1985 (NCA). Sem. plan. Degrees: A. Pres. Andrew Komar, Jr.
Enroll.: FTE 790
(816) 263-4110

NATIONAL EDUCATION CENTER, KANSAS CITY CAMPUS
1415 McGee, Kansas City 64106. Private junior business. 1964/1981 (AICS). Qtr. plan. Degrees: A, diplomas. Dir. Stephen M. Buchenot.
Enroll.: 1,031 (*f.t.* 216 m., 815 w.)
(816) 842-2374

NAZARENE THEOLOGICAL SEMINARY
Kansas City 64131. Private (Nazarene) professional; graduate only. Sem. plan. Degrees: P,M,D. *Prof. Accred.:* Theology (1970/1981, ATS). Pres. Terrell C. Sanders, Jr.
Enroll.: 457
(816) 333-6254

NORTHEAST MISSOURI STATE UNIVERSITY
Kirksville 63501. Public liberal arts and teachers. 1914/1985 (NCA). Sem. plan. Degrees: B,M. *Prof. Accred.:* Home Economics, Music, Nursing (B), Speech Pathology, Teacher Education (*e,s,p*). Pres. Charles J. McClain.
Enroll.: FTE 5,958
(816) 785-4000

NORTHWEST MISSOURI STATE UNIVERSITY
Maryville 64468. Public liberal arts and teachers. 1921/1978 (NCA). Sem. plan. Degrees: B,M. *Prof. Accred.:* Home Economics, Music, Teacher Education (*e,s*). Pres. Dean L. Hubbard.
Enroll.: FTE 4,428
(816) 785-1212

Park College
Parkville 64152. Private (Reorganized Church of Latter-Day Saints) liberal arts. 1913/1984 (NCA). 4-1-4 plan. Degrees: B,M. Pres. Harold L. Condit.
Enroll.: FTE 2,693
(816) 741-2000

Patricia Stevens Career College
1139 Olive St., St. Louis 63101. Private. 1968/1981 (AICS). Qtr. plan. Diplomas. Pres. John F. Klute.
Enroll.: 337 (*f.t.* 0 m., 337 w.)

Platt College
3131 Frederick Blvd., St. Joseph 64506-2911. Private business. 1965/1985 (AICS); 1980/1985 (NCA). Courses of varying lengths. Degrees: A, diplomas. Pres. Stanley L. Shaver.
Enroll.: FTE 182
(816) 233-9563

Branch Campus
6250 El Cajon Blvd., San Diego, CA 92115. Dir. Marshall Payn.
(714) 265-0107

Branch Campus
3400 Thomas Rd., Oklahoma City, OK 73179. Dir. George F. Gillard, III.
(405) 682-9222

Branch Campus
3105 Leopard, Corpus Christi, TX 78401. Dir. Louie Heerwagen.
(512) 883-5000

Branch Campus
3101 McArdle Rd., Corpus Christi, TX 78415. Dir. William P. Hefley.
(512) 582-1888

Professional Business School
1017 Olive, Suite 400, St. Louis 63101. Private. 1986 (AICS). Courses of varying lengths. Certificates. Exec. Dir. Richard Gans.
Enroll.: *f.t.*34
(314) 231-5266

Ranken Technical Institute
4431 Finney Ave., St. Louis 63113. Private. 1975/1980 (NATTS). Courses of varying lengths. Certificates, diplomas. Dir. Robert L. Garrett.
Enroll.: 1,175 (*f.t.* 632 m., 10 w.)
(314) 371-0233

Rockhurst College
5225 Troost Ave., Kansas City 64110. Private (Roman Catholic) liberal arts. 1934/1983 (NCA). Sem. plan. Degrees: A,B,M. *Prof. Accred.:* Physical Therapy. Pres. Rev. Robert F. Weiss, S.J.
Enroll.: FTE 1,877
(816) 926-4250

Rutledge College
625 N. Benton, Springfield 65806. Private junior. 1981 (AICS). Qtr. plan. Degrees: A. *Prof. Accred.:* Medical Assisting. Dir. Stephen Butler.
Enroll.: 662 (*f.t.* 196 m., 466 w.)
(417) 864-7220

St. Louis Christian College
1360 Grandview Dr., Florissant 63033. Private (Christian Churches) professional. 1977 (AABC). Sem. plan. Degrees: A,B. Pres. Thomas W. McGee.
Enroll.: 128
(314) 837-6777

St. Louis College of Health Careers
4477 Forest Park, St. Louis 63108. Private. 1986 (ABHES). Courses of varying lengths. Certificates. Pres. Rush L. Robinson.
(314) 652-0300

St. Louis College of Pharmacy
4588 Parkview Pl., St. Louis 63110. Private professional. 1967/1976 (NCA). Sem. plan. Degrees: B,P,D. *Prof. Accred.:* Pharmacy. Pres. Sumner M. Robinson.
Enroll.: FTE 704
(314) 367-8700

St. Louis Community College District
Central office. St. Louis 63110. Public 2-year institutions. Sem. plan. Degrees: A. Chanc. Michael E. Crawford.
(314) 644-9550

The following were formerly accredited as part of Junior College District—St. Louis, first accredited in 1966.

St. Louis Community College at Florissant Valley
St. Louis 63135. 1969/1979 (NCA). *Prof. Accred.:* Art, Engineering Technology (civil, electrical, electronic, mechanical), Nursing (A). Pres. David A. Harris.
Enroll.: FTE 4,955
(314) 595-4208

St. Louis Community College at Forest Park
St. Louis 63110. 1969/1981 (NCA). *Prof. Accred.:* Dental Assisting, Dental Hygiene, Diagnostic Medical Sonography, Medical As-

sisting, Medical Laboratory Technology (A), Nursing (A), Radiography, Respiratory Therapy Technology, Surgical Technology. Pres. Vernon O. Crawley.
Enroll.: FTE 3,189
(314) 644-9743

ST. LOUIS COMMUNITY COLLEGE AT MERAMEC
Kirkwood 63122. 1969/1983 (NCA). *Prof. Accred.:* Dental Assisting, Dental Laboratory Technician, Nursing (A). Pres. Ralph R. Doty.
Enroll.: FTE 5,839
(314) 966-7500

ST. LOUIS CONSERVATORY OF MUSIC
560 Trinity Ave., St. Louis 63130. Private professional. 1936/1978. Sem. plan. Degrees: B,M. *Prof. Accred.:* Music. Dean Joel Revzen.
Enroll.: 106 (*f.t.* 35 m., 49 w.)
(314) 863-3033

ST. LOUIS TECH
4144 Cypress Rd., St. Ann 63074. Private. 1977/1983 (NATTS). Courses of varying lengths. Certificates, diplomas. Dir. Henry L. Kemp.
Enroll.: 141 (*f.t.* 116 m., 25 w.)
(314) 427-3600

SAINT LOUIS UNIVERSITY
221 N. Grand Blvd., St. Louis 63103. Private (Roman Catholic). 1916/1982 (NCA). Sem. plan. Degrees: A,B,P,M,D. *Prof. Accred.:* Assistant to the Primary Care Physician, Business (B,M), Community Health/Preventive Medicine, Dietetics, Engineering (geophysical), Health Services Administration, Law, Medical Technology, Medicine, Nursing (B,M), Perfusion, Psychology, Social Work (B,M), Speech Pathology and Audiology, Teacher Education (*e,s,p*). Pres. Rev. Thomas F. Fitzgerald, S.J.
Enroll.: FTE 6,284
(314) 658-2474

ST. MARY COLLEGE OF O'FALLON
O'Fallon 63366. Private (Roman Catholic) junior. 1962/1984 (NCA). Sem. plan. Degrees: A. *Prof. Accred.:* Medical Record Technology, Nursing (A). Pres. Sister Elizabeth Weiman, C.P.P.S.
Enroll.: FTE 320
(314) 272-6171

SAINT PAUL SCHOOL OF THEOLOGY
Kansas City 64127. Private (United Methodist) professional; graduate only. 1976/1982 (NCA). Sem. plan. Degrees: P,M,D. *Prof. Accred.:* Theology (1964/1981, ATS). Pres. Lovett H. Weems, Jr.
Enroll.: FTE 181
(816) 483-9600

SANFORD-BROWN BUSINESS COLLEGE
4100 Ashby Rd., St. Ann 63074. Private. 1982 (AICS). Qtr. plan. Certificates, diplomas. Exec. Vice Pres. Larry Doyle.
Enroll.: 1,369 (*f.t.* 552 m., 817 w.)
(314) 427-7100

SCHOOL OF THE OZARKS
Point Lookout 65726. Private (Presbyterian, U.S.) liberal arts. 1961/1981 (NCA). Tri. plan. Degrees: B. *Prof. Accred.:* Music, Teacher Education (*e,s*). Pres. Stephen G. Jennings.
Enroll.: FTE 1,002
(417) 334-6411

SOUTHEAST MISSOURI STATE UNIVERSITY
Cape Girardeau 63701. Public liberal arts and teachers. 1915/1986 (NCA). Sem. plan. Degrees: A,B,M. *Prof. Accred.:* Music, Speech Pathology, Teacher Education (*e,s,p*). Pres. Bill W. Stacy.
Enroll.: FTE 8,019
(314) 651-2222

SOUTHWEST BAPTIST UNIVERSITY
Bolivar 65613. Private (Southern Baptist) liberal arts. 1957/1985 (NCA). Sem. plan. Degrees: B. *Prof. Accred.:* Medical Record Administration, Music. Chanc. James L. Sells.
Enroll.: FTE 1,773
(417) 326-5281

SOUTHWEST MISSOURI STATE UNIVERSITY
Springfield 65804. Public liberal arts and teachers. 1915/1986 (NCA). Includes branch campus at West Plains. Sem. plan. Degrees: B,M. *Prof. Accred.:* Home Economics, Music, Nurse Anesthesia Education, Nursing (B), Respiratory Therapy, Social Work (B), Teacher Education (*e,s,p*). Pres. Marshall Gordon.
Enroll.: FTE 11,790
(417) 836-5000

STATE FAIR COMMUNITY COLLEGE
Sedalia 65301. Public (district) junior. 1977/1982 (NCA). Sem. plan . Degrees: A. *Prof. Accred.:* Respiratory Therapy Technology. Pres. Marvin Fielding.
Enroll.: FTE 1,032
(816) 826-7100

STEPHENS COLLEGE
Columbia 65201. Private liberal arts primarily for women. 1918/1978 (NCA). Sem. plan. Degrees: A,B. *Prof. Accred.:* Medical Record Administration. Pres. Patsy H. Sampson.
Enroll.: FTE 932
(314) 442-2211

SULLIVAN EDUCATIONAL CENTERS
1617 McGee Ave., Kansas City 64108. Private. 1982 (NATTS). Courses of varying lengths. Diplomas. Dir. Phillip Sullivan.
Enroll.: 1,140 (*f.t.* 110 m., 4 w.)
(816) 471-1811

TARKIO COLLEGE
Tarkio 64491. Private (United Presbyterian) liberal arts. 1922/1984 (NCA). 4-1-4 plan. Degrees: B. Pres. Roy McIntosh.
Enroll.: FTE 981
(816) 736-4131

THREE RIVERS COMMUNITY COLLEGE
Poplar Bluff 63901. Public (district). 1974/1980 (NCA). Sem. plan. Degrees: A. *Prof. Accred.:* Dental Assisting, Medical Laboratory Technology, Nursing (A). Pres. Jack L. Bottenfield.
Enroll.: FTE 995
(314) 686-4101

TRANS WORLD TRAVEL COLLEGE
11500 Ambassador Dr., Kansas City 64195. Private home study. 1981 (NHSC). Dir. Sherry Huggins.
(816) 464-6303

TRENTON JUNIOR COLLEGE
Trenton 64683. Public (district). 1983 (NCA). Sem. plan. Degrees: A. Pres. Donald Gatzke.
Enroll.: FTE 622
(816) 359-3948

UNIFIED TECHNICAL COLLEGE
8800 Blue Ridge Blvd., Kansas City 64138. Private. 1985 (ABHES). Courses of varying lengths. Certificates, diplomas. *Prof. Accred.:* Medical Assisting. Dir. Bill Honeycutt.
(816) 761-8555

UNIVERSITY OF HEALTH SCIENCES/COLLEGE OF OSTEOPATHIC MEDICINE
Kansas City 64124. Private professional. 1916/1975. Sem. plan. Degrees: P. *Prof. Accred.:* Osteopathy. Pres. Rudolph S. Bremen.
Enroll.: 622 (*f.t.* 518 m., 104 w.)
(816) 283-2000

UNIVERSITY OF MISSOURI
Central office. Columbia 65211. Public (state). Sem. plan. Pres. Peter Magrath.
(314) 882-2011

UNIVERSITY OF MISSOURI—COLUMBIA
Columbia 65211. 1913/1985 (NCA). Degrees: B,P,M,D. *Prof. Accred.:* Accounting (Type A,C), Business (B,M), Cytotechnology, Dietetics, Engineering (agricultural, chemical, civil, computer, electrical, industrial, mechanical), Forestry, Health Services Administration, Histologic Technology, Home Economics, Interior Design, Journalism, Law, Librarianship, Medical Technology, Medicine, Music, Nuclear Medicine Technology, Nurse Anesthesia Education, Nursing (B,M), Occupational Therapy, Physical Therapy, Psychology, Radiography, Radiation Therapy Technology, Rehabilitation Counseling, Respiratory Therapy, Social Work (B,M), Specialist in Blood Bank Technology, Speech Pathology, Teacher Education (*e,s,p*), Veterinary Medicine. Chanc. Barbara S. Uehling.
Enroll.: FTE 20,171
(314) 882-3387

UNIVERSITY OF MISSOURI—KANSAS CITY
5100 Rockhill Rd., Kansas City 64110. 1938/1979 (NCA). Degrees: B,P,M,D. *Prof. Accred.:* Business (B,M), Dental Hygiene, Dentistry, Engineering (civil, electrical, mechanical), Law, Medicine, Music, Nurse Anesthesia Education, Nursing (B,M), Pharmacy, Teacher Education (*e,s,p*). Chanc. George A. Russell.
Enroll.: FTE 7,745
(816) 276-1107

UNIVERSITY OF MISSOURI—ROLLA
Rolla 65401. 1913/1979 (NCA). Degrees: B,M,D. *Prof. Accred.:* Engineering (aerospace, ceramic, chemical, civil, electrical, engineering management, engineering mechanics, geological, mechanical, metallurgical, mining, nuclear, petroleum). Chanc. Martin Jischke.
Enroll.: FTE 5,351
(314) 341-4114

UNIVERSITY OF MISSOURI—ST. LOUIS
8001 Natural Bridge, St. Louis 63121. 1960/1978 (NCA). Degrees: B,M,D. *Prof. Accred.:* Business (B,M), Nursing (B), Optometry, Psychology, Social Work (B), Teacher Education (*e,s,p*). Chanc. Marguerite Ross Barnett.

Enroll.: FTE 7,239
(314) 553-5252

VANDERSCHMIDT SCHOOL
4625 Lindell Blvd., St. Louis 63108. Private business. 1985 (AICS). Courses of varying lengths. Certificates, diplomas. Pres. Gretchen Vanderschmidt.
(314) 361-6000

VATTEROTT EDUCATIONAL CENTERS
3929 Industrial Dr., St. Ann 63074. Private. 1976 (NATTS). Courses of varying lengths. Certificates, diplomas. Pres. John C. Vatterott.
Enroll.: 125 (*f.t.* 115 m., 10 w.)
(314) 428-5900

VATTEROTT EDUCATIONAL CENTERS
3854 Washington Ave., St. Louis 63108. Private. 1976 (NATTS). Courses of varying lengths. Certificates, diplomas. Pres. John C. Vatterott.
(314) 534-2586

VOCATIONAL TRAINING CENTER
5027 Columbia Ave., St. Louis 63139. Private. 1977/1985 (NATTS). Courses of varying lengths. Diplomas. Dir. Jeannette Lasky.
Enroll.: 330 (*f.t.* 250 m., 10 w.)
(314) 776-3302

WASHINGTON UNIVERSITY
St. Louis 63130. Private. 1913/1984 (NCA). Sem. plan. Degrees: B,P,M,D. *Prof. Accred.:* Architecture (M), Art, Audiology, Business (B,M), Dentistry, Engineering (chemical, civil, computer science, electrical engineering and public policy, mechanical, systems science and engineering), Health Services Administration, Law, Medicine, Music, Nuclear Medicine Technology, Nurse Anesthesia Education, Occupational Therapy, Physical Therapy, Psychology, Radiation Therapy Technology, Radiography, Social Work (M), Teacher Education (*e,s,p*). Chanc. William H. Danforth.
Enroll.: FTE 8,056
(314) 889-5000

WEBSTER UNIVERSITY
470 E. Lockwood Ave., St. Louis 63119. Private liberal arts. 1925/1978 (NCA). Accreditation includes institutional operations at the following academic sites: Graduate Center at Little Rock, AR; Marine Corps Air Sta., Yuma, AZ; Camp Pendleton, CA; Marine Corps Air Sta., Tustin, Irvine, CA; Graduate Center at Colorado Springs, CO; Graduate Center at Denver, Aurora, CO; Graduate Center at Chicago, Northfield, IL; Scott AFB, IL; Graduate School at Jeffersonville, Jeffersonville, IN; McConnell AFB, KS; England AFB, LA; Graduate School at Kansas City, MO; Graduate Center at St. Louis, MO; Truman Education Ctr., Fort Leondard Wood, MO; Graduate Center at Albuquerque, Albuquerque, NM; Graduate Center at Santa Teresa, Santa Teresa, NM; Keflavik Naval Sta., FPO New York, NY; Naval Air Sta., Bermuda, FPO New York, NY; Pope AFB, NC; Altus AFB, OK; Fort Jackson, SC; Graduate Center at Charleston, SC; Myrtle Beach AFB, SC; U.S. Naval Hospital, Beaufort, SC; Fort Bliss, TX; Army Education Center, Fort Sam Houston, TX; Kingsville Naval Air Sta., Corpus Christi, TX; Vienna, Austria; London, England; Leiden, The Netherlands; Geneva, Switzerland. Sem. plan. Degrees: B,M. *Prof. Accred.:* Health Administration, Music. Pres. Leigh Gerdine.
Enroll.: FTE 6,321
(314) 968-6900

WENTWORTH MILITARY ACADEMY AND JUNIOR COLLEGE
Lexington 64067. Private junior college primarily for men. 1930/1976 (NCA). Sem. plan. Degrees: A. Supt. Col. James M. Sellers, Jr.
Enroll.: FTE 215
(816) 259-2221

WESTMINSTER COLLEGE
Fulton 65251. Private (Presbyterian, U.S.) liberal arts for men. 1913/1985 (NCA). Sem. plan. Degrees: B. Pres. J. Harvey Saunders.
Enroll.: FTE 614
(816) 453-4600

WILLIAM JEWELL COLLEGE
Liberty 64068. Private (Southern Baptist) liberal arts. 1915/1981 (NCA). 4-1-4 plan. Degrees: B. *Prof. Accred.:* Music, Nursing (B). J. Gordon Kingsley.
Enroll.: FTE 1,652
(816) 781-4120

WILLIAM WOODS COLLEGE
Fulton 65251. Private (Disciples of Christ) liberal arts for women. 1919/1977 (NCA). Sem. plan. Degrees: B. *Prof. Accred.:* Teacher Education (*e,s*) Pres. John M. Bartholomy.
Enroll.: FTE 741
(314) 642-2251

MONTANA

Billings Vocational-Technical Center
Billings 59102. Public (district) 2-year. 1979/1984 (NASC). Qtr. plan. Certificates. Dir. Jeffrey Dietz.
Enroll.: 439
(406) 652-1720

Blackfeet Community College
Browning 54117. Tribal junior. 1985 (NASC). Qtr. plan. Degrees: A. Pres. Donald Pepion.
Enroll.: 270
(406) 338-7755

Butte Vocational-Technical Center
Butte 59701. Public (district) 2-year. 1984 (NASC). Qtr. plan. Certificates. Pres. Harrison J. Freebourn.
Enroll.: 450
(406) 494-2894

Carroll College
Helena 59625. Private (Roman Catholic) liberal arts. 1949/1980 (NASC). Sem. plan. Degrees: B. *Prof. Accred.:* Dental Hygiene, Medical Record Administration, Nursing (B), Social Work (B). Pres. Francis J. Kerins.
Enroll.: 1,501
(406) 442-3450

College of Great Falls
Great Falls 59405. Private (Roman Catholic) liberal arts. 1935/1979 (NASC). Sem. plan. Degrees: B,M. Pres. William A. Shields
Enroll.: 1,339
(406) 761-8210

Dawson Community College
Glendive 59330. Public (district) junior. 1969/1984 (NASC). Qtr. plan. Degrees: A. Pres. Donald H. Kettner.
Enroll.: 786
(406) 365-3396

*Eastern Montana College
Billings 59101-0298. Public (state) liberal arts and teachers. 1932/1978 (NASC). Qtr. plan. Degrees: B,M. *Prof. Accred.:* Art, Music, Rehabilitation Counseling, Teacher Education (*e,s,p*). Pres. Bruce H. Carpenter.
Enroll.: 4,488
(406) 657-2011

Flathead Valley Community College
Kalispell 59901. Public (district) junior. 1970/1982 (NASC). Qtr. plan. Degrees: A. Pres. Howard L. Fryett.

*Member Montana University System

Enroll.: 2,031
406) 755-5222

Great Falls Vocational-Technical Center
Great Falls 59405. Public (district) 2-year. 1979/1984 (NASC). Qtr. plan. Certificates. *Prof. Accred:* Dental Assisting, Respiratory Therapy Technology. Dir. Willard R. Weaver.
Enroll.: 559
(406) 791-2100

Helena Vocational-Technical Center
Helena 59601. Public (district) 2-year. 1977/1982 (NASC). Qtr. plan. Certificates. Dir. Alex Capdeville.
Enroll.: 971
(406) 442-0060

May School of Broadcast
928 Broadway, P.O. Box 127, Billings 59103. Private. 1983 (NATTS). Courses of varying lengths. Diplomas. Pres. Michael May.
Enroll.: 17
(406) 248-4888

Miles Community College
Miles City 59301. Public (district) junior. 1971/1986 (NASC). Qtr. plan. Degrees: A. Pres. Judson H. Flower.
Enroll.: 720
(406) 232-3031

Missoula Vocational-Technical Center
Missoula 59801. Public (district) 2-year vocational-technical. 1974/1979 (NASC). Qtr. plan. Certificates. *Prof. Accred.:* Respiratory Therapy Technology, Surgical Technology. Dir. Dennis Lerum.
Enroll.: 595
(406) 721-1330

Montana University System
Central office. 33 S. Last Chance Gulch Rd., Helena 59601. Public (state). Commissioner of Higher Education Carroll Krause.
(406) 444-6570

*Montana College of Mineral Science and Technology
Butte 59701. Public (state) technological. 1932/1981 (NASC). Sem. plan. Degrees: B,M. *Prof. Accred.:* Engineering (engineering science, environmental, geological, geophysi-

*Member Montana University System

Montana

cal, metallurgical, mineral processing, mining, petroleum). Pres. Lindsay Norman, Jr.
Enroll.: 1,932
(406) 496-4101

*MONTANA STATE UNIVERSITY
Bozeman 59717. Public. 1932/1980 (NASC). Qtr. plan. Degrees: B,M,D. *Prof. Accred.:* Architecture (B), Art, Business (B), Engineering (agricultural, chemical, civil, electrical, industrial, mechanical), Engineering Technology (construction, electrical and electronic, mechanical), Home Economics, Music, Nursing (B,M), Teacher Education (*e,s,p*). Pres. William J. Tietz.
Enroll.: 10,710
(406) 994-0211

*NORTHERN MONTANA COLLEGE
Havre 59501. Public (state) teachers. 1932/1977 (NASC). Qtr. plan. Degrees: A,B,M. Pres. William C. Merwin.
Enroll.: 1,775
(406) 265-7821

ROCKY MOUNTAIN COLLEGE
Billings 59102. Private (United Methodist, United Presbyterian, and United Church of

*Member Montana University System

Christ) liberal arts. 1949/1977 (NASC). Sem. plan. Degrees: B. Pres. ———.
Enroll.: 404
(406) 657-1020

SALISH KOOTENAI COLLEGE
Pablo 59855. Tribal junior. 1984 (NASC). Qtr. plan. Degrees: A. Pres. Joseph F. McDonald.
Enroll.: 653
(406) 675-4800

*UNIVERSITY OF MONTANA
Missoula 59812. Public (state). 1932/1978 (NASC). Qtr. plan. (sem. plan in law school). Degrees: A,B,P,M,D. *Prof. Accred.:* Business (B,M), Forestry, Journalism, Law, Music, Pharmacy, Physical Therapy, Psychology, Social Work (B), Speech Pathology and Audiology, Teacher Education (*e,s,p*). Pres. James V. Koch.
Enroll.: 8,989
(406) 243-0211

*WESTERN MONTANA COLLEGE
Dillon 59725. Public (state) teachers. 1932/1978 (NASC). Qtr. plan. Degrees: A,B,M. Pres. Douglas M. Treadway.
Enroll.: 881
(406) 683-7251

*Member Montana University System

NEBRASKA

Barber College of Professional Arts
3504–08 Leavenworth St., Omaha 68105. Private. 1978 (NATTS). Courses of varying lengths. Diplomas. Pres. Eugene White.
Enroll.: 31 (*f.t.* 13 m., 18 w.)
(402) 346-7722

Bellevue College
Bellevue 68005. Private liberal arts. 1977/1982 (NCA). Sem. plan. Degrees: B. Pres. John B. Muller.
Enroll.: FTE 1,566
(402) 291-8100

Bishop Clarkson Memorial Hospital College of Nursing
333 S. 44th St., Omaha 68131. Private professional. 1984 (NCA). Sem. plan. Degrees: B, diplomas. Dean Patricia B. Perry.
Enroll.: FTE 339
(402) 559-3100

Central Community College Area
Grand Island 68802. Public (district) 2-year technical. Accreditation includes Central Technical Community College at Hastings 68901; Platte Technical Community College at Columbus 68601; Grand Island Education Center at Grand Island 68801; and community education centers throughout the twenty-five county service area. 1974/1980 (NCA). Qtr. plan. Degrees: A. *Prof. Accred.:* Dental Assisting, Dental Hygiene, Dental Laboratory Technology, Medical Assisting, Practical Nursing. Pres. Joseph W. Preusser.
Enroll.: FTE 1,100
(308) 384-5220

Chadron State College
Chadron 69337. Public liberal arts and teachers. 1915/1977 (NCA). Sem. plan. Degrees: B,M. *Prof. Accred.:* Teacher Education (*e,s,p*). Pres. Samuel H. Rankin, Jr.
Enroll.: FTE 1,610
(308) 432-4451

College of Hair Design
304 S. 11th St., Lincoln 68508. Private. 1977 (NATTS). Qtr. plan. Diplomas. Pres. Alyce Howard.
Enroll.: 19 (*f.t.* 4 m., 15 w.)
(402) 474-4244

College of Saint Mary
1901 S. 72nd St., Omaha 68124. Private (Roman Catholic) liberal arts for women. 1958/1978 (NCA). Sem. plan. Degrees: A,B. *Prof. Accred.:* Medical Record Administration, Nursing (A), Respiratory Therapy. Pres. Kenneth R. Nielsen.
Enroll.: FTE 661
(402) 399-2400

Concordia Teachers College
Seward 68434. Private (Lutheran-Missouri Synod) for training parish school teachers. 1953/1978 (NCA). Sem. plan. Degrees: B,M. *Prof. Accred.:* Teacher Education (*e,s*). Acting Pres. James H. Pragman.
Enroll.: FTE 858
(402) 643-3651

Creighton University
2500 California St., Omaha 68178. Private (Roman Catholic). 1916/1978 (NCA). Sem. plan. Degrees: B,P,M,D. *Prof. Accred.:* Accounting (Type A), Business (B,M), Dentistry, EMT-Paramedic, Law, Medical Technology, Medicine, Nurse Anesthesia Education, Nursing (B), Pharmacy, Respiratory Therapy, Teacher Education (*e,s,p*). Pres. Rev. Michael G. Morrison, S.J.
Enroll.: FTE 5,149
(402) 280-2770

Dana College
Blair 68008. Private (American Lutheran) liberal arts and professional. 1958/1982 (NCA). 4-1-4 plan. Degrees: B. *Prof. Accred.:* Teacher Education (*e,s*). Pres. Myrvin Christopherson.
Enroll.: FTE 401
(402) 426-4101

Doane College
Crete 68333. Private (United Church of Christ) liberal arts. 1913/1982 (NCA). Sem. plan. Degrees: B. *Prof. Accred.:* Teacher Education (*e,s,p*). Pres. Philip R. Heckman.
Enroll.: FTE 662
(402) 826-2161

Electronic Computer Programming Institute
The Center, 42nd and Center, Fourth Level, Omaha 68105. Private. 1971/1982 (NATTS). Courses of varying lengths. Certificates. Dir. Terry O'Shaughnessy.
Enroll.: 200 (*f.t.* 60 m., 40 w.)
(402) 345-1300

GATEWAY ELECTRONICS INSTITUTE
4001 S. 24th, Omaha 68107. Private. 1973/1978 (NATTS). Qtr. plan. Diplomas. Pres. Robert J. Ochs.
Enroll.: 325 (*f.t.* 230 m., 20 w.)
(402) 734-4420

GRACE COLLEGE OF THE BIBLE
1515 S. Tenth St., Omaha 68108. Private (Independent) professional. 1948/1984 (AABC). Sem. plan. Degrees: A,B. Pres. Warren Bathke.
Enroll.: 281
(402) 342-3377

HASTINGS COLLEGE
Hastings 68901. Private (United Presbyterian) liberal arts. 1916/1985 (NCA). 4-1-4 plan. Degrees: B. *Prof. Accred.:* Music, Teacher Education (*e,s*). Pres. Thomas J. Reeves.
Enroll.: FTE 794
(402) 463-2402

INSTITUTE OF COMPUTER SCIENCE, LTD.
808 S. 74th Plaza, Suite 220, Omaha 68114. Private. 1984 (NATTS). Courses of varying lengths. Certificates. Dir. Kenneth Carlson.
(402) 393-7064

KEARNEY STATE COLLEGE
Kearney 68849. Public liberal arts and teachers. 1916/1984 (NCA). Sem. plan. Degrees: B,M. Prof. Accred.: Nursing (B), Social Work (B), Speech Pathology, Teacher Education (*e,s,p*). Pres. William R. Nester.
Enroll.: FTE 6,441
(308) 236-4141

LINCOLN SCHOOL OF COMMERCE
1821 K St., P.O. Box 82826, Lincoln 68501-2826. Private; recognized candidate for junior college status. 1966/1979 (AICS). Qtr. plan. Degrees: A, diplomas. Dir. Ronald Anderson.
Enroll.: 914 (*f.t.* 116 m., 556 w.)
(402) 474-5315

METROPOLITAN TECHNICAL COMMUNITY COLLEGE AREA
P.O. Box 3777, Omaha 68103. Public 2-year. Accreditation includes Ft. Omaha, South Omaha, and Southwest Campuses. 1979/1983 (NCA). Qtr. plan. Degrees: A. *Prof. Accred.:* Dental Assisting, Respiratory Therapy Technology, Surgical Technology. Pres. J. Richard Gilliland.
Enroll.: FTE 3,510
(402) 449-8415

MIDLAND LUTHERAN COLLEGE
Fremont 68025. Private (Lutheran in America) liberal arts. 1947/1982 (NCA). 4-1-4 plan. Degrees: B. *Prof. Accred.:* Nursing (B), Teacher Education (*e,s*). Pres. Carl L. Hansen.
Enroll.: FTE 754
(402) 721- 5480

MID-PLAINS TECHNICAL COMMUNITY COLLEGE AREA
Central office. North Platte 69101. Public; accreditation includes McCook Community College and Mid-Plains Community College. 1980/1981 (NCA). Sem. plan. Degrees: A. *Prof. Accred.:* Dental Assisting, Medical Laboratory Technology (A). Area Pres. William G. Hasemeyer.
(308) 532-8740
Enroll.: Total FTE 1,460

North Platte 69101. Public 2-year. 1981 (NCA). Pres. Kenneth L. Aten.
Enroll.: 2,051 (*f.t.* 375 m., 326 w.)
(308) 532-8740

NEBRASKA CHRISTIAN COLLEGE
1899 Syracuse, Norfolk 68701. Private (Christian Churches) professional. 1985 (AABC). Sem. plan. Degrees: A,B. Pres. Richard Walmsley.
Enroll.: 156
(402) 371-5960

NEBRASKA COLLEGE OF BUSINESS
3636 California St., Omaha 68131. Private. 1968/1981 (AICS). Qtr. plan. Degrees: A, certificates, diplomas. Dir. Pamela Boehm.
Enroll.: 822 (*f.t.* 137 m., 548 w.)
(402) 553-8500

NEBRASKA WESLEYAN UNIVERSITY
Lincoln 68504. Private (United Methodist) liberal arts college. 1914/1980 (NCA). Sem. plan. Degrees: B. *Prof. Accred.:* Medical Technology, Music, Nursing (B), Social Work (B), Teacher Education (*e,s*). Pres. John W. White, Jr.
Enroll.: FTE 1,168
(402) 466-2371

NORTHEAST TECHNICAL COMMUNITY COLLEGE
Norfolk 68701. Public 2-year. 1979/1984 (NCA). Sem. plan. Degrees: A. Pres. Robert P. Cox.
Enroll.: FTE 1,316
(402) 371-2020

Omaha College of Health Careers
1052 Park Ave., Omaha 68105. Private. 1973/1978 (NATTS). Qtr. plan. Degrees; A, diplomas. *Prof. Accred.:* Dental Assisting, Dental Laboratory Technology, EEG Technology, Medical Assisting, Medical Assisting in Pediatrics. Pres. William J. Stuckey.
Enroll.: 120 (*f.t.* 8 m., 112 w.)
(402) 342-1818

Peru State College
Peru 68421. Public liberal arts and teachers. 1915/1981 (NCA). Sem. plan. Degrees: A,B. *Prof. Accred.:* Teacher Education (*e,s*). Pres. Jerry L. Gallentine.
Enroll.: FTE 1,020
(402) 872-3815

Southeast Community College Area
8800 O St., Lincoln 68505. Public 2-year. Area Pres. Robert S. Eicher.
Enroll.: FTE 1,578
(402) 471-3413

Southeast Community College Fairbury Campus
924 K St., Fairbury 68352. Public (district) 2-year. 1981 (NCA). Qtr. and sem. plans. Degrees: A, certificates *Prof. Accred.:* Medical Laboratory (A), Practical Nursing. Campus Dir. Daniel R. Gerber.
Enroll.: 323 (*f.t.* 114 m., 110 w.)
(402) 729-6148

Southeast Community College—Lincoln Campus
Lincoln 68505. Public (district) 2-year technical. 1977 (NCA). Qtr. plan. Degrees: A, certificates. *Prof. Accred.:* Dental Assisting, Medical Assisting, Medical Laboratory Technology (A), Practical Nursing, Radiography, Respiratory Therapy, Surgical Technology. Campus Dir. Jack Huck.
Enroll.: 3,692 (*f.t.* 476 m., 752 w.)
(402) 474-3333

Southeast Community College—Milford Campus
Buena Vista, S.E., Milford 68405. Public (district) 2-year. Accreditation includes the Joseph M. Montoya Attendance Center. 1979 (NCA). Qtr. plan. Degrees: A. Dir. Robert E. Klabanes.
Enroll.: 945 (*f.t.* 889 m., 53 w.)
(402) 761-2131

Spencer School of Business
410 W. Second St., P.O. Box 399, Grand Island 68802. 1985 (AICS). Qtr. plan. Diplomas. Dir. Connie J. Collins.
(308) 382-8044

Union College
Lincoln 68506. Private (Seventh-day Adventist) liberal arts. 1923/1980 (NCA). Sem. plan. Degrees: A,B. *Prof. Accred.:* Music, Nursing (B), Social Work (B), Teacher Education (*e,s*). Pres. John H. Wagner.
Enroll.: FTE 700
(402) 488-2331

Universal Technical Institute
902 Capitol Ave., Omaha 68102. Private. 1967/1977 (NATTS). Courses of varying lengths. Certificates, diplomas. Dir. Ivan Abdouch.
Enroll.: 250 (*f.t.* 212 m., 2 w.)
(402) 345-2422

University of Nebraska
Central administrative office, 3835 Holdrege, Lincoln 68583-0745. Public (state). Pres. Ronald W. Roskens.
(402) 472-2111

University of Nebraska—Lincoln
Lincoln 68588. 1913/1977 (NCA). Accreditation includes School of Technical Agriculture at Curtis. Sem. plan. Degrees: A,B,P,M,D. *Prof. Accred.:* Accounting (Type A,C), Architecture (B), Business (B,M), Construction Education, Dental Hygiene, Dentistry, Dietetics, Engineering (agricultural, chemical, civil, electrical, industrial, mechanical), Home Economics, Interior Design, Journalism, Law, Music, Psychology, Social Work, Speech Pathology and Audiology, Teacher Education (*e,s,p*). Chanc. Martin A. Massengale.
Enroll.: FTE 20,904
(402) 472-2116

University of Nebraska at Omaha
60th and Dodge Sts., Omaha 68182. 1939/1977 (NCA). Sem. plan. Degrees: A,B,M. *Prof. Accred.:* Business (B,M), Engineering (civil), Engineering Technology (construction, drafting and design, electronic, manufacturing), Interior Design, Music, Social Work (B,M), Speech Pathology, Teacher Education (*e,s,p*). Chanc. Del Weber.
Enroll.: FTE 9,767
(402) 554-2311

University of Nebraska Medical Center
Omaha 68105. Public (state). 1913/1977 (NCA). Sem. plan. Degrees: A,B,P,M,D. *Prof. Accred.:* Assistant to the Primary Care Physician, Medical Technology, Medicine, Nuclear Medicine Technology, Nursing (A,B,M), Pharmacy, Physical Therapy, Radiation Therapy, Radiation Therapy Technology, Radiography. Chanc. Charles E. Andrews.
Enroll.: FTE 2,569
(402) 559-4200

Wayne State College
Wayne 68787. Public liberal arts and teachers. 1917/1985 (NCA). Tri. plan. Degrees: B,M. *Prof. Accred.:* Teacher Education (*e,s,p*). Pres. Thomas A. Coffey.
Enroll.: FTE 2,245
(402) 375-2224

Western Technical Community College Area
Scottsbluff 69361. Public (district) 2-year. Area Pres. John N. Harms.
(308) 635-3606

Nebraska Western College
Scottsbluff 69361. Public (district) junior. 1973/1978 (NCA). Sem. plan. Degrees: A. *Prof. Accred.:* Practical Nursing. Pres. John N. Harms.
Enroll.: FTE 801
(308) 635-3606

Word Porcessing and Secretarial College
2900 Douglas, Omaha 68131. Private. 1984 (AICS). Courses of varying lengths. Certificates, diplomas. Dir. Terry W. Murphy.
(402) 346-4048

York College
York 68467. Private (Church of Christ) junior. 1970/1984 (NCA). Sem. plan. Degrees: A. Pres. Gary Bartholomew.
Enroll.: FTE 360
(402) 362-4441

NEVADA

AMERICAN ACADEMY FOR CAREER EDUCATION
953-35B E. Sahara, Suite 102, Las Vegas 89104. Private. 1977 (NATTS). Courses of varying lengths. Certificates. Dir. Yvonne Crosby.
Enroll.: 96 (*f.t.* 10 m., 86 w.)
(702) 732-7748

APOLLO BUSINESS AND TECHNICAL SCHOOL
2001 E. Flamingo Rd., Suite 228, Las Vegas 89109. Private. 1981 (AICS). Qtr. plan. Certificates. Dir. Gertie Johannsson.
Enroll.: 232 (*f.t.* 163 m., 69 w.)
(702) 737-1569

BRANCH CAMPUS
5400 Equity Ave., Reno 89502. Dir. William Burgess.
(702) 329-0904

BRANCH CAMPUS
6507 Fourth Ave., No. 450, Sacramento, CA 95817. Dir. Mike Conant.
(916) 456-5100

BRANCH CAMPUS
2800 South IH 35, Austin TX 78704. Dir. Don Myers.
(512) 440-8222

BRANCH CAMPUS
6994 S. Zarzamora, San Antonio, TX 78224. Dir. Fred Berrera.
(512) 927-3924

*CLARK COUNTY COMMUNITY COLLEGE
3200 E. Cheyenne Ave., North Las Vegas 89030. Public (district) junior. 1975/1980 (NASC). Sem. plan. Degrees: A. *Prof. Accred.:* Dental Hygiene, Respiratory Therapy, Respiratory Therapy Technology. Pres. Paul E. Meacham.
Enroll.: 10,029
(702) 643-6060

DANA MCKAY BUSINESS COLLEGE
953 E. Sahara, Las Vegas 89104. Private. 1985 (AICS). Courses of varying lengths. Certificates, diplomas. Dir. Dana McKay.
(702) 734-9449

EDUCATION DYNAMICS INSTITUTE
2635 N. Decatur Blvd., Las Vegas 89108. Private. 1973/1978 (NATTS). Courses of varying lengths. Diplomas. Pres. Michael L. Dawson.
Enroll.: 225 (*f.t.* 98 m., 7 w.)
(702) 648-1522

INTERNATIONAL DEALERS SCHOOL
1030 E. Twain Ave., Las Vegas 89109. Private. 1983 (NATTS). Courses of varying lengths. Certificates, diplomas. Pres. Gary Mahoney.
Enroll.: 235
(702) 733-9133

KROLAK BUSINESS INSTITUTE
2917 W. Washington Ave., Las Vegas 89107. Private. 1983 (AICS). Qtr. plan. Certificates. Pres. Barbara Paulus.
Enroll.: 359 (*f.t.* 54 m., 305 w.)
(702) 647-3446

NEVADA GAMING SCHOOL
3100 Sirius Rd., Las Vegas 89102. Private. 1976/1981 (NATTS). Courses of varying lengths. Certificates, diplomas. Pres. A. W. Morgan.
Enroll.: 638 (*f.t.* 586 m., 52 w.)
(702) 873-2343

NEVADA GAMING SCHOOL
881 E. Glendale Ave., Sparks 89431. Private. 1983 (NATTS). 24-week program. Diplomas. Pres. A. W. Morgan.
Enroll.: 60
(702) 359-2345

*NORTHERN NEVADA COMMUNITY COLLEGE
Elko 89801. Public (district) junior. 1974/1984 (NASC). Sem. plan. Degrees: A. Pres. William J. Berg.
Enroll.: 1,928
(702) 738-8493

RENO BUSINESS COLLEGE
140 Washington St., Reno 89502. Private. 1970/1983 (AICS). Qtr. plan. Degrees: A. Admin. Mary T. Morrison.
Enroll.: 1,091 (*f.t.* 360 m., 731 w.)
(702) 323-4145

SIERRA NEVADA COLLEGE
Incline Village 89450-4269. Private liberal arts. 1977/1982 (NASC). Sem. plan. Degrees: B. Pres. Ben Solomon.
Enroll.: 256
(702) 831-1314

*Member University of Nevada System

*Member University of Nevada System

STRIP DEALERS SCHOOL
2309 Las Vegas Blvd. S., Las Vegas 89104. Private. 1985 (NATTS). Courses of varying lengths. Certificates, diplomas. Pres. Gary Mahoney.
(702) 731-1010

*TRUCKEE MEADOWS COMMUNITY COLLEGE
7000 Dandini Blvd., Reno 89512. Public (district) junior. 1980/1985 (NASC). Sem. plan. Degrees: A. *Prof. Accred.:* Dental Assisting, Radiography. Pres. John W. Gwaltney.
Enroll.: 7,441
(702) 673-7025

UNIVERSITY OF NEVADA SYSTEM
Central office. 405 Marsh Ave., Reno 89507. Public (state). Sem. plan. Chanc. Robert M. Bersi.
(702) 784-4901

UNIVERSITY OF NEVADA, LAS VEGAS
4505 Maryland Parkway, Las Vegas 89154. 1964/1980 (NASC). Degrees: A,B,M. *Prof. Accred.:* Music, Nuclear Medicine Technology, Nursing (A,B), Radiography, Rehabilitation Counseling, Social Work (B), Teacher Education (*e,s,p*). Pres. Robert C. Maxson.
Enroll.: 9,402
(702) 739-3671

*Member University of Nevada System

UNIVERSITY OF NEVADA, RENO
Reno 89557-0002. 1938/1978 (NASC). Technical Institute at Stead. Degrees: A,B,M,D. *Prof. Accred.:* Basic Medical Sciences, Business (B,M), Engineering (civil, electrical, geological, mechanical, metallurgical, mining), Engineering Technology (architectural design, electronics), Home Economics, Journalism, Medical Technology, Music, Nursing (B), Psychology, Social Work (B), Teacher Education (*e,s,p*). Pres. Joseph N. Crowley.
Enroll.: 9,817
(702) 784-6865

*WESTERN NEVADA COMMUNITY COLLEGE
2201 W. Nye Lane, Carson City 89701. Public (district) junior. 1975/1980 (NASC). Sem. plan. Degrees: A. *Prof. Accred.:* Radiography. Pres. Anthony Calabro.
Enroll.: 3,381
(702) 887-3000

*Member University of Nevada System

NEW HAMPSHIRE

Castle Junior College
Searles Rd., Windham 03087 . Private. 1968/1981 (AICS); 1985 (NEASC-CVTCI). Five 6-week terms. Degrees: A. Pres. Sister Sheila L. Garvey, R.S.M.
Enroll.: 163 (*f.t.* 1 m., 159 w.)
(603) 893-6111

Colby-Sawyer College
New London 03257. Private for women. 1933/1984 (NEASC-CIHE). 4-1-4 plan. Degrees: A,B. *Prof. Accred.:* Medical Record Administration, Nursing (B). Pres. Peggy Leiterman-Stock.
Enroll.: 468
(603) 526-2010

Daniel Webster College
Nashua 03063. Private; New England Aeronautical Institute, a division. 1972/1986 (NEASC-CIHE). Tri. plan. Degrees: A,B. Pres. Hannah McCarthy.
Enroll.: 1,127
(603) 883-3556

Dartmouth College
Hanover 03755. Private liberal arts. 1929/1978 (NEASC-CIHE). Modified qtr. plan. Degrees: B,P,M,D. *Prof. Accred.:* Basic Medical Sciences, Business (M), Engineering, Medicine. Pres. David T. McLaughlin.
Enroll.: 4,626
(603) 646-1110

Franklin Pierce College
Rindge 03461. Franklin Pierce Law Center at Concord. Private liberal arts. 1968/1985 (NEASC-CIHE). Tri. plan. Degrees: B. *Prof. Accred.:* Law (ABA only). Pres. Walter R. Peterson.
Enroll.: 2,293
(603) 899-5111

Hawthorne College
Antrim 03440. Private liberal arts. 1971/1983 (NEASC-CIHE). Sem. plan. Degrees: A,B. Pres. Harry P. Weber.
Enroll.: 636
(603) 588-6341

Hesser College
25 Lowell St., Manchester 03101. Private junior business. 1962/1982 (AICS); 1985 (NEASC-CVTCI). Sem. plan. Degrees: A. Pres. Kenneth W. Galeucia.
Enroll.: 1,877
(603) 668-6660

*Keene State College
Keene 03431. Public liberal arts and teachers; member of University of New Hampshire System. 1949/1981 (NEASC-CIHE). Sem. plan. Degrees: A,B,M. *Prof. Accred.:* Teacher Education (*e,s*). Pres. Barbara J. Seelye.
Enroll.: 3,512
(603) 352-1909

†McIntosh College
23 Cataract Ave., Dover 03820. Private junior business. 1962/1984 (AICS). Sem. plan. Degrees: A, diplomas. Pres. Richard F. Waldo.
Enroll.: 555
369 (*f.t.* 891 m., (603) 742-3518

New England College
Henniker 03242. Private liberal arts. 1967/1984 (NEASC-CIHE). Accreditation includes British Campus in Arundel, Sussex. 4-1-4 plan. Degrees: B,M. *Prof. Accred.:* Engineering (civil). Pres. William R. O'Connell, Jr.
Enroll.: 1,260
(603) 428-2211

New England Technical Institute
750 Massabesic St., Manchester 03103. Private. 1981 (NATTS). Qtr. plan. Diplomas. Pres. Socrates Chaloge.
Enroll.: 180 (*f.t.* 70 m., 10 w.)
(603) 669-1231

New Hampshire Barber College
64 Merrimack St., Manchester 03101. Private. 1979 (NATTS). Courses of varying lengths. Diplomas. Pres. Roland Forcier.
Enroll.: 22 (*f.t.* 5 m., 17 w.)
(603) 623-9885

New Hampshire College
2500 North River Rd., Manchester 03104. Private. 1960/1985 (AICS); 1973/1985 (NEASC-CIHE). Sem. plan. Degrees: A, B,M. Pres. Edward M. Shapiro.
Enroll.: 7,175
(603) 668-2211

New Hampshire Technical Institute
Concord 03301. Public (state) 2-year technological. 1969/1985 (NEASC-CVTCI). Qtr.

* Member University System of New Hampshire
†Candidate for Accreditation by Regional Accrediting Commission

plan. Degrees: A. *Prof. Accred.:* Dental Assisting, Dental Hygiene, Engineering Technology (architectural, electronic, mechanical), Nursing (A), Radiography. Pres. David E. Larrabee.
Enroll.: 2,077
(603) 271-2531

New Hampshire Vocational-Technical College
Berlin 03570. Public (state) 2-year technological. 1974/1985 (NEASC-CVTCI). Qtr. plan. Degrees: A. Pres. Lawrence Twitchell.
Enroll.: 353
(603) 752-2221

New Hampshire Vocational-Technical College
Claremont 03743. Public (state) 2-year technological. 1973/1983 (NEASC-CVTCI). Qtr. plan. Degrees: A. *Prof. Accred.:*Medical Assisting, Medical Laboratory Technology (A), Medical Record Technology, Respiratory Therapy. Pres. Roland V. Stoodley, Jr.
Enroll.: 214
(603) 542-7744

New Hampshire Vocational-Technical College
Laconia 03246. Public (state) 2-year technological. 1974/1985 (NEASC-CVTCI). Qtr. plan. Degrees: A. Pres. George M. Strout.
Enroll.: 402
(603) 524-3207

New Hampshire Vocational-Technical College
Manchester 03102. Public (state) 2-year technological. 1974/1985 (NEASC-CVTCI). Qtr. plan. Degrees: A. Pres. Richard Edouard Mandeville.
Enroll.: 1,261
(603) 668-6706

New Hampshire Vocational-Technical College
Nashua 03063. Public (state) 2-year technological. 1974/1985 (NEASC-CVTCI). Qtr. plan. Degrees: A. Pres. Robert E. Bloomfield.
Enroll.: 356
(603) 882-6923

New Hampshire Vocational-Technical College
Stratham 03885. Public (state) 2-year technological. 1975/1985 (NEASC-CVTCI). Qtr. plan. Degrees: A. Pres. Charles H. Green.
Enroll.: 240 (*f.t.* (603) 772-1194

Notre Dame College
Manchester 03104. Private (Roman Catholic) liberal arts for women. 1970/1983 (NEASC-CIHE). Sem. plan. *Prof. Accred.:* Medical Technology. Degrees: A,B,M. Pres. Sister Carol Descoteaux, C.S.C.
Enroll.: 772
(603) 669-4298

*Plymouth State College
Plymouth 03264. Public liberal arts and professional. 1955/1984 (NEASC-CIHE). Sem. plan. Degrees: A,B,M. *Prof. Accred.:* Teacher Education (*e,s,p*). Pres. William J. Farrell.
Enroll.: 3,577
(603) 536-1550

Polytechnic Institute of New England
546 Amherst St., Nashua 03063. Private. 1983 (NATTS). Courses of varying lengths. Certificates, diplomas. Dir. Timothy Kolojay.
Enroll.: 36
(603) 881-8277

Rivier College
Nashua 03060. Private (Roman Catholic) liberal arts primarily for women. 1948/1983 (NEASC-CIHE). Sem. plan. Degrees: A,B,M. *Prof. Accred.:* Medical Laboratory Technology (A). Pres. Sister Jeanne Perreault.
Enroll.: 2,257
(603) 888-1311

Saint Anselm College
Manchester 03102. Private (Roman Catholic) liberal arts. 1941/1979 (NEASC-CIHE). Sem. plan. Degrees: A,B. *Prof. Accred.:* Nursing (B). Pres. Brother Joachim W. Froehlich, O.S.B.
Enroll.: 1,917
(603) 669-1030

*School for Lifelong Learning
Durham 03824. Public (state) adult education. 1980/1986 (NEASC-CIHE). Sem. plan. Degrees: A,B. Dean Alvin Hall.
Enroll.: 4,172
(603) 862-1692

Travel Education Center
402 Amherst St., Nashua 03063. Private. 1985 (NATTS). Courses of varying lengths. Certificates, diplomas. Dir. Linda Paresky.
(603) 880-7200

* Member University System of New Hampshire

University System of New Hampshire
Central office. Dunlap Center, Durham 03824-3563. Public (state). Chanc. Claire Van Ummersen.
(603) 868-1800

University of New Hampshire
Durham 03824. Public (state). 1929/1985 (NEASC-CIHE); accreditation includes Manchester campus (formerly Merrimack Valley College). Sem. plan. Degrees: A,B,M,D. *Prof. Accred.:* Engineering (chemical, civil, electrical, mechanical), Engineering Technology (electrical, mechanical), Forestry, Music, Nursing, Occupational Therapy, Social Work (B), Teacher Education (*e,s,p*). Pres. Gordon A. Haaland.
Enroll.: 13,602
(603) 862-1234

* Member University System of New Hampshire

White Pines College
Chester 03036. Private junior. 1975/1985 (NEASC-CIHE). Sem. plan. Degrees: A. Pres. Faith Preston.
Enroll.: 64
(603) 887-4401

NEW JERSEY

American Business Academy
66 Moore St., Hackensack 07601. Private. 1976/1982 (AICS). Qtr. plan. Diplomas. Pres. S. Theodore Takvorian.
Enroll.: 242 (*f.t.* 6 m., 236 w.)
(201) 488-9400

Associated Business Careers
1616 Pacific Ave., Suite 801, Atlantic City 08401. Private. 1984 (AICS). Qtr. plan. Certificates, diplomas. Dir. Stanley Wiley.
(609) 344-1954

Branch Campus
Cranbrook Professional Bldg., Whitehorse-Mercerville-Hamilton Township 08619.
(609) 581-0222

Associated Business Careers
106 W. Atlantic Ave., Roads B and C, Audubon Park 08106. Private. 1981/1984 (AICS). Qtr. plan. Certificates, diplomas. Exec. Dir. Marianne Tedesco.
Enroll.: 1,231 (*f.t.* 310 m., 921 w.)
(609) 546-0512

Assumption College for Sisters
Hilltop Rd., Mendham 07945-9998. Private (Roman Catholic) junior for training of sisters. 1965/1985 (MSA/CHE). Sem. plan. Degrees: A. Pres. Sister Mary Gerard Gebler, S.C.C.
Enroll.: 11 (*f.t.* 8 w.)
(201) 543-6528

Atlantic Community College
Mays Landing 08330. Public (county) junior. 1971/1986 (MSA/CHE). Sem. plan. Degrees: A. *Prof. Accred.:* Engineering Technology (electronic), Medical Laboratory Technology (A), Nursing (A), Respiratory Therapy, Respiratory Therapy Technology. Pres. Ronald W. Bush.
Enroll.: 4,164 (*f.t.* 455 m., 592 w.)
(609) 625-1111

Berdan Institute
265 Rt. 46 West, Totowa 07512. Private. 1980 (NATTS). Courses of varying lengths. Certificates, diplomas. *Prof. Accred.:* Dental Assisting. Dir. Ruth P. Lipka.
Enroll.: f.t. 100 w.
(201) 256-3444

Bergen Community College
Paramus 07652. Public (county). 1972/1986 (MSA/CHE). Sem. plan. Degrees: A. *Prof. Accred.:* Dental Hygiene, Medical Assisting, Medical Laboratory Technology (A), Nursing (A), Radiography, Respiratory Therapy, Surgical Technology. Pres. Jose Lopez-Isa.
Enroll.: 11,008 (*f.t.* 1,860 m., 1,944 w.)
(201) 447-7100

The Berkeley School
Drawer F, Little Falls 07424. Private junior. 1967/1981 (AICS); 1983 (MSA/CHE). Qtr. plan. Degrees: A, diplomas. Pres. Jack R. Jones.
Enroll.: 785 (*f.t.* 1 m., 614 w.)
(201) 278-5400

The Berkeley School
100 W. Prospect St., Waldick 07463. Private business. 1969/1981 (AICS). Qtr. plan. Diplomas. Vice Pres/Dir. Patricia Koch.
Enroll.: 425 (*f.t.* 0 m., 425 w.)
(201) 652-0388

Branch Campus
P.O. Box 815, White Horse Pike, Pomona 08240. Dir. Joette G. Dodds.
(609) 652-0444

The Berkeley School of Mt. Laurel
8000-A Greentree Industrial Pkwy., Mt. Laurel 08054. Private business 1981 (AICS). Qtr. plan. Diplomas. Dir. Samuel J. Morreale.
(609) 983-8307

Beth Medrash Govoha
617 Sixth St., Lakewood 08701. Private professional. 1974/1985. Degrees: B and M of Rabbinic and Talmudic Studies. *Prof. Accred.:* Rabbinical and Talmudic Education. Pres. Rabbi M. Kotler.
Enroll.: 960 (*f.t.* 894 m., 0 w.)
(201) 367-1060

Bi-Lingual Institute
571 Broad St., Newark 07102. Private business. 1982 (AICS). Courses of varying lengths. Certificates, diplomas. Dir. Eduardo L. Gonzalez.
Enroll.: 106 (*f.t.* 14 m., 92 w.)
(201) 624-3883

Bloomfield College
Franklin St., Bloomfield 07003. Private (United Presbyterian) liberal arts. 1960/1983 (MSA/CHE). 4-1-4 plan. Degrees: B. *Prof. Accred.:* Nursing (B). Pres. ———.
Enroll.: 1,463 (*f.t.* 301 m., 504 w.)
(201) 748-9000

Brick Computer Science Institute
525 Hwy. 70, Brick Office Park, Brick 08723. Private. 1974/1980 (NATTS). Courses of varying lengths. Diplomas. Dir. Edward Zapp.
Enroll.: 240 (*f.t.* 130 m., 110 w.)
(201) 477-0975

Brookdale Community College
Newman Springs Rd., Lincroft 07738. Public junior. Accreditation includes Learning Center at Long Branch 07740; (201) 224-8440. 1972/1985 (MSA/CHE). Tri. plan. Degrees: A. *Prof. Accred.* Medical Laboratory Technology (A), Nursing (A), Respiratory Therapy. Pres. Bob A. Barringer.
Enroll.: 10,973 (*f.t.* 1,446 m., 1,450 w.)
(201) 842-1900

Burlington County College
Pemberton 08068. Public junior. 1972/1983 (MSA/CHE). Sem. plan. *Prof. Accred.* Medical Laboratory Technology (A). Degrees: A. Pres. ———.
Enroll.: 6,704 (*f.t.* 903 m., 1,047 w.)
(609) 894-9311

Business Training Institute
Bergen Mall, Rte. 4, Paramus 07652. Private business. 1985 (AICS). Courses of varying lengths. Certificates, diplomas. Pres. James P. Mellett, Jr.
(201) 845-9300

Caldwell College
Caldwell 07006. Private (Roman Catholic) liberal art primarily for women. 1952/1985 (MSA/CHE). Sem. plan. Degrees: B. Pres. Sister Vivien Jennings, O.P.
Enroll.: 749 (*f.t.* 451 w.)
(201) 228-4424

Camden County College
Blackwood 08012. Public junior. 1972/1983 (MSA/CHE). Sem. plan. Degrees: A. *Prof. Accred.:* Dental Assisting, Dental Hygiene, Medical Laboratory Technology (A). Pres. Otto R. Mauke.
Enroll.: 8,130 (*f.t.* 1,241 m., 1,472 w.)
(609) 227-7200

Centenary College
400 Jefferson St., Hackettstown 07840. Private primarily for women. 1932/1979 (MSA/CHE). Sem. plan. Degrees: A,B. Pres. Stephanie Mitchell Bennett.
Enroll.: 1,063 (*f.t.* 546 w.)
(201) 852-1400

Century Institute of Court Reporting
270 State St., Hackensack 07602. Private. 1976/1982 (AICS). Courses of varying lengths. Certificates. Dir. John R. Squillace.
Enroll.: 202 (*f.t.* 5 m., 197 w.)
(201) 343-5330

Chubb Institute for Computer Technology
8 Sylvan Way, Box 342, Parsippany 07054-0342. Private. 1972/1977 (NATTS). Courses of varying lengths. Diplomas. Dir. Peter C. Enander.
Enroll.: 500 (*f.t.* 150 m., 130 w.)
(201) 285-9700

Cittone Institute
1697 Oak Tree Rd., Edison 08820. Private business. 1975/1984 (AICS). Courses of varying lengths. Certificates. Dir. Simon Cittone.
Enroll.: 1,693 (*f.t.* 340 m., 1,353 w.)
(201) 548-8798

Claire DeMarzo Institute of Professional Electrology
5 Park Ave., Westwood 07675. Private. 1983 (NATTS). 10-week courses. Certificates. Dir. Claire DeMarzo.
Enroll.: 10
(201) 664-0171

Clifton School of Business—Sawyer Campus
346 Lexington Ave., Clifton 07011. Private business. 1973/1985 (AICS). Courses of varying lengths. Certificates. Pres. Joseph McGlone.
Enroll.: 581 (*f.t.* 21 m., 560 w.)
(201) 546-3470

Branch Campus
2108 E. Thomas Rd., Phoenix, AZ 85016. Dir. Jack King.
(602) 277-0592

College of Saint Elizabeth
Convent Station 07961. Private (Roman Catholic) liberal arts for women. 1921/1984 (MSA/CHE). Sem. plan. Degrees: B. Pres. Sister Jacqueline Burns.
Enroll.: 991 (*f.t.* 3 m., 427 w.)
(201) 539-1600

Computer Learning Center
160 E. Route 4, Paramus 07652. Private business. 1985 (AICS). Courses of varying lengths. Certificates. Dir. Stuart Arnheim.
(201) 845-6868

County College of Morris
Route 10 and Center Grove Rd., Randolph 07869. Public (county) junior. 1972/1983 (MSA/CHE). Sem. plan. Degrees: A. *Prof. Accred.:* Dental Assisting, Engineering Technology (electronics, mechanical), Medical Laboratory Technology, Nursing (A). Pres. Edward J. Yaw.
Enroll.: 11,012 (*f.t.* 2,418 m., 2,024 w.)
(201) 361-5000

Cumberland County College
College Dr., P.O. Box 517, Vineland 08360. Public (county) junior. 1970/1981 (MSA/CHE). Sem. plan. Degrees: A. *Prof. Accred.:* Nursing (A). Pres. Philip S. Phelon.
Enroll.: 2,357 (*f.t.* 268 m., 546 w.)
(609) 691-8600

DeVry Technical Institute
479 Green St., Woodbridge 07095. Private 1971/1983 (NATTS); 1981 (NCA). Tri. plan. Certificates, diplomas. Pres. Robert Bocchino.
Enroll.: 2,353 (*f.t.* 2,063 m., 97 w.)
(201) 634-3460

Divers' Academy of the Eastern Seaboard
2500 Broadway, Camden 08104. Private. 1981 (NATTS). Courses of varying lengths. Diplomas. Pres. William Brown.
Enroll.: *f.t.* 30 m.
(609) 966-1871

Don Bosco College
Swartswood Rd., Newton 07860. Private (Roman Catholic, Salesian Society) seminary. 1966/1986 (MSA/CHE). Sem. plan. Degrees: B. Interim Pres. V. Rev. Joseph M. Occhio, S.D.B.
Enroll.: 62 (*f.t.* 50 m., 12 w.)
(201) 383-3900

Dorothy Aristone's School of Paramedical and Business Professions
Routes 73 & 38, Maple Shade 08052. Private. 1980 (NATTS). Courses of varying lengths. Diplomas. Pres. Dorothy Aristone.
Enroll.: 175 (*f.t.* 15 m., 160 w.)
(609) 234-5223

Dover Business College
15 E. Blackwell St., Dover 07801. Private. 1974/1981 (AICS). Qtr. plan. Certificates, diplomas. Dir. Fern K. Stone.
Enroll.: 191 (*f.t.* 0 m., 191 w.)
(201) 366-6700

Drake College of Business
9 Caldwell Pl., Elizabeth 07201. Private. 1982/1985 (AICS). Sem. plan. Certificates, diplomas. Pres. Frieda Kay.
Enroll.: 73 (*f.t.* 1 m., 72 w.)
(201) 352-5509

Drake Secretarial College
905 Bergen Ave., Jersey City 07306. Private. 1983 (AICS). Sem. plan. Certificates, diplomas. Dir. Catherine Palmer.
(201) 653-2875

Drew University
Route 24, Madison 07940. Private (United Methodist). 1932/1985 (MSA/CHE). 4-1-4 plan. Degrees: B,P,M,D. *Prof. Accred.:* Theology. Pres. Paul Hardin.
Enroll.: 2,354 (*f.t.* 712 m., 834 w.)
(201) 377-3000

du Cret School of the Arts
1030 Central Ave., Plainfield 07060. Private. 1979 (NATTS). Sem. plan. Certificates, diplomas. Dir. Frank J. Falotico.
Enroll.: 220 (*f.t.* 136 m., 84 w.)
(201) 757-7171

Electronic Computer Programming Institute
152 Market St., Paterson 07505. Private. 1969/1974 (NATTS). Courses of varying lengths. Certificates. Pres. John Tinnesz.
Enroll.: 149 (*f.t.* 70 m., 37 w.)
(201) 523-1200

Empire Technical Schools of New Jersey
576 Central Ave., East Orange 07018. Private. 1969/1980 (NATTS). Courses of varying lengths. Certificates. Dir. Timothy M. Rodgers.
Enroll.: 354 (*f.t.* 210 m., 144 w.)
(201) 675-0565

Engine City Technical Institute
Route 22 W., Box 3316, Union 07083. Private. 1984 (NATTS). Courses of varying lengths. Certificates. Dir. Larry Berlin.
(201) 964-1450

Essex College of Business
15 New St., Newark 07102. Private. 1970/1982 (AICS). Courses of varying lengths. Certificates. Pres. Jay M. Brill.
Enroll.: 1,654 (*f.t.* 415 m., 1,239 w.)
(201) 624-7300

Branch Campus
Routes 4 and 17, Paramus 07652. Dir. Ilse Nathan.
(201) 368-2920

Essex County College
303 University Ave., Newark 07102. Public (state) junior. 1974/1983 (MSA/CHE). Sem. plan. Degrees: A. *Prof. Accred.:* Radiography. Pres. A. Zachary Yamba.
Enroll.: 5,007 (*f.t.* 1,119 m., 1,646 w.)
(201) 877-3000

Branch Campus
Routes 4 and 17, Paramus 07652. Dir. Ilse Nathan.
(201) 368-2920

Fairleigh Dickinson University
Rutherford 07070. Private; campuses at Madison, Rutherford, Teaneck-Hackensack. 1948/1986 (MSA/CHE). Sem. plan. Degrees: (Florham-Madison) A,B,M; (Rutherford) B,M; (Teaneck) A,B,P,M,D. *Prof. Accred.:* Dental Hygiene, Dentistry, Engineering (electrical, industrial, mechanical), Nursing (B), Radiography, Respiratory Therapy, Social Work (B). Pres. Robert H. Donaldson.
Total
Enroll.: 14,305 (*f.t.* 3,601 m., 2,813 w.)
(201) 460-5000

Felician College
Lodi 07644. Private (Roman Catholic) liberal arts. 1974/1985 (MSA/CHE). Sem. plan. Degrees: A,B. *Prof. Accred.:* Medical Laboratory Technology, Nursing (A,B). Pres. Sister Theresa Mary Martin.
Enroll.: 574
(201) 778-1190

First School of Secretarial and Paralegal Studies
110 Main Ave., Passaic 07055. Private. 1977/1983 (AICS). Qtr. plan. Certificates, diplomas. Dir. Barbara Mongiello.
Enroll.: 1,062 (*f.t.* 84 m., 978 w.)
(201) 777-2121

Branch Campus
516 Main St., East Orange 07018. Dir. Beverlee J. Levy.
(201) 675-4300

Branch Campus
2200 Bergenline Ave., Union City 07087. Dir. James Jeffers.
(201) 867-3500

General Technical Institute
1118 Baltimore Ave., Linden 07036. Private. 1967/1977 (NATTS). Courses of varying lengths. Certificates, diplomas. Pres. Gregory G. Sytch, Jr.
Enroll.: 83 (*f.t.* 39 m., 3 w.)
(201) 486-9353

Georgian Court College
Lakewood Ave., Lakewood 08701. Private (Roman Catholic) liberal arts primarily for women. 1922/1984 (MSA/CHE). Sem. plan. Degrees: B,M. Pres. Sister Barbara Williams.
Enroll.: 1,608 (*f.t.* 23 m., 704 w.)
(201) 364-2200

Glassboro State College
Glassboro 08028. Public liberal arts and teachers. Accreditation includes Camden Campus, Camden 08102. 1958/1984 (MSA/CHE). Sem. plan. Degrees: B,M. *Prof. Accred.:* Music, Teacher Education (*e,s,p*). Pres. Herman D. James.
Enroll.: 9,436 (*f.t.* 2,657 m., 3,383 w.)
(609) 863-5000

Gloucester County College
Sewell 08080. Public junior. 1973/1978 (MSA/CHE). Sem. plan. Degrees: A. *Prof. Accred.:* Nuclear Medicine Technology, Nursing (A), Respiratory Therapy. Pres. Gary L. Reddig.
Enroll.: 3,383 (*f.t.* 571 m., 647 w.)
(609) 468-5000

HCA Institute
Cherry Hill Exec. Campus, 430 Cherry Hill Mall, Cherry Hill 08002. Private. 1978 (NATTS). Sem. plan. Diplomas. Gen. Mgr. Joseph D. Fuller.
Enroll.: 141 (*f.t.* 1 m., 140 w.)
(609) 663-8500

Harris School of Business
654 Longwood Ave., Cherry Hill 08002. Private. 1978/1982 (AICS). Courses of varying lengths. Certificates, diplomas. Pres. Ethel S. Harris.
Enroll.: 388 (*f.t.* 4 m., 384 w.)
(609) 662-5300

Branch Campus
3401 Blackhorse Pike, P.O. Box 1019, Turnersville. Dir. Gail Peterson.
(609) 728-1500

Branch Campus
301-B E. Lea Blvd., Wilmington, DE 19802. Dir. Gail Peterson.
(302) 764-4483

Hill Institute
21 Bloomfield Ave., Denville 07834. Private business. 1982 (AICS). Qtr. plan. Certificates, diplomas. Dir. Philip Fishman.
Enroll.: 62 (*f.t.* 3 m., 59 w.)
(201) 625-2660

Ho-Ho-Kus School
27 S. Franklin Tpk., Ramsey 07446. Private business. 1976/1985 (AICS). Courses of varying lengths. Certificates. Dir. Thomas Eastwick.
Enroll.: 86
(201) 327-8877

Hudson County Community College
168 Sip Ave., Jersey City 07306. Public (county) degree-granting agency, contracts for services from other colleges and schools; off-campus centers at Hoboken, Journal Square, Lafayette, North Hudson. 1981/1986 (MSA/CHE). Sem. plan. Degrees: A. *Prof. Accred.:* Engineering Technology (electronics), Medical Assisting, Medical Record Technology. Pres. Joseph F. Scott.
Enroll.: 3,365 (*f.t.* 837 m., 1,244 w.)
(201) 656-2020

Immaculate Conception Seminary of Seton Hall University
400 S. Orange Ave., South Orange 07079. Private (Roman Catholic) graduate school of theology. 1977/1982 (MSA/CHE). Sem. plan. Degrees: P,M. *Prof. Accred.:* Theology (1977/1982, ATS). Rector/Dean Richard M. Liddy.
Enroll.: 158
(201) 761-9575

Institute of Business and Technology
Three William St., Newark 07102. Private. 19791982 (AICS). Courses of varying lengths. Certificates. Pres. LeCogbill Friend.
Enroll.: 537 (*f.t.* 51 m., 486 w.)
(201) 624-0380

Branch Campus
3355 Lenox Road, N.E., No. 175, Atlanta, GA 30326. Dir. Doug Solomon.
(404) 262-1552

Branch Campus
400 Market St., Philadelphia, PA 10106. Dir. Michael Lowry.
(215) 592-8800

Institute of Business Careers
25 Scotch Rd., Suburban Shopping Center, Trenton 08628. Private. 1983 (AICS). Courses of varying lengths. Certificates. Pres. Andrew Dovi.
Enroll.: 225 (*f.t.* 34 m., 191 w.)
(609) 883-3943

Jersey City State College
2039 Kennedy Blvd., Jersey City 07305. Public liberal arts and teachers. 1959/1985 (MSA/CHE). Sem. plan. Degrees: B,P,M. *Prof. Accred.:* Art, Music, Nursing, Teacher Education (*e,s*). Pres. William J. Maxwell.
Enroll.: 7,450 (*f.t.* 1,535 m., 1,647 w.)
(201) 547-6000

Joe Kubert School of Cartoon and Graphic Art
37 Myrtle Ave., Dover 07801. Private. 1980 (NATTS). Sem. plan. Diplomas. Pres. Joe Kubert.
Enroll.: 99 (*f.t.* 60 m., 10 w.)
(201) 361-1327

Kane Business Institute
206 Haddonfield Rd., Cherry Hill 08002. Private. 1985 (AICS). Courses of varying lengths. Certificates, diplomas. Dir. Elma J. Kane.
(609) 488-1166

Branch Campus
319 Cooper St., Camden 08102.
(609) 963-1111

Katharine Gibbs School
33 Plymouth St., Montclair 07042. Private junior. 1967/1983 (AICS). Sem. plan. Certificates. Dir. Ann L. Maude.
Enroll.: 1,107 (*f.t.* 10 m., 1,097 w.)
(201) 744-2010

Branch Campus
80 Kingsbridge Rd., Piscataway 08854. Dir. Gloria Davis.
(201) 885-1580

Kean College of New Jersey
Union 07083. Public liberal arts and teachers. 1960/1985 (MSA/CHE). Sem. plan. Degrees: B,M. *Prof. Accred.:* Medical Record Administration, Music, Nursing (B), Occupational Therapy, Physical Therapy, Social Work (B), Teacher Education (*e,s,p*). Pres. Nathan Weiss.
Enroll.: 12,933 (*f.t.* 2,559 m., 3,487 w.)
(201) 527-2000

Lincoln Technical/Business Institute
Haddonfield Rd. at Rte. 130 N., Pennsauken 08110. Private. 1975/1980 (AICS); 1967/1978

(NATTS). Courses of varying lengths. Diplomas. Dir. Herman Solitrin.
Enroll.: 660 (*f.t.* 322 m., 28 w.)
(609) 665-3010

LINCOLN TECHNICAL INSTITUTE
2299 Vauxhall Rd., Union 07083. Private. 1967/1983 (NATTS). Courses of varying lengths. Diplomas. Dir. Michael R. Iannacone.
Enroll.: 1,100 (*f.t.* 1,095 m., 5 w.)
(201) 964-7800

LYONS INSTITUTE
16 Springdale Rd., Cherry Hill 08003. Private. 1971/1976 (NATTS). Courses of varying lengths. Diplomas. *Prof. Accred.:* Medical Assisting, Medical Laboratory Technology. Pres. Michael Dubroff.
Enroll.: 300 (*f.t.* 125 m., 100 w.)
(609) 424-5800

LYONS INSTITUTE
10 Commerce Pl., Clark 07066. Private. 1977/1984 (NATTS). Courses of varying lengths. Diplomas. *Prof. Accred.:* Medical Assisting, Medical Laboratory Technology. Dir. George T. Sappington.
Enroll.: 176 (*f.t.* 45 m., 70 w.)
(201) 574-2090

LYONS INSTITUTE
320 Main St., Hackensack 07601. Private. 1971/1977 (NATTS). Courses of varying lengths. Diplomas. *Prof. Accred.:* Medical Assisting, Medical Laboratory Technology. Pres. Michael Dubroff.
Enroll.: 340 (*f.t.* 136 m., 74 w.)
(201) 488-3790

MTA SCHOOL
1231 Rte. 22 W., Box 6807, Bridgewater 08807. Private. 1983 (NATTS). Courses of varying lengths. Certificates. Pres. Robert Antonelli.
(201) 526-7050

MERCER COUNTY COMMUNITY COLLEGE
P.O. Box B, Trenton 08690. Public (county) junior. Accreditation includes James Kerney Campus, Trenton O8608; (609) 586-4800. 1967/1985 (MSA/CHE). Sem. plan. Degrees: A. *Prof. Accred.:* Dental Assisting, Engineering Technology (civil, construction, electrical, mechanical), Medical Laboratory Technology, Nursing (A), Radiography. Pres. John P. Hanley.
Enroll.: 8,623 (*f.t.* 1,300 m., 1,237 w.)
(609) 586-4800

METROPOLITAN TECHNICAL INSTITUTE
400 Lyster Ave., Saddle Brook 07662. Private. 1982 (NATTS). Courses of varying lengths. Certificates. Dir. Frank Gergelyi.
(201) 843-4004

MIDDLESEX COUNTY COLLEGE
Edison 08818. Public (county) junior. 1970/1981 (MSA/CHE). Sem. plan. Degrees: A. *Prof. Accred.:* Dental Assisting, Dental Hygiene, Engineering Technology (civil/construction, electrical, mechanical), Medical Laboratory Technology, Nursing (A), Radiography. Pres. Flora Mancuso-Edwards.
Enroll.: 10,499 (*f.t.* 2,023 m., 2,065 w.)
(201) 548-6000

MONMOUTH COLLEGE
West Long Branch 07764. Private liberal arts. 1952/1986 (MSA/CHE). Sem. plan. Degrees: A,B,M. *Prof. Accred.:* Engineering (electronic), Medical Technology, Nursing (B), Social Work (B). Pres. Samuel H. Magill.
Enroll.: 4,414 (*f.t.* 1,054 m., 1,058 w.)
(201) 222-6600

MONTCLAIR STATE COLLEGE
Upper Montclair 07043. Public liberal arts and teachers. 1937/1982 (MSA/CHE). Sem. plan. Degrees: B,M. *Prof. Accred.:* Music, Teacher Education (*s,p*). Pres. Donald E. Walters.
Enroll.: 13,915 (*f.t.* 2,857 m., 4,599 w.)
(201) 893-4000

THE NASH ACADEMY OF ANIMAL ARTS
595 Anderson Ave., Cliffside Park 07010. Private. 1982 (NATTS). Courses of varying lengths. Certificates, diplomas. Dir. John Nash.
Enroll.: f.t. 12
(201) 945-2710

NATIONAL EDUCATION CENTER-BRYMAN CAMPUS
211 Route 18, East Brunswick 08816. Private. 1972/1978 (NATTS). Courses of varying lengths. Diplomas. *Prof. Accred.:* Medical Assisting. Dir. Warren P. Thompson.
Enroll.: f.t. 350 w.
(201) 249-9383

NATIONAL EDUCATION CENTER/R.E.T.S. ELECTRONIC SCHOOL CAMPUS
103 Park Ave., Nutley 07110. Private. 1977/1983 (NATTS). Qtr. plan. Certificates, diplomas. Dir. Martin Klangasky.
Enroll.: 569 (*f.t.* 317 m., 12 w.)
(201) 661-0600

Naval Air Technical Training Center
Lakehurst 08733. Public (federal). 1984 (SACS-COEI). Courses of varying lengths. Certificates. Commandant Capt. N. H. Lowery.
Enroll.: 926

Branch Campus
Naval Air Station, North Island, San Diego, CA 92135.

Branch Campus
Naval Air Station, Norfolk, VA 23511.

New Brunswick Theological Seminary
New Brunswick 08901. Private (Reformed) professional; graduate only. Sem. plan. Degrees: P,M. *Prof. Accred.:* Theology (1938/1973, ATS). Pres. Robert A. White.
Enroll.: 133
(201) 247-5241

New Jersey Institute of Technology
323 Martin Luther King, Jr. Blvd., Newark 07102. Public (state and city) technological. 1934/1982 (MSA/CHE). Sem. plan. Degrees: B,M,D. *Prof. Accred.:* Architecture (B), Engineering (chemical, civil, electrical, engineering science, industrial, mechanical), Engineering Technology (construction/contracting, electrical systems, environmental, manufacturing, mechanical). Pres. Saul K. Fenster.
Enroll.: 7,495 (*f.t.* 3,415 m., 545 w.)
(201) 596-3300

New York School of Dog Grooming
311 Hackensack St., Carlstadt 07072. Private. 1985 (NATTS). Courses of varying lengths. Certificates. Dir. Sam Kohl.
(201) 933-3636

Northeastern Bible College
12 Oak La., Essex Fells 07021. Private (Interdenominational) professional. 1958/1978 (AABC); 1974/1978 (MSA/CHE). Sem. plan. Degrees: A,B. Pres. Robert W. Benton.
Enroll.: 228 (*f.t.* 67 m., 42 w.)
(201) 226-1074

Ocean County College
Toms River 08753. Public junior. 1969/1984 (MSA/CHE). Sem. plan. Degrees: A. *Prof. Accred.:* Engineering Technology (civil, electronic), Nursing (A). Pres. Milton Shaw.
Enroll.: 5,538 (*f.t.* 1,109 m., 1,211 w.)
(201) 255-4000

Omega Institute
Rte. 130 S., Cinnaminson Mall, Cinnaminson 08077. Private business. 1982 (AICS). Courses of varying lengths. Certificates, diplomas. *Prof. Accred.:* Medical Assisting. Pres. Jeffrey H. Gitomer.
Enroll.: 294 (*f.t.* 29 m., 265 w.)
(609) 786-2200

Passaic County Community College
College Blvd., Paterson 07509. Public (state) junior. 1978/1984 (MSA/CHE). 4-1-4 plan. Degrees: A. *Prof. Accred.:* Nursing (A), Radiography, Respiratory Therapy. Pres. Kenneth E. Wright.
Enroll.: 2,940 (*f.t.* 500 m., 760 w.)
(201) 684-6800

Pennco Tech
Erial Rd., P.O. Box 1427, Blackwood 08012. Private. 1980 (NATTS). Courses of varying lengths. Diplomas. Dir. Donald S. Vandemark, Jr.
Enroll.: 748 (*f.t.* 547 m., 40 w.)
(609) 232-0310

Phillips Business School
137 Ellison St., Patterson 07505. Private. 1985 (AICS). Courses of varying lengths. Certificates. Dir. David Goehring.
(201) 279-9800

The Plaza School of Drafting
Garden State Plaza, Rtes. 4 and 17, Paramus 07652. Private business and technical. 1971/1978 (NATTS). Courses of varying lengths. Diplomas. Pres. Leslie Balter.
Enroll.: 120 (*f.t.* 45 m., 20 w.)
(201) 843-0344

Popkin School of Court Reporting
496 N. Kings Hwy., Cherry Hill 08034. Private. 1978/1984 (AICS). Courses of varying lengths. Certificates. Dir. Claire Popkin.
Enroll.: 126 (*f.t.* 8 m., 118 w.)
(609) 779-0045

Princeton Theological Seminary
Princeton 08542. Private (Presbyterian, U.S.A.), professional; graduate only. 1968/1984 (MSA/CHE). Sem. plan. Degrees: P,M,D. *Prof. Accred.:* Theology (1938/1978, ATS). Pres. Thomas W. Gillespie.
Enroll.: 854
(609) 921-8300

Princeton University
Princeton 08544. Private. 1921/1984 (MSA/CHE). Sem. plan. Degrees: B,M,D. *Prof. Accred.:* Architecture (M), Engineering (aerospace physics, geological, mechanical). Pres. William G. Bowen.

Enroll.: 6,293 (*f.t.* 4,030 m., 2,176 w.)
(609) 452-3000

Rabbinical College of America
226 Sussex Ave., Morristown 07960. Private professional. 1979/1985. Degrees: B of Rel. Studies. *Prof. Accred.:* Rabbinical and Talmudic Education. Pres. Rabbi M. Herson.
Enroll.: f.t. 230 m.
(201) 267-9404

Ramapo College of New Jersey
Mahwah 07430-1680. Public (state) liberal arts. 1975/1981 (MSA/CHE). Sem. plan. Degrees: B. *Prof. Accred.:* Social Work (B). Pres. Robert A. Scott.
Enroll.: 3,934 (*f.t.* 1,279 m., 970 w.)
(201) 825-2800

Rider College
2083 Lawrenceville Rd., Lawrenceville 08648-3099. Private, business, teacher and liberal arts. 1955/1986 (MSA/CHE). 5-1-5 plan. Degrees: A,B,M. *Prof. Accred.:* Teacher Education (*e,s*). Pres. Frank N. Elliott.
Enroll.: 4,971 (*f.t.* 1,479 m., 1,578 w.)
(609) 896-5000

Roberts-Walsh Business School
2343 Morris Ave., Union 07083. Private. 1968/1982 (AICS). Qtr. plan. Certificates. Pres. John P. Walsh.
Enroll.: 1,372 (*f.t.* 224 m., 1,148 w.)
(201) 964-3663

Rutgers, The State University of New Jersey
Central Office, New Brunswick 08903. Public (state). Sem. plan. Pres. Edward J. Bloustein.
(201) 932-1766

New Brunswick Campus
New Brunswick 08903. Cook College, Douglass College (women), Livingston College, Rutgers College, University College. 1921/1983 (MSA/CHE). Degrees: A,B,P,M,D. *Prof. Accred.:* Assistant to the Primary Care Physician, Engineering (agricultural, ceramic, chemical, civil, electrical, industrial, mechnical), Landscape Architecture, Librarianship, Music, Pharmacy, Psychology, Social Work (B,M). Provost Kenneth W. Wheeler.
Enroll.: 33,524 (*f.t.* 11,843 m., 12,301 w.)
(201) 932-1766

Newark Campus
Newark 07102. 1946/1983 (MSA/CHE). Degrees: B,P,M,D. *Prof. Accred.:* Business (B,M), Law, Music, Nursing (B,M), Psychology, Social Work (B). Provost Norman Samuels.
Enroll.: 9,400 (*f.t.* 2,519 m., 2,501 w.)
(201) 648-1766

Camden Campus
Camden 08102. 1950/1983 (MSA/CHE). Degrees: B,P,M. *Prof. Accred.:* Law, Nursing (B), Social Work (B). Provost Walter K. Gordon.
Enroll.: 4,722 (*f.t.* 1,419 m., 1,322 w.)
(609) 757-1766

Saint Peter's College
2641 Kennedy Blvd., Jersey City 07306. Private (Roman Catholic) liberal arts and business; accreditation includes Englewood Cliffs campus. 1935/1983 (MSA/CHE). Sem. plan (qtr. plan in night division). Degrees: A,B,M. *Prof. Accred.:* Nursing (B). Pres. Rev. Edward Glynn., S.J.
Enroll.: 3,757 (*f.t.* 1,119 m., 1,172 w.)
(201) 333-4400

Salem Community College
460 Hollywood Ave., Carneys Point 08069. Public 2-year. 1979/1984 (MSA/CHE). Sem. plan. Degrees: A. Pres. William Wenzel.
Enroll.: 1,002 (*f.t.* 170 m., 321 w.)
(609) 299-2100

Sawyer School
664 Newark Ave., Elizabeth 07208. Private business. 1972/1981 (AICS). Courses of varying lengths. Certificates. Pres. George Vomacka.
Enroll.: 614 (*f.t.* 36 m., 578 w.)
(201) 351-5151

Branch Campus
305 E. Front St., Plainfield 07060. Dir. Carol Kane.
(201) 757-5151

School of Business Machines
880 Bergen Ave., Jersey City 07306. Private. 1975/1982 (AICS). Courses of varying lengths. Certificates, diplomas. Pres. Albert Stine.
Enroll.: 505 (*f.t.* 121 m., 384 w.)
(201) 656-4949

Branch Campus
5918 Bergenline Ave., West New York 07093. Dir. Robert A. Gutkowski.
(201) 861-6800

School of Data Programming
1969 Morris Ave., Union 07083. Private. 1986 (AICS). 60-week program. Diplomas. Pres. Thomas Scalea.

Enroll.: 62
(201) 964-1144

BRANCH CAMPUS
295 Pierson Ave., Edison 08837.
(201) 494-5450

BRANCH CAMPUS
188 E. Bergen Pl., Red Bank 07701.
(201) 741-0800

SETON HALL UNIVERSITY
South Orange 07079. Private (Roman Catholic) 1932/1986 (MSA/CHE). Sem. plan. Degrees: B,P,M,D. *Prof. Accred.*: Business (B,M), Nursing (B), Rehabilitation Counseling, Social Work (B), Teacher Education (*e,s,p*). Chanc. Msgr. John J. Petillo.
Enroll.: 7,556 (*f.t.* 2,365 m., 2,482 w.)
(201) 761-9000

SETON HALL UNIVERSITY SCHOOL OF LAW
Newark 07102. Degrees: P. *Prof. Accred.*: Law. Dean Elizabeth F. Defeis.
Enroll.: 1,234 (*f.t.* 638 m., 442 w.)
(201) 761-9000

SOMERSET COUNTY COLLEGE
Somerville 08876. Public (county) junior. 1972/1984 (MSA/CHE). Sem. plan. Degrees: A. *Prof. Accred.*: Nursing (A). Pres. S. Charles Irace.
Enroll.: 4,663 (*f.t.* 746 m., 618 w.)
(201) 526-1200

SPECTRUM INSTITUTE FOR THE ADVERTISING ARTS, INC.
32 New Amwell Rd., Somerville 08876. Private. 1981 (NATTS). Sem. plan. Diplomas. Asst. Dir. James S. MacDonald.
Enroll.: 68 (*f.t.* 37 m., 31 w.)
(201) 359-5155

STAFFORD HALL SCHOOL OF BUSINESS
185 Summit Ave., Summit 07901. Private. 1975/1985 (AICS). Courses of varying lengths. Diplomas. Pres. Thomas Heaton.
Enroll.: 118 (*f.t.* 0 m., 118 w.)
(201) 273-3661

STAR TECHNICAL INSTITUTE
Cinnaminson Mall, Rte. 130 S., Cinnaminson 08077. Private. 1982 (NATTS). Courses of varying lengths. Diplomas. Dir. Harry Commisso.
Enroll.: 125 (*f.t.* 70 m., 30 w.)
(609) 786-8836

STAR TECHNICAL INSTITUTE
Road 5, Box 617-A, Blackhorse Pike, Williamstown 08094. Private. 1984 (NATTS). Courses of varying lengths. Diplomas. Dir. Karen Commisso.
(695) 629-0550

STAR TECHNICAL INSTITUTE
1386 S. Delsea Dr., Vineland 08360. Private. 1985 (NATTS). Courses of varying lengths. Diplomas. Dir. Michael Cable.
(609) 696-0500

STEVENS INSTITUTE OF TECHNOLOGY
Hoboken 07030. Private coeducational technological. 1927/1983 (MSA/CHE). Sem. plan. Degrees: B,M,D. *Prof. Accred.*: Engineering. Pres. Kenneth C. Rogers.
Enroll.: 2,700 (*f.t.* 1,727 m., 346 w.)
(201) 420-5100

STOCKTON STATE COLLEGE
Pomona 08240. Public (state) liberal arts. 1975/1981 (MSA/CHE). Qtr. plan. Degrees: B. *Prof. Accred.*: Nursing (B), Social Work (B). Pres. Vera King Farris.
Enroll.: 4,922 (*f.t.* 2,102 m., 1,807 w.)
(609) 652-1776

STUART SCHOOL OF BUSINESS ADMINISTRATION
2400 Belmar Blvd., Wall 07719. Private. 1967/1979 (AICS). Sem. plan. Diplomas. Dir. Letitia M. Cooper.
Enroll.: 217 (*f.t.* 1 m., 216 w.)
(201) 681-7200

TALMUDICAL ACADEMY OF NEW JERSEY
Route 524, Adelphi 07710. Private; graduate and professional only. 1986. Degrees: B of Talmudic Studies. *Prof. Accred.*: Rabbinical and Talmudic Education. Pres. B. Leff.
Enroll.: 40 m.
(201) 420-5100

TAYLOR BUSINESS INSTITUTE
250 Rte. 28, P.O. Box 6875, Bridgewater 08807. Private. 1969/1981 (AICS). Qtr. plan. Diplomas. Dir. Peter Carey.
Enroll.: 4895 (*f.t.* 117 m., 372 w.)
(201) 231-1249

TAYLOR BUSINESS INSTITUTE
2444 Rte. 34, Manasquan 08736. Private. 1978/1984 (AICS). Courses of varying lengths. Certificates, diplomas. Dir. James W. Lawlor.
Enroll.: 555 (*f.t.* 149 m., 406 w.)
(201) 528-7363

Taylor Business Institute
8000 A Greentree Industrial Pkwy., Mt. Laurel 08054. Private. 1981 (AICS). Qtr. plan. Diplomas. Acting Dir. Kathleen Mazzy.
Enroll.: 238 (*f.t.* 67 m., 171 w.)
(609) 983-8307

Taylor Business Institute
291Buehler Pl. at Route 17, Paramus 07652. Private. 1974/1981 (AICS). Qtr. plan. Diplomas. Dir. Sheila Bellini.
Enroll.: 1,136 (*f.t.* 448 m., 688 w.)
(201) 967-8880

Branch Campus
One Park Pl., Bloomfield 07003. Dir. Sharon Confessore.
(201) 748-7601

Branch Campus
86 River St., Hoboken 07030. Dir. Warner Smith.
(201) 656-6185

Teterboro School of Aeronautics
80 Moonachie Ave., Teterboro 07608. Private. 1973/1979 (NATTS). Courses of varying lengths. Certificates, diplomas. Dir. Anthony DiStefano.
Enroll.: 480 (*f.t.* 476 m., 4 w.)
(201) 288-6300

Thomas A. Edison State College
101 W. State St.,C.N.545, Trenton 08625. Public (state) nonteaching liberal arts. Established to administer New Jersey's external degree program. 1977/1982 (MSA/CHE). Degrees: A,B. Pres. George A. Pruitt.
Enroll.: 2,774 (*f.t.* 0)
(609) 984-1100

Trenton State College
Hillwood Lakes, P.O. Box 940,C.N.550, Trenton 08625. Public liberal arts and professional. 1938/1985 (MSA/CHE). Sem. plan. Degrees: B,M. *Prof. Accred.:* Engineering Technology (electronic, mechanical), Interior Design, Music, Nursing (B), Teacher Education (*e,s,p*). Pres. Harold W. Eickhoff.
Enroll.: 8,652 (*f.t.* 2,068 m., 3,068 w.)
(609) 771-1855

Union County College
1033 Springfield Ave., Cranford 07016. Public junior. 1957/1983 (MSA/CHE). Accreditation includes branches at Elizabeth 07206 and Scotch Plains 07076. Sem. plan. Degrees: A. Pres. Derek N. Nunney.
Enroll.: 8,395 (*f.t.* 1,708 m., 1,872 w.)
(201) 276-2600

Union Technical Institute
1117 Green Grove Rd., Neptune 07753. Private. 1965/1982 (NATTS). Courses of varying lengths. Diplomas. Pres. Lawrence Kraft.
Enroll.: 280
(201) 922-1100

U.S. Army Chaplain Center and School
Watters Hall, Fort Monmouth 07703. Public (federal) professional. 1978/1983 (SACS-COEI). Courses of varying lengths. Certificates. Commandant Chap. (Col.) Richard R. Tupy, Jr.
Enroll.: FTE 200
(201) 532-4537

University of Medicine and Dentistry of New Jersey
Newark 07103. Public (state) professional. 1979/1985(MSA/CHE). Degrees: A,B,P,M,D. Pres. Stanley S. Bergen, Jr.

New Jersey Dental School
Newark 07103. Public (state) professional. 1965. Tri. plan. Degrees: A,P. *Prof. Accred.:* Dental Assisting, Dental Hygiene, Dentistry. Dean Theodore E. Bolden.
Enroll.: 697 (*f.t.* 268 m., 418 w.)

New Jersey Medical School
100 Bergen St., Newark 07103. Public (state) professional. 1974. Degrees: A,B,M,P,D. *Prof. Accred.:* Cytotechnology, Medical Technology, Medicine, Radiography, Respiratory Therapy Technology, Surgical Technology. Dean Vincent Lanzoni.
Enroll.: 2,728 (*f.t.* 2,101 m., 561 w.)

New Jersey School of Osteopathic Medicine
401 Haddon Ave., Camden 08103. Public professional. 1977. Sem. plan. Degrees: P. *Prof. Accred.:* Osteopathy. Acting Dean Robert Fogel.
Enroll.: 139 (*f.t.* 110 m., 29 w.)
(609) 757-7706

Rutgers Medical School
Piscataway 08854. Public (state) professional. 1973. Sem. plan. Degrees: P,D. *Prof. Accred.:* Medicine, Psychology. Dean Richard C. Reynolds.
Enroll.: 422 (*f.t.* 297 m., 125 w.)
(609) 463-4705

Upsala College
Prospect St., East Orange 07019. Private (Lutheran in America) liberal arts. Accreditation includes Wirths Campus, Sussex 07461; (201) 875-7187. 1936/1984 (MSA/CHE). Sem. plan. Degrees: A,B,M. *Prof. Accred.:* Social Work (B). Pres. David E. Schramm.
Enroll.: 1,366 (*f.t.* 494 m., 421 w.)
(201) 266-7000

Welder Training & Testing Institute
7015 Westfield Ave., Pennsauken 08110. Private. 1980 (NATTS). Courses of varying lengths. Certificates, diplomas. Dir. Ray Moyer.
Enroll.: 105 (*f.t.* 91 m., 4 w.)
(609) 663-6313

Westminster Choir College
Princeton 08540. Private professional 1966/1976. (MSA/CHE). 4-1-4 plan. Degrees: B,M. *Prof. Accred.:* Music. Pres. Ray E. Robinson.
Enroll.: 349 (*f.t.* 131 m., 185 w.)
(609) 921-7100

William Paterson College of New Jersey
300 Pompton Rd., Wayne 07470. Public (state) liberal arts and teachers. 1958/1982 (MSA/CHE). Sem. plan. Degrees: B,M. *Prof. Accred.:* Music, Nursing (B), Speech Pathology, Teacher Education (*e,s,p*). Pres. Arnold Speert.
Enroll.: 10,931 (*f.t.* 3,100 m., 3,539 w.)
(201) 595-2000

NEW MEXICO

ALBUQUERQUE TECHNICAL-VOCATIONAL INSTITUTE
Albuquerque 87106. Public 2-year. 1978 (NCA). Tri. plan. Certificates. *Prof. Accred.:* Practical Nursing, Respiratory Therapy. Pres. Louis E. Saavedra.
Enroll.: FTE 7,158
(505) 842-1400

COLLEGE OF SANTA FE
Santa Fe 87501. Private (Roman Catholic) liberal arts. 1965/1985 (NCA). Sem. plan. Degrees: A,B,M. *Prof. Accred.:* Art, Nursing (A), Social Work (B). Pres. Brother Donald C. Mouton, F.S.C.
Enroll.: FTE 885
(505) 473-6234

*COLLEGE OF THE SOUTHWEST
Hobbs 88240. Private liberal arts. 1980/1986 (NCA). Sem. plan. Degrees: B. Pres. Robert R. Galvan.
Enroll.: FTE 154
(505) 392-7237

EASTERN NEW MEXICO UNIVERSITY
Portales 88130. Public (state). 1947/1977 (NCA). Sem. plan. Degrees: A,B,M. *Prof. Accred.:* Music, Teacher Education (*e,s,p*). Pres. Robert Matheny.
Enroll.: FTE 3,190
1,700 (*f.t.* 1,670 m., (505) 562-2121

EASTERN NEW MEXICO UNIVERSITY—ROSWELL
Roswell 88201. 1971/1982 (NCA). Degrees: A. *Prof. Accred.:* Nursing (A). Prov. Lloyd Hughes.
Enroll.: FTE 845
(505) 347-5441

INSTITUTE OF AMERICAN INDIAN ARTS
Santa Fes 875701. Public (federal). 1985 (NCA). Sem. plan. Degrees: A, certificates. Pres. John C. Wade.
Enroll.: FTE 213
(505) 988-6463

LUNA VOCATIONAL TECHNICAL INSTITUTE
Las Vegas 87701. Public. 1982 (NCA). Tri. plan. Certificates. Pres. Samuel F. Vigil.
Enroll.: FTE 418
(505) 454-1484

*Accreditation on Probation

NEW MEXICO HIGHLANDS UNIVERSITY
Las Vegas 87701. Public (state) liberal arts and professional college. 1926/1981 (NCA). Sem. plan. Degrees: A,B,M. *Prof. Accred.:* Social Work (B,M). Pres. Gilbert Sanchez.
Enroll.: FTE 1,805
(505) 425-7511

NEW MEXICO INSTITUTE OF MINING AND TECHNOLOGY
Socorro 87801. Public (state) technological. 1949/1985 (NCA). Sem. plan. Degrees: B,M,D. *Prof. Accred.:* Engineering (geological, metallurgical, mining, petroleum). Pres. Laurence Lattman.
Enroll.: FTE 1,041
(505) 835-5508

NEW MEXICO JUNIOR COLLEGE
Hobbs 88240. Public (district). 1970/1986 (NCA). Sem. plan. Degrees: A. *Prof. Accred.:* Medical Laboratory Technology, Nursing (A). Pres. Robert A. Anderson, Jr.
Enroll.: FTE 1,305
(505) 392-6526

NEW MEXICO MILITARY INSTITUTE
Roswell 88201. Public (state) junior college. 1938/1981 (NCA). Sem. plan. Degrees: A. Pres. Maj. Gen. Gerald Childress.
Enroll.: FTE 446
(505) 622-6250

NEW MEXICO STATE UNIVERSITY—CENTRAL OFFICE
Las Cruces 88003. Public (state). Pres. James E. Halligan.
Enroll.: FTE 12,613
(505) 437-6860

NEW MEXICO STATE UNIVERSITY—MAIN CAMPUS
Las Cruces 88003. Public. 1926/1978 (NCA). Accreditation includes 2-year branch at Grants. Sem. plan with 2-week interim. Degrees: A,B,M,D. *Prof. Accred.:* Business (B,M), Dental Hygiene, Engineering (agricultural, chemical, civil, electrical, industrial, mechanical), Engineering Technology (civil, electronic, mechanical), Home Economics, Music, Social Work (B), Teacher Education (*e,s,p*). Pres. James E. Halligan.
Enroll.: FTE 12,613
(505) 646-2035

New Mexico State University at Alamogordo
Alamogordo 88310. 1973/1983 (NCA). Degrees: A. *Prof. Accred.:* Medical Laboratory Technology (A). Dir. Charles R. Reidlinger.
Enroll.: FTE 796
(505) 437-6860

New Mexico State University at Carlsbad
Carlsbad 88220. Public 2-year. 1980/1985 (NCA). Sem. plan. Degrees: A. Dir. Sheldon W. Marlow.
Enroll.: FTE 491
(505) 885-8831

Northern New Mexico Community College
El Rito 87530. Public 2-year. 1982 (NCA). Sem. plan. Degrees: A, certificates. *Prof. Accred.:* Radiography. Pres. Sigfredo Maestas.
Enroll.: FTE 658
(505) 581-4501

Parks College
1023 Tijeras, N.W., Albuquerque 87102. Private business; recognized candidate for junior college status. 1981 (AICS). Qtr. plan. Degrees: A, certificates, diplomas. Pres. Cynthia Welch.
Enroll.: 509 (*f.t.* 161 m., 348 w.)
(505) 843-7500

Pima Medical Institute (Branch)
5509 Menaul Blvd. N.E., Albuquerque 87110. Private. 1985 (ABHES). Courses of varying lengths. Certificates, diplomas. *Prof. Accred.:* Medical Assisting. Pres. Richard L. Luebke.
(505) 881-2893

St. John's College
Santa Fe 87501. Private liberal arts branch of St. John's College, Md. 1969/1979 (NCA). Sem. plan. Degrees: B, M. Pres. Michael P. Riccards.
Enroll.: 330
(505) 982-3691

Sandia College
2403 San Mateo, N.E., Suite W-23, Albuquerque 87110. Private business. 1982/1985 (AICS). Qtr. plan. Certificates, diplomas. Dir. Sheila Maxon.
Enroll.: 50 (*f.t.* 2 m., 48 w.)
(505) 888-5406

Branch Campus
6992 E. Broadway, Tucson, AZ 85710. Dir. Kathleen Scharf.
(602) 886-7979

San Juan College
Farmington 87401. Public (state) 2-year. 1973/1984 (NCA). Sem. plan. Degrees: A. Dir. James C. Henderson.
Enroll.: FTE 1,298
(505) 326-3311

Santa Fe Business College
110 Delgado, Santa Fe 87501. Private. 1966/1985 (AICS). Courses of varying lengths. Diplomas. Dir. Agnes I. Williams.
Enroll.: 146 (*f.t.* 9 m., 137 w.)
(505) 983-8171

Southwestern Business College
100 North Pennsylvania, Roswell 88201. Private. 1978/1981 (AICS). Sem. plan. Diplomas. Pres. Florine Waugh.
Enroll.: 94 (*f.t.* 9 m., 85 w.)
(505) 622-8080

Southwestern Indian Polytechnic Institute
Albuquerque 87184. Public (federal) 2-year. 1975/1981 (NCA). Qtr. plan. Certificates. Pres. Bob Martin.
Enroll.: FTE 715
(505) 766-3197

University of New Mexico
Albuquerque 87131. Public (state). Accreditation includes 2-year branch campus at Gallup. 1922/1982 (NCA). Sem. plan. Degrees: B, P, M, D. *Prof. Accred.:* Architecture (M), Business (B, M), Dental Assisting, Dental Hygiene, Engineering (chemical, civil, computer, electrical, mechanical, nuclear), Journalism, Law, Medical Laboratory Technology, Medical Technology, Medicine, Music, Nuclear Medicine Technology, Nursing (A, B, M), Pharmacy, Physical Therapy, Psychology, Radiography, Speech Pathology and Audiology, Teacher Education (*e,s,p*). Pres. Tom J. Farer.
Enroll.: FTE 17,371
Gallup:
Enroll.: 1,449 (*f.t.* 149 m., 243 w.)
505) 277-2626

Western New Mexico University
Silver City 88061. Public (state) liberal arts and professional college. 1926/1984 (NCA).

Sem. plan. Degrees: A,B,M. *Prof. Accred.:* Teacher Education (*e,s,p*). Pres. Rudolph Gomez.
Enroll.: FTE 1,424
(505) 538-6238

NEW YORK

Academy of Aeronautics
LaGuardia Airport Station, Flushing 11371. Private 2-year technical. 1969/1982 (MSA/CHE). Tri. plan. Degrees: A. *Prof. Accred.:* Engineering Technology (design-option, electronics-option, maintenance-option). Pres. George W. Brush.
Enroll.: 1,366 (*f.t.* 1,098 m., 39 w.)
(718) 429-6600

Adelphi University
South Ave., Garden City 11530. Private. 1921/1981 (MSA/CHE). Sem. plan. Degrees: A,B,M,D. *Prof. Accred.:* Nursing (B,M), Psychology, Social Work (B,M), Speech Pathology. Pres. Peter Diamandopoulos.
Enroll.: 10,727 (*f.t.* 1,523 m., 3,212 w.)
(516) 294-8700

Adirondack Community College
Glens Falls 12801. Public (district) junior; under State University of New York supervision. 1971/1978 (MSA/CHE). Sem. plan. Degrees: A. Pres. Gordon C. Blank.
Enroll.: 2,687 (*f.t.* 506 m., 701 w.)
(518) 793-4491

Advanced Career Training
Eight W. 40th St., New York 10018. Private. 1968/1982 (NATTS). Qtr. plan and courses of varying lengths. Diplomas. Pres. Marilyn Bock
Enroll.: 201 (*f.t.* 176 m., 14 w.)
(212) 719-1450

Advanced Training Center
2829 Sheridan Dr., Tonawanda 14150. Private. 1974/1979 (NATTS). Courses of varying lengths. Certificates, diplomas. Dir. Marilyn Bock.
Enroll.: 113 (*f.t.* 32 m., 52 w.)
(716) 835-4410

Kenmore Branch
c/o ATC, 2829 Sheridan Dr., Tonawanda. Dir. Frederic J. Rambuss.
(716) 835-4410

Airco Technical Institute
476 Louisiana St., Buffalo 14204. Private. 1981 (NATTS). Courses of varying lengths. Certificates. Dir. Michael Seifert.
Enroll.: 320 (*f.t.* 290 m., 30 w.)
(716) 842-6420

Albany Business College
130 Washington Ave., Albany 12210. Private. 1953/1983 (AICS). Sem. plan. Degrees: A. Pres. Prentiss Carnell, III.
Enroll.: 1,290 (*f.t.* 385 m., 905 w.)
(518) 449-7163

***Albany College of Pharmacy**
106 New Scotland Ave., Albany 12208. 1981 (MSA/CHE). Degrees: B. *Prof. Accred.:* Medical Technology, Pharmacy. Pres. Kenneth W. Miller.
Enroll.: 643 (*f.t.* 229 m., 389 w.)
(518) 445-7211

Albany Law School
Albany 12208. Degrees: P,D. *Prof. Accred.:* Law. Dean Richard J. Bartlett.
Enroll.: 706 (*f.t.* 329 m., 277 w.)
(518) 434-0136

***Albany Medical College**
47 New Scotland Ave.,Albany 12208. Private. 1980 (MSA/CHE). Degrees: P,M,D. *Prof. Accred.:* Assistant to the Primary Care Physician, Medicine, Nurse Anesthesia Education, Physical Therapy. Pres. Robert L. Friedlander, M.D.
Enroll.: 597 (*f.t.* 387 m., 208 w.)
(518) 445-5544

Albert Merrill School
21 W. 60th St., New York 10023. Private. 1972/1977 (NATTS). Courses of varying lengths. Diplomas. Dir. H. J. Schoenfeld.
Enroll.: 518 (*f.t.* 182 m., 65 w.)
(212) 246-7130

Alfred University
Alfred 14802. Private; includes State University of New York College of Ceramics. 1921/1984 (MSA/CHE). 4-1-4 plan. Degrees: B,M,D. *Prof. Accred.:* Art, Engineering (ceramic, ceramic science, glass science), Nursing (B). Pres. Edward G. Coll, Jr.
Enroll.: 2,426 (*f.t.* 1,131 m., 883 w.)
(607) 871-2111

Allen School for Physicians' Aides
163-18 Jamaica Ave., Jamaica 11432. Private. 1981 (NATTS). Courses of varying lengths. Certificates, diplomas. Exec. Dir. Howard Zimmet.
Enroll.: 280 (*f.t.* 18 m., 159 w.)
(718) 291-2200

*Formerly accredited under the aegis of Union University

American Academy of Dramatic Arts
120 Madison Ave., New York 10016. Private 2-year professional. 1983 (MSA/CHE). Sem. plan. Degrees: A. Dir. George Cuttingham.
Enroll.: 503 (*f.t.* 122 m., 144 w.)
(212) 686-9244

American Business Institute
1657 Broadway, New York 10019. Private. 1978/1980 (AICS). Sem. plan. Certificates, diplomas. Dir. Philip E. Jakeway, III.
Enroll.: 6,907 (*f.t.* 1,434 m., 5,473 w.)
(212) 582-9040

Branch Campus
2432 Grand Concourse, Bronx 10458. Dir. John J. Boyle.
(212) 364-1101

Branch Campus
152 Court St., Brooklyn 11201. Dir. Stanley Gruveman.
(212) 875-3800

Branch Campus
133-35 Roosevelt Blvd., Flushing 11354. Dir. Stanley Gruverman.
(718) 353-1600

Branch Campus
2410 E. Bush Blvd., Tampa, FL 33612. Dir. Charles Ralph.
(813) 932-7879

Branch Campus
65 E. South Water St., Chicago, IL 60601. Dir. William Smith.
(312) 443-1445

Branch Campus
17 Winter St., Boston, MA 02108. Dir. Richard Brennan.
(617) 338-1033

Branch Campus
601 Broad St., Newark, NJ 07102. Dir. Bruce Deyong.
(201) 623-0082

Branch Campus
46 S. 11th St, Philadelphia, PA 19107. Dir. Mark Bohen.
(215) 923-2260

American Career School, Inc
One N. Broadway, White Plains 10601. Private. 1981 (NATTS). Courses of varying lengths. Certificates. *Prof. Accred.:* Medical Assisting. Pres. Lori L. Gross.
Enroll.: 73 (*f.t.* 3 m., 70 w.)
(914) 428-1960

Extension
130 Ontario St., Albany 12206. Dir. Marion D. Soupios.
(518) 462-6621

Apex Technical School
635 Sixth Ave., New York 10011. Private. 1968/1979 (NATTS). Courses of varying lengths. Certificates. Dir. Dorothy Cann.
Enroll.: 1,200 m.
(212) 924-7373

Bank Street College of Education
610 W. 112th St., New York 10025. Private teachers, graduate only. 1960/1983 (MSA/CHE). Sem. plan. Degrees: P,M. Pres. Richard R. Ruopp.
Enroll.: 631 (*f.t.* 13 m., 110 w.)
(212) 663-7200

Barclay Career Schools
105 Madison Ave., New York 10016. Private. 1983 (AICS). Courses of varying lengths. Certificates. Dir. David Schuchman.
Enroll.: 1,302 (*f.t.* 181 m., 1,121 w.)
(212) 532-4315

Branch Campus
3400 Wilshire Blvd., Suite 1111, Los Angeles, CA 90010. Dir. Roger Williams.
(213) 318-3504

Branch Campus
3555 Timmons La., Suite 200, Houston, TX 77027. Dir. Mac N. Callis.
(713) 963-9639

Bard College
Annandale-on-Hudson 12504. Private liberal arts. 1922/1986 (MSA/CHE). 4-1-4 plan. Degrees: B,M. Pres. Leon Botstein.
Enroll.: 710 (*f.t.* 315 m., 362 w.)
(914) 758-6822

Barnard College
606 W. 120th St., New York 10027. Private liberal arts for women; affiliate of Columbia University. 1921/1981 (MSA/CHE). Sem. plan. Degrees: B. Pres. Ellen V. Futter.
Enroll.: *f.t.* 2,114 w.
(212) 280-5262

Berk Trade and Business School
384 Atlantic Ave., Brooklyn 11217. Private. 1973/1978 (NATTS). Courses of varying lengths. Certificates. Dir. Irving Berk.
Enroll.: 497 (*f.t.* 490 m., 7 w.)
(212) 855-5603

BERKELEY SCHOOL
99 N. Broadway, Hicksville 11801. Private business. 1969/1981 (AICS). Qtr. plan. Degrees: A. Dir. Cynthia Marchese.
Enroll.: 528 (*f.t.* 2 m., 526 w.)
(516) 938-7272

BERKELEY SCHOOL
405 Lexington Ave., New York 10174. Private business. 1967/1979 (AICS). Qtr. plan. Degrees: A, diplomas. Dir. John C. Clow.
Enroll.: 1,058 (*f.t.* 22 m., 1,036 w.)
(212) 986-4343

*BERKELEY SCHOOL
West Red Oak La., White Plains 10604. Private business. 1967/1979 (AICS). Qtr. plan. Degrees: A. Pres. Laura B. Egatz.
Enroll.: 673 (*f.t.* 3 m., 568 w.)
(914) 694-1122

BETH HAMEDRASH SHAAREI YOSHER
4102 16th Ave., Brooklyn 11204. Private professional. 1982. Degrees: 1st Talmudic. *Prof. Accred.:* Rabbinical and Talmudic Education. Pres. Rabbi J. Mayer.
Enroll.: f.t. 71 m.

BETH HATALMUD RABBINICAL COLLEGE
2127 82nd St., Brooklyn 11214. Private professional. 1978/1983. Degrees: 1st Talmudic. *Prof. Accred.:* Rabbinical and Talmudic Education. Pres. Rabbi Yosef Kotler.
Enroll.: f.t. 121 m.
(718) 259-2525

BETH MEDRASH EMEK HALACHA RABBINICAL COLLEGE
1763 63rd St., Brooklyn 11219. Private professional. 1979. *Prof. Accred.:* Rabbinical and Talmudic Education. Pres. Rabbi T. Goldstein.
Enroll.: f.t. 54 m.
(718) 232-1600

BETH MEDRASH GOVOHA
Executive offices, 314 McDonald Ave., Brooklyn 11218.
(718) 438-8300. *See listing in* New Jersey.

BEXLEY HALL
Rochester 14620. Private (Episcopal) professional; graduate only by virtue of affiliation with Colgate Rochester Divinity School. Pres. Larry L. Greenfield.
(716) 271-1320

*Candidate for Accreditation by Regional Accrediting Commission

BLAKE BUSINESS SCHOOL
145-A Fourth Ave., New York 10003. Private. 1974/1984 (AICS). Courses of varying lengths. Certificates, diplomas. Pres. Barbara Marion.
Enroll.: 92 (*f.t.* 0 m., 92 w.)
(212) 254-1233

BRANCH CAMPUS
222 Middle Country Rd., Smithtown 11787. Pres. Thomas F. Bierne.
(516) 724-4433

BORICUA COLLEGE
3755 Broadway, New York 10032. Accreditation includes Brooklyn Campus, 186 N. Sixth St., Brooklyn 11211 (718) 782-2200. Private, nontraditional liberal arts. 1980/1983 (MSA/CHE). Sem. plan. Degrees: A,B. Pres. Victor G. Alicea.
Enroll.: 1,125 (*f.t.* 423 m., 702 w.)
(718) 865-9000

BRIARCLIFFE SCHOOL
55 N. Broadway, Hicksville 11801. Private business. 1977/1983 (AICS). Sem plan. Diplomas. Pres. Richard Turan.
Enroll.: 462 (*f.t.* 0 m., 462 w.)
(516) 681-1100

BRANCH CAMPUS
10 Peninsula Blvd., Lynbrook 11563. Dir. Richard Turan.
(516) 596-1313

BRANCH CAMPUS
10 Lake St., Patchogue 11772. Dir. Jack Turan.
(516) 654-5300

BROOKLYN LAW SCHOOL
Brooklyn 11201. Private professional. 1937 (ABA); 1973 (AALS). Sem. plan. Degrees: P. *Prof. Accred.:* Law. Dean Israel L. Glasser.
Enroll.: 1,310 (*f.t.* 481 m., 420 w.)
(718) 625-2200

BROOME COMMUNITY COLLEGE
Upper Front St., P.O. Box 1017, Binghamton 13902. Public (county) junior; under State University of New York supervision. 1960/1985 (MSA/CHE). Qtr. plan. Degrees: A. *Prof. Accred.:* Dental Hygiene, Engineering Technology (chemical, civil, electrical, mechanical), Medical Assisting, Medical Record Technology (A), Nursing (A), Radiography. Pres. Donald W. Beattie.
Enroll.: 6,186 (*f.t.* 1,627 m., 1,660 w.)
(607) 771-5000

Bryant and Stratton Business Institute
1028 Main St., Buffalo 14202. Private. 1953/1978 (AICS). Qtr. plan. Degrees: A. *Prof. Accred.:* Medical Assisting. Dir. Kenneth Konesco.
Enroll.: 10,611 (*f.t.* 3,408 m., 7,203 w.)
(716) 884-9120

Branch Campus
200 Bryant and Stratton Way, Williamsville 14221. Admin. Lora K. Vahue.
(716) 631-0260

Branch Campus
320 S. Kellogg Ave., Goleta, CA 93117. Dir. James N. Trebbin.
(805) 964-4896

Bryant and Stratton Business Institute
14 Franklin St., Rochester 14604. Private. 1975/1981 (AICS). Qtr. plan. Degrees: A, diplomas. *Prof. Accred.:* Medical Assisting. Dir. Paul L. Hossenlopp.
Enroll.: 2,041 (*f.t.* 203 m., 1,838 w.)
(716) 325-6010

Bryant and Stratton Business Institute
400 Montgomery St., Syracuse 13202. Private. 1968/1981 (AICS). Qtr. plan. Degrees: A, diplomas. *Prof. Accred.:* Medical Assisting. Dir. Barbara A. Dalto.
Enroll.: 1,617 (*f.t.* 370 m., 1,247 w.)
(315) 472-6603

Branch Campus
5775 S. Bay Rd., Clay 13041. Dir. Joel Beck.
(315) 458-1105

Canisius College
2001 Main St., Buffalo 14208. Private liberal arts. 1921/1985 (MSA/CHE). Sem. plan. Degrees: A, B, M. *Prof. Accred.:* Business (B,M), Teacher Education (*e,s,p*). Pres. Rev. James M. Demske, S.J.
Enroll.: 4,155 (*f.t.* 1,659 m., 1,275 w.)
(716) 883-7000

Cashier Training Institute
1540 Broadway, 15th Fl., New York 10036. Private. 1985 (NATTS). Courses of varying lengths. Certificates. Dir. Harry Lokos
(212) 869-3607

Cathedral College of the Immaculate Conception
7200 Douglaston Pkwy., Douglaston 11362. Private (Roman Catholic) liberal arts for men. 1971/1986 (MSA/CHE). Sem. plan. Degrees: B. Pres. Rev. James P. Grace.
Enroll.: f.t. 83 m.
(718) 631-4600

Cayuga County Community College
Auburn 13021. Public (city) junior; under State University of New York supervision. 1965/1986 (MSA/CHE). Sem. plan. Degrees: A. *Prof. Accred.:* Nursing (A). Pres. Lawrence H. Poole.
Enroll.: 2,746 (*f.t.* 682 m., 558 w.)
(315) 255-1743

Cazenovia College
Cazenovia 13035. Private junior for women. 1961/1981 (MSA/CHE). Sem. plan. Degrees: A. Pres. Stephen M. Schneeweiss.
Enroll.: 807 (*f.t.* 112 m., 682 w.)
(315) 655-8283

Center for the Media Arts
226 W. 26th St., New York 10001. Private. 1969/1981 (NATTS). Courses of varying lengths. Certificates. Dir. H. Scott Cannell.
Enroll.: 523
(212) 807-6670

Central Yeshiva Tomchei Tmimim—Lubavitch
841-853 Ocean Pkwy., Brooklyn 11230. Private professional. 1976/1982. Degrees: 1st Rabbinic and 1st Talmudic. *Prof. Accred.:* Rabbinical and Talmudic Education. Pres. Rabbi Eliyahu N. Sklar.
Enroll.: f.t. 397 m.
(718) 434-0784

Chauffeurs' Training School
12 Railroad Ave., Albany 12205. Private. 1980 (NATTS). Courses of varying lengths. Certificates. Pres. Albert V. Hanley, Jr.
Enroll.: 90 (*f.t.* 75 m., 15 w.)
(518) 482-8601

Extension
RR 2, Box 137, Charleston, IL 61920.
(217) 581-2019

Extension
4950 W. 55th St., Chicago IL 60638.
(312) 456-0300

Extension
Rte. 2, Box 508, Ashland, VA 23005.
(804) 798-7722

Cheryl Fell's School of Business
2541 Military Rd., Niagara Falls 14304. Private. 1981/1984 (AICS). Courses of varying lengths. Certificates, diplomas. Dir. Cheryl A. Fell.

Enroll.: 50 (*f.t.* 2 m., 48 w.)
(716) 297-2750

CHRIST THE KING SEMINARY
711 Knox Rd., P.O. Box 607, East Aurora 14052-0607. Private (Roman Catholic). 1974/1983 (MSA/CHE). Degrees: P,M. *Prof. Accred.:* Theology (1977/1983 ATS). Rector/Pres. Rev. Kevin E. Mackin, O.F.M.
Enroll.: 135
(716) 652-8900

CITY TECHNICAL INSTITUTE
64 W. 36th St., New York 10018. Private. 1972/1984 (NATTS). Courses of varying lengths. Certificates. Dir. Richard Devaney.
Enroll.: 310 (*f.t.* 14 m., 19 w.)
(212) 563-3636

CITY UNIVERSITY OF NEW YORK
Central Office, 535 E. 80th St., New York 10021. Public (city). (MSA/CHE). Chanc. Joseph S. Murphy.
(212) 794-5414

BERNARD M. BARUCH COLLEGE
17 Lexington Ave., New York 10010. Business and public administration. 1968/1984 (MSA/CHE). Degrees: B,M. *Prof. Accred.:* Accounting (Type A,B), Business (B,M), Health Services Administration. Pres. Joel Segall.
Enroll.: 15,167 (*f.t.* 3,645 m., 4,905 w.)
(212) 725-3000

BOROUGH OF MANHATTAN COMMUNITY COLLEGE
199 Chambers St., New York 10007. Junior. 1964/1979 (MSA/CHE). Degrees: A. *Prof. Accred.:* Medical Record Technology, Nursing (A), Respiratory Therapy. Acting Pres. Evangelos J. Gizis.
Enroll.: 12,626 (*f.t.* 2,182 m., 5,158 w.)
(212) 618-1000

BRONX COMMUNITY COLLEGE
University Ave. and 181st St., Bronx 10453. Junior. 1963/1983 (MSA/CHE). Degrees: A. *Prof. Accred.:* Engineering Technology (electrical), Nuclear Medicine Technology, Nursing (A). Pres. Roscoe C. Brown, Jr.
Enroll.: 6,856 (*f.t.* 1,618 m., 2,758 w.)
(212) 220-6920

BROOKLYN COLLEGE
Bedford Ave. and Avenue H, Brooklyn 11210. Liberal arts. 1933/1975 (MSA/CHE). Degrees: B,M. *Prof. Accred.:* Nurse Anesthesia Education, Speech Pathology and Audiology, Teacher Education (*e,s,p*). Pres. Robert L. Hess.
Enroll.: 15,568 (*f.t.* 4,198 m., 4,197 w.)
(718) 780-5485

CITY COLLEGE
Convent Avenue at 138th St., New York 10031. 1921/1982 (MSA/CHE). Degrees: B,M. *Prof. Accred.:* Architecture (B), Assistant to the Primary Care Physician, Engineering (chemical, civil, electrical, mechanical), Engineering Technology (electromechanical), Landscape Architecture (B), Nursing (B), Psychology, Speech Pathology, Teacher Education (*e,s,p*). Pres. Bernard W. Harleston.
Enroll.: 12,841 (*f.t.* 4,895 m., 2,975 w.)
(212) 690-6741

COLLEGE OF STATEN ISLAND
715 Ocean Ter., Staten Island 10301. Liberal arts and professional. 1963/1985 (MSA/CHE). Degrees: A,B,M. *Prof. Accred.:* Engineering (engineering science), Engineering Technology (civil, electrical, electro-mechanical, industrial management, mechanical), Medical Laboratory Technology (A), Nursing (A). Pres. Edmond L. Volpe.
Enroll.: 10,779 (*f.t.* 2,578 m., 2,560 w.)
(718) 390-7733

GRADUATE SCHOOL AND UNIVERSITY CENTER
33 W. 42nd St., New York 10036. Graduate only. 1961/1982 (MSA/CHE). Degrees: B,P,M,D. Pres. Harold Proshansky.
Enroll.: 3,609 (*f.t.* 1,482 m., 1,385 w.)
(212) 790-4395

HERBERT H. LEHMAN COLLEGE
Bedford Park Blvd. W., Bronx 10468. Liberal arts. 1968/1983 (MSA/CHE). Degrees: B,M. *Prof. Accred.:* Nursing (B,M), Social Work (B), Speech Pathology, Teacher Education (*e,s*). Pres. Leonard Lief.
Enroll.: 9,646 (*f.t.* 1,632 m., 3,350 w.)
(212) 960-8881

HOSTOS COMMUNITY COLLEGE
475 Grand Concourse, Bronx 10451. Junior. 1974/1985 (MSA/CHE). Modular plan. Degrees: A. *Prof. Accred.:* Dental Hygiene, Radiography. Acting Pres. Adriana Garcia de Aldridge.
Enroll.: 3,800 (*f.t.* 1,021 m., 2,168 w.)
(212) 960-1200

HUNTER COLLEGE
695 Park Ave., New York 10021. Liberal arts. 1921/1982 (MSA/CHE). Degrees: B,M.

Prof. Accred.: Community Health Education, Medical Record Administration, Nursing (B,M), Occupational Therapy, Physical Therapy, Rehabilitation Counseling, Social Work (M), Speech Pathology and Audiology, Teacher Education (*e,s,p*). Pres. Donna Edna Shalala.
Enroll.: 18,606 (*f.t.* 2,617 m., 6,551 w.)
(212) 772-4000

John Jay College of Criminal Justice
444 W. 56th St., New York 10019. Specialized. 1965/1984 (MSA/CHE). Degrees: A,B,M,D. Pres. Gerald W. Lynch.
Enroll.: 6,369 (*f.t.* 1,984 m., 1,916 w.)
(212) 489-3500

Kingsborough Community College
Oriental Blvd., Manhattan Beach, Brooklyn 11235. Junior. 1964/1986 (MSA/CHE). Degrees: A. *Prof. Accred.:* Nursing (A). Pres. Leon Goldstein.
Enroll.: 11,554 (*f.t.* 2,256 m., 4,188 w.)
(718) 934-5000

La Guardia Community College
30-10 Thomson Ave., Long Island City 11101. Comprehensive cooperative community. Qtr. plan. 1974/1984 (MSA/CHE). Degrees: A. Pres. Joseph Shenker.
Enroll.: 7,609
(718) 626-2700

Medgar Evers College
1150 Carroll St., Brooklyn 11225. Two-year community oriented college of 2-year and 4-year professional studies. 1976/1981 (MSA/CHE). Degrees: A,B. *Prof. Accred.:* Nursing (B). Pres. Jay C. Chunn, II.
Enroll.: 10,916 (*f.t.* 469 m., 9,397 w.)
(718) 735-1750

Mount Sinai School of Medicine
New York 10029. Professional; affiliated with City University of New York. 1966/1976 (MSA/CHE). Sem. plan. Degrees: P,D. *Prof. Accred.:* Health Services Administration, Medicine. Pres. Thomas C. Chalmers.
Enroll.: 483 (*f.t.* 316 m., 167 w.)
(212) 650-6500

New York City Technical College
300 Jay St., Brooklyn 11201. 1957/1982 (MSA/CHE). Degrees: A,B. *Prof. Accred.:* Dental Hygiene, Dental Laboratory Technology, Engineering Technology (civil, electrical, electromechanical, mechanical), Nursing (A), Radiography. Pres. Ursula Schwerin.
Enroll.: 11,115 (*f.t.* 3,279 m., 3,232 w.)
(718) 643-4900

Queens College
65-30 Kissena Blvd., Flushing 11367. Liberal arts. 1941/1986 (MSA/CHE). Degrees: B,P,M. *Prof. Accred.:* Librarianship, Speech Pathology and Audiology. Pres. Shirley Strum Kenny.
Enroll.: 15,827 (*f.t.* 3,905 m., 4,813 w.)
(718) 520-7000

Queensborough Community College
Springfield Blvd. and 56th Ave., Bayside 11364. Junior. 1963/1984 (MSA/CHE). Degrees: A. *Prof. Accred.:* Engineerying Technology (computer, electrical, electrical-electronic option, mechanical), Nursing (A). Pres. Kurt Schmeller.
Enroll.: 12,869 (*f.t.* 2,807 m., 3,175 w.)
(718) 631-6262

York College
150-14 Jamaica Ave, Jamaica 11451. Liberal arts and teachers. 1967/1982 (MSA/CHE). Degrees: B. *Prof. Accred.:* Occupational Therapy. Pres. Milton G. Bassin.
Enroll.: 6,292 (*f.t.* 1,674 m., 2,938 w.)
(718) 969-4040

Clarkson University
Potsdam 13676. Private technological. 1927/1983 (MSA/CHE). Sem. plan. Degrees: B,M,D. *Prof. Accred.:* Engineering (chemical, civil, electrical, mechanical). Pres. Allan H. Clark.
Enroll.: 4,145 (*f.t.* 3,119 m., 852 w.)
(315) 268-6590

Clinton Community College
Plattsburgh 12901. Public (county) junior; under State University of New York supervision. 1975/1986 (MSA/CHE). Sem. plan. Degrees: A. *Prof. Accred.:* Medical Laboratory Technology (A). Pres. Jay L. Fennell.
Enroll.: 1,553 (*f.t.* 395 m., 377 w.)
(518) 793-4491

Colgate Rochester Divinity School/
Crozer Theological Seminary
Rochester 14620. Private (Interdenominational) professional; graduate only; affiliated with Bexley Hall. Sem. plan. Degrees: P,M,D. *Prof. Accred.:* Theology (1938/1982, ATS). Pres. Larry L. Greenfield.
Enroll.: 231
(716) 271-1320

COLGATE UNIVERSITY
Hamilton 13346. Private liberal arts. 1921/1983 (MSA/CHE). Degrees: B,M. Pres. George D. Langdon, Jr.
Enroll.: 2,664 (*f.t.* 1,453 m., 1,180 w.)
(315) 824-1000

COLLEGE FOR HUMAN SERVICES
345 Hudson St., New York 10014. Private professional. 1984 (MSA/CHE). Sem. plan. Degrees: A,B. Pres. Audrey C. Cohen.
Enroll.: 486 (*f.t.* 139 m., 347 w.)
(212) 989-2002

COLLEGE OF INSURANCE
One Insurance Plaza, 101 Murray St., New York 10007. Private professional. 1967/1978 (MSA/CHE). Tri. plan. Degrees: A,B,M. Pres. Linda Lamel.
Enroll.: 1,006 (*f.t.* 110 m., 4 w.)
(212) 962-4111

COLLEGE OF MOUNT SAINT VINCENT
263rd St. and Riverdale Ave., Riverdale 10471. Private liberal arts. 1921/1986 (MSA/CHE). Accreditation includes Malcolm-King: Harlem College Extension. Sem. plan. Degrees: A,B. *Prof. Accred.:*Nursing (B). Pres. Sister Doris Smith.
Enroll.: 1,050 (*f.t.* 71 m., 654 w.)
(212) 549-8000

COLLEGE OF NEW ROCHELLE
New Rochelle 10801. Private liberal arts. 1921/1983 (MSA/CHE). Sem. plan. Degrees: B,M. *Prof. Accred.:*Nursing (B), Social Work (B). Pres. Sister Dorothy Ann Kelley, O.S.U.
Enroll.: 4,596 (*f.t.* 414 m., 2,732 w.)
(914) 632-5300

COLLEGE OF SAINT ROSE
432 Western Ave., Albany 12203. Private liberal arts. 1928/1984 (MSA/CHE). Sem. plan. Degrees: B,M.*Prof. Accred.:* Cytotechnology, Medical Technology. Pres. Louis Vaccaro.
Enroll.: 2,886 (*f.t.* 365 m., 944 w.)
(518) 454-5111

COLUMBIA UNIVERSITY
116th and Broadway, New York 10027. Private. College of Pharmaceutical Sciences affiliated. 1921/1985 (MSA/CHE). Sem. plan (tri. plan in business school). Degrees: B,P,M,D. *Prof. Accred.:* Architecture (M), Business (M), Dental Hygiene, Dentistry, Engineering (chemical, civil, electrical, engineering mechanics, industrial, mechanical, metallurgical, mining), Journalism, Law, Librarianship, Medicine, Nurse Anesthesia Education, Nursing (B,M), Occupational Therapy, Physical Therapy, Public Health, Social Work (M). Pres. Michael I. Sovern.
Enroll.: 17,523 (*f.t.* 8,236 m., 5,176 w.)
(212) 280-1754

COLUMBIA-GREENE COMMUNITY COLLEGE
P.O. Box 1000, Hudson 12534. Public (county) junior; under State University of New York supervision. 1975/1986 (MSA/CHE). Sem. plan. Degrees: A. Pres. Robert K. Luther.
Enroll.: 1,369 (*f.t.* 257 m., 338 w.)
(518) 828-4181

COMMERCIAL DRIVER TRAINING
600 Patton Ave., W. Babylon 11704. Private. 1984 (NATTS). Courses of varying lengths. Certificates. Pres. John B. Rayne.
(516) 249-1330

COMMERCIAL PROGRAMMING UNLIMITED
25 W. 17th St., New York 10011. Private. 1979/1985 (AICS). Courses of varying lengths. Certificates. Dir. Walter Small.
Enroll.: 2,592 (*f.t.* 1,258 m., 1,334 w.)
(212) 243-7800

COMMUNITY COLLEGE OF THE FINGER LAKES
Lincoln Hill, Canandaigua 14424. Public (city) junior; under State University of New York supervision. 1977/1982 (MSA/CHE). Sem. plan. Degrees: A. *Prof. Accred.:* Nursing (A). Pres. Charles J. Meder.
Enroll.: 3,111 (*f.t.* 646 m., 824 w.)
(716) 394-3500

COMPUTER LEARNING CENTER
900 Ellison Ave., Westbury 11590. Private. 1985 (AICS). Courses of varying lengths. Certificates. Dir. Robert R. Birkenmaier.
(516) 832-9200

CONCORDIA COLLEGE
Bronxville 10708. Private (Luthern-Missouri Synod). 1941/1985 (MSA/CHE). Sem. plan. Degrees: A,B. *Prof. Accred.:* Social Work (B). Pres. Ralph C. Schultz.
Enroll.: 542 (*f.t.* 197 m., 221 w.)
(914) 337-9300

CONTINENTAL HEALTH AND CAREER CENTER
55 Stone St., Rochester 14604. Private. 1983 (ABHES). Courses of varying lengths. Certificates. Pres. Arthur J. Resso.
(716) 473-7070

CONTROL DATA INSTITUTE
11 W. 42nd St., New York 10036. Private. 1970/1980 (NATTS). Courses of varying lengths. Certificates. Dir. Bruce B. Misiaszek.
(212) 944-4400

COOPER UNION
Cooper Square, New York 10003. Private art, architecture, engineering. 1946/1978 (MSA/CHE). Sem. plan. Degrees: B,M. *Prof. Accred.:* Architecture (B), Art, Engineering (chemical, civil, electrical, mechanical). Pres. Bill N. Lacy.
Enroll.: 1,079 (*f.t.* 670 m., 304 w.)
(212) 254-6300

COPE INSTITUTE
4419 18th Ave., Brooklyn 11204. Private business. 1981 (AICS). Qtr. plan. Degrees: A, certificates, diplomas. Dir. Rabbi Yerachmiel Barash.
Enroll.: 357 (*f.t.* 103 m., 254 w.)
(718) 436-1700

CORNELL UNIVERSITY
Ithaca 14853. Private; includes State University of New York College of Agriculture and Life Sciences, College of Human Ecology, Veterinary College, and School of Industrial and Labor Relations. 1921/1985 (MSA/CHE). Medical center at New York City. Sem. plan. Degrees: B,P,M,D. *Prof. Accred.:* Architecture (B), Business (M), Cytotechnology, Engineering (agricultural, applied and engineering physics, chemical, civil and environmental, electrical, material science and engineering, mechanical, operations research and industrial engineering), Health Services Administration, Landscape Architecture (B,M), Law, Medicine, Psychology, Radiography, Social Work (B), Surgeon's Assistant, Veterinary Medicine. Pres. Frank H. T. Rhodes.
Enroll: Endowed Colleges: 10,615 (*f.t.* 6,979 m., 3,606 w.); Medical Center: 568 (*f.t.* 367 m., 190 w.); Statutory Colleges: 7,552 (*f.t.* 3,003 m., 3,525 w.)
(607) 255-1000

CORNING COMMUNITY COLLEGE
Corning 14830. Public (city) junior; under State University of New York supervision. 1964/1985 (MSA/CHE). Sem. plan. Degrees: A. *Prof. Accred.:* Nursing (A). Pres. Donald H. Hangen.
Enroll.: 3,476 (*f.t.* 924 m., 932 w.)
(607) 962-9011

CROWN BUSINESS INSTITUTE
26 Court St., Brooklyn 11201. Private. 1981 (AICS). Qtr. plan. Certificates Diplomas. Dir. Robert Teich.
Enroll.: 1,790 (*f.t.* 49 m., 1,741 w.)
(718) 596-2600

BRANCH CAMPUS
100 Peachtree St., N.W., Atlanta GA 30303. Dir. Gaylinda Cuff.
(404) 577-3400

CROWN BUSINESS INSTITUTE
163-18 Jamaica Ave., Jamaica 11432. Private. 1981 (AICS). Qtr. plan. Certificates Diplomas. Dir. Loretta Teich.
Enroll.: 702 (*f.t.* 45 m., 657 w.)
(212) 291-1300

CROWN BUSINESS INSTITUTE
655 Third Ave., New York 10017-5617. Private. 1981 (AICS). Qtr. plan. Certificates Diplomas. Dir. Howard E. Zimmet.
Enroll.: 1,148 (*f.t.* 129 m., 1,019 w.)
(212) 575-1777

BRANCH CAMPUS
1223 S.W. Fourth St., Miami, FL 33135. Dir. Diego Valero.
(305) 643-1600

THE CULINARY INSTITUTE OF AMERICA
Route 9, Hyde Park 12538. Private. 1983 (NATTS). Courses of varying lengths. Diplomas. Dir. Ferdinand E. Metz.
Enroll.: 1,806 (*f.t.* 1,341 m., 465 w.)
(914) 452-9600

DAEMEN COLLEGE
4380 Main St., Amherst 14226-3592. Private liberal arts. 1956/1986 (MSA/CHE). Sem. plan. Degrees: B. *Prof. Accred.:* Medical Record Administration, Medical Technology, Nursing (B), Physical Therapy, Social Work (B). Pres. Robert S. Marshall.
Enroll.: 1,706 (*f.t.* 618 m., 825 w.)
(716) 839-3600

DOMINICAN COLLEGE OF BLAUVELT
Ten Western Hwy., Orangeburg 10962. Private liberal arts. 1972/1983 (MSA/CHE). Sem. plan. Degrees: A,B. *Prof. Accred.:* Nursing (B), Occupational Therapy, Social Work (B). Pres. Sr. Mary Eileen O'Brien.
Enroll.: 1,105 (*f.t.* 251 m., 580 w.)
(914) 359-7800

DOWLING COLLEGE
Oakdale 11769, Private liberal arts. 1971/1985 (MSA/CHE). Sem. plan. Degrees: B,M. Pres. Victor P. Meskill.

Enroll.: 2,773 (*f.t.* 828 m., 905 w.)
(516) 589-6100

DRAKE BUSINESS SCHOOL
2488 Grand Concourse, Bronx 10458. Private. 1974/1981 (AICS). Courses of varying lengths. Certificates. Admin. Dorothy Campbell.
Enroll.: 671 (*f.t.* 4 m., 667 w.)
(212) 295-6200

DRAKE BUSINESS SCHOOL
41-25 Kissena Blvd., Flushing 11355. Private. 1974/1980 (AICS). Courses of varying lengths. Certificates. Admin. Irmgard Gerbavsits.
Enroll.: 597 (*f.t.* 23 m., 574 w.)
(212) 353-3535

DRAKE BUSINESS SCHOOL
15 Park Row, New York 10038. Private. 1974/1980 (AICS). Courses of varying lengths. Certificates. Admin. Carol Martin.
Enroll.: 655 (*f.t.* 23 m., 632 w.)
(212) 349-7900

DRAKE BUSINESS SCHOOL
25 Victory Blvd., Staten Island 10301. Private. 1974/1980 (AICS). Courses of varying lengths. Certificates. Admin. Susan Lent.
Enroll.: 411 (*f.t.* 5 m., 406 w.)
(212) 447-1515

DUTCHESS COMMUNITY COLLEGE
Poughkeepsie 12601. Public (county) junior; under State University of New York supervision. 1966/1985 (MSA/CHE). Sem. plan. Degrees: A. *Prof. Accred.:* Dental Assisting, Medical Assisting, Medical Laboratory Technology, Nursing (A). Pres. Jerry A. Lee.
Enroll.: 6,591 (*f.t.* 1,414 m., 2,825 w.)
(914) 471-4500

D'YOUVILLE COLLEGE
320 Porter Ave., Buffalo 14201. Private liberal arts primarily for women. 1928/1985 (MSA/CHE). Sem. plan. Degrees: B,M. *Prof. Accred.:* Nursing (B). Pres. Sister Denise Roche, G.N.S.H.
Enroll.: 1,211 (*f.t.* 143 m., 761 w.)
(716) 881-3200

EASTERN TECHNICAL SCHOOL
85 Fifth Ave., New York 10003. Private. 1983 (ABHES). 12-month program. Diplomas. *Prof. Accred.:* Medical Assisting, Medical Laboratory Technology. Dean/Dir. Walter E. Cochrane.
Enroll.: 56
(212) 542-2330

ELIZABETH SETON COLLEGE
Yonkers 10701. Private, independent 2-year. 1965/1986 (MSA/CHE). Sem. plan. Degrees: A, certificates. *Prof. Accred.:* Nursing (A), Practical Nursing. Pres. Mary Ellen Brosnan, S.C.
Enroll.: 1,143 (*f.t.* 193 m., 656 w.)
(914) 969-4000

ELMIRA BUSINESS INSTITUTE
180 Clemens Center Pkwy., Elmira 14901. Private. 1969/1980 (AICS). Sem. plan. Certificates, diplomas. Dir. John Hyland.
Enroll.: 220 (*f.t.* 29 m., 191 w.)
(607) 733-7177

ELMIRA COLLEGE
Elmira 14901. Private liberal arts. 1921/1984 (MSA/CHE). Year of two 12-week and one 6-week terms. Degrees: A,B,M. *Prof. Accred.:* Nursing (B). Pres. Leonard T. Grant.
Enroll.: 2,016 (*f.t.* 341 m., 584 w.)
(607) 734-3911

EMPIRE CAREER CENTER
16 Weaver St., P.O. Box 208, Utica 13502. Private. 1985 (NATTS). Courses of varying lengths. Certificates. Dir. Kathleen Guerino.
(315) 732-0540

EMPIRE TECHNICAL SCHOOL
Empire State Building, 350 Fifth Ave., New York 10118. Private. 1969/1980 (NATTS). Courses of varying lengths. Certificates. Dir. Charles D. Kleinow.
Enroll.: 605 (*f.t.* 250 m., 280 w.)
(212) 563-3100

ERIE COMMUNITY COLLEGE
Central Administration, 121 Ellicott St., Buffalo 14203. Public (district) 2-year technological; under State University of New York supervision. 1981/1984 (MSA/CHE). Sem. plan. Degrees: A. Pres. L. T. Ricci.
(716) 842-2770

CITY CAMPUS
121 Ellicott St., Buffalo 14203. *Prof. Accred.:* Nursing (A). Vice Pres. Cassell A. Lawson.
Enroll.: 3,144 (*f.t.* 841 m., 1,039 w.)
(716) 842-2770

NORTH CAMPUS
Main St. and Youngs Rd., Williamsville 14221. 1972/1984 (MSA/CHE). Sem. plan. Degrees: A. *Prof. Accred.:* Dental Hygiene, Engineering Technology (civil, electrical, me-

chanical), Medical Laboratory Technology (A), Nursing (A), Radiation Therapy, Respiratory Therapy. Vice Pres. Janice Karlen.
Enroll.: 5,692 (*f.t.* 1,851 m., 1,438 w.)
(716) 634-0800

South Campus
4140 Southwestern Blvd., Orchard Park 14127. 1981 (MSA/CHE). Sem. plan. Degrees: (A). Vice Pres. John Rydzik.
Enroll.: 3,194 (*f.t.* 948 m., 746 w.)
(716) 648-5400

Fashion Institute of Technology
227 W. 27th St., New York 10001. Public (city) professional; under State University of New York supervision. 1957/1982 (MSA/CHE). Sem. plan. Degrees: A,B. *Prof. Accred.:* Art, Interior Design. Pres. Marvin J. Feldman.
Enroll.: 11,058 (*f.t.* 684 m., 2,307 w.)
(212) 760-7660

Fordham University
Fordham Rd., Bronx 10458, and at Lincoln Center, New York 10023. 1921/1985 (MSA/CHE). Accreditation includes Malcolm-King: Harlem College Extension. Sem. plan. Degrees: B,P,M,D. *Prof. Accred.:* Business (B,M), Law, Psychology, Social Work (M), Teacher Education (*e,s,p*). Pres. Rev. Joseph A. O'Hare, S.J.
Enroll.: 12,228 (*f.t.* 3,468 m., 3,505 w.)
(212) 579-2000

French Culinary Institute
600 Madison Ave., New York 10022. Private. 1985 (NATTS); a division of Apex Tech. Courses of varying lengths. Certificates. Dir. Dorothy Cann.
(212) 219-3074

French Fashion Academy
600 Madison Ave., New York 10022. Private. 1974/1979 (NATTS). Courses of varying lengths. Certificates. Dir. John Klamar.
Enroll.: 227 (*f.t.* 25 m., 200 w.)
(212) 421-7770

Fulton-Montgomery Community College
Johnstown 12095. Public (county) junior; under State University of New York supervision. 1969/1986 (MSA/CHE). 4-1-4 plan. Degrees: A. Pres. John G. Boshart.
Enroll.: 1,748 (*f.t.* 542 m., 476 w.)
(518) 762-4651

Gemological Institute of America
1180 Avenue of the Americas, New York 10036. Private. 1984 (NATTS). Courses of varying lengths. Certificates, diplomas. Mgr. Thomas C. Yonelunas.
(212) 944-5900

General Theological Seminary
175 Ninth Ave., New York 10011. Private (Episcopal) professional; graduate only. 1978/1984 (MSA/CHE). Sem. plan. Degrees: P,M,D. *Prof. Accred.:* Theology (1938/1983, ATS). Pres. and Dean James C. Fenhagen.
Enroll.: 136 (*f.t.* 78 m., 45 w.)
(212) 243-5150

Genesee Community College
College Rd., Batavia 14020. Public (district) junior; under State University of New York supervision. 1971/1981 (MSA/CHE). Sem. plan. Degrees: A. *Nursing (A). Pres. Stuart Steiner.*
Enroll.: 2,633 (*f.t.* 657 m., 956 w.)
(716) 343-0055

Global Business Institute
1931 Mott Ave., Far Rockaway 11691. Private. 1984 (AICS). Courses of varying lengths. Certificates. Dir. Michael J. Hatten.
(212) 327-2220

Branch campus
209 W. 125th St., New York 10027. Dir. Michael J. Hatten.
(212) 663-1500

Grumman Data Systems Institute
250 Crossways Park Dr., Woodbury 11797. Private. 1980 (AICS). Courses of varying lengths. Certificates. Dir. Charlene Russert.
Enroll.: 2,171 (*f.t.* 1,615 m., 556 w.)
(516) 364-2055

Branch campus
4170 Veterans Hwy., Bohemia 11716. Dir. Charlene Russert.
(516) 467-6690

Hamilton College
Clinton 13323. Private liberal arts. 1921/1986 (MSA/CHE). Sem. plan. Degrees: B. Pres. J. Martin Carovano.
Enroll.: 1,618 (*f.t.* 900 m., 683 w.)
(315) 859-4011

Hartwick College
Oneonta 13820. Private liberal arts. 1949/1984 (MSA/CHE). 4-1-4 plan. Degrees B. *Prof. Accred.:* Nursing (B). Pres. Philip S. Wilder, Jr.

Enroll.: 1,397 (*f.t.* 616 m., 737 w.)
(607) 432-4200

HAUSMAN COMPUTER ASSOCIATES SCHOOL OF COMPUTER PROGRAMMING
500 Eighth Ave., New York 10018. Private. 1984 (NATTS). Courses of varying lengths. Certificates. Dir. Leonard Hausman.
(212) 736-1117

HEBREW UNION COLLEGE—JEWISH INSTITUTE OF RELIGION
One W. Fourth St., New York 10012. Private (Union of Hebrew Congregations) school of religious studies primarily for men; parent institution at Cincinnati, Ohio. 1960/1982 (MSA/CHE). Qtr. plan. Degrees: B,P,M,D. Pres. Alfred Gottschalk.
Enroll.: 112 (*f.t.* 43 m., 40 w.)
(212) 674-5300

HEFFLEY AND BROWNE SECRETARIAL SCHOOL
188 Montague St., Brooklyn 11201. Private. 1972/1984 (AICS). Courses of varying lengths. Diplomas. Pres. Philip Tarr.
Enroll.: 332 (*f.t.* 13 m., 319 w.)
(718) 858-1600

HERKIMER COUNTY COMMUNITY COLLEGE
Herkimer 13350. Public (county) junior; under State University of New York supervision. 1972/1983 (MSA/CHE). Sem. plan. Degrees: A. Pres. Ronald F. Williams.
Enroll.: 1,989 (*f.t.* 594 m., 934 w.)
(315) 866-0300

HILBERT COLLEGE
5200 S. Park Ave., Hamburg 14075. Private junior. 1976/1985 (MSA/CHE). Sem. plan. Degrees: A. Pres. Sister Edmunette Paczesny, F.S.S.J.
Enroll.: 710 (*f.t.* 135 m., 328 w.)
(716) 649-7900

HOBART AND WILLIAM SMITH COLLEGES
Geneva 14456. Coordinate institutions sharing facilities and faculty but maintaining separate campuses. 1921/1984 (MSA/CHE). Degrees: B. 3-3 plan. Pres. Carroll W. Brewster.
Enroll.: 1,960 (*f.t.* 1,145 m., 809 w.)
(315) 789-5500

HOBART COLLEGE
Private (Episcopal) liberal arts for men.

WILLIAM SMITH COLLEGE
Private liberal arts for women.

HOFSTRA UNIVERSITY
Hempstead 11550. Private 1940/1984 (MSA/CHE). Sem. plan. (year of four 10-week terms in New College). Degrees: A,B,P,M,D. *Prof. Accred.:* Business (B,M), Engineering (engineering science), Law, Psychology, Rehabilitation Counseling, Speech Pathology and Audiology, Teacher Education (*e,s,p*). Pres. James M. Shuart.
Enroll.: 11,542 (*f.t.* 3,947 m., 3,854 w.)
(516) 560-6600

HOSPITAL FOR SPECIAL SURGERY-SCHOOL OF PRACTICAL NURSING
535 E. 70th St., New York 10021. Public vocational. 1960/1978. 1-year program. Certificates. *Prof. Accred.:* Practical Nursing. Asst. Dir. Joan Moscati.
(212) LE 5-5500

HOUGHTON COLLEGE
Houghton 14744. Private (Wesleyan) liberal arts. 1935/1985 (MSA/CHE). 4-1-4 plan. Degrees: A,B. *Prof. Accred.:* Music. Pres. Daniel R. Chamberlain.
Enroll.: 1,311 (*f.t.* 494 m., 701 w.)
(716) 567-2211

BUFFALO SUBURBAN CAMPUS
910 Union Rd., West Seneca 14224. 1969/1985 (MSA/CHE). Dean Charles E. Massey.
Enroll.: 80A
(716) 674-6363

HUDSON VALLEY COMMUNITY COLLEGE
Troy 12180. Public (county) junior; under State University of New York supervision. 1969/1985 (MSA/CHE). Sem. plan. Degrees: A. *Prof. Accred.:* Dental Assisting, Dental Hygiene, Engineering Technology (air conditioning, civil, electrical, mechanical), Nursing (A), Radiography, Respiratory Therapy. Pres. Joseph J. Bulmer.
Enroll.: 8,292 (*f.t.* 3,324 m., 2,208 w.)
(518) 283-1100

HUNTER BUSINESS SCHOOL
99 Railroad Sta. Plaza, Hicksville 11801. Private. 1982/1986 (AICS). Courses of varying lengths. Certificates, diplomas. Dir. Florence Goodman.
Enroll.: 272 (*f.t.* 22 m., 250 w.)
(516) 935-7420

INSTITUTE OF AUDIO RESEARCH
64 University Pl., Greenwich Village, New York 10003. Private. 1985 (NATTS). Courses

of varying lengths. Certificates. Dir. Phil Stein.
(212) 677-7580

Interboro Institute
450 W. 56th St., New York 10019. Private business, recognized candidate for junior college accreditation. 1968/1984 (AICS). Sem. plan. Degrees: A. Pres. Mischa Lazoff.
Enroll.: 1,384 (*f.t.* 656 m., 728 w.)
(212) 399-0091

International Career Institute
120 W. 30th St., New York 10001. Private. 1977 (NATTS); 1978/1981 (AICS). Courses of varying lengths. Certificates, diplomas. Dir. Andrew Edelman.
Enroll.: 4,089 (*f.t.* 1,173 m., 2,916 w.)
(212) 244-5252

Iona College
715 North Ave., New Rochelle 10801-1890. Private liberal arts. 1952/1986 (MSA/CHE); accreditation includes Rockland Campus, Orangeburg 10962. Sem. plan. Degrees: B,M. *Prof. Accred.:* Social Work (B). Pres. Brother John G. Driscoll.
Enroll.: 6,050 (*f.t.* 2,005 m., 1,561 w.)
(914) 633-2000

Island Drafting and Technical Institute
128 Broadway, Amityville 11701. Private. 1967/1982 (NATTS). Courses of varying lengths. Diplomas. Pres. Joseph P. DiLiberto.
Enroll.: 400 (*f.t.* 350 m., 50 w.)
(516) 691-8733

Ithaca College
Ithaca 14850. Private liberal arts and teachers. 1955/1982 (MSA/CHE). Sem. plan. Degrees: B,M. *Prof. Accred.:* Medical Record Administration, Music, Physical Therapy, Speech Pathology and Audiology. Pres. James J. Whalen.
Enroll.: 5,532 (*f.t.* 2,298 m., 2,984 w.)
(607) 274-3013

Jamestown Business College
7 Fairmount Ave., P.O. Box 429, Jamestown 14702-0429. Private. 1968/1983 (AICS). Sem. plan. Degrees: A. Pres. Tyler Swanson.
Enroll.: 340 (*f.t.* 16 m., 324 w.)
(716) 664-5100

Jamestown Community College
525 Falconer St., Jamestown 14701. Public (city) junior; under State University of New York supervision; accreditation includes branch campus at Olean 14760. 1956/1981 (MSA/CHE). Sem. plan. Degrees: A. *Prof. Accred.:* Nursing (A). Pres. Paul A. Benke.
Enroll.: 3,806 (*f.t.* 680 m., 805 w.)
(716) 665-5220

Jefferson Community College
Watertown 13601. Public (county) junior; under State University of New York supervision. 1969/1985 (MSA/CHE). Sem. plan. Degrees: A. *Prof. Accred.:* Nursing (A). Pres. John T. Henderson.
Enroll.: 1,875 (*f.t.* 397 m., 648 w.)
(315) 782-5250

Jewish Theological Seminary of America
3080 Broadway, New York 10027. Private (Conservative Jewish) teachers, professional, theological institution; coeducational except in rabbinical and cantors divisions. 1954/1986 (MSA/CHE). Sem. plan. Degrees: B,P,M,D. Chanc. Ismar Schorsch.
Enroll.: 375 (*f.t.* 158 m., 106 w.)
(212) 678-8000

Joseph Bulova School of Watchmaking
40-24 62nd St., Woodside 11377. Private. 1978 (NATTS). Courses of varying lengths. Certificates. Dir. Robert Allen.
Enroll.: 98 (*f.t.* 82 m., 16 w.)
(212) 424-2929

The Juilliard School
Lincoln Center Plaza, New York 10023. Private professional. 1956/1982 (MSA/CHE). Sem. plan. Degrees: B,M,D. Pres. Joseph W. Polisi.
Enroll.: 889 (*f.t.* 425 m., 436 w.)
(212) 799-5000

Katharine Gibbs School
535 Broad Hollow Rd., Melville 11747. Private business. 1973/1979 (AICS). Sem. plan. Degrees: A, certificates. Dir. Bruce Misiaszek.
Enroll.: 722 (*f.t.* 2 m., 720 w.)
(516) 293-2460

Katharine Gibbs School
200 Park Ave., New York 10017. Private business. 1967/1985 (AICS). Courses of varying lengths. Degrees: A. Dir. Diane Mazzarella.
Enroll.: 2,291 (*f.t.* 72 m., 2,919 w.)
(212) 867-9300

Kelley Business Institute
1601 Main St., Niagara Falls 14305. Private. 1975/1983 (AICS). Courses of varying lengths. Certificates. Dir. Philip G. Kearney.
Enroll.: 291 (*f.t.* 91 m., 200 w.)
(716) 284-9800

Kensington Business Institute
1085 Kensington Ave., Buffalo 14215. Private. 1976/1982 (AICS). Courses of varying lengths. Certificates. Pres. Amedeo J. Duke.
Enroll.: 673 (*f.t.* 205 m., 468 w.)
(716) 833-6611

Keuka College
Keuka Park 14478. Private liberal arts primarily for women. 1927/1973 (MSA/CHE). Qtr. plan. Degrees: B. *Prof. Accred.:* Nursing (B), Social Work (B). Pres. Arthur F. Kirk, Jr.
Enroll.: 435 (*f.t.* 46 m., 349 w.)
(315) 536-4411

The King's College
Briarcliff Manor. 10510. Private liberal arts. 1968/1984 (MSA/CHE). Sem. plan. Degrees: A,B. Pres. Friedhelm K. Radandt.
Enroll.: 647 (*f.t.* 252 m., 374 w.)
(914) 941-7200

Krissler Business Institute
P.O. Box 5070, Poughkeepsie 12602. Private. 1975/1984 (AICS). Courses of varying lengths. Diplomas. Exec. Dir. Edgar Hamilton Krissler.
Enroll.: 171 (*f.t.* 0 m., 171 w.)
(914) 471-0330

Laboratory Institute of Merchandising
12 E. 53rd St., New York 10022. Private. 1977/1982 (MSA/CHE). Sem. plan. Degrees: A,B. Pres. Adrian G. Marcuse.
Enroll.: 260 (*f.t.* 9 m., 249 w.)
(212) 752-1530

Latin American School
525 Eighth Ave., New York 10018. Private business. 1981 (AICS). Courses of varying lengths. Certificates, diplomas. Pres. Carlos Casulo.
Enroll.: 3,463 (*f.t.* 895 m., 2,568 w.)
(212) 391-0032

Le Moyne College
Le Moyne Heights, Syracuse 13214. Private liberal arts. 1953/1982 (MSA/CHE). Sem. plan. Degrees: B. Pres. Frank R. Haig, S.J.
Enroll.: 2,140
(315) 445-4100

Lehigh Technical School
91-14 Merrick Blvd., Jamaica 11432. Private. 1977/1984 (NATTS). Courses of varying lengths. Certificates. Dir. Barbara Kamholtz.
Enroll.: 134 (*f.t.* 110 m., 24 w.)
(212) 297-2722

Leone School of Dental Laboratory Technology
1120 Little East Neck Rd., West Babylon 11704. Private. 1982 (NATTS). Courses of varying lengths. Certificates. Pres. Gerard Leone.
Enroll.: 134 (*f.t.* 110 m., 24 w.)
(516) 661-4540

Lewis A. Wilson Technical Center
17 Westminster Ave., Dix Hills 11746. Public. 1981. 10-month program. Certificates. *Prof. Accred.:* Practical Nursing. Coord. Margaret A. Shields.
Enroll.: 172

Long Island Business Institute
6500 Jericho Tpk., Commack 11725. Private. 1978/1984 (AICS). Courses of varying lengths. Diplomas. Dir. Genevieve Baron.
Enroll.: 262 (*f.t.* 12 m., 250 w.)
(516) 499-7100

Long Island University
Greenvale 11548. Private liberal arts and professional. Pres. David J. Steinberg.
(516) 299-2501

Brooklyn Campus
University Plaza, Brooklyn 11201; accreditation includes College of Pharmacy and Health Sciences. 1955/1985 (MSA/CHE). Degrees: A,B,M,D. *Prof. Accred.:* Assistant to the Primary Care Physician, Medical Technology, Nursing (A,B), Physical Therapy, Pharmacy, Respiratory Therapy. Senior Vice Pres./Univ. Prov. Lester Wilson.
Enroll.: 5,750 (*f.t.* 1,225 m., 2,037 w.)
(718) 834-6000

Rockland Campus
Orangeburg 10962. 1981/1985 (MSA/CHE). Prov. Joram Warmund.
(914) 359-7200

Westchester Campus at Mercy College
Dobbs Ferry 10522. 1981/1985. Prov. Michael Gillan.
Enroll.: 911 (*f.t.* 29 m., 61 w.)
(914) 693-4500

C. W. Post Campus
Greenvale 11548. 1955/1985 (MSA/CHE). Degrees: B,P,M. *Prof. Accred.:* Librarianship, Nursing (B), Psychology. Senior Vice Pres/Univ. Prov. Edward J. Cook.
Enroll.: 9,670 (*f.t.* 2,391 m., 2,842 w.)
(516) 299-0200

Brentwood Campus
Brentwood 11717. 1981/1985 (MSA/CHE). Prov. Dennis Payette.
Enroll.: 1,162 (*f.t.* 124 m., 113 w.)
(516) 273-5112

Southampton Campus
Southampton 11968. 1963/1985 (MSA/CHE). Degrees: B,M. Prov. Dennis Murphy.
Enroll.: 1,224 (*f.t.* 504 m., 527 w.)
(516) 283-4000

MTI Business School
175 Remsen St., Brooklyn 11201. Private. 1980/1983 (AICS). Courses of varying lengths. Certificates. Dir. Milton Lang.
Enroll.: 919 (*f.t.* 103 m., 816 w.)
(718) 522-2100

Branch Campus
59-17 Junction Blvd., One LeFrak City Plaza, Queens 11368. Dir. Jay Eisner.
(718) 699-2828

MTI Business School
107 W. 37th St., New York 10018. 1985 (AICS). Courses of varying lengths. Certificates. Dir. Gloria Mino.
(212) 382-2340

Magna Institute of Dental Technology
360 West 31st St., New York 10001. Private. 1977/1983 (NATTS). Courses of varying lengths. Certificates. Pres. Richard E. Resk.
Enroll.: 140 (*f.t.* 62 m., 30 w.)
(212) 947-6066

Mandl School for Medical & Dental Assistants
254 W. 54th St., New York 10019. Private. 1967/1977 (NATTS). Courses of varying lengths. Diplomas. Dir. Frederick Hirsch.
Enroll.: 337 (*f.t.* 19 m., 252 w.)
(212) 247-3434

Manhattan Career Institute
351 E. 61st St., New York 10021. Private. 1975/1981 (NATTS); 1983 (AICS). Courses of varying lengths. Certificates, diplomas. Dir. Angelo Ingorvaia.
Enroll.: 1,250 (*f.t.* 448 m., 804 w.)
(212) 593-1231

Manhattan College
Manhattan College Pkwy., Riverdale, Bronx 10471. Private liberal arts and professional. 1921/1982 (MSA/CHE). Sem. plan. Degrees: A,B,M. *Prof. Accred.:* Engineering (chemical, civil, electrical, environmental, mechanical), Nuclear Medicine Technology. Pres. Brother J. Stephen Sullivan, F.S.C.
Enroll.: 4,550 (*f.t.* 2,318 m., 1,232 w.)
(212) 920-0100

Manhattan School of Music
120 Claremont Ave., New York 10027. Private professional. 1956/1982 (MSA/CHE). Sem. plan. Degrees: B,M,D. Dir. Gideon W. Waldrop.
Enroll.: 841 (*f.t.* 338 m., 309 w.)
(212) 749-2802

Manhattan School of Printing
88 W. Broadway, New York 10007. Private. 1979/1981 (NATTS). Courses of varying lengths. Certificates. Pres. John L. Kress, Jr.
Enroll.: 274 (*f.t.* 173 m., 16 w.)
(212) 962-4330

Manhattan Technical Institute
154 W. 14th St., New York 10011. Private. 1982 (NATTS). Courses of varying lengths. Certificates. Dir. Herbert K. Swarte.
(212) 989-2662

Manhattanville College
Purchase 10577. (Independent coeducational) liberal arts. 1926/1980 (MSA/CHE). Sem. plan. Degrees: B,M. *Prof. Accred.:* Music. Pres. Marcia A. Savage.
Enroll.: 1,306 (*f.t.* 257 m., 651 w.)
(914) 694-2200

Mannes College of Music
150 W. 85th St., New York 10024. Private conservatory. 1975/1981 (MSA/CHE). Sem. plan. Degrees: B,M. Pres. Charles H. Kaufman.
Enroll.: 439 (*f.t.* 88 m., 106 w.)
(212) 580-0210

Maria College
700 New Scotland Ave., Albany 12208. Private nonsectarian junior for women. 1973/1984 (MSA/CHE). Sem. plan. Degrees: A. *Prof. Accred.:* Nursing (A). Pres. Sister Laureen Fitzgerald.

Enroll.: 911 (*f.t.* 24 m., 339 w.)
(518) 438-3111

MARIA REGINA COLLEGE
Syracuse 13208. Private junior for women. 1972/1986 (MSA/CHE). Sem. plan. Degrees: A. Pres. Sister Stella Maris Zuccolillo, O.S.F.
Enroll.: 557 (*f.t.* 0 m., 178 w.)
(315) 474-4891

MARIST COLLEGE
82 North Rd., Poughkeepsie 12601. Private liberal arts. 1964/1984 (MSA/CHE). Sem. plan. Degrees: B,M. *Prof. Accred.:* Social Work (B). Pres. Dennis J. Murray.
Enroll.: 4,471 (*f.t.* 1,887 m., 1,329 w.)
(914) 471-3240

MARYKNOLL SCHOOL OF THEOLOGY
Maryknoll 10545. Private (Roman Catholic) professional; graduate only. 1962/1984 (MSA/CHE). Sem. plan. Degrees: P,M. *Prof. Accred.:* Theology (1968/1983, ATS). Pres. Gerard T. McCrane, M.M.
Enroll.: 89 (*f.t.* 52 m., 14 w.)
(914) 941-7590

MARYMOUNT COLLEGE
Tarrytown 10591. Private liberal arts. 1927/1984 (MSA/CHE). 4-1-4 plan. Degrees: B. *Prof. Accred.:* Social Work (B). Pres. Sr. Brigid Driscoll, R.S.H.M.
Enroll.: 1,233 (*f.t.* 36 m., 936 w.)
(914) 631-3200

MARYMOUNT MANHATTAN COLLEGE
221 E. 71st St., New York 10021. Private liberal arts. 1961/1982 (MSA/CHE). 4-1-4 plan. Degrees: A,B. Pres. Sister Colette Mahoney, R.S.H.M.
Enroll.: 1,551 (*f.t.* 26 m., 499 w.)
(212) 517-0400

MATER DEI COLLEGE
Riverside Dr., Ogdensburg 13669. Private (Roman Catholic) junior. 1974/1984 (MSA/CHE). Sem. plan. Degrees: A. Acting Pres. Rev. Robert Aucoin.
Enroll.: 607 (*f.t.* 121 m., 324 w.)
(315) 393-5930

MCCARTHY'S BUSINESS INSTITUTE
339 East Ave., Rochester 14604. Private. 1981 (AICS). Qtr. plan. Certificates, diplomas. Dir. Daryl C. Paxon.
Enroll.: 284 (*f.t.* 54 m., 230 w.)
(716) 546-5302

MEDAILLE COLLEGE
18 Agassiz Circle, Buffalo 14214. Private (coeducational) liberal arts, teachers and career. 1951/1983 (MSA/CHE). Sem. plan. Degrees: A,B. Pres. Leo R. Downey.
Enroll.: 926 (*f.t.* 322 m., 458 w.)
(716) 884-3281

MERCY COLLEGE
Dobbs Ferry 10522. Private (non-denominational) liberal arts. 1968/1984 (MSA/CHE). Sem. plan. Degrees: A,B,M. *Prof. Accred.:* Nursing (B), Social Work (B). Pres. Wilbert J. LeMelle.
Enroll.: 7,572 (*f.t.* 2,026 m., 2,333 w.)
(914) 693-4500

YORKTOWN CAMPUS
2651 Strang Blvd., Yorktown Heights 10598. 1978/1984 (MSA/CHE). Dean Ann E. Grow.
Enroll.: 802 (*f.t.* 121 m., 140 w.)
(914) 245-6100

MESIVTA OF EASTERN PARKWAY RABBINICAL SEMINARY
510 Dahill Rd., Brooklyn 11218. Private professional. 1986. Degrees: 1st Talmudic. *Prof. Accred.:* Rabbinical and Talmudic Education. Pres. Rabbi David Feinstein.
Enroll.: f.t. 71 m.

MESIVTA TIFERETH JERUSALEM OF AMERICA
141 E. Broadway, New York 10002. Private professional. 1979. Degrees: 1st Talmudic. *Prof. Accred.:* Rabbinical and Talmudic Education. Pres. Rabbi J. Epstein.
Enroll.: f.t. 71 m.
(212) 964-2830

MESIVTA TORAH VODAATH SEMINARY
425 E. Ninth St., Brooklyn 11218. Private professional. 1975/1983. Degrees: 1st Talmudic. *Prof. Accred.:* Rabbinical and Talmudic Education. Pres. H. Hirsch.
Enroll.: f.t. 105 m.
(212) 941-8000

METROPOLITAN CAREER INSTITUTE
203 Jackson St., Hempstead 11550. Private. 1976/1980 (NATTS). Courses of varying lengths. Certificates, diplomas. Dir. Henry L. Young.
Enroll.: 70 (*f.t.* 12 m., 58 w.)
(516) 538-0996

MIDLAND CAREER INSTITUTE
900 Wheeler Rd., Hauppauge 11788. Private. 1967/1983 (NATTS). Courses of varying lengths. Diplomas. Dir. Stanley Males.
(516) 361-7335

Branch Campus
175 Fulton Ave., Hempstead 11550. Private. 1985 (NATTS). Courses of varying lengths. Diplomas. Dir. Stanley Males.
(516) 481-2774

Midtown School of Business
19 W. 44th St., New York 10036. Private. 1974/1980 (AICS). Courses of varying lengths. Certificates, diplomas. Dir. Murray Wolkind.
Enroll.: 1,410 (*f.t.* 433 m., 977 w.)
(212) 730-1020

Mildred Elley School
227 Quail St., Albany 12203. Private business. 1982 (AICS). Sem. plan. Certificates, diplomas. Pres. Faith Ann Takes.
Enroll.: 85 (*f.t.* 1 m., 84 w.)
(518) 472-9227

Mirrer Yeshiva
1795 Ocean Pkwy., Brooklyn 11223. Private professional. 1975. Degrees: 1st Rabbinic and 1st Talmudic. *Prof. Accred.:* Rabbinical and Talmudic Education. Pres. Rabbi S. M. Kalmanowitz.
(718) 645-0536

Modern Welding School
1740 Broadway., Schenectady 12306. Private. 1985 (NATTS). Courses of varying lengths. Certificates. Dir. Dana J. Gillenwalters.
(518) 374-1216

Mohawk Valley Community College
Utica 13501. Public (county) junior; under State University of New York supervision; accreditation includes branch campus at Rome 13440. 1960/1980 (MSA/CHE). Qtr. plan. Degrees: A. *Prof. Accred.:* Engineering Technology (civil, electrical, mechanical, solar energy, surveying), Medical Record Technology, Nursing (A), Respiratory Therapy Technology. Pres. Michael I. Schafer.
Enroll.: 6,168 (*f.t.* 1,947 m., 1,812 w.)
(315) 792-5400

Molloy College
1000 Hempstead Ave., Rockville Centre 11570. Private (Roman Catholic) liberal arts. 1967/1982 (MSA/CHE). Sem. plan. Degrees: A,B. *Prof. Accred.:* Nursing (A), Social Work (B). Pres. Sister Janet A. Fitzgerald, O.P.
Enroll.: 1,593 (*f.t.* 110 m., 1,135 w.)
(516) 678-5000

Monroe Business Institute
29 E. Fordham Rd., Bronx 10468. Private. 1963/1980 (AICS). Sem. plan. Degrees: A, certificates, diplomas. Pres. Stephen J. Jerome.
Enroll.: 2,670 (*f.t.* 815 m., 1,855 w.)
(212) 933-6700

Branch Campus
434 Main St., New Rochelle 10801. Dir. Peter Neigler.
(914) 632-5400

Monroe Community College
Rochester 14623. Public (county) junior; under State University of New York supervision; 1965/1986 (MSA/CHE). Sem. plan. Degrees: A. *Prof. Accred.:* Dental Hygiene, Engineering Technology (electrical), Medical Laboratory Technology (A), Medical Record Technology, Nursing (A), Radiography. Pres. Peter A. Spina.
Enroll.: 11,686 (*f.t.* 2,703 m., 2,776 w.)
(716) 424-5200

Mount Saint Mary College
Newburgh 12550. Private liberal arts. 1968/1983 (MSA/CHE). Sem. plan. Degrees: B, M. *Prof. Accred.:* Medical Technology, Nursing (B). Pres. Sister Ann Sakac.
Enroll.: 1,399 (*f.t.* 142 m., 652 w.)
(914) 561-0800

Munson-Williams-Proctor Institute, School of Art
310 Genesee St., Utica 13502. Private professional. 1981. 2-year program. Certificates. *Prof. Accred.:* Art. Dir. Clyde E. McCulley.
(315) 797-0000

Nassau Community College
Garden City, L.I. 11530. Public (county) junior; under State University of New York supervision; 1967/1984 (MSA/CHE). Sem. plan. Degrees: A. *Prof. Accred.:* Engineering Technology (civil), Music, Nursing (A), Radiation Therapy, Radiography, Respiratory Therapy, Surgical Technology. Pres. Sean A. Fanelli.
Enroll.: 20,320 (*f.t.* 4,819 m., 5,450 w.)
(516) 222-7500

The Nassau School for Medical and Dental Assistants
Nassau Plaza, One Fulton Ave., West Hempstead 11550. Private, 1978/1984 (NATTS). Courses of varying lengths. Diplomas. Pres. Marvin Kornblau.
Enroll.: 125 (*f.t.* 23 w.)
(516) 483-0577

NATIONAL ELECTRONIC TECHNICAL SCHOOL
24 Montcalm Ave., Buffalo 14609. Private. 1985 (NATTS). Courses of varying lengths. Certificates. Dir. Donald Hain.
(716) 835-2033

NATIONAL SCHOOL OF LOCKSMITHING
152 W. 42nd St., New York 10036. Private. 1978/1984 (NATTS). Courses of varying lengths. Certificates. Dir. Bert Michaels.
Enroll.: 40 (*f.t.* 38 m., 2 w.)
(800) 223-6466

NATIONAL TAX TRAINING SCHOOL
8 Albert Dr., Monsey 10952. Private home study. 1965/1981 (NHSC). Dir. Ben D. Eisenberg.
(914) 352-3634

NATIONAL TRACTOR TRAILER SCHOOL
4650 Buckley Rd., Liverpool 13088. Private. 1984 (NATTS). Courses of varying lengths. Certificates. Pres. Harry Kowalchyk, Jr.
(315) 451-2430

NAZARETH COLLEGE OF ROCHESTER
4245 East Ave., Rochester 14610. Private liberal arts. 1930/1986 (MSA/CHE). Sem. plan. Degrees: B,M. *Prof. Accred.:* Music, Nursing (B), Social Work (B). Pres. Rose Marie Beston.
Enroll.: 2,620 (*f.t.* 333 m., 1,114 w.)
(716) 586-2525

NEW SCHOOL FOR SOCIAL RESEARCH
66 W. 12th St., New York 10011. Private specialized, upper division and graduate only. 1960/1982 (MSA/CHE). Sem. plan. Degrees: B,M,D. *Prof. Accred.:* Psychology. Pres. Jonathan F. Fanton.
Enroll.: 6,252 (*f.t.* 976 m., 1,647 w.)
(212) 741-5600

PARSONS SCHOOL OF DESIGN
66 W. 12th St., New York 10011. Private, art and design. 1971/1982 (MSA/CHE). Accreditation includes Otis Art Institute, Los Angeles, CA 90057. Sem. plan. Degrees: A,B,M. *Prof. Accred.:* Art. Dean David C. Levy.
Enroll.: 1,801 (*f.t.* 600 m., 1,111 w.)
(212) 741-8900

NEW SCHOOL OF CONTEMPORARY RADIO
50 Colvin Ave., Albany 12206. Private. 1981 (NATTS). Courses of varying lengths. Certificates. Dir. Thomas Browlie, III.
Enroll.: 21 (*f.t.* 8 m., 1 w.)
(518) 438-7682

NEW YORK BUSINESS SCHOOL
269 W. 40th St., New York 10018. Private business. 1974/1985 (AICS). Courses of varying lengths. Diplomas. Exec. Dir. Gary Kay.
Enroll.: 1,063 (*f.t.* 69 m., 994 w.)
(212) 944-9200

NEW YORK CAREER CENTER
1545 Middle Country Rd., Centereach 11720 Private business. 1977/1981 (AICS). Courses of varying lengths. Certificates, diplomas. Pres. Bradley Baran.
Enroll.: 733 (*f.t.* 106 m., 627 w.)
(516) 698-3000

BRANCH CAMPUS
133-35 Roosevelt Ave., Flushing 11354. Dir. Carol Sikowitz.
(212) 353-1600

BRANCH CAMPUS
600 Executive Blvd., Farmingdale 11735. Dir. Jerry Sikowitz.
(516) 752-1006

NEW YORK CHIROPRACTIC COLLEGE
P.O. Box 167, Glen Head 11545. Private professional. 1985 (MSA/CHE). Tri. plan. Degrees: P. *Prof. Accred.:* Chiropractic Education. Acting Pres. Neil Stern.
Enroll.: 869 (*f.t.* 554 m., 301 w.)
(516) 626-2700

NEW YORK COLLEGE OF PODIATRIC MEDICINE
53 E. 124th St., New York 10035. Private professional. 1922/1975. Sem. plan. Degrees: P. *Prof. Accred.:* Podiatry. Pres. Horace DeCotiis.
Enroll.: 504 (*f.t.* 401 m., 103 w.)
(212) 427-8400

NEW YORK FOOD AND HOTEL MANAGEMENT SCHOOL
154 W. 14th St., New York 10011. Private. 1973/1984 (NATTS). Sem. plan. Courses of varying lengths. Certificates. Dir. Beth A. Smith.
Enroll.: 187 (*f.t.* 39 m., 86 w.)
(212) 675-6655

NEW YORK INSTITUTE OF COMPUTER SCIENCE AND TEHNOLOGY
165 W. 46th St., Suite 305, New York 10036. Private business. 1986 (AICS). Courses of varying lengths. Certificates, diplomas. Pres. John Tzovolos.
(212) 354-2800

New York Institute of Technology
Wheatley Rd., Old Westbury, L.I. 11568. Accreditation includes branches at 1855 Broadway, New York 10023 and Central Islip 11722. Private professional. 1969/1981 (MSA/CHE). Sem. plan. Degrees: A,B,P,M. *Prof. Accred.:* Architecture, (B), Engineering Technology (aeronautical operations, electromechanical computer), Interior Design, Osteopathy. Pres. Matthew Schure.
Enroll.: 12,180 (*f.t.* 5,621 m., 1,636 w.)
(516) 686-7516

New York Law School
New York 10013. Private professional. 1954 (ABA); 1974 (AALS). Sem. plan. Degrees: P. *Prof. Accred.:* Law. Dean E. Donald Shapiro.
Enroll.: 1,528 (*f.t.* 655 m., 331 w.)
(212) 966-3500

New York Medical College
Valhalla 10595. Private professional. 1934/1976. Sem. plan. Degrees: P,M,D. *Prof. Accred.:* Medicine, Nurse Anesthesia Education. Pres. John J. Connolly.
Enroll.: 1,157 (*f.t.* 631 m., 261 w.)
(914) 347-5000

New York School for Medical and Dental Assistants
116-16 Queens Blvd., Forest Hills 11375. Private. 1973/1978 (NATTS). Courses of varying lengths. Certificates, diplomas. *Prof. Accred.:* Medical Assistant, Medical Laboratory Technology. Pres. E. Richard Schwabach.
Enroll.: 180 (*f.t.* 7 m., 173 w.)
(212) 793-2330

New York School of Dog Grooming
248 E. 34th St., New York 10016. Private. 1973/1978 (NATTS). Courses of varying lengths. Certificates. Dir. Sam Kohl.
Enroll.: 72 (*f.t.* 10 m., 48 w.)
(212) 685-3776

Branch Campus
265-17 Union Tpke., New Hyde Park 11040.
(718) 343-3130

New York School of Interior Design
155 E. 56th St., New York 10022. Private. 1978. Courses of varying lengths. Degrees: A, diplomas. *Prof. Accred.:* Interior Design. Dean Kerwin Kettler.
Enroll.: 713 (*f.t.* 32 m., 104 w.)
(212) PL3-5365

New York Theological Seminary
New York 10001. Private (Interdenominational) professional and graduate only. Sem. plan. Degrees: P, M,D. *Prof. Accred.:* Theology (1958/1984, ATS). Pres. Keith A. Russell.
Enroll.: 240
(212) 532-4012

New York University
Washington Square, New York 10012. Private. 1921/1984 (MSA/CHE). Sem. plan. Degrees: A,B,P,M,D. *Prof. Accred.:* Accounting (Type A,B,C), Business (B,M), Community Health Education, Dental Assisting, Dentistry, Diagnostic Medical Sonography, Engineering (aeronautics and astronautics, chemical, civil, electrical, industrial, mechanical, metallurgy and materials science), Health Administration, Journalism, Law, Medicine, Music, Nuclear Medicine Technology, Nursing (B,M), Occupational Therapy, Physical Therapy, Psychology, Radiation Therapy Technology, Rehabilitation Counseling, Respiratory Therapy, Social Work (B,M), Speech Pathology and Audiology, Teacher Education (*e,s,p*). Pres. John Brademas.
Enroll.: 32,266 (*f.t.* 8,712 m., 9,480 w.)
(212) 598-3131

New York Vocational School
331 Park Ave. S., New York 10010. Private. 1981 (NATTS). Courses of varying lengths. Certificates. Pres. Kevin A. O'Brien.
Enroll.: 31 (*f.t.* 23 m., 8 w.)
(212) 234-3440

Newspaper Institute of America
112 W. Boston Post Rd., Mamaroneck 10543. Private home study. 1961/1984 (NHSC). varying lengths. Pres. Lois Stuart.
(914) 698-7488

Writers Institute
Mamaroneck 10543. A division.

Niagara Community College
3111 Saunders Settlement Rd., Sanborn 14132. Public (county) junior; under State University of New York supervision; 1970/1986 (MSA/CHE). Sem. plan. Degrees: A. *Prof. Accred.:* Dental Assisting, EEG Technology, Nursing (A), Surgical Technology. Pres. Donald J. Donato.
Enroll.: 4,270 (*f.t.* 1,227 m., 1,485 w.)
(716) 731-3271

Niagara University
Niagara University 14109. Private (Roman Catholic). 1922/1983 (MSA/CHE). Sem. plan.

Degrees: A,B,M. *Prof. Accred.:* Nursing (B), Social Work (B), Teacher Education (*s, p*). Pres. Donald J. Harrington, C.M.
Enroll.: 3,618 (*f.t.* 1,297 m., 1,566 w.)
(716) 285-1212

NORTH COUNTY COMMUNITY COLLEGE
20 Winona Ave., P.O. Box 89, Saranac Lake 12983. Public (county) junior; under State University of New York supervision; accreditation includes branch campuses at Elizabethtown 12932, Malone 12953, and Ticonderoga 12833. 1975/1984 (MSA/CHE). Sem. plan. Degrees: A. *Prof. Accred.:* Engineering Technology (electrical, mechanical), Medical Laboratory Technology (A), Radiography. Pres. David W. Petty.
Enroll.: 1,655 (*f.t.* 372 m., 449 w.)
(518) 891-2915

NYACK COLLEGE
Nyack 10960. Private (Christian Missionary Alliance) liberal arts, teachers, and church-related professional. 1962/1978 (MSA/CHE). Sem. plan. Degrees: A,B,M. *Prof. Accred.:* Music. Pres. David L. Rambo.
Enroll.: 823 (*f.t.* 346 m., 300 w.)
(914) 358-1710

OLEAN BUSINESS INSTITUTE
301 N. Union St., Olean 14760. Private. 1969/1982 (AICS). Sem. plan. Degrees: A, diplomas. Dir. Patrick J. McCarthy.
Enroll.: 181 (*f.t.* 13 m., 168 w.)
(716) 372-7978

ONONDAGA COMMUNITY COLLEGE
Route 173, Syracuse 13215. Public (county) junior; under State University of New York supervision. 1972/1977 (MSA/CHE). Sem. plan. Degrees: A. *Prof. Accred.:* Dental Hygiene, Nursing (A), Respiratory Therapy, Respiratory Therapy Technology, Surgical Technology. Pres. Bruce H. Leslie.
Enroll.: 7,131 (*f.t.* 1,706 m., 1,515 w.)
(315) 469-7741

ORANGE COUNTY COMMUNITY COLLEGE
Middletown 10940. Public (county) junior; under State University of New York supervision. 1962/1983 (MSA/CHE). Sem. plan. Degrees: A. *Prof. Accred.:* Dental Hygiene, Engineering Technology (electrical), Medical Laboratory Technology, Nursing (A). Acting Pres. Murray H. Block.
Enroll.: 5,174 (*f.t.* 942 m., 1,190 w.)
(914) 343-1121

OUR LADY OF VICTORY SECRETARIAL SCHOOL
146 S. Catherine St., Plattsburgh 12901. Private. 1981 (AICS). Qtr. plan. Certificates, diplomas. Exec. Dir. Sister Theresa Martel.
Enroll.: 102 w.
(518) 563-0851

PSI INSTITUTE
269 W. 40th St., New York 10018. Private. 1971/1979 (NATTS). Courses of varying lengths. Certificates, diplomas. Pres. Irwin Mautner.
Enroll.: 601 (*f.t.* 304 m., 126 w.)
(212) 944-9200

PACE BUSINESS SCHOOL
45 Park Ave., Yonkers 10703. Private. 1980/1983 (AICS). Courses of varying lengths. Diplomas. Dir. Richard Pfundstein.
Enroll.: 385 (*f.t.* 102 m., 283 w.)
(914) 963-7945

PACE UNIVERSITY
One Pace Plaza, New York 10038. Private liberal arts and professional. 1957/1983 (MSA/CHE). Sem. plan. Degrees: A,B,P,M,D. Pres. William G. Sharwell.
Enroll.: 14,696 (*f.t.* 2,158 m., 2,589 w.)
(212) 488-1200

UNIVERSITY COLLEGE OF PACE UNIVERSITY
Pleasantville 10570. 1963/1983 (MSA/CHE). Sem. plan. Degrees: A,B,M,D. *Prof. Accred.:* Nursing (A,B,M). Exec. Vice Pres. Frank Falcone.
Enroll.: 4,998 (*f.t.* 1,308 m., 1,758 w.)
(914) 769-3200

PACE UNIVERSITY AT WHITE PLAINS
White Plains 10603. 1930/1983 (MSA/CHE). 4-1-4 plan. Degrees: B,P,D. *Prof. Accred.:* Law. Vice Pres. Arthur Antin.
Enroll.: 4,127 (*f.t.* 460 m., 590 w.)
(914) 681-4025

PAN AMERICAN SCHOOL
116 W. 14th St., Fifth Fl., New York 10011. Private. 1985 (AICS). Courses of varying lengths. Certificates, diplomas. Dir. Angelo Chavez.
(212) 675-6450

PARSONS SCHOOL OF DESIGN *See* NEW SCHOOL FOR SOCIAL RESEARCH

PAUL SMITH'S COLLEGE
Paul Smiths 12970. Private business, liberal arts and technical. 1977 (MSA/CHE). Sem. plan. Degrees: A. Pres. Harry K. Miller, Jr.

Enroll.: 720 (*f.t.* 458 m., 218 w.)
(518) 327-6211

PLAZA BUSINESS INSTITUTE
74-09 37th Ave., Jackson Heights 11372. Private. 1974/1980 (AICS). Tri. plan. Diplomas. Pres. Charles E. Callahan.
Enroll.: 856 (*f.t.* 69 m., 787 w.)
(212) 779-1430

POLYTECHNIC INSTITUTE OF NEW YORK
333 Jay St., Brooklyn 11201. Private liberal arts and technological. Accreditation includes campus at Farmingdale 11735 and Westchester Graduate Center, White Plains 10605. 1927/1982 (MSA/CHE). Sem. plan. Degrees: B,M,D. *Prof. Accred.:* Engineering (aerospace, chemical, civil, electrical, industrial, mechanical, metallurgical). Pres. George Bugliarello.
Enroll.: 5,013 (*f.t.* 1,847 m., 239 w.)
(718) 643-5000

PRACTICAL BIBLE TRAINING SCHOOL
Drawer A, Bible School Park 13737. Private (Interdenominational). 1985 (AABC). Sem. plan. Degrees: A,B. Pres. Woodrow M. Kroll.
Enroll.: 256
(607) 729-1581

PRATT INSTITUTE
200 Willoughby Ave., Brooklyn 11205. Private professional school. 1950/1986 (MSA/CHE). Sem. plan. Degrees: A,B,M. *Prof. Accred.:* Architecture (B), Art, Engineering (chemical, electrical, mechanical), Librarianship. Pres. Richardson Pratt, Jr.
Enroll.: 3,672 (*f.t.* 1,838 m., 1,189 w.)
(718) 636-3600

PRINTING TRADES SCHOOL
229 Park Ave., S., New York 10003. Private. 1975/1981 (NATTS). Courses of varying lengths. Certificates. Dir. Elizabeth G. Jenkins.
Enroll.: 87 (*f.t.* 51 m., 10 w.)
(212) 677-0505

PROFESSIONAL BUSINESS INSTITUTE
119 Main St., Nanuet 10954. Private. 1984 (AICS). Courses of varying lengths. Certificates, diplomas. Dir. Elayne Zinbarg.
(914) 623-3495

THE PROFESSIONAL DIVING SCHOOL OF NEW YORK
222 Fordham St., City Island, New York 10464. Private. 1982 (NATTS). Courses of varying lengths. Certificates. Dir. Glenn J. Butler.
(212) 885-0600

RABBINICAL ACADEMY MESIVTA RABBI CHAIM BERLIN
1593 Coney Island Ave., Brooklyn 11230. Private professional. 1975/1981. Degrees: 1st and 2nd Talmudic. *Prof. Accred.:* Rabbinical and Talmudic Education. Pres. Rabbi A. M. Schechter.
Enroll.: f.t. 447 m.
(718) 377-0777

RABBINICAL COLLEGE BETH SHRAGA
28 Saddle River Rd., Monsey 10952. Private professional. 1978/1983. Degrees: 1st Talmudic. *Prof. Accred.:* Rabbinical and Talmudic Education. Pres. Rabbi S. Schiff.
Enroll.: f.t. 46 m.
(914) 356-1980

RABBINICAL COLLEGE BOBOVER YESHIVA B'NEI ZION
1577 48th St., Brooklyn 11219. Private professional. 1979/1984. Degrees: 1st Rabbinic. *Prof. Accred.:* Rabbinical and Talmudic Education. Pres. Rabbi B. Grunfeld.
Enroll.: f.t. 330m.
(718) 438-2018

RABBINICAL COLLEGE CH'SAN SOFER
1876 50th St., Brooklyn 11204. Private professional. 1979/1985. Degrees: 1st Talmudic. *Prof. Accred.:* Rabbinical and Talmudic Education. Pres. S. Fischer.
Enroll.: f.t. 118 m.
(718) 236-1171

RABBINICAL COLLEGE OF LONG ISLAND
201 Magnolia Blvd., Long Beach 11561. Private professional. 1979/1984. Degrees: 1st Talmudic. *Prof. Accred.:* Rabbinical and Talmudic Education. Pres. Rabbi Y. Feigelstock.
Enroll.: f.t. 96 m.
(516) 431-7414

RABBINICAL SEMINARY ADAS YEREIM
185 Wilson St., Brooklyn 11211. Private professional. 1979/1985. Degrees: 1st Talmudic. *Prof. Accred.:* Rabbinical and Talmudic Education. Pres. A. Schonberger.
Enroll.: f.t. 114 m.
(718) 388-1751

RABBINICAL SEMINARY OF AMERICA
92-15 69th Ave., Forest Hills 11375. Private professional. 1976/1981. Degrees: 1st Tal-

mudic. *Prof. Accred.:* Rabbinical and Talmudic Education. Pres. A. H. Leibowitz.
Enroll.: f.t. 200 m.
(718) 268-4700

RABBINICAL SEMINARY M'KOR CHAIM
1571 55th St., Brooklyn 11219. Private professional. 1979/1984. Degrees: 1st Talmudic. *Prof. Accred.:* Rabbinical and Talmudic Education. Pres. Rabbi B. Paler.
Enroll.: f.t. 87 m.
(718) 851-0183

RENSSELAER POLYTECHNIC INSTITUTE
Troy 12180-3590. Private university. 1927/1986 (MSA/CHE). Sem. plan. Degrees: B,M,D. *Prof. Accred.:* Architecture (B,M), Business (B,M), Engineering (aeronautical, biomedical, chemical, civil, computer and systems, electric power, electrical, environmental, industrial, management, materials, mechanical, nuclear). Pres. Daniel Berg.
Enroll.: 6,873 (*f.t.* 4,975 m., 1,225 w.)
(518) 266-6000

RIDLEY-LOWELL SCHOOL OF BUSINESS
116 Front St., Binghamton 13905. Private. 1977/1983 (AICS). Courses of varying lengths. Diplomas. Dir. Anne E. Healy.
Enroll.: 398 (*f.t.* 33 m., 365 w.)
(607) 724-2941

RIVERSIDE SCHOOL OF AERONAUTICS
Riverside Airport, Box 444, Utica 13503. Private. 1972/1984 (NATTS). Qtr. plan. Diplomas. Dir. Gloria L. Santucci.
Enroll.: 93 (*f.t.* 91 m., 2 w.)
(315) 736-5241

ROBERT FIANCE BUSINESS INSTITUTE
401 Fifth Ave., New York 10016. Private. 1980 (AICS). Courses of varying lengths. Certificates. Dir. Claire J. Nyandoro.
Enroll.: 770 (*f.t.* 91 m., 679 w.)
(212) 889-8736

BRANCH CAMPUS
55 Willoughby St., Brooklyn 11201. Dir. William J. O'Shea.
(212) 855-7900

ROBERTS WESLEYAN COLLEGE
Rochester 14624. Private (Free Methodist) liberal arts. 1963/1985 (MSA/CHE). 3-3 plan. Degrees: A,B. *Prof. Accred.:* Music, Nursing (B), Social Work (B). Pres. William C. Crothers.
Enroll.: 715 (*f.t.* 217 m., 392 w.)
(716) 594-9471

ROCHESTER BUSINESS INSTITUTE
107 Clinton Ave., N., Rochester 14604. Private. 1966/1984 (AICS). Qtr. plan. Degrees: A, diplomas. Pres. Gerald J. Wright.
Enroll.: 806 (*f.t.* 248 m., 558 w.)
(716) 325-7290

BRANCH CAMPUS
165 E. Union St., Newark 14513. Dir. Gladys Robbins.
(315) 331-8820

ROCHESTER INSTITUTE OF TECHNOLOGY
One Lomb Memorial Dr., Rochester 14623. Private technological and professional. 1958/1978 (MSA/CHE). Qtr. plan. Degrees: A,B,M. *Prof. Accred.:* Art, Diagnostic Medical Sonography, Dietetics, Engineering (electrical, industrial, mechanical), Engineering Technology (architectural, civil-construction and environmental options, civil, electrical, electro-mechanical, industrial drafting, manufacturing, mechanical), Medical Record Technology, Nuclear Medicine Technology, Social Work (B). Pres. M. Richard Rose.
Enroll.: 14,786 (*f.t.* 5,708 m., 2,776 w.)
(716) 475-2400

ROCKLAND COMMUNITY COLLEGE
145 College Rd., Suffern 10901. Public (county) junior; under State University of New York supervision. 1968/1985 (MSA/CHE). Sem. plan. Degrees: A. *Prof. Accred.:* Dental Assisting, Medical Laboratory Technology (A), Nursing (A), Respiratory Therapy. Pres. F. Thomas Clark.
Enroll.: 8,978 (*f.t.* 2,232 m., 2,588 w.)
(914) 356-4650

ROYAL BUSINESS SCHOOL
250 W. 18th St., New York 10011. Private. 1978/1980 (AICS). Qtr. plan. Diplomas. Pres. Claude Hoyte.
Enroll.: 2,885 (*f.t.* 1,016 m., 1,869 w.)
(212) 807-1800

BRANCH CAMPUS
119-45 Union Tpk., Queens Hills 11412. Dir. Joan L. Rhodes.
(212) 793-8010

RUSSELL SAGE COLLEGE
45 Ferry St., Troy 12180. Private liberal arts primarily for women. 1928/1986 (MSA/CHE). Accreditation includes Junior College of Albany, 2-year coeducational branch campus at Albany. 4-1-4 plan. Degrees: A,B,M. *Prof. Accred.:* Art, Nursing (A,B,M), Physical

Therapy (at Albany). Pres. William Frederick Kahl.
Enroll.: 3,253 (*f.t.* 32 m., 1,302 w.)
Junior College: *Enroll.:* 983 (*f.t.* 303 m., 556 w.)
(518) 270-2000

SCS BUSINESS AND TECHNICAL INSTITUTE
57 Willoughby St., Brooklyn 11202. Private. 1985 (NATTS). Courses of varying lengths. Certificates. Exec. Dir. Nathan Kajawski.
(718) 237-3730

SCS BUSINESS AND TECHNICAL INSTITUTE
1472 Broadway, New York 10036. Private. 1980 (NATTS); 1984 (AICS). Courses of varying lengths. Certificates. Exec. Dir. Barbara Leroy.
Enroll.: 970 (*f.t.* 292 m., 438 w.)
(212) 921-5000

BRANCH CAMPUS
57 Willoughby St., Brooklyn 11202. (AICS). Dir. Nathan Kajawski.
(718) 237-3730

BRANCH CAMPUS
2467 Jerome Ave., Bronx 10468. (AICS). Dir. Alan Shikowitz.
(212) 733-5200

BRANCH CAMPUS
163-02 Jamaica Ave., Jamaica 11432. (AICS). Dir. Larry Pollock.
(718) 658-8855

SYRIT COMPUTER SCHOOL SYSTEMS
5220 13th Ave., Brooklyn 11219. Private 1981 (NATTS). Courses of varying lengths. Diplomas. Dir. Rabbi Elliot Amsel.
Enroll.: 250 (*f.t.* 75 m., 75 w.)
(718) 853-1212

ST. BERNARD'S INSTITUTE
1100 S. Goodman St., Rochester 14620. Private (Roman Catholic) professional; graduate only. Sem. plan. Degrees: M. *Prof. Accred.:* Theology (1970/1982, ATS). Accredited by virtue of affiliation with Colgate Rochester Divinity School. Pres. Sebastian A. Falcone.
Enroll.: 86
(716) 271-1320

ST. BONAVENTURE UNIVERSITY
St. Bonaventure 14778. Private. 1924/1984 (MSA/CHE). Sem. plan. Degrees: B,M. Pres. Rev. Mathias F. Doyle, O.F.M.
Enroll.: 2,658 (*f.t.* 1,212 m., 1,097 w.)
(716) 375-2000

ST. FRANCIS COLLEGE
180 Remsen St., Brooklyn 11201. Private liberal arts. 1959/1984 (MSA/CHE). Sem. plan. Degrees: A,B. Pres. Brother Donald Sullivan, O.S.F.
Enroll.: 2,436 (*f.t.* 798 m., 724 w.)
(718) 522-2300

ST. JOHN FISHER COLLEGE
3690 East Ave., Rochester 14618. Private (coeducational) liberal arts. 1957/1986 (MSA/CHE). Sem. plan. Degrees: B,M. Pres. William L. Pickett.
Enroll.: 3,273 (*f.t.* 846 m., 772 w.)
(716) 385-8000

ST. JOHN'S UNIVERSITY
Grand Central and Utopia Parkways, Jamaica 11439. Private (Roman Catholic). Accreditation includes campus at 300 Howard Ave., Staten Island 10301. 1921/1986 (MSA/CHE). Sem. plan. Degrees: A,B,P,M,D. *Prof. Accred.:* Business (B,M), Law, Librarianship, Pharmacy, Psychology. Pres. V. Rev. Joseph T. Cahill, C.M.
Enroll.: 19,248 (*f.t.* 7,266 m., 6,940 w.)
(718) 990-6161

ST. JOSEPH'S COLLEGE
245 Clinton Ave., Brooklyn 11205. Private, non-resident liberal arts. Accreditation includes branch campus at Patchogue 11772. 1928/1982 (MSA/CHE). Sem. plan. Degrees: B. Pres. Sister George Aquin O'Connor, C.S.J.
Enroll.: 2,318 (*f.t.* 287 m., 917 w.)
(718) 636-6800

ST. JOSEPH'S SEMINARY
Dunwoodie, Yonkers 10704. Private (Roman Catholic) professional; graduate only. 1961/1983 (MSA/CHE). Sem. plan. Degrees: P,M. *Prof. Accred.:* Theology (1973/1983, ATS). Rector/Pres. Rev. Edwin F. O'Brien.
Enroll.: 173
(914) 968-6200

ST. LAWRENCE UNIVERSITY
Canton 13617. Private. 1921/1983 (MSA/CHE). Sem. plan. Degrees: B,M. *Prof. Accred.:* Teacher Education (*p*). Pres. W. Lawrence Gulick.
Enroll.: 2,328 (*f.t.* 1,128 m., 1,049 w.)
(315) 379-5011

ST. THOMAS AQUINAS COLLEGE
Rte. 340, Sparkill 10976. Private (independent coeducational) liberal arts. 1972/1982

(MSA/CHE). 4-1-4 plan. Degrees: A, B. Pres. Donald T. McNelis.
Enroll.: 2,081 (*f.t.* 558 m., 658 w.)
(914) 359-9500

St. Vladimir's Orthodox Theological Seminary
Crestwood 10707. Private (Eastern Orthodox) professional; graduate only. Sem. plan. Degrees: P, M. *Prof. Accred.:* Theology (1973/1983, ATS). Dean John Meyendorff.
Enroll.: 80
(914) 961-8313

Sarah Lawrence College
Bronxville 10708. Private liberal arts coeducational. 1937/1984 (MSA/CHE). Sem. plan. Degrees: B, M. Pres. Alice Stone Ilchman.
Enroll.: 1,080 (*f.t.* 193 m., 777 w.)
(914) 337-0700

The Sawyer School
69 Linwood Ave., Buffalo 14209. Private. 1973/1986 (AICS). Courses of varying lengths. Certificates. Pres. Andrew H. Moorhead.
Enroll.: 828 (*f.t.* 60 m., 768 w.)
(716) 884-3982

Schenectady County Community College
78 Washington Ave., Schenectady 12305. Public (county) junior; under State University of New York supervision. 1974/1984 (MSA/CHE). Qtr. plan. Degrees: A. *Prof. Accred.:* Music. Pres. Peter F. Burnham.
Enroll.: 3,063 (*f.t.* 709 m., 595 w.)
(518) 346-6211

School of Visual Arts
209 E. 23rd St., New York 10010. Independent professional. 1978/1983 (MSA/CHE). 4-1-4 plan. Degrees: B, M. *Prof. Accred.:* Art. Pres. David J. Rhodes.
Enroll.: 5,087 (*f.t.* 1,211 m., 995 w.)
(212) 679-7350

Seminary of the Immaculate Conception
Huntington 11743. Private (Roman Catholic) professional; graduate only. 1976/1981 (MSA/CHE). Sem. plan. Degrees: P, M, D. *Prof. Accred.:* Theology (1976/1981, ATS). Rector/Pres. Msgr. John J. Strynkowski.
Enroll.: 176 (*f.t.* 72 m.)
(516) 423-0483

Sh'or Yoshuv Rabbinical College
1526 Central Ave., Far Rockaway 11691. Private professional. 1979. Degrees: 1st Talmudic. *Prof. Accred.:* Rabbinical and Talmudic Education. Pres. Rabbi S. Freifeld.
Enroll.: *f.t.* 120 m.
(718) 327-2048

Siena College
Loudonville 12211. Private liberal arts. 1943/1984 (MSA/CHE). Sem. plan. Degrees: B. *Prof. Accred.:* Pres. Rev. Hugh F. Hines, O.F.M.
Enroll.: 3,355 (*f.t.* 1,429 m., 1,320 w.)
(518) 783-2300

The Simmons School
190 E. Post Rd., White Plains 10601. Private business. 1983 (AICS). Qtr. plan. Certificates, diplomas. Dir./Vice Pres. Peggy H. Simmons.
Enroll.: 166 (*f.t.* 3 m., 163 w.)
(914) 761-2701

Skidmore College
Saratoga Springs 12866-0851. Private liberal arts. 1925/1983 (MSA/CHE). 4-1-4 plan. Degrees: B. *Prof. Accred.:* Art, Social Work (B). Pres. Joseph C. Palamountain, Jr.
Enroll.: 2,585 (*f.t.* 830 m., 1,346 w.)
(518) 584-5000

Skinner Business School
200 Garden City Plaza, Garden City 11530. Private. 1980 (AICS). Courses of varying lengths. Certificates. Dir. Diane Froment.
Enroll.: 400 (*f.t.* 22 m., 378 w.)
(516) 747-4443

Spencer's Business and Technical Institute
404 Union St., Schenectady 12305. Private. 1981 (AICS). Qtr. plan. Certificates, diplomas. Area Dir. Faith Takes-Wright.
Enroll.: 423 (*f.t.* 42 m., 381 w.)
(518) 374-7619

State University of New York
State University Plaza, Albany 12246. Public university comprising various units located throughout the state, including those at Alfred and Cornell universities and 38 locally sponsored community colleges. Chanc. Clifton R. Wharton, Jr.
(518) 473-1011

University Centers

State University of New York at Albany
1400 Washington Ave., Albany 12222. 1938/1986 (MSA/CHE). Sem. plan. Degrees: B, M, D. *Prof. Accred.:* Business (B, M), Li-

brarianship, Nursing (B), Psychology, Rehabilitation Counseling, Social Work (B,M). Pres. Vincent O'Leary.
Enroll.: 15,978 (*f.t.* 5,699 m., 6,064 w.)
(518) 442-5571

STATE UNIVERSITY OF NEW YORK AT BINGHAMTON
Binghamton 13901. Liberal arts and professional. 1952/1981 (MSA/CHE). Sem. plan. Degrees: B,M,D. *Prof. Accred.:* Engineering Technology (electrical, electromechanical, mechanical), Nursing (B,M), Psychology. Pres. Clifford D. Clark.
Enroll.: 12,191 (*f.t.* 4,484 m., 4,870 w.)
(607) 777-2000

STATE UNIVERSITY OF NEW YORK AT BUFFALO
Amherst 14260. 1921/1983 (MSA/CHE). Sem. plan. Degrees: A,B,P,M,D. *Prof. Accred.:* Accounting (Type A,B), Architecture (M), Art, Business (B,M), Dental Assisting, Dentistry, Engineering (aerospace, chemical, civil, electrical, industrial, mechanical), Law, Librarianship, Medical Technology, Medicine, Music, Nuclear Medicine Technology, Nurse Anesthesia Education, Nursing (B,M), Occupational Therapy, Pharmacy, Physical Therapy, Psychology, Rehabilitation Counseling, Social Work (M), Speech Pathology and Audiology. Pres. Steven B. Sample.
Enroll.: 22,896 (*f.t.* 9,947 m., 6,394 w.)
Health Science Center *Enroll.:* 2,978 (*f.t.* 1,120 m., 1,143 w.)
(716) 636-2901

STATE UNIVERSITY OF NEW YORK AT STONY BROOK
Stony Brook 11794. Liberal arts and engineering. 1957/1984(MSA/CHE). Sem. plan. Degrees: B,P,M,D. *Prof. Accred.:* Assistant to the Primary Care Physician, Dentistry, Engineering (electrical, engineering science, mechanical), Medical Technology, Medicine, Nursing (B,M), Physical Therapy, Psychology, Respiratory Therapy, Social Work (B,M). Pres. John H. Marburger, III.
Enroll.: 14,360 (*f.t.* 6,732 m., 5,172 w.)
Health Science Center
Enroll.: 1,589 (*f.t.* 487 m., 768 w.)
(516) 246-5000

MEDICAL CENTERS

COLLEGE OF OPTOMETRY
100 E. 24th St., New York 10010. 1976/1981 (MSA/CHE). 3-3-3 plan. Degrees: P,M,D. *Prof. Accred.:* Optometric Technology, Optometry. Pres. Edward R. Johnston.
Enroll.: 244 (*f.t.* 122 m., 116 w.)
(212) 420-4900

HEALTH SCIENCE CENTER AT BROOKLYN
450 Clarkson Ave., Brooklyn 11203. 1952/1986 (MSA/CHE). Year varies among programs. Degrees: B,P,M,D. *Prof. Accred.:* Medical Record Administration, Medicine, Nursing (B), Occupational Therapy, Physical Therapy. Pres. Donald J. Scherl, M.D.
Enroll.: 1,350 (*f.t.* 643 m., 603 w.)
(718) 270-1000

HEALTH SCIENCE CENTER AT SYRACUSE
155 Elizabeth Blackwell St., Syracuse 13210. 1952/1979 (MSA/CHE). Sem. plan. Degrees: A,B,P,M,D. *Prof. Accred.:* Cytotechnology, Medical Technology, Medicine, Nuclear Medicine Technology, Nursing (A), Perfusion, Physical Therapy, Psychology, Radiation Therapy, Radiography, Respiratory Therapy, Specialist in Blood Bank Technology. Pres. John Bernard Henry.
Enroll.: 907 (*f.t.* 487 m., 363 w.)
(315) 473-5540

STATE UNIVERSITY COLLEGES OF ARTS AND SCIENCE
Public liberal arts and teachers. Sem. plan. Degrees: B,M.

STATE UNIVERSITY COLLEGE AT BROCKPORT
Brockport 14420. 1952/1982 (MSA/CHE). *Prof. Accred.:* Nursing (B), Social Work (B). Pres. John E. Van de Wetering.
Enroll.: 7,421 (*f.t.* 2,484 m., 2,378 w.)
(716) 395-2121

STATE UNIVERSITY COLLEGE AT BUFFALO
1300 Elmwood Ave., Buffalo 14222. 1948/1982 (MSA/CHE). *Prof. Accred.:* Dietetics, Engineering Technology (electrical, mechanical), Social Work (B), Speech Pathology, Teacher Education (*e,s*). Pres. D. Bruce Johnstone.
Enroll.: 11,521 (*f.t.* 3,842 m., 4,517 w.)
(716) 878-4000

STATE UNIVERSITY COLLEGE AT CORTLAND
Cortland 13045. 1948/1982 (MSA/CHE). *Prof. Accred.:* Teacher Education (*e,s*). Pres. James M. Clark.
Enroll.: 6,491 (*f.t.* 2,238 m., 3,115 w.)
(607) 753-2001

Empire State College
Two Union Ave., Saratoga Springs 12866. 1974/1984 (MSA/CHE). External degree program. Degrees: A, B, M. Pres. James W. Hall.
Enroll.: 5,511 (*f.t.* 438 m., 626 w.)
(518) 587-2100

State University College at Fredonia
Fredonia 14063. 1952/1980 (MSA/CHE). *Prof. Accred.:* Art, Music. Pres. Donald A. MacPhee.
Enroll.: 4,831 (*f.t.* 1,933 m., 2,173 w.)
(716) 673-3111

State University College at Geneseo
Geneseo 14454. 1952/1981 (MSA/CHE). *Prof. Accred.:* Speech Pathology and Audiology. Pres. Edward B. Jakubauskas.
Enroll.: 5,425 (*f.t.* 1,770 m., 3,253 w.)
(716) 245-5210

State University College at New Paltz
New Paltz 12561. 1950/1986 (MSA/CHE). Degrees: B, M. *Prof. Accred.:* Music, Nursing (B), Teacher Education (*e,s,p*). Pres. Alice Chandler.
Enroll.: 7,392 (*f.t.* 2,015 m., 2,466 w.)
(914) 257-2121

State University College at Old Westbury
Old Westbury 11568. 1976/1981 (MSA/CHE). Degrees: B only. Pres. L. Eudora Pettigrew.
Enroll.: 3,558 (*f.t.* 1,109 m., 1,369 w.)
(516) 876-3000

State University College at Oneonta
Oneonta 13820. 1949/1983 (MSA/CHE). *Prof. Accred.:* Nursing, Teacher Education (*e,s,p*). Pres. Clifford J. Craven.
Enroll.: 5,751 (*f.t.* 2,113 m., 3,063 w.)
(607) 431-3730

State University College at Oswego
Oswego 13126. 1950/1982 (MSA/CHE). Degrees: B, M. *Prof. Accred.:* Music. Pres. Virginia L. Radley.
Enroll.: 7,810 (*f.t.* 2,972 m., 3,380 w.)
(315) 341-2500

State University College at Plattsburgh
Plattsburgh 12901. 1952/1982 (MSA/CHE). Degrees: B, M. *Prof. Accred.:* Nursing (B). Pres. ———.
Enroll.: 6,225 (*f.t.* 2,210 m., 2,995 w.)
(518) 564-2000

State University College at Potsdam
Potsdam 13676. 1952/1982 (MSA/CHE). Degrees: B, M. *Prof. Accred.:* Music. Pres. Humphrey Tonkin.
Enroll.: 4,249 (*f.t.* 1,694 m., 1,936 w.)
(936) 267-2000

State University College at Purchase
Purchase 10577. 1976/1982 (MSA/CHE). Degrees: B, M. Pres. Sheldon N. Grebstein.
Enroll.: 3,875 (*f.t.* 952 m., 1,208 w.)
(914) 253-5000

Specialized Colleges

College of Environmental Science and Forestry
Syracuse 13210. 1952/1982 (MSA/CHE). Sem. plan. Degrees: A, B, M, D. *Prof. Accred.:* Engineering (forest), Forestry, Landscape Architecture (M),. Pres. Ross S. Whaley.
Enroll.: 1,381 (*f.t.* 748 m., 279 w.)
(315) 470-6500

College of Technology
P.O. Box 3050, Utica 13504-3050. Upper division only. 1979/1983 (MSA/CHE). Degrees: B, M. *Prof. Accred.:* Engineering Technology (electrical, industrial, mechanical), Medical Record Administration, Nursing (B). Pres. Peter J. Cayan.
Enroll.: 2,407 (*f.t.* 753 m., 499 w.)
(315) 792-7400

Maritime College
Fort Schuyler, Bronx 10465. Professional. 1952/1986 (MSA/CHE). Sem. plan. Degrees: B, M. *Prof. Accred.:* Engineering (marine). Pres. RADM Floyd H. Miller, USN (Ret.).
Enroll.: 926 (*f.t.* 757 m., 56 w.)
(212) 409-7200

Agricultural and Technical Colleges

2-year institutions. 1952/1963 (MSA/CHE). Sem. plan.

SUNY Agricultural and Technical College at Alfred
Alfred 14802. 1952/1981 (MSA/CHE). Degrees: A. *Prof. Accred.:* Engineering Technology (air conditioning, construction, electrical, electro-mechanical, mechanical-internal combustion option, mechanical-product and machine design option, surveying), Medical Laboratory Technology (A), Medical Record Technology, Nursing (A). Pres. John O. Hunter.

Enroll.: 3,803 (*f.t.* 2,158 m., 1,386 w.)
(607) 871-7294

SUNY Agricultural and Technical College at Canton
Canton 13617. 1952/1982 (MSA/CHE). Degrees: A.*Prof. Accred.:* Engineering Technology (air conditioning, civil, construction, electrical, mechanical), Medical Laboratory Technology (A), Nursing (A). Pres. Earl W. MacArthur.
Enroll.: 2,234 (*f.t.* 1,191 m., 762 w.)
(315) 386-7011

SUNY Agricultural and Technical College at Cobleskill
Cobleskill 12043. 1952/1986 (MSA/CHE). Degrees: A,B. *Prof. Accred.:* Histologic Technology. Pres. Cornelius V. Robbins.
Enroll.: 2,706 (*f.t.* 1,258 m., 1,293 w.)
(518) 234-5011

SUNY Agricultural and Technical College at Delhi
Delhi 13753. 1952/1982 (MSA/CHE). Degrees: A. Pres. Seldon M. Kruger.
Enroll.: 2,378 (*f.t.* 1,284 m., 872 w.)
(607) 746-4111

SUNY Agricultural and Technical College at Farmingdale
Farmingdale 11735. 1952/1981 (MSA/CHE). Degrees: A,B. *Prof. Accred.:* Dental Hygiene, Engineering Technology (air conditioning, automotive, civil, construction-architectural, electrical, mechanical), Nursing (A). Pres. Frank A. Cipriani.
Enroll.: 11,975 (*f.t.* 3,249 m., 2,653 w.)
(516) 420-2000

SUNY Agricultural and Technical College at Morrisville
Morrisville 13408. 1952/1982 (MSA/CHE). Degrees: A. *Prof. Accred.:* Engineering Technology (electrical, mechanical), Nursing (A). Pres. Donald G. Butcher.
Enroll.: 3,066 (*f.t.* 1,498 m., 1,036 w.)
(315) 684-6000

Stenotype Academy
291 Broadway, New York 10007. Private. 1978/1984 (AICS). Courses of varying lengths. Certificates, diplomas. Pres. Melvin D. Eisner.
Enroll.: 248 (*f.t.* 13 m., 235 w.)
(212) 962-0002

Stenotype Institute
1780 Broadway, New York 10019. Private. 1984 (AICS). Qtr. plan. Degrees: A. Pres. Hubert Delapine.
Enroll.: 445
(212) 581-0270

Branch Campus
901B Mid-Island Plaza, Hicksville 11802, Admin. Jerri Fitzpatrick.
(516) 938-5535

The Stratford School
917 Main St., E., Rochester 14605. Private business. 1973/1984 (AICS). Courses of varying lengths. Certificates, diplomas. *Prof. Accred.:* Medical Assisting, Nursing (A). Vice Pres. Jo Ann C. Wheeler.
Enroll.: 947 (*f.t.* 322 m., 625 w.)
(716) 244-1290

Branch Campus
2697 Main St., Buffalo 14214. Dir. Simone Rockwell.
(716) 837-7900

Branch Campus
845 Central Ave., Albany 12206. *Prof. Accred.:* Medical Assisting. Dir. Gino Danese.
(518) 438-2022

Branch Campus
2301 James St., Syracuse 13206. *Prof. Accred.:* Medical Assisting. Dir. Frank Castiglia.
(315) 433-1500

Branch Campus
6776 Reisterstown Rd., Baltimore, MD 21215. Dir. Virginia Stockdale.
(301) 358-4700

Branch Campus
2801 Hennepin Ave., S., Minneapolis, MN 55408. *Prof. Accred.:* Medical Assisting. Dir. Christine M. Sage.
(612) 872-4663

Suburban Technical School
175 Fulton Ave., Hempstead 11550. Private 1972/1977 (NATTS). Courses of varying lengths. Diplomas. Dir. Annette Robb.
Enroll.: 631 (*f.t.* 332 m., 41 w.)
(516) 481-6660

Branch Campus
900 Wheeler Rd., Rte. 111, Hauppauge 11788. Dir. Robert Capon.
(516) 361-7336

Suffolk County Community College
System Office, Selden 11784. Public (county) junior; under State University of New York supervision. Sem. plan. Degrees: A. Pres. Robert T. Kreiling.
Enroll.: 18,115 (*f.t.* 3,163 m., 3,644 w.)
(516) 451-4110

Ammerman Campus at Selden
Selden 11784. 1966/1982 (MSA/CHE). Sem. plan. Degrees: A. *Prof. Accred.:* Dental Assisting, Nursing (A). Exec. Dean. William Hudson.
Enroll.: 11,357 (*f.t.* 2,333 m., 2,488 w.)
(516) 451-4110

Eastern Campus
Speonk-Riverhead Rd., Riverhead 11901. 1982 (MSA/CHE). Exec. Dean Steven Kenny.
Enroll.: 1,837 (*f.t.* 222 m., 312 w.)
(516) 369-2600

Western Campus
Crooked Hill Rd., Brentwood 11717. 1981 (MSA/CHE). Sem. plan. Degrees: A. *Prof. Accred.:* Nursing (A). Exec. Dean Salvatore LaLima.
Enroll.: 4,921 (*f.t.* 608 m., 844 w.)
(516) 434-6751

Suffolk Technical Institute
28 W. Main St., Bay Shore 11706. Private. 1983 (NATTS). Courses of varying lengths. Certificates, diplomas. Dir. Carmen Santana.
Enroll.: 27
(516) 665-8030.

Sullivan County Community College
College Rd., Loch Sheldrake 12759. Public (county) junior; under State University of New York supervision. 1968/1984 (MSA/CHE). Sem. plan. Degrees: A. Pres. John F. Walter.
Enroll.: 1,669 (*f.t.* 696 m., 597 w.)
(914) 434-5750

Superior Career Institute
116 W. 14th St., New York 10011. Private (NATTS). Courses of varying lengths. Certificates. Dir. Murray Bernstein.
Enroll.: 220
(212) 675-2140

Sutton Secretarial School
2149 Wantagh Ave., Wantagh 11793. Private. 1981/1984 (AICS). Sem. plan. Certificates, diplomas. Dir. Marcia Gold.
Enroll.: 94 (*f.t.* 1 m., 93 w.)
(516) 221-2149

Branch Campus
150 Nassau St., New York 10038. Dir. Frederick Hershinson.
(212) 619-6190

The Swedish Institute, Inc.
875 Avenue of the Americas, New York 10001. Private. 1981 (NATTS). Sem. plan. Diplomas. Dir. Patricia J. Eckardt.
Enroll.: 231 (*f.t.* 88 m., 143 w.)
(212) 695-3964

Syracuse University
Syracuse 13244. Private. 1921/1983 (MSA/CHE). Sem. plan. Degrees: A,B,P,M,D. *Prof. Accred.:* Architecture (B), Art, Business (B,M), Dietetics, Engineering (aerospace, chemical, civil, computer, electrical, engineering and operations research, industrial, mechanical, mechanical/aerospace), Home Economics, Interior Design, Journalism, Landscape Architecture, Law, Librarianship, Music, Nursing (B,M), Rehabilitation Counseling, Psychology, Social Work (B,M), Speech Pathology and Audiology, Teacher Education (*e,s,p*). Chanc.-Pres. Melvin A. Eggers.
Enroll.: 20,980 (*f.t.* 7,694 m., 7,130 w.)
(315) 423-1870

Talmudical Seminary Oholei Torah
417 Troy Ave., P,O Box 273, Brooklyn 11213. Private; graduate and professional only. 1985. Degrees: 1st Talmudic. *Prof. Accred.:* Rabbinical and Talmudic Education. Pres. Rabbi Teitelbaum.
Enroll.: 115 m.

Taylor Business Institute
One Penn Plaza, New York 10001. Private. 1962/1981 (AICS). Sem. plan. Degrees: A. Dir. William Wildish.
Enroll.: 2,604 (*f.t.* 1,194 m., 1,410 w.)
(212) 279-0510

Teachers College of Columbia University
525 W. 120th St., New York 10027. Private professional; graduate only; affiliate of Columbia University. 1921/1986 (MSA/CHE). Sem. plan. Degrees: M,D. *Prof. Accred.:* Community Health Education, Nursing (M), Psychology, Speech Pathology and Audiology, Teacher Education (*e,s,p*). Pres. P. Michael Timpane.

Enroll.: 4,155 (*f.t.* 449 m., 921 w.)
(212) 678-3000

TECHNICAL CAREER INSTITUTES
320 W. 31st St., New York 10001. Private. 1976 (NATTS). Qtr. plan. Degrees: A, certificates. *Prof. Accred.:* Engineering Technology (electronics). Pres. George E. Leelike.
Enroll.: 2,376 (*f.t.* 1,564 m., 186 w.)
(212) 594-4000

TECHNO-DENT SCHOOL OF DENTAL LAB TECHNOLOGY
265 W. 37th St., Fourth Fl., New York 10018. Private. 1983 (NATTS). Tri. plan. Certificates. Pres. George A. Nossa.
Enroll.: 40
(212) 840-0939

TOBE-COBURN SCHOOL FOR FASHION CAREERS
686 Broadway, New York 10012. Private. 1972/1983 (NATTS). Tri. plan. Degrees: A. Dir. Ann Z. Wareham.
Enroll.: 450 (*f.t.* 20 m., 430 w.)
(212) 460-9600

TOMPKINS CORTLAND COMMUNITY COLLEGE
170 North St., Dryden 13053. Public junior; under State University of New York supervision. 1973/1984 (MSA/CHE). Sem. plan. Degrees: A. *Prof. Accred.:* Nursing (A). Pres. Eduardo J. Marti.
Enroll.: 2,944 (*f.t.* 528 m., 837 w.)
(607) 844-8211

TOURO COLLEGE
30 W. 44th St., New York 10036. Independent, liberal arts and science. 1976/1982 (MSA/CHE). Sem. plan. Degrees: A,B,P,M. *Prof. Accred.:* Assistant to the Primary Care Physician, Law (ABA only), Medical Record Administration. Pres. Bernard Lander.
Enroll.: 4,297 (*f.t.* 1,238 m., 2,522 w.)
(212) 575-0190

TRAPHAGEN SCHOOL OF FASHION
257 Park Ave. S., New York 10010. Private. 1972/1978 (NATTS). Sem. plan. Certificates. Dir. Dorothy E. Hellman.
Enroll.: 134 (*f.t.* 24 m., 110 w.)
(212) 673-0300

TROCAIRE COLLEGE
110 Red Jacket Pkwy., Buffalo 14220. Private junior. 1974/1984 (MSA/CHE). Sem. plan. Degrees: A. *Prof. Accred.:* Radiography, Nursing (A). Pres. Sister Mary Carmina Coppola.
Enroll.: 1,009 (*f.t.* 50 m., 457 w.)
(716) 826-1200

ULSTER COUNTY COMMUNITY COLLEGE
Stone Ridge 12484. Public junior; under State University of New York supervision. 1970/1986 (MSA/CHE). Sem. plan. Degrees: A. Pres. Robert T. Brown.
Enroll.: 3,120 (*f.t.* 793 m., 705 w.)
(914) 687-7621

ULTRASOUND DIAGNOSTIC SCHOOL
30 E. 23rd St., New York 10010. Private. 1984 (ABHES). Courses of varying lengths. Certificates. Dir. Matthew Fenster.
(212) 420-0330

BRANCH CAMPUS
499 Jerico Tpke., Mineola 11501. Coord. Douglas Teague.
(516) 248-6060

BRANCH CAMPUS
170 E. Post Rd., White Plains 10601. Coord. Marie Buschel.
(914) 328-0003

UNION COLLEGE
Schenectady 12308. Private liberal arts. 1921/1985 (MSA/CHE); accreditation includes branch campus at Poughkeepsie 12603. Year of 3 10-week terms. Degrees: B,M,D. *Prof. Accred.:* Engineering (civil, electrical, mechanical), Health Administration. Pres. John S. Morris.
Enroll.: 3,283 (*f.t.* 1,353 m., 846 w.)
(518) 370-6000

UNION SETTLEMENT ASSOCIATION TRAINING SCHOOL
237 E. 104th St., New York 10029. Private. 1983 (ABHES). Courses of varying lengths. Certificates. Dir. Dorothea Hickman.
(212) 348-1822

UNION THEOLOGICAL SEMINARY
3041 Broadway, New York 10027. Private (Interdenominational) professional; graduate only. 1967/1983 (MSA/CHE). Sem. plan. Degrees: P,M,D. *Prof. Accred.:* Music, Theology (1938/1978, ATS). Pres. Donald W. Shriver, Jr.
Enroll.: 392 (*f.t.* 117 m., 140 w.)
(212) 662-7100

UNITED STATES MERCHANT MARINE ACADEMY
Kings Point 11024. Public (federal) technological. 1949/1985 (MSA/CHE). Qtr. plan.

Degrees: B. Supt. RADM Thomas A. King, USMS.
Enroll.: 1,014 (*f.t.* 926 m., 88 w.)
(516) 482-8200

UNITED STATES MILITARY ACADEMY
West Point 10996-5000. Public (federal) professional. 1949/1985 (MSA/CHE). *Prof. Accred.:* Engineering (civil, electrical, engineering management, mechanical), Sem. plan. Degrees: B. Supt. Lt. Gen. Dave Palmer, USA.
Enroll.: 4,600 (*f.t.* 4,150 m., 450 w.)
(914) 938-3122

UNITED TALMUDICAL ACADEMY
82 Lee Ave., Brooklyn 11211. Private professional. 1979. Degrees: 1st Talmudic. *Prof. Accred.:* Rabbinical and Talmudic Education. Pres. Rabbi S. Deutsch.
Enroll.: f.t. 669 m.
(718) 963-9260

UNIVERSITY OF ROCHESTER
River Blvd., Rochester 14627. Private. 1921/1986 (MSA/CHE). Sem. plan. Degrees: B,P,M,D. *Prof. Accred.:* Business (M), Community Health/Preventive Medicine, Engineering (chemical, electrical, mechanical), Medicine, Music, Nursing (B,M), Psychology. Pres. G. Dennis O'Brien.
Enroll.: 8,561 (*f.t.* 4,028 m., 2,546 w.)
(716) 275-2121

UNIVERSITY OF THE STATE OF NEW YORK REGENTS COLLEGE DEGREES
Albany 12230. Public (state) nonteaching. 1977/1982 (MSA/CHE). Degrees: A,B. *Prof. Accred.:* Nursing (A,B). Pres. Gordon M. Ambach.
Enroll.: 14,257 (*f.t.* 7,708 m., 6,549 w.)
(518) 474-3703

UTICA COLLEGE OF SYRACUSE UNIVERSITY
Utica 13502. Private liberal arts/sciences/business. 1946/1983 (MSA/CHE). Sem. plan. Degrees: A,B. *Prof. Accred.:* Medical Technology, Occupational Therapy, Surgical Technology. Pres. Lansing G. Baker.
Enroll.: 2,327 (*f.t.* 581 m., 733 w.)
(315) 792-3144

UTICA SCHOOL OF COMMERCE
201 Bleecker St., Utica 13501. Private. 1969/1981 (AICS). Qtr. plan. Degrees: A, diplomas. Pres. Philip M. Williams.
Enroll.: 645 (*f.t.* 108 m., 537 w.)
(315) 733-2307

VASSAR COLLEGE
Poughkeepsie 12601. Private liberal arts. 1921/1985 (MSA/CHE). Sem. plan. Degrees: B,M. Pres. Frances Daly Fergusson.
Enroll.: 2,317 (*f.t.* 875 m., 1,330 w.)
(914) 452-7000

VILLA MARIA COLLEGE OF BUFFALO
240 Pine Ridge Rd., Buffalo 14225. Private junior. 1972/1983 (MSA/CHE). 4-1-4 plan. Degrees: A. Pres. Sister Marcella Marie Garus, C.S.S.F.
Enroll.: 700 (*f.t.* 180 m., 350 w.)
(716) 896-0700

WADHAMS HALL SEMINARY/COLLEGE
Ogdensburg 13669. Private (Roman Catholic, Diocese of Ogdensburg) seminary/college. 1972/1982 (MSA/CHE). Sem. plan. Degrees: B. Pres. Rev. Leeward J. Poissant.
Enroll.: f.t. 52 m.
(315) 393-4231

WAGNER COLLEGE
631 Howard Ave., Staten Island 10301. Private (Lutheran in America) liberal arts. 1931/1985 (MSA/CHE). Sem. plan. Degrees: B,M. *Prof. Accred.:* Nursing. Pres. Sam H. Frank.
Enroll.: 1,980 (*f.t.* 764 m., 723 w.)
(718) 390-3100

WEBB INSTITUTE OF NAVAL ARCHITECTURE
Glen Cove 11542. Private technological. 1950/1985 (MSA/CHE). Sem. plan with 8-week winter work period. Degrees: B. *Prof. Accred.:* Engineering (naval architecture and marine). Pres. VADM Benedict L. Stabile USCG (Ret.).
Enroll.: 82 (*f.t.* 70 m., 12 w.)
(516) 671-2213

WELLS COLLEGE
Aurora 13026-0500. Private liberal arts for women. 1921/1984 (MSA/CHE). 4-1-4 plan. Degrees: B. Pres. Patti M. Peterson.
Enroll.: 433 (*f.t.* 420 w.)
(315) 364-3360

WESTCHESTER BUSINESS INSTITUTE
325 Central Ave., P.O. Box 710, White Plains 10602. Private. 1966/1979 (AICS). Qtr. plan. Degrees: A. Pres. Ernest H. Sutkowski.
Enroll.: 1,116 (*f.t.* 301 m., 815 w.)
(914) 948-4442

WESTCHESTER COMMUNITY COLLEGE
Valhalla 10595. Public junior; under State University of New York supervision. 1970/1985 (MSA/CHE). Sem. plan. Degrees: A.

Prof. Accred.: Radiography, Respiratory Therapy. Pres. Joseph N. Hankin.
Enroll.: 7,515 (*f.t.* 1,794 m., 1,413 w.)
(914) 285-6600

WESTCHESTER CONSERVATORY OF MUSIC
30 Burling Ave., White Plains 10605. Regional (public and private support) professional. 1977. Courses of varying lengths. Certificates. *Prof. Accred.:* Music. Exec. Dir. Michael Pollon.
Enroll.: 639 (*f.t.* 137)
(914) RO1-3715

WEYMOUTH BUSINESS INSTITUTE
196 Fulton Ave., Hempstead 11551. Private. 1973/1985 (AICS). Qtr. plan. Certificates, diplomas. Dir. W. T. Weymouth.
Enroll.: 193 (*f.t.* 64 m., 129 w.)
(516) 483-8855

WOOD SCHOOL
Eight E. 40th St., New York 10016. Private business. 1967/1982 (AICS). Qtr. plan. Degrees: A, diplomas. Pres. Rosemary Duggan.
Enroll.: 579 (*f.t.* 0 m., 579 w.)
(212) 686-9040

WRITERS INSTITUTE
112 Boston Post Rd., Mamaroneck 10543. Private home study. 1961/1984 (NHSC). Pres. Lois Stuart.
(9142) 698-7488

YESHIVA KARLIN STOLIN
1818 54th St., Brooklyn 11204. Private; graduate and professional only. 1984. Degrees: 1st Talmudic. *Prof. Accred.:* Rabbinical and Talmudic Education. Pres. Rabbi M. Pilchick.
Enroll.: 75 (*f.t.* 60 m., 0 w.)

YESHIVA UNIVERSITY
500 W. 185th St., New York 10033-3299. Private; coordinate undergraduate colleges, graduate schools coeducational. 1948/1981 (MSA/CHE). Sem. plan. Degrees: A,B, P,M,D. *Prof. Accred.:* Law, Medicine, Nuclear Medicine Technology, Psychology, Social Work (M). Pres. Norman Lamm.
Enroll.: 4,360 (*f.t.* 2,041 m., 1,787 w.)
(212) 960-5400

YESHIVAH AND MESIVTA TORAH TEMIMAH TALMUDICAL SEMINARY
555 Ocean Pkwy., Brooklyn 11218. Private; graduate and professional only. 1986. Degrees: 1st Talmudic. *Prof. Accred.:* Rabbinical and Talmudic Education. Pres. Rabbi L. Margulis.

YESHIVATH VIZNITZ
P.O. Box 446, Phyllis Ter., Monsey 10952. Private; graduate and professional only. 1986. Degrees: 1st Rabbinic. *Prof. Accred.:* Rabbinical and Talmudic Education. Pres. Rabbi J. Luria.
Enroll.: 95

YESIVATH ZICHRON MOSHE
Laurel Park Rd., South Fallsburg 12779. Private professional. 1979. Degrees: 1st Talmudic. *Prof. Accred.:* Rabbinical and Talmudic Education. Pres. Rabbi A. Gorelick.
Enroll.: *f.t.* 115 m.
(914) 434-5240

YORK INSTITUTE
23 E. 15th St., New York 10003. Private business. 1984 (AICS). 16-month program. Certificates. Pres. Kenneth F. Ostrom.
Enroll.: 273 (*f.t.* 265)
(212) 741-8820

BRANCH CAMPUS
212 Hicks St., Brooklyn 11201.
(212) 855-5010

NORTH CAROLINA

AMERICAN BUSINESS AND FASHION INSTITUTE
1515 Mockingbird La., Suite 600, Charlotte 28209. Private. 1978/1985 (AICS). Courses of varying lengths. Diplomas. Pres. William H. Hummel.
Enroll.: 274 (*f.t.* 11 m., 263 w.)
(704) 523-3738

ANSON TECHNICAL COLLEGE
Ansonville 28007. Public 2-year. 1977/1983 (SACS-Comm. on Coll.). Qtr. plan. Degrees: A. Pres. Edwin R. Chapman.
Enroll.: 1,106
(704) 826-8333

*APPALACHIAN STATE UNIVERSITY
Boone 28608. Public. 1942/1982 (SACS-Comm. on Coll.). Sem. plan. Degrees: B,M. *Prof. Accred.:* Business (B,M), Home Economics, Music, Rehabilitation Counseling, Teacher Education (*e,s,p*). Chanc. John E. Thomas.
Enroll.: 8,894
(704) 262-2000

ASHEVILLE-BUNCOMBE TECHNICAL COLLEGE
340 Victoria Rd., Asheville 28801. Public 2-year. 1969/1984 (SACS-Comm. on Coll.). Qtr. plan. Degrees: A. *Prof. Accred.:* Dental Assisting, Dental Hygiene, Medical Laboratory Technology (A), Radiography. Pres. Harvey L. Haynes.
Enroll.: 2,841
(704) 254-1921

ATLANTIC CHRISTIAN COLLEGE
Wilson 27893. Private (Disciples of Christ) liberal arts. 1955/1977 (SACS-Comm. on Coll.). Sem. plan. Degrees: B. *Prof. Accred.:* Medical Technology, Nursing (B), Teacher Education (*e,s*). Pres. James B. Hemby, Jr.
Enroll.: 1,233
(919) 237-3161

BARBER-SCOTIA COLLEGE
Concord 28025. Private (United Presbyterian) liberal arts and teachers. 1949/1984 (SACS-Comm. on Coll.). Sem. plan. Degrees: A,B. Pres. Mable Parker McLean.
Enroll.: 373
(704) 786-5171

*Member University System of North Carolina

BEAUFORT COUNTY COMMUNITY COLLEGE
P.O. Box 1069, Washington 27889. Public 2-year. 1973/1978 (SACS-Comm. on Coll.). Qtr. plan. Degrees: A, certificates. Pres. James P. Blanton.
Enroll.: 1,484
(919) 946-6194

BELMONT ABBEY COLLEGE
Belmont 28012. Private (Roman Catholic) liberal arts. 1957/1978 (SACS-Comm. on Coll.). Sem. plan. Degrees: B. Pres. John R. Dempsey.
Enroll.: 837
(704) 825-3711

BENNETT COLLEGE
Greensboro 27420. Private (United Methodist) liberal arts for women. 1935/1979 (SACS-Comm. on Coll.). Sem. plan. Degrees: A,B. Pres. Isaac H. Miller, Jr.
Enroll.: 575
(919) 273-4431

BLADEN TECHNICAL COLLEGE
Dublin 28332. Public (state) 2-year. 1976/1982 (SACS-Comm. on Coll.). Qtr. plan. Degrees: A. *Prof. Accred.:* Medical Laboratory Technology. Pres. Lynn G. King.
Enroll.: 729
(919) 862-2164

BLANTON'S JUNIOR COLLEGE
126 College St., Asheville 28801. Private business. 1972/1984 (AICS). Qtr. plan. Degrees: A, diplomas. Exec. Dir. Andrew Craig.
Enroll.: 395 (*f.t.* 134 m., 261 w.)
(704) 252-7346

BLUE RIDGE TECHNICAL COLLEGE
Rt. 2, Flat Rock 28731. Public 2-year. 1973/1978 (SACS-Comm. on Coll.). Qtr. plan. Degrees: A. Pres. William D. Killian.
Enroll.: 1,853
(704) 692-3572

BREVARD COLLEGE
Brevard 28712. Private (United Methodist) junior. 1949/1975 (SACS-Comm. on Coll.). Sem. plan. Degrees: A. *Prof. Accred.:* Music. Pres. William Thomas Greer, Jr.
Enroll.: 649
(704) 883-8292

Brookstone College of Business
101 S. Main St., High Point 27260. Private junior. 1984 (AICS). Qtr. plan. Degrees: A, certificates, diplomas. Dir. Linda Yokeley.
(919) 884-5515

Brunswick Technical College
P.O. Box 30, Supply 28462. Public 2-year. 1983 (SACS-Comm. on Coll.). Qtr. plan. Degrees: A. Pres. Joseph B. Carter.
Enroll.: 1,515
(919) 754-6900

Caldwell Community College and Technical Institute
1000 Hickory Blvd., Hudson 28638. Public (state) junior. 1969/1975 (SACS-Comm. on Coll.). Qtr. plan. Degrees: A. *Prof. Accred.:* Nuclear Medicine Technology. Pres. Eric McKeithan.
Enroll.: 2,220
(704) 728-4323

Cambridge Academy
Petti Bldg., Suite B, P.O. Box 1289, Banner Elk 28604. Private home study. 1985 (NHSC). CEO Tanzee Nahas.
1-(800) 327-4871

Campbell University, Inc.
Buie's Creek 27506. Private (Southern Baptist) liberal arts. 1966/1980 (SACS-Comm. on Coll.). Sem. plan. Degrees: A,B,M,P. *Prof. Accred.:* Law (ABA only). Teacher Education (*e,s*). Pres. Norman A. Wiggins.
Enroll.: 2,676
(919) 893-4111

Cape Fear Technical Institute
411 N. Front St., Wilmington 28401. Public 2-year. 1971/1975 (SACS-Comm. on Coll.). Qtr. plan. Degrees: A. Pres. E. Thomas Satterfield, Jr.
Enroll.: 5,764
(919) 343-0481

Carolina Beauty Systems
102 Chestnut Dr., High Point 27260. Private. 1984 (SACS-COEI). Courses of varying lengths. Certificats. Dir. Marion Fields.
Enroll.: FTE 1,249

Branch Campus
240-246 E. Front St., Burlington 27215.

Branch Campus
Cloverleaf Plaza, Concord 28025.

Branch Campus
776 Ninth St., Durham 27705.

Branch Campus
120 E. Main St., Elkin 28621.

Branch Campus
401 Cox Rd., Gastonia 28052.

Branch Campus
2001 W. Wendover Ave., Greensboro 27405.

Branch Campus
1105 E. Lexington Ave., High Point 27262.

Branch Campus
930 Floyd St., Kannapolis 28081.

Branch Campus
103 E. Center St., Lexington 27292.

Branch Campus
1201 Stafford St., Suite 132, Monroe 28110.

Branch Campus
501 S. South St., Mount Airy 27030.

Branch Campus
609 W. 20th St., Newton 28658.

Branch Campus
220 S. Main St., Salisbury 28144.

Branch Campus
231 N. Lafayette St., Shelby 28150.

Branch Campus
123 Berry St., Statesville 28677.

Branch Campus
5059 Country Club Rd., Winston-Salem 27104.

Carteret Technical College
3505 Arndell Street, Morehead City 28557. Public 2-year. 1974/1979 (SACS-Comm. on Coll.). Qtr. plan. Degrees: A. *Prof. Accred.:* Medical Assisting, Radiography, Respiratory Therapy, Respiratory Therapy Technology. Pres. Donald W. Bryant.
Enroll.: 1,454
(919) 247-6000

Catawba College
Salisbury 28144. Private (United Church of Christ) liberal arts. 1928/1984 (SACS-Comm. on Coll.). Sem. plan. Degrees: B. *Prof. Accred.:* Social Work (B). Pres. Stephen H. Wurster.
Enroll.: 865
(704) 637-4111

Catawba Valley Technical College
Hickory 28601. Public 2-year. 1969/1984 (SACS-Comm. on Coll.). Qtr. plan. Degrees: A. *Prof. Accred.* Assistant to the Primary Care Physician, Engineering Technology (ar-

chitectural, drafting and design, electro-mechanical, industrial, mechanical). Pres. Robert E. Paap.
Enroll.: 2,888
(704) 327-9124

CECILS JUNIOR COLLEGE OF BUSINESS
1567 Patton Ave., P.O. Box 6407, Asheville 28816. Private. 1971/1979 (AICS). Qtr. plan. Degrees: A, certificates, diplomas. Pres. John T. South.
Enroll.: 478 (*f.t.* 119 m., 359 w.)
(704) 252-2486

CENTRAL CAROLINA TECHNICAL COLLEGE
1105 Kelly Dr., Sanford 27330. Public 2-year. 1972/1976 (SACS-Comm. on Coll.). Qtr. plan. Degrees: A. Pres. Marvin R. Joyner.
Enroll.: 4,535
(919) 775-5401

CENTRAL PIEDMONT COMMUNITY COLLEGE
P.O. Box 35009, Charlotte 28235. Public (state) junior. 1969/1983 (SACS-Comm. on Coll.). Qtr. plan. Degrees: A. *Prof. Accred.:* Dental Assisting, Dental Hygiene, Engineering Technology (architectural, civil, electrical, electronics, manufacturing, mechanical), Medical Assistant, Medical Record Technology, Respiratory Therapy. Pres. Ruth G. Shaw.
Enroll.: 11,341
(704) 373-6633

CHOWAN COLLEGE
Murfreesboro 27855. Private (Southern Baptist) junior. 1956/1978 (SACS-Comm. on Coll.). Sem. plan. Degrees: A. Pres. Bruce E. Whitaker.
Enroll.: 899
(919) 398-4101

CLEVELAND TECHNICAL COLLEGE
Shelby 28150. Public 2-year. 1975/1981 (SACS-Comm. on Coll.). Qtr. plan. Degrees: A. *Prof. Accred.:* Radiography. Pres. James B. Petty.
Enroll.: 1,841
(704) 484-4000

COASTAL CAROLINA COMMUNITY COLLEGE
444 Western Blvd., Jacksonville 28540. Public junior. 1983/1976 (SACS-Comm. on Coll.). Qtr. plan. Degrees: A. *Prof. Accred.:* Dental Assisting, Dental Hygiene, Medical Laboratory Technology (A), Surgical Technology. Pres. James L . Henderson, Jr.
Enroll.: 3,577
(919) 455-1221

COLLEGE OF THE ALBEMARLE
Elizabeth City 27909. Public junior. 1968/1983 (SACS-Comm. on Coll.). Qtr. plan. Degrees: A. Pres. J. Parker Chesson, Jr.
Enroll.: 1,653
(919) 335-0821

CRAVEN COMMUNITY COLLEGE
Race Track Rd., New Bern 28560. Public 2-year. 1971/1975 (SACS-Comm. on Coll.) Qtr. plan. Degrees: A. Pres. Robert L. Phillips.
Enroll.: 2,135
(919) 638-4131

DAVIDSON COLLEGE
Davidson 28036. Private (Presbyterian, U.S.) Liberal arts, primarily for men. 1917/1975 (SACS-Comm. on Coll.). 3-3 plan. Degrees: B. Pres. John W. Kuykendall.
Enroll.: 1,369
(704) 892-2000

DAVIDSON COUNTY COMMUNITY COLLEGE
Lexington 27292. Public junior. 1968/1982 (SACS-Comm. on Coll.). Qtr. plan. Degrees: A. Pres. J. Bryan Brooks.
Enroll.: 2,878
(704) 249-8186

DUKE UNIVERSITY
Durham 27706. Private (Independent) liberal arts and professional. 1895/1977 (SACS-Comm. on Coll.). Sem. plan. Degrees: A,P,M,D. *Prof. Accred.:* Assistant to the Primary Care Physician, Business (M), EEG Technology, Engineering (biomedical, civil, electrical, mechanical), Forestry, Law, Medical Technology, Medicine, Nuclear Medicine Technology, Physical Therapy, Psychology, Radiography, Specialist in Blood Bank Technology, Teacher Education (*e,s,p*), Theology. Pres. H. Keith H. Brodie.
Enroll.: 9,753
(919) 684-8111

DURHAM TECHNICAL INSTITUTE
1637 Lawson St., Durham 27703. Public 2-year. 1971/1975 (SACS-Comm. on Coll.). Qtr. plan. Degrees: A. *Prof. Accred.:* Dental Laboratory Technology, Respiratory Therapy. Pres. Phail Wynn, Jr.
Enroll.: 3,467
(919) 598-9222

EAST COAST BIBLE COLLEGE
6900 Wilkinson Blvd., Charlotte 28214. Private (Church of God) professional. 1985

(AABC). Sem. plan. Degrees: A,B. Pres. Henry J. Smith.
Enroll.: 270
(704) 397-2307

*East Carolina University
Greenville 27834. Public. 1927/1982 (SACS-Comm. on Coll.). Qtr. plan. Degrees: B,P,M,D. *Prof. Accred.:* Art, Business (B,M), Dietetics, Home Economics, Medical Record Administration, Medical Technology, Medicine, Music, Occupational Therapy, Physical Therapy, Rehabilitation Counseling, Social Work (B), Teacher Education (*e,s,p*). Chanc. John M. Howell.
Enroll.: 13,331
(919) 757-6131

Edgecombe Technical College
2009 W. Wilson St.,P.O. Box 550, Tarboro 27886. Public 2-year. 1973/1978 (SACS-Comm. on Coll.). Qtr. plan. Degrees: A. *Prof. Accred.:* Radiography. Pres. Charles B. McIntyre.
Enroll.: 1,489
(919) 823-5166

*Elizabeth City State University
Elizabeth City 27909. Public liberal arts and teachers college. 1947/1982 (SACS-Comm. on Coll.). Sem. plan. Degrees: B. Chanc. Jimmy R. Jenkins.
Enroll.: 1,508
(919) 335-3230

Elon College
Elon College 27244. Private (United Church of Christ) liberal arts. 1947/1982 (SACS-Comm. on Coll.). 4-1-4 plan. Degrees: A,B,(candidate for M). *Prof. Accred.:* Cytotechnology, Medical Laboratory Technology (A). Pres. J. Fred Young.
Enroll.: 2,602
(919) 584-9711

*Fayetteville State University
Fayetteville 28301. Public liberal arts and teachers college. 1947/1981 (SACS-Comm. on Coll.). Sem. plan. Degrees: A,B,M. *Prof. Accred.:* Teacher Education (*e,s,*). Chanc. Charles A. Lyons, Jr.
Enroll.: 2,396
(919) 486-1111

Fayetteville Technical Institute
P.O. Box 35236, Fayetteville 28303. Public 2-year. 1967/1981 (SACS-Comm. on Coll.).

*Member University System of North Carolina

Qtr. plan. Degrees: A. *Prof. Accred.:* Dental Assisting, Dental Hygiene, Engineering Technology (civil, electronics), Nursing (A), Radiography, Respiratory Therapy, Surgical Technology. Pres. Robert Craig Allen.
Enroll.: 7,610
(919) 323-1961

Forsyth Technical College
2100 Silas Creek Pkwy., Winston-Salem 27103. Public 2-year. 1968/1982 (SACS-Comm. on Coll.). Qtr. plan. Degrees: A. *Prof. Accred.:* Engineering Technology (electronics, manufacturing, mechanical drafting and design), Radiography, Respiratory Therapy, Respiratory Therapy Technology, Nuclear Medicine Technology. Pres. Bob H. Greene.
Enroll.: 4,894
(919) 723-0371

Gardner-Webb College
Boiling Springs 28017. Private (Southern Baptist) liberal arts. 1971/1975 (SACS-Comm. on Coll.). Sem. plan. Degrees: A,B,M. *Prof. Accred.:* Music, Nursing (A,B). Pres. Christopher White.
Enroll.: 1,696
(704) 434-2361

Gaston College
Dallas 28034. Public junior. 1967/1981 (SACS-Comm. on Coll.). Qtr. plan. Degrees: A. *Prof. Accred.:* Engineering Technology (civil, electrical, electronics, industrial, mechanical and production). Pres. Wayne Scott.
Enroll.: 3,488
(704) 922-3136

Greensboro College
815 W. Market St., Greensboro 27401-1875. Private (United Methodist) liberal arts. 1926/1974 (SACS-Comm. on Coll.). Sem. plan. Degrees: B. Pres. William H. Likins.
Enroll.: 513
(919) 272-7102

Guilford College
Greensboro 27410. Private (Friends) liberal arts. 1926/1975 (SACS-Comm. on Coll.). Sem. plan. Degrees: A,B. Pres. William R. Rogers.
Enroll.: 1,461
(919) 292-5511

Guilford Technical Community College
P.O. Box 309, Jamestown 27282. Public 2-year. 1969/1984 (SACS-Comm. on Coll.).

Qtr. plan. Degrees: A. *Prof. Accred.:* Dental Assisting, Dental Hygiene, Engineering Technology (civil, electronics, mechanical drafting and design). Pres. Ray Needham.
Enroll.: 6,341
(919) 292-1101

THE HAIRSTYLING ACADEMY
232 Roanoke Ave., Roanoke Rapids 27870. Private. 1984 (SACS-COEI). 39-week program. Diplomas. Dir. George Campbell.
Enroll.: FTE 43

BRANCH CAMPUS
1108 Brandon Ave., S.W., Roanoke, VA 24012.

BRANCH CAMPUS
3024 Trinkle Ave., Roanoke, VA 24012.

BRANCH CAMPUS
109 E. Main St., Salem, VA 24153.

HAIRSTYLING INSTITUTE OF CHARLOTTE
3440 Wilkinson Blvd., Charlotte 28208. Private. 1983 (NATTS). 39-week program. Diplomas. Vice Pres. A. Eugene Spangler.
Enroll.: 50
(704) 394-9214

HAIRSTYLING INSTITUTE
936 Raleigh Rd., Rocky Mount 27850. Private. 1984 (SACS-COEI). 39-week program. Diplomas. Dir. Mary Richardson.
Enroll.: FTE 35

HALIFAX COMMUNITY COLLEGE
P.O. Drawer 809, Weldon 27890. Public 2-year. 1975/1980 (SACS-Comm. on Coll.). Qtr. plan. Degrees: A. *Prof. Accred.:* Medical Laboratory Technology. Pres. Phillip W. Taylor.
Enroll.: 1,350
(919) 536-2551

HARDBARGER JUNIOR COLLEGE OF BUSINESS
P.O. Box 2505, Raleigh 27602. Private. 1953/1982 (AICS). Qtr. plan. Degrees: A, diplomas. Pres. James W. Burnette.
Enroll.: 1,619 (*f.t.* 192 m., 1,427 w.)
(919) 828-7291

HAYWOOD TECHNICAL COLLEGE
Freelander Dr., Clyde 28721-9454. Public. 2-year. 1973/1978 (SACS-Comm. on Coll.). Qtr. plan. Degrees: A. Pres. Joseph H. Nanney.
Enroll.: 1,597
(704) 627-2821

HIGH POINT COLLEGE
High Point 27262. Private (United Methodist) liberal arts. 1951/1985 (SACS-Comm. on Coll.). 4-1-4 plan. Degrees: B. *Prof. Accred.:* Teacher Education (*e,s*). Pres. Jacob C. Martinson, Jr.
Enroll.: 1,259
(919) 885-5101

ISOTHERMAL COMMUNITY COLLEGE
Spindale 28160. Public junior. 1970/1974 (SACS-Comm. on Coll.). Qtr. plan. Degrees: A. Acting Pres. G. Herman Porter.
Enroll.: 2,262
(704) 286-3636

JAMES SPRUNT TECHNICAL COLLEGE
P.O. Box 398, Kenansville 28349. Public 2-year. 1973/1978 (SACS-Comm. on Coll.). Qtr. plan. Degrees: A. Pres. Carl D. Price.
Enroll.: 1,035
(919) 296-1341

JOHN ROBERT POWERS SCHOOL OF FASHION CAREERS
3522 Haworth Dr., Suite 101, Raleigh 27609. Private. 1978 (NATTS). Qtr. plan. Certificates. Dir. Vickie Wood.
Enroll.: 32 (*f.t.* 3 m., 26 w.)
(919) 787-7253

JOHN WESLEY COLLEGE
2314 N. Centennial St., High Point 27260. Private (Interdenominational) professional. 1982 (AABC). Sem. plan. Degrees: A,B. Pres. Clifford W. Thomas.
Enroll.: 71
(919) 889-2262

JOHNSON C. SMITH UNIVERSITY
100-152 Beatties Ford Rd., Charlotte 28216. Private (Presbyterian, U.S.) liberal arts and education college. 1933/1975 (SACS-Comm. on Coll.). Sem. plan. Degrees: B. Pres. Robert Albright.
Enroll.: 1,257
(704) 378-1000

JOHNSTON TECHNICAL COLLEGE
P.O. Box 2350, Smithfield 27577. Public 2-year. 1977/1982 (SACS-Comm. on Coll.). Qtr. plan. Degrees: A. Pres. John L. Tart.
Enroll.: 2,951
(919) 934-3051

KING'S COLLEGE
322 Lamar Ave., Charlotte 28204. Private business. 1954/1986 (AICS). Qtr. plan. De-

grees: A. *Prof. Accred.:* Medical Assisting. Pres. John A. Besser.
Enroll.: 441 (*f.t.* 7 m., 433 w.)
(704) 372-0266

LEES-MCRAE COLLEGE
Banner Elk 28604. Private (Presbyterian, U.S.) junior. 1953/1985 (SACS-Comm. on Coll.). Sem. plan. Degrees: A. Pres. Bradford L. Crain.
Enroll.: 668
(704) 898-5241

LENOIR COMMUNITY COLLEGE
P.O. Box 188, Kinston 28502-0188. Public junior. 1968/1983 (SACS-Comm. on Coll.). Qtr. plan. Degrees: A. *Prof. Accred.:* Surgical Technology. Pres. Jesse L. McDaniel.
Enroll.: 2,043
(919) 527-6223

LENOIR-RHYNE COLLEGE
P.O. Box 7163, Hickory 28603. Private (Lutheran in America) liberal arts. 1928/1982 (SACS-Comm. on Coll.). 4-1-4 plan. Degrees: B,M. *Prof. Accred.:* Nursing (B), Teacher Education (*e,s*). Pres. John E. Trainer, Jr.
Enroll.: 1,323
(704) 328-1741

LIVINGSTONE COLLEGE
Salisbury 28144. Private (African Methodist Episcopal Zion) liberal arts and theology. 1944/1982 (SACS-Comm. on Coll.). Sem. plan. Degrees: B. *Prof. Accred.:* Social Work (B). Pres. William H. Greene.
Enroll.: 650
(704) 633-7960

LOUISBURG COLLEGE
501 N. Main St., Louisburg 27549. Private (United Methodist) junior. 1952/1975 (SACS-Comm. on Coll.). Sem. plan. Degrees: A. Pres. J. Allen Norris, Jr.
Enroll.: 694
(919) 496-2521

MTA SCHOOL
1061 Boulder Rd., Greensboro 27410. Private. 1985 (NATTS). Courses of varying lengths. Certificates. Dir. C. M. Fike.
(919) 852-3044

MARS HILL COLLEGE
Mars Hill 28754. Private (Southern Baptist) liberal arts. 1967/1981 (SACS-Comm. on Coll.). 4-1-4 plan. Degrees: A,B. *Prof. Accred.:* Music, Social Work (B). Pres. Fred Blake Bentley.
Enroll.: 1,269
(704) 689-1141

MARTIN COMMUNITY COLLEGE
Williamston 27892. Public 2-year. 1972/1977 (SACS-Comm. on Coll.). Qtr. plan. Degrees: A. Pres. W. Travis Martin.
Enroll.: 634
(919) 792-1521

MAYLAND TECHNICAL COLLEGE
Spruce Pine 28777. Public 2-year. 1978/1984 (SACS-Comm. on Coll.). Qtr. plan. Degrees: A. Pres. O.M. Blake, Jr.
Enroll.: 1,803
(704) 765-7351

MCDOWELL TECHNICAL COLLEGE
Rt. 1, Box 170, Marion 28752. Public 2-year. 1975/1980 (SACS-Comm. on Coll.). Qtr. plan. Degrees: A. Pres. Robert M. Boggs.
Enroll.: 888
(704) 652-6021

MEREDITH COLLEGE
Raleigh 27607-5298. Private (Southern Baptist) liberal arts for women. 1921/1980 (SACS-Comm. on Coll.). Sem. plan. Degrees: B,M. *Prof. Accred.:* Music, Social Work (B). Pres. John E. Weems
Enroll.: 1,586
(919) 829-8600

METHODIST COLLEGE, INC.
Fayetteville 28301. Private (United Methodist) liberal arts. 1964/1979 (SACS-Comm. on Coll.). Sem. plan. Degrees: A,B. Pres. M. Elton Hendricks.
Enroll.: 726
(919) 488-7110

MILLER-MOTTE BUSINESS COLLEGE
606 S. College Rd., Wilmington 28403. Private. 1966/1984 (AICS). Qtr. plan. Diplomas. Pres. Richard Craig.
Enroll.: 456 (*f.t.* 85 m., 371 w.)
(919) 392-4660

BRANCH CAMPUS
160 W. Franklin Blvd., Gastonia 28503. Dir. Judy Reed.
(704) 861-0833

MITCHELL COMMUNITY COLLEGE
Statesville 28677. Public junior. 1955/1976 (SACS-Comm. on Coll.). 4-1-4 plan. Degrees: A. Pres. Charles C. Poindexter.

Enroll.: 2,083
(704) 873-2201

MONTGOMERY TECHNICAL COLLEGE
P.O.B. 787, Troy 27371. Public 2-year. 1978/1983 (SACS-Comm. on Coll.). Qtr. plan. Degrees: A. Pres. Benny B. Hampton.
Enroll.: 561
(919) 572-3691

MONTREAT-ANDERSON COLLEGE
Montreat 28757. Private (Presbyterian, U.S.) junior. 1960/1980 (SACS-Comm. on Coll.). Sem. plan. Degrees: A. Pres. Silas M. Vaughn.
Enroll.: 360
(704) 669-8011

MOUNT OLIVE COLLEGE
Mount Olive 28365. Private (Free Will Baptist) junior. 1960/1981 (SACS-Comm. on Coll.). Sem. plan. Degrees: A. Pres. W. Burkette Raper.
Enroll.: 574
(919) 658-2502

NASH TECHNICAL INSTITUTE
Rocky Mount 27801. Public (state) 2-year. 1976/1981 (SACS-Comm. on Coll.). Qtr. plan. Degrees: A. Pres. J. Reid Parrott.
Enroll.: 2,609
(919) 443-4011

*NORTH CAROLINA AGRICULTURAL AND TECHNICAL STATE UNIVERSITY
Greensboro 27411. Public (state). 1936/1980 (SACS-Comm. on Coll.). Sem. plan. Degrees: B,M. *Prof. Accred.:* Accounting (Type A), Business (B), Engineering (architectural, electrical, industrial, mechanical), Nursing (B), Social Work (B), Teacher Education (*e,s*). Chanc. Edward Fort.
Enroll.: 4,965
(919) 379-7500

*NORTH CAROLINA CENTRAL UNIVERSITY
Durham 27707. Public (state) liberal arts and professional. 1937/1979 (SACS-Comm. on Coll.). Sem. plan. Degrees: B,P,M. *Prof. Accred.:* Law (ABA only), Librarianship, Nursing (B), Teacher Education (*e,s,p*). Chanc Tyronza Richmond.
Enroll.: 4,731
(919) 683-6100

*NORTH CAROLINA SCHOOL OF THE ARTS
Winston-Salem 27107. Public (state) professional. 1970/1985 (SACS-Comm. on Coll.). Tri. plan. Degrees: B,M. Chanc Jane E. Milley.
Enroll.: 482
(919) 784-7170

*NORTH CAROLINA STATE UNIVERSITY AT RALEIGH
P.O. Box 7001, Raleigh 27695. Public (state). 1928/1984 (SACS-Comm. on Coll.). Sem. plan. Degrees: A,B,M,D. *Prof. Accred.:* Architecture (M), Engineering (aerospace, biological and agricultural, chemical, civil, construction, electrical, industrial, materials, mechanical, nuclear), Forestry, Landscape Architecture (M), Social Work (B), Teacher Education (*s,p*), Veterinary Medicine. Chanc. Bruce R. Poulton.
Enroll.: 20,277
(919) 737-2011

NORTH CAROLINA WESLEYAN COLLEGE
Rocky Mount 27801. Private (United Methodist) liberal arts. 1963/1980 (SACS-Comm. on Coll.). 4-1-4 plan. Degrees: B. Acting Pres. Stephen Fritz.
Enroll.: 845
(919) 977-7171

NORTHERN HOSPITAL OF SURRY COUNTY SCHOOL OF MEDICAL TECHNOLOGY
830 Rockford St., P.O. Box 1101, Mt. Airy 27030. Private. 1967/1980 (ABHES). 12-month program. Diplomas. *Prof. Accred.:* Medical Laboratory Technology. Dir. David A. McCullough.
Enroll.: 4
(919) 789-9541

OCONALUFTEE JOB CORPS CIVILIAN CONSERVATION CENTER
Great Smokey Mountains Nat'l. Park, Cherokee 28719. Public (federal). 1984 (SACS-COEI). Courses of varying lengths. Certificates. Dir. Delmar P. Robinson.
Enroll.: FTE 272

PAMLICO TECHNICAL COLLEGE
P.O. Box 185, Grantsboro 28529. Public 2-year. 1977/1982 (SACS-Comm. on Coll.). Qtr. plan. Degrees: A. Pres. Paul H. Johnson.
Enroll.: 234
(919) 249-1851

PEACE COLLEGE
Raleigh 27604. Private (Presbyterian, U.S.) junior for women. 1947/1985 (SACS-Comm.

*Member University System of North Carolina

*Member University System of North Carolina

on Coll.). Sem. plan. Degrees: A. Pres. S. David Frazier.
Enroll.: 487
(919) 832-2881

*PEMBROKE STATE UNIVERSITY
Pembroke 28372. Public (state) liberal arts and teachers college. 1951/1979 (SACS-Comm. on Coll.). Sem. plan. Degrees: B,M. *Prof. Accred.:* Music, Teacher Education (*e,s,p*). Chance. Paul R. Givens.
Enroll.: 1,874
(919) 521-4214

PFEIFFER COLLEGE, INC.
Misenheimer 28109. Private (United Methodist) liberal arts. 1959/1984 (SACS-Comm. on Coll.). Sem. plan. Degrees: B. *Prof. Accred.:* Music, Social Work (B). Pres. Cameron P. West.
Enroll.: 717
(704) 463-7343

†PIEDMONT BIBLE COLLEGE, INC.
716 Franklin St., Winston-Salem 27101. Private (Baptist) professional. 1956/1984 (AABC). Sem. plan. Degrees: B. Pres. Donald K. Drake.
Enroll.: 286
(919) 725-8344

PIEDMONT TECHNICAL COLLEGE
P.O. Box 1197, Roxboro 27573. Public 2-year. 1977/1982 (SACS-Comm. on Coll.). Qtr. plan. Degrees: A. Pres. Edward W. Cox.
Enroll.: 1,044
(919) 599-1181

PITT COMMUNITY COLLEGE
P.O. Drawer 7007, Greenville 27834. Public 2-year. 1969/1983 (SACS-Comm. on Coll.). Qtr. plan. Degrees: A. *Prof. Accred.:* Radiography. Pres. Charles E. Russell.
Enroll.: 2,072
(919) 756-3130

QUEENS COLLEGE
1900 Selwyn Ave., Charlotte 28274. Private (Presbyterian, U.S.) liberal arts primarily for women. 1932/1981 (SACS-Comm. on Coll.). 4-1-4 plan. Degrees: B,M. *Prof. Accred.:* Music, Nuclear Medicine Technology, Nursing (B). Pres. Billy O. Wireman.
Enroll.: 1,148
(704) 337-2200

RANDOLPH TECHNICAL COLLEGE
Asheboro 27204-1009. Public 2-year. 1974/1979 (SACS-Comm. on Coll.). Qtr. plan. Degrees: A. Pres. M. H. Branson.
Enroll.: 1,917
(919) 629-1471

RICHMOND TECHNICAL COLLEGE
P.O. Box 1189, Hamlet 28345. Public 2-year. 1969/1983 (SACS-Comm. on Coll.). Qtr. plan. Degrees: A. Pres. Joseph W. Grimsley.
Enroll.: 2,050
(919) 582-1980

ROANOKE BIBLE COLLEGE
P.O. Box 387, Elizabeth City 27909. Private (Christian Churches) professional. 1979 (AABC). Sem. plan. Degrees: A,B. Pres. George W. BonDurant.
Enroll.: 125
(919) 338-5191

ROANOKE-CHOWAN TECHNICAL COLLEGE
Route 2, Box 46-A, Ahoskie 27910. Public (state) 2-year. 1976/1982 (SACS-Comm. on Coll.). Qtr. plan. Degrees: A. Acting Pres. David W. Sink, Jr.
Enroll.: 1,515
(919) 332-5921

ROBESON TECHNICAL COLLEGE
Lumberton 28358. Public 2-year. 1975/1980 (SACS-Comm. on Coll.). Qtr. plan. Degrees: A. Pres. Frederick G. Williams, Jr.
Enroll.: 2,643
(919) 738-7101

ROCKINGHAM COMMUNITY COLLEGE
Wentworth 27375. Public junior. 1968/1983 (SACS-Comm. on Coll.). Qtr. plan. Degrees: A. Pres. N. Jerry Owens, Jr.
Enroll.: 1,660
(919) 342-4261

ROWAN TECHNICAL COLLEGE
P.O. Box 1595, Salisbury 28144. Public 2-year. 1970/1985 (SACS-Comm. on Coll.). Qtr. plan. Degrees: A. *Prof. Accred.:* Dental Assisting, Radiography. Pres. Richard L. Brownell.
Enroll.: 3,598
(704) 637-0760

RUTLEDGE COLLEGE
2600 First Union Plaza, Charlotte 28282. Private junior business. 1969/1984 (AICS).

*Member University System of North Carolina
†Candidate for Accreditation by Regional Accrediting Commission

Qtr. plan. Degrees: A, certificates, diplomas. Pres. Carl Settle.
Enroll.: 930 (*f.t.* 197 m., 733 w.)
(704) 376-6430

Rutledge College
410 W. Chapel Hill St., Durham 27701. Private junior business. 1980 (AICS). Courses of varying lengths. Degrees: A, certificates. Dir. Wayne Thompson.
Enroll.: 491 (*f.t.* 144 m., 347 w.)
(919) 682-5681

Rutledge College
603 Country Club Dr., Fayetteville 28301. Private junior business. 1973/1981 (AICS). Qtr. plan. Degrees: A, diplomas. CEO Robert Manor.
Enroll.: 801 (*f.t.* 305 m., 496 w.)
(919) 488-2527

Rutledge College
P.O. Box 21266, Greensboro 27420. Private junior business. 1972/1983 (AICS). Qtr. plan. Degrees: A, certificates, diplomas. Dir. Chauncey W. Lever.
Enroll.: 615 (*f.t.* 244 m., 371 w.)
(919) 272-6194

Rutledge College
211 W. Martin St., Raleigh 27601. Private junior business. 1953/1979 (AICS). Qtr. plan. Degrees: A, certificates, diplomas. Dir. Wayne Thompson.
Enroll.: 664 (*f.t.* 214 m., 450 w.)
(919) 833-6402

Rutledge College
820 W. Fourth St., P.O. Box 3138, Winston-Salem 27102. Private junior business. 1966/1980 (AICS). Qtr. plan. Degrees: A, certificates, diplomas. CEO J. Robert Middleton.
Enroll.: 894 (*f.t.* 298 m., 596 w.)
(919) 725-8701

Sacred Heart College
Belmont 28012. Private (Roman Catholic) liberal arts primarily for women. 1970/1975 (SACS-Comm. on Coll.). Sem. plan. Degrees: A,B. *Prof. Accred.:* Social Work (B). Pres. Sister Mary Michel Boulus, R.S.M.
Enroll.: 315
(704) 825-5146

St. Andrews Presbyterian College
Laurinburg 28352. Private (Presbyterian, U.S.A.) liberal arts. 1961/1980 (SACS-Comm. on Coll.). 4-1-4 plan. Degrees: B. Pres. Alvin P. Perkinson, Jr.
Enroll.: 703
(919) 276-3652

Saint Augustine's College
1315 Oakwood Ave., Raleigh 27611. Private (Episcopal) liberal arts. 1942/1981 (SACS-Comm. on Coll.). Sem. plan. Degrees: B. Pres. Prezell R. Robinson.
Enroll.: 1,610
(919) 828-4451

St. Mary's College
Raleigh 27603. Private (Episcopal) for women. 1927/1979 (SACS-Comm. on Coll.). Sem. plan. Degrees: A. Pres. Clauston L. Jenkins.
Enroll.: 273
(919) 828-2521

Salem College
Winston-Salem 27108. Private (Moravian) liberal arts for women. 1922/1980 (SACS-Comm. on Coll.). 4-1-4 plan. Degrees: B *Prof. Accred.:* Music, Teacher Education (*e,s*). Pres. Thomas V. Litzenburg, Jr.
Enroll.: 653
(919) 721-2600

Salisbury Business College
129 Corriher Ave., Salisbury 28144. Private. 1975/1981 (AICS). Qtr. plan. Certificates, diplomas. Pres. Wayne Abernethy.
Enroll.: 140 (*f.t.* 3 m., 137 w.)
(704) 636-4071

Sampson Technical College
P.O. Drawer 318, Clinton 28328. Public 2-year. 1977/1983 (SACS-Comm. on Coll.). Qtr. plan. Degrees: A. Pres. Clifton W. Paderick.
Enroll.: 1,422
(919) 592-8081

Sandhills Community College
Route 3, Box 182-C, Carthage 28327. Public junior. 1968/1983 (SACS-Comm. on Coll.). Qtr. plan. Degrees: A. *Prof. Accred.:* Medical Laboratory Technology (A), Nursing (A), Radiography, Respiratory Therapy. Pres. Raymond Stone.
Enroll.: 2,558
(919) 692-6185

Schenck Civilian Conservation Center
P.O. Box 98, Pisgah Forest 28768. Public (federal). 1985 (SACS-COEI). Courses of varying lengths. Certificates, diplomas. Dir. Raymond K. Ricketts.
Enroll.: FTE 224

SHAW UNIVERSITY
Raleigh 27611. Private (Independent) liberal arts college. 1943/1982 (SACS-Comm. on Coll.). Tri. plan. Degrees: A,B. Pres. Stanley H. Smith.
Enroll.: 1,718
(919) 755-4800

SOUTHEASTERN BAPTIST THEOLOGICAL SEMINARY
P.O. Box 712, Wake Forest 27587. Private (Southern Baptist) professional; graduate only. 1978/1982 (SACS-Comm. on Coll.). Sem. plan. Degrees: A,P,M,D. *Prof. Accred.:* Theology (1958/1981, ATS). Pres. W. Randall Lolley.
Enroll.: 1,183
(919) 556-3101

SOUTHEASTERN COMMUNITY COLLEGE
Whiteville 28472. Public junior 1967/1981 (SACS-Comm. on Coll.). Qtr. plan. Degrees: A. Pres. Dan W. Moore.
Enroll.: 1,724
(919) 642-7141

SOUTHWESTERN TECHNICAL COLLEGE
275 Webster Rd., Sylva 28779. Public 2-year. 1971/1975 (SACS-Comm. on Coll.). Qtr. plan. Degrees: A. *Prof. Accred.:* Medical Laboratory Technology. Pres. Norman K. Myers.
Enroll.: 1,665
(704) 586-4091

STANLY TECHNICAL COLLEGE
Route 4, Box 55, Albemarle 28001. Public 2-year. 1979 (SACS-Comm. on Coll.). Qtr. plan. Degrees: A. *Prof. Accred.:* Respiratory Therapy Technology. Pres. Charles H. Byrd.
Enroll.: 1,836
(704) 982-0121

SURRY COMMUNITY COLLEGE
Dobson 27017. Public (state) junior. 1969/1984 (SACS-Comm. on Coll.). Qtr. plan. Degrees: A. Pres. Swanson Richards.
Enroll.: 2,941
(919) 386-8121

TECHNICAL COLLEGE OF ALAMANCE
P. O. Box 623, Haw River 27258. Public 2-year. 1969/1983 (SACS-Comm. on Coll.). Qtr. plan. Degrees: A. *Prof. Accred.:* Dental Assisting, Engineering Technology (electronic engineering). Pres. W. Ronald McCarter.
Enroll.: 3,128
(919) 578-2002

TRI-COUNTY COMMUNITY COLLEGE
Murphy 28906. Public 2-year. 1975/1980 (SACS-Comm. on Coll.). Qtr. plan. Degrees: A. Pres. Vincent Crisp.
Enroll.: 841
(704) 837-6810

U.S. ARMY JOHN F. KENNEDY SPECIAL WARFARE CENTER
Attn: ATSU-DT, Fort Bragg 28307. Public (federal). 1976/1981 (SACS-COEI). Courses of varying lengths. Certificates. Commandant Brig. Gen. Robert D. Wiegand.
Enroll.: FTE 1,607
(919) 396-2109

UNIVERSITY SYSTEM OF NORTH CAROLINA
Central office, P.O. Box 309, Chapel Hill 27514. Public (state). Sem. plan (qtr. plan in medical units). Pres. C. D. Spangler, Jr.
(919) 962-2211

*UNIVERSITY OF NORTH CAROLINA AT ASHEVILLE
Asheville 28804. Public (state) 1966/1982 (SACS-Comm. on Coll.). Degrees: B. Chanc. David G. Brown.
Enroll.: 2,008
(704) 258-6600

*UNIVERSITY OF NORTH CAROLINA AT CHAPEL HILL
Chapel Hill 27514. Public (state) 1895/1985 (SACS-Comm. on Coll.). Degrees: B,P,M,D. *Prof. Accred.:* Business (B,M), Cytotechnology, Dental Assisting, Dental Hygiene, Dentistry, Engineering (environmental-programs in air and industrial hygiene and water resources), Health Administration, Journalism, Law, Librarianship, Medical Technology, Medicine, Nuclear Medicine Technology, Nursing (B,M), Occupational Therapy, Pharmacy, Physical Therapy, Psychology, Public Health, Radiography, Rehabilitation Counseling, Social Work (M), Surgeon's Assistant, Teacher Education (*e,s,p*). Chanc. Christopher C. Fordham, III.
Enroll.: 21,229
(919) 962-2211

*UNIVERSITY OF NORTH CAROLINA AT CHARLOTTE
UNCC, Charlotte 28223. Public (state). 1965/1982 (SACS-Comm. on Coll.). Sem. plan. Degrees: A,B,M. *Prof. Accred.:* Accounting (Type A), Architecture (B), Business (B,M),

*Member University System of North Carolina

Engineering (civil, electrical, mechanical), Engineering Technology (civil, electrical, mechanical), Nursing (B,M), Teacher Education (*e,s,p*). Chanc. E. K. Fretwell, Jr.
Enroll.: 10,842 (*f.t.* 3,880 m., 3,426 w.)
(704) 597-2000

*University of North Carolina at Greensboro
Greensboro 27412. Public (state). 1921/1983 (SACS-Comm. on Coll.). Degrees: A,B,M,D. *Prof. Accred.:* Business (B,M), Home Economics, Music, Librarianship, Nursing (M), Social Work (B), Teacher Education (*e,s,p*). Chanc. William E. Moran.
Enroll.: 8,837
(919) 379-5000

*University of North Carolina at Wilmington
601 South College Rd., Wilmington 28403. 1965/1982 (SACS-Comm. on Coll.). Degrees: A,B,M. *Prof. Accred.:* Teacher Education (*e,s,p*). Chanc. William Hampton Wagoner.
Enroll.: 5,014
(919) 395-3000

Vance-Granville Community College
P.O. Box 917, Henderson 27536. Public 2-year. 1977/1983 (SACS-Comm. on Coll.). Qtr. plan. Degrees: A. *Prof. Accred.:* Radiography. Pres. Ben F. Currin.
Enroll.: 1,531
(919) 492-2061

Wake Forest University
Winston-Salem 27109. Private (Southern Baptist). 1921/1975 (SACS-Comm. on Coll.). 4-1-4 plan. Degrees: B,P,M,D. *Prof. Accred.:* Accounting (Type A), Assistant to the Primary Care Physician, Business (B,M), Cytotechnology, Law, Medical Technology, Medicine, Nurse Anesthesia Education. Pres. Thomas K. Hearn, Jr.
Enroll.: 5,178
(919) 761-5000

Wake Technical College
9101 Fayetteville Rd., Raleigh 27603. Public 2-year. 1970/1985 (SACS-Comm. on Coll.). Qtr. plan. Degrees: A, certificates. *Prof. Accred.:* Engineering Technology (chemical, civil, computer, electronics, industrial), Radiography. Pres. Bruce I. Howell.
Enroll.: 4,351
(919) 772-0551

*Member University System of North Carolina

Warren Wilson College
701 Warren Wilson Rd., Swannanoa 28778-2099. Private (United Presbyterian) liberal arts. 1969/1984 (SACS-Comm. on Coll.). Sem. plan. Degrees: B,M. *Prof. Accred.:* Social Work (B). Pres. John Carey.
Enroll.: 458
(704) 298-3325

Wayne Community College
Goldsboro 27530. Public junior. 1970/1974 (SACS-Comm. on Coll.). Qtr. plan. Degrees: A. *Prof. Accred.:* Dental Assisting, Dental Hygiene. Pres. Clyde A. Erwin, Jr.
Enroll.: 2,868
(919) 735-5151

*Western Carolina University
Cullowhee 28723. Public (state). 1946/1975 (SACS-Comm. on Coll.). Sem. plan. Degrees: B,M. *Prof. Accred.:* Business (B,M), Engineering Technology (manufacturing), Home Economics, Medical Record Administration, Medical Technology, Nursing (B), Social Work (B), Teacher Education (*e,s,p*). Chanc. Myron L. Coulter.
Enroll.: 5,491
(704) 227-7211

Western Piedmont Community College
1001 Burkemont Ave., Morganton 28655. Public junior. 1968/1983 (SACS-Comm. on Coll.). Qtr. plan. Degrees: A. *Prof. Accred.:* Dental Assisting, Medical Assisting, Medical Laboratory Technology (A), Nursing (A). Pres. James A. Richardson.
Enroll.: 2,655
(704) 437-8688

Wilkes Community College
P.O. Drawer 120, Wilkesboro 28697. Public (state) junior. 1970/1985 (SACS-Comm. on Coll.). Qtr. plan. Degrees: A. Pres. David E. Daniel.
Enroll.: 2,643
(919) 667-7136

Wilson County Technical Institute
P.O. Box 4305, Wilson 27893. Public 2-year. 1969/1984 (SACS-Comm. on Coll.). Qtr. plan. Degrees: A. Pres. Frank L. Eagles.
Enroll.: 2,224
(919) 291-1195

*Member University System of North Carolina

WINGATE COLLEGE
Wingate 28174. Private (Southern Baptist) liberal arts. 1979/1985 (SACS-Comm. on Coll.). Sem. plan. Degrees: A,B. *Prof. Accred.:* Medical Assistant, Music. Pres. Paul R. Corts.
Enroll.: 1,446
(704) 233-4061

*WINSTON-SALEM STATE UNIVERSITY
1600 Wallace St., Winston-Salem 27110. Public liberal arts and teachers college. 1947/1980 (SACS-Comm. on Coll.). Sem. plan. Degrees: B. *Prof. Accred.:* Medical Technology, Music, Nursing (B), Teacher Education (*e,s*). Chanc. Cleon F. Thompson, Jr.
Enroll.: 2,194
(919) 761-2011

*Member University System of North Carolina

NORTH DAKOTA

AAKER'S BUSINESS COLLEGE
201 N. Third St., Grand Forks 58201. Private. 1966/1979 (AICS). Courses of varying lengths. Diplomas. Admin. R.C. Hadlich.
Enroll.: 251 (*f.t.* 36 m., 215 w.)
(701) 772-6646

*BISMARCK JUNIOR COLLEGE
Bismarck 58501. Public (city). 1966/1984 (NCA). Sem. plan. Degrees: A. *Prof. Accred.:* Medical Laboratory Technology. Pres. Kermit Lidstrom.
Enroll.: FTE 1,886
(701) 224-5400

*DICKINSON STATE COLLEGE
Dickinson 58601. Public liberal arts and teachers. 1928/1985 (NCA). Qtr. plan. Degrees: A,B. *Prof. Accred.:* Nursing (A), Teacher Education (*e,s*). Pres. Albert A. Watrel.
Enroll.: FTE 1,167
(701) 227-2326

INTERSTATE BUSINESS COLLEGE
3329 S. University Dr., Fargo 58103. Private. 1953/1983 (AICS). Courses of varying lengths. Certificates. Pres. Susan K. Jensen.
Enroll.: 638 (*f.t.* 124 m., 514 w.)
(701) 232-2477

BRANCH CAMPUS
520 E. Main, Bismarck 58505. Dir. Stephen M. Collins.
(701) 255-0779

JAMESTOWN COLLEGE
Jamestown 58401. Private (United Presbyterian) liberal arts. 1920/1979 (NCA). 4-1-4 plan. Degrees: B. *Prof. Accred.:* Nursing (B). Pres. James S. Walker.
Enroll.: FTE 438
(701) 253-2550

*LAKE REGION COMMUNITY COLLEGE
Devils Lake 58301. Public (district). Accreditation includes Little Hoop Community College, Fort Totten. 1974/1984 (NCA). Sem. plan. Degrees: A. Pres. James A. Horton.
Enroll.: FTE 478
(701) 662-4836

MARY COLLEGE
Bismarck 58501. Private (Roman Catholic) liberal arts. 1969/1973 (NCA). 4-1-4 plan. Degrees: A,B,P,M. *Prof. Accred.:* Nursing (B), Social Work (B). Pres. Sister Thomas Welder, O.S.B.
Enroll.: FTE 929
(701) 255-4681

*MAYVILLE STATE COLLEGE
Mayville 58257. Public liberal arts and teachers. 1917/1986 (NCA). Qtr. plan. Degrees: B. *Prof. Accred.:* Teacher Education (*e,s*). Pres. James A. Schobel.
Enroll.: FTE 657
(701) 786-2301

*MINOT STATE COLLEGE
Minot 58701. Public liberal arts and teachers. 1917/1978 (NCA). Qtr. plan. Degrees: A,B,M. *Prof. Accred.:* Music, Nursing (B), Social Work (B), Speech Pathology and Audiology, Teacher Education (*e,s*). Pres. Gordon B. Olson.
Enroll.: FTE 2,783
(701) 857-3303

NORTH DAKOTA STATE BOARD OF HIGHER EDUCATION
State Capitol Bldg., Bismarck 58505. Public. Commissioner John A. Richardson.
(701) 224-2960

*NORTH DAKOTA STATE SCHOOL OF SCIENCE
Wahpeton 58075. Public junior. 1971/1981 (NCA). Qtr. plan. Degrees: A. *Prof. Accred.:* Dental Assisting, Dental Hygiene, Medical Record Technology. Pres. Clair T. Blikre.
Enroll.: FTE 3,109
(701) 671-2221

*NORTH DAKOTA STATE UNIVERSITY
Fargo 58105. Public. 1915/1976 (NCA). Qtr. plan. Degrees: A,B,M,D. *Prof. Accred.:* Architecture (B), Construction Education, Dietetics, Engineering (agricultural, civil, construction, electrical, industrial, mechanical), Home Economics, Music, Nursing (A), Pharmacy, Teacher Education (*s*). Pres. Laurel D. Loftsgard.
Enroll.: FTE 8,292
(701) 237-7211

NORTH DAKOTA STATE UNIVERSITY—BOTTINEAU BRANCH
Bottineau 58318. 1971/1981 (NCA). Qtr. plan. Degrees: A. Dean Michael Smith.

*Member North Dakota State Board of Higher Education

*Member North Dakota State Board of Higher Education

Enroll.: FTE 339
(701) 228-2277

NORTHWEST BIBLE COLLEGE
1900 Eighth Ave., S.E., Minot 58701. Private (Church of God) professional. 1974/1985 (AABC). Sem. plan. Degrees: A,B. Pres. Donald M. Walker.
Enroll.: 103
(701) 852-3781

*STANDING ROCK COLLEGE
Fort Yates 58538. Tribally controlled. 1984 (NCA). Sem. plan. Degrees: A. Pres. William D. Phillips.
Enroll.: FTE 289
(701) 6854-3861

TRI-COLLEGE UNIVERSITY
306 Ceres Hall, North Dakota State University, Fargo 58105. Private consortium. 1979/1984 (NCA). The institution is an interstate consortium with programs in both MN and ND; one on qtr. plan; one on sem. plan. Degrees: M. Provost John McCune.
Enroll.: FTE 280
(701) 237-8170 or (218) 236-2844

TRINITY BIBLE COLLEGE
Ellendale 58436. Private (Assembly of God) professional. 1980 (AABC). Sem. plan. Degrees: A,B. Pres. Lowell Lundstrom.
Enroll.: 506
(701) 349-3621

*TURTLE MOUNTAIN COMMUNITY COLLEGE
Belcourt 58316-0340. Tribally controlled. 1984 (NCA). Sem. plan. Degrees: A. Pres. Gerald C. Monette.
Enroll.: FTE 357
(701) 662-4836

TURTLE MOUNTAIN SCHOOL OF PARAMEDICAL TECHNIQUE
Bottineau 58318. Private. 1972/1985 (ABHES). 12-month program. Certificates. *Prof. Accred.:* Medical Laboratory Technology. Dean M. Gale Feland.
Enroll.: 26
(701) 228-3390

UNITED TRIBES EDUCATIONAL TECHNICAL CENTER
3315 S. Airport Rd., Bismarck 58501. Tribally controlled. 1982/1985(NCA). Qtr. plan. Certificates. Pres. David Gipp.
Enroll.: FTE 222
(701) 255-3285

*UNIVERSITY OF NORTH DAKOTA
Grand Forks 58202. Public (state). 1913/1984 (NCA). Sem. plan. Degrees: A,B,P,M,D. *Prof. Accred.:* Art, Assistant to the Primary Care Physician, Business (B), Cytotechnology, Engineering (chemical, civil, electrical, mechanical), Histologic Technology, Home Economics, Journalism, Law, Medical Technology, Medicine, Music, Nurse Anesthesia Education, Nursing (B), Occupational Therapy, Physical Therapy, Psychology, Social Work (B), Speech Pathology, Teacher Education (*e,s,p*). Pres. Thomas J. Clifford.
Enroll.: FTE 9,724
(701) 777-2121

UNIVERSITY OF NORTH DAKOTA—WILLISTON CENTER
Williston 58801. Public junior. 1972 (NCA). Sem. plan. Degrees: A. Dean Garvin L. Stevens.
Enroll.: 547
(701) 572-6736

*VALLEY CITY STATE COLLEGE
Valley City 58072. Public liberal arts and teachers. 1915/1976 (NCA). Qtr. plan. Degrees: B. *Prof. Accred.:* Teacher Education (*e,s*). Pres. Charles B. House, Jr.
Enroll.: FTE 974
(701) 845-7100

*Member North Dakota State Board of Higher Education

*Member North Dakota State Board of Higher Education

OHIO

ACA College of Design
2528 Kemper La., Cincinnati 45206. Private. 1979 (NATTS). Qtr. plan. Certificates. Pres. Marion Allman.
Enroll.: 35 (*f.t.* 16 m., 19 w.)
(513) 751-1206

A.T.E.S. Technical School
2076-86 Youngstown-Warren Rd., Niles 44446. Private. 1968/1980 (NATTS). Courses of varying lengths. Degrees: A, diplomas. Pres. M. E. Riley, Jr.
Enroll.: 600 (*f.t.* 235 m., 61 w.)
(216) 652-9919

Academy of Court Reporting
1250 Superior Ave., Cleveland 44114. Private. 1980 (AICS). Courses of varying lengths. Certificates. Pres. Charles A. Kolak.
Enroll.: 310 (*f.t.* 13 m., 297 w.)
(216) 861-3222

Branch Campus
2930 W. Market St., Akron 44313. Dir. Michelle Endres
(216) 876-4030

Air Force Institute of Technology
Wright-Patterson Air Force Base 45433. Public (federal) technological; graduate only. 1960/1981 (NCA). Qtr. plan. Degrees: M,D. *Prof. Accred.:* Engineering (aeronautical, astronautical, electrical, engineering management, nuclear, systems). Commandant Brig. Gen. James T. Callaghan.
Enroll.: FTE 597
(513) 255-2079

Airco Technical Institute
1361 E. 55th St., Cleveland 44103. Private. 1971/1976 (NATTS). Courses of varying lengths. Certificates. Dir. Frank Colen.
Enroll.: 536 (*f.t.* 506 m., 30 w.)
(216) 431-1050

Extension
1201 W. Adams, Chicago, Il 60607.
(312) 666-5590

Akron Institute of Medical and Dental Assistants
733 W. Market St., Akron 44303. Private. 1977 (NATTS). Qtr. plan. Diplomas. Dir. Vincent J. Didato.
Enroll.: *f.t.* 170 w.
(216) 762-9788

Antioch University
Yellow Springs 45387. Private liberal arts and professional. 1927/1985 (NCA); accreditation includes Antioch College and Antioch International, Yellow Springs, OH; Antioch New England Graduate School, Keene, NH and additional sites at Bennington, VT and Hartford, CT; Antioch University, Philadelphia, PA; Antioch University West with sites at San Francisco, Los Angeles, and Santa Barbara, CA, Seattle, WA, Denver, CO, and Honolulu, HI; the E. W. Cook Institute, Faribault, MN; the George Meany Center for Labor Studies, Silver Spring, MD; and at various other sites in the United States and overseas. Qtr. plan. Degrees: B,P,M,D. *Prof. Accred.:* Law (ABA only). Pres. Alan E. Guskin.
Enroll.: 3,147
(513) 767-7331

Antonelli Institute of Art and Photography
124 E. Seventh St., Cincinnati 45202. Private. 1975/1980 (NATTS). Qtr. plan. Degrees: A. Dir. Randall P. Miller.
Enroll.: 160 (*f.t.* 65 m., 80 w.)
(513) 241-4338

Art Academy of Cincinnati
Eden Park, Cincinnati 45202. Private professional; museum affiliated. 1948/1980. Sem. plan. Degrees: B, certificates. *Prof. Accred.:* Art. Dir. Roger Williams.
Enroll.: 246 (*f.t.* 99 m., 110 w.)
(513) 721-5205

Art Advertising Academy
4343 Bridgetown Rd., Cincinnati 45211. Private. 1984 (NATTS). Courses of varying lengths. Certificates. Owner/Dir. Jerry E. Neff.
(513) 574-1010

Ashland College
Ashland 44805. Private (Brethren) liberal arts and theology. 1930/1980 (NCA). Sem. plan. Degrees: A,B,M,D. *Prof. Accred.:* Music, Teacher Education (*e,s*), Theology. Pres. Joseph Shultz.
Enroll.: FTE 2,596
(419) 289-4142

Athenaeum of Ohio
6616 Beechmont Rd., Cincinnati 45230. Private (Roman Catholic, Archdiocese of Cin-

cinnati) seminary; accreditation includes Mt. St. Mary's Seminary, Norwood. 1959/1983 (NCA). Qtr. plan. Degrees: B,P,M. *Prof. Accred.:* Theology (1972/1982, ATS). Pres. Rev. James J. Walsh.
Enroll.: FTE 138
(513) 231-2223

BALDWIN-WALLACE COLLEGE
Berea 44017. Private (United Methodist) liberal arts. 1913/1978 (NCA). Qtr. plan. Degrees: B,M. *Prof. Accred.:* Music, Teacher Education (*e,s*). Pres. Neal Malicky.
Enroll.: FTE 2,861
(216) 826-2424

BELMONT TECHNICAL COLLEGE
68094 Hammond Rd., St. Clairsville 43950. Public (state) 2-year. 1978/1984 (NCA). Qtr. plan. Degrees: A. Pres. Paul R. Ohm.
Enroll.: FTE 1,055
(614) 695-9500

BLISS COLLEGE
3770 N. High St., Columbus 43214. Private business. 1961/1981 (AICS). Qtr. plan. Degrees: A, certificates. Pres. James D. Tussing.
Enroll.: 1,208 (*f.t.* 344 m., 864 w.)
(614) 267-8355

BRANCH CAMPUS
145 E. Corwin St., Circleville 43113. Dir. Richard Bartlett.
(614) 833-0568

BRANCH CAMPUS
2989 Valley View Dr., Columbus 43204. Dir. Richard Bartlett.
(614) 276-8080

BLUFFTON COLLEGE
Bluffton 45817. Private (General Mennonite) liberal arts. 1953/1979 (NCA). 4-1-4 plan. Degrees: B. *Prof. Accred.:* Music, Nursing (B), Social Work (B). Pres. Elmer Neufeld.
Enroll.: FTE 553
(419) 358-8015

BOHECKER'S BUSINESS COLLEGE
161 E. Main St., Ravenna 44266-9998. Private. 1985 (AICS). Courses of varying lengths. Certificates, diplomas. Exec. Dir. Jean K. Wise.
(216) 297-7319

BORROMEO COLLEGE OF OHIO
Wickliffe 44092. Private (Roman Catholic, Diocese of Cleveland) liberal arts. 1963/1973 (NCA). Sem. plan. Degrees: B. Rector Pres. James Caddy.
Enroll.: FTE 91
(216) 585-5900

BOWLING GREEN STATE UNIVERSITY
Bowling Green 43403. Public. 1916/1983 (NCA); accreditation includes Firelands Campus. Sem. plan. Degrees: B,M,D. *Prof. Accred.:* Art, Business (B,M), Journalism, Medical Record Administration, Medical Record Technology, Medical Technology, Music, Nursing (B), Rehabilitation Counseling, Psychology, Social Work (B), Speech Pathology and Audiology, Teacher Education (*e,s,p*). Pres. Paul J. Olscamp.
Enroll.: TotalFTE 16,031
(419) 372-2211

BRADFORD SCHOOL
4807 Evanswood Dr., Columbus 43229. Private. 1960/1982 (AICS). Qtr. plan. Degrees: A, diplomas. Dir. Ralph R. Rutledge.
Enroll.: 543 (*f.t.* 187 m., 356 w.)
(614) 846-9410

BRYANT AND STRATTON BUSINESS INSTITUTE
26700 Brookpark Rd. Ext., North Olmstead 44070. Private. 1984 (AICS). Qtr. plan. Diplomas. Mgng. Dir. Richard Anderson.
Enroll.: 647 (*f.t.* 34 m., 613 w.)
(216) 777-3151

CAPITAL UNIVERSITY
East Main St., Columbus 43209. Private (American Lutheran) liberal arts and professional college. 1921/1983 (NCA). 4-1-4 plan. Degrees: B,P,M. *Prof. Accred.:* Law (ABA only), Music, Nursing (B), Social Work (B), Teacher Education (*e,s*). Pres. Harvey Stegemoeller.
Enroll.: FTE 2,220
(614) 236-6908

CAREERCOM COLLEGE OF BUSINESS
2572 Cleveland Ave., Columbus 43211. Private. 1985 (AICS). Courses of varying lengths. Certificates, diplomas. Dir. Robert Flynn.
(614) 268-8000

BRANCH CAMPUS
P.O. Box 36, Cameron 43914.
(614) 458-1246

CASE WESTERN RESERVE UNIVERSITY
2040 Adelbert, Cleveland 44106. Private. 1913/1985 (NCA). Sem. plan. Degrees: B,P,M,D. *Prof. Accred.:* Business (B,M), Dentistry, Dietetics, Engineering (biomed-

ical, chemical, civil, computer, electrical, engineering, fluid and thermal science, mechanical, metallurgy and materials science, polymer science, systems and control), Law, Librarianship, Medicine, Music, Nursing (B,M), Psychology, Social Work (M), Speech Pathology and Audiology. Pres. David V. Ragone.
Enroll.: FTE 6,700
(216) 368-2000

CEDARVILLE COLLEGE
Cedarville 45314. Private (Baptist) liberal arts. 1975/1980 (NCA). Qtr. plan. Degrees: B. *Prof. Accred.:* Nursing (B). Pres. Rev. Paul Dixon.
Enroll.: FTE 1,783
(513) 766-2211

CENTRAL OHIO TECHNICAL COLLEGE
Newark 43055. Public (district) 2-year. 1975/1978 (NCA). Qtr. plan. Degrees: A. *Prof. Accred.:* Nursing (A), Radiography. Pres. Julius S. Greenstein.
Enroll.: FTE 813
(614) 366-1351

CENTRAL STATE UNIVERSITY
Wilberforce 45384. Public. 1949/1979 (NCA). Qtr. plan. Degrees: A, B. *Prof. Accred.:* Music, Teacher Education (*e,s*). Pres. Arthur E. Thomas.
Enroll.: FTE 2,680
(216) 777-3151

CHATFIELD COLLEGE
St. Martin 45118. Private liberal arts. 1971/1983 (NCA). Sem. plan. Degrees: A. President Sister Xavier Ladrigan.
Enroll.: 72
(513) 875-3344

CINCINNATI BIBLE COLLEGE
2700 Glenway Ave., Cincinnati 45204. Private (Christian Churches) professional. 1966/1976 (AABC). Sem. plan. Degrees: A,B. Pres. Harvey C. Bream, Jr.
Enroll.: 560
(513) 244-8100

THE CINCINNATI COLLEGE OF MORTUARY SCIENCE
2220 Victory Pkwy., Cincinnati 45206. Private. 1982 (NCA). Qtr. and sem. plans. Degrees: A,B. Pres. David Fitzsimmons.
Enroll.: FTE 101
(513) 861-3240

CINCINNATI METROPOLITAN COLLEGE
4320 Bertus St., St. Bernard 45217. Private business. 1973/1980 (AICS). Qtr. plan. Degrees: A, certificates, diplomas. *Prof. Accred.:* Medical Assisting. Pres. Thomas F. Clay.
Enroll.: 1300 (*f.t.* 170 m., 1,130 w.)
(513) 242-0202

CINCINNATI SCHOOL OF COURT REPORTING AND BUSINESS
230 E. Ninth St., Cincinnati 45202. Private. 1982 (AICS). Courses of varying lengths. Certificates, diplomas. Pres. Adeline M. Womack.
Enroll.: 268 (*f.t.* 3 m., 265 w.)
(513) 241-1011

CINCINNATI TECHNICAL COLLEGE
3520 Central Pkwy., Cincinnati 45223. Public (state) 2-year technical. 1976/1981 (NCA). Qtr. plan. Degrees: A. *Prof. Accred.:* Engineering Technology (civil), Medical Assisting, Medical Laboratory Technology (A), Medical Record Technology, Respiratory Therapy, Respiratory Therapy Technology, Surgical Technology. Pres. Frederick B. Schlimm.
Enroll.: FTE 2,223
(513) 559-1520

CIRCLEVILLE BIBLE COLLEGE
P.O. Box 458, Circleville 43113. Private (Church of Christ in Christian Union) professional. 1976 (AABC). Sem. plan. Degrees: B. Pres. Douglas Carter.
Enroll.: 180
(614) 474-8896

CLARK TECHNICAL COLLEGE
Springfield 45505. Public (state) 2-year technological. 1974/1979 (NCA). Qtr. plan. Degrees: A. *Prof. Accred.:* Assistant to the Primary Care Physician, Medical Laboratory Technology (A), Medical Record Technology, Nursing (A). Pres. George H. Robertson.
Enroll.: FTE 1,385
(513) 325-0691

CLEVELAND INSTITUTE OF ART
Cleveland 44106. Private professional. 1970/1980 (NCA). Sem. plan. Degrees: B. *Prof. Accred.:* Art. Pres. Joseph McCullough.
Enroll.: FTE 469
(216) 421-4322

CLEVELAND INSTITUTE OF DENTAL-MEDICAL ASSISTANTS
5564 Mayfield Rd., Lyndhurst 44124. Private. 1979 (NATTS); 1986 (ABHES). Courses

of varying lengths. Diplomas. *Prof. Accred.:* Medical Assisting, Medical Laboratory Technology. Pres. Helen Davis.
Enroll.: 189 (*f.t.* 4 m., 165 w.)
(216) 473-6273

Branch
5733 Hopkins Rd., Mentor 44060. *Prof. Accred.:* Medical Assisting.
(216) 257-5524

Cleveland Institute of Electronics
1776 E. 17th St., Cleveland 44114. Private home study. 1956/1983 (NHSC). Degrees: A. Pres. John D. Drinko.
Enroll.: 2,280 (*f.t.* 0 m., 0 w.)
(216) 781-9400

Cleveland Institute of Music
Cleveland 44106. Private professional. 1980 (NCA). Sem. plan. Degrees: B,M,D. *Prof. Accred.:* Music. Pres. David Cerone.
Enroll.: FTE 225
(216) 791-5165

Cleveland Institute of Technology
6701 Rockside Rd., Suite 102, Independence 44131. Private. 1971/1985 (AICS); 1974/1979 (NATTS). Courses of varying lengths. Certificates. Dir. George E. Layne.
Enroll.: 486 (*f.t.* 451 m., 35 w.)
(216) 447-1095

Cleveland State University
Euclid Ave., at 24th St., Cleveland 44115. Public. 1940/1982 (NCA). Qtr. plan. Degrees: A,B,P,M,D. *Prof. Accred.:* Accounting (Type A,C), Business (B,M), Engineering (chemical, civil, electrical, industrial, mechanical), Law, Nursing (B), Occupational Therapy, Physical Therapy, Social Work (B), Speech Pathology and Audiology, Teacher Education (*e,s,p*). Pres. Walter B. Waetjen.
Enroll.: 12,428
(216) 687-3544

College of Mount St. Joseph on the Ohio
Mount St. Joseph 45051. Private (Roman Catholic) liberal arts primarily for women. 1932/1983 (NCA). Sem. plan. Degrees: A,B,M. *Prof. Accred.:* Medical Laboratory Technology, Music, Nursing (B), Respiratory Therapy, Respiratory Therapy Technology. Pres. Sister Jean P. Harrington.
Enroll.: FTE 1,120
(513) 244-4232

College of Wooster
Wooster 44691. Private (United Presbyterian) liberal arts. 1915/1973 (NCA). Qtr. plan. Degrees: B. *Prof. Accred.:* Music. Pres. Henry J. Copeland.
Enroll.: FTE 1,709
(216) 263-2311

*Columbus College of Art and Design
Columbus 43215. Private professional. 1976/1980. Sem. plan. Degrees: B. *Prof. Accred.:* Art. Pres. Joseph V. Canzani.
Enroll.: 1,125 (*f.t.* 470 m., 455 w.)
(614) 224-9101

Columbus Paraprofessional Institute East—Branch
70 Robinwood, Columbus 43213. Private. 1980 (NATTS). Qtr. plan. Degrees: A, diplomas. Pres. I. D. Voldness.
Enroll.: 197 (*f.t.* 50 m., 147 w.)
(614) 221-4481

Columbus Paraprofessional Institute North
4820 Indianola Ave., Columbus 43214. Private. 1972/1978 (NATTS). Qtr. plan. Certificates, diplomas. Dir. Hobert Van Hoose.
Enroll.: 246 (*f.t.* 79 m., 117 w.)
(614) 885- 9460

Extension
1077 Lexington Ave., Columbus 43201. Dir. Edward J. Schober.
(614) 294-4636

Columbus Technical Institute
Columbus 43216. Public 2-year technological. 1973/1984 (NCA). Qtr. plan. Degrees: A. *Prof. Accred.:* Dental Laboratory Technology, Engineering Technology (electronics), Medical Laboratory Technology (A), Nursing (A), Optometric Technology, Respiratory Therapy. Pres. Harold M. Nestor.
Enroll.: FTE 4,513
(614) 227-2400

Control Data Institute
1946 N. 13th St., Suite 392, Toledo 43624. Private. 1982 (NATTS). Courses of varying lengths. Certificates. Dir. Norman Cohen.
Enroll.: 150
(419) 255-5969

Cuyahoga Community College
700 Carnegie Ave., Cleveland 44115. Public (county) junior; accreditation includes East-

*Candidate for Accreditation by Regional Accrediting Commission

ern, Metropolitan, and Western Campuses. 1968/1985 (NCA). Qtr. plan. Degrees: A. *Prof. Accred.:* Assistant to the Primary Care Physician, Dental Hygiene, Dental Laboratory Technology, Medical Assisting, Medical Laboratory Technology (A), Medical Record Technology, Nursing (A), Radiography, Respiratory Therapy, Respiratory Therapy Technology, Surgeon's Assistant. Pres. Nolen M. Ellison.
Enroll.: FTE 12,597
(216) 241-5966

DAVIS JUNIOR COLLEGE OF BUSINESS
4747 Monroe St., Toledo 43623. Private. 1953/1986 (AICS). Courses of varying lengths. Certificates. Pres. John Lambert.
Enroll.: 884 (*f.t.* 175 m., 709 w.)
(419) 473-2700

DEFIANCE COLLEGE
Defiance 43512. Private (United Church of Christ) liberal arts. 1916/1983 (NCA). 4-1-4 plan. Degrees: B. *Prof. Accred.:* Social Work (B). Pres. Marvin J. Ludwig.
Enroll.: FTE 750
(419) 784-4010

DENISON UNIVERSITY
Granville 43023. Private (American Baptist) liberal arts college. 1913/1980 (NCA). 4-1-4 plan. Degrees: B. *Prof. Accred.:* Music. Pres. Andrew G. DeRocco.
Enroll.: FTE 2,126
(614) 587-0810

DEVRY INSTITUTE OF TECHNOLOGY
1350 Alum Creek Dr., Columbus 43209. Private. 1972/1983 (NATTS); 1981 (NCA). Tri. plan. Degrees: A,B, diplomas. *Prof. Accred.:* Engineering Technology (electronics). Pres. R. A. Czerniak.
Enroll.: 4,440 (*f.t.* 3,567 m., 585 w.)
(614) 253-7291

DYKE COLLEGE
112 Prospect Ave., Cleveland 44115. Private. 1978/1985 (NCA). Tri. plan. Degrees: A,B, diplomas. Pres. John C. Corfias.
Enroll.: 913
(216) 696-9000

EDISON STATE COMMUNITY COLLEGE
Piqua 45356. Public 2-year. 1981 (NCA). Qtr. plan. Degrees: A. Pres. Conrad W. Burchill.
Enroll.: FTE 1,541
(513) 778-8600

ELECTRONIC SERVICING INSTITUTE
3030 Euclid Ave., Suite 312, Cleveland 44115. Private. 1981 (NATTS). 26-week program. Certificates. Pres. Thomas Strong.
Enroll.: *f.t.*40 m.
(216) 391-5500

ELECTRONIC TECHNOLOGY INSTITUTE
4300 Euclid Ave., Cleveland 44103. Private. 1969/1979 (NATTS). Qtr. plan. Degrees: A, diplomas. Pres. A. Jablonski.
Enroll.: 1,069 (*f.t.* 1,014 m., 55 w.)
(216) 391-9696

FINDLAY COLLEGE
Findlay 45840. Private (Churches of God) liberal arts. 1933/1984 (NCA). 3-3 plan. Degrees: B. Pres. Kenneth E. Zirkle.
Enroll.: 1,000
(419) 422-8313

FRANCISCAN UNIVERSITY OF STEUBENVILLE
Steubenville 43952. Private (Roman Catholic) liberal arts. 1960/1985(NCA). Sem plan. Degrees: B,M. *Prof. Accred.:* Nursing (B). Pres. Rev. Michael Scanlan, T.O.R.
Enroll.: FTE 895
(614) 283-2771

FRANKLIN UNIVERSITY
Columbus 43215. Private liberal arts and technical. 1976/1981 (NCA). Tri. plan. Degrees: A,B. *Prof. Accred.:* Engineering Technology (electronics, mechanical), Nursing (B). Acting Pres. John A. DeSando.
Enroll.: FTE 2,752
(614) 224-6237

HAMMEL COLLEGE
885 E. Buchtel Ave., Akron 44305. Private business. 1953/1982 (AICS). Courses of varying lengths. Diplomas. Pres. William B. Carson.
Enroll.: 794 (*f.t.* 116 m., 678 w.)
(216) 762-7491

BRANCH CAMPUS
6500 Emory Dr., Brook Park 44142. Dir. Robert McBee.
(216) 433-7733

HARDING BUSINESS COLLEGE
1988 McCartney Rd., Youngstown 44505. Private. 1980/1983 (AICS). Qtr. plan. Degrees: A, certificates, diplomas. Dir. Kenneth Martin.
Enroll.: 921 (*f.t.* 255 m., 666 w.)
(216) 746-2424

Branch Campus
21007 Southgate Park Blvd., Maple Heights 44137. Dir. James M. Smith.
(216) 475-1736

Branch Campus
217 W. Center St., Marion 43302. Dir. Earsel W. Gillam.
(614) 383-3187

Hebrew Union College—Jewish Institute of Religion
3101 Clifton Ave., Cincinnati 45220. Private (Union of American Hebrew Congregations) school of religous studies primarily for men. Accreditation includes campus in Jerusalem. Branch U.S. campuses at New York, Los Angeles. 1960/1981 (NCA). Qtr. plan. Degrees: B,P,M,D. Pres. Alfred Gottschalk.
Enroll.: FTE 168
(513) 221-1875

Heidelberg College
Tiffin 44883. Private (United Church of Christ) liberal arts. 1913/1985 (NCA). Sem. plan. Degrees: B. *Prof. Accred.:* Music. Pres. William C. Cassell.
Enroll.: FTE 925
(419) 448-2202

Hickok Technical Institute
2012 W. 25th St., Cleveland 44113. Private. 1980 (NATTS). Qtr. plan. Diplomas. Dir. Lawrence Stone.
Enroll.: 265 (*f.t.* 202 m., 63 w.)
(216) 696-2626

Hiram College
Hiram 44234. Private (Disciples of Christ) liberal arts. 1914/1982 (NCA). Qtr. plan. Degrees: B. *Prof. Accred.:* Music, Teacher Education (*e,s*). Pres. Russell Aiuto.
Enroll.: FTE 1,074
(216) 569-3211

Hobart School of Welding Technology
Trade Square E., Troy 45373. Private. 1972/1984 (NATTS). Courses of varying lengths. Mgr. John Bird.
Enroll.: 223 (*f.t.* 231 m., 2 w.)
(513) 339-6000

Hocking Technical College
Nelsonville 45764. Public (state) 2-year. 1976/1981 (NCA). Qtr. plan. Degrees: A. *Prof. Accred.:* Medical Assisting, Medical Record Technology. Pres. John J. Light.
Enroll.: FTE 3,350
(614) 753-3591

ICM School of Business
1375 Euclid Ave., Cleveland 44115. Private. 1968/1981 (AICS). Courses of varying lengths. Certificates, diplomas. *Prof. Accred.:* Medical Assisting. Vice Pres. Robert P. Gioella.
Enroll.: 1,650 (*f.t.* 873 m., 777 w.)
(216) 241-3964

ITT Technical Institute
4920 Northcutt Pl., Dayton 45414. Private. 1969/1979 (NATTS). Qtr. plan. Degrees: A, certificates. Dir. Dennis W. Alspaugh.
Enroll.: 699 (*f.t.* 684 m., 15 w.)
(513) 278-8286

ITT Technical Institute
655 Wick Ave., P.O. Box 779, Youngstown 44501. Private. 1971/1983 (AICS). Courses of varying lengths. Degrees: A, certificates. Dir. Michael Thompson.
Enroll.: 1,175 (*f.t.* 501 m., 674 w.)
(216) 747-5555

Institute of Medical and Dental Technology
375 Glenspring Dr., Cincinnati 45246. Private. 1983 (ABHES). 520-hour courses. Diplomas. *Prof. Accred.:* Medical Assisting. Pres. J. Vincent Sofia.
Enroll.: 150
(513) 851-8500

Institute of Medical and Dental Technology
1100 Norse Rd., Columbus 43229. Private. 1985 (NATTS). Courses of varying lengths. Diplomas. Dir. Don Pargeon.
(614) 436-4820

International Broadcasting School
Six S. Smithville Rd., Dayton 45431. Private. 1976 (NATTS). Courses of varying lengths. Diplomas. Pres. Don Gingerich.
Enroll.: 150 (*f.t.* 118 m., 32 w.)
(513) 258-8251

Jane Addams School
4016 Woodbine, Cleveland 44113. Public (Cleveland Public Schools) vocational. 1-year program. Certificates. *Prof. Accred.:* Dental Assisting (1977). Dir. Helen Moonert.
(216) 621-2131

Jefferson Technical College
Steubenville 43952. Public (state) 2-year technical. 1973/1981 (NCA). Qtr. plan. Degrees: A. *Prof. Accred.:* Dental Assisting, Dental Technology, Medical Assisting, Med-

ical Laboratory Technology (A), Radiography. Pres. Edward L. Florak.
Enroll.: FTE 986
(614) 264-5591

JOHN CARROLL UNIVERSITY
University Heights, Cleveland 44118. Private (Roman Catholic) liberal arts and business college. 1922/1984 (NCA). Sem. plan. Degrees: B,M. *Prof. Accred.:* Teacher Education (*e,s,p*). Pres. Rev. Thomas P. O'Malley, S.J.
Enroll.: FTE 2,986
(216) 397-1886

KENT STATE UNIVERSITY
Kent 44242. Public. Accreditation includes Ashtabula, East Liverpool, Geauga, Salem, Stark, Trumbull, and Tuscarawas Campuses. 1915/1984 (NCA). Qtr. plan. Degrees: A,B,M,D. *Prof. Accred.:* Architecture (B,M), Art, Business (B,M), Engineering Technology (electrical/electronic, mechanical), Interior Design, Journalism, Librarianship, Music, Nursing (A,B,M), Psychology, Rehabilitation Counseling, Speech Pathology and Audiology, Teacher Education (*e,s,p*). Pres. Michael Schwartz.
Enroll.: FTE 16,258
(216) 672-2210

KENYON COLLEGE
Gambier 43022. Private (Episcopal) liberal arts. 1913/1981 (NCA). Sem. plan. Degrees: B. Pres. Philip Harding Jordan, Jr.
Enroll.: FTE 1,477
(614) 427-2244

KETTERING COLLEGE OF MEDICAL ARTS
Kettering 45429. Private (Seventh-day Adventist) junior. 1974/1984 (NCA). Sem. plan. Degrees: A. *Prof. Accred.:* Assistant to the Primary Care Physician, Diagnostic Medical Sonography, Medical Laboratory Technology, Radiography, Respiratory Therapy. Dean Robert A. Williams.
Enroll.: FTE 417
(513) 296-7218

LAKE ERIE COLLEGE
Painesville 44077. Private liberal arts for women. 1913/1985 (NCA). Year of three 11-week terms. Degrees: B,M. Pres. Edward Q. Moulton.
Enroll.: FTE 552
(216) 352-3361

LAKELAND COMMUNITY COLLEGE
Mentor 44060. Public (district) junior. 1973/1984 (NCA). 4-1-4 plan. Degrees: A. *Prof. Accred.:* Dental Hygiene, Medical Laboratory Technology (A), Nursing (A), Respiratory Therapy. Pres. James L. Catanzaro.
Enroll.: FTE 4,113
(216) 953-7118

LIMA TECHNICAL COLLEGE
Lima 45804. Public 2-year. 1979/1984 (NCA). Qtr. plan. Degrees: A. *Prof. Accred.:* Nursing (A), Radiography, Respiratory Therapy Technology. Dir. James S. Biddle.
Enroll.: FTE 1,373
(419) 227-5131

LORAIN BUSINESS COLLEGE
1907 N. Ridge Rd., Lorain 44055. Private. 1980 (AICS). Courses of varying lengths. Certificates. Dir. Jane McComb.
Enroll.: 501 (*f.t.* 121 m., 380 w.)
(216) 277-0021

BRANCH CAMPUS
1100 Cleveland Rd., Sandusky 44870. Dir. Jacquelyn Marshall.
(419) 627-8345

LORAIN COUNTY COMMUNITY COLLEGE
Elyria 44035. Public (district) junior. 1971/1984 (NCA). Qtr. plan. Degrees: A, certificates. *Prof. Accred.:* Medical Assisting, Medical Laboratory Technology (A), Nursing (A), Practical Nursing, Radiography. Pres. Richard R. Mellott.
Enroll.: FTE 3,442
(216) 365-4191

LOURDES COLLEGE
6832 Convent Blvd., Sylvania 43560. Private (Roman Catholic) liberal arts junior. 1964/1982 (NCA). Sem. plan. Degrees: A,B. Pres. Sister Ann Francis, O.S.F.
Enroll.: FTE 421
(419) 885-3211

MTA SCHOOL (EXTENSION)
445 Glade Run Rd., S.E., P.O. Box 24, West Jefferson 43162. Private. 1985 (NATTS). Courses of varying lengths. Certificates. Dir. William Antonelli.
(614) 852-1852

MTA SCHOOL (EXTENSION)
3440 East Main St., Columbus 43213. Private. 1985 (NATTS). Courses of varying lengths. Certificates. Dir. William R. Ritter.
(614) 236-1972

MTI BUSINESS SCHOOL
1901 E. 13th St., Suite 310, Cleveland 44114. Private. 1980/1983 (AICS). Courses of vary-

ing lengths. Certificates. Pres. Charles M. Kramer.
Enroll.: 393 (*f.t.* 6 m., 387 w.)
(216) 621-8228

MALONE COLLEGE
Canton 44709. Private (Friends) liberal arts. 1964/1984 (NCA). Sem. plan. Degrees: B. *Prof. Accred.:* Social Work (B). Pres. Gordon R. Werkema.
Enroll.: FTE 879
(216) 489-0800

MANSFIELD BUSINESS COLLEGE
523 Park Ave., E., Mansfield 44905. Private. 1968/1986 (AICS). Qtr. plan. Degrees: A, certificates, diplomas. Dir. Robert L. Trautwein.
Enroll.: 3,277 (*f.t.* 901 m., 2,376 w.)
(419) 526-4988

BRANCH CAMPUS
222 S. Main St., Sixth Fl., O'Neil's Plaza, Akron 44308. Dir. George Dupey.
(216) 762-3030

BRANCH CAMPUS
3011 Mahoning Rd., N.E., Canton 44705. Dir. Ronald A. Rountree.
(216) 452-8171

BRANCH CAMPUS
2525 W. Alameda Ave., Denver, CO 80219. Dir. Mary Sanford.
(303) 936-5951

BRANCH CAMPUS
3322 Olive St., St. Louis, MO 63103. Dir. E. Eugene Gray, Jr.
(314) 531-1768

BRANCH CAMPUS
2638 Two Notch Rd., Midland Shopping Center, Columbia, SC 29204. Dir. Kevin J. Daughtry.
(803) 771-6411

BRANCH CAMPUS
Nine S. 12th St., Philadelphia, PA 19107. Dir. Kay Wideman.
(215) 561-2226

BRANCH CAMPUS
714 N. Watson Rd., Arlington, TX 76011. Dir. James L. Howard.
(817) 261-1128

BRANCH CAMPUS
3615 Culebra Rd., San Antonio, TX 78228. Dir. Gene Troiano.
(512) 432-3100

MARIETTA COLLEGE
Marietta 45750. Private liberal arts. 1913/1976 (NCA). Sem. plan. Degrees: A,B,M. *Prof. Accred.:* Engineering (petroleum). Pres. Sherrill Cleland.
Enroll.: FTE 1,148
(614) 373-4700

MARION TECHNICAL COLLEGE
Marion 43302. Public (state) 2-year. 1977/1980 (NCA). Qtr. plan. Degrees: A. *Prof. Accred.:* Medical Laboratory Technology, Nursing (A). Pres. J. Richard Bryson.
Enroll.: FTE 852
(614) 389-4636

MCKIM TECHNICAL INSTITUTE
1791 S. Jacoby Rd., Akron/Copley 44321. Private. 1980 (NATTS). Courses of varying lengths. Certificates, diplomas. Pres. Nelson J. Rohac.
Enroll.: 158 (*f.t.* 103 m., 5 w.)
(216) 666-4014

MEDICAL COLLEGE OF OHIO AT TOLEDO
Toledo 43699. Public (state) professional. 1980/1986(NCA). Sem. plan. Degrees: A,B,P,D. *Prof. Accred.:* Medical Technology, Medicine, Nursing (B,M), Physical Therapy. Pres. Richard Ruppert.
Enroll.: FTE 763
(419) 381-4260

METHODIST THEOLOGICAL SCHOOL IN OHIO
Delaware 43015. Private (United Methodist) professional; graduate only. 1976/1982 (NCA). Qtr. plan. Degrees: P,M,D. *Prof. Accred.:* Theology (1965/1982, ATS). Pres. Norman E. Dewire.
Enroll.: FTE 147
(614) 363-1146

MIAMI-JACOBS JUNIOR COLLEGE OF BUSINESS
P.O. Box 1433, Dayton 45401. Private. 1957/1985 (AICS). Qtr. plan. Degrees: A. Pres. Charles G. Campbell.
Enroll.: 1,324 (*f.t.* 210 m., 1,114 w.)
(513) 461-5174

MIAMI UNIVERSITY
Oxford 45056. Public (state). 1913/1985 (NCA). Accreditation includes Hamilton and Middletown Campuses and Luxembourg Study Center. Sem. plan. Degrees: A,B,M,D. *Prof. Accred.:* Accounting (Type A), Architecture (M), Business (B,M), Home Economics, Music, Nursing (A,B), Psychology, Speech Pa-

thology, Teacher Education (*e,s,p*). Pres. Paul G. Pearson.
Enroll.: FTE 15,686
(513) 529-2345

MOUNT UNION COLLEGE
Alliance 44601. Private (United Methodist) liberal arts. 1913/1982 (NCA). Qtr. plan. Degrees: B. *Prof. Accred.:* Music. Pres. Harold M. Kolenbrander.
Enroll.: FTE 960
(216) 821-5320

MOUNT VERNON NAZARENE COLLEGE
Mt. Vernon 43050. Private (Nazarene) liberal arts. 1972/1979 (NCA). Qtr. plan. Degrees: A,B. Pres. William J. Prince.
Enroll.: FTE 969
(614) 397-1244

MUSKINGUM AREA TECHNICAL COLLEGE
Zanesville 43701. Public (state) 2-year technological. 1975/1978 (NCA). Qtr. plan. Degrees: A. *Prof. Accred.:* Medical Assisting, Medical Laboratory Technology (A), Radiography. Respiratory Therapy Technology. Pres. Lynn H. Willett.
Enroll.: FTE 932
(614) 454-2501

MUSKINGUM COLLEGE
New Concord 43762. Private (United Presbyterian) liberal arts. 1919/1983 (NCA). 4-1-4 plan. Degrees: B. *Prof. Accred.:* Music. Pres. Arthur J. De Jong.
Enroll.: FTE 1,006
(614) 826-8115

NHAW HOME STUDY INSTITUTE
North American Heating and Airconditioning Wholesalers Association. 1369 Dublin Rd., Box 16790, Columbus 43216. Private home study. 1969/1981 (NHSC). Dir. James H. Healy.
(614) 488-1835

NATIONAL EDUCATION CENTER/NATIONAL INSTITUTE OF TECHNOLOGY CAMPUS
1225 Orlen Ave., Cuyahoga Falls 44221. Private. 1969/1980 (NATTS). Qtr. plan. Diplomas. Dir. Richard A. Mills.
Enroll.: 610 (*f.t.* 393 m., 55 w.)
(216) 923-9959

NORTH CENTRAL TECHNICAL COLLEGE
Mansfield 44906. Public (state) 2-year. 1976/1981 (NCA). Qtr. plan. Degrees: A, certificates. *Prof. Accred.:* Nursing (A), Radiography. Pres. Byron E. Kee.
Enroll.: FTE 1,172
(419) 747-4999

NORTHEASTERN OHIO UNIVERSITIES COLLEGE OF MEDICINE
Rootstown 44272. Public (state) professional; consortium with campuses also at Akron, Kent, and Youngstown. 1981. Sem. plan. Degrees: P. *Prof. Accred.:* Medicine. Prov. and Dean Robert A. Liebelt.
Enroll.: 379 (*f.t.* 249 m., 130 w.)
(216)325-2511

NORTHWEST TECHNICAL COLLEGE
Archbold 43502. Public (state) 2-year. 1977/1982 (NCA). Qtr. plan. Degrees: A. Pres. James O. Miller.
Enroll.: FTE 560
(419) 267-5511

NORTHWESTERN BUSINESS COLLEGE AND TECHNICAL CENTER
1441 N. Cable Rd., Lima 45805. Private. 1958/1981 (AICS); 1976/1982 (NATTS). Qtr. plan. Degrees: A, certificates, diplomas. Pres. Loren R. Jarvis.
Enroll.: 1,618 (*f.t.* 1,120 m., 498 w.)
(419) 227-3141

NOTRE DAME COLLEGE
4545 College Rd., Cleveland 44121. Private (Roman Catholic) liberal arts for women. 1931/1985 (NCA). Sem. plan. Degrees: B. Pres. Sister Mary Marthe Reinhard, S.N.D.
Enroll.: FTE 500
(216) 381-1680

OBERLIN COLLEGE
Oberlin 44074. Private liberal arts and music. 1913/1978 (NCA). 4-1-4 plan. Degrees: B,M. *Prof. Accred.:* Art, Music. Pres. S. Frederick Starr.
Enroll.: FTE 2,724
(216) 775-8400

OHIO COLLEGE OF BARBER STYLING
5100 Pearl Rd., Cleveland 44129. Private. 1984 (NATTS). Courses of varying lengths. Certificates. Dir. Ralph J. Boothe.
(216) 741-0905

OHIO COLLEGE OF BUSINESS AND TECHNOLOGY
7601 Harrison Ave., Mt. Healthy 45231. Private 1975/1984 (AICS); 1978 (NATTS). Qtr. plan. Degrees: A, diplomas. *Prof. Accred.:* Medical Assisting. Pres. James L. Atkins.

Enroll.: 530 (*f.t.* 230 m., 300 w.)
(513) 521-0505

BRANCH CAMPUS
4420 Manchester Rd., Middletown 45042. *Prof. Accred.:* Medical Assisting. Dir. Mark Atkins.
(513) 424-3205

BRANCH CAMPUS
992 Lila La., U.S. 50, Milford 45150. *Prof. Accred.:* Medical Assisting. Dir. Ruth Hamilton.
(513) 831-6940

*OHIO COLLEGE OF PODIATRIC MEDICINE
10515 Carnegie Ave., Cleveland 44106. Private professional. 1922/1984. Qtr. plan. Degrees: P. *Prof. Accred.:* Podiatry. Pres. Thomas V. Melillo.
Enroll.: FTE 564
(216) 231-3300

OHIO DIESEL TECHNICAL INSTITUTE
1421 E. 49th St., Cleveland 44103. Private. 1973/1978 (NATTS). Courses of varying lengths. Certificates. Pres. Julius A. Brenner.
Enroll.: 642 (*f.t.* 641 m., 1 w.)
(216) 881-1700

OHIO DOMINICAN COLLEGE
Columbus 43219. Private (Roman Catholic) liberal arts. 1934/1978 (NCA). Sem. plan. Degrees: B. Pres. Sister Mary Andrew Matesich, O.P.
Enroll.: FTE 884
(614) 253-2741

OHIO INSTITUTE OF PHOTOGRAPHY
2029 Edgefield Rd., Dayton 45439. Private. 1976/1981 (NATTS). Sem. plan. Degrees: A, diplomas. Dir K. Terry Guthrie.
Enroll.: 195 (*f.t.* 112 m., 38 w.)
(513) 294-6155

OHIO NORTHERN UNIVERSITY
Ada 45810. Private (United Methodist). 1958/1985 (NCA). Qtr. plan. Degrees: B,P. *Prof. Accred.:* Engineering (civil, electrical, mechanical), Law, Music, Pharmacy, Social Work (B). Pres. DeBow Freed.
Enroll.: FTE 2,382
(419) 772-2000

OHIO SCHOOL OF BROADCAST TECHNIQUE
1737 Euclid Ave., Cleveland 44115. Private. 1975/1980 (NATTS). Courses of varying lengths. Certificates, diplomas. Gen. Mgr. Marge Bush.
Enroll.: 172 (*f.t.* 103 m., 21 w.)
(216) 861-1111

OHIO SCHOOL OF CAREER TECHNOLOGY
6655 Sharon Woods Blvd., Columbus 43229. Private. 1979 (NATTS). Qtr. plan, courses of varying lengths. Degrees: A, certificates, diplomas. Dir. David S. Brown.
Enroll.: 515 (*f.t.* 5 m., 38 w.)
(614) 891-1328

OHIO STATE COLLEGE OF BARBER STYLING
4602 E. Main St., Columbus 43213-9990. Private. 1977 (NATTS). Courses of varying lengths. Certificates. Pres. Louis G. Farber.
Enroll.: 58 (*f.t.* 24 m., 34 w.)
(614) 868-1011

OHIO STATE COLLEGE OF BARBER STYLING
4376 Karl Rd., Columbus 43224-9990. Private. 1979 (NATTS). Courses of varying lengths. Diplomas. Pres. Louis G. Farber.
(614) 267-4247

OHIO STATE COLLEGE/BARBER STYLING
329 Superior St., Toledo 43604. Private. 1983 (NATTS). Courses of varying lengths. Diplomas. Pres. Louis G. Farber.
(419) 241-5618

OHIO STATE UNIVERSITY—CENTRAL OFFICE
Columbus 43210. Public. Pres. Edward H. Jennings.
(614) 422-2424

OHIO STATE UNIVERSITY—MAIN CAMPUS
Columbus 43210. Public. 1913/1977 (NCA). Qtr. plan. Degrees: A,B,P,M,D. *Prof. Accred.:* Accounting (Type A,B), Architecture (M), Business (B,M), Dental Hygiene, Dentistry, Dietetics, Engineering (aeronautical and astronautical, agricultural, ceramic, chemical, civil, electrical, industrial and systems, mechanical, metallurgical, welding), Health Services Administration, Histologic Technology, Journalism, Landscape Architecture (B), Law, Medical Record Administration, Medical Technology, Medicine, Music, Nuclear Medicine Technology, Nurse Anesthesia Education, Nursing (B,M), Occupational Therapy, Optometry, Perfusionist, Pharmacy, Physical Therapy, Preventive Medicine and Public Health, Psychology, Radiography, Respiratory Therapy, Social Work (B,M), Speech Pathology and Audiology, Teacher Education (*e,s,p*), Veterinary Medicine. Pres. Edward H. Jennings.

*Candidate for Accreditation by Regional Accrediting Commission

Enroll.: FTE 52,156
(614) 422-2424

Ohio State University—Agricultural Technical Institute
Wooster 44691. 1978/1983 (NCA). Qtr. plan. Degrees: A, diplomas. Dir. Dan Garrison.
Enroll.: FTE 624
(216) 264-3911

Ohio State University—Lima Campus
Lima 45804. 1972/1982 (NCA). Degrees: A,B. Dean and Dir. J. S. Biddle.
Enroll.: FTE 919
(419) 228-2641

Ohio State University—Mansfield Campus
Mansfield 44906. 1972/1982 (NCA). Degrees: A,B. Dean and Dir. Laurine Fitzgerald.
Enroll.: FTE 869
(419) 755-4222

Ohio State University—Marion Campus
Marion 43302. 1972/1982 (NCA). Degrees: A,B. Dean and Dir. Francis E. Hazard.
Enroll.: FTE 654
(614) 389-2361

Ohio State University—Newark Campus
Newark 43055. 1972/1982 (NCA). Degrees: A,B. Dean and Dir. Julius S. Greenstein.
Enroll.: FTE 750
(614) 366-3321

Ohio University
Athens 45701. Public (state). 1913/1984 (NCA). Accreditation includes Ohio University Campuses at Belmont County, Chillicothe, Lancaster, Zanesville, and Ironton Branch. Qtr. plan. Degrees: A,B,P,M,D. *Prof. Accred.:* Business (B,M), Engineering (chemical, civil, electrical, industrial and systems, mechanical), Home Economics, Journalism, Music, Nursing (B), Osteopathy, Physical Therapy, Psychology, Social Work (B), Speech Pathology and Audiology, Teacher Education (*e,s,p*). Pres. Charles J. Ping.
Enroll.: FTE 15,535
(614) 594-5461

Ohio Valley Business College
500 Maryland St., P.O. Box 7000, East Liverpool 43920. Private. 1985 (AICS). Courses of varying lengths. Certificates, diplomas. Admin. Doris McKinnon.
(216) 385-1070

Ohio Wesleyan University
Delaware 43015. Private (United Methodist) liberal arts college. 1913/1979 (NCA). 4-1-4 plan. Degrees: B. *Prof. Accred.:* Music. Pres. David L. Warren.
Enroll.: FTE 1,510
(614) 369-4431

Otterbein College
Westerville 43081. Private (United Methodist) liberal arts. 1913/1985 (NCA). 3-3 plan. Degrees: B. *Prof. Accred.:* Music, Nursing (B), Teacher Education (*e,s*). Pres. C. Brent DeVore.
Enroll.: FTE 1,510
(614) 890-3000

Owens Technical College
Toledo 43699. Public (state) 2-year technical. 1976/1981 (NCA). Qtr. plan. Degrees: A. *Prof. Accred.:* Dental Hygiene, Engineering Technology (civil, electrical), Nursing (A), Respiratory Therapy Technology, Surgical Technology. Pres. Daniel H. Brown.
Enroll.: FTE 2,985
(419) 666-0580

PSI Institute
1858 Euclid Ave., Cleveland 44115. Private. 1983 (NATTS). Courses of varying lengths. Diplomas. Chairman Irwin Mautner.
Enroll.: 25
(216) 771-6680

Penn-Ohio College
3517 Market St., Youngstown 44507. Private business. 1971/1983 (AICS). Sem. plan. Certificates, diplomas. Pres. William M. Clark, Jr.
Enroll.: 431 (*f.t.* 42 m., 389 w.)
(216) 788-5084

Pontifical College Josephinum
Columbus 43085. Private (Roman Catholic) liberal arts and professional. 1977/1981 (NCA). Sem. plan. Degrees: B,P,M. *Prof. Accred.:* Theology (1970/1981, ATS). Pres./Rector Msgr. Dennis F. Sheehan.
Enroll.: FTE 181
(614) 885-5585

Professional Skills Institute
6711 Airport Hwy., Hillard 43528. Private. 1986 (ABHES). Curses of varying lengths. Certificates, diplomas. Dir. Patricia A. Finch.
(419) 865-1454

Progressive Fashion School
2012 W. 25th St., Room 612, Cleveland 44113. Private. 1977 (NATTS). Qtr. plan and

courses of varying lengths. Certificates, diplomas. Dir. Jean Dunn Salata.
Enroll.: 48 (*f.t.* 8 m., 25 w.)
(216) 781-4595

RETS INSTITUTE OF TECHNOLOGY
1606 Laskey Rd., Toledo 43612. Private. 1973/1980 (NATTS). Qtr. plan. Certificates, diplomas. Dir. Frank Reidy.
Enroll.: 500 (*f.t.* 380 m., 20 w.)
(419) 478-2674

RETS TECH CENTER
116 Westpark Rd., P.O. Box 130, Centerville 45459. Private. 1974/1979 (NATTS). Qtr. plan. Degrees: A, certificates. Pres. Michael Lemaster.
Enroll.: 826 (*f.t.* 687 m., 117 w.)
(513) 433-3410

RABBINICAL COLLEGE OF TELSHE
28400 Euclid Ave., Wickliffe 40092. Private professional. 1974/1981. Degrees: M and D of Talmudic and Theological Education. *Prof. Accred.:* Rabbinical and Talmudic Education. Pres. Rabbi M. Gifter.
Enroll.: f.t. 158 m.
(216) 943-5300

RIO GRANDE COLLEGE/COMMUNITY COLLEGE
Rio Grande 45674. Private liberal arts. 1969/1983 (NCA). 4-1-4 plan. Degrees: A, B. *Prof. Accred.:* Medical Laboratory Technology (A). Pres. Clodus R. Smith.
Enroll.: FTE 1,480
(614) 245-5353

SAINT MARY SEMINARY
Cleveland 44108 Private (Roman Catholic) professional; graduate only. 1981/1986 (NCA). Qtr. plan. Degrees: P, M. *Prof. Accred.:* Theology (1970/1985, ATS). Pres. Very Rev. Allan R. Laubenthanl.
Enroll.: FTE 61
(216) 721-2100

SAWYER COLLEGE OF BUSINESS
13027 Lorain Ave., Cleveland 44111. Private. 1982 (AICS). Qtr. plan. Degrees: A, diplomas. Pres. George W. King.
Enroll.: 296 (*f.t.* 25 m., 271 w.)
(216) 941-7666.

SAWYER COLLEGE OF BUSINESS
3150 Mayfield Rd., Cleveland Heights 44118. Private. 1973/1985. Qtr. plan. Degrees: A, diplomas. Pres. George W. King.
Enroll.: 548 (*f.t.* 18 m., 530 w.)
(216) 932-0911

SHAWNEE STATE COMMUNITY COLLEGE
940 Second St., Portsmouth 45662. Public 2-year. 1975/1983 (NCA). Qtr. plan. Degrees: A. *Prof. Accred.:* Dental Hygiene, Medical Laboratory Technology (A), Radiography, Respiratory Therapy, Respiratory-Therapy Technology. Pres. Frank C. Taylor.
Enroll.: FTE 1,888
(614) 345-3205

SINCLAIR COMMUNITY COLLEGE
Dayton 45402. Public (district) junior. 1970/1971 (NCA). Qtr. plan. Degrees: A. *Prof. Accred.:* Dental Hygiene, Engineering-Technology (electronic, mechanical), Medical Record Technology, Nursing (A), Radiography, Respiratory Therapy, Surgical Technology. Pres. David H. Ponitz.
Enroll.: FTE 7,225
(513) 226-2525

SOUTHEASTERN BUSINESS COLLEGE
1855 Western Ave., Chillicothe 45601. Private. 1976/1982 (AICS). Courses of varying lengths. Certificates. Pres./Dir. Sam C. Blackburn.
Enroll.: 251 (*f.t.* 95 m., 156 w.)
(614) 774-6300

BRANCH CAMPUS
529 Jackson Pike, Suite 312, Gallipolis 45631. Dir. Kenneth W. Christopher.
(614) 446-4367

BRANCH CAMPUS
1600 Sheridan Dr., Lancaster 43130. Dir. Nancy Taylor.
(614) 687-6126

BRANCH CAMPUS
P.O. Box 1382, Portsmouth 45662. Dir. Robert Shirey.
(614) 354-8811

SOUTHERN OHIO COLLEGE
1055 Laidlaw Ave., Cincinnati 45237. Private junior. 1964/1984 (AICS); 1983 (NCA). Qtr. plan. Degrees: A. *Prof. Accred.:* Medical Assisting. Pres. M. Douglas Reed.
Enroll.: FTE 4,449
(513) 242-3791

BRANCH CAMPUS
2791 Mogadore Rd., Akron 44312. Dir. Wayne Mullis.
(216) 733-8766

BRANCH CAMPUS
4430 State Rd., Cleveland 44109. Dir. Kenneth Jones.
(216)661-4300

BRANCH CAMPUS
9200 Wade Park Ave., Cleveland 44106. Dir. Carol Whitman-Imfeld
(216) 229-7190

BRANCH CAMPUS
979 S. James Rd., Columbus 43227. Dir. Karen Young.
(614) 231-8888

BRANCH CAMPUS
880 S. Wayne Ave., Columbus 43204. Dir. Karen Young.
(614) 274-9003

BRANCH CAMPUS
4271 W. Third St., Dayton 45417. Dir. Kimberly Alexander.
(513) 263-7666

BRANCH CAMPUS
4641 Bacher La., Fairfield 45014. Dir. Duane Hawkins.
(513) 829-7100

SOUTHERN STATE COMMUNITY COLLEGE
200 Hobart Dr., Hillsboro 45133. Public (state) 2-year technical. 1981/1985 (NCA). Qtr. plan. Degrees: A. Pres. Lewis C. Miller.
Enroll.: FTE 765
(513) 393-3431

SOUTHWESTERN COLLEGE OF BUSINESS
3700 Far Hills Ave., Kettering 45429. Private. 1973/1984 (AICS). Qtr. plan. Degrees: A. *Prof. Accred.:* Medical Assisting. Pres. Gary Wright.
Enroll.: 2,515 (*f.t.* 754 m., 1,761 w.)
(513) 294-2103

BRANCH CAMPUS
9910 Princeton-Glendale Rd., Cincinnati 45246. *Prof. Accred.:* Medical Assisting. Dir. of Ed. Sharon Winstead.
(513) 874-0432

BRANCH CAMPUS
717 Race St., Cincinnati 45202. Dir. of Ed. Brenda Dixon.
(513) 421-3212

BRANCH CAMPUS
1830 Yankee Rd., Middletown 45042. *Prof. Accred.:* Medical Assisting. Dir. of Ed. Bev Turner.
(513) 423-3346

BRANCH CAMPUS
Crestview Hills Shopping Mall, Dixie Hwy., Covington, KY 41017. Dir. Mendell Hodges.
(606) 261-6400

STARK TECHNICAL COLLEGE
Canton 44720. Public 2-year. 1976/1981 (NCA). Qtr. plan. Degrees: A. *Prof. Accred.:* Engineering Technology (civil construction, drafting and design, electrical, electronic, mechanical), Medical Assisting, Medical Laboratory Technology (A), Medical Record Technology, Respiratory Therapy Technology. Pres. John J. McGrath.
Enroll.: FTE 2,273
(216) 494-6170

STAUTZENBERGER COLLEGE
5355 Southwyck Blvd., Toledo 43614. Private business. 1962/1986 (AICS). Qtr. plan. Diplomas. *Prof. Accred.:* Medical Assisting. Vice Pres. Marge Yaney.
Enroll.: 2,738 (*f.t.* 566 m., 2,172 w.)
(419) 866-0261

BRANCH CAMPUS
309 S. Main St., Bowling Green 43402. *Prof. Accred.:* Medical Assisting. Dir. Connie Teare.
(419) 352-2162

BRANCH CAMPUS
1637 Tiffin Ave., Findlay 45840. *Prof. Accred.:* Medical Assisting. Dir. Gary A. Johnson.
(419) 423-2211

BRANCH CAMPUS
4404 Secor Rd., Toledo 43623. *Prof. Accred.:* Medical Assisting, Medical Laboratory Technology. Dir. James Edwards.
(419) 472-2115

BRANCH CAMPUS
4615 Woodville Rd., Toledo 43619. *Prof. Accred.:* Medical Assisting. Dir. Larry Mitchell.
(419) 693-9311

TECHNICRON VOCATIONAL INSTITUTE
4040 Spring Grove Ave., Cincinnati 45223. Private. 1973/1978 (NATTS). Qtr. plan, courses of varying lengths. Certificates, diplomas. Pres. Lee Spievack.
Enroll.: 146 (*f.t.* 5 m., 131 w.)
(513) 541-8111

TERRA TECHNICAL COLLEGE
Fremont 43420. Public (state) 2-year. 1975/1980 (NCA). Qtr. plan. Degrees: A. Pres. Richard M. Simon.

Enroll.: FTE 1,560
(419) 334-3886

TIFFIN UNIVERSITY
155 Miami St., Tiffin 44883. Private senior. 1953/1983 (AICS); 1985 (NCA). Sem. plan. Degrees: A,B. Pres. George Kidd, Jr.
Enroll.: FTE 500
(419) 447-6442

TOTAL TECHNICAL INSTITUTE (EXTENSION)
13505 West 130th St., North Royalton 44133. Private. 1985 (NATTS). Courses of varying lengths. Certificates. Dir. David E. Anderson.
(216) 237-0288

TRINITY LUTHERAN SEMINARY
Columbus 43209. Private (American Lutheran Church and Lutheran Church in America) professional; graduate only. 1974/1982 (NCA). Sem. plan. Degrees: P,M,D. *Prof. Accred.:* Theology (1940/1982, ATS). Pres. Frederick W. Meuser.
Enroll.: FTE 287
(614) 235-4136

TRUMBULL BUSINESS COLLEGE
3200 Ridge Rd., Warren 44484. Private. 1976/1982 (AICS). Courses of varying lengths. Certificates. Pres. Dennis R. Griffith.
Enroll.: 271 (*f.t.* 58 m., 213 w.)
(216) 369-3200

UNION FOR EXPERIMENTING COLLEGES AND UNIVERSITIES/UNIVERSITY WITHOUT WALLS AND UNION GRADUATE SCHOOL
Cincinnati 45201. Private. 1985 (NCA). Qtr. plan. Degrees: B,D. Pres. Robert T. Conley
Enroll.: FTE 730
(513) 621-6444

UNITED THEOLOGICAL SEMINARY
Dayton 45406. Private (United Methodist) professional; graduate only. 1975/1980 (NCA). Qtr. plan. Degrees: P,M,D. *Prof. Accred.:* Theology (1938/1980, ATS). Pres. Leonard I. Sweet.
Enroll.: FTE 228
(513) 278-5817

THE UNIVERSITY OF AKRON—CENTRAL OFFICE
302 E. Buchtel Ave., Akron 44325. Public (state). Pres. William V. Muse.
Enroll.: FTE 18,199
(216) 375-7074

THE UNIVERSITY OF AKRON—MAIN CAMPUS
302 E. Buchtel Ave., Akron 44325. Public (state). 1914/1977 (NCA). Sem. plan. Degrees: A,B,P,M,D. *Prof. Accred.:* Art, Business (B,M), Dietetics, Engineering (chemical, civil, electrical, mechanical), Engineering Technology (construction, electronic, mechanical), Home Economics, Law, Music, Nursing (B,M), Respiratory Therapy, Social Work (B), Speech Pathology and Audiology, Teacher Education *(e,s,p)*. Pres. William V. Muse.
Enroll.: FTE 17,994
(216) 375-7074

WAYNE GENERAL AND TECHNICAL COLLEGE
Orrville 44667. 1972/1984 (NCA). Degrees: A. Dean Tyrone M. Turning
Enroll.: FTE 462
(216) 683-2010

UNIVERSITY OF CINCINNATI—CENTRAL OFFICE
Cincinnati 45221. Public (state). Pres. Joseph A. Steger.
(513) 475-2201

UNIVERSITY OF CINCINNATI—MAIN CAMPUS
Cincinnati 45221. Public (state). Accreditation includes Evening College, University College, and Ohio College of Applied Science. 1913/1983 (NCA). Qtr. plan. Degrees: A,B,P,M,D. *Prof. Accred.:* Architecture(B), Art, Business (B,M), Community Health Planning/Administration, Construction Education, Cytotechnology, Engineering (aerospace, chemical, civil, electrical, environmental, industrial, mechanical, metallurgical, nuclear), Engineering Technology (arcitectural, chemical, civil, electrical, mechanical), Interior Design, Law, Medical Technology, Medicine, Music, Nuclear Medicine Technology, Nurse Anesthesia Education, Nursing (B,M), Pharmacy, Psychology, Radiation Therapy Technology, Radiography, Rehabilitation Counseling, Social Work (B,M), Speech Pathology and Audiology, Teacher Education *(e,s,p)*. Pres. Joseph A. Steger.
Enroll.: 24,680
(513) 475-2201

CLERMONT GENERAL AND TECHNICAL COLLEGE
Batavia 45103. 1978/1982 (NCA). Qtr. plan. Degrees: A. Dean Roger J. Barry.

Enroll.: FTE 605
(513) 732-2990

RAYMOND WALTERS GENERAL AND TECHNICAL COLLEGE
Cincinnati 45236. 1969/1984 (NCA). Degrees: A. *Prof. Accred.:* Dental Hygiene, Nursing (A), Radiation Therapy Technology. Dean Ernest Gordon Muntz.
Enroll.: FTE 1,606
(513) 745-4301

UNIVERSITY OF DAYTON
300 College Park Ave., Dayton 45469. Private (Roman Catholic). 1928/1978 (NCA). Tri. plan. Degrees: A,B,M,D. *Prof. Accred.:* Business (B), Engineering (chemical, civil, electrical, mechanical), Engineering Technology (electronic, industrial, mechanical), Law, Music, Social Work(B), Teacher Education *(e,s,p)*. Pres. Brother Raymond L. Fitz, S.M.
Enroll.: FTE 8,739
(513) 229-4122

UNIVERSITY OF TOLEDO
Toledo 43606. Public (state). 1922/1983 (NCA). Qtr. plan. Degrees: A,B,P,M,D. *Prof. Accred.:* Business (B,M), Engineering (chemical, civil, electrical, engineering physics, industrial, mechanical), Engineering Technology (civil, drafting, electronic, industrial, mechanical) Law, Medical Assisting, Music, Nursing (A,B), Pharmacy, Psychology, Respiratory Therapy Technology, Teacher Education *(e,s,p)*. Pres. James D. McComas.
Enroll.: 15,789
(419) 537-2211

URBANA UNIVERSITY
Urbana 43078. Private (Swedenborgian) liberal arts. 1975/1985 (NCA). Sem. plan. Degrees: B. Pres. Paul G. Bunnell.
Enroll.: FTE 515
(513) 652-1301

URSULINE COLLEGE
2550 Lander Rd., Pepper Pike 44124. Private (Roman Catholic) liberal arts primarily for women. 1931/1986 (NCA). Sem. plan. Degrees: B,M. *Prof. Accred.:* Nurse Anesthesia Education, Nursing (B). Pres. Sister M. Kenan Dulzer.
Enroll.: FTE 1,085
(216) 449-4200

VIRGINIA MARTI SCHOOL OF FASHION AND ART
11724 Detroit Ave., INA Bldg., Lakewood 44107. Private. 1975/1980 (NATTS). Qtr. plan, courses of varying lengths. Degrees: A, certificates, diplomas. Dir. Virginia Marti.
Enroll.: 160 (*f.t.* 7 m., 64 w.)
(216) 221-8584

WALSH COLLEGE
Canton 44720. Private (Roman Catholic) liberal arts. 1970/1985 (NCA). Sem. plan. Degrees: B,M. *Prof. Accred.:* Nursing (A). Pres. Brother Francis Blouin, F.I.C.A
Enroll.: FTE 1,088
(216) 499-7090

WASHINGTON TECHNICAL COLLEGE
Marietta 45750. Public 2-year. 1979/1982 (NCA). Qtr. plan. Degrees: A. *Prof. Accred.:* Medical Laboratory Technology (A). Acting Pres. Carson K. Miller.
Enroll.: FTE 578
(614) 374-8716

WEST SIDE INSTITUTE OF TECHNOLOGY
9801 Walford Ave., Cleveland 44102. Private. 1969/1978 (NATTS). Qtr. plan. Degrees: A, certificates. Dir. Richard R. Pountney.
Enroll.: 541 (*f.t.* 277 m., 1 w.)
(216) 651-1656

WILBERFORCE UNIVERSITY
Wilberforce 45384. Private (African Methodist Episcopal) liberal arts college and seminary. 1939/1982 (NCA). Tri. plan. Degrees: B. Pres. Yvonne Walker-Taylor.
Enroll.: FTE 797
(513) 376-6661

WILMINGTON COLLEGE
Wilmington 45177. Private (Friends) liberal arts. 1944/1982 (NCA). Qtr. plan. Degrees: B. Pres. Neil A. Thorburn.
Enroll.: FTE 1,210
(513) 382-6661

WITTENBERG UNIVERSITY
Springfield 45501. Private (Lutheran in America). 1916/1977 (NCA). 3-3 plan. Degrees: B,P. *Prof. Accred.:* Music, Radiography, Teacher Education *(e,s,p)*, Theology. Pres. William A. Kinnison.
Enroll.: FTE 2,132
(513) 327-7916

WOOSTER BUSINESS COLLEGE
201 E. Liberty St., Wooster 44691. Private. 1986 (AICS). Courses of varying lengths. Certificates, diplomas. Pres. Steven K. Knox.
(216) 264-4110

WRIGHT STATE UNIVERSITY—CENTRAL OFFICE
7751 Col. Glenn Hwy., Dayton 45435. Public (state). Pres. Paige E. Mulhollan.
(513) 873-2310

WRIGHT STATE UNIVERSITY—MAIN CAMPUS
7751 Col. Glenn Hwy., Dayton 45435. Public (state) liberal arts and teachers. 1968/1986(NCA). Qtr. plan. Degrees: B,P,M,D. *Prof. Accred.:* Business (B,M), Engineering (computer, materials science and engineering, systems), Medical Technology, Medicine, Music, Nursing (B,M), Psychology, Social Work (B). Pres. Paige E. Mulhollan.
Enroll.: FTE 11,732
(513) 873-2310

WRIGHT STATE UNIVERSITY—LAKE CAMPUS
Celina 45822. Public junior. 1974/1982 (NCA). Qtr. plan. Degrees: A. Dean Donald A. Carlson.
Enroll.: FTE 519
(419) 586-2365

XAVIER UNIVERSITY
Dana Ave. and Victoria Pkwy., Cincinnati 45207., Private (Roman Catholic). Accreditation includes Edgecliff College; the Lexington, KY program; and the Columbus, OH program. 1925/1978 (NCA). Sem. plan. Degrees: A,B,M. *Prof. Accred.:* Health Services Administration, Nursing (B,M), Radiography, Social Work (B). Pres. Rev. Albert J. DiUlio, S.J.
Enroll.: FTE 3,930
(513) 745-3501

YOUNGSTOWN STATE UNIVERSITY
Youngstown 44555. Public (state). 1945/1978 (NCA). Qtr. plan. Degrees: A,B,M. *Prof. Accred.:* Dental Hygiene, Dietetics, Engineering (chemical, civil, electrical, materials science, mechanical), Medical Laboratory Technology (A), Music, Nursing (A,B), Respiratory Therapy, Teacher Education *(e,s)*. Pres. Neil D. Humphrey.
Enroll.: FTE 11,203
(216) 742-3101

OKLAHOMA

AAA WELDING SCHOOL, INC.
9363 E. 46th St., S., Tulsa 74145. Private. 1982 (NATTS). Courses of varying lengths. Certificates. Vice Pres. Frances A. Sells.
(918) 627-2699

ACADEMY OF HAIR DESIGN
3420 South Sunnylane, P.O. Box 15157, Del City 73115. Private. 1981 (NATTS). Sem. plan. Certificates, diplomas. Pres. Gene Beavers.
Enroll.: 20 (*f.t.* 5 m., 15 w.)
(405) 677-8311

BACONE COLLEGE
Muskogee 74401. Private (American Baptist) junior. 1965/1983 (NCA). Sem. plan. Degrees: A. *Prof. Accred.:* Nursing (A), Radiography. Pres. Alfred O. Ginkel.
Enroll.: FTE 421
(918) 683-4581

BARTLESVILLE WESLEYAN COLLEGE
Bartlesville 74003. Private (Western Zone of the Wesleyan Church) liberal arts . 1978/1983 (NCA). Sem. plan. Degrees: B. Pres. Paul R. Mills.
Enroll.: FTE 355
(918) 333-6151

BETHANY NAZARENE COLLEGE
Bethany 73008. Private (Nazarene) liberal arts. 1956/1985 (NCA). Sem. plan. Degrees: B,M. *Prof. Accred.:* Teacher Education (*e,s*). Pres. Ponder Gilliand.
Enroll.: FTE 970
(405) 789-6400

BRYAN INSTITUTE
2843 E. 51st St., Tulsa 74105. Private. 1974/1979 (NATTS). Courses of varying lengths. Diplomas. *Prof. Accred.:* Medical Assisting. Dir. Ed Gough.
Enroll.: 305 (*f.t.* 140 m., 165 w.)
(918) 749-6891

CAMERON UNIVERSITY
2800 Gore Blvd., Lawton 73505. Public (state) liberal arts and professional. 1973/1984 (NCA). Sem. plan. Degrees: A,B. *Prof. Accred.:* Music, Nursing (A). Pres. Don Davis.
Enroll.: FTE 3,607
(405) 248-2200

CARL ALBERT JUNIOR COLLEGE
Poteau 74953. Public (state) 2-year. 1978 (NCA). Sem. plan. Degrees: A. *Prof. Accred.:* Nursing (A). Pres. Joe E. White.
Enroll.: FTE 1,015
(918) 647-8660

CENTRAL STATE UNIVERSITY
Edmond 73034. Public liberal arts and teachers. 1921/1986(NCA). Sem. plan. Degrees: B,M. *Prof. Accred.:* Nursing (B), Teacher Education (*e,s*). Pres. William J. Lillard.
Enroll.: FTE 8,684
(405) 341-2980

CLIMATE CONTROL INSTITUTE, INC.
708 S. Sheridan St., Tulsa 74112. Private. 1978 (NATTS). Qtr. plan. Certificates. Dir. Lawrence R. Gregory.
Enroll.: 93 (*f.t.* 90 m., 3 w.)
(918) 836-6656

CONNORS STATE COLLEGE
Warner 74469. Public junior. 1963/1985 (NCA). Sem. plan. Degrees: A. Pres. Carl O. Westbrook.
Enroll.: FTE 1,105
(918) 463-2931

DRAUGHON SCHOOL OF BUSINESS
4610 S. May, Oklahoma City 73119. Private. 1960/1980 (AICS). Qtr. plan. Certificates, diplomas. Dir. Richard A. McNeil.
Enroll.: 881 (*f.t.* 142 m., 739 w.)
(405) 682-4626

EAST CENTRAL UNIVERSITY
Ada 74820. Public liberal arts and teachers. 1922/1982 (NCA). Sem. plan. Degrees: B,M. *Prof. Accred.:* Medical Record Administration, Nursing (B), Teacher Education (*e,s*). Pres. Stanley P. Wagner.
Enroll.: FTE 3,448
(405) 332-8000

EASTERN OKLAHOMA STATE COLLEGE
Wilburton 74578. Public junior. 1954/1976 (NCA). Sem. plan. Degrees: A. *Prof. Accred.:* Nursing (A). Pres. James M. Miller.
Enroll.: FTE 1,381
(918) 465-2132

EL RENO JUNIOR COLLEGE
El Reno 73036. Public (state) 2-year. 1978/1983 (NCA). Sem. plan. Degrees: A. *Prof. Accred.:* Nursing (A). Pres. Bill S. Cole.
Enroll.: FTE 784
(405) 262-2552

FLAMING RAINBOW UNIVERSITY
419 N. Second St., Stilwell 74960. Private. 1985 (NCA). Sem. plan. Degrees: B. Pres. Dan Goehring.

Enroll.: FTE 193
(918) 696-3644

LANGSTON UNIVERSITY
Langston 73050. Public (state) liberal arts and professional college. 1948/1977 (NCA). Sem. plan. Degrees: A,B. *Prof. Accred.:* Teacher Education (*e,s*). Pres. Ernest L. Holloway.
Enroll.: FTE 1,367
(405) 466-2231

MID-AMERICA BIBLE COLLEGE
3500 S.W. 119th St., Oklahoma City 73170-9797. Private (Church of God) professional. 1968/1979 (AABC); 1985 (NCA). Sem. plan. Degrees: B. Pres. John W. Conley.
Enroll.: 249
(405) 691-3800

MURRAY STATE COLLEGE
Tishomingo 73460. Public junior. 1964/1984 (NCA). Sem. plan. Degrees: A. *Prof. Accred.:* Nursing (A). Pres. Clyde R. Kindell.
Enroll.: FTE 827
(405) 371-3500

NATIONAL COLLEGE OF TECHNOLOGY
3020 N. Stiles Rd., Oklahoma City 73105. 1984 (NATTS). Courses of varying lengths. Degrees: A, certificates, diplomas. Dir. Truman G. Smith.
(405) 528-2731

NATIONAL EDUCATION CENTER/SPARTAN SCHOOL OF AERONAUTICS CAMPUS
8820 E. Pine St., P.O. Box 582833, Tulsa 74151-2833. 1969/1981 (NATTS). Courses of varying lengths. Degrees: A, certificates, diplomas. Pres. Kenneth L. Tallman.
Enroll.: 2,050 (*f.t.* 1,408 m., 14 w.)
(918) 836-6886

NORTHEASTERN OKLAHOMA A & M COLLEGE
Miami 74354. Public (state) junior. 1925/1977 (NCA). Sem. plan. Degrees: A. *Prof. Accred.:* Medical Laboratory Technology (A), Nursing (A). Pres. Bobby R. Wright.
Enroll.: FTE 2,291
(918) 542-8441

NORTHEASTERN STATE UNIVERSITY
Tahlequah 74464. Public liberal arts and teachers. 1922/1982 (NCA). Sem. plan. Degrees: B,M. *Prof. Accred.:* Nursing (B), Optometry, Teacher Education (*e,s*). Pres. W. Roger Webb.
Enroll.: FTE 5,928
(918) 456-5511

NORTHERN OKLAHOMA COLLEGE
Tonkawa 74653. Public (state) junior. 1948/1978 (NCA). Sem. plan. Degrees: A. *Prof. Accred.:* Nursing (A). Pres. Edwin E. Vineyard.
Enroll.: FTE 1,148
(405) 628-2581

NORTHWESTERN OKLAHOMA STATE UNIVERSITY
Alva 73717. Public liberal arts and teachers. 1922/1984 (NCA). Sem. plan. Degrees: B,M. *Prof. Accred.:* Teacher Education (*e,s*). Pres. Joe J. Struckle.
Enroll.: FTE 1,550
(405) 327-1700

OKLAHOMA BAPTIST UNIVERSITY
Shawnee 74801. Private (Southern Baptist) liberal arts and professional college. 1952/1978 (NCA). 4-1-4 plan. Degrees: B. *Prof. Accred.:* Music, Nursing (B), Teacher Education (*e,s*). Pres. Bob R. Agee.
Enroll.: 1,321
(405) 275-2850

OKLAHOMA CHRISTIAN COLLEGE
Oklahoma City 73111. Private (Church of Christ) liberal arts. 1966/1986 (NCA). Tri. plan. Degrees: B. *Prof. Accred.:* Teacher Education (*e,s*). Pres. J. Terry Johnson.
Enroll.: FTE 1,483
(405) 478-1661

OKLAHOMA CITY COMMUNITY COLLEGE
Oklahoma City 73159. Public (district). 1977/1982 (NCA). 4-1-4 plan. Degrees: A. *Prof. Accred.:* Nursing (A). Pres. Donald L. Newport
Enroll.: FTE 2,972
(405) 682-7503

OKLAHOMA CITY UNIVERSITY
2501 N. Blackwelder, Oklahoma City 73106. Private (United Methodist). 1951/1983 (NCA). Sem. plan. Degrees: B,P,M. *Prof. Accred.:* Law (ABA only), Music. Pres. Jerald C. Walker.
Enroll.: FTE 2,293
(405) 521-5032

OKLAHOMA COLLEGE OF OSTEOPATHIC MEDICINE AND SURGERY
P.O. Box 2280, Tulsa 74101. Private professional. 1975. Tri. plan. Degrees: P. *Prof.*

Accred.: Osteopathy. Pres. Rodney T. Houlihan.
Enroll.: 259 (*f.t.* 182 m., 77 w.)
(918) 582-1972

OKLAHOMA FARRIERS' COLLEGE
Route 2, Box 88, Sperry 74073. Private. 1980 (NATTS). Courses of varying lengths. Diplomas. Pres. Bud Beaston.
Enroll.: 308 (*f.t.* 300 m., 8 w.)
(918) 288-7221

OKLAHOMA INSTITUTE OF HAIR DESIGN
5808 N.W. 36th, Oklahoma City 73122. Private. 1985 (NATTS). Courses of varying lengths. Certificates. Dir. Manly E. Jones.
(405) 946-2297

*OKLAHOMA JUNIOR COLLEGE
4821 S. 72nd East Ave., Tulsa 74145. Private. 1953/1980 (AICS). Tri. plan. Degrees: A, certificates. *Prof. Accred.:* Medical Assisting. Pres. David L. Stephenson.
Enroll.: 1,481 (*f.t.* 678 m., 803 w.)
(918) 663-9500

BRANCH CAMPUS
3232 Northwest 65th, Oklahoma City 73116. Dir. Jimmy Addison.
(405) 848-3400

OKLAHOMA PANHANDLE STATE UNIVERSITY
Goodwell 73939. Public liberal arts, teachers, technological. 1926/1985 (NCA). Sem. plan. Degrees: B. *Prof. Accred.:* Teacher Education (*e,s*). Pres. Thomas L. Palmer.
Enroll.: FTE 1,014
(405) 349-2610

OKLAHOMA STATE UNIVERSITY
Central administration, Stillwater 74078. Public. Pres. Lawrence L. Boger.
(405) 624-6384

OKLAHOMA STATE UNIVERSITY—MAIN CAMPUS
Stillwater 74078. Public. 1916/1976 (NCA). Sem. plan. Degrees: A,B,P,M,D. *Prof. Accred.:* Accounting (Type A,C), Architecture (M), Business (B,M), Dietetics, Engineering (aerospace, agricultural, architectural, chemical, civil, electrical, general, industrial, mechanical), Engineering Technology (construction management, electrical power, electronics, fire protection and safety, manufacturing, mechanical design, mechanical power, petroleum), Forestry, Home Economics, Interior Design, Journalism, Landscape Architecture (B), Music, Nursing (A) (Oklahoma City), Psychology, Rehabilitation Counseling, Speech Pathology, Teacher Education (*e,s,p*), Veterinary Medicine. Pres. Lawrence L. Boger.
Enroll.: FTE 18,167
(405) 624-6384

OKLAHOMA STATE UNIVERSITY—TECHNICAL BRANCH, OKLAHOMA CITY
Oklahoma City 73107. 1975/1985(NCA). Degrees: A. *Prof. Accred.:* Nursing (A). Dir. James E. Hooper.
Enroll.: FTE 1,467
(405) 947-4421

OKLAHOMA STATE UNIVERSITY—TECHNICAL BRANCH, OKMULGEE
Okmulgee 74447. 1975/1985(NCA). Degrees: A, certificates, diplomas. Dir. Robert Klabenes.
Enroll.: FTE 2,379
(918) 756-6211

ORAL ROBERTS UNIVERSITY
Tulsa 74171. Private liberal arts and professional. 1971/1981 (NCA). Sem. plan. Degrees: B,P,M,D. *Prof. Accred.:* Dentistry, Law (ABA only), Medicine, Music, Nursing (B,M), Social Work (B), Theology. Pres. G. Oral Roberts.
Enroll.: FTE 4,722
(918) 495-7349

PHILLIPS UNIVERSITY
Enid 73701. Private (Christian Church, Disciples of Christ). 1919/1978 (NCA). Sem. plan. Degrees: B,P,M. *Prof. Accred.:* Music, Teacher Education (*e,s*), Theology. Pres. Joe R. Jones.
Enroll.: FTE 804
(405) 237-4433

PLATT COLLEGE
3015 E. Skelley Dr., Suite 102, Tulsa 74105. Private. 1985 (NATTS). Courses of varying lengths. Certificates. Dir. George F. Gillard.
(918) 747-8057

ROGERS STATE COLLEGE
Claremore 74017. Public (state) junior. 1950/1980 (NCA). Sem. plan. Degrees: A. *Prof. Accred.:* Nursing (A). Pres. Richard H. Mosier
Enroll.: FTE 1,962
(918) 341-7510

*Candidate for Accreditation by Regional Accrediting Commission

Rose State College
Midwest City 73110. Public (state). 1975/1978 (NCA). Sem. plan. Degrees: A. *Prof. Accred.:* Dental Assisting, Dental Hygiene, Dental Laboratory Technology, Histologic Technology, Medical Laboratory Technology (A), Radiography, Respiratory Therapy, Respiratory Therapy Technology. Pres. Larry Nutter.
Enroll.: FTE 5,115
(405) 733-7311

St. Gregory's College
Shawnee 74801. Private (Roman Catholic) junior. 1969/1979 (NCA). Sem. plan. Degrees: A. Pres. Michael Roethler, O.S.B.
Enroll.: FTE 304
(405) 273-9870

Sayre Junior College
Sayre 73662. Private 2-year. 1971/1983 (ABHES). Degrees: A. *Prof. Accred.:* Medical Laboratory Technology. Dean Paul E. Conner.
Enroll.: 389 (*f.t.* 73 m., 115 w.)
(405) 928-5533

Seminole Junior College
Seminole 74868. Public (city). 1975/1980 (NCA). Tri. plan. Degrees: A. *Prof. Accred.:* Medical Laboratory Technology, Nursing (A). Pres. Gregory Fitch.
Enroll.: FTE 917
(405) 382-9950

Sooner Mechanical Trade School
1100 W. Main St., Oklahoma City 73106. Private. 1968/1979 (NATTS). Courses of varying lengths. Diplomas. Pres. Bob M. Culver.
Enroll.: 168 (*f.t.* 163 m., 5 w.)
(405) 235-8683

Southeastern Oklahoma State University
Durant 74701. Public liberal arts and teachers. 1922/1984 (NCA). Sem. plan. Degrees: B,M. *Prof. Accred.:* Music, Teacher Education (*e,s*). Pres. Leon Hibbs.
Enroll.: 3,045
(405) 924-0121

Southwest Technical College
1520 South Central, Oklahoma City 73129. Private. 1967/1977 (NATTS). Courses of varying lengths. Diplomas. Dir. George T. Elliott.
Enroll.: 250 (*f.t.* 196 m., 24 w.)
(405) 732-7785

Southwestern College of Christian Ministries
P.O. Box 340, Bethany 73008. Private (Pentecostal Holiness) liberal arts. 1973/1985 (NCA). Sem. plan. Degrees: A,B. Pres. Frank G. Tunstall
Enroll.: FTE 72
(405) 789-7661

Southwestern Oklahoma State University
Weatherford 73096. Public liberal arts and professional. 1922/1981 (NCA). Sem. plan. Degrees: B,M. *Prof. Accred.:* Medical Record Administration, Music, Nursing (B), Pharmacy, Teacher Education (*e,s*). Pres. Leonard G. Campbell.
Enroll.: FTE 4,372
(405) 772-6611

State Barber College
2514 S. Agnew, Oklahoma City 73108. Private. 1979 (NATTS). Courses of varying lengths. Diplomas. Pres. Bobby Lewis. *Enroll.:* *f.t.* 32 m.
(405) 631-8621

Tri-County Area Vocational-Technical School
6101 Nowata Rd., Box 3428, East Side Sta., Bartlesville 74006. Public practical nursing program. 1982. 12-month program. Diplomas. *Prof. Accred.:* Practical Nursing. Dir. Maxine Moulton.
(918) 333-2422

Tulsa Barber College
1314 East Third St., Tulsa 74120. Private. 1985 (NATTS). Courses of varying lengths. Certificates. Dir. Manly E. Jones.
(918) 599-0803

Tulsa Junior College
Tulsa 74135. Public (state). Accreditation includes both Metropolitan and Northeast Campuses. 1974/1983 (NCA). Sem. plan. Degrees: A. *Prof. Accred.:* Medical Assisting, Medical Laboratory Technology (A), Nursing (A), Radiography, Respiratory Therapy, Respiratory Therapy Technology. Pres. Alfred M. Philips.
Enroll.: FTE 6,270
(918) 664-5622

Tulsa Welding School
3038 Southwest Blvd., P.O. Box 9829, Tulsa 74107. Private. 1970/1980 (NATTS). Courses of varying lengths. Diplomas. Pres. Noel E. Adams.

Oklahoma

Enroll.: 229 (*f.t.* 226 m., 3 w.)
(918) 587-6789

UNITED ELECTRONICS INSTITUTE
3020 N. Stiles Ave., Oklahoma City 73105. Private. 1970/1980 (NATTS). Courses of varying lengths. Diplomas. Dir. Truman J. Smith.
Enroll.: 325 (*f.t.* 250 m., 75 w.)
(405) 528-2731

U.S. COAST GUARD INSTITUTE
P.O. Substation 18, Oklahoma City 73169. Public (federal) home study. 1981 (NHSC). Commander: Capt. Robert W. Davis.
(405) 686-4262

UNITED TECHNICAL INSTITUTE, INC.
4533 Enterprise Dr., Oklahoma City 73128. Private. 1979 (NATTS). Courses of varying lengths. Certificates, diplomas. *Prof. Accred.:* Medical Assisting, Medical Laboratory Technology. Pres. R. P. Cropper.
Enroll.: 125 (*f.t.* 95 m., 30 w.)
(405) 942-7700

UNIVERSITY OF OKLAHOMA
Norman 73069. Public (state). Accreditation includes Medical Center at Oklahoma City. 1913/1982 (NCA). Sem. plan. Degrees: A,B,P,M,D. *Prof. Accred.:* Accounting (Type A,C), Architecture (B,M), Assistant to the Primary Care Physician, Business (B,M), Cytotechnology, Dental Hygiene, Dentistry, Diagnostic Medical Sonographer, Dietetics, Engineering (aerospace, chemical, civil, electrical, engineering physics, industrial, mechanical, petroleum), Health Administration, Journalism, Law, Librarianship, Medical Technology, Medicine, Music, Nuclear Medicine Technology, Nursing (B), Occupational Therapy, Pharmacy, Physical Therapy, Psychology, Radiation Therapy, Radiography, Social Work (B,M), Speech Pathology and Audiology, Teacher Education (*e,s,p*). Pres. Frank E. Horton.
Enroll.: FTE 18,899
(405) 325-3916

UNIVERSITY OF SCIENCE AND ARTS OF OKLAHOMA
Chickasha 73018. Public (state) liberal arts and teachers. 1920/1983 (NCA). Tri. plan. Degrees: B. *Prof. Accred.:* Music, Teacher Education (*e,s,p*). Pres. Roy Troutt.
Enroll.: FTE 865
(405) 224-3140

UNIVERSITY OF TULSA
600 S. College, Tulsa 74104. Private (United Presbyterian). 1929/1978 (NCA). 4-1-4 plan. Degrees: A,B,P,M,D. *Prof. Accred.:* Business (B,M), Engineering (chemical, electrical, engineering physics, mechanical, petroleum), Law, Music, Nursing (B), Teacher Education (*e,s,p*). Pres. J. Paschal Twyman.
Enroll.: FTE 4,437
(918) 592-6000

WESTERN OKLAHOMA STATE COLLEGE
Altus 73521. Public (state) junior. 1976/1981 (NCA). Sem. plan. Degrees: A. Pres. W. C. Burris.
Enroll.: FTE 1,003
(405) 477-2000

OREGON

Apollo Collegeof Medical and Dental Careers Branch
2025 Lloyd Center, Portland 97232. Private. 1985 (ABHES). 7-month program. Certificates. *Prof. Accred.:* Medical Assisting. Pres. Margaret M. Carlson.
(503) 288-4400

Bassist College
2000 S.W. Fifth Ave., Portland 97201. Private 2-year technical. 1977/1982 (NASC). Qtr. plan. Degrees: A. Pres. Donald H. Bassist.
Enroll.: 223
(503) 228-6528

Blue Mountain Community College
Pendleton 97801. Public (district) junior. 1968/1984 (NASC). Qtr. plan. Degrees: A. *Prof. Accred.:* Dental Assisting, Engineering Technology (civil, electronic). Pres. Ronald L. Daniels.
Enroll.: 2,290
(503) 276-1260

Bradford School
921 S.W. Washington St., Suite 200, Portland 97205. Private. 1980/1986 (ABHES); 1985 (NATTS). Qtr. plan, courses of varying lengths. Certificates. *Prof. Accred.:* Medical Assisting. Dir. Richard Leesman.
Enroll.: 235 (*f.t.* 43 m., 192 w.)
(503) 222-3801

Central Oregon Community College
Bend 99701-5998. Public (district) junior. 1966/1982 (NASC). Qtr. plan. Degrees: A. *Prof. A ccred.:* Medical Record Technology. Pres. Frederick H. Boyle.
Enroll.: 2,067
(503) 385-5517

Chemeketa Community College
P.O. Box 14007, Salem 97309. Public (district) junior. 1972/1977 (NASC). Qtr. plan. Degrees: A. *Prof. Accred.:* Dental Assisting, Medical Assistant, Nursing (A). Pres. William Segura.
Enroll.: 9,700
(503) 399-5121

Clackamas Community College
Oregon City 97045. Public (district) junior. 1971/1986 (NASC). Qtr. plan. Degrees: A. Pres. John S. Keyser.
Enroll.: 5,154
(503) 657-8400

Clatsop Community College
Astoria 97103. Public (district) junior. 1965/1981 (NASC). Qtr. plan. Degrees: A. Pres. Philip L. Bainer.
Enroll.: 2,465
(503) 325-0910

Columbia Christian College
9101 E. Burnside, Portland 97216-1515. Private (Church of Christ) liberal arts. 1975/1980 (NASC). Sem. plan. Degrees: B. Pres. Gary D. Elliott.
Enroll.: 270
(503) 257-1365

Commercial Driver Training
2416 N. Marine Dr., Portland 97217. Private. 1973/1985 (NATTS). Courses of varying lengths. Certificates. Pres. Clifford Georgioff.
Enroll.: 37 (*f.t.* 32 m., 5 w.)
(503) 285-7542

Computer Career Institute
2104 S.W. Fifth Ave., Portland 97201. Private. 1969/1979 (NATTS). Courses of varying lengths. Certificates. Dir. Walter Peterson.
Enroll.: 220 (*f.t.* 72 m., 48 w.)
(503) 226-1241

Concordia College
2811 N.E. Holman St., Portland 97211. Private (Lutheran-Missouri Synod) liberal arts including business, education, and church professions. 1962/1981 (NASC). Qtr. plan. Degrees: A,B. Pres. Charles E. Schlimpert.
Enroll.: 481
(503) 288-9371

Court Reporting Institute
520 S.W. Sixth Ave., Suite 908, Portland 97204. Private. 1978/1984 (AICS). Courses of varying lengths. Certificates, diplomas. Dir. Billy P. Ellis.
Enroll.: 190 (*f.t.* 15 m., 175 w.)
(503) 223-5100

*Eastern Oregon State College
La Grande 97850. Public (state) liberal arts and teachers. 1931/1978 (NASC). Qtr. plan. Degrees: A,B,M. *Prof. Accred.:* Teacher Education *(e,s)*. Pres. David E, Gilbert.

*Member Oregon State Higher Education System

Enroll.: 1,532
(503) 963-2171

Eugene Bible College
2155 Bailey Hill Rd., Eugene 97405. Private (Open Bible Standard) professional. 1983 (AABC). Sem. plan. Degrees: B. Pres. Donald R. Bryan.
Enroll.: 120
(503) 485-1780

George Fox College
Newberg 97132. Private (Friends) liberal arts. 1959/1980 (NASC). Sem. plan. Degrees: B. *Prof. Accred.:* Music. Pres. Edward F. Stevens.
Enroll.: 699
(503) 538-8383

ITT Technical Institute
10822 S.E. Bush St., Portland 97266. Private. 1973/1983 (NATTS). Qtr. plan. Degrees: A,B, diplomas. Dir. Coy D. Ritchie.
Enroll.: 830 (*f.t.* 770 m., 60 w.)
(503) 760-5690

La Grande College of Business
Hwy. 82 N., La Grande 97850. Private. 1979/1982 (AICS). Courses of varying lengths. Certificates. Pres. Ronald L. Vincent.
Enroll.: 64 (*f.t.* 2 m., 62 w.)
(503) 963-6485

Lane Community College
Eugene 97405. Public (district) junior. 1968/1984 (NASC). Qtr. plan. Degrees: A. *Prof. Accred.:* Dental Assisting, Dental Hygiene, Nursing (A), Respiratory Therapy. Pres. Richard M. Turner, III.
Enroll.: 14,141
(503) 747-4501

Lewis and Clark College
0615 S.W. Palatine Hill Rd., Portland 97219. Private (United Presbyterian) liberal arts. 1943/1976 (NASC). Qtr. plan. Degrees: B,P,M. *Prof. Accred.:* Law, Music, Teacher Education (*e,s*). Pres. James A. Gardner.
Enroll.: 2,160
(503) 293-2650

Linfield College
McMinnville 97128. Private (American Baptist) liberal arts. 1928/1978 (NASC). 4-1-4 plan. Degrees: B,M. *Prof. Accred.:* Music. Pres. Charles U. Walker.
Enroll.: 1,800
(503) 472-4121

Linn-Benton Community College
Albany 97321. Public (district) junior. 1972/1977 (NASC). Qtr. plan. Degrees: A. *Prof. Accred.:* Dental Assisting, Nursing (A). Pres. Thomas Gonzales.
Enroll.: 10,831
(503) 967-6100

Marylhurst College for Lifelong Learning
Marylhurst 97036. Private (Roman Catholic) liberal arts. 1977/1986 (NASC). Qtr. plan. Degrees: B,M. *Prof. Accred.:* Music. Pres. Nancy A. Wilgenbusch.
Enroll.: 1,145
(503) 636-8141

Merritt Davis Business College
78 Centennial Loop, Suite F, Eugene 97401. Private. 1974/1985 (AICS). Courses of varying lengths. Diplomas. Dir. Maureen Gharrity.
Enroll.: 508 (*f.t.* 72 m., 436 w.)
(503) 342-5377

Merritt Davis College of Business
210 S.E. Liberty, Salem 97301. Private. 1970/1980 (AICS). Courses of varying lengths. Certificates. Dir. Pam Hartsoch.
Enroll.: 393 (*f.t.* 81 m., 312 w.)
(503) 581-1476

Branch Campus
400 Earhart St., Medford 97501. Dir. Terry Stauffer.
(503) 779-5581

Mount Angel Seminary
St. Benedict 97373. Private (Roman Catholic). 1929/1977 (NASC). Sem. plan. Degrees: B,M. *Prof. Accred.:* Theology (1978/1985, ATS). Pres. Rev. J. Terrence Fitzgerald.
Enroll.: 107
(503) 845-3243

Mount Hood Community College
26,000 S.E. Stark St., Gresham 97030. Public (district) junior. 1972/1977 (NASC). Qtr. plan. Degrees: A. *Prof. Accred.:* Dental Hygiene, Nursing (A), Respiratory Therapy, Surgical Technology. Pres. Paul E. Kreider.
Enroll.: 6,313
(503) 667-7211

Multnomah School of the Bible
8435 N.E. Glisan St., Portland 97220. Private (Interdenominational) professional. 1953/1983 (AABC). Sem. plan. Degrees: B. Pres. Joseph C. Aldrich.

Enroll.: 597
(503) 255-0332

Northwest Christian College
Eugene 97401. Private (Disciples of Christ) liberal arts and training for church service. 1962/1980 (NASC). Qtr. plan. Degrees: A,B. Pres. James E. Womack.
Enroll.: 255
(503) 343-1641

Northwest Schools
1221 N.W. 21st Ave., Portland 97209. Private home study. 1984 (NHSC). Pres. William A. Sawyer.
(503) 226-4811

Northwestern College of Business
1950 S.W. Sixth Ave., Portland 97201. Private. 1966/1983 (AICS). Qtr. plan. Certificates, diplomas. Dir. Letitia T. Underhill.
Enroll.: 635 (*f.t.* 93 m., 542 w.)
(503) 224-6410

Oregon Graduate Center
19600 N.W. Von Neuman Dr., Beaverton 97006-1999. Private; graduate only. 1973/1978 (NASC). Qtr. plan. Degrees: M,D. Pres. Stephen Kahne.
Enroll.: 243
(503) 690-1020

Oregon Polytechnic Institute
900 S.E. Sandy Blvd., Portland 97214. Private. 1974/1981 (NATTS). Qtr. plan. Degrees: A. Pres. E. L. Yakimchick.
Enroll.: 108 (*f.t.* 82 m., 11 w.)
(503) 234-9333

Oregon State Higher Education System Office
P.O. Box 3175, Eugene 97403-0175. Public (state). Chanc. William E. Davis.
(503) 686-4141

Oregon Health Sciences University
3181 S.W. Sam Jackson Park. Portland 97201. Public (state) professional. 1980/1985 (NASC). Degrees: A,B,P,M,D. *Prof. Accred.:* Cytotechnology, Dental Hygiene, Dentistry, Medical Technology, Medicine, Radiation Therapy Technology. Pres. Leonard Laster.
Enroll.: 1,226
(503) 225-8311

Oregon Institute of Technology
Klamath Falls 97601-8801. Public (state) technological. 1962/1982 (NASC). Qtr. plan. Degrees: A,B. *Prof. Accred.:* Dental Hygiene, Engineering Technology (civil-construction-public works, structural options; computer systems; electronics; engineering drafting; mechanical; public works; structural; surveying), Medical Technology, Radiography. Pres. Larry J. Blake.
Enroll.: 2,807
(503) 882-6321

Oregon State University
Corvallis 97331. Public. 1924/1980 (NASC). Qtr. plan. Degrees: B,P,M,D. *Prof. Accred.:* Accounting (Type A), Business (B,M), Construction Education, Engineering (agricultural, chemical, civil, electrical and computer, industrial, mechanical, nuclear), Engineering Technology (nuclear), Forestry, Home Economics, Journalism, Music, Pharmacy, Teacher Education (*e,s,p*). Pres. John V. Byrne.
Enroll.: 15,379
(503) 754-0123

Pacific Northwest College of Art
1219 S.W. Park Ave., Portland 97205. Private professional. 1961/1981 (NASC). Sem. plan. Degrees: B. *Prof. Accred.:* Art. Dir. Sally C. Lawrence.
Enroll.: 197
(503) 226-4391

Pacific University
Forest Grove 97116. Private (United Church of Christ). 1929/1977 (NASC). Sem. plan. Degrees: B,P.M,D. *Prof. Accred.:* Music, Optometry, Physical Therapy. Pres. Robert F. Duvall.
Enroll.: 1,136
(503) 357-6151

Portland Community College
12000 S.W. 49th St., Portland 97219. Public (district) junior. 1970/1985 (NASC). Qtr. plan. Degrees: A. *Prof. Accred.:* Dental Assisting, Dental Hygiene, Dental Laboratory Technology, Engineering Technology (electronic), Medical Assisting, Medical Laboratory Technology (A), Medical Record Technology, Nursing (A), Radiography. Pres. Daniel J. Moriarity
Enroll.: 19,135
(503) 244-6111

*Portland State University
P.O. Box 751, Portland 97207. Public. 1955/1985 (NASC). Qtr. plan. Degrees: B,M,D. *Prof. Accred.:* Business (B,M), Engineering

*Member Oregon State Higher Education System

(civil, electrical, mechanical), Music, Social Work (B,M), Speech Pathology and Audiology, Teacher Education (*e,s,p*). Pres. Natalie Sicuro.
Enroll.: 14,768
(503) 229-4433

REED COLLEGE
3203 S.E. Woodstock Blvd., Portland 97202. Private liberal arts. 1920/1978 (NASC). Sem. plan. Degrees: B,M . *Prof. Accred.:* Teacher Education (*s*). Pres. Paul E. Bragdon.
Enroll.: 1,072
(503) 771-1112

ROGUE COMMUNITY COLLEGE
Grants Pass 97527. Public (district) junior. 1976/1981 (NASC). Qtr. plan. Degrees: A. *Prof. Accred.:* Respiratory Therapy. Acting Pres. Harvey Bennett.
Enroll.: 4,489
(503) 479-5541

*SOUTHERN OREGON STATE COLLEGE
Ashland 97520. Public (state) liberal arts and teachers. 1928/1977 (NASC). Qtr. plan. Degrees: B,M. *Prof. Accred.:* Chemistry, Music, Nursing (A,B), Teacher Education (*e,s*). Pres. Natale A. Sicuro.
Enroll.: 4,587
(503) 482-6111

SOUTHWESTERN OREGON COMMUNITY COLLEGE
Coos Bay 97420. Public (district) junior. 1966/1982 (NASC). Qtr. plan. Degrees: A. Pres. Robert L. Barber.
Enroll.: 3,747
(503) 888-3234

TREASURE VALLEY COMMUNITY COLLEGE
Ontario 97914. Public (district) junior. 1966/1980 (NASC). Qtr. plan. Degrees: A. Pres. Glenn E. Mayle.
Enroll.: 1,532
(503) 889-6493

UMPQUA COMMUNITY COLLEGE
Roseburg 97470. Public (district) junior. 1970/1985 (NASC). Qtr. plan. Degrees: A. Pres. James M. Kraby.
Enroll.: 1,980
(503) 440-4600

*UNIVERSITY OF OREGON
Eugene 97403. Public (state). 1918/1977 (NASC). Qtr. plan. Degrees: B,P,M,D. *Prof. Accred.:* Architecture (B,M), Business (B,M), Dietetics, Interior Design, Journalism, Landscape Architecture (B), Law, Music, Nursing (B,M), Psychology, Teacher Education (*e,s,p*). Pres. Paul Olum.
Enroll.: 16,375
(503) 686-3036

UNIVERSITY OF PORTLAND
5000 N. Willamette Blvd., Portland 97203. Private. 1931/1980 (NASC). Sem. plan. Degrees: B,M. *Prof. Accred.:* Business (B,M), Engineering (civil, electrical, mechanical), Nursing (B,M), Teacher Education (*e,s,p*). Pres. Rev. Thomas C. Oddo, CSC.
Enroll.: 2,792
(503) 283-7911

WARNER PACIFIC COLLEGE
2219 S.E. 68th Ave., Portland 97215. Private (Church of God) liberal arts. 1961/1982 (NASC). Qtr. plan. Degrees: A,B,M. Pres. Marshall K. Christensen.
Enroll.: 392
(503) 775-4368

WESTERN BAPTIST COLLEGE
5000 Deer Park Dr., S.E., Salem 97301. Private (Regular Baptist) liberal arts and professional. 1959/1980 (AABC); 1971/1976 (NASC). Qtr. plan. Degrees: A,B. Pres. John G. Balyo.
Enroll.: 260
(503) 581-8600

WESTERN BUSINESS COLLEGE
505 S.W. Sixth Ave., Portland 97204 . Private. 1969/1981 (AICS). Qtr. plan. Diplomas. Pres. Donald H. Waldbauer.
Enroll.: 1,509 (*f.t.* 460 m., 1,049 w.)
(503) 222-3225

BRANCH CAMPUS
6625 E. Mill Plain Blvd., Vancouver, WA 98661. Pres. Donald H. Waldbauer.
(206) 694-3225

WESTERN CONSERVATIVE BAPTIST SEMINARY
5511 S.E. Hawthorne Blvd., Portland 97215. Private (Conservative Baptist), first professional and graduate. 1969/1983 (NASC). Sem. plan. Degrees: P,M,D. Pres. Earl D. Radmacher.
Enroll.: 588
(503) 233-8561

WESTERN EVANGELICAL SEMINARY
Portland 97267. Private (Interdenominational) professional; graduate only. 1976/1981

*Member Oregon State Higher Education System

(NASC). Qtr. plan. Degrees: P,M. *Prof. Accred.:* Theology (1974/1981, ATS). Pres. Leo M. Thornton.
Enroll.: 185
(503) 654-5466

*WESTERN OREGON STATE COLLEGE
Monmouth 97361. Public (state) teacher. 1924/1978 (NASC). Qtr. plan. Degrees: A,B,M. *Prof. Accred.:* Music, Rehabilitation Counseling, Teacher Education (*e,s*). Pres. Richard S. Meyers.
Enroll.: 4,180
(503) 838-1220

*Member Oregon State Higher Education System

†WESTERN STATES CHIROPRACTIC COLLEGE
2900 N.E. 132nd Ave., Portland 97230. Private professional. 1980. Qtr. plan. Degrees: P. *Prof. Accred.:* Chiropractic Education. Pres. ———.
Enroll.: 410
(503) 256-3180

WILLAMETTE UNIVERSITY
Salem 97301. Private (United Methodist). 1924/1980 (NASC). Sem. plan. Degrees: B,P,M. *Prof. Accred.:* Law, Music. Pres. Jerry E. Hudson.
Enroll.: 1,930
(503) 370-6200

†Candidate for Accreditation by Regional Accrediting Commission

PENNSYLVANIA

ACADEMY OF MEDICAL ARTS AND BUSINESS
279 Boas St., Harrisburg 17102. Private. 1983 (ABHES); 1983 (NATTS). Courses of varying lengths. Diplomas. *Prof. Accred.:* Medical Assisting. Dir. Margery A. Grove.
Enroll.: 95
(717) 233-2172

ACADEMY OF THE NEW CHURCH
P.O. Box 278, Bryn Athyn 19009. Private (General Church of New Jersusalem) coeducational liberal arts college and seminary for men. 1952/1984 (MSA/CHE). Sem. plan. Degrees: A,B,P. Pres. Rev. Peter M. Buss.
Enroll.: 155 (*f.t.* 72 m., 64 w.)
(215) 947-4200

ADELPHIA BUSINESS SCHOOL
63 W. Lancaster Ave., Ardmore 19003. Private. 1982 (AICS). Courses of varying lengths. Certificates, diplomas. CEO Robert A. Thomas.
Enroll.: 278 (*f.t.* 30 m., 248 w.)
(215) 896-8060

BRANCH CAMPUS
13th and Sansom Sts., Philadelphia 19107. Asst. Dir. Richard A. Thomas.
(215) 627-1188

AIRCO TECHNICAL INSTITUTE
4725 Chestnut St., Philadelphia 19139. Private. 1978/1984 (NATTS). Courses of varying lengths. Certificates. Dir. Charles F. Hamilton.
Enroll.: 275 (*f.t.* 260 m., 15 w.)
(215) 748-6101

ALBRIGHT COLLEGE
Reading 19603. Private (United Methodist) liberal arts. 1926/1983 (MSA/CHE). 4-1-5 plan. Degrees: B. *Prof. Accred.:* Nursing (B). Pres. David G. Ruffer.
Enroll.: 2,053 (*f.t.* 573 m., 774 w.)
(215) 921-2381

ALLEGHENY COLLEGE
Meadville 16335. Private (United Methodist) liberal arts. 1921/1984 (MSA/CHE). 3-3 plan. Degrees: B,M. *Prof. Accred.:* Music. Pres. Daniel F. Sullivan.
Enroll.: 1,903 (*f.t.* 964 m., 922 w.)
(814) 724-3100

ALLENTOWN COLLEGE OF ST. FRANCIS DE SALES
Center Valley 18034. Private (Roman Catholic) liberal arts. 1970/1985 (MSA/CHE). Sem. plan. Degrees: B,M. *Prof. Accred.:* Nursing (B). Pres. V. Rev. Daniel G. Gambet, O.S.F.S.
Enroll.: 1,407 (*f.t.* 430 m., 580 w.)
(215) 282-1100

ALTOONA SCHOOL OF COMMERCE
508 58th St., Altoona 16602. Private. 1971/1983 (AICS). Qtr. plan. Certificates. Pres. Robert A. Halloran.
Enroll.: 284 (*f.t.* 70 m., 214 w.)
(814) 944-6134

ALVERNIA COLLEGE
Reading 19607. Private (Roman Catholic) liberal arts. 1967/1975 (MSA/CHE). Sem. plan. Degrees: A,B. *Prof. Accred.:* Nursing (A). Pres. Sister Mary Dolorey, C.S.B.
Enroll.: 779 (*f.t.* 161 m., 270 w.)
(215) 777-5411

ALVERNIA SCHOOL OF PRACTICAL NURSING
ST. FRANCIS GENERAL HOSPITAL
45th St., Pittsburgh 15201. Public vocational. 1971. 1-year program. Certificates. *Prof. Accred.:* Practical Nursing. Dir. Anna Wagner.
(412) 683-6000

AMERICAN COLLEGE
270 Bryn Mawr Ave., Bryn Mawr 19010. Private professional; external degrees also offered nationally and through self-study. 1978/1983 (MSA/CHE). Sem. plan. Degrees: M. Pres. Edward G. Jordan.
Enroll.: 5,970 (*f.t.* 467 m., 103 w.)
(215) 896-4500

AMERICAN INSTITUTE OF DESIGN
1616 Orthodox St., Philadelphia 19124. Private. 1972/1977 (NATTS). Qtr. plan. Degrees: A, certificates. Dir. James M. Bell.
Enroll.: 350 (*f.t.* 260 m., 45 w.)
(215) 288-8200

ANTONELLI INSTITUTE OF ART AND PHOTOGRAPHY
2910 Jolly Rd., P.O. Box 570, Plymouth Meeting 19462., Private. 1975/1980 (NATTS). Sem. plan. Degrees: A. Pres. Dir. Gilbert Weiss.
Enroll.: 300 (*f.t.* 114 m., 75 w.)
(215) 275-3040

EXTENSION
625 E. Philadelphia St., P.O. Box 2505, York 17405. Dir. Severino Stefanon.
(717) 848-1447

ART INSTITUTE OF NEW KENSINGTON
401 Ninth St., New Kensington 15068. Private. 1980 (NATTS). Qtr. plan. Diplomas. Dir. William H. Breyak.
Enroll.: 13 (*f.t.* 5 m., 8 w.)
(412) 335-5336

ART INSTITUTE OF PHILADELPHIA
1622 Chestnut St., Philadelphia 19103. Private. 1973/1978 (NATTS). Qtr. plan. Degrees: A. Pres. Edward R. D'Alessio.
Enroll.: 927 (*f.t.* 390 m., 527 w.)
(215) 567-7080

ART INSTITUTE OF PITTSBURGH
526 Penn Ave., Pittsburgh 15222. Private. 1970/1980 (NATTS). Qtr. plan. Degrees: A. Pres. John T. Barclay.
Enroll.: 1,950 (*f.t.* 892 m., 952 w.)
(412) 263-6600

AUTOMOTIVE TRAINING CENTER
Pickering Creek Industrial Park, 114 Pickering Way, Lionville 19341. Private. 1973/1978 (NATTS). Courses of varying lengths. Certificates, diplomas. Dir. Qamarul A. Khan.
(215) 363-6716

BAPTIST BIBLE COLLEGE OF PENNSYLVANIA
538 Venard Rd., Clarks Summit 18411. Private (Baptist) professional. 1968/1984 (AABC); 1984 (MSA/CHE). Sem. plan. Degrees: A,B,M. Pres. Milo Thompson.
Enroll.: 694 (*f.t.* 287 m., 266 w.)
(717) 587-1172

BARBER STYLING INSTITUTE
3447 Simpson Ferry Rd., Camp Hill 17011. Private. 1983 (NATTS). Courses of varying lengths. Certificates. Dir. Richard Brennan.
Enroll.: 20
(717) 763-4787

BEAVER COLLEGE
Glenside 19038. Private (United Presbyterian) liberal arts. 1946/1984 (MSA/CHE). 4-1-4 plan. Degrees: A,B,M. *Prof. Accred.:* Art, Physical Therapy. Pres. Bette E. Landman.
Enroll.: 2,004 (*f.t.* 169 m., 602 w.)
(215) 572-2900

BEREAN INSTITUTE
1901 W. Girard Ave., Philadelphia 19130. Private business and technical. 1974/1980 (AICS); 1974/1979 (NATTS). Sem. plan. Degrees: A, certificates, diplomas. Exec. Admin. Lucille P. Blondin.
Enroll.: 452 (*f.t.* 109 m., 343 w.)
(215) 763-4833

*BLOOMSBURG UNIVERSITY OF PENNSYLVANIA
Bloomsburg 17815. Public liberal arts, business, and teachers. 1950/1984 (MSA/CHE). Sem. plan. Degrees: B,M. *Prof. Accred.:* Nursing (B), Teacher Education (*e,s,*). Pres. John P. Watkins.
Enroll.: 6,439 (*f.t.* 2,001 m., 3,240 w.)
(717) 389-4000

BRADFORD SCHOOL
Five Penn Center Plaza, 16th and Market Sts., Philadelphia 19103. Private business. 1984 (AICS). Courses of varying lengths. Certificates. Dir. Charles P. Scholer.
Enroll.: 267 (*f.t.* 2 m., 265 w.)
(215) 854-0788

BRADFORD SCHOOL
355 Fifth Ave., Pittsburgh 15222. Private business. 1970/1981 (AICS). Courses of varying lengths. Certificates. Pres. Carmen P. Sporio.
Enroll.: 989 (*f.t.* 63 m., 926 w.)
(412) 391-6710

BREEDEN SCHOOL OF WELDING
Central Ave.,P.O. Box 236, Genesee 16923. Private. 1982 (NATTS). Courses of varying lengths. Certificates. Pres. John Less, Jr.
Enroll.: f.t. 50 m.
(814) 228-3217

BRYN MAWR COLLEGE
Bryn Mawr 19010. Private liberal arts for women; graduate school coeducational. 1921/1983 (MSA/CHE). Sem. plan. Degrees: B,M,D. *Prof. Accred.:* Social Work (M). Pres. Mary Patterson McPherson.
Enroll.: 1,794 (*f.t.* 107 m., 1,367 w.)
(215) 645-5000

BUCKNELL UNIVERSITY
Lewisburg 17837. Private. 1921/1984 (MSA/CHE). 4-1-4 plan. Degrees: B,M. *Prof. Accred.:* Engineering (chemical, civil, electrical, mechanical), Music. Pres. Gary A. Sojka.
Enroll.: 3,404 (*f.t.* 1,702 m., 1,595 w.)
(717) 523-1271

BUCKS COUNTY COMMUNITY COLLEGE
Newtown 18940. Public junior. 1968/1982 (MSA/CHE). Sem. plan. Degrees: A. *Prof. Accred.:* Art, Nursing (A). Pres. Charles E. Rollins.

*Member Pennsylvania State System of Higher Education

Enroll.: 9,222 (*f.t.* 1,247 m., 1,330 w.)
(215) 968-8000

Business Careers Institute
33 W. Otterman St., Greensburg 15601. Private. 1972/1984 (AICS). Qtr. plan. Certificates, diplomas. Dir. Andrew Ogrodnik.
Enroll.: 237 (*f.t.* 7 m., 230 w.)
(412) 834-1258

Butler County Community College
Butler 16001. Public (county) junior. 1971/1981 (MSA/CHE). Sem. plan. Degrees: A. Pres. Frederick W. Woodward.
Enroll.: 2,068 (*f.t.* 442 m., 522 w.)
(412) 287-8711

Cabrini College
Radnor 19087. Private (Roman Catholic) liberal arts for women. 1965/1985 (MSA/CHE). Sem. plan. Degrees: B,M. Pres. Sister Eileen Currie, M.S.C.
Enroll.: 922 (*f.t.* 195 m., 527 w.)
(215) 687-2100

*California University of Pennsylvania
California 15419. Public liberal arts and teachers. 1951/1985 (MSA/CHE). Tri. plan. Degrees: A,B,M. *Prof. Accred.:* Nurse Anesthesia Education, Social Work (B), Teacher Education (*e,s,p*). Pres. John P. Watkins.
Enroll.: 5,063 (*f.t.* 2,180 m., 1,688 w.)
(412) 938-4000

Cambria-Rowe Business College
221 Central Ave., Johnstown 15902. Private. 1959/1981 (AICS). Qtr. plan. Degrees: A. Pres. Robert J. Mullen.
Enroll.: 479 (*f.t.* 96 m., 383 w.)
(814) 536-5168

The Career Institute
1724 John F. Kennedy Blvd., Philadelphia 19103. Private. 1984 (AICS). Qtr. plan. Certificates. Dir. Eve Cohen-Corey.
Enroll.: 131
(215) 561-7600

Carlow College
3333 Fifth Ave., Pittsburgh 15213. Private (Roman Catholic) liberal arts for women. 1935/1986(MSA/CHE). Sem. plan with winter interim. Degrees: B,M. *Prof. Accred.:* Nursing (B). Pres. Sister Marylouise Fennell.
Enroll.: 1,174 (*f.t.* 24 m., 708 w.)
(412) 578-6000

*Member Pennsylvania State System of Higher Education

Carnegie-Mellon University
5000 Forbes Ave., Pittsburgh 15213. Private. 1921/1982 (MSA/CHE). Sem. plan. Degrees: B,M,D. *Prof. Accred.:* Architecture, Art, Business (B,M), Engineering (chemical, civil, electrical, mechanical, metallurgy and materials science), Music. Pres. Richard M. Cyert.
Enroll.: 6,621 (*f.t.* 4,040 m., 1,677 w.)
(412) 268-2000

Cedar Crest College
Allentown 18104. Private (United Church of Christ) liberal arts for women. 1944/1983 (MSA/CHE). 4-1-4 plan. Degrees: B. *Prof. Accred.:* Nuclear Medical Technology, Nursing (B), Social Work (B). Pres. Gene S. Cesari.
Enroll.: 1,157 (*f.t.* 5 m., 577 w.)
(215) 437-4471

Central Pennsylvania Business School
College Hill Rd., Summerdale 17093-0309 Private. 1977/1983 (MSA/CHE). Tri. plan. Degrees: A. *Prof. Accred.:* Medical Assisting. Pres. Bart A. Milano.
Enroll.: 699 (*f.t.* 86 m., 582 w.)
(717) 732-0702

Centre Business School
105 Gerald St., State College 16801. Private. 1980/1982 (AICS). Qtr. plan. Certificates, diplomas. Dir. Lois H. Campbell.
Enroll.: 188 (*f.t.* 12 m., 176 w.)
(814) 238-4916

Centre County Vocational-Technical School of Practical Nursing
Pleasant Gap 16823. Public. 1981. 1-year program. Certificates. *Prof. Accred.:* Practical Nursing. Coord. Marian W. Weir.
Enroll.: 54

Chatham College
Pittsburgh 15232. Private liberal arts for women. 1924/1983 (MSA/CHE). 4-1-4 plan. Degrees: B. Pres. Rebecca Stafford.
Enroll.: 565 (*f.t.* 411 w.)
(412) 365-1100

Chestnut Hill College
Germantown and Northwestern Aves., Philadelphia 19118. Private (Roman Catholic) liberal arts for women. 1930/1982 (MSA/CHE). Sem. plan. Degrees: A,B,M. *Prof. Accred.:* Pres. Sister Matthew Anita MacDonald.
Enroll.: 925 (*f.t.* 1 m., 474 w.)
(215) 248-7000

*Cheyney University of Pennsylvania
Cheyney 19319. Public liberal arts and teachers. 1951/1971 (MSA/CHE). Sem. plan. Degrees: B,M. *Prof. Accred.:* Teacher Education (*e,s*). Pres. LaVerne McCummings.
Enroll.: 1,463 (*f.t.* 593 m., 591 w.)
(215) 399-2000

Churchman Business School
355 Spring Garden St., Easton 18042. Private. 1954/1981 (AICS). Tri. plan. Degrees: A. Pres. Charles W. Churchman, Jr.
Enroll.: 410 (*f.t.* 151 m., 259 w.)
(215) 258-5345

*Clarion University of Pennsylvania
Clarion 16214. Public liberal arts and professional. 1948/1982 (MSA/CHE). Sem. plan. Degrees: A,B,M. *Prof. Accred.:* Librarianship, Nursing (B), Teacher Education (*e,s,p*). Pres. Thomas Alden Bond.
Enroll.: 6,071 (*f.t.* 2,289 m., 2,616 w.)
(814) 226-2000

Venango Campus
Oil City 16301. 1962/1982 (MSA/CHE). *Prof. Accred.:* Nursing (A). Dir. Thomas Rookey.
Enroll.: 556 (*f.t.* 60 m., 117 w.)
(814) 676-6591

The Clarissa School of Fashion Design
107 Sixth St., Pittsburgh 15222. Private 1970/1982 (NATTS). Sem. plan. Certificates, diplomas. Pres. Penelope M. Smith.
Enroll.: 70 (*f.t.* 4 m., 57 w.)
(412) 471-4414

Clearfield County Technical Institute
Box 5, RD #1, Clearfield 16830. Public. 1981. 1-year program. Certificates. *Prof. Accred.:* Practical Nursing. Coord. Barbara A. Tubbs.
Enroll.: 32

College Misericordia
Dallas 18612. Private (Roman Catholic) liberal arts primarily for women. 1935/1984 (MSA/CHE). Sem. plan. Degrees: A,B,M. *Prof. Accred.:* Music, Nursing (B), Occupational Therapy, Radiography, Social Work (B). Pres. Joseph R. Fink.
Enroll.: 1,268 (*f.t.* 173 m., 738 w.)
(717) 675-2181

Combs College of Music
7500 Germantown Ave., Philadelphia 19119. Private professional. 1981 (MSA/CHE). Sem. plan. Degrees: B,M,D. Acting Pres. Bernard Guth.
Enroll.: 85 (*f.t.* 45 m., 24 w.)
(215) 248-7900

*Member Pennsylvania State System of Higher Education

Community College of Allegheny County
Central Office, 800 Allegheny Ave., Pittsburgh 15233-1895. Public (county) junior. Sem. plan. Degrees: A. Pres. John W. Kraft.
Enroll.: 22,740 (*f.t.* 6,432 m., 7,153 w.)
(412) 323-2323

Allegheny Campus
808 Ridge Ave., Pittsburgh 15212. 1970/1984 (MSA/CHE); accreditation includes Homewood-Brushton Center, Pittsburgh 15208. *Prof. Accred.:* Assistant to the Primary Care Physician, Medical Assisting, Medical Laboratory Technology (A, certificates), Medical Record Technology, Nuclear Medicine Technology, Nurse Anesthesia Education, Nursing (A), Radiation Therapy Technology, Respiratory Therapy, Respiratory Therapy Technology. Exec. Dean Julius Brown.
Enroll.: 6,871 (*f.t.* 1,604 m., 1,747 w.)
(412) 237-2525

Boyce Campus
595 Beatty Rd., Monroeville 15146. 1970/1984 (MSA/CHE). *Prof. Accred.:* Radiography, Surgical Technology. Acting Exec. Dean Carl A. DiSibio.
Enroll.: 4,260 (*f.t.* 779 m., 812 w.)
(412) 371-8651

College Center North
111 Pine Plaza, 1130 Perry Hwy., Pittsburgh 15237. 1979/1984 (MSA-CHE). Acting Exec. Dean Frank F. Bartok.
Enroll.: 2,891 (*f.t.* 267 m., 261 w.)
(412) 931-8500

South Campus
1750 Clairton Rd., Rte. 885, West Mifflin 15122. 1973/1984 (MSA/CHE). *Prof. Accred.:* Medical Laboratory Technology (A), Nursing (A). Exec. Dean Helen Smith.
Enroll.: 4,404 (*f.t.* 786 m., 938 w.)
(412) 469-1100

Community College of Beaver County
College Dr., Monaca 15061. Public junior. 1972/1985 (MSA/CHE). Sem. plan. Degrees: A. *Prof. Accred.:* Medical Laboratory Technology. Pres. William K. Bauer.
Enroll.: 2,373 (*f.t.* 682 m., 512 w.)
(412) 775-8561

Community College of Philadelphia
1700 Spring Garden St., Philadelphia 19130. Public (city) junior. 1968/1984 (MSA/CHE). Sem. plan. Degrees: A. *Prof. Accred.:* Assistant to the Primary Care Physician, Dental Assisting, Dental Hygiene, Medical Assisting, Medical Laboratory Technology (A), Medical Record Technology, Nursing (A), Radiography, Respiratory Therapy. Pres. Judith S. Eaton.
Enroll.: 20,575 (*f.t.* 1,922 m., 2,759 w.)
(215) 751-8000

Computer Learning Center
3607 Rosemont Ave., Camp Hill 17011. Private. 1985 (NATTS). Courses of varying lengths. Certificates. Dir. George Aversa.
(717) 761-1481

Computer Learning Center
30th and Market St., First Floor, PSFS, Philadelphia 19104. Private. 1985 (AICS). Courses of varying lengths. Certificates. Dir. Robert A. Dickinson.
(215) 222-6450

Computer Learning Center/Maxwell Campus
2860 De Kalb Pike, Norristown 19401. Private. 1985 (NATTS). Courses of varying lengths. Certificates. Dir. Mary Benson.
(215) 277-7920

Computer Systems Institute
900 Penn Ave., Pittsburgh 15222. Private. 1967/1985 (AICS). Qtr. plan. Degrees: A. Pres. Joseph R. Yorke.
Enroll.: 326 (*f.t.* 199 m., 127 w.)
(412) 261-6110

Branch Campus
996 S. Main St., Meadville 16335. Co-Dir. Ben Wilke.
(814) 336-5517

Consolidated School of Business
131 N. Duke St., York 17401. Private. 1984 (AICS). Courses of varying lengths. Certificates, diplomas. Dir. Robert L. Safran.
Enroll.: 35 (*f.t.* 26)
(717) 846-4076

Control Data Institute
Four Penn Center Plaza, Suite 600, Philadelphia 19103. Private. 1980 (NATTS). Courses of varying lengths. Certificates. Dir. James A. Cantrell.
Enroll.: 192 (*f.t.* 123 m., 30 w.)
(215) 854-1370

Extension
One Allegheny Center Mall, Pittsburgh 15212. Mgr. Mary L. Putman.
(412) 321-1300

Craft School of Tailoring
210 N. Broad St., Philadelphia 19102. Private. 1980 (NATTS). Courses of varying lengths. Certificates. Dir. Terry Focht.
Enroll.: 90 (*f.t.* 50 m., 40 w.)
(215) 665-8546

Crawford County Area Vocational-Technical School
Meadville 16335. Public practical nursing program. 1980. 12-month program. Diplomas. *Prof. Accred.:* Practical Nursing. Dir. Donald H. Dickey.
(814) 724-6028

The Curtis Institute of Music
1726 Locust St., Philadelphia 19103. Private professional. 1979. Sem. plan. Degrees: B,M, diplomas. *Prof. Accred.:* Music. Dir. John de Lancie.
Enroll.: 182 (*f.t.* 78 m., 64 w.)
(215) 893-5252

Danville Area School District
DeLong Bldg., Box 140, Washingtonville 17884. Public practical nursing program. 1980. 12-month program. Diplomas. *Prof. Accred.:* Practical Nursing. Dir. Marguerite J. Savidge.
(717) 437-3176

Dean Institute of Technology
1501 W. Liberty Ave., Pittsburgh 15226-9990. Private. 1969/1980 (NATTS). Qtr. plan. Degrees: A, certificates, diplomas. Dir. James S. Dean.
Enroll.: 380 (*f.t.* 124 m., 8 w.)
(412) 531-4433

Delaware County Community College
Media 19063. Public junior. 1970/1985 (MSA/CHE). Sem. plan. Degrees: A. *Prof. Accred.:* Nursing (A). Pres. Richard D. DeCosmo.
Enroll.: 7,638 (*f.t.* 1,313 m., 1,236 w.)
(215) 359-5000

Delaware County Institute of Training
615 Avenue of the States, Chester 19013. Private. 1984 (NATTS). Courses of varying lengths. Certificates. Pres. James Ricciardi.
(215) 874-1888

Delaware Valley College of Science and Agriculture
Doylestown 18901. Private (state-aided) professional primarily for men. 1962/1983

(MSA/CHE). Sem. plan. Degrees: B. *Prof. Accred.:* Pres. Joshua Feldstein.
Enroll.: 1,422 (*f.t.* 750 m., 335 w.)
(215) 345-1500

DELAWARE VALLEY SCHOOL OF TRADES, INC.
1210 Race St., 4th Floor, Philadelphia 19107. Private. 1981 (NATTS). Qtr. plan. Diplomas. Dir. D. E. Schollenberger.
Enroll.: 120 (*f.t.* 70 m., 5 w.)
(215) 568-1950

DICKINSON COLLEGE
Carlisle 17013. Private (United Methodist) liberal arts. 1921/1982 (MSA/CHE). Sem. plan. Degrees: B. Pres. Samuel A. Banks.
Enroll.: 1,937 (*f.t.* 832 m., 1,042 w.)
(717) 243-5121

DICKINSON SCHOOL OF LAW
Carlisle 17013. Private professional. 1931 (ABA); 1934 (AALS). Sem. plan. Degrees: P,M. *Prof. Accred.:* Law. Dean William L. Wilks.
Enroll.: 524 (*f.t.* 322 m., 195 w.)
(717) 243-4611

DOUGLAS SCHOOL OF BUSINESS
130 Seventh St., Monessen 15062. Private. 1977/1980 (AICS). Tri. plan. Diplomas. Pres. Andrew H. Solan.
Enroll.: 105 (*f.t.* 4 m., 101 w.)
(412) 684-7644

DREXEL UNIVERSITY
32nd and Chestnut Sts., Philadelphia 19104. Private (state-aided). 1927/1981 (MSA/CHE). Qtr. plan. Degrees: B,M,D. *Prof. Accred.:* Architecture (B), Business (B,M), Dietetics, Engineering (chemical, civil, electrical, materials, mechanical), Home Economics, Interior Design, Librarianship. Pres. William S. Gaither.
Enroll.: 12,386 (*f.t.* 5,580 m., 2,441 w.)
(215) 895-2000

DROPSIE COLLEGE
250 N. Highland Ave., Merion Station 19066. Private specialized, graduate only. 1954/1975 (MSA/CHE). Sem. plan. Degrees: M,D. Pres. David M. Goldenberg.
Enroll.: 47 (*f.t.* 44 m., 1 w.)
(215) 527-6900

DUBOIS BUSINESS COLLEGE
One Beaver Dr., P.O. Box 0, DuBois 15801. Private. 1954/1982 (AICS). Tri. plan. Degrees: A, certificates, diplomas. Pres. Robert G. Flanagan.
Enroll.: 443 (*f.t.* 15 m., 428 w.)
(814) 371-6920

DUFF'S BUSINESS INSTITUTE
110 Ninth St., Pittsburgh 15222. Private. 1961/1986 (AICS). Qtr. plan. Degrees: A, certificates, diplomas. Pres. Thomas W. Dillenburg.
Enroll.: 1,582 (*f.t.* 103 m., 1,479 w.)
(412) 261-4520

DUQUESNE UNIVERSITY
600 Forbes Ave., Pittsburgh 15282. Private (Roman Catholic). 1935/1983 (MSA/CHE). Sem. plan. Degrees: A,B,P,M,D. *Prof. Accred.:* Business (B,M), Law, Music, Nursing (B), Pharmacy. Pres. Donald S. Nesti, C.S.Sp.
Enroll.: 6,528 (*f.t.* 2,393 m., 2,457 w.)
(412) 434-6000

*EAST STROUDSBURG UNIVERSITY OF PENNSYLVANIA
East Stroudsburg 18301. Public liberal arts and teachers. 1950/1982 (MSA/CHE). Sem. plan. Degrees: A,B,M. *Prof. Accred.:* Nursing (B), Teacher Education (*e,s*). Pres. James E. Gilbert.
Enroll.: 4,223 (*f.t.* 1,697 m., 1,815 w.)
(717) 424-3211

EASTERN BAPTIST THEOLOGICAL SEMINARY
City Line and Lancaster Ave., Philadelphia 19151. Private (American Baptist) professional; graduate only. 1954/1985 (MSA/CHE). 4-1-4 plan. Degrees: P,M,D. *Prof. Accred.:* Theology (1954/1984, ATS). Pres. Robert A. Seiple.
Enroll.: 391
(215) 896-5000

EASTERN COLLEGE
Fairview Dr., St. Davids 19087. Private (American Baptist) liberal arts. 1954/1985 (MSA/CHE). Sem. plan. Degrees: B,M. *Prof. Accred.:* Social Work (B). Pres. Robert A. Seiple.
Enroll.: 960 (*f.t.* 268 m., 382 w.)
(215) 341-5810

*EDINBORO UNIVERSITY OF PENNSYLVANIA
Edinboro 16444. Public liberal arts and teachers. 1949/1983 (MSA/CHE). Sem. plan. Degrees: A,B,M. *Prof. Accred.:* Dental Laboratory Technology, Dietetics, Nursing (B), Nurse Anesthesia Education, Rehabilitation

*Member Pennsylvania State System of Higher Education

Counseling, Teacher Education (*e,s,p*). Pres. Foster Diebold.
Enroll.: 5,849 (*f.t.* 2,252 m., 2,493 w.)
(814) 732-2000

ELECTRONIC INSTITUTES
19 Jamesway Plaza, Middletown 17105. Private. 1985 (NATTS). Courses of varying lengths. Certificates. Dir. Donna Chalfant.
(717) 944-2731

ELECTRONIC INSTITUTES
4634 Browns Hill Rd., Pittsburgh 15217. Private. 1985 (NATTS). Courses of varying lengths. Certificates. Dir. Donna Chalfant.
(412) 521-8686

ELIZABETHTOWN COLLEGE
Elizabethtown 17022. Private (Church of Brethren) liberal arts. 1948/1984 (MSA/CHE). Sem. plan. Degrees: A,B. *Prof. Accred.*: Music, Occupational Therapy, Social Work (B). Pres. Gerhard E. Spiegler.
Enroll.: 1,681 (*f.t.* 516 m., 859 w.)
(717) 367-1151

*ERIE BUSINESS CENTER
246 W. Ninth St., Erie 16501. Private. 1954/1982 (AICS). Sem. plan. Degrees: A, certificates. Dir. Charles P. McGeary.
Enroll.: 380 (*f.t.* 32 m., 227 w.)
(814) 456-7504

ERIE INSTITUTE OF TECHNOLOGY
2221 Peninsula Dr., Erie 16506. Private. 1979 (NATTS). Courses of varying lengths. Certificates. Pres. Edward Grzelak.
Enroll.: 120 (*f.t.* 40 m., 2 w.)
(814) 838-2711

EVANGELICAL SCHOOL OF THEOLOGY
Myerstown 17067. Private professional; graduate only. 1984 (MSA/CHE). Sem. plan. Degrees: M. Pres. Ray Sielhamer.
Enroll.: 71 (*f.t.* 13 m., 0 w.)
(717) 866-5775

FPM DATA SCHOOL, INC.
1704 Fourth Ave., Arnold 15068. Private. 1980 (NATTS). Courses of varying lengths. Certificates, diplomas. Dir. Robert Nave.
Enroll.: 92 (*f.t.* 28 m., 64 w.)
(412) 339-3571

FRANKLIN AND MARSHALL COLLEGE
P.O.Box 3003., Lancaster 17604. Private (United Church of Christ) liberal arts. 1921/1983 (MSA/CHE). 4-1-4 plan. Degrees: A,B. Pres. James L. Powell.
Enroll.: 2,007 (*f.t.* 1,070 m., 897 w.)
(717) 291-3911

GANNON UNIVERSITY
University Sq., Erie 16541. Private (Roman Catholic) liberal arts. 1951/1977 (MSA/CHE). Sem. plan. Degrees: A,B,M. *Prof. Accred.*: Assistant to the Primary Care Physician, Engineering (electrical, mechanical), Medical Assisting, Respiratory Therapy, Social Work (B), Teacher Education (*s,p*). Pres. Joseph P. Scottino.
Enroll.: 4,096 (*f.t.* 1,469 m., 1,229 w.)
(814) 871-7000

GATEWAY TECHNICAL INSTITUTE
100 Seventh St., Pittsburgh 15222. Private. 1969/1980 (NATTS). Tri. plan. Diplomas. Dir. Wayne D. Smith.
Enroll.: 400 (*f.t.* 254 m., 18 w.)
(412) 281-4111

GENEVA COLLEGE
Beaver Falls 15010. Private (Reformed Presbyterian) liberal arts. 1922/1980 (MSA/CHE). Sem. plan. Degrees: A,B. Pres. Joseph McFarland.
Enroll.: 1,191 (*f.t.* 608 m., 388 w.)
(412) 846-5100

GETTYSBURG COLLEGE
N. Washington St., Gettysburg 17325. Private (Lutheran in America) liberal arts. 1921/1984 (MSA/CHE). Sem. plan. Degrees: B. Pres. Charles E. Glassick.
Enroll.: 1,978 (*f.t.* 978 m., 977 w.)
(717) 337-6000

GRATZ COLLEGE
10th St. and Tabor Rd., Philadelphia 19141. Private teachers. 1967/1977 (MSA/CHE). Sem. plan. Degrees: B,M. Pres. Gary S. Schiff.
Enroll.: 270 (*f.t.* 10 m., 26 w.)
(215) 329-3363

GREENSBURG INSTITUTE OF TECHNOLOGY
302 W. Otterman St., Greensburg 15601. Private. 1970/1976 (NATTS). Sem. plan. Diplomas. Pres. William F. Margut.
Enroll.: 200 (*f.t.* 168 m., 12 w.)
(412) 837-3330

GROVE CITY COLLEGE
Grove City 16127. Private (United Presbyterian) liberal arts. 1922/1985 (MSA/CHE). Sem. plan. Degrees: B. Pres. Charles S. MacKenzie.

*Candidate for Accreditation by Regional Accrediting Commission

Enroll.: 2,162 (*f.t.* 1,075 m., 1,065 w.)
(412) 458-6600

GWYNEDD-MERCY COLLEGE
Gwynedd Valley 19437. Private (Roman Catholic) liberal arts primarily for women. Accreditation includes Edmonda Campus, Darby 19023, (215) 237-0440. 1958/1983 (MSA/CHE). Sem. plan. Degrees: A,B,M. *Prof. Accred.:* Medical Laboratory Technology (A), Medical Record Technology, Nursing (A,B), Radiation Therapy, Radiography, Respiratory Therapy. Pres. Sister Isabelle Keiss, R.S.M.
Enroll.: 2,007 (*f.t.* 102 m., 664 w.)
(215) 646-7300

HAHNEMANN UNIVERSITY
230 N. Broad St., Philadelphia 19102-1192. Private for training in Health Sciences. 1978/1983 (MSA/CHE). Degrees: A,B,P,M,D. *Prof. Accred.:* Assistant to the Primary Care Physician, Cytotechnology, Medical Laboratory Technology (A), Medical Technology, Medicine, Nursing (A,B), Physical Therapy, Psychology, Radiography, Respiratory Therapy. Pres. Bertram S. Brown.
Enroll.: 2,119 (*f.t.* 753 m., 1,029 w.)
(215) 448-7000

HARCUM JUNIOR COLLEGE
Bryn Mawr 19010. Private for women. 1970/1985 (MSA/CHE). Sem. plan. Degrees: A. *Prof. Accred.:* Dental Assisting, Medical Assisting, Medical Laboratory Technology (A). Pres. Norma Furst.
Enroll.: 1,016 (*f.t.* 15 m., 857 w.)
(215) 525-4100

HARRISBURG AREA COMMUNITY COLLEGE
3300 Cameron Street Rd., Harrisburg 17110. Public (district) junior. 1967/1982 (MSA/CHE). Sem. plan. Degrees: A. *Prof. Accred.:* Medical Laboratory Technology, Respiratory Therapy, Respiratory Therapy Technology. Pres. Kenneth B. Woodbury, Jr.
Enroll.: 6,598 (*f.t.* 1,043 m., 1,075 w.)
(717) 780-2300

HARRISBURG BARBER SCHOOL
67 N. Fifth St., Lemoyne 17043. Private. 1982 (NATTS). 9-month program. Diplomas. Dir. Peter S. Otto.
Enroll.: 36
(717) 737-4544

HAVERFORD COLLEGE
Haverford 19041. Private (Friends) liberal arts. 1921/1985 (MSA/CHE). Sem. plan. Degrees: B. *Prof. Accred.:* Pres. Robert Bocking Stevens.
Enroll.: 1,101 (*f.t.* 616 m., 480 w.)
(215) 896-1000

HOLY FAMILY COLLEGE
Grant and Frankford Aves., Philadelphia 19114. Private (Roman Catholic) liberal arts. 1961/1986 (MSA/CHE). Sem. plan. Degrees: A,B. *Prof. Accred.:* Nursing (B). Pres. Sister M. Francesca Onley, CSFM.
Enroll.: 1,617 (*f.t.* 108 m., 574 w.)
(215) 637-7700

HUSSIAN SCHOOL OF ART
1010 Arch St., Philadelphia 19107. Private. 1972/1984 (NATTS). Sem. plan. Degrees: A. Pres.-Dir. Edward Grzelak, Jr.
Enroll.: 180 (*f.t.* 101 m., 62 w.)
(215) 238-9000

ICM SCHOOL OF BUSINESS
10 Wood St. at Ft. Pitt, Pittsburgh 15222. Private. 1967/1985 (AICS). Qtr. and Tri. plans. Degrees: A, certificates, diplomas. *Prof. Accred.:* Medical Assisting. Dir. of Ed. Deborah Begg.
Enroll.: 1,746 (*f.t.* 694 m., 1,052 w.)
(412) 261-2647

IMMACULATA COLLEGE
Immaculata 19345. Private (Roman Catholic) liberal arts for women. 1928/1984 (MSA/CHE). Sem. plan. Degrees: A,B,M. *Prof. Accred.:* Music. Pres. Sister Marian William Hoben, I.H.M.
Enroll.: 1,912 (*f.t.* 6 m., 552 w.)
(215) 647-4400

*INDIANA UNIVERSITY OF PENNSYLVANIA
Indiana 15705. Public liberal arts and teachers; accreditation includes branch campuses at Kittanning 16201 and Punxsutawney 15767. 1941/1973 (MSA/CHE). Sem. plan. Degrees: A,B,M,D. *Prof. Accred.:* Home Economics, Music, Nursing (B), Respiratory Therapy, Teacher Education (*e,s,p*). Pres. John D. Welty.
Enroll.: 12,938 (*f.t.* 4,979 m., 6,117 w.)
(412) 357-2100

INFORMATION COMPUTER SYSTEMS INSTITUTE
2201 Hangar Pl., Allentown 18103. Private. 1984 (NATTS). Courses of varying lengths. Certificates. Pres. William H. Barber, Jr.
(215) 264-8029

*Member Pennsylvania State System of Higher Education

INSTITUTE OF SECURITY AND TECHNOLOGY
955 Liberty Ave., Suite 301, Pittsburgh 15222. Private. 1985 (NATTS). Courses of varying lengths. Certificates. Dir. Victor S. Cianca.
(412) 765-3366

INSTITUTE OF SECURITY AND TECHNOLOGY
319 S. 69th St., Upper Darby 19082. Private. 1984 (NATTS). Courses of varying lengths. Certificates. Vice Pres. Walter E. Cochrane.
(215) 352-6100

INTERNATIONAL CORRESPONDENCE SCHOOLS
Scranton 18515. Private home study. A division of National Education Corportation, Scranton, PA. 1956/1979 (NHSC). Pres. David Crowther.
(717) 342-7701

ICS CENTER FOR DEGREE STUDIES
A division of National Education Corporation, Scranton, PA. Degrees: A.

NORTH AMERICAN CORRESPONDENCE SCHOOLS
A division of National Education Corporation, Scranton, PA.

J. H. THOMPSON'S ACADEMIES
2910-11 State St., Erie 16508. Private. 1979 (NATTS). Courses of varying lengths. Diplomas. Dir. Barbara L. Brairton.
Enroll.: f.t. 16 m.
(814) 456-6217

JAMES MARTIN SCHOOL
Adult Vocational Training Center, Richmond and Ontario Sts., Philadelphia 19134. Public (city). Courses of varying lengths. Diplomas. *Prof. Accred.:* Medical Laboratory Technology (1982 ABHES), Practical Nursing. Admin. Richard L. Brown.
(215) 739-1891

JOHNSON TECHNICAL INSTITUTE
3427 N. Main Ave., Scranton 18508. Private. 1979 (NATTS). Sem. plan. Degrees: A. Pres. John R. O'Hara.
Enroll.: 560 (*f.t.* 542 m., 18 w.)
(717) 342-6404

JOSEPH DONAHUE INTERNATIONAL SCHOOL OF HAIRSTYLING
2485 Grant Ave., Philadelphia 19114. Private. 1984 (NATTS). Courses of varying lengths. Certificates. Pres. Thomas J. Magrann.
(215) 969-1313

JUNIATA COLLEGE
1700 Moore St., Huntingdon 16652. Private liberal arts. 1922/1983 (MSA/CHE). 3-3 plan. Degrees: B. *Prof. Accred.:* Social Work (B). Pres. Robert W. Neff.
Enroll.: 1,274 (*f.t.* 691 m., 567 w.)
(814) 643-4310

JUNIATA-MIFFLIN COUNTIES AREA VOCATIONAL TECHNICAL SCHOOL
Pitt St. & Belle Vernon Ave., Lewistown 17044. Public vocational. 1980. 1-year program. Certificates. *Prof. Accred.:* Practical Nursing.
(717) 248-3933

KATHARINE GIBBS SCHOOL
Land Title Bldg., Chestnut at Broad, 10th Fl., Philadelphia 19110. Private business. 1985 (AICS). Courses of varying lengths. Certificates. Dir. Betsy S. Tougas.
Enroll.: 712 (*f.t.* 5 m., 707 w.)
(215) 564-5035

BRANCH CAMPUS
2550 Eisenhower Ave., P.O. Box 759, Valley Forge 19482. Dir. Janet Cegelka.
(215) 666-7910

KEYSTONE JUNIOR COLLEGE
La Plume 18440. Private. 1936/1983 (MSA/CHE). Sem. plan. Degrees: A. Acting Pres. Margaretta B. Chamberlin.
Enroll.: 1,198 (*f.t.* 350 m., 385 w.)
(717) 945-5141

KEYSTONE SECRETARIAL AND BUSINESS ADMINISTRATION SCHOOL
Baltimore Pk. and Lincoln Ave., Swarthmore 19081. Private. 1968/1980 (AICS). Sem. plan. Degrees: A, certificates, diplomas. Pres. Alfred B. Smith.
Enroll.: 195 (*f.t.* 2 m., 193 w.)
(215) 543-1747

KING'S COLLEGE
133 N. River St., Wilkes-Barre 18711. Private (Roman Catholic) liberal arts. 1955/1984 (MSA/CHE). Sem. plan. Degrees: A,B. *Prof. Accred.:* Assistant to the Primary Care Physician, Teacher Education (*s*). Pres. James R. Lackenmier, C.S.C.
Enroll.: 2,327 (*f.t.* 915 m., 797 w.)
(717) 826-5900

*KUTZTOWN UNIVERSITY OF PENNSYLVANIA
Kutztown 19530. Public liberal arts and teachers. 1944/1983 (MSA/CHE). Sem. plan.

*Member Pennsylvania State System of Higher Education

Degrees: B,M. *Prof. Accred.:* Teacher Education (*e,s,p*). Pres. Lawrence M. Stratton.
Enroll.: 6,252 (*f.t.* 2,317 m., 2,720 w.)
(215) 683-4000

LACKAWANNA JUNIOR COLLEGE
901 Prospect Ave., Scranton 18505. Accreditation includes Wilkes-Barre Center 18701. Private. 1973/1978 (MSA/CHE). 4-1-4 plan. Degrees: A. Pres. Allan Mensky.
Enroll.: 1,132 (*f.t.* 192 m., 464 w.)
(717) 961-7810

LAFAYETTE COLLEGE
Easton 18042. Private (United Presbyterian) liberal arts and engineering. 1921/1983 (MSA/CHE). Sem. plan. Degrees: B. *Prof. Accred.:* Engineering (chemical, civil, electrical, mechanical, metallurgical). Pres. David W. Ellis.
Enroll.: 2,375 (*f.t.* 1,228 m., 842 w.)
(215) 250-5000

LANCASTER BIBLE COLLEGE
901 Eden Rd., Lancaster 17601. Private (Interdenominational) professional. 1964/1984 (AABC); 1982 (MSA/CHE). Sem. plan. Degrees: A,B. Pres. Gilbert A. Peterson.
Enroll.: 342
(717) 569-7071

LANCASTER THEOLOGICAL SEMINARY
Lancaster 17603. Private (United Church of Christ) professional; graduate only. 1978/1984 (MSA/CHE). 4-1-4 plan. Degrees: P,M,D. *Prof. Accred.:* Theology (1938/1984, ATS). Pres. Rev. Peter Schmiechen.
Enroll.: 242 (*f.t.* 52 m., 31 w.)
(717) 393-0654

LANSDALE SCHOOL OF BUSINESS
Hancock St. and Church St., Lansdale 19446. Private. 1967/1983 (AICS). Courses of varying lengths. Diplomas. Pres. Eugene Speer.
Enroll.: 595 (*f.t.* 96 m., 499 w.)
(215) 855-4212

BRANCH CAMPUS
100 Porter Rd., Pottstown 19464. Dir. Sue Ricci.
(215) 326-4142

LA ROCHE COLLEGE
9000 Babcock Blvd., Pittsburgh 15237. Private liberal arts. 1973/1984 (MSA/CHE). Sem. plan. Degrees: B,M. *Prof. Accred.:* Nurse Anesthesia Education, Nursing (B). Pres. Sister Margaret Huber, C.D.P.
Enroll.: 1,751 (*f.t.* 249 m., 381 w.)
(412) 367-9300

LA SALLE UNIVERSITY
Olney Ave. at 20th St., Philadelphia 19141. Private (Roman Catholic) liberal arts. 1930/1986 (MSA/CHE). Sem. plan. Degrees: A,B,M. *Prof. Accred.:* Nursing (B), Social Work (B). Pres. Brother F. Patrick Ellis, F.S.C.
Enroll.: 6,408 (*f.t.* 1,947 m., 1,414 w.)
(215) 951-1000

LEARNING AND EVALUATION CENTER
479 Drinker St., P.O. Box 616, Bloomsburg 17815. Private home study. 1985 (NHSC). Dir. I. L. McCloskey.
(717) 784-5220

LEBANON VALLEY COLLEGE
N. College Ave., Annville 17003-0501. Private (United Methodist) liberal arts. 1922/1983 (MSA/CHE). Sem. plan. Degrees: B. *Prof. Accred.:* Music. Pres. Arthur L. Peterson.
Enroll.: 1,210 (*f.t.* 337 m., 422 w.)
(717) 867-6100

LEHIGH COUNTY COMMUNITY COLLEGE
Schnecksville 18078-9372. Public junior. 1972/1978 (MSA/CHE). Sem. plan. Degrees: A. *Prof. Accred.:* Dental Assisting, Medical Assisting, Respiratory Therapy Technology. Pres. Robert L. Barthlow.
Enroll.: 3,287 (*f.t.* 378 m., 608 w.)
(215) 799-2121

LEHIGH DATA PROCESSING INSTITUTE
833 N. Park Rd., Wyomissing 19610. Private. 1984 (NATTS). Courses of varying lengths. Certificates. Pres. William H. Barber, Jr.
(215) 372-1722

LEHIGH UNIVERSITY
Bethlehem 18015. Private university. 1921/1984 (MSA/CHE). Sem. plan. Degrees: B,M,D. *Prof. Accred.:* Accounting (Type A), Business (B,M), Engineering (chemical, civil, electrical, industrial, mechanical, metallurgy and materials), Teacher Education (*e,s,p*). Pres. Peter W. Likins.
Enroll.: 6,393 (*f.t.* 3,361 m., 1,663 w.)
(215) 861-3000

LINCOLN TECHNICAL INSTITUTE
5151 Tilghman St., Allentown 18104. Private. 1967/1978 (NATTS). Qtr. plan, sem. plan, courses of varying lengths. Degrees: A, diplomas. Dir. Donald R. Frey.
Enroll.: 872 (*f.t.* 831 m., 41 w.)
(215) 398-5300

Lincoln Technical Institute
9191 Torresdale Ave., P.O. Box 6229, Philadelphia 19136. Private. 1986 (NATTS). Qtr. plan, sem. plan, courses of varying lengths. Degrees: A, diplomas. Dir. Robert Wurst.
(215) 335-0080

Lincoln University
Lincoln University 19352. Private (state-related) liberal arts college. 1922/1984 (MSA/CHE). Sem. plan. Degrees: A,B,M. Acting Pres. Donald L. Mullett.
Enroll.: 1,181 (*f.t.* 532 m., 626 w.)
(215) 932-8300

*Lock Haven University of Pennsylvania
Lock Haven 17745. Public liberal arts and teachers. 1949/1985 (MSA/CHE). Sem. plan. Degrees: A,B. *Prof. Accred.:* Social Work (B), Teacher Education (*e,s,*). Pres. Craig D. Willis.
Enroll.: 2,682 (*f.t.* 1,310 m., 1,210 w.)
(717) 893-2011

Lutheran Theological Seminary at Gettysburg
Gettysburg 17325. Private (Lutheran Church in America) professional; graduate only. 1971/1986 (MSA/CHE). Qtr. plan. Degrees: P,M,D. *Prof. Accred.:* Theology (1938/1980, ATS). Pres. Herman G. Stuempfle, Jr.
Enroll.: 243 (*f.t.* 146 m., 67 w.)
(717) 334-6286

Lutheran Theological Seminary at Philadelphia
Philadelphia 19119. Private (Lutheran Church in America) professional; graduate only. 1971/1986 (MSA/CHE). Sem. plan. Degrees: P,M,D. *Prof. Accred.:* Theology (1938/1981, ATS). Pres. John W. Vannorsdall.
Enroll.: 259 (*f.t.* 77 m., 69 w.)
(215) 248-4616

Luzerne County Community College
Nanticoke 18634. Public (district) junior. 1975/1985 (MSA/CHE). Sem. plan. Degrees: A. *Prof. Accred.:* Dental Assisting, Dental Hygiene, Nursing (A), Respiratory Therapy Technology. Pres. Thomas J. Moran.
Enroll.: 4,524 (*f.t.* 730 m., 895 w.)
(717) 829-7000

Lycoming College
Williamsport 17701. Private (United Methodist) liberal arts. 1934/1986 (MSA/CHE). Sem. plan. Degrees: B. Pres. Frederick E. Blumer.
Enroll.: 1,239 (*f.t.* 592 m., 566 w.)
(717) 321-4000

*Member Pennsylvania State System of Higher Education

Lyons Technical Institute
D St. and Erie Ave., Philadelphia 19134. Private. 1968/1979 (NATTS). Courses of varying lengths. Degrees: A, diplomas. Dir. John R. O'Hara.
Enroll.: 350 (*f.t.* 200 m., 20 w.)
(215) 426-5500

Lyons Technical Institute
67 Long La., Upper Darby 19082. Private. 1975/1980 (NATTS). Courses of varying lengths. Degrees: A, diplomas. *Prof. Accred.:* Medical Assisting, Radiography. Dir. William G. Mark.
Enroll.: 300 (*f.t.* 150 m., 150 w.)
(215) 734-1250

MTA School, Inc.
1801 Oberlin Rd., Middletown 17057. Private; residence and home study. 1973/1981 (NHSC); 1982 (NATTS). NHSC accreditation includes resident training site at Elizabethtown, PA 17022. Courses of varying lengths. Certificates. Pres. Gabe Royer.
(717) 939-1981.

Main Line Paralegal Institute
100 E. Lancaster Ave., Wayne 19087. Private. 1985 (NATTS). Courses of varying lengths. Certificates. Admin. Diane T. Mankin.
(215) 687-4600

Manor Junior College
Jenkintown 19046-3393. Private (Ukranian Rite) for women. 1967/1985 (MSA/CHE). Sem. plan. Degrees: A. *Prof. Accred.:* Dental Assisting, Medical Laboratory Technology (A). Pres. Sister Mary Cecilia Jurasinski, O.S.B.M.
Enroll.: 513 (*f.t.* 14 m., 282 w.)
(215) 885-2360

*Mansfield University of Pennsylvania
Mansfield 16933. Public liberal arts and teachers. 1942/1985 (MSA/CHE). Sem. plan. Degrees: A,B,M. *Prof. Accred.:* Music, Radiography, Respiratory Therapy, Social Work (B), Teacher Education (*e,s,*). Pres. Rodney C. Kelchner.
Enroll.: 2,868 (*f.t.* 1,116 m., 1,160 w.)
(717) 662-4000

*Member Pennsylvania State System of Higher Education

MARY IMMACULATE SEMINARY
300 Cherryville Rd., P.O. Box 27, Northampton 18067. Private (Roman Catholic), professional; graduate only. 1960/1986 (MSA/CHE). Sem. plan. Degrees: P,M. *Prof. Accred.:* Theology (1971/1981, ATS). Pres. Thomas F. Hoar, C.M.
Enroll.: 55 (*f.t.* 48 m., 0 w.)
(215) 262-7866

MARYWOOD COLLEGE
2300 Adams Ave., Scranton 18509. Private (Roman Catholic) liberal arts primarily for women. 1921/1986 (MSA/CHE). 4-1-4 plan. Degrees: B,M. *Prof. Accred.:* Art, Dietetics, Music, Social Work (B,M), Teacher Education (*e,s*). Pres. Sister M. Coleman Nee.
Enroll.: 3,194 (*f.t.* 381 m., 1,729 w.)
(717) 348-6211

MCCANN SCHOOL OF BUSINESS
Main and Pine Sts., Mahanoy City 17948. Private. 1962/1985 (AICS). Tri. plan. Degrees: A, diplomas.(*e,s*). Dir. James Noone.
Enroll.: 400 (*f.t.* 128 m., 272 w.)
(717) 773-1820

MCCARRIE SCHOOLS OF HEALTH SCIENCES AND TECHNOLOGY
132 N. 12th St., Philadelphia 19107. Private technical. 1973/1984 (NATTS). Courses of varying lengths. Degrees: A, diplomas. *Prof. Accred.:* Dental Assisting, Medical Assisting, Medical Laboratory Technology. Dir. Robert Walder.
Enroll.: 293 (*f.t.* 64 m., 184 w.)
(215) 569-9155

MEDIAN SCHOOL OF ALLIED HEALTH CAREERS
121 Ninth St., Pittsburgh 15222. Private. 1970/1981 (NATTS). Qtr. plan. Degrees: A, certificates, diplomas. *Prof. Accred.:* Dental Assisting, Medical Assisting. Pres. Frank I. Gale.
Enroll.: 548 (*f.t.* 21 m., 500 w.)
(412) 391-7021

MEDICAL COLLEGE OF PENNSYLVANIA
Philadelphia 19129. Private professional. 1984 (MSA/CHE). Sem. plan. Degrees: P,M,D. *Prof. Accred.:* Medical Technology, Medicine, Nurse Anesthesia Education, Radiography. Pres. D. Walter Cohen.
Enroll.: 565 (*f.t.* 224 m., 304 w.)
(215) 842-6000

MERCYHURST COLLEGE
501 E. 38th St., Erie 16546. Private (Roman Catholic) liberal arts. 1931/1984 (MSA/CHE). Modified 3-3 plan; intersession. Degrees: A,B,M. *Prof. Accred.:* Dietetics, Social Work (B). Pres. William P. Garvey.
Enroll.: 1,765 (*f.t.* 532 m., 714 w.)
(814) 825-0200

MESSIAH COLLEGE
Grantham 17027. Private (Brethrenin Christ) liberal arts; accreditation includes branch campus at 2026 N. Broad, Philadelphia 19121. 1963/1983 (MSA/CHE). Sem. plan. Degrees: B. Pres. D. Ray Hostetter.
Enroll.: 1,612 (*f.t.* 611 m., 943 w.)
(717) 766-2511

*MILLERSVILLE UNIVERSITY OF PENNSYLVANIA
Millersville 17551. Public liberal arts and teachers. 1950/1985 (MSA/CHE). Sem. plan. Degrees: A,B,M. *Prof. Accred.:* Music, Respiratory Therapy, Social Work (B). Pres. Joseph A. Caputo.
Enroll.: 6,151 (*f.t.* 2,214 m., 2,613 w.)
(717) 872-3011

MONROEVILLE SCHOOL OF BUSINESS
337 W. Mall Blvd., Monroeville 15146. Private. 1979/1982 (AICS). Courses of varying lengths. Certificates, diplomas. Pres./Dir. Edward R. McNutt.
Enroll.: 209 (*f.t.* 21 m., 188 w.)
(412) 856-8040

MONTGOMERY COUNTY COMMUNITY COLLEGE
Blue Bell 19422. Public (county) junior. 1970/1985 (MSA/CHE). Sem. plan. Degrees: A. *Prof. Accred.:* Dental Hygiene, Medical Laboratory Technology. Pres. Edmond A. Watters, III.
Enroll.: 7,047 (*f.t.* 1,148 m., 1,107 w.)
(215) 641-6300

MOORE COLLEGE OF ART
20th and The Parkway, Philadelphia 19103. Private professional for women. 1958/1984 (MSA/CHE). Sem. plan. Degrees: B. *Prof. Accred.:* Art. Pres. Edward C. McGuire.
Enroll.: 534 (*f.t.* 437 w.)
(215) 568-4515

MORAVIAN COLLEGE
Bethlehem 18018. Private (Moravian) liberal arts and theology. 1922/1983 (MSA/CHE). 4-1-4 plan. Degrees: B,P,M. *Prof. Accred.:* Theology (1954/1977, ATS). Pres. Roger H. Martin.

*Member Pennsylvania State System of Higher Education

Enroll.: 1,734 (*f.t.* 655 m., 543 w.)
(215) 861-1300

MOUNT ALOYSIUS JUNIOR COLLEGE
Cresson 16630-1999. Private (Roman Catholic). 1943/1984 (MSA/CHE). Sem. plan. Degrees: A. *Prof. Accred.:* Medical Laboratory Technology, Nursing (A). Pres. Edward F. Pierce.
Enroll.: 852 (*f.t.* 161 m., 411 w.)
(814) 886-4131

MUHLENBERG COLLEGE
Allentown 18104. Private (Lutheran in America) liberal arts. 1921/1986 (MSA/CHE). Sem. plan. Degrees: B. Pres. Jonathan C. Messerli.
Enroll.: 1,669 (*f.t.* 806 m., 716 w.)
(215) 433-3191

NATIONAL EDUCATION CENTER/ALLENTOWN CAMPUS
11 N. Seventh St., Allentown 18101. Private business. 1968/1980 (AICS). Sem. plan. Degrees; A, certificates, diplomas. Dir. Russ O'Neill.
Enroll.: 872 (*f.t.* 118 m., 754 w.)
(215) 432-4371

NATIONAL EDUCATION CENTER/THOMPSON CAMPUS
5650 Derry St., Harrisburg 17111. Private business. 1962/1985 (AICS). Qtr. plan. Degrees: A, diplomas. Dir. Sherman Harlow.
Enroll.: 1,135 (*f.t.* 568 m., 567 w.)
(717) 564-4112

BRANCH CAMPUS
3440 Market St., Philadelphia 19104. Dir. Leon G. Yourgevidge.
(215) 387-1530

NATIONAL EDUCATION CENTER/VALE TECHNICAL INSTITUTE CAMPUS
135 W. Market St., Blairsville 15717. Private. 1967/1983 (NATTS). Courses of varying lengths. Degrees: A. CEO Edward R. Buhler.
Enroll.: 702 (*f.t.* 699 m., 3 w.)
(412) 459-9500

NATIONAL EDUCATION CORPORATION
Scranton 18515. Private home study. 1965/1985 (NHSC). Pres. David Crowther.
(717) 342-7701

NATIONAL SCHOOL OF HEALTH TECHNOLOGY
1819 J. F. Kennedy Blvd., Philadelphia 19103. Private. 1972/1979 (NATTS). Courses of varying lengths. Degrees A, diplomas. *Prof. Accred.:* Dental Assisting, Medical Assisting, Medical Laboratory Technology. Pres. William Lobel.
Enroll.: 430
(215) 561-5020

NEUMANN COLLEGE
Aston 19014. Private (Roman Catholic) liberal arts. 1972/1986 (MSA/CHE). Sem. plan. Degrees: B,M. *Prof. Accred.:* Medical Technology, Nursing (B). Pres. Sister Margarella O'Neill, O.S.F.
Enroll.: 1,016 (*f.t.* 115 m., 379 w.)
(215) 459-0905

NEW CASTLE BUSINESS SCHOOL
316 Rhodes Pl., New Castle 16101. Private. 1954/1981 (AICS). Qtr. plan. Degrees: A. Dir. Shirley M. Eliason.
Enroll.: 170 (*f.t.* 55 m., 115 w.)
(412) 658-9066

NEW CASTLE SCHOOL OF TRADES
R.D. No. 1, Pulaski 16143. Private. 1973/1978 (NATTS). Courses of varying lengths. Certificates, diplomas. Dir. Tony Mazatasta.
Enroll.: 325 (*f.t.* 315 m., 10 w.)
(412) 964-8811

NEW KENSINGTON COMMERCIAL SCHOOL
945 Greensburg Rd., New Kensington 15068. Private. 1959/1981 (AICS). Qtr. plan. Degrees: A, certificates, diplomas. Pres. Robert J. Mullen.
Enroll.: 324 (*f.t.* 48 m., 276 w.)
(412) 339-7542

NORTHAMPTON COUNTY AREA COMMUNITY COLLEGE
3835 Green Pond Rd., Bethlehem 18017. Public junior. 1970/1985 (MSA/CHE). Sem. plan. Degrees: A, diplomas. *Prof. Accred.:* Dental Assisting, Dental Hygiene, Medical Laboratory Technology (A), Nursing (A), Practical Nursing, Radiography. Pres. Robert J. Kopecek.
Enroll.: 4,041 (*f.t.* 558 m., 770 w.)
(215) 861-5300

NORTHEAST INSTITUTE OF EDUCATION
527-535 Linden St., Scranton 18503. Private business. 1982 (AICS). Courses of varying lengths. Certificates, diplomas. Pres. Gregory Walker.
Enroll.: 289 (*f.t.* 101 m., 188 w.)
(717) 342-1365

Northeastern Christian Junior College
1860 Montgomery Ave., Villanova 19085. Private (Church of Christ) liberal arts. 1978/1986 (MSA/CHE). Tri. plan. Degrees: A. Pres. Larry Roberts.
Enroll.: 190 (*f.t.* 83 m., 99 w.)
(215) 525-6780

Orleans Technical Institute
1330 Rhawn St., Philadelphia 19111. Private. 1981 (NATTS). Courses of varying lengths. Certificates, diplomas. Exec. Dir. Gail Zuckerman.
Enroll.: 130 (*f.t.* 92 m., 38 w.)
(215) 728-4700

Orthotics Technician Training Institute
Guys Run Rd., P.O. Box 11460, Pittsburgh 15328. Private. 1984 (ABHES). Courses of varying lengths. Certificates. Dir. Rick Blackburn.
(412) 838-2010

The PJA School
7900 West Chester Pike, Upper Darby 19082. Private. 1985 (NATTS). Courses of varying lengths. Diplomas. Dir. Peter J. Antenucci.
(215) 789-6700

PSI Institute
219 N. Broad St., Philadelphia 19107. Private. 1983 (NATTS). Courses of varying lengths. Diplomas. Dir. William A. Hart.
(215) 568-3140

PTC Career Institute
2207 Chestnut St., Philadelphia 19103. Private. 1985 (NATTS). Courses of varying lengths. Diplomas. Dir. Matthew Cyrelson.
(215) 567-3104

Pace Institute
606 Court St., Reading 19601. Private business. 1984 (AICS). Courses of varying lengths. Certificates. Pres. Rhoda Dersh.
Enroll.: 46 (*f.t.* 39)
(215) 375-1212

Palmer School
1118 Market St., Philadelphia 19107. Private business. 1979/1985 (AICS). Courses of varying lengths. Certificates, diplomas. Dir. Robert Roush.
Enroll.: 352 (*f.t.* 78 m., 274 w.)
(215) 568-3800

Branch Campus
3350 Paxton St., Harrisburg 17111. Dir. R. Ester Friskney.
(717) 561-1444

Peirce Junior College
1420 Pine St., Philadelphia 19102. Private. 1971/1977 (MSA/CHE). Sem. plan. Degrees: A. Pres. Raymond C. Lewin.
Enroll.: 1,492 (*f.t.* 190 m., 682 w.)
(215) 545-6400

Penn Commercial College
82 S. Main St., Washington 15301. Private. 1960/1982 (AICS). Qtr. plan. Degrees: A. Pres. S. S. Bazant.
Enroll.: 246 (*f.t.* 24 m., 222 w.)
(412) 222-5330

Penn Technical Institute
110 Ninth St., Pittsburgh 15222. Private. 1967/1983 (NATTS). Qtr. plan. Degrees: A. Dir. Louis A. Dimasi.
Enroll.: 538 (*f.t.* 430 m., 20 w.)
(412) 355-0455

Pennco Tech
3815 Otter St., Bristol 19007. Private. 1975/1980 (NATTS). Courses of varying lengths. Degrees: A, certificates, diplomas. Pres. John A. Hobyak.
Enroll.: 559 (*f.t.* 536 m., 23 w.)
(215) 824-3200

Pennsylvania Academy of the Fine Arts
Broad and Cherry Sts., Philadelphia 19102. Private professional. 1979. Four-year program. Certificates. *Prof. Accred.:* Art. Dir. Frederick S. Osborne, Jr.
(215) 972-7623

Pennsylvania College of Optometry
1200 W. Godfrey Ave., Philadelphia 19141. Private, upper division and professional only. 1954/1982 (MSA/CHE). Sem. plan. Degrees: B,P,M. *Prof. Accred.:* Optometry. Pres. Melvin D. Wolfberg.
Enroll.: 614 (*f.t.* 351 m., 236 w.)
(215) 276-6200

Pennsylvania College of Podiatric Medicine
Eighth at Race St., Philadelphia 19107. Private professional. 1964/1985. Tri. plan. Degrees: P,M. *Prof. Accred.:* Podiatry. Pres. James E. Bates.
Enroll.: 475 (*f.t.* 381 m., 94 w.)
(215) 629-0300

PENNSYLVANIA INSTITUTE OF TECHNOLOGY
Rose Valley-Notre Dame Campus, 800 Manchester Ave., Media 19063. Private. 1972/1984 (NATTS); 1983/1986 (MSA/CHE). Qtr. plan. Degrees: A, certificates, diplomas. Pres. Kenneth A. Miller.
Enroll.: 523 (*f.t.* 299 m., 51 w.)
(215) 565-7900

PENNSYLVANIA SCHOOL OF THE ARTS
264-W. Market St., Box 175, Marietta 17547. Private professional. 1984. Three-year program. Diplomas. *Prof. Accred.:* Art. Pres. Robert Brummett.
(717) 426-4166

PENNSYLVANIA STATE SYSTEM OF HIGHER EDUCATION
Central Office, 301 Market St., Harrisburg 17108. Public (state-related). Chanc. James H. McCormick.
(717) 783-8887

PENNSYLVANIA STATE UNIVERSITY CENTRAL OFFICE
University Park 16802. Public (state-related). Pres. Bryce Jordan.
Enroll.: 63,989 (*f.t.* (814) 865-4700

UNIVERSITY PARK CAMPUS
308 Old Main, University Park 16802. 1921/1982 (MSA/CHE). Sem. plan. Degrees: A,B,P,M,D. *Prof. Accred.:* Accounting (Type A,B,C), Architecture (B,M), Art, Assistant to the Primary Care Physician, Business (B,M), Dietetics, Engineering (aerospace, agricultural, architectural, ceramics science, chemical, civil, electrical, engineering science, environmental, industrial, mechanical, metchallurgy, mining, nuclear, petroleum and natural gas), Engineering Technology (at one or more Commonwealth campuses: air pollution control, architectural, bio-medical equipment, chemical, electrical, electrical design, energy, materials-metallurgical option, mechanical, mechanical design, metallurgical, mineral processing option, mining, mining-maintenance option, mining-production option, nuclear, solar heating and cooling, structural design and construction, surveying, telecommunications, water resources), Forestry, Health Planning Administration, Journalism, Landscape Architecture (B), Medicine, Music, Nursing (B,M), Psychology, Rehabilitation Counseling, Social Work (B), Speech Pathology and Audiology, Teacher Education (*e,s,p*). Exec. Vice Pres. and Prov. William C. Richardson.
Enroll.: 35,028 (*f.t.* 17,755 m., 13,475 w.)
(814) 865-4700

ALLENTOWN CAMPUS
Fogelsville 18051. 1947/1982 (MSA/CHE). Degrees: A. Campus Exec. Officer John V. Cooney.
Enroll.: 492 (*f.t.* 282 m., 106 w.)
(215) 285-4811

ALTOONA CAMPUS
Altoona 16603. 1939/1982 (MSA/CHE). Degrees: A. Campus Exec. Officer James A. Duplass.
Enroll.: 2,144 (*f.t.* 1,024 m., 736 w.)
(814) 946-4321

BEAVER CAMPUS
Monaca 15601. 1965/1982 (MSA/CHE). Degrees: A. Campus Exec. Officer David B. Otto.
Enroll.: 1,038 (*f.t.* 585 m., 277 w.)
(412) 775-8830

BEHREND COLLEGE
Station Rd., Erie 16563. 1948/1982 (MSA/CHE). Degrees: A,B,M. Campus Exec. Officer John M. Lilley.
Enroll.: 2,251 (*f.t.* 1,265 m., 644 w.)
(814) 898-6000

BERKS CAMPUS
Reading 19608. 1958/1982 (MSA/CHE). Degrees: A. Campus Exec. Officer Frederick H. Gaige.
Enroll.: 1,252 (*f.t.* 509 m., 180 w.)
(215) 320-4800

CAPITOL CAMPUS
Middletown 17057. 1966/1982 (MSA/CHE). Degrees: B,M. Prov. Ruth Leventhal.
Enroll.: 2,644 (*f.t.* 794 m., 344 w.)
(717) 948-6100

DELAWARE COUNTY CAMPUS
Media 19063. 1967/1982 (MSA/CHE). Degrees: A. Campus Exec. Officer John D. Vairo.
Enroll.: 1,491 (*f.t.* 686 m., 354 w.)
(215) 565-3300

DUBOIS CAMPUS
DuBois 15801. 1935/1982 (MSA/CHE). Degrees: A. Campus Exec. Officer Jacqueline L. Schoch.
Enroll.: 859 (*f.t.* 355 m., 175 w.)
(814) 371-2800

Fayette Campus
Uniontown 15401. 1965/1982 (MSA/CHE). Degrees: A. Campus Exec. Officer John D. Sink.
Enroll.: 742 (*f.t.* 298 m., 164 w.)
(412) 437-2801

Hazleton Campus
Hazleton 18201. 1934/1982 (MSA/CHE). Degrees: A. Campus Exec. Officer Harmon B. Pierce.
Enroll.: 1,093 (*f.t.* 603 m., 318 w.)
(717) 454-8731

King of Prussia Graduate Center
650 S. Henderson Rd., King of Prussia 19406. 1963/1982 (MSA/CHE). Degrees: M. Acting Campus Exec. Officer Lawrence S. Cote.
Enroll.: 659 (*f.t.* 20 m., 2 w.)
(215) 265-7640

McKeesport Campus
McKeesport 15132. 1948/1982 (MSA/CHE). Degrees: A. Campus Exec. Officer Casimir J. Kowalski.
Enroll.: 1,401 (*f.t.* 625 m., 285 w.)
(412) 678-9501

The Milton S. Hershey Medical Center
Hershey 17033. 1964/1982 (MSA/CHE). Degrees: A,P,M,D. Prov. and Dean Harry Prystowsky.
Enroll.: 720 (*f.t.* 280 m., 173 w.)
(717) 534-8521

Mont Alto Campus
Mont Alto 17237. 1963/1982 (MSA/CHE). Degrees: A. Campus Exec. Officer Vernon L. Shockley.
Enroll.: 773 (*f.t.* 442 m., 247 w.)
(717) 749-3111

New Kensington Campus
New Kensington 15068. 1958/1982 (MSA/CHE). Degrees: A. *Prof. Accred.:* Medical Assisting. Campus Exec. Officer Robert D. Arbuckle.
Enroll.: 1,267 (*f.t.* 506 m., 258 w.)
(412) 339-7561

Ogontz Campus
Abington 19001. 1950/1982 (MSA/CHE). Degrees: A. Campus Exec. Officer Robert A. Bernoff.
Enroll.: 3,499 (*f.t.* 1,224 m., 867 w.)
(215) 886-9400

Schuylkill Campus
Schuylkill Haven 17972. 1934/1982 (MSA/CHE). Degrees: A. Campus Exec. Officer Wayne D. Lammie.
Enroll.: 948 (*f.t.* 314 m., 240 w.)
(717) 385-4500

Shenango Valley Campus
147 Shenango Ave., Sharon 16146. 1965/1982 (MSA/CHE). Degrees: A. Campus Exec. Officer Vincent De Sanctis.
Enroll.: 1,076 (*f.t.* 301 m., 196 w.)
(412) 981-1640

Wilkes-Barre Campus
P.O. Box 1830, Lehman 18627. 1947/1982 (MSA/CHE). Degrees: A. Campus Exec. Officer James H. Ryan.
Enroll.: 750 (*f.t.* 424 m., 143 w.)
(717) 675-2171

Worthington-Scranton Campus
Dunmore 18512. 1951/1982 (MSA/CHE). Degrees: A. Campus Exec. Officer James D. Gallagher.
Enroll.: 1,086 (*f.t.* 519 m., 238 w.)
(717) 963-4757

York Campus
York 17403. 1949/1982 (MSA/CHE). Degrees: A. Campus Exec. Officer John J. Romano.
Enroll.: 1,156 (*f.t.* 456 m., 237 w.)
(717) 771-4586

Philadelphia College of Bible
Langhorne Manor, Langhorne 19047. Private (Interdenominational) professional. 1950/1977 (AABC); 1967/1986 (MSA/CHE). Sem. plan. Degrees: B. *Prof. Accred.:* Music, Social Work (B). Pres. W. Sherrill Babb.
Enroll.: 537
(215) 752-5800

†Philadelphia College of Osteopathic Medicine
4150 City Ave., Philadelphia 19131. Private professional. 1901/1975. Sem. plan. Degrees: P. *Prof. Accred.:* EEG Technology, Medical Assisting, Osteopathy. Pres. J. Peter Tilley.
Enroll.: 833 (*f.t.* 636 m., 197 w.)
(215) 581-6370

Philadelphia College of Pharmacy and Science
43rd St. and Kingsessing Mall, Philadelphia 19104. Private professional. 1962/1983 (MSA/

†Candidate for Accreditation by Regional Accrediting Commission

CHE). Sem. plan. Degrees: B,M,D. *Prof. Accred.:* Pharmacy. Pres. Allen Misher.
Enroll.: 1,243 (*f.t.* 542 m., 684 w.)
(215) 596-8800

PHILADELPHIA COLLEGE OF TEXTILES AND SCIENCE
School House Lane and Henry Ave., Philadelphia 19144. Private professional. 1955/1986 (MSA/CHE). Sem. plan. Degrees: A,B, M. *Prof. Accred.:* Pres. James P. Gallagher.
Enroll.: 2,974 (*f.t.* 494 m., 1,004 w.)
(215) 951-2700

*PHILADELPHIA COLLEGES OF THE ARTS
Broad and Pine Sts., Philadelphia 19102. Private professional. 1959/1979 (College of Art); 1969/l974 (College of Performing Arts) (MSA/CHE). Sem. plan. Degrees: A,B,M. *Prof. Accred.:* Art, Music.. Pres. Peter Solmssen.
Enroll.: 1,041 (*f.t.* 392 m., 515 w.)
(215) 875-4800

PHILADELPHIA SCHOOL OF OFFICE TECHNOLOGIES
1724 Chestnut St., Philadelphia 19103. Private. 1964/1981 (AICS). Courses of varying lengths. Certificates. Pres. Richard S. Ross, Jr.
Enroll.: 939 (*f.t.* 71 m., 868 w.)
(215) 567-7600

BRANCH CAMPUS
8001 Roosevelt Blvd., Philadelphia 19152. Dir. Carole Toby Lazowick.
(215) 338-1212

BRANCH CAMPUS
500 Chesterbrook Blvd., Wayne 19087. Dir. Marenda Campbell.
(215) 644-5800

PHILADELPHIA SCHOOL OF PRINTING AND ADVERTISING
928 Market St., Philadelphia 19107. Private. 1973/1985 (NATTS). Qtr. plan. Degrees: A, diplomas. Dir. John McGowan.
Enroll.: 282 (*f.t.* 207 m., 75 w.)
(215) 925-1115

PHILADELPHIA TECHNICAL INSTITUTE SCHOOL OF TRADES
231-33 N. Broad St., Philadelphia 19107. Private. 1982 (NATTS). Courses of varying lengths. Certificates. Dir. Gerasimo Harris.
(215) 563-4547

*Formed in l986 from consolidation of Philadelphia College of Art and Phildelphia College of the Performing Arts

PITTSBURGH BARBER SCHOOL
421 E. Ohio St., Pittsburgh 15212. Private. 1974/1980 (NATTS). 9-month course. Diplomas. Campus Exec. Officer Frank Quinio.
Enroll.: 38 (*f.t.* 11 m., 27 w.)
(412) 321-5457

PITTSBURGH INSTITUTE OF AERONAUTICS
P.O. Box 10897, Pittsburgh 15236. Private. 1970/1980 (NATTS). Qtr. plan, Sem. plan. Degrees: A, diplomas. Pres. Ivan Livi.
Enroll.: 650 (*f.t.* 522 m., 10 w.)
(412) 462-9011

PITTSBURGH TECHNICAL INSTITUTE
635 Smithfield St., Pittsburgh 15222. Private. 1976 (NATTS). Sem. plan. Degrees: A. Pres. William J. Vandemark.
Enroll.: 258 (*f.t.* 200 m., 50 w.)
(412) 471-1011

PITTSBURGH THEOLOGICAL SEMINARY
616 N. Highland Ave., Pittsburgh 15206. Private (Presbyterian, U.S.A.) professional; graduate only. 1970/1983 (MSA/CHE). Sem. plan. Degrees: P,M,D. *Prof. Accred.:* Theology (1938/1982, ATS). Pres. C. Samuel Calian.
Enroll.: 425 (*f.t.* 313 m., 112 w.)
(412) 362-5610

POINT PARK COLLEGE
201 Wood St., Pittsburgh 15222. Private liberal arts. 1968/1984 (MSA/CHE). Sem. plan. Degrees: A,B,M. Pres. J. Matthew Simon.
Enroll.: 2,762 (*f.t.* 601 m., 510 w.)
(412) 391-4100

READING AREA COMMUNITY COLLEGE
P.O. Box 1706, Reading 19603. Public (district). 1979/1983 (MSA/CHE). Tri. plan. Degrees: A. *Prof. Accred.:* Medical Laboratory Technology (A), Nuclear Medicine Technology. Acting Pres. Gust Zogas.
Enroll.: 1,279 (*f.t.* 100 m., 264 w.)
(215) 372-4721

R.E.T.S. ELECTRONIC SCHOOL
2641 West Chester Pike, Broomall 19008. Private. 1973 (NATTS). Courses of varying lengths. Diplomas. Dir. Arthur Kleinman.
(215) 352-5586

THE RESTAURANT SCHOOL
2129 Walnut St., Philadelphia 19103. Private. 1982 (NATTS). Courses of varying lengths. Diplomas. Campus Exec. Officer Daniel Liberatoscioli.

Enroll.: 68 (*f.t.* 36 m., 32 w.)
(215) 561-3446

ROBERT MORRIS COLLEGE
Narrows Run Rd., Moon Township, Coraopolis 15108. Private professional and liberal arts. Accreditation includes Pittsburgh Campus 15219. 1968/1983 (MSA/CHE). Sem. plan. Degrees: A,B,M. *Prof. Accred.:* Radiography. Pres. Charles L. Sewall.
Enroll.: 5,545 (*f.t.* 1,441 m., 1,621 w.)
(412) 262-8200

ROSEDALE TECHNICAL INSTITUTE
4634 Browns Hill Rd., Pittsburgh 15217. Private. 1974/1979 (NATTS). Qtr. plan. Diplomas. Exec. Vice Pres. David M. McCormic.
Enroll.: 387 (*f.t.* 378 m., 9 w.)
(412) 521-6200

ROSEMONT COLLEGE
Rosemont 19010. Private (Roman Catholic) liberal arts for women. 1930/1985 (MSA/CHE). Sem. plan. Degrees: B. Pres. Dorothy McKenna Brown.
Enroll.: 520
(215) 527-0200

ST. CHARLES BORROMEO SEMINARY
Overbrook, Philadelphia 19151. Private (Roman Catholic). 1971/1986 (MSA/CHE). Sem. plan. Degrees: B,P,M. *Prof. Accred.:* Theology (1970/1986, ATS). Pres. Rector Msgr. Francis X. DiLorenzo.
Enroll.: 504 (*f.t.* 175 m., (215) 839-3760

ST. FRANCIS COLLEGE
Loretto 15940. Private (Roman Catholic) liberal arts. 1939/1986 (MSA/CHE). Sem. plan. Degrees: A,B,M. *Prof. Accred.:* Assistant to the Primary Care Physician, Library Science, Medical Technology, Nursing (B), Social Work (B). Pres. Rev. Christian Oravec, T.O.R.
Enroll.: 1,604 (*f.t.* 498 m., 487 w.)
(814) 472-7000

ST. JOSEPH'S UNIVERSITY
5600 City Ave., Philadelphia 19131. Private (Roman Catholic) liberal arts. 1922/1984 (MSA/CHE). Sem. plan. Degrees: A,B,M. Pres. Rev. Nicholas S. Rashford.
Enroll.: 5,813 (*f.t.* 1,215 m., 1,135 w.)
(215) 879-7300

ST. VINCENT COLLEGE AND SEMINARY
Latrobe 15650. Private (Roman Catholic) liberal arts and seminary. 1921/1983 (MSA/CHE). Sem. plan. Degrees: B,P,M. *Prof. Accred.:* Theology (1984, ATS). Pres. V. Rev. John F. Murtha, O.S.B.
Enroll.: 1,176 (*f.t.* 628 m., 345 w.)
(412) 539-9761

SAWYER SCHOOL
717 Liberty Ave., Pittsburgh 15222. Private business. 1973/1985 (AICS). Courses of varying lengths. Certificates. *Prof. Accred.:* Medical Assisting. Pres. Thomas B. Sapienza.
Enroll.: 797 (*f.t.* 25 m., 772 w.)
(412) 261-5700

SCHOOL OF COMPUTER TECHNOLOGY
107 Sixth St., Pittsburgh 15222. Private. 1971/1983 (AICS). Courses of varying lengths. Certificates, diplomas. Pres. Alan Maglin.
Enroll.: 1,760 (*f.t.* 1,285 m., 475 w.)
(412) 391-4197

SCHUYLKILL BUSINESS INSTITUTE
2400 West End Ave., Pottsville 17901. Private. 1980 (AICS). Courses of varying lengths. Certificates. Pres. James Tarity, Jr.
Enroll.: 224 (*f.t.* 40 m., 184 w.)
(717) 622-4835

SETON HILL COLLEGE
Greensburg 15601. Private (Roman Catholic) liberal arts for women. 1921/1982 (MSA/CHE). Sem. plan. Degrees: B. *Prof. Accred.:* Dietetics, Music. Pres. Eileen Farrell.
Enroll.: 892 (*f.t.* 0 m., 570 w.)
(412) 834-2200

SHENANGO VALLEY SCHOOL OF BUSINESS
335 Boyd Dr., Sharon 16146. Private. 1977/1980 (AICS). Courses of varying lengths. Diplomas. Pres. Richard P. McMahon.
Enroll.: 351 (*f.t.* 23 m., 328 w.)
(412) 983-0700

BRANCH CAMPUS
500 S. Mill St., New Castle 16101
(412) 654-1976

*SHIPPENSBURG UNIVERSITY OF PENNSYLVANIA
Shippensburg 17257. Public liberal arts and professional. 1939/1985 (MSA/CHE). Early sem. plan. Degrees: B,M. *Prof. Accred.:* Business (B), Social Work (B), Teacher Education (*e,s,p*). Pres. Anthony F. Ceddia.
Enroll.: 6,219 (*f.t.* 2,363 m., 2,607 w.)
(717) 532-9121

*Member Pennsylvania State System of Higher Education

*SLIPPERY ROCK UNIVERSITY OF PENNSYLVANIA
Slippery Rock 16057. Public liberal arts and teachers. 1943/1981 (MSA/CHE). Sem. plan. Degrees: B,M. *Prof. Accred.:* Music, Nursing (B), Teacher Education (*e,s,p*). Pres. Robert N. Aebersold.
Enroll.: 6,496 (*f.t.* 2,723 m., 2,683 w.)
(412) 794-2510

SOUTH HILLS BUSINESS COLLEGE
901 Boalsburg Pk., P.O. Box 670, Boalsburg 16827. Private. 1976/1985 (AICS). Tri. plan. Certificates, diplomas. Dir. Marilyn J. Mazza.
Enroll.: 250 (*f.t.* 42 m., 208 w.)
(814) 466-7951

SPRING GARDEN COLLEGE
7500 Germantown Rd., Philadelphia 19119. Private science and technology. 1973/1984 (MSA/CHE). 4-1-4 plan. Degrees: A,B. *Prof. Accred.:* Engineering Technology (computer, electronics, mechanical), Medical Laboratory Technology (A). Pres. Thomas Patrick Melady.
Enroll.: 1,677 (*f.t.* 561 m., 133 w.)
(215) 248-7900

SUPERIOR TECHNICAL INSTITUTE, INC.
Deer Lake Campus, Box 9, Fleetville 18420. Private 1972/1977 (NATTS). Courses of varying lengths. Certificates. Dir. Larry Bergman.
Enroll.: 176 (*f.t.* 86 m., 90 w.)
(717) 945-5135

SUSQUEHANNA UNIVERSITY
Selinsgrove 17870. Private (Lutheran in America) liberal arts college. 1930/1984 (MSA/CHE). Sem. plan. Degrees: A,B. *Prof. Accred.:* Music, Nurse Anesthesia Education. Pres. Joel L. Cunningham.
Enroll.: 1,724 (*f.t.* 736 m., 652 w.)
(717) 374-0101

SWARTHMORE COLLEGE
Swarthmore 19081. Private liberal arts. 1921/1984 (MSA/CHE). Sem. plan. Degrees: B,M. *Prof. Accred.:* Engineering. Pres. David W. Fraser.
Enroll.: 1,322 (*f.t.* 692 m., 624 w.)
(215) 447-7000

TALMUDICAL YESHIVA OF PHILADELPHIA
6063 Drexel Rd., Philadelphia 19131. Private professional. 1975/1981. Degrees: 1st Rabbinic and 1st Talmudic. *Prof. Accred.:* Rabbinical and Talmudic Education. Pres. E. Weinberg.
Enroll.: *f.t.* 81 m.
(215) 473-1212

TECHNICIAN TRAINING SCHOOL
1000 Island Ave., McKees Rocks 15136. Private. 1975/1980 (NATTS). Courses of varying lengths. Diplomas. Campus Exec. Officer Richard J. Zaiden, Jr.
Enroll.: 496 (*f.t.* 480 m., 16 w.)
(412) 771-7590

TEMPLE UNIVERSITY
Broad St. and Montgomery Ave., Philadelphia 19122. Private (state-related). 1921/1982 (MSA/CHE). Branch campus at Ambler 19002. Sem. plan. Degrees: A,B,P,M,D. *Prof. Accred.:* Architecture (B), Art, Business (B,M), Dental Hygiene, Dentistry, Engineering Technology (biomedical, civil and construction, electrical, electronics, environmental, mechanical), Health Services Administration, Journalism, Law, Medical Record Administration, Medical Technology, Medicine, Music, Occupational Therapy, Nuclear Medicine Technology, Nursing (B), Pharmacy, Physical Therapy, Psychology, Public Health, Radiography, Social Work (B,M), Speech Pathology and Audiology, Teacher Education (*e,s,p*). Pres. Peter J. Liacouras.
Enroll.: 31,001 (*f.t.* 10,730 m., 9,432 w.)
(215) 787-7000

THIEL COLLEGE
Greenville 16125. Private (Lutheran in America) liberal arts. 1922/1984 (MSA/CHE). 4-1-4 plan. Degrees: A,B. *Prof. Accred.:* Respiratory Therapy Technology. Pres. Louis T. Almen.
Enroll.: 864 (*f.t.* 396 m., 394 w.)
(412) 588-7700

THOMAS JEFFERSON UNIVERSITY
11th and Walnut Sts., Philadelphia 19107. Private liberal arts and professional. 1976/1981 (MSA/CHE). 3-3-3 plan. Degrees: A,B,P,M,D. *Prof. Accred.:* Cytotechnology, Dental Hygiene, Diagnostic Medical Sonography, Medical Technology, Medicine, Nursing (B), Occupational Therapy, Physical Therapy, Radiography. Pres. Lewis W. Bluemle, Jr.
Enroll.: 2,016 (*f.t.* 776 m., 793 w.)
(215) 928-6000

*Member Pennsylvania State System of Higher Education

TRACEY-WARNER SCHOOL
401 N. Broad St., Philadelphia 19108. Private. 1972/1984 (NATTS). Sem. plan. Degrees: A. Pres. Lewis H. Warner.
Enroll.: 145 (*f.t.* 35 m., 110 w.)
(215) 574-0402

TRIANGLE TECH
I-80, Exit 16, P.O. Box 551, DuBois 15801. Private. 1981 (NATTS). Courses of varying lengths. Certificates. Dir. James Edwards.
Enroll.: 65
(814) 371-2090

TRIANGLE TECH
2000 Liberty St., Erie 16502. Private. 1978 (NATTS). Sem. plan. Degrees: A. Campus Exec. Officer Edward Petrunak.
Enroll.: 202 (*f.t.* 171 m., 16 w.)
(814) 453-6016

TRIANGLE TECH
Triangle Tech Plaza, Blank School Rd., Greensburg 15601. Private. 1970/1980 (NATTS). Sem. plan. Degrees: A, certificates. Pres. James Agras.
Enroll.: 260 (*f.t.* 185 m., 15 w.)
(412) 832-1050

TRIANGLE TECH
1940 Perrysville Ave., Pittsburgh 15214. Private. 1970/1980 (NATTS). Sem. plan. Degrees: A, certificates, diplomas. Pres. James R. Agras.
Enroll.: 228 (*f.t.* 177 m., 13 w.)
(412) 359-1000.

TRINITY EPISCOPAL SCHOOL FOR MINISTRY
311 11th St., Ambridge 15003. Private (Episcopal) professional; graduate only. Sem. plan. Degrees: P,M. *Prof. Accred.:* Theology (ATS, 1985). Pres. John H. Rodgers, Jr.
Enroll.: 125
(412) 978-2133

†UNITED WESLEYAN COLLEGE
1414 E. Cedar St., Allentown 18103. Private (Wesleyan Church) professional. 1972/1982 (AABC). Sem. plan. Degrees: A,B. Pres. John P. Ragsdale.
Enroll.: 201 (*f.t.* 107 m., 59 w.)
(215) 439-8709

UNIVERSITY OF PENNSYLVANIA
Philadelphia 19104. Private (state-aided); coordinate liberal arts colleges for men and women. 1921/1984 (MSA/CHE). Sem. plan. Degrees: A,B,P,M,D. *Prof. Accred.:* Architecture (M,D), Business (B,M), Dental Hygiene, Dentistry, Engineering (bioengineering, chemical, civil and urban, electrical engineering and science, materials science and engineering, mechanical engineering and applied mechanics, systems science and engineering), Health Services Administration, Landscape Architecture (M), Law, Medical Technology, Medicine, Nursing (B,M), Practical Nursing, Psychology, Social Work (M), Teacher Education (*e,s,p*), Veterinary Medicine. Pres. F. Sheldon Hackney.
Enroll.: 21,870 (*f.t.* 10,081 m., 7,420 w.)
(215) 898-5000

UNIVERSITY OF PITTSBURGH—CENTRAL OFFICE
4200 Fifth Ave., Pittsburgh 15260. Private (state-related). Chanc. Wesley W. Posvar.
(412) 624-4141

UNIVERSITY OF PITTSBURGH—PITTSBURGH CAMPUS
Fifth and Bigelow Sts., Pittsburgh 15260. Private (state-related). 1921/1986 (MSA/CHE). Tri. plan. Degrees: A,B,P,M,D. *Prof. Accred.:* Business (B,M), Dental Assisting, Dental Hygiene, Dentistry, Dietetics, Engineering (chemical, civil, electrical, industrial, mechanical, metallurgical and materials), Engineering Technology (civil, electrical, mechanical), Health Services Administration, Law, Librarianship, Medical Record Administration, Medical Technology, Medicine, Nursing (B,M), Occupational Therapy, Pharmacy, Physical Therapy, Psychology, Public Health, Rehabilitation Counseling, Respiratory Therapy, Social Work (B,M), Speech Pathology and Audiology, Teacher Education (*e,s,p*). Pres. Wesley W. Posvar.
Enroll.: 28,710 (*f.t.* 9,717 m., 8,088 w.)
(412) 624-4141

UNIVERSITY OF PITTSBURGH AT BRADFORD
Bradford 16701. 1963/1986 (MSA/CHE). Degrees: A,B. Pres. Richard E. McDowell.
Enroll.: 845 (*f.t.* 330 m., 285 w.)
(814) 362-3801

UNIVERSITY OF PITTSURGH AT GREENSBURG
Greensburg 15601. 1963/1986 (MSA/CHE). Certificates. Pres. George F. Chambers.

†Candidate for Accreditation by Regional Accrediting Commission

Enroll.: 1,395 (*f.t.* 502 m., 340 w.)
(412) 837-7040

UNIVERSITY OF PITTSBURGH AT JOHNSTOWN
Johnstown 15904. 1927/1986 (MSA/CHE). Degrees: B. *Prof. Accred.:* Nurse Anesthesia Education. Pres. Frank H. Blackington, III.
Enroll.: 3,214 (*f.t.* 1,432 m., 1,155 w.)
(412) 266-9661

UNIVERSITY OF PITTSBURGH AT TITUSVILLE
Titusville 16354. 1963/1986 (MSA/CHE). Degrees: A. Pres. L. Samuel Johnson.
Enroll.: 289 (*f.t.* 111 m., 73 w.)
(814) 827-2702

UNIVERSITY OF SCRANTON
Scranton 18510. Private (Roman Catholic). 1927/1983 (MSA/CHE). 4-1-4 plan. Degrees: A,B,M. *Prof. Accred.:* Physical Therapy, Rehabilitation Counseling, Teacher Education (*s,p*). Pres. Rev. Joseph A. Panuska, S.J.
Enroll.: 4,479 (*f.t.* 1,922 m., 1,502 w.)
(717) 961-7400

URSINUS COLLEGE
Collegeville 19426. Private (United Church of Christ) liberal arts. 1921/1984 (MSA/CHE). Sem. plan. Degrees: A,B. *Prof. Accred.:* Pres. Richard P. Richter.
Enroll.: 2,127 (*f.t.* 565 m., 585 w.)
(215) 489-4111

VALLEY FORGE CHRISTIAN COLLEGE
Charlestown Rd., Phoenixville 19460. Private (Assembly of God) professional. 1967/1977 (AABC). Sem. plan. Degrees: B. Pres. Wesley Smith.
Enroll.: 589
(215) 935-0450

VALLEY FORGE MILITARY JUNIOR COLLEGE
Wayne 19087. Private for men. 1954/1980 (MSA/CHE). Sem. plan. Degrees: A. Supt. Lt. Gen. Alexander M. Wayand, USA (Ret.)
Enroll.: *f.t.* 140 m.
(215) 688-1800

VILLA MARIA COLLEGE
Erie 16505. Private (Roman Catholic) liberal arts for women. 1933/1985 (MSA/CHE). 4-1-4 plan. Degrees: A,B. *Prof. Accred.:* Dietetics, Nursing (B). Pres. Sister M. Lawreace Antoun, S.S.J.
Enroll.: 597 (*f.t.* 6 m., 335 w.)
(814) 838-1966

VILLANOVA UNIVERSITY
Lancaster Pike, Villanova 19085. Private. 1921/1986 (MSA/CHE). Sem. plan. Degrees: A,B,P,M,D. *Prof. Accred.:* Accounting (Type A), Business (B,M), Engineering (chemical, civil, electrical, mechanical), Law, Nursing (B). Pres. Rev. John M. Driscoll, O.S.A.
Enroll.: 11,956 (*f.t.* 4,392 m., 3,437 w.)
(215) 645-4500

WASHINGTON AND JEFFERSON COLLEGE
Washington 15301. Private liberal arts. 1921/1983 (MSA/CHE). 4-1-4 plan. Degrees: A,B,M. *Prof. Accred.:* Pres. Howard J. Burnett.
Enroll.: 1,062 (*f.t.* 634 m., 404 w.)
(412) 222-4400

WASHINGTON INSTITUTE OF TECHNOLOGY, INC.
82 S. Main St., Washington 15301. Private. 1974/1979 (NATTS). Sem. plan and courses of varying lengths. Certificates, diplomas. Campus Exec. Officer Stanley S. Bazant.
Enroll.: 138 (*f.t.* 128 m., 10 w.)
(412) 222-1942

WAYNESBURG COLLEGE
51 W. College St., Waynesburg 15370. Private (United Presbyterian) liberal arts. 1950/1985 (MSA/CHE). Sem. plan. Degrees: A,B,M. Pres. J. Thomas Mills.
Enroll.: 869 (*f.t.* 368 m., 352 w.)
(412) 627-8191

WELDER TRAINING AND TESTING INSTITUTE
729 E. Highland, Allentown 18103. Private. 1973/1978 (NATTS). Courses of varying lengths. Certificates. Admin. Vincent Castelluci.
Enroll.: 125 (*f.t.* 120 m., 5 w.)
(215) 437-9720

WELDER TRAINING AND TESTING INSTITUTE
One Schuylkill Pkwy., Bridgeport 19405. Private. 1977 (NATTS). Courses of varying lengths. Degrees: A, certificates, diplomas. Campus Exec. Officer G. M. Orthaus.
Enroll.: 150 (*f.t.* 125 m., 5 w.)
(215) 277-5455

WELDER TRAINING AND TESTING INSTITUTE
439 N. 11th St., Philadelphia 19123. Private. 1978 (NATTS). Courses of varying lengths. Degrees: A, certificates, diplomas. Pres. Raymond M. Moyer.
(215) 765-7028

WELDER TRAINING AND TESTING INSTITUTE
Brown St. and Pennsylvania Ave., Selingsgrove 17870. Private. 1985 (NATTS). Courses of varying lengths. Degrees: A, certificates, diplomas.
(717) 743-5500

WELDER TRAINING AND TESTING INSTITUTE
230 Johnson St., Wilkes-Barre 18702. Private. 1978 (NATTS). Courses of varying lengths. Certificates. Pres. Robert K. Wiswesser.
Enroll.: 61 (*f.t.* 55 m.)
(717) 823-0109

*WEST CHESTER UNIVERSITY OF PENNSYLVANIA
West Chester 19383. Public liberal arts and teachers. 1946/1981 (MSA/CHE). Sem. plan. Degrees: A,B,M. *Prof. Accred.:* Music, Nursing (B), Social Work (B), Teacher Education (*e,s,p*). Pres. Kenneth L. Perrin.
Enroll.: 9,953 (*f.t.* 3,077 m., 3,988 w.)
(215) 436-1000

WESTERN PENNSYLVANIA SCHOOL OF HEALTH AND BUSINESS CAREERS, INC.
Ruben Bldg.-Second Fl., 221-225 Fifth Ave., Pittsburgh 15222. Private. 1982 (ABHES). Courses of varying lengths. Diplomas. *Prof. Accred.:* Medical Assisting. Dir. Ross Perilman.
Enroll.:
(412) 281-2600

WESTMINSTER COLLEGE
New Wilmington 16172. Private (United Presbyterian) liberal arts. 1921/1986 (MSA/CHE). Sem. plan. Degrees: B,M. *Prof. Accred.:* Music. Interim Pres. Jerry M. Boone.
Enroll.: 1,296 (*f.t.* 526 m., 631 w.)
(412) 946-8761

WESTMINSTER THEOLOGICAL SEMINARY
Church Rd. and Willow Grove Ave., Laverock: Mailing address; P.O. Box 27009, Philadelphia 19118. Private (Presbyterian) graduate and professional only. 1954/1974 (MSA/CHE). 4-1-4 plan. Degrees: P,M,D. *Prof. Accred.:* Theology (1986, ATS). Pres. Rev. George C. Fuller.
Enroll.: 502 (*f.t.* 229 m., 18 w.)
(215) 887-5511

* Member Pennsylvania State System of Higher Education

WESTMORELAND COUNTY COMMUNITY COLLEGE
Youngwood 15697. Public (district) junior. 1978/1983 (MSA/CHE). Sem. plan. Degrees: A, certificates. Interim Pres. N. Dean Evans.
Enroll.: 3,312 (*f.t.* 560 m., 784 w.)
(412) 836-1600

WIDENER UNIVERSITY
Chester 19013. Private independent coeducational liberal arts and science; affiliated Brandywine College and Delaware Law School—See Delaware. 1954/1986 (MSA/CHE). 4-1-4 plan. Degrees: A,B,M,D. *Prof. Accred.:* Engineering (chemical, electrical, mechanical), Health and Medical Services Administration, Nursing (B,M), Social Work (B). Prov. Joel M. Rodney. Pres. Robert J. Bruce.
Enroll.: 6,676 (*f.t.* 1,799 m., 1,490 w.)
(215) 499-4000

WILKES COLLEGE
P.O. Box 111, Wilkes-Barre 18766. Private liberal arts. 1937/1985 (MSA/CHE). Sem. plan. Degrees: B,M. *Prof. Accred.:* Engineering (electrical), Nursing (B). Pres. Christopher N. Breiseth.
Enroll.: 2,991 (*f.t.* 956 m., 802 w.)
(717) 824-4651

THE WILLIAMSON FREE SCHOOL OF MECHANICAL TRADES
Middletown Rd., Rt. 352, Media 19063. Private. 1970/1980 (NATTS). Sem. plan. Degrees: A, diplomas. Pres. Howard B. Maxwell.
Enroll.: f.t. 218 m.
(215) 566-1776

WILLIAMSPORT AREA COMMUNITY COLLEGE
Williamsport 17701. Public (district) junior. Accreditation includes branch campus at Wellsboro 16901. 1970/1984 (MSA/CHE). Sem. plan. Degrees: A. *Prof. Accred.:* Dental Hygiene, Radiography. Pres. Robert L. Breuder.
Enroll.: 3,576 (*f.t.* 1,792 m., 914 w.)
(717) 326-3761

WILLIAMSPORT SCHOOL OF COMMERCE
941 W. Third St., Williamsport 17701. Private. 1963/1980 (AICS). Qtr. plan. Degrees: A, diplomas. Dir. Benjamin H. Comfort, III.
Enroll.: 207 (*f.t.* 9 m., 198 w.)
(717) 326-2869

WILMA BOYD CAREER SCHOOLS
One Chatham Center, Pittsburgh 15219. Private. 1975/1984 (AICS); 1972/1984

(NATTS); 1979/1984 (NHSC). Qtr. plan. Certificates. Pres./Dir. Alfred McCloy.
Enroll.: 1,860 (*f.t.* 465 m., 1,395 w.)
(412) 456-1800

WILSON COLLEGE
Chambersburg 17201. Private (United Presbyterian) liberal arts for women. 1922/1978 (MSA/CHE). Sem. plan. Degrees: A, B. Pres. Mary-Linda S. Merriam.
Enroll.: 333 (*f.t.* 2 m., 178 w.)
(717) 264-4141

YESHIVA BETH MOSHE
930 Hickory St., P.O. Box 1141, Scranton 18505. Private professional. 1975/1983. Degrees: 1st and 2nd Rabbinic. *Prof. Accred.:* Rabbinical and Talmudic Education. Pres. D. Fink. *Enroll.: f.t.* 65 m.
(717) 346-1747

YORK COLLEGE OF PENNSYLVANIA
Country Club Road, York 17403-34265. Private liberal arts. 1959/1985 (MSA/CHE). Sem. plan. Degrees: A, B, M. *Prof. Accred.:* Nursing (B), Respiratory Therapy. Pres. Robert V. Iosue.
Enroll.: 4,638 (*f.t.* 998 m., 1,482 w.)
(717) 846-7788

YORK COUNTY AREA VOCATIONAL-TECHNICAL SCHOOL
2179 S. Queen St., York 17402. Public practical nursing program. 1982. 12-month program. Diplomas. *Prof. Accred.:* Practical Nursing. Dir. Barbara J. Garzon.
(717) 741-0820

YORK TECHNICAL INSTITUTE
3351 Whiteford Rd., York 17402. Private. 1979 (NATTS). Courses of varying lengths. Diplomas. Dir. Loren H. Kroh.
Enroll.: 58 (*f.t.* 37 m., 21 w.)
(717) 755-1100

YORKTOWNE BUSINESS INSTITUTE
W. Seventh Ave., York 17404. Private. 1985 (AICS). Courses of varying lengths. Certificates, diplomas. Pres. Gertrude K. Murphy.
Enroll.: 378 (*f.t.* 38 m., 340 w.)
(717) 846-5111

PUERTO RICO

ACADEMIA DE ESTETICA LANIN
752 Andalucia St., Puerto Nuevo, Rio Piedras 00921. Private technical. 1979 (NATTS). Courses of varying lengths. Certificates. Pres. Lanin Aponte de Santana.
(809) 781-7960

ALLIED SCHOOLS OF PUERTO RICO
Calle McKinley No. 2, Manati 00701. Private business. 1984 (AICS). Courses of varying lengths. Certificates, diplomas. Dir. Maria S. Pinto.
(809) 854-3785

BRANCH CAMPUS
Calle Del Carmen #6, Altos Morovis 00717. Dir. Zulma Martinez.
(809) 854-3785

BRANCH CAMPUS
Highway #2, Km. 11.1, Bayamon 00619. Dir. Gustavo Sanchez.
(809) 854-3785

BRANCH CAMPUS
Corozal Shopping Ctr., St. Rd. 159, Corozal 00643. Dir. Ligia Rivera.
(809) 859-1255

BRANCH CAMPUS
1342 Durazno Blvd., Levittown Toa Baja 00759. Dir. Licette Nazario Torres.
(809) 795-2240

AMERICAN COLLEGE OF PUERTO RICO
P.O. Box 2037, Bayamon 00621. Private liberal arts and business administration. 1975/1982 (AICS); 1982 (MSA/CHE). Sem. plan. Degrees: A,B, certificates, diplomas. Pres. Juan Nazario-Negron.
Enroll.: 3,515 (*f.t.* 1,396 m., 1,945 w.)
(809) 786-0090

BRANCH CAMPUS
P.O. Box 929, Dorado 00646. Dir. Juan Osorio.
(809) 796-2169

BRANCH CAMPUS
P.O. Box 708, Manati 00701. Dir. Jose Nazario.
(809) 854-2835

AMERICAN EDUCATIONAL COLLEGE
65th Infantry Ave., El Commandante Plaza Shopping Center, Second Floor, Carolina 00630. Private business. 1985 (AICS). Courses of varying lengths. Certificates, diplomas. Pres. Joaquin Gonzalez Pinto.
(809) 752-3230

ANA G. MENDEZ EDUCATIONAL FOUNDATION
Río Piedras 00929. Private. Sem. plan. Pres. José F. Méndez.
(809) 751-0178

PUERTO RICO JUNIOR COLLEGE
Apartado 21373, Rio Piedras 00928. 1959/1983 (MSA/CHE). Degrees: A. *Prof. Accred.:* Medical Record Technology. Acting Chanc. Luis Gonzalez-Vales.
Enroll.: 5,001 (*f.t.* 1,579 m., 2,749 w.)
(809) 758-7171

UNIVERSIDAD DEL TURABO
P.O. Box 1791, Caguas 00625. 1974/1984 (MSA/CHE). Degrees: A,B,M. Chanc. Gamaliel Perez-Santiago.
Enroll.: 7,388 (*f.t.* 2,556 m., 3,959 w.)
(809) 744-8791

UNIVERSIDAD METROPOLITANO
Box 2115, Rio Piedras 00928. 1980/1985 (MSA/CHE). Degrees: A,B. *Prof. Accred.:* Nursing (A). Chanc. Juan Gonzalez-Lamela.
Enroll.: 5,411 (*f.t.* 1,569 m., 3,118 w.)
(809) 766-1717

ANTILLES SCHOOL OF PRACTICAL NURSING
Calle Domenech No. 107, Hato Rey 00917; Postal address: GPO Box 1742, San Juan 00936. Private. 1985 (ABHES). 1-year program. Certificates, diplomas. *Prof. Accred.:* Practical Nursing. Admin. Pablo Guzman Peres.
(809) 764-7576

ANTILLIAN COLLEGE
P.O. Box 118, Mayaguez 00709-01188. Private (Seventh-Day Adventist) liberal arts. 1978/1983 (MSA/CHE). Sem. plan. Degrees: A,B. Pres. Angel M. Rodriquez.
Enroll.: 867 (*f.t.* 300 m., 483 w.)
(809) 834-9595

BAYAMON CENTRAL UNIVERSITY
P.O. Box 1725, Bayamón 00621. Private liberal arts college. 1971/1985 (MSA/CHE). Sem. plan. Degrees: A,B. Pres. Rev. P. Vincent A. M. van Rooij, O.P.
Enroll.: 2,801 (*f.t.* 1,037 m., 1,516 w.)
(809) 786-3030

BAYAMON REFRIGERATION INSTITUTE
Avenue Los Millones, No. 100, Bayamon 00619. Private. 1985 (NATTS). Courses of varying lengths. Certificates, diplomas. Dir. Gabriel Colon.
(809) 786-2468

BAYAMON TECHNICAL AND COMMERCIAL INSTITUTE
Calle Marti #9 Esq. Paseo Barbosa, P.O. Box 6008, Sta. #1, Bayamon 00619. Private. 1984 (AICS). Courses of varying lengths. Certificates, diplomas. Pres. Wilson Del Toro.
(809) 787-8805

BENEDICT SCHOOL OF LANGUAGE AND COMMERCE
403 Ponce de Leon Ave., Hato Rey 00917. Private. 1982 (AICS). Qtr. plan. Certificates, diplomas. Pres. Jose Luis Padial.
Enroll.: 842 (*f.t.* 160 m., 682 w.)
(809) 754-1499

CEDECA
1612 Ponce de Leon Ave., Fourth Floor, P.O. Box 8245, Fernandez Juncos Sta., San Juan, 00910. Private business. 1984 (AICS). Courses of varying lengths. Certificates, diplomas. Dir. Isabel Leon.
(809) 725-8718

CAGUAS BEAUTY, BARBER, AND HAIR STYLING ACADEMY
Calle Acosta No. 24, P.O. Box 8003, Caguas 00625. Private. 1982 (NATTS). Courses of varying lengths. Certificates. Dir. Feliciano Medina.
(809) 743-3679

CAGUAS CITY COLLEGE
Carr. 183, Km. 1.7, P.O. Box 8517, Caguas 00626. Private senior. 1976/1983 (AICS). Tri. plan. Degrees: A, certificates, diplomas. Pres. Alex A. De Jorge.
Enroll.: 1,230 (*f.t.* 547 m., 683 w.)
(809) 743-4041

BRANCH CAMPUS
San Jose St. in Front of Public Square, Rio Grande 00745. Dir. Loida Ramirez.
(809) 887-3352

CAGUAS COLLEGE OF TECHNOLOGY AND SCIENCE
Dr. Rufo #13, Box 351, Caguas 00626. Private. 1983 (AICS). Courses of varying lengths. Certificates. Dir. Esteban Lopez Lleras.
Enroll.: 1,071 (*f.t.* 604 m., 467 w.)
(809) 746-6575

BRANCH CAMPUS
Edificio Federal (Antiguo) Carretera #2, Km. 11.0, P.O. Box 2859, Bayamon 00621-2859. Dir. Luis Rafael Santiago.
(809) 798-0300

CARIBBEAN CENTER FOR ADVANCED STUDIES
Minillas Sta. (Apartado 41246), Santurce 00940. Independent, graduate only; accreditation includes Miami Campus, 1401 S.W. First St., Miami, FL 33135,
(305) 541-8970. 1974/1984 (MSA/CHE). Sem. plan. Degrees: P,M,D. Chanc. Salvador Santiago-Negron.
Enroll.: 486 (*f.t.* 128 m., 223 w.)
(809) 725-2451

CARIBBEAN UNIVERSITY COLLEGE
P.O. Box 493, Bayamon 00621. Independent liberal arts; accreditation includes branch campuses at Carolina, Vega Baja, and Ponce. 1977/1981 (MSA/CHE). Sem. plan. Degrees: A,B. Pres. Angel E. Juan-Ortega.
Enroll.: 3,497 (*f.t.* 829 m., 1,350 w.)
(809) 780-0070

CATHOLIC UNIVERSITY OF PUERTO RICO
Las Americas Ave., Ponce 00732. Private (Roman Catholic). 1953/1983 (MSA/CHE). Sem. plan. Degrees: A,B,P,M. *Prof. Accred.:* Law (ABA only), Medical Technology, Nursing (B), Social Work (B). Pres. F. Tosello Giangiacomo.
Enroll.: 12,627 (*f.t.* 3,315 m., 6,000 w.)
(809) 844-4150

ARECIBO BRANCH CAMPUS
P.O. Box 495, Arecibo 00613. Degrees: A,B.
(809) 881-1212

GUAYAMA BRANCH CAMPUS
P.O. Box 809, Guayama 00654. Degrees: A,B.
(809) 864-0550

MAYAGUEZ BRANCH CAMPUS
P.O. Box 1326, Mayaguez 00709. Degrees: A.
(809) 834-5151

CENTRO DE ESTUDIOS DE PUERTO RICO Y EL CARIBE
San Sebastian St. 1, Old San Juan 00904. Private graduate, with undergraduate programs in the humanities. 1982 (MSA/CHE). Sem. plan. Degrees: B,M. Dir. Ricardo E. Alegria.

Enroll.: 79 (*f.t.* 17 m., 12 w.)
(809) 723-4481

CENTRO DE ESTUDIOS MULTIDISCIPLINARIOS
Ave. Domenech 210, Hato Rey 00918. Public. 1981. 1-year program. Certificates. *Prof. Accred.:* Practical Nursing. Dir. Flor E. Saez.
Enroll.: 176

COLEGIO COMERCIAL DE CAYEY
Calle de Diego 164 (Altos), Box K, Cayey 00633. Private. 1983 (AICS). Qtr. plan. Certificates, diplomas. Pres. Mariano Garcia.
Enroll.: 216 (*f.t.* 72 m., 144 w.)
(809) 738-5555

BRANCH CAMPUS
Central Aguirre, Aguirre 00608. Dir. Sandra Suarez.
(809) 853-2050

CONSERVATORY OF MUSIC OF PUERTO RICO
P.O. Box 41227, Santurce 00940. Public conservatory. 1975/1985 (MSA/CHE). Sem. plan. Degrees: B. Chan. Jorge Perez Rolon.
Enroll.: 251 (*f.t.* 125 m., 48 w.)
(809) 751-0160

ELECTRONIC COLLEGE AND COMPUTER PROGRAMMING
Munoz Rivera No. 504 Altos, Box 202, Hato Rey 00918. Private. 1983 (AICS). Courses of varying lengths. Certificates. Pres. Cris Burgos Rodriguez.
Enroll.: 2,530 (*f.t.* 1,409 m., 1,121 w.)
(809) 753-1500

BRANCH CAMPUS
P.O. Box 1947, Arecibo 00612. Dir. Peter Martinez Gaud.
(809) 878-1500

ELECTRONIC DATA PROCESSING COLLEGE
P.O. Box 2303, Hato Rey 00918. Private senior. 1976/1983 (AICS). Courses of varying lengths. Degrees: A, certificates. Pres. Anibal Nieves.
Enroll.: 3,036 (*f.t.* 2,062 m., 974 w.)
(809) 765-3560

BRANCH CAMPUS
P.O. Box 1674, San Sebastian 00755. Dir. Juan S. Robles.
Enroll.: (809) 896-2137

EVANGELICAL SEMINARY OF PUERTO RICO
Hato Rey 00918. Private (interdenominational) professional; graduate only. Sem. plan. Degrees: P,M. *Prof. Accred.:* Theology (1982,ATS). Pres. Luis Fidel Mercado.
Enroll.: 177
(809) 765-1834

HUERTAS JUNIOR COLLEGE
P.O. Box 8429, Caguas 00626. Private junior. 1977/1983 (AICS). Qtr. plan. Degrees: A, diplomas. Pres. Ruben Lopez Huertas.
Enroll.: 2,124 (*f.t.* 1,104 m., 1,020 w.)
(809) 743-2156

HUMACAO COMMUNITY COLLEGE
101 Cruz Stella Ave., Humacao 00661. Private business. 1979/1982 (AICS). Courses of varying lengths. Diplomas. Pres. Jorge Mojica-Ramirez.
Enroll.: 319 (*f.t.* 37 m., 242 w.)
(809) 852-1430

ICPR JUNIOR COLLEGE
558 Munoz Rivera Ave., Box 304, Hato Rey 00919-0304. Private business. 1975/1981 (AICS); 1985 (MSA/CHE). Tri. plan. Degrees: A. Pres. Enrique Pineiro.
Enroll.: 1,356 (*f.t.* 322 m., 838 w.)
(809) 763-1010

BRANCH CAMPUS
Road 2, Km. 80.4, Bo. San Daniel Box 1606, Arecibo 00612-1606. Dir. Angel Curbelo Soto.
(809) 878-0524

BRANCH CAMPUS
Mendez Vigo 55, Box 1108, Mayaguez 00708-1108. Dir. Genoveva Christian.
(809) 832-2250

INSTITUTO DE BANCA Y PROGRAMACION
996 Munoz Rivera Ave., Rio Piedras 00925. Private business. 1978/1981 (AICS). Courses of varying lengths. Certificates, diplomas. Pres. Fidel Alonso Valls.
Enroll.: 4,592 (*f.t.* 2,270 m., 2,322 w.)
(809) 765-8687

BRANCH CAMPUS
Calle Post #154 Sur, Mayaguez 00708. Interim Dir. Carlos Rovira Burset.
(809) 833-4690

BRANCH CAMPUS
Edif. Torre de Oro, Ave. Las Americas, Ponce 00731. Dir. Carlos Rovira.
(809) 840-6119

INSTITUTE OF MULTIPLE TECHNOLOGY
P.O. Box 209, Mayaguez 00709. Private. 1985 (AICS). Courses of varying lengths. Certificates, diplomas. Pres. Angel L. Negron.
(809) 833-6305

BRANCH CAMPUS
163 Antonio R. Barcelo St., Esq., Arecibo 00612. Dir. Harold Mejia.
(809) 878-6844

INSTITUTO DE EDUCACION UNIVERSAL
Carr. 2, K. 16.2, Hato Tejas 00619. Private. 1984 (NATTS). Courses of varying lengths. Certificates. Pres. Angel Ruiz Rivera.
(809) 787-3215

INSTITUTO SUPERIOR ELECTRONICO
Kennedy Ave., Km. 34, Apartado 4379, Hato Rey Station 00919. Private. 1985 (NATTS). Courses of varying lengths. Certificates. Dir. Guillermo M. Ruiz.
(809) 781-3865

INSTITUTO TECNICO COMERCIAL JUNIOR COLLEGE
GPO Box 2527, San Juan 00936. Private. 1975/1985 (AICS). Courses of varying lengths. Degrees: A, diplomas. Pres. Carmen T. Ramirez.
Enroll.: 1,168 (*f.t.* 425 m., 743 w.)
(809) 767-4323

INTER AMERICAN UNIVERSITY OF PUERTO RICO
Central Office, Box 3255, San Juan 00936. Private (United Presbyterian). Pres. Ramón A. Cruz.
Enroll.: 37,822 (*f.t.* 11,159 m., 18,326 w.)
(809) 766-1912

SAN GERMÁN CAMPUS
San Germán 00753. 1944/1983 (MSA/CHE). Degrees: A,B,M. *Prof. Accred.:* Medical Technology. Vice Pres. and Exec. Dean Federico Matheu.
Enroll.: 6,300 (*f.t.* 2,196 m., 3,065 w.)
(809) 892-1095

METROPOLITAN CAMPUS
P.O. Box 1293, Hato Rey 00919. Accreditation includes School of Law, Santurce 00910, School of Optometry, San Juan 00936, and Bayamón Campus, Bayamón 00620. 1960/1983 (MSA/CHE). Degrees: A,B,P,M,D. *Prof. Accred.:* Law, Optometry, Social Work (B). Chanc. Rafael Cartagena.
Enroll.: 13,106 (*f.t.* 3,839 m., 5,526 w.)
(809) 758-8000
(809) 780-4040 Bayamón

REGIONAL COLLEGES ADMINISTRATION OFFICE
Box 4927, San Juan 00936. Chanc. Felix Torres Leon.
Enroll.: (890) 763-3393

AGUADILLA REGIONAL COLLEGE
P.O. Box 20000, Victoria St. Sta., Aguadilla 00605. 1957/1983 (MSA/ CHE). Degrees: A. Dean and Dir. Hilda M. Baco.
Enroll.: 3,093 (*f.t.* 928 m., 1,453 w.)
(809) 891-0925

ARECIBO REGIONAL COLLEGE
P.O. Box UI, Arecibo 00613. 1957/1983 (MSA/CHE). Degrees: A,B. Dir. Maria de los A. Ortiz de Leon.
Enroll.: 3,494 (*f.t.* 980 m., 1,989 w.)
(809) 878-6795

BARRANQUITAS REGIONAL COLLEGE
P.O. Box 517, Barranquitas 00618. 1957/1983 (MSA/CHE). Degrees: A. Dir. Vidal Rivera-Garcia.
Enroll.: 1,439 (*f.t.* 410 m., 803 w.)
(809) 857-3600

FAJARDO REGIONAL COLLEGE
P.O. Box 1029, Fajardo 00648. 1961/1983 (MSA/CHE). Degrees: A. Acting Dean and Dir. Jose Luis Larrieux.
Enroll.: 1,799 (*f.t.* 419 m., 933 w.)
(809) 863-2390

GUAYAMA REGIONAL COLLEGE
P.O. Box 1559, Carreterra Machete-Urb., Guayama 00655. 1957/1983 (MSA/CHE). Degrees: A. Dir. Pablo Rivera-Diaz.
Enroll.: 1,231 (*f.t.* 298 m., 730 w.)
(809) 864-2222

PONCE REGIONAL COLLEGE
P.O. Box 309, Ponce 00715. 1962/1983 (MSA/CHE). Degrees: A. Dean and Dir. Jose I. Correa.
Enroll.: 2,832 (*f.t.* 789 m., 1,601 w.)
(809) 840-9090

LICEO DE ARTE Y TECNOLOGIA
405 Ponce de Leon Ave., Hato Rey 00917. Private. 1978 (NATTS). Courses of varying lengths. Diplomas. Pres. Carlos M. Valencia.
(809) 754-8250

MBTI BUSINESS TRAINING INSTITUTE
1225 Ponce de Leon Ave., Santurce 00908. Private. 1974/1980 (AICS). Courses of varying lengths. Diplomas. Dir. Carlos Vega Lebron.
Enroll.: 1,211 (*f.t.* 138 m., 1,073 w.)
(809) 723-9403

METROPOLITAN INSTITUTE OF SCIENCE AND TECHNOLOGY
359 San Claudio St, Centro Commercial Cupey Hall, San Juan 00926. Private. 1985

(NATTS). Courses of varying lengths. Diplomas. Pres. Ruben Rivera.
Enroll.: 2774 (*f.t.* 220 m., 57 w.)
(809) 754-8250

NATIONAL COLLEGE OF BUSINESS AND TECHNOLOGY
P.O. Box 2036, Bayamon 00621. Private. 1983 (AICS). Qtr. plan. Certificates, diplomas. Pres. Jesus Siverio Orta.
(809) 780-5134

BRANCH CAMPUS
Ave. Gonzalo Marin #109, Arecibo 00612. Dir. Claribel Rodriguez Bernardi.
(809) 879-5044

NATIONAL COMPUTER COLLEGE
Calle Garrido Morales, Km. 44, Fajardo 00648. Private. 1986 (AICS). Courses of varying lengths. Certificates. Dir. Muhamed Musa Rabeh.
(809) 863-0593

PERCY BUSINESS COLLEGE
82 Salud St., Ponce 00733. Private. 1982 (AICS). Courses of varying lengths. Certificates, diplomas. Pres. Thelma Percy.
Enroll.: 971 (*f.t.* 306 m., 665 w.)
(809) 842-0121

BRANCH CAMPUS
Centro Educacional Mirador Echevaria, Los Almendros St., Box Q, Cayey 00633. Dir. Aida Ramos.
(809) 738-3114

BRANCH CAMPUS
105 E. Mendez Vigo St., P.O. Box 399, Mayaguez 00709-399. Interim Dir. Amado Pereira.
(809) 833-2424

PONCE SCHOOL OF MEDICINE
Ponce 00731. Private professional. 1981. Sem. plan. Degrees: *Prof. Accred.:* Medicine. Dean Jose N. Correa.
Enroll.: 177 (*f.t.* 130 m., 47 w.)
(809) 843-8288

PONCE TECHNICAL SCHOOL
16 Salud St., Ponce 00731. Private. 1985 (ABHES). Courses of varying lengths. Certificates, diplomas. *Prof. Accred.:* Practical Nursing. Pres. Fernando Torres.
Enroll.: 244
(809) 844-7940

PUERTO RICO BARBER, COSMETOLOGY, AND HAIRSTYLING COLLEGE
Apartado 849, Calle One, No. One Urbanizacion Isleta, Bayamón 00619. Private. 1980 (NATTS). Courses of varying lengths. Certificates, diplomas. Pres. Zenon Torres Contes.
(809) 785-3119

BRANCH CAMPUS
Avenida Eugenio Maria de Hostos #198, Arecibo 00612.
(809) 878-0164

RAMIREZ COLLEGE OF BUSINESS AND TECHNOLOGY
P.O. Box 8074, Santurce 00910. Private junior. 1975/1981 (AICS); 1977 (NATTS). Sem. plan. Degrees: A, certificates, diplomas. Acting Pres. Ludi Pinero.
Enroll.: 1,777 (*f.t.* 609 m., 1,168 w.)
(809) 763-3120

SAN JUAN CITY COLLEGE
818 Ponce de Leon Ave., Miramar, Santurce 00907. Private technical. 1984 (NATTS). Courses of varying lengths. Certificates. Pres. Americo Reyes, Jr.
(809) 725-4949

TECHNICAL COLLEGE OF THE MUNICIPALITY OF SAN JUAN
Jose Oliver St., Urb. Industrial Tres Monjitas, Hato Rey 00918. Public (municipal) 2-year. 1978 (MSA/CHE). Sem. plan. Degrees: A. Chanc. Rafael Farilla.
Enroll.: 1,027 (*f.t.* 537 m., 284 w.)
(809) 753-6678

UNIVERSIDAD CENTRAL DEL CARIBE ESCUELA DE MEDICINA DE CAYEY
P.O. Box 935, Cayey 00633. Private professional. 1982. Sem. plan. Degrees: P. *Prof. Accred.:* Medicine. Dean Raúl A. Marcial Rojas.
Enroll.: 318 (*f.t.* 228 m., 90 w.)
(809) 738-2330

UNIVERSIDAD POLITECNICA DE PUERTO RICO
Box 2017, Hato Rey 00919. Private technical. 1985 (MSA/CHE). Qtr. plan. Degrees: A,B. Pres. Ernesto Vazquez-Torres. *Enroll.:* 579 (*f.t.* 409 m., 30 w.)
(809) 754-8000

UNIVERSITY OF PUERTO RICO
Central office at Río Piedras. G.P.O. Box 4984-G, San Juan 00936. Public (commonwealth) multi-unit system. Sem. plan. *Prof. Accred.:* Architecture (M), Dental Assisting,

Dentistry, Dietetics, Engineering (chemical, civil, electrical, industrial, mechanical), Health Services Administration, Law, Medical Record Administration, Medical Technology, Nuclear Medicine Technology, Occupational Therapy, Physical Therapy, Public Health, Rehabilitation Counseling, Social Work (B,M), Teacher Education (*e,s,p*). Pres. Fernando Agraite.
(809) 765-6590

Río Piedras Campus
Ponce de Leon Ave., Río Piedras 00931. 1946/1985 (MSA/CHE). Degrees: A,B,P,M,D. Chanc. Juan Fernandez.
Enroll.: 21,699 (*f.t.* 5,016 m., 10,262 w.)
(809) 764-0000

Mayaguez Campus
Mayaguez 00708. 1946/1984 (MSA/CHE). Degrees: A,B,M,D. *Prof. Accred.:* Nursing (B). Chanc. Jose L. Martinez Pico.
Enroll.: 9,673 (*f.t.* 5,030 m., 3,480 w.)
(809) 832-4040

Medical Sciences Campus
P.O. Box 5067 San Juan 009361. 1949/1981 (MSA/CHE). Degrees: A,B,P,M,D. *Prof. Accred.:* Medicine, Nursing (B,M), Radiography, Speech Pathology. Chanc. Jose M. Saldana.
Enroll.: 3,364 (*f.t.* 1,023 m., 1,904 w.)
(809) 758-2525

Cayey University College
Cayey 00633. 1967/1985 (MSA/CHE). Degrees: B. Chanc. Margarita Benitez.
Enroll.: 3,519 (*f.t.* 1,057 m., 2,161 w.)
(809) 738-6161

Humacao University College
P.O. Box 428, Humacao 00661. 1962/1984 (MSA/CHE). Degrees: A,B. *Prof. Accred.:* Nursing (A), Social Work (B). Chanc. Elsa Berrios de Santos
Enroll.: 3,545 (*f.t.* 1,125 m., 1,934 w.)
(809) 852-2525

Regional Colleges
Administrative Office, P.O. Box 25189, Venezuela Contract Sta., Río Piedras 00928-5189. Chanc. William Riefkohl.
(809) 763-1600

Aguadilla Regional College
P.O. Box 160, Ramey, Aguadilla 00604. 1976/1981 (MSA/CHE). Degrees: A. Dean and Dir. Ricardo Villalon.
Enroll.: 1,500 (*f.t.* 594 m., 802 w.)
(809) 890-2681

Arecibo Technological University College
Call Box A-1806, Arecibo 00613. 1967/1984 (MSA/CHE). Degrees: A,B. Dean and Dir. Ana Pabelonia.
Enroll.: 3,685 (*f.t.* 1,046 m., 2,137 w.)
(809) 878-2830

Bayamón Technological University College
Bayamón 00620. 1960/1983 (MSA/CHE). Degrees; A,B. Dean and Dir. Aida Canals de Derra.
Enroll.: 4,036 (*f.t.* 1,512 m., 1,837 w.)
(809) 786-2885

Carolina Regional College
P.O. Box CR, Carolina 00630. 1978/1983 (MSA/CHE). Degrees: A. Dean and Dir. Andrea Rodriguez Rubio.
Enroll.: 1,337 (*f.t.* 477 m., 732 w.)
(809) 757-2000

La Montana Regional College
P.O. Box 1449, Utuado 00761. 1986 (MSA/CHE). Degrees: A. Dean and Dir. Carmen Gloria Ortiz.
Enroll.: 555 (*f.t.* 228 m., 283 w.)
(809) 894-2828

Ponce Technological University College
P.O. Box 7186, Ponce 00732. 1970/1985 (MSA/CHE). Degrees: A,B. Dean and Dir. Pedro La Boy.
Enroll.: 1,988 (*f.t.* 758 m., 1,127 w.)
(809) 844-8181

University of the Sacred Heart
Box 12383, Loíza Sta., Santurce 00914. Private liberal arts and teachers. 1950/1978 (MSA/CHE). Sem. plan. Degrees: A,B. Acting Pres. Candida R. Acosta.
Enroll.: 8,453 (*f.t.* 2,350 m., 4,145 w.)
(809) 728-1515

RHODE ISLAND

ALLIED TECHNICAL INSTITUTE
20 Marblehead Ave., North Providence 02904. Private. 1982 (NATTS). Courses of varying lengths. Certificates. Dir. Orrin Laferte.
(401) 353-8800

BROWN UNIVERSITY
Providence 02912. Private. 1929/1978 (NEASC-CIHE). Sem. plan. Degrees: B,P,M,D. *Prof. Accred.:* Engineering (biomedical, chemical, civil, electrical, materials, mechanical), Medicine, Psychology. Pres. Howard R. Swearer.
Enroll.: 7,198
(401) 863-1000

BRYANT COLLEGE
Smithfield 02917. Private business. 1964/1980 (NEASC-CIHE). Sem. plan. Degrees: A,B,M. Pres. William T. O'Hara.
Enroll.: 6,505
(401) 232-6000

COMMUNITY COLLEGE OF RHODE ISLAND
Warwick 02886. Accreditation includes Branch Campus at Providence. Public (state). 1960/1984 (NEASC-CIHE). Sem. plan. Degrees: A, certificates. *Prof. Accred.:* Dental Assisting, Medical Laboratory Technology, Nursing (A), Practical Nursing, Radiography. Pres. Edward J. Liston.
Enroll.: 12,317
(401) 825-1000

HALL INSTITUTE
120 High St., Pawtucket 02860. Private technical. 1980 (NATTS). Courses of varying lengths. Certificates. Charles K. Rodgers.
Enroll.: 200 (*f.t.* 150 m., 50 w.)
(401) 461-6000 and 722-2003

THE JEWELRY INSTITUTE
40 Sims Ave., Providence 02909. Private. 1982 (NATTS). Sem. plan. Diplomas. Pres. Larry Braids.
Enroll.: 210 (*f.t.* 15 m., 5 w.)
(401) 351-0700

JOHNSON AND WALES COLLEGE
8 Abbott Park Pl., Providence 02903. Private senior. 1954/1981 (AICS). Tri. plan. Degrees: A,B, certificates, diplomas. Pres. Morris J. W. Gaebe.
Enroll.: 7,626 (*f.t.* 4,984 m., 2,642 w.)
(401) 456-1000

BRANCH CAMPUS
701 E. Bay St., Charleston, SC 29403. Dir. Steve Nogle.
(803) 723-4638

KATHARINE GIBBS SCHOOL
178 Butler Ave., Providence 02906. Private business. 1967/1986 (AICS). Sem. plan. Certificates. Dir. Elaine Carroll.
Enroll.: 467 (*f.t.* 1 m., 466 w.)
(401) 861-1420

NATIONAL EDUCATION CENTER-RHODE ISLAND TRADES SHOP SCHOOL CAMPUS
361 W. Fountain St., Providence 02903. Private. 1971/1983 (NATTS). Courses of varying lengths. Diplomas. Dir. Joseph E. Bukowski.
Enroll.: 477 (*f.t.* 301 m., 11 w.)
(401) 331-3008

NEW ENGLAND INSTITUTE OF TECHNOLOGY
184 Early St., Providence 02907. Private. 1972/1984 (NATTS); 1982 (NEASC-CVTCI). Qtr. plan. Degrees: A. Pres. Richard I. Gouse.
Enroll.: 1,524 (*f.t.* 715 m., 224 w.)
(401) 467-7744

OCEAN STATE BUSINESS INSTITUTE
One High St., P.O. Box 377, Wakefield 02880. Private. 1979/1985 (AICS). Courses of varying lengths. Certificates. Dir. Assunta G. Pouliot.
Enroll.: 173 (*f.t.* 7 m., 166 w.)
(401) 789-0287

PROVIDENCE COLLEGE
Providence 02918. Private (Roman Catholic) liberal arts. 1933/1978 (NEASC-CIHE). Sem. plan. Degrees: B,M,D. *Prof. Accred.:* Social Work (B). Pres. V. Rev. John F. Cunningham, O.P.
Enroll.: 5,679
(401) 865-1000

RISE INSTITUTE OF ELECTRONICS
14 Third St., Providence 02906. Private. 1968/1978 (NATTS). Courses of varying length. Certificates, diplomas. Dean Thomas Carmody.
Enroll.: 347 (*f.t.* 226 m., 14 w.)
(401) 861-9664

RHODE ISLAND BUSINESS INSTITUTE
1080 Newport Ave., Pawtucket 02861. Private. 1980 (AICS). Courses of varying lengths. Certificates. Pres. Dennis J. Saccoia.

Enroll.: 193 (*f.t.* 54 m., 139 w.)
(401) 728-1570

RHODE ISLAND COLLEGE
Providence 02908. Public (state) liberal arts and teachers. 1958/1986 (NEASC-CIHE). Sem. plan. Degrees: B,M. *Prof. Accred.:* Art, Music, Nursing (B), Rehabilitation Counseling, Social Work (B,M), Teacher Education (*e,s,p*). Pres. Carol J. Guardo.
Enroll.: 8,530 (401) 456-8000

RHODE ISLAND SCHOOL OF DESIGN
Providence 02903. Private professional. 1949/1982 (NEASC-CIHE). Sem. plan. Degrees: B,M. *Prof. Accred.:* Architecture (B), Art, Interior Design, Landscape Architecture (B). Pres. Thomas F. Schutte.
Enroll.: 1,838
(401) 331-3511

RHODE ISLAND SCHOOL OF PHOTOGRAPHY
241 Webster Ave., Providence 02909. Private. 1982 (NATTS). 2-year courses. Diplomas. Pres. Donald Folgo.
Enroll.: 160
(401) 943-7722

ROGER WILLIAMS COLLEGE
Bristol 02809. Private liberal arts; second campus at Providence. 1972/1986 (NEASC-CIHE). Sem. plan. Degrees: A,B. *Prof. Accred.:*Architecture (B), Engineering Technology (electrical, mechanical). Pres. William H. Rizzini.
Enroll.: (Total) 3,718
(401) 253-1040

SALVE REGINA—THE NEWPORT COLLEGE
Newport 02840. Private (Roman Catholic) liberal arts and sciences. 1956/1981 (NEASC-CIHE). Sem. plan. Degrees: A,B,M. *Prof. Accred.:* Nursing (B). Pres. Sister Lucille McKillop, R.S.M.
Enroll.: 2,065
(401) 847-6650

SAWYER SCHOOL
101 Main St., Pawtucket 02860. Private business. 1973/1985 (AICS). Courses of varying lengths. Certificates. Pres. Thomas W. Kirkpatrick.
Enroll.: 756 (*f.t.* 94 m., 662 w.)
(401) 272-8400

BRANCH CAMPUS
1109 Warwick Ave., Warwick 02888. Dir. Dennis L. Byrnes.
(401) 781-2887

SCHOOL OF MEDICAL AND SECRETARIAL SCIENCES
60 Angell St., Providence 02906. Private. 1981 (NATTS). Courses of varying lengths. Certificates. Dir. Norma Casale.
Enroll.: 37
(401) 331-1711.

UNIVERSITY OF RHODE ISLAND
Kingston 02881. Public (state). 1930/1977 (NEASC-CIHE). Sem. plan. Degrees: A,B,M,D. *Prof. Accred.:* Business (B,M), Dental Hygiene, Engineering (chemical, civil, electrical, industrial, mechanical), Librarianship, Music, Nursing (B,M), Pharmacy, Psychology, Teacher Education (*p*). Pres. Edward D. Eddy.
Enroll.: 13,616
(401) 792-1000

SOUTH CAROLINA

AIKEN TECHNICAL COLLEGE
P.O. Drawer 696, Aiken 29802-0696. Public 2- year. 1975/1980 (SACS-Comm. on Coll.). Qtr. plan. Degrees: A. Dir. Paul L. Blowers.
Enroll.: 863
(803) 593-9231

ANDERSON COLLEGE
Anderson 29621. Private (Southern Baptist) junior. 1959/1980 (SACS-Comm. on Coll.). Sem. plan. Degrees: A. *Prof. Accred.:* Music. Pres. Mark L. Hopkins.
Enroll.: 1.070
(803) 231-2000

BAPTIST COLLEGE AT CHARLESTON
P.O. Box 10087, Charleston 29411. Private (Southern Baptist) liberal arts and teachers. 1970/1974 (SACS-Comm. on Coll.). Sem. plan. Degrees: A,B. *Prof. Accred.:* Music. Pres. Jairy C. Hunter, Jr.
Enroll.: 1,261
(803) 797-4011

BEAUFORT TECHNICAL COLLEGE
Beaufort 29902. Public 2-year. 1978/1984 (SACS-Comm. on Coll.). Qtr. plan. Degrees: A. Pres. George W. Goldsmith, Jr.
Enroll.: 916
(803) 524-3380

BENEDICT COLLEGE
Harden and Blanding Sts. , Columbia 29204. Private (Independent) liberal arts. 1946/1981 (SACS-Comm. on Coll.). Sem. plan. Degrees: B. *Prof. Accred.:* Social Work (B). Pres. Marshall C. Grigsby.
Enroll.: 1,486
(803) 256-4220

BETTY STEVENS COSMETOLOGY INSTITUTE
301 Rainbow Dr., Florence 29501. Private. 1985 (SACS-COEI). Courses of varying lengths. Certificates. Dir. Elizabeth Humphries.
Enroll.: 29

CENTRAL WESLEYAN COLLEGE
Central 29630. Private (Wesleyan Methodist) liberal arts and teachers. 1973/1978 (SACS-Comm. on Coll.). Sem. plan. Degrees: B. Pres. John M. Newby.
Enroll.: 367
(803) 639-2453

CHESTERFIELD-MARLBORO TECHNICAL COLLEGE
Cheraw 29520. Public 2-year. 1973/1978 (SACS-Comm. on Coll.). Qtr. plan. Degrees: A. Pres. Ronald W. Hampton.
Enroll.: 818
(803) 537-5286

THE CITADEL
Charleston 29409. Public (state) liberal arts and military college primarily for men. 1924/1984 (SACS-Comm. on Coll.). Sem. plan. Degrees: B,M. *Prof. Accred.:* Engineering (civil, electrical), Teacher Education (*s*). Pres. Maj. Gen. James A. Grimsley, Jr., USA.
Enroll.: 2,709
(803) 792-5000

CLAFLIN COLLEGE
Orangeburg 29115. Private (United Methodist) liberal arts. 1947/1981 (SACS-Comm. on Coll.). Sem. plan. Degrees: B. Pres. Oscar A. Rogers, Jr.
Enroll.: 639
(803) 534-2710

CLEMSON UNIVERSITY
Clemson 29631. Public (state) 1927/1982 (SACS-Comm. on Coll.). Sem. plan. Degrees: A,B,M,D. *Prof. Accred.:* Architecture (B,M), Business (B,M), Construction Education, Engineering (agricultural, ceramic, chemical, civil, electrical, environmental systems, mechanical), Engineering Technology, Forestry, Nursing (B,M), Teacher Education (*e,s,p*). Pres. Max M. Lennon.
Enroll.: 11,343
(803) 656-3311

COKER COLLEGE
Hartsville 29550. Private liberal arts primarily for women. 1923/1985 (SACS-Comm. on Coll.). Qtr. plan. Degrees: B. *Prof. Accred.:* Music. Pres. James D. Daniels.
Enroll.: 283
(803) 332-1381

COLLEGE OF CHARLESTON
66 George St., Charleston 29424. Public (state) liberal arts. 1916/1975 (SACS-Comm. on Coll.). Sem. plan. Degrees: B,M. Pres. Harry M. Lightsey, Jr.
Enroll.: 4,549
(803) 792-5507

Columbia Bible College
7435 Monticello Rd., P.O. Box 3122, Columbia 29230. Private (Interdenominational) professional. 1948/1982 (AABC); 1982 (SACS-Comm. on Coll.). Qtr. plan. Degrees: A,B,M. Pres. J. Robertson McQuilkin.
Enroll.: 885
(803) 754-4100

Columbia College
Columbia 29203. Private (United Methodist) liberal arts primarily for women. 1938/1981 (SACS-Comm. on Coll.). Sem. plan. Degrees: B,M. *Prof. Accred.:* Music, Social Work (B), Teacher Education (*e,s*). Pres. Ralph T. Mirse.
Enroll.: 1,057
(803) 786-3012

Columbia Graduate School of Bible and Mission
P.O. Box 3122, Columbia 29230. Private (nondenominational) professional. Sem. plan. Degrees: M,P. *Prof. Accred.:* Theology (ATS, 1985). Pres. Robert J. McQuilkin.
Enroll.: 348
(803) 754-4100

Columbia Junior College of Business
3810 Main St., P.O. Box 1196, Columbia 29202. Private. 1964/1981 (AICS). Qtr. plan. Degrees: A. Pres. Michael Gorman.
Enroll.: 783 (*f.t.* 178 m., 605 w.)
(803) 799-9082

Branch
800 Dutch Square Blvd., Suite 209, Columbia 29210.
(803) 798-1339

Converse College
Spartanburg 29301. Private liberal arts primarily for women. 1912/1975 (SACS-Comm. on Coll.). 4-1-4 plan. Degrees: B,M. *Prof. Accred.:* Music. Pres. Robert T. Coleman, Jr.
Enroll.: 881
(803) 596-9000

Denmark Technical College
Solomon Blatt Blvd., Box 327, Denmark 29042. Public 2-year. 1979/1984 (SACS-Comm. on Coll.). Qtr. plan. Degrees: A. Acting Pres. Marianna W. Davis.
Enroll.: 1,021 m.
(803) 793-3301

Erskine College
Due West 29639. Private (Associate Reformed Presbyterian) coeducational liberal arts college and seminary for men. 1925/1982 (SACS-Comm. on Coll.). Sem. plan. Degrees: B,P,M,D. *Prof. Accred.:* Theology (1981/1985, ATS). Pres. William Bruce Ezell, Jr.
Enroll.: 598
(803) 379-2131

Farah's Beauty School
P.O. Box 71673, Charleston Heights 29405. Private. 1985 (SACS-COEI). Courses of varying lengths. Certificates. Dir. Jeani M. Yarashus.
Enroll.: FTE 35

Florence-Darlington Technical College
Florence 29501-0057. Public 2-year. 1970/1974 (SACS-Comm. on Coll.). Qtr. plan. Degrees: A. *Prof. Accred.:* Dental Assisting, Dental Hygiene, Engineering Technology (electronics, engineering graphics), Medical Laboratory Technology, Nursing (A), Radiography, Respiratory Therapy Technology, Surgical Technology. Pres. Fred C. Fore..
Enroll.: 2,087
(803) 662-8151

Forrest College
601 E. River St., Anderson 29624. Private business. 1965/1982 (AICS). Qtr. plan. Certificates, diplomas. Pres. Charles E. Palmer, Jr.
Enroll.: 241 (*f.t.* 42 m., 199 w.)
(803) 225-7653

Francis Marion College
P.O. Box F-7500, Florence 29501. Public (state) liberal arts. 1972/1976 (SACS-Comm. on Coll.). Sem. plan. Degrees: A,B,M. Pres. Thomas C. Stanton.
Enroll.: 2,748
(803) 661-1362

Furman University
Poinsett Hwy., Greenville 29613. Private (Southern Baptist) liberal arts college. 1924/1976 (SACS-Comm. on Coll.). 3-2-3 plan. Degrees: B,M. *Prof. Accred.:* Music. Pres. John Edwin Johns.
Enroll.: 2,816
(803) 294-2000

Greenville Technical College
Sta. B, P.O. Box 5616, Greenville 29606. Public (state) 2-year. 1968/1982 (SACS-Comm. on Coll.). Qtr. plan. Degrees: A. *Prof. Accred.:* Dental Assisting, Dental Hygiene, Engineering Technology (architectural, elec-

tronic, industrial, mechanical), Medical Laboratory Technology (A), Medical Record Technology, Medical Technology, Nursing (A), Optometric Technology, Radiography, Respiratory Therapy, Surgical Technology. Dir. Thomas E. Barton, Jr.
Enroll.: 6,157
(803) 242-3170

HORRY-GEORGETOWN TECHNICAL COLLEGE
P.O. Box 1966, Conway 29526. Public 2-year. 1972/1977 (SACS-Comm. on Coll.). Qtr. plan. Degrees: A. Pres. D. Kent Sharples.
Enroll.: 1,497
(803) 347-3186

KENNETH SHULER SCHOOL OF BARBERSTYLING
6026 St. Andrews Rd., Columbia 29210. Private. 1980 (NATTS). Courses of varying lengths. Diplomas. Dir. Kenneth Shuler.
Enroll.: 24 (*f.t.* 10 m., 14 w.)
(803) 772-6098

LANDER COLLEGE
Greenwood 29646. Public (state) liberal arts. 1952/1975 (SACS-Comm. on Coll.). Sem. plan. Degrees: A, B, M. *Prof. Accred.:* Nursing (A). Pres. Larry A. Jackson.
Enroll.: 2,035
(803) 229-8300

LIMESTONE COLLEGE
1115 College Dr., Gaffney 29340. Private liberal arts. 1928/1979 (SACS-Comm. on Coll.). 4-1-4 plan. Degrees: B. *Prof. Accred.:* Music. Interim Pres. Francis Bonner.
Enroll.: 1,151
(803) 489-7151

LUTHERAN THEOLOGICAL SOUTHERN SEMINARY
4201 N. Main St., Columbia 29203. Private (Lutheran Church in America) professional; graduate only. 1983 (SACS-Comm on Coll.). Sem. plan. Degrees: P, M, D. *Prof. Accred.:* Theology (1944/1983, ATS). Pres. Mack C. Branham, Jr.
Enroll.: 178
(803) 786-5150

MANGUM'S BARBER AND HAIRSTYLING COLLEGE
137 Caldwell St., Rock Hill 29730. Private. 1985 (NATTS). Courses of varying lengths. Diplomas. Dir. Richard Mangum.
(803) 328-0809

MEDICAL TRAINING CENTER
4949 Two Notch Rd., #201, Columbia 29204-3211. Private. 1984 (NATTS). Courses of varying lengths. Certificates. Dir. Robert C. MacElhiney.
(803) 754-5580

MEDICAL UNIVERSITY OF SOUTH CAROLINA
171 Ashley Ave., Charleston 29425. Public (state) professional. 1971/1975 (SACS-Comm. on Coll.). Sem. and qtr. plan. Degrees: A, B, P, M, D. *Prof. Accred.:* Assistant to the Primary Care Physician, Cytotechnology, Dental Assisting, Dental Hygiene, Dental Laboratory Technology, Dentistry, Histologic Technology, Medical Laboratory Technology (A), Medical Record Administration, Medical Technology, Medicine, Nurse Anesthesia Education, Nursing (B), Occupational Therapy, Perfusionist, Pharmacy, Physical Therapy, Practical Nursing, Radiation Therapy Technology, Radiography, Specialist in Blood Bank Technology. Pres. James B. Edwards.
Enroll.: 1,926
(803) 792-2300

MIDLANDS TECHNICAL COLLEGE
P.O. Box 2408, Columbia 29202. Public (state) 2-year. 1974/1979 (SACS-Comm. on Coll.). Qtr. plan. Degrees: A, certificates. *Prof. Accred.:* Dental Assisting, Dental Hygiene, Engineering Technology (architectural, civil, electrical/electronics, mechanical), Medical Laboratory Technology (A), Nuclear Medicine Technology, Practical Nursing, Radiography, Respiratory Therapy, Respiratory Therapy Technology, Surgical Technology. Pres. James L. Hodgins.
Enroll.: 5,069
(803) 791-8281

MORRIS COLLEGE
Sumter 29150. Private (Baptist) liberal arts. 1978/1983 (SACS-Comm. On Coll.). Sem. plan. Degrees: B. Pres. Luns C. Richardson.
Enroll.: 600
(803) 775-9371

NEWBERRY COLLEGE
Newberry 29108. Private (Lutheran in America) liberal arts. 1936/1982 (SACS-Comm. on Coll.). 4-1-4 plan. Degrees: B. *Prof. Accred.:* Music, Teacher Education (*e*). Pres. John S. Ammarell.
Enroll.: 614
(803) 276-5010

NIELSEN ELECTRONICS INSTITUTE
1600 Meeting St., Charleston 29405. Private. 1974/1979 (NATTS). Qtr. plan. Degrees: A. Pres. Robert R. Nielsen, Sr.
Enroll.: 355 (*f.t.* 324 m., 31 w.)
(803) 722-2344

NORTH AMERICAN INSTITUTE OF AVIATION
P.O. Box 680, Conway-Horry County Airport, Conway 29526. Private. 1981 (NATTS). Courses of varying lengths. Certificates. Pres. Douglas Beckner.
Enroll.: 45 (*f.t.* 40 m., 5 w.)
(803) 397-9111

NORTH GREENVILLE COLLEGE
Tigerville 29688. Private (Southern Baptist). 1957/1979 (SACS-Comm. on Coll.). Sem. plan. Degrees: A. Pres. James D. Jordan.
Enroll.: 461
(803) 895-1410

ORANGEBURG-CALHOUN TECHNICAL COLLEGE
3250 St. Matthews Rd., N.E., Orangeburg 29115. Public 2-year. 1970/1985 (SACS-Comm. on Coll.). Qtr. plan. Degrees: A. *Prof. Accred.:* Medical Laboratory Technology (A), Radiography, Respiratory Therapy Technology. Pres. M. Rudy Groomes.
Enroll.: 1,329
(803) 536-0311

PIEDMONT TECHNICAL COLLEGE
P.O. Box 1467, Greenwood 29648. Public 2-year. 1972/1976 (SACS-Comm. on Coll.). Qtr. plan. Degrees: A. *Prof. Accred.:* Engineering Technology (electronic, engineering graphics), Radiography. Pres. Lex D. Walters.
Enroll.: 2,462
(803) 223-8357

PRESBYTERIAN COLLEGE
Clinton 29325. Private (Presbyterian, U.S.) liberal arts. 1949/1975 (SACS-Comm. on Coll.). Sem. plan. Degrees: B. Pres. Kenneth B. Orr.
Enroll.: 894
(803) 833-2820

RUTLEDGE COLLEGE
P.O. Box 98, Columbia 29202. Private junior. 1966/1984 (AICS). Qtr. plan. Certificates. CEO Doris Brozik.
Enroll.: 1,574 (*f.t.* 848 m., 726 w.)
(803) 779 -0360

RUTLEDGE COLLEGE
617 McBee Ave., Piedmont Ctr., Greenville 29601. Private junior. 1981 (AICS). Qtr. plan. Degrees: A, certificates. CEO Eugene Spiess.
Enroll.: 624 (*f.t.* 128 m., 496 w.)
(803) 232-8502

RUTLEDGE COLLEGE
5290 River Ave., Suite 400, N. Charleston 29418. Private junior. 1982 (AICS). Qtr. plan. Degrees: A. CEO W. D. John Almond.
Enroll.: 655 (*f.t.* 228 m., 427 w.)
(803) 554-5091

RUTLEDGE COLLEGE
366 N. Church St., Spartanburg 29303. Private junior. 1953/1981 (AICS). Qtr. plan. Degrees: A, certificates. Pres. Eugene Spiess.
Enroll.: 1,004 (*f.t.* 388 m., 616 w.)
(803) 585-3446

BRANCH CAMPUS
3838 W. Martin Luther King, Jr. Blvd., Los Angeles, CA 90008. Dir. Ray White.
(213) 299-2966

BRANCH CAMPUS
4019 Gaston Ave., Dallas, TX 75246. Dir. Tom Hopkins.
(214) 826-7925

BRANCH CAMPUS
105 San Pedro St., San Antonio, TX 78205. Dir. John Guzman.
(512) 226-9042

SHERMAN COLLEGE OF STRAIGHT CHIROPRACTIC
P.O. Box 1452, Spartanburg 29304. Private professional. 1984 (SACS-Comm. on Coll.). Qtr. plan. Degrees: P,D. Acting Pres. Leroy Moore.
Enroll.: 342
(803) 578-8770

SOUTH CAROLINA STATE COLLEGE
Orangeburg 29117. Public liberal arts and professional. 1941/1980 (SACS-Comm. on Coll.). Sem. plan. Degrees: B,M, (candidate for D). *Prof. Accred.:* Engineering Technology (civil, electrical, mechanical), Home Economics, Teacher Education (*e,s*). Pres. Albert E. Smith.
Enroll.: 3,654
(803) 536-7000

SPARTANBURG METHODIST COLLEGE
Spartanburg 29301. Private (United Methodist). 1957/1978 (SACS-Comm. on Coll.).

Sem. plan. Degrees: A. Pres. George D. Fields, Jr.
Enroll.: 836
(803) 576-3911

SPARTANBURG TECHNICAL COLLEGE
P.O. Drawer 4386, Spartanburg 29305. Public 2-year. 1970/1985 (SACS-Comm. on Coll.). Qtr. plan. Degrees: A. *Prof. Accred.:* Dental Assisting, Engineering Technology (civil, electronics, mechanical), Medical Laboratory Technology (A), Radiography, Respiratory Therapy Technology. Pres. Jack A. Powers.
Enroll.: 1,768
(803) 576-5770

SUMTER AREA TECHNICAL COLLEGE
506 N. Guignard Dr., Sumter 29150. Public 2-year. 1970/1985 (SACS-Comm. on Coll.). Qtr. plan. Degrees: A. *Prof. Accred.:* Engineering Technology (civil). Pres. ———.
Enroll.: 1,810
(803) 778-1961

TRI-COUNTY TECHNICAL COLLEGE
Pendleton 29670. Public (state) 2-year technological. 1971/1975 (SACS-Comm. on Coll.). Qtr. plan. Degrees: A. *Prof. Accred.:* Engineering Technology (electronics), Medical Laboratory Technology (A). Pres. Don C. Garrison.
Enroll.: 3,187
(803) 646-8361

TRIDENT TECHNICAL COLLEGE
P.O. Box 10367, Charleston 29411. Public 2-year. 1974/1980 (SACS-Comm. on Coll.). Qtr. plan. Degrees: A. *Prof. Accred.:* Engineering Technology (architectural, chemical, civil, electrical, electronics, mechanical). Pres. Charles W. Branch
Enroll.: 4,855
(803) 572-6111

UNIVERSITY OF SOUTH CAROLINA—CENTRAL OFFICE
Columbia 29208. Public (state). Pres. James B. Holderman.
(803) 777-0411

UNIVERSITY OF SOUTH CAROLINA—MAIN CAMPUS
Columbia 29208. Public (state). 1917/1981 (SACS-Comm. on Coll.). Sem. plan. Degrees: A,B,P,M,D. *Prof. Accred.:* Accounting (Type A,C), Business (B,M), Engineering (chemical, civil, electrical, mechanical), Journalism, Law, Librarianship, Medicine, Music, Nursing (B,M), Pharmacy, Psychology, Public Health, Rehabilitation Counseling, Social Work (M), Speech Pathology and Audiology, Teacher Education (*e,s,p*). Pres. James B. Holderman.
Enroll.: 18,096
(803) 777-0411

UNIVERSITY OF SOUTH CAROLINA AT AIKEN
171 University Pkwy., Aiken 29801. Public (state). 1977/1981 (SACS-Comm. on Coll.). Degrees: A,B. *Prof. Accred.:* Nursing (A). Chanc. Robert E. Alexander.
Enroll.: 1,532
(803) 648-6851

UNIVERSITY OF SOUTH CAROLINA AT BEAUFORT
P.O. Box 1007, Beaufort 29902. Public (state). 1959/1981 (SACS-Comm. on Coll.). Degrees: A. Dean Roland L. Tuttle.
Enroll.: 479
(803) 524-7112

UNIVERSITY OF SOUTH CAROLINA AT COASTAL CAROLINA
P.O. Box 1954, Conway 29526. Public (state). 1970/1981 (SACS-Comm. on Coll.). Degrees: A,B. *Prof. Accred.:* Nursing (A). Chanc. Roland G. Eaglin.
Enroll.: 2,246
(803) 347-3161

UNIVERSITY OF SOUTH CAROLINA AT LANCASTER
P.O. Box 370, Lancaster 29720. Public (state). 1959/1981 (SACS-Comm. on Coll.). Degrees: A. Dean John R. Arnold.
Enroll.: 637
(803) 285-7471

UNIVERSITY OF SOUTH CAROLINA AT SALKEHATCHIE
P.O. Box 617, Allendale 29810. Public (state). 1965/1981 (SACS-Comm. on Coll.). Degrees: A. Dean Carl A. Clayton.
Enroll.: 384
(803) 584-3446

UNIVERSITY OF SOUTH CAROLINA AT SPARTANBURG
Spartanburg 29303. Public (state). 1976/1981 (SACS-Comm. on Coll.). Degrees: A,B. *Prof. Accred.:* Nursing (A,B). Chanc. Olin B. Sansbury, Jr.
Enroll.: 1,988
(803) 578-1800

University of South Carolina at Sumter
Miller Rd., Sumter 29150. Public (state). 1976/1981 (SACS-Comm. on Coll.). Degrees: A. Dean Jack C. Anderson.
Enroll.: 886
(803) 775-6341

University of South Carolina at Union
P.O. Box 729, Union 29379. Public (state). 1965/1981 (SACS-Comm. on Coll.). Degrees: A. Dean Kenneth L. Davis.
Enroll.: 201
(803) 427-3681

Voorhees College
Denmark 29042. Private (Episcopal) liberal arts. 1968/1982 (SACS-Comm. on Coll.). Sem. plan. Degrees: A, B. Pres. Leonard Dawson.
Enroll.: 560
(803) 793-3351

Williamsburg Technical College
601 Lane Rd., Kingstree 29556. Public (state) community. 1977/1982 (SACS-Comm. on Coll.). Qtr. plan. Degrees: A. Pres. John T. Wynn.
Enroll.: 508
(803) 354-7423

Winthrop College
Rock Hill 29733. Public (state) liberal arts. 1923/1981 (SACS-Comm. on Coll.). Sem. plan. Degrees: B, M. *Prof. Accred.:* Art, Business (B, M), Dietetics, Music, Social Work (B), Teacher Education (*e,s*). Pres. Martha Kime Piper.
Enroll.: 4,510
(803) 323-2211

Wofford College
Spartanburg 29301. Private (United Methodist) liberal arts primarily for men. 1917/1975 (SACS-Comm. on Coll.). 4-1-4 plan. Degrees: B. Pres. Joab M. Lesesne, Jr.
Enroll.: 1,025
(803) 585-4821

York Technical College
U.S. 21-A By-Pass, Rock Hill 29730. Public 2-year. 1970/1985 (SACS-Comm. on Coll.). Qtr. plan. Degrees: A. *Prof. Accred.:* Dental Assisting, Engineering Technology (electronic, engineering graphics), Medical Laboratory Technology (A). Pres. Baxter M. Hood.
Enroll.: 1,839
(803) 324-3130

SOUTH DAKOTA

Augustana College
Sioux Falls 57197. Private (American Lutheran) liberal arts. 1931/1982 (NCA). 4-1-4 plan. Degrees: A,B,M. *Prof. Accred.:* Music, Nursing (B), Social Work (B), Teacher Education (*e,s*). Chanc. William C. Nelsen.
Enroll.: FTE 1,651
(800) 843-3370

Black Hills State College
Spearfish 57783. Public liberal arts and teachers. 1928/1983 (NCA). Sem. plan. Degrees: B,M. *Prof. Accred.:* Music, Teacher Education (*e,s*). Pres. Clifford Trump.
Enroll.: FTE 1,853
(605) 642-6111

Dakota State College
Madison 57042. Public liberal arts and teachers. 1920/1981 (NCA). Sem. plan. Degrees: B. *Prof. Accred.:* Medical Record Administration, Medical Record Technology, Respiratory Therapy, Respiratory Therapy Technology, Teacher Education (*e,s*). Pres. Richard Gowen.
Enroll.: FTE 752
(605) 256-5111

Dakota Wesleyan University
Mitchell 57301. Private (United Methodist) liberal arts college. 1913/1977 (NCA). 4-1-4 plan. Degrees: A,B. *Prof. Accred.:* Nursing (A), Social Work (B). Pres. James B. Beddow.
Enroll.: FTE 640
(605) 996-6511

Huron College
Huron 57350. Private (United Presbyterian) liberal arts. 1915/1985 (NCA). 4-1-4 plan. Degrees: B. Pres. R. John Reynolds.
Enroll.: FTE 366
(605) 352-8721

Kilian Community College
1600 S. Menlo Ave., Sioux Falls 57105. Private. 1986 (NCA). Qtr. Plan. Degrees: A, certificates, diplomas. Pres. Jim Schmidt.
Enroll.: FTE 117
(605) 336-5444

Lake Area Vocational-Technical Institute
Watertown 57201. Public (district). 1980/1985 (NCA). Qtr. plan. Certificates. *Prof. Accred.:* Dental Assisting, Dental Laboratory Technology, Medical Laboratory Technology, Practical Nursing. Dir. Leonard H. Timmerman.
Enroll.: FTE 988
(605) 886-5872

Mitchell Area Vocational-Technical School
821 N. Capitol St., Mitchell 57301. Public (district). 1980/1986 (NCA). Certificates. *Prof. Accred.:* Medical Laboratory Technology. Dir. Chris A. Paustian.
Enroll.: FTE 696
(605) 996-6671

Mount Marty College
Yankton 57078. Private (Roman Catholic) liberal arts. 1961/1973 (NCA). Sem. plan. Degrees: B. *Prof. Accred.:* Nurse Anesthesia Education, Nursing (B), Respiratory Therapy, Respiratory Therapy Technology, Social Work (B). Pres. Sister Jacquelyn Ernster.
Enroll.: FTE 602
(605) 668-1514

National College
321 Kansas City St., Rapid City 57701. Mailing address: P.O. Box 1780, Rapid City 57709. Private senior. 1953/1982 (AICS); 1985 (NCA). Qtr. plan. Degrees: A,B, diplomas. *Prof. Accred.:* Medical Assisting. Pres. and Chmn. of the board John W. Hauer.
Enroll.: FTE 2,973
(605) 394-4800

Branch Campus
3201 S. Kiwanis Ave., P.O. Box 1795, Sioux Falls 57105. Dir. Harold R. Cook.
(605) 334-5430

Branch Campus
2577 N. Chelton, Colorado Springs, CO 80909. Dir. Milo Wepking.
(303) 471-4205

Branch Campus
10958 E. Bethany Dr., Denver, CO 80014. Dir. Bill Willis.
(303) 337-3206

Branch Campus
330 Lake Ave., Pueblo, CO 81004. Dir. Diane Gallagher.
(303) 545-8763

Branch Campus
630 Minnesota Ave., Kansas City, KS 66101. Dir. James Galle.
(913) 371-0420

Branch Campus
1275 University Ave., St. Paul, MN 55104. Dir. Albert O'Donnell.
(612) 644-1265

Branch Campus
525 San Pedro, N.E., Box 8265, Albuquerque, NM 87198. Dir. Larry Weber.
(505) 265-7517

Nettleton College
Box 924, Sioux Falls 57101. Private business. 1953/1982 (AICS). Courses of varying lengths. Diplomas. Pres. Eugene Reinholt.
Enroll.: 563 (*f.t.* 84 m., 479 w.)
(605) 336-1837

Nettleton College—Technical Division
Ninth and Spring Ave., Sioux Falls 57102. Private. 1980 (NATTS). Qtr. plan. Diplomas. Pres. Eugene Reinholt.
Enroll.: 400 (*f.t.* 125 m., 375 w.)
(605) 336-1837

North American Baptist Seminary
Sioux Falls 57105. Private (North American Baptist General Conference) professional and graduate only. 1979/1984 (NCA). Sem. plan. Degrees: P,M,D. *Prof. Accred.:* Theology (1968/1984, ATS). Pres. Charles M. Hiatt.
Enroll.: FTE 133
(605) 336-6588

Northern State College
Aberdeen 57401. Public liberal arts and teachers. 1918/1977 (NCA). Sem. plan. Degrees: B,M. *Prof. Accred.:* Music, Teacher Education (*e,s,p*). Pres. Terence Brown.
Enroll.: 2,319
(605) 622-2521

Oglala Lakota Community College
P.O. Box 351, Kyle 57752. Tribally controlled. 1983 (NCA). Sem. plan. Degrees: A,B. Pres. Elgin Badwound.
Enroll.: FTE 540
(605) 455-2321

Presentation College
Aberdeen 57401. Private (Roman Catholic) junior. 1971/1981 (NCA). Sem. plan. Degrees: A. *Prof. Accred.:* Medical Laboratory Technology (A), Nursing (A). Pres. Sister Lynn Marie Welbig.
Enroll.: FTE 302
(605) 225-0420

Sinte Gleska College
Rosebud 57570. Tribally controlled. 1983 (NCA). Sem. plan. Degrees: A,B. Pres. Lionel R. Bordeaux.
Enroll.: FTE 422
(605) 747-2263

Sioux Falls College
Sioux Falls 57101. Private (American Baptist) liberal arts. 1931/1982 (NCA). 4-1-4 plan. Degrees: B,M. *Prof. Accred.:* Social Work (B), Teacher Education (*e,s*). Pres. Owen P. Halleen.
Enroll.: FTE 683
(605) 331-5000

South Dakota Barber College
1500 W. 41st St., Sioux Falls 57105. Private. 1984 (NATTS). Courses of varying lengths. Certificates. Pres. Chuck Huber.
(605) 338-3751

South Dakota School of Mines and Technology
Rapid City 57701. Public (state) technological. 1925/1981 (NCA). Sem. plan. Degrees: B,M,D. *Prof. Accred.:* Engineering (chemical, civil, electrical, geological, mechanical, metallurgical, mining). Pres. Richard A. Schleusener.
Enroll.: FTE 1,922
(605) 394-2411

South Dakota State University
Brookings 57007. Public. 1916/1985 (NCA). Sem. plan. Degrees: A,B,M,D. *Prof . Accred.:* Dietetics, Engineering (agricultural, civil, electrical, mechanical), Home Economics, Journalism, Music, Nursing (B), Pharmacy, Teacher Education (*s,p*). Pres. Robert T. Wagner.
Enroll.: FTE 6,416
(605) 688-4111

Southeast Vo-Technical Institute
701 Western Ave., Sioux Falls 57104. Public (district). 1981/1985 (NCA). Qtr. plan. Certificates. Dir. Ed Wood.
Enroll.: FTE 485
(605) 331-7631

Stenotype Institute of South Dakota
132 South Dakota Ave., Sioux Falls 57102. Private business. 1975/1984 (AICS). Courses of varying lengths. Diplomas. Pres. Linda Clauson.
Enroll.: 234 (*f.t.* 13 m., 221 w.)
(605) 336-1442

University of South Dakota
Vermillion 57069. Public (state). 1913/1985 (NCA). Sem. plan. Degrees: A, B,P,M,D. *Prof. Accred.:* Art, Business (B,M), Dental Hygiene, Law, Medicine, Music, Nurse Anesthesia Education, Nursing (A), Psychology, Social Work (B), Speech Pathology, Teacher Education (*e,s,p*). Pres. Joseph McFadden.
Enroll.: FTE 5,214
(605) 677-5641

Western Dakota Vocational-Technical Institute
Rapid City 57709. Public (district); accreditation includes center at Rapid City. 1983/1985 (NCA). Qtr. plan. Certificates. Dir. Bill Verbeck.
Enroll.: FTE 382
(605) 347-2611

TENNESSEE

AMERICAN BAPTIST COLLEGE
1800 White's Creek Pike, Nashville 37207. Private (Baptist) professional. 1971/1981 (AABC). Sem. plan. Degrees: B. Pres. Odell McGlothian, Sr.
Enroll.: 144
(615) 262-1369

AMERICAN INSTITUTE OF TECHNOLOGY
131 Eighth Ave. N., Nashville 37203. Private business. 1984 (AICS). Qtr. plan. Certificates, diplomas. Pres. Dave Davidson.
(615) 242-1674

AQUINAS JUNIOR COLLEGE
4210 Harding Rd., Nashville 37205. Private (Roman Catholic). 1971/1975 (SACS-Comm. on Coll.). 4-1-4 plan. Degrees: A. *Prof. Accred.:* Nursing (A), Radiography, Respiratory Therapy. Pres. Sister Robert Ann Britton, O.P.
Enroll.: 277
(615) 297-7545

ARNOLD'S BEAUTY SCHOOL
313 S. Second St., Milan 38358. Private. 1983 (SACS-COEI). 1,500 hours. Certificates. Dir. Norma Arnold.
Enroll.: FTE 31
(901) 686-7351

*AUSTIN PEAY STATE UNIVERSITY
Clarksville 37044. Public. 1947/1984 (SACS-Comm. on Coll.). Qtr. plan. Degrees: A,B,M. *Prof. Accred.:* Music, Nursing (B), Teacher Education (*e,s,p*). Pres. Robert O. Riggs.
Enroll.: 4,741
(615) 648-7011

BELMONT COLLEGE
1900 Belmont Blvd., Nashville 37203. Private (Southern Baptist) liberal arts. 1959/1980 (SACS-Comm. on Coll.). Sem. plan. Degrees: A,B. *Prof. Accred.:* Music, Nursing (A). Pres. William E. Troutt.
Enroll.: 2,125
(615) 383-7001

BETHEL COLLEGE
McKenzie 38201. Private (Cumberland Presbyterian) liberal arts. 1952/1978 (SACS-Comm. on Coll.). Qtr. plan. Degrees: B. Pres. William L. Odom.

*Member of State University and Community College System

Enroll.: 450
(901) 352-5321

BLAIR SCHOOL OF MUSIC
1208 18th Ave. S., Nashville 37212. Private professional. 1977. Courses of varying lengths. Certificates. *Prof. Accred.:* Music. Exec. Dir. John F. Sawyer.
(615) 327-8010

BRISTOL COLLEGE
P.O. Box 757, Bristol 37621-0757. Private senior. 1970/1982 (AICS). Qtr. plan. Degrees: A,B. Pres. Ronald H. Cosby.
Enroll.: 877 (*f.t.* 287 m., 590 w.)
(615) 968-1442

BRANCH CAMPUS
500 N. Boone St,. Johnson City 37601-5688. Dir. Bernie Young.
(615) 928-8142

BRANCH CAMPUS
1200 E. Center St., Kingsport 37660. Dir. Mitchell Davenport.
(615) 246-3721

BRYAN COLLEGE
Box 7000, Dayton 37321-7000. Private liberal arts. 1969/1984 (SACS-Comm. on Coll.). Sem. plan. Degrees: B. Pres. Theodore C. Mercer.
Enroll.: 484
(615) 775-2041

CARSON-NEWMAN COLLEGE
Jefferson City 37760. Private (Southern Baptist) liberal arts. 1927/1983 (SACS-Comm. on Coll.). Sem. plan. Degrees: B. *Prof. Accred.:* Home Economics, Music, Teacher Education (*e,s*). Pres. J. Cordell Maddox.
Enroll.: 1,622
(615) 475-9061

*CHATTANOOGA STATE TECHNICAL COMMUNITY COLLEGE
4501 Amnicola Hwy., Chattanooga 37406. Public 2-year. 1967/1981 (SACS-Comm. on Coll.). Qtr. plan. Degrees: A. *Prof. Accred.:* Dental Assisting, Dental Hygiene, Engineering Technology (civil; electrical/electronic: automated control systems technology option, instrumentation option, and power systems option; mechanical, engineering de-

*Member of State University and Community College System

sign option and mechanical option), Medical Record Technology, Nuclear Medicine Technology, Nursing (A), Radiography, Respiratory Therapy. Interim Pres. Harry Wagner.
Enroll.: 4,612
(615) 697-4400

CHRISTIAN BROTHERS COLLEGE
650 E. Parkway, S., Memphis 38104. Private (Roman Catholic) business, engineering, and liberal arts. 1958/1980 (SACS-Comm. on Coll.). Sem. plan. Degrees: B. *Prof. Accred.:* Engineering (civil, electrical, mechanical). Pres. Brother Theodore Drahmann.
Enroll.: 1,397
(901) 278-0100

THE CHURCH OF GOD SCHOOL OF THEOLOGY
900 Walker St., N.E., Cleveland 37311. Private (Church of God) professional; graduate only. 1984 (SACS-Comm. on Coll.). 4-1-4 plan. Degrees: P,M. Pres. Ray H. Hughes.
Enroll.: 158
(615) 478-1131

*CLEVELAND STATE COMMUNITY COLLEGE
Cleveland 37311. Public junior. 1969/1984 (SACS-Comm. on Coll.). Qtr. plan. Degrees: A. *Prof. Accred.:* Dental Laboratory Technology, Medical Laboratory Technology (A), Nursing (A). Pres. James T. Ford
Enroll.: 2,011
(615) 472-7141

*COLUMBIA STATE COMMUNITY COLLEGE
P.O. Box 1315, Hwy. 99 West, Columbia 38401. Public junior. 1968/1983 (SACS-Comm. on Coll.). Qtr. plan. Degrees: A. *Prof. Accred.:* Medical Laboratory Technology, Nursing (A), Optometric Technology, Radiography, Respiratory Therapy. Pres. L. Paul Sands.
Enroll.: 1,594
(615) 388-0120

CONTROL DATA INSTITUTE
5100 Poplar, Suite 132, Memphis 38137. Private. 1985 (NATTS). Courses of varying lengths. Diplomas.
(901) 458-0088

COOPER INSTITUTE
724 N. Fifth Ave., Knoxville 37917. Private junior. 1980/1984 (AICS). Qtr. plan. Degrees: A, certificates. Pres. David A. Cooper.
Enroll.: 299 (*f.t.* 77 m., 222 w.)
(615) 637-3573

*Member of State University and Community College System

COVENANT COLLEGE
Lookout Mountain 37350. *See listing under* Georgia.

CUMBERLAND SCHOOL OF MEDICAL TECHNOLOGY
321 N. Washington Ave., Cookeville 38501. Private 2-year. 1972/1983 (ABHES). Degrees: A, diplomas. *Prof. Accred.:* Medical Assisting, Medical Laboratory Technology, Medical Technology. Pres. LaVerne Floyd.
Enroll.: 63 (*f.t.* 17 m., 46 w.)
(615) 526-3660

EXTENSION
208 23rd Ave., N., Nashville 37203.
(615) 327-1256

EXTENSION
176-A Northwestern Ave., Oak Ridge 37830.

CUMBERLAND UNIVERSITY
Lebanon 37087. Private junior. 1985 (SACS-Comm. on Coll.). 4-1-4 plan. Degrees: A,B. Pres. Robert N.Clement.
Enroll.: 490
(615) 444-2562

DAVID LIPSCOMB COLLEGE
Nashville 37203. Private (Churches of Christ) liberal arts. 1954/1975 (SACS-Comm. on Coll.). Qtr. plan. Degrees: B, (candidate for M). *Prof. Accred.:* Teacher Education (*e,s*). Pres. Harold Hazelip.
Enroll.: 2,164
(615) 385-3855

DRAUGHONS JUNIOR COLLEGE
P.O.Box 4103 CRS, Johnson City 37601. Private. 1985 (AICS). Qtr. plan. Degrees: A. Dir. Jim Mullins.
(615) 282-3320

DRAUGHONS JUNIOR COLLEGE
315 Erin Dr., Knoxville 37919. Private. 1953/1984 (AICS). Qtr. plan. Degrees: A. Pres. Dewitt Shelton.
Enroll.: 2,875 (*f.t.* 553 m., 2,322 w.)
(615) 584-8621

BRANCH CAMPUS
1241 Volunteer Pkwy., Suite 600, Bristol 37620. Dir. Vickie Wilcox.
(615) 968-5000

BRANCH CAMPUS
202 W. Fourth St., Chattanooga 37402. Dir. Tony Clift.
(615) 756-1431

Branch Campus
444 E. Center St., Kingsport 37660. Dir. Clifton W. Phillips.
(615) 246-5182

Draughons Junior College
3200 Elvis Presley Blvd., Memphis 38116. Private. 1960/1984 (AICS). Qtr. plan. Degrees: A. Exec. Dir. John Pitts.
Enroll.: 2,424 (*f.t.* 606 m., 1,818 w.)
(901) 332-7800

Branch Campus
1776 Peachtree Rd., N.E., Atlanta, GA 30309. Dir. John Pitts.
(404) 892-0814

Draughons Junior College
Plus Park at Pavilion Blvd., Nashville 37217. Private business. 1954/1984 (AICS). Qtr. plan. Degrees: A, certificates, diplomas. Chmn. C. W. Davidson.
Enroll.: 2,380 (*f.t.* 693 m., 1,687 w.)
(615) 361-7555

*Dyersburg State Community College
Dyersburg 38024. Public junior. 1971/1975 (SACS-Comm. on Coll.). Qtr. plan. Degrees: A. *Prof. Accred.:* Nursing (A). Pres. Karen A. Bowyer.
Enroll.: 965
(901) 285-6910

*East Tennessee State University
Johnson City 37614. Public. 1927/1983 (SACS-Comm. on Coll.). Qtr. plan. Degrees: A,B,M,D. *Prof. Accred.:* Dental Assisting, Dental Hygiene, Dental Laboratory Technology, Engineering Technology (design graphics and modeling, electronic, manufacturing, surveying), Medical Assisting, Medical Laboratory Technology, Medicine, Music, Nursing (A,B), Radiography, Respiratory Therapy Technology, Social Work (B), Surgical Technology, Teacher Education (*e,s,p*). Pres. Ronald E. Beller.
Enroll.: 10,059
(615) 929-4112

Electronic Computer Programming Institute
3805 Brainerd Rd., Chattanooga 37411. Private. 1982 (NATTS). 8-month course. Certificates. Dir. JoAnn Pearson.
Enroll.: 110
(615) 624-0077

*Member of State University and Community College System

Emmanuel School of Religion
Rt. 6, Box 500,Johnson City 37601. Private (Christian Churches and Churches of Christ) professional; graduate only. Sem. plan. Degrees: P,M. *Prof. Accred.:* Theology (1981/1986, ATS). Pres. Calvin Phillips.
Enroll.: 142
(615) 926-1186

Excel Business College
620 Gallatin Rd., S., Madison 37115. Private. 1983 (ABHES). 36-week course. Diplomas. *Prof. Accred.:* Medical Assisting. Pres. Ira Vatandoost.
Enroll.: 15
(615) 865-1022

Fisk University
Nashville 37203. Private liberal arts college. 1930/1979 (SACS-Comm. on Coll.). 4-1-4 plan. Degrees: B,M. *Prof. Accred.:* Music. Pres. Henry Ponder.
Enroll.: 553
(615) 329-8500

Free Will Baptist Bible College
3606 West End Ave., Nashville 37205. Private (Free Will Baptist) liberal arts and professional. 1958/1978 (AABC). Sem. plan. Degrees: B. Pres. Charles A. Thigpen.
Enroll.: 358
(615) 383-1340

Freed-Hardeman College
Henderson 38340. Private (Church of Christ) liberal arts. 1956/1981 (SACS-Comm. on Coll.). Sem. plan. Degrees: A,B. *Prof. Accred.:* Art, Social Work (B), Teacher Education (*e,s*). Pres. E. Claude Gardner.
Enroll.: 1,135
(901) 989-4611

Harding Graduate School of Religion
1000 Cherry St., Memphis 38117. Branch of Harding College, Searcy, Ark. Private professional. 1972/1976 (SACS-Comm. on Coll.). Sem. plan. Degrees: P,M,D. Dean ———.
Enroll.: 132
(901) 761-1352

Health Care Training Institute
1378 Union Ave., Memphis 38104. Private. 1978/1984 (NATTS). Courses of varying lengths. Diplomas. Asst. Dir. Hope W. Tisdale.
Enroll.: 141 (*f.t.* 5 m., 136 w.)
(901) 722-2288

EXTENSION
1514 Church St., Nashville 37203. Dir. Ann Degasperis. (615) 320-0208

HIWASSEE COLLEGE
Madisonville 37354. Private (United Methodist) junior. 1958/1980 (SACS-Comm. on Coll.). Qtr. plan. Degrees: A. Pres. Curtis Schofield.
Enroll.: 603
(615) 442-2091

HUMBOLDT BEAUTY SCHOOL
1412 Main St., Humboldt 38343. Private. 1983 (SACS-COEI). 1,500 hours. Certificates. Dir. Gerri Ashmore.
Enroll.: FTE 24
(901) 784-9614

ITT TECHNICAL INSTITUTE (EXTENSION)
441 Donelson Pike, Nashville 37214. Private. 1985 (NATTS). Courses of varying lengths. Diplomas. Dir. David Sollie.
(615) 889-8700

INTERNATIONAL BARBER AND STYLE COLLEGE
619 S. Gallatin Rd, Madison 37115. Private. 1985 (NATTS). Courses of varying lengths. Diplomas. Dir. Edward L. Dunn.
(615) 865-7233

*JACKSON STATE COMMUNITY COLLEGE
Jackson 38302. Public junior. 1969/1984 (SACS-Comm. on Coll.). Qtr. plan. Degrees: A. *Prof. Accred.:* Medical Laboratory Technology (A), Radiography, Respiratory Therapy. Pres. Walter L. Nelms.
Enroll.: 1,900
(901) 424-3520

JETT COLLEGE OF COSMETOLOGY AND BARBERING
3744 N. Watkins, Memphis 38217. Private. 1983 (SACS-COEI). Courses of varying lengths. Certificates. Dir. Charles F. Holland.
Enroll.: FTE 244

BRANCH CAMPUS
524 S. Cooper, Memphis 38104.

BRANCH CAMPUS
3993 Jackson, Memphis 38128.

BRANCH CAMPUS
3740 N. Watkins, Memphis 38127.

*Member of State University and Community College System

BRANCH CAMPUS
5016 Navy Rd., Millington 38053.

JOHN A. GUPTON COLLEGE
2507 West End Ave., Nashville 37203. Private 2-year school of mortuary science. 1971/1975 (SACS-Comm. on Coll.). Qtr. plan. Degrees: A. Pres. John A. Gupton.
Enroll.: 45
(615) 327-3927

JOHNSON BIBLE COLLEGE
Knoxville 37998. Private (Christian Churches) professional. 1970/1979 (AABC); 1979/1985 (SACS-Comm. on Coll.). Sem. plan. Degrees:A,B. Pres. David L. Eubanks.
Enroll.: 397
(615) 573-4517

KING COLLEGE, INC.
Bristol 37620. Private (Presbyterian, U.S.) liberal arts. 1947/1977 (SACS-Comm. on Coll.). 4-1-4 plan. Degrees: B. Pres. Donald R. Mitchell.
Enroll.: 511
(615) 968-1187

KNOXVILLE BUSINESS COLLEGE
720 N. Fifth Ave., Knoxville 37917. Private junior. 1955/1983 (AICS). Qtr. plan. Degrees: A, certificates, diplomas. Dir. Jane Johnston.
Enroll.: 581 (*f.t.* 161 m., 420 w.)
(615) 524-3043

†KNOXVILLE COLLEGE
901 College St., Knoxville 37921. Private (United Presbyterian) liberal arts. Tri. plan. Degrees: A,B. 1948/1979 (SACS-Comm. on Coll.). Pres. Robert E. Shepherd.
Enroll.: 543
(615) 524-6511

KNOXVILLE INSTITUTE OF HAIR DESIGN
1221 N. Central, Knoxville 37917. Private. 1979 (NATTS). Courses of varying lengths. Certificates. Dir. Jack Rogers.
Enroll.: 57 (*f.t.* 8 m., 22 w.)
(615) 523-5541

KNOXVILLE STATE AREA-VOCATIONAL TECHNICAL SCHOOL
1100 Liberty St., Knoxville 37919. Public (state) technical. 1971/1981 (SACS-COEI). Courses of varying lengths. Certificates. Supt. Phillip W. Johnston.
Enroll.: FTE 444
(615) 546-5567

†Extraordinary Status

LAMBUTH COLLEGE
Jackson 38301. Private (United Methodist) liberal arts. 1954/1979 (SACS-Comm. on Coll.). 4-1-4 plan. Degrees: B. Pres. Harry W. Gilmer.
Enroll.: 557
(901) 427-1500

LANE COLLEGE
545 Lane Ave., Jackson 38301. Private (Christian Methodist Episcopal) liberal arts. 1949/1982 (SACS-Comm. on Coll.). Sem. plan. Degrees: B. Pres. Herman Stone, Jr.
Enroll.: 689
(901) 424-4600

LEE COLLEGE
Cleveland 37311. Private (Churches of God) liberal arts. 1969/1984 (SACS-Comm. on Coll.). Sem. plan. Degrees: A, B. Pres. Rev. R. Lamar Vest.
Enroll.: 1,154
(615) 472-2111

LEMOYNE-OWEN COLLEGE
807 Walker Ave., Memphis 38126. Private (United Church of Christ and Baptist) liberal arts. 1960/1983 (SACS-Comm. on Coll.). Sem. plan. Degrees: B. Pres. Walter L. Walker.
Enroll.: 835
(901) 774-9090

LINCOLN MEMORIAL UNIVERSITY
Harrogate 37752-0901. Private liberal arts college. 1936/1980 (SACS-Comm. on Coll.). Qtr. plan. Degrees: A, B, M. *Prof. Accred.:* Nursing (A). Pres. Gary J. Burchett.
Enroll.: 1,177 (*f.t.* (615) 869-3611

MARTIN COLLEGE
Pulaski 38478. Private (United Methodist) junior. 1952/1979 (SACS-Comm. on Coll.). Sem. plan. Degrees: A. Pres. Thomas S. Yow, III.
Enroll.: 268
(615) 363-7456

MARYVILLE COLLEGE
Maryville 37801. Private (United Presbyterian) liberal arts. 1922/1983 (SACS-Comm. on Coll.). 3-3 plan. Degrees: B. *Prof. Accred.:* Music. Pres. ———.
Enroll.: 521
(615) 982-6412

MCKENZIE COLLEGE
1000 Riverfront Pkwy., Chattanooga 37402. Private junior. 1953/1983 (AICS). Qtr. plan. Degrees: A. Pres. Roy McKenzie, III.
Enroll.: 650 (*f.t.* 174 m., 476 w.)
(615) 756-7042

MEDICAL CAREER COLLEGE
537 Main St., Nashville 37206. Private. 1978 (NATTS). Qtr. plan. Diplomas. Pres. N. T. Long.
Enroll.: 200 (*f.t.* 10 m., 190 w.)
(615) 255-7531

MEHARRY MEDICAL COLLEGE
1005 Dr. D. B. Todd Blvd., Nashville 37208. Private professional. 1972/1976 (SACS-Comm. on Coll.). Sem. plan. Degrees: A, B, P, M, D. *Prof. Accred.:* Dental Hygiene, Dentistry, Medical Technology, Medicine. Pres. David Satcher.
Enroll.: 808
(615) 327-6111

MEMPHIS COLLEGE OF ART
Overton Park, Memphis 38112. Private professional. 1963/1984 (SACS-Comm. on Coll.). Sem. plan. Degrees: B. *Prof. Accred.:* Art. Pres. John S. Slorp.
Enroll.: 208
(901) 726-4085

MEMPHIS AREA VOCATIONAL-TECHNICAL SCHOOL
620 Mosby Ave., Memphis 38105. Public (state) technical. 1970/1985 (SACS-COEI). Courses of varying lengths. Certificates. *Prof. Accred.:* Dental Assisting, Respiratory Therapy. Dir. Guy E. Treece.
Enroll.: FTE 499
(901) 527-8455

MEMPHIS INSTITUTE OF TECHNOLOGY
5100 Poplar Ave., Suite 132, Memphis 38137. Private. 1980/1985 (SACS-COEI); 1983 (NATTS). Courses of varying lengths. Certificates. Dir. I. D. Williams.
Enroll.: 111
(901) 761-9494

BRANCH CAMPUS
588 Vance St., Memphis 38126.

BRANCH CAMPUS
100 Kermit Dr., Nashville 37209.

*MEMPHIS STATE UNIVERSITY
Memphis 38152. Public. 1927/1984 (SACS-Comm. on Coll.). Sem. plan. Degrees: A, B, P, M, D. *Prof. Accred.:* Accounting (Type A), Art, Business (B, M), Engineering (civil,

*Member of State University and Community College System

computer systems, electrical, mechanical), Engineering Technology (architectural, computer systems, construction, electronics, manufacturing), Journalism, Law (ABA only), Medical Record Administration, Music, Nursing (B), Psychology, Rehabilitation Counseling, Social Work (B), Speech Pathology and Audiology, Teacher Education (*e,s,p*). Pres. Thomas G. Carpenter.
Enroll.: 16,512
(901) 454-2000

MEMPHIS THEOLOGICAL SEMINARY
Memphis 38104. Private (Cumberland Presbyterian) professional; graduate only. Sem. plan. Degrees: P,M. *Prof. Accred.:* Theology (1973/1978, ATS). Pres. J. David Hester.
Enroll.: 164
(901) 458-8232

MID-AMERICA BAPTIST THEOLOGICAL SEMINARY
P.O. Box 3624, Memphis 38173-0624. Private (Baptist) professional. 1981 (SACS-Comm. on Coll.). Sem. plan. Degrees: A,P,M,D. Pres. B. Gray Allison.
Enroll.: 372
(901) 726-9171

*MIDDLE TENNESSEE STATE UNIVERSITY
Murfreesboro 37132. Public. 1928/1985 (SACS-Comm. on Coll.). Sem. plan. Degrees: A,B,P,M,D. *Prof. Accred.:* Business (B,M), Home Economics, Music, Nursing (A), Social Work (B), Teacher Education (*e,s,p*). Pres. Sam H. Ingram.
Enroll.: 10,154
(615) 898-2300

†MID-SOUTH BIBLE COLLEGE
2485 Union Ave., Memphis 38112. Private (Interdenominational) professional. 1971/1981 (AABC). Sem. plan. Degrees: B. Pres. Robert J. Hilgenberg.
Enroll.: 190
(901) 458-7526

MILLER-HAWKINS BUSINESS COLLEGE
1399 Madison Ave., Memphis 38104. Private. 1965/1982 (AICS). Qtr. plan. Certificates, diplomas. Dir. L. E. Patrick.
Enroll.: 417 (*f.t.* 31 m., 386 w.)
(901) 725-6614

*Member of State University and Community College System
†Candidate for Accreditation by Regional Accrediting Commission

MILLIGAN COLLEGE
Milligan College 37682. Private liberal arts. 1960/1982 (SACS-Comm. on Coll.). Sem. plan. Degrees: A,B. Pres. Marshall J. Leggett.
Enroll.: 615
(615) 929-0116

MISTER WAYNE'S SCHOOL OF UNISEX HAIR DESIGN
170 S. Willow Ave., Cookeville 38501. Private. 1985 (NATTS). Courses of varying lengths. Diplomas. Dir. Charles W. Fletcher.
(615) 526-1478

*MOTLOW STATE COMMUNITY COLLEGE
Tullahoma 37388. Public junior. 1971/1975 (SACS-Comm. on Coll.). Qtr. plan. Degrees: A. *Prof. Accred.:* Nursing (A). Pres. R. Wade Powers.
Enroll.: 1,559
(615) 455-8511

NASHVILLE AUTO DIESEL COLLEGE
1524 Gallatin Rd., Nashville 37206. Private. 1967/1985 (NATTS). Courses of varying lengths. Diplomas. Pres. Thomas W. Balls.
Enroll.: 749 (*f.t.* 749 m., 0 w.)
(615) 226-3990

NASHVILLE COLLEGE
402 Plaza Professional Bldg., Madison 37115. Private. 1975/1982 (ABHES). Courses of varying lengths. Certificates. *Prof. Accred.:* Medical Assisting . Pres. A. Malek.
Enroll.: 44
(615) 868-2963

NASHVILLE STATE TECHNICAL INSTITUTE
120 White Bridge Rd., Nashville 37209. Public 2-year. 1972/1976 (SACS-Comm. on Coll.). Qtr. plan. Degrees: A. *Prof. Accred.:* Engineering Technology (architectural and building construction, chemical, civil, electrical, electronic, industrial, mechanical), Medical Laboratory Technology (A). Pres. Howard Lawrence.
Enroll.: 3,063
(615) 741-1236

NATIONAL INSTITUTE OF TECHNOLOGY
Plaza Professional Bldg., Suite 300, Madison 37115. Private. 1984 (AICS). Courses of varying lengths. Certificates, diplomas. Pres. Raymond Rotellini.
(615) 868-7444

*Member of State University and Community College System

NAVAL AIR TECHNICAL TRAINING CENTER
Naval Air Station Memphis (85), Millington 38054. Public (federal). 1976/1981 (SACS-COEI). Courses of varying lengths. Certificates. Cmdr. Capt. Joe A. McElmurry.
Enroll.: FTE 9,044
(901) 872-5306

NAVY LEADERSHIP AND ORGANIZATIONAL EFFECTIVENESS SCHOOL
Naval Air Station Memphis (96), Millington 38054. Public (federal) technical. 1983 (SACS-COEI). Courses of varying lengths. Certificates. Cmdg. Off. Capt. J. K. Taylor.
Enroll.: FTE 52
(901) 8872-5155

O'MORE SCHOOL OF INTERIOR DESIGN
319 W. Main St., Franklin 37064. Private professional. 1978. Sem. plan. Degrees: A,B. *Prof. Accred.:* Interior Design. Dir. Eloise Pitts O'More.
Enroll.: 131 (*f.t.* 14 m., 82 w.)
(615) 794-4254

PROFESSIONAL ACADEMY OF BROADCASTING
1809 Ailor Ave., P.O. Box 2411, Knoxville 37921. Private. 1979 (NATTS). Courses of varying lengths. Diplomas. Pres. Ernest Skinner.
Enroll.: 63 (*f.t.* 46 m., 17 w.)
(615) 546-5717

RHODES COLLEGE
2000 N. Parkway, Memphis 38112. Private (Presbyterian, U.S.A.) liberal arts college. 1911/1980 (SACS-Comm. on Coll.). Tri. plan. Degrees: B. *Prof. Accred.:* Music. Pres. James H. Daughdrill, Jr.
Enroll.: 1,027
(901) 726-3000

RICE COLLEGE
2829 Lamar Ave., Memphis 38114. Private business. 1952/1984 (AICS). Qtr. plan. Certificates, diplomas. Pres. Richard K. Rice.
Enroll.: 1,582 (*f.t.* 452 m., 1,130 w.)
(901) 743-3111

BRANCH CAMPUS
1621 Magnolia Ave., Knoxville 37917. Dir. Gerry Chapman.
(615) 637-9899

BRANCH CAMPUS
333 Laura St., Jacksonville, FL 32202. Dir. Jesse T. Garnett.
(904) 354-0773

BRANCH CAMPUS
1817 Terry Rd., Jackson, MS 39204. Dir. Billy W. Griffin.
(601) 373-7800

*ROANE STATE COMMUNITY COLLEGE
RFD, Harriman 37748. Public 2-year. 1974/1979 (SACS-Comm. on Coll.). Qtr. plan. Degrees: A. *Prof. Accred.:* Engineering Technology (electrical, mechanical), Medical Laboratory Technology (A), Medical Record Technology, Nursing (A), Radiography, Respiratory Therapy. Pres. Cuyler Dunbar.
Enroll.: 2,660
(615) 354-3000

RUTLEDGE COLLEGE
3495 Lamar Ave., Memphis 38118. Private junior. 1982 (AICS). Qtr. plan. Degrees: A. CEO Carl C. Brown.
Enroll.: 1,558 (*f.t.* 412 m., 1,146 w.)
(901) 362-9351

SCARRITT GRADUATE SCHOOL
1008 Nineteenth Ave., S., Nashville 37203. Private (United Methodist) liberal arts training for church service, graduate only. 1940/1975 (SACS-Comm. on Coll.). Sem. plan. Degrees: P,M. *Prof. Accred.:* Theology (1986, ATS). Pres. Donald J. Welch.
Enroll.: 8
(615) 327-2700

SEMINARY EXTENSION INDEPENDENT STUDY INSTITUTE
901 Commerce, Suite 500, Nashville 37203-3697. Private (Southern Baptist) home study. 1972/1983 (NHSC) . Dir. Raymond M. Rigdon.
Enroll.: (615) 242-2453

*SHELBY STATE COMMUNITY COLLEGE
P.O. Box 40568 , Memphis 38174. Public junior. 1974/1979 (SACS-Comm. on Coll.). Qtr. plan. Degrees: A. *Prof. Accred.:* EMT-Paramedic, Medical Laboratory Technology (A), Music, Nursing (A), Radiography. Pres. Raymond C. Bowen.
Enroll.: 3,384
(901) 528-6700

SOUTHEASTERN INSTITUTE FOR PARALEGAL EDUCATION
Suite 202, 112 21st Ave., S, Nashville 37203. Private. 1985 (SACS-COEI). Courses of vary-

*Member of State University and Community College System

ing lengths. Certificates. Dir. Katheryn L. Hearne.
Enroll.: FTE 9

SOUTHERN COLLEGE OF SEVENTH-DAY ADVENTISTS
Collegedale 37315. Private (Seventh-day Adventist) liberal arts. 1950/1982 (SACS-Comm. on Coll.). Sem. plan. Degrees: A,B. *Prof. Accred.:* Music, Nursing (A,B), Teacher Education (*e,s*). Pres. Donald R. Sahley.
Enroll.: 1,348
(615) 238-2111

SOUTHERN COLLEGE OF OPTOMETRY
1245 Madison Ave., Memphis 38104. Private professional. 1967/1982 (SACS-Comm. on Coll.). Qtr. plan. Degrees: A,B,P. *Prof. Accred.:* Optometric Technology, Optometry. Pres. William E. Cochran.
Enroll.: 432
(901) 725-0180

STATE AREA VOCATIONAL-TECHNICAL SCHOOL—ATHENS
P.O. Box 848, Athens 37303. Public (state) technical. 1971/1981 (SACS-COEI). Courses of varying lengths. Certificates. Dir. Robert E. Barnett.
Enroll.: FTE 161
(615) 745-6940

STATE AREA VOCATIONAL-TECHNICAL SCHOOL—COVINGTON
1600 Hwy. 51, S., Covington 38019. Public (state) technical. 1972/1982 (SACS-COEI). Courses of varying lengths. Certificates. Dir. Walter T. Fletcher, Jr.
Enroll.: FTE 114
(901) 476-8634

STATE AREA VOCATIONAL-TECHNICAL SCHOOL—CROSSVILLE
715 N. Miller Ave., Crossville 38555. Public (state) technical. 1971/1981 (SACS-COEI). Courses of varying lengths. Certificates. *Prof. Accred.:* Radiography. Dir. A. Burton Ingram.
Enroll.: FTE 190
(615) 484-7502

STATE AREA VOCATIONAL-TECHNICAL SCHOOL—DICKSON
Route 8, Box 420, Dickson 37055. Public (state) technical. 1974/1984 (SACS-COEI). Courses of varying lengths. Certificates. Dir. Robert Sullivan.
Enroll.: FTE 152
(615) 446-4710

STATE AREA VOCATIONAL-TECHNICAL SCHOOL—ELIZABETHTON
1500 Arney St., Elizabethton 37643. Public (state) technical. 1973/1983 (SACS-COEI). Courses of varying lengths. Certificates. *Prof. Accred.:* Medical Technology, Radiography. Dir. Kelly C. Yates.
Enroll.: FTE 178
(615) 542-4174

STATE AREA VOCATIONAL-TECHNICAL SCHOOL—HARRIMAN
P.O. Box 1109, Harriman 37748. Public (state) technical. 1973/1983 (SACS-COEI). Courses of varying lengths. Certificates. Dir. F. W. Kennedy.
Enroll.: FTE 154
(615) 882-6703

STATE AREA VOCATIONAL-TECHNICAL SCHOOL—HARTSVILLE
Hwy. 25 E., Hartsville 37074. Public (state) technical. 1971/1981 (SACS- COEI). Courses of varying lengths. Certificates. Dir. H. Dean Ward.
Enroll.: FTE 94
(615) 374-2147

STATE AREA VOCATIONAL-TECHNICAL SCHOOL—HOHENWALD
Route 1, Linden Hwy., Hohenwald 38462. Public (state) technical. 1972/1982 (SACS-COEI). Courses of varying lengths. Certificates. Dir. Billy F. Tucker.
Enroll.: FTE 121
(615) 796-5351

STATE AREA VOCATIONAL-TECHNICAL SCHOOL—JACKSBORO
P.O.Box 419, Jacksboro 37757. Public (state) technical. 1972/1982 (SACS-COEI). Courses of varying lengths. Certificates. Dir. C. H. Breeding.
Enroll.: FTE 151
(615) 562-8648

STATE AREA VOCATIONAL-TECHNICAL SCHOOL—JACKSON
McKellar Field, Jackson 38301. Public (state) technical. 1972/1982 (SACS-COEI). Courses of varying lengths. Certificates. Dir. Edwin H. Croom.
Enroll.: FTE 205
(901) 424-0691

STATE AREA VOCATIONAL-TECHNICAL SCHOOL—LIVINGSTON
Airport Rd., Livingston 38570. Public (state) technical. 1971/1981 (SACS-COEI). Courses

of varying lengths. Certificates. Dir. Ralph E. Robbins.
Enroll.: FTE 208
(615) 823-5525

State Area Vocational-Technical School—McKenzie
Hwy. 22 N., McKenzie 38201. Public (state) technical. 1971/1981 (SACS-COEI). Courses of varying lengths. Certificates. Dir. Kenneth D. Warren.
Enroll.: FTE 126
(901) 352-5364

State Area Vocational-Technical School—McMinnville
Hwy. 70 S., McMinnville 37110. Public (state) technical. 1971/1981 (SACS-COEI). Courses of varying lengths. Certificates. Dir. Jonah Fitch.
Enroll.: FTE 191
(615) 473-5587

State Area Vocational-Technical School—Morristown
821 W. Louise Ave., Morristown 37815. Public (state) technical. 1971/1981 (SACS-COEI). Courses of varying lengths. Certificates. Dir. Eugene G. Smith.
Enroll.: FTE 374
(615) 586-5771

Branch Campus
316 E. Main, Rogersville 37857.

State Area Vocational-Technical School—Murfreesboro
1303 Old Fort Pkwy., Murfreesboro 37130. Public (state) technical. 1985 (SACS-COEI). Courses of varying lengths. Certificates. Dir. Wallace E. Burke.
Enroll.: FTE 149
(615) 893-4095

State Area Vocational-Technical School—Nashville
100 White Bridge Rd., Nashville 37209. Public (state) technical. 1972/1982 (SACS-COEI). Courses of varying lengths. Certificates. Dir. Charles F. Malin.
Enroll.: FTE 387
(615) 741-1241

State Area Vocational-Technical School—Newbern
Hwy. 51 N., Newbern 38059. Public (state) technical. 1972/1982 (SACS-COEI). Courses of varying lengths. Certificates. Dir. Wallace E. Sexton.
Enroll.: FTE 179
(901) 627-2511

State Area Vocational-Technical School—Oneida
120 Elihare, Oneida 37841. Public (state) technical. 1973/1983 (SACS-COEI). Courses of varying lengths. Certificates. Dir. Arvis Blakley.
Enroll.: FTE 231
(615) 569-8338

State Area Vocational-Technical School—Paris
312 S. Wilson St., Paris 38242. Public (state) technical. 1974/1981 (SACS-COEI). Courses of varying lengths. Certificates. Dir. Jimmie R. Pritchard.
Enroll.: FTE 194
(901) 642-7552

State Area Vocational-Technical School—Pulaski
1233 E. Collage St., Pulaski 38478. Public (state) technical. 1973/1983 (SACS-COEI). Courses of varying lengths. Certificates. Dir. Henry H. Sims.
Enroll.: FTE 124
(615) 363-1588

State Area Vocational-Technical School—Ripley
South Industrial Park, Ripley 38063. Public (state) technical. 1973/1983 (SACS-COEI). Courses of varying lengths. Certificates. Dir. Jerry W. Little.
Enroll.: FTE 55
(901) 635-3368

State Area Vocational-Technical School—Savannah
P.O.Box 89, Crump 38327. Public (state) technical. 1974/1982 (SACS-COEI). Courses of varying lengths. Certificates. Dir. Sammie Smith.
Enroll.: FTE 138
(901) 632-3393

State Area Vocational-Technical School—Shelbyville
1405 Madison St., Shelbyville 37160. Public (state) technical. 1972/1982 (SACS-COEI). Courses of varying lengths. Certificates. Dir. R. E. Holden.
Enroll.: FTE 183
(615) 684-1828

State Area Vocational-Technical School—Whiteville
P.O. Box 489, Whiteville 30875. Public (state) technical. 1985 (SACS-COEI). Courses of varying lengths. Certificates. Dir. Verla Jacobs.
Enroll.: FTE 146
(901) 254-8521

State Technical Institute at Knoxville
3435 Division St., P.O. Box 19802, Knoxville 37919. Public 2-year. 1977/1982 (SACS-Comm. on Coll.). Qtr. plan. Degrees: A. *Prof. Accred.:* Engineering Technology (chemical, construction, electronic, mechanical). Pres. J. L. Goins.
Enroll.: 1,414
(615) 584-6103

State Technical Institute at Memphis
5983 Macon Cove at I-40, Memphis 38134. Public 2-year. 1969/1984 (SACS-Comm. on Coll.). Qtr. plan. Degrees: A. *Prof. Accred.:* Engineering Technology (architectural, biomedical, chemical, civil, computer, electrical, electronic, industrial, instrumentation, mechanical). Pres. Charles Temple.
Enroll.: 4,962
(901) 377-4111

State University and Community College System of Tennessee—System Office
Nashville 37219. Coordinating agency for 16 public universities and community colleges. Chanc. Roy S. Nicks.
(615) 741-4821

Tennessee Institute of Electronics
3203 Tazewell Pike, Knoxville 37918. Private. 1967/1977 (NATTS). Qtr. plan. Degrees: A, diplomas. Pres. Ronald R. Rackley.
Enroll.: 206 (*f.t.* 140 m., 6 w.)
(615) 688-9422

*Tennessee State University
3500 John Merritt Blvd., Nashville 37203. Public. 1946/1979 (SACS-Comm. on Coll.). Sem. plan. Degrees: A,B,M,D. *Prof. Accred.:* Engineering (architectural, civil, electrical, mechanical), Home Economics, Medical Record Administration, Music, Nursing (A,B), Social Work (B), Speech Pathology, Teacher Education (*e,s*). Pres. Roy P. Peterson.
Enroll.: 5,836
(615) 320-3131

*Member of State University and Community College System

*Tennessee Technological University
Cookeville 38505. Public (state) 1939/1985 (SACS-Comm. on Coll.). Qtr. plan. Degrees: A,B,M,D. *Prof. Accred.:* Accounting (Type A), Business (B,M), Engineering (chemical, civil, electrical, industrial, mechanical), Music, Nursing (B), Teacher Education (*e,s,p*). Pres. Wallace Prescott.
Enroll.: 6,851
(615) 528-3101

Tennessee Temple University
1815 Union Ave., Chattanooga 37404. Private (Independent Baptist) professional. 1984 (AABC). Sem. plan. Degrees: A,B. Pres. J. Don Jennings.
Enroll.: 1,888
(615) 698-6021

Tennessee Wesleyan College
P.O. Box 40, Athens 37303. Private (United Methodist) liberal arts . 1958/1981 (SACS-Comm. on Coll.). 4-1-4 plan. Degrees: B. Pres. James E. Cheek, II.
Enroll.: 376
(615) 745-7504

Tomlinson College
North Lee Hwy., P.O. Box 3030, Cleveland 37311. Private (Church of God of Prophecy) junior. 1983 (SACS-Comm. on Coll.). Tri. plan. Degrees: A., Pres. Emerson G. Hall.
Enroll.: 240
(615) 476-3271

Trevecca Nazarene College
Nashville 37203. Private (Church of Nazarene) liberal arts and teachers. 1969/1984 (SACS-Comm. on Coll.). Qtr. plan. Degrees: A,B,M. *Prof. Accred.:* Assistant to the Primary Care Physician, Medical Assisting, Music. Pres. Homer J. Adams.
Enroll.: 867
(615) 248-1200

Tri-Cities State Technical Institute—Blountville
P.O. Box 246, Blountville 37617. Public (state) (SACS-Comm. on Coll.). Qtr. plan. Degrees: A, certificates. *Prof. Accred.:* Engineering Technology (electronic, instrumentation, mechanical). Pres. H. James Owens.

*Member of State University and Community College System

Tennessee

Enroll.: 1,418
(615) 323-3191

TRI-CITY BARBER COLLEGE
113 South Central St., Knoxville 37902. Private. 1982 (NATTS). Courses of varying lengths. Diplomas. Dir. Walter E. McGinnis.
(615) 522-3736

TUSCULUM COLLEGE
Greeneville 37743. Private (United Presbyterian) liberal arts. 1926/1983 (SACS-Comm. on Coll.). Qtr. plan. Degrees: B. Pres. Earl R. Mezoff.
Enroll.: 382
(615) 638-1111

UNION UNIVERSITY
Jackson 38305. Private (Southern Baptist) liberal arts college. 1948/1975 (SACS-Comm. on Coll.). 4-1-4 plan. Degrees: A,B. *Prof. Accred.:* Music, Nursing (A,B). Interim Pres. Hyran E. Barefoot.
Enroll.: 1,268
(901) 668-1818

UNIVERSITY OF THE SOUTH
Sewanee 37375. Private (Episcopal) liberal arts college and theology. 1895/1985 (SACS-Comm. on Coll.). Sem. plan. Degrees: B,P,M,D. *Prof. Accred.:* Theology (1958/1985). Pres. Robert M. Ayres, Jr.
Enroll.: 1,140
(615) 598-5931

UNIVERSITY OF TENNESSEE SYSTEM
Central Office, Knoxville 37916. Public (state). Qtr. plan. Pres. Edward J. Boling.
(615) 974-0111

UNIVERSITY OF TENNESSEE AT CHATTANOOGA
Chattanooga 37402. Public (state) 1910/1981 (SACS-Comm. on Coll.). Degrees: B,M. *Prof. Accred.:* Business (B), Engineering, Music, Nursing (B), Social Work (B), Teacher Education (*e,s*). Chanc. Frederick W. Obear.
Enroll.: 6,356
(615) 755-4141

UNIVERSITY OF TENNESSEE AT KNOXVILLE
Knoxville 37996. Public (state) 1897/1981 (SACS-Comm. on Coll.). Degrees: A,B,M,D. *Prof. Accred.:* Accounting (Type A,B,C), Architecture (B), Art, Business (B,M), Community Health Education, Cytotechnology, Dietetics, Engineering (aerospace, agricultural, chemical, civil, electrical, engineering science and mechanics, industrial, mechanical, metallurgical, nuclear), Forestry, Home Economics, Interior Design, Journalism, Law, Librarianship, Medical Technology, Music, Nurse Anesthesia Education, Nursing (B,M), Physical Therapy, Psychology, Radiological Technology, Social Work (B,M), Speech Pathology and Audiology, Teacher Education (*e,s,p*), Veterinary Medicine. Chanc. Jack E. Reese.
Enroll.: 22,572
(615) 974-1000

UNIVERSITY OF TENNESSEE AT MARTIN
Martin 38238. Public (state) 1951/1982 (SACS-Comm. on Coll.). Degrees: A,B,M. *Prof. Accred.:* Engineering Technology (civil, electrical, mechanical), Home Economics, Music, Nursing (A), Social Work (B), Teacher Education (*e,s,p*). Chanc. Margaret N. Perry.
Enroll.: 5,453
(901) 587-7000

UNIVERSITY OF TENNESSEE CENTER FOR THE HEALTH SCIENCES
Memphis 38163. Public (state) 1897/1983 (SACS-Comm . on Coll.). Degrees: B,P,M,D. *Prof. Accred.:* Cytotechnology, Dental Hygiene, Dentistry, Medical Record Administration, Medical Technology, Medicine, Nursing (B,M), Pharmacy, Physical Therapy, Psychology, Radiography, Social Work (M), Specialist in Blood Bank Technology. Chanc. James C. Hunt.
Enroll.: 2,039
(902) 528-5500

VANDERBILT UNIVERSITY
21st Ave. and West End, Nashville 37240. Private. 1895/1975 (SACS-Comm. on Coll.). Accreditation includes George Peabody College for Teachers. Sem. plan. Degrees: B,P,M,D. *Prof. Accred.:* Business (M), Cytotechnology, Diagnostic Medical Sonography, Dietetics, Engineering (chemical, civil, electrical, mechanical), Law, Librarianship, Medical Technology, Medicine, Music, Nuclear Medicine Technology, Nursing (B,M), Perfusionist, Psychology, Radiation Therapy Technology, Respiratory Therapy, Specialist in Blood Bank Technology, Speech Pathology and Audiology, Teacher Education (*e,s,p*), Theology. Chanc. Joe B. Wyatt.
Enroll.: 8,538
(615) 322-7311

*Volunteer State Community College
Gallatin 37066. Public (state) 2-year. 1973/1978 (SACS-Comm. on Coll.). Qtr. plan. Degrees: A. *Prof. Accred.:* Dental Assisting, Medical Laboratory Technology (A), Medical Record Technology, Respiratory Therapy. Pres. Hal R. Ramer.
Enroll.: 2,084
(615) 452-8600

*Walters State Community College
500 South Davy Crockett Pkwy., Morristown 37813. Public junior. 1972/1976 (SACS-Comm. on Coll.). Qtr. plan. Degrees: A. *Prof. Accred.:* Engineering Technology (architectural, industrial), Nursing (A). Pres. Jack E. Campbell.
Enroll.: 2,578
(615) 581-2121

*Member of State University and Community College System

West Tennessee Business College
P.O. Box 1668, 1186 Hwy. 45 By-Pass, Jackson 38302. Private. 1953/1985 (AICS). Tri. plan. Diplomas. Pres. Barbara Turner.
Enroll.: 786 (*f.t.* 46 m., 740 w.)
(901) 668-7240

William R. Moore School of Technology
1200 Poplar Ave., Memphis 38104. Private technical. 1971/1981 (SACS-COEI). Courses of varying lengths. Certificates. Dir. Gaylon S. Hall.
Enroll.: FTE 83
(901) 726-1977

TEXAS

ABILENE CHRISTIAN UNIVERSITY
P.O. Box 8000, ACU Sta., Abilene 79699. Private (Church of Christ) liberal arts. 1951/1981 (SACS-Comm. on Coll.). Sem. plan. Degrees: A,B,P,M. *Prof. Accred.:* Music, Social Work (B), Teacher Education (*e,s*). Pres. William J. Teague.
Enroll.: 4,160oore
(915) 677-1911

ALAMO COMMUNITY COLLEGE DISTRICT—CENTRAL OFFICE
1300 San Pedro, San Antonio 78284. Chanc. Byron N. McClenny.
(512) 734-7311

ALLSTATE BUSINESS COLLEGE
6200 Maple Ave., Dallas 75235. Private. 1971/1982 (AICS). Courses of varying lengths. Diplomas. Dir. Jim Howard.
Enroll.: 996 (*f.t.* 59 m., 937 w.)
(214) 357-8453

ALVIN COMMUNITY COLLEGE
3110 Mustang Rd., Alvin 77511. Public (district). 1959/1980 (SACS-Comm. on Coll.). Sem. plan. Degrees: A. *Prof. Accred.:* Medical Laboratory Technology, Nursing (A), Respiratory Therapy, Respiratory Therapy Technology. Pres. A. Rodney Allbright.
Enroll.: 3,132
(713) 331-6111

AMARILLO COLLEGE
P.O. Box 447, Amarillo 79178. Public (district) junior. 1933/1982 (SACS-Comm. on Coll.). Sem. plan. Degrees: A. *Prof. Accred.:* Dental Assisting, Dental Hygiene, Medical Laboratory Technology (A), Music, Nursing (A), Radiation Therapy Technology, Radiography, Respiratory Therapy, Surgical Technology. Pres. H. D. Yarbrough.
Enroll.: 5,047
(806) 371-5000

AMBER UNIVERSITY
1700 Eastgate Dr., Garland 75041. Private (Church of Christ). 1981 (SACS-Comm. on Coll.). Sem. plan. Degrees: B,M. Pres. Douglas W. Warner.
Enroll.: 579
(214) 279-6511

AMERICAN COMMERCIAL COLLEGE
402 Butternut St., Abilene 79602. Private. 1970/1982 (AICS). Courses of varying lengths. Certificates, diplomas. Dir. W. I. Chandler.
Enroll.: 292 (*f.t.* 52 m., 240 w.)
(915) 672-8495

AMERICAN COMMERCIAL COLLEGE
2007 34th St., Lubbock 79411. Private. 1982 (AICS). Courses of varying lengths. Certificates, diplomas. Dir. Brent Sheets.
Enroll.: 443 (*f.t.* 78 m., 365 w.)
(806) 747-4339

AMERICAN COMMERCIAL COLLEGE
2115 E. Eighth St., Odessa 79761. Private. 1970/1982 (AICS). Courses of varying lengths. Certificates, diplomas. Dir. Raul Hernandez.
Enroll.: 307 (*f.t.* 30 m., 277 w.)
(915) 332-0768

AMERICAN COMMERCIAL COLLEGE
3177 Executive Dr., San Angelo 76904. Private. 1970/1982 (AICS). Courses of varying lengths. Certificates, diplomas. Dir. B. A. Reed.
Enroll.: 287 (*f.t.* 37 m., 250 w.)
(915) 942-6797

BRANCH CAMPUS
701 Professional Dr. N., Shreveport, LA 71105. Dir. Jerry W. Wood.
(318) 798-3333

AMERICAN TECHNICAL INSTITUTE
517 N. Bivins, Amarillo 79107. Private. 1983 (SACS-COEI). Courses of varying lengths. Certificates. Dir. Evey Ezell.
Enroll.: FTE 275
(806) 372-3868

BRANCH CAMPUS
2509 S. 32nd St., Muskogee, OK 74401.

BRANCH CAMPUS
6707 E. 12th St., Tulsa, OK 74112.

AMERICAN TECHNICAL INSTITUTE
U.S. Hwy. 190 W., Killeen 76542. Private. 1985 (SACS-COEI). Courses of varying lengths. Certificates. Dir. Don Mikles.
Enroll.: FTE 2,952

AMERICAN TECHNOLOGICAL UNIVERSITY
P.O. Box 1416, Killeen 76540. Private. 1976/1985 (SACS-Comm. on Coll.). Sem. plan. Degrees: B,M. Pres. L. Harlan Ford.
Enroll.: 291
(817) 526-1170

American Trades Institute
2608 Howes, Dallas 75235. Private. 1975/1980 (NATTS). Courses of varying lengths. Diplomas. Pres. Jim Craddock.
Enroll.: 331 (*f.t.* 147 m., 23 w.)
(214) 352-2222

Angelina College
P.O. Box 1768, Lufkin 75902-1768. Public (district) junior. 1970/1985 (SACS-Comm. on Coll.). Sem. plan. Degrees: A. *Prof. Accred.:* Nursing (A,B), Radiography. Pres. Jack W. Hudgins.
Enroll.: 1,772
(409) 639-1301

***Angelo State University**
2601 West Ave., N., San Angelo 76909. Public liberal arts college. 1967/1982 (SACS-Comm. on Coll.). Sem. plan. Degrees: A,B,M. *Prof. Accred.:* Music, Nursing (A,B). Pres. Lloyd D. Vincent.
Enroll.: 5,395
(915) 942-2131

Arlington Baptist College
3001 W. Division, Arlington 76012. Private (Baptist) professional. 1981 (AABC). Sem. plan. Degrees: B. Pres. Wayne Martin.
Enroll.: 210
(817) 461-8741

Art Institute of Dallas (Extension)
2829 W. Northwest Hwy., Dallas 75220. Private. 1985 (NATTS). Qtr. plan. Diplomas. Dir. William Mazur.
(214) 350-8874

Art Institute of Houston
3600 Yoakum Blvd., Houston 77006. Private. 1979 (NATTS). Qtr. plan. Diplomas. Dir. Charles P. Janssen.
Enroll.: 495 (*f.t.* 148 m., 230 w.)
(713) 523-2564

Austin College
Sherman 75090. Private (Presbyterian, U.S.) liberal arts. 1947/1977 (SACS-Comm. on Coll.). 2-2-1-4 plan. Degrees: B,M. Pres. Harry E. Smith.
Enroll.: 1,175
(214) 892-9101

Austin Community College
P.O. Box 2285, Austin 78768. Public 2-year. 1978/1983 (SACS-Comm. on Coll.). Sem. plan. Degrees: A. *Prof. Accred.:* Medical Laboratory Technology (A), Nursing (A), Radiography, Surgical Technology. Pres. Daniel D. Angel.
Enroll.: 11,782
(512) 495-7000

*Member Texas State University System

Austin Presbyterian Theological Seminary
Austin 78705-5797. Private. (Presbyterian, U.S.A.) professional; graduate only. 1973/1978 (SACS-Comm. on Coll.). Sem. plan. Degrees: P,M,D. *Prof. Accred.:* Theology (1940/1978, ATS). Pres. Jack L. Stotts.
Enroll.: 192
(512) 472-6736

BMI School of Business
710 S. Standard St., Longview 75604. Private. 1971/1984 (AICS). Courses of varying lengths. Certificates, diplomas. Pres. Leslie Roberts.
Enroll.: 329 (*f.t.* 2 m., 327 w.)
(214) 759-0001

Branch Campus
621 E. Ferguson St., Tyler 75702. Dir. Catharine Counts.
(214) 593-0166

Bauder Fashion College
508 S. Center St., Arlington 76010. Private. 1971/1984 (NATTS); 1985 (SACS-Comm. on Coll.). Qtr. plan. Degrees: A. Dir. Beverly Gooch.
Enroll.: 445 (*f.t.* (817) 277-6666

Baylor College of Dentistry
3302 Gaston Ave., Dallas 75246. Private; graduate and professional only. 1976/1980 (SACS-Comm. on Coll.). Qtr. plan. Degrees: B,M,D. *Prof. Accred.:* Dental Hygiene, Dentistry. Dean Richard E. Bradley.
Enroll.: 626
(214) 828-8100

Baylor College of Medicine
One Baylor Plaza, Houston 77030. Private; graduate and professional only. 1970/1985 (SACS-Comm. on Coll.). Qtr. plan. Degrees: B,P,M,D. *Prof. Accred.:* Assistant to the Primary Care Physician, Cytotechnology, Dietetics, Medical Technology, Medicine, Nuclear Medicine Technology, Nurse Anesthesia Education, Perfusionist, Psychology, Radiography. Pres. William T. Butler.
Enroll.: 899
(713) 799-4846

BAYLOR UNIVERSITY
Waco 76798. Private (Southern Baptist). 1914/1974 (SACS-Comm. on Coll.). Sem. plan. (qtr. plan in law school). Degrees: B, P, M, D. *Prof. Accred.:* Accounting (Type A), Business (B, M), Health Services Administration, Law, Medical Technology, Music, Nursing (B), Physical Therapy, Psychology, Social Work (B), Teacher Education (*e,s,p*). Pres. Herbert H. Reynolds.
Enroll.: 10,564
(817) 755-1011

BAYTOWN TECHNICAL SCHOOL
324 S. Airhart, Baytown 77520. Private. 1979/1984 (SACS-COEI). Courses of varying lengths. Certificates. Pres. Ruth Allison.
Enroll.: FTE 28
(713) 422-3656

BRANCH CAMPUS
3524 First Ave., S., Texas City 77590.

BRANCH CAMPUS
1575 W. Mockingbird La. Dallas 75235.

BEE COUNTY COLLEGE
3800 Charco Rd., Beeville 78102. Public (district) junior. 1969/1984 (SACS-Comm. on Coll.). Sem. plan. Degrees: A. *Prof. Accred.:* Dental Hygiene. Pres. Norman E. Wallace.
Enroll.: 1,900
(512) 358-3130

†BISHOP COLLEGE
3837 Simpson-Stuart Rd., Dallas 75241. Private (American Baptist) liberal arts. 1947/1971 (SACS-Comm. on Coll.). Sem. plan. Degrees: B. Pres. Wright L. Lassiter, Jr.
Enroll.: 1,136
(214) 372-8000

BLINN COLLEGE
902 College Ave., Brenham 77833. Public (district) junior. 1950/1984 (SACS-Comm. on Coll.). Sem. plan. Degrees: A. Pres. Walter Schwartz.
Enroll.: 3,157
(409) 836-9311

BRADFORD SCHOOL OF BUSINESS
4669 Southwest Freeway, Suite 350, Houston 77027. Private. 1980 (AICS). Courses of varying lengths. Certificates. Pres. Jo Ann Travis.
Enroll.: 996 (*f.t.* 9 m., 987 w.)
(713) 629-8940

†Accreditation on Probation

BRANCH CAMPUS
1681 S. Dayton St., Denver, CO 80231. Dir. Dennis Folden.
(303) 750-0742

BRANCH CAMPUS
5501 LBJ Freeway, #201, Dallas 75240. Dir. Judith A. Jacks.
(214) 458-1225

BRAZOS BUSINESS COLLEGE
1702 S. Texas Ave., Bryan 77803-1019. Private. 1986 (AICS). 10-month programs. Diplomas. Dir. Patty K. Reece.
(409) 822-6423

BRAZOSPORT COLLEGE
500 College Dr., Lake Jackson 77566. Public (district) junior. 1970/1985 (SACS-Comm. on Coll.). Sem. plan. Degrees: A. Pres. Wilbur A. Bass.
Enroll.: 2,247
(409) 265-6131

BROADWAY TECHNICAL INSTITUTE
8403 Broadway, San Antonio 78209. Private. 1982/1984 (SACS-COEI). Courses of varying lengths. Certificates. Dir. Bennie J. Orens.
Enroll.: FTE 13
(512) 826-3505

*BROOKHAVEN COLLEGE
3939 Valley View Lane, Farmers Branch 75234-5295. Public (district) junior. 1979/1983 (SACS-Comm. on Coll.). Sem. plan. Degrees: A. Pres. Patsy J. Fulton.
Enroll.: 4,775
(214) 206-4800

BROUSSARD'S TECHNICAL SCHOOL
2021 Savannah, Port Arthur 77640. Private. 1979/1984 (SACS-COEI). Courses of varying lengths. Certificates. Dir. B. E. Churchwell.
Enroll.: FTE 100
(713) 985-2555

BRANCH CAMPUS
1050 11th St., Beaumont 77704.
(409) 832-7703

BRANCH CAMPUS
10625 Stuebner, Airline Rd., Houston 77038.

BRANCH CAMPUS
8211 Channelside, Houston 77012.

BRANCH CAMPUS
835 Dal Sasso, Orange 77630.
(409) 886-3102

*Member Dallas County Community College District

Branch Campus
132 New Jersey, Mobile, AL 36603.

Bryan Institute
1719 W. Pioneer Pkwy., Arlington 76013. Private technical. 1980 (ABHES). Also recognized 1982 as an extension facility by (NATTS). 600-hour program. Diplomas. *Prof. Accred.:* Medical Assisting. Dir. Gerald E. Parr.
Enroll.: f.t. 6
(817) 265-5588

CBM Education Center
406 W. Durango, San Antonio 78207. Private. 1971/1982 (NATTS). Courses of varying lengths. Diplomas. Dir. Richard Jauregui.
Enroll.: 265 (*f.t.* 125 m., 75 w.)
(512) 224-9286

Extension
2550 W. Highway 83, San Benito 78586. Dir. Robert F. Stephens.
(512) 399-4007

Capitol City Trade and Technical School
205 E. Riverside Dr., Austin 78704. Private. 1977/1984 (NATTS); 1979/1984 (SACS-COEI). Courses of varying lengths. Diplomas. Pres./Dir. Gordon Blacketer.
Enroll.: FTE 325
(512) 444-3257

Branch Campus
4630 Westgate Blvd., Austin 78745. 1980/1984 (NATTS); 1979/1984 (SACS-COEI). Dir. David Darnell.
Enroll.: 130 (*f.t.* 6 m., 72 w.)
(512) 892-4270

Career Institute
1017 N. Main St., Suite 341, San Antonio 78212. Private. 1983 (SACS-COEI). Courses of varying lengths. Certificates. Dir. Sally Chapman.
Enroll.: FTE 156
(512) 271-0161

Branch Campus
2026 East Texas St., Bossier City, LA 71111.

*Cedar Valley College
3030 N. Dallas Ave., Lancaster 75134. Public (district) 2-year. 1979/1983 (SACS-Comm. on Coll.). Sem. plan. Degrees: A. Pres. Floyd S. Elkins.
Enroll.: 2,099
(214) 372-8200

Central Texas College
U.S. Hwy. 190 W., Killeen 76542. Public (district) junior. 1969/1984 (SACS-Comm. on Coll.). Sem. plan. Degrees: A. *Prof. Accred.:* Nursing (A). Pres. Phil Swartz.
Enroll.: 7,332
(817) 526-1211

Central Texas Commercial College
P .O. Box 1324, Brownwood 76801. Private. 1971/1983 (AICS). Qtr. plan. Diplomas. Dir. Martha Day.
Enroll.: 189 (*f.t.* 17 m., 172 w.)
(915) 646-0521

Cisco Junior College
Route 3, Box 3, Cisco 76437. Public (district). 1958/1979 (SACS-Comm. on Coll.). Sem. plan. Degrees: A, certificates. *Prof. Accred.:* Practical Nursing. Pres. Henry E. McCullough.
Enroll.: 1,265
(817) 442-2567

Clarendon College
P.O. Box 968, Clarendon 79226. Public (district) junior. 1970/1985 (SACS-Comm. on Coll.). Sem. plan. Degrees: A. Pres. Kenneth D. Vaughan.
Enroll.: 579
(806) 874-3571

College of the Hill Junior College District
P.O.Box 619, Hillsboro 76645. Public (district). 1963/1980 (SACS-Comm. on Coll.). Sem. plan. Degrees: A. Pres. W. R. Auvenshine.
Enroll.: 867
(817) 582-2555

College of the Mainland
8001 Palmer Hwy., Texas City 77591. Public (district) junior 1969/1984 (SACS-Comm. on Coll.). Sem. plan. Degrees: A. *Prof. Accred.:* Nursing (A). Pres. Larry Stanley.
Enroll.: 2,655
(713) 938-1211

Computer Learning Center
11200 Westheimer Rd., Houston 77042. Private. 1983 (NATTS). Courses of varying lengths. Diplomas. Dir. Craig Wood.
Enroll.: 100
(713) 781-6800

*Member Dallas County Community College District

CONCHO TRADE SCHOOL
706 Knickerbocker, San Angelo 76904. Private. 1983 (SACS-COEI). Courses of varying lengths. Certificates. Dir. Eugene Spann.
Enroll.: FTE 39
(915) 655-3420

BRANCH CAMPUS
14100 McCormick Dr., Tampa, FL 33625

CONCORDIA LUTHERAN COLLEGE
3400 N. I-35, Austin 78705. Private (Lutheran-Missouri Synod) liberal arts. 1982 (SACS-Comm. on Coll.). Sem. plan. Degrees: A,B. Pres. Ray Martens.
Enroll.: 448
(512) 452-7661

CONTROL DATA INSTITUTE
8585 N. Stemmons Frwy., Suite 201, Dallas 75247. Private. 1968/1978 (NATTS); 1980/1985 (SACS-COEI). Courses of varying lengths. Diplomas. Dir. Louis F. Griffin, Jr.
Enroll.: FTE 168
(214) 688-5900

CONTROL DATA INSTITUTE
2990 Richmond Ave., Suite 600, Houston 77098. 1981 (NATTS); 1981 (SACS-COEI). Private. Courses of varying lengths. Certificates. Dir. Kenneth Preston.
Enroll.: FTE 143
(713) 522-6115

COOKE COUNTY COLLEGE
P.O. Box 815, Gainesville 76240. Public (district) junior. 1961/1981 (SACS-Comm. on Coll.). Sem. plan. Degrees: A. *Prof. Accred.:* Nursing (A). Pres. Whitten Williams.
Enroll.: 1,195
(817) 688-7731

*CORPUS CHRISTI STATE UNIVERSITY
6300 Ocean Dr., P.O. Box 6010, Corpus Christi 78412. Public (state) liberal arts; upper level and graduate only. 1975/1980 (SACS-Comm. on Coll.). Sem. plan. Degrees: B,M. *Prof. Accred.:* Medical Technology, Music, Nursing (B). Pres. B. Alan Sugg.
Enroll.: 1,970
(512) 991-6810

COURT REPORTING INSTITUTE OF DALLAS
8585 N. Stemmons Freeway, #20050, Dallas 75247. 1979/1985 (SACS-COEI); 1986 (AICS). Private. Courses of varying lengths. Certificates. Dir. Carolyn S. Willard.
Enroll.: FTE 868
(214) 350-9722

CRISWELL COLLEGE
525 N. Ervay, Dallas 75201. Private (Baptist) professional. 1979 (AABC); 1985 (SACS-Comm. on Coll.). Sem. plan. Degrees: A,B,M. Pres. L. Paige Patterson.
Enroll.: 329
(214) 954-0012

DALLAS BAPTIST UNIVERSITY
7777 W. Kiest Blvd., Dallas 75211. Private (Southern Baptist) liberal arts. 1970/1977 (SACS-Comm. on Coll.). 4-1-4 plan. Degrees: B,M. *Prof. Accred.:* Nursing (B). Pres. W. Marvin Watson.
Enroll.: 1,029
(214) 331-8311

DALLAS CHRISTIAN COLLEGE
2700 Christian Pkwy., Dallas 75234. Private (Christian Churches) professional. 1978 (AABC). Sem. plan. Degrees: A,B. Pres. Gene Shepherd.
Enroll.: 121
(214) 241-3371

DALLAS COUNTY COMMUNITY COLLEGE DISTRICT—SYSTEMS OFFICE
701 Elm St., Room 712, Dallas 75202. Chanc. R. Jan LeCroy.
(214) 746-2237

DALLAS INSTITUTE OF FUNERAL SERVICES
3909 S. Buckner Blvd., Dallas 75227. Private 2-year. 1974/1984 (SACS-COEI). Certificates. Pres. Robert P. Kite.
Enroll.: FTE 198
(214) 823-6159

DALLAS THEOLOGICAL SEMINARY
3909 Swiss Ave., Dallas 75204. Private (nondenominational) for men. 1969/1984 (SACS-Comm. on Coll.). Sem. plan. Degrees: M,D. Pres. John F. Walvoord.
Enroll.: 1,083
(214) 824-3094

DEL MAR COLLEGE
Baldwin Blvd. and Ayers St., Corpus Christi 78404. Public (district) junior. 1946/1980 (SACS-Comm. on Coll.). Sem. plan. Degrees: A, certificates. *Prof. Accred.:* Dental Assisting, Dental Hygiene, Engineering Technology (electrical, electronic), Medical Laboratory Technology (A), Music, Nursing (A), Radiography, Respiratory Therapy, Sur-

*Member University System of South Texas

gical Technology. Pres. Edwin Biggerstaff, Jr.
Enroll.: 7,486
(512) 881-6200

DeVry Institute of Technology
4250 N. Beltline Rd., Irving 75038. Private. 1971/1984 (NATTS); 1981 (NCA). Tri. plan. Degrees: A,B, diplomas. *Prof. Accred.:* Engineering Technology (electronics). Pres. Thomas E. Colvin.
Enroll.: 2,306 (*f.t.* 1,715 m., 272 w.)
(214) 258-6767

Draughon's College of Business
2725 W. Seventh St., Fort Worth 76107. Private. 1970/1981 (AICS); 1983 (SACS-COEI). Courses of varying lengths. Certificates. Dir. John L. Roberts.
Enroll.: FTE 199
(817) 335-2381

Branch Campus
Walter Ctr., Suite 110, 1850 White Settlement Rd., Fort Worth 76107.

Durham College of El Paso
1801 Wyoming, El Paso 79902. Private. 1966/1980 (AICS). Courses of varying lengths. Certificates. Dir. Jim Giles.
Enroll.: 631 (*f.t.* 187 m., 444 w.)
(915) 533-9797

Durham College
4618 San Pedro Ave., San Antonio 78212. Private business. 1965/1982 (AICS). Courses of varying lengths. Certificates. Dir. Eugene Graygiles.
Enroll.: 872 (*f.t.* 198 m., 672 w.)
(512) 736-1566

Durham Nixon-Clay Business College
119 W. Eighth St., P.O. Box 1626, Austin 78767. Private. 1967/1985 (AICS); 1976/1983 (NATTS). Sem. plan. Certificates, diplomas. Pres. Orland W. Rury.
Enroll.: 1,087 (*f.t.* 450 m., 637 w.)
(512) 478-3446

Eason's Institute of Technology
1616 E. Commerce, San Antonio 78205. Private. 1981/1984 (SACS-COEI). Courses of varying lengths. Certificates. Dir. Oscar Eason.
Enroll.: FTE 262
(512) 223-2651

East Texas Baptist University
Marshall 75670. Private (Southern Baptist) liberal arts. 1957/1978 (SACS-Comm. on Coll.). Sem. plan. Degrees: A,B. *Prof. Accred.:* Music. Pres. Robert E. Craig.
Enroll.: 714
(214) 935-7963

East Texas State University
ETSU Sta., Commerce 75428. Public (state). 1925/1983 (SACS-Comm. on Coll.). Sem. plan. Degrees: B,M,D. *Prof. Accred.:* Business (B,M), Music, Social Work (B), Teacher Education (*e,s,p*). Pres. Charles J. Austin.
Enroll.: 5,366
(214) 886-5000

East Texas State University at Texarkana
P.O. Box 5518, Texarkana 75505-0518. Public (state) upper level only. 1979/1985 (SACS-Comm. on Coll.). Sem. plan. Degrees: B,M. Pres. John F. Moss.
Enroll.: 757
(214) 838-6514

*Eastfield College
3737 Motley Dr., Mesquite 75150. Public (district) junior. 1972/1983 (SACS-Comm. on Coll.). Sem. plan. Degrees: A. Pres. Eleanor D. Ott.
Enroll.: 5,583
(214) 324-7600

*El Centro College
Main at Lamar Sts., Dallas 75202. Public (district) junior. 1968/1983 (SACS-Comm. on Coll.). Sem. plan. Degrees: A, certificates. *Prof. Accred.:* Dental Assisting, Interior Design, Medical Assisting, Medical Laboratory Technology (A), Nursing (A), Radiography, Respiratory Therapy, Surgical Technology. Pres. ———.
Enroll.: 4,378
(214) 746-2200

El Paso County Community College
P.O. Box 20500, El Paso 79998. Public 2-year. 1978/1983 (SACS-Comm. on Coll.). Sem. plan. Degrees: A. *Prof. Accred.:* Dental Assisting, Dental Hygiene, Medical Assisting, Medical Laboratory Technology, Nursing (A), Radiation Therapy Technology, Radiography, Respiratory Therapy, Surgical Technology. Pres. Robert E. Shepack.
Enroll.: 11,793
(915) 594-2000

*Member Dallas County Community College District

Texas

EL PASO TRADE SCHOOL, INC.
1000 Texas Ave., P.O. Box "M," El Paso 79951. Private. 1979 (NATTS). Courses of varying lengths. Certificates. Pres. Randy Kuykendall.
Enroll.: 350 (*f.t.* 340 m., 10 w.)
(915) 532-3737

ELKINS INSTITUTE IN DALLAS
2603 Inwood Rd., Dallas 75235. Private. 1980 (NATTS). Courses of varying lengths. Certificates. Pres. David Liszt.
Enroll.: 175
(214) 350-1212

ELKINS INSTITUTE OF HOUSTON
7322 S.W. Freeway #1450, Houston 77074. Private. 1985 (NATTS). Courses of varying lengths. Certificates. Pres. Pat Sadler.
(713) 271-7722

THE EPISCOPAL THEOLOGICAL SEMINARY OF THE SOUTHWEST
P.O. Box 2247, Austin 78768. Private (Episcopal) professional; graduate only. 1983 (SACS-Comm. on Coll.). Sem. plan. Degrees: P,M. *Prof. Accred.:* Theology (1958/1983, ATS). Dean Rev. Durstan R. McDonald.
Enroll.: 91
(512) 472-4133

EXECUTIVE SECRETARIAL SCHOOL
2829 W. Northwest Hwy., Suite 226, Dallas 75220. Private. 1969/1981 (AICS); 1977/1982 (SACS-COEI). Tri. plan. Diplomas. Dir. Jan Eisenhour Friedheim.
Enroll.: FTE 226
(214) 350-0093

FORT WORTH TRADE SCHOOLS
3617 Collinwood, Fort Worth 76107. Private. 1979 (NATTS). Courses of varying lengths. Certificates. Dir. Gerald McEntire.
Enroll.: f.t. 95 m.
(817) 731-8423

FOUR-C COLLEGE
P.O. Box 4, Waco 76703. Private business. 1973/1985 (AICS). Courses of varying lengths. Diplomas. Dir. Camilla M. McKenzie.
Enroll.: 416 (*f.t.* 86 m., 330 w.)
(817) 756-7201

FRANK PHILLIPS COLLEGE
P.O. Box 5118, Borger 79007. Public (district) junior. 1958/1979 (SACS- Comm. on Coll.). Sem. plan. Degrees: A. Pres. Andy Hicks.
Enroll.: 940
(806) 274-5311

GALVESTON COLLEGE
4015 Ave. Q, Galveston 77550. Public (district) junior. 1969/1984 (SACS-Comm. on Coll.). Sem. plan. Degrees: A. *Prof. Accred.:* Nuclear Medicine Technology, Nursing (A), Radiography, Respiratory Therapy, Surgical Technology. Pres. John Pickleman.
Enroll.: 1,462
(409) 763-6551

GARY JOB CORPS CENTER
P.O.Box 967, Hwy. 21, San Marco 78667. Public (federal). 1985 (SACS-COEI). Courses of varying lengths. Certificates. Dir. Albert Perkins.
Enroll.: FTE 1,6921

GRAYSON COUNTY COLLEGE
6101 Hwy. 691, Denison 75020. Public junior. 1967/1981 (SACS-Comm. on Coll.). Sem. plan. Degrees: A. *Prof. Accred.:* Dental Assisting, Medical Laboratory Technology (A), Nursing (A). Pres. Jim M. Williams.
Enroll.: 2,835
(214) 465-6030

GULF COAST TRADE CENTER
P.O. Box 515, New Waverly 77358. Private. 1984 (SACS-COEI). Courses of varying lengths. Certificates. Dir. Thomas M. Buzbee.
Enroll.: FTE 126

HALLMARK INSTITUTE OF TECHNOLOGY
1130 99th St., San Antonio 78214. Private. 1971/1978 (NATTS). Courses of varying lengths. Certificates. Dir. Richard H. Fessler.
Enroll.: 220 (*f.t.* 212 m., 8 w.)
(512) 924-8551

EXTENSION
10401 I-10 West, San Antonio 78230.
(512) 690-9000

HARDIN-SIMMONS UNIVERSITY
P.O. Drawer A, HSU Sta., Abilene 79698. Private (Southern Baptist). 1927/1976 (SACS-Comm. on Coll.). Sem. plan. Degrees: B,M. *Prof. Accred.:* Music. Pres. Jesse C. Fletcher.
Enroll.: 1,803
(915) 677-7281

HARGEST VOCATIONAL AND TECHNICAL COLLEGE
4608 Main St., Houston 77002. Private. 1981/1984 (AICS). Courses of varying lengths. Certificates. Pres. Conard Hargest.

Texas

Enroll.: 1,436 (*f.t.* 98 m., 1,338 w.)
(713) 524-6882

HENDERSON COUNTY JUNIOR COLLEGE
Cardinal Dr., Athens 75751. Public (district). 1952/1975 (SACS-Comm. on Coll.). Sem. plan. Degrees: A. *Prof. Accred.:* Nursing (A). Pres. William J. Campion.
Enroll.: 2,575
(214) 675-6211

HOUSTON BAPTIST UNIVERSITY
7502 Fondren Rd., Houston 77074. Private (Southern Baptist) liberal arts college. 1968/1981 (SACS-Comm. on Coll.). Qtr. plan. Degrees: B,M. *Prof. Accred.:* Nursing (B), Social Work (B). Pres. W. H. Hinton.
Enroll.: 2,962
(713) 774-7661

HOUSTON COMMUNITY COLLEGE
P.O. Box 7849, Houston 77270-7849. Public (district) 2-year. 1977/1982 (SACS-Comm. on Coll.). Sem. plan. Degrees: A. *Prof. Accred.:* Dental Assisting, Engineering Technology (electronic), Medical Laboratory Technology (A), Nuclear Medicine Technology, Radiography, Respiratory Therapy. Pres. J. B. Whiteley.
Enroll.: 20,239
(713) 869-5021

HOWARD COUNTY JUNIOR COLLEGE DISTRICT
Eleventh Pl. and Birdwell La., Big Spring 79720. Public. 1955/1975 (SACS-Comm. on Coll.). Sem. plan. Degrees: A. *Prof. Accred.:* Dental Hygiene, Nursing (A). Pres. Bob E. Riley.
Enroll.: 1,138
(915) 267-6311

HOWARD PAYNE UNIVERSITY
Brownwood 76801. Private (Southern Baptist) liberal arts college. 1948/1984 (SACS-Comm. on Coll.). Sem. plan. Degrees: B. Pres. Ralph A. Phelps, Jr.
Enroll.: 873
(915) 646-2502

HUSTON-TILLOTSON COLLEGE
1820 E. Eighth St., Austin 78702. Private (United Methodist and United Church of Christ) liberal arts. 1943/1979 (SACS-Comm. on Coll.). Sem. plan. Degrees: B. Pres. John Q. Taylor King.
Enroll.: 540
(512) 476-7421

ITT TECHNICAL INSTITUTE
2202 Road to Six Flags, Arlington 76011. Private. 1983 (NATTS). Qtr. plan. Degrees: A, certificates. Dir. Don Wilkes.
(817) 640-7100

ITT TECHNICAL INSTITUTE (EXTENSION)
9421 Roark Rd., Houston 77099. Private. Qtr. plan. Degrees: A, certificates. Dir. Gene Feichtner.
(713) 270-1634

INCARNATE WORD COLLEGE
4301 Broadway, San Antonio 78209. Private (Roman Catholic) liberal arts. 1925/1985 (SACS-Comm. on Coll.). Sem. plan. Degrees: B,M. *Prof. Accred.:* Nuclear Medicine Technology, Nursing (B), Teacher Education (*e,s*). Pres. Louis J. Agnese, Jr.
Enroll.: 1,101
(512) 828-1261

INTERNATIONAL AVIATION AND TRAVEL ACADEMY
1201 N. Watson Rd., Suite 270, Arlington 76011. Private. 1979/1984 (SACS-COEI). Courses of varying lengths. Certificates. Dir. Kenneth Woods.
Enroll.: FTE 186
(214) 358-6511 or 358-7366

INTERNATIONAL BUSINESS COLLEGE
4121 Montana Ave., El Paso 79903. Private. 1969/1981 (AICS). Courses of varying lengths. Certificates. Dir. Robert Brown.
Enroll.: 1,588 (*f.t.* 144 m., 1,444 w.)
(915) 566-8644

BRANCH CAMPUS
3628 50th St., Lubbock 79413. Dir. Darold Russell.
(806) 797-1933

BRANCH CAMPUS
1201 Cuba St., Alamogordo, NM 88310. Dir. Louis Telles.
(505) 437-1854

BRANCH CAMPUS
4223 Montgomery NE, Albuquerque, NM 87109. Dir. William Kaltenbach.
(505) 883-0696

BRANCH CAMPUS
650-E Montana, Las Cruces, NM 88001. Dir. Lorry Foodrill.
(505) 526-5579

JACKI NELL EXECUTIVE SECRETARY SCHOOL
2538 S. Congress, Austin 78704. Private. 1978/1981 (AICS). Courses of varying lengths. Certificates. Exec. Dir. Nelda Brock.
Enroll.: 188 w.
(512) 447-9415

JACKSONVILLE COLLEGE
500 Pine St., Jacksonville 75766. Private (Baptist) 2-year. 1974/1979 (SACS-Comm. on Coll.). Sem. plan. Degrees: A. Pres. Curtis M. Carroll.
Enroll.: 221
(214) 586-2518

JARVIS CHRISTIAN COLLEGE
P.O. Drawer G, Hawkins 75765. Private (Disciples of Christ) liberal arts; affiliate of Texas Christian University. 1967/1983 (SACS-Comm. on Coll.). Sem. plan. Degrees: A,B. Pres. Charles A. Berry, Jr.
Enroll.: 524
(214) 769-2174

KD STUDIO
2600 Stemmons Freeway, Suite 117, Dallas 75207. Private. 1985 (SACS-COEI). Courses of varying lengths. Certificates. Dir. Kathy Tyner.
Enroll.: FTE 260
(817) 335-2381

KILGORE COLLEGE
1100 Broadway, Kilgore 75662. Public (district) junior. 1939/1979 (SACS-Comm. on Coll.). Sem. plan. Degrees: A. *Prof. Accred.:* Medical Laboratory Technology (A), Nursing (A). Pres. Stewart H. McLaurin.
Enroll.: 5,342
(214) 984-8531

LAMAR UNIVERSITY
Lamar Sta., Box 10001, Beaumont 77710. Public liberal arts and professional. 1955/1977 (SACS-Comm. on Coll.). Sem. plan. Degrees: A,B,M,D. *Prof. Accred.:* Business (B,M), Dental Hygiene, Engineering (chemical, civil, electrical, industrial, mechanical), Music, Nursing (A,B), Radiography, Respiratory Therapy, Respiratory Therapy Technology, Social Work (B), Speech Pathology, Teacher Education (*e,s,p*). Pres. Bill J. Franklin.
Enroll.: 14,151
(409) 880-7011

LAREDO JUNIOR COLLEGE
West End Washington St., Laredo 78040. Public (district). 1957/1978 (SACS-Comm. on Coll.). Sem. plan. Degrees: A, certificates. *Prof. Accred.:* Medical Laboratory Technology (A), Nursing (A), Practical Nursing, Radiography. Pres. Roger L. Worsley.
Enroll.: 3,779
(512) 722-0521

*LAREDO STATE UNIVERSITY
West End Washington St., Laredo 78040. Public (state). 1970/1980 (SACS-Comm. on Coll.). Sem. plan. Degrees: A,B,M. Pres. Manuel T. Pacheco.
Enroll.: 576
(512) 722-8001

LEE COLLEGE
P.O. Drawer 818, Baytown 77520. Public (district) junior. 1948/1985 (SACS-Comm. on Coll.). Sem. plan. Degrees: A. Pres. Robert C. Cloud.
Enroll.: 3,692
(713) 427-5611

LETOURNEAU COLLEGE
P.O. Box 7001, Longview 75607. Private liberal arts and professional. 1970/1974 (SACS-Comm. on Coll.). Sem. plan. Degrees: A,B. *Prof. Accred.:* Engineering (electrical, mechanical). Pres. Richard C. Berry.
Enroll.: 919
(214) 753-0231

LINCOLN TECHNICAL INSTITUTE
2227 Irving Blvd., Dallas 75207. Private. 1968/1979 (NATTS). Courses of varying lengths. Diplomas. Dir. Michael Thayer.
Enroll.: 225 (*f.t.* 223 m., 2 w.)
(214) 631-2780

LON MORRIS COLLEGE
Jacksonville 75766. Private (United Methodist) junior. 1927/1984 (SACS-Comm. on Coll.). Sem. plan. Degrees: A. Pres. W. Faulk Landrum.
Enroll.: 290
(214) 586-2471

LUBBOCK CHRISTIAN COLLEGE
5601 W. 19th St., Lubbock 79407. Private (Church of Christ) liberal arts. 1972/1977 (SACS-Comm. on Coll.). Sem. plan. Degrees: A,B. *Prof. Accred.:* Teacher Education (*e,s,p*). Pres. Steven S. Lemley.
Enroll.: 924
(806) 792-3221

*Member University System of South Texas

MASSEY BUSINESS COLLEGE
4916 Main, Houston 77002. Private. 1954/1985 (AICS); 1984 (SACS-COEI). Qtr. plan. Diplomas. Pres. P. E. Compton.
Enroll.: FTE 729
(713) 521-0426

BRANCH CAMPUS
1225 Agnes, Corpus Christi 78401. Dir. Jim Giles.
(512) 883-5700

BRANCH CAMPUS
3333 Fannin, Houston 77002.
(713) 524-2686

MASSEY BUSINESS COLLEGE
P.O. Box 444, Nacogdoches 75961. Private. 1966/1984 (AICS). Courses of varying lengths. Diplomas. Dir. Clarence E. Chandler.
Enroll.: 123 (*f.t.* 7 m., 116 w.)
(409) 564-3788

MCLENNAN COMMUNITY COLLEGE
1400 College Dr., Waco 76708. Public (district) junior. 1968/1982 (SACS-Comm. on Coll.). Sem. plan. Degrees: A. *Prof. Accred.:* Medical Laboratory Technology (A), Nuclear Medicine Technology, Nursing (A), Radiography. Pres. Wilbur A. Ball
Enroll.: 3,928
(817) 756-6551

MCMURRY COLLEGE
P.O. Box 98, McMurry Sta., Abilene 79697. Private (United Methodist) liberal arts. 1949/1978 (SACS-Comm. on Coll.). Sem. plan. Degrees: A,B. *Prof. Accred.:* Teacher Education (*e,s*). Pres. Thomas K. Kim.
Enroll.: 1,116
(915) 692-4130

METILS WELDING SCHOOL
7645 Gulf Freeway, Houston 77207. Private. 1985 (SACS-COEI). Courses of varying lengths. Certificates and Diplomas. Dir. Thomas C. Reed.
Enroll.: FTE 26

BRANCH CAMPUS
1625 E. Cardinal Dr.,Beaumont 77701.

BRANCH CAMPUS
2302 N. Port Ave., Beaumont 77701.

BRANCH CAMPUS
3502 Second Ave., S.,Texas City 77690..

METRO BARBER COLLEGE—AMARILLO
4123 W. 34th St., Amarillo 79109. Private. 1985 (NATTS). Courses of varying lengths. Certificates. Dir. Frances Clark.
Enroll.: 20 (*f.t.* 3 m., 17 w.)
(806) 355-7277

METRO BARBER COLLEGE—LUBBOCK
2806 Avenue Q, Lubbock 79405. Private. 1981 (NATTS). 9-month courses. Certificates. Owner Frances Clark.
Enroll.: 22 (*f.t.* 4 m., 18 w.)
(806) 744-8496

MICROCOMPUTER TECHNOLOGY INSTITUTE
6116 Windswept, Houston 77057. Private. 1983 (NATTS); 1984 (SACS-COEI). Courses of varying lengths. Certificates, diplomas. Pres. Robert E. Obenhaus.
Enroll.: 434
(713) 974-7181

BRANCH CAMPUS
211 E. Parkwood, Suite 112, Friends Wood, 77546.

MIDLAND COLLEGE
3600 N. Garfield St., Midland 79705. Public 2-year. 1975/1980 (SACS-Comm. on Coll.). Sem. plan. Degrees: A. *Prof. Accred.:* Nursing (A), Respiratory Therapy. Pres. Jess H. Parrish.
Enroll.: 2,565
(915) 684-7851

MIDWESTERN STATE UNIVERSITY
3400 Taft Blvd., Wichita Falls 76308. Public (state). 1950/1982 (SACS-Comm. on Coll.). Sem. plan. Degrees: A,B,M. *Prof. Accred.:* Dental Hygiene, Medical Laboratory Technology (A), Music, Nursing (A), Radiography, Teacher Education (*e,s*). Pres. Louis J. Rodriguez.
Enroll.: 3,510
(817) 692-6611

MISS WADE'S FASHION MERCHANDISING COLLEGE
Suite 6837, P.O. Box, 586343, Dallas 75258. Private. 1971/1982 (NATTS); 1985 (SACS-Comm. on Coll.). Qtr. plan. Degrees: A. Pres. Frank J. Tortoriello, Jr.
Enroll.: 335
(214) 637-3530

*MOUNTAIN VIEW COLLDGE
4849 W. Illinois Ave., Dallas 75211. Public (district) junior. 1972/1983 (SACS-Comm. on Coll.). Sem. plan. Degrees: A. William H. Jordan.
Enroll.: 3,474
(214) 333-8700

*Member Dallas County Community District

NATIONAL CENTER FOR CHILDCARE PROFESSIONALS
5322 W. Bellfort, Suite 103, Houston 77035. Private home study-internship. 1982 (NHSC). Pres. Marilyn M. Appelbaum.
(713) 723-9498

NATIONAL EDUCATION CENTER/BRYMAN CAMPUS
9724 Beechnut, Suite 300, Houston 77036. Private. 1973/1978 (NATTS). Courses of varying lengths. Diplomas. *Prof. Accred.:* Medical Assisting. Dir. Glensford L. Craig.
Enroll.: 150 (*f.t.* 5 m., 145 w.)
(713) 776-3656

NATIONAL EDUCATION CENTER/NATIONAL INSTITUTE OF TECHNOLOGY CAMPUS
3040 N. Bue.ckner Blvd., Dallas 75228. Private. 1981 (NATTS). Qtr. plan. Diplomas. Dir. Joe Kirkland.
Enroll.: 287 (*f.t.* 220 m., 67 w.)
(512) 324-2811

NATIONAL EDUCATION CENTER/NATIONAL INSTITUTE OF TECHNOLOGY CAMPUS
401 W. Byrd St., Universal City 78148. Qtr. plan. Diplomas. Dir. Jerry Templeton.
Enroll.: 168 (*f.t.* 137 m., 12 w.)
(512) 658-7078

NAVARRO COLLEGE
P.O. Box 1170, Corsicana 75110. Public (district) junior. 1954/1985 (SACS-Comm. on Coll.). Sem. plan. Degrees: A. *Prof. Accred.:* Medical Laboratory Technology. Pres. Kenneth P. Walker.
Enroll.: 1,683
(214) 874-6501

NORTH HARRIS COUNTY COLLEGE
Three Greenspoint Plaza, 233 Benmar Dr., Suite 150, Houston 77060. Public (district) 2-year. 1976/1981 (SACS-Comm. on Coll.). Sem. plan. Degrees: A. *Prof. Accred.:* Dental Assisting, Nursing (A). Pres. Joe A. Airola.
Enroll.: 8,023
(713) 875-1515

*NORTH LAKE COLLEGE
5001 N. MacArthur Blvd., Irving 75038. Public (district) 2-year. 1979/1983 (SACS-Comm. on Coll.). Sem. plan. Degrees: A. James F. Horton Jr.
Enroll.: 3,095
(214) 659-5229

*Member Dallas County Community District

NORTH TEXAS STATE UNIVERSITY
P.O. Box 13737, NT Sta., Denton 76203. Public. 1925/1985 (SACS-Comm. on Coll.). Sem. plan. Degrees: B,M,D. *Prof. Accred.:* Business (B,M), Interior Design, Journalism, Music, Librarianship, Psychology, Social Work (B), Speech Pathology and Audiology, Teacher Education (*e,s,p*). Chanc. and Pres. Alfred F. Hurley.
Enroll.: 17,869
(817) 565-2000

NORTHWOOD INSTITUTE—CEDAR HILL CAMPUS
Cedar Hill 75104. 1978 (NCA). Private business management. Qtr. and module plan. Degrees: A. Pres. Thomas J. Brown.
Enroll.: 1,653 (*f.t.* 1,153 m., 486 w.)
(214) 291-1541

OBLATE SCHOOL OF THEOLOGY
285 Oblate Dr., San Antonio 78216. Private (Roman Catholic), professional only. 1968/1982 (SACS-Comm. on Coll.). Sem. plan. Degrees: P,M. *Prof. Accred.:* Theology (ATS, 1982). Pres. Patrick Guidon, O.M.I.
Enroll.: 114
(512) 341-1366

ODESSA COLLEGE
201 West University, Odessa 79764. Public (district) junior. 1952/1982 (SACS-Comm. on Coll.). Sem. plan. Degrees: A. *Prof. Accred.:* Medical Laboratory Technology, Music, Nursing (A), Radiography, Respiratory Therapy, Respiratory Therapy Technology, Surgical Technology. Pres. Philip T. Speegle.
Enroll.: 3,429
(915) 335-6400

OUR LADY OF THE LAKE UNIVERSITY OF SAN ANTONIO
411 S.W. 24th St., San Antonio 78285. Private (Roman Catholic) liberal arts. 1923/1982 (SACS-Comm. on Coll.). Sem. plan. Degrees: B,M. *Prof. Accred.:* Social Work (B,M), Speech Pathology. Pres. Sister Elizabeth A. Sueltenfuss.
Enroll.: 1,330
(512) 434-6711

PAN AMERICAN UNIVERSITY
Edinburg 78539. Public (state) liberal arts college. 1956/1975 (SACS-Comm. on Coll.). Sem. plan. Degrees: A,B,M. *Prof. Accred.:* Business (B,M), Dietetics, Medical Technology, Nursing (A,B), Social Work (B),

Teacher Education (*e,s,p*). Pres. Miguel A. Nevarez.
Enroll.: 7,865
(512) 381-2011

Panola Junior College
Carthage 75633. Public (district). 1960/1980 (SACS-Comm. on Coll.). Sem. plan. Degrees: A. Pres. Gary D. McDaniel.
Enroll.: 1,231
(214) 693-2000

Paris Junior College
2400 Clarkville St., Paris 75460. Public (district). 1934/1982 (SACS-Comm. on Coll.). Sem. plan. Degrees: A. *Prof. Accred.:* Nursing (A). Pres. Dennis F. Michaelis.
Enroll.: 1,767
(214) 785-7661

Paul Quinn College
1020 Elm St., Waco 76704. Private (African Methodist Episcopal) liberal arts. 1972/1976 (SACS-Comm. on Coll.). Sem. plan. Degrees: B. *Prof. Accred.:* Social Work (B). Pres. Warren Morgan.
Enroll.: 339
(817) 753-6415

Pharr Vocational School
1006 E. Ferguson Rd., Pharr 78577. Private. 1982 (SACS-COEI). Courses of varying lengths. Certificates. Dir. David Coers, Jr.
Enroll.: FTE 62
(512) 781-1181

*Prairie View Agricultural and Mechanical University
Prairie View 77445. Public (state). 1934/1980 (SACS-Comm. on Coll.). Sem. plan. Degrees: A,B,M. *Prof. Accred.:* Engineering (civil, electrial, mechanical), Home Economics, Nursing (B), Social Work (B), Teacher Education (*e,s,p*). Pres. Percy A. Pierre.
Enroll.: 4,080
(409) 857-3311

R/S Institute
1210 Uvalde, Houston 77015. Private. 1984 (SACS-COEI). Courses of varying lengths. Certificates. Dir. Robert Saldivar.
Enroll.: FTE 26

*Member Texas A&M University System

Branch Campus
7122 Lawndale Ave., Houston 77023.

Ranger Junior College
College Cir., Ranger 76470. Public (district). 1968/1982 (SACS-Comm. on Coll.). Sem. plan. Degrees: A. Pres. Jack M. Elsom.
Enroll.: 685
(817) 647-3234

Rice University
P.O. Box 1892, Houston 77251. Private. 1914/1985 (SACS-Comm. on Coll.). Sem. plan. Degrees: B,M,D. *Prof. Accred.:* Architecture (B,M), Engineering (chemical, civil, electrical, materials science, mechanical). Pres. George E. Rupp.
Enroll.: 4,048 (*f.t.* (713) 527-8101

†Richland College
12800 Abrams Rd., Dallas 75243. Public (district) 2-year. 1974/1983 (SACS-Comm. on Coll.). Sem. plan. Degrees: A. Pres. Stephen K. Mittelstet.
Enroll.: 10,115
(214) 238-6194

Roffler College of Hair Design
4400 N. Shephard Dr., Houston 77018. Private. 1985 (NATTS). Courses of varying lengths. Diplomas. Dir. Marjorie F. Osborn.
(713) 695-9574

S.W. School of Business and Technical Careers
1103 E. Commerce, San Antonio 78205. Private. 1982 (SACS-COEI). Courses of varying lengths. Certificates. Dir. Armando M. Salazar.
Enroll.: FTE 76
(512) 226-2784

Branch Campus
265 Jefferson St., Eagle Pass 78852.

Saint Edward's University
3001 S. Congress, Austin 78704. Private liberal arts and teachers college. Maryhill College, women's coordinate. 1958/1976 (SACS-Comm. on Coll.). 4-1-4 plan. Degrees: B,M. *Prof. Accred.:* Social Work (B). Pres. Patricia A. Hayes.
Enroll.: 1,698
(512) 444-2621

St. Mary's University of San Antonio
One Camino Santa Maria, San Antonio 78284-0400. Private (Roman Catholic). 1949/1984

†Member Dallas County Community College District

(SACS-Comm. on Coll.). Sem. plan. Degrees: B,P,M. *Prof. Accred.:* Engineering (industrial), Law. Pres. Rev. John A. Leies.
Enroll.: 2,753
(512) 436-3011

†ST. PHILIP'S COLLEGE
2111 Nevada St., San Antonio 78203. Public (district) junior. 1951/1985 (SACS-Comm. on Coll.). Sem. plan. Degrees: A. *Prof. Accred.:* Medical Laboratory Technology, Medical Record Technology, Music, Nursing (A), Practical Nursing, Radiography, Respiratory Therapy, Surgical Technology. Acting Pres. Stephen Mitchell.
Enroll.: 2,765
(512) 531-3200

*SAM HOUSTON STATE UNIVERSITY
Huntsville 77341. Public liberal arts and teachers college. 1925/1979 (SACS-Comm. on Coll.). Sem. plan. Degrees: B,M,D. *Prof. Accred.:* Music, Teacher Education (*e,s,p*). Pres. Elliott T. Bowers.
Enroll.: 9,002
(409) 294-1111

†SAN ANTONIO COLLEGE
1300 San Pedro., San Antonio 78284. Public (district) junior. 1952/1985 (SACS-Comm. on Coll.). Sem. plan. Degrees: A. *Prof. Accred.:* Dental Assisting, Nursing (A). Pres. Max Castillo.
Enroll.: 12,904
(512) 733-2000

SAN ANTONIO COLLEGE OF MEDICAL AND DENTAL ASSISTANTS
4205 San Pedro, San Antonio 78212. Private. 1970/1980 (NATTS); 1984 (SACS-COEI). Courses of varying lengths. Diplomas. *Prof. Accred.:* Medical Assisting. Pres. Comer M. Alden.
Enroll.: FTE 165
(512) 733-0777

BRANCH CAMPUS
8375 Burnhan Dr., El Paso 79907. *Prof. Accred.:* Medical Assisting. Dir. Jay Tellock.
(915) 595-1935

BRANCH CAMPUS
3900 N. 23rd, McAllen 78501. *Prof. Accred.:* Medical Assisting. Dir. Bonita Mahannah.
(512) 630-1499

†Member Alamo Community College District
*Member Texas State University System

SAN ANTONIO TRADE SCHOOL
120 Playmoor, San Antonio 78210. Private. 1982 (SACS-COEI). Courses of varying lengths. Certificates. Dir. Charles Lee.
Enroll.: FTE 58
(512) 533-9126

BRANCH CAMPUS
117 W. Martin, Del Rio 78840.

SAN ANTONIO TRAINING DIVISION
9350 N. Presa, San Antonio 78223. Private. 1984 (SACS-COEI). Courses of varying lengths. Certificates. Dir. James Partain.
Enroll.: FTE 228

SAN JACINTO COLLEGE DISTRICT
System Office, 4624 Fairmont Pkwy., Suite 201. Pasadena 77504. Chanc. Thomas S. Sewell.
(713) 476-1501

SAN JACINTO COLLEGE—CENTRAL CAMPUS
8060 Spencer Hwy., Pasadena 77505. Public (district) junior. 1963/1979 (SACS-Comm. on Coll.). Sem. plan. Degrees: A. *Prof. Accred.:* Respiratory Therapy, Respiratory Therapy Technology. Pres. Monte Blue.
Enroll.: 8,698
(713) 476-1501

SAN JACINTO COLLEGE—NORTH CAMPUS
5800 Uvalde, Houston 77049. Public (district) junior. 1976/1982 (SACS-Comm. on Coll.). Sem. plan. Degrees: A. Pres. Edwin E. Lehr.
Enroll.: 2,213
(713) 458-4050

SCHREINER COLLEGE
Kerrville 78028. Private (Presbyterian, U.S.). 1984 (SACS-Comm. on Coll.). Sem. plan. Degrees: A,B. Pres. Sam M. Junkin.
Enroll.: 435
(512) 896-5411

SEBRING SCHOOL OF HAIR DESIGN
1406 S. Texas Ave., College Station 77840. Private. 1985(SACS-COEI). Courses of varying lengths. Certificates. Dir. Reese Moore.
Enroll.: FTE 97

SIMDEX TECHNICAL INSTITUTE
8110 LaPorte Rd., Houston 77012. Private. 1979 (NATTS). Courses of varying lengths. Certificates. Dir. Dion Padin.
Enroll.: 285 (*f.t.* 256 m., 29 w.)
(713) 923-1110

SOUTH PLAINS COLLEGE
Levelland 79336. Public (district) junior. 1963/1983 (SACS-Comm. on Coll.). Sem. plan. Degrees: A. *Prof. Accred.:* Medical Record Technology, Radiography, Respiratory Therapy, Respiratory Therapy Technology, Surgical Technology. Pres. Marvin Baker.
Enroll.: 3,141
(806) 894-9611

SOUTH TEXAS COLLEGE OF LAW
Houston 77002. Public professional. 1959. Sem. plan. Degrees: P. *Prof. Accred.:* Law (ABA only). Dean W. J. Williamson.
Enroll.: 1,164 (*f.t.* 392 m., 191 w.)
(713) 659-8040

SOUTH TEXAS VOCATIONAL-TECHNICAL INSTITUTE
2255 N. Coria, Brownsville 78520. Private. 1982 (SACS-COEI). Courses of varying lengths. Certificates. Dir. Elma Rodriguez.
Enroll.: FTE 82
(512) 546-0353

SOUTH TEXAS VOCATIONAL-TECHNICAL INSTITUTE
1120 Lindberg Ave., A-7, McAllen 78501. Private. 1982 (SACS-COEI). Courses of varying lengths. Certificates. Dir. Theodore D. Frasier.
Enroll.: FTE 129
(512) 631-1107

SOUTH TEXAS VOCATIONAL-TECHNICAL INSTITUTE
2419 E. Haggar Ave., P.O. Box 629, Weslaco 78596. Private. 1982 (SACS-COEI). Courses of varying lengths. Certificates. Dir. Darlene Leboeuf.
Enroll.: FTE 123
(512) 464-5519

SOUTHERN BIBLE COLLEGE
10950 Beaumont Hwy., Houston 77078. Private (Pentecostal Church of God) professional. 1973 (AABC). Sem. plan. Degrees: A,B. Pres. Charles B. Allen.
Enroll.: 126 (*f.t.* 60 m., 42 w.)
(713) 675-2351

SOUTHERN METHODIST UNIVERSITY
Dallas 75275. Private (United Methodist). 1921/1980 (SACS-Comm. on Coll.). Sem. plan. Degrees: B,P,M,D. *Prof. Accred.:* Business (B,M), Engineering (civil, electrical, engineering management, mechanical), Law, Music, Teacher Education (*e,s,p*), Theology. Pres. L. Donald Shields.
Enroll.: 8,347
(214) 692-2000

SOUTHWEST INSTITUTE OF MERCHANDISING AND DESIGN
9611 Acer Ave., El Paso 79925. Private. 1975/1980 (NATTS). 9-month course. Diplomas. Pres. Mary F. Simon.
Enroll.: 45
(915) 593-7328

SOUTHWEST SCHOOL OF ELECTRONICS
Oak Hill Office Park, 5424 Hwy. 290 W., Suite 200, Austin 78735. Private. 1978 (NATTS); 1982 (SACS-COEI). Courses of varying lengths. Certificates, diplomas. Dir. Nella V. Trisdale.
Enroll.: FTE 159
(512) 892-2640

SOUTHWEST SCHOOL OF MEDICAL ASSISTANTS
115 N. Broadway, San Antonio 78205. Private. 1974/1978 (NATTS). Courses of varying lengths. Certificates. *Prof. Accred.:* Medical Assisting, Medical Laboratory Technology. Dir. Denise Jauregui.
Enroll.: 132 (*f.t.* 8 m., 124 w.)
(512) 224-2296

SOUTHWEST TEXAS JUNIOR COLLEGE
Garnerfield Rd., Uvalde 78801. Public (district). 1964/1985 (SACS-Comm. on Coll.). Sem. plan. Degrees: A. Pres. Jimmy Goodson.
Enroll.: 1,754
(512) 278-4401

*SOUTHWEST TEXAS STATE UNIVERSITY
SWTSU Sta., Box 1002, San Marcos 78666. Public liberal arts and teachers college. 1925/1979 (SACS-Comm. on Coll.). Sem. plan. Degrees: A,B,M. *Prof. Accred.:* Health Care Administration, Home Economics, Music, Physical Therapy, Respiratory Therapy, Respiratory Therapy Technology, Social Work (B), Speech Pathology, Teacher Education (*e,s,p*). Pres. Robert L. Hardesty.
Enroll.: 17,202
(512) 245-2111

SOUTHWESTERN ADVENTIST COLLEGE
P.O. Box 567, Keene 76059-0567. Private (Seventh-day Adventist) liberal arts and teachers. 1970/1985 (SACS-Comm. on Coll.). Sem. plan. Degrees: A,B. *Prof. Accred.:* Nursing (A,B). Pres. Marvin E. Anderson.

*Member Texas State University System

Enroll.: 594
(817) 645-3921

SOUTHWESTERN JUNIOR COLLEGE OF THE ASSEMBLIES OF GOD
1200 Sycamore St., Waxahachie 75165. Private (Assembly of God) liberal arts and professional. 1948/1985 (AABC); junior college accredited 1968/1983 (SACS-Comm. on Coll.). Sem. plan. Degrees: A,B. Pres. J. Paul Savell.
Enroll.: 635
(214) 937-4010

SOUTHWESTERN BAPTIST THEOLOGICAL SEMINARY
Fort Worth 76122. Private (Southern Baptist). 1969/1981 (SACS-Comm. on Coll.). Sem. plan. Degrees: P,M,D. *Prof. Accred.:* Music, Theology (1944/1981, ATS). Pres. Russell H. Dilday.
Enroll.: 3,817
(817) 923-1921

SOUTHWESTERN CHRISTIAN COLLEGE
Terrell 75160. Private (Church of Christ) liberal arts. 1984 (SACS-Comm. on Coll.). Sem. plan. Degrees: A,B. Pres. Jack Evans.
Enroll.: 267
(214) 563-3341

SOUTHWESTERN UNIVERSITY
Georgetown 78626. Private, liberal and fine arts college. 1915/1982 (SACS-Comm. on Coll.). Sem. plan. Degrees: B. *Prof. Accred.:* Music. Pres. Roy B. Shilling, Jr.
Enroll.: 972
(512) 863-6511

STEPHEN F. AUSTIN STATE UNIVERSITY
SFA Sta., Box 6078, Nacogdoches 75962. Public liberal arts and teachers. 1927/1980 (SACS-Comm. on Coll.). Sem. plan. Degrees: B,M,D. *Prof. Accred.:* Business (B,M), Forestry, Home Economics, Interior Design, Music, Nursing (B), Social Work (B), Teacher Education (*e,s,p*). Pres. William R. Johnson.
Enroll.: 11,420
(713) 569-2011

*SUL ROSS STATE UNIVERSITY
Alpine 79832. Public liberal arts and teachers college. 1929/1977 (SACS-Comm. on Coll.). Sem. plan. Degrees: A,B,M. Pres. Jack W. Humphries.
Enroll.: 1,647
(915) 837-8011

SUPERIOR TECHNICAL INSTITUTE
13609 Industrial Rd., P.O. Box 24816, Houston 77231. Private. 1985 (NATTS). Courses of varying lengths. Certificates. Dir. Paul Morris.
(713) 455-4070

†TARLETON STATE UNIVERSITY
Stephenville 76402. Public liberal arts and professional. 1966/1980 (SACS-Comm. on Coll.). Sem. plan. Degrees: A,B,M. *Prof. Accred.:* Medical Technology, Social Work (B). Pres. Barry B. Thompson.
Enroll.: 4,122
(817) 968-9000

TARRANT COUNTY JUNIOR COLLEGE
1500 Houston St., Fort Worth 76102-6599. Public (district). 1969/1983 (SACS-Comm. on Coll.). Sem. plan. Degrees: A. *Prof. Accred.:* Dental Assisting, Dental Hygiene, Medical Laboratory Technology (A), Medical Record Technology, Nursing (A), Radiography, Respiratory Therapy, Surgical Technology. Chanc. Joe B. Rushing.
Enroll.: 17,326
(817) 336-7851

TEMPLE JUNIOR COLLEGE
2600 S. First St., Temple 76501. Public (district). 1959/1980 (SACS-Comm. on Coll.). Sem. plan. Degrees: A. *Prof. Accred.:* Medical Laboratory Technology (A), Medical Record Technology, Respiratory Therapy. Pres. Marvin R. Felder.
Enroll.: 1,777
(817) 773-9961

TEXARKANA COMMUNITY COLLEGE
2500 N. Robison Rd., Texarkana 75501. Public (district) junior. 1931/1985 (SACS-Comm. on Coll.). Sem. plan. Degrees: A. *Prof. Accred.:* Nursing (A). Pres. Carl M. Nelson.
Enroll.: 2,941
(214) 838-4541

**TEXAS A & I UNIVERSITY
Texas A & I Sta., Box 101, Kingsville 78363. Public (state). 1933/1984 (SACS-Comm. on Coll.). Sem. plan. Degrees: B,M,D. *Prof Accred.:* Engineering (chemical, electrical, mechanical, natural gas), Music, Teacher Education (*e,s,p*). Pres. Steve Altman.

*Member Texas State University System

†Member Texas A&M University System
**Member University System of South Texas

Enroll.: 4,620
(512) 595-2111

TEXAS A & M UNIVERSITY SYSTEMS OFFICE
College Station 77843. Chanc. Arthur G. Hansen.
(403) 845-4311

TEXAS A & M UNIVERSITY
College Station 77843. Public (state). 1924/1983 (SACS-Comm. on Coll.). Sem. plan. (tri. plan in school of veterinary medicine). Degrees: B,P,M,D. *Prof. Accred.:* Accounting (Type A,C), Architecture (M), Business (B,M), Construction Education, Engineering (aerospace, agricultural, bioengineering, chemical, civil, electrical, industrial, mechanical, mining, nuclear, ocean, petroleum), Engineering Technology, Forestry, Journalism, Landscape Architecture (B), Medicine, Psychology, Teacher Education (*e,s,p*), Veterinary Medicine. Pres. Frank E. Vandiver.
Enroll.: 34,242
(409) 845-1015

TEXAS A & M UNIVERSITY AT GALVESTON
P.O. Box 1675, Galveston 77553. Public (state). 1978/1983 (SACS-Comm. on Coll.). Sem. plan. Degrees: B. *Prof. Accred.:* Engineering (marine). Pres. William H. Clayton.
Enroll.: 571 (*f.t.* (409) 740-4400

TEXAS AERO TECH
7326 Aviation Pl., Dallas 75235. Private. 1979/1984 (SACS-COEI). Courses of varying lengths. Certificates. Dir. Melvin Kabler.
Enroll.: FTE 358
(214) 263-9780

TEXAS CHIROPRACTIC COLLEGE
5912 Spencer Hwy., Pasadena 77505. Private professional. 1984 (SACS-Comm. on Coll.). Sem. plan. Degrees: P. *Prof. Accred.:* Chiropractic Education. Interim CEO Hugh MacDonell.
Enroll.: 449
(713) 487-1170

TEXAS CHRISTIAN UNIVERSITY
University Dr., Fort Worth 76129. Private (Christian Church, Disciples of Christ). 1922/1984 (SACS-Comm. on Coll.). Jarvis Christian College, affiliated. Sem. plan. Degrees: B,P,M,D. *Prof. Accred.:* Business (B,M), Dietetics, Home Economics, Interior Design, Journalism, Music, Nursing (B), Social Work (B), Teacher Education (*e,s,p*), Theology. Chanc. William E. Tucker.
Enroll.: 5,723
(817) 921-7000

TEXAS COLLEGE
2404 N. Grand, Tyler 75701. Private (Christian Methodist Episcopal) liberal arts and teachers. 1970/1984 (SACS-Comm. on Coll.). Sem. plan. Degrees: B. Pres. David Johnson.
Enroll.: 561
(214) 593-8311

TEXAS COLLEGE OF MEDICAL & DENTAL CAREERS
4255 L.B.J. Freeway, Suite 242, Dallas 75234. Private. 1972/1978 (NATTS). Qtr. plan. Diplomas. Dir. L. Kent Langum.
Enroll.: 156 (*f.t.* 2 m., 154 w.)
(214) 387-8670

EXTENSION
1919 North Loop West, Suite 180, Houston 77008. Dir. Edward Todd.
(713) 863-0404

TEXAS COLLEGE OF OSTEOPATHIC MEDICINE
Camp Bowie at Montgomery St., Fort Worth 76107. Public (state) professional. 1970/1975. Sem. plan. Degrees: P. *Prof. Accred.:* Osteopathy. Pres. David M. Richards.
Enroll.: 363 (*f.t.* 262 m., 101 w.)
(817) 735-2000

TEXAS INSTITUTE, INC.
1440 Mockingbird, Suite 500, Dallas 75247. Private. 1969/1980 (NATTS); 1985(SACS-COEI). Courses of varying lengths. Certificates. Pres.-Dir. Stewart W. Swacker.
Enroll.: 176
(214) 637-5211

TEXAS LUTHERAN COLLEGE
Seguin 78155. Private (American Lutheran) liberal arts. 1953/1977 (SACS-Comm. on Coll.). 4-1-4 plan. Degrees: A,B. *Prof. Accred.:* Social Work (B). Pres. Charles H. Oestreich.
Enroll.: 1,152
(512) 379-4161

TEXAS SCHOOL OF BUSINESS
12620 Interstate 45 N., #117, Houstons 770605234. Private. 1985 (AICS). Courses of varying lengths. Certificates, diplomas. Pres./Dir. Judy Autman.
(713) 876-2888

TEXAS SCHOOLS
1308 35th St., Lubbock 79412. Private. 1983 (SACS-COEI). Courses of varying lengths. Certificates. Dir. Roy D. Hennen.

Enroll.: FTE 102
(806) 744-9194

TEXAS SOUTHERN UNIVERSITY
3100 Cleburne Ave., Houston 77004. Public (state). 1948/1980 (SACS-Comm. on Coll.). Sem. plan. Degrees: B,P,M,D. *Prof. Accred.:* Business (B,M), Law (ABA only), Pharmacy, Respiratory Therapy, Social Work (B), Teacher Education (*e,s,p*). Pres. ———.
Enroll.: 8,654
(713) 527-7011

TEXAS SOUTHMOST COLLEGE
80 Ft. Brown, Brownsville 78520. Public (district) junior. 1930/1981 (SACS-Comm. on Coll.). Sem. plan. Degrees: A. *Prof. Accred.:* Medical Laboratory Technology, Nursing (A), Radiography, Respiratory Therapy, Respiratory Therapy Technology. Pres. Juliet Garcia.
Enroll.: 4,298
(512) 544-8200

TEXAS STATE TECHNICAL INSTITUTE—SYSTEM OFFICE
Waco 76705. Public (state). Pres. Jack E. Tompkins.
(817) 799-3611

TEXAS STATE TECHNICAL INSTITUTE—AMARILLO
P.O. Box 11035, Amarillo 79111. Public 2-year. 1970/1985 (SACS-Comm. on Coll.) Qtr. plan. Degrees: A. *Prof. Accred.:* Interior Design. Campus Pres. Ronald Despain.
Enroll.: 1,430
(806) 335-2316

TEXAS STATE TECHNICAL INSTITUTE—HARLINGEN
Harlingen 78550. Public 2-year. 1968/1985 (SACS-Comm. on Coll.). Qtr. plan. Degrees: A. Campus Pres. J. Gilbert Leal.
Enroll.: 2,482
(512) 425-4922

TEXAS STATE TECHNICAL INSTITUTE—SWEETWATER
Route 3, Box 18, Sweetwater 79556. Public 2-year. 1979/1984 (SACS-Comm. on Coll.). Qtr. plan. Degrees: A. Campus Pres. Herbert Robbins.
Enroll.: 567
(915) 235-8441

TEXAS STATE TECHNICAL INSTITUTE—WACO
Waco 76705. Public 2-year. 1968/1983 (SACS-Comm. on Coll.). Year of three 15-week terms. Degrees: A. *Prof. Accred.:* Dental Assisting, Dental Laboratory Technology. Campus Pres. Robert D. Krienke.
Enroll.: 4,522
(817) 799-3611

TEXAS STATE UNIVERSITY SYSTEM
505 Sam Houston Bldg., Austin 78701. Exec. Dir. Lamar Urbanovsky.
(512) 475-3876

TEXAS TECH UNIVERSITY
P.O. Box 4349, Lubbock 79409. Public (state). 1928/1984 (SACS-Comm. on Coll.). Sem. plan. Degrees: B,P,M,D. *Prof. Accred.:* Accounting (Type A,C), Architecture (B), Art, Business (B,M), Dietetics, EMT-Paramedic, Engineering (agricultural, chemical, civil, electrical, engineering physics, industrial, mechanical, petroleum), Engineering Technology (construction, electrical, electronics, mechanical), Home Economics, Interior Design, Journalism, Landscape Architecture (B), Law, Medical Technology, Medicine, Music, Nursing (B), Physical Therapy, Psychology, Rehabilitation Counseling, Social Work (B), Speech Pathology and Audiology, Teacher Education (*e,s,p*). Pres. Lauro F. Cavazos.
Enroll.: 22,377
(806) 742-2011

TEXAS VOCATIONAL SCHOOL
1913 S. Flores St., San Antonio 78204. Private. 1982 (SACS-COEI); 1982 (NATTS). Courses of varying lengths. Certificates. Dir. Melvin Heitcamp.
Enroll.: FTE 317
(512) 225-3253

TEXAS VOCATIONAL SCHOOLS
201 E. Rio Grande, Victoria 77901. Private. 1983 (SACS-COEI). 615 clock hours. Certificates. Dir. Angie S. Boone.
Enroll.: FTE 105
(512) 575-4768

BRANCH CAMPUS
Rt. 1, Box 132-C, Pharr 78577.

TEXAS WESLEYAN COLLEGE
P.O. Box 50010, Fort Worth 76105. Private (United Methodist) liberal arts. 1949/1983 (SACS-Comm. on Coll.). Sem. plan. Degrees: B,M. *Prof. Accred.:* Music, Nurse Anesthesia Education, Teacher Education (*e,s*). Pres. Jerry G. Bawcom.
Enroll.: 1,088
(817) 534-0251

TEXAS WOMAN'S UNIVERSITY
TWU Sta., Box 23925, Denton 76204. Public (state) for women. 1923/1983 (SACS-Comm. on Coll.). Sem. plan. Degrees: B,M,D. *Prof. Accred.:* Dental Hygiene, Dietetics, Health Care Administration, Interior Design, Librarianship, Medical Record Administration (Dallas Center), Music, Nursing (B,M), Occupational Therapy, Physical Therapy, Social Work (B), Teacher Education (*e,s,p*). Pres. ———.
Enroll.: 5,588
(817) 383-1466

TOTAL TECHNICAL INSTITUTE (EXTENSION)
9205 Skilman St., Suite 116, Dallas 75243. Private. 1985 (NATTS) Courses of varying lengths. Certificates. Dir. Richard A. Gemmel.
(214) 340-9922

TRINITY UNIVERSITY
715 Stadium Dr., San Antonio 78284. Private. 1946/1976 (SACS-Comm. on Coll.). Sem. plan. Degrees: B,M. *Prof. Accred.:* Engineering (engineering science), Health Services Administration, Teacher Education (*e,s,p*). Pres. Ronald K. Calgaard.
Enroll.: 3,022
(512) 736-7011

TYLER JUNIOR COLLEGE
P.O. Box 9020, Tyler 75711. Public (district). 1931/1980 (SACS-Comm. on Coll.). Sem. plan. Degrees: A. *Prof. Accred.:* Dental Hygiene, Medical Laboratory Techmology (A), Radiography, Respiratory Therapy. Pres. Raymond M. Hawkins.
Enroll.: 5,541
(214) 531-2200

U.S. ARMY ACADEMY OF HEALTH SCIENCES
Fort Sam Houston 78234. Public (federal) professional. 1983 (SACS-COEI). Courses of varying lengths. Certificates. *Prof. Accred.:* Assistant to the Primary Care Physician, Cytotechnology, Medical Technology, Nurse Anesthesia Education, Radiography, Respiration Therapy Technology. Cmdr. Maj. Gen. William W. Winkler.
Enroll.: FTE 7,083
(512) 221-4325

BRANCH CAMPUS
Army Medical Equipment and Optical School, Aurora, CO 80045

BRANCH CAMPUS
School of Aviation Medicine, Ft. Rucker AL 36362.

U.S. ARMY AIR DEFENSE ARTILLERY SCHOOL
Fort Bliss 79916. Public (federal) technical. 1975/1985 (SACS-COEI). Courses of varying lengths. Certificates. Comdr. Maj. Gen. D. R. Infante.
Enroll.: FTE 3,719
(915) 568-4436

U.S. ARMY SERGEANTS MAJOR ACADEMY
Fort Bliss 79918. Public (federal) technical. 1975/1985 (SACS-COEI). Courses of varying lengths. Certificates. Cmdr. Col. Fitzhugh H. Chandler.
Enroll.: FTE 385
(915) 568-8619

BRANCH CAMPUS
7th ATC-FSC (McGraw-Kaserne), Munich, West Germany, APO, New York, NY 09407. Tel. Munich Military 7209

UNIVERSAL TECHNICAL INSTITUTE (EXTENSION)
721 Lockhave Dr., Houston 77073. Private. 1985 (NATTS). Courses of varying lengths. Certificates. Dir. Robert I. Sweet.
(713) 443-6262

UNIVERSITY OF DALLAS
University Sta., Irving 75061. Private (Roman Catholic). 1963/1984 (SACS-Comm. on Coll.) Sem. plan. Degrees: B,M,D. Pres. Robert Sasseen.
Enroll.: 1,712
(214) 721-5000

UNIVERSITY OF HOUSTON SYSTEM
Administration Office, 4600 Gulf Freeway, Suite 500, Houston 77023. Pres. Charles E. Bishop.
(713) 221-8000

UNIVERSITY OF HOUSTON—UNIVERSITY PARK
4800 Calhoun Blvd., Houston 77004. Public (state). 1954/1976 (SACS-Comm. on Coll.). Sem. plan. Degrees: A,B,P,M,D. *Prof. Accred.:* Accounting (Type A,B,C), Architecture (B,M), Business (B,M), Engineering (chemical, civil, electrical, industrial, mechanical), Engineering Technology (construction management, design drafting, electrical, electronics, manufacturing, mechanical environmental systems), Journalism, Law, Music, Optometry, Pharmacy, Psychology, Social Work (M), Speech Pathology, Teacher Education (*e,s,p*). Chanc. Richard Van Horn.

Enroll.: 24,077
(713) 749-1011

UNIVERSITY OF HOUSTON—CLEAR LAKE
2700 Bay Area Blvd., Houston 77058. Public (state) upper division and graduate only. 1976/1982 (SACS-Comm. on Coll.). Sem. plan. Degrees: B,M. *Prof. Accred.:* Accounting (Type A,C), Business (B,M), Health Services Administration, Teacher Education (*e,s,p*). Chanc. Thomas M. Stauffer.
Enroll.: 3,490
(713) 488-7170

UNIVERSITY OF HOUSTON—VICTORIA
2302-C Red River, Victoria 77901. Public (state) liberal arts; upper division only. 1978/1983 (SACS-Comm. on Coll.). Sem. plan. Degrees: B,M. Chanc. ———.
Enroll.: 531
(512) 576-3151

UNIVERSITY OF HOUSTON—DOWNTOWN
One Main St., Houston 77002. Public (state) liberal arts. 1979/1985 (SACS-Comm. on Coll.). Sem. plan. Degrees: A,B. *Prof. Accred.:* Engineering Technology (process and piping design). Chanc. Alexander F. Schilt.
Enroll.: 5,206
(713) 221-8000

UNIVERSITY OF MARY HARDIN—BAYLOR
MHB Sta., Belton 76513. Private (Southern Baptist) liberal arts primarily for women. 1926/1983 (SACS-Comm. on Coll.). Sem. plan. Degrees: A,B,M. *Prof. Accred.:* Music, Nursing (B). Pres. Bobby E. Parker.
Enroll.: 971
(817) 939-5811

UNIVERSITY OF ST. THOMAS
3812 Montrose Blvd., Houston 77006. Private (Roman Catholic) liberal arts college. 1954/1984 (SACS-Comm. on Coll.). Sem. plan. Degrees: B,P,M. *Prof. Accred.:* Nursing (B).Acting Pres. Rev. Frank Bredeweg.
Enroll.: 1,460
(713) 522-7911

UNIVERSITY OF TEXAS SYSTEM
Central Office, 601 Colorado St., Austin 78701. Public (state). Chanc. Hans M. Mark.
(512) 471-3434

UNIVERSITY OF TEXAS AT ARLINGTON
P.O. Box 19125, Arlington 76019.Public (state). Liberal arts and professional. 1964/1974 (SACS-Comm. on Coll.). Sem. plan. Degrees: A,B,M,D. *Prof. Accred.:* Accounting (Type A,B,C), Architecture (M), Business (B,M), Engineering (aerospace, civil, computer, electrical, industrial, mechanical), Engineering Technology (aeronautical, civil, electrical, mechanical), Interior Design, Music, Nursing (M), Social Work (B,M). Pres. Wendell H. Nedderman.
Enroll.: 19,275
(817) 273-2011

UNIVERSITY OF TEXAS AT AUSTIN
University Sta., Austin 78712. Public (state). 1901/1976 (SACS-Comm. on Coll.). Sem. plan. Degrees: B,P,M,D. *Prof. Accred.:* Architecture (B,M), Business (B,M), Dietetics, Engineering (aerospace, architectural, chemical, civil, electrical, engineering science, environmental health, mechanical, petroleum), Engineering Technology (aeronautical, civil, electrical, mechanical), Home Economics, Interior Design, Journalism, Law, Librarianship, Music, Nursing (B,M), Pharmacy, Psychology, Rehabilitation Counseling, Social Work (B,M), Speech Pathology and Audiology, Teacher Education (*e,s,p*). Pres. William H. Cunningham.
Enroll.: 44,781
(512) 471-3434

UNIVERSITY OF TEXAS AT DALLAS
P.O. Box 830688, Richardson 75083. Public (state). 1972/1977 (SACS-Comm. on Coll.). Sem. plan. Degrees: B,M,D. *Prof. Accred.:* Speech Pathology and Audiology. Pres. Robert H. Rutford.
Enroll.: 4,507
(214) 690-2111

UNIVERSITY OF TEXAS AT EL PASO
El Paso 79968. Public (state). Liberal arts and professional. 1936/1976 (SACS-Comm. on Coll.). Sem. plan. Degrees: B,M,D. *Prof. Accred.:* Engineering (civil, electrical, mechanical, metallurgical), Medical Technology, Music, Nursing (M). Pres. Haskell M. Monroe, Jr.
Enroll.: 12,753
(915) 747-5000

UNIVERSITY OF TEXAS AT SAN ANTONIO
San Antonio 78285. Public (state). 1974/1980 (SACS-Comm. on Coll.). Sem. plan. Degrees: A,B,M. *Prof. Accred.:* Art, Business (B,M), Medical Technology, Music, Occupational Therapy, Physical Therapy. Pres. James W. Wagener.
Enroll.: 9,863
(512) 691-4011

UNIVERSITY OF TEXAS AT TYLER
3900 University Blvd., Tyler 75701. Public, upper division and graduate only. 1974/1979 (SACS-Comm. on Coll.). Sem. plan. Degrees: B,M. *Prof. Accred.:* Medical Technology, Nursing (B). Pres. George F. Hamm.
Enroll.: 2,239
(214) 566-1471

UNIVERSITY OF TEXAS HEALTH SCIENCE CENTER AT DALLAS
5323 Henry Hines Blvd., Dallas 75235. Public (state). 1973/1978 (SACS-Comm. on Coll.). Qtr. plan. Degrees: B,P,M,D. *Prof. Accred.:* Assistant to the Primary Care Physician, Dietetics, Medical Technology , Medicine, Physical Therapy, Psychology, Rehabilitation Counseling. Pres. Charles C. Sprague.
Enroll.: 1,314
(214) 688-3111

UNIVERSITY OF TEXAS HEALTH SCIENCE CENTER AT HOUSTON
P.O. Box 20036, Houston 77225. Public (state). 1973/1979 (SACS-Comm. on Coll.). Qtr. plan. Degrees: B,P,M,D. *Prof. Accred :* Cytotechnology, Dental Assisting, Dental Hygiene, Dentistry, Dietetics, Histologic Technology, Medical Technology, Medicine, Nurse Anesthesia Education, Nursing (B,M), Perfusion, Psychology, Public Health, Respiratory Therapy Technology, Specialist in Blood Bank Technology. Pres. Roger J. Bulger.
Enroll.: 3,006
(713) 792-4975

UNIVERSITY OF TEXAS HEALTH SCIENCE CENTER AT SAN ANTONIO
7703 Floyd Curl Dr., San Antonio 78284. Public (state). 1973/1978 (SACS-Comm. on Coll.). Qtr. plan. Degrees: A,P,M,D. *Prof. Accred.:* Dental Assisting, Dental Hygiene, Dental Laboratory Technology, Dentistry, EMT-Paramedic, Medicine, Nursing (B,M), Psychology. Pres. John P. Howe, III.
Enroll.: 2,179
(512) 691-6011

UNIVERSITY OF TEXAS MEDICAL BRANCH
Galveston 77550. Public (state). 1973/1978 (SACS-Comm. on Coll.). Sem. plan. Degrees: B,P,M,D. *Prof. Accred.:* Assistant to the Primary Care Physician, Medical Record Administration, Medical Technology, Medicine, Nursing (B,M), Occupational Therapy, Physical Therapy, Psychology, Radiation Therapy Technology, Radiography, Specialist in Blood Bank Technology. Pres. William C. Levin.
Enroll.: 1,576
(409) 761-1011

UNIVERSITY OF TEXAS OF THE PERMIAN BASIN
Odessa 79762. Public (state) liberal arts; upper division only. 1975/1980 (SACS-Comm. on Coll.). Sem. plan. Degrees: B,M. Pres. Duane M. Leach.
Enroll.: 1,281
(915) 367- 2011

UNIVERSITY SYSTEM OF SOUTH TEXAS
Central Office, P.O. Box 1238, Kingsville 78363. Chanc. ———.
(512) 595-2215

VERNON REGIONAL JUNIOR COLLEGE
4400 College Dr., Vernon 76384. Public (district). 1974/1979 (SACS-Comm. on Coll.). Sem. plan. Degrees: A. Pres. Joe Mills.
Enroll.: 1,523
(817) 552-6291

VICTORIA COLLEGE
2200 E. Red River, Victoria 77901. Public (district) junior. 1951/1980 (SACS-Comm. on Coll.). Sem. plan. Degrees: A. *Prof. Accred.:* Medical Laboratory Technology (A), Nursing (A), Respiratory Therapy Technology. Pres. Roland Bing.
Enroll.: 2,069
(512) 573-3291

VIDEO TECHNICAL INSTITUTE
1806 Royal La., Dallas 75229. Private. 1978 (NATTS). Courses of varying lengths. Diplomas. Pres. Wayne C. Paul.
Enroll.: 95 (*f.t.* 65 m., 15 w.)
(214) 263-2613

BRANCH CAMPUS
2201 N. Collins, Suite 305, Arlington 76011. Dir. Richard Feldbush.
(817) 860-0741

WAYLAND BAPTIST UNIVERSITY
1900 W. Seventh St., Plainview 79072-6998. Private (Southern Baptist) liberal arts. 1956/1978 (SACS-Comm. on Coll.). Sem. plan. Degrees: A,B,M. Pres. David L. Jester.
Enroll.: 1,145
(806) 296-5521

WEATHERFORD COLLEGE
308 E. Park Ave., Weatherford 760 86. Public (district) junior. 1956/1981 (SACS-Comm. on

Coll.). Sem. plan. Degrees: A. Pres. E. W. Mince.
Enroll.: 1,285
(817) 594-5471

WEST TEXAS BARBER/STYLING COLLEGE
4001 Mockingbird La., Amarillo 79109. Private. 1975/1980 (NATTS). Qtr. plan. Certificates, diplomas. Vice Pres. James Watson.
Enroll.: 20 (*f.t.* 5 m., 15 w.)
(806) 355-9426

WEST TEXAS STATE UNIVERSITY
P.O. Box 998, Canyon 79016. Public liberal arts and professional college. 1925/1985 (SACS-Comm. on Coll.). Sem. plan. Degrees: B,M. *Prof. Accred.:* Music, Nursing (B), Social Work (B), Teacher Education (*e,s,p*). Pres. Ed D. Roach.
Enroll.: 5,301
(806) 656-0111

WESTERN TEXAS COLLEGE
Snyder 79549. Public (district) 2-year. 1973/1978 (SACS-Comm. on Coll.). Sem. plan. Degrees: A. Pres. Donald Newbury.
Enroll.: 872
(915) 573-8511

WHARTON COUNTY JUNIOR COLLEGE
911 Boling Hwy., Wharton 77488. Public. 1951/1977 (SACS-Comm. on Coll.). Sem. plan. Degrees: A. *Prof. Accred.:* Dental Hygiene, Medical Record Technology, Radiography. Pres. Elbert C. Hutchins.
Enroll.: 2,219
(409) 532-4560

WILEY COLLEGE
Marshall 75670. Private (United Methodist) liberal arts and teachers. 1933/1983 (SACS-Comm. on Coll.). Sem. plan. Degrees: A,B. Pres. Rev. Robert E. Hayes.
Enroll.: 536
(214) 938-8341

WOODCREST COLLEGE
Route 1, Box 106, Lindale 75771. Private (Interdenominational) professional. 1971/1984 (AABC). Sem. plan. Degrees: A,B. Pres. Thomas Houston.
Enroll.: 153
(214) 882-7566

UTAH

AMERICAN INSTITUTE OF MEDICAL-DENTAL TECHNOLOGY
1675 N. 200 West, Bldg. 9B, Provo 84604. Private. 1984 (ABHES). Courses of varying lengths. Certificates. *Prof. Accred.:* Medical Assisting. Admin. Keith T. Van Soest.
(801) 375-6717

AMERICAN TECHNICAL CENTER
445 S. 300th E., Salt Lake City 84111. Private. 1976/1982 (NATTS). Courses of varying lengths. Certificates. Dir. John S. Cowan.
Enroll.: 20 (*f.t.* 16 m., 4 w.)
(801) 355-3632

BRIGHAM YOUNG UNIVERSITY
Provo 84602. Private (Latter-day Saints). 1923/1986 (NASC); intern doctorate program in CA accredited 1983 (WASC-Sr.). Sem. plan. Degrees: A,B,P,M,D. *Prof. Accred.:* Business (B,M), Dietetics, Engineering (chemical, civil, electrical, mechanical), Engineering Technology (design and graphics, electronics, manufacturing), Journalism, Law, Librarianship, Medical Technology, Music, Nursing (B,M), Psychology, Social Work (B,M), Speech Pathology and Audiology, Teacher Education (*e,s,p*). Pres. Jeffrey R. Holland.
Enroll.: 26,894
(801) 378-2521

THE BRYMAN SCHOOL
445 S. Third E., Salt Lake City 84111. Private. 1973/1984 (NATTS). Courses of varying lengths. Certificates. Pres. John S. Cowan.
Enroll.: 125 (*f.t.* 11 m., 114 w.)
(801) 521-2830

*COLLEGE OF EASTERN UTAH
Price 84501. Public (state) junior. 1945/1981 (NASC). Qtr. plan. Degrees: A. Pres. Michael A. Petersen
Enroll.: 1,371
(801) 637-2120

*DIXIE COLLEGE
St. George 84770. Public (state) junior. 1945/1982 (NASC). Qtr. plan. Degrees: A. *Prof. Accred.:* Nursing (A). Pres. ———.
Enroll.: 2,232
(801) 673-4811

*Member Utah Higher Education System

ITT TECHNICAL INSTITUTE
4876 W. North Temple, Salt Lake City 84116. Private. 1985 (NATTS). Courses of varying lengths. Certificates. Pres. Larry Cammack.
(801) 537-5003

INTERMOUNTAIN COLLEGE OF COURT REPORTING
5258 Pinemont Dr., Suite B-160, Murray 84123. Private. 1981 (AICS). Qtr. plan. Certificates. Pres. Linda Smurthwaite.
Enroll.: 93 (*f.t.* 11 m., 82 w.)
(801) 268-9271

L.D.S. BUSINESS COLLEGE
411 E. South Temple St., Salt Lake City 84111. Private (Latter-day Saints). 1977/1982 (NASC). Qtr. plan. Degrees: A. Pres. Kenneth H. Beesley
Enroll.: 572
(801) 363-2765

MOUNTAINWEST COMPUTER SCHOOLS
3098 Highland Dr., Suite 100, Salt Lake City 84106. Private. 1985 (AICS). Courses of varying lengths. Certificates. Dir. Keith Green.
(801) 485-0221

SALT LAKE CITY COLLEGE OF MEDICAL AND DENTAL CAREERS
12 W. Malvern Ave., P.O. Box 15625, Salt Lake City 84115. Private. 1969/1979 (NATTS). Courses of varying lengths. Diplomas. *Prof. Accred.:* Medical Assisting. Dir. H. Max Seal.
Enroll.: f.t. 42 w.
(801) 487-0657

*SNOW COLLEGE
Ephraim 84627. Public (state) junior. 1953/1982 (NASC). Qtr. plan. Degrees: A. Pres. Steven D. Bennion.
Enroll.: 1,162
(801) 283-4021

*SOUTHERN UTAH STATE COLLEGE
Cedar City 84720. Public (state) liberal arts and teachers. 1933/1983 (NASC). Qtr. plan. Degrees: A,B,M. *Prof. Accred.:* Nursing (A), Social Work (B), Teacher Education (*e,s*). Pres. Gerald R. Sherratt.
Enroll.: 2,584
(801) 586-4411

*Member Utah Higher Education System

THE STEVENS-HENAGER COLLEGE OF BUSINESS
2351 Grant Ave., Ogden 84401. Private junior. 1962/1986 (AICS). Qtr. plan. Degrees: A, certificates, diplomas. Pres. Frank Johnson.
Enroll.: 1,775 (*f.t.* 592 m., 1,193 w.)
(801) 394-7791

BRANCH CAMPUS
250 W. Center St., Provo 84601. Dir. John Montrose.
(801) 375-5455

BRANCH CAMPUS
4555 S. 2300 East, Salt Lake City 84117. Dir. Blair K. Carruth.
(801) 272-8881

*UNIVERSITY OF UTAH
Salt Lake City 84112. Public (state). 1933/1976 (NASC). Qtr. plan. Degrees: A,B,P,M,D. *Prof. Accred.:* Accounting (Type A,C), Architecture (M), Assistant to the Primary Care Physician, Business (B,M), Community Health/Preventive Medicine, Engineering (chemical, civil, electrical, geological, materials science and engineering, mechanical, metallurgical, mining), Journalism, Law, Medical Technology, Medicine, Music, Nursing (B,M), Pharmacy, Physical Therapy, Psychology, Rehabilitation Counseling, Respiratory Therapy Technology, Social Work (M), Speech Pathology and Audiology, Teacher Education (*e,s,p*). Pres. Chase N. Peterson.
Enroll.: 25,646
(801) 581-7200

UTAH HIGHER EDUCATION SYSTEM OFFICE
807 E. South Temple, Salt Lake City 84102. Public (state). Commissioner of Higher Education Arvo Van Alstyne.
(801) 533-5617

*UTAH STATE UNIVERSITY
Logan 84322. Public. 1924/1978 (NASC). Qtr. Plan. Degrees: A,B,M,D. *Prof. Accred.:* Business (B,M), Dietetics, Engineering (agricultural and irrigation, civil, electrical, manufacturing, mechanical), Forestry, Home Economics, Landscape Architecture (B), Music, Nursing (A), Psychology, Social Work (B), Speech Pathology and Audiology, Teacher Education (*e,s,p*). Pres. Stanford Cazier.
Enroll.: 12,571
(801) 750-1000

*UTAH TECHNICAL COLLEGE AT PROVO
Provo 84603. Public (state) 2-year vocational-technical. 1969/1984 (NASC). Qtr. plan. Degrees: A. *Prof. Accred.:* Dental Assisting. Pres. J. Marvin Higbee.
Enroll.: 6,013
(801) 226-5000

*UTAH TECHNICAL COLLEGE AT SALT LAKE
P.O. Box 30808, Salt Lake City 84131. Public (state) 2-year vocational-technical. 1969/1984 (NASC). Qtr. plan. Degrees: A. *Prof. Accred.:* Nursing (A), Practical Nursing. Pres. Orville D. Carnahan.
Enroll.: 8,307
(801) 967-4111

*WEBER STATE COLLEGE
3750 Harrison Blvd., Ogden 84408. Public liberal arts and teachers. 1932/1984 (NASC). Qtr. plan. Degrees: A,B,M. *Prof. Accred.:* Dental Hygiene, Diagnostic Medical Sonography, Engineering Technology (electronic, manufacturing), Medical Laboratory Technology (A), Medical Technology, Music, Nuclear Medicine Technology, Nursing (A), Practical Nursing, Radiation Therapy, Radiography, Respiratory Therapy, Respiratory Therapy Technology, Social Work (B), Teacher Education (*e,s*). Pres. Stephen D. Nadauld.
Enroll.: 11,117
(801) 626-6114

WESTMINSTER COLLEGE OF SALT LAKE CITY
1840 S. 1300 East, Salt Lake City 84105. Private (United Methodist, United Presbyterian, United Church of Christ) liberal arts and professional. 1936/1983 (NASC). 4-1-4 plan. Degrees: B,M. *Prof. Accred.:* Nursing (B). Pres. Charles H. Dick.
Enroll.: 1,336
(801) 488-4298

*Member Utah Higher Education System

*Member Utah Higher Education System

VERMONT

Bennington College
Bennington 05201. Private liberal arts. 1935/1984 (NEASC-CIHE). Year of two 14-week and one 9-week terms. Degrees: B,M. Interim Pres. John Williams.
Enroll.: 584
(802) 442-5401

Burlington College
Burlington 05401. Private. 1982 (NEASC-CIHE). Tri. plan. Degrees: A,B. Pres. Steward LaCasce.
Enroll.: 167
(802) 862-9616

*Castleton State College
Castleton 05735. Public liberal arts and teachers. 1960/1985 (NEASC-CIHE). Sem. plan. Degrees: A,B,M. *Prof. Accred.:* Nursing (A), Social Work (B). Pres. Thomas K. Meier.
Enroll.: 2,043
(802) 4684-5611

Champlain College
Burlington 05402. Private junior. 1972/1980 (NEASC-CVTCI). Sem. plan. Degrees: A. *Prof. Accred.:* Dental Assisting. Pres. Robert A. Skiff.
Enroll.: 1,798
(802) 658-0800

College of St. Joseph
Rutland 05701. Private (Roman Catholic) teachers. 1972/1986 (NEASC-CIHE). Sem. plan. Degrees: A,B,M. Pres. Frank G. Miglorie, Jr.
Enroll.: 387
(802) 773-5900

*Community College of Vermont
Waterbury 05676. Public (state) junior. 1975/1982 (NEASC-CIHE). Tri. plan. Degrees: A. Pres. Kenneth G. Kalb.
Enroll.: 2,344
(802) 241-3535

Goddard College
Plainfield 05667. Private liberal arts. 1959/1986 (NEASC-CIHE). Modified sem. plan. Degrees: B,M. Pres. Jack Lindquist.
Enroll.: 1,416
(802) 454-8311

*Member Vermont State Colleges System

Green Mountain College
Poultney 05764. Private (United Methodist) liberal arts. 1934/1985 (NEASC-CIHE). 4-1-4 plan. Degrees: A,B. *Prof. Accred.:* Medical Assisting. Pres. James M. Pollock.
Enroll.: 385
(802) 287-9313

*Johnson State College
Johnson 05656. Public liberal arts and teachers. 1961/1986 (NEASC-CIHE). Sem. plan. Degrees: A,B,M. Pres. Eric R. Gilbertson.
Enroll.: 1,128
(802) 635-2356

*Lyndon State College
Lyndonville 05851. Public liberal arts and teachers. 1965/1983 (NEASC-CIHE). Sem. plan. Degrees: A,B,M. Pres. Clive C. Veri.
Enroll.: 1,014
(802) 626-9371

Marlboro College
Marlboro 05344. Private liberal arts. 1965/1984 (NEASC-CIHE). Year of two 11-week and one 10-week terms. Degrees: B. Pres. Roderick M. Gander.
Enroll.: 190
(802) 257-4333

Middlebury College
Middlebury 05753. Private liberal arts. 1929/1980 (NEASC-CIHE). Sem. plan. Degrees: B,M,D. Pres. Olin C. Robison.
Enroll.: 2,012
(802) 388-3711

New England Culinary Institute
250 Main St., R.R. 1, Box 1255, Montpelier 05602. Private. 1984 (NATTS). Courses of varying lengths. Certificates. Pres. Francis Voigt.
(802) 223-6324

Norwich University
Northfield 05663. Private liberal arts and engineering military college. 1933/1984 (NEASC-CIHE). Sem. plan. Degrees: A,B,M,D. *Prof. Accred.:* Engineering (civil, electrical, mechanical), Engineering Technology (environmental), Medical Laboratory Technology (A). Pres. W. Russell Todd.
Enroll.: 2,528
(802) 485-5011

*Member Vermont State Colleges System

VERMONT COLLEGE
Montpelier 05602. Division of Norwich University. *Prof. Accred.:* Nursing (A,B).
Enroll.: 880 (*f.t.* 194 m., 641 w.)
(802) 229-0522

SAINT MICHAEL'S COLLEGE
Winooski 05404. Private (Roman Catholic, Society of St. Edmund) liberal arts and theology. 1939/1980 (NEASC-CIHE). Sem. plan. Degrees: B,M. Pres. Paul J. Reiss.
Enroll.: 1,774
(802) 655-2000

SCHOOL FOR INTERNATIONAL TRAINING
Brattleboro 05301. Private liberal arts. 1974/1986 (NEASC-CIHE). Modular plan. Degrees: B,M. Dir. Edward Heneveld.
Enroll.: 439
(802) 257-7751

SOUTHERN VERMONT COLLEGE
Bennington 05201. Private. 1979/1986 (NEASC-CIHE). Sem. plan. Degrees: A,B, certificates, diplomas. Pres. William A. Glasser.
Enroll.: 482
(802) 442-5427

TRINITY COLLEGE
Burlington 05401. Private (Roman Catholic) liberal arts for women. 1952/1985 (NEASC-CIHE). Sem. plan. Degrees: B. *Prof. Accred.:* Social Work (B). Pres. Sister Janice E. Ryan, R.S.M.
Enroll.: 945 (802) 658-0337

U.S. SCHOOL OF PROFESSIONAL PAPERHANGING
16 Chaplin Ave., Rutland 05701. Private. 1976/1982 (NATTS). Sem. plan. Certificates. Pres. Stanley Warshaw.
Enroll.: 62 (*f.t.* 52 m., 10 w.)
(802) 773-2455

UNIVERSITY OF VERMONT
Burlington 05405. Public (state). 1929/1979 (NEASC-CIHE). Sem. plan. Degrees: A,B,P,M,D. *Prof. Accred.:* Business (B,M), Dental Hygiene, Engineering (civil, electrical, mechanical), Forestry, Medical Technology, Medicine, Music, Nuclear Medicine Technology, Nursing (A,B), Physical Therapy, Psychology, Radiation Therapy, Radiography, Social Work (B), Speech Pathology, Teacher Education (*e,s,p*). Pres. Lattie F. Coor.
Enroll.: 10,908
(802) 656-3480

VERMONT LAW SCHOOL
South Royalton 05068. Private professional. 1980/1985 (NEASC-CIHE). Sem. plan. Degrees: P. *Prof. Accred.:* Law. Dean Jonathon B. Chase.
Enroll.: 382
(802) 763-8303

VERMONT STATE COLLEGES SYSTEM
Central Office, P.O. Box 359, Waterbury 05676-0359. Public (state). Chanc. Charles I. Bunting.
(802) 241-2520

*VERMONT TECHNICAL COLLEGE
Randolph Center 05061. Public (state) 2-year technical. 1970/1985 (NEASC-CVTCI). Sem. plan. Degrees: A. *Prof. Accred.:* Engineering Technology (architectural and building, civil, electrical and electronics, manufacturing, mechanical, surveying). Pres. Robert G. Clark.
Enroll.: 761
(802) 728-3391

WOODBURY COLLEGE
Montpelier 05602. Private one-year program. 1984 (NEASC-CVTCI). Qtr. plan. Certificates. Pres. Lawrence H. Mandell.
Enroll.: 73
(802) 229-0516

*Member Vermont State Colleges System

VIRGIN ISLANDS

COLLEGE OF THE VIRGIN ISLANDS
Charlotte Amalie, St. Thomas 00802. Public (territorial) liberal arts and professional. Accreditation includes branch campus at St. Croix 00820. 1971/1986 (MSA/CHE). Sem. plan. Degrees: A,B,M. *Prof. Accred.:* Nursing (A). Pres. Arthur A. Richards.
Enroll.: 3,035 (*f.t.* 229 m., 581 w.)
(809) 774-9200

VIRGINIA

APPRENTICE SCHOOL—NEWPORT NEWS SHIPBUILDING
4101 Washington Ave., Newport News 23607. Private. 1982 (SACS-COEI). Courses of varying lengths. Certificates. Dir. James H. Hughes.
Enroll.: FTE 868
(804) 380-2723

ARMED FORCES SCHOOL OF MUSIC
Naval Amphibious Base, Little Creek, Norfolk 23521. Public (federal). 1983 (SACS-COEI). Courses of varying lengths. Certificates. Cmdg. Off. Lt. Comdr. Philip H. Field.
Enroll.: FTE 417
(804) 464-7501

AUTOMOTIVE TRAINING INSTITUTE
5700 Southern Blvd., Virginia Beach 23462. Private. 1980 (NATTS); 1984 (SACS-COEI). Courses of varying lengths. Diplomas. Pres./Dir. William A. Wagner.
Enroll.: FTE 122
(804) 490-1241

AVERETT COLLEGE
Danville 24541. Private (Southern Baptist) liberal arts. 1971/1976 (SACS-Comm. on Coll.). Tri. plan. Degrees: A,B,M. *Prof. Accred.:* Social Work (B). Pres. Frank R. Campbell.
Enroll.: 831
(804) 793-7811

*BLUE RIDGE COMMUNITY COLLEGE
P.O. Box 80, Weyers Cave 24486. Public (state) junior. 1969/1984 (SACS-Comm. on Coll.). Qtr. plan. Degrees: A. Pres. James C. Sears.
Enroll.: 1,143
(703) 234-9261

BLUEFIELD COLLEGE
Bluefield 24605. Private (Southern Baptist) liberal arts. 1977/1984 (SACS-Comm. on Coll.). Sem. plan. Degrees: A,B. Pres. Charles Tyer.
Enroll.: 301
(304) 327-7137

BRANDON SECRETARIAL COLLEGE
3139 Williamson Rd., N. E., Roanoke 24012. Private. 1972/1984 (AICS). Courses of varying lengths. Diplomas. Pres. Emmett Hanger.
Enroll.: 138 (*f.t.* 10 m., 128 w.)
(703) 366-1613

*Member of Virginia Community College System

BRIDGEWATER COLLEGE
Bridgewater 22812. Private (Church of Bretheren) liberal arts. 1925/1981 (SACS-Comm. on Coll.). 3-3-1-3 plan. Degrees: B. Pres. Wayne F. Geisert.
Enroll.: 769
(703) 828-2501

CBN UNIVERSITY
1000 Centerville Tnpk., Virginia Beach 23463. Private professional; graduate only. 1984 (SACS-Comm. on Coll.). Qtr. plan. Degrees: M. Pres. Bob G. Slosser.
Enroll.: 715
(804) 424-7000

CAREER DEVELOPMENT CENTER
9705 Warwick Blvd., Newport News 23601. Private. 1983 (SACS-COEI). Courses of varying lengths. Certificates. Dir. Patricia Dolan Ettuo.
Enroll.: FTE 79
(804) 599-4088

*CENTRAL VIRGINIA COMMUNITY COLLEGE
3506 Wards Rd., Lynchburg 24502. Public (state) junior. 1969/1984 (SACS-Comm. on Coll.). Qtr. plan. Degrees: A. *Prof. Accred.:* Medical Laboratory Technology, Medical Record Technology, Radiography, Respiratory Therapy. Pres. Johnnie E. Merritt.
Enroll.: 2,094
(804) 239-0321

CHRISTOPHER NEWPORT COLLEGE
50 Shoe Lane, Newport News 23606. Public (state) liberal arts. 1971/1975 (SACS-Comm. on Coll.). Sem. plan. Degrees: B. *Prof. Accred.:* Social Work (B). Pres. John E. Anderson.
Enroll.: 3,019
(804) 599-7000

COLLEGE OF WILLIAM AND MARY IN VIRGINIA SYSTEM
Central Office, Williamsburg 23185. Public (state). Pres. Paul R. Verkuil.
(804) 253-4000

*Member of Virginia Community College System

College of William and Mary in Virginia
Williamsburg 23185. Public (state) liberal arts and law. 1921/1985 (SACS-Comm. on Coll.). Sem. plan. Degrees: A,B,P,M,D. *Prof. Accred.:* Accounting (Type A), Business (B,M), Law, Teacher Education (*e,s,p*). Pres. Paul R. Verkuil.
Enroll.: 6,229
(804) 253-4000

Richard Bland College
Route 1, Box 77-A, Petersburg 23805. Public (state) liberal arts. 1961/1978 (SACS-Comm. on Coll.). Sem. plan. Degrees: A. Pres. Clarence Maze, Jr.
Enroll.: 673
(804) 732-0111

Commonwealth College
1120 W. Mercury Blvd., Hampton 23666-3319. Private business. 1984 (AICS); 1984 (SACS-COEI). Courses of varying lengths. Certificates, diplomas. Dir. Ted Morris.
Enroll.: FTE 317
(804) 838-2122

Commonwealth College
300 Boush St., Norfolk 23510. Private business. 1964/1981 (AICS); 1984 (SACS-COEI). Courses of varying lengths. Certificates, diplomas. Dir. Marilyn Helms.
Enroll.: 563
(804) 625-5891

Commonwealth College
4000 W. Broad St., Richmond 23230. Private business. 1984 (AICS); 1984 (SACS-COEI). Courses of varying lengths. Certificates, diplomas. Dir. Robert C. Hodge.
Enroll.: FTE 218
(804) 353-2424

Commonwealth College
4160 Virginia Beach Blvd., Virginia Beach 23452. Private business. 1970/1982 (AICS); 1984 (SACS-COEI). Courses of varying lengths. Certificates. Dir. Julia Heffernan.
Enroll.: 496
(804) 340-0222

Branch Campus
3431 Carlin Springs Rd., Bailey's Crossroads 22041. Dir. James V. Foran.
(703) 845-8600

Computer Learning Center
6666 Commerce St., Springfield 22150. Private. 1979/1985); 1984 (SACS-COEI). Courses of varying lengths. Diplomas. Dir. Samuel D. Aven.
Enroll.: 475
(703) 971-0500

Control Data Institute
3717 Columbia Pike, Arlington 22204. Private. 1968/1979 (NATTS); 1979/1984 (SACS-COEI). Courses of varying lengths. Certificates. Dir. John J. Lantzy.
Enroll.: FTE 322
(703) 533-2050

*Dabney S. Lancaster Community College
Route 60 West, Clifton Forge 24422. Public (state) junior. 1969/1984 (SACS-Comm. on Coll.). Qtr. plan. Degrees: A. Pres. John F. Backels.
Enroll.: 723
(703) 862-4246

*Danville Community College
1008 South Main St., Danville 24541. Public (state) junior 1970/1985 (SACS-Comm. on Coll.). Qtr. plan. Degrees: A. Pres. Walter S. DeLany, Jr.
Enroll.: 1,363
(804) 797-3553

Defense Mapping School
Fort Belvoir 22060. Public (federal) technical. 1975/1985 (SACS-COEI). Courses of varying lengths. Certificates. Commandant Col. David F. Maune.
Enroll.: FTE 356
(703) 664-2182

Dominion Business Schools
3139 Williamson Rd., N.E., Roanoke 24012. Private business. 1972 (AICS). Courses of varying lengths. Certificates. Pres. E. W. Hanger.
(703) 366-1613

Early Learning Center for Montessori Education
National Center for Montessori Education, 9912 Cockrell Rd., Manassas 22110. Private home study-internship. 1982 (NHSC). Pres. Dennis A. Laskin.
(703) 631-0352

*Member of Virginia Community College System

EASTERN MENNONITE COLLEGE AND SEMINARY, INC.
Harrisonburg 22801. Private (Mennonite) liberal arts and theology. 1959/1980 (SACS-Comm. on Coll.). Sem. plan. Degrees: A,B. *Prof. Accred.:* Nursing (B), Social Work (B), Teacher Education (*e,s*), Theology (1985, ATS). Pres. Richard C. Detweiler.
Enroll.: 890
(703) 433-2771

*EASTERN SHORE COMMUNITY COLLEGE
Route One, Box 6, Melfa 23410. Public 2-year. 1973/1978 (SACS-Comm. on Coll.). Qtr. plan. Degrees: A. Pres. John C. Fiege.
Enroll.: 300
(804) 787-3972

EASTERN VIRGINIA MEDICAL AUTHORITY
P.O. Box 1980, Norfolk 23501. Private professional. 1984 (SACS-Comm. on Coll.). Sem. plan. Degrees: P. *Prof. Accred.:* Medicine. Pres. William D. Mayer.
Enroll.: 359
(804) 446-5600

ELECTRONIC COMPUTER PROGRAMMING INSTITUTE OF TIDEWATER
3661 E. Virginia Beach Blvd., Norfolk 23502. Private. 1971/1978 (NATTS); 1984 (SACS-COEI). Courses of varying lengths. Certificates. Pres. Alfred Dreyfus.
Enroll.: FTE 587
(804) 461-6161

BRANCH CAMPUS
4303 W. Broad St., Richmond 23230. Dir. Robb Moss.
(804) 359-3535

EMORY AND HENRY COLLEGE
Emory 24327. Private (United Methodist) liberal arts. 1925/1975 (SACS-Comm. on Coll.). Tri. plan. Degrees: B. Pres. Charles W. Sydnor, Jr.
Enroll.: 753
(703) 944-3121

FERRUM COLLEGE
Ferrum 24088. Private (United Methodist) liberal arts. 1976/1981 (SACS-Comm. on Coll.). Sem. plan. Degrees: A,B. *Prof. Accred.:* Social Work (B). Pres. Joseph T. Hart.
Enroll.: 1,464
(703) 365-2121

*Member of Virginia Community College System

GEORGE MASON UNIVERSITY
Fairfax 22030. Public (state). 1957/1981 (SACS-Comm. on Coll.). Sem. plan. Degrees: B,M,D. *Prof. Accred.:* Law (ABA only), Nursing (B,M), Social Work (B), Teacher Education (*e,s,p*). Pres. George W. Johnson.
Enroll.: 11,731
(703) 323-2000

*GERMANNA COMMUNITY COLLEGE
Box 339, Locust Grove 22508. Public (state) junior. 1972/1976 (SACS-Comm. on Coll.). Qtr. plan. Degrees: A. *Prof. Accred.:* Nursing (A). Pres. Marshall W. Smith.
Enroll.: 903
(703) 399-1333

HAMPDEN-SYDNEY COLLEGE
Hampden-Sydney 23943. Private (Presbyterian, U.S.) liberal arts for men. 1919/1975 (SACS-Comm. on Coll.). Sem. plan. Degrees: B. Pres. Josiah Bunting, III.
Enroll.: *f.t.* 753
(804) 223-4381

HAMPTON UNIVERSITY
Hampton 23668. Private liberal arts, teachers and technological. 1932/1977 (SACS-Comm. on Coll.). 4-1-4 plan. Degrees: B,M. *Prof. Accred.:* Architecture (B), Music, Nursing (B,M), Speech Pathology. Pres. William R. Harvey.
Enroll.: 3,786
(804) 727-5000

HOLLINS COLLEGE
Hollins College 24020. Private liberal arts primarily for women. 1932/1975 (SACS-Comm. on Coll.). 4-1-4 plan. Degrees: B,M. Pres. Paula Pimlott Brownlee.
Enroll.: 895
(703) 362-6000

INSTITUTE OF BUSINESS AND TECHNOLOGY
300 W. Grace St., Richmond 23220. Private. 1983 (AICS). Qtr. plan. Certificates, diplomas. Acting Dir. Charlene Peters.
Enroll.: 277 (*f.t.* 20 m., 251 w.)
(804) 644-5627

*J. SARGEANT REYNOLDS COMMUNITY COLLEGE
P.O. Box C32040, Richmond 23261. Public 2-year; accreditation includes three campuses in Richmond. 1974/1979 (SACS-Comm. on Coll.). Qtr. plan. Degrees: A. *Prof. Accred.:* Dental Assisting, Dental Laboratory

*Member of Virginia Community College System

Technology, Medical Assisting, Medical Laboratory Technology, Nursing (A), Respiratory Therapy, Respiratory Therapy Technology. Pres. S. A. Burnette.
Enroll.: 5,047
(804) 264-3200

JAMES MADISON UNIVERSITY
Harrisonburg 22807. Public (state) liberal arts and teachers. 1927/1982 (SACS-Comm. on Coll.). Sem. plan. Degrees: B,M. *Prof. Accred.:* Accounting (Type A,C), Art, Business (B,M), Home Economics, Music, Social Work (B), Speech Pathology and Audiology, Teacher Education (*e,s,p*). Pres. Ronald E. Carrier.
Enroll.: 9,088
(703) 568-6211

*JOHN TYLER COMMUNITY COLLEGE
Chester 23831. Public (state) junior. 1969/1983 (SACS-Comm. on Coll.). Qtr. plan. Degrees: A. *Prof. Accred.:* Engineering Technology (architectural, electronic), Nursing (A). Pres. Freddie W. Nicholas, Sr.
Enroll.: 1,894
(804) 796-4000

JUDGE ADVOCATE GENERAL'S SCHOOL, U.S. ARMY
Charlottesville 22901. Public (federal) professional; post J.D. programs only. 1965. Sem. plan. Certificates. *Prof. Accred.:* Law (ABA only). Dean William Sherman Fulton, Jr.
Enroll.: 87 (*f.t.* 82 m., 5 w.)
(804) 293-2028

KATHARINE GIBBS SCHOOL
2070 Chain Bridge Rd., Suite 6-100, Vienna 22180. Private. 1985 (AICS). Courses of varying lengths. Degrees: A. Dir. Noel Jablonski.
(703) 821-8100

KEE BUSINESS COLLEGE
803 Diligence Dr., Newport News 23606. Private business. 1955/1982 (AICS); 1984 (SACS-COEI). Qtr. plan. Certificates, diplomas. Dir. Kitty Heffington
Enroll.: 311
(804) 873-1111

KEE BUSINESS COLLEGE
1510 Norview Ave., Norfolk 23513. Private. 1967/1983 (AICS); 1984 (SACS-COEI). Qtr. plan. Degrees: A, certificates, diplomas. Dir. Lois P. Parks.

*Member of Virginia Community College System

Enroll.: 173
(804) 855-3311

KEE BUSINESS COLLEGE
810 Airline Blvd., Portsmouth 23707. Private. 1984 (SACS-COEI); branch of (AICS). Qtr. plan. Degrees: A, certificates, diplomas. Dir. Yvonna Santos.
Enroll.: FTE 361
(804) 397-0776

KEE BUSINESS COLLEGE
6301 Midlothian Tpke., Richmond 23225. Private. 1984 (SACS-COEI); branch of (AICS). Qtr. plan. Degrees: A, certificates, diplomas. Dir. Zoe S. Thompson.
Enroll.: FTE 272
(804) 745-5660

LIBETY UNIVERSITY
P.O. Box 20000, Lynchburg 24506. Private (Baptist) liberal arts. 1980 (SACS-Comm. on Coll.). Sem. plan. Degrees: A,B,M. Pres. A. Pierre Guillermin.
Enroll.: 4,239
(804) 237-5961

LONGWOOD COLLEGE
Farmville 23901. Public (state) liberal arts and teachers for women, graduate school coeducational. 1927/1983 (SACS-Comm. on Coll.). Sem. plan. Degrees: B,M. *Prof. Accred.:* Music, Social Work (B), Teacher Education (*e,s,p*). Pres. Janet D. Greenwood.
Enroll.: 2,606
(804) 392-9211

*LORD FAIRFAX COMMUNITY COLLEGE
P.O. Box 47, U.S. Rt. 11, Middletown 22645. Public (state) junior. 1972/1976 (SACS-Comm. on Coll.). Qtr. plan. Degrees: A. Pres. William H. McCoy.
Enroll.: 871
(703) 869-1120

LYNCHBURG COLLEGE
Lynchburg 24501. Private (Disciples of Christ) liberal arts. 1927/1983 (SACS-Comm. on Coll.). Sem. plan. Degrees: B,M. Pres. George N. Rainsford.
Enroll.: 1,716
(804) 522-8100

MARY BALDWIN COLLEGE
Staunton 24401. Private (Presbyterian, U.S.) liberal arts for women. 1931/1976 (SACS-Comm. on Coll.). Sem. plan. Degrees: B. Pres. Cynthia H. Tyson.

*Member of Virginia Community College System

Enroll.: 879
(703) 887-7000

Mary Washington College
Fredericksburg 22401. Public (state) liberal arts. 1930/1983 (SACS-Comm. on Coll.). Sem. plan. Degrees: B,M. *Prof. Accred.:* Music. Pres. William M. Anderson, Jr.
Enroll.: 2,629
(703) 899-4100

Maryland Drafting Institute
8001 Forbes Place, Springfield 22151. Private. 1985 (NATTS). Certificates.
(703) 321-9777

Marymount College of Virginia
2807 N. Glebe Rd., Arlington 22207. Private for women; 3-year baccalaureate. 1975/1978 (SACS-Comm. on Coll.). Sem. plan. Degrees A,B,M. *Prof. Accred.:* Interior Design, Nursing (A,B,M.), Teacher Education (*e,s*). Pres. Sister M. Majella Berg, R.S.H.M.
Enroll.: 1,499
(703) 522-5600

*Mountain Empire Community College
P.O. Drawer 700, Big Stone Gap 24219. Public (state) 2-year. 1974/1979 (SACS-Comm. on Coll.). Qtr. plan. Degrees: A. *Prof. Accred.:* Nursing (A), Respiratory Therapy. Pres. Victor B. Ficker.
Enroll.: 1,370
(703) 523-2400

National Business College
1813 E. Main St., Salem 24153. Private junior. 1954/1980 (AICS). Qtr. plan. Degrees: A. Dir. Irwin S. Monsein.
Enroll.: 2,196 (*f.t.* 995 m., 1,201 w.)
(703) 986-1800

Branch Campus
100 Logan St., Bluefield 24605. Dir. Mary Ann Thorn.
(703) 326-3621

Branch Campus
615 W. Main St., Charlottesville 22901.
(804) 295-0136

Branch Campus
401 Main St., Danville 24541. Dir. Rupert Jenkins.
(804) 793-6822

National Business School
3108 Mount Vernon Ave., Alexandria 22305. Private. 1982 (AICS). Qtr. plan. Certificates, diplomas. *Prof. Accred.:* Medical Assisting. Exec. Dir. Judith Colen.
Enroll.: 1,387 (*f.t.* 846 m., 541 w.)
(703) 683-6554

Branch Campus
1444 P St., N.W., Washington, DC 20005. Dir. Horris L. Johnson.
(202) 232-1800

Branch Campus
510 N. Hilton St., Baltimore, MD 21229. Dir. David S. Beard.
(301) 945-1800

Naval Guided Missiles School
Dam Neck, Virginia Beach 23461. Public (federal) technical. 1983 (SACS-COEI). Courses of varying lengths. Certificates. Cmdg. Off. Cmdr. Capt. John M Drustrup.
Enroll.: FTE 812
(804) 425-4628

*New River Community College
Drawer 1127, Dublin 24084. Public (state) junior. 1972/1976 (SACS-Comm. on Coll.). Qtr. plan. Degrees: A. Pres. H. Randall Edwards.
Enroll.: 1,561
(703) 674-4121

Norfolk State University
2401 Corprew St., Norfolk 23504. Public liberal arts and teachers. 1967/1977 (SACS-Comm on Coll.). Sem. plan. Degrees: A,B,M. *Prof. Accred.:* Medical Record Administration, Medical Technology, Music, Nursing (A,B), Psychology, Social Work (B,M), Teacher Education (*e,s*). Pres. Harrison B. Wilson.
Enroll.: 7,746
(804) 623-8600

*Northern Virginia Community College
4001 Wakefield Chapel Rd., Annandale 22003. Public (state) junior; other campuses at Alexandria, Manassas, Sterling, and Woodbridge. 1968/1982 (SACS-Comm. on Coll.). Qtr. plan. Degrees: A. *Prof. Accred.:* Dental Assisting, Dental Hygiene, Dental Laboratory Technology, EMT-Paramedical Training, Medical Laboratory Technology (A), Medical Record Technology, Nursing (A), Radiography, Respiratory Therapy. Pres. Richard J. Ernst.
Enroll.: 18,549
(703) 323-3000

*Member of Virginia Community College System

*Member of Virginia Community College System

Old Dominion University
Norfolk 23508. Public (state) liberal arts and professional. 1961/1982 (SACS-Comm. on Coll.). Sem. plan. Degrees: A,B,M,D. *Prof. Accred.:* Accounting (Type A), Business (B,M), Dental Assisting, Dental Hygiene, Engineering (civil, electrical, mechanical), Engineering Technology (civil, electrical, mechanical), Medical Technology, Music, Nursing (B,M), Physical Therapy, Teacher Education (*e,s,p*). Pres. Joseph M. Marchello.
Enroll.: 12,738
(804) 440-3000

Page Business School
11260 Roger Bacon Dr., Suite 203, Reston 22090. Private. 1984 (AICS). Qtr. plan. Diplomas. Dir. Sondra Lee Abbott.
Enroll.: 30
(703) 435-4440

*Patrick Henry Community College
P.O. Drawer 5311, Martinsville 24115. Public (state) junior. 1972/1976 (SACS-Comm. on Coll.). Qtr. plan. Degrees: A. Pres. Max F. Wingett.
Enroll.: 1,037
(703) 638-8777

*Paul D. Camp Community College
P.O. Box 737, Franklin 23851. Public (state) junior. 1973/1978 (SACS-Comm. on Coll.). Qtr. plan. Degrees: A. Pres. Michael B. McCall.
Enroll.: 829
(804) 562-2171

Phillips Business College
P.O. Box 169, Lynchburg 24505. Private. 1953/1984 (AICS). Qtr. plan. Diplomas. Acting Pres. Eunice Hall.
Enroll.: 1,483 (*f.t.* 514 m., 969 w.)
(804) 847-7701

Branch Campus
3823 Mt. Vernon Ave., Alexandria 22305. Dir. Jendra Combs.
(703) 549-9131

Branch Campus
60 Evergreen Pl., East Orange, NJ 07018. Dir. Craig F. Johnson.
(201) 673-6009

*Piedmont Virginia Community College
Route 6, Box 1-A, Charlottesville 22901. Public 2-year. 1974/1979 (SACS-Comm. on Coll.). Qtr. plan. Degrees: A. *Prof. Accred.:* Nursing (A), Respiratory Therapy. Pres. George B. Vaughan.
Enroll.: 1,970
(804) 977-3900

*Member of Virginia Community College System

Presbyterian School of Christian Education
1205 Palmyra Ave., Richmond 23227. Private (Presbyterian, U.S.A.); graduate only. 1951/1977 (SACS-Comm. on Coll.). 4-1-4 plan. Degrees: M,D. *Prof. Accred.:* Theology (1964/1977, ATS). Pres. Heath K. Rada.
Enroll.: 138
(804) 359-5031

Radford University
Radford 24142. Public liberal arts and teachers. 1928/1983 (SACS-Comm. on Coll.). Qtr. plan. Degrees: B,M. *Prof. Accred.:* Music, Nursing (B), Social Work (B), Teacher Education (*e,s,p*). Pres. Donald N. Dedmon.
Enroll.: 5,941
(703) 731-5000

Randolph-Macon College
Ashland 23005. Private (United Methodist) liberal arts. 1904/1976 (SACS-Comm. on Coll.). 4-1-4 plan. Degrees: B. Pres. Ladell Payne.
Enroll.: 958
(804) 798-8372

Randolph-Macon Woman's College
Lynchburg 24503. Private (United Methodist) liberal arts for women. 1902/1980 (SACS-Comm. on Coll.). Sem. plan. Degrees: B. Pres. Robert A. Spivey.
Enroll.: 779
(804) 846-7392

*Rappahannock Community College
Glenns 23149. Public (state) 2-year. 1973/1978 (SACS-Comm. on Coll.). Qtr. plan. Degrees: A. Pres. John H. Upton.
Enroll.: 551
(804) 758-5324

Roanoke College
Salem 24153. Private (Lutheran in America) liberal arts. 1927/1981 (SACS-Comm. on Coll.). 4-1-4 plan. Degrees: B. Pres. Norman D. Fintel.
Enroll.: 1,318
(703) 389-2351

*Member of Virginia Community College System

RUTLEDGE COLLEGE
613 N. Lombardy St., Richmond 23220. Private business. 1978/1981 (AICS). Qtr. plan. Diplomas. Dir. Richard Wilson.
Enroll.: 709 (*f.t.* 212 m., 497 w.)
(804) 353-9294

S.T.O.P. VOCATIONAL SCHOOL
411 St. Pauls Blvd., Norfolk 23501. Public (state) technical. 1984 (SACS-COEI). Courses of varying lengths. Certificates. Dir. Lorraine Brinkley-Skeeter.
Enroll.: FTE 51

BRANCH CAMPUS
1514 Brambleton Ave., Norfolk 23504.

SAINT PAUL'S COLLEGE
406 Winsor Ave., Lawrenceville 23868. Private (Episcopal) liberal arts and teachers. 1950/1980 (SACS-Comm. on Coll.). Sem. plan. Degrees: B. Pres. Marvin B Scott.
Enroll.: 683
(804) 848-3111

SHENANDOAH COLLEGE AND CONSERVATORY OF MUSIC
Winchester 22601. Private (United Methodist). 1973/1978 (SACS-Comm. on Coll.). Sem. plan. Degrees: A,B,M. *Prof. Accred.:* Music, Nursing (A). Pres. James Davis.
Enroll.: 773
(703) 665-4500

SOUTHERN SEMINARY JUNIOR COLLEGE
Buena Vista 24416. Private for women. 1962/1983 (SACS-Comm. on Coll.). Sem. plan. Degrees: A. Pres. Joyce O. Davis.
Enroll.: f.t. 243 w.
(703) 261-6181

*SOUTHSIDE VIRGINIA COMMUNITY COLLEGE
Rt.1, P.O.Box 60, Alberta 23821. Public (state) junior; accreditation includes campus at Keysville. 1972/1976 (SACS-Comm. on Coll.). Qtr. plan Degrees: A. Pres. John J. Cavan.
Enroll.: 866
(804) 949-7111

*SOUTHWEST VIRGINIA COMMUNITY COLLEGE
P.O. Box SVCC, Richlands 24641. Public (state) junior. 1970/1985 (SACS-Comm. on Coll.). Qtr. plan. Degrees A. *Prof. Accred.:* Nursing (A), Radiography, Respiratory Therapy. Pres. Charles R. King.
Enroll.: 1,997
(703) 964-2555

SWEET BRIAR COLLEGE
Sweet Briar 24595. Private liberal arts for women. 1920/1980 (SACS-Comm. on Coll.). 4-1-4 plan. Degrees: B. *Prof. Accred.:* Pres. Nenah E. Fry.
Enroll.: 654
(804) 381-6100

TECC SCHOOL OF ELECTRONICS
P.O. Box 10378, Alexandria 22310. Private. 1985(SACS-COEI). Courses of varying lengths. Certificates. Dir. Homer R. Belche.
Enroll.: FTE 8l

TEMPLE SCHOOL
5832 Columbia Pike, Baileys Crossroads 22041. Private business. 1971/1984 (AICS); 1984 (SACS-COEI). Qtr. plan. Certificates, diplomas. *Prof. Accred.:* Medical Assisting, Medical Laboratory Technology. Dir. Marvin Carter.
Enroll.: 213
(703) 671-7100

*THOMAS NELSON COMMUNITY COLLEGE
P.O. Box 9407, Hampton 23670. Public (state) junior. 1970/1985 (SACS-Comm. on Coll.). Qtr. plan. Degrees: A . *Prof. Accred.:* Medical Laboratory Technology (A). Pres. Thomas S. Kubala.
Enroll.: 3,774
(804) 825-2700

*TIDEWATER COMMUNITY COLLEGE
Portsmouth 23703. Public (state) junior; accreditation includes campuses at Chesapeake and Virginia Beach. 1971/1975 (SACS-Comm. on Coll.). Qtr. plan. Degrees: A. *Prof. Accred.:* Medical Record Technology, Nursing (A), Radiography, Respiratory Therapy, Respiratory Therapy Technology. Pres. George B. Pass.
Enroll.: 8,512
(804) 484-2121

UNION THEOLOGICAL SEMINARY IN VIRGINIA
3401 Brook Rd., Richmond 23227. Private (Presbyterian, U.S.A.) professional; graduate only. 1971/1975 (SACS-Comm. on Coll.). 5 terms. Degrees: P,M,D. *Prof. Accred.:* Theology (1938/1976, ATS). Pres. Rev. T. Hartley Hall, IV.
Enroll.: 211
(804) 355-0671

*Member of Virginia Community College System

*Member of Virginia Community College System

Virginia

U.S. Army Engineer School
Fort Belvoir 22060. Public (federal) technical. 1975/1985 (SACS-COEI). Courses of varying lengths. Certificates. Commander Col. Don W. Barber.
Enroll.: FTE 1,938
(703) 664-3170

U.S. Army Institute for Professional Development
Bldg. P-5000, Fort Eustis 23604. Public (federal) home study. 1978/1984 (NHSC). Deputy Commander Col. Dennis D. Frink.
(804) 878-4774

U.S. Army Quartermaster School
Bldg. P-500, Fort Lee 23801. Public (federal) technical. 1975/1985 (SACS-COEI). Courses of varying lengths. Certificates. Commander Maj. Gen. Eugene L. Stillions.
Enroll.: FTE 3,801
(804) 734-2950

U.S. Army Transportation and Aviation Logistics Schools
Fort Eustis 23604. Public (federal) technical. 1975/1982 (SACS-COEI). Courses of varying lengths. Certificates. Commander Maj. Gen. Fred E. Elam.
Enroll.: FTE 2,618
(804) 878-2694

Branch Campus
Western Nebraska Technical College, Sidney, NE 69162.

University of Richmond
Richmond 23173. Private (Southern Baptist); Richmond College for men, Westhampton College for women, others coeducational. 1910/1975 (SACS-Comm. on Coll.). Sem. plan. Degrees: A,B,P,M. *Prof. Accred.:* Business (B,M), Law. Pres. E. Bruce Heilman.
Enroll.: 3,814
(804) 289-8000

University of Virginia
Central Office, Charlottesville 22903. Public (state). Pres. Robert M. O'Neil.
(804) 924-0311

University of Virginia
Charlottesville 22903. Public (state) primarily for men, graduate and professional schools coeducational. 1904/1975 (SACS-Comm. on Coll.). Sem. plan. Degrees: B,P,M,D. *Prof. Accred.:* Accounting (Type A,C), Architecture (M), Business (B,M), Engineering (aerospace, chemical, civil, electrical, mechanical, nuclear, systems), Landscape Architecture (M), Law, Medical Technology, Medicine, Music, Nuclear Medicine Technology, Nursing (B,M), Psychology, Radiation Therapy Technology, Radiography, Speech Pathology and Audiology, Teacher Education (*e,s,p*). Pres. Robert M. O'Neil.
Enroll.: 18,518
(804) 924-0311

Clinch Valley College
Wise 24293. Liberal arts and teachers; branch of University of Virginia. Public. 1970/1985 (SACS-Comm. on Coll.). Sem. plan. Degrees: B. Chanc. W. Edmund Moomaw.
Enroll.: 844
(703) 328-2431

Virginia Commonwealth University
910 W. Franklin St., Richmond 23284. Public (state). 1953/1984 (SACS-Comm. on Coll.). Qtr. plan in medical units; sem. plan in others. Degrees: A,B,P,M,D. *Prof. Accred.:* Accounting (Type A,C), Art, Business (B,M), Dental Hygiene, Dentistry, Dietetics, Health Services Administration, Interior Design, Journalism, Medical Record Administration, Medical Technology, Medicine, Music, Muclear Medicine Technology, Nursing (B,M), Occupational Therapy, Pharmacy, Physical Therapy, Psychology, Radiation Therapy Technology, Radiography, Rehabilitation Counseling, Social Work (B,M), Teacher Education (*e,s,p*). Pres. Edmund F.Ackell.
Enroll.: 15,586
(804) 257-0100

Virginia Community College System
James Monroe Bldg., 101 N. 14th St., P.O. Box 23212, Richmond 23212. Administrative office for 23 community colleges. Chanc. Johnas F. Hockaday.
(804) 225-2117

Virginia Hair Academy
3312 Williamson Rd., N.W., Roanoke 24012. Private. 1981 (NATTS). Courses of varying lengths. Certificates, diplomas. Pres. Linwood Locklear.
Enroll.: 36 (*f.t.* 7 m., 29 w.)
(703) 563-2015

*Virginia Highlands Community College
P.O. Box 828, Abingdon 24210. Public (state) junior. 1972/1976 (SACS-Comm. on Coll.).

*Member of Virginia Community College System

Qtr. plan. Degrees: A. *Prof. Accred.:* Nursing (A). Pres. N. DeWitt Moore, Jr..
Enroll.: 1,101
(703) 628-6094

VIRGINIA INSTITUTE OF TECHNOLOGY
5425 RobinHood Rd., Gateway One, Norfolk 23513. Private. 1980/1982 (NATTS). Qtr. plan. Certificates, diplomas. Senior Vice Pres. J. D. Hall.
Enroll.: 126 (*f.t.* 2 m., 124 w.)
(804) 855-9300

BRANCH
1118-B W. Mercury Blvd., Hampton 23666. Dir. Gwendolyn D. Kerbush..
Enroll.: f.t. 139 w.
(804) 827-5000

VIRGINIA INTERMONT COLLEGE
Bristol 24201. Private (Southern Baptist) 4-year primarily for women. 1972/1976 (SACS-Comm. on Coll.). Sem. plan. Degrees: A,B. *Prof. Accred.:* Music, Social Work. Pres. Gary Poulton.
Enroll.: 493
(703) 669-6101

VIRGINIA MILITARY INSTITUTE
Lexington 24450. Public (state) liberal arts and engineering college for men. 1926/1975 (SACS-Comm. on Coll.). Sem. plan. Degrees: B. *Prof. Accred.:* Engineering (civil, electrical). Supt. Gen. Sam S. Walker.
Enroll.: f.t. 1,340 m.
(703) 463-6201

VIRGINIA POLYTECHNIC INSTITUTE AND STATE UNIVERSITY
Blacksburg 24061. Public 1923/1977 (SACS-Comm. on Coll.). Qtr. plan. Degrees: B,M,D. *Prof. Accred.:* Accounting (A,C), Architecture (B,M), Business (B,M), Dietetics, Engineering (aerospace and ocean, agricultural, chemical, civil, electrical, engineering science and mechanics, industrial engineering and operations research, materials, mechanical, metallurgical, mining, sanitary), Forestry, Home Economics, Landscape Architecture (B), Psychology, Teacher Education (*e,s,p*), Veterinary Medicine. Pres. William E. Lavery.
Enroll.: 21,962
(703) 961-6000

(VIRGINIA) PROTESTANT EPISCOPAL THEOLOGICAL SEMINARY IN VIRGINIA
Alexandria 22304. Private (Episcopal) professional; graduate only. Sem. plan. Degrees: P,M,D. *Prof. Accred.:* Theology (1938/1983, ATS). Dean Richard Reid.
Enroll.: 229
(703) 370-6600

VIRGINIA SCHOOLS
14341 Jefferson Davis Hwy., Woodbridge 22191. Private. 1984 (SACS-COEI). Courses of varying lengths. Certificates. Dir. Sharon K. Shirk.
Enroll.: FTE 84

BRANCH CAMPUS
1101 Westbank Expressway, Gretna LA 70058.

VIRGINIA STATE UNIVERSITY
Petersburg 23803. Public liberal arts and professional. 1933/1978 (SACS-Comm. on Coll.). Sem. plan. Degrees: A,B,M. *Prof. Accred.:* Music, Social Work (B), Teacher Education (*e,s,p*). Pres. Wilbert Greenfield.
Enroll.: 3,911
(804) 520-5000

VIRGINIA UNION UNIVERSITY
1500 N. Lombardy St., Richmond 23220. Private (American Baptist) liberal arts college and graduate theology. 1935/1981 (SACS-Comm. on Coll.). Sem. plan. Degrees: B,P. *Prof. Accred.:* Social Work (B), Theology. Pres. S. Dallas Simmons.
Enroll.: 1,128
(804) 257-5600

VIRGINIA WESLEYAN COLLEGE
Norfolk 23502. Private (United Methodist) liberal arts and teachers. 1970/1985 (SACS-Comm. on Coll.). Sem. plan. Degrees: B. Pres. Lambuth M. Clarke.
Enroll.: 884
(804) 461-3232

*VIRGINIA WESTERN COMMUNITY COLLEGE
P.O. Box 14045, Roanoke 24038. Public (state) junior. 1969/1983 (SACS-Comm. on Coll.). Qtr. plan. Degrees: A. *Prof. Accred.:* Dental Assisting, Dental Hygiene, Nursing (A), Radiography. Pres. Charles L. Downs.
Enroll.: 3,377
(703) 982-7200

WASHINGTON BUSINESS SCHOOL OF NORTHERN VIRGINIA
8233 Old Courthouse Rd., Vienna 22180. Private. 1969/1984 (AICS). Qtr. plan. Diplomas. Dir. Maria C. Blase.
Enroll.: 622 (*f.t.* 13 m., 609 w.)
(703) 566-8888

*Member of Virginia Community College System

Washington and Lee University
Lexington 24450. Private primarily for men. 1895/1978 (SACS-Comm. on Coll.). Tri. plan. Degrees: B,P. *Prof. Accred.:* Business (B), Journalism, Law. Pres. John D. Wilson.
Enroll.: 1,702
(703) 463-8400

The Westmoreland Davis Equestrian Institute at Morven Park
Route 3, Box 50, Leesburg 22075. Private 2-year. 1975/1985 (SACS-COEI). Sem. plan. Certificates. Dir. Raul de Leon.
Enroll.: FTE 32
(703) 777-2414

Woodrow Wilson Rehabilitation Center
P.O. Box 81, Fisherville 22939. Private. 1983 (SACS-COEI). Courses of varying lengths. Certificates. Dir. Ken Kuester.
Enroll.: FTE 321
(804) 885-9618

*Wytheville Community College
1000 E. Main St., Wytheville 24382. Public (state) junior. 1970/1985 (SACS-Comm. on Coll.). Qtr. plan. Degrees: A. *Prof. Accred.:* Dental Assisting, Nursing (A). Pres. William F. Snyder.
Enroll.: 1,126
(703) 228-5541

*Member of Virginia Community College System

WASHINGTON

ART INSTITUTE OF SEATTLE (EXTENSION)
905 E. Pine St., Seattle 98122. Private. 1983 (NATTS). Qtr. plan. Degrees: A, diplomas. Dir. George Pry.
(206) 322-0596

BAILIE SCHOOL OF BROADCAST
2517 Eastlake Ave., Seattle 98101. Private. 1972/1984 (NATTS). Courses of varying lengths. Diplomas. Dir. Dick Curtis.
Enroll.: 66 (*f.t.* 55 m., 11 w.)
(206) 328-2900

BAILIE SCHOOL OF BROADCAST
W. 621 Mallon, The Old Flour Mill, Spokane 99201. Private. 1974/1980 (NATTS). Courses of varying lengths. Diplomas. Dir. Jerry Anderson.
Enroll.: 80 (*f.t.* 50 m., 30 w.)
(509) 326-6229

BELLEVUE COMMUNITY COLLEGE
3000 Landerholm Cir., S.E., Bellevue 98009-2037. Public (district) junior. 1970/1985 (NASC). Qtr. plan. Degrees: A. *Prof. Accred.:* Nursing (A), Radiography. Pres. Paul N. Thompson.
Enroll.: 10,140
(206) 641-2271

BIG BEND COMMUNITY COLLEGE
Moses Lake 98837. Public (district) junior. 1965/1982 (NASC). Qtr. plan. Degrees: A. Pres. Peter D. DeVries.
Enroll.: 1,963
(509) 762-5351

CAPITOL BUSINESS COLLEGE
815 E. Olympia Ave., Olympia 98506. Private. 1972/1983 (AICS). Courses of varying lengths. Certificates. Dir. Ken Warden.
Enroll.: 313 (*f.t.* 35 m., 278 w.)
(206) 357-9313

CASCADE BUSINESS COLLEGE
205 W. Holly, Bellingham 98225. Private. 1972/1981 (AICS). Courses of varying lengths. Diplomas. Pres. Pete Augusztiny.
Enroll.: 211 (*f.t.* 39 m., 172 w.)
(206) 733-3869

CENTRAL WASHINGTON UNIVERSITY
Ellensburg 98926. Public liberal arts and teachers. 1918/1979 (NASC). Qtr. plan. Degrees: B,M. *Prof. Accred.:* Music, Teacher Education (*e,s,p*). Pres. Donald L. Garrity.
Enroll.: 6,993
(509) 963-1401

CENTRALIA COLLEGE
Centralia 98531. Public (district) junior. 1948/1980 (NASC). Qtr. plan. Degrees: A. Pres. ———.
Enroll.: 2,929
(206) 736-9391

CHASE BUSINESS COLLEGE
2700 N.E. Andersen Rd., Vancouver 98661. Private. 1970/1980 (AICS). Courses of varying lengths. Certificates. Dir. Dick Lee.
Enroll.: 361 (*f.t.* 33 m., 328 w.)
(206) 693-4717

CITY UNIVERSITY
16661 Northup Way, Bellevue 98008. Private. 1978/1981 (NASC). Qtr. plan. Degrees: A,B,M. Pres. Michael A. Pastore.
Enroll.: 3,447
(206) 643-2000

CLARK COLLEGE
Vancouver 98663. Public (district) junior. 1948/1980 (NASC). Qtr. plan. Degrees: A. *Prof. Accred.:* Dental Hygiene, Nursing (A) Pres. Earl P. Johnson.
Enroll.: 6,223
(206) 699-0100

COLUMBIA BASIN COLLEGE
2600 N. 20th Ave., Pasco 99301. Public (district) junior. 1960/1980 (NASC). Qtr. plan. Degrees: A. Pres. Fred L. Esvelt.
Enroll.: 4,977
(509) 547-0511

COMMERCIAL DRIVER TRAINING
24325 Pacific Hwy. S., Kent 98031. Private. 1973/1985 (NATTS). Courses of varying lengths. Certificates. Pres. Clifford Georgioff.
Enroll.: 12 (*f.t.* 11 m., 1 w.)
(206) 824-3970

CORNISH INSTITUTE
710 E. Roy St., Seattle 98112. Private professional. 1977/1982 (NASC). Sem. plan. Degrees: B. Acting Pres. Robert Funk.
Enroll.: 457
(206) 323-1400

CROWN SCHOOL OF HAIR DESIGN
4821 Evergreen Way S., Everett 98203. Private. 1979 (NATTS). 8-month course. Diplomas. Dir. Neil Hanson.

Enroll.: 30 (*f.t.* 18 m., 12 w.)
(206) 252-6695

DIVERS INSTITUTE OF TECHNOLOGY, INC.
4601 Shilshole Ave., N.W. , P.O. Box 70312, Seattle 98107. Private. 1973/1978 (NATTS). Courses of varying lengths. Certificates, diplomas. Pres. John W. Manlove.
Enroll.: 200 (*f.t.* 198 m., 2 w.)
(206) 783-5542

EASTERN WASHINGTON UNIVERSITY
Cheney 99004. Public liberal arts and teachers. 1919/1978 (NASC). Qtr. plan. Degrees: B,M. *Prof. Accred.:* Business (B,M), Dental Hygiene, Dietetics, Music, Social Work (B,M), Teacher Education (*e,s,p*). Pres. H. George Frederickson.
Enroll.: 8,102 (*f.t.* 3,385 m., 3,405 w.)
(509) 359-2371

EDMONDS COMMUNITY COLLEGE
Lynnwood 98036. Public (district) junior. 1973/1978 (NASC). Qtr. plan. Degrees: A. *Prof. Accred.:* Dental Assisting, Medical Assistant. Pres. Thomas Nielsen.
Enroll.: 6,635
(206) 771-5000

ETON COLLEGE
812 Sixth St., Bremerton 98310. Private business. 1979/1985 (AICS). Courses of varying lengths. Certificates, diplomas. Pres. Walter C. Greenly.
Enroll.: 101 (*f.t.* 5 m., 96 w.)
(206) 373-7171

BRANCH CAMPUS
1516 Second Ave., Second Fl., Seattle 98111.
(206) 622-3866

EVERETT COMMUNITY COLLEGE
Everett 98201. Public (district) junior. 1948/1979 (NASC). Qtr. plan. Degrees: A, certificates. *Prof. Accred.:* Nursing (A), Practical Nursing. Acting Pres. Robert Drewel.
Enroll.: 6,341
(206) 259-7151

THE EVERGREEN STATE COLLEGE
Olympia 98505. Public liberal arts. 1974/1979 (NASC). Qtr. plan. Degrees: B,M. Pres. Joseph P. Olander.
Enroll.: 2,980
(206) 866-6400

GONZAGA UNIVERSITY
Spokane 99258. Private (Roman Catholic) 1927/1984 (NASC). Sem. plan. Degrees: B,P,M,D. *Prof. Accred.:* Engineering (civil, electrical, mechanical), Nursing (B), Law (ABA only), Teacher Education (*e,s,p*). Pres. Rev. Bernard J. Coughlin, S.J.
Enroll.: 3,194
(509) 328-4220

GRAYS HARBOR COLLEGE
Aberdeen 98520. Public (district) junior. 1948/1981 (NASC). Qtr. plan. Degrees : A. Pres. Joseph A. Malik.
Enroll.: 2,593
(206) 532-9020

GREEN RIVER COMMUNITY COLLEGE
Auburn 98002. Public (district) junior. 1967/1983 (NASC). Qtr. plan. Degrees: A. Pres. Richard Rutkowski.
Enroll.: 6,354
(206) 833-9111

GRIFFIN BUSINESS COLLEGE
2005 Fifth Ave., Seattle 98121. Private. 1972/1983 (AICS); 1984 (NASC). Modified Tri. plan. Degrees: A,B, diplomas. Pres. J. Michael Griffin.
Enroll.: 698
(206) 624-7154

BRANCH CAMPUS
10833 N.E. Eighth, Bellevue 98004. Dir. Michael Tenore.
(206) 455-3636

BRANCH CAMPUS
955 Commerce St., Tacoma 98402. Dir. Susan Bergsten.
(206) 383-2236

HERITAGE COLLEGE
Rte. 3, Box 3540, Toppenish 98948-9527. Private (Roman Catholic) liberal arts and teachers. 1986 (NASC). Sem. plan. Degrees: A,B,M. Pres. Sister Kathleen Ross, S.N.J.M.
Enroll.: 331
(509) 865-2244

HIGHLINE COMMUNITY COLLEGE
Midway 98032-0424. Public (district) junior. 1965/1983 (NASC). Qtr. plan. Degrees: A. *Prof. Accred.:* Dental Assisting, Medical Assistant, Nursing (A), Respiratory Therapy. Pres. Shirley B. Gordon.
Enroll.: 7,272
(206) 878-3710

ITT/PETERSON SCHOOL OF BUSINESS—TECHNICAL DIVISION
130 Nickerson St., Seattle 98109. Private. 1977/1983 (NATTS). Courses of varying lengths. Diplomas. Dir. Dennis E. Griffin.

Enroll.: 396 (*f.t.* 220 m., 160 w.)
(206) 285-2600

INTERNATIONAL AIR ACADEMY
2901 E. Mill Plain Blvd., Vancouver 98661. Private technical. 1983 (NATTS). Courses of varying lengths. Certificates. Pres. Arch Miller.
(206) 695-2500

EXTENSION
2326 Millpark Dr., St. Louis, MO 63043. Dir. Leo J. Appelbaum.
(314) 429-7860

KINMAN BUSINESS UNIVERSITY
N. 214 Wall St., Spokane 99201. Private. 1953/1980 (AICS). Courses of varying lengths. Diplomas. *Prof. Accred.:* Dental Assisting. Dir. Carol L. A. Menck.
Enroll.: 1,112 (*f.t.* 99 m., 1,013 w.)
(509) 838-3521

BRANCH CAMPUS
1721 Hewill, 6th Fl., Everett 98201. Dir. Melissa Chrysler.
(206) 258-6787

BRANCH CAMPUS
230 Grant Rd., Wenatchee 98801. Dir. Marcia Henkle.
(509) 884-1587

KNAPP COLLEGE OF BUSINESS
1001 North J St., Tacoma 98403. Private. 1956/1984 (AICS). Courses of varying lengths. Certificates. Pres. Michael G. Lockwood.
Enroll.: 1,851 (*f.t.* 833 m., 1,018 w.)
(206) 572-3933

BRANCH CAMPUS
8 Auburn Way, Auburn 98002. Dir. Ed Tarry.
(206) 833-4560

LAKE WASHINGTON VOCATIONAL TECHNICAL INSTITUTE
11605 132nd Ave., N.E., Kirkland 98034. Public (district). 1981 (NASC). Sem. plan. Certificates. Dir. Donald W. Fowler.
Enroll.: FTE 1,610
(206) 828-3311

LONGVIEW BUSINESS COLLEGE
1260 Commerce, Longview 98632. Private. 1973/1985 (AICS). Courses of varying lengths. Certificates, diplomas. Dir. Mary Mizrahi.
Enroll.: 253 (*f.t.* 35 m., 218 w.)
(206) 425-4790

LOWER COLUMBIA COLLEGE
Longview 98632. Public (district) junior. 1948/1980 (NASC). Qtr. plan. Degrees: A. *Prof. Accred.:* Nursing (A), Practical Nursing. Pres. Vernon R. Pickett.
Enroll.: 3,829
(206) 577-2300

LUTHERAN BIBLE INSTITUTE OF SEATTLE
Providence Heights, Issaquah 98027. Private (Lutheran) professional. 1978 (AABC); 1982 (NASC). Qtr. plan. Degrees: A,B. Pres. C. Jack Eichhorst.
Enroll.: 160
(206) 392-0400

METROPOLITAN BUSINESS COLLEGE
1331 Third Ave., Seattle 98101. Private. 1976/1982 (AICS). Tri. plan. Certificates, diplomas. CEO Allen L. Vernon.
Enroll.: 266 (*f.t.* 77 m., 189 w.)
(206) 624-3773

BRANCH CAMPUS
3649 Frontage Rd., Gorst 98337. Dir. Dickie D. Stephens.
(206) 377-8978

BRANCH CAMPUS
2390 Pacific Ave., Long Beach, CA 90806. Dir. Jana Cloward.
(213) 426-6258

MILLER INSTITUTE
1050 Argonne Rd., Spokane 99212. Private. 1985 (NATTS). Courses of varying lengths. Diplomas. Dir. Rose M. Borchers.
(509) 926-2900

MODERN BUSINESS COLLEGE
3311 W. Clearview Ave., Suite 1201, Kennewick 99336. Private. 1973/1983 (AICS). Courses of varying lengths. Diplomas. Dir. Loretta McDaniel.
Enroll.: 219 (*f.t.* 21 m., 198 w.)
(509) 735-8515

NORTHWEST COLLEGE OF THE ASSEMBLIES OF GOD
P.O. Box 579, Kirkland 98033-0579. Private (Assemblies of God) liberal arts and training for church service. 1952/1982 (AABC); 1973/1978 (NASC). Qtr. plan. Degrees: A,B. Pres. Donald V. Hurst.
Enroll.: 671
(206) 822-8266

OLYMPIC COLLEGE
Bremerton 98310-1699. Public (district) junior. 1948/1981 (NASC). Qtr. plan. Degrees: A. Pres. Henry M. Milander.

Enroll.: 5,655
(206) 478-4551

PACIFIC LUTHERAN UNIVERSITY
Tacoma 98447-0003. Private (American Lutheran). 1936/1979 (NASC). 4-1-4. plan. Degrees: B,M. *Prof. Accred.:* Accounting (Type A), Business (B,M), Music, Nursing (B), Social Work (B), Teacher Education (*e,s,p*). Pres. William O. Rieke.
Enroll.: 3,758
(206) 535-7125

PENINSULA COLLEGE
Port Angeles 98362. Public (district) junior. 1965/1977 (NASC). Qtr. plan. Degrees: A. Pres. Paul G. Cornaby.
Enroll.: 2,793
(206) 452-9277

PERRY TECHNICAL INSTITUTE
P.O. Box 9457, Yakima 98909. Private. 1969/1980 (NATTS). Courses of varying lengths. Certificates. Dir. Fred J. Iraola.
Enroll.: 325 (*f.t.* 300 m., 25 w.)
(509) 453-0374

PIERCE COLLEGE
9401 Farwest Dr., Tacoma 98498. Public (district) junior. 1972/1977 (NASC). Qtr. plan. Degrees: A. *Prof. Accred.:* Dental Hygiene. Pres. Brent Knight.
Enroll.: 8,142
(206) 964-6500

PUGET SOUND CHRISTIAN COLLEGE
410 Fourth Ave. N., Edmonds 98020-8686. Private (Christian Churches) professional. 1979 (AABC). Sem. plan. Degrees: B. Pres. Glen Basey.
Enroll.: 104
(206) 775-8686

PUGET SOUND INSTITUTE OF TECHNOLOGY
1116 Summit, Seattle 98101-2884. Private. 1982 (ABHES). Tri. plan. Diplomas. *Prof. Accred.:* Medical Assisting. Pres. Walter C. Greenly.
Enroll.: 87 (*f.t.* 23 m., 64 w.)
(206) 323-1810

EXTENSION
555 108th Ave., N.E., Bellevue 98004.
(206) 451-8534

EXTENSION
Center Plaza, 2016 S. 320th St., Federal Way 98003.

RENTON VOCATIONAL-TECHNICAL INSTITUTE
3000 fourth St., N.E., Renton 98056. Public (district). 1978/1983 (NASC). Sem. plan. Certificates. Dir. Robert C. Roberts.
Enroll.: 26,700
(206) 235-2352

ST. MARTIN'S COLLEGE
Lacy 98503. Private (Roman Catholic) liberal arts. 1933/1982 (NASC). Sem. plan. Degrees: B,M. *Prof. Accred.:* Engineering (civil). Pres. David R. Spangler.
Enroll.: 875
(206) 438-4307

SEATTLE COMMUNITY COLLEGE DISTRICT
Central Office, P.O. Box C-19105, Seattle 98119. Public (state). Chanc. Donald Phelps.
(206) 587-3876

NORTH SEATTLE COMMUNITY COLLEGE
Seattle 98103. Public (district) junior. 1973/1978 (NASC). Qtr. plan. Degrees: A. *Prof. Accred.:* Medical Assisting. Pres. Barbara R. Daum.
Enroll.: 6,546
(206) 634-4444

SEATTLE CENTRAL COMMUNITY COLLEGE
1701 Broadway, Seattle 98122. Public (district) junior. 1970/1985 (NASC). Qtr. plan. Degrees: A. *Prof. Accred. :* Dental Assisting, Dental Laboratory Technology, Respiratory Therapy. Pres. Ernest A. Martinez.
Enroll.: 7,839
(306) 587-4144

SOUTH SEATTLE COMMUNITY COLLEGE
6000 16th St., S.W., Seattle 98106. Public (district) junior. 1975/1980 (NASC). Qtr. plan. Degrees: A. Pres. Jerry M. Brockey.
Enroll.: 4,612
(206) 764-5300

SEATTLE OPPORTUNITIES INDUSTRIALIZATION CENTER
315 22nd Ave. S., Seattle 98144. Private technical. 1978 (NATTS). Courses of varying lengths. Certificates. Exec. Dir. James Williams.
Enroll.: 1,802 (*f.t.* 1,117 m., 685 w.)
(206) 223-2858

SEATTLE PACIFIC UNIVERSITY
3307 Third Ave. W., Seattle 98119. Private (Free Methodist) liberal arts. 1933/1978 (NASC). Qtr. plan. Degrees: B,M. *Prof. Accred.:* Music, Nursing (B), Rehabilitation

Counseling, Teacher Education (*e,s,p*). Pres. David C. LeShana.
Enroll.: 2,975
(206) 281-2111

SEATTLE UNIVERSITY
Seattle 98122. Private (Roman Catholic). 1935/1979 (NASC). Qtr. plan. Degrees: B,M,D. *Prof. Accred.:* Business (B,M), Diagnostic Medical Sonography, Engineering (civil, electrical, mechancial), Medical Record Administration, Nuclear Medicine Technology, Nursing (B), Teacher Education (*e,s,p*). Pres. Rev. William J. Sullivan, S.J.
Enroll.: 4,406
(206) 626-6868

SHORELINE COMMUNITY COLLEGE
Seattle 98133. Public (district) junior. 1966/1982 (NASC). Qtr. plan. Degrees: A. *Prof. Accred.:* Dental Hygiene, Medical Record Technology, Nursing (A). Pres. Ronald E. Bell.
Enroll.: 5,337
(206) 546-4551

SKAGIT BUSINESS COLLEGE
821 Cleveland, Mount Vernon 98273. Private. 1976/1982 (AICS). Courses of varying lengths. Certificates. Pres. Karen Sather.
Enroll.: 129 (*f.t.* 16 m., 113 w.)
(206) 336-3119

SKAGIT VALLEY COLLEGE
Mount Vernon 98273. Public (district) junior. 1948/1979 (NASC). Qtr. plan. Degrees: A, certificates. *Prof. Accred.:* Practical Nursing, Respiratory Therapy Technology. Pres. James M. Ford.
Enroll.: 4,374
(206) 428-1150

SOUTH PUGET SOUND COMMUNITY COLLEGE
Olympia 98502. Public (district) 2-year technical. 1975/1980 (NASC). Qtr. plan. Degrees: A. *Prof. Accred.:* Dental Assisting. Pres. Kenneth J. Minnaert.
Enroll.: 3,730
(206) 754-7711

*SPOKANE COMMUNITY COLLEGE
Spokane 99207-5399. Public (district) junior. 1967/1983 (NASC). Qtr. plan. Degrees: A. *Prof. Accred.:* Dental Assisting, Medical Record Technology, Optometric Technology. Pres. Donald Bressler.
Enroll.: 4,531 (*f.t.* (509) 536-7042

*Member Washington State Community College District 17

*SPOKANE FALLS COMMUNITY COLLEGE
Spokane 99204-5288. Public (district) junior. 1967/1983 (NASC). Qtr. plan. Degrees: A. *Prof. Accred.:* Interior Design, Medical Record Technology, Respiratory Therapy. Pres. Phyllis Everest.
Enroll.: 5,221
(509) 459-3535

SPOKANE TECHNICAL INSTITUTE
E. 5634 Commerce, Spokane 99212. Private. 1975/1981 (NATTS). Courses of varying lengths. Certificates, diplomas. Pres. William L. Bieber.
Enroll.: 108 (*f.t.* 98 m., 10 w.)
(509) 535-7771

TACOMA COMMUNITY COLLEGE
Tacoma 98465. Public (district) junior. 1967/1984 (NASC). Qtr. plan. Degrees: A. *Prof. Accred.:* Medical Record Technology, Nursing (A), Radiography, Respiratory Therapy, Respiratory Therapy Technology. Pres. Carleton M. Opgaard.
Enroll.: 4,668
(206) 756-5050

UNIVERSITY OF PUGET SOUND
Tacoma 98416. Private (United Methodist). 1923/1979 (NASC). 4-1-4 plan. Degrees: B,P,M. *Prof. Accred.:* Law, Music, Occupational Therapy, Physical Therapy, Teacher Education (*e,s,p*). Pres. Philip M. Phibbs.
Enroll.: 4,134
(206) 756-3201

UNIVERSITY OF WASHINGTON
Seattle 98195. Public (state). 1918/1983 (NASC). Qtr. plan. Degrees: B,P,M,D. *Prof. Accred.:* Accounting (Type A), Architecture (M), Art, Assistant to the Primary Care Physician, Business (B,M), Cytotechnology, Dentistry, Engineering (aeronautics and astronautics, ceramic, chemical, civil, electrical, mechanical, metallurgical), Forestry, Health Services Administration, Journalism, Landscape Architecture (B), Law, Librarianship, Medical Technology, Medicine, Music, Nursing (B,M), Occupational Therapy, Pharmacy, Physical Therapy, Psychology, Public Health, Social Work (B,M), Speech Pathology and Audiology, Teacher Education (*e,s,p*). Pres. William P. Gerberding.
Enroll.: 34,771
(206) 543-6616

*Member Washington State Community College District 17

WALLA WALLA COLLEGE
College Place 99324. Private (Seventh-day Adventist) liberal arts. 1932/1982 (NASC). Qtr. plan. Degrees: A,B,M. *Prof. Accred.:* Engineering, Music, Nursing (B), Social Work (B). Pres. H. Jack Bergman.
Enroll.: 1,480
(509) 527-2122

WALLA WALLA COMMUNITY COLLEGE
Walla Walla 99362. Public (district) junior. 1969/1985 (NASC). Qtr. plan. Degrees: A. *Prof. Accred.:* Nursing (A). Pres. Steven L. Van Ausdle.
Enroll.: 4,584
(509) 527-4222

WASHINGTON STATE COMMUNITY COLLEGE DISTRICT 17
Central Office, N. 2000 Greene St., Spokane 99207. Public (state). Dist. C.E.O.,C. Nelson Grote.
(509) 456-2936

WASHINGTON STATE UNIVERSITY
Pullman 99164-1046. Public. 1918/1980 (NASC). Sem. plan. Degrees: B,P,M,D. *Prof. Accred.:* Accounting (Type A), Architecture (B), Business (B,M), Dietetics, Engineering (agricultural, chemical, civil, electrical, geological, mechanical, physical metallurgy), Forestry, Interior Design, Landscape Architecture (B), Music, Pharmacy, Psychology, Speech Pathology, Teacher Education (*e,s,p*). Pres. Samuel Smith.
Enroll.: 16,139
(509) 335-3564

WENATCHEE VALLEY COLLEGE
Wenatchee 98801. Public (district) junior. 1948/1980 (NASC). Qtr. plan. Degrees: A. *Prof. Accred.:* Medical Laboratory Technology, Medical Technology. Pres. James R. Davis.
Enroll.: 2,350
(509) 662-1651

WESTERN WASHINGTON UNIVERSITY
Bellingham 98225. Public liberal arts and teachers. 1921/1978 (NASC). Qtr. plan. Degrees: B,M. *Prof. Accred.:* Music, Nursing (B), Speech Pathology and Audiology, Teacher Education (*e,s,p*). Pres. G. Robert Ross.
Enroll.: 9,200
(206) 676-3111

WHATCOM COMMUNITY COLLEGE
Bellingham 98226. Public (district) junior. 1976/1981 (NASC). Qtr. plan. Degrees: A. Pres. Harold G. Heiner.
Enroll.: 2,102
(206) 676-2170

WHITMAN COLLEGE
Walla Walla 99362. Private liberal arts. 1918/1978 (NASC). Sem. plan. Degrees: B. *Prof. Accred.:* Music. Pres. Robert A. Skotheim.
Enroll.: 1,186
(509) 527-5132

WHITWORTH COLLEGE
Spokane 99251-0002. Private (United Presbyterian) liberal arts. 1933/1978 (NASC). 4-1-4 plan. Degrees: B, M. *Prof. Accred.:* Medical Record Administration, Music, Teacher Education (*e,s*). Pres. Robert H. Mounce.
Enroll.: 1,803
(509) 466-1000

YAKIMA BUSINESS COLLEGE
112 Pierce Ave., Yakima 98902. Private. 1972/1983 (AICS). Courses of varying lengths. Diplomas. Dir. Judi Gilmore.
Enroll.: 426 (*f.t.* 46 m., 380 w.)
(509) 248-4806

YAKIMA VALLEY COMMUNITY COLLEGE
Yakima 98907. Public (district) junior. 1948/1981 (NASC). Qtr. plan. Degrees: A, certificates. *Prof. Accred.:* Dental Hygiene, Nursing (A), Practical Nursing, Radiography. Acting Pres. James E. Brooks.
Enroll.: 4,583
(509) 575-2612

WEST VIRGINIA

ALDERSON-BROADDUS COLLEGE
Philippi 26416 Private (American Baptist) liberal arts. 1959/1983 (NCA). Qtr. plan. Degrees: B. *Prof. Accred.:* Assistant to the Primary Care Physician, Nursing (B), Social Work (B). Pres. W. Christian Sizemore.
Enroll.: FTE 712
(304) 457-1700

APPALACHIAN BIBLE COLLEGE
Bradley 25818. Private (Independent) professional. 1967/1977 (AABC). Sem. plan. Degrees: B. Pres. Daniel Anderson.
Enroll.: 180
(304) 877-6428

BECKLEY COLLEGE
Beckley 25801. Private junior. 1981/1985 (NCA). Sem. plan. Degrees: A. Pres. John W. Saunders.
Enroll.: FTE 1,119
(304) 253-7351

BETHANY COLLEGE
Bethany 26032. Private (Disciples of Christ) liberal arts. 1926/1979 (NCA). Sem. plan. Degrees: B. *Prof. Accred.:* Social Work (B), Teacher Education (*e,s*). Pres. Todd H. Bullard.
Enroll.: FTE 769
(304) 829-7111

B. M. SPURR SCHOOL OF PRACTICAL NURSING
800 Wheeling Ave., Glen Dale 26038. Public vocational. 1953. 1-year course. Certificates. *Prof. Accred.:* Practical Nursing. Asst. Dir. Dorothy McCulley.
(304) 845-3211

*BLUEFIELD STATE COLLEGE
Bluefield 24701. Public liberal arts and teachers. 1951/1982 (NCA). Sem. plan. Degrees: A,B. *Prof. Accred.:* Engineering Technology (architectural, civil, electrical, mechanical, mining), Nursing (A), Radiography, Respiratory Therapy. Pres. Jerold O. Dugger.
Enroll.: 1,637
(304) 325-7102

BOONE COUNTY CAREER CENTER
P.O. Box 50 B, Danville 25053. Private. 1980 (ABHES). Courses of varying lengths. Certificates. *Prof. Accred.:* Medical Laboratory Technology. Dir. Jimmy H. Dolan.
(304) 369-4585

*Under Supervision West Virginia Board of Regents

CENTURY COLLEGE
536 Fifth Ave., Huntington 25701. Private business. 1969/1982 (AICS). Qtr. plan. Degrees: A, diplomas. Pres. Philip G. Niebergall.
Enroll.: 1,566 (*f.t.* 395 m., 1,171 w.)
(304) 529-2451

BRANCH CAMPUS
1050 N. Beach St., Daytona Beach, FL 32014. Dir. Lawrence Del Vecchio.
(904) 253-8888

BRANCH CAMPUS
2192 N. U.S 1, Fort Pierce, FL 33450. Dir. Lawrence Del Vecchio.
(305) 461-3586

BRANCH CAMPUS
2301 W. Sample Rd., Bldg. 4, 6-B, Pompano Beach, FL 33067. Dir. Linda K. Zeitzer.
(305) 975-8922

BRANCH CAMPUS
2520 N. Monroe St., Tallahassee, FL 32301. Dir. Philip G. Niebergall.
(904) 386-7035

CHARLESTON BARBER COLLEGE
1030 Quarrier St., Charleston 25301. Private. 1979 (NATTS). Courses of varying lengths. Diplomas. Pres. Raymond R. Lindquist.
Enroll.: 18 (*f.t.* 10 m., 8 w.)
(304) 346-1366

*CONCORD COLLEGE
Athens 24712. Public (state) liberal arts and teachers. 1931/1978 (NCA). Sem. plan. Degrees: B. *Prof. Accred.:* Social Work (B), Teacher Education (*e,s*). Pres. Jerry L. Beasley.
Enroll.: FTE 2,032
(304) 384-3115

DAVIS AND ELKINS COLLEGE
Elkins 26241. Private (Presbyterian, U.S. and United Presbyterian) liberal arts. 1946/1980 (NCA). 4-1-4 plan. Degrees: B. Pres. Dorothy I. MacConkey.
Enroll.: FTE 855
(304) 636-1900

*Under Supervision West Virginia Board of Regents

*FAIRMONT STATE COLLEGE
Fairmont 26554. Public liberal arts and professional. 1928/1982 (NCA). Sem. plan. Degrees: A,B. *Prof. Accred.:* Medical Laboratory Technology, Medical Record Technology, Nursing (A), Teacher Education (*e,s*). Pres. Wendell G. Hardway.
Enroll.: FTE 4,037
(304) 367-4151

*GLENVILLE STATE COLLEGE
Glenville 26351. Public liberal arts and teachers. 1949/1982 (NCA). Sem. plan. Degrees: A,B. *Prof. Accred.:* Teacher Education (*e,s*). Pres. William K. Simmons.
Enroll.: FTE 1,365
(304) 462-7361

HUNTINGTON BARBER COLLEGE
338 Washington Ave., Huntington 25701. Private. 1976/1980 (NATTS). Courses of varying lengths. Diplomas. Dir. Bernadine Pinson.
Enroll.: 25 (*f.t.* 13 m., 12 w.)
(304) 523-6311

HUNTINGTON JUNIOR COLLEGE OF BUSINESS
900 Fifth Ave., Huntington 25701. Private. 1969/1982 (AICS). Qtr. plan. Degrees: A, certificates, diplomas. Dir. Carolyn Smith.
Enroll.: 910 (*f.t.* 257 m., 653 w.)
(304) 697-7550

*MARSHALL UNIVERSITY
Huntington 25701. Public (state). 1928/1981 (NCA). Sem. plan. Degrees: A,B,P,M. *Prof. Accred.:* Engineering (civil), Journalism, Medical Laboratory Technology (A), Medicine, Music, Nursing (A,B), Teacher Education (*e,s,p*). Pres. Dale F. Nitzschke.
Enroll.: FTE 8,092
(304) 696-2300

MOUNTAIN STATE COLLEGE
Spring at 16th St., Parkersburg 26101. Private business. 1977/1979 (AICS). Qtr. plan. Certificates, diplomas. Dir. Judith Sutton.
Enroll.: 325 (*f.t.* 40 m., 285 w.)
(304) 485-5487

NATIONAL EDUCATION CENTER/NATIONAL INSTITUTE OF TECHNOLOGY CAMPUS
5514 Big Tyler Rd., Cross Lanes 25313. Private 2-year. 1977 (NATTS). Sem. plan. Degrees: A, diplomas. Dir. Teresa Arrington.
Enroll.: 400 (*f.t.* 320 m., 80 w.)
(304) 776-6290

*Under Supervision West Virginia Board of Regents

NORTHEASTERN BUSINESS COLLEGE
18 Tenth St., Wheeling 26003. Private. 1972/1984 (AICS). Courses of varying lengths. Certificates, diplomas. Dir. Richard L. West.
Enroll.: 474 (*f.t.* 75 m., 399 w.)
(304) 232-5790

BRANCH CAMPUS
1145 Dunbar Ave., Dunbar 25064. Dir. Edna Houchins.
(304) 766-6178

OHIO VALLEY COLLEGE
Parkersburg 26101. Private junior. 1978 (NCA). Sem. plan. Degrees: A,B, certificates. Pres. Keith Stotts.
Enroll.: FTE 234
(304) 485-7384

PARKERSBURG COMMUNITY COLLEGE
Parkersburg 26101. Public (state) junior. 1971/1980 (NCA). Degrees: A. *Prof. Accred.:* Medical Laboratory Technology (A), Nursing (A). Pres. Eldon L. Miller.
Enroll.: 1,678
(304) 424-8200

*POTOMAC STATE COLLEGE OF WEST VIRGINIA UNIVERSITY
Keyser 26726. Public (state) junior. 1926/1984 (NCA). Sem. plan. Degrees: A. Exec. Dean James McBee, Jr.
Enroll.: 729
(304) 788-3011

SALEM COLLEGE
Salem 26426. Private liberal arts. 1963/1985 (NCA). Sem. plan. Degrees: A,B,M. *Prof. Accred.:* Social Work (B) Pres. Ronald Ohl.
Enroll.: 763
(304) 782-5389

*SHEPHERD COLLEGE
Shepherdstown 25443. Public (state) liberal arts and teachers. 1950/1982 (NCA). Sem. plan. Degrees: A,B. *Prof. Accred.:* Nursing (A), Social Work (B), Teacher Education (*e,s*). Pres. James A. Butcher.
Enroll.: 2,650
(304) 876-2511

SOUTHERN WEST VIRGINIA COMMUNITY COLLEGE
Logan 25601. Public (state) junior. 1971/1984 (NCA). Accreditation includes campus at Williamson. Sem. plan. Degrees: A. Pres. Gregory D. Adkins.

*Under Supervision West Virginia Board of Regents

Enroll.: 1,488
(304) 752-5900

UNIVERSITY OF CHARLESTON
Charleston 25304. Private liberal arts. 1958/1985 (NCA). Sem. plan. Degrees: A ,B,M. *Prof. Accred.:* Nursing (A), Radiography, Respiratory Therapy. Pres. Richard D. Breslin.
Enroll.: 989
(304) 357-4713

WEBSTER COLLEGE
412 Fairmont Ave., Fairmont 26554. Private business. 1968/1980 (AICS). Qtr. plan. Degrees: A, diplomas. Exec. Dir. Milton A. Metheny.
Enroll.: 325 (*f.t.* 61 m., 264 w.)
(304) 363-8824

BRANCH CAMPUS
529 13th St., W., Bradenton, FL 33505. Dir. Michael Callen.
(813) 748-6172

BRANCH CAMPUS
2002 N. W. 13th St., Gainesville, Fl. 32601. Dir. Stephen J. Alan.
(904) 375-8014

BRANCH CAMPUS
5623 U.S. Hwy. 19. New Port Richey, FL 33552. Dir. Thomas Crouse.
(813) 849-4993

BRANCH CAMPUS
1530 S.W. Third Ave., Ocala, FL 32674. Dir. Stephen J. Callen.
(904) 629-1941

*WEST LIBERTY STATE COLLEGE
West Liberty 26074. Public liberal arts and professional. 1942/1978 (NCA). Sem. plan. Degrees: A,B. *Prof. Accred.:* Dental Hygiene, Medical Technology, Music, Teacher Education (*e,s*). Pres. Clyde D. Campbell.
Enroll.: FTE 2,468
(304) 336-8000

WEST VIRGINIA BOARD OF REGENTS
950 Kanawha Blvd., E., Charleston 25301. Public (state) Chanc. ———.
(304) 348-2101

WEST VIRGINIA BUSINESS COLLEGE
215 W. Main St., Clarksburg 26301. Private. 1966/1984 (AICS). Qtr. plan. Degrees: A, certificates, diplomas. Dir. Eugenia L. Boord.

*Under Supervision West Virginia Board of Regents

Enroll.: 414 (*f.t.* 94 m., 320 w.)
(304) 624-7695

BRANCH CAMPUS
360 Broadway, Paintsville, KY 41240. Dir. John E. Bland.
(606) 789-2099

WEST VIRGINIA CAREER COLLEGE
1000 Virginia St., E., Charleston 25301. Private. 1971/1983 (AICS). Qtr. plan. Degrees: A, diplomas. Vice Pres. Thomas A. Crouse.
Enroll.: 655 (*f.t.* 173 m., 482 w.)
(304) 345-2820

WEST VIRGINIA CAREER COLLEGE
148 Willey St., Morgantown 26505. Private. 1953/1982 (AICS). Qtr. plan. Degrees: A, diplomas. Assoc. Dir. Patricia A. Callen.
Enroll.: 471 (*f.t.* 84 m., 387 w.)
(304) 296-8282

*WEST VIRGINIA COLLEGE OF GRADUATE STUDIES
Institute 25112. Public (state) liberal arts and professional. 1972/1981 (NCA). Sem. plan. Degrees: B,M. *Prof. Accred.:* Teacher Education (*e,s,p*). Pres. James W. Rowley.
Enroll.: FTE 896
(304) 768-9711

*WEST VIRGINIA INSTITUTE OF TECHNOLOGY
Montgomery 25136. Public (state) liberal arts and professional. 1956/1985 (NCA). Sem. plan. Degrees: A,B,M. *Prof. Accred.:* Dental Hygiene, Engineering (chemical, civil, electrical, mechanical), Engineering Technology (civil, drafting and design, electrical, electronic, fluid power, mechanical, mining), Teacher Education (*s*). Pres. Leonard C. Nelson.
Enroll.: FTE 2,900
(304) 442-3146

WEST VIRGINIA NORTHERN COMMUNITY COLLEGE
Wheeling 26003. Public (state) junior. 1972/1986 (NCA). Accreditation includes Wierton campus. Degrees: A. *Prof. Accred.:* Medical Laboratory Technology (A), Nursing (A), Respiratory Therapy, Surgical Technology. Pres. Barbara Guthrie-Morse.
Enroll.: FTE 1,473
(304) 233-5900

*Under Supervision West Virginia Board of Regents

*WEST VIRGINIA SCHOOL OF OSTEOPATHIC MEDICINE
400 N. Lee St., Lewisburg 24901. Public (state) professional. 1976. Sem. plan. Degrees: P. *Prof. Accred.:* Osteopathy. Pres. Clyde B. Jensen.
Enroll.: 232 (*f.t.* 183 m., 49 w.)
(304) 645-6270

*WEST VIRGINIA STATE COLLEGE
Institute 25112. Public liberal arts and professional. 1927/1978 (NCA). Sem. plan. Degrees: A,B. *Prof. Accred.:* Nuclear Medicine Technology, Social Work (B), Teacher Education (*e,s*). Pres. Thomas W. Cole, Jr.
Enroll.: FTE 2,913
(304) 766-3000

*WEST VIRGINIA UNIVERSITY
Morgantown 26506. Public (state). 1926/1984 (NCA). Sem. plan. Degrees: A,B,P,M,D. *Prof. Accred.:* Art, Business (B,M), Dental Hygiene, Dentistry, Engineering (aerospace, chemical, civil, electrical, industrial, mechanical, mining), Forestry, Journalism, Landscape Architecture (B), Law, Medical Technology, Medicine, Music, Nursing (B,M), Pharmacy, Physical Therapy, Psychology, Rehabilitation Counseling, Social Work (B,M), Speech Pathology and Audiology, Teacher Education (*e,s,p*). Pres. Neil S. Bucklew.
Enroll.: FTE 16,461
(304) 293-0111

*Under Supervision West Virginia Board of Regents

WEST VIRGINIA WESLEYAN COLLEGE
Buckhannon 26201. Private (United Methodist) liberal arts. 1927/1985 (NCA). 4-1-4 plan. Degrees: B,M. *Prof. Accred.:* Music, Nursing. Pres. ———.
Enroll.: FTE 1,352
(304) 473-8181

WHEELING BARBER COLLEGE
1107 Main St., Wheeling 26003. Private. 1978 (NATTS). Courses of varying lengths. Certificates. Mgr. Harry Adams.
Enroll.: 71 (*f.t.* 34 m., 68 w.)
(304) 232-0100

WHEELING COLLEGE
Wheeling 26003. Private (Roman Catholic) liberal arts. 1962/1979 (NCA). Sem. plan. Degrees: B,M. *Prof. Accred.:* Nuclear Medicine Technology, Nursing (B), Respiratory Therapy. Pres. Fr. Thomas S. Acker.
Enroll.: FTE 847
(304) 243-2233

WISCONSIN

ACME INSTITUTE OF TECHNOLOGY
5101 S. 116th St., Hales Corners 53130. Private. 1967/1984 (NATTS). Courses of varying lengths. Diplomas. Pres. William W. Warren.
Enroll.: 61 (*f.t.* 60 m., 1 w.)
(414) 529-0705

ACME INSTITUTE OF TECHNOLOGY
1122 Washington St., Manitowoc 54220. Private. 1967/1985 (NATTS). Courses of varying lengths. Diplomas. Pres. William W. Warren.
Enroll.: 189 (*f.t.* 188 m., 1 w.)
(414) 682-6144

ALVERNO COLLEGE
3401 S. 39th St., Milwaukee 53215. Private (Roman Catholic) liberal arts primarily for women. 1951/1977 (NCA). 4-1-4 plan. Degrees: A,B. *Prof. Accred.:* Music, Nuclear Medicine Technology, Nursing (B), Teacher Education (*e,s*). Pres. Sister Joel Read.
Enroll.: FTE 1,257
(414) 647-3999

BELOIT COLLEGE
Beloit 53511. Private liberal arts. 1913/1977 (NCA). Sem. plan. Degrees: B,M. Pres. Roger H. Hull.
Enroll.: FTE 1,004
(608) 365-3391

BLACKHAWK TECHNICAL INSTITUTE
Janesville 53545. Public (district) 2-year; accreditation includes Beloit Campus. 1978/1986 (NCA). Sem. plan. Degrees: A. *Prof. Accred.:* Dental Assisting, Nursing (A). Dist. Dir. James C. Catania.
Enroll.: FTE 1,650
(608) 756-4121

CARDINAL STRITCH COLLEGE
6801 N. Yates Rd., Milwaukee 53217. Private (Roman Catholic) liberal arts. 1953/1984 (NCA). Sem. plan. Degrees: A,B,M. *Prof. Accred.:* Nursing (A), Teacher Education (*e,s*). Pres. Sister M. Camille Kliebhan, O.S.F.
Enroll.: FTE 1,433
(414) 352-5400

CARROLL COLLEGE
Waukesha 53186. Private (United Presbyterian) liberal arts. 1913/1985 (NCA). 4-1-4 plan. Degrees: B. *Prof. Accred.:* Social Work (B). Pres. Robert V. Cramer.
Enroll.: FTE 1,365
(414) 547-1211

CARTHAGE COLLEGE
Kenosha 53141. Private (Lutheran in America) liberal arts. 1916/1985 (NCA). 4-1-4 plan. Degrees: B,M. *Prof. Accred.:* Music, Social Work (B). Pres. Erno Dahl, Jr.
Enroll.: FTE 1,092
(414) 551-8500

CONCORDIA COLLEGE WISCONSIN
12800 N. Lakeshore Rd., 9W, Mequon 53092. Private (Lutheran-Missouri Synod). 1964/1985 (NCA). 4-1-4 plan. Degrees: A,B. Pres. R. John Buuck.
Enroll.: FTE 751
(414) 243-5700

DIESEL TRUCK DRIVER TRAINING SCHOOL
Hwy. 151 and Elder La., R.R. #2, Sun Prairie 53590. Private. 1973/1978 (NATTS). Courses of varying lengths. Certificates, diplomas. Pres. Jerry Klabacka.
Enroll.: 60 (*f.t.* 47 m., 3 w.)
(608) 837-7800

DISTRICT ONE TECHNICAL INSTITUTE
Eau Claire 54701. Public 2-year technical. 1973/1978 (NCA). Sem. plan. Degrees: A. *Prof. Accred.:* Histologic Technology, Medical Laboratory Technology (A), Medical Record Technology, Radiography. Dist. Dir. Norbert Wurtzel.
Enroll.: FTE 1,420
(715) 836-3911

EDGEWOOD COLLEGE
855 Woodrow St., Madison 53711. Private (Roman Catholic) liberal arts. 1958/1985 (NCA). 4-1-4 plan. Degrees: B,M. *Prof. Accred.:* Nursing (B), Teacher Education (*e,s*). Pres. Sister Mary Ewens.
Enroll.: FTE 600
(608) 257-4861

FOX VALLEY TECHNICAL INSTITUTE
Appleton 54913. Public (district) 2-year technical. 1974/1986 (NCA). Sem. plan. Degrees: A. *Prof. Accred.:* Dental Assisting, Nursing (A), Respiratory Therapy Technology. Dist. Dir. Stanley Spanbauer.
Enroll.: FTE 2,800
(414) 735-5731

GATEWAY TECHNICAL INSTITUTE
Kenosha 53141. Public (district) technical. 1970/1980 (NCA). Accreditation includes Ke-

nosha and Elkhorn Campuses; Gateway Technical Institute, Racine. Sem. plan. Degrees: A. *Prof. Accred.:* Dental Assisting, Medical Assisting, Nursing (A). Dist. Dir. and Pres. John R. Birkholz.
Enroll.: FTE 2,398
(414) 656-6900

THE INSTITUTE OF PAPER CHEMISTRY
Appleton 54911. Institute offering graduate programs in pulp and paper science. 1970/1980 (NCA). Degrees: M,D. Pres. Richard A. Matula.
Enroll.: FTE 102
(414) 734-9251

LAKELAND COLLEGE
Sheboygan 53081. Private (United Church of Christ) liberal arts. 1961/1982 (NCA). 4-1-4 plan. Degrees: B. Pres. Richard E. Hill.
Enroll.: 746
(414) 565-1201

LAKESHORE TECHNICAL INSTITUTE
Cleveland 53015. Public (district) 2-year. 1977/1982 (NCA). Sem. plan. Degrees: A, certificates. *Prof. Accred.:* Dental Assisting, Medical Assisting, Nursing (A), Practical Nursing. District Dir. Frederick J. Nierode.
Enroll.: FTE 753
(414) 458-4183

LAWRENCE UNIVERSITY
Appleton 54912. Private liberal arts college. 1913/1979 (NCA). Qtr. plan. Degrees: B. *Prof. Accred.:* Music. Pres. Richard Warch.
Enroll.: FTE 1,026
(414) 739-3681

MBTI BUSINESS TRAINING INSTITUTE
820 N. Plankinton Ave., Milwaukee 53203. Private. 1969/1981 (AICS). Courses of varying lengths. Diplomas. Pres. J. Michael Bartels.
Enroll.: 1,356 (*f.t.* 567 m., 789 w.)
(414) 272-2192

MADISON AREA TECHNICAL COLLEGE
Madison 53703. Public (district) junior. 1969/1973 (NCA). Sem. plan. Degrees: A, certificates. *Prof. Accred.:* Dental Assisting, Dental Hygiene, Medical Assistant, Medical Laboratory Technology, Nursing (A), Practical Nursing, Respiratory Therapy. District Dir. Norman P. Mitby.
Enroll.: FTE 5,914
(608) 266-5050

MADISON BUSINESS COLLEGE
1110 Spring Harbor Dr., Madison 53705. Private junior. 1953/1984 (AICS). Tri. plan. Degrees: A. Pres. Stuart E. Sears.
Enroll.: 525 (*f.t.* 139 m., 386 w.)
(608) 238-4266

MARIAN COLLEGE OF FOND DU LAC
Fond du Lac 54935. Private (Roman Catholic) liberal arts. 1960/1984 (NCA). Sem. plan. Degrees: B. *Prof. Accred.:* Nursing (B), Teacher Education (*e,s*). Pres. Leo Krzywkowski.
Enroll.: FTE 347
(414) 921-3900

MARQUETTE UNIVERSITY
615 N. 11th St., Milwaukee 53233. Private (Roman Catholic). 1922/1983 (NCA). Sem. plan. Degrees: B,P,M,D. *Prof. Accred.:* Business (B,M), Dental Hygiene, Dentistry, Engineering (biomedical, civil, electrical, mechanical), Law, Nursing (B,M), Physical Therapy, Social Work (B), Speech Pathology, Teacher Education (*e,s*). Pres. Rev. John P. Raynor, S.J.
Enroll.: FTE 10,030
(414) 224-7223

MEDICAL COLLEGE OF WISCONSIN
Box 26509, Milwaukee 53226. Private graduate only. 1922/1979 (NCA). Sem. plan. Degrees: P,M,D. *Prof. Accred.:* Medicine, Radiation Therapy. Pres. Edward J. Lennon.
Enroll.: FTE 931
(414) 257-8225

MID-STATE VOCATIONAL, TECHNICAL, AND ADULT EDUCATION DISTRICT
Wisconsin Rapids 54494. Public (district) 2-year. Accreditation includes centers at Marshfield and Stevens Point. 1979/1984 (NCA). Sem. plan. Degrees: A, certificates. *Prof. Accred.:* Medical Assisting, Practical Nursing, Surgical Technology. District Dir. M. H. Schneeberg.
Enroll.: FTE 1,620
(715) 423-5650

MILWAUKEE AREA TECHNICAL COLLEGE
1015 N. 6th St., Milwaukee 53203. Public (city) junior: accreditation includes North Campus, Mequon; South Campus, Oak Creek; West Campus, West Allis. 1959/1985 (NCA). Sem. plan. Degrees : A, certificates. *Prof. Accred.:* Dental Assisting, Dental Hygiene, Dental Laboratory Technology, Medical Assisting, Nursing (A), Practical Nursing, Ra-

diography, Respiratory Therapy, Surgical Technology. District Dir. Rus F. Slicker.
Enroll.: FTE 11,946
(414) 278 -6320

MILWAUKEE INSTITUTE OF ART AND DESIGN, INC.
207 N. Milwaukee St., Milwaukee 53202. Private professional. 1981. Degrees: B, diplomas. *Prof. Accred.:* Art. Dir. Jack White.
Enroll.: 405 (*f.t.* 154 m., 179 w.)
(414) 276-7889

MILWAUKEE SCHOOL OF ENGINEERING
1025 N. Milwaukee St., P.O. Box 644, Milwaukee 53201. Private professional. 1971/1984 (NCA). Qtr. plan. Degrees: B,M. *Prof. Accred.:* Engineering (electrical, mechanical), Engineering Technology (air conditioning, architectural and building construction, biomedical engineering, computer, electrical, electrial construction, electrical power, electronic communications, fluid power, industrial, internal combustion engines, manufacturing, mechanical, mechanical design), Perfusion. Pres. Robert R. Spitzer.
Enroll.: FTE 2,153
(414) 277-7300

MORAINE PARK TECHNICAL INSTITUTE
Fond du Lac 54935. Public (district) 2-year technological. Accreditation includes centers at Beaver Dam and West Bend. 1975/1985 (NCA). Sem. plan. Degrees: A, certificates. *Prof. Accred.:* Medical Record Technology, Nursing (A), Practical Nursing. District Dir. John J. Shanahan.
Enroll.: FTE 2,103
(414) 922-8611

MOUNT MARY COLLEGE
2900 N. Menomonee River Pkwy., Milwaukee 53222. Private (Roman Catholic) liberal arts primarily for women. 1926/1973 (NCA). Sem. plan. Degrees: B. *Prof. Accred.:* Dietetics, Occupational Therapy, Social Work (B), Teacher Education (*e,s*). Pres. Sister Ellen Lorenz.
Enroll.: FTE 857
(414) 258-4810

MOUNT SENARIO COLLEGE
Ladysmith 54848. Private liberal arts. 1975/1985 (NCA). Sem. plan. Degrees: B. Pres. Robert E. Powless.
Enroll.: FTE 546
(715) 532-5511

NASHOTAH HOUSE
Nashotah 53058. Private (Episcopal) professional; graduate only. Sem. plan. Degrees: P,M. *Prof. Accred.:* Theology (1954/1979, ATS). Dean Jack C. Knight.
Enroll.: 73
(414) 646-3371

NICOLET COLLEGE AND TECHNICAL INSTITUTE
Rhinelander 54501. Public (district) junior. 1975/1983 (NCA). Sem. plan. Degrees: A. District Dir. Jack T. Lundy.
Enroll.: FTE 948
(715) 369-4410

NORTH CENTRAL TECHNICAL INSTITUTE
Wausau 54401. Public (district) 2-year technical. 1970/1978 (NCA). Sem. plan. Degrees: A. *Prof. Accred.:* Dental Hygiene, Medical Technology. District Dir. Donald L. Hagen.
Enroll.: FTE 2,475
(715) 675-3331

NORTHEAST WISCONSIN TECHNICAL INSTITUTE
Green Bay 54303. Public (district) 2-year technological. Accreditation covers centers at Marinette and Sturgeon Bay. 1970/1981 (NCA). Sem. plan. Degrees: A. *Prof. Accred.:* Dental Assisting, Dental Hygiene, Medical Assisting, Nursing (A), Respiratory Therapy Technology, Surgical Technology. District Dir. Gerald Prindiville.
Enroll.: FTE 1,849
(414) 497-3111

NORTHLAND COLLEGE
Ashland 54806. Private (United Church of Christ) liberal arts. 1957/1981 (NCA). 4-1-4 plan. Degrees: B. Pres. Malcolm McLean.
Enroll.: 508
(715) 682-4531

NORTHWESTERN COLLEGE
Watertown 53094. Private (Evangelical Lutheran Synod) liberal arts. 1981/1984 (NCA). Sem. plan. Degrees: B. Pres. Carleton Toppe.
Enroll.: FTE 210 m.
(414) 261-4352

PATRICIA STEVENS CAREER COLLEGE AND FINISHING SCHOOL
161 W. Wisconsin Ave., Milwaukee 53203. Private. 1969/1981 (AICS). Courses of varying lengths. Diplomas. Pres. Milton Parlow.
Enroll.: *f.t.* 377
(414) 272-4736

Ripon College
Ripon 54971. Private liberal arts. 1913/1980 (NCA). Sem. plan. Degrees: B. Pres. William R. Stott, Jr.
Enroll.: FTE 847
(414) 748-8118

Sacred Heart School of Theology
7335 S. Lovers Lane Rd., Hales Corners 53130. Private (Roman Catholic) professional; graduate only. Sem. plan. Degrees: P. *Prof. Accred.:* Theology (1981/1983, ATS). Rector John A. Kasparek, S.C.J.
Enroll.: 106
(414) 425-8300

Saint Francis Seminary, School of Pastoral Ministry
3257 S. Lake Dr., Milwaukee 53207. Private (Roman Catholic) professional; graduate only. 1963/1980 (NCA). Sem. plan. Degrees: P,M. *Prof. Accred.:* Theology (1976/1980, ATS). Rector Rev. Daniel J. Pakenham.
Enroll.: FTE 62
(414) 744-1730

St. Norbert College
De Pere 54115. Private (Roman Catholic) liberal arts. 1934/1982 (NCA). Sem. plan. Degrees: B. Pres. Thomas A. Manion.
Enroll.: 1,705
(414) 337-3165

Silver Lake College
Manitowoc 54220. Private (Roman Catholic) liberal arts. 1959/1978 (NCA). Sem. plan. Degrees: B. *Prof. Accred.:* Music, Teacher Education (*e,s*). Pres. Sister Anne Kennedy.
Enroll.: FTE 317
(414) 684-6691

Southwest Wisconsin Vocational-Technical Institute
Fennimore 53809. Public (district) 2-year. 1976/1981 (NCA). Sem. plan. Degrees: A, certificates. *Prof. Accred.:* Practical Nursing. Dist. Dir. Ronald H. Anderson.
Enroll.: FTE 897
(608) 822-3262

Stratton College
1300 N. Jackson St., Milwaukee 53202. Private junior. 1966/1981 (AICS). Qtr. plan. Degrees: A, diplomas. Pres. Maritza Samoorian.
Enroll.: 983 (*f.t.* 232 m., 751 w.)
(414) 276-5200

Technical Institute of Milwaukee
804 N. Milwaukee St., Milwaukee 53302. Private. 1985 (NATTS). Courses of varying lengths. Diplomas. Pres. Elmer F. Haas.
(414) 223-0223

Trans American School of Broadcasting
108 Scott St., Wassau 54401. Private. 1972/1977 (NATTS). Sem. plan. Diplomas. Pres. Raymond J. Szmanda.
Enroll.: 100 (*f.t.* 60 m., 40 w.)
(715) 842-1000

University of Wisconsin
Central Office, Madison 53706. Public (state). Sem. plan (qtr. plan at River Falls and Superior; mod. plan at Oshkosh). Pres. Kenneth A. Shaw.
(608) 262-2321

University of Wisconsin—Eau Claire
Eau Claire 54701. Public liberal arts and teachers. 1950/1980 (NCA). Degrees: B,M. *Prof. Accred.:* Business (B), Journalism, Music, Nursing (B,M), Social Work (B), Speech Pathology. Acting Chanc. Larry Schnack.
Enroll.: FTE 10,121
(715) 836-2326

University of Wisconsin—Green Bay
Green Bay 54302. Public liberal arts and teachers. 1972/1984 (NCA). 4-1-4 plan. Degrees: B,M. *Prof. Accred.:* Music. Chanc. Edward W. Weidner.
Enroll.: FTE 3,607
(414) 465-2207

University of Wisconsin—La Crosse
La Crosse 54601. Public liberal arts and teachers. 1928/1986 (NCA). Degrees: B,M. *Prof. Accred.:* Business (B), Music, Physical Therapy, Social Work (B), Teacher Education (*e,s,p*). Chanc. Noel J. Richards.
Enroll.: FTE 8,826
(608) 785-8000

University of Wisconsin—Madison
Madison 53706. 1913/1979 (NCA). Degrees: A,B,P,M,D. *Prof. Accred.:*
Assistant to the Primary Care Physician, Business (B,M), Cytotechnology, Dietetics, Engineering (agricultural, chemical, civil and environmental, electrical, engineering mechanics, industrial, mechanical, metallurgical, mining, nuclear, surveying-option in civil and environmental), Forestry, Health Services Administration, Interior Design, Jour-

nalism, Landscape Architecture (B), Law, Librarianship, Medical Technology, Medicine, Music, Nursing (B,M), Occupational Therapy, Pharmacy, Physical Therapy, Psychology, Radiation Therapy, Radiography, Rehabilitation Counseling, Social Work (B,M), Speech Pathology and Audiology, Veterinary Medicine. Chanc. Irving Shain.
Enroll.: FTE 39,639
(608) 262-9946

University of Wisconsin—Milwaukee
Milwaukee 53201. 1969/1985 (NCA). Degrees: B,M,D. *Prof. Accred.:* Architecture (M), Business (B,M), Engineering (civil, electrical, industrial, materials, mechanical), Librarianship, Medical Record Administration, Music, Nursing (M), Occupational Therapy, Psychology, Rehabilitation Counseling, Social Work (B,M), Speech Pathology, Teacher Education (*p*). Chanc. Clifford V. Smith.
Enroll.: FTE 18,621
(414) 963-4331

University of Wisconsin—Oshkosh
Oshkosh 54901. Public liberal arts and teachers. 1915/1977 (NCA). Degrees: B,M. *Prof. Accred.:* Business (B,M), Journalism, Music, Nursing (B,M), Social Work (B), Teacher Education (*e,s,p*). Chanc. Edward M. Penson.
Enroll.: FTE 9,875
(414) 424-0200

University of Wisconsin—Parkside
Kenosha 53141. Public liberal arts and teachers. 1972/1983 (NCA). Degrees: B,M. Chanc. Sheila Kaplan.
Enroll.: 3,474
(414) 553-2345

University of Wisconsin—Platteville
Platteville 53818. Public liberal arts and teachers. 1918/1977 (NCA). Degrees: B,M. *Prof. Accred.:* Engineering (civil, mining). Chanc. William W. Chmurny.
Enroll.: FTE 5,279
(608) 342-1234

University of Wisconsin—River Falls
River Falls 54022. Public liberal arts and teachers. 1935/1978 (NCA). Degrees: B,M. *Prof. Accred.:* Journalism, Teacher Education (*e,s,p*). Chanc. Gary Thibodeau.
Enroll.: FTE 4,954
(715) 425-3911

University of Wisconsin—Stevens Point
Stevens Point 54481. Public liberal arts and teachers college. 1916/1978 (NCA). Degrees: B,M. *Prof. Accred.:* Forestry, Home Economics, Music, Speech Pathology and Audiology. Chanc. Philip R. Marshall.
Enroll.: FTE 8,482
(715) 346-2123

University of Wisconsin—Stout
Menomonie 54751. Public liberal arts and teachers. 1928/1976 (NCA). Degrees: B,M. *Prof. Accred.:* Teacher Education (*e,s,p*). Chanc. Robert Sterling Swanson.
Enroll.: FTE 7,465
(715) 232-2441

University of Wisconsin—Superior
Superior 54880. Public liberal arts and teachers college. 1916/1983 (NCA). Degrees: B,M. *Prof. Accred.:* Music, Social Work (B). Chanc. Karl W. Meyer.
Enroll.: FTE 1,823
(715) 394-8101

University of Wisconsin—Whitewater
Whitewater 53190. Public liberal arts and teachers college. 1915/1976 (NCA). Degrees: B,M. *Prof. Accred.:* Business (B,M), Music, Social Work (B), Speech Pathology, Teacher Education (*e,s,p*). Chanc. James R. Connor.
Enroll.: FTE 9,783
(414) 472-1918

University of Wisconsin Center System
Madison 53706. Public (state). 1913/1983 (NCA). Accreditation includes the following 2-year lower division centers at Baraboo, Barron County, Fond du Lac, Fox Valley, Manitowoc, Marathon, Marinette, Marshfield, Medford, Richland, Rock County, Sheboygan, Washington, and Waukesha. Executive Dean Norman Ratner.
Enroll.: FTE 7,062
(608) 262-1783

Viterbo College
La Crosse 54601. Private (Roman Catholic) liberal arts. 1954/1979 (NCA). Sem. plan. Degrees: B. *Prof. Accred.:* Dietetics, Medical Record Administration, Music, Nursing (B), Teacher Education (*e,s*). Pres. Robert E. Gibbons.
Enroll.: 816
(608) 784-0040

WAUKESHA COUNTY TECHNICAL INSTITUTE
Pewaukee 53072. Public (district) 2-year technological. 1975/1980 (NCA). Sem. plan. Degrees: A, certificates. *Prof. Accred.:* Medical Assisting, Nursing (A), Practical Nursing, Surgical Technology. Dist. Dir. Richard T. Anderson.
Enroll.: FTE 1,488
(414) 548-5201

WESTERN WISCONSIN TECHNICAL INSTITUTE
La Crosse 54601. Public (district) 2-year technical. 1972/1982 (NCA). Qtr. plan. Degrees: A, certificates. *Prof. Accred.:* Dental Assisting, EEG Technology, Medical Assisting, Medical Laboratory Technology (A), Medical Record Technology, Nursing (A), Practical Nursing, Radiography, Respiratory Therapy Technology, Surgical Technology. District Dir. Charles G. Richardson.
Enroll.: FTE 3,375
(608) 785-9101

WISCONSIN INDIANHEAD TECHNICAL INSTITUTE
Shell Lake 54871. Public (district) 2-year. 1979/1984 (NCA). Sem. plan. Degrees: A. *Prof. Accred.:* Nursing (A). District Dir. David Hildebrand.
Enroll.: FTE 2,231
(715) 468-2815

WISCONSIN SCHOOL OF ELECTRONICS
1601 N. Sherman Ave., Madison 53704. Private. 1970/1980 (NATTS). Qtr. plan. Degrees: A, certificates. Dir. Thomas A. Byrnes.
Enroll.: 317 (*f.t.* 303 m., 14 w.)
(608) 249-6611

WYOMING

CASPER COLLEGE
Casper 82601. Public (district) junior. 1960/1979 (NCA). Sem. plan. Degrees: A, certificates. *Prof. Accred.:* Music, Nursing (A), Practical Nursing, Radiography. Pres. Lloyd H. Loftin.
Enroll.: FTE 2,568
(307) 268-2548

CENTRAL WYOMING COLLEGE
Riverton 82501. Public (district) junior. 1976/1981 (NCA). Sem. plan. Degrees: A. Pres. Edward L. Donovan.
Enroll.: FTE 900
(307) 856-9291

CERTIFIED WELDING & TRADE SCHOOL
7030 Salt Creek Rt., Box 7, Casper 82601. Private. 1980 (NATTS). Courses of varying lengths. Certificates, diplomas. Pres./Dir. Ernest E. Ashley.
Enroll.: 41 (*f.t.* 25 m., 2 w.)
(307) 266-2066

CHEYENNE AERO TECH
3801 Morrie Ave., Cheyenne 82001. 1983 (NATTS). Courses of varying lengths. Certificates. Pres. Owen Johnson.
(307) 632-1090

EASTERN WYOMING COLLEGE
Torrington 82240. Public (district) junior. 1976/1981 (NCA). Sem. plan. Degrees: A. Pres. Guido Smith.
Enroll.: FTE 859
(307) 532-7111

LARAMIE COUNTY COMMUNITY COLLEGE
Cheyenne 82001. Public (state) junior. 1975/1980 (NCA). Sem. plan. Degrees: A. *Prof. Accred.:* Medical Technology, Practical Nursing, Radiography. Pres. Timothy G. Davies.
Enroll.: FTE 2,252
(307) 634-5853

NORTHWEST COMMUNITY COLLEGE
Powell 82435. Public (district) junior. 1964/1984 (NCA). Sem. plan. Degrees: A. *Prof. Accred.:* Medical Laboratory Technology (A), Practical Nursing. Pres. SinClair Orendorff.
Enroll.: 1,297
(307) 754-6200

SHERIDAN COLLEGE
Sheridan 82801. Public (district) junior. Accreditation includes Gillette Campus. 1968/1978 (NCA). Sem. plan. Degrees: A. *Prof. Accred.:* Dental Hygiene, Practical Nursing. Pres. Gordon A. Ward.
Enroll.: FTE 1,264
(307) 672-6446

UNIVERSITY OF WYOMING
Laramie 82071. Public (state). 1915/1980 (NCA). Sem. plan. Degrees: B,P,M,D. *Prof. Accred.:* Business (B,M), Engineering (agricultural, chemical, civil, electrical, mechanical, petroleum), Law, Medical Technology, Music, Nursing (B,M), Pharmacy, Psychology, Social Work (B), Speech Pathology and Audiology, Teacher Education (*e,s,p*). Pres. Donald L. Veal.
Enroll.: FTE 10,840
(307) 766-4121

WESTERN WYOMING COLLEGE
Rock Springs 82901. Public (district) junior. 1976/1981 (NCA). Sem. plan. Degrees: A. *Prof. Accred.:* Medical Laboratory Technology (A), Radiography, Respiratory Therapy Technology. Pres. Terrance R. Brown.
Enroll.: 1,231
(307) 382-2121

WYOMING TECHNICAL INSTITUTE
Box 906, Laramie 82070. Private. 1969/1979 (NATTS). Courses of varying lengths. Diplomas. Pres. Tim Schutz.
Enroll.: 398 (*f.t.* 395 m., 3 w.)
(307) 742-3776

INSTITUTIONS OUTSIDE THE UNITED STATES

AUSTRALIA

PHILLIP INSTITUTE OF TECHNOLOGY, SCHOOL OF CHIROPRACTIC
Plenty Rd., Bundoora, Victoria 3083. Private professional. 1985. Sem. plan. Degrees: P. *Prof. Accred.:* Chiropractic Education. Head Andries M. Kleynhaus.
(03) 468-2200

BAHAMAS

BAHAMAS HOTEL TRAINING COLLEGE
P.O. Box N-4896, College Ave., Oakes Field, Nassau. Public technical. 1977/1982 (SACS-COEI). Courses of varying lengths. Certificates. Dir. Lincoln H. Marshall.
Enroll.: FTE 101
(809) 323-5804

BRANCH CAMPUS
P.O. Box F-1679, Freeport, Grand Bahamas.
(809) 323-5804

BELGIUM

INTERNATIONAL CORRESPONDENCE INSTITUTE
Chaussee de Waterloo 45, 1640 Rhode-St. Genese (Brussels). Private home study. 1977 (NHSC). Courses of varying lengths. Degrees: A,B. Pres. George M. Flattery.
(02) 358-59-46

CANADA

ACADIA DIVINITY COLLEGE
Wolfville, Nova Scotia B0P 1X0. Private (Baptist) professional; graduate only. Sem. plan. Degrees: P,M. *Prof. Accred.:* Theology (1984/1985, ATS). Principal Andrew MacRae.
Enroll.: 115
(902) 542-2285

ATLANTIC SCHOOL OF THEOLOGY
640 Francklyn St., Halifax, N.S., B3H 3B5. Private (Interdenominational) professional; graduate only. Sem. plan. Degrees: P,M. *Prof. Accred.:* Theology (1976/1983, ATS). Interim Pres. C. D. Edward Aitken.
Enroll.: 153
(902) 423-6801

BRIERCREST BIBLE COLLEGE
Caronport, Sask. S0H 0S0. Private (Interdenominational) professional. 1976 (AABC). Sem. plan. Degrees: A,B. Pres. Henry H. Budd.
Enroll: 773
(306) 756-2321

CANADIAN BIBLE COLLEGE
4400 Fourth Ave., Regina, Sask. S4T 0H8. Private (Christian and Missionary Alliance) professional. 1961/1980 (AABC). Sem. plan. Degrees: B. Pres. Rexford A. Boda.
Enroll.: 408
(306) 545-1515

EMMANUEL BIBLE COLLEGE
100 Fergus Ave., Kitchener, Ont. N2A 2H2. Private (Missionary Church) professional. 1982 (AABC). Sem. plan. Degrees: A,B. Pres. E. A. Lageer.
Enroll.: 220
(519) 742-3572

EMMANUEL COLLEGE OF VICTORIA UNIVERSITY
75 Queen's Park Crescent, E., Toronto, Ont., M5S 1K7. Private (United Church of Canada) professional; graduate only. Sem. plan. Degrees: P,M,D. *Prof. Accred.:* Theology (1938/1980, ATS). Principal C. Douglas Jay.
Enroll.: 210
(416) 978-3811

FACULTÉ DE MÉDECINE VETERINAIRE, UNIVERSITÉ DE MONTRÉL
St. Hyacinthe, Que. J2S 7C6. Public professional. 1948/1982 Sem. plan. Degrees: P. *Prof. Accred.:* Veterinary Medicine. Dean Raymond S. Roy.
Enroll.: 277
(514) 773-8521

Granton Institute of Technology
263 Adelaide St., W., Toronto, Ont. M5H 1Y3. Private home study. 1985 (NHSC). Pres. Christopher Hope.
(416) 977-3929

Huron College Faculty of Theology
London, Ont., N6G 1H3. Private (Anglican) professional; graduate only. Sem. plan. Degrees: P,M. *Prof. Accred.:* Theology (1981/1985, ATS). Acting Principal F. W. Burd.
Enroll.: 66
(519) 438-7224

Knox College
59 St. George St., Toronto, Ont., M5S 2E6. Private (Presbyterian) professional; graduate only. Sem. plan. Degrees: P,M,D. *Prof. Accred.:* Theology (1948/1980, ATS). Principal Donald J. M. Corbett..
Enroll.: 145
(416) 978-4500

Lutheran Theological Seminary
114 Seminary Crescent, Saskatoon, Sask. S7N 0X3. Private (Lutheran) professional; graduate only. Sem. plan. Degrees: P,M. *Prof. Accred.:* Theology (1976, ATS). Pres. Roger Nostbakken.
Enroll.: 123
(306) 343-8204

McGill University
3520 University St., Montreal, Quebec, H3A 2A7. Private. Sem. plan. Degrees: P,M,D. *Prof. Accred.:* Physical Therapy, Psychology, Theology (1952/1979, ATS).
(514) 392-4828

McMaster Divinity College
Hamilton, Ont., L8S 4K1. Private (Baptist) professional; graduate only. Sem. plan. Degrees: P,M. *Prof. Accred.:* Theology (1954/1977, ATS). Principal Melvyn R. Hillmer.
Enroll.: 122
(416) 525-9140

Ner Israel Yeshiva College of Toronto
625 Finch Ave., W., Willowdale, Ont., M2R 1N8. Private professional. 1980. Degrees: B of Talmudic Law. *Prof. Accred.:* Rabbinical and Talmudic Education. Pres. Rabbi N. Friedler.
(416) 636-2360

North American Baptist College
11525 23rd Ave., Edmonton, Alta., T6J 4T3. Private (Baptist) professional. 1969/1979 (AABC). Sem. plan. Degrees: A,B. Pres. J. Walter Coltz.
Enroll.: 166
(403) 437-1960

Ontario Bible College
25 Ballyconnor Ct., Willowdale, Ont., M2M 4B3. Private (Interdenominational) professional. 1966/1978 (AABC). Sem. plan. Degrees: B. Pres. William McRea.
Enroll.: 373
(416) 226-6380

Ontario Veterinary College University of Guelph
Guelph, Ont. N1G 2W1. Public professional. 1925/1982. Sem. plan. Degrees: P. *Prof. Accred.:* Veterinary Medicine. Dean D. C. Maplesden.
Enroll.: 475
(519) 824-4120

Queen's Theological College
Kingston, Ont., K7L 3N6. Private (United Churches of Canada) professional; graduate only. Sem. plan. Degrees: P,M. *Prof. Accred.:* Theology (1986, ATS). Principal Clifford G. Hospital.
Enroll.: 100
(613) 547-2788

Regent College
2130 Westbrook Mall, Vancouver, B.C., V6T 1W6. Private (Transdenominational) professional; graduate only. Sem. plan. Degrees: P,M. *Prof. Accred.:* Theology (1985, ATS). Principal Carl E. Armerding.
Enroll.: 382
(604) 224-3245

Regis College
15 St. Mary St., Toronto, Ont., M4Y 2R5. Private (Roman Catholic) professional; graduate only. Sem. plan. Degrees: P,M,D. *Prof. Accred.:* Theology (1970/1980, ATS). Pres. Jacques Monet.
Enroll.: 140
(416) 922-5474

St. Augustine's Seminary of Toronto
2661 Kingston Rd., Scarborough, Ont., M1M 1M3. Private (Roman Catholic) professional; graduate only. Sem. plan. Degrees: P,M. *Prof. Accred.:* Theology (1980/1985, ATS). Pres. Peter Somerville.
Enroll.: 61
(416) 261-7207

St. Peter's Seminary
1040 Waterloo St., London, Ont., N6A 3Y1. Private (Roman Catholic) professional; graduate only. Sem. plan. Degrees: P,M. *Prof. Accred.:* Theology (1985, ATS). Rector Rev. Patrick Fuerth.
Enroll.: 86
(519) 432-1824

Toronto School of Theology
47 Queen's Park Crescent, E., Toronto, Ont. M5S 2C3. Private (Interdenominatio nal) professional; graduate only; consortium. Sem. plan. Degrees: P,M,D. *Prof. Accred.:* Theology (1980/1985, ATS). Dir. Iain G. Nicol.
(416) 978-4039

Trinity College Faculty of Divinity
Hoskin Ave., Toronto, Ont., M5S 1H8. Private (Anglican) professional; graduate only. Sem. plan. Degrees: P,M,D. *Prof. Accred.:* Theology (1938/1980, ATS). Dean Peter Slater.
Enroll.: 132
(416) 978-3609

Universite de Montreal
Department d'Administration de la Sante, 2375 Chemin de la Cote Ste. Catherine, Montreal, P.Q., H3T 1A8. Private. Sem. plan. Degrees: M. *Prof. Accred.:* Health Services Administration. Dir. Roger Gosselin.
(514) 343-6175
School of Optometry, Case Postale 6128, Succursale "A", Montreal, P.Q. H3c 3J7. Sem. plan. Degrees: P. *Prof. Accred.:* Optometry. Dir. David Forthomme.
(514) 343-6948

University of Alberta
Department of Health Services Administration, 13-103 Clinical Sciences Bldg., Edmonton, Alta., T6G 2G3. Public. Sem. plan. Degrees: M. *Prof. Accred.:* Health Services Administration. Chairman Clarke Hazlett.
(403) 432-6407

University of British Columbia
Department of Health Services and Epidemiology, James Mather Bldg., 5804 Fairview Crescent, Vancouver, B.C., V6T 1W5. Public. Sem. plan. Degrees: B. *Prof. Accred.:* Health Services Administration. Dir. T. W. Anderson.
(604) 228-2375

University of Guelph
Guelph, Ont., N1G 2W1. Public. Sem. plan. Degrees: B,M. *Prof. Accred.:* Landscape Architecture (B,M).
(519) 824-4120

University of Manitoba
Winnipeg, Man., L8S 4L8. Public. Sem. plan. Degrees: B. *Prof. Accred.:* Psychology.

University of Ottawa
Ottawa, Ont., K1N 9A9. Public. Sem. plan. Degrees: B,M. *Prof. Accred.:* Health Services Administration, Psychology.
(613) 564-4999

University of St. Michael's College Faculty of Theology
81 St. Mary St., Toronto, Ont., M5S 1J4. Private (Roman Catholic) professional; graduate only. Sem. plan. Degrees: P,M,D. *Prof. Accred.:* Theology (1972/1980, ATS). Dean Anthony Ceresko.
Enroll.: 324
(416) 926-1300

University of Toronto
Department of Health Administration, 12 Queens Park Crescent W., McMurrich Bldg., 2nd Fl., Toronto, Ont., M5S 1A8. Public. Sem. plan. Degrees: M. *Prof. Accred.:* Health Services Administration. Dir. Peggy Leatt.
(416) 978-2047

University of Waterloo
University Ave., Waterloo, Ont., N2L 3G1. Private liberal arts. Sem. plan. Degrees: B,M. *Prof. Accred.:* Psychology.
(519) 885-1211

Vancouver School of Theology
6000 Iona Dr., Vancouver, B.C. V6T 1L4. Private (Interdenominational) professional; graduate only. Sem. plan. Degrees: P,M. *Prof. Accred.:* Theology (1976/1981, ATS). Principal Arthur Van Seters.
Enroll.: 113
(604) 228-9031

Waterloo Lutheran Seminary
75 University Ave., W., Waterloo, Ont., N2L 3C5. Private (E. Canada Synod of LCA) professional; graduate only. Sem. plan. Degrees: P,M. *Prof. Accred.:* Theology (1982, ATS). Principal Richard C. Crossman.
Enroll.: 127
(519) 884-1970

Western College of Veterinary Medicine University of Saskatchewan
Saskatoon, Sask. S7N 0W0. Public professional. 1967/1983. Qtr. plan. Degrees: P. *Prof. Accred.:* Veterinary Medicine. Dean Gavin F. Hamilton.
Enroll.: 273
(306) 343-2634

Western Pentecostal Bible College
Box 1000, Clayburn, B. C., V0X 1E0. Private (Pentecostal) professional. 1980 (AABC). Sem. plan. Degrees: A,B. Pres. L. Thomas Holdcroft.
Enroll.: 221
(604) 853-7491

Winnipeg Bible College
Otterburne, Man., R0A 1C0. Private (Interdenominational) professional. 1973/1983 (AABC). Sem. plan. Degrees: A,B. Pres. William R. Eichhorst.
Enroll.: 309
(204) 284-2923

Wycliffe College
5 Hoskin Ave., Toronto, Ont., M5S 1H7. Private (Anglican) professional; graduate only. Sem. plan. Degrees: P,M,D. *Prof. Accred.:* Theology (1978, ATS). Principal Peter Mason.P,M,D. *Prof. Accred.:* Theology (1978, ATS). Principal Peter Mason.
Enroll.: 111
(416) 979-2870

EGYPT

American University in Cairo
Cairo, Egypt. U.S. address: 866 United Nations Plaza, New York, NY 10017. Private. 1982 (MSA/CHE). Sem. plan. Degrees: B,M. Pres. Richard F. Pedersen.
Enroll.: 2,782 (*f.t.* 920 m., 1,377 w.)
(212) 421-6320

ENGLAND

Richmond College
Queens Rd., Richmond, Surrey TW10 6JP, and One St. Albans Grove, Kensington, London W8 5PN. Private liberal arts. 1981/1986 (MSA/CHE). Sem. plan. Degrees: A,B. Pres. William Petrek.
Enroll.: 828 (*f.t.* 336 m., 483 w.)
01-940-9762 USA: (203) 869-9090

Schiller International University
Royal Waterloo House, 51-55 Waterloo Rd., SE1 8TX London. Private. 1983 (AICS). Sem. plan. Degrees: A,B,M. Dir. Richard Taylor.
(01) 928- 1372

Branch Campus
Wickman Court, Kent BR4 9HH (Greater London Area). Dir. May Rugg.
(01) 777-8069

FRANCE

American College in Paris
31 Avenue Bosquet, 75007 Paris. Private liberal arts. 1973/1983 (MSA/CHE). Sem. plan. Degrees: A,B. Pres. Daniel J. Socolow.
Enroll.: 969 (*f.t.* 244 m., 525 w.)
44.55.91.73

Schiller International University
103 rue de Lille, 75007 Paris. Private. 1983 (AICS). Sem. plan. Degrees: A,B,M. Dir. David Holmberg.
551-2893

Schiller International University
Chateau Portales, 161 rue Melanie, 67000 Strausbourg. Private. 1983 (AICS). Sem. plan. Degrees: A,B,M. Acting Dir. Walter Leibrecht.
(08) 8.3.10.07 or 8.31.07.65

GREECE

Deree College
c/o The American College of Greece, Box 60018 GR-153, 10 Agnia Paraskevi Attikis. U.S. office: 79 Milk St., Suite 710, Boston, MA 02109. Private liberal arts. 1981 (NEASC-CIHE). 4-1-4 plan. Degrees: A,B. Pres. John S. Bailey.
Enroll.: FTE 1,634
Greece: (301) 659-3250
United States: (617) 542-7872

MEXICO

INSTITUTO TECNOLOGICO Y DE ESTUDIOS SUPERIORES DE MONTERREY
Sucursal de Correos J, Monterrey, N.L. 64849. Private university. 1950/1978 (SACS-Comm. on Coll.). Degrees: B,M,D. Pres. Fernando Garcia Roel.
Enroll.: FTE 15,995
58-20-00

UNIVERSIDAD DE LAS AMERICAS (UNIVERSITY OF THE AMERICAS)
Apto Postal 100, Catarina Martir, Puebla 72820. Private university. 1959/1984 (SACS-Comm. on Coll.). Degrees: B,M. Pres. Fernando Macias-Rendon.
Enroll.: FTE 4,311
47-00-00

NIGERIA

NIGERIAN BAPTIST THEOLOGICAL SEMINARY
Ogbomoso. Private (Southern Baptist) professional; branch of Southern Baptist Theological Seminary, Louisville, KY. 1983 (SACS-Comm. on Coll.). Sem. plan. Degrees: P. Pres. Osaldolar Imasogie.
Enroll.: 162
71-0011

REPUBLIC OF PANAMA

PANAMA CANAL COLLEGE
DoDDS, Panama Region, APO Miami 34002 Public (federal) junior. 1941/1983 (MSA/CHE). Sem. plan. Degrees: A, (B). Dean Harold C. Brown.
Enroll.: 1,320 (*f.t.* 146 m., 165 w.)
507-52-3107

SPAIN

SCHILLER INTERNATIONAL UNIVERSITY
Calle de Rodriguez San Pedro, 10 Madrid 15. Private. 1983 (AICS). Sem. plan. Degrees: A,B,M. Dir. William O. Reiners.
446-2349

SWITZERLAND

AMERICAN COLLEGE OF SWITZERLAND
CH 1854 Leysin. U.S. office: 30 Colpitts Rd., P.O. Box 425, Weston, MA 02193. Private liberal arts and business administration. 1980/1986 (MSA/CHE). Sem. plan. Degrees: A,B. Pres. Daniel Queudot.
Enroll.: 326 (*f.t.* 140 m., 171 w.)
Switzerland: (025) 34-22-23 Telex 453227 AMCO-CH United States: (617) 891-4753

FRANKLIN COLLEGE
Via Ponte Tresa 29, 6924 Lugano-Sorengo. U.S. office: 866 United Nations Plaza, New York 10017 . Private liberal arts junior. 1975/1983 (MSA/CHE). Sem plan. Degrees: A. Pres. Theo. E. Brenner.
Enroll.: 169 (*f.t.* 59 m., 106 w.)
(41-91)55.01.01
NYC/USA (212) 832-7775

TRUST TERRITORY OF THE PACIFIC ISLANDS

COMMUNITY COLLEGE OF MICRONESIA
P.O. Box 159, Kolonia, Pohnpei, Eastern Caroline Islands, FSM 96941. Public junior. 1978/1982 (WASC-Jr.). Sem. plan. Degrees: A. Pres. Catalino L. Cantero.
Enroll.: 291
Overseas Ponape 480

MICRONESIAN OCCUPATIONAL COLLEGE
P.O. Box 9, Koror, Republic of Palau 96940. Public vocational. 1977/1982 (WASC-Jr.) Sem. plan. Degrees: A. Pres. Wilhelm R. Rengiil.
Enroll.: 411
Overseas Koror 471

NORTHERN MARIANAS COLLEGE
Box 1250, Saipan CM 96950. Public junior. 1985 (WASC-Jr.). Degrees: A. Pres. Agnes M. McPhetres.
Enroll.: 172
(670) 000-7542

WEST GERMANY

SCHILLER INTERNATIONAL UNIVERSITY
Friedrich-Ebert-Anlage #4, 6900 Heidelberg. Private senior. 1983 (AICS). Sem. plan. Degrees: A,B,M. Pres. Walter Leibrecht. *Enroll.*: 814 (*f.t.* 542 m., 272 w.) (Telex: 461435 SIU D) (06221) 12046 USA: (612) 871-6988

WEST INDIES

INTERNATIONAL COLLEGE OF THE CAYMAN ISLANDS
P.O. Box 136, Newlands, Grand Cayman. Private senior. 1979/1984 (AICS). Qtr. plan. Degrees: A,B,M, diplomas. Pres. J. Hugh Cummings. *Enroll.*: 265 (*f.t.* 25 m., 92 w.) (809) 947-2150

Major Changes in Four-Year Institutions

Alabama Christian College changed its name to Faulkner University fall 1985
Aurora College, IL changed its name to Aurora University, January 1985
Barrington College, RI, merged with Gordon College, MA, fall 1985
Cardinal Newman College, MO, closed January 1985
Clarkson College of Technology, NY, changed its name to Clarkson University spring 1984
Dallas Bible College, Dallas, TX, changed its name to Woodcrest College and moved to Lindale, TX, summer 1985
DeAndreis Seminary, IL, closed June 1984
Down State Medical Center, SUNY, changed its name to Health Science Center at Brooklyn February 1986
East Central Oklahomas State University changed its name to East Central University winter 1985
George Williams College, IL, closed 1986
Gulf Coast Bible College, TX, changed its name to Mid-America Bible College and moved to Oklahoma City, OK summer 1985
Hampton Institute, VA, changed its name to Hampton University fall 1984
Indiana Central University changed its name to University of Indianapolis May 1986
Mount Saint Alphonsus Seminary, NY, closed May 31, 1985
Philadelphia College of Art, PA, and Philadelphia College of the Performing Arts, PA, merged to form the Philadelphia Colleges of the Arts February 1986
Saint Mary's Dominican College, LA, closed August 1984
University of Albuquerque, NM, closed 1986
University of Santa Clara, CA, changed its name to Santa Clara University winter 1985
University of the State of New York Regents External Degree Program changed its name to University of the State of New York Regents College Degrees summer 1984
Urbana College, OH, changed its name to Urbana University fall 1984
Upstate Medical Center, SUNY, changed its name to Health Science Center at Syracuse February 1986
Yankton College, SD closed winter 1984

Major Changes in Two-Year Institutions

College of Marin and Indian Valley Colleges, CA, merged to form Marin Community College spring 1985
Freeman Junior College, SD, closed spring 1986
Gadsden State Technical College, AL, merged with Alabama State Technical College fall 1984
Golden Valley Lutheran College, MN, closed June 1985
Los Angeles Metropolitan College, CA, closed January 1984
Morristown College, TN, closed fall 1986
Morven Park International Equestrian Institute, VA, changed its name to The Westmoreland Davis Equestrian Institute at Morven Park fall 1984
Olympia Technical Community College, WA, changed its name to South Puget Sound Community College fall 1984
Saint Paul's College, MO, closed June 1986
South Oklahoma City Junior College changed its name to Oklahoma City Community College summer 1984

Candidates

Candidates for Accreditation

Candidate for Accreditation is a status of affiliation with a recognized accrediting commission which indicates that an institution has achieved initial recognition and is progressing toward, but does not assure, accreditation.

The Candidate for Accreditation classification is designed for postsecondary institutions which may or may not be fully operative. In either case the institution must provide evidence of sound planning, the resources to implement these plans, and appear to have the potential for attaining its goals within a reasonable time.

To be considered for Candidate for Accreditation status the applicant organization must be a postsecondary educational institution with the following characteristics.

1. Have a charter and/or formal authority from an appropriate governmental agency to award a certificate, diploma, or degree.
2. Have a governing board which includes representation reflecting the public interest.
3. Have employed a chief administrative officer.
4. Offer, or plan to offer, one or more educational programs of at least one academic year in length, or the equivalent at the postsecondary level, with clearly defined and published educational objectives as well as a clear statement of the means for achieving them.
5. Include general education at the postsecondary level as a prerequisite to or an essential element in its principal educational programs.
6. Have admission policies compatible with its stated objectives.
7. Have developed a preliminary survey or evidence of basic planning for the development of the institution.
8. Have established an adequate financial base of funding commitments and have available a summary of its latest audited financial statement.

ALABAMA

AMERICAN INSTITUTE OF PSYCHOTHERAPY
2611 Leeman Ferry Rd.,Huntsville 35801. Private professional. Cand. Dec. 1983 (SACS-Comm. on Coll.). Degrees: D. Pres. Robert A. Webb.
Enroll.: 30

INTERNATIONAL BIBLE COLLEGE
P.O. Box 1BC, Florence 35630. Private (Church of Christ) professional. Cand. 1984 (AABC). Degrees: A,B. Pres. Charles R. Coil.
Enroll.: 132

SELMA UNIVERSITY
Selma 36702. Private (Baptist) teachers. Cand. June 1985 (SACS-Comm. on Coll.). Degrees: A,B. Pres. Wilson Fallin.
Enroll.: 216

T. L. FAULKNER AREA VOCATIONAL CENTER
33 W. Elm, Pritchard 36610. Public (state). 1984 (SACS-COEI). Certificates. Dir. Richard D. Davis, Jr.

ALASKA

PRINCE WILLIAM SOUND COMMUNITY COLLEGE
Valdez 99686. Public junior; member of University of Alaska System. Cand. June 1984 (NASC). Sem. plan. Degrees: A. Pres. John Devens.
Enroll.: 574
(907) 835-2421

ARIZONA

AMERICAN INDIAN BIBLE COLLEGE
10020 N. Fifteenth Ave., Phoenix 85021. Private. Cand. June 1982 (Aug. 1984) (NCA). Degrees: A,B. Pres. Carl E. Collins.
Enroll.: FTE 96

FRANK LLOYD WRIGHT SCHOOL OF ARCHITECTURE, TALIESIN WEST
Scottdale 85261. Private. Cand. Aug. 1985 (NCA). Degrees: M. Managing Trustee Richard Carney.
Enroll.: FTE 28

Southwestern College
2625 E. Cactus Rd., Phoenix 85032. Private. Cand. Feb. 1986 (NCA). Degrees: A,B, diplomas. Pres. Wesley A. Olsen.
Enroll.: FTE 123

ARKANSAS

Arkansas Baptist College
1600 Bishop St., Little Rock 72202. Private (Baptist) liberal arts. Cand. June 1981 (June 1984) (Mar. 1986) (NCA). Degrees: B. Pres. W. Thomas Keaton.
Enroll.: 189

Capital City Junior College
7723 Asher St., P.O. Box 4818, Little Rock 72214. Private. Cand. Aug. 1985 (NCA). Degrees: A, diplomas. Pres. Kenneth Sullivan.
Enroll.: 430

Central Baptist College
Conway 72032. Private (Baptist) Cand. June 1985 (NCA). Degrees: A,B,M. Pres. James Ray Raines.
Enroll.: 185

Rich Mountain Community College
6001 Bush St., Mena 71953. Public. Cand. June 1984 (NCA). Degrees: A. Pres. Mary Louise Spencer.
Enroll.: FTE 224

CALIFORNIA

Academy of Art College
540 Powell St., San Francisco 94108. Proprietary. Cand. Feb. 1982 (June 1984) (WASC-Sr.). Degrees: B. *Prof. Accred.:* Art, Interior Design. Pres. Donald A. Haight.
Enroll.: FTE 1,345

American Baptist Seminary of the West
2515 Hillegass St., Berkeley 94704. Private (American Baptist Convention) Cand. Feb. 1986 (WASC-Sr.). Degrees: P,M,D. *Prof. Accred.:* Theology. Pres. Wesley H. Brown.
Enroll.: FTE 125

Condie Junior College
One West Campbell Ave., Campbell 95008. Private. Cand. Jan. 1986 (WASC-Jr.). Degrees: A. diplomas. Pres. Wayne P. Wilson.
Enroll.: FTE 197

Humphreys College
6650 Inglewood St., Stockton 95202. Private. Cand. June 1985 (WASC-Sr.). Degrees: A,B,P. certificates, diplomas. Pres. Robert G. Humphreys.
Enroll.: FTE 400

Irvine Valley College
5500 Irvine Center Dr., Irvine 92714. Public (district) junior. Cand. June 1985 (WASC-Jr.). Degrees: A. Pres. Edward A. Hart.

Life Chiropractic College West
2005 Via Barrett, P.O. Box 367, San Lorenzo 94580. Private professional. Cand. Feb. 1983. Degrees: P. *Prof. Accred.:* Chiropractic Education. Pres. Gerard Clum.
Enroll.: 212

Los Angeles College of Chiropractic
16200 E. Amber Valley Dr., P.O. Box 1166, Whittier 90609-1166. Private professional. Cand. Feb. 1986 (WASC-Sr.). Degrees: P. *Prof. Accred.:* Chiropractic Education. Pres. E. Maylon Drake.
Enroll.: 862

Naval Technical Training Center
Treasure Island, San Francisco 94130. Public (federal). Cand. Jan. 1986 (WASC-Jr.). Certificates. Commanding Officer M. J. Evans.

Pacific Graduate School of Psychology
431 Burgess Dr., Menlo Park 94025. Independent professional. Cand. June 1980 (June 1984) (WASC-Sr). Degrees: D. Pres. Allen Calvin.
Enroll.: FTE 105

Pasadena College of Chiropractic
1505 N. Marengo Ave., Pasadena 91103. Private professional. Cand. Dec. 1981. Degrees: P. *Prof. Accred.:* Chiropractic Education. Pres. Arthur Garrow.
Enroll.: 181 (*f.t.* 36 m., 45 w.)

COLORADO

Beth-El College of Nursing
10 N. Farragut Ave., Colorado Springs, 80907. Private. Cand. June 1986 (NCA). Degrees: B. Dean Jean Johns.
Enroll.: 128

Blair Junior College
828 Wooten Rd., Colorado Springs 80915. Private junior. Cand. Feb. 1984 (June 1986)

(NCA). Degrees: A. Dir. Thomas J. Twardowski.
Enroll.: FTE 496

COMMUNITY COLLEGE OF AURORA
East Park Plaza, 791, Chambers Rd., Aurora 80011. Public (state) junior. Cand. Aug. 1984 (NCA). Degrees: A. Pres. Nai-Kwang Chang.
Enroll.: FTE 804

NAROPA INSTITUTE
Boulder 80302. Private professional. Cand. July 1978 (May 1980) (Jan. 1983) (Aug. 1984) (NCA). Degrees: M. Chanc. Barbara Dilley.
Enroll.: FTE 202

NATIONAL TECHNOLOGICAL UNIVERSITY
P.O.Box 700, Fort Collins 80522. Private. Cand. Aug. 1985 (NCA). Degrees: M. Pres. Lionel Baldwin.
Enroll.: 617

PARKS COLLEGE
7350 N. Broadway, Denver 80221. Private. Cand. July 1979 (Oct. 1981) (Oct. 1983) (June 1985) (NCA). Degrees: A, certificates, diplomas. *Prof. Accred.:* Medical Assisting. Pres. Morgan Landry.
Enroll.: FTE 713

CONNECTICUT

BETH BENJAMIN ACADEMY OF CONNECTICUT
132 Prospect St., Stamford 06901. Private professional. Cand. 1978 (1984). Degrees: B. of Talmudic Studies. *Prof. Accred.:* Rabbinical and Talmudic Education. Pres. Rabbi D. Mayer.

FLORIDA

FLORIDA BIBLE COLLEGE
3150 N. Poinciana Blvd., Kissimmee 32758 Private (Interdenominational) professional. Cand. July 1984 (AABC). Degrees: B. Pres. Mark G. Cambron.
Enroll.: 132

FLORIDA TECHNICAL COLLEGE OF TAMPA
4308 56th St., N., Tampa 33610. Private. Cand. 1985 (SACS-COEI). Certificates. Dir. Neil Euliano.

GARCES COMMERCIAL COLLEGE
1301 S.W. First St., Miami 33135. Private. Cand. Dec. 1983 (SACS-COEI). Diplomas. Pres. Robert Medell.
Enroll.: 1,035 (*f.t.* 342 m., 686 w.)

HOBE SOUND BIBLE COLLEGE
P.O. Box 1065, Hobe Sound 33455. Private (Interdenominational) professional. Cand. July 1981 (AABC). Degrees: A,B. Pres. Robert Whitaker
Enroll.: 205

JOHN AMICO'S SCHOOL OF HAIR DESIGN
4956 E. Busch Blvd., Tampa 33617. Private. Cand. 1985 (SACS-COEI). Certificates. Dir. Karen Varuda.

JOHN AMICO'S SCHOOL OF HAIR DESIGN
8803 N. Florida Ave., Tampa 33604. Private. Cand. 1985 (SACS-COEI). Certificates. Dir. Terri Showinard.

JOHN AMICO'S SCHOOL OF HAIR DESIGN
2710 W. Hillsborough, Tampa 33614. Private. Cand. 1985 (SACS-COEI). Certificates. Dir. Pauline Nicholson.

LOYOLA BUSINESS SCHOOL
10375 Coral Way, Miami 33165. Private. Cand. Dec. 1984 (SACS-COEI). Certificates. Dir. Carlos Benitez.

MIAMI JOB CORPS CENTER
660 S.W. Third St., Miami 331305. Private. Cand. Dec. 1984 (SACS-COEI). Certificates. Dir. Don E. DeJarnett.

SOUTHEASTERN COLLEGE OF THE ASSEMBLIES OF GOD
1000 Longfellow Blvd., Lakeland 33801. Private (Assembly of God) professional. Cand. Dec. 1984 (SACS-Comm. on Coll.). Degrees: B. Pres. James L. Hennesy.
Enroll.: 984

TALMUDICAL COLLEGE OF FLORIDA
4014 Chase Ave., Miami Beach 33140. Private professional. Cand. 1977 (1983). Degrees: B. of Talmudic Law. *Prof. Accred.:* Rabbinical and Talmudic Education. Pres. Rabbi J. Zweig.
Enroll.: f.t. 43 m.

WINTER PARK ADULT VOCATIONAL CENTER
901 Webster Ave., Winter Park 32789. Public (county). Cand. Dec. 1984 (SACS-COEI). Certificates. Dir. Richard Miglione.
Enroll.: FTE 169

GEORGIA

THE AMERICAN COLLEGE FOR THE APPLIED ARTS
3330 Peachtree Rd., N.E., Atlanta 30326. Private. Cand. Dec. 1984 (SACS-Comm. on Coll.). Degrees: A,B. Dir. Rafael A. Lago.
Enroll.: 395

Branch Campus
1651 Westwood Blvd., Los Angeles, CA 90024.

Gwinnett Area Technical School
1250 Atkinson Rd., Lawrenceville 30246. Public (county). Cand. 1984 (SACS-COEI). Certificates. Dir. J. Alvin Wilbanks.

Heart of Georgia Vocational-Technical School
Route 5, Box 136A-1, Dublin 31021. Public (federal). Cand. 1984 (SACS-COEI). Certificates. Dir. W. R. Stewart.

The Morehouse School of Medicine
720 Westview Dr., S.W., Atlanta 30310. Private professional. Cand. Dec. 1983 (SACS-Comm. on Coll.). Degrees: P. Pres. and Dean Louis W. Sullivan.
Enroll.: 127

IDAHO

Boise Bible College
8695 Marigold St., Boise 83714. Private (Christian Churches) professional. Cand. 1982 (AABC). Degrees: A,B. Pres. J. Richard Ewing.
Enroll.: 75

ILLINOIS

American Islamic College
Chicago 60613. Private. Cand. Feb. 1985 (NCA). Degrees: B. Acting Pres. Ahmad Sakr.
Enroll.: FTE 42

Brisk Rabbinical College
2965 W. Peterson Ave., Chicago 60659. Private professional. Cand. 1981. Degrees: B. of Hebrew Literature. *Prof. Accred.:* Rabbinical and Talmudic Education. Pres. Rabbi A. Soloveichik.
Enroll.: *f.t.* 32 m.

Saint Augustine College
133 W. Argyle St., Chicago 60604. Private 2-year. Cand. Jan. 1983 (Feb. 1985) (NCA). Degrees: A, certificates. Pres. Carlos A. Plazas.
Enroll.: FTE 724

Shimer College
438 N. Sheridan Rd., Waukegan 60085. Private liberal arts. Cand. Nov. 1980 (Jan. 1983) (Aug. 1984) (Feb. 1986) (NCA). Degrees: B. Pres. Don P. Moon.
Enroll.: 72

West Suburban College of Nursing
Erie at Austin, Oak Park 60302. Private. Cand. Aug. 1984 (NCA). Degrees: B. Dean Sharon Bolin.
Enroll.: FTE 180

INDIANA

Holy Cross Junior College
Notre Dame 46556. Private. Cand. June 1985 (NCA). Degrees: A. Pres. Bro. John Driscoll.
Enroll.: 354

Martin Center College
3553 N. College Ave., Indianapolis 46205. Private. Cand. May 1980 (June 1984) (Oct. 1985) (NCA). Degrees: B. Pres. Rev. Boniface Hardin.
Enroll.: 96

IOWA

Emmaus Bible College
2570 Asbury Rd., Dubuque 52001. Private (Interdenominational) professional. Cand. 1982 (AABC). Degrees: A,B. Pres. Daniel H. Smith.
Enroll.: 182

University of Osteopathic Medicine and Health Sciences
3200 Grand Ave., Des Moines 50312. Private professional. Cand. April 1982 (Aug. 1984) (NCA). Degrees: P. *Prof. Accred.:* Osteopathy, Physician's Assistant, Podiatry. Pres. J. Leonard Azneer.
Enroll.: 777 (*f.t.* 604 m., 173 w.)

KENTUCKY

Clear Creek Baptist School
Pineville 40977. Private (Baptist) professional. Cand. July 1981 (AABC). Degrees: A,B. Pres. Leon D. Simpson.
Enroll.: 203

Mid-Continent Baptist Bible College
Route 2, Mayfield 42066 Private (Baptist) professional. Cand. Dec. 1984 (SACS-Comm. on Coll.). Degrees: B. Pres. Raymond E. Lawrence.
Enroll.: 84

PJ's College of Cosmetology
Western Gateway Shopping Center, Russellville Rd., Bowling Green 42101. Private. Cand. 1985 (SACS-COEI). Certificates. Dir. Judith Stewart.

Trend Setters' Academy of Beauty Culture.
7283 Dixie Hwy., Louisville 40258. Private. Cand. 1985 (SACS-COEI). Certificates. Dir. Donna L. Dunn.

LOUISIANA

Acadiana Technical College
102 Savonne Dr. Scott 70583. Private. Cand. Dec. 1984 (SACS-COEI). Certificates. Phillip J. Vinciquerra.

American College
2804 Florida Blvd. Baton Rouge 70802. Private. Cand. 1985 (SACS-COEI). Certificates. Dir. Monty G. Miller.

American College
2025 Canal St., Suite 210, New Orleans 70112. Private. Cand. 1985 (SACS-COEI). Certificates. Dir. Ron K. Witt.

Louisiana School of Professions
4140 Hollywood Ave., Shreveport 71109. Private. Cand. 1985 (SACS-COEI). Certificates. Dir. Earnest H. Lampkins.

New Orleans Regional Vocational-Technical Institute
980 Navarre Ave., New Orleans, 70124. Public (state). Cand. Dec. 1984 (SACS-COEI). Certificates. Dir. Em Tampke.

Rutledge College of New Orleans
2609 Canal St., New Orleans 70119. Private. Cand. 1985 (SACS-COEI). Certificates. Dir. Carl E. Settle.

MAINE

Beal College
Bangor 04401. Private junior business. Cand. April 1979 (NEASC-CVTCI). Degrees: A, diplomas. *Prof. Accred.:* Medical Assisting. Pres. Allen T. Stehle.
Enroll.: 359

YDI Schools
Main St., Blue Hill 04614. Private residential technical. Cand. May 1984 (NEASC-CVTCI). Degrees: A., certificates, diplomas. Dir. Robert E. Wallstrom.

MASSACHUSETTS

Bay State Junior College
122 Commonwealth Ave., Boston 02116. Private. Cand. May 1982 (NEASC-CVTCI). Degrees: A, diplomas. *Prof. Accred.:* Medical Assisting. Pres. Thomas E. Langford.
Enroll.: 664

Chamberlayne Junior College
128 Commonwealth Ave., Boston 02116. Private. Cand. May 1982 (NEASC-CVTCI). Degrees: A. *Prof. Accred.:* Interior Design. Pres. Matthew J. Malloy.
Enroll.: 759

Conway School of Landscape Design
Delabarre Ave., Conway 01341. Private. Cand. May 1983/1985 (NEASC-CIHE). Degrees: M. Dir. Walter Cudnohufsky.
Enroll.: 18

Kodaly Center of America
295 Adams St., Newton 02158. Private nonprofit. Cand. May 1984 (NEASC-CVTCI). Certificates, diplomas. Dir. Denise Bacon.

MICHIGAN

Cleary College
2170 Washtenaw Rd., Ypsilanti 48197. Private. Cand. Feb. 1984 (Oct. 1985) (NCA). Degrees: A,B, diplomas. *Prof. Accred.:* Medical Assisting. Pres. Harry Howard.
Enroll.: 563

Detroit College of Business
4801 Oakman Blvd., Dearborn 48126. Private. Cand. Apr. 1981 (June 1984) (NCA). Degrees: A,B, diplomas. Pres. Frank Paone.
Enroll.: 2,046

Grace Bible College
P.O. Box 910, Grand Rapids 49509. Private (Grace Gospel Fellowship) professional. Cand. Feb. 1984 (NCA). Sem. plan. Degrees: A,B. Pres. Samuel R. Vinton, Jr.
Enroll.: FTE 114

Yeshiva Gedolah of Greater Detroit
24600 Greenfield, Oak Park 48237. Private professional. Cand. June 1986. Degrees B. of Hebrew Letters, M. and D. of Talmudic Law. *Prof. Accred.:* Rabbinic and Talmudic Education. Pres. Saul Weingarten.

MINNESOTA

Kotz Graduate School of Management
1450 Energy Park Dr., Ste. 112, St. Paul 55018. Private. Cand. June 1986 (NCA). Degrees: M. Pres. Eugene Kotz.
Enroll.: 68

Northwestern College of Chiropractic
2501 W. 84th St., Bloomington 55431. Private professional. Cand. June 1986 (NCA). Degrees: P. Pres. Donald M. Cassata.
Enroll.: 455 (*f.t.* 331 m., 124 w.)

MISSISSIPPI

Hattiesburg School of Cosmetology
132 New Orleans St., Hattiesburg 39401. Private. Cand. 1985 (SACS-COEI). Certificates. Dir. Jack R. Davis.

Phillips Business College
Gulfport 39501. Private. Cand. 1985 (SACS-Comm. on Coll.). Degrees: A. Dir. Ann Gibson.

Phillips College of Jackson
2680 Insurance Center at Lakeland, Jackson 39216. Private. Cand. 1985 (SACS-Comm. on Coll.). Degrees: A. Dir. Nan Thompson.

Southeastern Baptist College
4229 Hwy. 15 N., Laurel 39440. Private (Baptist). Cand. 1983 (AABC). Degrees: A,B. Pres. A. M. Wilson.
Enroll.: 81

MISSOURI

International Graduate School
55 Maryland Plaza, St. Louis 63108. Private professional. Cand. April 1981 (Oct. 1984) (NCA). Degrees: D. Exec. Dean Stephen L. Nichols.
Enroll.: FTE 55

Logan College of Chiropractic
P.O. Box 100, Chesterfield 63017. Private professional. Cand. Feb. 1984 (June 1986) (NCA). Degrees: P. *Prof. Accred.:* Chiropractic Education. Pres. Beatrice B. Hagen.
Enroll.: FTE 686

Ozark Christian
1111 N. Main St., Joplin 64801. Private (Christian Church) professional. Cand. 1985 (AABC). Degrees: A,B. Pres. Ken Idleman.
Enroll.: 498

Research College of Nursing
2316 E. Meyer Blvd., Kansas City 64132. Private professional. Cand. June 1980 (Oct. 1982) (Aug. 1985) (NCA). Degrees: B. Dean Barbara Clemence.
Enroll.: FTE 239

St. Louis Rabbinical College
7400 Olive Street Rd., St. Louis 63230. Private professional. Cand. 1980. Degrees: 1st Rabbinic. *Prof. Accred.:* Rabbinical and Talmudic Education. Pres. Rabbi Y. Kleiman.

MONTANA

Big Sky Bible College
Rt. 3, Lewistown 59457. Private (Interdenominational) professional. Cand. Oct. 1977 (AABC). Degrees: A,B. Pres. Rodric H. Pence.
Enroll.: 33 (*f.t.* 22 m., 11 w.)

Fort Peck Community College
Poplar 59255. Tribally controlled junior. Cand. June 1986 (NASC). Degrees: A. Pres. James E. Shanley.
Enroll.: 172

Little Big Horn College
Crow Agency 59022. Tribally controlled junior. Cand. June 1984/1986 (NASC). Degrees: A. Pres. Janine Pease-Windy Boy.
Enroll.: 142

NEBRASKA

Nebraska Indian Community College
Winnebago 68071. Public (federal). Cand. June 1981 (Oct. 1982) (Oct. 1984) (NCA). Degrees: A. Pres. James E. Bealer.
Enroll.: FTE 162

Western Nebraska Technical College
Sidney 69162. Public (district). Cand. June 1983 (Oct. 1985) (NCA). Degrees: A, certificates. Campus Dir. Gary Lund.
Enroll.: FTE 186

NEVADA

Old College
401 W. Second Ave., Reno 89503. Private liberal arts and law. Cand Dec. 1981 (1984) (NASC). Degrees: B,P. Pres. Allan DeGuilio.
Enroll.: 89

NEW HAMPSHIRE

McIntosh College
23 Cataract Ave., Dover 03820. Private junior. Cand. Oct. 1983 (NEASC-CVTCI). Degrees: A, diplomas. Pres. Richard F. Waldo.
Enroll.: 555

NEW MEXICO

Santa Fe Community College
P.O. Box 4187, Santa Fe 87502. Public (state). Cand. Aug. 1984 (NCA) (June 1986). Degrees: A. Pres. William C. Witter.
Enroll.: FTE 587

NEW YORK

Berkeley School
Westchester Campus, West Red Oak La., White Plains 10604. Private business. Cand. June 1981 (MSA/CHE). Degrees: A. Pres. Warren T. Schimmel.
Enroll.: 805 (*f.t.* 0 m., 700 w.)

Beth Hillel Rabbinical Seminary
1366 42nd St., Brooklyn 11219. Private; graduate and professional only. Cand. 1976 (1983). Degrees: lst Talmudic. *Prof. Accred.:* Rabbinical and Talmudic Education. Pres. J. Tauber.

Beth Medrash L'Torah Rabbinical College
23 Union St., Spring Valley 10977. Administrative office: 15 Meadow La., Monsey 10952. Private; graduate and professional only. Cand. 1985. Degrees: lst Talmudic. *Prof. Accred.:* Rabbinical and Talmudic Education. Pres. Rabbi S. Faivelson.

Bramson ORT Technical Institute
304 Park Ave.,S., New York 10010. Private technical college. Cand. June 1981 (MSA/CHE). Degrees: A, certificates. Dir. Ira L. Jaskoll.
Enroll.: 166 (*f.t.* 70 m., 8 w.)

Darkei No'am Rabbinical College
1535 49th St., Brooklyn 11219. Private; graduate and professional only. Cand. 1982. Degrees: 1st Rabbinic. *Prof. Accred.:* Rabbinical and Talmudic Education. Pres. J. Sitorsky.
Enroll.: 44 (*f.t.* 41 m., 0 w.)

Five Towns College
2165 Seaford Ave., Seaford 11783. Private professional. Cand. June 1981 (MSA/CHE). Degrees: A, certificates. Pres. Stanley G. Cohen.
Enroll.: 402 (*f.t.* 253 m., 91 w.)

Friends World College
Plover La., Huntington 11743. Private, nontraditional liberal arts. Cand. Feb. 1984 (MSA/CHE). Degrees: B. Pres. Lawrence Weiss.
Enroll.: 141

Helene Fuld School of Nursing
Joint Diseases North General Hospital, 1919 Madison Ave., New York 10035. Private. Cand. June 1984 (MSA/CHE). Degrees: A. *Prof. Accred.:* Nursing (A). Dir. and Dean Margaret Wines.
Enroll.: 153 (*f.t.* 5 m., 84 w.)

Kehillath Yakov Rabbinical Seminary
206 Wilson St., Brooklyn 11211. Private; graduate and professional only. Cand. 1980. Degrees: 1st Rabbinis. *Prof. Accred.:* Rabbinical and Talmudic Education. Pres. Rabbi S. Schwartz.
Enroll.: *f.t.* 180 m.

Kol Yakov Torah Center
29 W. Maple Ave., Monsey 10952. Private; graduate and professional only. Cand. 1984. *Prof. Accred.:* Rabbinical and Talmudic Education. Pres. Rabbi Leib Tropper.

Machzikei Hadrath Rabbinical College
5407 16th Ave., Brooklyn 11204. Private; graduate and professional only. Cand. 1980 (1983). Degrees: 1st Talmudic. *Prof. Accred.:* Rabbinical and Talmudic Education. Pres. Ch. Hertz.
Enroll.: *f.t.* 83 m.

Ohr Hameir Theological Seminary
Furnace Woods Rd., P.O. Box 2130, Peekskill 10566. Private; graduate and professional only. Cand. 1979 (1984). Degrees: 1st Rabbinic. *Prof. Accred.:* Rabbinical and Talmudic Education. Pres. Rabbi I. Kanarek.
Enroll.: *f.t.* 34 m.

Ohr Somayach Institutions
142 Rte. 306, P.O. Box 334, Monsey 10952. Private; graduate and professional only. Cand. 1984. Degrees: 1st Talmudic. *Prof. Accred.:* Rabbinical and Talmudic Education. Pres. Rabbi A. Braun.

Talmudical Institute of Upstate New York
769 Park Ave., Rochester 14607. Private; graduate and professional only. Cand. 1984.

Degrees: 1st Talmudic. *Prof. Accred.:* Rabbinical and Talmudic Education. Pres. Mayer Lebovics.

YESHIVA AND KOLLEL HARBOTZAS TORAH
4407 12th Ave., Brooklyn 11219691. Private; graduate and professional only. Cand. 1985. Degrees: 1st Rabbinic and 1st Talmudic. *Prof. Accred.:* Rabbinical and Talmudic Education.

YESHIVA B'NEI TORAH
737 Elvira Ave., Far Rockaway 11691. Private; graduate and professional only. Cand. 1984 Degrees: 1st Rabbinic and 1st Talmudic. *Prof. Accred.:* Rabbinical and Talmudic Education. Pres. Rabbi I. Chait.
Enroll.: 26 (*f.t.* 22 m., 0 w.)

YESHIVA DERECH CHAIM
4907 18th Ave., Brooklyn 11204. Private; graduate and professional only. Cand. 1984. Degrees: 1st and Advanced Talmudic. *Prof. Accred.:* Rabbinical and Talmudic Education.

YESHIVA GEDOLAH BAIS YISROEL
1719 Avenue P, Brooklyn 11229. Private; graduate and professional only. Cand. 1985. Degrees: 1st Talmudic. *Prof. Accred.:* Rabbinical and Talmudic Education. Pres. David Pollack.

YESHIVA MIKDASH MELECH
1326 Ocean Pkwy., Brooklyn 11230. Private; graduate and professional only. Cand. 1984. Degrees: 1st Rabbinic. *Prof. Accred.:* Rabbinical and Talmudic Education.

YESHIVA OF THE TELSHE ALUMNI
4904 Independence Ave., Riverdale 10471. Private; graduate and professional only. Cand. 1985. Degrees: 1st Talmudic. *Prof. Accred.:* Rabbinical and Talmudic Education. Pres. Rabbi A. Ausband.
Enroll.: f.t. 116 m.

YESHIVA OHEL SHMUEL
Haines Rd., Bedford Hills 10507. Private; graduate and professional only. Cand. 1977 (1983). Degrees: 1st Talmudic. *Prof. Accred.:* Rabbinical and Talmudic Education. Pres. A. Fischer.

YESHIVA SHAAR HATORAH TALMUDIC RESEARCH INSTITUTE
83-96 117th St., Kew Gardens 11415. Private; graduate and professional only. Cand. 1984. Degrees: 1st Rabbinic and 1st Talmudic. *Prof. Accred.:* Rabbinical and Talmudic Education. Pres. Rabbi Z. Epstein.

NORTH CAROLINA

CECILS JUNIOR COLLEGE
P.O. Box 6407, 1567 Patton Ave., Asheville 28801. Private. Cand. Dec. 1984 (SACS-Comm. on Coll.). Degrees: A. Pres. John T. South.
Enroll.: 172

EAST COAST BIBLE COLLEGE
6900 Wilkinson Blvd., Charlotte 28214. Private (Church of God) professional. Cand. Dec. 1985 (SACS-Comm. on Coll.). Degrees: A,B. Pres. Henry J. Smith.
Enroll.: 228

PIEDMONT BIBLE COLLEGE
716 Franklin St., Winston-Salem, 27101. Private. (Baptist) Cand. Dec. 1985 (SACS-Comm. on Coll.). Degrees: B. Pres. Donald K. Drake.
Enroll.: 352

RUTLEDGE COLLEGE OF NORTH CAROLINA
2600 First Union Plaza, Charlotte 28282. Private. Cand. Dec. 1984 (SACS-Comm. on Coll.). Degrees: A. Pres. Carl Settle.
Enroll.: 1,904

NORTH DAKOTA

FORT BERTHOLD COMMUNITY COLLEGE
New Town 58763. Tribally controlled. Cand. June 1981 (Oct. 1983) (Aug. 1985) (NCA). Degrees: A. Pres. Bennett Yellow Bird.
Enroll.: FTE 57

LITTLE HOOP COMMUNITY COLLEGE
P.O. Box 149, Fort Totten 59335. Tribally controlled (Devil's Lake Sioux Indian Tribe). Cand. Oct. 1982 (Feb. 1984) (June 1986) (NCA). Degrees: A, certificates. Pres. Myrna DeMarce. *Enroll.:* FTE 84

OHIO

CLEVELAND COLLEGE OF JEWISH STUDIES
26500 Shaker Blvd., Beachwood 44122. Private. Cand. April 1975 (April 1979) (Aug. 1985) (NCA). Degrees: M. Pres. David Ariel.
Enroll.: FTE 106

COLUMBUS COLLEGE OF ART AND DESIGN
47 N. Washington Ave., Columbus 43215. Private professional. Cand. June 1980 (Jan. 1983) (Aug. 1984) (NCA). Degrees: B. *Prof. Accred.:* Art. Dean Joseph V. Canzani.
Enroll.: FTE 987

God's Bible School
1810 Young St., Cincinnati 45210. Private (Interdenominational) professional. Cand. 1982 (AABC). Degrees: B. Pres. Bence C. Miller.
Enroll.: 271

Ohio College of Podiatric Medicine
10515 Carnegie Ave., Cleveland 44106. Private professional. Cand. Oct. 1982 (Oct. 1985) (NCA). Degrees: P. *Prof. Accred.:* Podiatry. Pres. Thomas V. Melillo.
Enroll.: FTE 564

Winebrenner Seminary
701 E. Melrose Ave., P.O. Box 478, Findlay 45840-0478. Private. Cand. Feb. 1984 (NCA). Degrees: P,M. Pres. George Weaver.
Enroll.: FTE 33

OKLAHOMA

Oklahoma Junior College of Business and Technology
4821 S. 72nd East Ave., Tulsa 74145. Private. Cand. Feb. 1986 (NCA). Degrees: A, diplomas. Pres. David Stephenson.
Enroll.: 1,015

OREGON

Western States Chiropractic College
2900 N.E. 132nd Ave., Portland 97230. Private professional. Cand. Dec. 1982 (1984) (NASC). Degrees: P. *Prof. Accred.:* Chiropractic Education. Pres. ———.
Enroll.: 410

PENNSYLVANIA

Biblical Theological Seminary
200 N. Main St., Hatfield 19440. Private (nondenominational) professional. Cand. Dec. 1983 (MSA/CHE). Degrees: P,M. Pres. David Dunbar
Enroll.: 167 (*f.t.* 62 m., 0 w.)

Erie Business Center
246 W. Ninth St., Erie 16501. Private. Cand. Dec. 1981 (MSA/CHE). Degrees: A, certificates. Dir. Charles P. McGeary
Enroll.: 665 (*f.t.* 66 m., 248 w.)

Naval Damage Control Training Center
Naval Base, Philadelphia 19112. Public (federal) technical. Cand. Dec. 1984 (SACS-COEI). Certificates. Commandant CDR B. F. Antrim.

Philadelphia College of Osteopathic Medicine
4150 City Ave., Philadelphia 19131. Private professional. Cand. Dec. 1983 (June 1983) (MSA/CHE). Degrees: P. *Prof. Accred.:* EEG Technology, Medical Assisting, Osteopathy. Pres. Jon P. Tilley.
Enroll.: 833 (*f.t.* 636 m., 197 w.)

Reconstructionist Rabbinical College
Greenwood Ave. and Church Rd., Wyncote 19095. Private professional. Cand. June 1984 (MSA/CHE) Degrees: M. Pres. Ira Silverman.
Enroll.: 65 (*f.t.* 29 m., 34 w.)

Thaddeus Stevens State School of Technology
750 E. King St., Lancaster 17602. Public. Cand. June 1983 (MSA/CHE). Degrees: A, certificates. Pres. Alan K. Cohen.
Enroll.: 467 (*f.t.* 415 m., 19 w.)

United Wesleyan College
1414 E. Cedar St., Allentown 18103. Private (Wesleyan Church) professional. Cand. March 1980 (MSA/CHE). Degrees: A,B. Pres. John P. Ragsdale.
Enroll.: 201

SOUTH CAROLINA

Alpha Beauty School of Greenville
Liberty Lane - Pleasantburg Shopping Ctr., Greenville 29607. Private. Cand. 1985 (SACS-COEI). Certificates. Dir. Kenneth W. Lochridge.

Charleston Cosmetology Institute
3211 E. Dorchester Rd., Summerville 29483. Private. Cand. 1985 (SACS-COEI). Certificates. Dir. Jerry R. Poer, Jr..

Charzanne Beauty College
Rt. 2, Box 9, Greenwood 29646. Private. Cand. 1985 (SACS-COEI). Certificates. Dir. Walker Byrd.

SOUTH DAKOTA

Sisseton-Wahpeton Community College
P.O. Box 209, Sisseton 57262. Tribally controlled 2-year. Cand. Aug. 1984 (NCA). Degrees: A. Pres. Phyllis Howard.
Enroll.: FTE 151

TENNESSEE

EMMANUEL SCHOOL OF RELIGION
Rte. 6, Box 500, Johnson City 37601. Private (Christian Churches and Churches of Christ) Cand. 1985 (SACS-Comm. on Coll.). Degrees: B. Pres. Calvin L. Phillips.
Enroll.: 85

MID-SOUTH BIBLE COLLEGE
2485 Union Ave., Memphis 38112. Private (Interdenominational) professional. Cand. 1984 (SACS-Comm. on Coll.). Degrees: A. Pres. Robert J. Hilgenberg.
Enroll.: 144

TEXAS

BAPTIST MISSIONARY ASSOCIATION THEOLOGICAL SEMINARY
P.O. Box 1797, Jacksonville 75766. Private (Baptist) professional; graduate only. Cand. Dec. 1982 (SACS-Comm. on Coll.). Degrees: B,P,M. Pres. Philip R. Bryan.
Enroll.: 70

CORPUS CHRISTI BUSINESS SCHOOL
1801 S. Staples, #202, Corpus Christi 78404. Private. Cand. 1985 (SACS-COEI). Certificates. Dir. Edna M. Bradley.

DOOLIN TECHNICAL COLLEGE
5646 Navigation, Houston 77011. Private. Cand. Dec. 1983 (SACS-COEI). Certificates. Dir. Julian R. Doolin.

EL PASO JOB CORPS CENTER
11155 Gateway West, El Paso 79935. Public (federal). Cand. Dec. 1984 (SACS-COEI). Certificates. Dir. David L. Carrasco.

HOUSTON GRADUATE SCHOOL OF THEOLOGY
1129 Wilkins, Suite 202, Houston 77030. Private. Cand. Dec. 1985 (SACS-Comm. on Coll.). Degrees: M. Pres. Delbert P. Vaughn.

INSTITUTE FOR CHRISTIAN STUDIES
1909 University Ave., Austin 78705. Private. Cand. Dec. 1985 (SACS-Comm. on Coll.). Degrees: B. Pres. James W. Thompson.

LAMAR UNIVERSITY ORANGE CENTER
410 Front St., Orange 77630. Public. Cand. Dec. 1985 (SACS-Comm. on Coll.). Degrees: A. Pres. Joe Ben Welch.

LAMAR UNIVERSITY AT PORT ARTHUR
P.O.Box 310, Port Arthur 77640. Public. Cand. Dec. 1985 (SACS-Comm. on Coll.). Degrees: A. Pres. Sam Monroe.

MCKINNEY JOB CORPS CENTER
1501 N. Church St., P.O. Box 750, Mckinney 75069. Public (federal). Cand. Dec. 1984 (SACS-COEI). Certificates. Dir. John O. Crosby.

NORTHEAST TEXAS COMMUNITY COLLEGE
P.O.Drawer 1307, Mt. Pleasant 754550. Public. Cand. Dec. 1985 (SACS-Comm. on Coll.). Degrees: A. Pres. Wayland DeWitt.

PALO ALTO COLLEGE
P.O.Box 3800, San Antonio 78284. Public. Cand. Dec. 1985 (SACS-Comm. on Coll.). Degrees: A. Pres. Terry L. Dicianna.

PARKER COLLEGE OF CHIROPRACTIC
300 E. Irving Blvd., Irving 75060. Private. Cand. Dec. 1985 (SACS-Comm. on Coll.). Degrees: P. Pres. James W. Parker.

PLATT CAREER SCHOOLS
3101 McArdle, Corpus Christi 78415. Private. Cand. 1985 (SACS-COEI). Certificates. Dir. Nancy Turner.

TEMPLE ACADEMY OF COSMETOLOGY
5 S. First St., Temple 76501. Private. Cand. Dec. 1985 (SACS-COEI). Certificates. Dir. David Tuck.

VERMONT

THE CENTER FOR NORTHERN STUDIES
Wolcott 05680. Private nonprofit. Cand. Oct. 1983 (NEASC-CVTCI). Diplomas. Pres. Oran R. Young.
Enroll.: 22

STERLING COLLEGE
Craftsbury Common 05827. Private 2-year. Cand. Feb. 1980 (NEASC-CVTCI). Degrees: A, certificates. Pres. A. Perry Whitmore.
Enroll.: 73

VIRGINIA

BUCKROE SKILL CENTER
710 Buckroe Ave., Hampton 23664. Public (state). Cand. Dec. 1983 (SACS-COEI). Certificates. Dir. Karen C. Strovink.

CHRISTENDOM COLLEGE
Route 3, Box 87, Front Royal 22630. Private. Cand. Dec. 1983 (SACS-Comm. on Coll.). Degrees: B. Pres. Damian Fedoryka.
Enroll.: 126

Fleet Anti-Submarine Warfare Training Center
Norfolk Station, Norfolk 23511. Public (federal) technical. Cand. Dec. 1981 (SACS-COEI). Certificates. Cmdg. Off. Capt. Ray Sharpe.
Enroll.: 7,499

Institute of Textile Technology
Charlottesville 22902. Private. Cand. Dec. 1985 (SACS-Comm. on Coll.). Degrees: M,D. Pres. Charles Tewksbury.

Naval Amphibious School
Naval Amphibious Base, Little Creek, Norfolk 23521. Public (federal). Cand. 1985 (SACS-COEI). Certificates. Dir. Capt. V. Dekshenieks.

Norfolk Skills Center
1830 Lindsay Ave., Norfolk 23504. Private. Cand. 1985 (SACS-COEI). Certificates. Dir. Raymond L. Murray.

Southside Training Skill Center
P.O.Box 258, Hwy. 460, E. Crewe 23930. Private. Cand. 1985 (SACS-COEI). Certificates. Dir. Allen S. Bridgeforth.

Total Action Against Poverty Adult Education Center
702 Shenandoah Ave., N.W., Roanoke 24001. Public (state). Cand. Dec. 1983 (SACS-COEI). Certificates. Dir. Theodore J. Edlich, III.

WASHINGTON

John Bastyr College
144 N.E. 54th St., Seattle 98105. Private professional. Cand. June 1983 (1985) (NASC). Degrees: P. Pres. Joseph E. Pizzorno, Jr.
Enroll.: 154

L. H. Bates Vocational Technical Institute
1101 S. Yakima Ave., Tacoma 90405. Public (district). Cand. June 1984 (NASC). Certificates. Dir. William Mohler.
Enroll.: 1,680

WISCONSIN

Bellin College of Nursing
744 S. Webster, P.O.Box 1700, Green Bay 54305. Private. Cand. Aug.1985 (NCA). Degrees: B. Dean Diane Koller.
Enroll.: FTE 132

Columbia College of Nursing
2121 E. Newport Ave., Milwaukee 53211. Private. Cand. June 1984 (NCA). Degrees: B. Vice Pres./Dean Marian Snyder.
Enroll.: FTE 230

Wisconsin Lutheran College
Milwaukee 53226. Private junior. Cand. April 1979 (April 1981) (Jan. 1983) (June 1985) (NCA). Degrees: A,B. Pres. Gary J. Greenfield.
Enroll.: FTE 102

Wisconsin School of Professional Psychology
4143 S. 13th St., Milwaukee 53226. Private professional. Cand. Oct. 1981 (June 1983) (June 1985) (NCA). Degrees: D. Dean Marc J. Ackerman.
Enroll.: FTE 14

INSTITUTIONS OUTSIDE THE UNITED STATES

CANADA

Aldersgate College
Box 460, Moose Jaw, Sask. S6H 4P1. Private (Free Methodist) professional. Cand. 1981 (AABC). Degrees: A,B. Acting Pres. G. Merrill.
Enroll.: 72

Bethany Bible College-Canada
Main St., Sussex, N.B. E0E 1P0. Private (Wesleyan) professional. Cand 1982 (AABC). Degrees: A,B. Pres. Ronald E. Mitchell.
Enroll.: 159

Bethany Bible Institute
Box 160, Hepburn, Sask. S0K 1Z0. Private (Mennonite Bretheren) professional. Cand. 1982 (AABC). Degrees: A,B. Pres. Clifford Jantzen.
Enroll.: 154

Columbia Bible Institute
2940 Clearbrook Rd., Clearbrook, B.C. V2T 2Z8. Private (Mennonite Bretheren) professional. Cand. 1985 (AABC). Degrees: A. Pres. Walter Unger.
Enroll.: 181

Hillcrest Christian College
2801 13th Ave., S.E., Medicine Hat, Alta. T1A 3R1. Private (Evangel Churches in Canada) professional. Cand. 1983 (AABC). Degrees: A,B. Pres. Arvid J. Lindley.
Enroll.: 78

Northwest Baptist Theological College
3358 S.E. Marine Dr., Vancouver. V5S 3W3. Private (Baptist) professional. Cand. 1985 (AABC). Degrees: A,B. Pres. Doug Harris.
Enroll.: 159

Appendixes

A. The Accrediting Process

Accreditation is a system for recognizing educational institutions and professional programs affiliated with those institutions for a level of performance, integrity, and quality which entitles them to the confidence of the educational community and the public they serve. In the United States this recognition is extended primarily through nongovernmental, voluntary institutional or professional associations. These groups establish criteria for accreditation, arrange site visits, and evaluate those institutions and professional programs which desire accredited status, and publicly designate those which meet their criteria.

In most other countries, the establishment and maintenance of educational standards is the responsibility of a central government bureau. In the United States, however, public authority in education is constitutionally reserved to the states. The system of voluntary nongovernmental evaluation, called accreditation, has evolved to promote both regional and national approaches to the determination of educational quality. While accreditation is basically a private, voluntary process, accrediting decisions are used as a consideration in many formal actions—by governmental funding agencies, scholarship commissions, foundations, employers, counselors, and potential students. Accrediting bodies have, therefore, come to be viewed as quasi-public entities with certain responsibilities to the many groups which interact with the educational community.

In America, accreditation at the postsecondary level performs a number of important functions, including the encouragement of efforts toward maximum educational effectiveness. The accrediting process requires institutions and programs to examine their goals, activities, and achievements; to consider the expert criticism and suggestions of a visiting team; and to determine internal procedures for action on recommendations from the accrediting body. Since accreditation status is reviewed on a periodic basis, recognized institutions and professional programs are encouraged to maintain continuous self-study and improvement mechanisms.

Types of Accreditation

Institutional accreditation is granted by the regional and national accrediting commissions of schools and colleges, which collectively serve most of the institutions chartered or licensed in the United States and its possessions. These commissions and associations accredit total operating units only.

Specialized accreditation of professional or occupational schools and programs is granted by national professional organizations in such fields as business, dentistry, engineering, and law. Each of these groups has its distinctive definitions of eligibility, criteria for accreditation, and operating procedures, but all have undertaken accreditation activities primarily to provide quality assurances concerning educational preparation of members of the profession or occupation. Many of the specialized accrediting bodies will consider requests for accreditation reviews only from programs affiliated with institutions holding comprehensive accreditation. Some specialized agencies, however, accredit professional programs at institutions not otherwise accredited. These are generally independent institutions which offer only the particular specified discipline or course of study in question.

Procedures in Accreditation

The accrediting process is continuously evolving. The trend has been from quantitative to qualitative criteria, from the early days of simple checklists to an increasing interest and emphasis on measuring the outcomes of educational experiences.

The process begins with the institutional or programmatic self-study, a comprehensive effort to measure progress according to previously accepted objectives. The self-study considers the interests of a broad cross-section of constituencies—students, faculty, administrators, alumni, trustees, and in some circumstances the local community.

The resulting report is reviewed by the appropriate accrediting commission and serves as the basis for evaluation by a site-visit team from the accrediting group. The site-visit team normally consists of professional educators (faculty and administrators), specialists elected according to the nature of the institution, and members representing specific public interests. The visiting team assesses the institution or program in light of the self-study and adds judgments based on its own expertise and its external perspective. The team prepares an evaluation report, which is reviewed by the institution or program for factual accuracy.

The original self-study, the team report, and any response the institution or program may wish to make are forwarded to the accreditation commission. The review body uses these materials as the basis for action regarding the accreditation status of the institution or program. Negative actions may be appealed according to established procedures of the accrediting body.

Although accreditation is generally granted for a specific term (e.g., five or ten years), accrediting bodies reserve the right to review member institutions or programs at any time for cause. They also reserve the right to review any substantive change, such as an expansion from undergraduate to graduate offerings. Such changes may require prior approval and/or review upon implementation. In this way, accrediting bodies hold their member institutions and programs continually responsible to their educational peers, to the constituents they serve, and to the public.

Accreditation's Functions

Throughout the evolution of its procedures, the aims of postsecondary accreditation have been and are to:

- foster excellence in postsecondary education through the development of uniform national criteria and guidelines for assessing educational effectiveness;
- encourage improvement through continuous self-study and review;
- assure the educational community, the general public, and other agencies or organizations that an institution or program has clearly defined and appropriate objectives, maintains conditions under which their achievement can reasonably be expected, is in fact accomplishing them substantially, and can be expected to continue to do so;
- provide counsel and assistance to established and developing institutions and programs; and
- endeavor to protect institutions against encroachments which might jeopardize their educational effectiveness or academic freedom.

Postsecondary education in the United States derives its strength and excellence from the unique and diverse character of its many individual institutions. Such qualities are best sustained and extended by the freedom of these institutions to determine their own objectives and to experiment in the ways and means of education within the framework of their respective authority and responsibilities.

Public as well as educational needs must be served simultaneously in determining and fostering standards of quality and integrity in the institutions and such specialized programs as they offer. Accreditation, through nongovernmental institutional and specialized agencies, provides a major means for meeting those needs.

Role of the Council on Postsecondary Accreditation

The Council on Postsecondary Accreditation (COPA) is a nongovernmental organization that works to foster and facilitate the role of accrediting bodies in promoting and insuring the quality and diversity of American postsecondary education. The accrediting bodies, while established and supported by their membership, are intended to serve the broader interests of society as well. To promote these ends, COPA recognizes, coordinates, and periodically reviews the work of its member accrediting bodies, and the appropriateness of existing or proposed accrediting bodies and their activities, through its granting of recognition and performance of other related functions.

B. Accrediting Groups Recognized by COPA

COPA periodically evaluates the accrediting activities of institutional and professional associations. Upon determining that those activities meet or exceed COPA provisions, the accrediting organizations are publicly recognized through this listing. Groups that are regional in nature are identified with their geographical areas; all others are national in their activities.

NATIONAL INSTITUTIONAL ACCREDITING BODIES

AMERICAN ASSOCIATION OF BIBLE COLLEGES
Randall E. Bell, *Executive Director*
130-F North College Street
P.O. Box 1523
Fayetteville, Arkansas 72701
(501) 521-8164

ASSOCIATION OF INDEPENDENT COLLEGES AND SCHOOLS
James M. Phillips, *Executive Director*
Accrediting Commission
One Dupont Circle, Suite 350
Washington, D. C. 20036
(202) 659-2460

ASSOCIATION OF THEOLOGICAL SCHOOLS IN THE UNITED STATES AND CANADA
Leon Pacala, *Executive Director*
42 East National Road
P.O. Box 130
Vandalia, Ohio 45377-0130
(513) 898-4654

NATIONAL ASSOCIATION OF TRADE AND TECHNICAL SCHOOLS
Dorothy Coyne Fenwick, *Executive Secretary*
Accrediting Commission
2251 Wisconsin Avenue, N.W.
Washington, D.C. 20007
(202) 333-1021

NATIONAL HOME STUDY COUNCIL
William A. Fowler, *Executive Secretary*
Accrediting Commission
1601 Eighteenth Street, N.W.
Washington, D.C. 20009
(202) 234-5100

REGIONAL INSTITUTIONAL ACCREDITING BODIES

MIDDLE STATES ASSOCIATION OF COLLEGES AND SCHOOLS
Delaware, District of Columbia, Maryland, New Jersey, New York, Pennsylvania, Puerto Rico, the Republic of Panama, Virgin Islands, and several institutions in Europe serving primarily U.S. students
Robert Kirkwood, *Executive Director*
Commission on Higher Education
3624 Market Street
Philadelphia, Pennsylvania 19104
(215) 662-5606

NEW ENGLAND ASSOCIATION OF SCHOOLS AND COLLEGES
Connecticut, Maine, Massachusetts, New Hampshire, Rhode Island, Vermont
The Sanborn House, 15 High Street
Winchester, Massachusetts 01890
(617) 729-6762
Charles M. Cook, *Director of Evaluation*
Commission on Institutions of Higher Education

Daniel S. Maloney, *Director of Evaluation*
Commission on Vocational, Technical, Career Institutions

NORTH CENTRAL ASSOCIATION OF COLLEGES AND SCHOOLS
Arizona, Arkansas, Colorado, Illinois, Indiana, Iowa, Kansas, Michigan, Minnesota, Missouri, Nebraska, New Mexico, North Dakota, Ohio, Oklahoma, South Dakota, West Virginia, Wisconsin, Wyoming
Thurston E. Manning, *Director*
Commission on Institutions of Higher Education
159 North Dearborn Street
Chicago, Illinois 60601
(312) 263-0456

NORTHWEST ASSOCIATION OF SCHOOLS AND COLLEGES
Alaska, Idaho, Montana, Nevada, Oregon, Utah, Washington
James F. Bemis, *Executive Director*
Commission on Colleges
3700-B University Way, N.E.
Seattle, Washington 98105
(206) 543-0195

SOUTHERN ASSOCIATION OF COLLEGES AND SCHOOLS
Alabama, Florida, Georgia, Kentucky, Louisiana, Mississippi, North Carolina, South Carolina, Tennessee, Texas, Virginia
795 Peachtree Street, N.E.
Atlanta, Georgia 30365
James T. Rogers, *Executive Director*
Commission on Colleges
(404) 897-6126

Kenneth W. Tidwell, *Executive Director*
Commission on Occupational Education Institutions
(404) 897-6163

WESTERN ASSOCIATION OF SCHOOLS AND COLLEGES
American Samoa, California, Guam, Hawaii, Trust Territory of the Pacific

Kay J. Andersen, *Executive Director*
Accrediting Commission for Senior Colleges and Universities
c/o Mills College, Box 9990
Oakland, California 94613
(415) 632-5000

John C. Petersen, *Executive Director*
Accrediting Commission for Community and Junior Colleges
P.O. Box 70
9053 Soquel Drive
Aptos, California 95003
(408) 688-7575

SPECIALIZED ACCREDITING BODIES

ALLIED HEALTH (Through the American Medical Association)
COPA recognizes the Committee on Allied Health Education and Accreditation (CAHEA) as an umbrella agency for 17 review committees representing 3 collaborating professional organizations in the accreditation of programs in the following areas of allied health. All questions concerning accreditation of these programs should be directed to CAHEA at the address given.
The review committees are: Committee on Accreditation (AABB), *Specialist in Blood Bank Technology;* Joint Review Committee on Education in *Cardiovascular Technology; Cytotechnology* Programs Review Committee; Joint Review Committee on Education in *Diagnostic Medical Sonography;* Joint Review Committee on Education in *EEG Technology;* Joint Review Committee on Educational Programs for *the EMT-Paramedic;* National Accrediting Agency for Clinical Laboratory Sciences, *Histologic Technician, Medical Laboratory Technician (associate degree and certificate programs), Medical Technologist;* Curriculum Review Board (AAMA), *Medical Assistant;* Council on Education (AMRA), *Medical Record Technician, Medical Record Administrator;* Joint Review Committee on Educational Programs in *Nuclear Medicine Technology;* Accreditation Committee (AOTA), *Occupational Therapy;* Joint Review Committee on Educational Programs for the *Ophthalmic Medical Assistant;* Joint Review Committee for *Perfusion Education;* Joint Review Committee on Educational Programs for *Physician's Assistant, Surgeon's Assistant;* Joint Review Committee on Education in Radiologic Technology, *Radiation Therapy Technologist, Radiographer;* Joint Review Committee for Respiratory Therapy Education, *Respiratory Therapist, Respiratory Therapy Technician;* Joint Review Committee on Eductional Programs for the *Surgical Technologist.*

American Medical Association Committee on Allied Health Education and Accreditation
John J. Fauser, *Director*
Division of Allied Health Education and Accreditation, AMA
535 North Dearborn Street
Chicago, Illinois 60610
(312) 645-4660

ARCHITECTURE
First professional degree programs

National Architectural Accrediting Board
John Maudlin-Jeronimo, *Executive Director*
1735 New York Avenue, N.W.
Washington, D.C. 20006
(202) 783-2007

ART AND DESIGN
Institutions and units within institutions offering degree programs in art, design, and art/design related disciplines; also nondegree-granting institutions

National Association of Schools of Art and Design
Samuel Hope, *Executive Director*
Commission on Accreditation
11250 Roger Bacon Drive, Suite 5
Reston, Virginia 22090
(703) 437-0700

BUSINESS ADMINISTRATION, MANAGEMENT, and ACCOUNTING
Bachelor's and master's degree programs in administration, management, and accounting

American Assembly of Collegiate Schools of Business

William K. Laidlaw, Jr. *Executive Vice President*
605 Old Ballas Road, Suite 220
St. Louis, Missouri 63141
(314) 872-8481

CHIROPRACTIC EDUCATION
Institutions offering first professional degrees
The Council on Chiropractic Education
Ralph G. Miller, *Executive Vice President*
3209 Ingersoll Avenue
Des Moines, Iowa 50312
Tel. (515) 255-2184

CONSTRUCTION EDUCATION
Baccalaureate programs in construction, construction science, construction management, and construction technology
American Council for Construction Education
Robert M. Dillon, *Executive Vice President*
1015 15th Street, N.W., Suite 700
Washington, D.C. 20005
Tel. (202) 347-5875 or (301) 593-7284

DENTISTRY AND DENTAL AUXILIARY PROGRAMS
First professional programs in dental education; advanced specialty programs; general practice residency; and degree and certificate programs in dental auxiliary education
American Dental Association
Mario V. Santangelo, *Secretary*
Commission on Dental Accreditation
211 East Chicago Avenue
Chicago, Illinois 60611
Tel. (312) 440-2708

DIETETICS
Coordinated baccalaureate programs and post-baccalaureate internship programs
The American Dietetic Association
Barbara Bobeng, *Assistant Executive Director*
Division of Education and Research
430 North Michigan Avenue
Chicago, Illinois 60611
Tel. (312) 280-5093

ENGINEERING
Professional engineering programs at the basic (baccalaureate) and advanced (master's) level; baccalaureate programs in engineering technology; and two-year (associate degree) programs in engineering technology
Accreditation Board for Engineering and Technology
David R. Reyes-Guerra, *Executive Director*
345 East 47th Street
New York, New York 10017
Tel. (212) 705-7685

FORESTRY
First professional degree programs, baccalaureate or higher
Society of American Foresters
P. Gregory Smith, *Coordinator, Educational and Professional Standards*
5400 Grosvenor Lane
Bethesda, Maryland 20814
Tel. (301) 897-8720

HEALTH SERVICES ADMINISTRATION
Graduate programs in health services administration, health planning, and health policy analysis
Accrediting Commission on Education for Health Services Administration
David F. Bergwall, *Executive Secretary*
1911 North Fort Myer Drive, Suite 503
Arlington, Virginia 22209
Tel. (703) 524-0511

HOME ECONOMICS
Baccalaureate degree programs
American Home Economics Association
Helen Grove, *Director*
Office of Professional Education
2010 Massachusetts Avenue, N.W.
Washington, D.C. 20036
Tel. (202) 862-8355

INTERIOR DESIGN
Programs from the junior college through the graduate level in interior design and interior architecture
Foundation for Interior Design Education Research
Edna Kane, *Executive Director*
322 Eighth Avenue, Room 1501
New York, New York 10001
Tel. (212) 929-8366

JOURNALISM
Units and programs leading to undergraduate and graduate (master's) degrees
Accrediting Council on Education in Journalism and Mass Communication
Susanne Shaw, *Executive Director*
Accrediting Council
School of Journalism, University of Kansas
Stauffer-Flint Hall

Lawrence, Kansas 66045
Tel. (913) 864-3973

LANDSCAPE ARCHITECTURE
First professional programs at the bachelor's or master's level
American Society of Landscape Architects
Gayle L. Berens, *Acting Director of Education and Research*
Landscape Architectural Accreditation Board
1733 Connecticut Avenue, N.W.
Washington, D.C. 20009
Tel. (202) 466-7730

LAW
Programs leading to the first professional degree and advanced degrees in law
American Bar Association
James P. White, *Consultant on Legal Education*
Indianapolis Law School
Indiana University—Purdue University at Indianapolis
735 West New York Street, Room 237
Indianapolis, Indiana 46202
Tel. (317) 264-8071
and
Programs leading to the first professional degree
Association of American Law Schools
Millard H. Ruud, *Executive Director*
One Dupont Circle, N.W., Suite 370
Washington, D.C. 20036
Tel. (202) 296-8851

LIBRARIANSHIP
First professional degree programs
American Library Association
Elinor Yungmeyer, *Accreditation Officer*
Committee on Accreditation
50 East Huron Street
Chicago, Illinois 60611
Tel. (312) 944-6780

MEDICAL ASSISTANT AND MEDICAL LABORATORY TECHNICIAN
Diploma, certificate, and associate degree programs
Accrediting Bureau of Health Education Schools
Hugh A. Woosley, *Administrator*
Oak Manor Offices
29089 U.S. 20 West
Elkhart, Indiana 46514
Tel. (219) 293-0124

MEDICINE
Programs leading to first professional degree and programs in the basic medical sciences
Liaison Committee on Medical Education
(in odd-numbered years beginning each July 1st, contact)

Edward S. Petersen, *Secretary*
Council on Medical Education, AMA
535 North Dearborn Street
Chicago, Illinois 60610
Tel. (312) 751-6310
or
(in even-numbered years beginning each July 1st, contact)
J. R. Schofield, *Secretary*
Association of American Medical Colleges
One Dupont Circle, N.W., Suite 200
Washington, D.C. 20036
Tel. (202) 828-0670

MUSIC
Institutions and units within institutions offering degree programs in music and music related disciplines, also nondegree-granting institutions
National Association of Schools of Music
Samuel Hope, *Executive Director*
11250 Roger Bacon Drive, Suite 5
Reston, Virginia 22090
Tel. (703) 437-0700

NURSE ANESTHESIA EDUCATION
Nurse Anesthesia Programs within institutions offering baccalaureate and master's degrees in nurse anesthesia education
Council on Accreditation of Nurse Anesthesia Education Programs/Schools
Doris A. Stoll, *Executive Secretary*
216 Higgins Rd.
Park Ridge, Illinois 60068
Tel. (312) 692-7050

NURSING
Associate, baccalaureate, and higher degree programs; also diploma and practical nurse programs
National League for Nursing
Carl H. Miller, *Director of Accreditation Services*
10 Columbus Circle
New York, New York 10019
Tel. (212) 582-1022

OPTOMETRY
Professional programs in optometry and optometric technology
American Optometric Association
Ellis Smith, *Executive Secretary*
Council on Optometric Education
243 North Lindbergh Boulevard
St. Louis, Missouri 63141
Tel. (314) 991-4100

OSTEOPATHIC MEDICINE
First professional degree programs
American Osteopathic Association
Douglas Ward, *Director*
Office of Osteopathic Education
212 East Ohio Street
Chicago, Illinois 60611
Tel. (312) 280-5800

PHARMACY
First professional degree programs (baccalaureate or doctoral)
American Council on Pharmaceutical Education
Daniel A. Nona, *Executive Director*
311 West Superior Street, Suite 512
Chicago, Illinois 60610
Tel. (312) 664-3575

PHYSICAL THERAPY
First professional degree programs for the physical therapist and programs for the physical therapy assistant
American Physical Therapy Association
Patricia Yarbrough, *Director*
Department of Educational Affairs
Transpotomac Plaza, 1111 North Fairfax Street
Alexandria, Virginia 22314
Tel. (703) 684-2782

PODIATRY
First professional degree programs
American Podiatric Medical Association,
Warren G. Ball, *Director*
Council on Podiatric Medical Education
20 Chevy Chase Circle, N.W.
Washington, D.C. 20015
Tel. (202) 537-4970

PSYCHOLOGY
Doctoral programs in professional specialties of psychology and pre-doctoral internship training programs in professional psychology
American Psychological Association
Paul D. Nelson, *Director of Accreditation*
1200 Seventeenth Street, N.W.
Washington, D.C. 20036
Tel. (202) 955-7671

PUBLIC HEALTH
Graduate schools of public health and master's degree programs in community health education and community health preventive medicine
Council on Education for Public Health
Patricia P. Evans, *Executive Director*
1015 Fifteenth Street, N.W., Suite 403
Washington, D.C. 20005
Tel. (202) 789-1050

RABBINICAL AND TALMUDIC EDUCATION
Rabbinical and Talmudic schools offering rabbinical degrees, ordination, and appropriate undergraduate and graduate degrees
Association of Advanced Rabbinical and Talmudic Schools
Bernard Fryshman, *Executive Director*
175 Fifth Avenue, Room 711
New York, New York 10010
Tel. (212) 477-0950 or 645-1814

REHABILITATION COUNSELING
Master's degree programs
Council on Rehabilitation Education
Charline McGrath, *Executive Director*
185 North Wabash Street, Room 1617
Chicago, Illinois 60601
Tel. (312) 346-6027

SOCIAL WORK
Baccalaureate and master's degree programs
Council on Social Work Education
Nancy Randolph, *Director*
Division of Education Standards and Accreditation
1744 R St., N.W.
Washington, D.C. 20036
Tel. (202) 667-2300

SPEECH PATHOLOGY AND AUDIOLOGY
Master's degree programs
American Speech—Language—Hearing Association
Billie Ackerman, *Director*
Education Division
10801 Rockville Pike
Rockville, Maryland 20852
Tel. (301) 897-5700

TEACHER EDUCATION
Baccalaureate and graduate degree programs for the preparation of teachers and other professional school personnel

National Council for Accreditation of Teacher Education
Richard C. Kunkel, *Director*
1919 Pennsylvania Avenue, N.W., Suite 202
Washington, D.C. 20006
Tel. (202) 466-7496

VETERINARY MEDICINE
First professional degree programs

Council on Education
American Veterinary Medical Association
R. Leland West, *Director of Scientific Activities*
930 North Meacham Road
Schaumburg, Illinois 60196
Tel. (312) 885-8070

(This listing current as of August 1, 1986)

C. Joint Statement on Transfer and Award of Academic Credit

The following set of guidelines were developed by the three national associations in higher education whose member institutions are directly involved in the transfer and award of academic credit. It is one in a series of policy guidelines developed through the American Council on Education to respond to issues in higher education by means of voluntary self-regulation. Each statement is developed through a process of wide review among representatives of different types of institutions and professional responsibilities in higher education. They are intended to summarize general principles of good practice that can be adapted to the specific circumstances of each college and university.

Transfer of credit is a concept that now involves transfer between dissimilar institutions and curricula and recognition of extra-institutional learning, as well as transfer between institutions and curricula of similar characteristics. As their personal circumstances and educational objectives change, students seek to have their learning, wherever and however attained, recognized by institutions where they enroll for further study. It is important for reasons of social equity and educational effectiveness, as well as the wise use of resources, for all institutions to develop reasonable and definitive policies and procedures for acceptance of transfer credit. Such policies and procedures should provide maximum consideration for the individual student who has changed institutions or objectives. It is the receiving institution's responsiblity to provide reasonable and definitive policies and procedures for determining a student's knowledge in required subject areas. All institutions have a responsibility to furnish transcripts and other documents necessary for a receiving institution to judge the quality and quantity of the work. Institutions also have a responsibility to advise the students that the work <reflected> on the transcript *may or may not* be accepted by a receiving institution.

Inter-Institutional Transfer of Credit

Transfer of credit from one institution to another involves at least three considerations:

(1) the educational quality of the institution from which the student transfers;
(2) the comparability of the nature, content, and level of credit earned to that offered by the receiving institution; and
(3) the appropriateness and applicability of the credit earned to the programs offered by the receiving institution, in light of the student's educational goals.

Accredited Institutions

Accreditation speaks primarily to the first of these considerations, serving as the basic indicator that an institution meets certain minimum standards. Users of accreditation are urged to give careful attention to the accreditation conferred by accrediting bodies recognized by the Council on Postsecondary Accreditation (COPA). COPA has a formal process of recognition which requires that any accrediting body so recognized must meet the same standards. Under these standards, COPA has recognized a number of accrediting bodies, including:

(1) regional accrediting commissions (which historically accredited the more traditional colleges and universities but which now accredit proprietary, vocational-technical, and single-purpose institutions as well);

(2) national accrediting bodies that accredit various kinds of specialized institutions; and
(3) certain professional organizations that accredit free-standing professional schools, in addition to programs within multi-purpose institutions. (COPA annually publishes a list of recognized accrediting bodies, as well as a directory of institutions accredited by these organizations.)

Although accrediting agencies vary in the ways they are organized and in their statements of scope and mission, all accrediting bodies that meet COPA's standards for recognition function to assure that the institutions or programs they accredit have met generally accepted minimum standards for accreditation.

Accreditation affords reason for confidence in an institution's or a program's purposes, in the appropriateness of its resources and plans for carrying out these purposes, and in its effectiveness in accomplishing its goals, insofar as these things can be judged. Accreditation speaks to the probability, but does not guarantee, that students have met acceptable standards of educational accomplishment.

Comparability and Applicability

Comparability of the nature, content, and level of transfer credit and the appropriateness and applicability of the credit earned to programs offered by the receiving institution are as important in the evaluation process as the accreditation status of the institution at which the transfer credit was awarded. Since accreditation does not address these questions, this information must be obtained from catalogues and other materials and from direct contact between knowledgeable and experienced faculty and staff at both the receiving and sending institutions. When such considerations as comparability and appropriateness of credit are satisfied, however, the receiving institution should have reasonable confidence that students from accredited institutions are qualified to undertake the receiving institution's educational program.

Admissions and Degree Purposes

At some institutions there may be differences between the acceptance of credit for admission purposes and the applicability of credit for degree purposes. A receiving institution may accept previous work, place a credit value on it, and enter it on the transcript. However, that previous work, because of its nature and not its inherent quality, may be determined to have no applicability to a specific degree to be pursued by the student.

Institutions have a responsibility to make this distinction, and its implications, clear to students before they decide to enroll. This should be a matter of full disclosure, with the best interests of the student in mind. Institutions also should make every reasonable effort to reduce the gap between credits accepted and credits applied toward an educational credential.

Unaccredited Institutions

Institutions of postsecondary education that are not accredited by COPA-recognized accrediting bodies may lack that status for reasons unrelated to questions of quality. Such institutions, however, cannot provide a reliable, third-party assurance that they meet or exceed minimum standards. That being the case, students transferring from such institutions may encounter special problems in gaining acceptance and transferring credits to accredited institutions. Institutions admitting students from unaccredited institutions should take steps to validate credits previously earned.

Foreign Institutions

In most cases, foreign institutions are chartered and authorized by their national governments, usually through a ministry of education. Although this provides for a standardization within a country, it does not produce useful information about comparability from one country to another. No other nation has a system comparable to voluntary accreditation. The Division of Higher Education of the United Nations Educational, Scientific, and Cultural Organization (UNESCO) is engaged in a project to develop international compacts for the acceptance of educational credentials. At the operational level, four organizations—the Council on International Educational Exchange (CIEE), the National Council on the Evaluation of Foreign Student Credentials (CEC), the National Association for Foreign Student Affairs (NAFSA), and the National Liaison Committee on Foreign Student Admissions (NLC)—often can assist institutions by distributing general guidelines on admission and placement of foreign students. Equivalency or placement recommendations are to be evaluated in terms of the programs and policies of the individual receiving institution.

Validation of Extra-Institutional and Experiential Learning for Transfer Purposes

Transfer-of-credit policies should encompass educational accomplishment attained in extra-institutional settings as well as at accredited postsecondary institutions. In deciding on the award of credit for extra-institutional learning, institutions will find the services of the American Council on Education's Office of Educational Credit and Credentials helpful. One of the Office's functions is to operate and foster programs to determine credit equivalencies for various modes of extra-institutional learning. The Office maintains evaluation programs for formally structured courses offered by the military and civilian noncollegiate sponsors such as business, corporations, government agencies, and labor unions. Evaluation services are also available for examination programs, for occupations with validated job proficiency evaluation systems, and for correspondence courses offered by schools accredited by the National Home Study Council. The results are published in a Guide series. Another resource is the General Education Development (GED) Testing Program, which provides a means for assessing high school equivalency.

For learning that has not been validated through the ACE formal credit recommendation process or through credit-by-examination programs, institutions are urged to explore the Council for Adult and Experiential Learning (CAEL) procedures and processes.

Uses of this Statement

This statement has been endorsed by the three national associations most concerned with practices in the area of transfer and award of credit—the American Association of Collegiate Registrars and Admissions Officers, the American Council on Education/Commission on Educational Credit, and the Council on Postsecondary Accreditation.

Institutions are encouraged to use this statement as a basis for discussions in developing or reviewing institutional policies with regard to transfer. If the statement reflects an institution's policies, that institution might want to use this publication to inform faculty, staff, and students.

It is recommended that accrediting bodies reflect the essential precepts of this statement in their criteria.

Approved by the COPA Board
October 10, 1978

Approved by the American Council on Education/Commission on Educational Credit
December 5, 1978

Approved by the Executive Committee, American Association of Collegiate Registrars and Admissions Officers
November 21, 1978

Institutional Index